# DIMENSIONS OF
# Human Sexuality

**6TH EDITION**

# DIMENSIONS OF
# Human Sexuality

REVISED BY SHARON P. SHRIVER
The Pennsylvania State University

CURTIS O. BYER
Mt. San Antonio College

LOUIS W. SHAINBERG
Mt. San Antonio College

GRACE GALLIANO
Kennesaw State University and Monroe Community College

Boston   Burr Ridge, IL   Dubuque, IA   Madison, WI   New York   San Francisco   St. Louis
Bangkok   Bogotá   Caracas   Kuala Lumpur   Lisbon   London   Madrid   Mexico City
Milan   Montreal   New Delhi   Santiago   Seoul   Singapore   Sydney   Taipei   Toronto

# McGraw-Hill Higher Education

*A Division of The McGraw-Hill Companies*

DIMENSIONS OF HUMAN SEXUALITY, SIXTH EDITION

This book is printed on acid-free paper.

1 2 3 4 5 6 7 8 9 0 QPV/QPV 0 9 8 7 6 5 4 3 2 1

ISBN 0–07–241278–X

Editorial director: *Jane E. Karpacz*
Senior sponsoring editor: *Rebecca H. Hope*
Developmental editor: *Rita Lombard*
Senior marketing manager: *Chris Hall*
Project manager: *Christine Walker*
Production supervisor: *Enboge Chong*
Coordinator of freelance design: *David W. Hash*
Cover designer: *Jay E. Bensen*
Cover image: *©The Stock Illustration Source, Inc./Andy Levine*
Senior photo research coordinator: *Lori Hancock*
Photo research: *Denise Simmons/Amy Bethea/Amelia Ames Hill Associates*
Supplement producer: *Tammy Juran*
Media technology lead producer: *David Edwards*
Compositor: *GAC–Indianapolis*
Typeface: *10.5/12 Sabon*
Printer: *Quebecor World Versailles Inc.*

The credits section for this book begins on page 533 and is considered an extension of the copyright page.

**Library of Congress Cataloging-in-Publication Data**

Dimensions of human sexuality / Curtis O. Byer, . . . [et al.]. — 6th ed.
    p. cm.
  Rev. ed. of: Dimensions of human sexuality / Curtis O. Byer, Louis W. Shainberg, Grace Galliano. 5th ed. 1999.
  Includes bibliographical references and indexes.
  ISBN 0–07–241278–X (acid-free paper)
  1. Sex.  I. Byer, Curtis O.  II. Byer, Curtis O.  Dimensions of human sexuality.  III. Title.
HQ21.B97 2002
306.7—dc21
                                      2001032709
                                      CIP

## ABOUT THE AUTHORS

**Curtis Byer** earned his B.S. degree from Goshen College and M.A. degree from the Claremont Graduate University. He completed thirty years of teaching in the Biological Sciences Department at Mt. San Antonio College in Walnut, CA. Initially working with the late Kenneth Jones, he and Louis Shainberg co-authored many college texts for Human Sexuality and the Health Sciences. More recently, Grace Galliano joined the team as a co-author for *Dimensions of Human Sexuality*. Curtis' teaching has included Human Sexuality and various Biology courses. His avocations include backpacking, travel, and genealogical work.

**Louis (Lou) Shainberg** earned his B.S. and Ph.D. at the University of California at Davis. He is now in his fortieth year in the Biological Sciences Department at Mt. San Antonio College in Walnut, CA. Working with Curtis Byer since 1965, and more recently with Grace Galliano, Lou has co-authored numerous college texts for Human Sexuality and Health Science courses. Lou's teaching includes Human Sexuality, Microbiology, and General Biology. Lou is an avid traveler, skier, and jazz fan.

**Grace Galliano** is a social psychologist who received her advanced degrees from the New School for Social Research and Georgia State University. Her professional passions continue to be writing and the day-to-day classroom interactions with students. She pursues both passions in the context of the complexities and cross-cultural aspects of gender and sexuality. After more than two delightful decades at Kennesaw State University, Grace recently returned to her home state of New York and is now involved in teaching at the community college level. Her greatest life adventure is about to begin as she contemplates an upcoming adoption.

**Sharon Shriver** is a biomedical researcher and full-time educator at the Pennsylvania State University. She received her B.A. degree in psychology from Indiana University, with a minor in education, before beginning graduate work in biology. After earning her Ph.D. from Case Western Reserve University, she held research positions at M.D. Anderson Cancer Institute and the University of Pittsburgh Cancer Institute, where her research focused on the genetics of lung cancer. She has published numerous scientific articles, including important studies addressing the increased risk of women for developing lung cancer. In addition to her ongoing research, she teaches courses at Penn State in sexuality, bioethics, and human genetics. In developing her sexuality courses, Dr. Shriver has done extensive research into effective pedagogical techniques, with a goal of making her courses interesting and practical as well as educational.

## DEDICATION

*To all of the world's hard-working college students.*
- **CB** *and* **LS**

*To Linda, who always inspires me.*
- **GG**

*To Mark, Carly, and Evan, for your support and boundless patience.*
- **SS**

# BRIEF CONTENTS

# CONTENTS

# BOXES

## SELF-ASSESSMENT: WHERE DO I STAND?

## CASE STUDIES

# PREFACE

## A PERSONAL NOTE FROM SHARON SHRIVER

I have been delighted to work on this new, updated edition of *Dimensions of Human Sexuality*. As a biologist and sexuality educator, I appreciate the solid foundation of the text in empirical research, and I find that the strong biological perspective of the book provides an understandable and accessible starting point for undergraduates in my sexuality classes. My background in health science research allowed me to update the text with the most recent research findings, a process that was educational and rewarding. I have also used my experiences as an instructor of undergraduates to revise the text to reflect current issues in a practical way, with examples and exercises that students can use in real-life situations. The result is a text that is current, accurate, and accessible, and I am pleased to have had the opportunity to contribute to it and continue the shared goals of the author team:

▌ To provide students with the most current perspectives and information about human sexuality in order to assist them in wiser sexual decision-making.

▌ To broaden the students' conceptualization of sexuality well beyond the notion of genital arousal, so that they might recognize that many aspects of living are expressions of our sexuality.

▌ To guide students in appreciating and celebrating the diversity of human sexual expression.

▌ To facilitate higher levels of sexual health and sexual well-being among students, as well as their partners, spouses, and families.

▌ To facilitate students' exploration and articulation of their personal sexual values and attitudes.

▌ To offer students sound critical thinking skills that are useful for comprehending and evaluating new sexuality-related information.

▌ To make optimal use of well-established pedagogical principles to assist the students to both master and evaluate important

information in the light of new findings and understandings.

▌ To make a contribution toward creating an environment of sexual understanding, sexual respect and personal sexual enrichment for the next generation and their children.

## WHAT'S NEW AND DIFFERENT IN THIS EDITION

The text has been reorganized and condensed into **18 chapters** for a more clear and concise presentation. Important topics are highlighted and expanded, and updated material is incorporated throughout the text:

▌ Chapters 1 and 2 have been combined.

▌ Chapter 12 on Sexual Dysfunctions has been deleted and the relevant material has been moved into chapter 8 on Sexual Response.

▌ Chapter 17 on Sexuality and Aging has been deleted and the relevant material has been moved into chapters 8, 11, and 14.

▌ Chapters 21 and 22 have been combined and condensed. Relevant material has been moved into the Sexually Transmitted Infections chapter.

Topics of social importance, such as infant male circumcision, have been updated to reflect the most recent information and changes. When appropriate, these topics are placed in a historical context so that the sources of change in society can be evaluated.

The chapter on Sexually Transmitted Diseases has been thoroughly updated and renamed Sexually Transmitted Infections, a more accurate term reflecting recent information about these infections and their causes. There is a strong emphasis in the text on understanding the biological basis of these infections, their transmission, and their prevention.

Critical Thinking Challenges have been incorporated into the end of each chapter. These encourage students to develop critical thinking skills through the thoughtful review of chapter material and to apply new concepts to relevant situations in their own lives.

Links to sites on the World Wide Web have been added to boxed material where appropriate. These links encourage students to pursue interesting topics on their own.

The text style has been modified for ease in reading and clear organization. All headings have been numbered to show the relationship between various topics in the text. Indexing of topics and headers at the beginning of each chapter using a scientific numbering system provide a clear outline of the presentation of material.

The text is fully accessible to students of all sexual orientations. Where relevant, similarities and differences between same-sex and other-sex partnering are fully discussed, and presented as normal variations in sexual behavior.

The overall physical appearance of the text has been modernized and updated to reflect the current topics and research that the text presents. Illustrations and figures throughout the text have also been updated and revised. Figures represent the diversity of human sexual expression among people of all ethnicities and sexual orientations. Whenever appropriate, illustrations provide detailed photographs, rather than artistic renderings, which support material presented in the text.

## WHAT HAS BEEN RETAINED

The text continues to cover major aspects of human sexuality, including communication about sexuality, critical thinking about sexual research and information, sexual anatomy and physiology, social aspects of sexuality (including sexually transmitted infections, prostitution, and pornography), sexual response and pleasure, and a comprehensive presentation of reproductive sexuality.

A life-span approach to understanding sexuality has been incorporated throughout the text. Material about sexual development in the prenatal period, sexuality in childhood, adolescence, and adult life, and during the aging process is presented.

There continues to be a strong emphasis on empirical research findings as the basis for the information presented in the text. The most up-to-date research findings are incorporated whenever available.

The text presents practical information to students to aid in dealing with sexuality issues: How to conduct breast or testicular self-examinations, making informed decisions about sexual activity, negotiating condom use, and complete information regarding contraceptive options. The Critical Thinking Challenges in each chapter ask students to consider the practical application of this information in various situations.

Topics of high personal interest continue to be covered throughout the text. These include such issues as sexuality education in the home and school, parenthood, communication in relationships, and destructive elements in relationships.

There are numerous opportunities throughout the book and in the "Where Do I Stand" boxes for self-reflection and self-assessment regarding one's personal sexual values, attitudes, and behaviors.

A multi-cultural perspective permeates virtually every topic or issue discussed in the text. The material is fully integrated and highlighted in a special feature called "Dimensions of Diversity."

A separate chapter is devoted to the most recent scientific data regarding HIV and AIDS, utilizing both a national and global perspective on this issue. Because this is a rapidly changing area, these topics are presented with a full appreciation that significant developments are occurring constantly, and the text aims to provide students with the background and skills necessary to evaluate new information as it arises throughout their lives.

Valuable pedagogical tools such as the running glossary and detailed end of chapter summary are included in this edition.

All the boxed features of the fifth edition have been retained with web links added as appropriate.

- *Go Ask Alice*—In most chapters there is at least one real student-generated question which Alice (spokesperson for the Healthwise Office at Columbia University in New York City) answers in plain language. These are real questions asked by real students in their own words. Students too shy to voice their questions in class are encouraged to contact the Alice Website, where they can submit their questions anonymously. These questions and Alice's responses then become part of the retrievable *Go Ask Alice* archive.

- *Where Do I Stand?*—These boxes allow the student/reader to explore his or her own values, attitudes, or opinions regarding a number of sexually-related issues.

- *Dimensions of Diversity*—These boxes examine some aspect of sexuality across several cultures or historical periods. They allow the student to see how differently various societies may regard a particular sexual behavior or issue.

- *At Issue*—These boxes provide a closer examination of some controversial issue in human sexuality. Many are followed by critical thinking questions, which may serve as the basis for classroom discussion or written papers.

■ *Case Study*—Several case studies interspersed throughout the book look at a sexuality-related issue as it is manifested in a single individual. They allow for the student or reader to experience how a particular behavior or issue is represented in a real individual.

■ *Healthy Sexuality*—This feature deals with sexuality-related issues with the goal of enhancing sexual health and well-being.

The text continues to represent a collaborative effort among teachers and scholars in the areas of biology, health, and social psychology. This provides a balance of perspective that makes the text suitable for sexuality courses taught in biology, human development, health science, psychology, sociology, anthropology, or physical education departments. Beyond the end of their sexuality course, students may keep the text for use as a personal and family reference book for sexuality-related questions.

## SUPPLEMENTS

The following items are available with this text. Some restrictions may apply. Please consult your local McGraw-Hill Sales Representative for policies, prices, and availability.

The updated **Student Workbook and Study Guide** continues to be a collection of valuable and interesting student activities that provoke an examination of sexual values, attitudes, and behavior. For every chapter, this ancillary provides learning objectives, a self-test of key terms and major concepts, an opportunity for students to assess their own sexuality, exercises in applying and integrating sexuality information to real-life situations, a reference section providing further readings and resources, and a self-quiz.

A combined **Instructor's Manual/Test Bank** is designed as a planning guide to accompany *Dimensions of Human Sexuality, Sixth Edition,* and is keyed to the text's 18 chapters. The Instructor's Manual provides learning objectives (keyed to those in the outline for each chapter in the main text), teaching strategies, and a detailed outline for each chapter. The fully updated Test Bank offers multiple choice, true/false, matching, and short answer questions designed to test basic knowledge as well as to challenge the student in the application, synthesis, and analysis of the text material. The Test Bank is also available on CD-ROM [a testing program], both in Windows and/or Mac format.

**The Dimensions of Human Sexuality Website** is the official website for the text. It contains Chapter Outlines, Practice Quizzes, Interactive Exercises, Links to Relevant Psychology sites, an Internet Primer, Career Appendix, and more. Visit us at www.mhhe.com/byer6

**McGraw-Hill's Sexuality Drop-In Center Supersite** provides a superstructure that organizes and houses all of our human sexuality text websites. It acts as a place where faculty and students can access a multitude of resources to support our human sexuality titles. In addition to book-specific resources, an Activity Center contains interesting online activities and exercises, a Counseling Room provides links to the popular *Go Ask Alice* site as well as many other counseling sites, and a Resource Room provides still more links to useful sexuality-related resources. Visit us at www.mhhe.com/sexuality

*The Aids Booklet* by Frank D. Cox contains the latest information on AIDS.

*Sources: Notable Selections in Human Sexuality* provides interesting further reading for students.

*Annual Editions: Human Sexuality* is a compilation of current articles from over 300 public press sources.

*Taking Sides: Clashing Views on Controversial Issues in Human Sexuality* is designed to introduce students to controversial issues in an area of study. The pro and con format is particularly effective for developing critical thinking skills and generating classroom discussion and debate.

## ACKNOWLEDGMENTS

We would like to thank our colleagues for all their support during the preparation of this edition, especially the following:

Lori Dawson, Worcester State College; John Duncan, University of Delaware; Matt Hobson, University of Northern Iowa; Donald Matlosz, California State University; Andrea Parrot, Cornell University; Brenda Soto-Torres, University of Wisconsin, La Crosse; and Beverly Tremain, Truman State University; we would also like to especially thank Mickey Elaison at the University of Iowa for her contribution to this edition.

We appreciate the strong support we have had from our publisher. We would like to express our special thanks to Jane Vaicunas Karpacz, editorial director; Rebecca Hope, senior sponsoring editor; Rita Lombard, developmental editor; Christine Walker, project manager; David Hash, design coordinator; Lori Hancock, photo research coordinator, and Tammy Juran, senior supplement producer.

We welcome and appreciate comments from readers, which help us continue to improve *Dimensions of Human Sexuality.*

*Curtis O. Byer*
*Louis W. Shainberg*
*Grace Galliano*
*Sharon P. Shriver*

# VISUAL WALKTHROUGH

## GO ASK ALICE

In most chapters there is at least one real student-generated question which Alice (spokesperson for the Healthwise Office at Columbia University in New York City) answers in plain language. These are real questions asked by real students in their own words. Students too shy to voice their questions in class are encouraged to contact the Alice Website, where they can submit their questions anonymously. These questions and Alice's responses then become part of the retrievable *Go Ask Alice* archive.

*All appropriate boxes indicate a link to the text's website.*

---

TYPES OF SEXUAL DYSFUNCTIONS: ORIGINS AND INTERVENTIONS    **227**

### GO ASK ALICE

Dear Alice,

What are the long-term effects of taking *Prozac*? I've been taking 20 mg/day for almost a year.

Happy but at what cost?

Dear Happy but at what cost?,

In the last several years, *Prozac* has become the most widely prescribed antidepressant in the United States. Besides treating depression, *Prozac* is used to treat obsessive-compulsive and panic disorders. *Prozac* is the oldest drug of this kind, with 20 years of research behind it showing no known long-term side effects. *Prozac* has few side effects when compared to other antidepressant drugs. These side effects may include dry mouth, constipation, urinary retention, sedation, and weight gain.

*Prozac*, however, is associated with insomnia, restlessness, nausea, and tension headaches, which normally go away within one to two weeks from when it was first taken. One possible side effect, which remains for the time *Prozac* is taken, is *Prozac's* affect on your sex life. It often reduces desire, and can delay or interfere with orgasm, in both women and men. Fatigue and memory loss are other possible problems. These side effects subside when you stop taking the drug. In some people, the effectiveness of *Prozac* seems to diminish with time, and an increase in dosage is necessary. In these cases, talk with your prescribing doctor, who may alter your medication.

Stopping *Prozac's* use needs to be supervised by a physician. It is not advised to take this drug if you are pregnant or breastfeeding. So, talk with your doctor for an alternative.

 http:www.mhhe.com/byer6

---

172    CHAPTER 7  HIV AND AIDS

## DIMENSIONS OF DIVERSITY

### THE 100% CONDOM PROGRAM IN THAILAND

Asia in general has lagged behind most of the world in the AIDS epidemic, but it is seen by many as poised for an outbreak that could equal or exceed the AIDS disaster in sub-Saharan Africa. Two areas in Asia—India and Cambodia-Myanmar-Thailand—already have massive amounts of HIV infection. Thailand responded in 1992 with the 100% Condom Program.

Thailand has a large and well-established network of government registered commercial sex establishments, but little "freelance" prostitution, an ideal situation for regulation of prostitution. In April 1992 the 100% Condom Program was fully implemented in all provinces.

The program mandates withholding sexual services for any customer who declines to use a condom. To ensure compliance, males diagnosed with any STI at government-run clinics are interviewed about their sexual contacts. Any sex establishment named as a source of infection is served notice of a potential government-imposed closure if there is continued noncompliance with the 100% Condom Program.

This program has been very successful. The total number of men diagnosed with an STI dropped from 199,000 in 1989 to 27,500 in 1994. The prevalence of HIV infection in military draftees declined from 12.5 percent in 1993 to 6.5 percent in 1995. (Induction into the Royal Thai Army is by lottery among twenty-one-year-old men and does not exclude individuals based on sexual orientation, drug use, or HIV status.) The prevalence of HIV in men who did not have sex with a prostitute until after 1992 was only 0.7 percent. The incidence of syphilis in inductees dropped by almost two-thirds following the passage of the condom law.

Several conclusions can be drawn from this situation: (1) HIV can become a major problem in Asia; (2) heterosexual prostitution can be a significant source of HIV in males; (3) condoms are effective in blocking HIV transmission; and (4) open, regulated prostitution allows enforcement of condom use.

**Source:** Data from K. Nelson, E. Celentano, S. Eiumtrakol, D. Hoover, C. Beyrer, S. Suprasert, S. Kuntolbutra, and C. Khamboonruang, "Changes in Sexual Behavior and a Decline in HIV Infection among Young Men in Thailand," *New England Journal of Medicine* 335:297–303.

## DIMENSIONS OF DIVERSITY

boxes examine some aspect of sexuality across several cultures or historical periods. They allow the student to see how differently various societies may regard a particular sexual behavior or issue.

### CASE STUDY

## AN INTERVIEW WITH GREG LOUGANIS

Four-time gold medal winning Olympic diver Greg Louganis stunned the world with his 1994 book, *Breaking the Surface*, coauthored with Eric Marcus, in which Louganis revealed that he was already HIV positive when he competed in the 1988 Seoul Olympics. Here are some excerpts from an interview with Greg Louganis by Daniel Wolfe, director of communications at Gay Men's Health Crisis in New York City, published in *The Volunteer*.

*Wolfe:* The press spent much of their time after your announcement obsessed with the possibility that your blood might have infected another diver. Readers of *The Volunteer* are more likely wrestling with the dynamics of what can seem like a different kind of impossibility: telling a parent, friend, or loved one that you have HIV. Why did you go public?

*Louganis:* Secrets can be really imprisoning. I had HIV, but I didn't have anybody to talk to. . . . I started thinking about all that when it came time to write the book, about breaking the sense of loneliness.

*Wolfe:* There's been a lot of attention to the public aspect of your disclosure. Did you talk with people close to you about having HIV before you went public?

*Louganis:* I told my dad when he was diagnosed with cancer. That was back in 1989 or 1990. It became a crusade for life for both of us—him with cancer and me with HIV. I didn't come out to my mom until later. . . . Once I told her, things were so much easier. She was there for me, providing me with unconditional love.

*Wolfe:* Do you think she knew already?

*Louganis:* She wasn't surprised, because she knew that two of my ex's had passed away. But once it penetrated, she started crying. "Mothers aren't supposed to outlive their sons," she said. Then, almost in the same breath, she said, "you know, Greg, you have beaten some incredible odds before."

**Source:** Excerpted from Daniel Wolfe. "An Interview with Greg Louganis," *The Volunteer,* published by Gay Men's Health Crisis, New York City, May/June, 1996.

# THINKING ABOUT HUMAN SEXUALITY

**AFTER STUDYING THIS CHAPTER, YOU SHOULD BE ABLE TO**

[1] Describe the components of human sexuality.

[2] List and describe the traditional sources of sexual knowledge and describe how science can expand such understanding.

[3] List and describe social institutions that influence our sexuality.

[4] List recent social changes and describe how they have an influence on our sexuality.

[5] Contrast the typical person's ways of trying to understand sexuality with the three major ways utilized by the sexuality scholar.

[6] Summarize some of what scholars know about sexuality in ancient cultures of Mesopotamia, the Middle East, Asia, and Greece and Rome.

[7] Describe the historical events and Christian traditions that influence modern Western concepts of sexuality.

[8] Describe those aspects of Victorianism that influence contemporary North American sexuality.

[9] Summarize the impact of the second wave of feminism on contemporary North American sexuality.

[10] Summarize the environmental and technical problems involved in conducting sexuality research.

[11] Explain why people should understand the methods used to study human sexuality.

[12] Describe the strengths and weaknesses of surveys, observation, experiments, correlational studies, and clinical studies.

[13] List the major ethical principles that guide sexuality research, practice, and education and explain their purpose.

[14] Define critical thinking and describe nine general guidelines for thinking critically about sexual information.

## 1.1 WHAT IS SEXUALITY?

Examining a thorough definition of *sexuality* will tell you about what follows in this book.

The term *sex* has two general meanings. First, it refers to genetic endowment, anatomical features, and physiological functions. Specifically it refers to whether one is female or male. This may seem simple enough, but you will learn that this is sometimes not as clear-cut as most of us believe. The term also refers to lovemaking or genital contact between two people, as in "having sex."

Depending on our anatomical sex, we secrete eggs or produce sperm, and can either impregnate or gestate and birth offspring. All of this constitutes another facet of our sexuality, namely our *reproductive role.* All of these aspects of sexuality are covered in chapter 4 ("Female Sexual Anatomy and Physiology"), chapter 5 ("Male Sexual Anatomy and Physiology"), chapter 11 ("Biological Sexual Development"), chapter 15 ("Fertility Management"), and chapter 16 ("Conception, Pregnancy, and Childbirth").

At the moment of birth, we are labeled according to our biological category (female or male) and then assigned to a social category (girl or boy; in some societies there may be more than two such social categories). At that point, culture takes over to shape us into an appropriately feminine or masculine person for that particular society. This very profound aspect of our sexuality is called our *gender role* and will be discussed in chapter 12 ("Gender Identity and Gender Roles").

An additional aspect of our sexuality is our pursuit of the *sensual and physical pleasures* that accompany human sexual behavior. How we go about pleasuring ourselves when alone or with others is another important aspect of our sexuality. These will be discussed in chapter 8 ("Patterns of Sexual Response") and chapter 9 ("Sexual Pleasuring").

For most human beings, reproduction and sexual pleasure take place in the context of relatively lasting *emotional relationships.* In our society, romantic love and monogamy are ideals for these relationships. You will find a thorough exploration of this complex facet of our sexuality in chapter 2 ("Communication and Sexuality") and chapter 3 ("Love and Intimacy").

The sexual relationships of those with certain types of *physical and mental challenges* are discussed in chapter 10 ("Sexuality in Disability and Illness"). Other kinds of difficulties arise when an individual's preferred type of sexual expression is in conflict with socially approved norms. We discuss *problematic sexual expression* in chapter 17 ("Variations in Sexual Behavior") and chapter 18 ("Commercial and Coercive Sex").

As we move from infancy through childhood, adulthood, and ultimately old age, our sexuality might be expressed in different ways. Chapter 13 ("Childhood and Adolescent Sexuality") and chapter 14 ("Adult Sexuality") deal with *sexual development over the course of life.*

To fully enjoy and express our sexual selves, we must attend to the troublesome issue of *sexually transmitted infections* (STIs). These are discussed in chapter 6 ("Sexually Transmitted Infections") and chapter 7 ("HIV and AIDS").

Our sexuality is both broad and complex, and it consists of all of the aspects mentioned: sex, reproductive roles, gender roles, sensual and sexual pleasure, romantic and intimate relationships, sexual expression throughout the life span, sexual dysfunctions, problematic sexual expression, and concerns regarding sexually transmitted infections.

## 1.2 SOURCES AND FOUNDATIONS OF OUR PERSONAL SEXUALITY

Where did you obtain your present knowledge and understanding of sexual behavior? If you are typical of most people in North America, your initial information (and perhaps misinformation) came from your *peers.* Later on, all sorts of *media* brought you models of how sexual expression is "supposed to be." For example, in children's books and movies you may have learned that males *do brave and exciting things and select their princesses,* while females *look pretty and wait until their princes select them.* Living in the "Information Age," we are engulfed by sexuality-related information from the media and some of it isn't very accurate or honest. When most people encounter sexual "information" in our society, they often find it in magazine articles with titles such as "Keeping the Ecstasy Alive" or "Sexual Secrets of the South Seas Islanders." Movies show scenes of perfect, "seamless" sex in which no one fumbles, worries about bad breath, or stops to put on a condom. Television talk shows seem to be overrun with "cross-dressing grandfathers" and "mother-daughter prostitutes." Much of this material is designed to be entertaining or arousing rather than informative.

If you were exposed to a formal program of sexuality education in your *school,* it probably emphasized the reproductive aspects of sexuality, rather than the complex socioemotional side of sex. Nor was the course likely to dwell on sensitive issues such as sexual values or sexual diversity (American Public Health Association, 1994).

Somewhere in all of this, our *parents* got lots of sexual information across to us. For some of us, one or both of our parents tried to talk with us about sex, or perhaps they gave us a book or video. For *all* of us, our parents' *behavior* was a powerful source of all kinds of data. For example, we might have learned that long-married couples kiss, fondle, and flirt with each other. Or we may have learned that long-married couples barely speak to each other, let alone engage in romantic or sexual acts. We may have learned that fathers and mothers share the care of their children equally, or observed the challenges that face single parents. Can you think of some other examples of what you learned about sexuality from your parents?

As we grow older, we look to our own *personal experiences and preferences* for more understanding about sexuality. For example, we might learn that we get aroused from a gentle kiss on the neck, or that alcohol helps us feel less anxious about behaving sexually. We learn that in our culture it might be okay to tell someone else about how great it felt to touch so-and-so, but it's probably *not* okay to tell anyone how great it was to touch yourself in a warm bath or shower.

For many people all over the world, *religious or philosophical teachings* are also an important source for understanding and guiding sexual behavior. These teachings differ from faith to faith and from culture to culture. Religious or philosophical traditions can sometimes be incomplete or restrictive, especially if they are the only source of information about sexuality. But an awareness of one's values and beliefs can help put sexual feelings, information, and behavior into the context of your life as a whole person.

In this book and in your course, you will be exposed to one more source of sexual information: *science*. In fact, this text will emphasize scientific knowledge. This might conjure up visions of computer screens, confusing graphs, and people in white lab coats, but that's not really what it's about at all. Science is really nothing more than a method that Western society has developed of asking and answering certain kinds of questions according to agreed-upon rules.

What are some of these rules? One has to do with the *type of questions* the scientist asks. For example, the sexuality scientist does not ask if living together before marriage is *right or wrong*. This is a moral question, best left to philosophers and theologians. The sexuality scientist might ask if there is a relationship between premarital cohabitation (living together) and divorce rates or "reported levels of marital satisfaction." Thus, the scientist does not ask if some aspect of sexuality is right or wrong, good or bad. Rather, she or he might ask how that factor is *related* to other factors. Second, the sexuality scientist answers questions about sex by collecting and examining **empirical data**. The third rule is that the knowledge must be *public*. That is, any new knowledge

must be submitted to other scientists for their examination and criticism. Most often this is done by presenting this new knowledge at a professional conference or by publishing it in a scientific journal or book. Other scientists then attempt to **replicate** the first scientist's findings, to see if his or her conclusions were justified.

Much of the information in this text will come from scholarly books, and from journals such as these:

> *American Journal of Public Health*
> *Annual Review of Sex Research*
> *Archives of Sexual Behavior*
> *Chinese Mental Health Journal*
> *Gender and Society*
> *International Journal of Law and Psychiatry*
> *Journal of Homosexuality*
> *Journal of Sex Education and Therapy*
> *Psychology of Women Quarterly*
> *Sexual and Marital Therapy*

You may want to take a look at a recent issue of one or more of these journals in your library or online to see the kinds of things sexuality scientists and practitioners are writing about. It is important for you to understand how our knowledge and understanding of sexuality develops and where you can go to increase your knowledge about a particular sexuality-related issue.

## 1.2.1 Social and Cultural Forces That Influence Our Sexuality

We normally think of our sexual expression as something private and personal. We experience our sexual preferences and behaviors as arising from within us and expressing a central aspect of our personality or personhood. However, we should recognize that there are also many environmental forces that have a great influence on how we express our sexual selves. That is, our biological potentials are filtered through and interact with many external forces that shape our sexuality (Nichols & Schwartz, 1995). Of course, human beings are not just passive recipients and responders to these external forces; we actively use them to create our sexual reality (Kelly, 1996). Let's look at some specifics.

| | |
|---|---|
| **empirical data** | knowledge derived from observation or experimentation |
| **replicate** | to redo or reproduce a study to determine if the findings are dependable or occurred by chance |

## Social Institutions That Affect Our Sexuality

Various *cultures* shape their members' sexuality in very diverse ways. For example, the nineteenth-century Victorian ideal of "true femininity" implied that sexual desires and intense sexual pleasure in a woman might call for medical intervention to reduce them (Mason, 1994). Ejaculation within a minute of vaginal insertion would be considered a sexual problem in our culture (we call it "premature ejaculation"), but this behavior is quite acceptable and expected in other cultures. Cultural influences are so pervasive and run so deep inside people, they often lead a society's members to view the sexual norms of their own culture as the only "natural" ones. This sexual **ethnocentrism** is pervasive and gets in the way of appreciating the true variety of human sexual expression.

The concept of *family* differs from culture to culture. A family may consist of a mother and her children, an adult male and an adult female and their offspring (biological, adopted, or **blended**), or an extended group, consisting of offspring, parents, grandparents, and various other parental siblings or relatives. Sometimes a whole village or clan might be considered family. Or a family might be defined by whoever inhabits a particular dwelling. The definition of family affects such issues as learning the proper roles for a "woman" or "man," how mates are selected, who instructs youngsters about sexual matters, and who is considered a desirable sexual or marriage partner.

*Religious teachings* affect many aspects of our sexuality. For example, our religious orientation might determine who we consider to be a suitable sexual or marital partner, what sexual behaviors we are willing to engage in, our attitude toward fertility control, and our acceptance of differences in sexual behavior both in ourselves and in others. Religious traditions can affect our attitude toward masturbation, how we relate to our sexual partners, the importance we place on sexual behavior in marriage, and what sexual teachings and attitudes we pass on to our children.

## Recent Social Changes That Affect Our Sexuality

Our time in history also affects our sexuality. As we enter the twenty-first century, our sexual expression will be influenced by certain changes that have recently occurred. Some of these changes have occurred only in our own society, while others are truly global in scale.

One ongoing social change in North American society is the acceptance of *premarital sexual behavior.* Some see this new norm as destructive and harm-

In light of social change, we might need to broaden our idea of what a "family" looks like.

ful to our society, believing that it has contributed to sexual callousness, the spread of sexually transmitted infections, and unwanted pregnancies. Others see it as bringing an end to the sexual *double standard,* and as an adaptive response to the strong economic pressures to postpone marriage. How do you view (or live out) this relatively new social norm?

It is difficult for most students to imagine a world in which *contraceptive devices* are illegal or inaccessible, or where knowledge regarding fertility control is considered "obscenity," but this was social reality just a few decades ago. It is still reality for many people all over the world.

Although the majority of Americans tend to select partners of their own or similar ethnicity (Laumann et al., 1994), there is now a greater acceptance of *interethnic sexual relationships.* Interethnic relationships have always existed in our society, but they were often based on exploitive or unequal social power. There was a time when relationships between people of different ethnic groups elicited ostracism, violence, or even murder. Today such relationships might still be disapproved of by many, but attitudes have become more egalitarian and accepting in many segments of our society.

While societies have a diversity of attitudes toward those who engage in sexual activities with those of their own sex, there is now *greater openness regarding homosexuality and bisexuality* in many cultures. In some segments of our society there is more toleration of this form of sexual expression; in others, very negative attitudes and behaviors prevail. However, issues related to gay men and lesbian women are now frequently examined in the headlines, mass media, courtrooms, and classrooms of our society.

Recent years have brought an *increased awareness regarding coercive and violent sexual behavior.* It is difficult for most of us to realize that up until about

Greater openness regarding same-sex relationships has resulted in advertising that openly markets to this segment of our population.

twenty-five years ago concepts such as "date rape" and "sexual harassment" did not exist. This is a good example of how knowledge or understanding about sexual phenomena may be "constructed" within a culture (Gergen, 1985). Rape, child sexual abuse, and incest were once believed to be extremely rare events, perpetrated by deranged deviants. Today, descriptions of these acts permeate our novels, movies, and news media. Sexuality researchers study them, and therapists try to help persons who are recovering from such trauma. Sexuality educators attempt to prevent such acts from occurring.

The twentieth century has been characterized by *migrations of people and their cultures* to other parts of the world (Hoerder, 1994). North America is just one of the places where large numbers of diverse people have newly settled. There may be groups in your school and community with vastly different sexual customs. You may encounter African women who have undergone—or who are fighting not to undergo—"female circumcision" (more commonly known as **female genital mutilation**). You might meet an attractive classmate who knows little about our custom of dating. You might have new neighbors who have radically different expectations for their daughters' behavior and their sons' behavior.

The *mass media* has inundated North American society with sexual images and sexual material. Much of it is frivolous and designed to sell, titillate, or entertain. Some of it seeks to enhance our sexual lives, whereas some communicates harmful or violent norms and false notions about human sexuality. Today, sexually explicit and pornographic materials are available to anyone with a television or a modem. Many believe that these materials have a very negative effect on interpersonal relationships as well as on sexual attitudes and behaviors. Others celebrate the greater openness about sexual matters.

With the *increase in affluence and leisure* in our society, many more people can afford to pursue the more pleasure-oriented aspects of sexuality. They can buy or rent videos that demonstrate exotic sexual techniques, pay to learn how to increase their orgasmic capacities, purchase penile implants to experience erections well into old age and so forth.

Thirty years after the "sexual revolution" of the 1960s, the *AIDS epidemic* has changed the way most of us view casual sexual encounters. Certainly the sexual norms of the North American gay male community have been radically altered in response to this health crisis. Today, researchers, educators, and political leaders are attempting to reach other communities, especially teenagers, intravenous drug users, and ethnic minority groups, in order to facilitate lifesaving changes in sexual behavior.

All of these forces have a direct or indirect impact on our personal sexual attitudes and behaviors. They influence our sexual thoughts, fantasies, and concerns as well as our sexual decision-making. Ultimately they affect our behavior. The ideas and information presented in this book help you deal with all of these influences as you live your life as a sexual person in the twenty-first century.

## 1.3 WAYS WE SEEK TO UNDERSTAND HUMAN SEXUALITY

### 1.3.1 The Typical Person

Because our society both idealizes sexuality and also keeps the reality of sexuality very private, most adults are very curious about sex. The average person seeks to satisfy this curiosity through several means. One's own personal sexual fantasies and experiences are a primary, but limited, source of insight into sexuality. We might also talk with others about their sexual interests or experiences, but in this day and time we also depend upon electronic and print media, literature, art, and television to fill in our "understanding."

| | |
|---|---|
| **ethnocentrism** (eth′-nō-cen′-trizm) | the belief that one's own ethnic group is superior to others |
| **blended family** | family unit made up of adults and their offspring from previous marriages or relationships |
| **female genital mutilation** | surgical removal of the clitoris and all or part of the labia (a cultural ritual) |

### 1.3.2   The Sexuality Scholar

The sexuality scholar uses three approaches to understand this aspect of living. *Historical accounts* are very useful in providing a picture of human sexual behavior (Bullough, 1990). Sexologists also find *cross-cultural comparisons* very useful because they remind us of all the different shapes human sexuality can take, and they also serve to place our society's version of human sexual expression in perspective. Lastly, sexologists apply *scientific methods* to understanding sexuality. This could involve *observations and comparisons across species;* asking people questions about their sexual attitudes and behaviors (*surveys*); watching, describing, and measuring behavior in the real world or in the laboratory (*naturalistic or laboratory observation*); studying groups of individuals who have some sexuality-related problem (*clinical studies*); or conducting carefully controlled *experiments* in the laboratory or in the field (i.e., in the real world).

These various approaches often overlap. For example, a researcher might examine and compare nudes that appear in sixteenth-, eighteenth-, and twentieth-century paintings to determine what physical features were considered attractive or ideal for men and women in each of these centuries. This combines a historical approach with a scientific one. Another researcher might survey college students in Canada, Argentina, Italy, Ethiopia, and Malaysia about their attitudes and behavior regarding premarital sex, thus combining a scientific technique with a cross-cultural approach. In section 1.4, we will examine each of the three major approaches (historical, cross-cultural, and scientific) that sexologists use to understand human sexual expression.

## 1.4   SELECTIONS FROM THE KNOWN HISTORY OF HUMAN SEXUAL BEHAVIOR

Like Jell-O, (human) sexuality has no shape without a . . . sociohistorical container of meaning and regulation. And, like Jell-O, once it is formed it appears quite fixed and difficult to re-form. A kiss is not a kiss; in this perspective, your orgasm is not the same as George Washington's, premarital sex in Peru is not premarital sex in Peoria, abortion in Rome at the time of Caesar is not abortion in Rome at the time of John Paul II, and rape is neither an act of sex nor an act of violence—all of these actions remain to be defined by individual experience within one's period and place.

   Leonore Tiefer, *Sex Is Not a Natural Act and Other Essays*, 1995, Westview Press, Boulder, CO.

### 1.4.1   Earliest Human Cultures (Mesopotamia)

Between ten thousand and thirty thousand years ago, human beings fashioned the first objects that did *not* have a direct use for physical survival (arrows, scrapers, etc., were clearly needed for survival). These objects were carefully carved statuettes of females with exaggerated secondary sex characteristics (breasts, hips, rounded buttocks), and they were often covered with markings that seemed to have symbolic significance. They have been found in many locations throughout the Middle and Near East and are often referred to as "Venus statuettes." It seems that early humans were in awe of the powers of the female body in terms of fertility and nourishment, and it is likely that some form of worship of the Great Mother prevailed in most human groups (Bullough, 1976).

As humans were transformed from hunter-gatherers into farmers and keepers of animals, the male role in fertility became recognized. The sex act itself became the symbol of fertility, so many fertility festivals involved sexual acts with priests and priestesses. Some human groups began worshiping the **phallus.**

The Venus of Willendorf (Austria), sculpted about 30,000 years ago. Note the exaggerated breasts, abdomen, and genital area. What do her armlessness and facelessness suggest to you?

## 1.4.2  North Africa and the Middle East

In ancient Egypt, women had relatively high status. They could own property, bring lawsuits, and pay taxes, but men were dominant in affairs of social and public life. Monogamy was the rule in marriage. There were also instances of marriages between brother and sister, especially among royalty (Ackerman, 1994). Temples were still dedicated to the Great Mother (now incarnated in the goddesses Cybele, Ishtar, and Isis). At these temples, sexual fertility rites included same-sex and other-sex couplings. The Egyptians recognized a place for nonprocreative sex and even developed some contraceptive technologies, such as inserting crocodile or elephant dung into the vagina and tampons made of honey and various other substances (Bullough, 1990).

Among the ancient Hebrews who wandered throughout the Middle East about 1000 B.C., quite another view of sexuality prevailed. Recognizing that social and military power came through sheer numbers, these tribes developed the biblical prescription to "be fruitful and multiply." This led to an emphasis on procreative sexuality and a proscription against any sexual expression that would not result in reproduction. Solomon's erotic *Song of Songs,* written at approximately 300 B.C., describes a guiltless approach to sensuality and a celebration of sexual expression within marriage. The Hebrew laws, as recorded in the Torah (or Old Testament) addressed a number of sex-related issues. Concerns about paternity resulted in adultery becoming a crime punishable by death for women. For men, adultery was merely a property crime against another man, and the adulterous man had only to compensate the wronged husband. Hebrew laws condemned male homosexuality and bestiality, although there was no mention of lesbian relationships in the Old Testament. No mention was made of abortion or contraception, with the exception of Onan's sin of "dropping his seed on the ground," which appears to be a condemnation of **coitus interruptus.** Later, this passage was misinterpreted as referring to masturbation (Tissot, 1766/1985).

Islam also originated in the Middle East and is based on the teachings of Muhammad, who was born in the city of Mecca around A.D. 570 or 580. Like the Bible, the Quran (Koran) is considered to be the revealed word of God. It is also a book of prescriptions and proscriptions that regulates many aspects of Muslim life. In terms of sexuality, there is a strong emphasis on controlling female sexuality, which is seen as dangerous and insatiable (Sabah, 1984). Between men and women there must be no public interactions, no dancing, and no handshakes.

Fauziya Kacinga fled to the United States from Togo to escape an arranged marriage and genital mutilation. She sought political asylum and was imprisoned here for eighteen months before being granted asylum.

Nonetheless, Islam has a tradition of treasuring marriage and marital sex (Farah, 1984). Other Muslim traditions include proscriptions against masturbation, sodomy, coitus interruptus, and intercourse with a menstruating woman. Pleasurable marital relations are seen as preventing adultery (Farah, 1984).

## 1.4.3  Asian Traditions

In Asia, a tradition of associating sexuality with spirituality arose. In Taoism, sex is seen as a sacred duty or a form of worship that could lead to immortality. The first "sex manual," *The Pillow Book,* written in Japan in about 200 B.C., encouraged frequent and extended intercourse, so that a husband could absorb his wife's *yin* (female energy) and thus enhance his own *yang* (male energy). Masturbation was acceptable for women, but not for men. Oral and anal sexual acts were acceptable as long as no ejaculation occurred, so that no semen was wasted. Chinese literature dating back to the seventh century describes same-sex relationships in terms of "the cut sleeve"—a reference to a famous ancient king who preferred to cut the sleeve of his own silken garment rather than awaken his male lover who lay upon it. Lesbian love poems were

| | |
|---|---|
| **phallus** (fa'-lus) | the penis |
| **coitus interruptus** (kō'-ih-tus ihn-ter-rup'-tus) | withdrawal of the penis from the vagina before ejaculation |

*The Kama Sutra,* a Hindu sex manual, contains many graphic illustrations of sexual techniques. Most scholars believe it was written between the third and the fifth century A.D.

Carvings from the façade of the Kandarya-Mehadeva Temple in India. The eroticism is overt and unabashed.

Same-sex sexual activities in classical Greece had a meaning that was quite different from in our own society.

written by Buddhist nuns from 520 to 480 B.C. (Bullough & Bullough, 1994) and there are records of formal associations for lesbians in nineteenth-century Shanghai (Ruan & Bullough, 1992). Under communism, the Chinese sustained decades of sexual repression. Today, new issues arise in China due to confrontations between ancient traditions and the modern world (Pan, 1993).

In India, another sex manual, the *Kama Sutra,* was written by Vatsyayana sometime between 300 and 500 A.D. This work is a compendium of descriptions and illustrations of sexual positions. It includes recipes for supposed **aphrodisiacs,** ways of kissing, and ways of touching and caressing to ensure maximum pleasure. Eleventh-century religious temples contain statuary demonstrating combinations of people engaging in remarkable sexual acts. A series of social and political upheavals led Hindu society to become much more sexually restrictive after about A.D. 1000 (Tannahill, 1980).

### 1.4.4 Greco-Roman Society

The ancient Greeks, like their Egyptian neighbors, were very tolerant of most sexual activities, as long as they did not disrupt families. Classical Athenian society idealized masculine beauty and male sexuality.

Women had virtually no rights and were confined to their homes to rear children (Ackerman, 1994).

Men engaged in many types of same-sex relationships, but, in contrast to contemporary Western society, they did not have a *social identity* as "homosexual." In Greek society, men learned their "manliness" through social and sexual contact with older men. This tradition of **pederasty,** or sexual activity between older men and adolescent males, often occurred in the context of a student-teacher relationship. The teacher-student norm may have been paralleled by Sappho, a teacher and poet. She was apparently happily married and lived on the Greek island of Lesbos with her affluent women students during the sixth century B.C.

Some other Greek sexual norms bear mentioning. Masturbation was seen as appropriate for young men who had not yet begun having intercourse, and a great many ancient writings discuss the great interest of girls and young women in acquiring *olisbos*

**TABLE 1.1**   DIMENSIONS OF DIVERSITY: GLOBAL EROTICS

From the beginning of human culture, some have devoted themselves to the creation of erotic works. Like much of today's sexuality-related material, some of it is instructive and some is entertaining. All of it attempts to celebrate an enjoyable and intense part of life.

### EARLY EROTIC WORKS

| Title | Author | Culture of Origin |
|---|---|---|
| Six Chapters of a Floating Life | Shen Sanpo | Chinese |
| Reminiscences under the Lamplight | Chiang T'an | Chinese |
| The Pillow Book | Sei Shonagon | Japanese |
| Song of Solomon | Solomon, King of Israel | Hebrew |
| Ars Amatoria | Ovid | Roman |
| Ecclesiazusae, Lysistrata | Aristophanes | Greek |
| The Perfumed Garden | Shaykh Nefzawi | Arabian |
| The Arabian Nights | unknown | Persian |
| Kama Sutra, Kama Kalpa | Vatsyayana | Indian |
| Aranga Ranga | Kalyana Malla | Indian |

**Source:** Donald McCormick, *Erotic Literature: A Connoisseur's Guide* (New York: Continuum Books, 1992).

## GO ASK ALICE

*Dear Alice,*
   *What exactly is tantric yoga and how does it affect love making?*
   *Guru*

Dear Guru,
   The tantric tradition is found in both Hinduism and Buddhism and it emphasizes both sexual and cosmic energy. Tantric yoga stresses the idea that a great vein runs from the lowest part of the spine, where the serpent power, Kundalini, rests, to the highest center, the mind (symbolized by the lotus). In Tantra, the greatest source of energy is sexual and ritualized intercourse, and orgasm is considered a cosmic and divine experience. The tantric practice called Karezza involves prolonged intercourse without ejaculation. It involves breathing control, meditation, postures, and finger pressure to prolong the state of climax without ejaculating. It is described in the *Kama Sutra* and is not learned easily. However, it can be learned with practice on your own and/or with a partner.

 http://www.mhhe.com/byer6

(self-satisfiers) either for solitary use or for sharing with a friend (Bullough, 1976). The ancient Greeks had a large slave population, and what we would now call a major "sex industry" with brothels and street prostitutes in great supply. One class of educated and refined prostitutes, the **hetaerae,** tended to be the only women viewed as suitable social companions for affluent men, and some enjoyed considerable respect and affluence through their connection with powerful men.

   The early Romans were considerably more conservative about some aspects of sexuality, and more progressive about others. Marriage by age twelve for girls and fourteen for boys was the norm. Prostitution was commonplace and, again, large populations of slaves provided these services. While Romans seemed to have many traditions of phallus worship (Priapus was a popular god), their artwork shifted from an earlier emphasis on male nudes to female nudes. Ovid's *Art of Love* was basically a handbook for extramarital seduction (McCormick, 1992). Table 1.1 lists examples of classic erotic literature from all over the ancient world.

| | |
|---|---|
| **aphrodisiac** (ah-frŏ-dē′-sē-ak) | a substance believed to increase sexual capacity or pleasure |
| **pederasty** (pe′-der-as′-tee) | sexual contact between adult men and adolescent boys |
| **hetaerae** (heh-tir′-ī) | courtesans; an educated and cultured class of female sexual companions for affluent Greek men in ancient Greece |

## 1.4.5 Christianity

Early ideas that there was something inherently shameful about sex may have come from important contemporaries of the early Christians—Greek Stoic philosophers who advocated **asceticism.** Their philosophy included the idea that the repression of emotions and pleasure was inherently virtuous. This was reflected in Augustine's (A.D. 354–430) writings that all sexual experience was lustful and shameful and would lead one to burn in hell for all eternity. Celibacy was considered the ideal, but for the weak-willed it was "better to marry than to burn." Augustine himself saw intercourse as an animal lust to be tolerated for the sake of procreation. He confessed to an erotic element in his friendships with men, and this led to his declaring same-sex relationships to be "unnatural."

Thomas Aquinas (1225–1274) condemned any sexual activity that was not procreative, and continued the tradition of sex as a "necessary evil." "Lust in the heart" became an additional sin, and led to our traditions of guilt and shame about sexual thoughts and fantasies. Aquinas' ideas became official church **dogma** in 1563 and dominated until the end of the Middle Ages. Masturbation or engaging in intercourse while unclothed, or during daylight, or in forbidden postures became sexual crimes that had to be confessed (Bullough & Bullough, 1994). By the fifteenth century, antisexual and especially antiwoman sentiments reached their apex (Bullough, 1990). In 1486, two German monks, Jakob Sprenger and Heinrich Kramer, wrote the *Malleus Mallificarum* (The Witches' Hammer)—a handbook devoted to finding evidence of witchcraft in women.

In the Eastern Christian church, established in Constantinople, castrated men, or **eunuchs,** were highly valued during the eighth and ninth centuries. Parents who were ambitious for a son's success would seek to have him castrated during boyhood. If he were smart and competent, he was likely to be appointed to high posts in the government, military, or church. Castration guaranteed that an appointee could never seek to pass on his position, property, or wealth to his own children (Bullough & Brundage, 1982).

By the seventeenth century several herbal abortive agents were known (McLaren, 1981). A woman could legally terminate her pregnancy up until she could feel the fetus move ("quickening"), and the church held that a fetus was not "ensouled" until about fourteen weeks. However, all abortion was made illegal in England in 1803; in the United States it became illegal in 1821 (Degler, 1980).

Other important events in Western history had significant effects on the practice and perception of human sexual behavior: the Renaissance, the Protestant Reformation, European colonization of the Americas, and the importation of African slaves to the West (see "Dimensions of Diversity: Sexuality and Family Life Under American Slavery"), the Age of Enlightenment, and the beginning of the Industrial Revolution. More recent events in England and the United States at the beginning of the nineteenth century had impacts on our sexuality that are still felt today, and some of these are summarized here.

## 1.4.6 Our Victorian Legacy

The Victorian era was a time of great sexual contradiction and hypocrisy. By the second half of the nineteenth century, ideas about "the true nature" of male and female sexuality had reversed. "Women" (specifically middle- and upper-class white women) were now viewed as delicate, passive, asexual, passionless creatures who were concerned only with their "proper sphere," the home (Marcus, 1966). Men were now seen as continually under the influence of their brutish lusts. Many of these ideas about the "nature" of female and male sexuality persist in some form in the West to this day. In general, our society still prescribes that women should be indirect about their sexual interests. It is generally believed that sexual drive and interest are more intense among men, that it is "natural" for men to have to persuade women to engage in intercourse, and that it takes effort to get women aroused and orgasmic. Stereotypes regarding the overly sexual nature of nonwhites also continue today (Nettles & Scott-Jones, 1987).

In England, Dr. William Acton (1814–1875) wrote a very popular book about "functions and disorders of the reproductive organs." The book is about male sexuality and contains only two passages about women, but these two passages are the ones ensconced in history: Acton declared that the normal, healthy woman was in a state of "sexual anesthesia" and that "the majority of women (happily for them) are not very much troubled with sexual feeling of any kind" (Acton, 1841, as cited in Marcus 1966, p. 31).

Meanwhile, the Reverend Sylvester Graham (1794–1851) and John Harvey Kellogg (1852–1943) became wealthy by selling graham crackers and corn flakes. These bland foods were recommended to control the masturbatory and other lustful appetites of

| | |
|---|---|
| **asceticism** (as-cet′-i-sizm) | a philosophy advocating extreme self-denial and self-discipline |
| **dogma** | a principle or doctrine believed by its advocates to be absolutely true |
| **eunuch** (ū′nuck) | a castrated male (testicles removed) |

# DIMENSIONS OF DIVERSITY

## SEXUALITY AND FAMILY LIFE UNDER AMERICAN SLAVERY

The lives and bodies of slaves belonged to their masters. Slaves were totally at the mercy and whim of their owners, and this reality permeated every aspect of their existence.

The slave-owners' norms of white female purity were based on the need to establish the paternity of heirs to property, but slaves had no property, so in that sense premarital chastity made little sense for them. However, settled, monogamous, marital unions were a powerful norm among slaves, and this was deeply ingrained in slave culture, especially by the churches. One remnant of African culture that slaves managed to keep intact was their very strong ties to an extended family. This led to strong prohibitions against marriage among cousins, a norm that did not exist among the white planter class. Among slaves, this norm often meant marriage between slaves living on different plantations—which were called "broad" marriages. The children resulting from these marriages remained with the mother and were considered the property of her master. The fathers had to obtain a pass to visit their wives and children.

Among slaves, courtship rituals varied, but it was expected that men would initiate courtship and ask the master's permission to marry. These marriages had absolutely no legal recognition, but were accompanied by a ceremony. Most common was the tradition of "jumping the broom," with a black preacher or white overseer presiding. The vows taken offer insight into the reality of the slave's life: "until death or distance do you part," or "till death or buckra (the master) part you" (Degler, 1980). After marriage, monogamy or serial monogamy was a typical pattern, largely because spouses often died or were sold away.

Two realities overshadowed the slave woman's life. Laws made it legitimate for the slave owner to "work out" his sexual desires with slave women (Katz, 1968). Mulatto children accounted for over one-fifth of the children born out of wedlock in Virginia in the early 1800s (D'Emilio & Freedman, 1988). Second, many slave women had additional roles as "breeders" who could increase their masters' wealth by producing children who could then be sold. This was especially true after the overseas slave trade was abolished in 1807. One rice planter gave some "rest" privileges to slave women who had six children alive at any one time (Gutman, 1976). See the photo of an announcement of a sale of slaves, to understand the prevalence of all of these sexual norms.

---

BY

## HEWLETT & BRIGHT.

### SALE OF

### VALUABLE

# SLAVES,

### *(On account of departure)*

The Owner of the following named and valuable Slaves, being on the eve of departure for Europe, will cause the same to be offered for sale, at the NEW EXCHANGE, corner of St. Louis and Chartres streets, on *Saturday,* May 16, at Twelve o'Clock, *viz.*

1. SARAH, a mulatress, aged 45 years, a good cook and accustomed to house work in general, is an excellent and faithful nurse for sick persons, and in every respect a first rate character.

2. DENNIS, her son, a mulatto, aged 24 years, a first rate cook and steward for a vessel, having been in that capacity for many years on board one of the Mobile packets; is strictly honest, temperate, and a first rate subject.

3. CHOLE, a mulatress, aged 36 years, she is, without exception, one of the most competent servants in the country, a first rate washer and ironer, does up lace, a good cook, and for a bachelor who wishes a house-keeper she would be invaluable; she is also a good ladies' maid, having travelled to the North in that capacity.

4. FANNY, her daughter, a mulatress, aged 16 years, speaks French and English, is a superior hair-dresser, (pupil of Guillac,) a good seamstress and ladies' maid, is smart, intelligent, and a first rate character.

5. DANDRIDGE, a mulatto, aged 26 years, a first rate dining-room servant, a good painter and rough carpenter, and has but few equals for honesty and sobriety.

6. NANCY, his wife, aged about 24 years, a confidential house servant, good seamstress, mantuamaker and tailoress, a good cook, washer and ironer, etc.

7. MARY ANN, her child, a creole, aged 7 years, speaks French and English, is smart, active and intelligent.

8. FANNY or FRANCES, a mulatress, aged 22 years, is a first rate washer and ironer, good cook and house servant, and has an excellent character.

9. EMMA, an orphan, aged 10 or 11 years, speaks French and English, has been in the country 7 years, has been accustomed to waiting on table, sewing etc.; is intelligent and active.

10. FRANK, a mulatto, aged about 32 years speaks French and English, is a first rate hostler and coachman, understands perfectly well the management of horses, and is, in every respect, a first rate character, with the exception that he will occasionally drink, though not an habitual drunkard.

All the above named Slaves are acclimated and excellent subjects; they were purchased by their present vendor many years ago, and will, therefore, be severally warranted against all vices and maladies prescribed by law, save and except FRANK, who is fully guaranteed in every other respect but the one above mentioned.

TERMS:—One-half Cash, and the other half in notes at Six months, drawn and endorsed to the satisfaction of the Vendor, with special mortgage on the Slaves until final payment. The Acts of Sale to be passed before WILLIAM BOSWELL, *Notary Public,* at the expense of the Purchaser.

*New-Orleans, May 13, 1835.*

PRINTED BY BENJAMIN LEVY.

---

An advertisement for the sale of slaves in New Orleans in 1835. Note the high number of slaves of mixed ethnicity. Note also the absence of any indication that young children would remain with their parents. Dandridge, Nancy, and Mary Ann might well all be separated by this sale.

---

Contributed by Theresa Meyers

# AT ISSUE

## WHO WERE THE MOTHERS AND FATHERS OF MODERN SEXOLOGY?

**HENRY HAVELOCK ELLIS (1859–1939):** Ellis, an unconventional English physician, established the sexological tradition of challenging unfounded ideas about human sexuality. In his *Studies in the Psychology of Sex,* he suggested that lovemaking could be pleasurable for both partners, homosexual interests might be inborn, masturbation could serve as means of mental relaxation, and there were *erogenous zones* of the body.

**SIGMUND FREUD (1846–1939):** Freud highlighted the centrality of sexuality in normal human development. He emphasized how important it was to not repress sexual energy (libido), but to channel it appropriately (his ideas about what was appropriate were quite conservative). Because psychoanalytic ideas dominated thinking about sexuality from about 1930 to 1960, one of the tasks of modern sexologists has been to disprove many of the ideas that originated with Freud and his disciples. Some of these harmful ideas were that (a) his patients' accounts of childhood sexual abuse were mere "fantasies" (Kilpatrick, 1992), (b) only immature women experienced orgasms through stimulation of the clitoris (Masters & Johnson, 1966), and (c) sexual attraction to persons of one's own sex implied immaturity and psychological maladjustment (Strickland, 1995).

**CLELIA DUEL MOSHER (1863–1940):** Mosher's life stands in sharp contrast to Victorian norms. Mosher showed that the severe menstrual pains that "naturally" incapacitated Victorian women were caused by the then-fashionable constrictive corsets worn by middle- and upper-class women (see figure 1.1). These corsets damaged women's internal organs and

deformed their bone structure. Mosher also determined that fear of menopause was more psychological than physical. It was Mosher rather than Kinsey who conducted the first known sexuality survey (Bullough & Bullough, 1994; Jacob, 1981). Her questions inquired about such intimate issues as reasons for intercourse, frequency of orgasm, whether contraception was used, and desired and actual frequency of intercourse. Contrary to prevailing beliefs, Mosher found that her middle-class respondents desired intercourse and experienced relatively frequent orgasms with their husbands. About two-thirds of her respondents used some form of contraception; methods included withdrawal, douching, "male sheaths," and the use of various ineffective substances, including cocoa butter (Jacob, 1981).

**MAGNUS HIRSCHFELD (1868–1935):** Hirschfeld is considered to be the founder of scientific sexology (Bul-

lough & Bullough, 1994; Vyras, 1996). His works dealt with topics such as love, sex crimes, and even the impact of maternal alcoholism on the developing fetus. He was the first to distinguish between homosexuality and *transvestism.* Hirschfeld established the first scientific journals devoted to sexuality in general, and then to homosexuality. He was both consultant and actor in the first film aimed at educating the public about homosexuality (*Different from the Others*). In Berlin, his Institute for Sexual Science housed the first marital counseling clinic, medical and research facilities, and an impressive library devoted to sexuality. This internationally recognized institute provided lectures for professionals and informational sessions for the general public. It offered treatment for sex-related problems such as infertility and sexually transmitted infections. While Hirschfeld was on an international tour, Nazis destroyed the institute and publicly burned its 20,000 volumes,

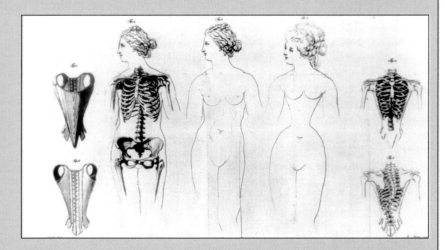

**FIGURE 1.1**   To be attractive and fashionable, Victorian women permanently damaged their bodies with tight corsets. Can you think of any current fashion statements that are dangerous and damaging to the body?

*Who Were the Mothers and Fathers of Modern Sexology—continued*

Magnus Hirschfeld, a man whose work was threatening to the forces of authoritarianism and bigotry in Nazi Germany.

35,000 photographs, and 40,000 biographical documents. Some irreplaceable documents were smuggled out of the country, but their location is still a mystery. A few other materials made it to the Kinsey Institute for Sex Research in Bloomington, Indiana.

### MARGARET SANGER (1879–1966):

Two events shaped Margaret Higgins-Sanger's attitudes toward sexuality. She attributed her mother's early death to her seven miscarriages and eleven live births. Secondly, while working as a nurse among the immigrant poor of New York City, she witnessed the death of one of her penniless patients after repeated self-induced abortions. Sanger thereafter devoted herself to achieving reproductive rights for women. She attempted to provide poor women with information about the safest and most effective contraceptives then known, and published articles about female sexuality in the journal *The Woman Rebel.* When she mailed contraceptive information to married couples, she was indicted under the infamous Comstock Laws, which classified her pamphlets and booklets as "obscene material." She and her sister opened the first American birth control clinic in Brooklyn,

New York. Police raided the center, and imprisoned both women. The trial was a public spectacle and Sanger became widely known, nationally and internationally. Sanger was convicted, and when she successfully appealed the conviction, she won the right for doctors to provide contraceptive information (but only to cure and prevent disease). She established the organization that later became the Planned Parenthood Federation of America. In 1936, Sanger initiated the case *United States v. One Package,* which resulted in freedom for physicians to send and receive contraceptives through the mail.

### EVELYN HOOKER (1907–1996):

In 1992, Dr. Evelyn Hooker won an American Psychological Association award for distinguished contributions to psychology in the public interest. Her work was a major factor in the decision of the American Psychiatric Association to no longer consider "homosexuality" a mental disorder (Hooker, 1993). Hooker (1957) matched a group of gay men with a group of heterosexual men in terms of age, education, and IQ levels. She took detailed life histories, administered several personality inventories, and a battery of psychological tests. She then asked several professionals to distinguish the heterosexual men from the homosexual men based on their psychological profiles and test results. Their inability to do so showed that there were no psychological differences between the two groups, demonstrating that gay men were neither more nor less psychologically healthy than heterosexual men.

A flyer distributed to poor immigrant women in the neighborhood surrounding Sanger's birth control clinic. The languages represented are Yiddish, Italian, and English.

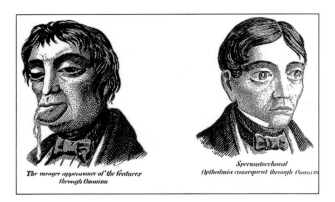

The results of "self-pollution" dramatically illustrated in a nineteenth-century text.

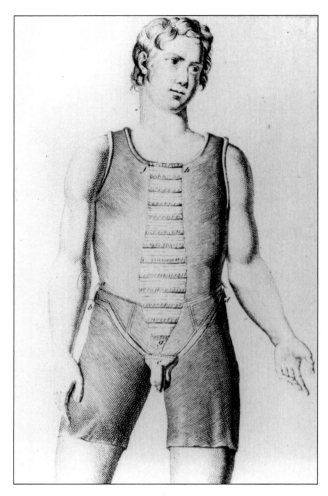

Antimasturbatory technology.

young men. According to many popular medical writers and moral leaders of the day, masturbation was clearly the cause of epilepsy, a pale complexion, pimples, blindness, memory loss, and even insanity. Quack medicinals and cruel and humiliating devices were sold to prevent the "vice of self-pollution" in adolescent boys. Girls found to be masturbating might be subjected to clitoridectomy (Mason, 1994). It was in this world of extreme sexual prudery and hypocrisy that Sigmund Freud developed his theory that conflicts about sex lay at the core of mental illness.

In the United States, the leaders of the Social Purity movement began to support sexual abstinence as the only way to better the health of women. This eventually led to support of the Comstock Laws, which classified contraceptive information and devices as "obscene materials" (Gordon, 1976).

In spite of all of the public posturing regarding sexual virtue and restraint, prostitution flourished in both England and the United States. Some historians estimated that during the late nineteenth century London was home to about eighty thousand prostitutes; authorities counted twenty thousand prostitutes in Manhattan in 1830 (D'Emilio & Freedman, 1988; Gilfoyle, 1992).

The Victorian era was also characterized by extreme ambivalence toward homosexuality. While such activity had previously been considered merely a sin, it was now criminalized. At the same time, homosexual activity flourished in the all-male English educational institutions, where, in a very repressive atmosphere, it took on a sadistic flavor. To this day, flagellation (whipping associated with erotic arousal) is known as the "English vice."

This brief history suggests that control of sexuality is an issue of power. In the West, the *church* controlled sexual expression up until about the beginning of the Renaissance. Attempts to control sexuality then gradually passed over to an increasingly powerful *state*

(Harrison, 1978). Beginning in the eighteenth century, and up through the present, *science* (and all too often **pseudoscience**) began to assert itself as the last word on human sexual expression (Bullough, 1990).

### 1.4.7 Feminism

The term **feminism** properly refers to political, social, and economic equality for both sexes (McCormick, 1996). While many tend to see the feminist movement as beginning during the 1960s, the first wave of organized feminism in the United States came in the early twentieth century with the fight to win the vote (Bullough, 1996). It soon became apparent that unless women could control their fertility, they could never really manage their lives and improve life for their children. In the United States, the fight for the right to obtain and use contraceptive information and services persisted into the 1950s. In the 1960s, feminists (both women and men) began a second struggle for economic, social, and sexual equality. The fight for **reproductive rights** (David, 1994) was one facet of this new wave of feminism. Contraceptive options were critical, and the right to abort an unwanted pregnancy was seen as a key issue in giving women control over their own fertility. This debate regarding the rights of women versus protection of the developing fetus has yet to be resolved. But once again, technological innovation is likely to change this debate forever, as RU-486 and similar drugs become easily available (see chapter 15).

A second aspect of the impact of feminism on the history of sexuality involved revelations regarding the many ways girls and women are sexually exploited: the virtual enslavement of many poor young girls into lives of prostitution, as well as the biases in the traditional laws surrounding rape, sexual assault, sexual abuse, and sexual harassment. Feminist women and men around the world have helped change both laws and attitudes concerning these behaviors.

A third aspect of feminism's impact on twentieth-century Western sexuality is increased acceptance of differences in human sexuality: the view that there are many "human sexualities" and that they all are legitimate means of sexual self-expression as long as there is no harm or exploitation of self or others. Thus, celibacy, bisexuality, homosexual relationships, heterosexual relationships, marriage, coparenting, single parenthood, cohabitation, childlessness, and remaining single are all viewed as acceptable life choices. What are your attitudes about this perspective?

## 1.5 THE SCIENTIFIC APPROACH TO UNDERSTANDING SEXUALITY

An important approach to understanding human sexuality involves the application of scientific methods to answering questions about sexuality. A "scientific approach" involves trying to answer questions about sexuality according to certain agreed-upon rules (the scientific method). This is called scientific **research.** These rules have to do with what kinds of questions are asked, how information is collected to answer those questions, how to evaluate and interpret that information, and how to communicate that information to other scholars and to those who will use the knowledge to help other people (**applied practitioners**). Physicians, sex therapists, marriage and family counselors, and nurses are all applied practitioners who might use new information about sexuality.

We should begin by noting that there are lots of problems in conducting sexuality research. There are *environmental* problems. For example, people with certain political views are opposed to scientific investigations of sexual behavior (Udry, 1993). They believe that sexual behavior is a moral issue or a very private act, and simply should not be examined. Cer-

tain religions hold that clergy, not scientists, should be in control of sexual knowledge. In addition, there are many cultural taboos against asking people questions about their sexual behavior or attitudes.

Even if these are somehow overcome, there are many *technical* problems. For the moment we'll just list them, and then later we'll take a closer look at these issues as we learn about the specific methods used to study sexual behavior.

1. Obviously, a researcher cannot question all the people on the planet about their sexual behavior or attitudes, so information is gathered from a **sample** of respondents. But how can one be sure that the sample *represents* an accurate cross section of people in terms of age, ethnicity, marital status, educational level, sexual orientation, and so forth? Accurate *sampling* is always an important technical problem. Other related problems have to do with respondents' poor memory, inadequate vocabulary, and misinterpretation of questions.

2. How can the researcher be sure that just the *act of measuring* some attitude or behavior doesn't influence the behavior? For example, if a couple knew that the amount of time they spent stimulating each other before joining in coitus were being measured, might they increase (or decrease) that time just because it was being measured? Some political leaders believe that questioning adolescents about their sexual activities results in an increase in teen sex, and so they oppose surveys of teen sexuality (Holden, 1994).

3. People have a tendency to present themselves in the best possible way. When people are asked if they have ever used force or trickery to get someone to be sexual, are they likely to accurately report this? What if they simply forget that they have ever done so? This problem is called **self-report bias.**

| | |
|---|---|
| pseudoscience (sū′-dō-sī′-ens) | a theory or practice that has no scientific basis |
| feminism | belief in the social, economic, and political equality of the sexes |
| reproductive rights | legal and political control over various aspects of reproduction |
| research | scholarly or scientific investigation or study |
| applied practitioner | a professional who applies scientific knowledge to assist others |
| sample | a portion that represents a whole population |
| self-report bias | a tendency to offer a generally favorable description of one's own behavior or attitude |

4. Later on you will read how William Masters and Virginia Johnson got volunteers to come to their laboratory and engage in various sexual acts while connected to electrodes and probes. How likely is "a regular person" to volunteer for such research? How likely is your partner to volunteer? See the problem? Are people who volunteer for such research different in some important way from people who refuse to volunteer (Clement, 1990)? What about people who respond to the "sex questionnaires" that appear in *Cosmo* or *Playboy*? Are their sexual attitudes and behaviors likely to be different from those who never read magazines or from those who subscribe to *Scientific American*? The sex researcher is forever dealing with the issue of **volunteer bias** (Bogaert, 1996).

5. Here's another tough one. If research participants show a particular response in the laboratory, or if thousands of college students answer a sexual question a particular way, is it safe to conclude that this response also occurs outside the lab? What about the responses of everybody who is not attending college? In other words, can the findings in one situation or the responses of one population group be **generalized** (applied) to other situations or groups?

6. Scientists depend on their own creativity and available technology to study what intrigues them. Just as scientists could not study bacteria until they had microscopes to make microbes visible, sexuality scientists could not study the process of physiological arousal until they had the proper instruments to do so. You will learn more about **plethysmography** later. Understanding of sexuality is constrained by *technological limitations*. *Psychological pleasure* is clearly an important aspect of human sexuality. What kinds of technological innovation would allow researchers to be able to compare how much psychological pleasure is felt during different kinds of kissing or during various fantasies?

7. Scientists, and therefore sexologists, cannot go around doing whatever they please to satisfy their curiosity. Researchers, applied practitioners, and educators are all guided by a set of **ethical principles** designed to *safeguard the welfare* of research participants, patients or clients, and students.

## 1.5.1   Why You Should Understand the Specific Methods Used to Study Human Sexuality

While it is unlikely that you will become a *producer* of scientific sexual information, virtually every reader of this text will become a *consumer* of such knowledge. At various points in our lives, we all have to make decisions about some aspect of our sexuality. For example, how does a heterosexual couple decide which type of contraception makes the most sense for them? What kind of information would help a lesbian couple decide whether to adopt a child or try artificial insemination? What's the best way to proceed if your supervisor or professor is making annoying sexual comments, or touching you in ways that scare or intimidate you? To make better decisions, people often need information, and not all information is equally valid or useful. By understanding the specific methods used to collect or produce information, as well as the strengths and weaknesses of each of those methods, you can determine how much weight to place on various types of information or data.

## 1.5.2   The Survey: Taking a "Photograph" of Patterns of Sexual Behavior

**Surveys** involve asking people questions, recording their answers, and analyzing groups of responses to uncover patterns of behavior or attitudes. It is like taking a photograph, because a good survey offers a still picture of sexual attitudes, behaviors, and values at one particular moment in time. Sometimes written questionnaires are used and sometimes face-to-face or telephone interviews. To get accurate data, survey researchers have to deal with quite a few issues. Failure to deal effectively with these problems results in a useless collection of numbers. One of the biggest problems is *sampling*. Here's a real-life example. Shere Hite (1976) set out to learn about the sexual attitudes and behaviors of American women. She sent out over 100,000 questionnaires to readers of women's magazines, members of feminist groups, and women frequenting university centers. (Does this sound like a cross section of American women to you?) Only 3 percent of the questionnaires were ever returned. This study clearly did not survey a representative sample, and it was further flawed by a terribly low **response rate**. Thus, this information tells us virtually nothing about the sexual behavior and attitudes of American women. Yet *The Hite Report* became a best-seller and popular writers still make reference to it.

In spite of the many weaknesses of surveys, the pioneering work of Alfred Kinsey (1894–1956) deserves special mention. In the 1940s and 50s, Alfred Kinsey and his associates interviewed 16,000 Americans about their sexual behavior. The responses of 5,300 men and 5,940 women formed the basis for *Sexual Behavior in the Human Male* (1948) and *Sexual Behavior in the Human Female* (1953). (Note that in spite of their titles, neither of these surveys looked at *human* sexual behavior in general; the researchers *merely attempted to describe American sexual behavior in the 1950s*). Rather than a representative sample, Kinsey interviewed a **sample of convenience,** and this resulted in the overrepresentation of certain groups (educated people) and the underrepresentation of other groups (Jews, Catholics, and African Americans). In spite of its many flaws, the work of Kinsey and his associates will always have a special place in the history of sex research. Before these efforts, literally no one knew how Americans conducted their sexual lives.

Kinsey and his colleagues tried to take a verbal and statistical photograph of American sexual life in the 1950s. Three findings caused particular upset. First, about half the women interviewed were sexually active before marriage and were enjoying non-procreative sex as much as men were. Second, the incidence of masturbation far exceeded polite predictions and popular assumptions. Actual rates were 90 percent for men and 62 percent for women. Most startling of all, Kinsey found that 4 percent of men described themselves as exclusively homosexual, while many others reported occasional or intermittent same-sex contact. Kinsey and his colleagues developed a seven-point scale on which to graph the incidence of same-sex behavior and concluded that it was inaccurate to believe that most men could be classified as *either* homosexual or heterosexual: sexual orientation seemed to exist along a continuum.

Some other surveys worth mentioning include Bell, Weinberg, and Hammersmith's (1981) ground-breaking survey of the sexual attitudes and behavior of gay men and lesbian women: their sample was limited to those living in the San Francisco area. Blumstein and Schwartz (1983) conducted a very intriguing survey, *American Couples,* describing and comparing a large and diverse sample of heterosexual, gay, and lesbian couples. Gail Wyatt and colleagues (Wyatt, Peters, & Guthrie, 1988a, 1988b; Wyatt & Dunn, 1991) explored the sexuality of white and African American women in three small studies. Most recently, Laumann et al. (1994) completed the National Health and Social Life Survey (known as the NHSLS, for short). These researchers used the most sophisticated survey methodology available to obtain a **representative sample** of 4,369 *households.* Eventually 3,432 *individuals* completed interviews, for a remarkable response rate of 80 percent. While their sampling and methodology are not perfect, their photograph seems as clear and detailed as scientists can presently make it (see "At Issue: Patterns of Contemporary American Sexual Expression"). Like the Kinsey report, the NHSLS caused an uproar, but for different reasons. This survey found that although Americans clearly engage in a wide array of sexual activities, they are much less sexually active than is generally believed. They also found that the vast majority of respondents are quite satisfied with their sexual lives.

Alfred C. Kinsey, a true pioneer who changed our understanding of American sexual behavior.

| | |
|---|---|
| **volunteer bias** | behavioral and attitudinal differences that exist between those likely to volunteer and those who are not |
| **generalization** | the degree to which a characteristic or claim is applicable to other individuals or groups |
| **plethysmography** (pleh-thiz-mah'-gra-fee) | measurement of the size or state of an organ based on the amount of blood flowing through it |
| **ethical principles** | guidelines for moral or correct conduct in a relationship |
| **survey** | a method of studying a topic by forming specific questions and asking them of a specific group |
| **response rate** | the proportion of those contacted in a survey who respond |
| **sample of convenience** | a survey target group that is easily available or from whom it is easy to collect data |
| **representative sample** | a survey target group that has the important characteristics of the whole population |

### 1.5.3   Naturalistic and Laboratory Observation

Obviously, **observation** refers to watching people's behavior. Some observational research is carried out in the *field,* that is, it involves watching people in their *natural environment.* A fair amount of sexuality-related behavior takes place in public. For example, a person's gender will affect all sorts of public behaviors, and one can observe flirting behavior in bars, at social gatherings, or even in the student center.

The work of William H. Masters (a gynecologist) and Virginia E. Johnson (a psychologist) represents the best-known examples of laboratory observation in the area of human sexuality. The goal of their research was to reveal the actual physiology of sexual arousal and response. They recruited 700 volunteers who agreed to have intercourse while connected to an electrocardiograph (heart monitor), an electromyograph (which measures changes in muscle activity), and other devices. Penile erection and vaginal changes were measured with a **penile strain gauge** and a **vaginal photoplethysmograph.** Their pioneering work resulted in remarkable insights into the physiology of sexual activity. Thousands of such laboratory observations formed the basis for their book *Human Sexual Response* (1966), and also their well-known and highly accepted four-stage model called the *human sexual response cycle.*

Although most sexologists view the work of Masters and Johnson as a major contribution to the understanding of sexuality, a few critics see their work as unethical. Others have found fault with their methodology (Tiefer, 1995). How would you evaluate their work in terms of what you now know about *measurement effects, volunteer bias,* and *generalizability?* Some insist that a more accurate title for their book might have been "Sexual Responses of Relatively Affluent Americans Who Volunteer to Have Orgasms while Monitored by Scientists."

### 1.5.4   The Experiment: Searching for Causes

To investigate **cause-and-effect relationships,** sexual researchers turn to the **experiment.** This technique often involves taking a sample of volunteers and **randomly assigning** each of them to one of two or more groups. Because the groups are formed randomly, there should be no important differences between the two groups on most factors. One group, the **experimental group,** is then exposed to some **variable** while the other group (the **control group**) is not. After exposure to this variable, the two groups are compared again on some factor of interest. Let's describe a simplified version of a series of experiments carried out to answer the important

The research of William Masters and Virginia Johnson resulted in another level of understanding of sexual response.

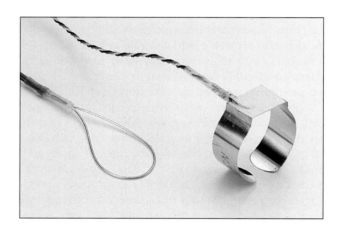

**(a)**

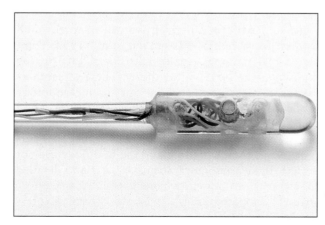

**(b)**

**a:** A penile strain gauge, and **b:** a vaginal photoplethysmograph. These devices are used to measure blood flow to the genitals, thus giving an indication of level of arousal.

question of whether exposure to violent pornography could *cause* men to behave more aggressively toward women. Donnerstein, Linz, and Penrod (1987) *randomly assigned* college men to one of three groups. Because of random assignment, it was assumed that all three groups were initially equivalent in their aggressiveness. One group was exposed to mildly erotic films, a second was exposed to explicit but nonviolent pornography, and the third was exposed to pornography that showed high levels of sexual violence toward women. Later, supposedly in the context of another study, *all* of the men had the opportunity to "deliver painful shocks" to a woman whom they believed to be another research participant. (Actually no shocks were ever administered.) The men who were exposed to the violent pornography "administered" the highest level of shocks. Since all three groups were assumed to be equivalent in aggressiveness before the experiment, it was concluded that the increase in aggressiveness on the part of members of one group (the one exposed to violent pornography) was *caused by* exposure to the violent pornography. Experiments offer a high degree of control, precision, and the opportunity to learn about which factors cause effects in other factors. However, experiments have been soundly criticized for being very artificial and therefore having little *generalizability.* Just because these male students behaved this way in the highly unusual setting of a psychology laboratory, can we safely conclude that men in the real world would behave this way too?

### 1.5.5 Examining Correlational Studies

Almost every week one hears a news story about how researchers have found a *relationship* or *association* between two factors or variables relevant to sexuality. For example, the likelihood of developing cervical cancer is *related to* (or **correlated** *with*) the number of different male sex partners a woman has had over the years she has been sexually active (Sikstrom et al., 1996). That is, the more male partners a woman has, the greater her likelihood of getting cervical cancer. Many people don't understand that just because researchers found a *relationship* between these two factors, it does not mean that having more sexual partners *caused* women to develop cervical cancer. Women who have many sexual partners might also engage in many other behaviors that result in cervical cancer. Or some unknown factor might lead some women to have many sexual partners *and* to develop cervical cancer. Recently, it has been shown that cervical cancer is not *caused* by "many sex partners." It is actually caused by infection with the human papilloma virus, or HPV. An increased number of coital partners or beginning sexual intercourse at an earlier age

increases the odds that a woman will be infected with HPV at some point in her life (Associated Press, 4 April 1996, as cited in "Cervical Cancer Deaths Preventable," 1996, p. 5). When you read or hear a report about a relationship between two factors, you need to know if the researcher was describing the findings of a *correlational study* or an *experimental study.* As we saw, experiments can tell us if a factor could *cause* some *effect,* but correlational studies cannot.

### 1.5.6 Clinical Research

Sexuality researchers often study groups of individuals who manifest some type of disorder or dysfunction. Because they come to the researcher or practitioner for help or treatment, they are described as a **clinical population** (an in-depth study of a single *patient* is called a **clinical case study**). For example,

| | |
|---|---|
| observation | the describing or recording of ongoing, visible behavior |
| penile strain gauge | a device used to measure penile engorgement during arousal |
| vaginal photoplethysmograph (fō′-tō′-pleh-thiz′-moh-graf) | a device used to measure engorgement of the vaginal walls during arousal |
| cause-and-effect relationships | how changes in one variable affect or cause change in a second variable |
| experiment | a research method in which one of two or more equivalent groups is exposed to a treatment to measure its effect on some variable of interest |
| random assignment | assigning research participants to groups in such a way that each participant has an equal chance of being in any group |
| experimental group | the group in an experiment that is exposed to some treatment or variable |
| variable | any factor that can vary in level, size, or intensity |
| control group | the group in an experiment that is *not* exposed to some treatment or variable |
| correlation | a relationship or association between two naturally occurring variables |
| clinical population | patients/group seeking, or identified as needing, treatment |
| clinical case study | an in-depth study of an individual patient |

## AT ISSUE

### PATTERNS OF CONTEMPORARY AMERICAN SEXUAL EXPRESSION: SOME FINDINGS FROM THE 1994 NATIONAL HEALTH AND SOCIAL LIFE SURVEY (LAUMANN ET AL., 1994)

#### WHO PARTICIPATED IN THE SURVEY?

Making use of the latest thinking about scientific sampling, 3,432 individuals were surveyed. They ranged from 18 to 59 years of age. This final sample represented an 80 percent response rate.

#### SOME INTERESTING (AND SOME UNEXPECTED) FINDINGS

- Eighty percent of those interviewed had one or no sexual partner in the year preceding the interview.
- Ninety percent of women and slightly more than 75 percent of men surveyed reported marital fidelity.
- Married people have more sex than singles do, but cohabiting singles have the most sex.
- About 75 percent of the married women reported they usually or always had an orgasm during intercourse. Ninety-five percent of the men reported orgasms during intercourse.
- The size of the population who identified themselves as having a same-sex orientation was found to be smaller than previously estimated (2.8 percent of male respondents and 1.4 percent of female respondents).

- Asking relevant questions differently brought different responses regarding same-sex orientation. About 9 percent of men and 5 percent of women had at least one same-sex experience. Forty percent of the men in this category had their experience before age 18. The majority of the women in this category had their same-sex experience after age 18.
- The three most preferred sexual activities for self-identified heterosexuals were (in order of preference) vaginal intercourse, *watching a partner undress,* and oral sex.
- More than half the men, but only 19 percent of the women, reported they thought about sex every day.
- About half of all cohabiting relationships last less than one year.
- Masturbation was generally regarded as a normal and healthy sexual outlet, particularly among males.
- Masturbation was more common among those between 24 and 34 compared to younger age groups.
- Contrary to the myth that adults masturbate if they do

not have an available sexual partner, those who had the most sex with others also tended to masturbate the most.
- About 80 percent of the white college-educated male respondents regularly engaged in oral-genital stimulation, but only 51 percent of the African American respondents (regardless of education) did.
- Men engaged in more overall sexual behavior with more partners (median number was 6) compared to women (median number was 2). However, the range was great, with 26 percent reporting one lifetime partner. One woman reported 1,009 partners and one man reported 1,016.

#### CRITICAL THINKING QUESTIONS

1. Which of the above findings are most and least in keeping with popular beliefs about American sexuality?
2. Which findings are most surprising to you?
3. Which findings would you guess would be very different if this survey were conducted in 1954 or in 2044?

you might read about clinical studies that involve older men who suffer from erection problems, or women who experience pain during intercourse.

Clinical studies are invaluable for helping scientists understand the problematic aspects of sexuality,

but such studies have an important weakness. Failure to understand that a clinical population is *not representative* of a whole population can lead to terrible biases and injustices. For example: As the idea of seeking psychotherapy or counseling for psychological or emotional problems became more socially acceptable, many lesbian women and gay men sought help with their personal problems. During these years homosexuality was so hidden and considered so mysterious in our society, these gay men and lesbians (as well as those in prison and mental hospital populations) were the only ones available for scientific study. Because this clinical population demonstrated psychological problems, many practitioners concluded that *all* gay men and lesbian women were poorly adjusted. This is simply not true, as Evelyn Hooker clearly showed in her research (see, p. 12, "At Issue: Who Were the Mothers and Fathers of Modern Sexology?").

## 1.6 ETHICAL ISSUES IN SEXUALITY RESEARCH, PRACTICE, AND EDUCATION

Ethics serve as guides about how people should treat each other, and set limits on what is acceptable behavior between people. What goes on between the sexuality researcher and the research participant, between the counselor or therapist and the client or patient, and between the educator or supervisor and the student, all constitute a real human relationship. However, these are relationships of unequal power and influence, so there must be safeguards to protect the rights and welfare of the person in the more vulnerable role. You may recall that sexology is a multidisciplinary field, and so professionals will be guided by the ethical principles developed by their respective professional groups such as the American Medical Association or the American Psychological Association. In addition, the American Association of Sex Educators, Counselors and Therapists has developed its own set of ethical principles to guide its members (AASECT, 1993). These principles exist primarily for the benefit of the consumer of sexual knowledge and society in general. As students, and as potential counseling/therapy consumers or research participants, you should be aware of these ethical guidelines.

First, the sex educator, counselor, therapist, or supervisor should have adequate *competence and integrity* in the area of sexuality to perform their tasks optimally. Competence in the area of sexuality is acquired through formal education, training, and practice and through supervision by a more qualified person. Integrity includes knowing the limits of one's competence and relating to the consumer in a way that benefits the consumer.

Second, sexologists will adhere to the recognized professional *moral, ethical, and legal standards* of their usual profession. This includes rejecting any inhumane practices and avoiding dual relationships that could harm the consumer or reduce the consumer's rights.

Third, recognizing that the consumer is vulnerable, the sexological professional acts in a way that *promotes the welfare of the consumer*. This principle covers issues such as appropriate confidentiality, the safety of the consumer and others to whom the consumer relates, dealing with minors and their parents, rejecting any sexual involvements with the consumer, and informed consent. Informed consent means that the student, client, or research participant understands the nature of what will happen in the relationship and voluntarily agrees to participate.

The fourth principle deals with the *welfare of students, trainees, and others*. This includes maintaining high standards of scholarship, not coercing or requiring students or trainees to become participants in research, and also rejecting any dual relationship that could harm the student or trainee. The sexuality scholar must also be concerned with the *welfare of research participants*. This means that any research proposal must be reviewed by qualified peers to be sure that the study follows accepted ethical standards and protects participants from harm. Researchers must be qualified to carry out the proposed study, protect the confidentiality of participants, and be honest and accurate with participants and consumers about the nature and results of the research conducted.

## 1.7 CRITICAL THINKING ABOUT HUMAN SEXUALITY

There are many definitions of critical thinking. For our purposes, **critical thinking** is *the avoidance of biases and preconceptions as we evaluate information, claims, and arguments* (Smith, 1995; Wade & Tavris, 1996). A lot of information about sex is available, but a fair proportion of it is *misinformation*. How can you separate the useful from the useless, the truth from the trash? Critical thinking is a tool to help you do just that. To take a look at some of your own attitudes, see "Where Do I Stand? Attitudes and Personal Sexual Expression."

---

**critical thinking**    awareness and avoidance of biases and presumptions in evaluating information, claims, and arguments; using facts and logical reasoning to reach conclusions

# WHERE DO I STAND?
## ATTITUDES AND PERSONAL SEXUAL EXPRESSION

All through this text you will find references to *sexual attitudes* and how they influence a person's sexuality. In the spirit of the first principle of critical thinking (*understanding terms and concepts*), it seems wise to take a moment to explore exactly what attitudes are and how they are related to our actual behavior or our evaluation of others' behavior.

An **attitude** is a positive or negative evaluation of an object. The "object" could be a person or group of people, things, events, or issues. Attitudes are related to a person's *beliefs, feelings, and behavior* toward the attitude object (Franzoi, 1996). For example, your attitude toward anal intercourse probably comes from your beliefs about whether such activity is normal, healthy, or moral (do these criteria sound familiar?). You might also consider whether this behavior is legal or illegal where you live. Your feelings might be based on your personal experiences around such behavior.

Use the scale below to describe your attitude toward the following sexuality-related "objects." On what beliefs, feelings, and behaviors are your attitudes based?

If so inclined, you can compare the attitudes of various subgroups in your class on these items: women versus men, students of traditional college age (18–22) versus those who are over 35, married versus unmarried, the various ethnic groups represented in your class, etc.

My attitude toward each of the following is best described as

| 1 | 2 | 3 | 4 | 5 |
|---|---|---|---|---|
| Very Favorable | Unfavorable | Neither Unfavorable nor Favorable | Favorable | Very Favorable |

Masturbation                                                     _____

Intercourse in the absence of a caring relationship            _____

Male genitals                                                    _____

Female breasts                                                   _____

Commitment to a monogamous relationship                         _____

Breast-feeding infants in a public place                         _____

The **sexual double standard**                                  _____

Sex toys                                                         _____

Pornography                                                      _____

Love and romance                                                 _____

Sexual attraction to a blind person                             _____

Same-sex relationships                                          _____

You may want to consider how your attitudes about these affect your sexual behavior.

---

## 1.7.1   Some General Guidelines for Thinking Critically About Human Sexuality

1. *Understand the meaning of terms and concepts.* Some chapters in this book contain a section called "What's in a Name?" In science and sexuality, it is very important to know what we are naming. For example, what is a person's **gender** and is that different from a person's **sex?** Scholars have found it useful to distinguish between the two. What's the difference, if any, between a **transvestite** and a **transsexual?** In order to examine information or discuss a controversial issue in sexuality, we must agree on what we mean by particular terms.

2. *Adopt an attitude of healthy skepticism.* When advertisers, researchers, or even sexuality instructors make claims, be wary. One of the benefits of depending on science for understanding the "truth about the world" is that our understanding can change. It was once said to be

"true" that an advanced education for women led to shrunken breasts, a withered uterus, and deformed children (Hall, 1904). Our society sees the relationship between women's education and fertility quite differently today.

3. *Question conventional wisdom.* The idea that "Everyone knows . . ." can be dangerous. For example, "everyone knows" that in the United States, the *number* of births to unmarried teenagers is alarmingly high. However, what is not conventionally known is that the *proportion of sexually active teens who become parents is lower than it has ever been* (Kantor & Haffner, 1995). Why? More sexually active teens use contraceptives, and more teens terminate their unwanted pregnancies. As you proceed through this course and through this book, be on the lookout for information that challenges conventional wisdom about sexuality.

4. *Identify the assumptions and biases behind claims and arguments.* This is tough, because it goes back to the very roots of how we know what we think we know. For example, during the last several decades, male infants born in the United States were routinely circumcised. Many assumed that because this practice was so prevalent, there must be an important health benefit from removal of the foreskin. Many parents wanted their sons circumcised so that their child wouldn't appear "different." But in 1999, following an analysis of numerous scientific and medical studies, the American Academy of Pediatrics issued the following statement: "Existing scientific evidence demonstrates potential medical benefits of newborn male circumcision; however these data are not sufficient to recommend routine neonatal circumcision" (American Academy of Pediatrics, 1999). Since then, the frequency of circumcision in the United States has declined, but for years, the practice was based on mistaken assumptions and cultural biases.

5. *Develop a solid knowledge base so you have reasons and information to support your own beliefs and values.* Do you believe that men who like to dress in women's clothing are homosexual? Do you believe that most married men have extramarital affairs? Do you believe that access to condoms encourages teenagers to have intercourse? Are these beliefs based on dinner table conversation or talk-show programs? Or perhaps amusing stories from an uncle or a neighbor? Did you read about this in *Cosmo* or *Playboy?* This book will attempt to offer you the most *current scientific knowledge* about these issues and many others. The goal is for you to have a current, solid knowledge base for your beliefs and values.

6. *Try to evaluate the quality of arguments, evidence, or claims.* In 1990, a physician in Atlanta and a second in Mexico City claimed that they could cure HIV (human immunodeficiency virus) infections by heating and replacing the blood of infected individuals ("Once Rejected AIDS Treatment Resurfaces," 1994). At what point should AIDS patients, physicians, the general public, and you accept this claim? The Atlanta patient was later found not to have HIV, the Mexico City patient died, and no other physicians could duplicate their results. However, recently (Steinhart et al., 1996), a variation of this treatment was tried again with fairly good results. Should this claim be accepted now? At what point, and under what circumstances, should other scientists or you accept any claims of a cure or improvement due to new procedures or technologies?

7. *Be open-minded: make room for new information that contradicts old beliefs.* Many people assume that gay men and lesbian women do not have children. However, researchers found that about 25 percent of lesbian women have children from previous relationships with men. More recently, with the greater availability of artificial insemination, changing values within the lesbian and gay communities, and new adoption policies (including easier international adoptions), the

| | |
|---|---|
| **attitude** | a positive or negative evaluation of some "object" (person, group, idea, behavior, etc.) |
| **sexual double standard** | belief that certain behaviors are acceptable for one gender but not for the other |
| **gender** | a societally constructed status to which one is assigned (boy or girl, woman or man) |
| **sex** | a biological status (female or male), typically based on the appearance of one's genitals |
| **transvestism** | dressing in the clothing and ornamentation usually associated with the other gender |
| **transsexualism** | intense and prolonged psychological discomfort with one's sexual anatomy, often to the degree that one seeks surgery to "correct" the condition |

percentage of lesbian women and gay men who have children is rising substantially (Patterson, 1994, 1995). What about the popular belief that rapists are mentally ill? Or the belief that men cannot care for infants as adequately as women can?

8. *Don't oversimplify or overgeneralize.* We all rely on our own personal experience to make judgments and come to conclusions. However, this can lead to erroneous thinking and even dangerous behavior. In the past, many believed that the most common rape scenario was when a deranged stranger attacked a woman in a dark, deserted area. We now know that most rapes are committed by dates and acquaintances (Koss, 1992, 1993).

What about the following examples of knowledge gained by personal experience? "My neighbor Jane is only thirteen years old and is pregnant. Nowadays, teenagers tend to be very promiscuous." Or what about the women and men on a recent talk show: "They all had terrible eating disorders and they all said they were sexually abused when they were kids. People with eating disorders have been sexually abused when they were children." It is important not to generalize from these personal "stories." These are **anecdotal reports**; they might be very vivid and personally meaningful, but they do not tell us what is happening to *most* people.

| | |
|---|---|
| **anecdotal reports** | stories of individual experiences or observations that may or may not be representative |

## SUMMARY

1. Our sexuality includes our biological sex, reproductive roles, gender roles, sensual and sexual pleasure, the initiation and maintenance of intimate relationships, lifelong sexual expression, problematic sexual expression, and concern about sexually transmitted infections.

2. Typical sources for our personal sexual knowledge are our peers, parents, media, and schools, and our own experiences. This text will emphasize scientific inquiry as a useful source for learning about sexuality.

3. Although our sexuality emerges from our biological and psychological selves, it is shaped by many environmental forces. These include various social institutions (cultural norms, family, religion), and social changes.

4. The sexuality scholar depends on historical accounts, cross-cultural comparisons, and scientific research methods to understand human sexuality.

5. Historical information from Mesopotamia, North Africa, the Middle East, Asia, ancient Greece and Rome, the Christian West, the Victorian Age, and the decades since the second wave of feminism reveals a wide variety of prescriptions and proscriptions for sexual behavior.

6. The scientific methods used to study sexuality include surveys, naturalistic and laboratory observation, experimentation, correlational studies, and clinical research. Each method has its own strengths and weaknesses.

7. There are several important ethical principles that guide the activities of sexuality educators, practitioners (counselors, therapists and supervisors), and researchers. The welfare of the student, trainee, client/patient, and research participant is protected through standards for such things as professional competence, avoidance of harm, informed consent, no sexual intimacies, freedom from coercion, confidentiality, accuracy in instruction, and institutional approval for research projects.

8. Critical thinking involves the avoidance of biases and preconceptions in evaluating information, claims, and arguments.

9. Some general guidelines for critical thinking involve
   a. understanding the meaning of terms;
   b. healthy skepticism;
   c. questioning conventional wisdom;
   d. identifying assumptions and biases;
   e. developing a solid knowledge base;
   f. evaluating the quality of arguments, evidence, or claims;
   g. open-mindedness;
   h. looking for alternative explanations; and
   i. not oversimplifying or overgeneralizing.

## CRITICAL THINKING CHALLENGES

1. How have your attitudes about sexuality been influenced by your family? Your religion? Your friends? Your culture? Try to identify ideas you hold where more information might affect your thoughts or opinions.

2. Locate a recent article about a sex-related topic in a newspaper, magazine, or the Internet. Read it critically, asking yourself the following questions: What is the purpose of the article? Does it provide accurate information? What could I do to confirm its accuracy? How will this information be used?

3. Imagine that you are a sexuality researcher. What type of study would you plan? How would you present your project to a granting agency? To the public? What are some of the technical difficulties with your method that you should consider?

# COMMUNICATION AND SEXUALITY

**AFTER STUDYING THIS CHAPTER, YOU SHOULD BE ABLE TO**

[1] List and explain seven principles that apply to all communication.

[2] Describe some gender differences in communication styles.

[3] Explain how communication between people of different ethnicities can be enhanced.

[4] Explain nonverbal communication and how verbal and nonverbal messages can conflict.

[5] Describe common flirting behaviors.

[6] Explain some ways to meet potential partners.

[7] Explain the differences between sexual coercion and sexual consent.

[8] Describe the communications that are appropriate when it appears that a relationship will become sexual.

[9] Explain effective ways to say no to unwanted sex.

[10] Describe several ways in which communication in gay and lesbian couples might differ from communication in heterosexual couples.

[11] Distinguish "I" statements from "You" statements and explain the likely outcome of each kind.

[12] Explain effective ways of resolving conflicts in relationships.

[13] Describe how an adequate sexual vocabulary can enhance sexual communication.

[14] Explain techniques of effective speaking and listening.

[15] Contrast passive, assertive, and aggressive behavior.

[16] Distinguish and explain sexist communication and nonsexist communication.

[17] Explain the content of effective home and school sexuality education.

Placing communication among the first topics in this text reflects the significance of effective communication in relationships, whether or not sex is a part of them. The quality of your relationships is central to the quality of your life. Rewarding relationships enable you to learn more about yourself, build your self-esteem, and grow. Clear and open communication between people helps build richer, closer, and more effective and rewarding relationships where growth can take place.

## 2.1  PRINCIPLES OF COMMUNICATION

Certain principles apply to all of our communication, whether sexual or nonsexual. Understanding these principles of communication can help us improve our sexual communication habits. Weaver (1993) has identified some principles that affect all interpersonal communication.

Words are only part of our communication. Look at all of the nonverbal clues visible as these people talk together.

- **Communication can be verbal or nonverbal.** The words we use convey only part of our message—often the smallest part. Nonverbal communication includes such behaviors as facial expressions, posture, and gestures. Furthermore, the same words can take on very different meanings when conveyed by different voice qualities, such as different volume, pitch, speed, and inflection. For example, the phrase *I love you, too* can have entirely different meanings when spoken sincerely and when spoken sarcastically.

- **You cannot *not* communicate.** Communication is more than just the exchange of words. Even without making any sound, you communicate through your body language—your facial expression, posture, manner of dress, grooming, and other visible clues. Even your silence can carry a powerful message. A single touch can communicate a lot. Without opening your mouth, you reveal far more about yourself to others than you may realize. For example, gazing into a person's eyes for even a few seconds longer than your culture considers "normal" can convey sexual interest, curiosity, anger, or other nonverbal messages (Razack, 1994).

- **Every communication contains information and defines relationships.** The *content dimension* in communication involves the information carried through the words used. The *relationship dimension* involves the feelings conveyed through both words and our many nonverbal symbols. For example, a message stated in a very factual way might be interpreted as being "cold." The same message could be stated more "warmly" by changing a facial expression or putting a different inflection on a word or two.

- **Communication relationships can be equal or unequal.** The way we communicate with people is influenced by whether we see our status as basically equal or unequal. In relationships based on equality, both people usually try to minimize the differences and emphasize the similarities between them. People in unequal relationships (in terms of age, occupation, wealth, or other status factors) might do just the opposite. Weaver (1993) notes that neither type of relationship is necessarily better than the other. Some people function best in equal relationships, others in unequal relationships. For example, Jennifer's interest in Christopher is mainly sexual: Christopher's main interest in Jennifer is that she pays his rent while he is in school. The patterns of communication in this relationship would probably reflect Jennifer's sexual dependency upon Christopher and Christopher's financial dependency upon Jennifer. Each partner might or might not feel comfortable with the arrangement.

- **Communication in relationships develops over time.** Patterns of communication within a relationship gradually change over a period of time as changes occur in the way the participants think of each other and define the rules governing their relationship. Each partner learns the meaning of a particular tone on a certain word, the meaning of a particular facial expression or gesture. Even a simple raised eyebrow can convey a huge message to a knowing person. Conversely, some couples maintain a communication (or perhaps we ought to say noncommunication) style that depends mainly on mind reading and guessing. Every couple is unique, and over time its style of communication becomes similarly unique. For example, to a couple who know each other well, "Do you feel like a nap?" might mean "I'm horny. Let's have some sex."

- **Communication is an ongoing process.** Our communication experiences are cumulative; each communication is influenced by what has preceded it. To fully understand any single communication, we need to know all that has come before it. A casual observer could easily misinterpret a conversation taking place between two long-term friends.

- **Communication is irreversible.** "Think before you speak" remains very important if you are to develop and maintain valuable relationships. Is there anyone who has never, in anger or frustration, said something that he or she later wished had remained unsaid? But remarks can never be taken back, and it is difficult to undo the damage done by a careless remark. When the occasional slip does occur, every effort can be made to minimize its impact. A sincere, honest explanation of the frustration, anger, or other feeling that motivated the remark can lead to a productive conversation. For example, "I feel really bad about what I said today. Nothing had gone right at school all day long, and I guess I just had to take my frustration out on someone. I chose you because I feel the most comfortable with you. I hope you will be able to forgive me."

## 2.2 THE CONTEXT OF COMMUNICATION

Communication never takes place in a social "vacuum." Every instance of communication is influenced by characteristics of each participant, such as their age, gender, education, and ethnicity. Here we will explore the effects of gender and culture on communication.

### 2.2.1 Gender and Communication

Problems in relationships at home, at work, and in other settings, often are direct results of the different communication styles of the genders (Tannen, 1990; Glass, 1992). Lillian Glass (1992) lists *105* communication differences between men and women, including differences in body language, facial language,

speech and voice patterns, language content, and behavioral communication patterns. Gender differences have even been reported in how we use e-mail (Allen, 1995).

A Canadian study (Kolaric & Galambos, 1995) suggests that communication differences between the genders might be narrowing as a new generation grows up. Observation of verbal and nonverbal communication in adolescents fourteen to sixteen years old indicated much more similarity than difference between the genders.

Deborah Tannen (1990) believes that gender-related communication differences reflect the different ways in which members of each gender tend to view relationships. Comparing the sexes, Tannen states that men tend to be more concerned with their independence and status in the social order. Their conversations are negotiations in which they try to achieve and maintain the upper hand if they can, while protecting themselves from others' attempts to put them down and push them around.

Tannen says that women, on the other hand, tend to approach the world as individuals in a network of connections. In their world, conversations are negotiations for closeness in which people try to seek and give confirmation and support, and to reach consensus. They try to protect themselves from others' attempts to push them away. Life is seen as a struggle to preserve intimacy and avoid isolation.

Tannen concludes that women, like men, are concerned with achieving status and avoiding failure, but these are not primary goals on which they constantly focus. Similarly, men, like women, are concerned with achieving intimacy and avoiding isolation, but they are more focused on attaining and maintaining status and independence.

If it is true that women tend to speak and hear a language of connection and intimacy, while men tend to speak and hear a language of status and independence, then the stage is set for misunderstandings and misinterpretations. Not seeing style differences for what they are, people draw faulty conclusions about each other, such as "You don't listen," "You are putting me down," or "You don't care about me."

Women are more likely than men to use *tag questions*. A tag question is a short phrase that turns a statement into a question. For example, "That was a hard test, wasn't it?" Instead of simply saying "That was a hard test." One interpretation of this is that women's tendency to use tag questions reflects uncertainty. A tag question is seen as weakening the statement being made. Another interpretation, however, is that the tag question encourages the other person to express an opinion. Rather than reflecting uncertainty, women's use of tag questions might reflect a greater sensitivity and warmth. This is an illustration of how different interpretations, one favoring men and the other favoring women, can be made of the same information.

Women and men tend to use somewhat different *intonation patterns* (Hyde, 1991). Women are more likely to communicate surprise, cheerfulness, and politeness and to use a wider range of pitches. Though this allows women to express a wider range of emotions, some men interpret women's speech as being overly emotional and high-pitched.

The final verbal difference we will mention might come as a surprise. Though we stereotype women as talking more than men, in terms of total talking time, *men talk more than women* (Hyde, 1991). This is especially true in a mixed-gender group, where men will often dominate the conversation.

There are also some gender-related differences in nonverbal communication. For example, *women tend to smile more than men* (Hyde, 1991). We can only speculate on why this is, but smiling appears to be a part of the stereotypical female role. People tend to expect women to smile. A woman's smile does not necessarily reflect happiness or friendliness and can even be associated with fear or other negative feelings.

Another nonverbal communication difference noted by Hyde (1991) is that women tend to prefer to *stand or sit closer* to other people while men tend to prefer a greater distance. The reason for this difference is unclear.

Also uncertain is the relationship between gender and *touching*. Most studies (e.g., Hall, 1996) have shown that, while talking, men touch women slightly more often than women touch men. Whether touching relates to power and dominance issues, sexual interest, or expression of warmth, solidarity, or caring is not always clear. In another study on gender and touching, Guerrero and Anderson (1994) explored touching in dating and married heterosexual couples. Touching behavior was similar between seriously dating or married partners, but not between casual daters. In the same study, women reported less-positive attitudes toward other-sex touch than did men. Finally, men initiated touch more in casual relationships, but women initiated touch more in married relationships.

How can couples learn to communicate with each other in ways that avoid misinterpretation? Since it seems unlikely that the two genders will soon adopt the same style of communication, the most realistic "fix" for this problem is for us to learn to speak clearly and to listen carefully. We must try to phrase our own messages in ways that people can understand and accept. We must learn how to interpret each other's messages accurately.

Some researchers maintain that men have, since the 1960s, been getting unfair criticism on their communication styles (Wood & Inman, 1993). Women's styles have been equated with intimacy and praised while men's have been equated with activity and devalued. Woods and Inman contend that men's communication styles are valid and that the greater legitimacy awarded to women's styles impairs research, teaching, and interpersonal contact.

In a similar tone, Twohey and Ewing (1995) express an opinion that men do have a "voice of intimacy," but that listening for evidence of intimacy in men's communication with ears attuned for how women express intimacy prevents understanding or even hearing the male voice of intimacy.

Simply knowing that the genders have different conversational styles helps us to recognize and accept differences without blaming ourselves, our partners, or our relationships. Neither communication style need be seen as superior to the other; they are just different. We can ask for clarifications or rephrase our statements without implying that either party is to blame for the communication difficulty. Understanding each other's ways of communicating is a big step toward smoother relationships.

One last point involves gender bias rather than gender-based communication differences. As women in many organizations have long suspected, research has shown that women's ideas can be devalued in a mixed-gender decision-making group (Propp, 1995). An idea introduced by a man has a higher probability of acceptance and use than if it were introduced by a woman. Female-introduced ideas are likely to be evaluated more stringently. Until the day comes when gender equity is achieved, if women in mixed-gender groups want their ideas to be taken seriously, they should speak with authority and demonstrate their competence clearly.

## 2.2.2  Culture and Communication

More than through any other characteristic, the nature of a culture is revealed through its traditions of communication. In fact, one definition of culture is that it is a "metacommunication system." Effective communication, and thus understanding, between people of different cultures involves much more than simply speaking the same language.

**Cultural diversity** refers to people with a variety of histories, ideologies, traditions, values, lifestyles, and languages living and interacting together. The United States is increasingly a nation with large populations of people representing many different ethnic groups. Many partnerships involve people of different ethnicities. Communication difficulties between ethnic groups might involve language barriers, but they also can reflect basic cultural differences that impair communication even when language differences are not a

# DIMENSIONS OF DIVERSITY

## SOME EXAMPLES OF CULTURAL COMMUNICATION DIFFERENCES

The following is a survey of some published cultural differences in communication styles. Keep in mind that while these individual studies can be informative, they should not be used to create or perpetuate cultural stereotypes.

- It has been reported that African Americans are more tolerant of people talking about their own accomplishments (boasting) than are white Americans (Kochman, 1981).

- The British, in contrast, tend to find *all* Americans annoyingly boastful (Tannen, 1994).

- In greeting, Americans often ask "How are you?" while Burmese ask "Have you eaten yet?" and people in the Philippines often ask "Where are you going?" To outsiders, each of these questions might seem intrusive. But to the last

question, the expected reply is simply "Over there," just as the expected reply to "How are you?" is simply "Fine" (Tannen, 1994).

- Americans tend to value direct communication, while the Japanese hold in high regard those who communicate indirectly, implicitly, subtly, and even nonverbally (Lebra, 1986).

- Greeks or Greek Americans are more likely than other Americans to interpret a question as being an indirect way of making a request. "Do you want to take your break now?" would be interpreted as "Take your break now" (Tannen, 1994).

- British conversations tend to move at a slower pace with longer silent periods than is

characteristic of American conversations (Tannen, 1994).

- Samoan mothers do not talk down to their children in the way that American mothers do, but talk to them just as they would to an adult (Ochs, 1992).

- In India a compliment is interpreted as meaning that the complimenter is asking for the admired item because custom dictates that an admired item be given as a gift (Holmes, 1989).

- Japanese adults rarely say no, considering the use of the word *no* to represent immaturity and weakness, something characteristic of children. Saying no is avoided by using silence, ambiguity, or expressions of regret, doubt, and apology (Clancy, 1986).

---

factor. In culture A, for example, communication might tend to be very direct and to the point. In culture B, the same topics might be approached indirectly, via allusions and inferences, without actually stating the message in any direct way. Members of culture A will probably not understand what members of culture B are trying to say, while members of culture B will perceive members of culture A as being overbearing or rude. For more examples, see "Dimensions of Diversity: Some Examples of Cultural Communication Differences."

In sexual communication, an understanding of cultural differences in communication habits is essential. Many relationships involve people of different cultures who may have very different approaches to sexual communication. If we are not careful to make ourselves very clear and to ask for clarification of ambiguous messages, serious misunderstandings can result.

For example, with the increasing numbers of international students and faculty on United States

college and university campuses have come increased accusations of sexual harassment. Tyler and Boxer (1996) studied the reactions of U.S. undergraduates and international teaching assistants (TAs) to twelve classroom scenarios. They found that language and behavior that is perceived as sexual in the United States might not be so perceived in other societies. They also found that certain sexually suggestive verbal and nonverbal behaviors might be more tolerated in societies outside of the United States, given the present sensitivity to sexual harassment in this country.

Here are some suggestions to enhance sexual communication between members of different cultures:

---

| **cultural diversity** | people with a variety of histories, ideologies, traditions, values, lifestyles, and languages living and interacting together |

▮ Develop an understanding of your own cultural values and biases. Most of us tend to be somewhat **ethnocentric,** assuming that the ways of our own culture are "best" and judging other cultures by how closely they approximate our own.

▮ Develop an understanding of the cultural values, beliefs, and customs of the other ethnic group(s) with which you interact.

▮ Be respectful of, interested in, and nonjudgmental about cultures other than your own.

▮ Speak in a way that promotes understanding and shows respect for someone from a different ethnic group. Be especially careful to avoid statements that could be interpreted or misinterpreted as disparaging a partner's ethnic group.

▮ Avoid using sexual slang or idioms that might be misunderstood by someone from a different ethnic group.

▮ Remember that the same gestures can carry different meanings in different cultures. Observe closely the use of gestures by people in different cultures and try to avoid body language that might be offensive or misunderstood.

▮ If you are conversing in English with someone who is fairly new at speaking English, listen very carefully to what she or he says. If you don't understand a certain word, you might ask to have it spelled or written out for you.

▮ Don't assume that someone who speaks less-than-perfect English or speaks English with an accent is not intelligent or has nothing important to say. Remember that he or she speaks at least two languages, even though at least one of them might be spoken with an accent.

## 2.3  NONVERBAL COMMUNICATION

Effective communication requires being alert to the many nonverbal signals we receive from others. Nonverbal communication includes what we commonly call "body language," meaning posture, gestures, and facial expressions. How we speak—the tone, force, tempo, and inflection we give to each word—is a part of nonverbal communication, as is how we dress and how close to someone we stand while speaking. Even information we might prefer not to reveal is readily conveyed nonverbally.

Nonverbal communication is influenced by numerous factors. It reflects the personality of the individual, the setting, how she or he feels in respect to others present, and to some degree, her or his cultural or ethnic background (Kenner, 1993). Kenner found that some hand movements are culture-specific, while others are common to a wide range of different cultures.

Cultures differ not only in the appearance of their nonverbal signals, but also in how they interpret the same nonverbal signal (Schimmack, 1996). For example, in one study, Japanese and American (U.S.) subjects interpreted the same smiling and nonsmiling faces differently (Matsumoto & Kudoh, 1993). Each culture made different assumptions about the social-personality characteristics associated with smiling faces; Americans associated more positive characteristics with the smiling faces than did the Japanese.

The better you know an individual, the better you are able to read his or her nonverbal signals. Close friends often carry on complex exchanges of information without the use of a single audible word. When people are less familiar with each other, and especially when they represent different cultures, misperceptions can easily occur.

There are major cultural differences in the use of eye contact. In some ethnic groups, such as European Americans, eye contact during communication is valued and expected. People who make eye contact are rated favorably and those who avoid it are viewed with suspicion (Droney & Brooks, 1993). Eye contact is the most frequently used courtship initiation tactic (deWeerth & Kalma, 1995; Kleinke & Taylor, 1991). And rightly so, because eye contact often leads to romantic attraction (Williams & Kleinke, 1993). In other groups, such as some Native American and some Asian cultures, eye contact is generally avoided or used quite minimally, and members of those cultures are offended when people who are unaware of this look into their eyes (Razack, 1994).

One area where misperceptions occur is in the use of touching as a form of nonverbal communication. Usually touching is a positive gesture, such as a pat on the back, a hug, a high five, a handshake, or a kiss. A simple touch can convey affection, caring, joy, empathy, sympathy, or many other emotions. Humans have a basic need for the touch of other humans, and touching is considered important for maintaining emotional health.

Occasionally, touching is, or is interpreted as, an expression of power or domination over a person. Different people might respond quite differently to the same touch. One person might appreciate it as a symbol of closeness or caring; another might view it as an invasion of her or his private space. Like most nonverbal communication, touching is interpreted differently by people of different cultures. People from cultures, such as some Asian cultures, where very little touching is practiced, can be very disturbed by a well-intentioned touch. Also, as described earlier in this chapter, there are gender-related differences in touching habits.

### 2.3.1 When Verbal and Nonverbal Messages Conflict

We have all had the experience of talking to someone whose nonverbal messages clearly contradict the person's words. Which message are we to believe? With only rare exceptions, the nonverbal message will be more accurate. It is easy to control our choice of words, but very difficult to control our tone of voice, facial expression, posture, and other nonverbal signals.

## 2.4 COMMUNICATION IN NEW RELATIONSHIPS

Communication patterns vary in the different stages of a relationship. Here we discuss communication in the early stages of relationships.

### 2.4.1 Flirting

**Flirting** is using nondirect tactics to signal interest in a potential partner. The word *flirting* probably has somewhat different meanings for different people. One Merriam Webster dictionary defines *flirt* as "to behave amorously without serious intent." Whether or not there is "serious intent" probably depends on the individual and the circumstances.

Setting is important in how people perceive flirting. In a study of university undergraduates, the same behavior was more likely to be perceived as flirting when it occurred in a bar than when it occurred in a classroom. Also, the same behavior was considered more flirtatious when more effort was expended, as in crossing a room to speak to someone (Downey & Damhave, 1991).

In almost every culture, specific flirting behaviors are common in each gender. Flirtation behavior can be verbal or nonverbal. A certain subtle facial expression, posture, gesture, or comment can, by most people within a culture, be instantly identified as flirtation (Moore, 1995).

Some of the most common ways of signaling interest in someone include gazing, smiling, eye contact, and leaning toward the person (Grammer, 1990; Kleinke & Taylor, 1991; deWeerth & Kalma, 1995). Males, more than females, also tend to use verbal tactics to express interest. Males also have a greater tolerance for nonverbal signals of interest from a stranger (Kleinke & Taylor, 1991). This probably reflects a woman's greater risk of being coerced or forced into unwanted sexual activity.

Flirting behavior in the workplace, although an old tradition, has become somewhat problematic today, as the line between flirting and sexual harass-ment can be blurry (Cooper, 1990). Many fine relationships do develop among coworkers. Most of us spend of lot of time at work, and people who work together have at least that much in common with each other (see section 2.4.2). But proceed cautiously. Any approach behavior that is both *unwanted* and *repeated* qualifies as being sexual harassment.

### 2.4.2 Meeting and Getting to Know Someone

Some people, especially those who think of themselves as "shy," find that meeting and getting to know a potential new partner is a challenge to their communication skills. In addition to feeling awkward about initiating a conversation, there can be an underlying fear of being rejected.

In general, the most productive places to meet potential partners are places where people share common interests. Many relationships form on the job, at school, at a church or temple, at a gym or fitness center, or in an organization or group pursuing a shared interest such as hiking, bicycling, art, music, acting, or computers. It's also common for relationships to form between "friends of friends."

People with more limited opportunities for meeting others help support the huge "singles industry," including singles bars, cruises, resorts, tours, clubs, and apartments. Also increasingly popular are ads in magazines and classified advertising sections. Note the older age range typical in the ads in figure 2.1. Note also that the women's ads more often emphasize attractiveness while the men's ads more often emphasize success (Davis, 1990).

The Internet plays a major role in the social and sexual communication of millions of people. For some, it is an excellent way to meet intimate partners; for others, anonymous cybersexual experiences provide a way to avoid intimacy (American Association of Sex Educators, Counselors, and Therapists, 1996b). A high degree of anonymity and deception is possible. For example, some researchers estimate that as many as one-third of the "women" having cybersex with people in Internet chat rooms are actually men (American Association of Sex Educators, Counselors, and Therapists, 1996b).

| | |
|---|---|
| **ethnocentric** (eth-no-cen′trik) | assuming that the ways of one's own culture are "best" and judging other cultures by how closely they approximate one's own |
| **flirting** | using nondirect tactics to signal interest to a potential partner |

| Women Seeking Men | Men Seeking Women | Women Seeking Women | Men Seeking Men |
|---|---|---|---|
| **CAPTIVATING** Exceptional woman for exceptional man. SWF, 33, 5'7", health-oriented, seeks professional SWM, 40s, 6'+. | **AFFLUENT** Man of the world looking for petite, slim, attractive South American 38–45. | **COULD U B** The one? ISO full-figured, honest, decent LF. Me: same. Any race, kids OK. | **CLEAN-CUT** Masc, good-looking, handsome, straight acting, GWM, HIV–, healthy ISO mature, stable, masc, straight acting WM, 35–55. |
| **ALL NIGHT LONG** SWF, 34, 5'9", 125#, sharp, sexy, intelligent, ISO SWM, 35–47, successful, brainy, fearless. | **NO WHINING** In shape, funny, SJ prof, 42, ISO trim, understanding SJF. | **SECURE** Very good-looking, masculine, 32, ISO very fem, fun-loving LF for special relationship. | **HANDSOME** GBM, 34, passionate, new in town, passive, 6', slender, ISO assertive GM, 25–40, any race, for fun and friendship. |
| **CAN'T HELP IT** Brainy, good-looking, trim DJF, red hair ISO outstanding DJM, 57–65 for an exceptional journey. | **VERY GOOD LKNG** SWM exec, 52, 5'10" ISO young attractive F 4 fun, travel, romance. | **BI HAWAIIAN** I'm 38, petite, activist. ISO Hawaiian, African American, or Pac Islander sister to chill with. | **FIREMAN** GWM, 28, coll educ, athletic, in top shape, ISO buddy, no G scene. |
| **LIFE PARTNER WNTD** SF, 35, active, fit, fin. sec. ISO marriage-minded man, 33–40 w/no kids. | **SEXY** Very good looking, 39, successful, prof, SWM, 6'3", love to sail, ski, travel, ISO beautiful, tall, athletic F, 26–39, for adventure and romance. | **LOVELY/LOVING** HLF, 24, beautiful body, ISO feminine LF, any race, 18–30, to be more than just friends. | **SINCERE** GWM, 25, 5'7", 140#, professional, ISO straight acting, sincere, in shape, GHM, 25–35, for long-term relationship. |

**Abbreviations:** A: Asian; B: Black; C: Christian; D: Divorced; F: Female; G: Gay; H: Hispanic; J: Jewish; L: Lesbian; M: Male; S: Single; W: White; ISO: In search Of

**FIGURE 2.1**   Some "personals" classified ads—real ads, modified just enough to make it legal to reproduce them.

More positively, the Internet is an excellent way for people to meet. People who have difficulty connecting with others often find it easier to communicate through the Internet. It provides a comfortable forum for saying those first few words and taking the first steps toward knowing each other. So long as the interaction remains strictly on-line, it is physically safe, and it forces people to take turns in communicating and not interrupt each other.

If you are going to meet in person someone you "know" through the Internet, some safety precautions are advised. Meet for the first time in a public place, and don't share your address, phone number, or last name until you have gotten to know each other better.

## 2.5  NEGOTIATING SEXUAL BEHAVIOR

Almost everyone has values defining when sexual activity is acceptable and desirable. Sexual values and the process of deciding whether to engage in a particular sexual experience are discussed in several other chapters in this text. Here we will discuss sexual coercion and saying yes or no to sex.

### 2.5.1  Sexual Coercion Versus Sexual Consent

Potential sexual partners need to discuss past sexual histories, expectations, commitment or noncommitment, sexual limit-setting, and disease control *before* becoming sexually involved; other-sex partners must also discuss fertility management. It is not always easy to communicate openly and honestly about such issues. But it takes such communication to ensure that a relationship is consensual, honest, and mutually pleasurable.

The essence of sexual consent is honest, direct communication about desires, hopes, expectations, and consequences. But seldom is this concept portrayed in the popular media. In TV programs, movies, and music the message is that sexual interactions should be spontaneous and instantaneous in the heat of passion. Rarely do the media portray people having discussions about their decision to have sex or to set sexual limits or discussing how they will prevent pregnancy or the transmission of disease. Unfortunately, many members of the public follow this media example in their own lives, letting sex "just happen." Their lack of planning and communication lead to our nation's high rates of unplanned pregnancy and sexually transmitted diseases, and cause many people to feel that they have been sexually coerced or exploited.

The media aren't entirely at fault for our lack of sexual communication. Some people avoid discussing sex with a potential partner because they are afraid that it will decrease their chances of having sex. Others might like to talk to a potential partner about sex-related issues but lack the confidence or vocabulary or just don't know how to get the discussion started.

Let's focus now on the issue of sexual *consent* versus sexual **coercion**. This is an important issue, as nearly one-quarter of all women and about 2 percent of men state that they have been forced against their will to do something sexual at some time (Haffner, 1995/96).

Charlene Muehlenhard (1995/96) points out that sexual consent requires adequate knowledge as well as freedom from coercion. "Consent is meaningless unless given freely."

The knowledge necessary to give consent comes from many sources, including sexuality education from parents, schools, and the media. Information is also needed from the partner involved. Some people lie in order to encourage a partner to agree to sexual activity. In one survey, 35 percent of men who held traditional sexual values reported lying to women to obtain sex (Muehlenhard, 1995/96). In such situations, there is no way the woman can give informed consent.

"Freely given consent" implies that there is no penalty for failure to give consent. For example, if one partner is financially or emotionally dependent on the other and the dependent partner's saying no to sex would mean the end of the relationship, then an element of coercion is present. On a societal level, the cultural rewards for heterosexual activity (marriage, child custody, insurance benefits, etc.) and sanctions against homosexual activity (family and career difficulties, for example) represent coercion toward heterosexual activity.

### Mental Versus Verbal Consent

Serious misunderstandings can arise when one partner considers consent to be a mental act (wanting sexual activity) while the other partner believes that consent should be verbal (telling someone else that you are ready for sexual activity). If consent is just a mental activity, then one person can never be certain that another person has consented. Someone who thinks of consent as a mental act can easily misjudge a partner's intent. Dressing seductively, drinking alcohol, going to a date's apartment, or allowing a date to pay for an evening's activities might be assumed to signal willingness to have sex even though no such intent has been verbally communicated and, in fact, no

About one-fourth of all women have been forced to do something sexual against their will. Men often misinterpret women's sexual boundaries or believe that a woman "owes" them sex.

such intent might exist (Muehlenhard, 1995/96). Date rape, or acquaintance rape, is the frequent outcome of such an assumption.

Further adding to the risk of serious misunderstanding and unwanted sexual aggression is the fact that many men believe that women often say no to sex when they really mean yes and are hoping to be taken forcefully. This might be true of a few women, but research shows that most women never do this and their no really means no (Muehlenhard & Hollabaugh, 1988).

Verbal consent—specifically stating willingness to engage in a specific sexual behavior—might not seem very romantic, is seldom portrayed in the media, and might actually be difficult for some people to communicate, but insisting upon it can prevent some very unpleasant situations. This is especially true in a

---

**coercion** (ko-ur'zhun)　to bring about by force, threat, or deceit rather than by informed free choice

# GO ASK ALICE

*Dear Alice,*

*Can you please suggest some appropriate ways to ask a person with whom you're about to have sex if he or she has any sexually transmitted infections? A few months ago I met a girl with whom I had sex and as I found later she had herpes. We did use condoms anyway, but there was still some risk in catching herpes since we didn't use condoms all the time. Sorry about my writing style.*

*Getting Smarter*

Dear Getting Smarter:

There is no A-B-C method of how to ask a partner if s/he has a sexually transmitted infection (STI). In fact, even if you find a comfortable way to ask, and your partner's been sexually active, s/he may have contracted an STI and not even know it.

One of the most common symptoms of an STI is **no symptom.**

Make a decision yourself about when and how you're comfortable bringing up the STI discussion. Be as direct as possible, knowing that it's probably going to be awkward. Be yourself! Pick a time and place where you won't be interrupted or disturbed and when you're not sexually engaged. Talk freely and openly, and have some suggestions ready for how you can learn more about your sexuality and sexual choices together as a couple. Many couples say that they use condoms regardless of their partner's history, and that that's how they avoid the awkwardness of this discussion.

 http://www.mhhe.com/byer6

---

new relationship that is progressing into new sexual territory. Partners who have been together for a time often don't routinely exchange verbal consent before having sex (although some do). In ongoing relationships, each partner is likely to have a pretty good idea what sexual activities are enjoyed by the other and under what circumstances. In such relationships, partners often assume the answer is yes unless no is stated. But, once again for emphasis, early in a relationship it is best to "assume no unless yes is stated" (Muehlenhard, 1995/96).

## 2.5.2   Saying Yes to Sex

How can you best communicate to a potential sexual partner your interest in having a sexual relationship? Many people are uncertain just how to communicate their readiness to begin a sexual relationship. The unfortunate outcome of this uncertainty is that, too often, people let sex "just happen," with little or no discussion of issues such as commitment, contraception, and disease prevention.

Letting sex "just happen" can result from inadequate communication skills, or it can reflect a person's ambivalence about entering into a particular sexual relationship. Still another possibility is fear of rejection. If you feel reluctant to discuss the issues regarding sex with a potential partner, it is important to determine the cause of your reluctance. If your concern is fear of rejection, you might want to make efforts to increase your self-esteem and self-confidence. If you haven't developed enough of a relationship

with the other person to feel comfortable discussing sex, perhaps it's not yet time to have sex in that relationship. If your problem is communication skills, read on.

This is one time for direct communication. The issues surrounding a sexual relationship are too important to be left to chance. Don't worry about offending or scaring away your partner with discussion of commitment, contraception, and disease prevention. If he or she isn't ready to talk about these issues, then he or she isn't ready to have a sexual relationship with you. If *you* are afraid to face these issues, then *you* aren't ready for the relationship to become sexual.

If you're uncomfortable with discussing sex, you might practice with a friend. In doing so, you might also be able to clear up some of your uncertainties about your relationship. If you can't talk about sex even with a friend, then this again would suggest that you are not ready for the relationship to become sexual.

The following are examples of ways to open the discussion:

"I think it's time to talk about having sex together."

"I'm really turned on to you, and I'd like to talk about us having sex together."

"Are you as turned on to me as I am to you?"

"I think there are some things we need to talk about, because it looks to me like we're going to be having sex pretty soon."

## NEGOTIATING CONDOM USE

Many people who want to use condoms or want their partner to use condoms meet with adamant resistance. This is especially true when condoms are not needed for birth control and their use would be for disease prevention only. Assertiveness and excellent communication skills are necessary in such cases.

In order to effectively counter someone's resistance to condom use, you need to know the basis of that resistance, which might be revealed only reluctantly, if at all. Some of the possible bases include denial of the possibility of catching or transmitting a disease, a religious objection, a belief that condoms reduce pleasure, inexperience in condom use, concern over the cost of condoms, fear of being hurt by a condom, and desire for a pregnancy. Here are a few ways to deal with these objections:

*Objection:* "I'm offended that you think I might have a disease (or) I'm sure that you don't have any disease. Why do we need condoms?"

*Your response:* "Actually, I doubt that either one of us has any disease, but neither you nor I know that for sure. If I really thought you had some disease, you can be sure that I wouldn't want to have sex with you even with a condom. But it's so easy to use condoms and I just don't believe in taking a chance with your health or mine."

*Objection:* "My religion doesn't allow me to use condoms."

*Your response:* "I certainly do respect your religious beliefs. In fact, your religion probably doesn't approve of you and I having sex, with or without a condom. If you really want to practice your religious beliefs, I'll understand if we don't have sex at this time."

*Objection:* "Sex is not pleasurable with a condom."

*Your response:* "For me, sex is not pleasurable without a condom. How do you expect me to enjoy sex when I'm worrying about catching some disease? It's nothing personal against you, but I am just very careful with my health. And I disagree with your idea that sex is not pleasurable with a condom. Millions of people are using condoms with great pleasure. What makes you so different from them?"

*Objection (seldom stated):* "I have no experience with condoms and am not sure exactly how to use them."

*Your response:* "Maybe you haven't had much experience with condoms; lots of people haven't. I'm no expert, but I know a little bit about them and we could learn together. Practice makes perfect, you know."

*Objection:* "Condoms are too expensive."

*Your response:* "I know where to get condoms at a good price. I'll make sure that we always have some available. Besides, condoms are a lot less expensive than getting a disease."

*Objection:* "I'm afraid that a condom might hurt me in some way."

*Your response:* "Condoms are very safe. Millions of people have been using them for many years. If they were dangerous, we would know about it. There are many types of condoms. I'm sure that there are kinds that you will be comfortable with."

*Objection (unstated):* "I want to get pregnant (or) I want to father a child."

*Your response:* Is it possible that you really want to (get pregnant) (get me pregnant)? I don't think that either one of us is really ready for that at this time. I would want our baby to be planned and mutually agreed upon, not just an accident. Don't you agree?"

*Objection:* "You must not really love me if you want me to use a condom."

*Your response:* "I could just turn that right around and say that you must not love me if you don't want us to use a condom. If you really love me, you wouldn't want to take any chances with my health and you wouldn't want to worry me. Well, having sex without a condom worries me. Don't you care about that?"

Some concessions might be necessary in this negotiation, but the bottom line must be: *no condom = no sex.* Anyone who won't respect your desire to protect yourself (as well as protect him or her) just isn't very concerned with your well-being. He or she is not the partner you've been looking for.

Once the discussion is opened, be very direct. If you expect commitment, ask for your partner's exact feelings about that. Don't assume that commitment will automatically follow if the relationship becomes sexual; your partner might not make that association. If *you* don't plan to make any commitment to your partner, communicate that fact. Don't assume that your partner will take care of contraception; he or she might be assuming that you will take care of it. Don't assume that there is no risk of disease transmission; even the "cleanest" and "nicest" people often have sexual diseases. All of these topics need to be openly discussed. (See "Healthy Sexuality: Negotiating Condom Use.")

### 2.5.3 Saying No to Sex

From time to time many of us receive requests or even demands for undesired sexual activity. People can be very aggressive in the pursuit of sex, and sometimes we must be quite assertive in order to avoid participating in sexual activity that is unwanted, inappropriate, or dangerous. We must learn to say no in a firm and effective way.

Not everyone shows respect for others' values, and many people believe that exerting considerable pressure on a person in order to initiate sexual activity is acceptable. For example:

▌ Someone you met at a nightclub only two hours ago is coming on strong to you.

▌ Your former girlfriend or boyfriend keeps pushing you to have sex "just one more time."

▌ You are exhausted from a long, difficult day at work and your partner is determined to have some sex.

▌ You are being pressured for sex at a time in your life when you choose celibacy.

Refusing unwanted sexual advances is not always easy. Even people who are quite assertive in other areas of their lives can have difficulty saying no to sex. Often we "give in," and hate ourselves for doing it. In addition to whatever risks the sexual activity might carry, we suffer from a loss of self-esteem. Why is it so hard to effectively say no to sex? There are many possible reasons (Zimmerman et al., 1995). For instance:

▌ All of us want acceptance and approval. We might believe that refusing a sexual request will lead to our being disliked, rejected, ignored, or ridiculed. People with lower self-esteem find it more difficult to say no.

▌ We might be trying to meet everyone's needs. We might "feel sorry for" someone who seems lonely, sad, or unable to find another partner.

▌ We might lack assertiveness skills.

The best way to say no is firmly and directly. One study (Motley & Reeder, 1995) showed that some women use the kind of vague resistance messages that are least understood by most men. Those women avoid the more direct messages that males understand best because they anticipate that those messages would have negative consequences for the relationship. Yet the study suggests that direct resistance messages do not usually lead to a negative outcome for the relationship.

If the person wanting sex is important in your life, explain honestly why you don't want sex at that time. If the person is only a casual acquaintance, no explanation is due. In either case, made-up excuses are not necessary or desirable. If it's someone you never want to have sex with, rape prevention experts caution you not to give tentative answers such as "Not now." Such answers might be taken to mean that sex later will be okay. Examples of direct ways to say no include these:

"No. I don't know you well enough."
"No. You need to find someone new."
"No. I'm just not attracted to you."

Remember, anyone who doesn't respect your wishes or values probably doesn't have a lot of respect for you. Don't worry about protecting the other person's feelings. Sexual freedom includes the freedom to say no.

### 2.6 GAY AND LESBIAN COMMUNICATION

How does communication in lesbian and gay couples compare with communication in heterosexual couples? While all couples face many of the same communication challenges, differences do exist. Lesbian and gay couples face some different issues, sometimes respond to similar issues differently, and might use somewhat different styles of communication in daily life (Steen & Schwartz, 1995).

The common expectation that a homosexual couple will include one dominant member and one supportive member, an extension of the stereotype of heterosexual couples, is not necessarily valid. Many gay and lesbian couples don't fit this stereotype, just as many heterosexual couples don't (Steen & Schwartz, 1995).

One big communication difference between homosexual and heterosexual couples is in the way the partners have been socialized. Two heterosexual partners have been socialized differently—one as a female and one as a male—causing them to communicate differently from each other, as discussed earlier in this chapter. But two gay or lesbian partners have been

Homosexual couples often communicate effectively because both partners have been socialized in a similar manner and they don't have to deal with gender differences in communication styles.

socialized in similar ways. They "speak the same language," as far as gender is concerned (Steen & Schwartz, 1995).

One other difference noted by Steen and Schwartz (1995) is in how homosexual couples use power in their communication. In heterosexual couples the more powerful partner is likely to exert his or her power in communication. In gay and lesbian couples the opposite is frequently observed; the more powerful partner uses less powerful conversational techniques, which brings more equality to the partnership.

Heterosexual people sometimes wonder how homosexual people find each other, with their relatively smaller numbers and some still being "in the closet." Can gay and lesbian people spot other gay and lesbian people just by their appearance or behavior? Studies show that physical appearance is not a reliable indicator of sexual orientation, whether the observer is heterosexual or homosexual (Rudd, 1996). Some lesbian women and gay men do make an effort to conform to some stereotypical concept of lesbian or gay appearance and/or behavior. But most don't and wouldn't be identified by either a heterosexual or homosexual observer as being lesbian or gay on the basis of their appearance. Gay men and lesbian women who are "out" have no trouble meeting each other within the gay or lesbian social structure. Those who remain closeted sometimes have very lonely existences.

## 2.7 COMMUNICATION IN CONFLICT

In even the best of relationships there are times when partners have conflicting needs, opinions, desires, or interests. Dealing effectively with conflict is essential to maintaining the quality of a relationship and, often, to the very survival of the partnership.

### 2.7.1 Clarify Your Thoughts

Before we can resolve conflicts, we have to understand just what it is that is bothering us. Often our emotions, especially those involving our closest relationships, are intense, but unclear. For example, we can feel a mixture of emotions such as jealousy, anger, fear, and sadness, which can be difficult to express in words until we sort out just what we are feeling.

We need to spend a little time analyzing what we are really feeling. Is it really anger, or is it actually fear? If it is fear, why do we have that fear? Or is it the need to feel more control over our lives? Is it an uncomfortable feeling of dependency? Often an effective way to clarify thoughts and emotions is to talk them through with an emotionally uninvolved person, such as a friend.

### 2.7.2 Use "I" Statements

When communicating in conflict situations, it is more effective to use "I" statements, rather than "you" statements. An **"I" statement** merely expresses the emotions that you are feeling, without blaming the other person for your feeling that way. **"You" statements** can put blame on the listener. This tends to force the listener into a defensive position, in which he or she has to justify a particular behavior. "I" statements, in contrast, encourage a more open discussion. Consider the likely response to each of the following statements:

| | |
|---|---|
| **"I" statements** | statements of how a person is feeling without placing blame for those emotions |
| **"You" statements** | statements that accuse or place blame on another person |

*"You really made me mad when you let him stay overnight at your place."*

*"I felt hurt when I came to your apartment and found him there."*

*"You never talk to me; you always go running to someone else."*

*"I felt rejected when you called her instead of talking over your feelings with me."*

*"You must not love me if you want to talk to other women."*

*"I feel unloved when you talk to other women."*

In each case, the "you" statement is an accusation or placement of blame, closing the door to a meaningful sharing of feelings and encouraging an angry response and escalating hostility. The "I" statement reveals feelings without placing blame for causing those feelings. The next time you find yourself in a conflict, try using "I" statements and see if you don't get an entirely different response.

### 2.7.3 Constructive Criticism

Sometimes it is appropriate to offer constructive criticism, a positive suggestion on how a partner, friend, or coworker might behave or perform some task in a more thoughtful or effective manner. Making effective constructive criticism is an art. We need to clearly communicate the desired behavior, but in a way that doesn't offend, hurt, or elicit a defensive response.

Some *don'ts* include statements like these:

"You should have. . . ."
"Why didn't you. . . ."
"You should. . . ."
"How could you have. . . ."

Statements like these force others to defend what they have done rather than enabling them to consider another approach. They portray the speaker as the all-knowing expert and the listener as stupid and inferior. They build hostility and resentment and seldom result in the desired behavioral change.

More effective are questions like these:

"Have you considered trying . . .?"
"Have you ever tried . . .?"
"What would happen if you . . .?"
"Would it work to . . .?"

By phrasing your suggestion as a question, it gives the listener a sense of equal power and status as the speaker, suggesting a relationship based on equality, rather than a master-subordinate relationship. It will encourage the listener to try out the desired behavior, rather than maintaining the undesired behavior as a way of saving face and maintaining some sense of control.

Don't risk becoming known as a "complainer." Restrict your criticisms to situations where the problem is really troubling to you *and* where there is a reasonable expectation that the problem could be resolved. In one study (Alicke et al., 1992) over 75 percent of all complaints registered over a period of time by a group of 160 college students were not directed at changing any situation, but were expressed merely to vent frustration or to solicit sympathy. If you complain about every trivial irritation in your partnership, then when you have a serious cause for complaint you might very well be "tuned out."

### 2.7.4 Receiving Criticism

One of the most essential skills in maintaining partnerships as well as in other life situations is the ability to gracefully receive criticism. Effectively giving and receiving criticism are both important learned social skills (Piccinin, Chislett, & McCarrey, 1989)

In addition to its impact on your partnership, how you handle criticism has powerful effects on your own physical and emotional health. Excessive criticism and poorly handled criticism have been associated with clinical depression, lowered self-esteem, loss of motivation, impaired task performance, and avoidance of opportunities to receive critical feedback (Atlas, 1994; Franks et al., 1992; Gruen, Gwadz, & Morrobel, 1994; Kirschenbaum & Wittrock, 1990). The most damaging response to criticism is a combination of emotional arousal with behavioral passivity—to become angry, but not to confront the critic (Atlas et al., 1994).

What causes people to offer humiliating or degrading criticism, commonly known as "put-downs?" Understanding where a critic is coming from helps us to deal with the criticism. The people who put us down probably don't consciously know why they do it, but they are usually motivated by one of the following feelings:

▌ *Low self-esteem.* People with low self-esteem try to devalue other people so that they can feel superior by comparison.

▌ *Feelings of powerlessness.* Sometimes put-downs are an effort to put the recipient into a weaker position by destroying his or her self-confidence.

▌ *Feelings of dependency.* A partner who feels dependent might use put-downs to "equalize" the relationship.

▌ *Feelings of envy.* People often react to their envy by disparaging the thing, person, or trait that they would actually like to have for themselves (Buss & Dedden, 1990).

## 2.7.5   Conflict Resolution

**Conflict** is any situation in which our wants, needs, or intentions are incompatible with the wants, needs, or intentions of another person. Conflict is a part of every relationship. No two people can have exactly the same desires, tastes, and ways of doing things. It might seem that conflicts destroy relationships, and they certainly do have the potential to do so. The needs and tastes of some people are so different that they really are incompatible with each other. But more often it is not conflict, but how conflict is handled, that destroys a relationship. Many complex elements, including power, trust, fear, cultural attitudes, and gender differences, determine how we handle conflict.

Power differences and power struggles are at the heart of many conflicts. All of us need to feel that we have control over our lives. Often what we seem to be fighting about isn't really the issue, but we're actually trying to gain a feeling of power. When people feel about equally powerful or when the more powerful individual doesn't use his or her power in a coercive way, conflicts are more easily resolved (deDreu, Nauta, & Van de Vliert, 1995).

Fear and trust are common issues in conflict resolution. When fear is high and trust is low, conflicts are not easily resolved (Parks, Henager, & Scamahorn, 1996; Parks & Hulbert, 1995). Effective conflict resolution in our relationships requires that we be perceived as kind and trustworthy.

Many of today's partnerships are cross-cultural. Partners of different ethnicities might handle conflict differently. A key issue is whether a culture is more individualistic, such as in the United States, or collectivistic, as in many Asian cultures. People from the collectivistic cultures are more likely to take a cooperative stance in conflict resolution (Parks & Vu, 1994).

Some gender differences have been identified in conflict resolution (Ball, Cowan, & Cowan, 1995). For example, in married heterosexual couples, women tend to raise issues first and engage men in discussion. But men tend to control the content and emotional depth of later discussion phases and largely determine the outcome. In a study by Ball, Cowan, & Cowan (1995), the women felt frustrated by their husbands' domination of the discussion process.

Conflict can be either constructive or destructive, depending on how we deal with it. In destructive conflict, neither person listens to the other. Both talk and scream at the same time. Reactions are highly emotional. Name-calling sometimes escalates to shoving and other physical abuse. But none of this is necessary.

One reason disputes tend to escalate is that all parties tend to evaluate their own behaviors in terms favorable to themselves (deDreu, Nauta, & Van de Vliert, 1995). Even though this might be "human nature," it doesn't help resolve conflicts. Self-serving evaluation of conflict behavior leads to increased frustration, reduced problem solving, and escalates the dispute. If we are going to resolve our conflicts, we have to consider the possibility that our own behavior is at least a partial cause of conflict.

Conversely, some people idealize their partners to the extent that they perceive their faults as virtues (Murray & Holmes, 1993). This can be a useful adaptation in some situations, but it can prevent a couple from dealing with what might eventually prove to be a highly destructive trait, harming the relationship or one or both individuals in it.

## 2.7.6   Styles of Handling Conflict

Conflict is often handled in one of five common ways, reflecting differing degrees of passive, aggressive, assertive, or cooperative behavior. Think about the last time you were in a conflict situation. Which of the following seems to most closely describe what took place?

### Avoiding

Avoiding results from behavior that is both passive and uncooperative on the part of one or both parties. There is no attempt to resolve the conflict or to address each other's needs and concerns. *Example: Tom*

Avoidance is a conflict-managing style that is both passive and uncooperative. There is no attempt to resolve the conflict, and unresolved conflict eventually damages or destroys the relationship.

| | |
|---|---|
| **conflict** | any situation in which the wants, needs, or intentions of one person are incompatible with the wants, needs, or intentions of another person |

*and Tina are both busy in their careers and spend lit-tle time in shared activities. Each feels neglected by the other, but neither mentions it. Lately Tina has started seeing a man she met at work, while Tom re-treats further into his job.*

Avoidance may be okay as a temporary measure until there is time to discuss a conflict or the means of dealing with it. But conflicts that go unresolved over a long period often destroy or damage a relationship. Even though conflicts are not discussed, they influence how the partners feel about each other and can even have physical effects. For example, an unre-solved conflict over how a couple manages their money or disciplines their children can lead to loss of sexual interest or problems in sexual response.

## Accommodating

Accommodating behavior is cooperative, but passive. One person gives up the satisfaction of her or his needs in order to accommodate the other's conflicting needs. If the yielding person really isn't too concerned about the situation, this might be fine. But if one partner is frequently accommodating the needs of the other, this is likely to lead to resentment, loss of self-esteem, and even loss of the other's respect. *Example: Rich prefers to have sex in the morning when he is re-freshed, but usually accommodates Mark, who likes to have sex at night. Rich seldom is able to reach or-gasm at night, which Mark views as indicating a lack of interest in him. Lately they have been having sex less and less often.*

## Competing

Competing takes place when both partners are ag-gressively trying to fulfill their own needs, with each person doing everything possible to assert power over the other. Competition consumes a lot of energy and, except for the few relationships that seem to thrive on competition, tends to eliminate the possibility of any true intimacy. *Example: Lisa and Cindy are both sales reps for similar product lines. On a morning when one has an important presentation to make, it can be predicted that the other will start a fight about some trivial complaint. They often go to work tired and upset.*

## Compromising

Compromising requires a moderate degree of both cooperativeness and assertiveness by each person. A mutually acceptable solution to the conflict is found, partially satisfying each person's needs. Though it is not ideal, a compromise may be the best solution for a conflict. Any ongoing relationship requires a certain amount of compromise. *Example: Shari likes to wake up at 6 A.M. on weekends and go running. Bill would prefer to sleep until 10 A.M., but cannot sleep after Shari wakes him up at 6. As a compromise, they de-cide to try waking up at about 8 A.M., enjoy sex to-gether, and Bill will read the paper while Shari runs.*

## Collaborating

**Collaborating** means working together to satisfy the needs of both partners through a maximum use of both cooperation and assertiveness. Weaver (1993) identifies a series of steps that enable collaborative conflict resolution:

1. Acknowledge that there really is a conflict (no avoidance).
2. Clearly define what the conflict is (some couples fight for years without knowing what their basic conflict really is).
3. View the conflict as a joint problem (the only approach that can lead to a win-win resolution).
4. Identify and acknowledge each person's needs.
5. Identify a number of possible resolutions for the conflict.
6. Speculate on the likely consequences of each resolution for each person.
7. Reach a mutually acceptable decision on which alternative best meets the needs of each party.
8. Implement the decision and set a date to review its effectiveness.
9. Evaluate the results and if either party is dissatisfied, return to step 5 or possibly even to step 2.

This is a time-consuming process that cannot be carried out if either partner is rushed or upset. Set a time, ideally within twenty-four hours of when the conflict emerges, to talk. When the couple sits down to talk, there must be no distractions—no TV, no mu-sic, no phone calls, no children, etc. If the discussion is not going well, either partner may feel free to call a time-out. Stop talking about the conflict and set an-other time to continue the talk, again within twenty-four hours. If one person absolutely refuses to talk, the relationship might be deeply troubled and in need of the help of a qualified counselor. Ideally, both part-ners will visit the counselor, but if one refuses, the other may feel free to consult a therapist by him- or herself.

## 2.8 BECOMING A BETTER COMMUNICATOR

This important section of the chapter offers practical advice on ways to become a more effective communi-cator. You might wish to take a few minutes at this point to assess your own sexual communication abilities—see "Where Do I Stand? An Assessment of Sexual Communication."

## 2.8.1 Sexual Vocabulary

Effective communication involves choosing the words that best convey both the factual and the emotional content of our intended message. For every part of the sexual anatomy and for every sexual activity there are usually a number of possible choices of terms, ranging from those that may seem quite technical or clinical to those that may seem endearing, clever, or even vulgar.

When talking about sex, we tend to choose different words for the same body part or sexual function, depending on the circumstances. Often we are uncertain just which terms to use. One unfortunate result of this uncertainty is that we sometimes simply fail to communicate at all. On the one hand, we don't want to appear impersonal by using too formal or technical a term, but on the other hand, we don't want to risk appearing crude or vulgar by using a slang term that might prove offensive. *Example: In human sexuality class you would like to ask a question about oral sex, but you're not sure whether to say "blowing" or "giving head" or "fellatio," so you just don't ask your question.*

There are no clear answers. The most acceptable terms vary with the context, the region of the nation, and the tastes of the individuals communicating. Further, the same term might gain or lose acceptability over time as changes occur in the general intellectual, moral, and cultural climate of an era.

When you are uncertain about which terms to use, simply ask which terms are most acceptable. This approach is especially valuable in close friendships, it helps guide communication and often leads to a very productive discussion in which values and attitudes are revealed and explored.

## 2.8.2 Effective Speaking

Do you ever believe that people don't seem to understand what you are saying or, worse still, just aren't interested in what you have to say? Becoming an interesting, effective speaker (and anyone can do this) greatly improves the quality of your relationships.

For starters, you need to *have something interesting to say.* This means being familiar with a broad range of topics and being sensitive to the interests of your listener. Even though the pressures of school or work might dictate where much of your attention is directed, you need to reserve time to broaden your interests and expand your awareness of a variety of subjects. If you are highly knowledgeable about your major field but have little awareness of other subjects, there will be relatively few people who find you a stimulating conversational partner.

If you frequently find yourself being misunderstood, you may need to *improve the exactness of your communication.* Vocabulary building might be necessary. Communication is often hindered by a lack of the precise word to express a particular idea or feeling. This is especially true in sexual communication. Knowing what you want to say, but lacking the words that would convey that thought, can be very frustrating. Books, tapes, computer programs, and other media are available to help expand your vocabulary. And don't forget to take advantage of the new terms introduced in this book!

To ensure the clarity of your communication, *think through what you intend to say before you say it.* This might create a slight pause in the flow of the conversation, but it reduces your risk of being misinterpreted. To further reduce this risk, when you have something important to say, repeat it several times, phrased in different ways.

*Try to get the "ums" out.* "Um" is so commonly used as a hesitant speech filler that we scarcely notice its use unless someone is extremely hesitant. But at some level we do notice. Research in which tapes were played with the *ums* left in or edited out (Christenfeld, 1995) has shown that speakers make a better impression when they speak without using *um* or similar fillers such as "like" or "you know."

*Be very alert to the verbal and nonverbal feedback* you get from your listener, and use this feedback to guide your communication. For example, you might sense the need to speak more slowly or to rephrase your message.

## 2.8.3 Effective Listening

An effective listener is just as actively involved in communication as the speaker. In fact, effective listening requires greater effort and concentration than speaking does. Your attention must remain focused on the speaker and not wander. Any momentary inattention can cause you to miss the meaning of what is being said.

In any important discussion, distractions need to be minimal so that your full attention can be focused on the speaker. Turn off the TV or stereo; close the door; suggest moving to a less distracting location; ask the other person to speak louder. If you can't eliminate distractions, at least make every effort to concentrate on the discussion.

Often the speaker's nonverbal communication reveals more than her or his actual words. Be very alert to posture, gestures, facial expressions, eye

---

**collaborating**   working together

# WHERE DO I STAND?
## AN ASSESSMENT OF SEXUAL COMMUNICATION

Communication skills contribute to rewarding relationships in many ways. Many of the problems couples experience could be avoided or easily resolved with more effective communication skills. How are your communication skills?

For each statement, circle the appropriate number of points:

|  | | Usually | Sometimes | Seldom |
|---|---|---|---|---|
| 1. | I find it easy to express my nonsexual needs and feelings to others. | 2 | 1 | 0 |
| 2. | I find it easy to express my sexual needs and feelings to others. | 2 | 1 | 0 |
| 3. | I am sensitive to the needs and feelings expressed by others, and especially their nonverbal expressions. | 2 | 1 | 0 |
| 4. | My relationships with other people are pleasant and rewarding. | 2 | 1 | 0 |
| 5. | When a conflict arises in one of my relationships, it is resolved with ease. | 2 | 1 | 0 |
| 6. | I find it easy to communicate with people of both genders. | 2 | 1 | 0 |
| 7. | I can communicate effectively with people of various ethnic groups. | 2 | 1 | 0 |
| 8. | I can find the right words to express the ideas I want to convey. | 2 | 1 | 0 |
| 9. | I am good at interpreting nonverbal messages from other people. | 2 | 1 | 0 |
| 10. | I try very hard not to interrupt someone who is speaking to me. | 2 | 1 | 0 |
| 11. | I try very hard to be nonjudgmental in my responses when people share their ideas and feelings with me. | 2 | 1 | 0 |
| 12. | When a discussion is causing me to feel uncomfortable, I try hard not to withdraw from the discussion or change the subject. | 2 | 1 | 0 |
| 13. | I try to help people open up by asking open-ended, rather than yes-or-no, types of questions. | 2 | 1 | 0 |
| 14. | When I want to express my feelings, I try to phrase them as "I" statements, rather than "you" statements. | 2 | 1 | 0 |
| 15. | I feel that I am adequately assertive. | 2 | 1 | 0 |
| 16. | I let someone know when they are not respecting my rights or feelings. | 2 | 1 | 0 |
| 17. | I find it easy to say no to pressure for unwanted sexual activity. | 2 | 1 | 0 |
| 18. | I find it easy to talk to a potential sexual partner about prevention of sexually transmitted infections. | 2 | 1 | 0 |
| 19. | When conflicts arise in my relationships, I am, if necessary, willing and able to make a compromise in order to resolve the conflict. | 2 | 1 | 0 |
| 20. | When conflicts arise in my relationships, I try to find a resolution that satisfies the needs of both persons involved. | 2 | 1 | 0 |

**Total points:** _____

## Interpretation:

36–40 points: You have developed highly effective patterns of communication and assertiveness.

32–35 points: You have above-average communication and assertiveness skills.

28–31 points: You have about average communication and assertiveness skills. Sharpening these skills will improve your relationships and need fulfillment.

27 points or less: It would be very rewarding for you to improve your communication skills. Your relationships would function much better and you would experience much greater need fulfillment.

movements, and the tone and inflection in the speaker's voice.

Listeners often misinterpret what they hear. For instance, people sometimes interpret messages as being hostile or critical when they were not intended that way. Major misunderstandings in relationships can develop when we fail to ask for clarification of a vague or seemingly hurtful statement. If you have any doubt about the meaning of what you have just been told, immediately ask for clarification.

Here are seven proven ways to improve listening abilities:

1. **Take time to listen.** Many people aren't sure just what they need to say or the best way to express their message. They think as they speak and might modify their message as they go. Though you might wish they would hurry up and get to the point, effective listening requires your patiently allowing them to finish their message. *Example: "Take your time, I'm listening to you. There's no rush."*

2. **Don't interrupt.** Even though you think you know what the speaker is leading to and you are impatient for him or her to make a point, resist the temptation to interrupt and finish sentences for the speaker. Doing so implies a sense of superiority and can break down communication. If you have the habit of interrupting, as many of us do, try breaking that habit by making yourself apologize every time you interrupt. *Example: "Excuse me for interrupting you. It's a habit I'm trying to break."*

3. **Teach yourself to concentrate.** One reason we sometimes have trouble concentrating on a speaker is that we can think much faster than a person can speak. We get bored and begin to think about something else. To remain focused on the speaker, keep analyzing what she or he is saying.

4. **Disregard speech mannerisms.** Don't focus on a person's accent, speech impediment, or delivery style; you will lose track of his or her message.

5. **Suspend judgment.** We tend to listen to the ideas we want to hear and to shut out others. We unconsciously do this because ideas that conflict with our own are threatening. But by listening to what others have to say, we can come to understand our own line of reasoning better and may even change our mind.

6. **Listen between the lines.** Much of the important content in some of the messages we receive is unstated or only indirectly implied. Focusing only on the message actually verbalized may lead us to miss the true message. Be sensitive to what the speaker is feeling and the true message might become evident. *Example: Lori says, "Are you hungry?" Lori means, "I'm hungry!"*

7. **Listen with your eyes.** Pay attention to the speaker's nonverbal signals. Sometimes the full message can't be gained from words alone. *Example: "How are you feeling today." "I'm fine." "Well, the sad look on your face and the way you're wringing your hands tells me that something is bothering you. Would you like to talk about it?"*

## 2.8.4 Responding

When you receive any message, your first response is internal. Your emotions, knowledge, and past experiences cause you to feel a particular way in response to what you have just heard. Your own particular style of feedback will then determine how or whether you communicate this feeling back to the speaker. Weaver (1993) has identified some common styles of feedback, which we discuss in the following sections.

### Withdrawing

The withdrawing response can occur when the topic under discussion creates uncomfortable feelings. The listener just ignores what the speaker has said or perhaps changes the subject. Withdrawing from an unpleasant topic does not contribute to a rewarding relationship. Even though the motivation for withdrawing might be to take the other person's mind off a problem, withdrawing tends to be taken as evidence of callousness or lack of concern. *Example: Your partner is trying to tell you that she or he would like more freedom within your relationship, but you start talking about going to the movies tonight.*

### Judging

One of the quickest ways to cut off open communication is to make a judgmental response. Bluntly telling someone that her or his idea or action is good or bad implies that you know more than that person does. You will seem to have already made up your mind and seem uninterested in hearing the whole story. *Example: "You've got it all wrong. Anyone with half a brain could see it's not like that."*

Judgmental responses can be very damaging to relationships, especially when someone is judged in a negative way. The judged person is placed in the position of having to defend his or her opinion, belief, or behavior. This leads to rejection of and resistance to the "judge." A common result is withdrawal from communication, if not from the entire relationship.

## Analyzing

Analyzing is very similar to judging. When you explain to people why they feel, believe, or act as they do, once again you have set yourself up as the expert, the superior person. And the results are the same: people are made to feel defensive and become less likely to reveal their thoughts and feelings. *Example: "The reason you believe that way is because you just haven't been around very much."*

## Questioning

Depending on your choice of questions, asking questions can either enhance or inhibit communication. Helpful questions are those that are neither threatening nor judgmental. They encourage a person to express ideas and feelings and often to gain insights previously overlooked. Damaging questions express a negative value judgment and force a person into a defensive position. Weaver suggests that "Why" questions are best avoided for that reason. *"Why did you do that?" might really mean "You shouldn't have done that."* Helpful questions tend to begin with "What," "Where," "When," "How," or "Who." These questions encourage people to open up, rather than to try to defend themselves.

Try to avoid questions that can be answered with a simple yes or no. These are closed-ended questions that don't usually lead to a very revealing answer. Ask open-ended questions that encourage self-disclosure. Where would you expect each of these questions to lead?

▌ "Do you have any sexual diseases?" (closed-ended)

▌ *Better:* "If we are going to be having sex, what precautions will we take to prevent disease transmission?" (open-ended)

▌ "Would it turn you on if I talked dirty to you?" (closed-ended)

▌ *Better:* "What are some things we could do that would really turn you on when we make love?" (open-ended)

You can see that, in each case, the open-ended question is more likely to lead to a productive discussion than a yes/no question.

## Reassuring

One important thing that friends do for each other is provide emotional support. This often takes the form of reassuring a friend who is feeling upset that she or he has someone who cares and who shares her or his concern. A reassuring response acknowledges the validity of the other person's feelings by expressing "I'm on your side." *Example: "I'm really sorry to hear*

*about your miscarriage. You were so excited about being pregnant."* When appropriate, more positive ways of viewing the troubling situation can be pointed out. Care must be taken, however, not to imply that the friend should not feel as he or she does, because that would be a judging response. We own our emotions and they are valid.

## Paraphrasing

Paraphrasing is an effective listening device. **Paraphrasing** is simply restating what has just been said, and putting it into the listener's own words. The speaker then knows that the listener has really heard what has been said and is given the chance to correct any misinterpretations. Paraphrasing makes certain that you have understood what has been said by encouraging the other person to expand and clarify his or her message. *Example: Maria says, "I just feel the need for a little more space right now. I still want to be your friend." Carlos responds, "You're saying that you don't want to spend as much time together as we have been, but you still want to spend some time together."*

## 2.8.5 Assertiveness

**Assertiveness** is making your needs and desires known to others and, when necessary, defending your rights. Rather than passively sitting back and wishing that other people would recognize and help fulfill your needs, you actively work toward fulfilling your own needs. Most of us have, at times, allowed someone to take advantage of us in some situation and later on felt extremely resentful for letting it happen. Other times we act aggressively to try to dominate a situation, but end up fearing retaliation from those who were repressed.

We need to be able to distinguish among three types of behavior in ourselves:

1. **Passive behavior** is when you fail to express your true feelings and desires. As a result, you fail to reach your goals or to fulfill your needs. You feel resentful toward others, but even more resentful toward yourself for being so passive. As a result, your self-esteem is reduced and your relationships with others can become strained. You are exhibiting passive behavior when you

   a. seldom speak up in groups;

   b. avoid taking a stand on issues;

   c. allow others to make decisions for you;

   d. avoid forming friendships because you fear rejection;

   e. speak in a soft voice and avoid making eye contact when speaking;

f. just agree with other people in order to avoid having a confrontation;

g. consider yourself weaker and less capable than others; or

h. avoid assuming responsibilities.

2. **Aggressive behavior** is when we attempt to accomplish our goals or fulfill our needs at the expense of others' rights, needs, or feelings. Aggressive behavior can hurt and humiliate others, or it can put them on the defensive. Aggressive behavior alienates other people, who, in reaction to our aggressive behavior, might avoid us or go out of their way to see that we don't achieve our goals. Internally, we feel guilt, remorse, fear of retaliation, and personal anxiety. Aggressive behavior does not contribute to rewarding relationships; in fact, it can ruin relationships (Cloven & Roloff, 1993). Partners of people with aggressive tendencies tend to withhold complaints about controlling behaviors out of fear of repercussions. The outcome is increasing resentment and hostility until the relationship is destroyed.

   You are being aggressive when you

   a. interrupt others before they finish speaking;

   b. try to force your position on others;

   c. make decisions for other people;

   d. take advantage of friendships by using people;

   e. speak loudly and say or do things to call attention to yourself;

   f. have little regard for other's feelings;

   g. aren't always honest with other people; or

   h. act as if you are superior to other people.

3. **Assertive behavior** is when we make our needs and desires known to others and when we stand up for our right to have our needs fulfilled. We make our own choices and achieve our goals without infringing upon the rights of other people. As a result, we feel good about ourselves and others, and others respect us. Assertive behavior results in maximum need fulfillment, increased self-esteem (Temple & Robson, 1991), a feeling of autonomy, good feelings about others, and healthy interpersonal relationships. Assertive behavior is sometimes confused with aggressive behavior, but there are distinct differences. You are being assertive when you

   a. allow others to complete their statements without interrupting them;

   b. stand up for your beliefs;

   c. think for yourself;

   d. enjoy meeting people and forming new friendships;

   e. are comfortable speaking to others and make eye contact with them;

   f. try to understand others' feelings and make your own feelings clear to them;

   g. face problems and confidently make decisions; and

   h. consider yourself equal to other people.

Assertiveness certainly pays off sexually. David Hurlbert (1991) compared fifty married sexually assertive women (as measured by a written self-assessment) with fifty sexually passive women. The assertive women reported higher frequencies of sexual activity, higher frequency of orgasm, greater sexual desire, greater overall sexual satisfaction, and greater happiness in their marriages than the passive women.

Why are some people too passive or too aggressive? Part of the answer can be found in the conflicting messages we get from our culture. On the one hand, tact, diplomacy, politeness, modesty, and self-denial are often praised. On the other hand, "getting ahead" is also valued, and in some circles "stepping on" or exploiting others is considered a necessary part of the process. As a result, some people have never learned to distinguish among the three types of behavior.

Furthermore, passive or aggressive behavior is the result of lifelong influences. Even though we might know that our behavior is sometimes inappropriate, overcoming well-established behavior patterns can be quite difficult.

## 2.8.6 Nonsexist Communication

Despite years of effort by those who strive for gender equity, there are still plenty of examples of **sexism** in communication. Use of sexist language marks a person as being unaware and uneducated about issues of gender equity.

| | |
|---|---|
| **paraphrasing** | restating what has just been said, and putting it into the listener's own words |
| **assertiveness** | making your needs and desires known to others |
| **passive behavior** | denying your own needs and rights |
| **aggressive behavior** | attempting to accomplish your goals or fulfill your needs at the expense of others' rights, needs, or feelings |
| **sexism** | behavior, conditions, or attitudes that foster stereotypes of social roles based on gender |

Several factors lead to sexism in communication. One is that in the English language, male terminology has traditionally been regarded as the standard form and the male pronoun is often used to refer to both genders. *"I want each student to bring his book to class next week."* A related factor introducing sexism into communication is when people in a certain category are assumed to be one gender or the other, reflecting gender-role stereotypes. *Example: "Every vice-president has his own secretary who has her own private office."* Still another form of sexism is the infantilization of females. Words like *chick* and *babe* imply immaturity and incompetence. The acceptability of using girl in reference to an adult female varies with the region, ethnic group, and context. While it is often acceptable among peers, it is seldom if ever acceptable for a manager or professor to refer to women in as "girls."

What can we do to eliminate sexism in our own communication? We can practice the following:

▌ Use "his or her" or "she or he" rather than just "his" or "he" when we mean to include both genders. This gets redundant, however, if done often.

▌ Pluralize possessives and other gendered terms. *"I'd like everyone to bring their books to class next week."*

▌ Avoid gendered terms. *"Please bring your book to class next week."*

▌ Use "one" as a third-person pronoun when appropriate. *When one studies, one's grades will surely improve."*

▌ Use gender-neutral titles for occupations. *Firefighter, not fireman. Police officer, not policeman.*

## 2.9  SEXUALITY EDUCATION: VITAL SEXUAL COMMUNICATION

Educating young people about sexuality is one of the most important applications of communication skills. There is no question of *whether* young people receive sexuality education, only one of *how*. They are constantly bombarded with sexual information from peers, the media, and the entire cultural environment (see "Dimensions of Diversity: Sexuality Education around the World"). In one way or another, an informal sexuality education is obtained, but often with much confusion and misinformation. With effective home and school sexuality education, young people are provided the factual information they need so that they can make their sexual decisions wisely and knowledgeably.

### 2.9.1  Goals of Sexuality Education

Adequate sexuality education has many lifelong benefits. First, quality sexuality education helps people develop a positive attitude about their sexual nature. This in turn contributes to total self-esteem and leads to more rewarding sexual relationships (Gordon, 1992).

Second, a sound, factual background of sexual information enables young people to recognize and ignore the sexual misinformation they so often receive from peers and other sources. Many sexual problems, such as sexually transmitted infections and unwanted pregnancies, can be prevented through the knowledge and positive attitudes that result from sexuality education. *Attitudes* are emphasized here because factual knowledge does not result in healthful behavior unless accompanied by healthy attitudes (Sheer & Cline, 1995).

Sexuality education also helps to develop the skills needed for effective communication of sexual ideas and feelings. The ability to freely communicate sexual needs and feelings is important at all ages, but it is a difficult ability to develop without a lifelong history of open sexual communication. When sexuality education has been an ongoing process from an early age, the communication of sexual information seems no different than any other form of communication.

There is yet another reason why sexuality education is essential. In years gone by, there were very few "respectable" options for sexual behavior or sexual lifestyles. Now people feel free to choose from many sexual alternatives with less concern about social condemnation. Unless at an early age children learn tolerance for others and develop adaptability in their own lives, they are likely to encounter many problems in their relationships with other people.

Effective sexuality education also includes training in critical thinking and decision-making skills. Knowledge and attitudes are not enough. Underlying values need to be explored and ways of clarifying personal values explained. People need to learn how to translate their knowledge and attitudes into well-grounded decisions based on a clear understanding of their personal values. Indecisiveness and impulsiveness are common symptoms of poorly developed decision-making abilities. Many people have simply never been taught how to make valid decisions—sexual or otherwise.

Finally, when we speak of sexuality education, it must be understood that sexuality includes more than reproductive physiology and data on sexually transmitted infections. Although it is important that people have a knowledge of these things, it is even more important that they understand the relationships between people and that they value themselves and respect others as well. Sexuality education should reflect the fact that sexuality is an integral part of the whole being.

## 2.9.2  Home Sexuality Education

Giving one's children a sound factual and attitudinal basis for their sexual decisions is among the most important aspects of parenting. Sadly, it is often mishandled. Little in our educational experience prepares us to be parents, and we are especially unprepared for conveying sexual information to our children (Kyman, 1995; Hockenberry-Eaton et al., 1996). For parents who feel uncomfortable with the prospect of sexuality education, parent education groups exist to help parents learn how to talk about sex with their children.

Effective sexuality education is an ongoing process throughout childhood and is well integrated with other life education. It cannot be accomplished in one lesson. It is planned, and it anticipates, as well as responds to, the needs of the child.

A child's sexual questions demand answers—immediately, honestly, and as fully as the child's level of understanding will allow. In their embarrassment or sexual discomfort, parents often make mistakes. One is to put off answering a question—"I'm busy right now; I'll tell you later" or "I'll tell you when you get older." Another mistake is to be dishonest—"The stork brought you" or "Babies come from hospitals." Perhaps the worst mistake of all is to chide or scold the child for having asked a question—"Nice little girls don't ask such questions." The child feels guilty for having asked, learns that sex is shameful, and suffers a loss of self-esteem for possessing shameful interests and feelings.

Parents who honestly answer their child's original question often find that the answer usually stimulates further questions. Children's questions are usually a good indicator of their capacity to understand the answers and thus should guide parents in how detailed they should make their explanations. While it may be appropriate to save some topics for when the child is older, often a brief, less detailed answer will satisfy a child's curiosity. For example, *"There are many different ways that adults can use their bodies to show their love for each other, and when you're older you'll learn about some of those ways."*

Parents need not always wait for a child's questions. Many other good opportunities for sexuality education present themselves. A pregnancy or birth within the family or among family friends is an excellent discussion opener. Perhaps the child has observed dogs or other animals mating or engaging in other sexual behavior. What the child sees can be explained

Educating their children about sexuality is one of parents' most important duties.

and related to human behavior with age-appropriate (but accurate!) descriptions.

Parents should also make sure that potential anxiety-causing events in the life of the child are understood well in advance of their taking place. Parents can anticipate the kinds of information their child will need and can develop a pool of knowledge and plan for the presentation of this information. Appropriate books can also be made available to children. With males, ejaculation and nocturnal emission should be anticipated and explained before they occur. With females, breast development and the first menstrual period need to be discussed in advance. In particular, the wide range of ages at which these events normally occur should be discussed, since many young people feel quite concerned if their sexual development seems to be happening earlier or later than that of their friends.

A group of 157 ninth-grade girls who had been menstruating for one to three years were asked how they would advise parents to prepare their daughters for menstruation (Koff & Rierdan, 1995). Their responses suggested a shift in focus from the biology of menstruation to the more personal, subjective, and immediate aspects of the experience. Responses also encouraged menstrual education to be a long-term, continuous process, beginning well before a girl's first period and continuing long after.

A sometimes troublesome source of anxiety in both genders is concern over various physical proportions or anatomical details. Girls worry about their breast size, boys worry about penis size. Young people need to know that sexual adequacy is not determined by details of body size or shape. It is also very helpful for a child to understand the physical changes that will be occurring in children of the other gender.

# DIMENSIONS OF DIVERSITY

## SEXUALITY EDUCATION AROUND THE WORLD

Every nation (and within the United States, every state) takes its own approach to sexuality education, reflecting local attitudes on sexuality. At one extreme in the approach to sexuality education is Japan; at the other extreme are the Scandinavian nations and Brazil.

Older Japanese seem embarrassed to discuss sex. Parents seldom discuss the subject with their children, although young people discuss sex together. School sexuality education is mandated, but the curriculum is very limited and is more like a biology class. Young people learn about sex mainly from friends and magazines. The Ministry of Education details the following guidelines for HIV/AIDS education in schools:

1. Grade schools must teach that HIV is a blood-borne disease.
2. Middle schools will teach about HIV in the context of other sexually transmitted diseases.
3. High schools are permitted to mention condoms as protection against HIV infection.

In short, the Ministry of Education intends that schools should teach HIV prevention without mentioning sexual intercourse and other high-risk sexual activities.

Japanese teens are less sexually active than their American peers. Although there are no religious prohibitions against nonmarital sex, Japanese culture urges people to wait until marriage. Also, young people in Japan are extremely involved with their education and have little time for dating and relationships.

In contrast to Japanese youth, Scandinavian teens take sex for granted. Although older adolescents are quite sexually active, there is not much talk about sex between teenagers. Schools have well-developed programs of sexuality education, and sexual matters are discussed whenever appropriate in any course. In Finnish schools, all 15-year-olds receive kits containing a brochure, a condom, and a cartoon love story. Younger Scandinavian adolescents are less likely to be sexually active than their counterparts in the United States. In Sweden, where sexuality education starts at age 7, first intercourse usually occurs at age 17, with contraception almost always used. The message to us in the United States is that effective sexuality education can help young people postpone sexual involvement.

In Brazil, like the Scandinavian nations, very open heterosexual expression prevails. The unabashed sexuality of Carnival reflects the character of Brazilian sexuality. At the same time, rigid gender roles, patriarchy, and homophobia are powerful forces. Child prostitution is common, HIV is epidemic, and many illegal abortions are performed. Most people (86 percent) believe that sexuality education is the job of the schools, and 50 percent of parents have never discussed sex with their children.

Brazilian schools' sexuality education programs emphasize sex as one of the most important sources of pleasure. There is little political opposition to sexuality education. The Catholic Church, which is the largest religion in Brazil, has similarly offered little opposition to sexuality education. Many Brazilians identify as Catholic but don't follow Catholic dictates on sexual matters.

**Sources:** Anastasia Toufexis, "Sex Has Many Accents," *Time,* 24 May, 1993, p. 66; Kyoko Kitazawa, "Sexuality Issues in Japan," *SIECUS Report,* December 1993/January 1994, pp. 7–10; Marta Suplicy, "Sexuality Education in Brazil," *SIECUS Report,* December 1993/January 1994, pp. 1–6.

Fertility, fertility management, and STIs are all essential topics to include in home sexuality education. Much misinformation is exchanged among children on these vital topics. Even though it might be some time before a child is expected to become sexually active, it is more effective to explain these matters progressively over time rather than in one major session. In one study of Hispanic adolescent females (Baumeister, Flores, & Marin, 1995) the young women who reported receiving more information from their parents about sexuality were the least likely to have been pregnant.

Parents also need to discuss with their children the possibility of sexual molestation (see "At Issue: Warning Your Child about Sexual Abuse"). Children need to be aware of the general dangers involved in sexual advances from adults. They also need to know of the possibility of sexual exploitation by adults or older children. Parents should encourage children to report any unusual occurrences.

Above all else, home sexuality education should convey a strongly positive view of sexuality. Children need to perceive their parents as being happy and comfortable with their own sexuality. Here nonverbal

# AT ISSUE

## WARNING YOUR CHILD ABOUT SEXUAL ABUSE

A few basic facts:

- An estimated 30 to 46 percent of all children are sexually assaulted in some way by age eighteen.
- Children of both sexes appear to be at about equal risk of sexual assault.
- Probably 85 to 90 percent of sexual abuse is perpetrated by someone the child knows, not a stranger.

Obviously, most parents want to provide their children with personal safety training designed to prevent sexual abuse. Yet they do not want their children to view the world as an evil place where the people they love and trust are likely to hurt them. A balanced, positive approach to child safety might include the following ideas:

1. Useful parental ideas about the abilities of children:
   - Children can and must be responsible for their own well-being at times.
   - Children can and should speak up for themselves.
   - Children as young as age three are able to understand and apply rules and guidelines.
   - Children are capable of making correct judgments.
2. The best overall defenses for children:
   - Having a sense of their own power.
   - Having experience in handling a wide variety of situations.
   - Knowing where and how to get help.
   - Knowing that they will be believed.
3. Make your child aware of potentially hazardous situations, such as overtures from strangers.
4. Rehearse dealing with dangerous situations by playing "what if" games with children: "What if a stranger tells you that I sent her to bring you home. What would you do?"
5. Parents and child should have a secret code word to be used by anyone who actually has been sent to pick up the child.

**Sources:**  Charles Schaefer, *How to Talk to Your Kids about Really Important Things,* (Jossey-Bass, 1994); Doris Sanford, *I Can't Talk About It* (Questar, 1986).

---

communication is often more meaningful than what is expressed in words. Children will perceive that their parents are at ease with their sexuality, just as they will be aware if this is not the case.

## 2.9.3 School Sexuality Education

Not everyone in our society is in agreement as to what the content of school sexuality education programs should be or even whether these programs should exist. But virtually all authorities in the fields of human sexuality, psychology, and sociology believe that effective school sexuality education benefits both the individual and the society. They further agree that an adequate program goes beyond sexual biology to encompass the emotional, cultural, and ethical aspects of sexuality. The goal of sexuality education is not to make students' decisions for them, but to provide them with a sound basis for making their own decisions.

Some critics of school sexuality education argue that today's high rates of adolescent pregnancy and sexually transmitted infections are evidence of the ineffectiveness of sexuality education. Actually, relatively few of the nation's schools have provided more than a token amount of sexuality education. And studies show that sexuality education does motivate students toward safer sex practices, having fewer sex partners, and using condoms (Feigenbaum, Weinstein, & Rosen, 1995). Currently, primarily in response to AIDS and high teen pregnancy rates, many more schools are implementing sexuality education programs.

People teaching human sexuality at any level should be carefully chosen and adequately trained for this important job. They need, first of all, to be comfortable with their own sexuality. They should also be objective about controversial issues and able to understand and appreciate the views of other people. A good sense of humor is also helpful. Sexuality educators need the broadest possible kind of knowledge, including familiarity with the biological, psychological, and cultural bases of sexuality.

The Sexual Information and Education Council of the United States (SIECUS, 1995a) has compiled a list of the characteristics of effective sexuality education programs. Among other things, effective programs:

Virtually all authorities in the human behavioral sciences agree that effective school sexuality education programs benefit both individuals and society. Adequate sexuality education must go beyond biology to include the emotional, cultural, and ethical aspects of sexuality.

▌ Are experiential and skill-based.

▌ Are taught by well-trained teachers and leaders.

▌ Discuss controversial issues.

▌ Are relevant to all young people, regardless of sexual orientation.

▌ Are culturally specific and culturally sensitive.

▌ Are linguistically appropriate.

▌ Discuss social influences and pressures.

▌ Reinforce values and group norms against unprotected sexual behaviors.

▌ Provide age- and experience-appropriate messages and lessons.

▌ Teach skill-building, including refusal skills.

▌ Use peer counseling and peer support when appropriate.

Does this sound like the sexuality education in the schools you attended? If not, perhaps you will want to become an active supporter for effective sexuality education in your community.

## SUMMARY

1. Rewarding relationships depend on effective communication.

2. Some of the difficulties in communication between women and men result from gender-related differences in communication styles.

3. People from different cultures have communication differences that go far beyond language differences. Communication problems between ethnic groups might reflect cultural differences more than language differences.

4. Effective communication requires being alert to the many nonverbal signals we receive from others. When people are unfamiliar with each other and especially when they represent different cultures, misperceptions can easily occur.

5. When verbal and nonverbal messages conflict, the nonverbal message is more often accurate.

6. Flirting is using nondirect tactics to signal interest to a potential partner.

7. The most productive places to meet potential partners is where people share common interests.

8. Before becoming sexually involved, potential sex partners need to discuss past sexual histories, expectations, commitment or noncommitment, sexual limit-setting, and disease prevention; heterosexual partners also need to discuss fertility management.

9. The distinction between sexual coercion and sexual consent relates to communication: the essence of sexual consent is honest, direct communication about desires, hopes, expectations, and consequences.

10. Gay and lesbian partners "speak the same language" because they have been socialized the same with regard to their gender, whereas other-sex partners must deal with gender differences in their communication.

11. Every relationship has conflicts that are best resolved with effective communication. How we deal with conflict can either destroy or strengthen a relationship.

12. Sexual communication is sometimes impaired by uncertainty over which terms to use.

13. Assertiveness is making your needs and desires known to others and defending your rights. It can be contrasted to passive behavior (denying your own needs and rights) and aggressive behavior (not respecting the needs, rights, or feelings of others).

14. Sexism (stereotyping based on gender) is common in many forms of communication.

15. Sexuality education is a vital application of sexual communication skills. Home sexuality education is an ongoing process beginning very early in childhood. There is also a need for well-developed school sexuality education programs.

## CRITICAL THINKING CHALLENGES

1. Think back to a recent conversation. What was your listening style? Do you feel that you were "heard"? What were the nonverbal messages being sent? Replay the conversation in your mind, incorporating some of the effective speaking, listening, and responding techniques described in this chapter.

Do you think the outcome would have been different?

2. Write a "personals" ad for yourself. What does the ad say about you? Do you think the reader would get an accurate impression of you from the ad? What aspects of your personality cannot be communicated in this type of ad?

3. What is your usual style of handling conflict? How would this style affect your ability to communicate about sexual behavior? How would you discuss sexual activity in a new relationship, or handle differing opinions about condom use?

# ATTRACTION, LOVE, AND PARTNERSHIPS

**AFTER STUDYING THIS CHAPTER, YOU SHOULD BE ABLE TO**

[1] Contrast secure, ambivalent, and avoidant attachment styles.

[2] Explain the factors that attract one person to another.

[3] List five unrealistic beliefs about romantic relationships.

[4] Explain the basis of infatuation and how infatuation differs from love.

[5] Explain the nature and benefits of intimate relationships.

[6] Explain the behavioral, psychoanalytic, and humanistic views of love.

[7] List and describe John Lee's six love styles.

[8] Contrast passionate love with companionate love.

[9] Explain how culture and gender influence views on love.

[10] Explain Sternberg's "triangle of love."

[11] Describe differences and similarities among gay, lesbian, bisexual, and heterosexual relationships.

[12] Describe relationships between love and honesty and between love and sex.

[13] Explain why some people are unable to love.

[14] Explain how excessive dependency and jealousy destroy relationships.

[15] List the common steps in the disintegration of relationships.

[16] Explain how breakups of relationships can be handled to minimize distress for each partner.

Previously, sexual attraction and love were thought to be the province of poets, song writers, and novelists. The topics included in this chapter have, by and large, been subjects of scientific study only in recent years. Even now, funding for research on relationships is limited, compared to the importance of relationships to our lives.

Enjoyable sexual activity and rewarding interpersonal relationships are often intertwined. In this chapter we will explore attachment styles, sexual attraction, love and partnerships, dependency and jealousy, and how relationships terminate.

## 3.1 ATTACHMENT STYLES

Current theory on attachment styles is valuable background information for the topics of this chapter. According to attachment theory, a behavioral attachment system resulting from natural selection acts to maintain closeness between infants and their caregivers. When the caregiver is perceived to be insufficiently available, the infant's attachment behaviors are activated to bring the caregiver closer. Over time, different forms of infant behavior emerge based on the caregiver's responsiveness and dependability (Ainsworth, 1978; Bowlby, 1969, 1973, 1980). Attachment styles developed in infancy carry over into adulthood and in many ways influence our relationships with our adult partners (Hazen & Shaver, 1987).

Three different attachment styles have been described: secure, ambivalent (which has also been called anxious/ambivalent or resistant), and avoidant (Ainsworth, 1978). *Secure* attachment, at any age, is characterized by trust in the availability and responsiveness of the attachment figure (person to whom you are attached). Adults with a secure attachment style feel comfortable in romantic relationships. They don't feel threatened by their dependency on their partner or by their partner's dependency on them. They don't worry about being abandoned because they have been conditioned to trust in the availability of their attachment figure (Shaver, Hazen, & Bradshaw, 1988).

*Ambivalent* and *avoidant* attachment styles both result from lack of trust in attachment figures. **Ambivalence** is associated with feelings of anxiety and a desire for greater interpersonal closeness. Anxious/ambivalent people want very close relationships and might be perceived by their partners as being too dependent and "clinging." They fall in love easily, perhaps indiscriminately, and become very possessive of their partners. The intensity of their dependency and jealousy might drive away their loved one (Shaver, Hazen, & Bradshaw, 1988).

Attachment theory holds that how we relate to our adult partners—with security, ambivalence, or avoidance—stems from how responsive and dependable our caretakers were when we were infants.

*Avoidance* is characterized by feelings of anxiety and a preference for maintaining interpersonal distance. Avoidant adults are distrustful and do not feel comfortable in a close romantic relationship. When avoidant adults are in a relationship, their distrust can give rise to severe jealousy (Shaver, Hazen, & Bradshaw, 1988).

Attachment styles have been shown to be reliably related to many aspects of our adult relationships, with some gender differences (Kirkpatrick & Hazen, 1994; Kirkpatrick & Davis, 1994). For example, for both men and women a secure attachment style is associated with relatively long-term and satisfying relationships. The relationships of ambivalent women are as long-term as those of secure women, but, at least initially, they are less rewarding. The relationships of ambivalent men, in contrast, are relatively unstable and short-term. Surprisingly, the relationships of avoidant men are as enduring as those of secure men (Kirkpatrick & Davis, 1994). The latter is not true for avoidant women.

Although it is commonly believed that attachment styles developed in infancy immutably carry over to adult relationships, newer research has shown that, given the right circumstances, attachment styles can change at any age, and can change rapidly during even a brief period of adult life (Kirkpatrick & Hazen, 1994). Such a change might be associated with an especially rewarding or unpleasant relationship, for example. Nevertheless, the tendency to maintain the same attachment style, with the same kinds of relationships, appears to be more common.

## 3.2 WHAT GETS PEOPLE TOGETHER: ATTRACTION

Later in this chapter we will discuss love and what keeps people together. But first, let's take a look at what initially attracts people to each other in the first place. Why, of the hundreds of people you see on a typical day, do you feel attracted to some and neutral or even repelled by others? Is attraction a strictly individual phenomenon? Or are there certain features that more universally attract people?

### 3.2.1 Physical Traits

Physical traits make our "first impression." These are the traits you might notice in someone "across a crowded room." To some extent, experts have been able to identify certain traits that are universally considered to be attractive, such as symmetry. People with more symmetrical features, especially of the face, are usually rated as more attractive than people with less symmetrical features (Gangestad, Thornhill, & Yeo, 1994; Grammer & Thornhill, 1994).

In heterosexual attraction, members of each gender are usually more attracted to people of the other gender who show average or slightly above-average gender-specific traits (e.g., large upper body in males, small waist in females) (Singh, 1995). More **androgynous** people are often rated as less sexually attractive by heterosexuals.

Senior citizens still rate attractiveness largely on the basis of physical appearance. A study of females and males from age 55 to 85 compared the importance of four characteristics: pleasing physical appearance, sociability (someone pleasant to be with), task-orientation (someone desirable to work with), and communication desirability (someone pleasant to converse with) (Portnoy, 1993). Physical attractiveness was rated most important of these four variables by both women and men.

### 3.2.2 Age

Much research has documented age-associated partner preferences, perhaps because age is easy to quan-

tify. In heterosexuals, women tend to prefer men about their own age or a little older. Young men tend to prefer women ranging from a little younger to a little older than they are, but as men grow older they often prefer women progressively younger than themselves. The more financially successful older men are, the younger the women they prefer. These preferences appear to be fairly universal, according to studies in the United States, Europe, India, and the Philippines (Kenrick & Keefe, 1992). Partner age preferences are usually explained in sociobiological terms as indicating that men look for a woman who will provide them with healthy babies and have the energy to take care of them, while women look for a man who can provide security for them and their children (Kenrick & Keefe, 1992).

Partner age preferences in homosexual people are similar to those of heterosexuals. Lesbian women, like heterosexual women, prefer partners about their own age. With increasing age, gay men, like heterosexual men, prefer partners progressively younger than themselves (Bailey et al., 1994; Hayes, 1995; Kenrick et al., 1995).

### 3.2.3 Gender Differences

Study after study has shown a consistent gender difference in what is most highly valued by heterosexuals in mate selection. And these differences are consistent with our cultural stereotypes of what each gender is looking for in a relationship. Simply put, heterosexual men are looking for women who are sexually attractive and willing to have sex with them. Heterosexual women are looking for men who have achieved high status and financial success and who are willing to share that status and success with them (Fischer & Heesacker, 1995; Hatfield & Sprecher, 1995; Perusse, 1994; Sprecher, Sullivan, & Hatfield, 1994; Singh, 1995; Suman, 1990; Townsend, 1993; Wiederman, 1993; Wiederman & Allgeier, 1992).

Cross-cultural studies (e.g., Hatfield & Sprecher, 1995) indicate that this distinction is true not only in the United States culture, but in other Western and Eastern cultures as well. But it doesn't mean that women aren't interested in sex. Studies of female sexuality in many cultures indicate that women in general are definitely concerned with their sexual satisfaction and have sexual needs and responses

| | |
|---|---|
| **ambivalence** (am-biv′a-lents) | being simultaneously attracted to and repulsed by a person, object, or action |
| **androgynous** (an-dra′ja-nus) | exhibiting both male and female traits; being both masculine and feminine |

parallel to those of males. Physical attractiveness is definitely one of most women's mate selection criteria (Small, 1992).

## 3.2.4 Do Likes or Opposites Attract?

In response to the age-old question whether opposites attract, we are usually said to be attracted to those who are similar to us in age, intelligence, education, ethnicity, religion, attitudes, socioeconomic level, and smoking and drinking habits (Brehm, 1992; Rytting, Ware, & Hopkins, 1992). But there are many exceptions to the rule. The following are a few areas where the rule does not always hold true.

### Ethnicity

When people of different ethnicities interact, a high rate of interethnic dating and marriage commonly results. In multiethnic southern California, where there is plenty of opportunity for interethnic dating, a telephone survey of over nine hundred people of several ethnicities (African American, Latino, and white) revealed that over half of the members of each group surveyed had done some interethnic dating (Tucker & Mitchell-Kernan, 1995). The rate was higher for males than for females, who more often reported family criticism for interethnic dating. Higher rates of interethnic dating were also associated with being younger, having more education, being less lonely, holding the perception of having more mating opportunities, and being African American or Latino rather than white.

### Attitudes and Values

Research indicates that discovering that we share similar attitudes with another person generates an attraction to that person (Aube & Koestner, 1995; Weaver, 1993). Interaction with someone whose attitudes are similar to our own acts to confirm the validity of our beliefs. Also, people who have similar attitudes find it easier to "get along" with each other and report more satisfactory partnerships (Aube & Koestner, 1995).

Yet we all know of couples who don't seem to have similar values and attitudes. What draws them together? Are people in a state of infatuation blind to differences in attitudes between themselves and the objects of their infatuation? Evidence indicates that people do recognize the differences in their attitudes. Their apparent blindness is more accurately described as a more favorable evaluation of the differing attitudes of the other person than would be made by an unbiased person (McClanahan et al., 1990). Sexual attraction in these cases may be based on traits other than attitudes, such as physical attractiveness.

## 3.2.5 Some Unrealistic Beliefs

Many individuals hold unrealistic beliefs about romantic relationships, which may hamper their search for a mate. Unrealistic beliefs are also associated with difficulty in maintaining a relationship. Jeffry Larson (1992) has identified many of these unrealistic beliefs, which include the following:

- *"The One and Only."* This belief, that each of us has our "one and only" ideal lover out there somewhere, is most typical of younger and less socially experienced people. The fact is that for every one of us, there are *many* potential partners with whom we could have a very rewarding relationship. Perhaps surprisingly, people who hold the "one and only" belief often have very little problem finding that person but have a very hard time letting go of their "one and only" when the relationship has run its course.

- *"The Perfect Partner."* People who believe that there is a "perfect partner" out there for them are often overly critical of the potential partners they meet, holding out for the "perfect" one. Perfection is an impossible standard to meet, so any potential partner is going to fall short by this standard. When a relationship does develop, it is not likely to be very happy for either the partner who expects perfection or the one who is supposed to be perfect.

- *"The Perfect Relationship"* (or) "And they lived happily ever after." This is the belief in the fairy tale expectation of a conflict-free partnership in which every day is "bliss." Even the finest relationship has its tense moments and long-term fluctuations in the partners' closeness. Anyone who judges their relationship by the impossible standard of perfection is going to evaluate it to be a failure. This can cause the termination of a very good relationship.

- *"Try Harder."* This is the belief that any relationship can be made to work if only the partners try harder. It's the opposite of the myth of the perfect relationship. The fact is that some people just aren't compatible, no matter how hard they try to be.

- *"Love Is Enough."* People who believe that "love is enough" are likely to enter a partnership with an inappropriate partner, or to begin a relationship under circumstances where it will be difficult or impossible to maintain. The fact is that love can't overcome every obstacle, and when the problems are severe enough, love itself soon disappears.

## 3.3    INFATUATION

**Infatuation** is a state of strong sexual attraction to someone based mainly on her or his resemblance to a lover fantasy. The origins of this fantasy lie in a person's life experiences, such as prior love relationships, and in powerful cultural influences.

For example, various physical and behavioral traits of the objects of your early love—usually your parents—can become a part of the mental picture that you have of a hoped-for lover. Appearances or characteristics of your real lovers also contribute to your fantasy of the ideal lover. In addition, the mass media shape your lover fantasy, by telling you in books and movies and on TV what kinds of people should turn you on sexually.

Infatuation is strong sexual attraction to someone based on their resemblance to a fantasy lover. The media help shape our unconscious image of our ideal lover.

This unreal lover fantasy that each of us develops is the key to the big difference between love and infatuation. Love is based on a long history of actual emotional reward or reinforcement that occurs *with* the specific loved person. In infatuation, however, we immediately associate with the object of our infatuation our early love relationships and cultural influences that occurred *prior* to meeting that person. Before we even get to know this person, we already perceive him or her as fitting our fantasy of an ideal lover. Thus, in contrast to love, which develops over time and with the specific loved person, infatuation is an immediate response to someone we have just met.

## 3.4    WHAT KEEPS PEOPLE TOGETHER: INTIMACY

Once two people are attracted to each other, then what happens? Will they be "two ships passing in the night" or will a long term partnership develop? Intimacy and love are two closely related concepts that can change attraction into a valued, lasting partnership. First we will examine intimacy.

### 3.4.1    What Is Intimacy?

Many of us misuse the word *intimacy*. For example, we might use it as a synonym for sexual activity ("We were intimate a few times"). Perhaps this misunderstanding reveals how little true intimacy we allow ourselves to enjoy. Sexual activity certainly involves physical closeness, but it might not include any other aspects of intimacy.

Throughout this text, the word **intimacy** implies not only physical closeness, but emotional, intellectual, social, and spiritual bonds as well. As integrated, whole people, we can form intimate relationships with others who are also whole people. In our intimate relationships, sex might or might not play a role, just as intimacy might or might not accompany sexual activity.

One definition of intimacy is "the sense that a partner understands and appreciates oneself" (Reis & Franks, 1994). Intimate relationships are characterized by feelings of closeness, interdependence, warmth, affection, caring, and sharing, especially the sharing of innermost feelings. Thoughts, needs, and feelings can be freely expressed without fear of a

| infatuation | a state of strong sexual attraction to someone based mainly on his or her resemblance to a lover fantasy |
|---|---|
| intimacy | a sense of closeness including emotional, intellectual, social, and spiritual bonds |

judgmental response. Thus, freedom of communication is an essential characteristic of an intimate relationship (Cloven & Roloff, 1994).

Relationships without the ongoing reinforcement of effective, sensitive communication eventually disintegrate because the individuals' needs are not fulfilled. In some relationships, for example, communication centers around "safe" topics, such as who is going to take care of what (pick up the laundry, fix dinner, etc.); rarely, if ever, are the individuals' feelings about their lives and each other a topic of discussion. Emotionally, the individuals gradually drift apart until, other than for convenience and security, there is little reason to continue the relationship.

### 3.4.2 Risking Intimacy

Intimacy is a risk-taking proposition—it means exposing our true emotions to another person. When our defenses are lowered, it is easy for others, as part of their own defensiveness, to attack one of our vulnerable areas. Without this risk taking, however, intimacy can never develop.

Risk taking is easier if both partners in a relationship remain as nonjudgmental as possible, have a mutual concern for each other's welfare and happiness, and accept each other for who they are. Such an atmosphere allows for continued and growing honesty and provides assurance that the vulnerability inherent in openness will not be exploited. Both partners can thus feel free to present themselves as they truly are, not as they would like to be or would like others to perceive them as being.

Some people, unfortunately, view intimacy with distrust and as something to be avoided. Research has shown that people who perceive more risk in intimacy have measurably less rewarding social lives (Nezlek & Pilkington, 1994). Concerns about the risk inherent in intimacy were greatest for women in their interactions with men and for men in their interactions with men. Interactions of either gender with women were less threatening.

### 3.4.3 Benefits of Intimacy

The benefits of intimacy easily outweigh the risks. If you are unaccustomed to emotional intimacy, the thought of revealing so much of yourself to another person can seem quite threatening. Many of us must learn to allow intimacy to develop. Intimacy, however, is well worth the risk involved.

Intimacy provides the foundation for social life and contributes to both intra- and interpersonal well-being (Nezlek & Pilkington, 1994). Intimacy contributes to physical and emotional health by enhancing our social support system (Reis & Franks,

1994). Intimate relationships with friends or lovers help to satisfy our needs to belong, to give and receive affection, and to develop self-esteem. Intimate friends help us to deal with anxiety by lending us their support. They also enable us to keep our problems in perspective by sharing their troubles with us. Sometimes, just by listening to us in a nonjudgmental manner, intimate friends help us to reduce our emotional stress level; they allow us to verbalize our internal conflicts and sort out possible solutions.

### 3.4.4 Trust and Intimacy

Intimacy requires a high level of trust, and many people have been conditioned through life experiences not to trust. Although trust in a partner means different things to different people—loyalty, honesty, dependability, fidelity—its essence is emotional safety. Trust enables us to expose our deepest feelings, knowing that they will be handled with care. The challenge for most of us in developing intimacy is not letting mutual distrust block the process.

How can two people, in a cynical, defensive world, come to trust each other enough to become emotionally intimate? Psychological theory suggests that the key to being trusted is to demonstrate trust—the more trusting you are, the more likely you are to be trusted by others. Mutual trust must be developed over time, by gradually sharing innermost thoughts and feelings. If each person's thoughts, feelings, and values are well received, trust and intimacy develop.

## 3.5   WHAT KEEPS PEOPLE TOGETHER: LOVE

As a society, we can be said to be "in love with love," to quote an old song. Love is a frequent theme in the arts and entertainment media. Literature, movies, TV, and the stage all rely heavily on love, but the public never seems to tire of the theme.

Some people have said that love defies explanation. Some have stated that love should remain mysterious, that to explain love scientifically would destroy its beauty. Some even doubt that love really exists as a valid phenomenon, but most authorities feel that love is a reality and that it can be explained in scientifically acceptable terms. They further believe that the study of love is highly worthwhile because a better understanding of love should help people develop more rewarding relationships.

How do you feel about love? Take a minute now and complete the assessment in "Where Do I Stand? How Realistic Are Your Attitudes about Love?"

# WHERE DO I STAND?
## HOW REALISTIC ARE YOUR ATTITUDES ABOUT LOVE?

By now you probably understand that *love* does not mean the same thing to everyone, even professionals in the field of human sexuality. As individuals, we carry concepts of love that range from romantic to realistic to cynical, depending largely upon our life experiences.

For each of the following statements, circle the number that most closely approximates your response:

|  |  | Strongly Agree | Somewhat Agree | Strongly Disagree |
|---|---|---|---|---|
| **1.** | I don't believe that research should be done on love, because love should remain mysterious. | 3 | 2 | 1 |
| **2.** | Love is the most important thing in my life. | 3 | 2 | 1 |
| **3.** | My life is very unhappy when I am not in love. | 3 | 2 | 1 |
| **4.** | I am able to function very well without someone to love. | 1 | 2 | 3 |
| **5.** | Love is a fantasy that is popular with 13-year-old girls. | 1 | 2 | 3 |
| **6.** | Each of us has our "one and only" somewhere out there, if only we can find that person. | 3 | 2 | 1 |
| **7.** | Once you find your "one and only," you will never feel attracted to anyone else. | 3 | 2 | 1 |
| **8.** | If you love too much, you will only get hurt. | 1 | 2 | 3 |
| **9.** | I am able to function very well without someone loving me. | 1 | 2 | 3 |
| **10.** | The smartest people don't get hung up on someone. | 1 | 2 | 3 |
| **11.** | You can tell when you first see someone if you are going to love that person. | 3 | 2 | 1 |
| **12.** | The best relationships have some basis more important than love. | 1 | 2 | 3 |
| **13.** | If you love someone enough, any kind of problem in the relationship can be overcome. | 3 | 2 | 1 |
| **14.** | If I had to choose between living in poverty or living without love, I would choose to love in poverty. | 3 | 2 | 1 |
| **15.** | As soon as someone thinks you love them, they will start to take advantage of you. | 1 | 2 | 3 |
| **16.** | You're a sucker if you fall in love with someone who has no money. | 1 | 2 | 3 |

**Total points:** _____

**Interpretation:**

40–48 points: You have very romantic ideas about love. You might put too much emphasis on love as a basis for a partnership while ignoring other important considerations.

24–39 points: You have more realistic ideas about love. Love is important to you, but you also are aware of the many other bases of a smoothly functioning partnership.

16–23 points: You appear to be pretty cynical about love. Maybe you previously have been hurt or come from a family where romance was not emphasized. Your attitudes might insulate you from getting hurt again, but could also be preventing you from enjoying the benefits of a loving relationship.

## 3.5.1 Professional Views on Love

Love has been studied from many perspectives, including behavioral, developmental, psychoanalytic, humanistic, and sociological viewpoints. The perceptions and terminology of each researcher are, of course, influenced by the researcher's areas of expertise. Sometimes the same phenomenon is given different names by different authorities. Each of these approaches contributes to our understanding of love. Here are a few theories about love.

### The Behavioral View of Love (The Dependence Model)

One of the less romantic but highly functional views of love is supported by the **behavioral psychologists** or **learning theorists,** who see behavior as conditioned by reward and punishment. In this context, love is viewed as a learned response. By "learned," behavioral psychologists mean that love is largely a product of experience: *"The ability to love is not something we are born with, but something that we must learn"* (McConnell, 1989).

Behaviorists believe that we approach a loved person because we have learned to associate that person with many different kinds of rewarding or reinforcing experiences. That person signals the possibility of some kind of reward at any time, and thus we enjoy a state of pleasant expectation just by being near that person.

It follows from this line of thinking that "true" love can develop only after a rather long period of experience with someone. We cannot develop a history of reinforcement from someone instantly.

This behavioral concept of varied reinforcement covers all kinds of love relationships. We reinforce each other in many different ways, leading to many different kinds of love.

In sexually loving relationships, for example, the physical pleasure of sex is a powerful reward. Sometimes, though, a more important source of reinforcement in the development of sexual love is the interest exhibited in us by an attractive person. Our culture and the media emphasize the importance of sexual attractiveness as part of our personal worth and adequacy. We are taught from infancy that the attention of a suitably attractive person makes us adequate and worth something. If a very attractive person seems to be attracted to us, it is flattering, it makes us feel good, and it helps to relieve any feelings of inferiority or inadequacy we have. This encourages us to approach this person and to seek her or his company. The more strongly other people view this person as desirable, the more rewarding it is for us to "capture" her or him and the more this person's interest in us becomes a powerful reinforcing agent.

The behaviorists' *dependence model* of love suggests that your commitment to a relationship is based on judgments about three main factors (Drigotas & Rusbult, 1992):

1. The degree to which fulfillment of each of various needs seems important to you. Examples of needs you might hope to fulfill through a relationship include needs for self-esteem, intimacy, sex, companionship, security, and intellectual stimulation.

2. The degree to which you perceive that each of your important needs is being satisfied in the relationship.

3. The degree to which you perceive people other than your partner as being able to fulfill these needs.

Not a very romantic view of love, perhaps, but according to this model we will feel love for the person we perceive as able to provide us with the most fulfillment of our needs. The fact that this model is based on perceptions, rather than realities, helps explain some of the inappropriate or unrewarding relationships that we see in those around us.

### The Psychoanalytic View of Love

Also called the analytic or psychodynamic approach to psychology, **psychoanalysis** was developed and popularized by Sigmund Freud. Freud regarded sex as a primary human motivating force and love as merely an expression of sexual desire—a mechanism in the service of sex. Freud also saw love of self and love of others as incompatible. He believed that a person has only so much love available and that whatever is reserved for the self reduces the amount that is available for others.

Analysts who were active in the field after Freud, sometimes called neo-Freudians, defined love much more broadly than Freud did. Erich Fromm (1956), for example, explained love as a striving to overcome the basic state of human loneliness.

In his classic book *The Art of Loving* (1956), Fromm proposed five different kinds of love: *brotherly love* (love for all humanity), *parental love* (parents' love for their child), *erotic love* (craving for sexual union with another person), *self-love* (love for one's own being), and *love of God* (religious love). Thus, unlike Freud, Fromm believed that sexual love is but one of many forms of love. To Fromm, people become human through loving and cannot love others if they do not first love themselves. Fromm conceptualized love not just in terms of need gratification, but as a caring and giving process. According to Fromm, loving people feel and demonstrate concern for the welfare of their partner and act

Erich Fromm (1900–1980) taught that people become more human through loving. We cannot love others if we do not first love ourselves. This is in sharp contrast to Freud's belief in love as self-serving striving for sexual satisfaction. Freud also thought that too much self-love (narcissism) used up one's ability to love others.

**TABLE 3.1**    COMPARISON OF SIGMUND FREUD'S AND ERICH FROMM'S VIEWS ON LOVE

| *Freud* | *Fromm* |
| --- | --- |
| Love is an expression of sexual desire. | Love is striving to overcome the basic state of human loneliness. |
| Love is an effort to relieve sexual tension. | People become human through loving. |
| Love of self and love of others are incompatible. | It is impossible to love others if we do not first love ourselves. |
| Love is a selfish process. | Love is a caring and giving process. |

Humanists value love for the emotional satisfaction and human growth it provides. They define love in much broader terms than just sexual and other need fulfillment. They emphasize the giving aspects of love rather than just the rewards. The concept of love is extended beyond lovers and family to encompass a love of all humanity.

Humanist Rollo May (1969) viewed love as the direct opposite of the depersonalized, dehumanized life in a modern technological society. He saw modern people as becoming just more machines in a machine age and thereby losing their identity. According to May, when people lose their identity, they deny the value of love, which results in a search for substitutes. This might characterize some of the people who haunt singles bars. These people seek, but fail to find, fulfillment in superficial, depersonalized relationships.

### 3.5.2    Love Styles

In evidence of the many shades of meaning given to the term *love,* John Lee (1988) described six very different love styles. His concept has been well accepted

in ways that foster the growth of their partner toward **self-actualization.** Fromm believed that a loving relationship, then, is based on giving as well as receiving. Table 3.1 compares and contrasts Freud's and Fromm's views on love.

### *The Humanistic View of Love*

**Humanistic psychology** integrates physiological, behavioral, emotional, and intellectual aspects of psychology. In contrast to much research in other types of psychology, humanistic psychologists typically study emotionally healthy people rather than people with problems.

Feelings and emotions are extremely important in humanistic psychology. Emotions are viewed as valid in and of themselves, regardless of how or whether they influence behavior. Individual happiness and personal fulfillment (self-actualization) are highly valued by humanists.

| | |
| --- | --- |
| **behavioral psychologists** or **learning theorists** | psychologists who see behavior as conditioned by reward and punishment |
| **psychoanalysis** (sī-kō-a-na´-la-sus) | a psychological model that emphasizes past experiences and the unconscious mind as motivating forces for human feelings and behavior |
| **self-actualization** | using our full inherent potential as human beings |
| **humanistic psychology** | a psychological model that emphasizes a person's conscious feelings and intellectual processes and the development of one's maximum potential |

among professionals who study various aspects of relationships. In any particular relationship, each partner displays some combination of these love styles. The love styles of an individual vary from partner to partner and from time to time with the same partner. The six styles, named using Greek terms, are as follows:

1. **Eros,** the erotic love style. Erotic love is intense, passionate, and sensual; it is discussed in this text as passionate love.

2. **Mania,** the obsessive love style. Manic lovers experience swings of mood ranging from ecstasy, when they feel that their relationship is going well, to despair when they are afraid that it is not.

3. **Ludus,** the playful love style. Ludus is associated with lack of commitment. Love is just for fun, a game to be played. Relationships are casual and seldom long lasting.

4. **Storge,** the companionate love style. Storge is a slowly developing, "comfortable" form of love, discussed in this text as companionate love.

5. **Agape,** the giving love. Agape is the generous love that puts others before self. It expects nothing in return.

6. **Pragma,** the practical love. Pragma is pragmatic and logical, rather than emotional.

Research studies associate the various love styles with other traits. For example, in one study females rated higher than males on erotic, pragmatic, and storgic love styles, while males rated higher than females on ludic and agapic styles (Rotenberg & Korol, 1995). A study of California Hispanic undergraduates also found that males were more ludic and agapic than females (Leon et al., 1995). Still another study associated higher stress levels with agapic interactions, higher identity enhancement with mania, higher levels of both social expectations and aging fears with pragma, and higher levels of sexual desire with eros (Jacobs, 1992). The same study rated women higher than men on pragma. Finally, one study associated love styles with qualities of relationships (Morrow, Clark, & Brock, 1995). High ratings on eros, ludus, and agape were more associated with rewarding relationships that were other love styles. Partners tended to have similar love styles. Partners' having different love styles was viewed negatively by women but not by men.

### 3.5.3 Passionate Love and Companionate Love

Another system of classifying love distinguishes between two different forms of love: passionate love and companionate love (Aron & Aron, 1994):

- **Passionate love** is a strong emotional state of confused feelings: tenderness and sexuality, elation and pain, anxiety and relief, altruism and jealousy.
- **Companionate love** is less emotionally intense and involves friendly affection and deep attachment.

Passionate and companionate love form a continuum, with all degrees between the two extremes possible.

Those who follow the passionate versus companionate love dichotomy believe that most love relationships start out as passionate love (which some people might call "infatuation") and later might develop into companionate love (which some people might call "true love"). During the passionate stage, the loved person is idealized—any faults she or he might possess are overlooked. Everything about the loved person is sexually exciting, even characteristics that will later be viewed as undesirable. Being in the passionate stage of love is a genuine peak emotional experience, and measurable physiological changes occur during this time. Many people report feeling more "alive" when in the passionate stage of love than during more normal circumstances.

Companionate love is the strong affection we feel for those with whom our lives are deeply intertwined. It includes shared experiences, understand-

| | |
|---|---|
| **eros** (air´ōs) | the erotic love style; erotic love is intense, passionate, and sensual |
| **mania** (mã´nē-a) | the obsessive love style; manic lovers experience swings of mood ranging from ecstasy to despair |
| **ludus** (lū´dus) | the playful love style; *ludus* is associated with lack of commitment; love is just for fun, a game to be played |
| **storge** (stōr´gāy) | the companionate love style; *storge* is a slowly developing, "comfortable" form of love |
| **agape** (a-ga´pāy) | the giving love; *agape* is the generous love that puts others before self |
| **pragma** | the practical love; *pragma* is pragmatic and logical, rather than emotional |
| **passionate love** | a strong emotional state of confused feelings: tenderness and sexuality, elation and pain, anxiety and relief, altruism and jealousy |
| **companionate love** | a less emotionally intense form of love involving friendly affection and deep attachment |

ings, emotions, and habits, and is less immediately intense than passionate love. Though the companionate couple usually still maintain an active sexual relationship, their lovemaking probably is not as frequent or as consistently intense as it was during the passionate stage. By this time, each individual's imperfections are no longer being overlooked by the other, and some conflict situations are likely to arise.

Fortunately, the decline of passionate love in long-term couples is not necessarily as dramatic or as inevitable as some people expect. Aron and Aron (1994) report that many couples maintain a reasonable level of passionate love for thirty years or longer.

### 3.5.4 Cultural and Gender Views on Love

Most of the research on love has been conducted in the United States or other Westernized societies. For some research in China, see "Dimensions of Diversity: Marriage in China."

Research reveals that attitudes on love are greatly influenced by culture and gender. (Sprecher et al., 1994). Through survey research, Susan Sprecher and her associates compared views on love of male and female university students in three major nations (the United States, Japan, and Russia). Some of the results of this survey are summarized in table 3.3.

Many apparent cultural and gender differences are evident from this study. For example, the Russian students placed considerably less emphasis on love as a basis for marriage than did the United States or Japanese students. The U.S. students apparently felt more secure in their attachments than did either the Russian or the Japanese students. Note that in two of the three cultures studied, the male students rated physical appearance as the highest predictor of who they would love, although the female students in none of the three cultures rated physical appearance

## DIMENSIONS OF DIVERSITY

### MARRIAGE IN CHINA

China is among the nations with a tradition of arranged marriages, in which spouses are chosen for young people by their parents on the basis of family status, wealth, or other criteria. But throughout the world a revolution has been taking place in how mates are selected. Arranged marriage is, in many places, gradually giving way to "love matches," in which young people choose their own spouses based on attraction. Table 3.2 illustrates some of the changes that have occurred in China.

People in nations with arranged marriages debate the merits of arranged marriages versus love matches. The two sides in the debate usually consist of the older generation, favoring arranged marriage, versus the younger generation, favoring love matches. The traditional belief in countries with arranged marriage is that "love matches start out hot and grow cold, while arranged marriages start out cold and grow hot." Xu

Xiaohe and Martin Whyte (1990) studied 586 ever-married women in the People's Republic of China to test that hypothesis.

The data did not support the hypothesis. It turned out that women in love-match marriages were more satisfied with their marriages than women in arranged marriages, regardless of the length of the marriage. The study did not survey men, but we might guess that they also would find more satisfaction in a love-match marriage.

**TABLE 3.2**    CHANGES IN ASPECTS OF MATE CHOICE IN CHENGDU, SICHUAN, CHINA FROM 1933 TO 1987

|  | YEAR OF FIRST MARRIAGE | |
| --- | --- | --- |
|  | 1933–48 | 1977–87 |
| Had traditional arranged marriage | 69% | 0% |
| Who played the dominant role in mate choice? | | |
| Parents | 56% | 5% |
| Parents and individual | 15% | 6% |
| Individual | 28% | 89% |
| Couple had never dated before marriage | 73% | 5% |
| Wife had never had a romance before marriage, including with her spouse | 73% | 5% |
| Wife saw herself as completely in love at time of marriage | 17% | 67% |

**Source:** X. Xiaohe and M. Whyte, "Love Matches and Arranged Marriages: A Chinese Replication," *Journal of Marriage and the Family* 52 (August 1990): 709–22.

**TABLE 3.3** VIEWS ON LOVE OF MALE AND FEMALE UNIVERSITY STUDENTS IN THREE NATIONS

| | UNITED STATES | | JAPAN | | RUSSIA | |
|---|---|---|---|---|---|---|
| | *Males* | *Females* | *Males* | *Females* | *Males* | *Females* |
| ***Love Experiences:*** | | | | | | |
| In love now | 53% | 63% | 41% | 63% | 61% | 73% |
| Number of times ever in love | 1.91 | 1.75 | 2.06 | 2.31 | 1.82 | 1.56 |
| Have never been in love | 13% | 10% | 30% | 14% | 12% | 14% |
| ***Attachment type:*** | | | | | | |
| Secure | 47% | 50% | 25% | 49% | 39% | 31% |
| Avoidant | 37% | 38% | 53% | 43% | 36% | 57% |
| Anxious-ambivalent | 16% | 12% | 23% | 9% | 25% | 12% |
| Agree that "love should be a basis of marriage" | 87% | 91% | 80% | 81% | 70% | 59% |
| ***To what degree is each of these items a predictor of love for you? (scale of 1–6; 6 is strongest)*** | | | | | | |
| Personality of an individual | 4.83 | **5.21** | **4.23** | **4.78** | 3.97 | 4.09 |
| Reciprocal liking | 4.55 | 4.77 | 4.08 | 4.32 | 3.96 | **4.37** |
| Physical appearance | **4.91** | 4.51 | 4.17 | 3.84 | **4.39** | 3.59 |
| Familiarity with an individual | 3.85 | 4.14 | 3.80 | 3.74 | 3.87 | 4.03 |
| "Something specific" | 4.06 | 4.28 | 3.75 | 3.57 | 3.97 | 3.77 |
| Similarity | 4.05 | 4.06 | 3.57 | 3.41 | 3.20 | 3.09 |
| Social standing | 2.97 | 3.26 | 2.77 | 3.28 | 2.69 | 2.84 |
| Family and friend approval | 3.08 | 3.41 | 3.10 | 2.88 | 2.93 | 3.07 |

**Source:** S. Sprecher, A. Aron, E. Hatfield, A. Cortese, E. Potapova, and A. Levitskaya. "Love: American style, Russian style, and Japanese style," *Personal Relationships* 1: 349–69, 1994.

any higher than third in importance as a predictor of who they would love.

Other research, conducted among students at the University of Hawaii by R. William Doherty and his associates (1994), compared the attitudes toward love of European Americans, Japanese Americans, Pacific Islanders, and Chinese Americans. Even though the groups differed significantly in their general orientations toward life (European Americans were most individualistic, Chinese Americans the most collectivist, and the other groups intermediate), these four groups *did not differ significantly* in their likelihood of being in love, or in the intensity or type of the love they felt. These results might or might not be valid for the same ethnic groups in other states or nations, as the various ethnic groups in Hawaii have a long history of interaction, which would tend to reduce the differences in their beliefs and behaviors.

### 3.5.5 Love as Growth

Psychiatrist M. Scott Peck, in his classic book *The Road Less Traveled* (1978), defined love as "the will to extend one's self for the purpose of nurturing one's own or another's spiritual (mental) growth." Note that this definition includes self-love along with love for the other. Like many others, Peck has emphasized that we cannot love another unless we love ourselves. He also points out that nurturing the growth of an-

other invariably contributes to our own growth. Love is a permanently self-enlarging experience; we grow by loving.

Nurturing, in this case, means allowing and encouraging the loved person to achieve her or his potential and giving the loved person time and space in which to grow. Nurturing means giving the loved person our full attention when she or he is communicating with us. It means having the courage to expand ourselves into new and unknown areas and encouraging our loved one to do the same. It means living our own lives autonomously and independently and encouraging our loved one to do the same.

Above all else, love means commitment. Peck (1994) reminds us that couples cannot resolve in any healthy way the universal issues in relationships—such as dependency and independence, dominance and submission, and freedom and fidelity—without the security of knowing that the act of struggling over these issues will not destroy the relationship. People who are unable to commit are unable to love.

### 3.5.6 "Falling in Love"

In a comparison of concepts similar to passionate versus companionate love, Peck makes a distinction between "falling in love" and love. He emphasizes the erotic sexual nature of "falling in love." We don't "fall in love" with our children, though we love them very much. Further, "falling in love" is always temporary, as is passionate love. We may continue to love the person, as in companionate love, but the emotionally charged, highly sexual feeling of "falling in love" always fades.

Peck goes on to explain "falling in love" in psychiatric terms. He points out that we all know our physical and mental limits, our boundaries. But the experience of "falling in love" includes a sudden collapse of some of our boundaries, allowing us to merge our identity with that of another person. We and our beloved become "one," an ecstatic experience. But sooner or later the individuals begin to assert themselves. One wants sex; the other doesn't. One wants to rent a video; the other wants to go out to the movies. Gradually or suddenly, we realize that the two of us are not one, but are two individuals with different likes, dislikes, and needs. Our boundaries snap back into place; we are two separate individuals; we fall out of love. At this point, either the relationship dissolves or it progresses to real love.

Relating this to growth, "falling in love" is not an extension of one's limits or boundaries, it is a partial and temporary collapse of them. Real love, which permanently extends boundaries, requires effort. "Falling in love" is effortless. Real love is dedicated to the growth of each individual, but someone we "fall in love" with is seen as perfect, certainly not in need of any growth.

"Falling in love" is not a bad way to start a relationship. Often it leads to the development of love. We do need to understand that the ecstasy of "falling in love" is only a temporary condition, and that if we are ever going to have any lasting love relationship, it will not be at this peak emotional level. Although "falling in love" is not love itself, if the people who have fallen in love are well matched, a growth-producing love relationship can be the outcome.

### 3.5.7 The Triangle of Love

Yale University psychology professor Robert Sternberg (1988), after extensive research on love, formulated a very logical and workable view of love that he termed the triangle of love (fig. 3.1). Sternberg conceives love as the interaction of three important components—*intimacy, passion,* and *decision/commitment.* For a complete, lasting, adult love relationship, all three elements must be present.

In the context of the triangular theory, *intimacy* refers to those feelings in a relationship that promote emotional closeness and bonding. Sternberg and his associates found that intimacy includes at least ten elements:

1. Desiring to promote the welfare of the loved one
2. Experiencing happiness with the loved one

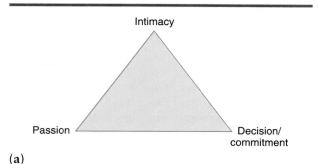

(a)

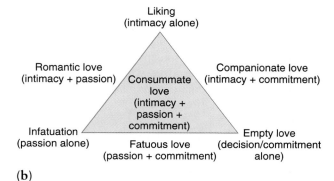

(b)

**FIGURE 3.1** The triangle of love, as conceived by Robert Sternberg. **a:** the three components of love, **b:** the kinds of loving as different combinations of the three components of love.

3. Holding the loved one in high regard
4. Being able to count on the loved one in times of need
5. Having mutual understanding with the loved one
6. Sharing oneself and one's possessions with the loved one
7. Receiving emotional support from the loved one
8. Giving emotional support to the loved one
9. Communicating intimately with the loved one
10. Valuing the loved one

These would seem to be excellent criteria for judging the level of intimacy in any relationship.

The *passion* component of the triangle of love includes the expression of one's needs and desires. In addition to (or instead of) the need for sexual fulfillment, there may be needs for self-esteem, nurturance, belonging, and dominance or submission. Passion and intimacy are often interdependent in a relationship—intimacy arouses passion, while the fulfillment of passion contributes to the sense of intimacy. Sternberg emphasizes, however, that intimacy and passion often develop separately.

The *decision/commitment* component of the love triangle usually consists of two phases, short-term and long-term. The short-term phase is the decision to love the other person; the long-term phase is the commitment to maintain that love. In some cases, one of these phases can occur without the other. Sometimes the decision to love is not followed by any long-term commitment. And sometimes a long-term commitment to a relationship is made without any conscious decision to love.

The commitment component of love interacts with both intimacy and passion. For most people, commitment results from the combination of intimate involvement and passionate attraction. Above all, commitment is what keeps a relationship going during those inevitable times when intimacy and/or passion wane. Without commitment, we would have few lasting love relationships.

### 3.5.8  Love at First Sight?

Is there such a thing as love at first sight? Most of us carry some mental image of a desirable mate. The picture may be incomplete, or vague, and include characteristics that would make such a person a poor choice for a long-term partner. Regardless, this image forms a large part of our basis for judging the sexual attractiveness of the people we meet each day. "Love at first sight" is possibly nothing more than the immediate, unconscious perception that a particular person fits our unconscious image of a desirable lover (Lykken & Tellegen, 1993). If such a person shows an interest in us, we immediately feel more sexually attractive and adequate.

This is not necessarily a poor basis for the beginning of love. It is, however, only a beginning. A couple must build up a substantial record of making each other happy, comfortable, and emotionally rewarded. Eventually, through enjoying each other in a variety of shared activities, the couple might develop a genuine love for each other. They might then look back at the origin of their relationship as having been love at first sight, though a more accurate description of the early stage of such a relationship is probably mutual sexual attraction or infatuation.

## 3.6  PARTNERSHIPS

Most of this chapter's content applies equally to all partnerships, whether individuals are **heterosexual** (having partners of the other sex), **homosexual** (having partners of one's own sex), or **bisexual** (having partners of both sexes).

### 3.6.1  Sexual Orientation

**Sexual orientation** means whether a person is attracted to people of the same, other, or both sexes. How a person's sexual orientation develops will be examined in chapter 13.

In describing a person's sexual orientation, it can be debated whether it is more meaningful to emphasize his or her perceived attractions, his or her current sexual partners, his or her lifetime sexual partners, or what description the person prefers for him- or herself (Laumann et al., 1994). Some people, for example, would prefer partners of their same sex, but for social or professional reasons, or as a result of religious training, restrict themselves to relationships with people of the other sex. Conversely, people who are more attracted to members of the other sex sometimes, in a restrictive environment such as a prison, have relationships with members of the same sex.

In interviews of 3,432 people randomly selected to represent a cross section of the United States population (the National Health and Social Life Survey, or NHSLS), Edward Laumann and his associates (1994) found that many popular beliefs about American sexuality were faulty. One apparently erroneous belief concerned the percentage of people who are gay or lesbian (formerly thought to be about 10 percent). The NHSLS found a somewhat lower percentage, which varied depending on how homosexuality is defined.

About 6 percent of men and 4 percent of women interviewed stated that they were sexually attracted to people of their same sex. About 9 percent of the men and 4 percent of the women had had sex with someone of their own sex at some time in their life. But only about 2 percent of the men and less than 2 percent of the women had had sex with someone of their own sex during the previous twelve months. Fairly low percentages of those interviewed—2.8 percent of the men and 1.4 percent of the women—thought of themselves as being homosexual or bisexual. Self-identification as homosexual or bisexual was positively associated with having a college degree: Three percent of college-educated men identified themselves as gay, compared to 1.5 percent of high-school-educated men. Four percent of female college graduates thought of themselves as lesbian, compared with less than half a percent of female high-school graduates.

Different survey techniques can provide different answers. A group from the Harvard School of Public Health surveyed the prevalence of homosexuality in three nations (Sell, Wells, & Wypij, 1995). Their somewhat different results are presented in table 3.4.

**TABLE 3.4** THE PREVALENCE OF HOMOSEXUAL ATTRACTION AND BEHAVIOR IN THE UNITED STATES, THE UNITED KINGDOM, AND FRANCE: RESULTS OF A SURVEY OF 2,158 WOMEN AND 3,931 MEN USING INTERVIEW AND QUESTIONNAIRES.

1. Percentage of subjects who reported homosexual attraction, but *no* homosexual behavior, since age 15:

|  | *Women* | *Men* |
|---|---|---|
| **United States** | 11.1 | 8.7 |
| **United Kingdom** | 8.6 | 7.9 |
| **France** | 11.7 | 8.5 |

2. Percentage of subjects who reported homosexual attraction *or* homosexual behavior since age 15:

|  | *Women* | *Men* |
|---|---|---|
| **United States** | 17.8 | 20.8 |
| **United Kingdom** | 18.6 | 16.3 |
| **France** | 18.5 | 18.5 |

3. Percentage of subjects who reported sexual contact with someone of the same sex within the past 5 years:

|  | *Women* | *Men* |
|---|---|---|
| **United States** | 3.6 | 6.2 |
| **United Kingdom** | 2.1 | 4.5 |
| **France** | 3.3 | 10.7 |

**Source:** R. Sell, J. Wells, and D. Wypij. "The Prevalence of Homosexual Behavior and Attraction in the United States, the United Kingdom, and France: Results of National Population-Based Samples," *Archives of Sexual Behavior,* 24 (1995): 235–48.

## 3.6.2 Gay and Lesbian Partnerships

Those who are unfamiliar with gay or lesbian relationships often imagine that in these relationships one partner assumes a stereotypical "male" role and the other a stereotypical "female" role. Not only is this *not* true of most gay or lesbian partnerships, it isn't even true of all heterosexual partnerships. Gay and lesbian partnerships are subject to all of the individual variations characteristic of straight partnerships.

Some differences, however, have been noted between gay and lesbian partnerships (Nichols, 1990). Lesbian women, on average, tend to recognize and act on their homosexual attractions at a later age than gay males. Higher percentages of lesbian women than gay men have had heterosexual relationships and have been married.

Lesbian women often first feel emotional attraction and love for another woman, then feel sexual attraction for her, while gay men tend to feel sexual attraction for another man first (Cass, 1990). This distinction is often true of heterosexual women and men as well.

Lesbian women often feel emotional attraction to a woman before they feel sexual attraction to her, while gay men more commonly feel sexual attraction before they feel emotional attraction. The same distinction is true for many heterosexual women and men.

In a somewhat limited study (34 lesbian women and 34 heterosexual women), the homosexual women demonstrated greater dependency, greater compatibility, and greater intimacy in their partnerships. The heterosexual women revealed more use of sexual fantasy, greater sexual assertiveness, stronger sexual desire, and higher frequencies of sexual activity. Both groups reported about equal sexual satisfaction (Hurlbert & Apt, 1993). Another study, comparing lesbian and bisexual women with regard to sexual attraction and behavior, found more similarities than differences between the two groups (Rust, 1992).

Even in this era of AIDS, gay men tend to be less monogamous than either lesbian women or straight men or women. When they have outside relationships, males, whether gay or straight, tend to have brief sexual encounters, while females, whether lesbian or heterosexual, tend to have longer-term relationships (Nichols, 1990).

| **heterosexual** | having or desiring partners of the other sex |
|---|---|
| **homosexual** | having or desiring partners of one's own sex |
| **bisexual** | having or desiring partners of both sexes |
| **sexual orientation** | whether a person is attracted to people of the same, the other, or both sexes |

A study of gay and lesbian couples related individuals' satisfaction with their relationships with whether they were "out of the closet" (open about their sexual orientation) or "passing" (presenting themselves to the world as being heterosexual). Those who were out were more likely to report satisfaction with their relationships, although there was no difference in the degree of love for their partners (Berger, 1990).

### 3.6.3 Bisexuality

Bisexuality, like other sexual orientations, is subject to various definitions, based on perceived attractions, current partnerships, past partnerships, or how an individual self-identifies. Bisexuality is generally defined as being sexually attracted to and/or having sexual relationships with people of both sexes. It does not necessarily mean being equally attracted to both.

There is evidence that more men are bisexual based on their behavior than based on their self-identity. In other words, some men who have sex with both men and women don't think of themselves as bisexual.

Relatively little is known with certainty about bisexual people. We don't know exactly how many there are, how they define themselves, or how their relationships differ from exclusively homosexual or exclusively heterosexual people.

Even sexual researchers disagree on what constitutes bisexuality. Some interpret the difference between reported bisexual behavior and bisexual identity as evidence that bisexuality is a temporary state that is subject to change. They believe that people who have sex with both males and females are either attempting to deny a homosexual orientation, experimenting, or responding to circumstantial reasons such as partner availability. According to this theory, in time an individual will replace bisexuality with exclusively homosexual or exclusively heterosexual behavior.

Other sexuality researchers (e.g., Lever et al., 1992; Hyde, 1991) disagree with this idea. Lever and colleagues (1992) point out that many men have long-term bisexual behavior patterns that indicate that bisexuality is not temporary. Hyde reports that women often become bisexual at relatively late ages after a long history of either exclusive heterosexuality or exclusive homosexuality.

It has been hypothesized that, for bisexual people, the choice of a sex partner is based less on gender than on other traits. This hypothesis was supported by research in Australia (Ross & Paul, 1992). Bisexual men and women were found to be attracted to potential sex partners based on specific personality traits, physical dimensions unrelated to gender, and

interaction styles more than on the gender of the potential partners. This can be interpreted as supporting the view that bisexuality is an enduring trait rather than merely a matter of expedience or convenience.

It has been suggested that few people identify themselves as bisexual because it is not a well-defined social category. In many cities, for example, there is no well-developed bisexual community comparable to the gay, lesbian, and heterosexual communities with their networks, support systems, and traditions (Rust, 1992). Many self-identified gay and lesbian people receive their major emotional support within the gay and lesbian communities and feel that they might lose this support if they adopt a bisexual identity. Some gay and lesbian people do, in fact, view bisexual people with suspicion or hostility, seeing their heterosexual involvement as revealing a lack of commitment to the gay or lesbian community (Rust, 1992).

## 3.7 LOVE AND HONESTY

Love thrives on being honest about who and what you are and also being honest about your feelings for your partner. Many of us have difficulty accepting the idea that someone can love us despite all of our inadequacies. This is why we sometimes find it difficult to disclose ourselves fully and honestly to another person. However, we usually find that we are our own worst critics. What we perceive as personal weakness is rarely judged so harshly by others. When we fully reveal ourselves to others and find that they still approve of us, it is a great boost to our self-esteem, which is an extremely rewarding and comforting feeling.

Similarly, honesty in revealing our true feelings about our partner is also essential to a loving relationship. Insincere compliments, even though well intended, soon become transparent, and the insincere complimenter quickly loses credibility. A person who knows that our compliments and expressed interest are not always genuine never knows when it is safe to believe us. Behaviorists would say that we have lost our power to reward that person and, in doing so, have lost our ability to be loved by that person.

When we react honestly to our partner and our partner's behavior, we give our partner the ability to predict the circumstances in which we will be pleased or displeased. When both partners have this knowledge, it may be possible to avoid conflict-creating situations. At least, there is a sound basis for deciding whether or not the relationship should be maintained. Knowing and accepting this early can prevent years of destructive interaction.

## 3.8  LOVE AND SEX

Sex offers many potential rewards capable of reinforcing a love relationship. First, a sexual orgasm is certainly among the great human pleasures and likely reinforces our approach behavior to the person who helps provide the orgasm. A second important reward in sexual activity is touching. Skin contact is a very basic source of human pleasure dating back to infant-mother interaction (Ward, 1990). In addition, sex offers many psychological rewards, such as the satisfaction of feeling wanted and accepted and reinforcement of feelings of personal worth. With so many rewards, sexual relations can certainly contribute to the development of love for our sexual partner.

Does it matter in a sexual encounter whether or not the two people involved are in love with each other? Most people believe that sexual pleasure is enhanced by a feeling of love for one's partner. Remember that one characteristic of love is a strong desire to approach and be close to the loved person (Giles, 1994). The satisfaction of emotional needs associated with love adds to the physical pleasure of the sexual activity. In addition, since many people hold the belief that love justifies sex, being in love relieves some of the guilt or anxiety that sexual activity might otherwise evoke in these people.

What about sex without love? There appears to be a gender difference in how we feel about sex without love. A research study with college undergraduates found that the women preferred partners who are willing to make some emotional investment in the relationship. This was true even of women with very permissive attitudes and multiple sex partners (Townsend, Kline, & Wasserman, 1995). The same study found that the men were more likely to pursue sex partners who require the least emotional investment from them. In other research, also conducted with college undergraduates, men were found to select dating partners on the basis of physical qualities while women preferred nurturing qualities (Fischer & Heesacker, 1995).

What people perceive as sexual needs are often actually other human needs mistaken for sexual desire. For example, we might mistake the need for companionship, belonging, security, self-esteem, or something else for a sexual need. Further, we might assume that sex is the only way to express happiness or love or that sex can relieve anger, anxiety, or boredom. Though this concept applies to people of all ages, these misconceptions especially contribute to premature adolescent sexual activity. Programs designed to reduce adolescent pregnancy try to help young people distinguish nonsexual from sexual

Love and sex are mutually reinforcing. Sexual pleasure is enhanced by a feeling of love for one's partner; sex offers many potential rewards capable of reinforcing a love relationship. Thus, it is not surprising that love and sex are so closely associated in our culture.

needs and to provide examples of appropriate ways of fulfilling these various needs.

## 3.9  INABILITY TO LOVE

Some unfortunate people are virtually incapable of sustaining a loving relationship. Time after time, relationships that initially seem to have the potential for being rewarding end before love really develops.

The ability to love is *learned,* usually early in life. Some people, however, had a childhood that neither provided examples of loving behavior nor helped to develop the personal characteristics necessary to love (Hazen & Shaver, 1987). Thus, they grow up without the ability to love.

Love requires commitment, and *commitment involves risk* (Fromm, 1956). Some of us are unable or unwilling to take the risk necessary to form a genuine love relationship. This inability to "take a chance" on love can result from childhood or adult experiences of betrayal. Perhaps as children we were frequently let down by the parents we had trusted (Bergmann, 1995). Perhaps as adults we have been badly hurt by someone whom we loved. We start to play "I'll reject you first," also known as "I'll desert you before you desert me." We keep our relationships superficial, not daring to trust or make a commitment. We might avoid the risk of losing someone we love or being rejected, but we suffer greater losses—the personal growth and other rewards of love.

Another common cause of the inability to love is *low self-esteem*. A person with low self-esteem cannot accept the interest of an attractive potential lover (Jeffries, 1993). Rather than concluding that being desired affirms her or his value, this person immediately devalues the person showing interest. The response is, "If she wants *me,* there must be something wrong with her."

## 3.10 DESTRUCTIVE ELEMENTS IN RELATIONSHIPS

Unfortunately, not every relationship we form lives up to its potential for contributing to our emotional fulfillment. Some relationships are destructive, in that they limit our emotional or other growth and development, diminish our self-esteem, restrict our self-actualization or involve physical abuse.

Destructive elements in relationships can originate from our own personality traits or those of our partner, or in the specific and often subtle ways partner's personalities interact. If the same type of problem seems to arise in each of our relationships, this tends to point to our own traits as the principal cause of trouble.

Let's explore two common and related destructive patterns of interaction that appear in relationships: excessive dependency and jealousy.

### 3.10.1 Excessive Dependency

Throughout this chapter, we have discussed love in terms of growth and need fulfillment—such that each partner contributes to the growth of the other and the fulfillment of one or more of the other's needs. However, partners do not necessarily fulfill the same needs for each other. In fact, each might be having very different needs fulfilled by the other. Trades of sex for sex, and companionship for companionship, are examples of trades fulfilling the same need for each partner. Trades of sex for security, sex for ego reinforcement, or sex for companionship are examples of situations where different needs are being fulfilled for each partner.

Relationships can be evaluated in terms of their perceived benefits and costs (Townsend, Kline, & Wasserman, 1995). Companionship, happiness, and feeling loved are common benefits; stress and worry about the relationship, social and personal sacrifices, and dependence on the partner are common costs. There appear to be gender differences in our perceptions of the benefits and costs of relationships. Compared to males, females regard intimacy, growth, self-understanding, and increased self-esteem as more important benefits, but regard loss of identity and disillusionment about love and relationships as more important costs. Compared to females, males regard sexual satisfaction as a more important benefit and monetary losses as a more serious cost (Sedikides, Oliver, & Campbell, 1994).

Many relationships are very unequal and involve such an extreme degree of dependency on the part of one partner that the relationships may be viewed as destructive. For many people, the basic problem is a form of emotional immaturity. As children, we were of necessity highly dependent on others for the satisfaction of most of our needs. As we grew up, most of us gradually assumed more and more responsibility for our own well-being. Some people, though, never develop such autonomy (Hazen & Shaver, 1987). Even as adults, they delegate the responsibility for their emotional or physical well-being to others. These are the people who are likely to become overly dependent on those they love.

Above all, a dependency is not a true love relationship. You will remember from earlier in this chapter that love promotes the growth of both individuals. *Dependency prevents growth.* Dependency is a matter of necessity rather than love. There is no freedom in such a relationship. Love is the free exercise of choice. People love each other because they want to, not because they have to.

If lasting relationships always involve mutual need fulfillment, how much dependency is too much? Psychiatrist Scott Peck (1994) defined dependency as "the inability to experience wholeness or to function adequately without the certainty that one is being actively cared for by another." We all feel some need to be taken care of by another. But for most of us, this feeling does not rule our lives. When this feeling does rule our lives, we have more than the normal need to rely on others—we are dependent. When one relationship ends and we must immediately begin another, no matter with whom, we are dependent. When we cling to someone, demanding more and more evidence of their affection, seeking to be with them constantly, hating to be alone, we are dependent.

An excessively dependent partner is likely to be perceived by the other partner as a burden. Although lovers normally enjoy doing things for each other, there is a limit to the amount of time and energy most people are willing to devote to even someone they love very much. If demands are made beyond that limit, resentment and hostility are almost certain to develop. Even if the true cause of the hostility is not communicated to the dependent partner, the hostility will still make itself felt—perhaps in fights, sexual problems, or termination of the relationship.

Excessive dependency can be overcome. The basic steps in the process are (1) recognizing or admitting to the nature of the problem, (2) developing an understanding of *why* such dependency exists, and (3) initiating a program leading to the goal of increased independence.

As adults, we must assume responsibility for our own well-being and not let other people determine whether or not we can be happy. We must see ourselves as capable of charting the course of our own lives, of making plans and carrying them out. Although it is certainly desirable to enjoy the love and companionship of others as we go through life, we must relate to each other as equal adults, not as children relating to parents. Our happiness is too important to delegate responsibility for it to anyone else.

## 3.10.2   Jealousy

**Jealousy** is fear of losing someone's exclusive love. The essential, defining characteristic of jealousy is that it is a response to a perceived threat to an existing relationship. (The threat might or might not be real.) Most people do experience some degree of jealousy, but usually it does not disrupt of the love relationship. There is, however, a type of demanding, obsessive, and unrealistic jealousy that can severely damage or even destroy a relationship. Jealousy of this magnitude commonly results in alienating the one person that we want so desperately to hold on to.

### *Causes of Jealousy*

Jealousy is more complex than just a response to a perceived threat to an existing relationship. It is perfectly possible to perceive such a threat and simply ignore it, believing that the existing relationship is strong enough to withstand the threat. It is also possible to perceive such a threat, but not be bothered by the possibility that the relationship will change. After all, you could always start a new relationship. Thus, jealousy is based on *dependency and insecurity*—insecurity about maintaining a relationship and insecurity about the ability to cope with a loss of the relationship. The more you *depend* on a relationship to make you happy, the more susceptible to jealousy you will be.

Most research on jealousy emphasizes the causative role of *insecurity* (McIntosh & Tate, 1990). Jealous people perceive their partner as being a highly desirable "possession," and they doubt that their own attractiveness or sexual adequacy is enough to hold on to such a person. They tend to idealize their partner and underestimate their own worth.

One way to deal with our jealousy is to build self-esteem. Another is to see relationships in a different light, to learn that our personal lives would be more satisfying and our professional lives more creative and productive if we and our partners felt free to interact (not necessarily sexually) with a great number of people. (See "Healthy Sexuality: Overcoming Jealousy.")

## 3.11   THE DISINTEGRATION OF PARTNERSHIPS

We might hope that a valued partnership will last "forever," but one of the realities of life is that most partnerships don't last indefinitely. Partnerships disintegrate for many different reasons. Some partnerships have weak foundations from the very beginning, as when a couple have little in common with each other. Sometimes one partner grows while the other stagnates. Sometimes partners both grow, but in different directions. Sometimes one or both partners become too involved in school or work to be able to devote enough time and energy into maintaining the partnership. Sometimes a career move geographically separates partners. The list goes on and on.

Disintegrating partnerships often pass through predictable stages (Weaver, 1993). The process can be reversed at any time if circumstances change or if the couple understand what is taking place and feel that it is worth the effort to put their relationship back on course. Partners, of course, don't always "fall out of love" or lose interest in each other at the same time. Often one partner holds on to hope for maintaining a relationship after the other partner has become disinterested. Weaver identifies the following stages in a disintegrating relationship.

## 3.11.1   Differentiating

**Differentiating** partners begin to focus more on themselves and less on the other and on the partnership. Shared possessions, shared friends, and shared times become less important. If too much of a partner's individuality has been lost in a relationship,

| | |
|---|---|
| **jealousy** | fear of losing someone's exclusive love |
| **differentiating** | in partnership disintegration, moving from a strongly shared identity to a more individual identity |

## HEALTHY SEXUALITY

### OVERCOMING JEALOUSY

Jealousy is such a prevalent disorder that special "jealousy clinics" are held in many cities to help people deal with this destructive emotion. Here is a sample of the advice they give (de Silva and Marks 1994):

1. Try to find out exactly what is making you jealous. Are you upset that other people find your partner attractive? Or is that OK? Are you upset that your partner is going out to lunch with someone else? Or is that OK too? Is it that your partner is having sexual relations with someone else? Is it that your partner might think this other person is a better lover than you? Or is it that the other person might think so? Is it that your partner might leave you? Are you so dependent on your partner that you could not make it if your partner left? Are you afraid you could never find someone else? Do you feel that you are no longer "number one" and that everyone knows it? Do you feel powerless because you realize that you cannot control your partner or your life? Do you feel emotionally, sexually, or intellectually deprived? Do you feel that your territory has been invaded? Do you feel that your property rights have been violated? Do you feel that you want more time with your partner? The first step, then, is to understand what you are feeling and why you feel that way.

2. Try to put your feelings in perspective. Emotional problems are primarily caused by irrational attitudes and beliefs. People who suffer excessive jealousy can be childishly insistent upon having the unattainable. Is it really so awful that your partner is interested in someone else? Don't you have such interests yourself? Is it true that you could not function without your current partner? Although you might never be able to eliminate all jealousy from your life, you can gain control over your emotions by viewing your situation more realistically.

3. Maintain some separate friends and interests of your own. Many counselors have found that it is easier for couples to maintain a close, although not excessively possessive, love relationship if they each maintain some separate friends and interests. It is much easier to have confidence in your desirability if you have an independent identity and if there are others who like and admire you. You are far less likely to fear being abandoned by your partner. It will also be a lot easier for you to cope if your partner does break off the relationship.

---

some degree of differentiating might actually benefit both partners and, in the long term, the relationship.

### 3.11.2 Circumscribing

**Circumscribing,** in this context, means restricting areas of communication to the "safe" topics. Partners avoid discussion of emotion-laden or conflict-laden topics. Should one partner attempt to open discussion of one of the "taboo" areas, the response will be "I don't care to talk about that right now," a sudden change of topics, or simply silence.

### 3.11.3 Stagnating

When a relationship is **stagnating,** hardly anything is discussed. The partners have learned that almost any discussion will lead to an unpleasant disagreement. There is certainly no discussion of the relationship. People who stay with a partnership at this point are either too insecure to break free or are gaining some degree of need fulfillment outside of the relationship, perhaps through work, with family members, or with another relationship partner.

### 3.11.4 Avoiding

When partners are avoiding, not only do they not speak to each other, they don't even want to see each other. They avoid doing so as much as possible. Their few exchanges are hostile. In addition to the unhappiness and stress that are inevitable in such a situation, one's self-esteem severely suffers. One or both partners might start to believe that perhaps they really aren't worthy of a rewarding relationship.

### 3.11.5 Final Termination

In the last stage of partnership disintegration—termination—the partners accept that their relationship is over. Practical matters, such as division of property or custody of children, are settled. Psychological "letting go" takes place, though much more slowly for some partners than for others. Sometimes the termination is never truly complete. A partnership that has been important to us for a long time is never forgotten and its residual effects go on for years. Each of our relationships changes us to some extent, in ways that can be positive or negative. Relationships alter our expectations, values, attitudes, and how we will interact with future partners. They influence our choice of future partners. We might avoid someone who is in any way similar to a prior partner or search for someone who is as much like him or her as possible. Even the most troubled relationship can serve as a growth experience, teaching us about ourselves, other people, and the nature of relationships.

## 3.12  BREAKING UP

One of life's more difficult situations is the breakup of a romantic partnership. Few people on either side of a breakup—rejector or rejectee—get through the breakup without at least some emotional difficulty. Both partners typically feel incomprehension of what has happened and struggle with issues of emotional interdependence (Baumeister, Wotman, & Stillwell, 1993).

Very few of us are going to get through our lives without a few situations of being on one side or the other of a rejection. How can we experience a break with a minimum of emotional turmoil for both ourselves and our partners? If you are the rejector, you probably would like to end the relationship with a minimum of guilt and annoyance for yourself and a minimum of emotional conflict for your partner. You don't want to be hated; you just want to be free.

The first advice is this: from the very beginning, don't behave in any way that could be interpreted as misleading ("leading on") someone with whom you're really not interested in having a committed relationship. Communicate your lack (or loss) of interest very clearly and obtain feedback from the other person to ensure that he or she has understood your message. Remember that people tend to hear what they want to hear, not necessarily what you are saying (Baumeister, Wotman, & Stillwell, 1993). Give a clear and honest explanation of why you are terminating the relationship. Vague or dishonest explanations don't really protect the rejectee from being hurt, and they can make the recovery more prolonged and more difficult.

If you are the rejectee, don't dwell upon whose "fault" the breakup was. There doesn't have to be someone at fault because a relationship didn't thrive. We all have our unique needs and expectations for re-

The end of a relationship can be very difficult for the rejected person. Expressing feelings to others and learning how to handle them can be a positive step toward accepting the loss of a partner and moving on.

lationships, and we all have our unique traits and abilities to offer to a relationship. That what one person needs and what the other person offers don't match up is no one's fault. Some people just aren't made for each other. But for every person, there are others with whom she or he would have a compatible relationship.

You're not the first person who was ever rejected. Most partnerships do end with a breakup and most people do successfully recover and get on with their lives. If your emotions are interfering with your education or your job or if you just can't seem to pull yourself together, consider getting some counseling to help you understand your feelings (Moss, 1995). Expressing your feelings and learning how to handle them can be a positive step toward accepting the loss of a partner and moving on.

| | |
|---|---|
| **circumscribing** | restricting areas of communication to the "safe" topics |
| **stagnating** | not advancing or developing; hardly anything is discussed in a stagnating relationship |

## SUMMARY

1. Secure, ambivalent, and avoidant attachment styles are thought to result from our relationships with our caretakers when we were infants. Our attachment styles affect our adult relationships.

2. Sexual attraction can be influenced by physical traits, age, attitudes, values and similarities and differences. In general, likes attract.

3. Five unrealistic beliefs or expectations that interfere with relationships are these: "the one and only," "the perfect partner," "the perfect relationship," "try harder," and "love is enough."

4. Infatuation is a powerful instant sexual attraction to someone based on her or his resemblance to a lover fantasy. It differs from love in that love takes time to develop.

5. Intimacy is a holistic concept that includes emotional, intellectual, social, spiritual, and, sometimes, sexual bonds. Intimate relationships are characterized by caring and sharing. Freedom of communication is an essential characteristic of an intimate relationship.

6. Intimacy requires risk taking, as it means lowering our defenses and exposing our true emotions to another person.

7. The word *love* means many different things to different people. Attitudes on love are influenced by culture and gender.

8. Sexual orientation means whether a person is attracted to people of the same sex (homosexuality), the other sex (heterosexuality), or both sexes (bisexuality). Some researchers believe that sexual orientation is fixed for life; some believe that it can change over time.

9. Gay and lesbian partners don't necessarily follow stereotypical gender roles, just as heterosexual partners don't.

10. Love thrives on honesty about who we are and our feelings about our partner.

11. Love and sex are mutually reinforcing: love enhances sexual relationships; rewarding sex strengthens love.

12. Some people are unable to love. Love requires commitment, and commitment involves risk that some people are unable to take. Low self-esteem can also interfere with ability to love.

13. Excessive dependency destroys many relationships.

14. Jealousy is fear of losing someone's exclusive love. It is a measure not of love, but of one's insecurity.

15. Disintegrating relationships pass through predictable stages. Breaking up is seldom easy for either partner.

## CRITICAL THINKING CHALLENGES

1. Rank the following in order of importance to you when feeling attraction to someone: physical traits, age, similar interests, ethnicity, similar attitudes and values. List one feature in each category that you would find attractive and one that you would find unattractive. Do you think attraction can be quantified in this way? What are some elements that cannot be categorized?

2. Do you think that infatuation can lead to love? What must occur for infatuation to lead to a long-term relationship?

3. Is an "equal" relationship possible? What qualities would each partner need to possess in order for an unequal partnership to be maintained? List some things that you feel would result in such an extreme degree of inequality that the relationship would dissolve.

# FEMALE ANATOMY, PHYSIOLOGY, AND SEXUAL HEALTH

**AFTER STUDYING THIS CHAPTER, YOU SHOULD BE ABLE TO**

[1] List and describe the woman's external and internal sex organs, including the breast.

[2] Describe the regulatory control of hormones.

[3] List and describe the sex glands.

[4] List six major sex hormones and describe their actions.

[5] Describe how the reproductive cycle changes over a woman's life.

[6] Explain how the sex hormones are involved in ovulation and menstruation.

[7] Describe the two types of menstrual difficulties.

[8] Describe the important features of the gynecological examination, including what is required for self-examination.

[9] List and describe four types of gynecological infections.

[10] List and describe the types of gynecological cancers.

[11] List and describe two types of breast conditions and summarize the important aspects of the treatment for these conditions.

[12] Describe the steps of breast self-examination.

In our culture, the female body is on display virtually everywhere. Idealized versions of women's bodies advertise everything from automobiles to zippers. The female nude is a central preoccupation of Western art. Even a woman's clothing is designed to display and accentuate the secondary sex characteristics of her body; shapely legs are available for all to see, the size and contours of the breasts exaggerated, tight-fitting clothing shows off the hips, and high heels make the buttocks more prominent. The female body is the very symbol of sexuality in Western culture (it may be the phallus in other cultures).

In this chapter and the next one, we will describe the sexual and reproductive structures (*anatomy*) of women and men, and how they function alone and together (*physiology*) both sexually and reproductively. An understanding of all these parts and processes helps to demystify our bodies and those of our partners. Such an understanding can help us keep health problems to a minimum, and it also gives us a sense of personal power in coping with disease or dysfunction.

As we explore the sexual body, keep in mind that we are really looking at two systems. Some of the structures we will examine are part of the *reproductive system*, that is, they are involved in procreation. Other structures are involved in the *sensory pleasure* that accompanies sexual activity. Those structures concerned with reproduction and sexual pleasuring are the *genitals*. Some of these, the external genitals, can be seen visually, whereas others are internal, located inside the body.

## 4.1 EXTERNAL SEX ORGANS

The **external sex organs**, or **genitals**, of the female are often referred to collectively as the **vulva**. The structures of the vulva surround the vaginal opening and include the mons pubis, labia majora, labia minora, perineum, clitoris, vestibule, and vaginal opening (figs. 4.1 and 4.2).

### 4.1.1 Mons Pubis

In the adult woman, the **mons pubis** is the area of the lower front abdomen over the pubic bone. It is covered with pubic hair in a somewhat triangular pattern (fig. 4.1). The mounded softness of the mons consists of a pad of fat lying between the skin and the pubic bone, which cushions the pubic bone during sexual activity. The numerous nerve endings in the mons make caressing this area a pleasurable experience for most women.

### 4.1.2 Labia Majora

The **labia majora** (singular, *labium majus*), or outer lips, enclose and protect the other external reproductive structures. These rounded structures are softened by adipose (fat) tissue. The outer skin of the labia majora is pigmented, covered with pubic hair, and contains sweat and oil glands, along with numerous nerve endings. The inner surfaces of the labia majora are smooth and hairless.

The labia majora lie close together and extend back from either side of the mons (figs. 4.1 and 4.2). They are separated by the *pudendal cleft* (the slitlike opening between the lips). Toward the rear, they taper and merge into the *perineum* (the area between the vagina and the anus). The labia majora are formed from the same tissue that forms the scrotum in a male.

### 4.1.3 Labia Minora

The inner lips, or **labia minora** (singular, *labium minus*), are longitudinal folds of tissue located between the labia majora (figs. 4.1 and 4.2). The labia minora begin as the hoodlike covering over the clitoris, then extend back along either side of the vestibule until they merge with the labia majora at the perineum. Thin and hairless, these folds of tissue are well supplied with nerve endings, sweat glands, and oil glands. The labia minora protect the vaginal and urethral openings.

### 4.1.4 Perineum

The **perineum** is the smooth skin that extends from the merged labia to the anus (fig. 4.1). The perineal tissue contains numerous nerve endings and is sensitive to touch and pressure.

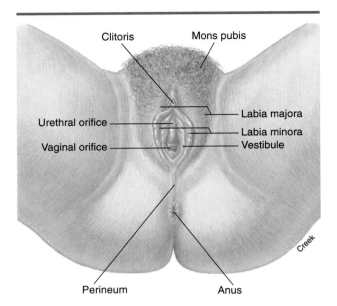

**FIGURE 4.1** The woman's external genitals.

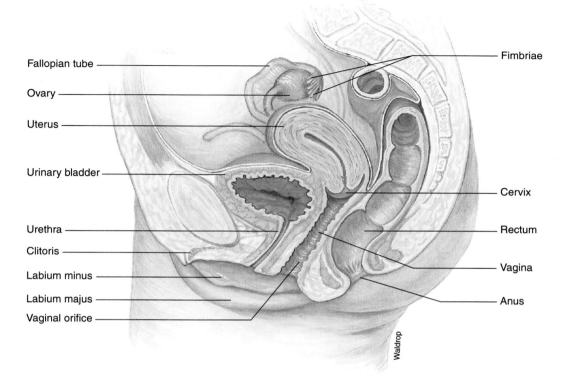

Fallopian tube

Ovary

Uterus

Urinary bladder

Urethra

Clitoris

Labium minus

Labium majus

Vaginal orifice

Fimbriae

Cervix

Rectum

Vagina

Anus

Waldrop

**FIGURE 4.2**    Side view of the female reproductive organs. The thick, muscular wall of the uterus stretches and thins during pregnancy.

## 4.1.5   Clitoris

The **clitoris** is a small projection located at the front end of the vestibule where the labia merge (figs. 4.1 and 4.2). The labia minora fold into a covering over the clitoris known as the *clitoral hood* or *prepuce*. The clitoris itself is a small erectile shaft embedded in the surrounding tissues, capped by an exposed pea-shaped **glans.** Commonly less than an inch long and one-quarter inch in diameter, it contains erectile tissue.

Although much smaller than the man's penis, the clitoris has as many nerve endings as the penis and is formed from the same tissues during development.

The only function of the clitoris is sexual pleasure. Erectile tissues of the woman, like those of the man, respond to sexual stimulation. Sexual stimulation of the clitoris and the nearby labia causes arteries leading to these structures to expand, or dilate. The resulting inflow of blood causes erection of the clitoris and swelling of the labia. Continued stimulation usually culminates in orgasm. In some cultures, the clitoris and surrounding tissues might be excised (see "Dimensions of Diversity: Female Genital Mutilation").

The clitoris can be seen if the labia are gently parted and the prepuce is pushed back. However, it might be easier for a woman to find her clitoris the first time by touch rather than by sight, because the nerve endings on the clitoris are very sensitive to touch.

| external sex organs | sex organs on the outside of the body |
| --- | --- |
| genitals (jen´i-talz) | external and internal sex organs |
| vulva (vul´va) | a woman's external sex organs |
| mons pubis (monz pū´bis) | fatty, hairy pad over the pubic bone |
| labia majora (lā´bē-ah mah-jor´ah) | outer genital lips |
| labia minora (lā´bē-ah mi-nor´ah) | inner genital lips |
| perineum (per-i-nē´um) | area between the vaginal opening and the anus |
| clitoris (clit´ō-ris) | erectile projection in the front part of the vestibule |
| glans (glanz´) | tip of the clitoris |

# GO ASK ALICE

Hi,
    *I have a stupid question. Where is the clitoris located exactly in the female's genitalia? If it differs per woman, what is the easiest way to locate it? Thanks,*
    *Can't find*

Dear Can't find,
    The clitoris is an extremely sensitive erectile organ located below the pubic bone, within and close to the top of the labia. The clitoris is sometimes called the "joy button." The size and shape of the clitoris varies in each woman, although its location is pretty much the same for all women.
    Although some women like direct touching on the glans of the clitoris to become aroused, for others it is so sensitive that direct touching hurts, even with lubrication. Try different kinds of pressure and timing. Talk with your partner. Ask her to show you her clitoris in a sensual way (you don't need to make it an issue). Ask her how she likes it to be touched. Ask her to show you how she touches it herself, or to put her hand on top of yours to guide you. If it's embarrassing, just remember, your (and her) knowledge is her pleasure!

Dear Alice,
    *I am (still!) a virgin and have a question about the hymen. I know mine is not entirely intact, because I did a lot of horseback riding as a child. But as I'm not a tampon-user (nor wish to become one), I'm not exactly sure how painful intercourse will be, for the first time, nor what will happen to the hymen. Yours,*
    *Tawanda*

Dear Tawanda,
    The hymen is a thin membrane with a space or spaces for periods to flow through. Hymens are stretched or torn during the first experience of sexual penetration, or with tampon use or other nonsexual activity. It can also be stretched with fingers. Once torn or stretched, the hymen becomes an irregular ring of tissue around the vaginal opening.
    You could also stretch your hymen yourself. Place a finger into your vagina and apply pressure on the vaginal entrance. Keep the pressure on for a few minutes, then release it. Repeat this procedure several times, each time with a little more pressure. This whole process can be repeated over several days and usually reduces discomfort during a first experience of intercourse.

 http://www.mhhe.com/byer6

## 4.1.6 Vestibule

The area between the labia minora is called the vaginal **vestibule** (fig. 4.1), and includes the urethra, vagina orifice, and openings of several ducts into the vestibule.

In women, the **urethra** is a short tube used for urinating. It connects the urinary bladder to the *urethral orifice*—the opening of the urethra to the outside of the body. On either side of the orifice are the openings of the ducts of the *Skene's (paraurethral) glands*. Embedded in the wall of the urethra, these glands secrete mucus. Note that in women the urinary system and the reproductive system are separate tracts, whereas in men these systems use the same structures.

## 4.1.7 Vaginal Orifice

The **vaginal orifice**, or opening of the vagina to the outside of the body, occupies the greater portion of the vestibule (figs. 4.1 and 4.2). At birth, the vaginal opening may be bordered by the **hymen** (see "At Issue: The Hymen, Symbolic Anatomy").

On either side of the vaginal opening, beneath the skin of the labia, are the *vestibular bulbs,* each consisting of elongated masses of erectile tissue. During sexual arousal the bulbs become engorged with blood. This narrows the vaginal orifice, which produces pressure on the penis during sexual intercourse. Located inside the walls of the vaginal orifice are *Bartholin's (vestibular) glands*. The ducts of these glands open into the vestibule near the vaginal orifice and, during sexual arousal, release a mucus secretion which helps lubricate the orifice.

## 4.2 INTERNAL SEX ORGANS

A woman's **internal sex organs** include the vagina, cervix, uterus, fallopian tubes, and ovaries, as shown in figures 4.2, 4.3, and 4.5.

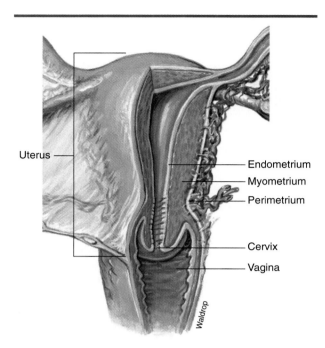

**FIGURE 4.3** The three tissue layers of the uterus. The endometrium is the layer that is partially shed with each menstrual period. The myometrium is the uterine muscle that contracts during labor. The perimetrium is the protective outer coating.

## 4.2.1   Vagina

The **vagina** is a fairly tubular structure that extends upward and inward from the vestibule in the direction of the small of the back. As shown in figure 4.2, the vagina is located behind the urinary bladder and urethra and in front of the anus and rectum. About four inches in length, its walls consist of a series of folds, allowing it to expand to accommodate an erect penis or a newborn in childbirth. The vagina also serves to receive the semen following ejaculation during intercourse, and as the passageway for the monthly menstrual flow. Only the outer third of the vagina has sensory nerve endings.

The mucous membranes lining the walls of the vagina produce clear, white, or yellow secretions. During sexual arousal, additional secretions arise from the cervix of the uterus and from the area of the vaginal opening. A woman's vaginal secretions may vary in color, consistency, and quantity depending on the phase of her menstrual period and her health.

The vagina has several natural features that help prevent infection. These will be discussed later in this chapter.

## 4.2.2   Cervix

Internally the upper vagina connects with the **cervix,** which extends downward into the vagina (figs. 4.2, 4.3, and 4.5). The cervix is the lower one-third of the uterus and surrounds the **os,** or cervical orifice, which is the opening to the uterus.

## 4.2.3   Uterus

The **uterus** is a hollow, thick-walled, pear-shaped organ; before pregnancy it is about three inches long and two inches wide (figs. 4.2, 4.3, and 4.5). The uterus serves as a part of the pathway for sperm to reach the fallopian tubes. It is also the site where the fertilized egg implants and is nourished during its development into an embryo and fetus during pregnancy. The muscles of the uterus expel the fetus in childbirth. Located above the vagina, the uterus appears to be bent forward over the urinary bladder (fig. 4.2). Uterine ligaments hold the uterus in place, so its position changes somewhat according to the fullness of the urinary bladder and rectum.

The muscular uterus has three parts: the fundus, the body, and the cervix. The upper two-thirds, or *body,* of the uterus has a dome-shaped top, or *fundus.* The lower third, or *cervix,* connects with the vagina. The uterine walls are made up of three layers (fig. 4.3). The outer layer, the *perimetrium,* covers the uterus and holds it together and in place. The middle layer, the *myometrium,* is composed of muscle that contracts during childbirth, orgasm, and during the menstrual flow. The innermost layer of the uterus, the **endometrium,** lines the uterine cavity and is the layer that is partially shed during menstruation, as will be discussed later in this chapter.

| | |
|---|---|
| vestibule (ves´ti-būl) | cavity between the genital lips |
| urethra (ū-rē´thra) | duct from urinary bladder to vestibule |
| vaginal orifice (vaj´in-al or´i-fis) | opening of vagina |
| hymen (hī´men) | membrane that might surround the vaginal opening |
| internal sex organs | sex organs inside of the body |
| vagina (va-jī´nah) | internal genital structure leading from vestibule to uterus |
| cervix (ser´viks) | neck of uterus |
| os (ŏss) | opening in cervix leading to uterus |
| uterus (ū´ter´us) | organ in which embryo-fetus develops |
| endometrium (en-dō-mē´trē-um) | inner lining of uterus |

# DIMENSIONS OF DIVERSITY

## FEMALE GENITAL MUTILATION

A standard practice in some countries is *female genital mutilation,* the medically unnecessary modification of the female genitals. Sometimes referred to as female circumcision, the procedure is practiced throughout Africa and the Middle East, and in Muslim populations of Indonesia and Malaysia. With an estimated 80 to 110 million women affected worldwide, the procedure is most often practiced in areas of poverty and illiteracy and where women hold low social status. Due to the influx of students and young couples from these countries, health care providers in the United States and Europe are seeing increasing numbers of these women in college health services, clinics, and hospitals.

There are different types of surgical modification of the female genitals. The least extreme is *sunna circumcision,* in which the clitoral prepuce is removed. This is most analogous to male circumcision as practiced in the United States. A more severe type of modification, called *excision,* consists of *clitoridectomy* (removal of the clitoris), along with the removal of parts or all of the labia minora.

A third and the most extreme form of female genital mutilation is *infibulation,* which is the removal of the entire clitoris, the whole of the labia minora, and at least two-thirds of the labia majora. After this the two sides of the vulva are stitched together. A small opening, sometimes created by inserting a matchstick-sized reed, is left open for the passage of urine and menstrual blood.

Female genital mutilation most typically is performed on girls around age seven, although it may be done at any time from infancy to puberty. The surgery is usually performed without anesthesia by a village woman or midwife using primitive instruments, and it carries a high risk of infection. In some African and Middle Eastern cities it is performed by physicians using modern surgical procedures, including hospitalization. Considered an initiation into adult society, the practice may be accompanied by ritual or ceremony.

The risks to the girl are many. Most severe is bleeding to death, but risks also include shock, urethral or anal damage, scar formation, and infections such as hepatitis B and HIV from the use of unsterilized "instruments."

Often on wedding nights midwives are called to cut open the scar so sexual intercourse can take place. During childbirth the scar must be opened further or else it can obstruct labor and lead to severe vaginal tearing and fetal damage.

Infibulated women tend to retain their urine due to the narrowed urinary opening. Tightly infibulated women must urinate drop by drop, often taking up to 15 minutes, and menstruation is painful and can take ten or more days. Many infibulated women experience years of crippling pain and are never able to enjoy orgasm.

Yet in some cultures the practice continues, for these reasons:

▪ It ensures protection of the family lineage by ensuring that wives are virgins before marriage, and it protects the female's value in societies where a bride is purchased from her father.

▪ It is an important source of income for those who perform the operation.

▪ False beliefs persist, such as that if the clitoris touches the baby's head during childbirth, the infant will die.

▪ It is often dictated by religious beliefs and traditions.

▪ Some believe that the clitoris, if not removed, will grow to the size of a penis, or that its removal is a reaffirmation of a girl's femininity.

Internationally, medical people agree that the procedures of excision and infibulation have no medical value and create unnecessary risks and complications. The practice has been condemned by the World Health Organization and the World Medical Association. Egypt, Great Britain, France, and some American states have laws forbidding its practice.

**Sources:** Council on Scientific Affairs, American Medical Association, "Female Genital Mutilation," *Journal of the American Medical Association* 274 (1995): 1714–16; E. Shaw, "Female Circumcision," *American Journal of Nursing* (June 1985): 684–87. A. Wittich and E. Salminen, "Genital Mutilation of Young Girls Traditionally Practiced in Militarily Significant Regions of the World." *Military Medicine* (October 1997): 677–79; M. Ghalwash (Associated Press), "Egyptian Court Bans Operation on Females." *Inland Valley Daily Bulletin* (29 December 1997): A–9.

## AT ISSUE

### THE HYMEN: SYMBOLIC ANATOMY

The *hymen* is a thin membrane that borders the vaginal orifice of most females. Hymens vary in size and shape, and in the extent to which they narrow the orifice. Of no known function, the hymen is often referred to in slang as "the cherry," implying that if pressure is placed on the hymen during first intercourse, it will bleed. In some cultures the hymen has assumed significance as a symbol of virginity. The hymen's importance in this respect has been exaggerated to the point where, in some cultures, a woman without an intact hymen has been devalued as a marriage partner.

Just what is the relationship of the hymen to virginity? It is not as reliable an indicator as some cultures have assumed. Virtually every female has some degree of hymen at birth, yet rarely does the hymen completely close the vaginal opening (fig. 4.4). Such a complete (imperforate) hymen would block the menstrual flow. Most hymens congenitally have an opening or openings large enough to admit a finger or narrow tampon.

If present, the hymen may be stretched by vigorous exercise, horseback riding, use of tampons, or the insertion of fingers or objects into the vagina. A common myth is that first sexual intercourse may be painful for the woman due to the rupture or stretching of the hymen. Although that might be true if the hymen is especially thick and blocking the vaginal entrance, most women have little pain, discomfort, or bleeding with first intercourse. Thus the presence of the hymen is not a reliable indicator of virginity and its absence is not a reliable indicator of sexual experience.

If a young woman's hymen seems tough and its opening small, and she is concerned that her first intercourse may be too difficult or painful, she can gradually widen the opening with her fingers. In extreme cases, a physician can slightly cut it with a scalpel.

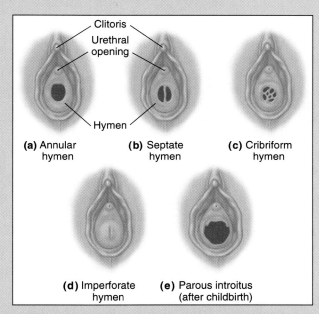

**(a)** Annular hymen   **(b)** Septate hymen   **(c)** Cribriform hymen

**(d)** Imperforate hymen   **(e)** Parous introitus (after childbirth)

**FIGURE 4.4**   Appearance of various types of hymens and the vaginal introitus as it appears after the delivery of a child.

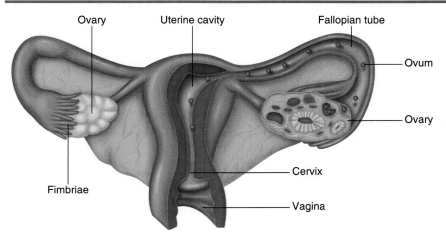

**FIGURE 4.5**   Relationship of ovaries, fallopian tubes, and uterus. An ovum is shown moving down one fallopian tube, a journey requiring several days.

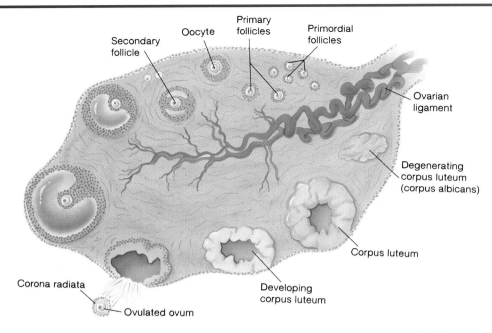

**FIGURE 4.6**    Structure of an ovary. The ovary has been sectioned to reveal the follicles in its interior. Note that not all of these structures would appear in the ovary at the same time.

Mucus in the opening of the cervix acts as a plug that prevents bacterial invasion into the uterus and beyond. A woman can touch her cervix. By inserting one or two fingers deep into her vagina, she reaches it when she touches a rounded projection that feels like the tip of the nose.

## 4.2.4    Fallopian Tubes

The two **fallopian tubes,** also called the *uterine tubes* or *oviducts,* are about four inches in length and one-third inch in diameter. One extends from each side of the uterus. The far end of each tube is funnel shaped and lies very close to an ovary, although not attached to it. This tubular ending is surrounded by a fringe of fingerlike projections called the *fimbriae* (figs. 4.2 and 4.5). Lining the inside of the tubes are hairlike cells called *cilia* that beat and help move any objects in the tubes toward the uterus.

Once in about every 28 days in a sexually mature woman, a mature ovum erupts from the surface of an ovary near the fallopian tube. Following this eruption of the ovum, called **ovulation,** the ovum is drawn into the fallopian tube by the sweeping movements of the fimbriae. Once the ovum is inside the tube, the cilia and rhythmic muscular contractions of the walls of the fallopian tube move the ovum down toward the uterus. If sperm are present in the fallopian tube, fertilization of the ovum may occur—usually in the upper third of the fallopian tube.

## 4.2.5    Ovaries

The two **ovaries,** or *female gonads,* are a pair of glands resembling almonds in size and shape. Each ovary is located near the end of a fallopian tube; thus, there is one ovary on either side of the uterus (figs. 4.2, 4.5, and 4.6). Each ovary is attached to several ligaments that help hold it in position. The ovaries have two functions. They produce and release **ova** (singular, *ovum*), or eggs, and female sex hormones. Each ovum is surrounded by a cellular sac called a *follicle.*

### Ovum Production and Release

There are approximately two million immature ova in the ovaries at birth, the only supply the woman will ever have. These gradually decline in number as they mature or degenerate with age. Only 300,000–400,000 remain in the ovaries at sexual maturity. Of these, only about 400 ova actually mature during a woman's reproductive life (Cunningham et al., 1993).

At *puberty,* the female becomes sexually mature, and her ovaries begin to mature and release the ova. During each menstrual cycle (approximately every 28 days), a number of follicles in one of the two ovaries begin to grow. Typically, however, only a single follicle matures to the point where it releases an ovum (fig. 4.6). The other developing follicles and the potential ova within them degenerate. After release of

**TABLE 4.1**    FEMALE REPRODUCTIVE STRUCTURES

| ORGAN | FUNCTION |
|---|---|
| *Internal* | |
| Vagina | Receives the penis, finger, vibrator, or similar object during sexual activity; receives sperm during intercourse; conveys menstrual flow to the outside of the body; serves as the birth canal for the fetus |
| Cervix | Lower part of uterus that opens into the vagina; contains gland that produces secretions during sexual arousal |
| Uterus | Receives and nurtures the embryo during development |
| Fallopian tubes | Convey ovum to uterus |
| Ovaries | Produce and release ova and female sex hormones |
| *External* | |
| Mons pubis | Physical stimulation associated with feeling of pleasure during sexual arousal and orgasm |
| Labia majora | Enclose and protect other external genitals |
| Labia minora | Protect the vaginal and urethral openings; react by swelling during sexual arousal |
| Perineum | The region between the vagina and anus; sensitive to touch and pressure |
| Clitoris | Sexual pleasure |
| Vaginal vestibule | Encloses the vaginal, urethral openings, and clitoral glans |
| Bartholin's glands | Secrete fluids that moisten and lubricate vestibule and outer portion of vagina |
| Vaginal orifice | Opening of the vagina; may be partly closed by thin membrane of connective tissue called the hymen |
| Urethral orifice | Opening of the urethral duct |
| Skene's glands | Secrete mucus |

the ovum, the follicle is converted into the **corpus luteum** ("yellow body"), which produces additional hormones.

This process continues during each cycle until all of the ova have either dissolved or been ovulated (usually when the woman is between the ages of 45 and 50), at which time the woman passes through menopause. Thus, the postmenopausal woman has used up or dissolved all of the ova in her ovaries.

Unlike the male, who produces fresh sperm every day, the female carries her lifetime supply of immature ova from birth. Any unused ova age as the woman ages, which is why an older woman has a greater risk of having a child with a genetic disorder (Cunningham et al., 1993).

Table 4.1 summarizes a woman's internal and external reproductive structures and their functions.

## 4.3    THE BREASTS

The breasts are not actually organs of the woman's reproductive system. Rather, they are *secondary sex characteristics*, those characteristics that develop after birth that distinguish females from males. Yet the breasts clearly play a part in a woman's sexuality.

### 4.3.1    Breast Structure

The breasts lie atop the chest muscles, extending from the second to the sixth rib, and from the central breastbone to the armpits. The breasts are specialized organs to produce and secrete milk following pregnancy.

Figure 4.7 shows the structures of the breast and the stages of breast development throughout the life of a woman. The **nipple** is located near the tip of each breast and is surrounded by a circular area of pigmented skin called the **areola.** (During pregnancy, the areola becomes even darker.) The nipple may stick out from the areola, or it may be flush with or even seem to sink into the areola.

Each breast contains 15 to 25 irregularly shaped lobes of milk-secreting **mammary glands,** connected to the nipple by *milk ducts* (fig. 4.8). These groups of glands are separated by *adipose* (fatty) tissue; the amount of adipose tissue determines the size of the

| | |
|---|---|
| **fallopian tubes** (fal-lō´pē-an) | ducts connecting ovaries to uterus |
| **ovulation** (ov-ū-lā´shun) | discharge of ovum from ovary |
| **ovaries** (ō´va-rēz) | female gonads |
| **ova** (ō´va) | female sex cells |
| **corpus luteum** (kor´pus loo´tē-um) | "yellow body" formed from follicle after ovulation |
| **nipple** (nip´l) | tip of breast |
| **areola** (a-rē´ō-lah) | darkened ring around nipple |
| **mammary glands** (mam´-a-rē glandz) | milk-producing glands in breast |

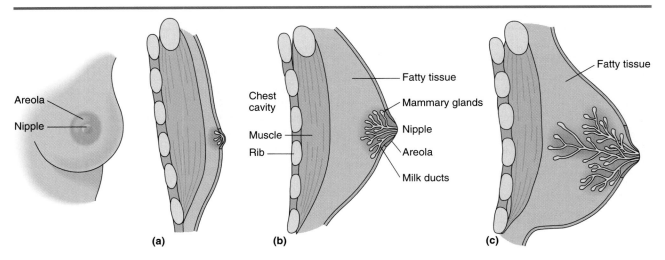

**FIGURE 4.7** Structures of the female breast at various ages: **a:** child; **b:** adolescent; **c:** adult. The main difference between smaller and larger breasts is in the amount of fatty tissue, not the amount of glandular tissue.

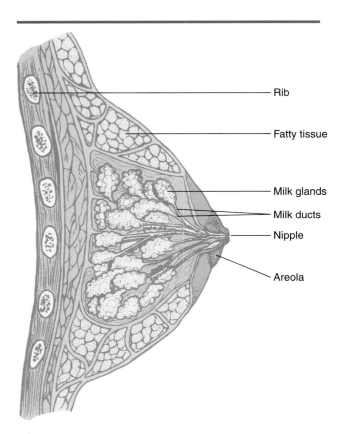

**FIGURE 4.8** Sagittal (side) view of the structure of a lactating breast.

breast. Each duct conveys milk from one of the lobes to the outside, although some join together before reaching the surface.

The breasts are undeveloped at birth and remain so until the onset of puberty. Under the influence of the hormones estrogen and progesterone, the breasts begin to develop, the duct system matures, and extensive fat deposition occurs. The nipple and areola grow and become pigmented.

An adult woman may occasionally notice a slight nipple secretion. This secretion, coming from the milk ducts inside the breast, is normal. When a nipple is exposed to cold temperature or is sexually aroused, small muscles around the nipple contract, causing the nipple to become more erect than usual.

The areola may have small bumps on its surface. These are _sebaceous_ (oil) _glands_ that help lubricate the nipples during breast-feeding. It is also quite common for hairs to grow around the areola. These may appear suddenly due to normal hormonal changes that take place during aging. Some women may notice an increase in hair growth during or following their use of birth control pills; this is also normal.

## 4.3.2 Variations in Shape and Size

Women's breasts normally vary in size and shape from one woman to the next. Breasts may be large, small, lumpy, firm, or saggy. One breast may be of a different shape and size than the other. Breast size and shape change with age and menstrual cycles.

The milk-producing glandular tissue is very sensitive to hormonal changes throughout a woman's life, and size may increase or decrease during events such as adolescence development, the menstrual cycle, the starting and stopping of birth control pills, and pregnancy.

However, when hormonal changes are not occurring, the amount of milk-producing glandular tissue in the breast varies little from woman to woman.

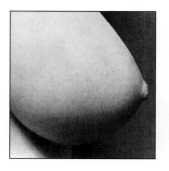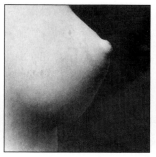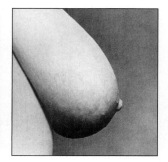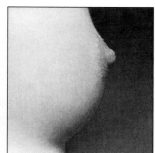

Breasts vary in size and shape from woman to woman.

Thus, the usual size of a woman's breast has little or nothing to do with the amount of milk that she is capable of producing after childbirth. Small-breasted women can produce as much milk as large-breasted women.

Variations in breast size and shape are due primarily to the amount of fatty tissue that lies over, under, and within the glandular tissue. The amount of fatty tissue present in a breast is determined partly by a woman's body weight and partly by heredity.

## 4.4 HORMONES AND THEIR ACTIONS

Like many other bodily processes, reproductive and sexual processes are under the control of a group of highly potent chemical regulators called **hormones.** Produced by cells in the **endocrine glands,** these chemical agents are released into nearby cells or into the bloodstream, where they are carried throughout the body. The action of a hormone is limited to its **target cells,** which possess specific receptors for that hormone. Hormones control the activities of their target cells. Some sexual and reproductive hormones are unique to the female or the male, whereas others are found in both females and males.

### 4.4.1 Regulatory Control of Hormones

Hormones are potent substances that function to regulate the chemical activities of the body, so they must be carefully produced in the proper amounts. Hormonal secretions are regulated in two ways, through a feedback system and a nerve control system.

*Feedback Control*

In the process of *feedback control,* the body system regulates itself, provided it has a sensing device. A simple example of how such a system works is the furnace and thermostat in a home (fig. 4.9). The fur-

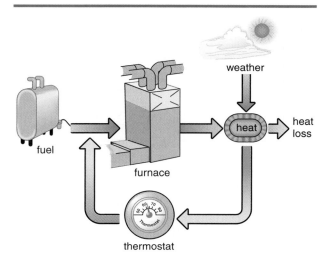

**FIGURE 4.9** Feedback control. A furnace produces heat, and when the heat reaches a certain level, the thermostat (a sensing device) turns off the furnace. When heat is needed, the thermostat turns on the furnace. Since the product (heat) is controlling its own production, this is termed feedback control.

nace produces heat, but when the temperature in a room reaches the temperature indicated on the thermostat (the sensing device), the furnace is automatically shut off. When the temperature in the room once again falls below the temperature level indicated on the thermostat, the furnace again turns on and heats up the room. Such an arrangement allows us to keep our homes at a comfortable temperature.

In the same way, the hormone-producing tissues continuously monitor and are sensitive to the hormone levels in the blood. When the level of a

| **hormones** (hor-mōnz) | internal chemical regulators |
| **endocrine glands** (en´dō-krin glandz) | glands that produce hormones |
| **target cells** | cells with specific receptors for a hormone |

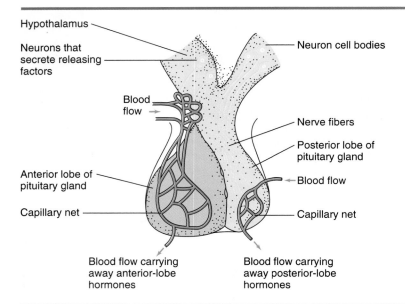

**FIGURE 4.10**   Neurons (nerve fibers) carry on the regulation of some endocrine glands. Neurons from the hypothalamus of the brain secrete releasing factors that flow to the anterior lobe of the pituitary gland, inducing the release of anterior-lobe hormones. Two hormones associated with the posterior lobe of the pituitary are actually produced in the hypothalamus and travel down nerve fibers into the posterior lobe of the pituitary gland, where they are stored until released into the blood.

hormone becomes too high, the producing endocrine gland responds by decreasing the amount of hormone being produced. This is "negative feedback." In other cases, the feedback system stimulates the producer gland to secrete greater amounts of the hormone by "positive feedback." Feedback control allows hormone concentrations to fluctuate slightly above and below their optimal levels, yet remain relatively stable within given ranges.

### Nerve Control

A second form of hormonal control involves the *nervous system*. Some endocrine glands secrete hormones only in response to nerve impulses. For example, nerve impulses can signal the ends of neurosecretory cells in the posterior lobe of the pituitary gland to release the hormone oxytocin (fig. 4.10).

## 4.5   THE SEX GLANDS

Six glands participate in sexual functioning: the hypothalamus, the pituitary gland, the two adrenal glands, the two ovaries (in males, the two testes). In addition, during pregnancy the placenta functions as a gland (fig. 4.11).

### 4.5.1   The Hypothalamus

The hypothalamus, a portion of the lower brain, is considered a sex gland because it produces certain hormones that control the pituitary gland. The hypothalamus produces the hormone **gonadotropin-**

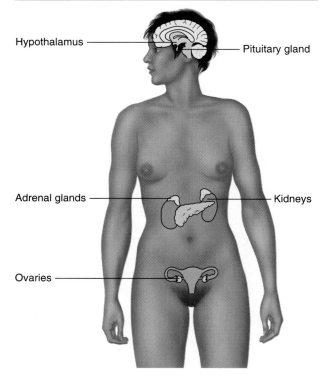

**FIGURE 4.11**   The endocrine glands. The figure shows the location of the hypothalamus, pituitary gland, adrenal glands, and the ovaries.

**releasing hormone (GnRH)**, which prompts the anterior pituitary gland to release its sex hormones, and the **prolactin-inhibiting hormone (PIH)**, which, by inhibiting prolactin secretion by the anterior pituitary,

**TABLE 4.2**    HORMONES IMPORTANT TO THE FEMALE REPRODUCTIVE PROCESSES

| HORMONE | SOURCE | ACTION |
|---|---|---|
| GnRH | Hypothalamus | Stimulates anterior pituitary to secrete FSH and LH |
| FSH | Anterior pituitary | Stimulates ovaries to develop mature follicles (with ova); follicles produce increasingly high levels of estrogen |
| LH | Anterior pituitary | Stimulates the release of the ovum by the follicle; follicle then converted into a corpus luteum that secretes progesterone |
| Estrogen | Ovary (follicle); placenta | Stimulates repair of endometrium of uterus; negative feedback effect inhibits hypothalamus production of GnRH |
| Progesterone | Ovary (corpus luteum); placenta | Stimulates thickening of and maintains endometrium; negative feedback effect inhibits pituitary production of LH |
| Prolactin | Anterior pituitary | Stimulates milk production after childbirth |
| Oxytocin | Posterior pituitary | Stimulates milk "letdown" |
| Androgens | Adrenal glands | Stimulates sexual drive |
| hCG | Embryo (if pregnant) | Stimulates production of progesterone |

inhibits the production of milk by the mammary glands in the breast. The hypothalamus also produces **oxytocin,** which travels to the pituitary for release.

### 4.5.2   The Pituitary

Located just beneath the hypothalamus of the brain, the **pituitary gland** is composed of two parts (lobes), called the *anterior* and *posterior* pituitary (figs. 4.10 and 4.11). Connected to the hypothalamus by a tiny stalk, the pituitary gland is under its control. The anterior pituitary produces two *gonadotropic hormones* (or gonad-stimulating hormones), **follicle-stimulating hormone (FSH)** and **luteinizing hormone (LH).** These hormones are so named because of their actions in women, yet they are also produced in men, stimulating the appropriate gonads in each sex. In men LH is called *interstitial cell stimulating hormone (ICSH).*

The other hormones released by the pituitary are **prolactin** and oxytocin. Prolactin, produced by the anterior pituitary, stimulates the female breast to produce milk following childbirth. Oxytocin, produced by the hypothalamus but released by the posterior pituitary, stimulates the release of the milk from a lactating woman's breasts. Oxytocin also can cause the muscles in the uterine wall to contract, which is important during and following childbirth.

### 4.5.3   The Ovaries

The ovaries in the woman (fig. 4.11), and the testes in the man, are controlled by the gonadotropic hormones. In a woman, FSH prompts the ovaries to develop a follicle, and LH signals the mature follicle to release its ovum, a process called *ovulation.* FSH and LH also stimulate the ovary to produce the female sex hormones **estrogen** and **progesterone.** In the male, FSH stimulates the testes to produce sperm, and ICSH stimulates the production of the male sex hormones called androgens, of which testosterone is the most important.

The hormones important to female sexual development and function are summarized in table 4.2.

| | |
|---|---|
| **hypothalamus** (hī-pō-thal´a-mus) | lower portion of front of brain |
| **gonadotropin-releasing hormone (GnRH)** (gon-a-dō-trō´pin, hor-mōn) | hormone that directs the release of pituitary sex hormones |
| **prolactin-inhibiting hormone (prō lak´ tin)** | hormone produced by hypothalamus that regulates prolactin secretion |
| **oxytocin (ok-sē-to´ sin)** | hormone that promotes release of milk |
| **pituitary gland** (pi-tū´i-tār-ē gland) | endocrine gland beneath hypothalamus |
| **follicle-stimulating hormone (FSH)** (fol´lik-kl, hor-mōn) | pituitary sex hormone affecting ovarian follicles |
| **luteinizing hormone (LH)** (lū´tē-in-īz-ing hor-mōn) | pituitary sex hormone affecting corpus luteum |
| **prolactin (prō-lak´tin)** | hormone that promotes milk production |
| **estrogens (es´trō-jenz)** | ovarian sex hormones that promote development of female reproductive tract |
| **progesterone** (prō-jes´te-rōn) | ovarian sex hormone that promotes repair of the uterus to receive the fertilized ovum |

### 4.5.4 The Adrenal Glands

There are two **adrenal glands,** one atop each kidney (fig. 4.11). Each gland has an outer cortex, which, in females and males, produces small amounts of both female and male sex hormones.

## 4.6 SEX HORMONES IN WOMEN

Sexual functioning in women involves a number of hormones and hormone-like substances. An understanding of these hormones helps us to understand the normal menstrual cycle, menstrual difficulties that may occur, female fertility and infertility, and how certain fertility control methods, such as oral contraceptives, prevent pregnancy.

### 4.6.1 Estrogens

Estrogens are female sex hormones that are responsible for the development and maintenance of feminine body characteristics (table 4.2). The primary source of estrogens in a nonpregnant woman is the ovaries. (However, during pregnancy the placenta also produces a large amount of estrogens.) During puberty the ovaries, under the influence of gonadotropic hormones from the pituitary gland, begin secreting estrogens. Estrogens stimulate the enlargement and maturity of the woman's sexual and reproductive organs, such as the uterus, vagina, fallopian tubes, and vulva. Estrogens are responsible for the following secondary sexual characteristics:

- Development of the breasts and the system of glands within the breasts
- Increased deposits of fat tissue below the skin, especially in the breasts, thighs, and buttocks
- Increased blood supply to the skin

Following each menstrual period, estrogens stimulate the rebuilding of the uterine lining (*endometrium*). The production of estrogens by the ovaries is greatly reduced at menopause. After this time a small amount continues to be available from the woman's adrenal glands.

### 4.6.2 Progesterone

Progesterone is the hormone that prepares a woman's body for pregnancy and continues to be important during her pregnancy (table 4.2). In a nonpregnant woman, the main source of progesterone is the ovaries. Progesterone is released from the corpus luteum ("yellow body"), the remains of the ruptured ovarian follicle after ovulation has occurred. Immediately following ovulation the cells inside the follicle wall enlarge to nearly fill the space formerly filled with liquid. When this happens, the developing corpus luteum secretes an increased amount of progesterone.

During each menstrual cycle, progesterone acts on the endometrium of the uterus, making it a spongy bed rich in blood and nutrients to provide a favorable site for the implantation of the blastocyst (fertilized egg). If no pregnancy occurs, the recently developed corpus luteum degenerates after about ten days. With this, progesterone production declines, and a menstrual discharge begins. On the other hand, if pregnancy has occurred, the corpus luteum persists and continues to produce progesterone. By about the twelfth week of pregnancy, the supply of progesterone will have increased greatly, to ensure a successful pregnancy.

### 4.6.3 Human Chorionic Gonadotropin (hCG)

**Human chorionic gonadotropin (hCG)** is a hormone present only when a woman is pregnant (table 4.2). In fact, most pregnancy tests are designed to detect the presence of hCG in the urine. Its source is the *chorion,* an outgrowth of the embryo. Human chorionic gonadotropin production by the chorion begins soon after fertilization and peaks in about fifty to sixty days; hCG causes the corpus luteum to be maintained and to continue secreting estrogen and progesterone, which allows the uterine lining to continue to grow and develop. Human chorionic gonadotropin is also responsible for stopping the menstrual periods in pregnancy.

The secretion of hCG, which declines by the tenth week of pregnancy, is actually required only for the first five to six weeks of pregnancy. During the remainder of the pregnancy, secretions of estrogen and progesterone by the developing placenta maintain the endometrium.

### 4.6.4 Androgens

It may be surprising to find androgens mentioned here, since they are known as male hormones. The explanation is that the *cortex* (outer part) of the adrenal gland secretes **androgens** in both sexes, though in very low concentrations in adults. Some androgens are converted to estrogens by skin, liver, and adipose tissue.

In women, the adrenal androgens are largely responsible for maintaining sex drive (Spence & Mason, 1992). Androgen levels also influence bone structure; women's low levels promote narrow shoulders and broad hips, the more typical female skeletal shape (Hole, 1994), whereas men's high levels of androgens (mainly from the testes) promote broad shoulders and narrow hips, and increase the relative amount of skeletal (body) muscle.

## 4.6.5    Other Female Sex Hormones

### Inhibin

Produced by the corpus luteum in the ovaries, **inhibin** reduces the secretions of FSH and GnRH, and to a lesser extent LH, toward the end of the menstrual cycle. Inhibin is also present in the human placenta at term, where its role is to inhibit the secretion of FSH and perhaps regulate the secretion of hCG.

### Relaxin

Just before the birth of a baby, the corpus luteum and placenta produce the hormone **relaxin.** This hormone relaxes the *pubic symphysis* (the tissue connecting the front portion of the hipbones) and helps dilate the uterine cervix, which eases the baby's passage through the birth canal.

## 4.7    HORMONAL CONTROL OF THE WOMAN'S REPRODUCTIVE CYCLE

During her reproductive years, a woman normally experiences a cyclic sequence of changes in her ovaries and uterus. Each cycle lasts about a month and involves changes in the ovary, maturation of an ovum (the *ovarian cycle*), and the repair and shedding of the endometrium of the uterus (the *menstrual,* or *uterine, cycle*). All of these monthly events, along with the changes in the breasts, are known as the **female reproductive cycle.** These events are all hormonally controlled.

## 4.7.1    Monthly Reproductive Cycle

As described previously, the hypothalamus controls sex hormones (fig. 4.10). Each female reproductive cycle begins when the hypothalamus secretes GnRH, which in turn stimulates the anterior pituitary to secrete the gonadotropins FSH and LH (fig. 4.12). FSH acts on the ovaries to stimulate the maturation of some ovum-containing *follicles,*(fig. 4.12). The follicles produce increasing amounts of estrogens, which stimulate repair of the endometrium.

By about the fourteenth day of the cycle, one follicle has matured into a *Graafian follicle,* which appears as a blister on the surface of the ovary. Since ordinarily only a single ovum is released each month, any other follicles that may also have begun maturing will degenerate. On rare occasions more than one mature ovum is released, which can result in a multiple pregnancy. Note that the *proliferative phase* of the uterine cycle corresponds to the *follicular phase* of the ovarian cycle (fig. 4.13).

Following ovulation, the empty follicle fills with cells to become the corpus luteum, which now secretes estrogens and progesterone. Because high levels of these hormones feed back to the pituitary and hypothalamus, inhibiting the release of GnRH, no other follicles are stimulated to develop while the corpus luteum remains active. Unless the ovum is fertilized, the corpus luteum begins to degenerate about the twenty-fourth day of the cycle.

As the corpus luteum degenerates, estrogen and progesterone levels fall rapidly, causing the outer portions of the endometrium to break down. Blood and cellular debris from the disintegrating endometrium form the **menstrual flow** (*period, menses*). This flow begins around the twenty-eighth day of the cycle and continues for three to five days. The low levels of estrogen and progesterone also signal the hypothalamus to release GnRH, and a new cycle begins. The "typical" or "average" 28-day reproductive cycle is most characteristic of a woman in her late twenties or older. Younger women more typically experience a longer cycle of perhaps 32 days, and tend to ovulate about 14 days prior to the onset of the next menstrual flow—not necessarily at midcycle. The complete cycle usually ranges from 21 to 35 days in length. Cycles longer than 35 days or shorter than 21 days are considered irregular.

Table 4.3 reviews the hormonal actions of the menstrual cycle in a slightly expanded fashion. Compare this table with figure 4.13.

## 4.7.2    Menarche and Menopause

The first menstruation a young woman experiences is her **menarche,** whereas the cessation of ovulation and menstruation is **menopause.** The average age for menarche is between 12 and 13 years of age,

| | |
|---|---|
| **adrenal glands** (ad-rē′nal glandz) | endocrine glands atop the kidneys |
| **human chorionic gonadotropin (hCG)** (kō-rē-on′ik gon-a-dō-trō′pin) | hormone produced by the chorion of the embryo-fetus |
| **androgens** (an′drō-jenz) | male sex hormones |
| **inhibin** (in-hib′in) | hormone that inhibits FSH, LH, and GnRH |
| **relaxin** (rē-lak′sin) | hormone that relaxes uterine contractions |
| **female reproductive cycle** | monthly events occurring in the ovaries and uterus |
| **menstrual flow** (men′stroo-al) | menstrual discharge, menses |
| **menarche** (men-ar′kē) | beginning of menses |
| **menopause** (men′ō-pawz) | cessation of menses |

The hypothalamus produces GnRH (gonadotropic-releasing hormone).

GnRH stimulates the anterior pituitary to produce FSH (follicle-stimulating hormone) and LH (luteinizing hormone).

FSH stimulates the follicle to produce estrogen and LH stimulates the corpus luteum to produce progesterone.

Estrogen and progesterone affect the sex organs (e.g., uterus) and the secondary sex characteristics, and they exert feedback control over the hypothalamus and the anterior pituitary.

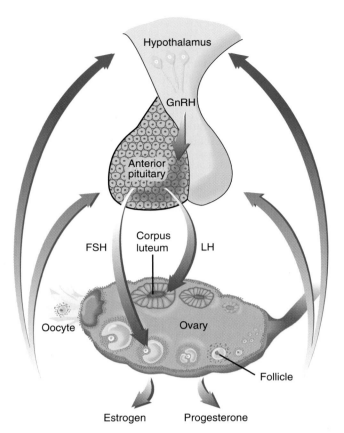

**FIGURE 4.12**   Hormones important to female sexual development and function. The ultimate control of hormones in both genders lies in the hypothalamus of the brain. Its gonadotropin-releasing hormone (GnRH) stimulates the pituitary gland to release the gonadotropins FSH and LH, which in turn stimulate the ovaries to release estrogen and progesterone. The hypothalamus is quite sensitive to one's emotional state, explaining why emotional upsets can affect fertility and disrupt the normal menstrual cycle.

although it may occur as early as the tenth year or as late as the sixteenth year (Cunningham et al., 1993).

There is wide variation in age at menopause. Many women experience menopause between the ages of 50 and 52 years, although it may occur as early as age 35 and as late as 55. There is often a transitional phase lasting several years, characterized by an increasing irregularity in the length of the menstrual cycle and in the bleeding pattern (Cutler, Garcia, & McCoy, 1987). This transitional phase is commonly known as the woman's *climacteric,* or her "change of life." The climacteric has a similar relation to the menopause as puberty has to the menarche. Just as menarche is one of several events of puberty, menopause is only one of several events of the climacteric.

A woman's age at menopause is unrelated to her race, body size, or the age when she began to menstruate (Willis, 1994). Until her menstrual cycles completely stop, its possible for a woman to conceive and become pregnant. Menopause is determined to

have occurred when menstrual periods have ceased for twelve months. This is good evidence that fertility has ended (Hatcher et al., 1994).

The cause of menopause appears to be an aging of the ovaries. After about thirty-five years of menstrual cycles, few, if any, primary follicles remain to be stimulated by the pituitary gonadotropins. With no follicles maturing, ovulation no longer occurs, and levels of estrogens in a woman's body decrease greatly. At the same time, FSH and LH secretions from the pituitary are elevated, because there is no negative feedback of estrogens to the pituitary to reduce their production. Although small amounts of estrogens may still be converted from the adrenal androgens, the total amount of postmenopausal estrogens is far less than was produced in the ovaries before menopause.

Due to the reduced supply of estrogens and the loss of progesterone, various changes occur in a woman during the climacteric. There may be *vasomotor* (control of blood vessel walls) disturbances that produce "hot flashes." *Atrophy* (shrinking) of

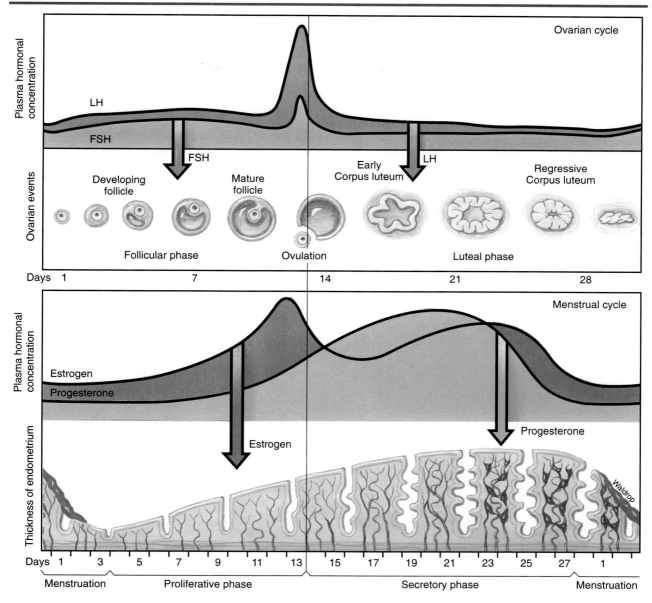

**FIGURE 4.13**    Phases of the menstrual cycle in relation to ovarian events, hormonal secretion, and the condition of the endometrium. Numbers 1 to 28 refer to the days of the cycle, with day 1 being the first day of menstruation. From top to bottom: levels of gonadotropic hormones; development of the ovarian follicle and, after ovulation, its conversion to a corpus luteum; estrogen and progesterone levels throughout the cycle; and changes occurring in the endometrium (uterine lining) during the cycle.

the uterus and vaginal walls may also occur, and the vaginal walls can become quite dry due to the loss of natural lubrication. Underarm and pubic hair thins, and the breasts might grow smaller. The skin thins and there is increased *osteoporosis* (loss of bone matrix) (Whitney & Rolfes, 1996).

Of the women who reach menopause, about 20 percent have no symptoms—they merely stop menstruating. About 50 percent of menopausal women experience unpleasant symptoms, such as sensations of heat in the face, neck, and upper body ("hot flashes"). About half of all women who experience "hot flashes" display a patchy reddish flush or visible blush on the skin (Willis, 1994). These sensations may last for thirty seconds to five minutes and may be accompanied by chills or sweating. Some menopausal women experience varying degrees of headache, backache, and fatigue. The causes for these symptoms are not well understood, but may involve changes in the rhythms of secretion of GnRH by the hypothalamus due to a lack of feedback of the sex hormones by the follicles.

**TABLE 4.3**    HORMONAL ACTIONS DURING THE MENSTRUAL CYCLE

| HORMONE | SOURCE | ACTIONS OF HORMONE |
|---|---|---|
| GnRH | Hypothalamus | Stimulates pituitary to secrete FSH and LH above a basal level |
| FSH | Pituitary | Stimulates ovaries to develop mature follicles (with ova); follicles produce increasingly high levels of estrogens |
| LH | Pituitary | Surge of LH stimulates follicle to break open and discharge ovum and follicular fluid (containing estrogens); follicle converted into corpus luteum, which secretes estrogens and gradually increasing amounts of progesterone |
| Estrogens | Ovary (follicle) | Causes rapid growth of endometrium of uterus; causes the breast sensitivity that often accompanies menstrual flow to disappear; rising level of estrogens have negative feedback effect on hypothalamus and GnRH; GnRH output reduced, and secretion of FSH and LH inhibited; very high level of estrogens reverses effect on hypothalamus, stimulating it to suddenly release large dose of GnRH; GnRH causes pituitary to release sudden surge of FSH and LH |
| Progesterone | Ovary (corpus luteum) | Causes endometrium to become thick, spongy, glandular, and receptive to a fertilized ovum (zygote); causes breast engorgement (may be sensitive or painful); has a negative feedback on pituitary; causing a drop in LH production, which results in the degeneration of the corpus luteum and a drop in progesterone and estrogen production; lack of progesterone initiates menstrual flow |

## 4.7.3    Menstrual Concerns and Myths

### A Woman's Feelings about Menstruating

Some young women are embarrassed when they start to menstruate. They might have grown up with little or no knowledge about where the menstrual discharge comes from or why, and when it occurs they might be frightened or wonder if they are hemorrhaging. Some might be afraid that boys will detect something out of the ordinary or that their bleeding will show. Menstruation is not something that most young women will discuss with their male friends.

Other young women feel inadequate if their first period is late, especially when most of their female friends have already started menstruating. Some believe that when a young woman "gets her period," it is physical confirmation that she has become a "true" woman.

There is no reason for a woman to limit her activities during menstruation unless she is experiencing severe discomfort (see "Dysmenorrhea," p. 94). The menstrual fluid (about 2 to 5 tablespoons for a whole menstrual period) can be absorbed using various products. Sanitary napkins are absorbent pads of various sizes worn in the panties. Tampons are absorbent cylinders that are worn internally, in the vagina. Many women prefer tampons because of their comfort and convenience. However, tampons should be used carefully since improper use can lead to toxic shock syndrome, a serious disease (see "Infections of the Reproductive System: Toxic Shock Syndrome").

As a young woman comes to know her own body well, she can respond to her period with confidence, as creative proof that she has the power to create life. If she becomes a parent she can model for her children an openness toward menstruation, including a willingness to talk about it so that her children are able to feel comfortable about it.

### Cultural Attitudes toward Menstruation

Attitudes about menstruation affect a woman's personal experience with menstruation and may reflect how her culture feels about women in general. Personal attitudes about menstruation have cultural and religious roots going back thousands of years (see "Dimensions of Diversity: Menarche and Menstruation in Three Cultures"). More often than not, attitudes about menstruation are primarily negative. Rather than being seen as a normal physiological function relating to femininity and fertility, menstruation is too often viewed as a "curse" a woman could well do without.

Negative attitudes toward menstruation can become "self-fulfilling prophecies." If a woman believes that menstruation will be an unpleasant experience, it probably will be for her.

Taboos have long surrounded menstruation and some still hold today. Certain cultures and religions have entirely isolated menstruating women or have confined them to the company of other women. Some cultures believe that menstrual blood is "unclean"; yet others believe that menstruating women have supernatural powers.

More current taboos (all lacking any factual basis) include avoiding exercise, showers, or sexual intercourse during menstruation. There is also a tendency to hide the fact of menstruation entirely.

# DIMENSIONS OF DIVERSITY

## MENARCHE AND MENSTRUATION IN THREE CULTURES

***ISRAEL AND ELSEWHERE:** Ortho-dox Judaism* The book of Leviticus (15:19–24) of the Old Testament de-mands that menstruating women be isolated from the rest of the commu-nity for seven days. It also proclaims that anyone and anything that touches her is unclean, so inter-course was forbidden during this time. At the end of the menstrual pe-riod a married woman was to bathe in the *mikvah,* a ritualized cleansing. Among Russian Jews, a sharp and painful slap was considered the ap-propriate mother-daughter ritual upon menarche. As recently as 1972 the chief rabbi of Israel issued a statement that called for punishment for married couples who violated the Torah (Jewish religious laws) by hav-ing intercourse during menstruation (Delaney, Lupton, & Toth, 1988).

***JAMAICA:*** Traditional rural Ja-maicans believe that menstrual blood has positive power. At the core of these traditional beliefs is the idea that toxins must be washed out of the body periodically ("washout"). Women are believed to take in men's

wastes or toxins when they take in semen. Women dirtied by semen ("discharge") must rid their bodies of it by menstruating. If left in the womb, this discharge will rot. While gravity runs some of the unused se-men out, the rest of it must be flushed out of the body. Menstrua-tion is thus considered a sign of health, and Jamaicans refer to men-struation as "seeing the health." Some Jamaicans believe that inter-course brings on menarche because it exposes women's bodies to men's discharge. They consider menstrual irregularities or excessively heavy menstrual flow as a sign of "too many lovers." Because of this, some Jamaican women reject contracep-tives that shut down the menstrual cycle. This system of beliefs holds that postmenopausal women do not need to menstruate because their wombs are "closed up" and are no longer susceptible to the dangerous effects of semen (Sobo, 1994).

***UNITED STATES: APACHE, NAVAJO, AND NOOTKA TRIBES:*** Among the Mescalero Apache, the pubertal rites

that accompany menarche are a cel-ebration of a woman's power and fertility. Each year there is a four-day celebration for all the young women who began menstruating that year. Some of this celebration is commu-nity wide, with the story of the tribe being told by young boys, and some of it involves the young women pri-vately contemplating their new power (Kelly, 1996).

Among the Navajo, the menar-chal *Kinaalda* ceremony is the most important religious ritual. Its pur-pose is to make sexual relations holy, and to ensure that they will be effec-tive in producing children who will carry out the work of the tribe. There is a large tribal celebration after a pe-riod of seclusion and instruction (Delaney, Lupton, & Toth, 1988).

The Nootka Indians of the Pa-cific Northwest celebrate a girl's menarche or "moontime" with a gi-gantic party. Part of the celebration involves her swimming to shore from a boat out at sea to demon-strate her courage and endurance.

Even advertisements for menstrual products tend to avoid using the term *menstruation*. Ads might refer to absorbency, but never state what the product is in-tended to absorb.

Worst of all, misconceptions about menstruation can contribute to job discrimination against women. Some people believe that the menstrual cycle makes women unstable or less capable, that women's effi-ciency decreases during their periods, or that men-struating women are unreasonable or unpleasant. Both men and women experience mood swings, yet when a woman has changes in mood, some immedi-ately see this as an inherent instability. There is also a myth that menstrual complications result in a higher absentee rate for women. But the reality is that women do not miss much work because of menstrual problems, and their job performance during men-struation is not measurably different than from other

times. A menstruating woman is just as able to per-form tasks and think constructively (Boston Women's Health Book Collective, 1992).

### Premenstrual Syndrome (PMS)

Most women who experience normal ovulatory cyclic patterns are able to identify changes in their sense of well-being, energy level, tendency for fluid retention, and so forth in relation to their menstrual cycles. **Premenstrual syndrome (PMS)** is a group of symptoms experienced by 20 to 50 percent of women before their menstrual periods (American Psychiatric

---

**premenstrual syndrome**  physical discomforts
(prē-men´stroo-al sin´drōm)  before menstruation

Association, 1994). PMS symptoms can be physical, emotional, and/or behavioral, and can occur in any combination. Three to 5 percent of women experience symptoms severe enough (markedly depressed mood, marked anxiety, marked affective lability [instability], and marked irritability) to meet the criteria for *premenstrual dysphoric disorder* (American Psychiatric Association, 1994). PMS symptoms occur for several days before and sometimes during the first day of the period.

The most common PMS symptoms are these (Hatcher et al., 1994):

- Dysphoria (depression, irritability, anxiety, nervousness, tension, inability to concentrate)
- Breast tenderness
- Fluid retention (bloating, edema, weight gain of two to five, or as much as ten, pounds)
- Headache
- Fatigue or exhaustion
- Food cravings (especially for salt, sugar, or chocolate)

The basic cause of PMS is unknown. Various theories have been proposed, including nutritional deficiency, excess levels of prostaglandins, abnormal fluid balances, progesterone deficiency, and central nervous system endorphin abnormalities (Lurie & Borenstein, 1990). Some believe that PMS is a cluster of syndromes rather than a single syndrome (Hatcher et al., 1994).

A woman who experiences PMS can follow some simple measures that may reduce potential PMS problems. She might consider:

- Following a diet of regular meals that are high in complex carbohydrates, moderate in protein, but low in refined sugars and salt
- Minimizing or eliminating her consumption of caffeinated beverages and foods (e.g., colas, tea, coffee, chocolate), alcohol, and tobacco (Hatcher et al., 1994; Rossignol & Bonnlander, 1990)
- Pursuing a regular program of aerobic exercise for at least 30 minutes, three to four times weekly, especially during the premenstrual interval
- Learning relaxation response techniques (Goodale, Domar, & Benson, 1990)

An awareness of her body's reactions to cyclical hormonal changes can help a woman understand and treat any accompanying symptoms. (See "Healthy Sexuality: Relief for PMS.") Many of these diet and lifestyle changes may not only reduce PMS symptoms but are likely to improve overall well-being.

## Dysmenorrhea

**Dysmenorrhea** refers to pain associated with menstruation, which usually begins slightly before or during menstrual discharge. Some women experience mild cramping, and some experience menstrual pain severe enough to prevent them from functioning normally for one or more days each month. If pain is not limited to the menstrual phase, and if its severity increases over time, then a more extensive medical evaluation is needed.

Dysmenorrhea can be described as primary or secondary. *Primary dysmenorrhea* is painful menstruation in which there is no detectable organic disease. It commonly begins during adolescence as soon as the young woman's ovulatory pattern is first established. Primary dysmenorrhea is caused by high levels of **prostaglandins,** fatlike substances that are produced in the uterine lining and released into the bloodstream as the lining is shed. Progesterone, which is present during the last half of each menstrual cycle, blocks the effects of prostaglandins. If the woman is pregnant, progesterone levels are maintained, but if not, progesterone levels drop rapidly and prostaglandin activity increases. This causes the uterus to contract and shed its lining, and may result in dysmenorrhea. Drugs that inhibit prostaglandins may be used to treat severe primary dysmenorrhea. *Secondary dysmenorrhea* is pelvic cramping caused by a disorder or disease, such as uterine tumors, ovarian cysts, pelvic inflammatory disease (PID), or endometriosis.

Dysmenorrhea can be an incapacitating problem. For many women with dysmenorrhea, simple treatments such as taking aspirin or ibuprofen, resting, or applying a heating pad may relieve the symptoms. For a woman with severe dysmenorrhea, stronger measures may be indicated by her health care practitioner.

## Amenorrhea

**Amenorrhea** is the absence of menstruation, ranging from a single missed period to a chronic condition. *Primary amenorrhea* is the condition of never having had a period, in women who are beyond sixteen years of age. *Secondary amenorrhea* is missing three to six consecutive menstrual cycles. Two to 5 percent of women have been reported to experience amenorrhea (Yeager et al., 1993).

A rather common cause of amenorrhea is eating disorders—amenorrhea can accompany extreme obesity, very low body weight, or malnutrition. Emotional causes can include anxiety or even the excitement associated with some special event (e.g., vacation, final exams, or marriage). Many cases involve hormonal conditions, especially those associated with

# RELIEF FOR PMS

*Bloated? Irritable? Despite what you might have heard, there's little evidence herbs can relieve your PMS symptoms. But calcium, magnesium, and vitamin E just might.*
*By Christie Aschwanden*
*WebMD Medical News*

May 22, 2000—As a physician, Mary Hardy, M.D., was trained to view herbal medicine with a healthy dose of skepticism. But her patients kept gushing about the remedies they were using for premenstrual syndrome (PMS). "I'd had so many patients come in with dramatic stories," she says. "One woman told me 'these herbs are like magic.' "

So when she herself fell victim to a bad case of PMS, Hardy decided to try the two herbs most commonly used for the problem—evening primrose oil and chaste tree berry (also known as vitex). To her delight, they eased her symptoms, and when Hardy praised the herbs at a March 2000 conference of the American Pharmaceutical Association, national news reports carried her remarks.

Hardy was more open than many physicians to the idea of herbal remedies; as the medical director of the Cedars-Sinai Integrative Medicine Medical Group in Los Angeles, her clinic melds conventional Western medicine with complementary methods like herbs, osteopathy, and acupuncture. After discovering that herbs relieved her own symptoms, Hardy hit the library to see what researchers had learned.

What she found highlights the dilemma of many women seeking alternative treatments to ease PMS. While self-help books and Internet sites trumpet the power of herbal remedies, there's scant scientific evidence to support the claims.

Fortunately, herbs aren't the only treatment available for PMS sufferers who want to avoid hormones and antidepressants with their side effects. Researchers have found solid evidence for some vitamins and minerals—so much that the American College of Obstetricians and Gynecologists (ACOG) in April revised its recommendations on PMS to include them.

## The Truth about Herbs

Most of the evidence for botanical PMS remedies is made up of individual anecdotes like Hardy's. And many studies have suggested that the placebo effect—a patient's belief in the power of a medicine—may be the reason so many women report relief from these herbs.

For example, PMS sufferers have reported feeling much better in studies using evening primrose oil. But in the August 1990 issue of the *Medical Journal of Australia,* researchers reported a more careful approach. They divided 38 women in two groups. One took primrose oil and one took a placebo. But groups reported the same improvement.

As for chaste tree berry, most tests haven't compared it to a placebo. And scientists have yet to scrutinize dong quai, another herb said to offer PMS relief.

## Vitamins and Minerals to the Rescue

Does this mean women must rely on hormones and antidepressants—the standard treatments—for PMS? No, says Susan Johnson, a gynecologist at the University of Iowa, who helped develop the new ACOG standards. If you're in the throes of PMS and in search of supplements that work, Johnson says you may benefit from calcium, magnesium, and vitamin E.

Here's the evidence:

▌ Calcium. Many PMS symptoms resemble those of calcium deficiency, says Susan Thys-Jacobs, an endocrinologist at St. Lukes Roosevelt Hospital in New York City. Though no one fully understands what causes PMS, Thys-Jacobs hypothesizes that for many women the problem may signal an underlying calcium shortage.

In a study of 466 PMS sufferers, published in the August 1998 issue of the *American Journal of Obstetrics and Gynecology,* Thys-Jacobs and her colleagues found that calcium supplements of 1,200 milligrams per day—the calcium equivalent of four glasses of milk—significantly eased PMS symptoms.

Calcium was no instant cure; the results only kicked in after about two months of use. But by the third month of treatment, women taking the supplements had only about half the PMS symptoms of those who took a placebo. The only symptoms calcium didn't curb, says Thys-Jacobs, were fatigue and insomnia.

*Relief for PMS—continued*

Thys-Jacobs recommends that women concentrate first on boosting the calcium in their diets. But if you can't stomach that much yogurt or tofu, go ahead and take a supplement. Aim for a total calcium intake of 1,200 to 1,500 milligrams per day, and be sure you take the supplements along with food so they're properly absorbed, says Thys-Jacobs.

▌ Magnesium. In March of this year, nutritionist Ann Walker and her colleagues at the University of Reading in England published a study in the *Journal of Women's Health and Gender-Based Medicine* comparing magnesium to a placebo. The results suggest that modest amounts—200 milligrams per day—could reduce water retention and bloating. A follow-up study, Walker says, showed that the same dose of magnesium paired with 50 milligrams of vitamin B-6 reduced mood symptoms like anxiety.

▌ Vitamin E. A dose of 400 IU of vitamin E per day allayed PMS symptoms more than a placebo in at least one small study published in the June 1987 *Journal of Reproductive Medicine*. Because vitamin E is an antioxidant with other health benefits and minimal side effects, Johnson says there's little harm in women trying this supplement.

▌ Vitamin B-6. In the May 22 issue of the *British Medical Journal*, researchers reviewed nine published studies of vitamin B-6 for PMS and concluded that a dose of 100 milligrams per day may relieve a wide range of symptoms, including depression. However, Johnson warns that B-6 is harmful in doses above 100 milligrams per day.

In addition to calcium, magnesium, and vitamin E, ACOG recommends lifestyle changes such as aerobic exercise and a complex carbohydrate diet to help relieve PMS symptoms.

As for Hardy, she readily agrees with these recommendations. But she still stands by her suggestion that PMS sufferers give herbs a try, too. "There isn't any one thing that's going to solve this," she says.

---

the ovaries, pituitary, thyroid, or adrenal glands. A few cases of amenorrhea relate to anatomical abnormalities present from birth.

Amenorrhea is not a normal adaptation to strenuous physical training, although vigorous training combined with low body fat or various life stresses may trigger it (Whitney & Rolfes, 1996). Amenorrhea is characterized by low blood estrogen, infertility, and often bone mineral losses. As many as 66 percent of female athletes might have amenorrhea (Yeager et al., 1993).

Unsuspected pregnancy often causes amenorrhea, so an immediate medical evaluation is important for any sexually active woman who develops the condition. If amenorrhea involves more than an occasional missed period, the underlying cause should be determined and corrected. Cases relating to hormonal deficiencies are often treated by hormone therapy.

### HIV and Menstruation

Some women with human immunodeficiency virus (HIV) report heavy bleeding, irregular periods, and premenstrual syndrome. The medications given for HIV and emotional stress may also contribute to these symptoms (Denenberg, 1993).

If a woman is infected with HIV, the presence of blood in the vagina during menstruation may increase the risk that a sexual partner could become infected. A woman diagnosed as HIV positive should always insist that her partner use a condom (along with nonoxynol-9), dental dam, or other protective measures. This is especially important if any blood is present in the vagina.

### Sexual Activity during Menstruation

Avoiding sexual activity during menstruation is an old tradition in Western and other cultures. This taboo has its roots in ancient beliefs that menstrual blood is "impure" and that menstruation is associated with illness.

Some women experience variation in their sexual drive during various parts of their menstrual cycle, yet no general pattern has been shown to be typical for women (Meuwissen & Over, 1992).

Generally, there are no health risks associated with a woman engaging in sexual intercourse during her menstrual period, if it feels comfortable for her. Heterosexual partners who do not wish to have intercourse when the woman is having her period can explore other sexual intimacies that can provide both of them with satisfaction.

### 4.7.4  Endometriosis

**Endometriosis** is a condition in which bits of endometrial tissue, normally found lining the uterus, spread and attach to other parts of the body. Affecting up to 15 percent of premenopausal women, endometriosis generally involves the pelvic cavity, but it can also involve the ovaries, external surface of the uterus, colon, abdominal wall, urinary bladder, and kidneys (Wallis, 1986).

The transplanted endometrial tissue may reduce the mobility of internal structures by forming adhesions. The transplanted tissue engorges with blood during the proliferative phase of the menstrual cycle each month, and breaks down with each menstrual period. But since the tissue cannot be expelled to the outside, the products remain in the pelvic cavity, causing painful menstruation, lower backache, and pain during intercourse (Barbieri, 1988). Untreated endometriosis is a major cause of infertility.

The cause of endometriosis is still uncertain. Symptoms include pelvic pain, often intense, abnormal menstrual bleeding, and a feeling of fullness during each menstrual period. The most reliable diagnosis of the disorder is made by direct visual examination of the internal pelvic organs by *laparoscopy,* in which a slender viewing device is inserted through a small incision in the abdomen. Treatment usually involves hormones or, in severe cases, surgery (Madaras & Patterson, 1984). In some cases, birth control pills are prescribed to prevent and treat endometriosis (Speroff & Darney, 1992).

## 4.8  THE SEXUAL BODY: PROMOTING HEALTH AND TREATING ILLNESS

A woman's body is designed to engage in sexual, as well as, reproductive functions. Women are at risk for conditions and diseases of the reproductive organs because of the cyclic nature of their reproductive physiology, the complexities of pregnancy, and hormonal changes throughout life. The medical specialty known as **gynecology** deals with women's reproductive health.

### 4.8.1  Gynecological Examinations

An important part of a woman's self-care is regular **gynecological examinations.** It is generally recommended that these exams begin at about age eighteen or whenever the woman becomes sexually active, whichever comes first. Many potentially serious reproductive problems in women can be detected in the early, often curable, stages during routine examinations. The specific schedule for periodic exams is influenced by several variables, such as the woman's age, the type of contraception she may be using, and findings of previous exams. Thus, the frequency of exams might range anywhere from once every six months to once a year or even less often.

In choosing her practitioner, a woman should make sure that the practitioner is well qualified and is someone she feels comfortable with and confident about. Various health care providers including family medicine specialists, certified nurse-midwives, and gynecologists, can perform gynecological exams. Practitioners can be either male or female. Many colleges have women's health services available through their student health clinics or will refer a woman to a qualified practitioner.

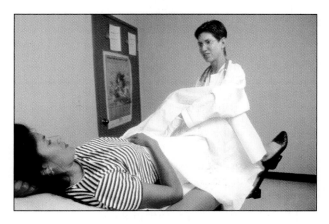

Gynecological exams and Pap smears are important for every woman. It is generally recommended that exams begin at age 18 or when a woman becomes sexually active, whichever comes first.

| | |
|---|---|
| **dysmenorrhea**<br>(dis-men-ō-rē′a) | painful menses |
| **prostaglandins**<br>(pros-ta-glan′din) | substances that cause uterine muscle contractions |
| **amenorrhea**<br>(a-men-ō-rē′a) | absence of menses |
| **endometriosis**<br>(en-dō-mē-trēō′-sis) | growth of endometrial tissue outside of the uterus |
| **gynecology**<br>(gī-ne-kol′ō-jē) | medical specialty that deals with female reproductive health |
| **gynecological examination**<br>(gī-ne-ko-loj′i-kal) | a medical exam that focuses on female reproductive health |

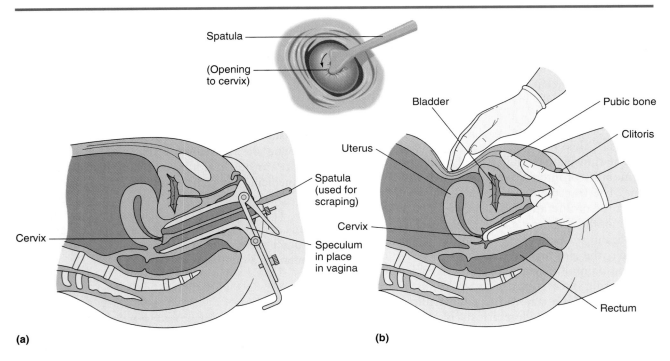

**FIGURE 4.14**  Types of pelvic examinations: **a:** Insertion of speculum for a pelvic exam, with spatula for cell removal. **b:** Bimanual pelvic exam.

If a woman has never had a gynecological exam, it is natural for her to wonder what to expect. While the details may vary, the following are typically part of the exam:

- Questions about family and personal medical history
- Listening to the heart and lungs with a stethoscope
- Checking of blood pressure and pulse
- Weight check
- Blood tests for blood count and blood sugar count
- Urinalysis
- Breast examination, with instruction on breast self-examination
- Abdominal exam
- Pelvic exam, including rectal exam
- Pap smear
- Mammogram (when the practitioner recommends it)

If the health care provider is male, a female nurse should be present during the exam. If this is not the case, a woman should feel free to request the presence of a nurse.

## Pelvic Examination

A **pelvic examination** typically includes four phases: examination of the external genitals, visual internal examination, bimanual internal examination, and rectovaginal examination.

In examining the external genitals, the practitioner looks for swelling, irritation, discoloration, unusual discharges, or other signs of infection. Then she or he will insert a *speculum* (spreading device) into the vagina to hold the walls open (fig. 4.14). The vaginal walls and cervix will be examined for any infection or other abnormalities, and at this time a Pap smear is taken. If a woman has never seen her cervix, she might ask for a hand mirror to take a look.

The speculum is then removed and the bimanual examination performed (fig. 4.14). The practitioner will insert two gloved fingers into the vagina while placing the other hand on the lower abdomen. By pressing in various locations, the size, shape, and firmness of the uterus, ovaries, and fallopian tubes can be determined, and the practitioner can check for unusual growths or pain.

The rectovaginal exam involves insertion of one finger into the rectum and two into the vagina. This reveals more information on the internal pelvic organs and might detect rectal disorders.

Self-examination of the external sex organs is recommended for people of both genders. This helps us to know ourselves, to be able to instruct our partners regarding where stimulation feels best, and to detect any unusual conditions.

## Self-Examination

Women can benefit from regular vulval, vaginal and cervical self-examinations. By examining herself regularly, a women can learn more about what the "normal" vulval and vaginal structures look like, what the normal discharges look like, and the changes in the mucus during different stages of the menstrual cycles.

The external genitals can best be viewed using a mirror, either holding it near the vulva or by placing it on the floor. Through use of a speculum (pharmacies carry inexpensive plastic ones) and mirror, a woman, by herself or with the help of a friend, can examine the color and appearance of her vaginal walls and cervix. She can learn what is normal for her so that any changes from pregnancy, infection, or ovulation can be more readily detected.

### 4.8.2   Infections of the Reproductive System

All women secrete moisture and mucus from membranes that line the vulva. Under conditions such as sexual arousal these secretions increase. Many bacteria grow in these secretions, even in a healthy woman.

### Vulvitis and Vaginitis

An inflammation of the vulva, or **vulvitis,** can be caused by oral sex or sensitivity to commonly used products like soaps, sanitary napkins, powders, deodorants, synthetic underwear, pantyhose, and medications. Vulvitis often occurs with other infections such as herpes or vaginitis. Poor diet, inadequate hygiene, and stress can make a woman more susceptible to vulvitis. Diabetic women often experience it more commonly, and postmenopausal women often encounter it due to lowered hormone levels, which can cause the vulvar tissue to become drier, thinner, and less elastic, thus leaving the vulva more susceptible to irritation and infection.

Women with vulvitis may experience itching, redness, and swelling. The surface skin may even form blisters, which may break open and ooze. Scratching these may lead to further irritation. Overcleaning an inflamed vulva can lead to further irritation.

Vaginal infections, or *vaginitis,* can result from lowered resistance, excessive douching, pregnancy, birth control pills, antibiotics, diabetes, cuts, abrasions, irritations due to the use of tampons, insufficient lubrication during sexual intercourse, placing other devices into the vagina, and sex with an infected partner. After menopause, women are especially susceptible to vaginal infections.

The vagina has several characteristics that help prevent infection. The normal acidity of the vaginal secretions, aided by the presence of beneficial vaginal bacteria, helps keep yeast and other organisms under control. Infection-fighting antibodies are also secreted in the vagina.

Vulvitis and vaginitis can be prevented by regular washing of the vulva; keeping the area dry; using clean towels and washcloths; avoiding feminine hygiene sprays, soaps, and talcum powders; wearing clean, all-cotton underpants rather than nylon; avoiding tight pants; wiping the genital area from front to

| | |
|---|---|
| **pelvic examination** | a medical examination of a |
| (pel´vik) | woman's genital-rectal organs |
| **vulvitis** (vul-vī´tis) | an inflammation of the vulva |

back (to avoid spreading bacteria from the anus); making sure the sexual partner and sex toys are clean; using a water-soluble lubricant if needed for intercourse; avoiding douching of any kind; eating well; getting sufficient rest; and avoiding tampon use if there is a history of vaginal infections. These infections can be treated with antibiotics and sulfa drugs.

## Candida (Yeast Infection)

Some of the more troublesome infections of the female sexual organs, especially the vagina, are caused by a yeast called **Candida albicans.** This yeast is a normal inhabitant of the mouth, skin, digestive tract, and vagina of about 20 percent of people at any given time. *Candida* is present in the vagina of 30 percent of pregnant women (Black, 1966). It is usually held in check by the other organisms present at these sites and by the body's natural defenses. *Candida* infection is technically called **candidiasis,** and is commonly called a *"yeast infection."* About 75 percent of women will experience vaginal yeast infection at some time (Tortora et al., 1998).

Factors that can allow *Candida* to become a problem include the following:

- Antibiotic use, which can destroy beneficial acid-forming vaginal bacteria
- Diabetes, of which infections are often an early indication
- Pregnancy or oral contraceptives that can reduce vaginal acidity
- Poor diet, especially a diet that is high in sugar
- Moisture buildup caused by wearing nylon panties, pantyhose, or other synthetic fabrics (cotton "breathes" much better)
- Douching

Characteristic symptoms of vaginal candidiasis include burning and itching and a thick, whitish discharge that can be quite abundant. There also can be patches of white pseudomembrane (false membrane) on the vaginal lining.

In treating vaginal candidiasis, there are several considerations. The vaginal area needs to be kept dry, and any contributing conditions, such as poor nutrition, need to be corrected. Also, a variety of effective medications are available at pharmacies and grocery stores or by prescription. If self-medicating, it is important to be sure that the problem is really *Candida* and not something else such as gonorrhea that would not be cured by medications intended for *Candida.*

## Toxic Shock Syndrome

**Toxic shock syndrome (TSS)** is a disease condition caused by *toxins* (poisons) released from some types of the bacterium *Staphylococcus aureus.* Only about 56 percent of cases of TSS are associated with menstruation (Farley, 1994), yet with these it often occurs in previously healthy, young women who use tampons during their periods. Nonmenstrual TSS has been known to occur after medical incidents such as surgery or a deep wound, or in women who use vaginal barrier methods of contraception (Schwartz et al., 1989).

TSS symptoms appear quickly and are often severe. Symptoms include temperatures of up to 105 degrees Fahrenheit, often accompanied by vomiting and diarrhea. Some patients have aching muscles, bloodshot eyes, or a sore throat, symptoms that resemble the flu. A sunburn-like rash might not develop until a person is very ill, and even this might not be noticed if it affects only a small area. Still later, some patients report a flaking or peeling of the skin on the palms of the hands and soles of the feet.

As many as 10 percent of TSS cases are fatal. The danger occurs with a sudden drop in blood pressure, which, without timely treatment, can lead to shock. Treatment usually involves large amounts of fluids and drugs administered to raise blood pressure and lower temperature, along with specific antibiotics to reduce the risk of recurrence. With proper treatment, patients usually recover within three weeks. An initial episode of TSS may be mild and go unnoticed, whereas a recurrent case may be severe. An initial episode increases a woman's chances of repeat symptoms. Risk can be reduced by stopping the use of tampons or by not leaving them in for an extended period of time.

The National Institutes of Health have shown that the risk of TSS is 19 to 48 times greater for women who use tampons than for those who do not (Farley, 1994). The Food and Drug Administration (FDA) requires tampon containers to be labeled *junior, regular, super,* and *super plus* to conform to specific absorbency ranges. The FDA recommends that women choose the *lowest* absorbency needed to control menstrual flow, since the risk of TSS increases with higher tampon absorbency. Women should be aware of the symptoms of TSS and should report any suspicious symptoms to their health practitioner immediately.

## Urinary Tract Infections

Although the urinary bladder is not a reproductive organ, **urinary tract infections** (UTI, or **cystitis**) are a common problem for women and are often related to sexual activity. The most common cause is the intestinal organism *E. coli,* although any of a variety of bacterial pathogens can cause this problem. The symptoms include frequent, burning, or painful urination and cloudy or bloody urine. Bladder infections occur more often in females than in males because the shorter urethra of the female makes it easier for bacteria to reach the bladder.

Cystitis needs to be treated promptly with medically prescribed drugs. Untreated, it can become a chronic problem or spread to the kidneys. Cleanliness, frequent urination, and drinking adequate water help to prevent this infection. Females may cleanse the genital area from front to back to avoid carrying intestinal bacteria from the anus to the urethra.

Cystitis may or may not be related to sexual activity. Vigorous vaginal intercourse tends to force bacteria through the urethra to the bladder, especially in women. Some people call this "honeymoon cystitis." Urinating immediately following sexual activity might help to prevent cystitis arising from this cause.

## 4.8.3  Gynecological Cancers

Cancers of a woman's reproductive organs, or *gynecological cancers,* may involve the vulva, vagina, cervix of the uterus, uterine (endometrial) lining, uterus, fallopian tubes, or ovaries. The three most common are cancers of the cervix, endometrium, and ovaries. In addition to discussing gynecological cancers, we will discuss breast cancer, an important cancer in women (American Cancer Society, 2000).

### Cervical Cancer

Abnormal cell growth, or cervical *dysplasia,* is relatively common on or near the cervix (Jolles, 1989). Such cell growth, usually detected by a Pap test, is often harmless, with the cells returning to normal spontaneously. In some cases, however, such abnormal cell growth develops into *cervical cancer.* At first, cervical cancer is *localized (in situ)* and confined to the cervix. If the abnormal cells spread beyond the upper, or surface, layer of the cervix into the underlying connective tissues, *invasive* cervical cancer has developed.

A woman's risks of developing cervical cancer can be increased by certain factors, some of which can be controlled. The most important *risk factor* is infection with human papillomavirus (HPV). HPV is transmitted during sex, so unprotected sex (especially starting at a young age), or having many sexual partners, makes HPV infection more likely. HIV infection is also a risk factor for cervical cancer, as is smoking. Cigarette smoking doubles a female smoker's risk of cervical cancer compared to that of a nonsmoker (American Cancer Society, 2000).

Risk factors that cannot be controlled include age and ethnic background. The risk for cervical can-

cer is greatest for women between their late teens and mid-thirties. Death rates from cervical cancer are higher among African American, Hispanic American, and Native American women, compared to the national average in the United States. This is probably because more affluent segments of the population are more likely to have their cancer detected and treated early. Factors that have no effect on cervical cancer risk include a history of herpes simplex virus infection, whether male partners have been circumcised, or the number of pregnancies a woman has had (Schiffman, 1992).

The course of treatment of cervical cancer depends on the stage of its development when it is detected. In its early stages, abnormal cell growth in the cervix can be treated with various therapies or surgery, often preserving the possibility of future pregnancy. More advanced cases may require the surgical removal of part or all of the uterus (a hysterectomy), radiation treatment, or a combination of the two.

### Pap Tests

In addition to avoiding risk factors for cervical cancer, a woman can monitor the condition of her cervix with a regular **Pap test.** In this test, developed by Dr. George Papanicolaou, cervical cells are sampled using a small swab or brush, and examined by a skilled technician. The Pap test should be performed annually (usually as part of a regular pelvic exam) in women who are, or have been, sexually active or who have reached the age of eighteen. After three or more consecutive normal Pap tests, a woman's practitioner may recommend less frequent exams (American Cancer Society, 2000). Most cervical cancers remain localized as small lesions for several years before spreading into surrounding tissues and organs. Thus, annual Pap tests can detect these lesions while they are still easy to remove.

Pap tests are simple, painless, highly effective, and lifesaving. Routine Pap tests have reduced deaths from cervical cancer by over 70%.

| | |
|---|---|
| *Candida albicans* (kan´ di-da al´ bi-kans) | a yeast that causes common vaginal infections |
| **candidiasis** (kan-di-di´ a-sis) | infection by *Candida albicans* |
| **toxic shock syndrome (TSS)** | condition caused by toxins of a certain bacterium |
| **urinary tract infection (UTI)** | inflammation of the urinary bladder |
| **Pap test** (pap) | diagnostic exam of cervical cells |

## Uterine Cancer

We have just discussed cancer of the lower part of the uterus, the cervix. Cancers of the upper part, or body, of the uterus can occur in the uterine lining (endometrial cancer) or in the muscle and connective tissue (uterine sarcomas). An estimated 36,000 new cases of cancer of the uterine body were diagnosed in the United States during 2000, and over 95% of these were endometrial cancer (American Cancer Society, 2000).

*Endometrial cancer* is the most common cancer of the female reproductive organs. Normally, the endometrium responds to a woman's changing levels of estrogen and progesterone, producing the monthly menstrual cycle. Factors that shift the balance of these hormones toward relatively more estrogen increase a woman's risk for developing endometrial cancer. These risk factors include early menarche (before age 12), late menopause (after age 52), no pregnancies, obesity, diabetes, and a family history of breast or ovarian cancer. Most cases of endometrial cancer occur in women over the age of 40, and whites are 70% more likely than African Americans to develop the disease (American Cancer Society, 2000).

In order to reduce her risk for endometrial cancer, a woman can control obesity and diabetes, and eat a diet low in animal fats. Being 30 pounds overweight triples endometrial cancer risk, since fat tissue can convert other hormones into estrogens. Long-term use of birth control pills can also reduce a woman's risk, though a woman should discuss her choice of contraceptive with her practitioner. Estrogen replacement therapy (ERT) is often recommended to offset some of the effects of menopause, such as hot flashes, osteoporosis (bone mineral loss), and increased risk of heart disease. Because estrogen alone increases a woman's endometrial cancer risk, estrogen and progesterone are used together for the same benefits without increasing the risk of endometrial cancer (often called hormone replacement therapy, HRT).

Endometrial cancer risk factors may increase a woman's risk for certain types of *uterine sarcoma*, but most cases of uterine sarcoma are not due to known risk factors. The primary symptom of uterine or endometrial abnormalities is unusual vaginal bleeding, particularly in postmenopausal women. Uterine sarcoma may also be signaled by other abnormal vaginal discharge or abdominal pain. Diagnosis of these diseases is by endometrial biopsy or dilation and curettage (D and C), both of which are outpatient procedures with minimal discomfort. Uterine sarcoma may additionally be diagnosed by ultrasound. Although the Pap test is very effective in detecting early cervical cancer, it is only partially effective in detecting endometrial cancer or uterine sarcoma.

Treatment for endometrial cancer and uterine sarcoma includes radiation therapy, hormones, chemotherapy, and **hysterectomy** (removal of the uterus). A *partial hysterectomy* involves removal only of the body of the uterus, leaving the cervix and lower uterus intact. With a *total (complete) hysterectomy* the entire uterus (with cervix) is removed.

## Ovarian Cancer

Less common than cervical cancers, ovarian cancer is the sixth most common cancer (other than skin cancer) in women. Ovarian cancer causes more deaths than any other cancer of the woman's reproductive system. Most cases of ovarian cancer are not due to any known *risk factors*. However, incidence increases with age and might be related to a family history of ovarian cancer, no pregnancies, and a personal history of breast cancer (American Cancer Society, 2000). Women who have used combined oral contraceptives are less likely to develop ovarian cancer than those who have not (Grimes, 1992).

Ovarian cancer is difficult to detect, as early cancers often have no symptoms. During a woman's annual pelvic exam, the practitioner will feel the size and shape of the ovaries. Any abnormalities detected during the exam (or suggested by symptoms such as pelvic or abdominal pain or swelling, or unusual vaginal bleeding) will be followed by ultrasound or biopsy of the ovaries. The treatment of ovarian cancer usually includes surgical removal of one or both ovaries, and may include removal of the fallopian tubes and uterus. This may result in significantly reduced estrogen levels. Women with lowered estrogen levels produce less vaginal lubrication during arousal, and may require more time for lubrication to occur. Aids to lubrication, such as K-Y jelly, can provide effective lubrication for the sexually active women. In addition, hormone replacement therapy is often prescribed, which can help alleviate some of the symptoms of estrogen loss.

### 4.8.4    Breast Conditions

It is very important for a woman to examine her breasts for changes that could indicate breast tumors, growths, or cancer. Many breasts normally feel lumpy, and few of these lumps are dangerous when they persist throughout life. A woman who starts examining her breasts in her teens and becomes familiar with them can notice changes as she becomes older. Any change should be reported to her practitioner.

Every woman should inspect her breasts monthly, immediately after the end of her menstrual period. Examination during the menstrual period is not recommended because the breasts can be somewhat swollen and tender at that time.

## Benign Changes

Some of the changes that may affect the breasts are *benign*, or noncancerous. Some women are fearful that any pain, change, or lump might be breast cancer. Information on typical breast conditions can dispel some of this anxiety. Here are some benign conditions:

*Fibrocystic conditions* (also known as cystic mastitis, or fibrocystic breast disease). Most breast lumps are caused by fibrocystic changes. *Cysts* (fluid-filled sacs) may swell, and connective tissue may grow (fibrosis) during the monthly cycle. These changes usually occur and subside regularly each month, and they may be mild or they may become severe and even painful over the years. Benign lumps do not usually develop into cancer, and a history of fibrocystic changes does not increase a woman's risk for developing breast cancer.

*Fibroadenoma.* A lump that does not fluctuate in size during a woman's monthly cycle may be a fibroadenoma. Such lumps are more common in teenagers and women in their twenties, and they are unlikely to develop after a woman has reached her forties. Those that appear may remain permanently. Although these lumps may feel like a cancerous growth, they cannot spread outside the breast and are not life-threatening (American Cancer Society, 2000).

It is important for a woman to consult her health care provider whenever any lumps or changes are noticed in the breast. Further diagnostic testing can distinguish benign changes from cancerous conditions. In *needle aspiration* a fine needle is inserted into the lump to learn if there is any fluid inside. If so, it is likely a cyst, which can be drained. If it is not a cyst, the lump can be *biopsied,* which is a microscopic surgical examination of the tissue, to determine whether the tissue is benign or malignant (Crowley & Rosenberg, 1992).

## Breast Cancer

Cancer of the breast is the most common form of cancer in women, and is the second leading cause of cancer death, after lung cancer. Fortunately, the overall mortality rates from breast cancer have decreased, probably due to earlier detection and improved treatment. If detected early, the survival rate is nearly 100% for some forms of breast cancer (American Cancer Society, 2000).

Breast cancer may be associated with known *risk factors,* some of which can be controlled and some that cannot be changed. Factors that cannot be changed include gender (breast cancer occurs in men but is 100 times more common in women), age, a family history of breast cancer, and a personal history of breast cancer (which increases the risk of a new cancer developing in the other breast). Radiation treatment of the chest (following childhood cancer, for example), and a long menstrual history also increase risk. There are some factors known to increase risk that women can avoid. Women who consume two to five alcoholic drinks a day have about 1.5 times the risk of women who drink no alcohol. Obesity is also associated with an increased risk of developing breast cancer, particularly in postmenopausal women.

Research studies have provided inconclusive or conflicting results about a number of potential risk factors for breast cancer. Physical inactivity, environmental pollutants (such as pesticides), oral contraceptives, dietary fat intake, and long-term hormone replacement therapy may slightly increase risk, though more research is needed to confirm these links. Some concerns that have been raised about other risk factors have been conclusively disproven by research. There is no link between induced abortion, antiperspirants, underwire bras, smoking, or silicone breast implants and breast cancer risk (American Cancer Society, 2000).

For cancers such as breast cancer, for which early screening tests are available, early detection and treatment can increase survival. Monthly breast self-examination, annual clinical breast exams, and annual mammograms (for women 40 and older) are recommended by the American Cancer Society. Although white American women are slightly more likely to develop breast cancer than African American women, African Americans are more likely to die from breast cancer because their cancer is often diagnosed at a later stage, when it is more difficult to cure. This is probably due to economic factors that can limit access to health care, as well as cultural factors affecting awareness and attitudes about self-exams and early screening detection.

Women's breasts are often viewed as a symbol of femininity and, as such, have been idealized. The cultural significance assigned to breasts often goes beyond their functions of lactation and tactile erotic stimulation. Some women in Western societies take their breasts to be a measure of their physical attractiveness, and any breast disfigurement can seriously damage their self-image. The symbolic value of the breasts for some women is evident in their reaction to learning they have breast cancer. While all cancer

---

**hysterectomy** (his-ta-rek´tō-mē)     removal of the uterus

diagnoses hold the fear of being fatal, breast cancer, and the fear of breast removal, seems to hold greater terror for some women (Boston Women's Health Book Collective, 1992). Yet many breast cancer survivors have a survivor's personality buttressed by newly discovered attitudes and perceptions (see "Healthy Sexuality: Breast Cancer Survivors").

### Breast Self-Examination

*Breast self-examination (BSE)* is a method that, when used regularly, can help a woman detect suspicious lumps in her breasts (American Cancer Society, 2000). Such lumps, though most often harmless, can be early indicators of cancer.

Eighty to 90 percent of all breast lumps are benign (noncancerous). Such lumps tend to disappear or fluctuate in size during the menstrual cycle, being more common during the first few days of the period or around ovulation. Thus, it is best to conduct a BSE about a week after menstruation. Women past menopause should perform the exam at the same time each month, such as on the first of the month. Consistent, regular exams will help a woman become familiar with the shapes, colors, texture, and consistency of her own breasts.

*In the shower:* Examine your breasts during your bath or shower, because hands glide more easily over wet skin. Keeping your fingers flat, move them with firm pressure over every part of each breast. Use the right hand to examine the left breast, and the left hand for the right breast. Check for any lump, hard knot, or thickening (fig. 4.15a).

*Before a mirror:* Inspect your breasts with your arms at your sides, facing the mirror (fig. 4.15b). Next raise your arms high overhead. Look for any changes in the contour of each breast: a swelling, dimpling of skin, or changes in the nipple.

Next, rest your palms on your hips and press down firmly to flex your chest muscles. Left and right breast will not exactly match—few women's breasts do. Again, look for changes and irregularities. Regular inspection shows what is normal for you and will give you confidence in your examination.

*Lying down:* To examine your right breast, while lying down put a pillow or folded towel under your right shoulder. Place your right hand behind your head—this distributes breast tissue more evenly on the chest. With your left hand, fingers flat, press firmly in small circular motions around an imaginary clock face. Begin at the outermost top of your right breast for twelve o'clock, then move to one o'clock, and so on around the circle back to twelve. (A ridge of firm tissue in the lower curve of each breast is normal.) Then move one inch inward, toward the nipple,

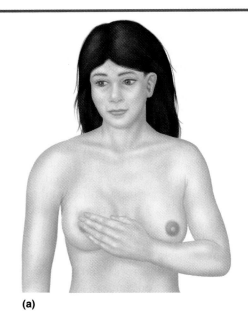

(a)

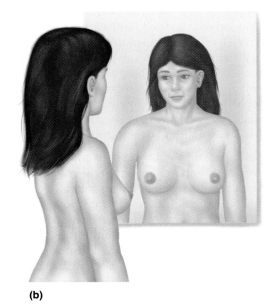

(b)

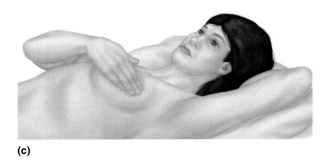

(c)

**FIGURE 4.15**  Self-examination of the breast. **a:** During your bath or shower. **b:** Standing before a mirror. **c:** While lying down.

## HEALTHY SEXUALITY

## BREAST CANCER SURVIVORS

Fortunately, with breast cancer, the rate of survivorship has been increasing, yet this increased survivorship highlights a concern for survivors' needs. A recent study described a "survivor personality" in which successful handling of adversity came from the victim's determination to survive. At the same time an awareness of vulnerability reshaped the survivor's life. The major fear was recurrence of cancer. In adjusting to living with cancer, these women described positive aspects of their cancer experiences in statements such as these:

■ On family and friends:
   *"You find out who your real friends are."*
■ A hopeful attitude:
   *"I took control and went right on with my life."*

■ Self-perception of survivorship:
   *"Everyone should know that you can survive physically and emotionally."*
■ What having cancer meant to them:
   *"There are gifts of cancer. I appreciate what is of value now."*
   *"The will to pick up and go on was the major factor in survival."*
   *"I did not deny. I confronted it."*

The survivor was found to be an individual who no longer defines existence in terms of a cancer diagnosis, has gained a perspective on life and death, may have discovered a new or reborn faith, chooses battles carefully, and is not afraid of risk.

**Source:** S. Fredette, "Breast Cancer Survivors: Concerns and Coping," *Cancer Nursing* 18 (1995): 35–46. Copyright © 1995 Lippincott Raven Press, Philadelphia, PA. Reprinted by permission.

and keep circling to examine every part of your breast, including the nipple. Use light, moderate, and firm pressure to feel deep regions of the breast as well as areas near the surface. Now slowly repeat the procedure on your left breast with a pillow under your left shoulder and your left hand behind your head. Notice how your breast structure feels (fig. 4.15c).

Finally, squeeze the nipple of each breast gently between the thumb and index finger. Any discharge, clear or bloody, should be reported to your physician immediately.

Regular monthly BSE is critical because malignant lumps are usually painless and early detection is essential for successful treatment.

### *Mammography*

The clinical detection of breast cancer can be done by **mammography,** a low-dose X-ray examination that can find cancers too small to be felt by the most experienced examiner. The mammogram involves placing the breast on a clear plastic surface, then another sheet of plastic is laid on top of the breast, which is then X-rayed. The breast is then placed between two vertical plastic sheets and again X-rayed. The pressure placed on the breast might be quite uncomfortable, but it lasts only for the few seconds needed to take the diagnostic photographs.

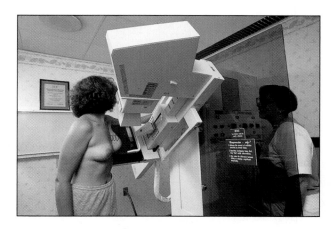

Mammograms are low-dose X-ray examinations that reveal fine details of internal breast tissue and detect cancers too small to be felt.

It is believed that routine screening every one to two years with mammography and clinical breast examination can reduce breast cancer mortality by about one-third for women age 50 and over. Various schedules for mammography have been proposed.

| | |
|---|---|
| **mammography** (mam-og´ra-fē) | X-ray examination of a woman's breast |

The American Cancer Society (2000) recommends a mammogram every year for all women age 40 and over. In addition, they recommend a clinical breast examination every three years for women ages 20 to 39, and every year for women over age 40.

When selecting a facility to provide the mammography, women should find out if it is accredited by the American College of Radiology (ACR) and certified by Medicare. Accreditation and certification are based on an evaluation of equipment, film processing, and the credentials and experience of the technologists who take the mammograms and the radiologists who interpret them. The National Cancer Institute (NCI) Cancer Information Service (800)4-CANCER and local chapters of the American Cancer Society can provide names of ACR-accredited facilities.

### Treatment and Recovery

Lumps that are first identified during a self-exam or by a clinician will probably be examined by mammography or ultrasound. Suspicious lumps should be *biopsied*. About half of all breast cancers develop in the upper outer quadrant of the breast (Segal, 1994b) (fig. 4.16). Treatment of confirmed cases of breast cancer includes radiation therapy, chemotherapy, hormone-blocking therapy, and surgery, which varies

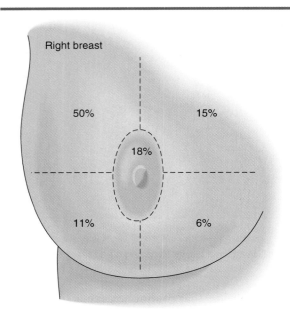

**FIGURE 4.16** Breast quadrants and breast cancers. About half of all breast cancers develop in the upper outer quadrant of the breast.

**Source:** Data from *Current Issues in Women's Health*, 2nd edition, DHHS Publ. #(FDA) 94–1181, Public Health Service, Washington, D.C.

from *lumpectomy* (partial removal of the breast) to *mastectomy* (full removal).

If surgical removal of cancerous breast tissue is the indicated treatment, the least disfiguring method is a lumpectomy in which the malignant lump and varying amounts of surrounding tissue are excised. Scarring can be reduced by making the smallest incision possible, and breast disfigurement might be only slightly more than that caused by an exploratory biopsy to confirm the malignancy.

As with other illnesses that affect sexuality, the patient's partner plays a critical role in her emotional recovery. If a woman who has had a breast removed believes she is no longer sexually desirable, she might find excuses to avoid sexual activity. This avoidance might then affect her partner's reaction to her. Even when her partner continues to accept her sexually as before the operation, her self-acceptance, or lack of it, can affect her emotional health, and thus, the relationship as well.

The partner, too, might have some difficulty accepting the woman's altered appearance. Some sexual partners, however, adjust more easily to the mastectomy if they are also partners in dealing with the problem—that is, if they are involved in the decision to have surgery, in caring for the incision after surgery, and in postsurgical therapy.

### Breast Reconstruction

Following a mastectomy a woman has several options: leaving her chest as it is and doing nothing, using an external breast prosthesis, or having one of several types of breast reconstruction. Not every woman who has had a mastectomy chooses reconstruction. Depending on the type and stage of her cancer, and the extent of surgery, reconstruction can be performed immediately or after a waiting period to allow time to complete any radiation or chemotherapy treatments.

Many women who have had a mastectomy wear an *external prosthesis,* an artificial removable breast-shaped device. Held in place by a bra, the prosthesis gives a natural appearance. This new "breast" might shift and feel hot and heavy (especially in warm weather), and the surgical scars on the chest will be visible when it is removed, but it does not require additional surgery.

Since the 1960s, advances in plastic surgery have made breast reconstruction an increasingly successful and popular procedure. Breast reconstruction can help a woman adjust to breast removal, although nursing and sexual functions of the breasts cannot be restored. Breast reconstruction is done by either an implant or a surgical reconstruction.

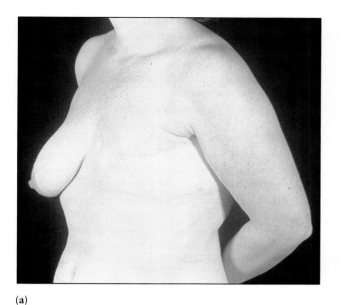

(a)

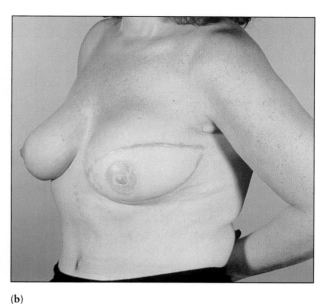

(b)

Current improvements in breast reconstruction are resulting in more natural-looking breasts. These photographs are of the same woman: **a:** taken after the mastectomy was performed, and **b:** after the reconstructive surgery. This woman's left breast has been reconstructed from lower abdominal tissue and her right breast has been reduced to match her reconstructed breast.

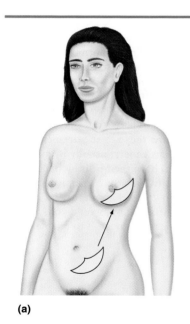

(a)

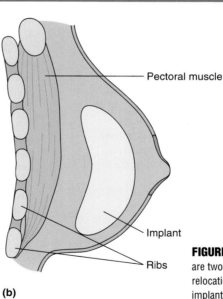

(b)

Pectoral muscle

Implant

Ribs

**FIGURE 4.17**   Breast reconstruction. There are two major surgical approaches: **a:** tissue relocation (such as from the abdomen), and **b:** implants.

In one surgical implant technique, a sac filled with saline is placed into a pocket created between the skin and the underlying muscle (fig. 4.17). The alternative method—surgical reconstruction of the breast—involves relocating muscle, fat, blood vessels, and other tissue from the back or abdomen (fig. 4.17). An implant, if needed, is then placed under the new muscle.

## SUMMARY

1. The woman's external genitals, or vulva, include the mons pubis, labia majora, labia minora, vestibule, perineum, and clitoris.

2. The internal sexual organs include the vagina, cervix, uterus, fallopian tubes, and ovaries.

3. The vagina functions as the receiving organ during copulation and similar sexual activity, and also as the birth canal during childbirth. The uterus consists of the fundus, body, and cervix. The three walls of the uterus are the perimetrium, myometrium, and endometrium.

4. The fallopian tubes carry ova from the ovaries to the uterus. Each tube ends in fimbriae and each tube contains cilia that wave the ova toward the uterus.

5. The ovaries (female gonads) produce ova and several hormones. During each menstrual cycle, usually one follicle matures and erupts.

6. Breast structure consists of the central nipple, surrounded by the pigmented areola, and the underlying mammary glands.

7. The sexual processes of the body are under the control of substances called hormones. Hormones are regulated by a feedback system.

8. The sex glands secrete hormones, and consist of the hypothalamus, the pituitary gland, the adrenal glands, and the ovaries. The developing placenta also secretes hormones.

9. There are six major sex hormones in women. Estrogen develops and maintains a woman's secondary sexual characteristics. Progesterone prepares the body for pregnancy and maintains any developing pregnancy. Androgens regulate a woman's sexual drive. Gonadotropin-releasing hormone (GnRH) stimulates the pituitary to secrete follicle-stimulating hormone (FSH) and luteinizing hormone (LH), both of which are involved in the ovulatory cycle.

10. Dysmenorrhea is menstrual pain (primary or secondary). Amenorrhea is the absence of menstruation. Endometriosis is the transplantation of endometrial tissue within the abdominal cavity.

11. Gynecological examinations include a medical history, a breast examination, an evaluation of lung and heart function, tests for blood composition, pulse, blood pressure, tests for STIs, a urinalysis, a Pap smear, an abdominal examination, and pelvic and rectal examinations.

12. Infections of the woman's reproductive system include vulvitis, vaginitis, yeast infections, toxic shock syndrome, and urinary tract infections.

13. Reproductive cancers include cervical cancer and uterine cancer (which includes endometrial cancer and uterine sarcoma) and ovarian cancers.

14. Breast self-examination and mammography are important for the early detection of breast cancer.

15. Medical interventions in women's reproductive diseases, such as mastectomy, have significant psychological effects on a woman's body image and self-esteem.

## CRITICAL THINKING CHALLENGES

1. What are your attitudes toward menstruation? Have they changed since you were young? Were you provided with adequate knowledge about the process? Describe how you would explain menstruation to a young person.

2. For a complete understanding of hormones and their actions, use a flow chart format to diagram a woman's monthly hormonal cycle. Include all hormones, target cells, effects, and regulatory feedback loops. How do the names of all the hormones relate to their function?

3. Some women who know they are at extremely high risk of developing breast cancer (usually by a known genetic predisposition) have their healthy breast(s) removed as a preventative measure (prophylactic mastectomy). How do you feel about this procedure? In a similar situation, would you consider doing this, or recommend it to a female family member?

# MALE SEXUAL ANATOMY, PHYSIOLOGY, AND SEXUAL HEALTH

# 5

**AFTER STUDYING THIS CHAPTER, YOU SHOULD BE ABLE TO**

[1]    List and describe a man's external and internal sexual organs.

[2]    Describe the internal structure of the penis.

[3]    Summarize the important aspects of the current controversy surrounding male circumcision.

[4]    Explain the mechanisms of the erection of the penis.

[5]    Trace the passage of sperm from the testes to the end of the penis and name the ducts and glands involved in its production.

[6]    Describe how semen is formed and what occurs during ejaculation and orgasm.

[7]    Summarize what is known about nocturnal emissions.

[8]    Discuss the similarities and differences between a man's and woman's breasts.

[9]    List and describe all of the sex glands of the man's reproductive system.

[10]    Explain the hypothalamus-pituitary-testes connection.

[11]    Discuss the ways in which prostate cancer is diagnosed.

In our culture the male body is valued in terms of what it can do, in addition to how it looks. Is he strong? Can he lift or carry? Can he exert force and have an impact on the world? Is he sufficiently athletic? In terms of sexuality: Can he have an erection easily and maintain it for as long as he wants to? Can he control his ejaculation? Can he impregnate? For many, if not most, men, hesitations or problems in any of these relatively mechanical functions deal a serious blow to both their self-esteem and their sense of masculinity. Yet many people know relatively little about how the male body actually functions. Due to our cultural norms prohibiting nudity, many women and men are unaware of the variety possible in male genitals.

As in the previous chapter on women's sexual physiology, we will begin with a tour of the male reproductive structures (*anatomy*) and how they function in the sexual system (*physiology*), both reproductive and sensual. The structures mentioned here are involved, variously, in the male *reproductive system, sensory pleasure,* and excretion. Then we will discuss care of the man's sexual body in health, aging, and in illness.

## 5.1    EXTERNAL SEX ORGANS

The male external sex organs consist of the penis, through which the urethra passes, and the scrotum, which encloses the testes (fig. 5.1).

### 5.1.1    The Penis

The **penis** is the male organ that conveys both urine and semen to the outside of the body. Cylindrical and hanging from the lower abdomen, it is attached to the pubic bone, or *pubis,* in front and to the floor of the pelvic cavity (fig. 5.1). The penis consists of fibrous tissue, nerves, blood vessels, and three cylinders of spongy erectile tissue specialized to elongate and stiffen in the process of *erection.* There is no significant amount of muscle in the penis, nor does it contain a bone. Muscles around the base of the penis help to eject both urine and semen through the urethra. Pubic hair covers the skin around the base of the penis.

The regions of the penis consist of the *root* (base), the *shaft* (body), and the *glans penis* (head) (fig. 5.1). The root, which extends back into the body, consists of the *bulb of the penis* and the *crura* (singular is *crus*), which are attached to the pubic bones. When his penis is erect, a man can feel these parts by pressing his fingers into the **perineum,** the area between his anus and scrotum.

The visible, long, external portion of the penis is the *shaft,* or body. The slightly enlarged, acorn-shaped end of the penis is the **glans penis,** or head. It may be slightly darker in color than the rest of the penis. At the tip of the glans is the opening of the urethra, called the *urethral orifice,* or *meatus.* The slightly enlarged rim, or *corona,* at the back part of the glans possesses a high concentration of sensitive nerve endings. The corona is separated from the shaft by a groove called the coronal *sulcus* (fig. 5.2).

Running through the penis are three cylinders of spongy, erectile tissue, and the **urethra,** the duct that passes urine from the bladder and semen through the penis to the outside of the body (fig. 5.1). The three cylinders, or **erectile bodies,** each consists of irregular cavities and vascular, spongy spaces that can fill with blood. The two larger cylinders, called the **corpora cavernosa (cavernous bodies),** lie in the upper part of the penis and extend the length of the root and shaft. The third cylinder, called the **corpus spongiosum (spongy body)** and lying beneath the other two cylinders, extends the length of the penis and forms the glans. The urethra passes through the corpus spongiosum (fig. 5.1).

When the penis is **flaccid** (not erect), the cylinders of erectile tissue cannot be seen or felt as distinct structures. However, when the penis is erect, the spongy body stands out as a distinct ridge along the underside of the penis (fig. 5.1).

The penis is covered by skin and a thin layer of connective tissue. The skin covering the shaft is hairless and quite loose, which allows for the enlargement of the penis when it becomes erect. A loose fold of skin called the **prepuce** (*foreskin*) is attached just behind the glans and extends forward, covering the glans as a sheath (figs. 5.1 and 5.2). The glans is anchored to the foreskin by a thin fold of tissue called the *frenulum* (fig. 5.2). As with the corona, the

| | |
|---|---|
| **penis** (pē´nis) | the external male reproductive organ |
| **perineum** (per-i-nē´um) | the area between the anus and scrotum |
| **glans penis** (glanz´ pē´nis) | the head of the penis |
| **urethra** (ū-rē´thra) | the urine duct through the penis |
| **erectile bodies** (e-rek´tīl) | cylinders of erectile tissue in the penis |
| **corpora cavernosa** (kor´pe-ra kav-er-nōs´ah) | see *cavernous bodies* |
| **cavernous bodies** (kav´er-nus) | the upper two erectile bodies in the penis |
| **corpus spongiosum** (kor´pus spon-jē-ō´sum) | see *spongy body* |
| **spongy body** | the lower erectile body in the penis |
| **flaccid** (flass´-id) | relaxed, not erect |
| **prepuce** (pre´pūs) | the foreskin of the penis |

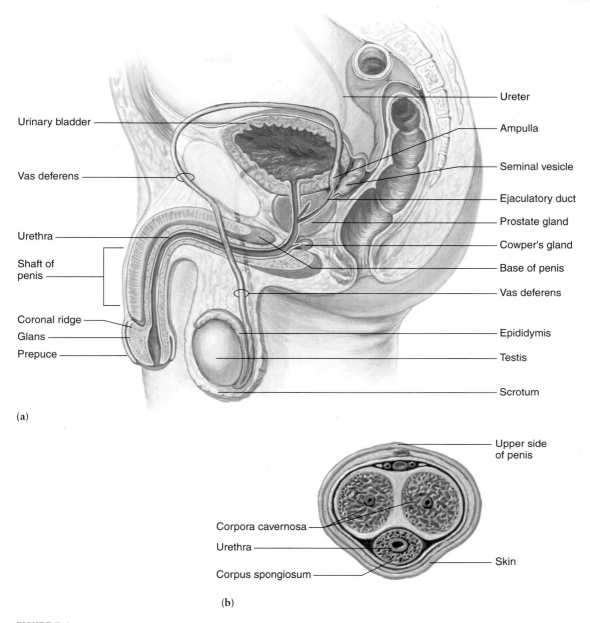

Urinary bladder

Vas deferens

Urethra

Shaft of penis

Coronal ridge
Glans
Prepuce

(a)

Ureter

Ampulla

Seminal vesicle

Ejaculatory duct

Prostate gland

Cowper's gland

Base of penis

Vas deferens

Epididymis

Testis

Scrotum

Upper side of penis

Corpora cavernosa

Urethra

Corpus spongiosum

Skin

(b)

**FIGURE 5.1**    The male genitals. In order to understand our genitals and how they respond to stimuli, we need to know their internal anatomy. **a:** A sagittal (front to back) section of the penis and scrotum. **b:** Cross section of the penis.

frenulum possesses a high concentration of sensitive nerve endings. The prepuce varies in the extent to which it covers the glans; in some men it covers the entire glans, whereas in others it covers only a small portion. In the United States, the prepuce is frequently surgically removed in newborn male infants (see "Dimensions of Diversity: Infant Male Circumcision"). If not previously removed, the prepuce can be drawn back from the glans to expose it.

The entire penis is sensitive to physical stimulation, but the greatest concentration of nerve endings is in the glans and prepuce. Two specific areas on the glans that are particularly responsive to stimulation are the corona and frenulum (fig. 5.2).

### Penis Size

Penile size is a common source of concern among men. Some men believe that penis size determines a man's sexual prowess. Many men hope that their sex partners will be impressed by the size of their penis. The average adult penis is 3 to 4 inches long when flaccid and 5 inches long when erect, although the

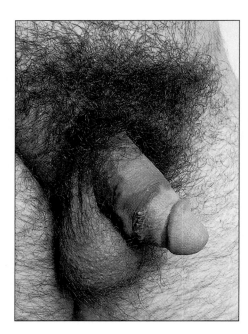

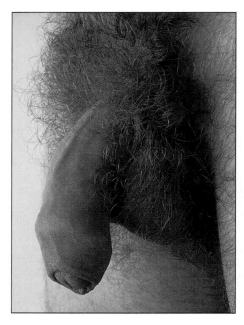

The penis. The tip of the penis is shaped to allow it to perform a variety of functions. It is partially covered with the foreskin (prepuce), which is anchored to the penis. The loose foreskin can readily be retracted from the glans of the penis when the penis is erect, exposing the highly sensitive glans to the stimuli it needs to induce ejaculation. Glands beneath the foreskin produce and secrete an oily substance called smegma. While easily washed away, its accumulation harbors bacteria. The penis on the left is circumcised; the penis on the right has an intact foreskin.

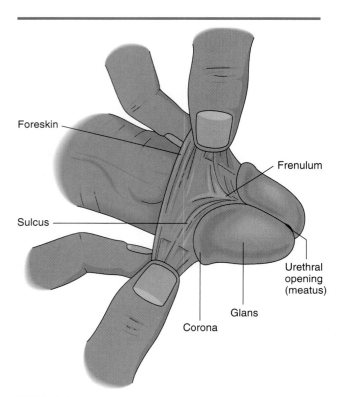

Foreskin

Frenulum

Sulcus

Urethral opening (meatus)

Glans

Corona

**FIGURE 5.2** The corona and frenulum are two areas of the penis that are especially sensitive to touch due to their high concentration of sensitive nerve endings.

erect penis may range from 3 to 7 inches long (McAninch & Wessels, 1995). A penis does not grow with frequent intercourse or decrease in size because of lack of intercourse. Nothing can be done through exercise to change its size.

Masters and Johnson found that erection tends to have an equalizing effect on long and short penises: penises that are smaller when flaccid tend to increase more in size when erect than do penises that are larger when flaccid (Masters & Johnson, 1966). Jamison and Gebhard (1988) found that erection causes a shorter flaccid penis to become proportionately longer and a narrower flaccid penis to become proportionately thicker. The size and shape of the penis are not related to a man's build, race, or ability to give or receive sexual satisfaction.

A man might wonder whether during sexual intercourse a woman's vagina can receive the full size of his erect penis. A woman's vagina is highly elastic and, when sufficiently sexually aroused, can easily accommodate any size penis. After all, during childbirth the vagina expands to serve as the passageway for the child. On the other hand, since the majority of nerve endings are located in the outer third of the vagina, shorter penises can stimulate the vagina as well as longer penises. For male-female intercourse, penile length is relatively unimportant.

Concern over penile size has led to surgical procedures to increase penis size. In one such procedure, the surgeon lengthens the penis by cutting the ligaments at the base of the penis that are responsible for its stability. This causes the portion of the penis normally hidden inside the body to emerge, giving the penis the appearance of being longer. Additional girth is given by injecting fat taken by liposuction from the abdominal areas. Unfortunately, this has sometimes resulted in lumpy, misshapen, and disfigured penises that have left some patients bitter and embarrassed (Shuit, 1996). Some men are sufficiently concerned

# GO ASK ALICE

*Dear Alice,*

*I have a problem with my penis. Even in the midst of excitement, it is not erect but it is curved. Is that a problem or something to be concerned about? Signed,*

*Straight and Narrow*

Dear Straight and Narrow,

Like other physical characteristics, penises come in different shapes and sizes. Some are longer, some are shorter, some are broader, some are narrower, some curve to the left, some to the right, some not at all. Erection is caused during arousal by more blood flowing into the penis than flows out. However, erect does not mean exactly straight as an arrow, hard as nails, perpendicular to your body, and parallel to the floor. Each person's erection is unique as well.

Do you experience orgasm and ejaculate when you masturbate? If your answers are "yes," then you don't have a problem—your penis seems to be behaving normally. It may only be your expectations that are a problem.

 http://www.mhhe.com/byer6

over penis size that they purchase "penis enlargement" devices, such as a plastic suction chamber. These devices might create erections, but they have also been known to cause injury to the penis.

## Erection

The tissue within the erectile bodies of the penis contains networks of vascular spaces that are separated from each other by smooth muscle and connective tissue. Usually the vascular spaces remain small as a consequence of a partial contraction of the muscle fibers that surround them. But during sexual arousal these smooth muscles become relaxed and the blood vessels in the penis *dilate* (expand), allowing more blood to enter the vascular spaces of the erectile bodies. At the same time, the increasing pressure of the arterial blood entering the vascular spaces of the penis compresses the veins of the penis, thus partially *occluding* (reducing the size of) them and reducing the flow of venous blood away from the penis. As blood accumulates in the erectile tissue, the penis swells in girth and length and becomes firm, and this is referred to as an **erection** (fig. 5.4). There is no bone in the human penis to contribute to the "hardness" of an erection.

During erection the three erectile columns in the penis can be felt distinctly. The erection often occurs in several phases as it becomes increasingly rigid and as stimulation continues. Not all erect penises are exactly straight. Sometimes there is a slight curvature of the erect penis to the side. If there is no disease or injury responsible for this, such curvature will not interfere with sexual intercourse.

Psychic and physical sexual stimuli can act cooperatively in producing or inhibiting erection, or they can act alone. An erection can result from psychic stimuli (visual, auditory, olfactory, memory, or fantasy) originating in the brain, which connects to "erection centers" along the lower spinal cord. Erection can also result from physical stimuli, such as from touching the penis and surrounding skin areas, or even from the vague sensations of a full urinary bladder or a full rectum. Even in individuals whose spinal cords have been accidently severed, breaking the connection between the brain and erection center, erection may be produced through physical stimulation (stroking) alone of the penis, even though the brain has no awareness of the sensation being received by the penis (Sporer, 1991). Psychic stimuli can greatly enhance the effectiveness of the physical stimuli. On the other hand, under adverse psychological conditions, physical stimulation of the penis may not be strong enough to result in an erection (Kennedy & Over, 1990).

Unwanted erections can occasionally occur in nonsexual situations and from nonsexual stimuli. In the well-regarded Kinsey studies of males (Kinsey, Pomeroy, & Martin, 1948), it was found that some young men reported erections from such events as being chased by the police or hearing the national anthem. Erections can also occur in the rapid eye movement (REM), or dream, stage of sleep (Chung & Choi, 1990). Occasionally men awaken with a "morning erection" just after having completed an REM period.

| | |
|---|---|
| **erection** (e-rek´shun) | the firming, swelling, and elevation of the penis |

# DIMENSIONS OF DIVERSITY

## INFANT MALE CIRCUMCISION

Infant male circumcision is a practice that has become a major source of controversy in the United States over the last thirty years. The decision to circumcise an infant is not merely a medical one; the religious, cultural, and emotional issues involved make this issue complex and personal. Once performed routinely in the United States, rates of circumcision have declined substantially due to new information and a new awareness on the part of parents.

**Circumcision** is the surgical removal of the prepuce (foreskin) of a penis to near the coronal sulcus. At birth, the prepuce in a male is still developing and is usually attached to the glans. The foreskin is retractable (able to be pulled away from the glans) in only 4 percent of newborns at birth. If the foreskin is left intact, it can be retracted in 80 to 90 percent of uncircumcised males by the age of three (Schoen et al., 1989). Circumcision of male infants is performed on the first or second day after birth in this country (fig 5.3).

Circumcision has historically been mandated by Jewish and Moslem peoples as fulfilling an ancient promise to God. In some African cultures it marks a "rite of passage" into adulthood. Nonreligious circumcision was first proposed in England and the United States as a remedy for masturbation, and one of its first supporters in the United States was Dr. John H. Kellogg, M.D., the inventor of cornflakes. Dr. Kellogg recommended treatment of both boys and girls:

A remedy for masturbation which is almost always successful in small boys is circumcision. The operation should be performed by a surgeon without administering an anesthetic, as the brief pain attending the operation will have a salutary ef-

fect upon the mind, especially if it be connected with the idea of punishment. In females, the author has found the application of pure carbolic acid to the clitoris an excellent means of allaying the abnormal excitement. (Kellogg, 1888)

Since that time, circumcision has been "a procedure in search of a reason." The current medical rationales for infant circumcision developed after the operation was in wide practice. They include: to make boys look like their fathers and peers; to improve hygiene; to prevent tight/nonretractile foreskin; to prevent urinary tract infections, sexually

transmitted infections, and cancer of the penis or cervix.

Currently, the United States is the only country in the world that routinely circumcises most of its male infants for nonreligious reasons. Over 80 percent of the world's males are intact. Although more than 90 percent of American males were circumcised in the 1960s, that number declined to approximately 60 percent in 1988 (The Circumcision Information Resource, 1999).

In 1999, the American Academy of Pediatrics (AAP) Task Force on Circumcision conducted an extensive analysis of the medical literature.

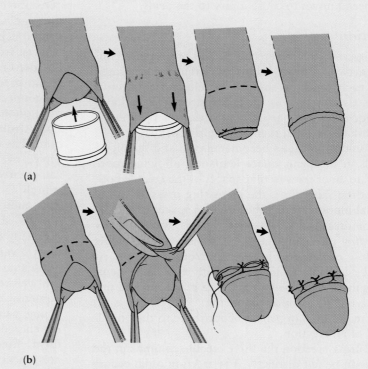

(a)

(b)

**FIGURE 5.3**    Methods of performing circumcision. **a:** In this method, a piece of plastic is placed over the glans and the foreskin is stretched over the plastic and trimmed off. **b:** In this method, the foreskin is carefully cut "freehand" and then stitched.

**Source:** Data from *Pediatrics*, Vol. 84, Page 388. Copyright 1989 American Academy of Pediatrics.

*Infant Male Circumcision—continued*

With the sole exception of studies that showed an increased risk of *urinary tract infections* in uncircumcised male infants, no consistent or significant associations were found between circumcision status and *penile problems, hygiene issues, sexual practice and sensation, penile cancer,* and *STI and HIV infection.* The AAP concluded that incidence of these potential medical problems was either not related to circumcision status, or too low in both circumcised and intact men to justify the procedure.

Although studies show the relative risk of developing a urinary tract infection (UTI) in the first year of life is higher for baby boys who are uncircumcised, research indicates that during the first year of life an intact male infant has at most about a 1 in 100 chance of developing a UTI, while a circumcised male has about a 1 in 1,000 chance.

The AAP subsequently issued the following Circumcision Policy Statement (1999):

> Existing scientific evidence demonstrates potential medical benefits of newborn male circumcision; however, these data are not sufficient to recommend routine neonatal circumcision. In circumstances in which there are potential benefits and risks, yet the procedure is not essential to the child's current well-being, parents should determine what is in the best interest of the child. To make an informed choice, parents of all male infants should be given accurate and unbiased information and be provided the opportunity to discuss this decision. If a decision for circumcision is made, procedural analgesia should be provided. (AAP, 1999)

For the first time, the AAP has recommended that analgesia (pain relief) should be used for infant male circumcision. They cite considerable new evidence that shows that newborns circumcised without analgesia experience pain and stress, and may respond more strongly to pain during future immunization than those who are uncircumcised. In response to this data, the AAP policy states that analgesia has been found to be safe and effective in reducing the pain associated with circumcision, and should be provided if the procedure is performed.

**Sources:** The Circumcision Information and Resource Pages (www.cirp.org); John Harvey Kellogg, M.D., (1888), "Treatment for self-abuse and its effects," Plain fact for old and young, Burlington, IA: F. Segner & Co., p. 295; Douglas Gairdner, D.M., M.R.C.P. (1949), The fate of the foreskin: A study of circumcision, *British Medical Journal,* Vol. 2, 1433–1437; American Academy of Pediatrics Task Force on Circumcision. *Circumcision Policy Statement Pediatrics,* Vol. 103, No. 3, (March 1, 1999) 686–693; Circumcision Resource Center, Boston (www.circumcision.org), The Circumcision Information Resource, Montréal, Québec (www.infocirc.org).

The practice of circumcision is a focus of controversy in the U.S., as new data fuels the anti-circumcision movement.

**Source:** Steve Breen, Asbury Park Press © 1999, www.injersey.com/breen, reprinted with permission.

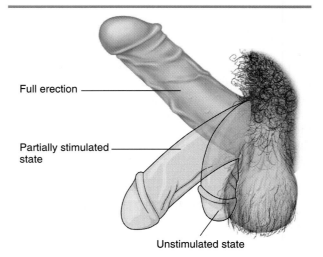

Full erection

Partially stimulated state

Unstimulated state

**FIGURE 5.4** Penile response. In response to stimulation, the penis changes in length, circumference, firmness, and position.

| circumcision (sur-kum-si´shun) | surgical removal of the foreskin of the penis |
|---|---|

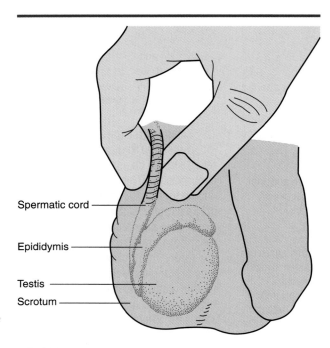

Spermatic cord

Epididymis

Testis

Scrotum

**FIGURE 5.5** The scrotal structures. The structures within the scrotum can be easily located by exerting pressure with the fingers. A thorough understanding of the testes is essential to regular self-examination of them for any abnormal conditions, such as testicular cancer (see section 5.6.1 "Testicular Disorders").

## 5.1.2 The Scrotum

The **scrotum** (scrotal sac) is a thin-walled loose pouch that hangs from the lower pelvic region behind the penis. Its surface is lightly covered with hair, contains many sweat glands, and is usually darker than the skin color of other body parts (fig. 5.1). The scrotum is divided into two compartments, each of which contains a *testis*. The inner wall of each chamber is lined with a smooth serous tissue that allows movement of the testis within the scrotum. As shown in figure 5.5, the spermatic cord, testis, and epididymis can be located by feeling the scrotal sac.

## 5.2 INTERNAL SEX ORGANS

The internal sex organs include the *testes,* which produce sperm and sex hormones, the *genital ducts,* which carry the semen, and the *fluid-producing glands* (table 5.1).

### 5.2.1 Testes

The two **testes** (*testicles* or *male gonads*) are located in the sac-like scrotum (figs. 5.1 and 5.6). They have the function of producing sperm and the sex hormones *testosterone* and *inhibin.* Oval shaped and about 2 inches long and 1.5 inches wide in adults (fig 5.1), they are suspended by the **spermatic cord,** which contains a vas deferens, blood vessels, and nerves (fig. 5.5). A firm, rubbery tube, the spermatic cord can be located by pinching the scrotum with the thumb and forefinger above the testis. In most men, the left testis hangs somewhat lower than the right one, although the opposite may sometimes occur. On the surface of each testis is an *epididymis,* which feels like a small elevation at the base of the spermatic cord (fig. 5.6).

### Descent of the Testes

Usually between the seventh and ninth months of fetal development, the fetal testes, which during pregnancy have developed on the back abdominal wall, begin their descent into the lower abdominal-pelvic cavity, to then pass through the abdominal wall into the scrotum. Stimulated by the male sex hormone *testosterone,* which they are secreting, they move through the *inguinal canal* of the abdominal wall and into the scrotum. During its descent, each testis carries with it a developing vas deferens, blood vessels, and nerves.

Failure of the testes to descend is known as **cryptorchidism.** In about 3 percent of full-term infants and 30 percent of premature infants, one or both testes fail to descend. Since the cells involved in the development of sperm cells are destroyed by the higher temperatures of the pelvic cavity, the male is infertile if both testes are affected. In about 80 percent of boys with cryptorchidism, the testes descend spontaneously during the first year of life. For undescended testes, injections of hCG given at two-and-a-half years of life may stimulate descent. If this fails, the condition can be corrected surgically at about age five. If the testes remain undescended, they will eventually *atrophy* (waste away).

In some men the opening through the abdominal wall remains more or less open after the passage of the testes, creating a structural weakness. This opening provides a potential passageway through which a loop of the small intestine could be forced by excessive abdominal pressure, such as with straining during heavy lifting or pushing. This would produce an **inguinal hernia,** which, if severe enough, could cause constriction and strangulation of that portion of the intestine, requiring prompt treatment.

### Position of the Testes

The position of the testes in the scrotum can be critical to the viability of the sperm, since too high a testicular temperature can lead to infertility; the temperature of the testes must be maintained at a relatively constant level 3 to 4 degrees Fahrenheit lower than body temperature. In fact, men who take frequent hot showers or baths, or sit in the hot water of

**TABLE 5.1**   STRUCTURES AND FUNCTIONS OF THE MALE REPRODUCTIVE SYSTEM

| ORGAN | FUNCTION |
|---|---|
| *External* | |
| Penis | Male organ for urination and the release of semen; richly supplied with nerve endings; associated with feelings of pleasure during sexual stimulation |
| Scrotum | Encloses the two testes; maintains the testes at a temperature suitable for sperm production |
| *Internal* | |
| Testes | |
|    Seminiferous tubules | Produce sperm |
|    Interstitial cells (Leydig cells) | Produce and secrete the male hormone testosterone |
| Epididymis | Stores slowly maturing sperm until sperm are released into the vas deferens for ejaculation or until they disintegrate or are reabsorbed |
| Vas deferens | Carries sperm upward from epididymis to the ejaculatory duct |
| Fluid-producing glands | |
|    Seminal vesicles | Secrete fluid with a high fructose content to nourish sperm; fluid also contains a prostaglandin to stimulate muscular contractions in the female that assist in sperm movement |
|    Prostate gland | Secretes fluid that initiates the movement of sperm and nutritionally sustains sperm |
|    Cowper's (bulbourethral) glands | Secrete fluid that neutralizes the acidity of any urine in the urethra prior to the passage of semen |

spas or whirlpools, and men (such as foundry workers) whose occupations involve subjecting the body to high temperatures might temporarily have reduced sperm count because their scrotum and testes have been exposed to such high temperatures (Tanagho, Lue, & McClure, 1988). Jockey shorts and tight pants can also suppress sperm production because the testes are held close to the body.

Testicular position is determined by several factors. One factor is the temperature of the testis inside the scrotum. The **cremaster muscle,** a skeletal muscle that surrounds the spermatic cord, contracts when the environmental temperature is low, moving the testis closer to the warmth of the body, and relaxes when the temperature is high to allow the testis to move away from the body. The **dartos muscle** forms the middle layer of the scrotum, just under the skin. Contraction of this muscle also moves the testis closer to the body for warmth, tightening and wrinkling the skin of the scrotum. When the temperature is warm, the dartos muscle relaxes, providing more surface (skin) area for cooling.

Another factor in the position of the testes is sexual arousal. During sexual excitement, the testes elevate toward the perineum and increase 50 to 100 percent in size. Orgasm in a man never occurs without at least a partial elevation of his testes (Masters & Johnson, 1966). The cremaster muscle is responsible for this rise in position. It is also possible to induce an elevation of the testis on the same side of the body by stroking the inside of the thigh, a response called the *cremaster reflex.*

## Structure of the Testes

Each testis is enclosed within a tough, white, fibrous capsule. This capsule extends inward as *septa* (partitions), which internally subdivide each testis into about 250 **lobules** (internal compartments) (fig. 5.6).

| | |
|---|---|
| **scrotum** (skrō′tum) | the loose pouch behind the penis that holds the testes |
| **testes** (tes′tēz) | male sex glands that produce sperm and testosterone; male gonads |
| **spermatic cord** (sper-mat′ik) | the cord that suspends the testes in the scrotum |
| **cryptorchidism** (krip-tor′ki-diz-um) | failure of testes to descend into scrotum during development |
| **inguinal hernia** (ing′gwi-nul hur′nē-a) | a portion of small intestine is forced through abdominal wall |
| **cremaster muscle** (crē-mǎs′ter) | surrounds spermatic cord |
| **dartos muscle** (dar′tōs) | muscle in scrotum |
| **lobules** (lŏ′byūlz) | compartments in testis |

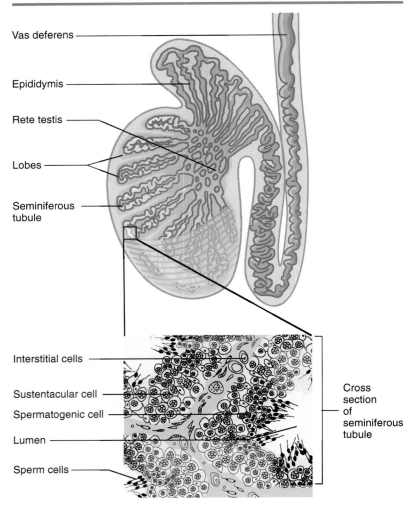

Vas deferens

Epididymis

Rete testis

Lobes

Seminiferous tubule

Interstitial cells

Sustentacular cell

Spermatogenic cell

Lumen

Sperm cells

Cross
section
of
seminiferous
tubule

**FIGURE 5.6** The testes serve double duty. The internal structures of the testes explain their remarkable capacity to produce millions of sperm daily. This sectional view of a testis shows the tubal structure where the sperm are produced. These glands also contain interstitial cells, which are the basic source of the major male sex hormone testosterone.

ulus of certain hormones, occurs within these tubules at the rate of several thousand **spermatozoa** (sperm cells) per second in the sexually mature male.

In the seminiferous tubule, sustentacular cells stimulate spermatogenic cells to begin the process of spermatogenesis (fig. 5.6). Spermatogenic cells in the earliest stages of development are closest to the outside of the seminiferous tubule. As the cells develop (becoming *spermatocytes*), they migrate toward the center of the tubule, so that the most completely formed sperm (called *spermatids*) are located closest to the center. Sperm cells then migrate into the lumen (space inside the tubule), and migrate to the **epididymis,** where they complete their maturation in ten to fourteen days.

A mature sperm cell is a microscopic, tadpole-shaped structure that consists of a flattened head, cylindrical midpiece, and elongated tail (fig. 5.7). The cell is highly adapted for reaching and penetrating the female ovum. The oval-shaped head, which contains 23 *chromosomes* (genetic material), is capped with an *acrosome,* a structure that releases enzymes that help the sperm penetrate the egg at the time of fertilization. The midpiece contains *mitochondria,* structures that produce the energy needed for the movement of the sperm cell. The tail, which contains much stored energy, propels the sperm.

## 5.2.2   Genital Ducts

After being released into the lumen of the seminiferous tubules, the sperm and fluid flow to the *rete testis* (a network of channels) and flow into the epididymis. Newly forming sperm and fluid in the seminiferous tubules creates a pressure that pushes the already released sperm along into the **genital ducts,** which carry sperm to the outside of the body. The genital ducts provide for both transport and storage. The genital ducts include the *epididymis, vas deferens, ejaculatory duct,* and *urethra* (figs. 5.1 and 5.8).

Each lobule contains one to four tightly coiled, convoluted **seminiferous tubules,** each about 28 inches long if uncoiled (fig. 5.6). These tubules are lined with **spermatogenic cells** that give rise to sperm cells (*spermatozoa*) and supporting cells called **sustentacular cells** (Sertoli's cells), which help nourish the new sperm cells by producing a rich fluid. Located in the spaces between the seminiferous tubules are other specialized cells called **interstitial cells** (Leydig cells), which secrete sex hormones (fig. 5.6).

*Sperm Cell Production*

Beginning with puberty and continuing into old age, *spermatogenesis* (sperm production), under the stim-

*Epididymis*

The epididymis is a long flattened organ attached to the upper surface of each testis (figs. 5.5, 5.6 and

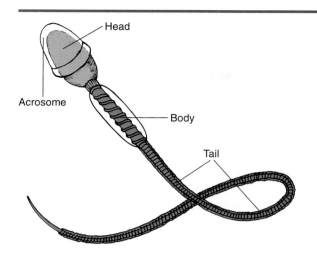

**FIGURE 5.7** Sperm cell. The streamlined, microscopic sperm cell carries a complete copy of the genetic code, enzymes for penetration of the ovum, an energy source, and a tail to direct its own propulsion. A sperm cell is highly adapted for reaching and penetrating a female ovum.

5.8). It contains a thin, tightly coiled tubule, the *ductus epididymis*. About 20 feet long, this tubule forms a continuous link between the network of ducts in each testis and the vas deferens. The epididymis is the site of sperm maturation and storage, and contains millions of sperm. During the several weeks the sperm are in the epididymis, they become increasingly *motile* (self-moving) as they mature into cells that are able to move independently and are capable of fertilizing ova. About two months is required for sperm cells to reach full maturity after initial cell division. Mature sperm cells are stored in the epididymis until released into the vas deferens. The contractions of the smooth muscles in the walls of the tubules help propel the spermatozoa forward. Any sperm that are not expelled from the epididymis degenerate and are reabsorbed.

## Vas Deferens

As shown in figures 5.1 and 5.8, the **vas deferens** (*ductus deferens*) is a small muscular tube about 18 inches long through which sperm are carried upward as they leave each epididymis. The vas deferens becomes a part of the *spermatic cord* (by which the testes are suspended in the scrotum) along with blood vessels and nerves. As the spermatic cord leaves the scrotum, it enters the *inguinal canal* and passes through the body wall into the pelvic cavity. Near its termination, each vas deferens becomes expanded to form an area called the **ampulla**. The ampulla joins with the duct from the *seminal vesicle* to form the

*ejaculatory duct*. Contractions within the tubes forcefully propel the stored sperm toward the ejaculatory duct. The surgical removal, or interruption, of a section of the vas deferens, followed by sealing or tying of each cut end is called a **vasectomy** (a male sterilization procedure that is usually done in the portion of the vas deferens that lies within the scrotum) (see chapter 15).

## Ejaculatory Duct

The two **ejaculatory ducts,** each about 0.8 inches long and formed from the union of the ampulla and the seminal vesicle duct, pass through the prostate gland to terminate at the *urethra* (figs. 5.1 and 5.8). Both of the ejaculatory ducts receive secretions from the seminal vesicles and prostate gland before the contents are ejected into the prostatic urethra.

## Urethra

The urethra is a small tube extending from the floor of the urinary bladder to the outside of the body (figs. 5.1 and 5.8). About 8 inches long, its course is S-shaped due to the curve of the penis. Immediately below the bladder, the urethra passes through the center of the *prostate gland,* where it receives the contents of the two ejaculatory ducts, as well as

| | |
|---|---|
| **seminiferous tubules** (sem-in-if´er-us tū´būlz) | ducts in the testes along which sperm are produced |
| **spermatogenic cells** (sper-mat-ō-jen´ik) | cells in the testes that produce sperm cells |
| **sustentacular cells** (sus-ten-tăk´yū-lar) | cells in the testes that nourish developing sperm cells |
| **interstitial cells** (in-ter-stish´al) | cells in the testes that produce testosterone |
| **spermatozoa** (sper-mat-ō-zō´a) | sperm cells; male sex cells |
| **epididymis** (ep-i-did´i-mus) | a genital duct located on the side of each testis in which sperm are stored |
| **genital ducts** (jen´i-tal) | ducts that carry sperm and semen |
| **vas deferens** (vas def´er-enz) | a genital duct that carries sperm to the inside of the man's body |
| **ampulla** (am-pŭl´a) | expansion near end of vas deferens |
| **vasectomy** (vas-ek´tō-mē) | surgical interruption of the vas deferens |
| **ejaculatory duct** (ē-jak´ū-la-tō-rē) | the last section of the vas deferens before it joins the urethra |

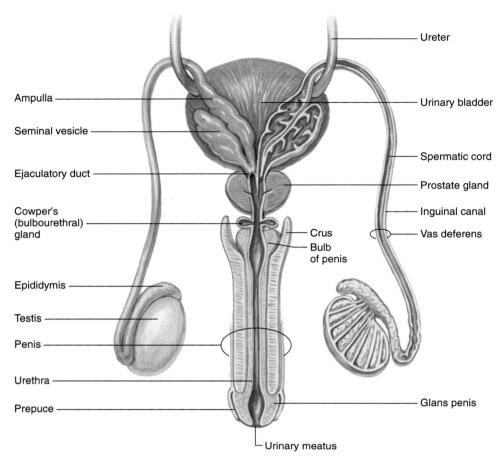

Ampulla

Seminal vesicle

Ejaculatory duct

Cowper's
(bulbourethral)
gland

Epididymis

Testis

Penis

Urethra

Prepuce

Ureter

Urinary bladder

Spermatic cord

Prostate gland

Inguinal canal

Vas deferens

Crus

Bulb
of penis

Glans penis

Urinary meatus

**FIGURE 5.8**   The ducts and glands of the male reproductive system as seen from a posterior view. This remarkable system produces great amounts of sperm cells and seminal fluid in structures occupying a minimum of space. It also provides for the delivery of the sperm through the penis during intercourse.

secretions from the prostate gland. Immediately below the prostate gland the ducts from the two *Cowper's glands* (*bulbourethral glands*) join the urethra. The remaining 6 inches of the urethra pass through the spongy erectile body of the shaft and glans of the penis. The opening of the urethra as it terminates at the outside of the body is called the **urinary meatus.** The function of the urethra is to convey both urine and semen, each at different times.

## 5.2.3   Accessory Glands

The **accessory,** or *fluid-producing*, **glands** include the seminal vesicles, the prostate gland, and the Cowper's glands. All produce secretions that become part of the **seminal fluid** and provide sperm with a liquid in which to swim, nutrients for energy, and the proper alkalinity for survival (figs. 5.1 and 5.8).

### Seminal Vesicles

The paired **seminal vesicles** (fig. 5.8) are pouchlike structures about 2 inches long, attached to the vas

deferens near the base of the urinary bladder, that secrete *seminal vesicle fluid*. The seminal vesicle fluid is secreted directly into the ejaculatory ducts at the time of ejaculation. It is a slightly alkaline fluid that helps neutralize the acid pH of the vas deferens, which would kill sperm if not corrected. The seminal vesicle fluid possesses a high fructose (sugar) content, which provides the sperm with energy and helps the sperm cells propel themselves. The fluid also contains **prostaglandins,** fatty acid substances that stimulate muscular contractions in the female reproductive tract that help sperm cells move toward the ovum. The seminal vesicle fluid makes up about 60 percent of the total volume of semen.

### Prostate Gland

The **prostate gland** is a single, doughnut-shaped gland about 1.5 inches across and 1.25 inches thick that surrounds the neck of the *urinary bladder* and urethra (figs. 5.1 and 5.8). The prostate gland is enclosed by a fibrous capsule, and is divided into lobules, whose ducts open in to the urethra. Directly behind the penis and the urethra, and in front of the rectum, it can be easily felt by the physician's gloved fingers during a rectal examination.

The thin, milky, alkaline *prostatic fluid* is released into the urethra during ejaculation, where it mixes with the fluids coming from the ejaculatory duct. Making up about 25 percent of the total volume of semen, the prostatic fluid helps to further neutralize the sperm-containing fluid, thus enhancing the motility of the sperm cells. The prostatic fluid also helps neutralize the acid secretion of the vagina, thus helping sustain the sperm cells entering the female reproductive tract.

## Cowper's Glands

The two **Cowper's glands** (*bulbourethral glands*), each about the size of a pea, are located beneath the prostate gland on either side of the urethra (figs. 5.1 and 5.8). Upon sexual excitement and just prior to ejaculation, a small amount of *preejaculatory fluid* (or *Cowper's gland fluid*) is released into the urethra. Usually, a drop or two of the clear, sticky secretion appears at the tip of the penis. The fluid coats the lining of the urethra to neutralize the pH of any urine residue in the urethra. A summary of the glands and structures of the male reproductive system is found in table 5.1.

## 5.2.4    Semen

**Semen** is a thick, whitish substance consisting of sperm and secretions from the fluid-producing glands, which is conveyed by the urethra to the outside of the body during ejaculation. Rather thick when ejaculated, it soon liquefies. The nutrients in semen aid sperm survival and movement through a woman's reproductive tract. There are usually 100 to 750 million sperm in one ejaculation, which has a volume of around 2 to 5 milliliters (about one teaspoonful). A large number of sperm are required for fertilization because only a tiny fraction of them are able to reach the ovum. Semen analysis is an important tool in finding answers for couples troubled by infertility (see "Healthy Sexuality: Semen Analysis").

### Sperm Capacitation

Although they are activated by secretions from the accessory glands before ejaculation, once released into a woman's vagina, sperm cells are unable to immediately fertilize an ovum. Over a period of several hours they acquire this ability through a process called **sperm capacitation**. Although this process is not completely understood, there is some evidence that as sperm move through the acidic environment of the woman's vagina, the acrosomal membrane on the tip of the sperm head weakens (fig. 5.7). When the sperm reaches the ovum, the acrosomal membrane is more likely to break, releasing the enzymes necessary for fertilization to occur.

### Frozen Semen

Although able to survive for many weeks in the ducts of a man's reproductive tract, sperm cells survive for only a day or two after being expelled in ejaculation. However, if frozen in liquid nitrogen at temperatures below −100 degrees centigrade, semen can be stored and kept viable for years. Some men who have no immediate prospects of fathering a child, or who want to store their viable sperm until after they die, are having their semen frozen for future use. Some sperm banks provide financial compensation to men who deposit their semen, which is made available (on an anonymous basis) to women seeking to become pregnant.

### Semen and Oral Sex

Some couples engage in **fellatio**, in which one partner uses their mouth to stimulate a man's penis. The man may withdraw his penis before ejaculation, or he may ejaculate within the mouth of the partner, who may choose to spit the semen out or swallow it. Sex partners may have some concerns about receiving semen into their mouths, and it is important for couples to discuss their plans before engaging in fellatio. Semen

| | |
|---|---|
| **urinary meatus** (yoor´i-nar-ē mē-ā´tus) | opening of urethra on glans |
| **accessory glands** | glands that produce the seminal fluid portion of the semen |
| **seminal fluids** (sem´i-nal) | fluids produced by accessory glands |
| **seminal vesicles** (sem´i-nal ves´i-kl) | two accessory glands near the prostate gland that produce seminal fluid |
| **prostaglandins** (pros´ta-gland-ins) | fatty acid substances that stimulate muscle contraction |
| **prostate gland** (pros´tāt) | in males, a gland surrounding the neck of the urinary bladder that produces prostatic fluid |
| **Cowper's glands** (Cow´perz) | two glands beneath the prostate that produce preejaculatory fluid |
| **semen** (sē´men) | the male ejaculate |
| **sperm capacitation** (kah-pas-i-tā´shun) | the process in which sperm acquire the capacity to fertilize an ovum |
| **fellatio** (fe-lā´shē-ō) | oral stimulation of the penis |

## HEALTHY SEXUALITY

### SEMEN ANALYSIS

An evaluation of a man's fertility often requires a semen analysis. This can indicate whether infertility is due to problems in sperm production. It can also be used to confirm the success of a vasectomy and to detect sperm in the body or on the clothing of a rape victim.

| NORMAL RANGE (ANALYSIS) | FUNCTION |
| --- | --- |
| *Volume*—2.0 ml (cc) or more | Over 95% of semen is accessory gland fluid supplying energy, enzymes, proper pH, and viscosity (stickiness) |
| *Motility*—50% or more sperm show good forward movement within the first three hours after ejaculation | Sperm must travel a great distance to the ovum |
| *Count*—20 million or more sperm per ml; 20–40 million is borderline; below 20 million may mean infertility | Combined action of great number of sperm required to digest covering around ovum |
| *Liquefaction*—ejaculate coagulates, becomes liquid-like within one hour | Prompt liquefaction allows sperm to travel |
| *Morphology*—14% or more of sperm have normally shaped heads and tails | Normally formed sperm are able to travel and unite with ovum |
| *pH*—slightly alkaline (pH 7.2 to 7.8) | To neutralize the acidity of the vagina, which will kill sperm |
| *Fructose*—sugar present | Major energy source; sperm cell contains little stored food |

does not have a distinctive taste and is not harmful in itself, but it can contain microorganisms, such as HIV. Because it is possible to contract HIV orally from infected semen, a condom should be worn during fellatio (see chapter 7).

### 5.2.5   Ejaculation

Ejaculation, like erection, is a spinal reflex. Effective manual, oral, or coital stimulation of the penis results in the buildup of neural excitement to a critical level, or threshold, which triggers several internal events. **Ejaculation** (fig 5.9), the process by which semen is ejected from the body, takes place in two stages. The first stage, **emission,** starts with the ejaculatory center in the lower spinal cord. Nerve impulses that originate in this center cause rhythmic contractions within the walls of the testicular ducts, epididymis, vas deferens, and ampulla (fig 5.8). At the same time, other nerve impulses stimulate the rhythmic contractions of the seminal vesicles and prostate gland. These contractions move the contents of the glands and ducts into the *urethral bulb,* the portion of the urethra within the prostate.

There are two urethral muscles, or **sphincters,** that encircle the urethra (fig. 5.9). The *internal urethral sphincter* is located above the prostate at the base of the urinary bladder, preventing the release of

urine. The *external urethral sphincter* at the base of the prostate also closes, trapping the semen in the urethral bulb. As fluids from the ducts and glands enter the bulb, it expands like a balloon. This expansion is perceived by the man as the feeling that ejaculation is inevitable (that he is "about to come").

As the urethral bulb fills with semen, sensory impulses are carried to the spinal cord, initiating the second stage of ejaculation, called **expulsion.** In response, motor impulses are transmitted from the spinal cord to skeletal muscles around the urethral bulb, causing them to contract rhythmically. This creates pressure within the bulb. The external sphincter muscle relaxes, and contractions along the entire urethra force the release of the semen from the penis in forcible spurts. The first several contractions are quite strong and occur closely together, followed by several more contractions of diminishing intensity and frequency. The expulsion stage takes place in three to ten seconds.

An average volume of semen per ejaculate is about 2 to 5 ml (one-half to one teaspoonful). The amount of semen ejaculated depends on various factors, such as age, general health, intensity of sexual stimulation, and length of time since the last ejaculation. Often, the more intense the sensation of orgasm, the more semen ejaculated and the greater the force of propulsion.

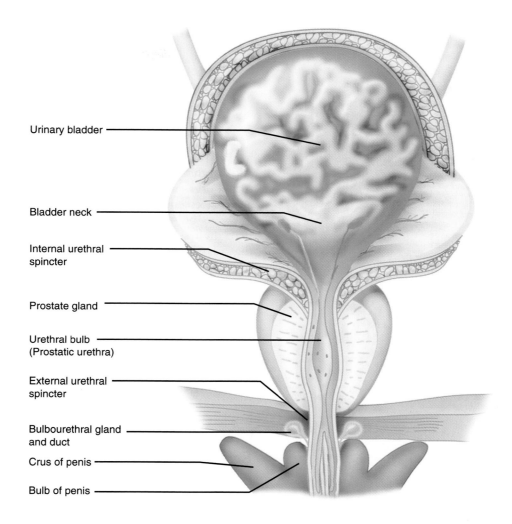

Urinary bladder

Bladder neck

Internal urethral
spincter

Prostate gland

Urethral bulb
(Prostatic urethra)

External urethral
spincter

Bulbourethral gland
and duct

Crus of penis

Bulb of penis

**FIGURE 5.9**    Structures involved in ejaculation. Contraction of the internal and external urethral sphincter muscles during emission allows the urethral bulb to fill with semen. During the expulsion stage, the external urethral sphincter relaxes and muscular contractions along the urethra force the release of semen.

## Ejaculation and Orgasm

The rhythmic contractions that cause ejaculation are usually accompanied by intensely pleasurable sensations of physiological and psychological release called **orgasm.** Although ejaculation in the adult male is generally accompanied by orgasm, the two processes do not always occur simultaneously. Before puberty, a boy might experience orgasm without ejaculation of semen. It is also possible for a man to experience more than one orgasm, but with little or no expulsion of semen with the second and third orgasm.

| | |
|---|---|
| **ejaculation** (ē-jak-ū-lā´shun) | expulsion of semen from the penis |
| **emission** (ē-mish´on) | a discharge of seminal fluid from the accessory glands |
| **sphincter** (sfingk´ter) | muscle that surrounds an opening which closes when muscle contracts |
| **expulsion** (eks-pul´shun) | the ejection of semen from the penis |
| **orgasm** (or´gazm) | the peak of sexual arousal; sexual climax |

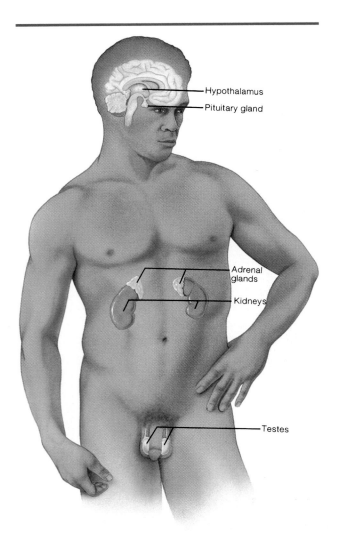

**FIGURE 5.10** The endocrine glands. This figure shows the location of the adrenal glands, the pituitary gland, the hypothalamus, and the testes.

Also, some men may experience one or more nonejaculatory orgasms before a last orgasm with ejaculation.

Ejaculation is a reflex phenomenon, yet it is possible for a man to learn how to control its onset. This may involve a conditioned learning of how to reduce sexual excitement or to control the triggering of the reflex, so that when ejaculation seems imminent, stimulation can be reduced until the sensation subsides.

### Nocturnal Emissions

Puberty signals the full development of the prostate gland, seminal vesicles, Cowper's glands, and sperm production; before this time a boy is incapable of ejaculation. However, by age 13 or 14 the young man typically experiences his first ejaculation (Thornburg

& Aras, 1986), though for some first ejaculation may occur as early as age 8, and for others as late as the early twenties (Reinisch, 1990). Although sperm may be present in the first ejaculate, sperm often do not appear in the ejaculate until about a year after the first ejaculation. About one year after first ejaculation, young men may begin having **nocturnal emissions** ("wet dreams").

There is evidence that both men and women experience *nocturnal orgasms* (orgasms during sleep), although the percentage of occurrence is higher for men. In the Kinsey studies (1948, 1953), virtually all of the men and 70 percent of the women reported having sexual dreams, with 90 percent of the men and less than 40 percent of the women reporting nocturnal orgasms. Some of this may be due to the size and placement of genitals; a man's penis is more likely to be stimulated by bedding and nightwear than the less exposed clitoris. Beyond this, the fact that a man has had a wet dream is plain to see, whereas the evidence for a women's nocturnal orgasm is more elusive.

The percentage of women reporting nocturnal orgasm may be increasing. In the interval of time between the Kinsey study (1953) and the Wells study (1986), nocturnal orgasms among a comparably aged group of young women had increased from 8 percent in 1953 to 37 percent in 1986. Knowledge of and positive feelings about the body, along with liberalized sexual attitudes, may be associated with a woman's experiencing and acknowledging nocturnal orgasm (Wells, 1986).

### Retrograde Ejaculation

As a consequence of certain illnesses, the effects of some tranquilizing drugs, or surgeries such as prostate surgery, the two urethral sphincter muscles might work in reverse. If this occurs, the semen may be ejected backward into the urinary bladder, a condition known as **retrograde ejaculation.** There is a full sensation of orgasm, but no semen is released from the penis. The semen in the bladder is later voided painlessly with the urine. The condition in itself is not harmful, but it might indicate some other medical problem if it persists.

## 5.3 THE BREASTS

There are significant structural, functional, and cultural differences between men's and women's breasts. Structurally, a man's breasts have the same basic components as a woman's—nipples, areolae, fat, and glandular tissue, although a man's breasts contain much less fat and glandular tissue. However, the man's breasts have no function, even though they have the same embryologic origin as the woman's.

Culturally, men's breasts are viewed and spoken of differently in our culture than women's are. We use different language for a man—he has a chest, not breasts. In public settings, such as the beach, it's expected that the man expose his breasts ("chest"), yet it is often deemed indecent for a woman to entirely expose her breasts. Some men report that their breasts are erotically responsive to stimulation, whereas others do not.

Some men experience a temporary swelling of their breasts during adolescence and adulthood called *gynecomastia*. Its occurrence in adolescence is probably due to hormonal changes during puberty. In adult men the appearance of such a condition may relate to cancers, alcohol, or liver or thyroid disease.

## 5.4 THE SEX GLANDS

As we saw in chapter 4, all processes of the body are under the control of a group of chemical regulators called **hormones**. These body chemicals are the products of the **endocrine glands** (fig. 5.10). Hormones from the endocrine glands are released into the bloodstream and carried to cells all over the body. Yet the action of any given hormone is restricted to its *target cells,* whose membranes contain *receptors* that allow only specific hormones to enter the cell and perform their functions.

Some of these glands in men are similar to female glands, whereas others are unique to men. Male endocrine glands involved in the reproductive process, or the **sex glands,** include the hypothalamus, the anterior pituitary gland, the testes, and the adrenal glands. Their hormones are responsible for sperm cell production and for the development and maintenance of male sexual characteristics.

Male hormones play a very important part in the prenatal formation and placement of the male urogenital system. As puberty begins, with the flow of hormones from the hypothalamus to the pituitary gland, the male reproductive system produces hormones to develop secondary sex characteristics and to enable erection, ejaculation, and sensual pleasure, to occur. This series of changes that cause the boy to become a sexually functional adult involve the hypothalamus.

### 5.4.1 Hypothalamus

The **hypothalamus,** which is a portion of the lower brain, contains cells that produce and secrete substances that maintain control of the *pituitary gland,* located just beneath it (fig. 5.10). The hypothalamus secretes **gonadotropin-releasing hormone (GnRH),** which is carried by blood vessels to the anterior, or front, lobe of the pituitary (table 5.2).

### 5.4.2 Pituitary Gland

The dual-lobed **pituitary gland** is attached to the hypothalamus by a tiny stalk (fig. 5.10). The *anterior lobe* of the pituitary responds to GnRH by secreting **gonadotropins,** or hormones that stimulate activity in the *gonads,* or sex glands. A man's gonadotropins include **interstitial cell-stimulating hormone (ICSH),** which is the same substance as *luteinizing hormone (LH)* in females, and **follicle-stimulating hormone (FSH).** The target cells for these hormones are in the two testes (table 5.2).

### 5.4.3 Testes

In the testes, the ICSH stimulates the development of the interstitial cells, so they, in turn, secrete the *androgens,* male sex hormones. The primary androgen is *testosterone.* FSH (from the pituitary) and testosterone (from the interstitial cells) stimulate the

| | |
|---|---|
| **nocturnal emission** | the harmless involuntary discharge of semen during sleep; a "wet dream" |
| **retrograde ejaculation** (ret´rō´grād ē-jak-ū-lā´shun) | reverse ejaculation into the urinary bladder |
| **hormone** (hor´mōn) | a chemical produced by and released into the blood from an endocrine gland |
| **endocrine gland** (en´dō-krin) | a gland that secretes hormones into the bloodstream |
| **sex glands** | glands that produce sex hormones |
| **hypothalamus** (hī-pō-thal´a-mus) | a lower portion of brain that suspends the pituitary gland and produces sex hormones |
| **gonadotropin-releasing hormone (GnRH)** (gon-a-dō-trō´pin) | a hypothalamic hormone that acts on the pituitary gland |
| **pituitary gland** (pi-tū´i-tār-ē) | a sex gland attached to the brain that produces gonadotropins |
| **gonadotropins** (gon-a-dō-trō´pinz) | pituitary hormones that act on the testes |
| **interstitial cell-stimulating hormone (ICSH)** (in-tēr-stish´al) | a pituitary hormone that acts on the interstitial cells of the testes to produce testosterone |
| **follicle-stimulating hormone (FSH)** (fol´li-kl) | a pituitary hormone that acts on sperm-producing cells of the testes |

**TABLE 5.2** HORMONES THAT AFFECT MALE REPRODUCTIVE PROCESSES

| HORMONE | SOURCE | ACTION |
|---|---|---|
| GnRH | Hypothalamus | Stimulates pituitary gland to secrete the gonadotropins FSH and ICSH |
| ICSH (LH) | Pituitary | Stimulates interstitial cells in the testes to produce androgens, especially testosterone; same as luteinizing hormone (LH) in females |
| FSH | Pituitary | Along with testosterone, stimulates sustentacular cells in seminiferous tubules to induce sperm development |
| Testosterone | Testes (interstitial cells) | Stimulates development of a man's primary and secondary sex characteristics and affects his sexual behavior; along with FSH, stimulates spermatogenic cells to undergo spermatogenesis; feeds back to hypothalamus and pituitary, where it inhibits GnRH secretion to pituitary and LH production by the pituitary gland |
| Inhibin | Testes (sustentacular cells) | Maturing sperm cause sustentacular cells in seminiferous tubules to secrete inhibin, which feeds back to the pituitary, inhibiting its production of FSH |

*sustentacular cells* of the seminiferous tubules. These cells in turn cause the spermatogenic cells lining the tubules to undergo *spermatogenesis,* the formation of new sperm cells. The sustentacular cells also secrete the hormone **inhibin,** which feeds back and inhibits the anterior pituitary from overproducing FSH.

## 5.4.4 Adrenal Glands

There are two **adrenal glands,** one atop each kidney (fig. 5.10). Each has an outer cortex that produces small amounts of *androgens.* Some of these are converted into estrogens by the skin, liver, and adipose tissue. The adrenal androgens in a man are an insignificant supplement to the far greater supply of androgens coming from his testes. This differs from the woman, whose adrenal glands provide her only supply of androgens.

## 5.5 SEX HORMONES IN MEN

As a group, a man's sex hormones are termed **androgens.** Most of these hormones are produced by the interstitial cells that line the spaces between the seminiferous tubules in the testes, although a small amount is produced in the adrenal cortex (fig. 5.10). The principal and most abundant androgen is **testosterone** (table 5.2).

## 5.5.1 Testosterone Production

The secretion of testosterone by the testes begins during fetal development, well before birth. The early testosterone stimulates the fetal formation of the male reproductive organs (the penis, scrotum, prostate gland, seminal vesicles, and ducts). These are the boy's *primary sexual characteristics*—or those with which he is born. Testosterone also stimulates

the descent of the testes into the scrotum. At birth, male babies normally have testosterone blood levels close to those of young adult men (Flieger, 1995).

Several weeks following birth, testosterone production falls and remains low until early adolescence. Between the ages of thirteen and fifteen (typically), production resumes, increases rapidly, and then continues throughout the man's remaining lifetime (Flieger, 1995) (fig. 5.11). The resumption of testosterone secretion marks the beginning of *puberty,* the time when the young man becomes reproductively functional. During this sexual maturation, or development of *secondary sex characteristics,* the boy notices the enlargement of his sex organs, growth of body hair, and voice change. With advancing age, testosterone levels decline, although some men retain youthful testosterone levels into their eighties (Flieger, 1995) (fig 5.11).

Far more testosterone is produced per day in a man than in a woman. Six to 8 milligrams (mg) are produced daily in the average man, compared to approximately 0.5 mg in a woman (Masters, Johnson, & Kolodny, 1988). Men secrete testosterone in a daily cycle, with the highest levels typically occurring at night (Dabbs, 1990).

Questions continue to be raised regarding the relationship, if any, between aggressive behavior and levels of testosterone. Aggressive behavior is not consistently related to higher plasma testosterone levels, yet persons with chronic low levels of testosterone, due to abnormal steroid synthesis before puberty, exhibit reduced aggression and diminished sexual drive (Hadley, 1996).

Beyond its sexual functions, testosterone and other androgens are *anabolic hormones;* that is, they stimulate protein synthesis. Thus men tend to have greater muscle mass and heavier bones than women, due to their greater supply of testosterone. The potency of testosterone has been a source of fascination

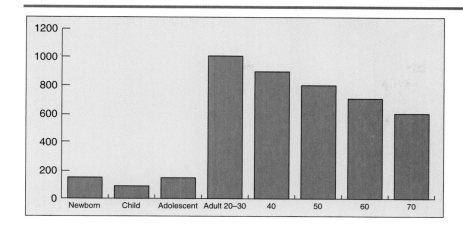

**FIGURE 5.11** Testosterone production throughout life. Approximate testosterone blood levels in human males (in nanograms per deciliter of blood).

**Source:** Data from Flieger, "Testosterone: Key to Masculinity and More" in *FDA Consumer,* May, 1995.

for people wanting to gain the benefits of added strength. This has led some athletes to use synthetic steroids (see "At Issue: 'Winning' with Anabolic Steroids?").

### 5.5.2 The Hypothalamus-Pituitary-Testes Connection

The development of male secondary sexual characteristics relates directly to the amount of testosterone produced by the interstitial cells in the testes. The amount produced is regulated by a negative feedback system involving the hypothalamus.

As already explained, the hypothalamus continually releases *gonadotropin-releasing hormone (GnRH)* (table 5.2), which stimulates the pituitary production and secretion of the gonadotropins *FSH* and *ICSH*. Whereas FSH, sensed by the sustentacular cells, stimulates the production of sperm cells, ICSH stimulates the interstitial cells to produce *testosterone* (fig. 5.12). As the supply of testosterone in the blood rises and feeds back to the hypothalamus and pituitary, the production of ICSH is inhibited (fig. 5.12). Likewise, the maturing sperm in the testes stimulate the sustentacular cells to secrete the hormone *inhibin,* which also feeds back to the hypothalamus and pituitary to cause a drop in FSH production. Once the production of FSH and ICSH drops, the amount of testosterone in the blood is reduced, which reduces the inhibition of the hypothalamus. This reversal starts the original cycle all over again. By this system of self-regulation in the man's body, the level of testosterone remains more or less constant. Table 5.2 and figure 5.12 summarize this process.

This system of self-regulation operates continuously in both men and women, though on different time scales. Whereas women have a cyclic production of estrogens and progesterone over the course each month due to the menstrual cycle, men maintain a relatively constant supply of testosterone throughout the month.

### 5.5.3 The Male Climacteric

For all living things, aging is a natural process, and eventual physical changes in the human body are predictable. Some of these changes are due to the normal wear and tear of people living active lives, whereas other changes are thought to be triggered by the actions of genes. The rate of aging varies widely between individuals due to their experiences, personal health habits, the environments in which they live, as well as their heredity. Individuals also age sexually. Our society places importance on sexual attractiveness and youthfulness, and we might naturally have some sense of fear as we see and feel ourselves getting older. Yet in the context of the life cycle, aging can be viewed with a sense of satisfaction gained from having lived a productive life.

As we saw in chapter 4, a woman is genetically programmed to begin and cease her menstrual periods at certain general ages. The years during which she ceases menstruation are known as her climacteric. Men do not have such well-defined changes in hormonal balance. For instance, they have no expected cutoff of sperm cell production, but continue to produce sperm into old age. Yet many men begin to notice changes in their sexual responsiveness in their

| | |
|---|---|
| **inhibin** (in-hib'in) | a hormone that inhibits FSH production |
| **adrenal glands** (ad-rē'nal) | glands located atop each kidney |
| **androgens** (an'drō-jenz) | male sex hormones |
| **testosterone** (tes-tos'ter-ōn) | the primary male sex hormone |

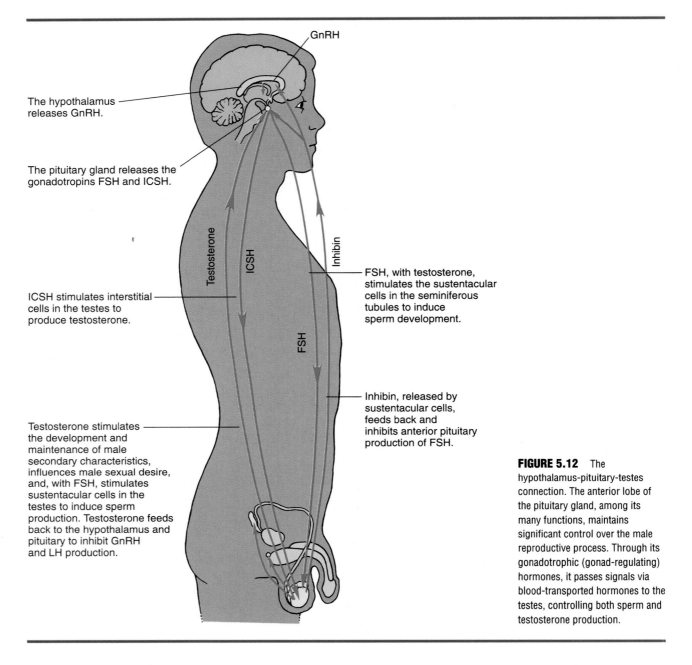

GnRH

The hypothalamus releases GnRH.

The pituitary gland releases the gonadotropins FSH and ICSH.

Testosterone

ICSH

Inhibin

FSH

ICSH stimulates interstitial cells in the testes to produce testosterone.

FSH, with testosterone, stimulates the sustentacular cells in the seminiferous tubules to induce sperm development.

Inhibin, released by sustentacular cells, feeds back and inhibits anterior pituitary production of FSH.

Testosterone stimulates the development and maintenance of male secondary characteristics, influences male sexual desire, and, with FSH, stimulates sustentacular cells in the testes to induce sperm production. Testosterone feeds back to the hypothalamus and pituitary to inhibit GnRH and LH production.

**FIGURE 5.12**    The hypothalamus-pituitary-testes connection. The anterior lobe of the pituitary gland, among its many functions, maintains significant control over the male reproductive process. Through its gonadotrophic (gonad-regulating) hormones, it passes signals via blood-transported hormones to the testes, controlling both sperm and testosterone production.

forties and fifties, a period some refer to as the male **climacteric** (also midlife crisis or transition). Although symptoms are variable and not predictable, many men experience some degree of sleeplessness, a decreased interest in sex, an inability to concentrate, depression, loss of appetite, and fatigue (Kolodny, Masters, & Johnson, 1979).

As a man ages, the gaining of erection takes more stimulation and time, the erection may be less firm, ejaculation takes longer and might not occur every time the penis is stimulated, there is less force behind the ejaculation, and the amount of ejaculate declines (Zilbergeld, 1992). Frequency of sexual activity declines with age, although sexual interest and enjoy-

ment need not decrease (Schiavi et al., 1990). Many of these changes are due to gradual declines in testosterone levels (fig. 5.11). Other changes can result from diseases that are more commonplace as the man ages. The state of a man's general health, the effects of poor health habits, and, gradual atherosclerosis are a part of this aging process. Yet because the decline in hormonal levels is gradual and not abrupt, and there is no loss of reproductive capacity, there is no "male menopause."

Along with physical changes, many men experience psychological stresses related to children growing up and leaving home, professional goals having been reached, and the prospects and adjustments of

# AT ISSUE

## "WINNING" WITH ANABOLIC STEROIDS?

In the past decade some athletes, particularly in competitive sports, have subscribed to the motto Win At Any Cost. To gain that competitive edge they have turned to **anabolic steroids,** a synthetic version of human testosterone. Although steroids are banned in competitive sports and it is illegal to obtain them without a prescription, they have been widely available. Men who are steroid abusers might take 10 to 40 times per day more anabolic steroids than the amount of testosterone their body normally produces (Mishra, 1991).

Why do athletes decide to use steroids? These are some of the things that steroid use does for athletes:

- Promotes protein synthesis, thus building the muscles that are key to strength and endurance
- Creates a sense of explosive power
- Improves one's physique through muscular weight gain
- Increases aggressiveness
- Appeals to a basic tendency to go for quicker results

without concern for the long-term adverse effects of drug abuse

Anabolic steroid users commonly are athletes (both men and women) who specialize in power events, such as weight lifters, football linemen, and body builders, and participants in track events such as shot put, discus, javelin throwing, and sprinting.

Being disqualified from competition or losing a medal is only one price an athlete may pay for steroid abuse. The large doses needed to produce a significant effect can have dangerous and damaging side effects, including liver cancer, kidney damage, increased risk of heart disease, stunted growth in young people, increased irritability, aggressive and antisocial behavior, and severe mood swings. In men the adverse effects of steroid use can include permanent shrinkage of the testes, reduced sperm production, loss of fertility, prostate enlargement with increased risk of cancer, diminished hormone production, unwanted and painful erection, and baldness. Adverse effects in women include loss of menstruation and fertility, fetal damage if pregnant, and masculin-

ization including male-pattern baldness, increased growth of face and body hair, irreversible deepening of the voice, permanent enlargement of the clitoris, and atrophy of the breast and uterus.

Adding to these hazards is the way in which anabolic steroids have been made and distributed. Many steroids have been made outside the United States and smuggled into the country. Their potency, purity, and strength are neither known nor regulated (Mishra, 1991).

Athletic organizations such as the United States Olympic Committee, the National Football League, and the National Collegiate Athletic Association maintain strict testing policies and discipline steroid users rigorously. Body-building authorities now advise readers of muscle magazines that the best body-building gains come with serious training and good nutrition, rather than steroid use.

Being fit is certainly a healthful lifestyle, and developing muscular strength for successful competition is certainly an acceptable goal, but does steroid use help a person reach that goal? You decide.

**Sources:** K. Ropp, "No-Win Situation for Athletes," *FDA Consumer* (December 1992): 8–12; R. Mishra, "Steroids and Sports Are a Losing Proposition," *FDA Consumer* (September 1991): 25–27; R. Miller, "Athletes and Steroids: Playing a Deadly Game," *FDA Consumer* (November 1987): 17–21; National Academy of Sports Medicine policy statement and position paper "Anabolic Steroids, Growth Hormones, Stimulants, Ergogenics, and Drug Use in Sports," in *Death in the Locker Room II: Drugs and Sports,* ed. B. Goldman and R. Klatz (Chicago: Elite Sports Medicine, 1992), pp.328–73.

nearing retirement. For some men these changes bring discouragement and worry, although many people approach this period of life with a sense of accomplishment and fulfillment. Because menopause brings distinct changes, menopausal women often receive support and understanding of the physical and psychological changes they are going through. It is important for a man's family or friends to realize that he, too, needs support. It may be wise for a man to

**climacteric** (klī-mak´ter-ik)    the period of life when sexual functions decline

**anabolic steroids** (a-na-bol´ik ster´oydz)    synthetic forms of testosterone that stimulate the growth of muscle mass

seek counseling, and to make major life changes only cautiously, realizing that these changes are a normal part of growing older.

## 5.6 THE SEXUAL BODY: PROMOTING HEALTH AND TREATING ILLNESS

A man's sexual and reproductive system, although not as complex as that of a woman, is subject to certain significant conditions and infections. Because his reproductive and urinary systems are located close to each other and have some of the same structures and ducts in common, the system is collectively referred to as the **urogenital system**. The medical specialty dealing with this system is **urology**. A discussion of several of these conditions follows.

### 5.6.1 Testicular Disorders

*Hypogonadism*

In some young males, problems can arise due to failure of the testes to function normally. Referred to as *hypogonadism,* such failure may be due to genetic defect, illness, or to injury. Unless there is a readily detectable sexual abnormality at birth, delayed puberty might be the first indication that the testes are not producing a sufficient supply of testosterone. Insufficient secretions of testosterone prior to puberty can result in the boy's beginning puberty late or not at all. Symptoms might include reduced genital growth and sparse body hair, retention of his boyish high-pitched voice, and atypical bone growth and body proportions (Hadley, 1996; Flieger, 1995). Too little testosterone after puberty can lead to a reduced sex drive, low sperm production, and reduced overall strength. In severe cases it can even lead to the atrophy (withering away) of the testes.

An estimated 150,000 to 200,000 boys and men in the United States are receiving replacement testosterone to treat hypogonadism, and there may be many more undiagnosed cases (Flieger, 1995). Most patients receiving replacement testosterone do so by injections that they must take throughout their lifetime; testosterone is not readily absorbed into the body when taken by mouth.

*Testicular Cancer*

It is very important for men to become familiar with their testicles and to check monthly for irregularities. In some men the cells of the seminiferous tubules give rise to *testicular cancer.* Testicular cancer occurs most often between the ages of fifteen and forty. The American Cancer Society (2000) predicted an esti-

mated 6,900 new cases of testicular cancer in 2000, with 300 expected deaths.

Although the cause is unknown, the *risk factors* for this type of cancer include cryptorchidism, ethnic background, and a personal or family history of the disease. Men who had cryptorchidism (undescended testicle) as an infant have an increased risk of developing cancer in the normally descended testicle. White American men have a five-fold increased risk of testicular cancer compared to African American men, with Asian and Hispanic Americans having an intermediate risk. A family history of testicular cancer increases a man's risk, and having cancer in one testicle increases the risk of developing cancer in the other testicle. Testicular injury, maternal use of hormones (such as DES) during pregnancy, and vasectomy do not increase the risk of testicular cancer (American Cancer Society, 2000).

Although risk factors are unavoidable, testicular cancer is one of the most curable forms of cancer, reinforcing the importance of early detection. The first sign of testicular cancer is a painless enlargement of one of the testes, or a scrotal mass that appears attached to a testis. When this condition is suspected, the physician does a *biopsy* (removal of a small piece of tissue for microscopic examination). If cancer cells are confirmed, the affected testis is surgically removed (*orchidectomy*). Depending on the nature of the cancerous tissue and the extent of the disease, the patient may be treated with radiation or with chemotherapy. As a result of such treatment, the cure rate for testicular cancer (for all stages combined) exceeds 90 percent (American Cancer Society, 2000).

The loss of one or both testes can have a psychological effect on the man's sexual functioning. Some men, feeling they have lost their masculinity or feeling self-conscious about their sexual performance, may experience sexual dysfunction. If only a single testis is removed, the remaining testis can still produce sufficient sperm and androgens to compensate for the removed testis. If both testes are removed (*castration*), the man might lose sexual desire and be unable to have erection. Testosterone replacement therapy can help him maintain both desire and erection, and implants resembling the missing testes can be surgically placed inside his scrotum.

*Testicular Self-Examination*

Breast self-examination has received wide publicity, yet many men do not know of the importance of *testicular self-examination* (TSE). It is recommended that a man examine himself when the skin of his scrotum is relaxed, as after a warm shower or bath. Roll each testicle between the thumb and fingertips. The testicle should feel smooth, except for the raised,

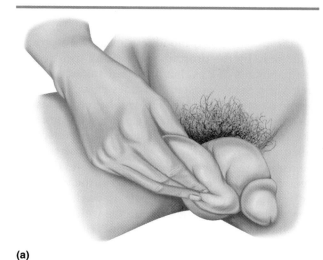

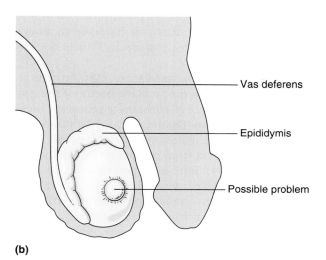

- Vas deferens
- Epididymis
- Possible problem

**FIGURE 5.13** Testicular self-examination.

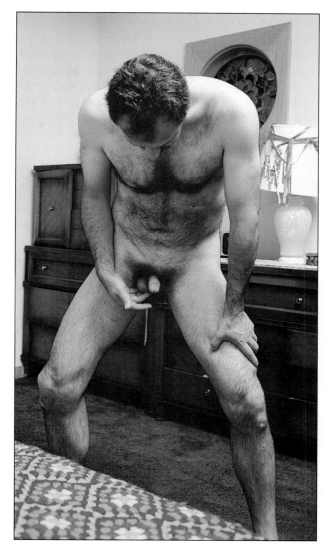

The sexual comfort of all individuals is increased as they understand and accept their own bodies. Such satisfaction can be increased if we feel free to thoroughly examine our genitals directly or by using a mirror.

wormlike epididymis on the back side of each (fig. 5.13). Feel the entire surface of each testis for any lump, hardening, or enlargement. You should report any lump, enlargement, or contour change to your health care practitioner immediately (fig. 5.13). All men, especially young men, should learn and practice regular TSE on a monthly basis. It is one important step a man can take to ensure early discovery of testicular cancer and to take responsibility for his own health.

### 5.6.2  Prostate Disorders

*Prostatitis*

Inflammation of the prostate gland due to bacterial infections is common in young, postpubescent men. Chronic infections (prostatitis) are common in middle-aged and elderly men. Symptoms include fever, chills, lower back or anal pain, urinary difficulties, and painful ejaculation. Prostatitis can be treated effectively with antibiotics.

| | |
|---|---|
| **urogenital system** (ū-rō-jen´i-tal) | the system of urinary and reproductive organs |
| **urology** (ū-rol´ō-jē) | a medical specialty treating urogenital organs and their conditions |

## Benign Prostatic Hyperplasia

Enlargement of the prostate is another common disorder. The prostate gland is small in male children, begins to grow during adolescence, reaches adult size at about twenty years of age, and then remains relatively unchanged in size until about fifty years of age, when it often starts to enlarge again. When this happens, the gland may squeeze the urethra and interfere with urination. Enlargement of the prostate to 2 to 4 times the normal size occurs in more than half of all men in their sixties (Henkel, 1994). Such *benign prostatic hyperplasia (BPH)* can cause a decreased force of urine flow, bedwetting, and sense of incomplete emptying of the bladder. Detection of such enlargement can be done by a *digital rectal examination (DRE),* in which the physician *palpates* (feels with the fingers) the prostate through the wall of the rectum. Surgical correction of the prostate can be done through *transurethral resection of the prostate (TURP),* in which excessive tissue is removed via the urethra. Other treatment options include balloon dilation to stretch the narrowed urethra, and medications to relax the prostatic pressure on the urethra.

## Prostate Cancer

Prostate cancer is the second leading cause of cancer death among men in the United States, exceeded only by lung cancer. Over 80 percent of all prostate cancer is diagnosed in men over age sixty-five (American Cancer Society, 2000).

Prostate cancer is twice as common in African American men compared to white American men, and their mortality rate is more than twice as high. Although common in North America and northwestern Europe, prostate cancer is rare in the Near East, Africa, and South America (American Cancer Society, 2000). In addition to age and ethnic background, other risk factors include having a father or brother with prostate cancer, and a diet high in fats and low in fruits and vegetables (American Cancer Society, 2000).

Growths within the prostate put pressure on the urethra, creating problems with urination. Prostate cancer often develops with no noticeable symptoms. Warning signs include weak or interrupted urine flow, pain or burning on urination, frequent need to urinate (especially at night), difficulty starting or stopping urine flow, blood in the urine, and back or pelvic pain. Most of these symptoms are nonspecific and can also occur with prostate infection or benign enlargement of the prostate.

Prostate cancer can be detected by several methods. The traditional screening test is the *digital rectal exam (DRE),* in which a physician inserts a lubricated rubber-gloved finger into the rectum to probe the prostate for lumps or enlargements that might indicate prostatic tumors. Another test, the *prostate specific antigen (PSA)* blood test, measures a protein made only by the prostate. All healthy men secrete small amounts of PSA, but increased amounts are secreted if a man's prostate becomes enlarged due to benign or malignant growths, or if he has a prostate infection (*prostatitis*). With an elevated PSA or a positive DRE, a more definitive test is a rectal probe called a *transrectal ultrasound (TRUS).* Inserted into the rectum, the probe produces sound waves that create a video image of the prostate. If suspicious areas are found, a small-gauge needle is used to take a biopsy of prostate tissue through the wall of the rectum. If cancer is diagnosed, other tests can determine whether the tumor has spread beyond the prostate.

Every man age forty and older should have a DRE as a part of his regular annual physical checkup. In addition, all men aged fifty and older, as well as high-risk men over age forty, should have an annual DRE and PSA blood test (American Cancer Society, 1997).

Treatment for prostate cancer may involve removal of all or part of the prostate, hormone therapy, or radiation therapy. For early-stage prostate cancer, some physicians now recommend a "wait-and-see" attitude for men in their sixties or older who could suffer adverse effects from surgery or radiation therapy (Henkel, 1994). Fifty-eight percent of all prostate cancers are diagnosed while they are still localized, and for these the five-year survival rate is 100 percent. The overall survival rate for prostate cancer is 92 percent (American Cancer Society, 2000).

## Urethritis

Both men and women are subject to inflammation of the urethra (*urethritis*). Symptoms of the condition in men include painful urination, frequent need to urinate, an urgency to urinate, and penile discharge. Feelings of urinary urgency may occur even though the person has little urine to void. Urethral inflammation can lead to constriction of the urethra, which can slow down or halt urination.

Various bacteria can cause urethritis. A laboratory test can determine the appropriate antibiotic for treatment. Drinking extra fluids and limiting alcohol and caffeine are also recommended to alleviate symptoms.

## Penile Cancer

Penile cancer is a very rare disorder in North America and Europe, occurring in about 1 of every 100,000 men in the United States, and accounting for about 0.2% of all cancers in men. In some parts of Africa and South America, however, penile cancer represents up to 10% of cancers in men (American Cancer Society, 2000). When detected early, penile cancer can be treated effectively and with a minimum of side effects or complications.

The most common type of penile cancer develops in the skin cells of the glans or foreskin, though lesions can develop elsewhere on the penis. Because these are slow-growing tumors, they can usually be cured when treated in the early stages. Signs of possible penile cancer development include any abnormal growths on the penis, such as warts, blisters, sores, white patches, or any abnormal swelling of the glans area. The most important *risk factor* for penile cancer is infection with human papillomavirus (HPV). Since HPV is transmitted sexually, beginning sexual activity later in life, and having few sex partners, are ways to reduce risk. Warts due to HPV can develop into cancer, so removal of these at an early stage is an important preventative measure. Cigarette smoking is another factor that increases the risk of penile cancer, as is age (most cases occur in men over fifty years of age; American Cancer Society, 2000).

It was previously thought that circumcision was a factor in reducing the risk of penile cancer. However, recent studies have suggested that in the absence of other risk factors, penile cancer risk is not significantly different between circumcised and uncircumcised men. Uncircumcised men should keep the penis free from smegma (oily secretions that accumulate under the foreskin) by retracting the foreskin and cleaning the glans regularly. While the presence of smegma is unlikely to affect penile cancer risk, it can lead to inflammation and irritation of the glans, which might mask early signs of cancer or other disorders.

## SUMMARY

1. A man's external sex organs consist of the penis (glans and shaft) and the scrotum, which contains the testes, spermatic cords, and epididymis.

2. Internally, the penis consists of the urethra, corpus spongiosum, and the corpora cavernosa.

3. Vasocongestion results in penile erection. Arousal can occur through either direct stimulation or thoughts and fantasy.

4. A man's internal sex organs include the two testes, the epididymis, the vas deferens, and several fluid-producing glands.

5. The testes contain seminiferous tubules in which spermatogenic cells produce sperm cells. The interstitial cells produce and secrete testosterone. Testosterone initiates and maintains the development of man's secondary sex characteristics and also influences male sexual interest.

6. The genital ducts, which store and transport sperm and seminal fluids, include the epididymis, vas deferens, ejaculatory duct, and urethra. The urethra also carries urine out of the body.

7. Sperm require a capacitation period in the woman's reproductive tract before they are able to fertilize an ovum.

8. Ejaculation is the sudden ejection of semen from the erect penis and consists of two phases: emission, which is the discharge of seminal fluid from the fluid-producing glands, and expulsion, which is the release of the semen from the penis.

9. In retrograde ejaculation, semen is ejaculated back into the urinary bladder instead of being expelled from the body.

10. The male breast is similar to the female breast in its embryologic origin and structure, yet it is regarded differently in our culture.

11. The sex glands include the hypothalamus, the pituitary gland, the two testes, and the two adrenal glands.

12. Testosterone is the hormone responsible for the sex drive in both men and women.

13. A man's hormone system includes GnRH from the hypothalamus, which stimulates the pituitary to produce ICSH and FSH. A man's sexual hormones are produced continuously, rather than cyclically as they are in women.

14. The period in life when sex hormone production and sex organ function begin to decline is called the climacteric.

15. One of the most common types of cancers in young men is testicular cancer.

16. Prostate gland disorders are common in older men. Prostate gland growths may be benign (noncancerous) or malignant (cancerous). Prostate cancer is the second leading cause of death among men in the United States.

17. Penile disorders include urethritis and penile cancer.

## CRITICAL THINKING CHALLENGES

1. Views toward infant male circumcision have changed in the Unites States in recent years. What is your opinion of this procedure? Based on your knowledge, would you circumcise your infant son, and why or why not? What additional information would you need to be comfortable with your decision?

2. A friend says to you, "I don't care what your book says, penis size *does* matter!" List some of the reasons, whether rational or irrational, why penis size matters (or should not matter) to various people. How would you answer your friend?

# SEXUALLY TRANSMITTED INFECTIONS

## 6

**AFTER STUDYING THIS CHAPTER, YOU SHOULD BE ABLE TO**

[1] Explain the general nature of communicable disease.

[2] Describe the general categories of pathogens and relate the possibilities for treating diseases caused by each category.

[3] Outline the steps in the typical progress of a communicable disease.

[4] Explain why STI rates are high and which individuals are at high risk of STIs.

[5] Explain why STI rates are high in young people and the attitudes that contribute to these high rates.

[6] Relate the special concerns that STIs present for each gender.

[7] Outline all personal and public health measures for reducing the risk of STI.

[8] Explain the symptoms (or lack of symptoms), progression, and possible harmful effects of each STI.

[9] Explain the steps a person should take if she or he suspects a possible STI.

[10] Describe the psychological aspects of STIs and explain how they contribute to the STI problem.

[11] Outline the social issues related to STIs.

The possibility of contracting an infectious disease is a factor that must be considered in making decisions regarding potential sexual partners and practices. Today, the prevention of disease is (or ought to be) a concern of every sexually active person.

Direct person-to-person contact of warm, moist body surfaces and exposure to fresh body fluids are ideal means of transmitting certain disease-causing agents. It is not surprising, therefore, that some diseases can be transmitted by sexual contact. These diseases are caused by **sexually transmitted infections,** or **STIs.**

An older term for these diseases, still in common use, is **venereal disease,** or **VD.** This name, derived from *Venus,* the name of a goddess of love, is not entirely accurate because love often plays little or no role in the transmission of such diseases. This term was used until the early 1970s, when the phrase *sexually transmitted disease (STD)* was first used. Recently, new information about these diseases and their causes has led to a more accurate term, **sexually transmitted infection (STI),** which reflects the fact that many of these infections have a period with no symptoms. In this chapter, we examine the various STIs—their symptoms, their prevention, and their treatment.

## 6.1 BASICS OF COMMUNICABLE DISEASES

Sexually transmitted infections all fall into the general category of **communicable diseases**—those that can be transmitted from one person to another—so there are various general concepts that apply to all of these diseases. A brief review of some of these concepts is helpful before we discuss the specific characteristics of each STI.

### 6.1.1 Pathogens

Communicable diseases are caused by infectious agents called **pathogens** (table 6.1 and fig. 6.1). Pathogens are commonly called "germs." Pathogens include microscopic living organisms, such as bacteria, fungi, yeasts, and protozoa (one-celled animal-like organisms), and larger parasites, such as worms and certain insects. Other important pathogens are viruses, which are extremely small and are usually

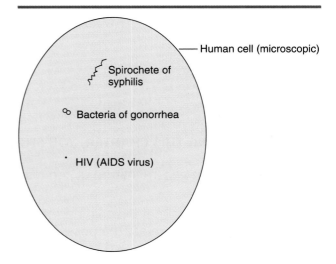

**FIGURE 6.1** A size comparison of some STI pathogens. The largest oval represents, for comparison, the size of a human cell, which is itself microscopic. From the top down: a syphilis spirochete, a pair of gonorrhea bacteria, and one particle of HIV, the virus that causes AIDS.

**TABLE 6.1** PATHOGEN GROUPS CAUSING SEXUALLY TRANSMITTED INFECTIONS

| Name of Group and Size | Sexually Transmitted Examples | Description | Comments |
|---|---|---|---|
| **Viruses** (10–250 nanometers;* visible only with electron microscope at hundreds of thousands of times magnification) | HIV, herpes simplex, hepatitis B, genital warts | Minute particles of nucleic acid and protein | Semiliving pathogens not controlled by antibiotics; specific antiviral drugs have only limited effectiveness |
| **Bacteria** (1–10 micrometers;** barely visible with light microscope at 1,000 times magnification) | Gonorrhea, syphilis, chlamydia | Microscopic cells in rodlike, spherical, or spiral shapes | Produce toxins and enzymes that damage human cells; most are controllable with antibiotic drugs |
| **Yeasts** (a few micrometers; clearly visible with 1,000 times magnification) | Candida | Microscopic oval cells; reproduce by budding | Release enzymes that damage human cells; controllable with special antibiotic drugs |
| **Protozoa** (a few to 250 micrometers; seen with 100 to 1,000 times magnification) | Trichomoniasis, amoebiasis | Microscopic single-celled animals | Release enzymes and toxins that destroy human cells |

*A nanometer is one one-billionth of a meter. It takes 25,400,000 nanometers to make one inch.

**A micrometer is one one-millionth of a meter. It takes 25,400 micrometers to make an inch.

considered to be semiliving particles. Sexually transmitted infections are caused by pathogens found in all of these groups.

## 6.1.2  Transmission of Pathogens

**Transmission** is the transfer of a pathogen from one person to another. It can be accomplished in many ways, including direct contact, or through contaminated objects (indirect contact), airborne dust or droplets, insect bites, and contaminated food and water. A disease that can be transmitted directly from person to person is said to be **contagious.** Sexually transmitted infections are transmitted almost exclusively through direct contact, including oral, anal, and vaginal sex, and are highly contagious.

## 6.1.3  Incubation Period

Following exposure to a communicable disease, a period of time called the **incubation period** passes before symptoms appear. During this time, the pathogen is increasing in number and commencing the process of disease production. Incubation periods for the various diseases range from hours to years, but the most common incubation time is usually a matter of days or weeks. During the latter part of the incubation period, many diseases become contagious to other people before symptoms are apparent in the infected person.

## 6.1.4  Communicable Period

Every disease has its own particular time during which it can be transmitted to other people. This **communicable period** often begins during the incubation period before the appearance of symptoms. Also, for some diseases a recovering patient continues to be a source of infection even after symptoms have disappeared.

## 6.1.5  Asymptomatic Carriers

For many diseases, it is possible to be a source of infection to others even though you are **asymptomatic—** you have never experienced any symptoms. People who are sources of infection in this way are called **asymptomatic carriers.** The pathogen colonizes some part of their body and can infect other people, but they experience no discomfort. At some later date, however, the asymptomatic infection might erupt into the disease.

## 6.1.6  Body Defenses against Diseases

Our bodies have many built-in mechanisms for protection against pathogens. The unbroken skin and mucous membranes, for example, form barriers against many pathogens. In addition, white blood cells are often able to engulf and destroy pathogens

that do enter the body. Our main defense against specific pathogens is immunity.

### *Immunity*

One of the most amazing abilities of the human body is that it can detect invasion by something harmful, such as a pathogen, and act to destroy or inactivate the invader. Without this ability, our lives would be very short, as evidenced by the early deaths of those few infants that are born without it.

Protection against harmful invaders is provided by a complex array of highly specific body defenses collectively called **immunity.** Immunity is developed against a specific pathogen upon exposure to the pathogen or exposure to a vaccine derived from the pathogen or some portion of it. Because immunity develops only *after* exposure to the pathogen or vaccine, it's complete name is *acquired immunity.*

The foreign substance that stimulates an immune response is called an **antigen.** Various chemical components of pathogens, such as the protein coat of a virus, can act as antigens.

| | |
|---|---|
| **sexually transmitted infections (STIs)** | infections that can be transmitted by sexual contact; other methods of transmission are sometimes possible |
| **venereal disease (VD)** (venē´real) | an older term for sexually transmitted infection |
| **communicable diseases** | diseases that can be transmitted from person to person (also called infectious diseases) |
| **pathogens** | disease-causing agents, commonly called "germs" |
| **transmission** | the transfer of a pathogen from one person to another |
| **contagious** | capable of being transmitted readily from one person to another |
| **incubation period** | interval between infection and appearance of disease symptoms |
| **communicable period** | the period when a disease is transmissible from person to person |
| **asymptomatic** (ā´´-simp-tō-mat´ik) | having no symptoms |
| **asymptomatic carrier** | a person who harbors a pathogen without experiencing symptoms |
| **immunity** | an array of highly specific bodily defenses against pathogens |
| **antigen** (an´ti-jen) | any substance that stimulates an immune response |

Lifelong immunity often results from a single experience with a disease or from proper immunization against the pathogen. However, some pathogens do not stimulate an effective immune response and the disease that results can be experienced repeatedly, or chronically. Unfortunately, most sexually transmitted infections are in this category.

Immunity (see fig. 6.2) is produced by two kinds of specialized white blood cells called **lymphocytes**—the *B lymphocytes* and *T lymphocytes*. B lymphocytes produce **antibodies** (Y-shaped proteins) that attach to a pathogen and interfere with its ability to cause infection (*antibody-mediated immunity*). T lymphocytes attack pathogens directly (*cell-mediated immunity*) and also regulate the activity of B lymphocytes. Certain T lymphocytes, called *T4* or *CD4 lymphocytes,* play a key role in antibody-mediated immunity by presenting antigens from pathogens to B lymphocytes and other T lymphocytes. Unfortunately, T4 lymphocytes are infected and destroyed by HIV (the virus that causes AIDS), thus crippling the entire immune system.

### Vaccines

For any disease, prevention is preferable to treatment, and the most effective prevention is usually through immunization. Immunization is accomplished by use of **vaccines**, preparations of one or more antigens. Vaccines typically contain either killed pathogens, living modified pathogens, or chemical parts of pathogens, such as the protein of a virus. The vaccine itself does not cause the disease, but when the same pathogen is encountered later, the immune system remembers the previous exposure and reacts to prevent disease (*immunity*). Many diseases, such as polio, diphtheria, and measles, have been largely eradicated by means of vaccines. With the exception of hepatitis B, vaccines are not yet available for any of the major sexually transmitted infections, although efforts to develop them are under way.

### 6.1.7 Treatment of Communicable Diseases

Effective drugs are now available to combat most categories of pathogens. Bacteria, fungi, yeasts, and protozoa all respond to drug therapy. Viruses, in contrast, present a greater challenge because they lack most of the enzymes or structures attacked by antibacterial drugs. None of the antibiotics or sulfa drugs, for example, are effective against viruses. Specific antiviral drugs have been developed, with limited safety and effectiveness. Some of the more successful examples are drugs used against herpes or HIV infections. Typically, antiviral drugs moderate symptoms but fail to cure viral infections, and some

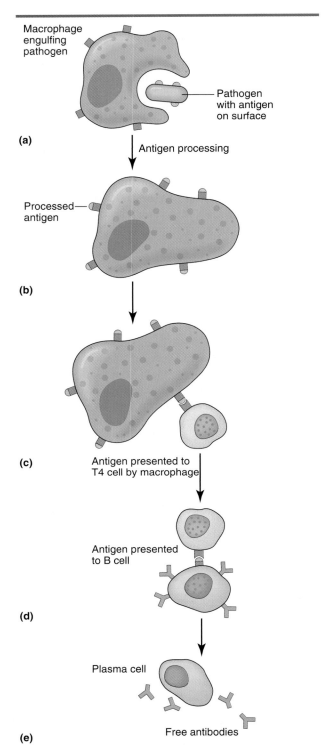

(a) Macrophage engulfing pathogen — Pathogen with antigen on surface

Antigen processing

(b) Processed antigen

(c) Antigen presented to T4 cell by macrophage

(d) Antigen presented to B cell

(e) Plasma cell — Free antibodies

**FIGURE 6.2** The sequence of events leading to an immune response. **a:** A large white blood cell known as a macrophage engulfs a pathogen. The semicircles on the pathogen's surface represent immunity-stimulating antigen. **b:** Antigen from the pathogen is moved onto the surface of the macrophage. **c:** Antigen is presented to a T4 (CD4) cell. **d:** The T4 cell presents the antigen to a B cell. **e:** The B cell, now called a plasma cell, releases Y-shaped antibodies to attack pathogens. Destruction of T4 (CD4) cells by HIV impairs a person's immune responses.

can have severe side effects. With time, better antiviral drugs are becoming available. The need to develop anti-HIV drugs has been a great stimulus in the development of antiviral drugs such as the protease inhibitors discussed in the next chapter.

### 6.1.8   Drug Resistance

Often after a drug has been successfully used against a certain pathogen for a period of time, the pathogen changes so that it is no longer affected by that drug. Drug resistance is caused by the naturally high rate of mutation of microorganisms. Drugs may destroy most of the pathogens present in an infection, but some can survive which have mutated to be resistant to the drug. These resistant strains multiply and can sometimes transmit their resistance to other pathogens. We can delay the onset of drug resistance by avoiding unnecessary use of antimicrobial drugs and using them properly when we must use them (e.g., being sure to use an antibiotic for its entire prescribed course, thus minimizing the number of individual pathogens that survive the dosage).

## 6.2   INCIDENCE OF STIs

Sexually transmitted infections are a major world problem. The World Health Organization (WHO) estimates that 125 million cases occur each year (Alexander, 1996). This amounts to about 356,000 new cases *every day*. In the United States, more than sixty-five million people are living with an incurable STI. An additional fifteen million Americans are infected each year (Cates, 1999).

Accurate incidence figures for most sexually transmitted infections are somewhat elusive. In the United States, many of the STIs are classified as *re-*

Who carries an STI? There is no way to know who they are by looking, but millions of people in the United States carry at least one STI.

*portable diseases;* that is, every case diagnosed must be reported to public health authorities. This does not mean, however, that the published incidence figures for reportable diseases are accurate. In the first place, many infected people fail to seek treatment, either because they are *asymptomatic* (experience no symptoms) or because they just ignore their symptoms. Further, many cases diagnosed by private physicians are not reported, in defiance of the laws. Some physicians wish to protect their patients' privacy, some may be too busy to deal with reporting paperwork.

Other common STIs, such as chlamydia, are reportable in some states but not in others. Some are not reportable anywhere. For these diseases, we can only guess the number of cases. Here are some reported and estimated numbers of STIs for the United States (Cates, 1999):

- *AIDS:* About 58,000 new cases reported in 1997; the CDC (U.S. Centers for Disease Control and Prevention, Atlanta, Georgia) has received reports that about 750,000 Americans are infected with HIV.
- *Chlamydia:* The most common STI; not reportable in most states; estimates average about three million new cases per year.
- *Gonorrhea:* An estimated 650,000 new cases per year.
- *Genital herpes:* A lifelong infection; not reportable in most states; an estimated forty-five million Americans are infected, and about one million new infections occur annually.
- *Papillomaviruses (genital warts and cervical cancer):* Approximately twenty million infected; estimated 5.5 million new cases per year (Alexander, 1996).
- *Syphilis:* About 70,000 new cases each year.

What is obvious, even from our incomplete statistics, is that every year millions of new cases of STIs develop in the United States, in addition to the pool of millions of existing untreated cases from previous years. In practical terms, when making your sexual decisions it is wise to assume that anyone who has a variety of sexual partners may be infected with one or more of the STIs.

| | |
|---|---|
| **lymphocytes** (lim´fō-sītz) | white blood cells involved in producing immunity |
| **antibodies** | Y-shaped protein molecules produced by B lymphocytes to destroy or inactivate antigens |
| **vaccine** | a preparation composed of one or more antigens used to stimulate the development of immunity |

## 6.2.1   Why Are STIs So Common?

No single explanation accounts for today's high incidence of STIs. Pathogen-related factors, such as mutations that give rise to entirely new or changed disease organisms play a role. HIV and drug-resistant strains of existing pathogens are examples of the results of such mutations.

Once new pathogens or newly drug-resistant strains of pathogens develop, world travel becomes a major factor in their spread. A new pathogen or strain of an existing pathogen can arise in any corner of the world and in a very short time be carried to every nation.

According to some authorities, one important factor in the current STI epidemic is the birth control pill. The pill has largely eliminated fear of pregnancy, thus encouraging greater freedom of sexual activity. Furthermore, it has reduced the use of condoms, a birth control method that is also of value in reducing the risk of transmission of some STIs. The pill increases the alkalinity and moisture of the female genital tract, encouraging the rapid growth of gonorrheal organisms and other pathogens. Other contraceptive aids for women, such as spermicidal jelly and foam, are acidic or toxic to pathogens, providing an environment antagonistic to the growth of infectious organisms. But motivating people who don't need condoms or spermicidal chemicals for birth control to use these products for lowering the risk of disease is often difficult (see "Healthy Sexuality: Negotiating Condom Use").

Some lifestyle choices are favorable to the spread of infections. Beginning sexual relationships at an early age and having a number of different sex partners have certainly contributed to the increased incidence of STIs. As the number of partners increases, the STI risk increases in direct proportion. In recent years, in response to the rise first of herpes and then of HIV, many people have modified their sexual habits. The tendency has been to reduce the number of partners, to more openly discuss the risks of disease transmission, and to take greater precautions, such as condom use, to reduce the risk of infection. Unfortunately, not everyone takes the risk of sexually transmitted infection seriously (Rekart 1996).

Attitudes and beliefs can also contribute to the STI problem:

▪ The belief that an STI is a disgrace or a deserved punishment for "sin" can discourage an individual from seeking treatment or from discussing STI prevention with sex partners.

▪ The attitude "It can't happen to me" is prevalent in all age groups, but it is especially common in younger people.

▪ The belief that a person who looks clean and attractive is unlikely to carry any STI is also prevalent, but incorrect.

## 6.2.2   Who Contracts STIs?

STIs have permeated American society. Infections cross all lines of age, education, income level, and ethnicity. Even so, some incidence differences are evident. Important differences in STI incidence are found among ethnic groups, age groups, and between men and women.

### Ethnic Distribution of STIs

Although STIs occur in every ethnic group in the United States, they don't occur uniformly. STI rates tend to be higher among African Americans than among white Americans, as much as thirty times higher for some infections. Explaining ethnic differences in STI rates between ethnic groups is difficult, as many cultural and socioeconomic influences come into play. Some of the difference may be due to sampling errors, as African Americans are more likely to seek care in public clinics that report STIs more completely than private medical providers. Other important factors include differences in affluence, access to health care, differences in prevention education and behavior, and level of drug use. Some notable differences in STI incidence include the following (all data is from the Centers for Disease Control, 2000):

▪ *Gonorrhea.* Reported rates of gonorrhea among African Americans are thirty times higher than rates among white Americans and more than eleven times higher than rates among Hispanic Americans (fig. 6.3).

▪ *Syphilis.* Even though syphilis is easily treated and cured, the reported incidence of syphilis is thirty times higher for African Americans than for white Americans.

▪ *Herpes.* Genital herpes infection is more common among African Americans (45 percent have a positive blood test for the virus) compared to white Americans (17 percent are positive).

▪ *Hepatitis B.* African Americans are four times more likely to test positive for hepatitis B infection than white Americans.

### STIs and Young People

Although sexually transmitted infections occur in all age groups, a disproportionate percentage occurs in people under the age of eighteen. Most young people have expectations of long, healthy lives including eventual parenthood, and their STI often makes parenthood difficult or impossible, and may result in a shortened life span.

## NEGOTIATING CONDOM USE

Many people who want to use condoms or want their partner to use condoms meet with adamant resistance. This is especially true when condoms are not needed for birth control and their use would be for disease prevention only. Assertiveness and excellent communication skills are necessary in such cases.

In order to effectively counter someone's resistance to condom use, you need to know the basis of that resistance, which might be revealed only reluctantly, if at all. Some of the possible bases include denial of the possibility of catching or transmitting a disease, a religious objection, a belief that condoms reduce pleasure, inexperience in condom use, concern over the cost of condoms, fear of being hurt by a condom, and desire for a pregnancy. Here are a few ways to deal with these objections:

*Objection:* "I'm offended that you think I might have a disease (or) I'm sure that you don't have any disease. Why do we need condoms?"

*Your response:* "Actually, I doubt that either one of us has any disease, but neither you nor I know that for sure. If I really thought you had some disease, you can be sure that I wouldn't want to have sex with you even with a condom. But it's so easy to use condoms and I just don't believe in taking a chance with your health or mine."

*Objection:* "My religion doesn't allow me to use condoms."

*Your response:* "I certainly do respect your religious beliefs. In fact, your religion probably doesn't approve of you and I having sex, with or without a condom. If you really want to practice your religious beliefs, I'll understand if we don't have sex at this time."

*Objection:* "Sex is not pleasurable with a condom."

*Your response:* "For me, sex is not pleasurable without a condom. How do you expect me to enjoy sex when I'm worrying about catching some disease? It's nothing personal against you, but I am just very careful with my health. And I disagree with your idea that sex is not pleasurable with a condom. Millions of people are using condoms with great pleasure. What makes you so different from them?"

*Objection (seldom stated):* "I have no experience with condoms and am not sure exactly how to use them."

*Your response:* "Maybe you haven't had much experience with condoms; lots of people haven't. I'm no expert, but I know a little bit about them and we could learn together. Practice makes perfect, you know."

*Objection:* "Condoms are too expensive."

*Your response:* "I know where to get condoms at a good price. I'll make sure that we always have some available. Besides, condoms are a lot less expensive than getting a disease."

*Objection:* "I'm afraid that a condom might hurt me in some way."

*Your response:* "Condoms are very safe. Millions of people have been using them for many years. If they were dangerous, we would know about it. There are many types of condoms. I'm sure that there are kinds that you will be comfortable with."

*Objection (unstated):* "I want to get pregnant (or) I want to father a child."

*Your response:* Is it possible that you really want to (get pregnant) (get me pregnant)? I don't think that either one of us is really ready for that at this time. I would want our baby to be planned and mutually agreed upon, not just an accident. Don't you agree?"

*Objection:* "You must not really love me if you want me to use a condom."

*Your response:* "I could just turn that right around and say that you must not love me if you don't want us to use a condom. If you really love me, you wouldn't want to take any chances with my health and you wouldn't want to worry me. Well, having sex without a condom worries me. Don't you care about that?"

Some concessions might be necessary in this negotiation, but the bottom line must be: *no condom = no sex.* Anyone who won't respect your desire to protect yourself (as well as protect him or her) just isn't very concerned with your well-being. He or she is not the partner you've been looking for.

Rate (per 100,000 population)

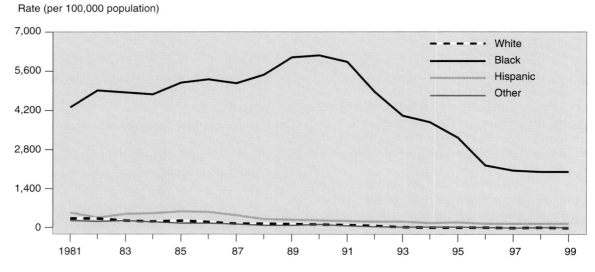

**FIGURE 6.3**    Gonorrhea, reported rates for 15- to 19-year-old males by race/ethnicity: United States, 1987–1999.

Chlamydia and gonorrhea are the most common STIs among teens. Five to 10 percent of teens are infected with chlamydia, and gonorrhea rates are highest among women aged fifteen to nineteen years and men aged twenty to twenty-four years (fig. 6.4). These infections are curable, but if left untreated can have severe health effects later in life. Between 15 and 20 percent of young men and women have become infected with herpes (an incurable STI) by the time they reach adulthood (CDC, 2000).

Many factors are known to contribute to the high STI rates among young people. Teens and young adults are more likely than other age groups to engage in unprotected sex and to have multiple partners. Young people might feel that nothing really serious or irreversible could happen to them. They might believe that precautions against infection are unnecessary because none of their friends have STIs. But many of these diseases have no symptoms, or have a long latency period before appearing. Many young people are uninformed about STI transmission, prevention, and symptoms, or are unwilling or unaware of how to seek medical care. Parents may lack information about STIs or the communication skills to pass it on. Many schools and teachers are unwilling or unable to teach about STIs (see "At Issue: What Direction for STI Prevention?").

Even if provided with an awareness and information about STIs, young people may lack the communication skills needed to discuss sexual histories, known STIs, and prevention strategies with prospective sexual partners. Many young people are unequipped to discuss such topics, either due to embarrassment, inadequate vocabulary, or as part of a pattern of sex without communication between partners. Young people need to be provided with a sound factual understanding of all STIs and the communication skills necessary to effectively reduce the risk of transmission of these diseases (see "Healthy Sexuality: Negotiating Condom Use").

## Gender Issues And STIs

STIs impact each gender in some special ways. First we'll look at some of the special risks and problems that STIs pose to women.

Because many of the STIs are asymptomatic in women, women are at increased risk of suffering from chronic (long-term) untreated cases that lead to severe complications. Further, the "open" reproductive system of women (the fallopian tubes flare open near the ovaries) allows infections to spread from a woman's reproductive organs into her abdominal cavity.

Unique to women are problems such as pelvic inflammatory disease (PID, see p. 158), tubal pregnancy, and spontaneous abortion, stillbirth, and preterm delivery. An infected woman can pass syphilis, herpes, HIV, gonorrheal eye infection, and chlamydial pneumonia to her infant.

Most cases of cervical cancer, one of the most common cancers in women, are caused by sexually transmitted papillomaviruses. HIV (the "AIDS virus") is now the fourth leading cause of death among women aged twenty-five to forty-four in the United States and a leading killer of women worldwide. Most HIV infections in women are the result of sexual transmission (Alexander, 1996).

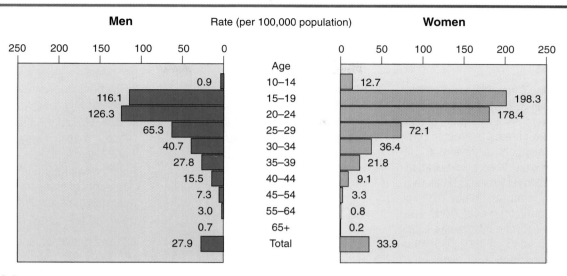

**FIGURE 6.4**    Gonorrhea, White Non-Hispanic race/ethnicity, age, and gender specific, United States, 1999.

Women are more susceptible to infection by some of the STIs. A single unprotected mating with a gonorrhea-infected partner will result in infection of about two-thirds of women, but only about one-third of men (Alexander, 1996). This is attributed to the greater surface area of the vaginal mucosa and cervix compared to that of the glans and shaft of the penis. Also, semen remains in contact with the vaginal and cervical membranes longer than vaginal fluid remains on the penis. These factors are also thought to explain the higher incidence of herpes among women (25% of American women are infected) compared to men (20%).

All of these factors add up to a strong argument for use of barrier contraceptives such as male or female condoms or dental dams (thin sheets of rubber) when there is any chance of STI transmission. Barrier contraceptives are currently the only methods that can protect a woman against STIs. Specifically, only male latex condoms have been proven to be an effective barrier against HIV in clinical trials (Alexander, 1996). For women who have difficulty negotiating condom use by their partners, female condoms are available. Although not as effective as male condoms, they do offer some protection against HIV and other pathogens.

Many women assume that their routine pelvic examinations and Pap smears will identify any STI they have. Unfortunately, some of the STIs present no visible symptom and are not detected by Pap smears. If a woman has any reason to suspect that she might be infected with an STI, she should mention this to her practitioner and ask for specific tests for STIs.

Men have some special STI concerns as well. Like women, men with untreated chlamydia or gon- orrhea can become sterile. Symptoms may be more difficult to detect in uncircumcised men. Lacking the tradition and experience of routine genital exams, men might feel reluctant to seek diagnosis and treatment of genital symptoms or might not know where to go for such professional help. A urologist or even a general practitioner can perform the tests needed to evaluate whether a man has an STI.

In the United States, though not everywhere, HIV has been more prevalent in men than in women. One factor is that injection drug users, who have been hard hit by HIV, are more often male than female. Another factor is that, in the United States, gay men have been another hard-hit group. Again, this is not true in all nations. But here, HIV entered the gay male community early and spread rapidly because of the ease with which HIV is transmitted during anal sex and the tendency for some gay men to have many sex partners.

## 6.3  PREVENTING SEXUALLY TRANSMITTED INFECTIONS

The emergence of HIV has added a new urgency to the need to control STIs. Preventing STIs involves both personal and public health efforts. We will consider personal risk reduction first.

### 6.3.1  Personal Risk Reduction

As with most other diseases, the ultimate responsibility for avoiding STIs lies with the individual (see "Where Do I Stand? STI-Related Behavior and Attitude Assessment"). The best way to avoid contracting sexually transmitted infections is abstinence. In

## AT ISSUE

### WHAT DIRECTION FOR STI PREVENTION?

Many schools have been rocked with controversy over what direction their STI prevention programs should take. Some parents and other community members believe that the emphasis should be on sexual abstinence and postponing sexual relationships until an older age or perhaps until marriage. Other parents and community members believe that effective STI prevention requires teaching the "safer sex" guidelines and possibly distributing condoms to students, because young people are likely to have sex no matter how much emphasis is placed on abstinence. Let's examine some of the arguments offered on each side of the issue.

#### SOME ARGUMENTS IN FAVOR OF TEACHING ABSTINENCE

- Abstinence is the only entirely effective way of preventing STIs. Condoms and other safer-sex techniques are never perfect.
- Teaching the safer-sex guidelines or distributing condoms is promoting teen sexual activity; it is saying that having sex is OK.
- Distributing condoms without parental consent is taking away the authority of parents over their children.
- Nonmarital sex is immoral and doing anything to encourage nonmarital sex is also immoral.

#### SOME ARGUMENTS IN FAVOR OF TEACHING SAFER-SEX PRACTICES AND DISTRIBUTING CONDOMS IN SCHOOLS

- The STI rate among adolescents is high.
- The pregnancy rate among adolescents is also high.
- Many HIV infections initially occur in people under age twenty.
- By the twelfth grade, the majority of students have at least some experience with partner sex.

A World Health Organization review of thirty-five studies on the effectiveness of sex education programs found no evidence that sex education increased sexual activity or experimentation. Six studies showed that sex education led to a delay or decrease in sexual activity, and ten studies showed that education programs increased safer-sex practices among young people who were already sexually active (Centers for Disease Control, 1997).

recent years, the threat of HIV and other STIs has encouraged many people to reevaluate their sexual habits and place new emphasis on *abstinence or long-term, monogamous relationships.*

If you choose not to be abstinent, it is essential to *minimize the number of sexual partners you have,* because the more partners you have, the greater your risk of contracting diseases. STIs can be transmitted through heterosexual or homosexual contact, including genital-genital, oral-genital, and anal-genital activities.

Another basic step is to *avoid high-risk activities or sexual partners who engage in high-risk activities.* High-risk activities include unprotected (no condom or other protection used) vaginal, oral, or anal intercourse. The risk increases with the number of partners.

With today's high incidence of STIs, partners to be avoided include anyone who has a variety of partners and anyone who has one regular partner who, in turn, has had many partners. Considering the methods of transmission of HIV and hepatitis B, it is unwise to choose for a sexual partner anyone who abuses drugs by injection or who has another partner who does so. People who have histories of many sexual partners or of drug abuse may be reluctant to reveal their entire personal histories out of fear of rejection. Thus, you might not be aware of someone's sexual or drug-abuse history after only a few dates. *It is best to move into a sexual relationship very slowly, getting to know a potential partner very well before becoming sexually involved.*

For someone who insists on sexual activity outside of long-term relationships, it is essential to make maximum use of other personal preventive methods to reduce the chances of infection. We use the word *reduce* rather than *eliminate* because none of the following methods is totally effective.

During sex activity, *be aware of any signs of possible infection in your partner,* such as urethral discharge or genital lesions of any kind. If such signs are present, immediately discontinue sexual activity with that partner until he or she has been examined by a physician and, if necessary, treated for the condition.

# WHERE DO I STAND?
## STI-RELATED BEHAVIOR AND ATTITUDE ASSESSMENT

STIs don't just strike people at random. Each of us largely determines our own risk of becoming infected with an STI. Where do you stand in regard to the risk of HIV infection? Circle the number that most closely approximates your answer.

| | | Almost Always | Sometimes | Almost Never |
|---|---|:---:|:---:|:---:|
| 1. | I am sexually abstinent or maintain a mutually monogamous relationship. | 10 | 2 | 0 |
| 2. | I move very slowly into a new sexual relationship. | 4 | 2 | 0 |
| 3. | In developing a new sexual partnership, I consider the risk of STI transmission. | 4 | 1 | 0 |
| 4. | I hold the number of my different sexual partners to a minimum. | 4 | 1 | 0 |
| 5. | I avoid sexual relationships with people who have had many sexual partners. | 4 | 1 | 0 |
| 6. | If a new relationship is becoming sexual, I discuss the topic of STIs with that person before engaging in sexual contact. | 4 | 1 | 0 |
| 7. | In anything but a long-term monogamous relationship, I insist on condom use. | 4 | 1 | 0 |

| | | Yes | No | |
|---|---|:---:|:---:|---|
| 8. | I know the symptoms (or know that there may be no symptoms) for: | | | |
| | Genital herpes | 2 | 0 | |
| | Genital warts | 2 | 0 | |
| | Gonorrhea | 2 | 0 | |
| | Chlamydia | 2 | 0 | |
| | Syphilis | 2 | 0 | |

| | | Almost Always | Sometimes | Almost Never |
|---|---|:---:|:---:|:---:|
| 9. | If I suspected that I had an STI, I would immediately see a physician or go to a health center. | 4 | 1 | 0 |
| 10. | If I learned that I had an STI, I would immediately inform my sex partner(s). | 4 | 1 | 0 |

**Total points:** _____

### Interpretation:

48–52 points: Your risk of STI is very low.
44–47 points: Your risk of STI is low.
40–43 points: Your risk of STI is average.
36–39 points: Your risk of STI is above average.
Less than 35 points: Your risk of STI is very high. These are dangerous infections that are very common. Read this chapter carefully and apply its suggestions to your own life.

## Male Condoms

Male condoms are highly recommended for disease risk reduction. They help prevent transmission of HIV, herpes, gonorrhea, chlamydia, and most other STIs. Condoms do have to be used carefully and consistently to achieve this purpose. Condom failure usually results from inconsistent or incorrect use, rather than condom breakage.

The following recommendations will ensure the proper use of condoms:

- *Always* use a condom.
- Condom use can be eroticized by incorporating the application of the condom into sex play.
- Use latex condoms, rather than natural "skins." Natural "skin" condoms are not useful for disease protection because their pores are large enough to allow passage of viruses.
- Don't store condoms in hot places such as a car's glove compartment.
- Use a new condom every time you have sex.
- Handle the condom carefully to avoid damaging it with fingernails, teeth, or other sharp objects.
- The condom must be applied to the erect penis *before any genital contact is made.*
- Ensure that no air is trapped at the end of the condom.

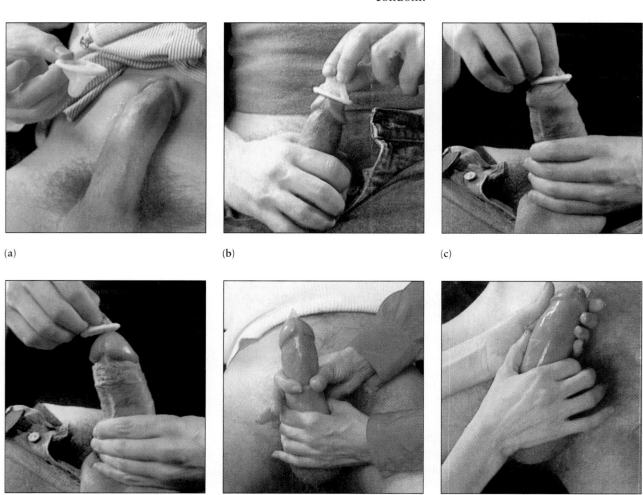

(a)    (b)    (c)

(d)    (e)    (f)

How to put on a male condom. **a:** If the condom is not prelubricated, put a small amount of water-based lubricant inside its tip to make the penis feel better during sex. Keep the shaft of the penis free of lubricant to help keep the condom from slipping off. **b:** Unroll about a half inch of the condom to make a space for the semen to go. **c:** Put the condom against the head of the erect penis. Squeeze any air out of the tip of the condom. **d:** If uncircumcised, pull back the foreskin of the penis. **e:** Roll the condom all the way down to the base of the penis. **f:** Gently smooth out any air trapped inside.

- Ensure that there is adequate lubrication throughout the sexual activity, always applying a lubricant for anal sex and, when needed, for vaginal sex.

- Use only water-based lubricants such as K-Y Jelly, ForPlay, Wet, or Kimono Aqua Lube. Oil-based products such as petroleum jelly, massage oils, body lotions, shortening, or cooking oil will weaken latex and should never be used.

- Hold the condom firmly against the base of the penis during withdrawal, and withdraw while the penis is still erect to prevent the condom from slipping off.

Even when condoms are not required for birth control purposes, a wise person will insist on their use in any situation other than in a long-term, monogamous relationship (see "Healthy Sexuality: Negotiating Condom Use"). Condoms are available with the spermicide nonoxynol-9 included as part of the lubricant. Although nonoxynol-9 can kill HIV and the pathogens of most STIs, some people are allergic to it. In addition, some individuals are allergic or sensitive to latex, which is the only condom material effective in blocking STI pathogens. These individuals can still obtain the STI protection of latex condoms if the man (if he is the one who is allergic) uses a natural skin condom under a latex condom. If the woman is sensitive to latex, a natural skin condom can be used over the latex one.

## Female Condoms

Female condoms, sold as *Reality* brand, are lubricated polyurethane sheaths with a ring on each end inserted into the vagina prior to vaginal intercourse, in a manner similar to inserting a diaphragm. The woman simply squeezes the inner ring and inserts it as far as possible into her vagina (fig. 6.5). The other ring, at the open end of the condom, remains outside the vagina to cover the labia. Her male partner must be careful that his penis actually enters into the condom. Although female condoms are prelubricated, some people prefer to use additional water-soluble lubricant. Female condoms conduct heat well and provide a pleasant sensation for both partners.

Laboratory studies indicate that female condoms form an effective barrier against HIV and hepatitis B virus. Female condoms are significant in that they are the only female-controlled method of reducing risks of both pregnancy and STIs. They provide an option for a woman whose male partner refuses to use a condom and for a woman who prefers to have more personal control over contraception and infection risk reduction.

Female condoms have had slow sales because they seem to some people to be large, awkward, inconvenient, and complicated to use. But many people of both sexes who have actually used them like them. Their cost averages about $2.50 each, and a new condom must be used for each occasion, so their cost is a concern for some people.

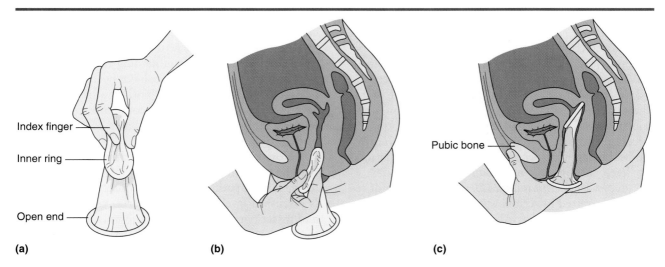

**FIGURE 6.5** How to insert a female condom. **a:** Hold the condom with the open (outer) end hanging down. Squeeze the inner ring with your thumb and middle finger. Place your index finger between your thumb and middle finger and keep squeezing the inner ring. **b:** With your other hand, spread your labia and insert the squeezed condom. **c:** Push the inner ring way up into your vagina, using your index finger inserted into the condom. The ring must be pushed beyond your pubic bone. *This may take some practice, but it becomes easy with experience.* Make sure your male partner inserts his penis into the condom and not outside of it. After finishing intercourse, twist the outer ring to keep the sperm inside the pouch, pull out the condom, and discard it. Don't reuse it and don't flush it (it could plug the toilet).

### Dental Dams

A dental dam is a rectangle of thin latex about 6 inches by 8 inches that can be used as a barrier to pathogens during oral sex on a woman (cunnilingus). The dam is stretched across her genitals to prevent her partner's tongue from touching her fluids. Dams can also be used for oral-anal sex (anilingus). Dams are effective in disease risk reduction, but can be difficult to hold in place. A latex male condom cut down one side with scissors can also serve as a dam.

### Spermicides

Many sources have recommended spermicides, such as nonoxynol-9, for disease prevention. The CDC (1993a) states, however: "No data exist to indicate that condoms lubricated with spermicides are more effective than other lubricated condoms in protecting against the transmission of HIV infection and other STDs." The CDC also states: "Protection of women against HIV infection should not be assumed from the use of vaginal spermicides. . . ."

### Other Preventive Measures

Even when a condom is used, it is still important for both partners to *wash with soap and water* immediately after contact because the condom covers only the penis. The pathogens of diseases such as syphilis and herpes, which can enter the body through the skin, can often be removed with soap and water.

*Urinating* immediately after sexual contact may help to reduce the chance of urethral infection by diseases such as gonorrhea and chlamydia. It also helps to prevent bladder infection (cystitis).

*Douching* (flushing the vagina with a liquid) is *not* recommended for STI prevention. Research in Indonesia (Joesoef, 1996) shows that douching before and/or after vaginal intercourse actually increases the risk of contracting an STI by 2 to 5 times. The investigators speculate that irritating substances in some douches make the vaginal lining more susceptible to infection and that douching agents kill or wash away the beneficial acid-forming vaginal bacteria that usually keep pathogens from becoming established.

*Avoid fecal contamination.* The incidence of fecally transmitted infections such as hepatitis A, *Giardia,* and other intestinal infections is very high among people who practice anilingus (oral-anal stimulation). Also, the male genitals need to be thoroughly washed when going from anal intercourse to vaginal or oral sex, and any sex toys that have entered the anus need to be well cleansed before any other use.

*Antibiotics* are occasionally used as a preventive measure after possible exposure to an STI. This might be useful for people who have been sexually involved with someone who has been diagnosed as having a bacterial STI. Antibiotics, however, are not effective for a viral infection such as herpes or HIV. Antibiotics should be used only when prescribed by a physician.

The most effective personal preventive measure, other than abstinence, would be a *vaccine* for each disease. Few communicable diseases have ever really been controlled until effective vaccines have been developed against them. So far, the only STI for which a vaccine is available is hepatitis B.

## 6.3.2   Public Health Measures

Even though preventing STIs is mainly an individual responsibility, public health agencies play an important role in STI control. Public health prevention of STIs is based on four major concepts:

1. Education of those at risk on the means for reducing the risk of transmission
2. Detection of infected people who exhibit no symptoms or who do experience symptoms but fail to seek treatment
3. Diagnosis and effective treatment of those who are infected
4. Evaluation, treatment, and counseling of sex partners of people who have an STI

Most public health departments sponsor STI education programs in schools and other locations and operate clinics for diagnosing and treating STIs at little or no cost to the individual. Laws in most states have been revised to allow for treatment of minors, often as young as twelve years of age (see "At Issue: Parental Consent for STI Therapy"), without parental permission or notification.

Another important public health function in STI control is finding and treating as many active cases of STIs as possible. It is urgent that people under treatment for STIs cooperate in naming their sexual contacts. Many individuals who have been infected can be asymptomatic, and unless notified, they will suffer severe consequences. Many people are sterile today because their infected partners failed to inform them of their exposure to an STI.

Now we will survey the specific STIs, arranged by type of pathogen. We will work from the smallest to the largest pathogens—viruses (except HIV, which is discussed in chapter 7), bacteria, yeast, protozoa, and insect parasites. Table 6.2 presents a summary of the STIs.

## 6.4   VIRAL INFECTIONS

Viral diseases are currently the most challenging of the STIs because we don't yet have drugs that can cure viral infections in the same way that antibiotics cure bacterial infections. The drugs currently used against HIV and herpes infections, for example, can

# AT ISSUE

## PARENTAL CONSENT FOR STI THERAPY

Health care for minors under age eighteen usually requires parental consent. An exception in most states is treatment for a sexually transmitted infection. Laws in virtually every state allow diagnosis and treatment of STIs for minors without parental consent or notification. Such laws were passed to encourage early diagnosis and treatment of these serious illnesses in order to protect infected young people from the consequences of chronic, untreated STIs and to help stop the spread of disease to others.

Not everyone believes that these laws are a good idea. The political right wing proposes "parental rights" legislation that would take away the states' rights to ensure confidential STI treatment to minors. The language of this proposed federal legislation is quite simple: "No federal,

state, or local government, or any official of such a government acting under color of law, shall interfere with or usurp the right of a parent to direct the upbringing of the child of the parent."

With such broad wording, a law like this would effectively end comprehensive sexuality education (the lawsuit of a single unhappy parent could block a school district's program) and the ability of adolescents to obtain confidential health care, including prenatal care, birth control, drug abuse treatment, suicide prevention counseling, as well as STI diagnosis and treatment.

In an ideal family situation, adolescents would feel free to involve their parents in their health care needs because the parents could be counted upon to be supportive and encouraging in any situation. But in

the real world, many parents are not that understanding of their children. Many young people will go untreated for STIs if their treatment requires parental consent. In one study, 25 percent of high school students said that they would not seek treatment if there was any chance that their parents would find out ("Some Teenagers Say . . ." 1993).

The "parental rights" issue pits the desire of some parents to maintain maximum control over their minor children against the need of minors to have confidential access to a variety of needed health services. Whose rights seem more important here? What would have happened in your family if you, as a minor, had to ask your parent(s)' permission to receive treatment for an STI? Do you believe that the laws need to be changed?

reduce the severity of symptoms, but they fail to eradicate the viruses from a person's body. At this point we will discuss genital herpes infections, hepatitis B, and papillomavirus infections (genital warts). Human immunodeficiency virus (HIV, the AIDS virus) will be the subject of an entire chapter (chapter 7).

## 6.4.1 Genital Herpes Infections

Prior to the emergence of HIV, genital herpes was one of the most feared STIs in the United States. It still warrants plenty of concern and precaution. Herpes infections are often lifelong, and there is currently no real cure.

As with all STIs, there are no exact figures on numbers of infected people. It was estimated in 1997 that one in five Americans (about 45 million people) are infected with genital herpes, though less than 10 percent of them knew about it (Fleming, 1997). The prevalence of herpes increased 30 percent from the late 1970s to the early 1990s, with the most dramatic increase among white teens aged twelve to nineteen years old. During the same period, prevalence increased twofold among white adults twenty to twenty-nine years of age. It is clear that genital herpes is or should be influencing the sexual decisions of a great many people.

Two types of viruses are associated with genital herpes infections: *herpes simplex virus type 1 (HSV-1)* and *herpes simplex virus type 2 (HSV-2)*. HSV-1 more typically attacks the upper parts of the body. About 85 percent of oral herpes infections (commonly called cold sores or fever blisters) are caused by HSV-1; about 15 percent are caused by HSV-2. Genital herpes infections are the converse: about 85 percent are caused by HSV-2, while about 15 percent are caused by HSV-1. Herpes viruses are freely transmitted by oral sex (in either direction), so either virus can attack either the oral or genital region. Laboratories can distinguish between the two viruses on the basis of cultures and blood tests.

In addition to oral and genital **lesions** (sores), herpes viruses are associated with skin lesions (often on the thighs or buttocks), corneal (eye) infection, infection of the membranes covering the brain and spinal cord (meningitis), and brain infection (encephalitis), especially in newborns. The latter two possibilities lead to the greatest concern over genital herpes.

**lesion** (lē´zhun)   an area of damaged tissue; a wound or infection

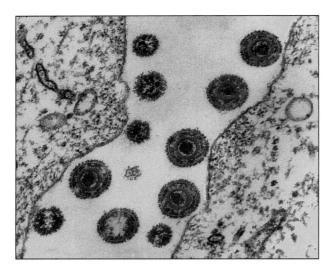

Herpes simplex virus particles. Called "submicroscopic" because they can be seen only with an electron microscope, these tiny particles cause persistent genital infections.

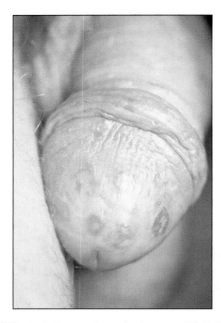

**FIGURE 6.6** Genital herpes. Herpes begins as small fluid-filled blisters that soon break, leaving painful, pitted spots. The surrounding area is usually inflamed and swollen.

## Transmission of Herpes

Herpes lesions shed virus from their surface, and thus any contact with a lesion carries the risk of transmission of the disease. Genital herpes is definitely contagious to others whenever an active lesion is present. Further, it is well documented that transmission can occur when no visible lesion is present (Mertz, 1992). This points out the importance of using latex condoms or dental dams for all sexual activity, even if neither partner shows signs of any infection.

## Long-Term Infection

Following initial infection, herpes simplex viruses remain as lifelong infections in most cases, although most of the time they remain in a state of latency (dormancy). Infected people carry antibodies against the viruses, as indicated by blood tests, but these antibodies do not prevent occasional reactivation of the virus (Drew, 1994b).

Between active attacks, the virus stays in the nerves serving the site of infection. This is why people tend to have repeated infections at the same site. In the case of genital herpes, the virus travels to the sacral ganglia nerve bundles located just outside of the spinal cord in the lower back. The immune mechanism is apparently unable to reach the virus at this site.

Following the first attack of either oral or genital herpes lesions, about 88 percent of those people with HSV-2 and about 50 percent of those with HSV-1 will have recurrences. If a person is going to have recurrences, the first will usually appear within about six months after the primary infection (Tortora et al., 1998). The frequency of recurrences ranges from once every several years to many times each year.

The virus seems to be reactivated by various stimuli, such as mechanical irritation, stress, hormonal changes, and certain foods. The infection is contagious whenever lesions are present; sometimes the virus can be transmitted to others even when no symptoms are visible, especially when infection is on the cervix of the uterus.

## 6.4.2   Symptoms of Herpes

In females, genital herpes sores can occur on the labia or, less commonly, within the vagina. In males they can be on the penis or within the urethra. They can also occur on the inside of the thighs or on the buttocks in either sex.

In someone not already carrying the virus, the symptoms of genital herpes usually appear between two and twelve days after sexual contact with an infected person. Subsequent attacks are caused by reactivation of the virus.

The first noticeable sign of a developing herpes attack is a tingling, itching, or burning sensation near the site of the developing infection. Usually within hours, small red marks appear that, within a few more hours, develop into red-rimmed, fluid-filled blisters (fig. 6.6). The entire area around the sores may be swollen and inflamed. The pain may be quite sharp, radiating out to adjacent areas. Many people will also experience more general symptoms, including swollen lymph nodes, aching muscles, fever, and a generally unwell feeling.

Over the next two to ten days, the blisters break and begin to "weep." Before a scab forms, the sores may appear ulcerlike (depressed or cratered). Scab formation indicates that healing is under way. A person's first herpes attack can take as long as four weeks to completely heal, although subsequent attacks usually heal within two weeks. The scabs simply fall off, usually without scarring.

### Herpes in Infants

If a pregnant woman has active herpes lesions at the time of the birth of her baby, and often even if no visible lesions are present (Mertz, 1992), there is a good chance that the infant will contract the disease during the vaginal birth process. Because the immune system of an infant is poorly developed, the baby is unable to fight the virus, which can spread throughout his or her body. The affinity of herpes simplex virus for nerve tissue often leads to brain infection (**encephalitis**) in the infant, with severe brain damage often being the result of the infection.

About two-thirds of infants who are infected at birth suffer systemic (bodywide) infection; about one-third have more localized infections, usually involving sores around the mouth or infection of the eyes. Of those with systemic infection, as many as 60 percent die, even with aggressive treatment with newly developed antiviral drugs (Drew 1994b). About half of the survivors have permanent brain damage. Eye infections can cause partial or complete loss of sight.

Some infected women shed the virus even in the absence of any visible lesion. Because of the great risk to infants whenever herpes is suspected, many physicians and medical centers do weekly herpes viral cultures on all infected pregnant women during the final six weeks of pregnancy (Tortora et al., 1998). If the mother has a positive herpes culture, they will deliver by cesarean section, as they do when a woman exhibits visible lesions.

### Diagnosis of Genital Herpes

Diagnosing herpes simplex virus can be a challenge. There are dozens of kinds of lab tests for herpes, each having some limitations (American Social Health Association, 1995). Lab tests are rated on *sensitivity*—the ability to detect a certain disease if it is present; and on *specificity*—the ability to distinguish that disease from other diseases. Poor sensitivity will result in false negative tests, while poor specificity will result in false positives. There are two approaches to diagnosing herpes infection: analyzing lesions for the presence of virus, and blood tests to determine if an infection is present.

Viral culture has long been one of the standard diagnostic methods. To perform a culture, an active lesion is swabbed to obtain a sample of the virus. The virus is grown in living human cells in the laboratory until it causes changes characteristic of herpes simplex. One of the newer methods of viral culture is

ELVIS, short for enzyme linked virus inducible system. This type of test is most successful early in the outbreak, when a large amount of virus is present in the lesion. ELVIS can only be used when active lesions are present and it cannot distinguish between HSV-1 and HSV-2 (Rice, 1995).

Another widely used test is antigen detection. Also performed by swabbing an active lesion, this test detects antigens—portions of viruses—which can persist after whole viruses have disappeared. Antigen detection works better than viral culture in the later stages of an attack.

An older approach to diagnosing herpes simplex is to microscopically examine cells scraped from a lesion and stained. Called the Tzanck test, this is rapid and inexpensive, but only 30 to 80 percent as sensitive as a culture.

All of the tests mentioned so far are valid only during an attack. The several kinds of blood tests can be used at any time and some have the advantage of distinguishing between HSV-1 and HSV-2. One test with that ability is the Western blot, which is almost 100 percent specific in distinguishing between HSV-1 and HSV-2. One disadvantage of blood tests is that, although they can tell whether or not a person is infected with herpes simplex, they cannot tell if a specific lesion is herpes.

### Relationship of Herpes to HIV Infection

Herpes and HIV are two separate diseases, caused by different viruses, but a disturbing relationship between them has been found (Fackelmann, 1992a). In a study of 471 heterosexual men and women that controlled for the influence of known risk factors for HIV infection, such as having multiple sexual partners, analysis revealed that men and women who have genital herpes face double the risk of HIV infection than people who do not have genital herpes.

Such studies suggest that HIV can find its way into the body through the open lesions produced when herpes blisters break. A similar association with HIV is believed to exist for any infection that causes lesions of the skin or mucous membranes. Another factor may be that the same high-risk behaviors that lead to herpes infection also increased the likelihood of HIV infection.

### Treatment of Genital Herpes

Although herpes infection cannot be cured, the painful blisters associated with the infection can be treated. Acyclovir (Zovirax) and the newer valacyclovir (Valtrex) are the drugs most used for treating genital

---

**encephalitis** (en-sef´a-lī´tis)    inflammation of the brain

**TABLE 6.2**   SUMMARY OF MAJOR SEXUALLY TRANSMITTED INFECTIONS

| Disease | Type of Pathogen | Incubation Period | Contagious Period |
|---|---|---|---|
| **HIV/AIDS** (see chapter 7) | Retrovirus (RNA virus that converts to DNA in human cells) | 1–8 weeks to brief primary illness; usually many years until AIDS | Begins 1–2 weeks after infection and continues for duration of life |
| **Genital herpes** | Herpes simplex viruses, types 1 and 2 | 2–12 days after initial infection; most attacks are from reactivation of latent infection | Whenever lesions (sores) are present, but virus is also sometimes shed in absence of lesions |
| **Hepatitis B** | Virus | Usually 45–180 days | Duration of infection, which is chronic for 5–10 percent of people infected as adults |
| **Genital warts** | Human papillomaviruses (at least 70 types) | 1–20 months | Unknown; probably at least as long as visible lesions persist |
| **Genital chlamydia** | Intracellular bacterium | 7–14 days or longer | Unknown; probably long-term |
| **Gonorrhea** | Bacterium (the gonococcus) | 2–7 days or longer | May extend for months in untreated people |
| **Syphilis** | A spirochete (spiral bacterium) | 10–90 days | By contact: whenever external lesions are present Transplacental: at any time |
| **Candidiasis (yeast infection)** | A yeast | Variable; usually develops when douching or antibiotics have damaged vaginal bacterial flora or from diabetes or impaired body defenses | As long as infection is present |
| **Trichomoniasis** | A protozoan | 4–20 days | Duration of infection (can be years) |

*PID is pelvic inflammatory disease, infection in the uterus, fallopian tubes, and abdominal cavity of a woman. There is abdominal pain, often severe, usually accompanied by nausea and vomiting.

**Sources:**   Data from A. Benenson, *Control of Communicable Diseases Manual,* 16th ed. (Washington, DC: American Public Health Association, 1995); K. Talaro, and A. Talaro, *Foundations in Microbiology,* 2nd ed. (McGraw-Hill Company, Inc., 1996); G. Tortora, et al., *Microbiology,* 6th ed. (Menlo Park, CA: Benjamin-Cummings, 1998); L. Prescott, J. Harley, and D. Klein, *Microbiology,* 3rd ed. (McGraw-Hill Company, Inc., 1996).

| Symptoms | Potential Damages | Treatment |
|---|---|---|
| Enlarged lymph nodes, weight loss fever, diarrhea, fatigue, mental changes | Loss of immune function causes severe infections and increased cancers; often fatal | Combinations of antiviral drugs are are prolonging lives |
| Itching, small fluid-filled blisters break to leave pitted areas surrounded by inflammation, fever, urethral discharge | Fetal or newborn infection is severe and can cause death or disability | Acyclovir reduces attack frequency and severity but does not cure the infection |
| Fatigue, loss of appetite, nausea, pain in joints, headache, jaundice, dark urine | Chronic cases may result in liver failure, cirrhosis, or liver cancer | No cure; effective vaccine will prevent infection |
| Cauliflower-like fleshy growths on genitals or around anus; flat lesions on cervix | Most cases of cervical cancer are caused by either of two types of papilloma viruses | Removal by physician or injection of interferon into each wart |
| Women: cervical discharge and possible bleeding, swelling<br>Men: Urethral itching, burning urination, urethral discharge<br>Both sexes: often no symptoms | Women: sterility, tubal pregnancy, PID*<br>Men: sterility | Specific antibiotics prescribed by physician |
| Women: burning urination, vaginal discharge, painful intercourse<br>Men: Burning urination, thick yellow urethral discharge<br>Both sexes: throat and rectal infection is common; asymptomatic cases are common | Women: sterility, tubal pregnancy, PID*<br>Men: sterility<br><br>Both sexes: arthritis, heart damage if untreated infection becomes systemic | Specific antibiotics prescribed by physician |
| Primary: one or more elevated, open lesions (chancres) at point of infection<br>Secondary: variable rash, oral and genital lesions, falling hair, general aching<br>Tertiary: paresis (psychosis and paralysis) | Permanent damage to central nervous system, circulatory system, and other organs | Specific antibiotics prescribed by physician |
| Can infect mouth, esophagus, skin other organs.<br>In vaginal infection: burning; itching; thick, white discharge | HIV-infected people often have severe problems with Candidiasis | Prescription or nonprescription drugs; keep vaginal area dry |
| Women: vaginal irritation; thin, foamy, greenish-yellow discharge with foul odor<br>Men: possible burning urination<br>Both sexes: asymptomatic infections are common, especially in males | Vaginal bleeding | Metronidazole or other prescribed medication |

## LIVING WITH HERPES

Herpes can create a heavy emotional burden. Sores on the lips or face are unattractive. A genital outbreak causes worry for the infected person as well as for his or her sexual partners. Some infected people view themselves as "sexual lepers" and withdraw entirely from the sexual arena. However, this seems to be an overreaction to the problem.

During an active outbreak and when symptoms are just beginning to appear, oral and genital herpes are quite contagious. A few commonsense precautions can reduce the risk of spread and lessen the risks of herpes complications.

1. Individuals can avoid direct contact with oral or genital herpes lesions by not kissing or having sexual contact with someone who is in the midst of an attack. The infected person should not kiss or have sexual contact with others until his or her sores are completely gone. Some authorities recommend the use of condoms or dental dams if either partner has

genital herpes but is between attacks. Since herpes is not confined to the penis or vagina, condoms provide only limited protection.

2. The infected area should be dried thoroughly to prevent secondary infections, and the virus should not be carried to the eyes by hands, towels, or similar means.

3. Individuals infected with herpes will want to maintain general good health and nutrition, and they should avoid inadequately lubricated sexual activity as this seems to precipitate repeated attacks. Emotional stress is also thought to stimulate new attacks in some people.

4. Infected people may wish to talk to their physicians about taking acyclovir (Zovirax) or valacyclovir (Valtrex) to reduce the frequency and severity of their attacks. Individuals with herpes might consider joining one of the many national or local herpes support groups.

---

herpes. Several forms are used: oral (capsules), topical (cream), and, for hospitalized patients, intravenous solutions.

Oral acyclovir is the most commonly used drug. It has been shown to reduce the frequency and length of outbreaks. Acyclovir can also reduce the shedding of virus by asymptomatic women from 5.8 percent of days to 0.4 percent, possibly reducing the risk of transmission to an uninfected partner (Wald, 1996).

Acyclovir appears to be quite safe as far as short-term side effects. The long-term side effects are relatively unknown, however, because the drug has not yet been in use for very long. Currently, there is no evidence connecting acyclovir to either cancer formation or birth defects. It is nonetheless advisable to avoid becoming pregnant or fathering a child until several weeks after use of the drug has been discontinued.

Other treatment of recurring attacks of genital herpes centers on relief of pain, itching, and burning. Astringent and drying agents, such as Burow's solution or Epsom salts, might help. A good diet, including a variety of fresh fruits, vegetables, and whole grains, helps maintain a strong immune mechanism, but no special diet has been scientifically proven to eliminate herpes attacks (American Social Health Association, 1994b). As with any disorder, unproved remedies are best avoided.

A diagnosis of genital herpes is no reason to abandon hope (see "Healthy Sexuality: Living with Herpes"). Understanding how herpes infections are transmitted and how symptoms can be successfully treated can help reduce both the pain and the anxiety that can accompany the disease.

### 6.4.3 Viral Hepatitis

**Hepatitis** means inflammation of the liver. It can have many causes, including excess alcohol consumption or other chemical exposure. Many viruses cause hepatitis; seven different viruses cause a series of diseases called hepatitis A through hepatitis G. Each of these might be to some degree sexually transmissible (Drew, 1994a).

Three of the viruses—hepatitis A, hepatitis B, and hepatitis C—account for over 90 percent of viral hepatitis. *Hepatitis A* is most commonly transmitted by contamination of food or water by feces of an infected person, often a food handler who fails to thoroughly wash his or her hands after using the toilet. It is also easily transmitted during anilingus (oral stimulation of the anus) or any other form of anal stimulation that can lead to traces of feces being ingested if the person being stimulated is infected.

*Hepatitis B* is the most common and most dangerous sexually transmitted viral hepatitis. Hepatitis B is a serious viral infection of the liver. After the initial illness, characterized by jaundice (yellowing of the skin), loss of appetite, nausea, and abdominal discomfort, the virus can remain in a person's blood for many years. The greatest danger associated with hepatitis B is the high incidence of liver cancer among those chronically carrying the virus (Franchis et al., 1993).

Methods of transmission of hepatitis B are similar to those of HIV. It is transmitted easily by blood, blood products, or penetration of the skin by any item contaminated with blood, such as an injection needle. It is also present in semen. Most sexual transmission of hepatitis B has been among gay men (Drew 1994a). Hepatitis B is also very prevalent in intravenous drug abusers, who tend to share injection equipment, and in the sex partners of drug abusers, due to sexual transmission.

Because of the extreme ease with which hepatitis B is transmitted through nonsexual blood-associated means, it actually presents a greater threat than HIV to health care workers who are exposed to blood. The same "standard precautions for health care workers" serve to protect against both hepatitis B and HIV, as well as other blood-borne viruses. The precautions are "standard" because they must be applied equally to every client, regardless of how likely or unlikely it seems that she or he might be infected with HIV, hepatitis B virus, or other disease agents.

Vaccines effectively prevent hepatitis A and B. Hepatitis B vaccine (Heptavax) is highly recommended for people whose occupation involves exposure to blood and for people who have multiple sexual partners. In 1992 this vaccine became a standard infant immunization. Hepatitis A vaccine is mainly used before travel into countries with poor sanitation.

*Hepatitis C* is transmitted in ways similar to hepatitis B, although it is apparently not as highly contagious. One study correlated transmission between spouses with frequency of sexual activity, sharing of toothbrushes, and increasing duration of marriage. After twenty years of marriage, however, only 22 percent of spouses of infected persons had become infected (Kao, 1996). There is currently no vaccine available to prevent hepatitis C.

## 6.4.4 Papilloma Virus Infection (Genital Warts)

At any one time, an estimated twenty million people (about 75 percent of the reproductive-age population) in the United States are infected with *human papillomavirus (HPV;* Cates, 1999; Koutsky, 1997). 5.5 million new cases are estimated to occur annually, though most cases have no visible symptoms. Young women are particularly at risk: between 28

and 46 percent of women under the age of twenty-five are infected, and about 14 percent of female college students become infected each year (Burk, 1996; Ho, 1998). Infection with certain types of HPV accounts for 80 percent of cervical cancers. HPV infection can also lead to cervical, anal, and penile cancer.

It was formerly believed that most cases of genital warts were caused by strains of HPV that do not produce cancers. Newer research casts doubt on this concept of "low-risk" HPV infection (Friis, 1997). In this Danish study, about 9,500 women with severe genital warts were tracked for an average of 7.4 years. During this time these women developed cervical cancer at a rate 2.6 times higher than the general population, anogenital cancer at a rate 3.0 times higher, and vulvar cancer at a rate 40 times higher. They also developed lung and other smoking-related cancers at a rate 3.8 times higher, due to the fact that smoking is an important contributor to cervical cancer risk.

In addition to genital and anal warts (which look quite similar to warts on the hands) (fig. 6.7), papillomaviruses cause inconspicuous or even invisible lesions on the vulva, vaginal wall, and penis. Even when these lesions aren't visible, as is often the case, they actively produce and shed viral particles that are easily transmissible through sexual contact. Forty to 85 percent of men and 60 to 90 percent of women

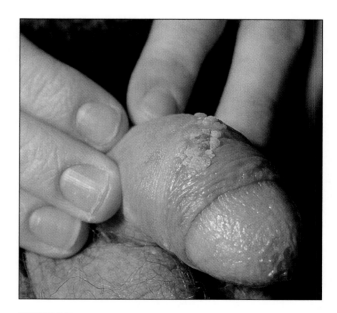

**FIGURE 6.7**  A case of genital warts. Several strains of papilloma viruses, the cause of genital warts, have been implicated as causing cervical cancer.

---

**hepatitis** (hep-a-tī′tis)    inflammation of the liver

---

who are exposed to genital HPV will become infected (Los Angeles County Department of Health Services, 1996).

Physicians can remove genital warts in a variety of ways. Between 25 and 60 percent of cases of treated genital warts reappear within three months (Los Angeles County Department of Health Services, 1996). There is no way yet to eliminate the virus from the body. Also, there is still no vaccine available to prevent papillomavirus infection. The best prevention is to limit the number of one's sexual partners and to use latex condoms. Women are advised to have regular Pap smears for early detection of cervical cancer.

## 6.5 BACTERIAL INFECTIONS

### 6.5.1 Genital Chlamydia

**Chlamydia** is the most commonly reported infectious disease in the United States and may be the most dangerous sexually transmitted infection among women today (Centers for Disease Control, 2000). It is estimated that there are two million people in the United States currently infected with chlamydia, and another three million are infected each year. The high prevalence of chlamydia, which is easily cured with anitbiotics, is due to the fact that 75 percent of women and 50 percent of men who are infected have no symptoms (see "Case Study: One More Case of Chlamydia"). Even asymptomatic cases, if untreated, progress to serious complications for women and men.

Chlamydia is particularly devastating for women. If left untreated, infected women can develop **pelvic inflammatory disease (PID)**, and one in five women with PID become infertile (see "Healthy Sexuality: Pelvic Inflammatory Disease"). If exposed to HIV, women infected with chlamydia are three to five times more likely to become infected. Young people of both sexes are particularly at risk, as 40 percent of chlamydia cases are reported among people aged fifteen to nineteen years.

Chlamydiae are unusually small bacteria (fig. 6.8), visible only with an electron microscope. They live as intracellular parasites. The same species that causes genital infections also causes the eye infection **trachoma.**

Chlamydia is usually transmitted through vaginal or anal intercourse. Although most cases are asymptomatic, when symptoms are present they can include painful urination and a thin urethral discharge in males. In females, symptoms can include painful urination, vaginal discharges, abdominal pain, and bleeding between menstrual periods. The long-term effects of untreated chlamydia infection cause the

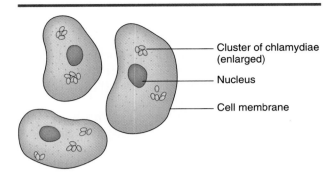

**FIGURE 6.8** Genital chlamydia, probably the most prevalent STI in the United States, is an intracellular infection by the bacterium *Chlamydia trachomatis.* If untreated, chlamydia can cause sterility in either sex.

greatest concern. In either sex, fertility problems are the likely outcome of this genital infection. In males, the vas deferens are blocked by scar tissue, which prevents the movement of sperm from the testes to the urethra. The male is then sterile. In females, there are numerous effects on childbearing:

- The fallopian tubes may be blocked, making conception impossible. More than 20,000 young women in the United States become sterilized by chlamydia each year (Talaro & Talaro, 1996). Seventy-five percent of women with fallopian tube blockage test positive for antibodies indicating chlamydia infection at some time.

- The risk of ectopic (tubal or abdominal) pregnancy is greatly increased. Most of the 80,000 tubal pregnancies each year are caused by chlamydia (Talaro & Talaro, 1996).

- The risk of premature delivery is tripled (Alger, 1989).

- In an estimated 100,000 cases annually, infants are infected during the birth process, developing eye infections or pneumonia (Talaro & Talaro, 1996).

Because chlamydiae are intracellular parasites that are invisible with the light microscope and fail to grow on culture media, their diagnosis is somewhat difficult. Genital samples are taken with a swab inserted into the cervix or urethra, rotated, and removed. A variety of technical lab tests, including enzyme immunoassay (EIA), and polymerase chain reaction (PCR), can be performed with this specimen. There is no self-test available for chlamydia. Anyone who has anything other than a mutually monogamous sexual partnership is urged to be tested for chlamydia every six months. Once diagnosed, the

## ONE MORE CASE OF CHLAMYDIA

Janet was well informed on STIs and the safer-sex guidelines. Her school district does a decent job of STI education. Janet was sexually cautious and was one of the last of her group of friends to begin vaginal intercourse.

At age eighteen and in her first semester of college, Janet fell in love for the first time. She decided that vaginal sex would be okay because Vince, the young man she loved, seemed so nice and so safe. They didn't even talk about STIs.

After a couple of months, Janet found out that Vince was much more sexually experienced than she had believed. It seemed that everyone she talked to knew of someone who had had sex with Vince. The relationship deteriorated, and Janet and Vince went their separate ways.

Because of all of the stories Janet had heard about Vince, she decided to get tested for STIs. Her school health center tested her for gonorrhea, chlamydia, and HIV. The several days of waiting for

her test results were awful. She couldn't study and barely slept.

When Janet returned to the health center for her results, there was "good news and bad news." The good news was that Janet was not infected with either gonorrhea or HIV. The bad news was that she did have chlamydia. She was given an antibiotic that effectively cured her chlamydia infection. The unanswered question was whether her fallopian tubes had been scarred by the infection, which might increase her chances of infertility or tubal pregnancy if she should ever desire to become pregnant.

As Janet told her human sexuality class, "He seemed to love me and I know that I loved him. I guess I thought that love would protect me. Boy, was I wrong."

**Source:** Student report to human sexuality class, names changed.

---

organism can be killed by a week-long treatment with a prescribed antibiotic, often azithromycin, doxycycline, or erythromycin (Los Angeles County Department of Health Services, 1995). Sex partners should be simultaneously treated. *No person with chlamydia or any other STI can be considered adequately treated until all of his or her sex partners have also been treated* (Los Angeles County Department of Health Services, 1995).

### 6.5.2   Gonorrhea

**Gonorrhea** is caused by the bacterium *Neisseria gonorrhoeae,* also called the *gonococcus. Neisseria gonorrhoeae* is extremely selective about where it grows, requiring just the right temperature, humidity, and nutrients. It dies or is inactivated when exposed to cold or dryness. For this reason, the transmission of gonorrhea requires contact between warm, moist body surfaces. Inanimate objects such as toilet seats can harbor the gonococcus for a few seconds, but they account for very few cases of gonorrhea.

The number of estimated cases of gonorrhea, as published by the Centers for Disease Control and Prevention, is 650,000 per year. Many infected people do not seek treatment, either because they are asymptomatic or experiencing relatively mild symptoms that they choose to ignore. The true incidence of gonorrhea may be over a million cases each year.

Gonorrhea rates are highest among teens and young adults (fig. 6.4), and rates of gonorrhea infection are increasing (a 9 percent increase was reported from 1997 to 1999), particularly among gay and bisexual men (Centers for Disease Control, 2000).

### Source and Transmission

Humans are the only natural source of gonorrhea. The organism occurs in the moist mucous membranes of infected people. The gonococcus can be

| | |
|---|---|
| **Chlamydia** (kla-mid´ē-ah) | the bacterium that causes genital chlamydia infections |
| **trachoma** (tra-kō´ma) | a chronic eye infection caused by *Chlamydia trachomatis* |
| **pelvic inflammatory disease (PID)** | extensive bacterial infection of the female pelvic organs, particularly the uterus, cervix, fallopian tubes, and ovaries |
| **gonorrhea** (gon-ō-rē´ah) | infection with *Neisseria gonorrhoeae* |
| ***Neisseria gonorrhoeae*** (nī-sē´rē-ah gon-ō-rē´ah) | the bacterium that causes gonorrhea |

**HEALTHY SEXUALITY**

## PELVIC INFLAMMATORY DISEASE (PID)

Pelvic inflammatory disease (PID) is a collective name for any extensive bacterial infection of the female pelvic organs, particularly the uterus, cervix, fallopian tubes, and ovaries. Symptoms of PID include severe pain, fever, and sometimes vaginal discharge.

Chlamydia and gonorrhea are two leading causes of PID—alone or in combination with each other or with other kinds of bacteria. It is theorized that in heterosexually active women these bacteria, which have no form of motility (movement) of their own, attach themselves to sperm and are transported by sperm to the fallopian tubes and on into the abdominal cavity (Tortora et al., 1998). Women using barrier-type contraceptives have lower rates of PID than other heterosexually active women. PID rates are lower still for homosexually active or sexually inactive women. Even in the absence of sexual activity, there is some risk of PID from nonsexually transmitted bacteria.

The past twenty-five years have brought a tremendous increase in the number of cases of PID. Although in 1970 there were only 17,800 cases of PID, now there are about one million per year. During their reproductive years, one in ten women suffers from PID (Tortora et al., 1998). Tens of thousands of women have been rendered sterile by PID in recent years. One case of PID causes sterility in 10 to 15 percent of women, and 50 to 75 percent become sterile after three or more infections.

PID is usually treated with the simultaneous administration of two powerful antibiotics—one for chlamydia and one for gonorrhea. This combination is recommended because many women who are infected with one of these diseases are also infected with the other. Moreover, to determine which pathogen caused a particular case of PID before treatment started would delay treatment and increase the risk of permanent damage to reproductive organs.

---

transmitted through various kinds of sexual contact—heterosexual or homosexual—including genital, oral-genital, and anal-genital contact.

### Nature of the Disease

The gonococcus has an affinity for various body membranes. It most commonly infects the mucous membranes of the genitals, throat, rectum, or the eye and is usually a local infection of one or more of these areas. However, if the organism enters the blood, it can infect the membranes lining the heart or the joints.

### Gonorrhea in Men

In most men, symptoms of gonorrhea appear within two days to a week after exposure. Unlike women, who are often asymptomatic, infected men usually do experience symptoms of gonorrhea (Lim, 1998).

The disease begins with a painful inflammation of the urethra, a condition termed **urethritis**. This causes a burning pain during urination. The inflammation begins at the tip of the penis and works up the urethra. The result is a "drip" of pus from the penis (fig. 6.9). In early infection, this discharge tends to be watery or milky. Later, it becomes thick greenish-yellow and is often tinged with blood.

The burning sensation upon urination may subside after two or three weeks. By this time, the infec-

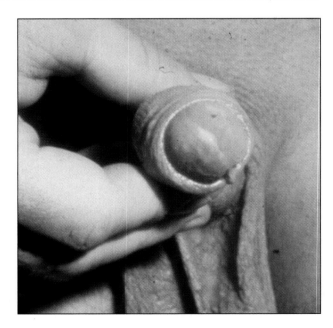

**FIGURE 6.9**  Gonorrhea in a male is characterized by burning urination and a discharge of pus from the penis.

tion may have reached the prostate gland, testicles, bladder, and kidneys. Permanent damage can include urinary obstruction, inflammation and abscesses of the prostate, and sterility. Sterility is caused by

# GO ASK ALICE

*Dear Alice,*
*I have a burning sensation when I pee. Is this bad?*
*Burning*

Dear Burning,

It's not bad, any more than a cough or sneeze is bad in and of itself. Burning when you pee is usually a symptom of an infection, a urinary tract infection (UTI), or an STI that's usually easily treated. Make an appointment to get this checked out, the sooner the better for your own personal health. It needs to be treated soon because if left untreated, it could cause permanent damage. Symptoms may include: needing to pee every few minutes; burning when you try to pee; needing to pee with hardly anything coming out; some blood in your pee (pink pee); pain just above your pubic bone; strong odor to your morning's first pee.

*Dear Alice,*
*I have been seeing my boyfriend for four weeks. He has told me all about his past relationships. Is it safe to stop using condoms now?*
*One at a Time*

Dear One at a Time,

You sound like you have a classic case of serial monogamy. That's only having sex with one person at a time, for a limited period of time, and then having sex with someone else—a pretty common pattern in high school and college. But, the drawback of this pattern is thinking you're safe, simply be-cause you're monogamous, so you stop using condoms. But, the truth is that this kind of monogamy lasts a relatively short period of time—four weeks, two months, a year—and then you start dating someone else. You feel safe and comfortable with her/him, so you stop using condoms again. And, with each time, you are subjecting yourself to the risk of contracting or transmitting HIV, as well as other STIs.

A few things to think about. . . . You are not only having sex with that person, but with everyone s/he has had sex with, and everyone those people have had sex with, etc. The actual number of potential virus transmitters is exponential. Also, everyone is not 100% truthful with each other. One's partner may say that s/he is a virgin, but not tell you that s/he has had oral sex, a potential route of HIV and other STI transmission. Someone saying s/he has been tested is not a tried and true safe proposition either. A person's test for the HIV antibodies will be negative from anytime up to three to six months after viral transmission. This period is called the window period, when the virus unknowingly can be transmitted to sexual partners.

One last thing to think about: if you two stop using condoms and either you or your boyfriend has an extra-relationship affair, think about what a pain it will be to start using condoms again. Clearly, these are decisions to make, while paying attention to your own comfort level, as well as your partner's.

 http://www.mhhe.com/byer6

---

blockage of the vas deferens and epididymis. Infection of the throat occasionally occurs following oral-genital contact, usually fellatio. This feels much like any sore throat. Rectal gonorrhea, which can be painful or asymptomatic, can follow anal-genital intercourse.

## Gonorrhea in Women

The early symptoms of gonorrhea in women are often so slight that they might be ignored. In fact, up to 80 percent of infected women do not realize they have the disease until their male partners discover their own infections (Tortora et al., 1998).

The symptoms of gonorrhea in a woman are different from those in a man. Usually a woman experiences irritation of the vagina, accompanied by a discharge. Unfortunately, such discharge is an unreliable sign in a woman, since she might ordinarily experience vaginal discharges unrelated to gonorrhea. In a woman, the gonococcus prefers the cervix and fallopian tubes. Cervical infection can cause pain during vaginal intercourse. As with men, the infection can also occur in the rectum or throat.

Gonorrhea in a woman becomes a more serious matter as it moves up through the genital tract. As it reaches the uterus and fallopian tubes, the pus discharge can increase. Sterility or ectopic pregnancy often results because of scar tissue left in the fallopian

---

**urethritis** (ū´´rē-thrī´tis)    inflammation of the urethra tubes following gonorrhea. Like chlamydia, gonorrhea also can cause *pelvic inflammatory disease (PID)* (Benenson, 1995).

### Gonorrhea in Newborns

When a woman with gonorrhea gives birth, there is a chance that the baby's eyes will be infected during the delivery process. Unless promptly treated, a gonorrheal eye infection can lead to blindness. To prevent this infection, laws require that an antiseptic or antibiotic be placed in the eyes of every newborn infant. Infants might also acquire genital infections during birth.

### Systemic Gonorrhea

Gonorrhea occasionally progresses into a serious, even fatal, **systemic** (blood-borne) infection. Systemic gonorrhea can attack the joints (causing a form of arthritis), heart lining (endocardium), heart muscle, brain, membranes covering the brain (meninges), lungs, kidneys, veins, and skin. A common group of symptoms of systemic gonorrhea includes fever, arthritis, and sores on the skin. Even though the gonococcus is fragile outside the human body, its potential for tissue destruction within the body is great.

### Diagnosis of Gonorrhea

The traditional tests for gonorrhea are cultures and stained microscope slides. For either cultures or slides, swabs are rubbed over the possibly infected tissue (urethra, cervix, throat, etc.). The swab is then rubbed over agar (the culture medium) or a glass microscope slide. A newer ELISA test detects gonorrhea in urethral pus or on cervical swabs within three hours (Tortora et al., 1998; Benenson, 1995).

### Treatment of Gonorrhea

Gonorrhea is treated with prescribed antibiotic drugs. Drug resistance has been a severe problem in gonorrhea treatment. Contrary to popular belief, drug resistance develops in pathogens, not humans. Thus, someone who has never used any penicillin might be infected with a strain of gonorrhea that is resistant to penicillin. So far, no totally drug-resistant gonococcus has been identified, though some strains are resistant to multiple drugs.

## 6.5.3   NSU/NGU

NSU (nonspecific urethritis) and **NGU** (nongonococcal urethritis) are labels that are becoming obsolete. Either term (they are synonymous) means that a person has urethritis of an unknown cause. When a client appears complaining of symptoms of urethritis (typically burning or difficult urination and a urethral discharge), tests are done to detect gonorrhea and chlamydia infection. If both of these tests prove negative, then the diagnosis of NSU or NGU is sometimes applied. As improved technology allows identification of additional urethra-infecting pathogens, there will be less and less need for the diagnosis of NSU or NGU.

## 6.5.4   Syphilis

Although less common than gonorrhea (about 70,000 new cases are estimated to occur each year by Centers for Disease Control and Prevention), **syphilis** is a more serious disease because it always spreads to the bloodstream and is a life-threatening systemic infection. The introduction of penicillin and public health programs in the 1940s led to an initial decrease in the incidence of syphilis, which has been followed by cyclic national epidemics every seven to ten years (St. Louis, 1998). The current reported rate of syphilis is the lowest in the United States since monitoring began in 1941, and in 1999 the CDC launched the National Plan to Eliminate Syphilis in the United States (CDC, 2000).

The pathogen causing syphilis is the **spirochete** (spiral bacterium) *Treponema pallidum*. This organism cannot survive drying or chilling. Since it dies within a few seconds after exposure to air, it must be transmitted by sexual contact, kissing, or other intimate body contact. The germ requires warm, moist skin or mucous membranes to penetrate the body (Prescott, Harley, & Klein, 1996).

Syphilis is contagious to a sexual partner only when external lesions (sores) are present (primary and secondary syphilis). Often these lesions, which swarm with spirochetes, are hidden inside the rectum or vagina, out of sight of a sexual partner. A condom offers some, though not total, protection from infection in such cases.

### Primary Syphilis

After infection with syphilis, there is a symptomless incubation period of ten to ninety days. Then, the first symptom that appears is the primary lesion, or **chancre** (fig. 6.10). This sore appears at the exact spot where infection took place. There can be one or several of these sores. The typical chancre is pink to red in color, raised, firm, and painless. It is usually the size of a dime, but it can be so small that it resembles a pimple. *The chancre is swarming with spirochetes.* Any contact with it is likely to result in the transmission of syphilis. The usual location of the chancre is on or near the sex organs, but it can be on the lip, tongue, finger, or any part of the body. In females, the chancre is often within the vagina, and since it is painless, it goes unnoticed.

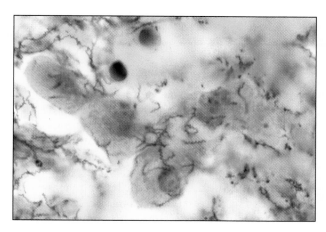

*Treponema pallidum,* the spirochete that causes syphilis. Spirochetes are long, slender bacteria in the form of a corkscrew.

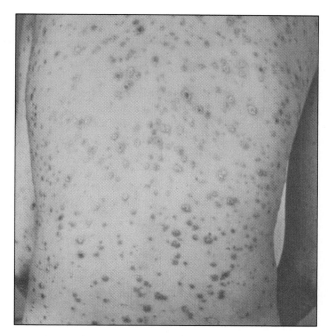

**FIGURE 6.11**  Rash of secondary syphilis. This rash can range from slight to severe, can cover any part of the body, and is often present on the palms of the hands and soles of the feet. It does not itch.

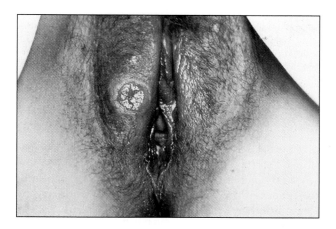

**FIGURE 6.10**  A chancre, usually the first symptom of syphilis. It can be anywhere on the body and can be hidden within the vagina or rectum. There can be more than one chancre.

Even if primary syphilis is not treated (which it definitely needs to be), the chancre will disappear spontaneously in three to six weeks. But disappearance of the chancre does not mean that the disease is cured. It is just progressing to the next stage. At about the time the chancre disappears, blood tests for syphilis become positive.

### Secondary Syphilis

In secondary syphilis, the true systemic nature of syphilis becomes obvious. Symptoms may appear throughout the body, starting one to six months after the appearance of the chancre. The most common symptom of secondary syphilis is a *rash* that does not itch (fig. 6.11). This rash is variable in appearance and can cover the entire body or any part of it. Common sites of this rash are the palms of the hands or the soles of the feet. Large, moist sores may develop on or around the sex organs or in the mouth. Such sores are loaded with spirochetes, and contact with them, through sexual contact or even kissing, can cause infections. Secondary syphilis is extremely contagious. Other symptoms of secondary syphilis can include sore throat, headache, slight fever, red eyes, pain in the joints, and patches of hair falling out.

The symptoms of secondary syphilis last from several days to several months. Then, like the chancre of primary syphilis, they disappear even without treatment. Syphilis has then entered the latent stage.

| | |
|---|---|
| **systemic** | pertaining to the whole body |
| **NSU or NGU** | urethritis of an unknown cause |
| **syphilis** (sif´i-lis) | infection of the body by the spirochete *Treponema pallidum* |
| **spirochete** (spi´rō-kēt) | a spiral bacterium |
| ***Treponema pallidum*** (trep˝ō-nē´ma pal´i-dum) | the spirochete that causes syphilis |
| **chancre** (shang´ker) | a lesion that appears at the exact spot where infection with syphilis took place |

## CASE STUDY

# THREE INTERSECTING EPIDEMICS

Crack cocaine, syphilis, and HIV are three epidemics that are more interrelated than you might suspect. From 1993 to 1995, while syphilis was declining throughout most of the United States, there was a 97 percent increase in new syphilis cases in Baltimore, Maryland. When this increase was studied by epidemiologists from the CDC and the state and local public health departments, some interesting relationships were discovered. Of people newly diagnosed with syphilis during 1995:

- 27 percent of the men and 15 percent of the women reported having given money or drugs in exchange for sex.
- 26 percent of the men and 28 percent of the women were cocaine users.
- 35 percent of the women who were cocaine users regularly worked as prostitutes.
- 18 percent were positive for HIV.

What are the connections among these statistics? There are several. First, among crack-cocaine users, there is a thriving exchange of sex for money or drugs and vice versa. Second, many crack-cocaine users are polydrug abusers—they use other drugs as well, including injection drugs with their high risk of HIV exposure. And third, syphilis causes an open genital lesion that facilitates HIV transmission in either direction. In a separate epidemic (Otten et al., 1994) 18 percent of all documented HIV cases were associated with syphilis infection. Thus, three epidemics—crack cocaine, syphilis, and HIV—intersect at the STI clinic.

**Source:** Data from Centers for Disease Control, "Outbreak of Primary and Secondary Syphilis—Baltimore City, Maryland, 1995," *Morbidity and Mortality Weekly Report* 45 (1 March 1996): 166–69.

## *Latent Syphilis*

**Latent** syphilis can last from a few months to a lifetime. Only a blood test can show that a person has latent syphilis, because there are *no external signs of disease*. Except during recurrences of secondary lesions, which can take place during the first two years of latent syphilis, the disease is no longer contagious by person-to-person contact. It can, however, still be transmitted at any time from a pregnant woman to her fetus. Some people spontaneously recover from latent syphilis when their body defenses overcome the spirochetes. There are no reliable statistics on the percentage of people who do so. In other people with latent syphilis, progressive degeneration of the brain, spinal cord, and other organs can be occurring unnoticed. When the symptoms of this degeneration appear, the late stage of syphilis has begun.

## *Late (Tertiary) Syphilis*

Late or tertiary syphilis is characterized by *permanent damage to vital organs*. Although almost any part of the body can be affected, the most common manifestations occur in the circulatory and nervous systems. In the circulatory system, the damage from syphilis in most cases is located in the aorta, the large artery carrying blood from the heart to the body. The elastic tissue is destroyed, and the aorta stretches, producing an **aneurysm** (saclike bulge). The infection can also

involve the aortic heart valve, causing an insufficient flow of blood.

In the nervous system, widespread destruction of the tissues of the brain and spinal cord is inflicted by large numbers of spirochetes. The term **paresis** encompasses all of the mental and physical effects of syphilitic degeneration of the nervous system. There is progressive deterioration of the mental state and gradually progressive paralysis. Death can eventually result.

## *Congenital Syphilis*

If a woman has syphilis during a pregnancy, infection of the fetus takes place when the spirochetes cross the placental membranes. This fetal infection apparently does not occur before the fifth month of development. Consequently, adequate treatment of an infected pregnant woman before the fifth fetal month will usually ensure the child's safety. The most extreme outcome of **congenital** syphilis is stillbirth (the fetus dies prior to birth). Infants born with congenital syphilis often experience many different types of damage. Thus, all pregnant women are advised to receive blood tests for syphilis detection.

## *Diagnosis and Treatment of Syphilis*

Early diagnosis followed by prompt and adequate treatment can completely cure syphilis. Diagnosis can be made through microscopic examinations or blood tests.

**TABLE 6.3**  CHARACTERISTICS OF THREE COMMON TYPES OF VAGINITIS

|  | *Candida albicans* | *Gardnerella vaginalis* | *Trichomonas vaginalis* |
|---|---|---|---|
| Type of organism | Yeast | Bacterium | Protozoan |
| Amount of discharge | Varies | Abundant | Varies |
| Consistency of discharge | Curdy | Frothy | Frothy |
| Color of discharge | White | Gray-white | Greenish-yellow |
| Odor of discharge | Yeasty | Fishy | Foul |
| Vaginal lining | Dry, red | Pink | Tender, red |

After many years of use, penicillin remains the most common treatment for syphilis. Larger doses of penicillin are needed to treat syphilis than for most other diseases. A more prolonged period of treatment is required for syphilis than for gonorrhea (Tortora et al., 1998).

### 6.5.5  Bacterial Vaginitis

**Vaginitis** is vaginal inflammation. Most vaginal inflammations are caused by organisms that can become abundant only when the normal vaginal microorganisms are disturbed by antibiotics or other factors such as diabetes, pregnancy, or contraceptive pills that change the acidity or sugar concentration in the vagina (Black, 1996). Vaginal infections have various causes, but three pathogens—*Candida, Trichomonas,* and *Gardnerella*—account for the majority of cases. Table 6.3 compares the three. The bacterium called *Gardnerella vaginalis* accounts for about a third of all vaginal infections, excluding gonorrhea and chlamydia (Black, 1996). *Trichomonas* causes about 20 percent and *Candida* causes most of the remaining cases.

Because there is relatively little inflammation, bacterial vaginitis (caused by *Gardnerella*) is referred to by some authorities as *bacterial vaginosis*. Bacterial vaginitis is characterized by a frothy vaginal discharge that has a fishy odor. Gardnerella infection is treated by drugs such as metronidazole that spare the vagina's acid-forming bacteria. Untreated bacterial vaginosis is associated with pelvic inflammatory disease in women, and in pregnant women this infection may lead to premature birth or low birth weight.

Over 90 percent of male partners of women with bacterial vaginitis have urethral colonization by *Gardnerella*, suggesting that sexual transmission of this organism may occur (Spiegel, 1991). Males also occasionally get lesions (sores) on the penis after having sex with a woman who has vaginitis. Lesbian pleasuring techniques also carry the potential for transmitting *Gardnerella*.

## 6.6  OTHER TYPES OF INFECTIONS

### 6.6.1  Candida (Yeast Infection)

Yeast infections (**candidiasis**) of the vagina are a common problem for women, and were described in detail in chapter 4. Because yeast infections, like bacterial vaginitis, often develop from nonsexually transmitted causes, they are not usually considered sexually transmitted infections. However, yeast infections can be passed between men and women during intercourse, so condoms should be used to prevent transmission.

Characteristic symptoms of vaginal candidiasis include burning and itching and a thick, whitish discharge that can be quite abundant. There also can be patches of white pseudomembrane (false membrane) on the vaginal lining.

In treating vaginal candidiasis, there are several considerations. The vaginal area needs to be kept dry, and any contributing conditions, such as poor nutrition, need to be corrected. Also, a variety of effective medications are available at pharmacies and grocery stores or by prescription. If self-medicating, it is important to be sure that the problem is really *Candida* and not something else such as gonorrhea that would not be cured by medications intended for *Candida*.

| | |
|---|---|
| **latent** (lā´tent) | dormant |
| **aneurysm** (an´ū-rizm) | saclike bulge in an artery |
| **paresis** (pa-rē´sis) | a term denoting all of the mental and physical effects of syphilitic degeneration of the nervous system |
| **congenital** (kon-jen´ĭ´tal) | present at birth |
| **vaginitis** (vaj-in-i´tis) | vaginal inflammation |
| **candidiasis** (kan-di-dī´a-sis) | infection by *Candida albicans* |

## HEALTHY SEXUALITY

### PREVENTING VAGINITIS

Because much *vaginitis* (vaginal inflammation) is caused by organisms already present in the vagina, rather than being "caught" from a partner, there are many things a woman can do to help prevent vaginitis:

1. Do not douche. Douching can actually contribute to the development of vaginitis by damaging the vagina's protective mucous layer and harming the beneficial, acid-forming bacteria (Ryan, 1994). Also to be avoided are vaginal deodorant products. They are irritating and not necessary.

2. Wash your genital and anal region thoroughly every day and dry the area carefully. Don't use other people's towels or washcloths. Wash from front to back to avoid carrying rectal bacteria to the genital area. Avoid irritating soaps or sprays.

3. Wear cotton panties. Avoid nylon panties or panty hose. If purchasing panty hose with a cotton crotch, be sure it is really a cotton inset and not just cotton sewn over the nylon.

4. Avoid pants that fit so tightly in the crotch that they "cut" or irritate the genitals.

5. Make sure your sexual partners are clean. It is a good idea for a man to wash his penis before vaginal intercourse.

6. If lubrication is needed for vaginal intercourse, use a water-soluble lubricant such as *K-Y Jelly* rather than petroleum jelly.

7. Avoid any sexual practice that is painful or abrasive to your vagina.

8. Try to eat a proper diet. The body's defenses against infection work much more effectively with adequate nutrition.

### 6.6.2   Trichomonas

*Trichomonas vaginalis* is a protozoan (one-celled animal-like organism) that is a frequent cause of genital infections in both sexes. At any given time, about 3 to 15 percent of the United States adult population is infected, though not all exhibit symptoms (Talaro & Talaro, 1996). *Trichomonas* is usually transmitted sexually, though nonsexual transmission is possible. One study showed that 13 percent of infected women left contaminated material on toilet seats after use, with the organisms surviving for forty-five minutes. *Trichomonas vaginalis* can also survive on wet towels for twenty-four hours (Martens & Faro, 1989).

About 50 to 75 percent of infected women suffer symptoms of vaginitis. Vaginal discharge is the most frequent symptom. This discharge varies in color from gray to yellow-green; it is usually thin and can be frothy. In about 10 percent of cases, there is a foul odor. Many infected women also experience irritation of the vagina and vulva, and about half find sexual vaginal intercourse to be painful. Untreated cases can spread upward into the fallopian tubes and other pelvic organs, causing infertility and complications of pregnancy.

Male infections can involve the urethra, glans of the penis, prostate gland, and epididymis. Symptoms in males include urethral irritation, with a thin milky

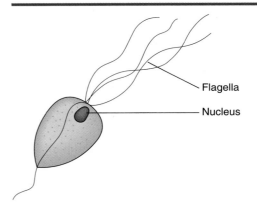

*Trichomonas vaginalis.* This microscopic, one-celled, animal-like parasite causes vaginitis. In males, it causes asymptomatic infection of the prostate and seminal vesicles.

discharge, and occasionally prostatitis. Often no symptoms occur, but the infection is still highly contagious to a sexual partner.

Trichomonas can be successfully treated by medically prescribed oral or vaginal medications. Simultaneous treatment of sexual partners is important in preventing reinfection. Even though a partner might be asymptomatic, he or she might be carrying the organism.

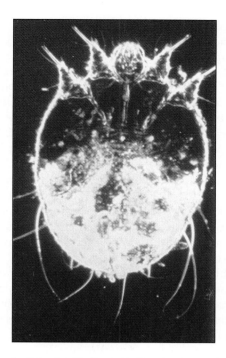

A scabies mite (itch mite). The tiny, spiderlike mites burrow through the skin, causing intense itching. Actual size is about 0.3 mm (smaller than the dot at the end of this sentence). They are extremely contagious by sexual or other contact.

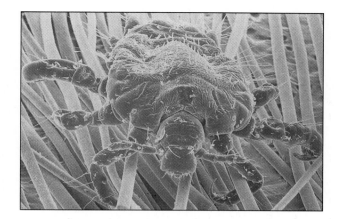

A pubic louse (crab louse). These small, gray insects live in coarse body hair such as pubic hair and feed on human blood. Their actual size is less than 2 mm.

### 6.6.3   Scabies

**Scabies** is infection of the skin by tiny burrowing mites. Scabies is highly contagious and is often sexually transmitted. It is also spread by freshly contaminated clothing or bedding. Symptoms include burrows that appear as discolored lines on the skin, welts, and water- or pus-filled blisters. Extreme itching is typical. In addition to the genital area, scabies might appear under the breasts, in the armpits, between the fingers, and elsewhere. Scabies does not occur above the neck. Scabies can be easily cured by using Kwell or other insecticide-containing soaps, lotions, or ointments.

### 6.6.4   Pubic Lice

Commonly called "crab lice" or "crabs" because of their crablike appearance, **pubic lice** are small, gray insects (one-sixteenth-inch long) that live as external parasites on the body. They usually live in pubic hair, but will also live in underarm hair and in eyebrows, eyelashes, and beards; they rarely live in scalp hair (which is too fine in texture). Crab lice do not really pinch with their claws. They feed on human blood, causing intense itching and discoloration of the skin.

Female lice attach eggs, called **nits**, to the body hair. These eggs hatch in six to eight days. Because the sexual maturity of pubic lice is reached in only fourteen to twenty-one days and each female lays up to fifty eggs, a crab louse infection can grow to alarming proportions in just a short time. Heavy infestations can result in fever and other disorders caused by toxins injected by the feeding lice.

Pubic lice can be transmitted through sexual contact. They can also be spread through other physical contact with infested people or by use of contaminated clothing, toilet seats, bedding, or other materials.

Crabs can usually be killed by washing the affected body parts with a special insecticide-containing shampoo, such as Kwell. Several applications of this shampoo usually are required, as any remaining nits can start a new lifecycle.

| | |
|---|---|
| *Trichomonas vaginalis* (trik-ō-mōn´as vaj´i-nal-is) | a protozoan that causes vaginal infection |
| scabies (skā´bēz) | infection of the skin by tiny burrowing mites |
| **pubic lice** | small, gray insects that live as external parasites on the body, especially in the pubic hair |
| **nits** | the eggs of lice |

## 6.7 WHERE CAN A PERSON GO FOR STI TESTING AND TREATMENT?

If you are still enrolled in a college or university, your school's student health center is usually a good choice. Wherever you go, don't expect a judgmental response from health care providers. They see many, many cases of STIs and will regard your case in the same way as they would regard any kind of infection—as a health problem that needs to be dealt with promptly before any serious damage is done.

If you have health insurance or belong to an HMO, your primary care physician is another good resource for STI diagnosis and treatment. If you are no longer enrolled in a college and have no health insurance or HMO coverage, your local city or county health department usually offers diagnosis and treatment for STIs for little or no cost. Their interest is in maintaining the health of the entire population of their area, and prompt treatment of people with infectious diseases is essential to prevent diseases from spreading to others.

## 6.8 PSYCHOLOGICAL ASPECTS OF STIs

**Denial** plays a big role in the spread of STIs, causing people to take chances with becoming infected and to delay seeking treatment. Here are some examples of denial:

> *"It couldn't happen to me."*
>
> *"If I bring up the topic of STIs, then he/she won't want to have sex with me."*
>
> *"A nice person like him/her couldn't have any disease."*
>
> *"He/she looks very clean."*
>
> *"He/she looks very healthy."*
>
> *"No one who dresses that nice could have any disease."*
>
> *"If he/she does have some disease, I probably won't catch it."*
>
> *"I've got some kind of discharge, but it probably doesn't mean anything."*
>
> *"If I just ignore that discharge, it'll probably go away."*
>
> *"I know that I caught something from him/her, but it doesn't seem too bad."*

**Anger** is another psychological component of STIs. The presumed source of a person's infection is likely to be the target of considerable anger: *"How could you have done that to me? You knew (should have known) that you were infected. Don't you care anything about me? Don't you have a brain? I hate you."* Even more destructive is the anger that many infected people feel toward themselves: *"How could I have done that? I knew that there was a chance that he/she had some disease. How could I have trusted him/her? What was I thinking? I hate myself."*

**Depression** is a predictable result of any kind of loss, and becoming infected with an STI involves many real or potential losses. Some real losses include a sense of "loss of innocence," a loss of self-esteem, and a loss of regard for the person who was the source of the infection. Some potential losses include loss of a relationship, loss of fertility, and, if the infection is by HIV, possible loss of life.

**Withdrawal** from social contact is an unfortunate outcome of many STIs. Resulting from depression, loss of self-esteem, embarrassment, and fear of infecting others, this withdrawal cuts off a person's sources of social support just when they are most needed. Like any of life's unfortunate events, STI is more easily dealt with when there are supportive friends. Most larger cities offer support groups for people with various STIs, especially those such as herpes or HIV, for which there is still no cure. These groups are highly recommended for anyone who is having a hard time dealing with an STI.

## 6.9 SOCIAL ISSUES SURROUNDING STIs

As is true with many other diseases, STIs carry social implications ranging beyond just the infected individual. Societies have always tried to protect themselves from infectious diseases. But conflicts arise between the rights of society and the rights of the individual, the rights of those who have STIs and the rights of those who might be affected: spouses, partners, infants, and health care providers. Many controversies surround the STIs. What are some of these issues?

### 6.9.1 Confidentiality

Many issues of confidentiality arise regarding STIs. To name just a few:

- Should a minor need parental consent for STI testing or treatment?
- Should spouses or other sex partners be informed of positive STI tests?
- Should health care workers dealing with HIV-positive clients know of their HIV status?
- Conversely, should clients know the HIV status of their health care providers?

Confidentiality is an important issue. On the one hand, people want to be able to protect themselves from infection. On the other hand, if people are not confident that their privacy will be respected, they won't seek HIV or other STI testing.

## 6.9.2 Partner Notification

As we mentioned earlier, it is urgent that people diagnosed with STIs inform their sexual contacts. Many infected individuals might be asymptomatic, and unless they are notified, they will suffer severe consequences. Many people are sterile today because their infected partners failed to inform them of their exposure to an STI.

There are two additional beneficiaries when an infected person's sex partners are notified and treated. One is the original patient, who does not become reinfected from an untreated partner. The other is the entire community, whose members come in contact with a smaller pool of infected people (Los Angeles County Department of Health Services, 1995). Partner identification reduces the number of people with open lesions of various STIs, thus reducing the likelihood of HIV transmission. It also provides an opportunity for STI education, including suggestions for behavioral changes and condom use.

## 6.9.3 Liability Issues

More and more people are seeking damages against those who infected them with herpes, HIV, and other STIs. Some have won substantial awards, which may include compensatory damages for lost earnings, medical expenses, and pain and suffering, as well as punitive damages far in excess of actual losses experienced.

An individual's decision to tell or not to tell a partner about having an STI has become more than a moral mandate: It's the *law*. The legal consensus is now clear: A person has a *right* to know about the health of a sex partner. Anyone who ignores this fact does so at great risk of being sued and losing. Further, in an increasing number of states, anyone who fails to inform a sex partner that he or she is infected with HIV faces criminal prosecution in addition to civil liability. Penalties include jail terms and large fines.

How do you protect yourself from lawsuit or prosecution? Even if the idea makes you uncomfortable, you must make a complete disclosure to a potential sex partner. Your disclosure needs to include your sexual history—including number of sexual partners, whether any of your partners were in a high-risk group or had any symptoms of an STI, and whether you are bisexual. You also need to disclose your medical history—including whether you have ever had symptoms of an STI, and if so, when, how,

and by whom it was treated—and information about any blood transfusions you have received. If you currently have an STI, make sure your disclosure is full and complete. Your legal duty can be met with three simple words—for example, "I have herpes."

| | |
|---|---|
| **denial** | keeping anxiety-producing realities out of one's conscious awareness |
| **anger** | a feeling of extreme displeasure or exasperation |
| **depression** | a feeling of sadness and apathy |
| **withdrawal** | as used here, shutting off from social contacts |

## SUMMARY

1. Every year millions of new cases of STIs develop in the United States, in addition to the pool of millions of untreated cases from previous years.

2. All kinds of people get STIs, but a major risk factor is having multiple sex partners.

3. A disproportionate number of cases of STIs occur in people under age eighteen.

4. Preventing STIs involves both personal and public health efforts.

5. Viral STIs are the most challenging because there are currently no cures.

6. Genital herpes infections are characterized by recurring blisterlike lesions.

7. Hepatitis viruses infect the liver. Hepatitis A, B, and C all have potential for sexual transmission.

8. Sexually transmitted papillomavirus infection causes genital warts, and two forms of papillomavirus have been associated with cervical cancer.

9. Genital chlamydia, gonorrhea, and syphilis are caused by bacteria.

10. Genital chlamydia is probably the most common STI in the United States. In either sex, infertility can result.

11. Gonorrhea most commonly infects membranes of the genitals, throat, rectum, or eye. Untreated cases can become systemic. Untreated cases in males can cause sterility by blockage of the vas deferens and epididymis.

12. Syphilis, caused by a spirochete, is always a systemic infection. It has definite stages and, if untreated, can be fatal.

13. Bacterial vaginitis is often caused by *Gardnerella vaginalis*.

14. Vaginal yeast infection (candidiasis) can be sexually transmitted.

15. *Trichomonas vaginalis* is a protozoan that causes male and female genital infections.

16. Scabies is infection of the skin by tiny, burrowing, spiderlike mites. Extreme itching is typical.

17. Pubic lice (crabs) are small insects that live in the pubic hair, causing itching and discoloration of the skin.

18. STI testing and treatment can be obtained at your college's student health center, a private physician or HMO, or a local public health department.

## CRITICAL THINKING CHALLENGES

1. List some of the factors that you think would be necessary and important to control STIs among adolescents. Design a hypothetical sex education program that incorporates these elements. What obstacles might you face in implementing your program?

2. Imagine that you've been dating someone you're really interested in, but you don't know much about their background. How would you go about discovering their sexual history? Write a "script" for a conversation you might realistically initiate in order to get this information.

3. Suppose you have just been diagnosed with chlamydia and are taking antibiotics. How would you disclose this information to a prospective sexual partner? To a current partner? To a former partner? What would you say, and what action would you recommend they take?

# HIV AND AIDS

7

**AFTER STUDYING THIS CHAPTER, YOU SHOULD BE ABLE TO**

[1] Explain what is known of the history of HIV.

[2] Describe the uneven distribution of HIV in the world.

[3] Describe trends in HIV incidence in the United States.

[4] Describe the human immune mechanism.

[5] Explain the role of T4 lymphocytes in immunity.

[6] Explain how HIV interferes with the immune mechanism.

[7] Explain the significance of HIV's being a retrovirus.

[8] Outline the methods of transmission of HIV.

[9] Describe the five important time periods associated with HIV infection.

[10] Explain the difference between HIV infection and AIDS.

[11] Describe the life-threatening conditions that often result from AIDS.

[12] Explain current screening tests for HIV and their limitations.

[13] Explain how HIV infection is currently treated and why HIV has been difficult to eradicate from the body.

[14] Explain why early treatment of HIV infection is advantageous.

[15] Describe some factors that put women at risk for HIV infection.

[16] Explain how a person can manage dating and courtship in the era of HIV.

[17] Explain the impact HIV is having on families, the health care system, the workplace, and schools.

[18] Outline some important laws regarding HIV.

[19] Outline how an individual can prevent HIV infection.

[20] Explain the relationship between alcohol and HIV infection.

So small it requires an electron microscope to be seen, so simple in its structure that it offers few vulnerabilities for its control, the human immunodeficiency virus (HIV) has profoundly changed the lives of individuals and families the world over. Throughout this chapter, our discussion of HIV will emphasize its impact on infected individuals, their families and friends, and all of society. Everyone is affected by HIV.

This chapter contains the fastest-changing information in this book. It could actually be updated every week with much new information. We can't do that in hard copy, but after reading this chapter you will be able to understand and appreciate the advances in HIV research that appear in the media almost daily.

## 7.1 HISTORY OF HIV: THE GLOBAL PERSPECTIVE

### 7.1.1 Early History

In 1981, reports began to appear of a new, unnamed disease causing severe illness and death in the United States. Most of the people affected at that time were either homosexual males or intravenous drug abusers. Massive research efforts in France and the United States soon revealed that this disease was a viral infection, which was given the name **acquired immune deficiency syndrome (AIDS)**.

In 1983 at the Pasteur Institute in Paris, the virus that causes AIDS was isolated by Luc Montagnier and given the name lymphadenopathy associated virus (LAV). At about the same time, Robert Gallo, at the National Cancer Institute in the United States, isolated an identical virus and named it human T-cell lymphotropic virus III (HTLV III). Apparently an isolate of Montagnier's LAV that had been sent to Gallo somehow contaminated Gallo's cultures, so Montagnier is usually given the distinction of finding the virus that causes AIDS (Stine, 1993). Because the same virus now had several different names, the Committee on the Taxonomy of Viruses subsequently named the virus that causes AIDS human immunodeficiency virus (HIV) (Stine, 1993).

In addition to the original HIV (HIV-1), a second AIDS-causing virus (HIV-2) was identified in 1985. It appears that almost all HIV in the United States is HIV-1. The discovery of HIV-2 suggests that other HIVs may exist or may appear through future mutations (Centers for Disease Control and Prevention [CDC], 1990b).

How and where HIV first entered the human population is unclear. Similar viruses infect monkeys and other mammals. HIV belongs to a group of viruses with an unusually high mutation rate. A mutation could have changed a nonhuman immunodeficiency virus into a human-infecting form. Africa has been the continent hardest hit by HIV infection and it is possible that this is where humans first became infected with HIV (Stine, 1993).

Although it wasn't identified until 1983, HIV may have been present in humans for a much longer time, possibly even a hundred years (Turgeon, 1996). This speculation is based on the presence of HIV in old blood samples that physicians kept in their freezers from patients who died of mysterious causes, and on reports dating back to 1902 of illnesses with symptoms identical to those of AIDS. HIV was identified in the stored tissue of a British sailor who died in Manchester in 1959 (Corbitt, 1990). It was present in the frozen blood of a fifteen-year-old boy who died of what we would now call AIDS in St. Louis, Missouri, in 1969 (Garry, 1988). Interestingly, the boy dated his illness to an instance of having sex with a neighborhood girl. Based on symptoms, it is believed that at least one case of AIDS occurred in New York City in 1952 and another in 1959 (Katner, 1987).

Among the American groups first severely impacted by HIV were intravenous drug abusers who shared unsterilized injection equipment, hemophiliacs who received clotting factor derived from contaminated blood, and gay men who had many sex partners. Currently, HIV is often transmitted through unprotected heterosexual intercourse.

### 7.1.2 Current Status of HIV

HIV is now **pandemic**—present at a high level throughout the world. The World Health Organization (WHO) estimated in 1996 that 21 million people worldwide had been infected by HIV (American Association of Sex Educators, Counselors, & Therapists, 1996a). WHO further estimated that another 11 to 14 million people would become infected by the year 2000.

For many nations accurate statistics are nonexistent. Some nations have apparently downplayed their HIV problem, so as not to discourage tourism or to protect their national images (Stine, 1993). And in some nations, health care systems are so deficient that the true incidence of HIV is unknown.

Three patterns of HIV infection have appeared in different parts of the world:

1. Pattern 1 is found in North and South America, Western Europe, Scandinavia, Australia, and New Zealand. In these areas, HIV has mainly occurred in gay males and intravenous drug abusers, and the ratio of infected males to infected females ranges from 10:1 to 15:1.

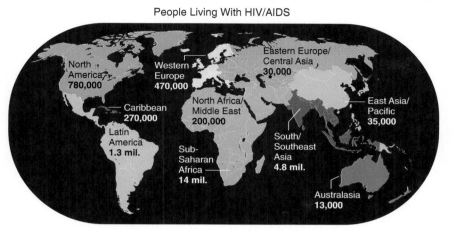

People Living With HIV/AIDS

- ▨ North America
- ■ Caribbean
- □ Latin America
- □ Western Europe
- ▨ Eastern Europe/Central Asia
- ▨ North Africa/Middle East
- ▨ Sub-Saharan Africa
- ▨ East Asia/Pacific
- ■ South/Southeast Asia
- ■ Australasia

**FIGURE 7.1**   Estimated numbers of HIV-infected people as of 1996.

**Source:** Data from the Joint United Nations Program on HIV/AIDS, 1996.

2.  Pattern 2 is found in Africa, the Caribbean, and some areas of South America. Here HIV is primarily transmitted by heterosexual intercourse and the number of infected males and females is about equal.

3.  Pattern 3 is found in Eastern Europe, North Africa, the Middle East, and Asia. These countries have relatively few cases of HIV and most of the infected individuals have had contact with pattern 1 or pattern 2 countries (Turgeon, 1996).

HIV has hit some countries much harder than others. Of the 21 to 22 million people infected with HIV in the world, 90 percent live in nonindustrialized countries (De Cock, 1996) (see fig. 7.1). These people have essentially no chance to benefit from the new drug combinations that are so effectively prolonging lives in the United States, because the cost of these drugs (US $15,000 or more per patient per year) is prohibitive for all but the most wealthy nations.

According to figures from the Joint United Nations Program on HIV/AIDS, sub-Saharan Africa is home to more than 60 percent of all the world's infected adults. For a single nation, the greatest number of HIV-infected adults is in India, with over 3 million. The nation with the highest rate of HIV infection is Botswana, where 18 percent of adults are infected. Eastern Europe and Central Asia have some of the lowest HIV rates. For information on HIV in Thailand, see "Dimensions of Diversity: The 100% Condom Program in Thailand."

## Recent United States Trends

Recent years have seen two encouraging trends in HIV in the United States. First, HIV is spreading more slowly in the United States than previously. There are now about 40,000 new infections per year, down from about 100,000 a few years ago. The total number of infected people in the nation is probably about 750,000.

The second trend is toward increased life spans for those who are infected. As discussed later in this chapter, new drug combinations are allowing many infected people to remaining healthy for long (perhaps indefinite) periods of time, and many who were previously quite ill have returned to high levels of health.

HIV is, however, still a major cause of illness and death in the United States. AIDS is the leading cause of death among American men ages 25 to 44, and the third leading cause of death among women in this age group (CDC, 1996f). Because of the young

| acquired immune deficiency syndrome (AIDS) | a severe disruption of the body's immune mechanism caused by viral infection of certain lymphocytes (white blood cells) needed to initiate immune responses |
| --- | --- |
| pandemic (pan-dem´ik) | a disease that is epidemic at the same time in many parts of the world |

# DIMENSIONS OF DIVERSITY

## THE 100% CONDOM PROGRAM IN THAILAND

Asia in general has lagged behind most of the world in the AIDS epidemic, but it is seen by many as poised for an outbreak that could equal or exceed the AIDS disaster in sub-Saharan Africa. Two areas in Asia—India and Cambodia-Myanmar-Thailand—already have massive amounts of HIV infection. Thailand responded in 1992 with the 100% Condom Program.

Thailand has a large and well-established network of government registered commercial sex establishments, but little "freelance" prostitution, an ideal situation for regulation of prostitution. In April 1992 the 100% Condom Program was fully implemented in all provinces.

The program mandates withholding sexual services for any customer who declines to use a condom. To ensure compliance, males diagnosed with any STI at government-run clinics are interviewed about their sexual contacts. Any sex establishment named as a source of infection is served notice of a potential government-imposed closure if there is continued noncompliance with the 100% Condom Program.

This program has been very successful. The total number of men diagnosed with an STI dropped from 199,000 in 1989 to 27,500 in 1994. The prevalence of HIV infection in military draftees declined from 12.5 percent in 1993 to 6.5 percent in 1995. (Induction into the Royal Thai Army is by lottery among twenty-one-year-old men and does not exclude individuals based on sexual orientation, drug use, or HIV status.) The prevalence of HIV in men who did not have sex with a prostitute until after 1992 was only 0.7 percent. The incidence of syphilis in inductees dropped by almost two-thirds following the passage of the condom law.

Several conclusions can be drawn from this situation: (1) HIV can become a major problem in Asia; (2) heterosexual prostitution can be a significant source of HIV in males; (3) condoms are effective in blocking HIV transmission; and (4) open, regulated prostitution allows enforcement of condom use.

**Source:** Data from K. Nelson, E. Celentano, S. Eiumtrakol, D. Hoover, C. Beyrer, S. Suprasert, S. Kuntolbutra, and C. Khamboonruang, "Changes in Sexual Behavior and a Decline in HIV Infection among Young Men in Thailand," *New England Journal of Medicine* 335:297–303.

average age at which people die of AIDS relative to most other deaths, this represents a huge loss in terms of potential years of life lost. By 1995, over 500,000 people had reached the stage of HIV infection defined as AIDS. Sixty-two percent of them (over 300,000) had died from their illness (CDC, 1995a). The highest incidence has occurred in the state of New York and in the District of Columbia. Other states with high incidence of AIDS include Massachusetts, Connecticut, Maryland, Georgia, Florida, Texas, California, and New Jersey (CDC, 1996f).

Some demographic trends are evident when reported AIDS cases are analyzed. Since 1981, the proportion of reported AIDS cases occurring in females increased from 8 percent of reported cases to 18 percent by 1995 (CDC, 1995b).

During the same period, the percentage of those persons newly diagnosed with AIDS who were white dropped from 60 to 43, the percentage who were African Americans increased from 25 to 38, and the percentage who were Hispanic increased from 14 to 18. Other ethnicities accounted for only 1 percent of the new cases. Based on cases per 100,000 population, AIDS is now six times as prevalent among African Americans and three times as prevalent among Hispanic Americans as in white Americans. Native Americans and Asian/Pacific Islander Americans have lower rates than other ethnic groups (CDC, 1995a).

There is no known biological reason why race or ethnicity should be risk factors for HIV infection. More likely, the differences in incidence between various ethnic groups relate to social, economic, and/or cultural factors that influence risk behaviors.

Although gay males continue to account for the largest number of cases of AIDS, the HIV epidemic is shifting toward intravenous drug abusers and persons infected through heterosexual contact. Cases associated with intravenous drug abuse increased from 17 percent of reported AIDS cases in 1981 to 27 percent in 1995. During the same period, the proportion of cases attributed to heterosexual transmission increased from 3 percent to 10 percent, while cases attributed to male homosexual transmission decreased from 64 percent to 45 percent (CDC, 1995a).

In interpreting the incidence of AIDS by age group, remember that adults generally are not diagnosed with AIDS until at least ten years after they

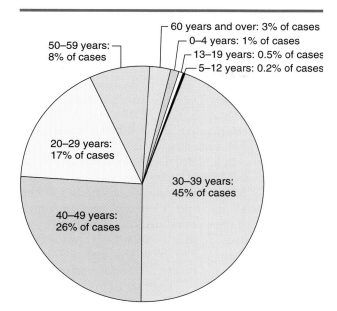

**FIGURE 7.2** Age at the time of first diagnosis of AIDS. Note that, except for infants infected before birth, this diagnosis follows HIV infection by an average of ten years. Thus, 62 percent of HIV infections take place between ages 10 and 29.

**Source:** Data from Centers for Disease Control and Prevention, "First 500,000 AIDS Cases—United States, 1995," *Morbidity and Mortality Weekly Report* 44 (1995): 849–53.

were infected with HIV. AIDS in infants and children is usually caused by transplacental transmission (congenital HIV) or infection by medical procedures such as administration of blood or blood products. The CDC (1995a) puts age distribution at the time of first AIDS diagnosis as follows (fig. 7.2):

▌ 0–4 years: 1% of cases
▌ 5–12 years: 0.2%
▌ 13–19 years: 0.5%
▌ 20–29 years: 17%
▌ 30–39 years: 45%
▌ 40–49 years: 26%
▌ 50–59 years: 8%
▌ 60 years and over: 3%

Note that 62 percent of AIDS diagnoses occur in people between the ages of 20 and 39. Subtracting the average 10-year interval between HIV infection and AIDS diagnosis, this means that 62 percent of HIV infections take place in people between the ages of 10 and 29. One in every four people becoming infected with HIV is a teenager. This fact needs to be effectively communicated to the many young people who believe that HIV is not a concern to members of their age group.

## 7.2  HUMAN IMMUNE MECHANISM

Because HIV infects the human immune system, we need to understand this vital part of our bodies in order to understand how HIV inflicts its damage. In fact, much of what is currently known about human immunity has been learned through efforts to understand and control HIV.

The immune mechanism centers in our **lymphatic system** (fig. 7.3). One function of the lymphatic system is to collect excess fluid from the tissues of the body and return this fluid, then called **lymph**, to the bloodstream. Because bacteria, viruses, or other pathogens might be present in lymph, our lymph vessels contain mazelike **lymph nodes** ("glands") where pathogens are destroyed by numerous white blood cells, usually preventing pathogens from being dumped into the bloodstream. It is these lymph nodes and other lymphatic tissues, such as the spleen, that house the immunity-producing white blood cells called lymphocytes.

### 7.2.1  Antigens

The purpose of the immune mechanism is to detect the invasion of the body by some harmful outside agent and to destroy or inactivate that agent. Any substance that stimulates an immune response is called an **antigen**. Chemically, most antigens are large molecules such as proteins, carbohydrates, and nucleic acids. Smaller molecules can become antigenic when they enter the body and attach to proteins in the blood.

Antigens occur in many forms. They can be parts or products of pathogens, such as the protein coats of viruses or the toxins of bacteria. Any vaccine is a preparation of antigens. Anything causing an allergic reaction is acting as an antigen (the allergic symptoms result from the immune response). Also,

| | |
|---|---|
| **lymphatic system** (lim-fat´ik) | the body system that conveys excessive fluid from the tissues to the bloodstream and houses the immunity-producing white blood cells called lymphocytes |
| **lymph** (limf) | the fluid found in the lymphatic system |
| **lymph nodes** | rounded structures along lymph vessels that produce certain white blood cells and serve as filters to keep pathogens and cancer cells from entering the bloodstream |
| **antigen** (an´ti-jen) | any substance that stimulates an immune response |

every cell in your body contains chemicals that would be antigenic to someone else, as in organ transplants.

## 7.2.2   Immune Responses

Immune responses are carried out by special white blood cells called **lymphocytes.** These lymphocytes originate in the bone marrow as immature **stem cells,** not yet capable of an immune response (see fig. 7.4). Some of the stem cells are processed by the thymus (a gland lying just under the sternum, or breastbone, in the chest). These stem cells become **T lymphocytes (T cells),** which produce a type of immunity called **cell-mediated immunity.** Other stem cells are processed by the bone marrow. These stem cells become **B lymphocytes (B cells),** which produce another form of immunity called **humoral** (or antibody-mediated) **immunity** (Turgeon, 1996).

## 7.2.3   Cell-Mediated Immunity

T cells respond to antigens by producing cell-mediated immunity. The target of a cell-mediated immune response may be the cell of a pathogen, or a human body cell that has been infected with an intracellular pathogen such as a virus.

Five different kinds of T cells act in various ways. Some—called T-helper, CD4, or T4 lymphocytes (three names for the same cells)—activate B cells and other T cells by presenting them with antigen from a pathogen (see table 7.1 and fig. 7.5). *T4 lymphocytes are of special significance because they are the cells infected and destroyed by HIV.* This loss of T4 lymphocytes impairs the function of both humoral and cell-mediated immunity (Turgeon, 1996).

Other T cells, called T-suppressor lymphocytes, suppress the activity of the B cells, preventing undesirable immune responses. A third kind of T cells, called T-killer or T-cytotoxic cells, dissolve abnormal cells, such as cancerous cells or virus-infected cells. A fourth type of T cells (T-dth cells) release inflammation-producing chemicals in response to specific antigens. And memory T cells retain the memory of how to fight a specific pathogen so that if that pathogen reinvades the body, the immune response can be rapid (Turgeon, 1996).

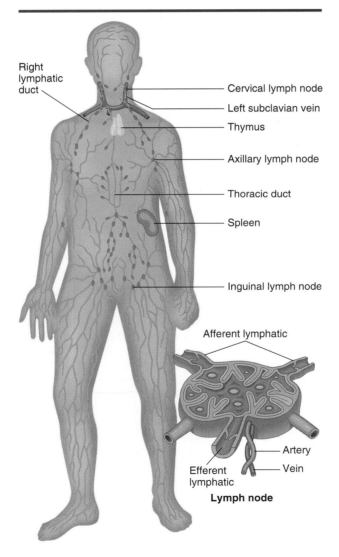

Right lymphatic duct

Cervical lymph node

Left subclavian vein

Thymus

Axillary lymph node

Thoracic duct

Spleen

Inguinal lymph node

Afferent lymphatic

Artery

Vein

Efferent lymphatic

**Lymph node**

**FIGURE 7.3**   The human lymphatic system, home of our immune mechanism.

| **TABLE 7.1** | SUMMARY OF WHITE BLOOD CELLS INVOLVED IN BODILY DEFENSES |
| --- | --- |

| KIND OF WHITE BLOOD CELL | FUNCTION |
| --- | --- |
| *T lymphocytes (T cells) of 5 types* | Produce cell-mediated immunity. Attack pathogens and abnormal body cells such as cancerous cells or cells infected by viruses. |
| T-helper cells (also called T4 or CD4 cells) | Present antigen to other lymphocytes to initiate immune responses. These cells are destroyed by HIV. |
| T-suppressor cells | Prevent undesirable immune responses. |
| T-cytotoxic cells | Dissolve cancer cells or virus-infected cells. |
| T-dth (delayed type hypersensitivity) cells | Release inflammation-causing chemicals to help fight pathogens. |
| T-memory cells | Settle down in lymph nodes and retain memory of how to fight a specific pathogen. |
| *B lymphocytes (B cells)* | Produce humoral immunity. Release pathogen-fighting antibodies that circulate with the blood. |
| *Phagocytes* | Engulf (consume) pathogens and destroy them. |

## 7.2.4 Humoral Immunity

The word *humoral* refers to a fluid. This form of immunity is called humoral because, upon exposure to antigens, B cells release **antibodies**, also called **immunoglobulins**, to circulate in the blood and to be present on the surface of mucous membranes. Antibodies are Y-shaped proteins that chemically bond to specific antigens and inactivate or destroy antigens (fig. 7.6). For example, viruses and bacterial toxins

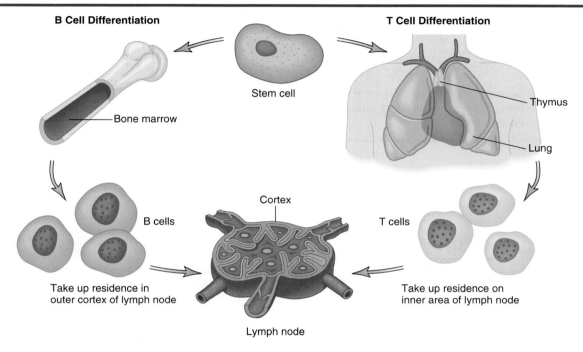

**B Cell Differentiation**

Stem cell

Bone marrow

B cells

Take up residence in outer cortex of lymph node

Cortex

Lymph node

**T Cell Differentiation**

Thymus

Lung

T cells

Take up residence on inner area of lymph node

**FIGURE 7.4** Development of the immune mechanism. Stem cells are undifferentiated lymphocytes produced in bone marrow. Before they can produce immunity, they must be processed either by the bone marrow into B cells or by the thymus into T cells. The B and T cells then settle down in our lymph nodes to wait for our bodies to be invaded by pathogens.

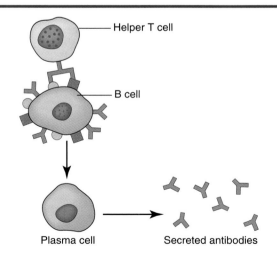

Helper T cell

B cell

Plasma cell

Secreted antibodies

**FIGURE 7.5** T-helper cells (also called T4 or CD4 cells) initiate the production of antibodies by presenting antigen to B cells. Activated B cells, called plasma cells, then release antibodies to circulate in the blood or to be secreted on the surface of our membranes to fight infections. The T-helper cells are destroyed by HIV, greatly reducing a person's ability to produce antibodies and fight diseases.

| | |
|---|---|
| **lymphocytes** (lim´fō-sītz) | special white blood cells that produce immunity |
| **stem cells** | immature lymphocytes not yet capable of an immune response |
| **T lymphocytes (T cells)** | lymphocytes that produce a type of immunity called cell-mediated immunity |
| **cell-mediated immunity** | immunity produced by T cells; its target is usually the cell of a pathogen or an abnormal human cell |
| **B lymphocytes (B cells)** | lymphocytes that produce a type of immunity called humoral immunity |
| **humoral immunity** | the immune response produced by the release of antibodies by B lymphocytes |
| **antibodies (immunoglobulins)** (im´´ū-nō-glob´u-linz) | Y-shaped protein molecules produced by B lymphocytes to destroy or inactivate specific antigens |

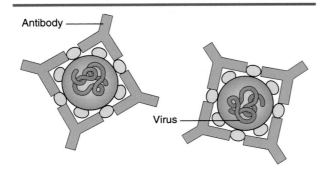

**FIGURE 7.6** These measles viruses have been inactivated by the attached Y-shaped antibodies. Now unable to penetrate a human cell, the viruses have been effectively neutralized.

can be inactivated by antibodies. Other types of antibodies clump bacteria together, making it easier for **phagocytes** to clean up an infection (Turgeon, 1996).

## 7.3  BIOLOGY OF HIV

The virus that causes AIDS is the **human immunodeficiency virus (HIV)** (fig. 7.7). Two primary variants of the virus have been identified and named HIV-1 and HIV-2. Within each of these general categories of HIV are essentially infinite strains (variations) of HIV because of the high mutation rate characteristic of HIV. Specific strains are often associated with specific parts of the world. For example, subtypes A, C, and D of HIV-1 dominate in sub-Saharan Africa, E dominates in Thailand, and B dominates in the United States and Western Europe (Soto-Ramirez, 1996).

The great majority of AIDS cases in the United States are caused by HIV-1. Both HIV-1 and HIV-2 are unusual pathogens in that they infect the immunity-producing T lymphocytes. Thus, HIV directly attacks the cells that should be defending our bodies against viral infection.

The effects of this attack on the immune mechanism are devastating. Both cell-mediated and humoral immune mechanisms are impaired. Pathogens that are normally held in check by one's immunity escape control and cause potentially lethal infections. Certain cancers, which are also usually destroyed in their early stages by the immune mechanism, spread unchecked through the body. Moreover, the virus can infect brain cells, causing neurological impairment. As of 1998, some very effective drugs were in use, but it was not believed that they were actually curing HIV infections.

### 7.3.1  Retrovirus

HIV belongs to a group of viruses called **retroviruses**. The genetic material of retroviruses is RNA, but once these viruses enter a host (human) cell, their genes are reproduced in the form of DNA, which is then incorporated into the chromosomes of the human cell (fig. 7.8). It is extremely difficult for the bodily defenses of the infected person to eradicate the virus as the viral DNA now appears indistinguishable from the human DNA.

The life cycle of HIV consists of five phases:

1.  The virus attaches to and penetrates into its target host cells. In addition to the CD4 lymphocytes, HIV is known to infect certain brain cells and believed to infect certain

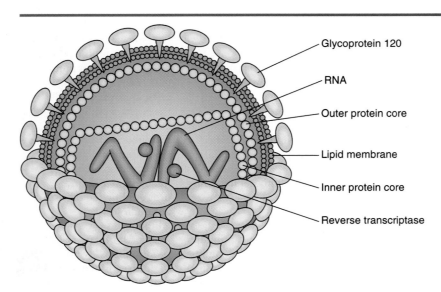

**FIGURE 7.7** Human immunodeficiency virus (HIV), the cause of AIDS. As a retrovirus, it carries the enzyme reverse transcriptase, which can produce viral DNA from viral RNA. The viral DNA is then incorporated into the chromosomes of the human host cell, creating an infection that is very difficult to eliminate.

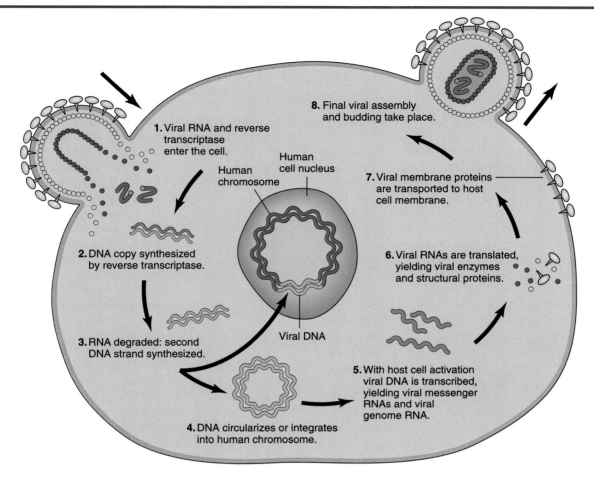

**FIGURE 7.8** Life cycle of HIV. **1:** Virus enters a human cell. **2–4:** Viral RNA converts to DNA and enters the human chromosome. **5–7:** New virus particles are produced with the aid of the host cell. **8:** The completed virus leaves the human cell, taking part of the cell membrane to form its outer layer.

intestinal cells (Turgeon, 1996). The intestinal infection might be what causes the weight loss characteristic of HIV infection.

2. Viral RNA converts into viral DNA (HIV carries a special enzyme for this purpose).

3. The viral DNA is integrated into one of the chromosomes of the host cell.

4. New virus particles are produced within the infected host cell.

5. These new viral particles bud from the host cell one by one, taking some of the host cell's membrane along as their envelope (fig. 7.8). Unlike the many viruses that quickly kill their host cell, HIV can continue to replicate in the same host cell for a long time.

## 7.3.2 High Mutation Rate

Further complicating the fight against HIV is its high mutation rate. **Mutations** are inheritable changes in

genes; the new genes are passed on to future generations. If the mutant form of virus or organism has a survival advantage over the original form, it will replace the original form. All viruses and organisms experience mutations, but the mutation rate for HIV is unusually high.

Through mutations, HIV is able to change its structure, enabling it to elude detection by our immune system or to avoid the effects of drugs and

| **phagocytes** | white blood cells that engulf and kill pathogens |
| **human immunodeficiency virus (HIV)** | the virus that causes AIDS |
| **retroviruses** | viruses containing RNA that converts to DNA upon entering a host cell |
| **mutation** | an inheritable change in a nucleic acid (gene) |

vaccines. Any effective vaccine will have to produce immunity against some stable part of the virus that is not affected by mutations. It is unclear at this time whether this will be possible.

## 7.4 TRANSMISSION OF HIV

One of the greatest public health tasks of all time has been alerting the public to the methods of HIV transmission and appropriate precautions. It has also been necessary to educate the public about how HIV is *not* transmitted in order to prevent irrational panic.

Although traces of HIV can be detected in most body fluids of infected people, it is apparently present in adequate quantities (an infective dosage) for disease transmission only in blood, vaginal or cervical secretions, breast milk, and semen.

Infection almost invariably can be traced to one of the following: virus crossing the placenta from mother to fetus, breast-feeding, sexual contact with an infected person, sharing an injection needle with an infected person, or receiving a blood transfusion or blood product from an infected person.

Before donor screening was implemented in 1985, there was some transmission of HIV to organ and tissue recipients. Today, transmission of HIV from screened, HIV-antibody-negative organ or tissue donors is rare.

There is no documented case of someone being infected by food prepared or served by an infected person or by working with or simply being around an infected person. Also, you cannot get HIV when donating blood. No one has ever been infected with HIV through a mosquito bite. The life cycle of a mosquito-borne pathogen is intimately involved with the anatomy and physiology of the mosquito, and this is not the case for HIV (Talaro & Talaro, 1996).

### 7.4.1 Sexual Transmission

About 75 percent of the world's HIV transmission is by sexual means (Stein, 1993). The most efficient mode of sexual transmission appears to be heterosexual or homosexual anal intercourse, with the most likely direction of transmission being from the inserter to the recipient. The membrane lining the rectum is a delicate membrane that suffers tears and abrasions, providing a ready portal of entry for HIV. Bleeding from these tears and abrasions can also infect the inserter, should the recipient already be infected (Stine, 1993).

Vaginal intercourse has also been documented as a method of transmitting HIV, from either male to female or female to male. The greater risk of transmission, however, is from male to female. In many parts of the world, heterosexual vaginal intercourse is the main means of transmission of HIV (Soto-Ramirez, 1996).

Oral sex has not been identified as a frequent means of transmission of HIV in either homosexual or heterosexual populations, though there are growing numbers of cases where it has been documented to have been the only possible method of transmission (Baba et al., 1996; Stine, 1993). It is highly advisable to use condoms or dental dams during oral sex.

It must be emphasized that not everyone who is infected will display symptoms. *A great many people are asymptomatic carriers. Even though these people are not experiencing any symptoms themselves, they are capable of infecting others.* Consequently, the potential for the spread of the disease is considerable. One sexually promiscuous or needle-sharing person could infect many people over a period of years.

### 7.4.2 Blood-Borne Transmission

In the early stages of the HIV epidemic, before HIV screening of donated blood became routine, hundreds of recipients became infected through contaminated transfusions of blood-derived products such as the clotting factor needed by hemophiliacs. Since blood banks began HIV testing in 1985, the risk of getting infected blood has become very small. Meticulous research by Dr. Eve Lackritz, director of HIV/AIDS prevention at the Centers for Disease Control and Prevention, indicates a risk of only one case of HIV transmission for every 450,000 to 660,000 donations of properly screened blood in the United States. Out of about 12 million blood donations a year, only about 18 to 27 HIV-infected ones fail to be detected by the screening process (Lackritz, 1995).

Even this rate could be lowered if potential donors were more honest in answering questions about high-risk behaviors that should result in deferral of their blood donation. An anonymous survey of 50,162 people who had donated blood revealed that 2 percent failed to reveal such risk behaviors as a history of intravenous drug use, sexual contact with a homosexually active male or an IV drug user, or having paid women for sex within the past year (Williams, 1997).

#### *Sharing Injection Equipment*

The blood-borne transmission that has not yet been controlled is through sharing of injection equipment by injection drug users. Currently, about 10 percent of world HIV infections occur by this route (Stine, 1993). The actual percentage of HIV infections related to shared injection equipment becomes larger if

## GO ASK ALICE

Dear Alice,

 *What is the risk of HIV transmission when performing oral sex on a man without a condom and without ejaculation?*

 *Safe*

Dear Safe,

 If there is truly no ejaculation, you have greatly reduced your risk of HIV transmission. However, drops of semen (pre-ejaculate or sometimes called "love-drops") are usually emitted while the penis is erect and being stimulated before ejaculation. These love drops can transmit the virus (as well as viable sperm), so to be as close as possible to 100% safe, use a condom.

Hi Alice,

 *I am sure this question of mine may sound stupid and you have been asked a number of times. However, for me it is a very important question relating to my sex life. My question is:*

*does kissing, with sucking your partner's tongue and lips, transmit HIV? For me sex without such kissing is no fun! Lately my girlfriend was told by someone that such kissing is risky, and therefore she refuses to give kisses during sex. Waiting anxiously for your reply.*

 *No kiss no fun*

Dear No kiss no fun,

 There have been no documented cases of HIV transmission through mouth-to-mouth kissing. Alice is not saying, however, NO KISSING. For example, risks exist in people with serious gum diseases, if one is HIV infected or has open sores on the lips or in the mouth, or has other diseases (i.e., mono, herpes). Be as informed as you can be, make your choices, and enjoy them.

 http://www.mhhe.com/byer6

---

we include subsequent sexual transmission of HIV to partners of infected drug users and transplacental transmission to infants of drug users or their partners. Thirty-six percent of United States HIV infections are thus directly or indirectly associated with injection drug use (CDC, 1996b).

 Several factors complicate the elimination of equipment sharing by injection drug users. One is that in almost every locality, obtaining sterile needles and syringes is difficult because these items are controlled on a prescription basis. Another is the low regard that many injection drug users have for their health. Injection of drugs like heroin carries many health hazards, such as the risk of overdose and damage to veins. People who engage in self-destructive behavior on a daily basis can't be expected to worry very much about the added risk of HIV infection.

### Health Care Personnel

Health care personnel face ongoing risk of HIV infection from the blood of their clients. The risk is not confined to any specific group, such as emergency room physicians or nurses, but extends to just about anyone involved in health care. Some examples of the risks include infected client blood contaminating a skin lesion on the worker or a sharp object contaminated with client blood penetrating the skin of the worker (Stine, 1993). The risk of infection by HIV has been identified by operating-room nurses as their

fourth most pressing ethical issue (King & Miskovic, 1996).

 Health care personnel are urged to follow a set of rules called the "Standard Precautions" (formerly "Universal Precautions") for preventing infection by HIV or hepatitis viruses in clients' blood (Garner, 1996). The "Standard" refers to the need for applying these precautions to *every* client, not just those who are judged to be at high risk of being HIV positive. The Standard Precautions include handwashing, gloving, masking, gowning, proper handling of medical devices such as syringes, and proper handling and processing of soiled laundry.

### Transplacental Transmission

In 20 to 30 percent of the pregnancies of HIV-infected women, the virus is transmitted **transplacentally** (it crosses the placenta into the blood of the fetus). In one study, the transmission rate of HIV from infected mothers to their fetuses was cut to about 8 percent when the drug AZT was taken during pregnancy. Although there were no serious short-term effects on the infants, any possible long-term effects are still unknown (Fackelmann, 1994).

---

**transplacental** across the placenta

In a study of 124 pregnancies in HIV-positive women, 14 pregnancies (11 percent) terminated in spontaneous abortions (miscarriages), a rate no higher than in uninfected women. Fifty percent of the aborted fetuses were positive for HIV. All of the HIV-infected aborted fetuses had thymus gland defects. Only 13 percent of the live-born babies were HIV positive, suggesting that fetal HIV infection increases the risk of miscarriage (Langston, 1995).

Infected mothers can transmit HIV to their newborn infants by breast-feeding (Turgeon, 1996). In a study of breast-fed HIV-positive infants of HIV-infected mothers in Zaire, only 22 percent of those infants were born infected with HIV; the remaining 78 percent became infected during their infancy (Bertolli, 1996). This suggests that transmission across the placenta is less important than breast-feeding as a source of infant HIV infection. Although breast-feeding of infants is usually recommended, HIV-positive mothers are cautioned not to breast-feed their babies.

Not every infant born with HIV infection remains infected. In one study, 2.7 percent of infants who were definitely confirmed (by viral cultures, rather than antibody tests) as infected at birth went on to later become free of the virus (Newell, 1996). Although this means that 97.3 percent of the infected infants did remain infected (and most of those went on to develop AIDS), it does indicate that the human body has some potential to eradicate HIV. Research on how this takes place may lead to methods of preventing or curing HIV infection.

## 7.5 DEVELOPMENT OF HIV DISEASE

Being infected with HIV is *not* synonymous with having AIDS. AIDS is the end result of a long process following HIV infection.

### 7.5.1 Five Important Time Periods

There are five significant time periods related to HIV infection.

1. The time from when the virus enters the body until it is circulating in the blood in quantities that make the infected person *contagious to others*. This period is only one to three weeks, following which the individual is able to infect others for the remainder of his or her life. Remember that an infected person can infect others even though he or she is completely free of any symptoms of HIV infection.

2. The time from when the virus enters the body until a *short-term illness* called the acute viral syndrome develops. This period ranges from one to eight weeks. The illness might be mild and flu-like or more severe. Symptoms can include fever, fatigue, rash, aching muscles and joints, sore throat, and enlarged lymph nodes. This early illness is often severe enough that the infected individual visits a physician or hospital emergency room (Turgeon, 1996).

3. The time from when the virus enters the body until the infected person has a *positive HIV antibody test* (the standard blood test for HIV infection). This is usually about six weeks, but it can be up to six months longer. A person with a negative test is sometimes referred to as **seronegative**; someone with a positive test is referred to as **seropositive**, and the process of becoming positive is referred to as **seroconversion**. The sero- in these terms refers to blood serum, in which antibodies are carried.

4. The time from when the virus enters the body until the onset of any sort of *longer-lasting (chronic) symptoms*. It is often about two years.

5. The time from when the virus enters the body until the *development of AIDS*. This ranges from six months to more than fifteen years and averages about ten years. People whose health is weakened by a preexisting medical condition before HIV infection usually progress toward AIDS more rapidly than others.

### 7.5.2 Typical Progression of HIV Infection

The first symptoms of HIV infection, the acute viral syndrome, develop from one to eight weeks after infection. The illness can be mild and flu-like or more severe. Symptoms can include fever, sore throat, fatigue, rash, oral and genital ulcers, aching muscles and joints, sore throat, and enlarged lymph nodes (Lapins, 1996).

If aggressive treatment with a combination of modern drugs begins within ninety days of being infected with HIV, further progression of illness might be prevented or at least delayed. In one of the first studies of such early drug therapy, after a year of treatment no trace of virus could be found in the blood of any of nine subjects (Richardson, 1997). Subsequent research suggests that current drugs cannot completely free an infected person of HIV.

Chronic symptoms, often developing about two years after untreated HIV infection, include enlarged lymph nodes, loss of appetite, diarrhea, weight loss, sweating, fever, and fatigue. Neurological symptoms that might appear include slurred speech, loss of peripheral sensation (loss of feeling in hands and feet), memory loss, and general mental deterioration (Turgeon, 1996).

Early in the course of an HIV infection the number of CD4 T cells (commonly referred to as "T cells") begins to decrease. Starting with a normal count of about 2,000 to 4,000 per microliter, the number of CD4 cells declines to a critically low level at which the body can no longer fight opportunistic infections and cancers. People with less than 200 CD4 cells per microliter meet the definition of AIDS, have very poor immune function, and are at great risk of illness.

In full-blown AIDS cases, one or both of two conditions usually appear: **opportunistic infections** (those that the body defenses would normally hold in check) and/or cancer. The opportunistic infection most closely associated with AIDS deaths in both sexes is pneumonia caused by the fungus *Pneumocystis carinii*.

The form of cancer most closely associated with AIDS in men is **Kaposi's sarcoma (KS)**, a cancer of the connective tissues (Turgeon, 1996). Kaposi's sarcoma is rare in the general population but common among men with AIDS. Most people who have developed AIDS have, in time, died of some type of infection or cancer. The interval between diagnosis of AIDS and death varies greatly. Without aggressive combination drug treatment, 50 percent of patients die within 18 months of diagnosis and 80 percent die within 36 months (Turgeon, 1996). As previously mentioned, recent improvements in treatment are extending the survival of AIDS patients.

### 7.5.3   Current Definition of AIDS

The official definition of a case of AIDS, as determined by the Centers for Disease Control and Prevention (CDC) at Atlanta, has evolved over the years. The definition currently, in use since 1 January 1993, includes people who test positive for HIV infection and who have at least 1 of about 26 listed opportunistic infections or cancers that are especially common in HIV-infected people. Even in the absence of any of these conditions, an HIV infection is defined as a case of AIDS when the count of CD4 lymphocytes, destroyed by HIV, drops below 200 per microliter (cubic millimeter) of blood. The addition of this latter criterion more accurately reflects the health status of people at this advanced stage of HIV infection, some of whom did not previously qualify as cases of AIDS, even though they were quite ill.

### 7.5.4   Kaposi's Sarcoma

From its description in 1872 by Moritz Kaposi until the emergence of AIDS in the early 1980s, Kaposi's sarcoma (KS) remained a rare form of cancer. Now KS is common among men with AIDS. People with intact immune mechanisms are usually able to suc-

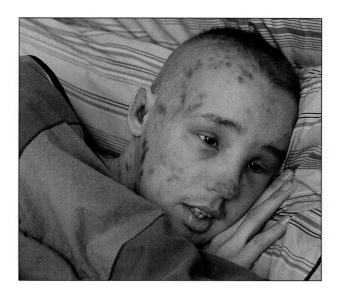

**FIGURE 7.9**   Kaposi's sarcoma. This form of cancer, now believed to be caused by a herpes virus (herpesvirus 8), is common among men with advanced HIV disease.

cessfully ward off KS. Women with AIDS only rarely experience KS, but have increased rates of invasive cervical cancer and cancers of the skin, mouth, rectum, brain, and lymphatic systems (Talaro & Talaro, 1996; Turgeon, 1996).

KS typically appears as one to many red, purple, or brown patches or nodules on the skin or in the mouth (fig. 7.9). It is most common on the legs, ankles, and feet. Although KS usually progresses slowly in people who do not have HIV, it can develop rapidly and severely in AIDS patients. KS in the mouth can result in painful chewing and swallowing. If present in the stomach or intestine, it can cause

| | |
|---|---|
| seronegative | having a negative test for HIV antibodies |
| seropositive | having a positive test for HIV antibodies |
| seroconversion | the process of becoming positive on an HIV antibody test |
| **opportunistic infections** | infections that the bodily defenses would normally hold in check; these pathogens require a special opportunity to produce disease |
| *Pneumocystis carinii* (nū″mō-sis′tis ca-rin′ē-ī) | a fungus that causes pneumonia in many AIDS patients |
| **Kaposi's sarcoma (KS)** (kap′ō-sēz sar-kō′ma) | a cancer of the connective tissues |

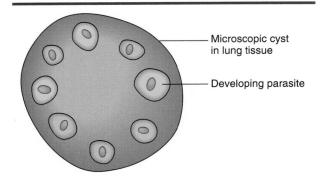

Microscopic cyst in lung tissue

Developing parasite

**FIGURE 7.10** *Pneumocystis carinii.* This microscopic fungus, formerly classified as a protozoan, frequently causes pneumonia in people with advanced HIV illness, but seldom in others. Within each oval parasite develops eight new parasites.

pain or bleeding. In the lungs, it can cause shortness of breath. KS is treated by chemotherapy or by removal of individual lesions.

### 7.5.5 *Pneumocystis carinii* Pneumonia

*Pneumocystis carinii* (fig. 7.10) is a fungus (previously classified as a protozoan) that can be found in the lungs of many healthy people. In advanced HIV cases, however, *Pneumocystis carinii* causes a form of pneumonia that is very difficult to control and often leads to death. It is, in fact, the most frequent opportunistic infection in AIDS patients, most of whom will develop one or more attacks (Talaro & Talaro, 1996). Symptoms include fever, cough, shallow breathing, and cyanosis (skin turning blue from lack of oxygen). Attacks of *Pneumocystis carinii* pneumonia tend to recur. Untreated attacks have a fatality rate of 50 to 100 percent, and even with treatment many AIDS patients die from this infection (Bozzette, 1995).

### 7.5.6 Tuberculosis

In recent years tuberculosis (TB) has emerged as a special threat to people infected with HIV, as well as to those who care for infected persons. Tuberculosis is a bacterial infection, usually in the lungs, but possibly in any part of the body. Tuberculosis can kill by destroying vital lung tissue. At one time it was the leading cause of death in the United States. It still infects 20 percent of the world's population—one billion people—and kills over 3 million people a year (Talaro & Talaro, 1996).

In many hospitals, strains of tuberculosis have emerged that are both highly virulent and resistant to many of the important tuberculosis-fighting drugs. TB is usually transmitted by airborne droplets discharged when infected people cough.

Because their immune systems are so impaired, many HIV-infected people who have tuberculosis fail to show a positive skin test for TB (Webster, 1995). Like an HIV antibody test, the TB skin test detects an immune response against the pathogen, not the pathogen itself. Chest X rays and sputum samples provide more reliable detection of TB for HIV patients. Treatment requires taking a combination of three or four drugs for six months or longer (Perriens, 1995).

### 7.5.7 Other Opportunistic Infections

Almost any infection becomes more serious in people infected with HIV. The following are some of the opportunistic infections found in HIV patients:

- *Candida.* This organism causes the common vaginal "yeast infection" but becomes much more serious in HIV patients, who experience severe yeast infections of the mouth, esophagus, and anal area.
- **Cytomegalovirus (CMV).** Although this virus infects up to 100 percent of the population of some nations (about 80 percent by age 30 in the United States), it seldom produces symptoms or does any damage. In HIV patients, disseminated (bodywide) CMV infection can create a medical crisis with fever, severe diarrhea, hepatitis, pneumonia, and a high death rate (Talaro & Talaro, 1996). It often attacks the retina of the eye of HIV patients, causing blindness.
- **Herpes simplex.** Although herpes simplex can be troublesome for anyone (see chapter 6), HIV patients are subject to severe and frequent or ongoing attacks.
- **Herpes zoster (shingles).** Anyone who has ever had chicken pox might carry its virus (another herpes virus) as a lifelong, latent infection. Reactivation of this virus causes shingles, an extremely painful eruption of lesions on the skin and peripheral nerves. As with the other herpes viruses, this is more likely to occur and to be severe in HIV-infected people.
- **Diarrhea-causing infections.** As we have mentioned, HIV infection alone appears capable of causing chronic diarrhea. But many additional causes of diarrhea plague HIV patients, causing considerable weight loss and wasting as a result of chronic diarrhea.

## 7.6 DETECTING HIV INFECTION

Several types of tests are available for detecting HIV infection. Screening tests actually detect antibodies against HIV rather than the virus itself. Initial tests

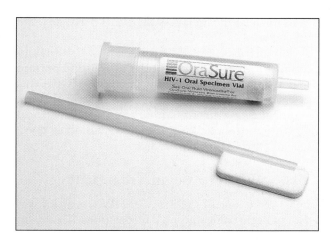

**FIGURE 7.11** OraSure, the first oral HIV test. Available only through physicians and clinics, the collection pad is placed between the cheek and gum for two minutes to absorb any HIV antibodies present, then placed in the vial and sent to a clinical lab to be tested for antibodies using ELISA and, if necessary, Western blot tests.

are usually by the ELISA (enzyme-linked immunosorbent assay) method, which gives some false positive results. A positive ELISA is, therefore, followed up with the more expensive but more specific Western blot test. False positive Western blot tests are extremely rare (Turgeon, 1996).

A newer variation on HIV testing is OraSure. OraSure, available only through physicians and clinics, is a collection pad (fig. 7.11) placed between the cheek and gum for two minutes to absorb any anti-HIV antibodies present. It is then sent to a laboratory for an ELISA test and, if necessary, a Western blot. It offers the advantage of using saliva instead of blood as a source of antibodies, thereby reducing the risk of accidental needle-stick injuries to health care workers.

HIV testing can be obtained under confidential or anonymous circumstances. *Confidential* testing is not the same as anonymous testing. Confidential medical records do contain your name and information from them can be disclosed under some circumstances, such as statistical reporting to public health agencies. Such information is very important for epidemiological monitoring of the spread of HIV and the effectiveness of public health initiatives. In anonymous testing, a random number is used for conveying test results only; no personal information is recorded.

The fact that current tests detect antibodies rather than the virus creates several problems:

- A newly infected person might continue to test negative on such tests for a period of one to twelve months yet carry the virus and be able to infect others.

- Current tests are unable to predict whether an infected person will, in time, develop AIDS.

- A positive antibody test in a newborn infant does not reveal whether the infant is HIV infected or just carrying antibodies that have crossed the placenta from its mother.

- The immune mechanisms of some people are so severely impaired by HIV that they test negative for antibodies even though they are quite ill with AIDS.

Tests that could reliably and economically detect the actual virus, rather than antibodies against it, would be ideal.

### 7.6.1 Counseling in Association with HIV Testing

Experts concerned with the behavioral aspects of HIV strongly emphasize the importance of expert one-on-one counseling in association with HIV testing. Counseling is appropriate both before and after HIV testing, and can be included in both confidential and anonymous testing settings.

During pretest counseling, the counselor will usually conduct a personalized risk assessment for the client, explain the principles of HIV testing, explain the meaning of both positive and negative test results, obtain "informed consent" for the test, and help the client to develop an effective risk-reduction plan.

Someone being notified of a positive HIV test needs counseling on many fronts. Foremost is help in dealing with what many patients will interpret as a death sentence. A newly diagnosed HIV-positive patient needs to know that healthful living habits (see "Healthy Sexuality: Living with HIV") and medication can greatly delay the onset of severe health problems. He or she also needs to know the risk of infecting others and be motivated to protect the health of other people.

Someone being notified of a negative HIV test also needs counseling. Most people who test negative feel relieved. This is a perfect time to stop any behavior that could put you at further risk of infection. HIV-negative people need to know that although they might not yet be infected, they could become infected if they participate in high-risk behavior. Also, they are usually counseled that a recent HIV infection might not yet have shown up on an HIV antibody test, so they should still practice precautions to

| | |
|---|---|
| **cytomegalovirus** (sī-tō-meg′a-lō-vī-rus) | a common virus that causes mild or asymptomatic infections in most people, but severe infections in HIV patients |

prevent infecting a partner. They should be tested again in about six months to confirm the negative result.

## 7.7   TREATING HIV AND ITS COMPLICATIONS

In many patients, new drug combinations have eliminated all symptoms of HIV infection and lowered the amount of the virus circulating in the bloodstream to undetectable levels. The circulating virus count has emerged as the best predictor of how HIV illness will progress, so in some cases it might now be possible to indefinitely postpone the onset of AIDS.

### 7.7.1   Available Treatments

Medications taken by HIV patients fall into two categories: those to fight HIV itself and those to fight the many opportunistic infections resulting from HIV's destruction of bodily defenses. Treatment for HIV has greatly improved as new drugs with new modes of action have appeared.

Earlier anti-HIV drugs such as AZT (azidothymidine; also known as zidovudine or *Retrovir*) and ddI (dideoxyinosine) interfere with replication of the virus's nucleic acid. Newer anti-HIV drugs—**protease inhibitors** such as ritonavir, saquinavir, and indinavir—block the enzyme **protease,** which is needed to split a protein molecule produced during HIV replication. Without this enzyme, a complete HIV particle cannot be assembled. These newer drugs tend to have milder side effects than the more toxic AZT and related drugs. Drug resistance, in which the virus no longer is affected by a drug, has been a problem with any drug used against HIV over a long period of time (Danner, 1995; Markowitz, 1995; Schmit, 1996).

Protease inhibitors have been most effective when used in combination with several other drugs, such as AZT and 3TC (lamivudine). The treatment involves from 14 to 20 carefully timed pills per day, requiring tremendous discipline and motivation from the patient.

These drug combinations sharply reduce the amount of HIV (viral load) circulating in the fluid portion (plasma) of an infected person's blood. Viral load has been found to be a more reliable predictor of the development of AIDS and of death than the number of T4 (CD4) lymphocytes in the blood (Mellors, 1996; Galetto-Lacour, 1996). Some experts predict that life can be prolonged for as much as twenty years, but at an annual cost for medicines of $12,000 to $16,000 (Paul et al., 1996). To put this in perspective, most of the people in the world who have HIV infection are in nations whose total per capita expenditure for health care is less than $10 per year (Paul et al., 1996).

Another aspect of HIV treatment is fighting opportunistic infections. One of the most important drugs against opportunistic infections in HIV patients has been pentamidine, given, often in aerosol form, to combat *Pneumocystis carinii* pneumonia. Medications to fight tuberculosis, *Candida,* and other infections are also frequently needed.

### 7.7.2   When to Begin Treatment

In past years, one of the issues in HIV treatment was *when* to begin using anti-HIV medications. Treatment was often delayed until HIV illness became quite advanced. As better drugs with milder side effects have become available, the trend has been toward initiating treatment sooner, often before any symptoms appear. Many experts now like to see treatment begin within 90 days of infection. Reasons include these:

- HIV is **homogeneous** early in an infection, making it easier to successfully treat people who are recently infected. With time, mutations cause increased variability of the virus (Richman, 1996).
- The early period of HIV infection is now recognized as a period of much hidden destruction. For example, irreversible damage to lymph nodes occurs during the early phase of HIV infection. Once destroyed, the immune system never regenerates its previous strength (Pantaleo, 1996).
- Stopping HIV replication early decreases the risk of its developing resistance to anti-HIV drugs.
- In 9 out of 12 people who started triple therapy (AZT, lamivudine [3TC], and ritonavir) within 90 days of HIV infection, the virus was reduced to an undetectable level in their blood and CD4 counts improved (Markowitz et al., 1996). Long-term follow-up will be necessary to learn the ultimate outcome of these cases.

| | |
|---|---|
| **protease inhibitors** | drugs that block the action of the enzyme protease, which is needed to complete the assembly of new HIV particles |
| **protease** (prō′tē-āce) | an enzyme that splits a protein molecule |
| **homogeneous** (hō-mō-gē′nē-us) | uniform in structure; all of the same kind |

## HEALTHY SEXUALITY

### LIVING WITH HIV

Abundant evidence indicates that the attitudes and health habits of people who are HIV positive can powerfully influence the progression of their infection. Here are some ways an infected person can stay healthier longer and enjoy the best possible quality of life.

The first step is to get beyond the stage of denial. Although denial is a predictable response to bad news, being in a state of denial prevents a person from taking the steps necessary to deal most successfully with a serious health threat. If you learn that you are infected with HIV, acknowledge that you have a problem, at least to yourself, if not immediately to others. Then you can begin to live in the most healthful ways.

As discussed on page 184, early, aggressive treatment with a combination of anti-HIV medications can greatly reduce the viral load in a person's body and delay the onset of illness. Some experts even believe that the virus can be eliminated from a person's body if treatment begins within ninety days of infection. You have to get out of denial to seek such treatment.

*Attitude* is the key to effective action. It's perfectly natural for anyone with a life-threatening condition to experience powerful negative feelings such as anxiety, depression, anger, mistrust, despair, hopelessness, and withdrawal. But such emotions, along with denial, eliminate the motivation to live in healthful, life-prolonging ways. Further, psychological factors can also influence physical health directly. The immune mechanism is quite sensitive to a person's mental state, and the survival of an HIV patient is closely associated with the strength of her or his immune system.

*Know your enemy.* If you are HIV positive, learn as much as possible about HIV and its treatment options. You might start by calling the National AIDS Hotline at (800) 342-AIDS or a local HIV/AIDS organization. Your physician, local library, or bookstore can also be a good source of literature.

*Diet* is important to optimum immune functioning. No known diet can cure an HIV infection, and some diets that have been suggested for HIV-infected people are so extreme that they probably actually shorten lives. But there is evidence that a well-balanced diet with plenty of fresh fruits and vegetables delays the appearance of severe illness.

*Maintain emotional support.* Knowing that they are HIV positive, some people isolate themselves from the people they need most—those who love them and could provide emotional and practical support. It's better to inform those close to you of your situation and accept their support and help. Most major cities also have specific self-help and support groups for people infected with HIV.

*Insist on quality health care.* Find a physician who keeps up-to-the-minute on rapidly changing HIV treatments. If you find that your physician or other health care provider is losing interest in your care, insist on obtaining better service or, if necessary, find a more dedicated provider. When to begin treatment with anti-HIV medications needs to be discussed with your primary physician. Many experts now believe that treatment should begin within ninety days of infection. If you want to try any of the many unconventional (alternative) treatments promoted for HIV, discuss this with your physician. And don't let your use of unproven treatments cause you to forgo more conventional treatments that might be of value to you.

*Prepare a "living will" and "durable power of attorney for health care."* These documents, which should be completed while you are in good health, will help ensure that your wishes regarding your health care will be followed should you become severely ill. The living will spells out your preferences on how specific health situations should be dealt with. The durable power of attorney for health care designates a trusted person to make decisions for you in situations not covered by your living will if you are too ill to make these decisions at the time.

---

All of this can be taken as evidence of the value of frequent HIV testing for people who engage in high-risk practices. Although only time will tell if a complete cure is possible, aggressive early treatment will at least delay symptoms and extend life.

### 7.7.3  Caring for Advanced HIV Illness

When HIV disease progresses into "full-blown" AIDS, the need for medical attention becomes more intense. Crises of various types, often opportunistic infections, become progressively more frequent and more severe. Periodic hospitalization is often required. Increasing kinds and dosages of expensive medications become necessary.

Most AIDS patients continue to live at home, although a few become residents in specialized facilities. Costs soar, and ability to pay can become an issue. Various government assistance programs apply to AIDS patients. For example, all fifty states have programs that help low- and middle-income people obtain expensive medications. These AIDS Drug Assistance Programs (ADAP) are federally mandated and operated by the states. Each state sets its own eligibility requirements. Information on programs available for AIDS patients is available through the National AIDS Hotline at (800) 342-AIDS.

In advanced AIDS cases, hospice care may become appropriate. A hospice is a program or organization dedicated to assisting dying people and their families. Hospice care can be provided in a specific facility or at home. Most commonly, hospices support the home care of the dying person by aiding family members and providing support for the dying person and his or her caregivers.

A hospice openly accepts that a person is probably going to die. The goal of the hospice is to keep the patient free of pain, comfortable, and alert throughout the final stages of life. Heroic life-sustaining measures such as resuscitations and heart stimulation are not part of the hospice concept.

## 7.8   HIV AND WOMEN

Because most of the early cases of AIDS in the United States occurred in males, the impact of HIV on women was largely ignored for some years (Corea, 1992). Even now, the risk of women becoming infected with HIV isn't fully understood by everyone. As mentioned earlier, the proportion of AIDS patients who are female has steadily grown from about 8 percent in 1981 to about 18 percent in 1997 and continues to grow (CDC, 1995a).

The median age of women at the time of diagnosis with AIDS is about 35 years, and women aged 15 to 44 years account for 84 percent of female AIDS cases (CDC, 1995b). Subtracting the 10 years on the average that it takes to move from first HIV infection to AIDS, we can see that the average age for women becoming infected with HIV is about 25 years.

The ethnic distribution of AIDS cases in women is even more disproportionately nonwhite than it is in males. Based on the actual number of people in each ethnic group, the incidence of AIDS is 16 times higher among African American women and 7 times

The proportion of HIV-infected people in the United States who are female has increased to 18 percent and continues to increase. Women become HIV positive at an average age of about 25 years.

higher among Hispanic American women than among white American women (CDC, 1995b).

AIDS in women is primarily associated with two modes of HIV transmission: sharing drug-injection equipment (41 percent of cases) and sexual contact with infected male partners (38 percent of cases) (CDC, 1995b). Women at highest risk for heterosexually transmitted HIV include those whose male partners have high-risk behaviors such as sharing drug injection equipment, having multiple sex partners, or having sex with men.

A woman's contraceptive method influences her likelihood of insisting on condom use for a male partner (CDC, 1996c). Results of a study of 952 women who had more than one sex partner are presented in table 7.2. Compared with women using condoms as their principle contraceptive method, women using hormonal methods such as pills were much less likely to use condoms for disease prevention.

Each year about 7,000 HIV-positive women deliver infants in the United States. Given HIV's transplacental transmission rate of 20 to 30 percent, this means that about 1,000 to 2,000 infants are born with HIV infection each year. The need is evident for effective HIV prevention programs for women and for counseling of HIV-positive women concerning the risk that their infants will also be infected. Aggressive drug therapy for infected women can greatly reduce the risk that their infants will be born infected.

In many cultures, male sexual privilege contributes to the spread of HIV. Men in these cultures feel free to enjoy many sex partners, including prostitutes. Their female partners have little voice in sexual decisions, including condom use.

**TABLE 7.2** FAILURE TO USE CONDOMS, RELATIVE TO CONTRACEPTIVE METHOD USED, AMONG WOMEN WITH MORE THAN ONE SEX PARTNER

| TYPE OF CONTRACEPTIVE USED | DID NOT USE CONDOM FOR LAST SEX WITH MAIN PARTNER | DID NOT USE CONDOM FOR LAST SEX WITH CASUAL PARTNER |
|---|---|---|
| Condoms | 39% | 22% |
| Hormonal methods | 70% | 42% |
| Sterilization | 73% | 37% |
| All methods combined | 56% | 29% |

**Source:** Data from Centers for Disease Control and Prevention, "Contraceptive Method and Condom Use among Women at Risk for HIV Infection and Other Sexually Transmitted Diseases—Selected U. S. Sites, 1993–1994," *Morbidity and Mortality Weekly Report* 45(1996): 820–23.

## 7.9 PSYCHOLOGICAL IMPLICATIONS OF HIV

Few, if any, diseases carry as heavy a psychological burden for those infected as HIV. In addition to the very real threat to one's life, HIV infection carries a stigma not present with most other diseases. Even though heart disease and cancer also relate to lifestyle factors, people tend to view them differently than they do HIV infection. Many people who are not infected have unrealistic fears regarding HIV.

### 7.9.1 Fear of HIV

Throughout this chapter you are encouraged to gain a healthy respect for HIV. But you don't want to be so afraid of HIV/AIDS that you can't enjoy life. How can you tell if your fear of HIV is excessive? Here are some signs of excessive fear (Bloom & Shernoff, 1986):

- You were previously sexually active, but you have entirely stopped having sex out of fear of HIV.

- You aren't as social as you once were because of your fear of HIV.

- You avoid interacting with gay or bisexual friends because you are afraid of HIV.

- You refuse to believe the results of your negative HIV antibody test.

- You refuse to be tested, but you assume that you are HIV positive.

- You have been tested, you are positive, and because you are HIV seropositive you have withdrawn from most of the activities you used to enjoy, even though you are in good health.

If you do have an unrealistic fear of HIV, what can you do about it? If you haven't had an HIV antibody test lately, get one. If you are HIV negative, make sure that you understand how HIV is and is not transmitted. Follow the safer-sex guidelines. Don't share injection equipment or anything that penetrates your skin. If you are HIV seropositive, don't give up on life. Medical advances are coming rapidly and now offer a long, productive life for someone who is HIV positive.

### 7.9.2 Dating and Courtship in the Age of HIV

Responses to the threat of becoming infected with HIV range from total indifference at one extreme to panic at the other. Neither extreme is an appropriate reaction to the HIV epidemic.

Some of those who ignore the possibility of becoming infected with HIV make heavy use of denial. The fact is that HIV is a real threat to people who have many sex partners or who choose their partners indiscriminately. Some people have a pattern of engaging in many high-risk or self-destructive behaviors such as smoking, heavy drinking or other substance abuse, and having many sex partners. AIDS awareness messages tend to fall on deaf ears with these people (Witte & Morrison, 1995).

At the other extreme are people who totally withdraw from all partnership-forming activities out of fear of HIV. Although this certainly reduces one's chances of acquiring HIV, it is an unnecessary overreaction. There is a middle ground that allows us to develop worthwhile relationships while still facing little risk of HIV infection.

Section 7.11 "Effectively Preventing HIV Infection" suggests ways to reduce your risk of HIV infection. Each of us needs to evaluate our approach to dating, courtship, and relationships in this era of HIV and AIDS. In the age of HIV, sexual activity needs to take place in the context of a stable, ongoing relationship rather than in a series of brief, casual acquaintances. This is not easy for some people, especially those who have a fear of commitment or who desire the novelty of the "attractive stranger." But in a stable, emotionally intimate, long-term relationship, many people find a level of satisfaction and reward that had always been missing from their brief attachments.

The threat of HIV is not to be ignored. But neither is it a reason to become a hermit. It is a good reason to put a new emphasis on stable, long-term relationships.

### 7.9.3 Getting the News: Learning That You're HIV Positive

HIV infection is closely associated with death in the minds of many people. So it is not surprising that, upon learning that they are infected with HIV, people often go through predictable stages similar to those of someone who is dying:

1. *Denial.* Denial is a natural response to hearing any bad news. It can keep a newly diagnosed HIV-seropositive person from seeking the modern drug treatment that could keep her or him healthy for a long time and possibly eliminate the infection.

2. *Anger.* Following denial, there is often anger—anger at the person who was the source of the virus, anger at oneself for becoming infected. Anger can prevent constructive action or cause counterproductive behaviors.

3. *Depression.* Depression is a predictable psychological state associated with any loss. People who learn that they are HIV positive are often sad, but they are not often depressed to the point of suicide or needing psychiatric hospitalization (Brown & Rundell, 1993; Dannenberg, 1996).

4. *Acceptance.* Acceptance shouldn't mean sitting around waiting to die. People who accept their HIV status can manage their lives in ways that help them to remain healthy.

### 7.9.4 HIV Disclosure

If you are HIV positive, one of the more difficult aspects can be disclosing your HIV status to someone in whom you are sexually or romantically interested. But for both ethical and legal reasons this is something that you must do, before there is any activity that could expose that person to risk of HIV transmission.

As to when to disclose, every case is unique—but in general, sooner is better than later. Fear often prevents or delays disclosure and the result can be viral transmission. One common fear is fear of rejection, which is realistic because some potential partners won't want to continue a relationship with anyone they know to be infected with HIV. But, in a positive view, someone who still wants you, knowing that you are seropositive, probably has some genuine caring feelings for you. Another fear is that after disclosure you will be related to as if you were ill. Sometimes that happens (Cyrus, 1996). And sometimes the person you disclose to breaks down and you have to take care of him or her.

How do you make this important disclosure? The direct approach is best. "There is something I need to tell you before our relationship goes any further. I have been tested and I am infected with HIV. I want to talk to you about what that means to each of us." Attending a support group for seropositive people can help you to disclose. For starters, just by attending the group, you are disclosing. Then, by participating, you see how others handle disclosure and learn techniques that you might use in other situations (Cyrus, 1996).

Disclosure of HIV status has become a little easier because of the openness of some prominent infected people such as Magic Johnson and Greg Louganis (see "Case Study: An Interview with Greg Louganis").

---

## 7.10 SOCIAL ASPECTS OF HIV

Some diseases have the power to bring about major social changes. You may be familiar, for example, with the impact that epidemics such as the plague and smallpox have had on human history. HIV has the potential to have a similar effect.

### 7.10.1 HIV in Families

As in other places in this book, we define "family" in a broad manner to include related and unrelated people whose lives are closely intertwined. The presence of HIV in a family affects every family member in many ways.

Disclosure of an HIV-seropositive status to other family members can be extremely intimidating to the infected family member, depending on the interpersonal dynamics of the family. The disclosure of HIV often involves a second disclosure regarding sexual orientation or drug abuse of which family members might be unaware. Cultural factors influence the ease

The presence of HIV in a family affects every family member in many ways. Family cohesiveness might be tested as various crises arise.

## CASE STUDY

### AN INTERVIEW WITH GREG LOUGANIS

Four-time gold medal winning Olympic diver Greg Louganis stunned the world with his 1994 book, *Breaking the Surface*, coauthored with Eric Marcus, in which Louganis revealed that he was already HIV positive when he competed in the 1988 Seoul Olympics. Here are some excerpts from an interview with Greg Louganis by Daniel Wolfe, director of communications at Gay Men's Health Crisis in New York City, published in *The Volunteer*.

> *Wolfe:* The press spent much of their time after your announcement obsessed with the possibility that your blood might have infected another diver. Readers of *The Volunteer* are more likely wrestling with the dynamics of what can seem like a different kind of impossibility: telling a parent, friend, or loved one that you have HIV. Why did you go public?
>
> *Louganis:* Secrets can be really imprisoning. I had HIV, but I didn't have anybody to talk to. . . . I started thinking about all that when it came time to write the book, about breaking the sense of loneliness.

> *Wolfe:* There's been a lot of attention to the public aspect of your disclosure. Did you talk with people close to you about having HIV before you went public?
>
> *Louganis:* I told my dad when he was diagnosed with cancer. That was back in 1989 or 1990. It became a crusade for life for both of us—him with cancer and me with HIV. I didn't come out to my mom until later. . . . Once I told her, things were so much easier. She was there for me, providing me with unconditional love.
>
> *Wolfe:* Do you think she knew already?
>
> *Louganis:* She wasn't surprised, because she knew that two of my ex's had passed away. But once it penetrated, she started crying. "Mothers aren't supposed to outlive their sons," she said. Then, almost in the same breath, she said, "you know, Greg, you have beaten some incredible odds before."

**Source:** Excerpted from Daniel Wolfe. "An Interview with Greg Louganis," *The Volunteer*, published by Gay Men's Health Crisis, New York City, May/June, 1996.

---

with which disclosure can be made. For example, in a Southern California study, Spanish-speaking Hispanic men were less likely than either English-speaking Hispanic men or non-Hispanic white men to make the disclosure of HIV infection to family (Mason et al., 1995). Both Hispanic and non-Hispanic men were more likely to withhold their diagnosis from their parents in order to prevent worrying them than in order to avoid personal rejection. Regardless of the reason for nondisclosure, people who are HIV positive and do not reveal this to family and friends deprive themselves of much-needed social support in a time of great need.

Family responses to the disclosure typically include many emotions. There might be denial; the infected family member might be urged to be retested. There might be grief in anticipation of the loss of a loved one. There might be anger—anger at the loved one for engaging in whatever behavior resulted in infection, anger at the person who was the source of the virus, anger at the government for not finding a solution to the HIV problem, and so on. There might be fear—fear of infection with HIV, fear of the economic impact the disease may have on the family, and fear of social rejection or prejudice from people outside of the family.

As HIV infection progresses to and into AIDS, family cohesiveness can be put to the test as stressful situations arise. Ultimately, many families feel closer and more united than previously, but few ever feel that they have fully recovered from the loss of a loved one at what is often a young age.

### 7.10.2   HIV and the Health Care System

HIV impacts the nation's health care system in many ways. So far, the system as a whole has been adequate for the task of caring for HIV patients, whose numbers remain small relative to the numbers of patients with cardiovascular disorders, cancers, and other problems. In many major cities, however, the large number of medically indigent HIV patients has overwhelmed the resources of publicly supported hospitals and clinics.

HIV transmission to health care workers occurs at a relatively low rate, even when workers are accidentally stuck with contaminated injection needles. Other diseases, especially hepatitis B, are much more contagious to health care workers. But the threat of HIV infection is real and ever-present to those employed in health care. Some workers have left health care entirely because of fear of HIV, and some people who might have sought careers in health care have made other choices out of the same fear.

The opposite situation—HIV transmission from health care worker to patient—has also been rare, despite an estimated 50,000 American health care workers with HIV (Burris, 1996). There have been a few documented cases of this happening, such as the Florida dentist who apparently infected several patients, but so few that you have little need for concern. Even so, you shouldn't hesitate to say something if you observe a health care worker bleeding from an injury, failing to wash his or her hands between patients, or breaching other rules intended to prevent disease transmission.

### 7.10.3  Organizations Helping People with HIV/AIDS

People with advanced HIV illness and those who love them and assist them have need for many types of support services. Most major metropolitan areas have responded to this need by developing various types of assistance programs. Social service agencies in your area can direct you to local organizations. Almost all of these programs rely heavily on volunteer workers and provide opportunities for rewarding service for caring individuals.

### 7.10.4  HIV in the Workplace

Even now, many years after HIV/AIDS became prevalent in the United States, people who are known or suspected of being infected with HIV are often discriminated against in their place of employment. This discrimination can take the form of refusal to hire, finding excuses to fire, giving undesirable assignments, denying advancement, or isolating infected workers from social contact.

Much of this discrimination is based on fear and ignorance. Despite massive public education efforts, many people still fear transmission of HIV through the air, drinking fountains, nonsexual contact, or simply being around an infected person. The fact is, that the presence of an HIV-positive worker presents no threat of HIV infection to coworkers.

If a coworker, whether HIV positive or not, has active tuberculosis, there is a risk of airborne transmission of TB when she or he coughs or sneezes. Anyone with active TB should be excluded from the workplace until medication eliminates the discharge of the TB bacillus, usually a period of 4 to 8 weeks (Benenson, 1995).

Many state and federal laws protect people from discrimination in the workplace because of their HIV

Even today, people who are known or suspected to be infected with HIV might experience discrimination in the workplace, based on fear and ignorance. HIV status is not a legal basis for refusing to hire or promote a person.

status. Persons with HIV disease, at any stage, are considered "disabled" under state and federal civil rights laws. Some laws also provide protection to people who are merely thought or "perceived" to be infected, such as a gay employee who is fired by an employer who believes, because of the employee's sexual orientation, that the employee might be infected. The laws also extend to family members, friends, significant others, and caregivers of persons with HIV.

Under these laws, employers are prohibited from making employment-related decisions based on HIV status, unless the employee's medical condition impairs his or her ability to perform the job duties. Therefore, an employer cannot refuse to hire, discharge, isolate, or demote an employee because the person has HIV.

An employer is *not* required to hire or retain an employee whose health condition interferes with the employee's ability to work efficiently and safely. However, an employer must first make reasonable efforts to accommodate an employee's disability. This might mean flexible work hours or different duty assignments.

An employer is forbidden from using prehire tests to screen out people with HIV. Once a person has been offered a job, the employer may require a physical. Since being HIV positive usually does not interfere with job performance, HIV status is not a legal basis to refuse to hire a person.

Anyone discriminated against because of real or perceived HIV status or because of association with a person with HIV may file a complaint with the appropriate state or federal agency. This needs to be done within 180 days of the violation. If the person is a union member, the union may assist with the complaint.

Not all employers are subject to these laws. In general, federal antidiscrimination laws apply to employers with fifteen or more employees. The number of employees making an employer subject to state laws varies from state to state.

### On-The-Job HIV Infection

Although not a common event, occasionally someone with on-the-job blood exposure becomes infected with HIV. Under some circumstances, the employee might be entitled to worker's compensation or other legal remedies for that infection. The claims in this situation are very complex. Anyone who believes that she or he has been infected with HIV on the job should consult with an attorney immediately upon confirmation of HIV-positive status.

## 7.10.5   HIV in Schools

HIV is the sixth leading cause of death among children from one to four years of age (Singh, Kochanek, & MacDorman, 1996). The majority of children in this age group with HIV infection have acquired it prenatally from their infected mothers. HIV takes a special toll on children of color. Table 7.3 compares the HIV death rates per 100,000 African American, Hispanic American, and white American children.

Reported deaths from childhood HIV underestimate the actual number of children infected with HIV. Children who develop symptoms before age two have a short life expectancy and many may never begin school. Others, however, do not become ill until after the age of five or six years and, with aggressive medical treatment, might live and attend school for a number of additional years.

Children infected with HIV can have very difficult times at school. When their HIV status becomes known, they are likely to experience isolation from other children, who might be encouraged by their parents to avoid an HIV-infected child. Further, as many as 90 percent of children with HIV infections have developmental disabilities that result in physical and/or mental impairment and learning difficulties. Time lost from school during periods of illness further reduces their progress. And many children infected with HIV have parents with problems of their own, such as AIDS and chemical dependencies, who are unable to provide much support and assistance to their children in dealing with difficulties at school. Other children with HIV infection are cared for by members of their extended family or by foster or adoptive families, who might not have access to needed resources.

**TABLE 7.3**   HIV DEATHS PER 100,000 AFRICAN AMERICAN, HISPANIC AMERICAN, AND NON-HISPANIC WHITE AMERICAN CHILDREN FOR 1994

|  | DEATHS PER 100,000 CHILDREN PER YEAR | |
| --- | --- | --- |
|  | Age 1–4 | Age 5–14 |
| African American children | 4.8 | 1.6 |
| Hispanic American children | 1.3 | 0.7 |
| Non-Hispanic white American children | 1.1 | 0.3 |

**Source:** Data from G. Singh, K. Kochanek, and M. MacDorman, "Advance Report of Final Mortality Statistics, 1994," *Monthly Vital Statistics Report* 45 (1, supp.), (Hyattsville, MD: National Center for Health Statistics, 30 Sept. 1996).

Early in the HIV epidemic, the frightened parents of other children sometimes made efforts to prevent children who are HIV positive from attending schools. As with HIV in the workplace, federal and state laws clearly allow infected children to attend school, and there have been extremely few cases of HIV transmission from child to child.

## 7.10.6   Laws Concerning HIV

A multitude of laws cover various aspects of HIV. Those concerning HIV in the workplace were mentioned previously.

### Injection Equipment

As of the beginning of 1997, over one-third (36 percent) of all the 573,000 AIDS cases that had ever been reported to the CDC had been directly or indirectly associated with injecting-drug use (CDC, 1997). This includes injection drug users and their sexual partners. As we have discussed, sharing nonsterile injection equipment is one of the most efficient ways of transmitting HIV.

In many states, access to sterile injection equipment is limited by laws requiring a prescription for the purchase of such equipment. Existing laws and regulations limit the sale of sterile syringes and needles and establish criminal penalties for possession of such equipment. Although this apparently seems like a good idea to many lawmakers, there is no evidence that such laws assist in the fight against drug abuse and plenty of evidence that they contribute to the spread of HIV.

In an effort to reduce HIV transmission, over 101 syringe exchange programs in 71 cities within 29 states are active in the United States, and their number is increasing (CDC, 1997). Eighty-seven of those programs responded to a survey that found that those 87 programs had exchanged about 14 million syringes during 1996.

Most of the 87 syringe-exchange programs also provide information about using bleach to disinfect injection equipment, make referrals to substance-abuse recovery programs, and offer instruction in the use of condoms and dental dams to prevent disease transmission.

Some syringe-exchange programs (53 percent) either operate in states where no prescription is required to purchase a syringe or operate under exemptions to state prescription laws. Some (23 percent) are "illegal but tolerated" by the formal vote of a local elected body such as a city council. And finally, some (24 percent) operate "underground" with no legal sanction (CDC, 1997).

Recognizing that their laws might have actually contributed to the spread of HIV, increasing numbers of states are making it easier to obtain sterile syringes and needles. For example, in May, 1997, the legislatures of Maine and Minnesota removed criminal penalties for possession of up to ten syringes (CDC, 1997). Many organizations, such as the National Commission on AIDS, support removal of all legal barriers to the purchase of sterile injection equipment.

### Housing

Federal and state laws forbid discrimination in the sale or rental of housing based upon disability, which includes HIV infection. Illegal acts include harassment, refusal to sell or rent, denial of insurance, and threats, intimidation, or coercion by neighbors. HUD (United States Department of Housing and Urban Development) will investigate complaints of violations, and civil lawsuits may also be filed.

Low-income HIV-infected people may qualify for federal rent assistance, commonly called "Section 8" housing. The classification of HIV infection as a disability might give some priority for this housing, but in most areas there will still be a waiting list for the limited amount of Section 8 housing available.

### Confidentiality

Because of the great potential for discrimination and persecution, as well as the tradition of confidentiality of medical records, most information on a person's HIV status is supposed to remain confidential. Breeches of confidentiality do occur. Once a person enters the health care system for HIV-related care, maintaining confidentiality becomes problematic. Many employers handle insurance claims internally, so there is a potential for leaks of information within the company. If, however, any adverse action were taken against an employee because of information received in this manner, it would constitute unlawful discrimination (Hansell, 1993).

### Victims of Crimes

One case where confidentiality might not apply involves victims of crimes such as rape or other crimes where an exchange of body fluids takes place. Fear of contracting HIV is a major concern for victims of such crimes. About forty states have laws requiring that people arrested and charged with sexual assaults be tested for HIV and the results of those tests be disclosed to the victims.

Required tests may be paid for by various government agencies in different states. Often HIV testing of the victim is paid for as well. In some states, the defendant may be required to reimburse the state for the costs of HIV testing and counseling.

## 7.10.7 Impact of HIV on Communities

Both within the United States and around the world, HIV has impacted some communities more severely than others. Here in the United States, one severely affected community has been the gay male population. The great loss of life and productivity within this community has resulted in a massive mobilization and unification of what was previously a more loosely organized population. Many highly effective organizations based primarily in the gay male community help affected people deal with the social and personal effects of HIV. An outstanding job of community education by these groups has reduced the high-risk practices of many gay and heterosexual people. In contrast with the gay community, the injection-drug-using population has made virtually no progress in organizing to defeat HIV. Most efforts in their behalf, such as needle exchange programs, have come from concerned people who are not drug users.

Perhaps the most affected populations of all are in sub-Saharan Africa, where it is estimated that 14 million people are infected with HIV (United Nations data). The impact on these already-struggling African nations has been staggering. Few or no health care services are available there for infected people.

## 7.11 EFFECTIVELY PREVENTING HIV INFECTION

As with other sexually transmitted infections, preventing HIV infections requires both individual efforts and the efforts of public health agencies. From a public health point of view, the task is not easy, because it requires people to make changes in areas of their lives, such as sexuality and drug use, where people are often reluctant to make changes. Take a moment now to rate your HIV-risk behavior with "Where Do I Stand? My Risk of HIV."

## 7.11.1 Risk-Reducing Strategies

Here are some suggested strategies to reduce your risk of sexually transmitted HIV infection:

- *Sexual abstinence.* Sexual abstinence is the one sure way of preventing sexually transmitted HIV infection. Sexual freedom includes the freedom to say no to sex. Increasing numbers of people are choosing to limit their sexual activity to committed relationships and remaining abstinent before and between such relationships.

- *Reduced number of sex partners.* Very simply put, the more sex partners you have, the greater your risk of acquiring HIV and other STIs. Wise people today restrict their sexual activity to long-term, committed relationships, avoiding sex with strangers or casual friends.

- *Careful selection of sex partners.* Not just anyone can be considered a good choice as a sex partner, at least in terms of risk of disease transmission. Traits like being physically attractive, dressing well, or having a pleasant personality don't necessarily make a person a wise choice as a sexual partner. More important are traits like *not* having a history of injection drug use, *not* having a history of many sex partners, and *not* recently having had a sex partner who fell into one of those categories. However, Stebleton and Rothenberger (1993) found that people will lie to get sex, and men do this more often than women. Their study of 169 college students found that 36 percent of the male subjects and 21 percent of the women had been sexually "unfaithful" in supposedly monogamous relationships. So even in a "monogamous" relationship, and even if a potential partner has all the right answers to your questions, you should still want to use condoms and follow all of the safer-sex practices.

- *Move slowly into a sexual relationship.* How can you know a person's history regarding drug abuse and multiple sex partners? These are areas of behavior that someone who would like to have sex with you may not be very honest about. Take plenty of time to get to know a potential sex partner. Consider his or her general lifestyle. Get to know his or her friends. Many partners today go together for HIV antibody tests before having sex. If this person is reluctant to be tested, you may wonder what he or she has to hide. Be suspicious of anyone who is rushing you into a sexual relationship. A big percentage of HIV infections occur from casual sex with a little-known partner.

- *Safer-sex practices.* Safer (not *safe*, because there is still some risk) sex practices include everything you can do to minimize exposure to potentially infectious body fluids such as semen, blood, and cervical or vaginal secretions. Some couples practice "outercourse," meaning that nothing is inserted into either person. Outercourse can include hugging, massage, mutual masturbation, and rubbing bodies together, for example. No lips, tongue, finger, or penis goes into or onto any mouth, rectum, or vagina, at least until HIV antibody tests are completed. Even then, condoms for vaginal or anal sex and condoms or dental dams for oral sex are considered a must today. The more casual the relationship, the more important the safer-sex practices become.

- *No sex with prostitutes.* With their numerous sex partners and high incidence of intravenous drug abuse, male and female prostitutes are simply unacceptable as sex partners in today's world.

## 7.11.2 Effective Barrier Use

Much of the following was previously discussed in chapter 6, but it's important enough to bear repeating:

- *Always* use a barrier such as a latex condom, cut-open condom, or dental dam for vaginal, oral, or anal sex. If your partner balks at barrier use, chapter 6 has a section on how to negotiate condom use. The same approaches are valid for other forms of barriers as well. There are issues of power and responsibility here that need to be addressed if your partner will not use or allow use of a barrier.

- Use latex condoms, rather than natural "skins." Natural "skin" condoms are not useful for disease protection, as their pores are large enough to allow passage of viruses. See chapter 6 for further information on condom selection.

- Dental dams (or condoms cut open lengthwise with scissors) are ideal for oral sex performed on a female.

- Use a new barrier every time you have sex, and check the expiration date.

- Handle the barrier carefully to avoid damaging it with fingernails, teeth, or other sharp objects.

- The male condom must be applied to the erect penis *before any genital or anal contact is made*.
- Ensure that no air is trapped at the end of the male condom.
- Ensure that there is adequate lubrication throughout the sexual activity, always applying a lubricant for anal sex and, when needed, for vaginal sex.
- Use only water-based lubricants such as *K-Y Jelly*. Oil based products, such as petroleum jelly, massage oils, body lotions, shortening, or cooking oil, will weaken latex and should never be used.

# WHERE DO I STAND?
## MY RISK OF HIV

How seriously do you take the threat of HIV infection? About 1 in every 350 Americans is currently infected, many of those are people much like yourself. HIV doesn't always happen to "someone else." Let's rate your behavior as it affects your chance of becoming infected with HIV. Circle the appropriate number for each question.

| | | Almost Always | Sometimes | Almost Never |
|---|---|---|---|---|
| 1. | I restrict my sexual activity to long-term, mutually monogamous relationships. | 4 | 2 | 0 |
| 2. | I move very slowly into a new sexual relationship. | 4 | 2 | 0 |
| 3. | I get to know a prospective sex partner and his or her friends very well before I have sex with that person. | 4 | 2 | 0 |
| 4. | I discuss sexual histories, drug use histories, and the possibility of HIV and other disease transmission with a potential sex partner. | 4 | 2 | 0 |
| 5. | I avoid having sex with someone who may have had a lot of previous sex partners. | 4 | 2 | 0 |
| 6. | I insist on mutual HIV antibody testing before beginning a new sexual relationship. | 4 | 2 | 0 |
| 7. | I strictly avoid sharing the use of any injection, piercing, tattooing, or other item that penetrates my skin. | 4 | 2 | −10 |
| 8. | I avoid entering into a sexual relationship with anyone who uses or may have used street drugs by injection. | 4 | 2 | −4 |
| 9. | I insist on condom or dental dam use in any sexual activity that might expose me to my partner's semen or vaginal secretions. | 4 | 2 | 0 |
| 10. | I avoid anal sex in anything other than a long-term, monogamous relationship and then only with the use of a condom. | 4 | 2 | −4 |

**Total points:** _____

**Interpretation:**

40 points: Congratulations! You should have very little risk of HIV infection.

36–39 points: Your risk of HIV infection appears to be relatively low.

32–35 points: You are placing yourself at some risk of HIV infection.

Less than 32 points: You are taking some unnecessary risks of infection with a potentially fatal virus. Please examine your values and attitudes carefully before it's too late.

▌ Hold the condom firmly against the base of the penis during withdrawal, and withdraw while the penis is still erect to prevent the condom from slipping off.

Even when barriers are not required for birth control purposes, a wise person will insist on their use in any situation other than in a long-term, monogamous relationship.

## 7.11.3   The Alcohol and Other Drugs/HIV Connection

In addition to the injection-drug, needle-sharing, HIV connection, there is a second important drug-HIV relationship. This one holds true of all mood-modifying drugs, including alcohol. Much research (and the personal experience of many people) shows that, after drinking or using other drugs, sexual judgment is impaired (Anderson & Mathieu, 1995; Leigh & Aramburu, 1996; Lemp et al., 1994). After a few drinks, or other drug use, we might become more likely to engage in HIV-risk behavior than when we are sober. We might have sex with someone whom we normally wouldn't consider having sex with. We might not insist on condom use, when under other circumstances we would. For example, a survey of 474 young gay and bisexual males showed a strong association between unprotected anal intercourse and being under the influence of alcohol or nitrites (Lemp et al., 1994).

Gender differences were shown in several studies. Leigh and Aramburu (1996) found that, among college students participating in an interactive computer game, the men, with or without alcohol, were much more likely than the women to choose responses leading to sexual activity and expressed more sexual

Alcohol increases the risk of HIV infection by increasing the likelihood of casual sexual relationships and high-risk practices such as failure to use condoms.

attraction and desire throughout the game. In women only, those in drinking scenarios were more likely than those in nondrinking scenarios to choose to have sex at the end of the scenario.

## 7.11.4   Injection Drug Users

Injection (intravenous) drug users are an extremely difficult group to motivate toward more healthful behavior. The risk of becoming infected with (or passing on) HIV is of little concern to many people whose general lifestyle is self-destructive and shows little regard for their own well-being or that of anyone else. The following messages are appropriate for injection drug users (CDC, 1993a):

▌ Enroll or continue in a drug recovery program (unfortunately in many cities the waiting lists for recovery programs are long).

▌ Do not, under any circumstances, use injection equipment that has already been used by another person.

▌ If you must use injection equipment that has been used by another person, first clean it with bleach and water (which is not certain to remove all HIV, but does reduce the risk of HIV transmission).

## 7.11.5   HIV Prevention Programs

If HIV prevention programs are to be effective, they must reflect the reasons why people engage in high-risk behaviors. Their reason is not usually ignorance, because most people today do know how HIV is transmitted and how to prevent its transmission. Here are some of the things that are known about why people continue to take risks with HIV:

▌ Alcohol and other drugs impair judgment even in people who know the facts of HIV prevention. A study of gay male substance abusers associated sexual risk taking with amount of drug use, difficulty avoiding high-risk sex when aroused, and testing positive for HIV (Paul et al., 1994).

▌ Lack of peer support for safer sex was associated with high-risk behaviors among young gay and bisexual men (Lemp et al., 1994).

▌ One disturbing survey revealed that among 156 HIV-positive gay and bisexual men, those who engaged in high-risk sexual behaviors that placed others at risk of infection showed lower levels of depression and distress and higher feelings of control over their lives than did those who didn't engage in high-risk behaviors. Those with risky behavior were also more likely to report using recreational drugs to reduce tension caused by thoughts about HIV (Robins et al., 1994).

■ A study of lesbian and bisexual women showed that they were aware of how HIV is transmitted, but respond with increased HIV testing, rather than safer-sex practices (Einhorn & Polgar, 1994).

Motivating people to modify their behavior in ways that reduce risk of HIV infection has not proven to be an easy task. The same program will not work with every group of people and in every region. For example, it is unlikely that a prevention program that is effective for the gay male community would be effective for intravenous drug users or heterosexual high school students. A review of HIV prevention programs has shown that effective programs must be based on the underlying social, economic, and cultural factors that influence HIV risk behaviors (CDC, 1995a). Research by the Centers for Disease Control and Prevention suggests that effective programs

■ need to be directed at the local level,

■ need to collect and analyze information regarding the specific and unique aspects of HIV transmission in their communities,

■ should have strong social and behavioral science bases, and

■ should reflect the cultures and needs of the communities for which they are intended.

## 7.11.6  Vaccine Development

Prevention of a disease is always preferable to trying to cure it. The ideal prevention for any disease is an effective vaccine. Vaccines stimulate development of immune responses that destroy or inactivate pathogens as soon as they enter the body.

Vaccines offer the advantages of stopping a disease before it even starts and of being much more cost effective than treating illnesses. Highly effective vaccines have been developed against a wide range of dangerous viral diseases, including polio, measles, rabies, hepatitis A and B, and many more. Smallpox was eliminated from the entire world by immunization.

One complicating factor in developing an HIV vaccine has been the mutability of HIV. An effective anti-HIV vaccine needs to produce immunity against some stable, universally present portion of the HIV particle. Many approaches to producing an HIV vaccine are being or have been tried. Active ingredients in various HIV vaccines include the following:

■ protein from the HIV surface

■ genes for HIV surface proteins incorporated into other viruses

■ proteins from the viral interior

■ the whole virus, after one gene necessary for disease production has been removed

■ dead HIV

■ selected isolated genes from HIV (Boyer, 1997)

It is uncertain at this time whether an effective vaccine will ever be produced, although many scientists are optimistic about the possibility. Many vaccines are currently being tested for the prevention of HIV, but it will still take years of testing to ensure that a vaccine is both safe and effective before it can be released to the general public.

---

## SUMMARY

1. HIV is now present at some level throughout the world.

2. United States trends: decreasing total number of new HIV infections; decreasing numbers of AIDS cases; decreasing numbers of HIV-related deaths; increasing percentages of cases occurring in females, African Americans, Hispanic Americans, and intravenous drug abusers, and through heterosexual transmission. Overall, fewer people are infected in the United States each year than previously.

3. Sixty-two percent of new HIV infections take place between the ages of 10 and 29.

4. HIV is a retrovirus: after entering a human host cell, its RNA genes are reproduced in the form of DNA, which is then incorporated into the chromosomes of the human cell. This is why it is difficult for bodily defenses to eradicate HIV.

5. HIV has a very high mutation rate.

6. Transmission of HIV is almost always by sexual contact with an infected person, sharing injection equipment with an infected person, receiving blood or a blood product from an infected person, virus crossing the placenta, or breast-feeding.

7. About 75 percent of the world's HIV is sexually transmitted. Both homosexual and heterosexual contact can transmit HIV. Anal, vaginal, and oral sex all can transmit HIV.

8. Even people who show no symptoms can be a source of virus to others.

9. Currently, about 10 percent of the world's HIV and 36 percent of new U.S. HIV infections can be directly or indirectly traced to shared injection equipment.

10. Chronic symptoms of HIV infection include enlarged lymph nodes, loss of appetite, diarrhea, weight loss, sweating, fever, and fatigue. Neurological symptoms can include slurred speech, loss of peripheral sensation, memory loss, and general mental deterioration.

11. The number of CD4 (T-helper) cells gradually declines. People with less than 200 CD4 cells per microliter (normal is 2,000 to 4,000) meet the definition of AIDS, have very poor immune function, and are at greater risk for opportunistic infections and cancers.

12. Current HIV screening tests ("AIDS tests") detect antibodies against HIV, not the actual virus.

13. HIV testing should always be accompanied with counseling.

14. Treatment of HIV is directed at suppressing the virus and fighting opportunistic infections.

15. Prevention of HIV infection includes risk-reducing strategies such as sexual abstinence, reduced number of sex partners, careful selection of sex partners, moving slowly into a sexual relationship, applying the safer-sex practices, not having sex with prostitutes, effective use of condoms and other barriers, and not using alcohol or other drugs in a way that impairs sexual judgment. Injection drug users must avoid sharing injection equipment. Vaccines are currently being tested, but it will take years before any vaccine is available to the public.

# CRITICAL THINKING CHALLENGES

1. List the five important time periods of HIV infection. For each interval, state whether an infected person would have a positive HIV test at that time. What would be the likelihood that they could transmit the virus to someone else? What would their health status most likely be?

2. What do you think would be an effective HIV/AIDS education program for the students on your campus? How would you reach the drug users in your city? What approach to HIV education would be most effective for *you?*

3. Do you think anyone—such as health care workers, drug abusers, those applying for insurance or a marriage license, those being admitted to a hospital—should be required to undergo HIV testing? Should everyone be tested? Who should have access to the results? Who should pay for the testing you suggest?

# SEXUAL RESPONSE, DYSFUNCTION, AND THERAPY

## AFTER STUDYING THIS CHAPTER, YOU SHOULD BE ABLE TO

[1] Describe the sources of sexual arousal and explain which parts of the central nervous system are important in the process of sexual arousal.

[2] Describe the characteristics of each of the phases of Masters and Johnson's sexual response cycle, and briefly summarize the criticisms surrounding this model.

[3] Describe Kaplan's triphasic model of sexual response and summarize the advantages of this model.

[4] Contrast the scientific models of human sexual response with the experiences of real people.

[5] List and describe the influences of culture and gender on sexual response.

[6] Summarize the findings regarding the controversial issues of simultaneous and multiple orgasms, female ejaculation, and the existence of a G spot on the wall of the vagina.

[7] Summarize the results of the human search for aphrodisiacs, and describe what is known about those factors that seem to truly enhance sexual response.

[8] Explain how the concept of "sexual dysfunction" is connected to cultural and subjective sexual norms and expectations.

[9] Distinguish among lifelong, acquired, situational, and generalized dysfunctions.

[10] Summarize what is known about hypoactive sexual desire disorder (HSD) and sexual aversion, and briefly describe the general approach to treating these disorders.

[11] Describe the hypothesized origins of the arousal disorders and their likely origins, emphasizing the psychological and physiological factors involved.

[12] List and describe the various treatments for the arousal disorders.

[13] Describe the important features of female and male orgasmic disorders, and summarize what is known about their likely origins.

[14] List and describe two common pain-producing sexual dysfunctions and summarize what is known about their likely origins.

[15] List some of the common medical conditions and medical treatments that can affect sexual desire, arousal, and orgasm.

[16] Summarize the important factors and issues to consider when seeking help for sexual dysfunctions.

[17] Summarize the important points to consider in a critical evaluation of sex therapy.

In this chapter and the next, we will be exploring some of the most intense psychological and physiological aspects of human sexuality. We will discover how the mind and body interact within a cultural context to produce the profound pleasure associated with sexual behavior. This chapter will describe the bodily bases of sexual responsiveness, and the models that sexologists have developed to help us understand what happens to our bodies during sexual arousal. We will also explore several of the issues and controversies that surround sexual arousal and response, and some of the problems that can occur in sexual functioning.

## 8.1 THE PHYSICAL BASES OF SEXUAL RESPONSE

How does sexual arousal begin? The originating stimulus is external and at other times it's internal. Sometimes it's difficult to separate the two. For example, you might see someone or something that has erotic charge for you, or you might hear a romantic song or poem. Perhaps someone you care for holds your hand or kisses your lips. You might even respond to a particular odor—the billion-dollar scent industry certainly hopes so. Some external stimulus like one of these enters your nervous system via your senses and is combined with a whole array of personal memories, learned associations, cultural norms, and uniquely individual reactions to produce the physiological responses of sexual arousal. Or you might be doing something completely nonsexual—waiting for a history lecture to begin or sitting in traffic—and suddenly you begin a sexual fantasy that results in physiological arousal (Tortora & Grabowski, 1993). Human beings find sexual arousal pleasant, yet no one requires sexual activity in order to live or even to be healthy.

### 8.1.1 The Central Nervous System: The Brain and Spinal Cord

#### The Brain

Whether sexual arousal begins from internal or external stimuli, the brain is really at the center of our experience of sexual arousal or pleasure.

The brain consists of three parts: hindbrain, midbrain, and forebrain (fig. 8.1). Many parts of the brain are involved in various aspects of sexual behavior (for example, the hypothalamus with the pituitary regulates menstruation, ovulation, and sperm production), but when we are concerned with sexual responsiveness, the **limbic system** (a group of structures encircling the inner brain) and the **cerebral cortex**

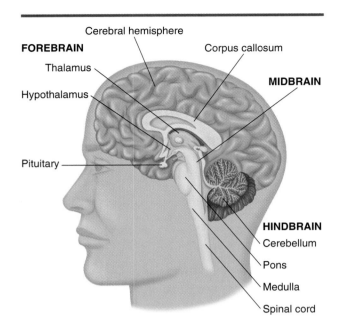

**FIGURE 8.1** A view of the middle of the brain, split from top to bottom.

(the outermost part of the forebrain) are most central to our discussion. The limbic system plays an important role in producing and modifying emotional behavior and is active in regulating sexual behavior (fig. 8.2). Because the limbic system has a primary function in emotions, such as sexual feelings, pleasure, affection, anger and rage, it is sometimes called the emotional brain. And because stimulation of some parts of the limbic system produces sexual arousal, some regard these parts as pleasure centers (Tortora & Grabowski, 1993). The cerebral cortex controls thinking, language, memory, and fantasy. It is also associated with conscious behavior and interprets sensory input as sexual turn-ons or turn-offs.

There are extensive connections between the cerebral cortex and the limbic system, which explains the sometimes difficult interactions between emotions and rationality. Sexuality is one of several areas of life where emotions sometimes overcome logic, or vice versa. Thus, there is no single sex center in the brain, but it is clear that both the limbic system and the cerebral cortex play important roles in initiating, organizing, and controlling sexual arousal and response (Carlson, 1995).

One important thing to keep in mind as we discuss the neural bases of sexual responsiveness: While the language used tends to make it sound as though some kind of automatic machinery is at work, our individual sexual responses are more like an original work of art. That is, even though all paintings are made up of the same basic materials—canvas, oil

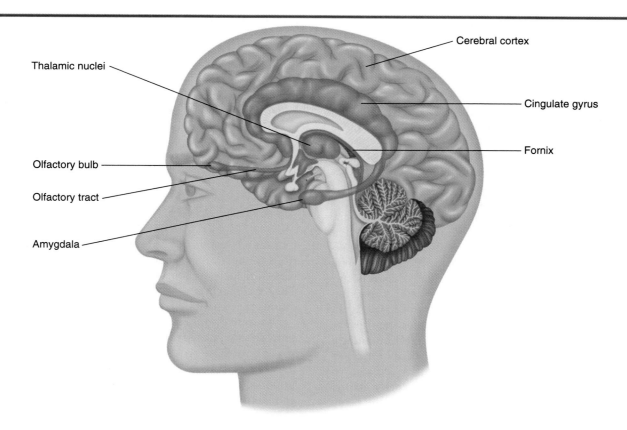

**FIGURE 8.2** Inside the brain are structures known as the limbic system (shown in purple). The parts of the limbic system that are involved in sexual arousal are known as the pleasure centers.

paints, mixed paint colors, well-established techniques for applying them to the canvas, and so on—*a painting is an original, one-of-a-kind creation with its own essence*. Similarly, your or a partner's particular sexual preferences, or combinations of responses, are part of your uniqueness. A very important and rewarding aspect of a loving sexual relationship is to discover and share a partner's unique responses as well as your own. Does he or she become more aroused by a gentle kiss on the small of the back, or by the sight of nicely rounded buttocks? Explicit sexual language can be a turn-on to one person but a turn-off to someone else. Human sexual arousal is truly a celebration of human diversity, because not only are each person's arousal preferences highly individual, but virtually any stimulus can potentially become arousing.

## The Spinal Cord

The spinal cord generates, transmits, and receives impulses from peripheral nerves and the brain. The nerves in the spinal cord are ordered into a scheme in which higher centers control lower centers. Vaginal

lubrication, erection, and ejaculation reflex centers, for example, are located in lower centers that are controlled by nerves located near the base of the spinal cord. This is relevant for understanding sexual functioning in the presence of a spinal cord injury (see chapter 10). Some reflexes operate only on an involuntary level. Erection of the penis, vulva, or breasts occurs involuntarily: we have little control over these responses. Nor can we "will" an erection by thinking about it intensely enough. Other reflexes, such as ejaculation, can be influenced by thought processes and then brought under some voluntary control; for example, some men think about recent sports statistics to delay ejaculation and thus prolong their lovemaking.

| limbic system (lim′bik) | a group of structures in the brain involved with emotions and motivation |
|---|---|
| cerebral cortex | a part of the brain involved in thinking, memory, and language |

## 8.1.2   The Autonomic Nervous System

The **autonomic nervous system (ANS)** is a special network of nerves that connects the central nervous system to internal organs such as the heart, stomach, and glands. Our sexual response is closely tied to the two subdivisions of the ANS: the *sympathetic* division and the *parasympathetic* division. Nerve fibers from each of these two divisions can affect the same organ. For instance, an organ might be activated by impulses from one division and inhibited by impulses from the other.

During sexual arousal, parasympathetic impulses cause the arteries in the penis and around the vaginal walls to relax, or dilate, so blood can rush in. The rise in internal blood pressure in the penis compresses the veins that normally drain the penis, and the penis becomes enlarged and erect. A parallel process occurs in women. The parasympathetic division causes arteries associated with erectile tissue to dilate. As the inflow of blood increases, erectile tissues engorge and swell, ultimately resulting in clitoral erection and the lubrication that prepares the genital tissue for possible insertion. Parasympathetic impulses are also responsible for contractions of the Cowper's glands, providing a small amount of lubrication to the penis. However, ejaculation and orgasm are produced by the actions of the sympathetic system.

## 8.1.3   Hormones and Sexual Interest

**Androgens** play a complex role in sexual interest and motivation (**libido**). Testosterone is the hormone associated with sexual interest and desire in both men and women. In men, 6 to 8 milligrams of testosterone are produced daily, mostly by the testes and partly by the adrenal glands. In women, 0.5 milligram of testosterone is produced daily, primarily by the adrenal glands. This difference does not mean that women have less sexual drive compared to men. Women's bodies appear to be much more sensitive to the effects of testosterone (Bancroft, 1984; Persky et al., 1982).

A minimal amount of testosterone appears necessary to "turn on," or activate, the sexual response systems of men and women. Increased levels of testosterone do not increase sexual desire and can have a variety of negative physical effects (Alexander et al., 1997).

Levels of testosterone *below* the minimum amount needed for arousal can lead to reduced sexual interest. Men who have been **castrated**, and thus have a significantly lowered testosterone level, usually show a gradual loss of sexual desire. Men who were sexually experienced before castration show a more gradual decline in sexual activity compared to those who were sexually inexperienced at the time of castration. Thus, learning, attitudes, and memory are important aspects of sexual interest among men (Leshner, 1978). Drugs that reduce levels of androgens, such as testosterone, in the blood (antiandrogens) also lead to reduced sexual desire (Money, 1987). In women, the removal of the adrenal glands and ovaries leads to a gradual loss of sexual interest. When these women are administered androgens, they experience heightened sexual desire (Kaplan & Owett, 1993; Sherwin, Gelfand, & Brender, 1985).

---

## 8.2   MODELS OF HUMAN SEXUAL RESPONSE

Our sexual responses are both fascinating and mysterious to most of us. They are a source of intense sensual satisfaction and unique personal pleasuring. They are also important in creating some of the conditions that facilitate reproduction.

In spite of our fascination with human sexual responsiveness, until recently little was actually known about how these processes actually occurred. Early in the century, Havelock Ellis (1906) summarized sexual response only with the terms **tumescence** (swelling) and **detumescence**. Freud and his followers wrote about female orgasm, but their ideas were not based on any scientific evidence. During the 1950s, there were controversies over whether women could have more than one orgasm at a time, and over the true nature of vaginal lubrication. But it was not until the 1960s that William Masters and Virginia Johnson offered the first scientific understanding of the details of the physiological processes involved in sexual response.

### 8.2.1   Masters and Johnson's Research

In their landmark work *Human Sexual Response* (1966), Masters and Johnson described how they monitored and measured the physiological responses of 694 volunteers as they experienced sexual arousal and orgasm in a specially equipped laboratory. Based on their observations and measurements, they developed their model of the **sexual response cycle**. Their study of over 10,000 response cycles in women and 2,500 response cycles in men led to the conclusion that the sexual responses of both sexes are basically quite similar. In their later works, including one dedicated to sexual response among those with a homosexual or bisexual orientation (*Homosexuality in Perspective*, 1979), Masters and Johnson were able to conclude that the sexual response cycle is the same whether due to oral or anal stimulation, self-stimulation by the hand or vibrator, or stimulation during intercourse. Nor does it matter if a partner is of the same or the other sex.

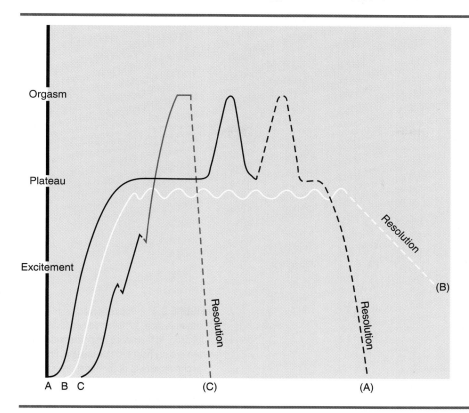

**FIGURE 8.3**    Typical sexual response pattern in women, as observed by Masters and Johnson. Three basic patterns are possible in a woman's sexual response. Pattern A resembles the man's pattern (fig. 8.4) except for the possibility of multiple orgasms without falling below the plateau level. Variations on this are Pattern B, which represents the nonorgasmic arousal, and Pattern C, which represents intense female orgasm that most resembles the male pattern in its intensity and rapid resolution.

The Masters and Johnson findings have been widely accepted and often serve as a standard against which other comparable research is measured (Adams, 1980). Their work has also provided a glossary of descriptive terms for sexual arousal that is now in near-universal usage. Yet despite Masters and Johnson's attention to scientific rigor, their work has been subject to a number of criticisms.

First, some critics contend that their research represents a narrow and incomplete view of human sexual response. It is seen as male-centered and tends to overemphasize the importance of the male sexual organs (Chalker, 1994; Tiefer, 1991). Other critics see Masters and Johnson's work as conceptually and scientifically invalid because they had the concept of a "sexual response cycle" in mind *before* the research began, and volunteers were selected only if they were sexually experienced and were easily orgasmic, that is, if their responses already "fit" the concept of the sexual response cycle model. Many scholars believe their work tends to reduce or ignore other important aspects of sexuality, such the influences of culture, love, and motivation on sexual responsiveness (Tiefer, 1994). As was stated earlier in this text, some believe that Masters and Johnson's first work should be more accurately entitled *The Sexual Responses of Relatively Affluent Americans Who Volunteer to Have Orgasms while Monitored by Scientists.* Yet there is no doubt that the work of Masters and John-

son has increased our knowledge of sexual response tremendously.

## 8.2.2    Masters and Johnson's Four-Phase Model

Masters and Johnson divided the sexual response cycle into four phases: *excitement, plateau, orgasm,* and *resolution* (figs. 8.3 and 8.4). Although these phases are described separately, a person experiencing sexual arousal perceives no break or gap between

| | |
|---|---|
| **autonomic nervous system (ANS)** (o-tō-nom'ik) | the part of the nervous system that controls glands and involuntary muscles |
| **androgens** | any of the male hormones, including testosterone |
| **libido** (li-be'do) | the sexual drive |
| **castration** | removal of the testicles |
| **tumescence** | swelling, such as that caused by vasocongestion |
| **detumescence** | the subsiding of tumescence, or swelling |
| **sexual response cycle (SRC)** | the cycle of sexual arousal and response |

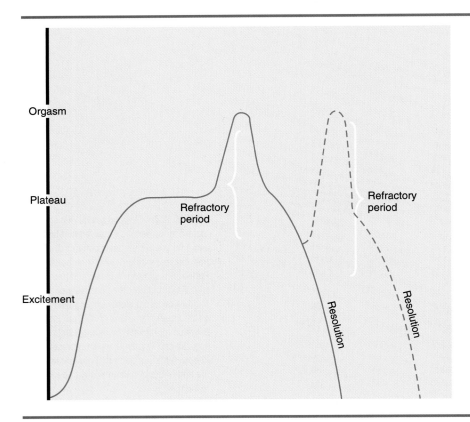

Orgasm

Plateau

Refractory period

Refractory period

Excitement

Resolution

Resolution

**FIGURE 8.4** Typical sexual response pattern in men, as observed by Masters and Johnson. In their basic response pattern, men usually have a single orgasm. For a second orgasm to occur during the same arousal, a refractory period must separate the two orgasms.

the phases. Both in perceived feeling and in physical response, the phases blend together to form a continuum.

The changes that take place in women and men during sexual arousal are due to two major processes that begin early in the response cycle: vasocongestion and myotonia. **Vasocongestion** is the engorgement of blood vessels from an increased flow of blood into the genital organs and nipples of both sexes, as well as the female breast. Because of this pooling of blood, congested tissue becomes swollen, red, and warm, and these areas feel full.

Most noticeable is the swelling of those organs containing erectile tissue—the clitoris, labia, vaginal opening, and penis (figs. 8.5–8.7). Vasocongestion in women will also lead to nipple erection and increased breast size (fig. 8.8). Vasocongestion occurs at about the same rate in men and women.

The increased muscle tension of **myotonia** leads to voluntary and involuntary muscle contractions. During sexual arousal myotonia becomes widespread and produces facial grimaces, spasms in the feet and hands, and finally the spasms of orgasm. Myotonia occurs somewhat slower than vasocongestion. Now let's take a look at the specific changes associated with these two processes all through the sexual response cycle.

### Excitement Phase

Both physiological and psychological stimuli can lead to widespread vasocongestion involving both superficial and deep tissue, especially in the pelvic area (tables 8.1 and 8.2).

In women, the first changes occur in the vagina, where the buildup of blood causes the vaginal walls to darken in color and vaginal lubrication to begin, often within ten to thirty seconds of the onset of stimulation. A **transudate**, or plasma fluid, seeps through the walls of the vagina. This is not a glandular secretion. Beads of droplets appear first, and these combine to cover the inner lining of the vagina, the labia, and the vaginal opening. Lubrication takes longer if a woman is lying down. The consistency of the lubricant varies and the amount produced ranges from very slight to copious. Women beyond menopause produce less lubricant because the vaginal walls have become thinner. The amount of lubricant does *not* indicate a woman's psychological readiness for penetration.

Vasocongestion in women causes the clitoris to swell and elongate, the labia majora to flatten, and the labia minora to expand and extend outward. The vaginal canal begins to elongate and the uterus begins to elevate. Women who have had children have more rapid vasocongestion. Women who have breast-fed

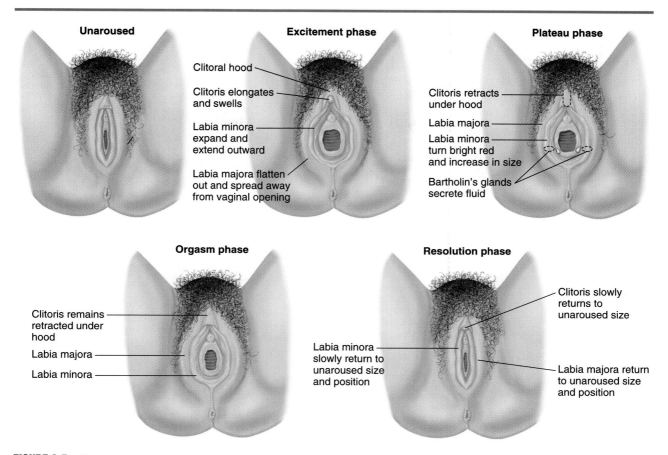

**Unaroused**

**Excitement phase**

Clitoral hood
Clitoris elongates and swells
Labia minora expand and extend outward
Labia majora flatten out and spread away from vaginal opening

**Plateau phase**

Clitoris retracts under hood
Labia majora
Labia minora turn bright red and increase in size
Bartholin's glands secrete fluid

**Orgasm phase**

Clitoris remains retracted under hood
Labia majora
Labia minora

**Resolution phase**

Clitoris slowly returns to unaroused size
Labia minora slowly return to unaroused size and position
Labia majora return to unaroused size and position

**FIGURE 8.5** Changes in a woman's external genitals during the sexual response cycle.

infants typically undergo a breast enlargement of up to 25 percent of their unaroused state. Those who have not breast-fed have comparatively little breast size change.

In men, vasocongestion produces penile erection. For both men and women, the rate of erection is affected by factors such as age, alcohol intake, and fatigue. In young men, erection can begin as quickly as three to eight seconds after stimulation begins. An erection might occur, subside, and reoccur as stimulation varies. The scrotal sac pulls upward from the body, and the testes enlarge and become elevated within the scrotum (fig. 8.7). Penile response has been of concern to men, and various cultures have developed some rather imaginative recommendations regarding ways to keep the penis erect and hard (see "Dimensions of Diversity: Maximizing Penile Arousal").

Nipple erection occurs in both sexes, especially in response to direct stimulation, but it is more noticeable in women (fig. 8.8). About 75 percent of women and some men develop a rosy **sex flush**, which begins on the upper abdomen and spreads over the chest. This might be more noticeable in the plateau phase.

Myotonia increases all through the body. There is increase in heart rate and blood pressure.

### Plateau Phase

The **plateau phase** is a continuation of the events of the excitement phase, and it involves the advanced state of arousal that precedes orgasm. The plateau phase might last a few seconds, several minutes, or longer. If protracted for a long period of time, the

| | |
|---|---|
| **vasocongestion** (vas-ō-kon-jest'shun) | the filling of blood vessels in response to sexual arousal |
| **myotonia** (mi-ō-tō′nē-ah) | muscle tension |
| **transudate** (trăns′ū-dāt) | a plasma fluid |
| **sex flush** | a temporary reddish color of the skin resulting from sexual excitement |
| **plateau phase** | the second phase of Masters and Johnson's sexual response cycle, the phase of sustained sexual arousal |

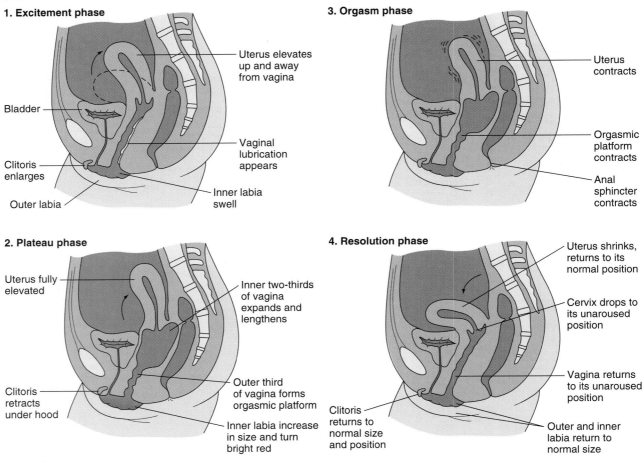

**FIGURE 8.6**  Changes in the vagina and uterus during the sexual response cycle.

plateau phase can be of major enjoyment in lovemaking. During sensual play, the intensity of plateau may rise and fall somewhat, but for most individuals the buildup of sexual tension will trigger orgasm (climax).

There is no clear physical sign in either sex that indicates the onset of plateau. The signs of excitement merely become more pronounced: pulse rate, blood pressure, and breathing rate continue to increase. The sex flush, or rashlike discoloration, spreads from the center of the lower chest out to the breasts, upper chest, neck, and head.

Vasocongestion continues and intensifies. In women, this engorgement results in the formation of the **orgasmic platform**, a narrowing of the outer third of the vagina. The inner two-thirds of the vagina expands in width and depth ("balloons out") and the uterus becomes fully elevated ("tented"). As the clitoris swells, it becomes erect and hard, and it changes position. As it becomes erect, it pulls up (retracts) under the hood. This is expected because the shaft of the clitoris is embedded in tissue and is unable to swing away from the body as does an erect penis. The

labia minora tend to develop a bright red color in women who have not borne children and a deep wine color in those who have. The size of the vaginal opening may become smaller and "grips" whatever might penetrate the vagina. As the areolae of the breasts further engorge, they tend to hide the erect nipples. The Bartholin's glands secrete a mucuslike fluid.

In men there is little change in the penis, except for an increase in the size of the coronal ridge, and the glans might turn a purplish color. The testes increase in size by 50 to 100 percent, and preejaculatory fluid from the Cowper's gland might be secreted by the penis (sometimes referred to as "love drops" or "pre-cum").

In both women and men, myotonia intensifies during the plateau phase and becomes quite marked throughout the body, especially in the face, neck, arms, and legs. **Carpopedal spasms** may occur. These are spastic contractions of the muscles of the hands and feet that cause these appendages to appear clawlike. Pelvic thrusting becomes involuntary late in the plateau phase. Pulse rates, blood pressure, and breathing rate continue to rise.

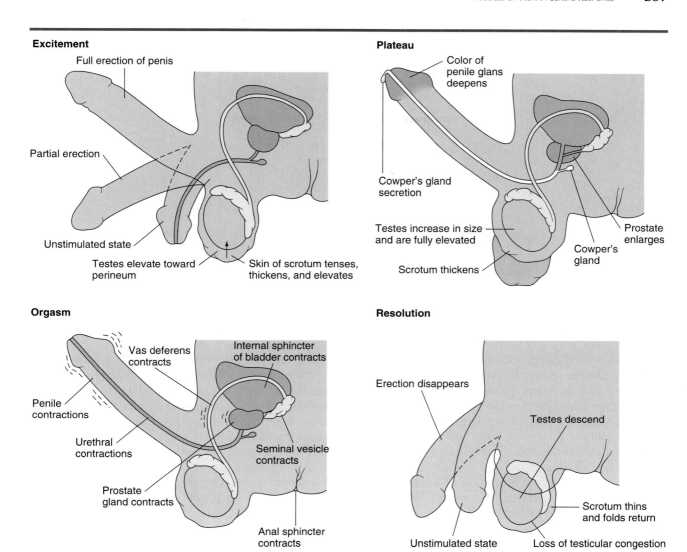

**Excitement**

Full erection of penis

Partial erection

Unstimulated state

Testes elevate toward perineum

Skin of scrotum tenses, thickens, and elevates

**Plateau**

Color of penile glans deepens

Cowper's gland secretion

Testes increase in size and are fully elevated

Scrotum thickens

Prostate enlarges

Cowper's gland

**Orgasm**

Vas deferens contracts

Internal sphincter of bladder contracts

Penile contractions

Urethral contractions

Prostate gland contracts

Seminal vesicle contracts

Anal sphincter contracts

**Resolution**

Erection disappears

Testes descend

Unstimulated state

Loss of testicular congestion

Scrotum thins and folds return

**FIGURE 8.7**    Changes in the man's genitals during the sexual response cycle.

## Orgasmic Phase

**Orgasm** (or *climax*) is perceived by both women and men as an intense, highly pleasurable experience in which the person might feel that time is standing still. Thought is momentarily suspended, and there is a rush of physical sensations. These feelings come from the sudden discharge of neuromuscular tensions accumulated from intensive pelvic vasocongestion and skeletal myotonia. This release occurs in a series of involuntary and pleasurable muscular contractions of the vaginal barrel, uterus, and anus in a woman, and the urethral bulb, urethra, penis, and anus in a man. Orgasms are the shortest phase of the sexual response cycle, and typically last longer in women than in men. This is probably because the woman's whole pelvic area is engorged, rather than just the genitals, as occurs in men.

For both sexes orgasm is accompanied by *tachycardia*, an excessively rapid heart action. The pulse rate can be 100 to 180 beats per minute (compared with a resting state of 70 to 80 beats per minute).

| | |
|---|---|
| **orgasmic platform** | the narrowing of part of the vagina during sexual arousal due to vasocongestion |
| **carpopedal spasms** | contractions of the muscles of the hands and feet during sexual arousal |
| **orgasm** (orˊgasm) | the climax of sexual excitement, characterized by intensely pleasurable sensations, muscle contractions, and, in males, ejaculation |

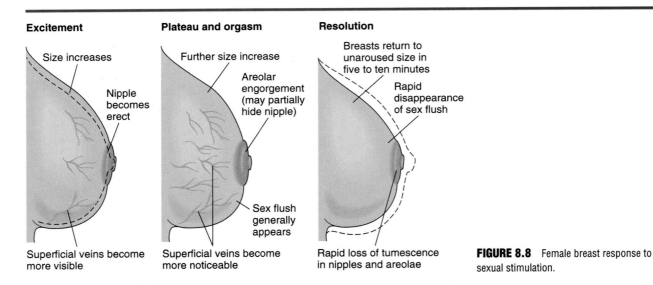

**Excitement**

Size increases

Nipple becomes erect

Superficial veins become more visible

**Plateau and orgasm**

Further size increase

Areolar engorgement (may partially hide nipple)

Sex flush generally appears

Superficial veins become more noticeable

**Resolution**

Breasts return to unaroused size in five to ten minutes

Rapid disappearance of sex flush

Rapid loss of tumescence in nipples and areolae

**FIGURE 8.8** Female breast response to sexual stimulation.

Under usual conditions, such tachycardia would be abnormal; during orgasm it is quite normal. Partly as a result of this increased pulse rate, both men and women experience **hypertension** (an increase in blood pressure). Orgasm also causes **hyperventilation**, in which breathing becomes faster and deeper (40 breaths per minute, compared to 18 to 20 breaths per minute when unaroused).

Another physical manifestation of orgasm is intense myotonia in many body muscles. The hands and feet contract and grasp in carpopedal spasms. The person might frown, scowl, or grimace as the facial muscles contract involuntarily. The mouth might open involuntarily in response to the body's need for more oxygen. Severe spastic contractions of the arms, legs, back, and lower abdomen are sometimes apparent. Sometimes these spasms result in backache or aches in the buttocks that are felt the next day. The sex flush also peaks at this time.

Several classic studies have demonstrated that the subjective experience of orgasm is virtually the same for both sexes (Vance & Wagner, 1976; Wiest, 1977). Research participants could not distinguish between experiences described by men or by women, and women and men used the same words to describe their sensations.

It is relatively difficult for men to "fake" orgasms; women can do so more easily. Although Victorian women might have been alarmed if they *had* an orgasm, today orgasm is too often stressed as the sign of a lover's "performance" and a mark of "liberated" femininity. With the recent emphasis on female sexual pleasure, some women report feelings of guilt if they do not "produce" an orgasm (Davidson & Moore, 1994b).

*Women's Orgasms:* Women's orgasms always consist of contractions of the orgasmic platform and the muscles around the vagina. The place of the eliciting stimulation does not appear to matter; orgasm can occur from breast stimulation alone. Women's orgasms start as an intense sensation in the clitoris that then moves through the pelvis. There are then three to fifteen contractions of the pelvic muscles around the vaginal barrel. Occurring in 0.8-second intervals, these contractions produce a release of sexual tension. These initial contractions might be followed by three to six slower, weaker ones. The uterus also contracts with wavelike contractions that move from its dome to the cervix. Some women describe a feeling of "falling," "opening up," or of "labor pains." A warmth spreading from the pelvis through the rest of the body may follow. Some women feel sensations of throbbing in the pelvis:

> First tension builds in my body and head, my heart beats, then I strain against my lover, and then there is a second or two of absolute stillness, nonbreathing, during which I know orgasm will come in the next second or two. Then waves, and I rock against my partner and cannot hold him tight enough. It's all over my body, but especially in my abdomen and gut. Afterwards, I feel suffused with warmth and love and absolute happiness. (Hite, 1976, pp. 162–63)

Organs that contain a greater number of nerve endings are more sensitive to sexual stimulation, and in women these nerve endings are most heavily concentrated in the clitoris, especially the glans of the clitoris. There are relatively few nerve endings in the vaginal walls. Sometimes called the "joy button," the clitoris connects to a complex of erectile tissue that extends throughout a woman's genital area.

# DIMENSIONS OF DIVERSITY

## MAXIMIZING PENILE AROUSAL

The responsiveness of the penis to arousal has undoubtedly been a preoccupation of men for ages. To the ancient followers of Islam, the solution was to be found in certain substances that they considered essential to *erotology,* the study of love.

According to Bouhdiba (1985), a traditional treatment to keep the *member* (penis) erect consisted of "steeping (soaking) leeches in good oil and smearing it on the penis." The effectiveness of the treatment is increased if "one leaves the mixture to steep in a bottle that is itself buried in warm manure; this produces a homogenous liniment."

A more demanding assignment was finding ways to make the erection last longer. To accomplish this, the recommended recipe was this:

Five measures of nitrated borax, five measures of lavender seed, dried or powdered, five measures of honey, and five measures of milk. Pound well. Smear the member with a little oil of the product. Massage the member well, sprinkle hot water on it from time to time. When the member is red, wash it and massage it again. This recipe is guaranteed, well tried and effective.

To make an erection especially firm:

One takes the testicles of three (or eight or fourteen) male chickens. One adds green ginger, nutmeg, walnut essence, pimento essence, tubipore, cloves, cinnamon, dried earth from India, palm seeds known as the seeds of intelligence, an ounce of salt from Hyderabad and quarter of an ounce of saffron. Grind, work together and pound with a good skimmed honey. Put the mixture into a glass container. Seal hermetically with a stopper made of a little clay of wisdom.

Leave the mixture to simmer near a fire for three nights and three days until it thickens. Leave it to cool. Form into small balls, the size of chick peas and take the equivalent of a lentil grain whenever one wishes to make love. The member then becomes erect and nothing will be able to soften it unless one drinks a little vinegar.

And finally, another method for a man "acquiring a virile firmness [of the penis] that will win the congratulations of his partner":

A diet of thick honey, almonds, pine kernels or a mixture of onion seeds pounded with honey. One may also rub the member with ass's milk or camel fat, which is a very effective lubricant.

**Source:** Abdelwahab Bouhdiba, *Sexuality in Islam* (London: Routledge & Kegan Paul, 1985) Reprinted by permission.

While some women desire the glans of the clitoris to be touched directly, for others it is so sensitive that direct touching hurts, even when the glans is lubricated. Some women find that stimulating the clitoris for too long a time can actually lead to a drop in arousal.

During vaginal penetration, the swollen inner lips serve as an extension of the vagina. During movement in and out of the vagina the swollen inner lips are pulled, which pulls on the clitoral hood and provides further stimulation to the swollen, retracted glans.

To reach orgasm, most women prefer direct and extended clitoral stimulation. This stimulation may come from masturbation, partner hand-genital caressing, or oral-genital stimulation, or during a coital position that facilitates clitoral stimulation (see chapter 9). One advantage of manual or oral stimulation is that it focuses more directly on clitoral rather than vaginal stimulation. A recent survey of women who use vibrators in both autoerotic and partnered activity reported that vibrator-induced orgasms were more intense than other types (Davis et al., 1996). More-over, over 50 percent of the respondents reported multiple orgasms with vibrator use.

*Men's Orgasms:* For men, orgasm generally includes ejaculation. Although the two are not the same process, they usually occur together. Physiologically, **ejaculation** consists of two phases: **emission** and **expulsion.**

Emission begins with contractions of the genital ducts, accessory glands, and urethral sphincters causing semen to collect in the *urethral bulb,* that portion

| | |
|---|---|
| hypertension | high blood pressure |
| hyperventilation | breathing that is faster and deeper than usual |
| ejaculation (ē-jak-ū-lā´shun) | the expulsion of semen from the penis |
| emission | the first stage of ejaculation, when sperm and semen fill the urethral bulb |
| expulsion | the second stage of ejaculation, when semen is released from the penis |

**TABLE 8.1** PHYSICAL REACTIONS OF A WOMAN DURING THE SEXUAL RESPONSE CYCLE

### Excitement

Onset of vaginal lubrication

Outer lips flatten out and spread away from the vaginal opening

Inner lips engorge with blood and extend outward

Clitoris elongates and widens; glans expands

Uterus begins to elevate (pulls up and away from the vagina)— becomes "tented"

Breasts begin to increase in size late in phase; areolae noticeably swell, and nipples become erect

Sex flush begins to develop

Increase in skeletal muscular tension; increase in respiratory and pulse rates, and in blood pressure

### Plateau

Vaginal barrel increases slightly in width and depth ("balloons"); further engorgement reduces the opening to the outer third of the vagina, which along with the engorged labia minora creates the orgasmic platform

Inner lips increase in size and turn bright red

Uterus fully elevated, creating a "tented" effect with the upper vagina

Noticeable engorgement of areolae

Sex flush may spread over stomach, back, and thighs

Increase in muscle tension; pulse rate, blood pressure, and breathing rates increase

### Orgasm

Strong vaginal contractions of the orgasmic platform (three to five contractions in a mild orgasm; eight to twelve in an intense one); beginning at 0.8-second intervals, contractions gradually diminish in strength and duration

Uterus undergoes contractions, moving from top of uterus downward

Anal sphincter contracts rhythmically and involuntarily

Muscle contractions throughout body; peak hyperventilation, peak pulse rate, and peak blood pressure occur

### Resolution

Orgasmic platform, or outer third of vagina, quickly returns to normal; inner two-thirds of vagina returns to normal more slowly

Outer lips rapidly return to unaroused size and position

Return of inner lips to unstimulated size and unaroused coloration within five to fifteen seconds after orgasm

Return of clitoris to normal position within five to fifteen seconds

Uterus returns to its normal unstimulated position and drops the cervix into the seminal pool on the vaginal floor

Nipples and areolae rapidly lose engorgement; breasts return to normal size more slowly

Sex flush rapidly disappears

Return to normal of breathing and heart rates, and of blood pressure

Relaxation of body muscles

Some women begin perspiring

**TABLE 8.2** PHYSICAL REACTIONS OF THE MAN DURING THE SEXUAL RESPONSE CYCLE

### Excitement

Penis increases in size and becomes erect

Skin of scrotum tenses, thickens, and elevates

Testes elevate and begin to increase in size

Nipples may become erect

Sex flush may occur over chest, neck, face, and forehead

Generalized skeletal muscular tension; increased respiratory and pulse rates, and blood pressure

### Plateau

Slight increase in coronal size due to engorgement; glans may turn reddish-purple

Testes fully elevated against body with marked increase in size (from 50 to 100 percent)

Escape of two to three drops of Cowper's fluid

Feeling of ejaculatory inevitability

Sex flush spreads with higher levels of sexual tension

Further elevation in pulse and breathing rates, and blood pressure

### Orgasm

Ejaculatory contractions along entire length of penile urethra, with expulsion of semen; expulsive contractions start at 0.8-second intervals, and after three to four contractions reduce in frequency and expulsive force

General loss of voluntary muscle control

### Resolution

Rapid loss of about half of erection, slower loss of remainder

Testes rapidly lose enlargement and descend to normal position

Slow loss of nipple erection

Sex flush rapidly disappears

Return of heart and respiratory rates, and blood pressure to prearousal levels

General muscle relaxation

Perspiration reaction in about a third of men

---

of the urethra within the prostate gland. This movement of semen into the urethral bulb causes it to expand, giving the man the feeling he is about to ejaculate. This is called **ejaculatory inevitability** and it lasts for about two to three seconds. At this point, a man cannot be stopped from "coming."

Expulsion begins when the external urethral sphincter relaxes and the muscles at the base of the penis and around the anus contract rhythmically in 0.8-second intervals, propelling the milky semen through the urethra to the outside. This occurs in four to five rhythmic contractions, followed by several weaker and slower ones, though the pattern can differ substantially between men (Masters & Johnson, 1966). The first contractions expel most of the semen and are usually the most pleasurable. Orgasm without ejaculation occurs in certain types of spinal cord injuries and in boys prior to puberty. Some neurological disorders result in ejaculation without the sensation of orgasm.

# GO ASK ALICE

*Dear Alice,*

*When my girlfriend and I make love, she says she gets too wet. She doesn't like it and would like to know if there is anything she can do to lessen the wetness just a bit.*

*Caring*

Dear Caring,

There are two possibilities here. First, it may be that your partner is suffering from cervicitis, an inflammation that is known to cause a copious discharge. Also, if you engage in oral genital sex, it would be wise to have the condition of your own mouth and throat checked medically. Does she wear an IUD? This could also cause a hypersecretion of vaginal fluids.

If a medical exam shows no problem, there is a second set of possibilities. Some women just naturally "ejaculate" lots of fluid upon orgasm. There are some men and women who are incontinent when highly aroused. Keep in mind that for most people, juiciness means sexiness and many would consider this much wetness a blessing. Try keeping a towel nearby and incorporate some sensual drying off into your lovemaking. Make this part of your loveplay.

*Dear Alice,*

*Should a normal man's penis become erect for a certain number of times throughout one day (without any external stimulus)? Or do these erections occur only while a man is sleeping? Plus I have been waking up with no morning erection during the past week. Have I been masturbating too much?*

*Worried*

Dear Worried,

Teenage boys have reflex erections (with no external stimulus) during any time of the day or night. As men get older, these reflex erections become less frequent and direct touching becomes necessary to produce erections. It is not clear how old you are, but you may just be experiencing part of the maturation process, and soon you will start to have erections at more "appropriate" times. And, masturbation may or may not affect your morning erections—you'll see what happens with your own body.

    http:www.mhhe.com/byer6

---

Many men find orgasm from self-stimulation to be stronger, but there are important psychological factors to consider.

> I like intercourse more psychologically than physically. I get a lot of physical pleasure from intercourse, but I can also get that from masturbating. The physical feeling of moving my penis back and forth inside my lover is pleasurable, but probably not as intense as a good hand job or fellatio combined with hands. Psychologically though, there's much to want—the anticipation of putting my penis inside my lover, knowing I'm going to be surrounded by her, warmed by the inside of her. Then, when I first slowly enter her, I want the instant to last and last. (Hite, 1982, p. 322)

## Resolution Phase

After orgasm, the body enters the **resolution phase** and returns to an unaroused state. Orgasm triggers the release of neuromuscular tension, which results in a state of deep body relaxation. Vasoconstriction of blood vessels gives way to vasodilation, so that blood flows out through the veins faster than it flows in through the arteries. The penis, labia, clitoris, nipples, and breasts rapidly lose their vasocongestion and re-

turn to their unaroused state. Within a few minutes, blood pressure and respiration return to their prearousal levels. Most muscle tension has dissipated within five minutes and both women and men feel relaxed and satisfied. In 30 to 40 percent of men and women, perspiration appears on their palms, the soles of their feet, and in some cases over much of their body. Resolution, then, is the reversal of the arousal processes that occurred during the excitement and plateau stages. If there is no additional sexual stimulation, resolution begins immediately after orgasm.

For those who do not experience orgasm, the resolution of myotonia and vasocongestion may be much slower. Some men use the term *blue balls* to refer to the heaviness or discomfort they feel in the

| | |
|---|---|
| **ejaculatory inevitability** | the point at which ejaculation must occur |
| **resolution phase** | the fourth phase of Masters and Johnson's sexual response cycle, in which the body returns to the unaroused state |

**TABLE 8.3**    COMPARISON OF SEX RESPONSE MODELS

| Masters and Johnson | | Excitement | Plateau | Orgasm | Resolution |
|---|---|---|---|---|---|
| Kaplan | Desire | Excitement | | Orgasm | |

testicles when pelvic vasocongestion persists. Women may also experience an uncomfortable pelvic throbbing if arousal is not followed by orgasm. For both men and women, the discomfort will dissipate over time, or can be relieved more quickly by masterbating to orgasm.

In women, orgasm releases the sexual tension. Myotonia and vasocongestion are reversed. The swelling of the areolae and nipples decreases. The sex flush is lost rapidly; the clitoris, vagina, uterus, and labia return to their prearoused sizes; and the bright red color of the labia minora disappears in ten to fifteen seconds.

During resolution in men, erection is lost in two stages. Within the first minute, half of the erection is lost. During the last several minutes the rest of the erection is lost, as the erectile tissue loses its excess of pooled blood. The testes and scrotum return to their prearoused sizes and descend away from the body wall. The scrotum once again regains its wrinkled appearance.

Men experience a **refractory period**, during which they cannot be aroused again. It is not clearly understood why men have a refractory period. It may be due to the depletion of seminal fluids from the fluid-producing glands (prostate and seminal vesicles) or to some neurological inhibition. The length of the refractory period varies according to age, mood, and type of stimulation available. A typical finding is that men in their late thirties cannot be stimulated to erection again until about thirty minutes have passed.

Individuals vary in their reactions during the resolution phase. Some people experience a profound need to rest and sleep. Others feel relaxed but energized. Some want solitude; others want physical closeness. Some want to talk about intimate feelings; others don't. Some people want to eat, others want to drink, and still others might crave the stereotypical cigarette. Couples might need to negotiate carefully what happens during the "afterglow."

### 8.2.3    Kaplan's Triphasic Model

Helen Singer Kaplan is a psychiatrist and sex therapist with decades of experience treating problems in sexual functioning. Informed by her clinical work, Kaplan (1974, 1979) developed a three-phase model: *sexual desire*, *excitement*, and *orgasm* (table 8.3).

Kaplan's model offers several important advantages over that of Masters and Johnson. First, she begins with *desire*, a most important psychological component of sexual response. Also, such a labeling more accurately reflects a person's subjective experience of sexual arousal. In the second phase (*excitement*), she emphasizes the largely physiological changes that involve *vasocongestion* and *myotonia*. She eliminates the plateau stage because it cannot be clearly distinguished as different from increasing excitement. Finally, *orgasm* is marked by the rapid loss of vasocongestion and myotonia. This model does not include a "resolution" phase because these processes do not involve *sexual response*.

The most significant advantage of Kaplan's model is that it is very useful in identifying, classifying, and treating problems in sexual functioning. Problems of *sexual desire* include a very low level of sexual desire, or sexual aversion. Problems involving *excitement* would include inability to have or maintain a penile erection or insufficient vaginal lubrication. *Orgasm*-related problems might include male premature ejaculation or female orgasmic dysfunction (see "Thinking about Sexual Dysfunctions, p. 217).

### 8.2.4    Sexual Response Models and Real People

Some students who read about the processes of sexual arousal and response find that their responses are rather different from what is described. Remember that sexual response is just one more expression of our individuality and uniqueness, so don't expect your responses or those of a partner to follow a prescribed stereotypical model. Here are a few things to keep in mind as you consider these models.

First, people do not all respond alike. Variations from the model do not imply a sexual problem. The models described here are the combined description of many research participants, and no two of them were exactly alike. A composite or average of the volunteers' behavior is being described here.

Second, an individual's responses can fluctuate considerably. These responses depend on what else is going on in our lives and how we are feeling. Stresses, strong feelings, anxieties, and our moods can all influence our sexual responsiveness. Some couples have more trouble than others getting their amorousness "in sync." One partner might feel romantic after a candlelight dinner and a walk in the moonlight. The other feels sexiest the first thing in the morning. Not being "in the mood" will surely affect our responsiveness, and that's perfectly understandable and normal.

Third, our sexual responses occur as a continuum, and we move through the sexual response cycle without interruption. The idea of distinct phases is another example of those "constructions" that are useful to researchers and practitioners but are not a part of the actual experience of our eroticism.

Fourth, one loses out by focusing on the mechanics of sex rather than the totality of the experience. Some individuals engage in **spectatoring** (like *spectators* at a performance). Here, a person carefully watches, monitors, grades, and compares his or her sexual performance. Such individuals set up certain standards of performance that they expect to meet or exceed. Spectatoring interferes with becoming lost in an erotic experience.

Fifth, sexual experiences vary considerably. To expect "mind-blowing" responses every time we engage in sexual behavior is unrealistic.

## 8.3 ISSUES AND CONTROVERSIES ABOUT SEXUAL RESPONSIVENESS

### 8.3.1   Culture and Sexual Response

Aside from the many individual and situational factors involved in sexual response (level of intimacy, the emotional context of the sexual act, etc.), our physical responses are also influenced by our culture.

A traditional Dani (New Guinea) married couple typically would not engage in intercourse for five or more years after the birth of a child (Heider, 1992), and the Dani seem to have no tension about this cultural norm. Among the Samoans, men get ready for sexual activity by reading poetry to their lovers or by singing them romantic songs, even before any touching begins. In parts of New Guinea, a sexual encounter begins with partners scratching and biting each other in a rather aggressive manner.

In many societies female orgasm is completely unknown, and in others vaginal lubrication is considered "unfeminine" and husbands will complain about it (Ecker, 1993).

In some Asian cultures, the goal of sexual activity is to postpone orgasm by extending sexual arousal for hours. These sexual practices are part of the spiritual traditions of yoga, Buddhism, Hinduism, and Taoism (Stubbs, 1992). By contrast, in our culture there seems to be a striving for sexual satisfaction and gratification by concentrating on genital response. This makes orgasm "the goal," so whatever a couple does before orgasm is called "foreplay"—that is, it is

"merely play" before the orgasm. In this cultural construction of the sex act, orgasm marks the "end" of the sexual experience. Notice that we do not really have a word to describe what we do after orgasm. The contrived word *afterplay* continues the theme that orgasm is the goal.

Within our own society, ethnicity appears to affect sexual response, especially for women. According to the National Health and Social Life Survey (Laumann et al., 1994), 26 percent of white American women reported they *always* had an orgasm during sex with their primary partner, compared to 38 percent of African-American women and 34 percent of Latinas. Regardless of ethnicity, about 75 percent of men reported they always had orgasms (Laumann et al., 1994).

### 8.3.2   Gender and Sexual Response

It is a commonly held belief in our culture that sex is more often on the minds of men than of women. Now there's some evidence to support this. According to the National Health and Social Life Survey (NHSLS), 54 percent of the American men surveyed stated they thought about sex every day, while only 19 percent of the women did. Also, in a sample of college students, Beck, Bozman, and Qualtrough (1991) found that male respondents experienced overt sexual desire more often compared to female respondents.

It is also a commonly held belief in our culture that women "take longer" to become aroused to the point of orgasm. This belief is not supported by the evidence. When women masturbate, they typically reach orgasm in under four minutes, which is very close to the length of time that men require (Masters & Johnson, 1966). During self-stimulation a woman can provide exactly the type and intensity of stimulation she needs at any moment.

Women with premarital orgasmic experience, whether through self-stimulation or with a partner, had orgasms more than twice as often during their first year of marriage. About 4 to 10 percent of adult women have never reached orgasm (Davidson & Darling, 1989). Nevertheless, most of these women report high levels of sexual and marital satisfaction (Jayne, 1981). Thus, we see that for some women the

| | |
|---|---|
| **refractory period** | for men, a period after orgasm during which they cannot have an erection or an orgasm |
| **spectatoring** | a process whereby a person monitors or evaluates his or her sexual performance |

occurrence of orgasm is not a defining feature of whether a sexual encounter or relationship is satisfying.

It is known that women show greater variability in their sexual response patterns than do men, and this has led to a number of speculations about the nature of the female orgasm. Sigmund Freud (1905) claimed there are two types of female orgasm: *clitoral orgasm* and *vaginal orgasm*. He wrote that that "sexually mature" woman reached orgasm through the deep penile thrusting of intercourse, and that "sexually immature" women reached orgasm through direct clitoral stimulation. Some women spent years in psychoanalysis hoping to mature sufficiently to have vaginal orgasms during intercourse.

Masters and Johnson (1966) clearly established three important facts about women's sexual response: (a) The clitoris is a female sex organ whose sole purpose is providing orgasmic pleasure, (b) effective clitoral stimulation is always involved in producing orgasm, and (c) all female orgasms are physiologically the same regardless of the location of the stimulation. In other words, an orgasm always consists of contractions of the orgasmic platform, whether stimulation is clitoral, vaginal, anal, or at the breast. While a woman (or a man, for that matter) might psychologically *prefer* one type of stimulation to another (e.g., oral stimulation of the clitoris, or penile thrusting in the vagina), the physiological events that define an orgasm are always the same.

### 8.3.3 Simultaneous Orgasm

Some couples strive for both partners to have orgasms at the same time (*simultaneous orgasm*), in the belief that this provides a unique level of gratification. Some partners do reach orgasm at about the same time, either by coincidence or by adjusting the level of arousal by having one partner hold back and pace his or her response until both partners can come together. However, most couples find this difficult, especially because individuals differ in the type of stimulation they prefer just prior to orgasm (Masters & Johnson, 1966). In a study of female nurses (Darling, Davidson, & Cox, 1991), only 17 percent of those surveyed experienced orgasm at about the same time as their partner. Simultaneous orgasm, separate orgasms, or even whether orgasm occurs at all seem to have little to do with sexual compatibility. Mutual enjoyment of the sexual activities is a much more reliable indicator of compatibility.

### 8.3.4 Multiple Orgasms

Kinsey et al. (1953) found that 14 percent of women reported experiencing multiple orgasms. Masters and Johnson (1966) defined multiple orgasms as the oc-currence of one or more additional orgasms within a short period of time, *before* the body's return to a "normal" state of arousal. Women might enjoy a series of orgasms if effective stimulation continues (Chalker, 1994). A recent study (Darling, Davidson, & Jennings, 1991) of 720 women found that 47 percent reported single orgasms as being most usual, while 43 percent reported having experienced multiple orgasms during some form of sexual activity (masturbation, manual or oral stimulation, or intercourse). Because many women are able to maintain a high level of sexual arousal following an orgasm, they can experience several orgasms in succession. The use of vibrators can increase this substantially. If a woman can direct the location or pressure of stimulation on the clitoris (most likely during masturbation, or by directing manual or oral stimulation by a partner), she is more likely to experience repeated orgasms. Researchers have shown that women who masturbate and women with female partners are more likely to reach initial orgasm and to continue to additional orgasms (Athanasiou, Shaver, & Tavris, 1970).

Masters and Johnson also found that some men below the age of thirty experienced multiple orgasm and ejaculation, without a refractory period. Other men reported reaching two to ten orgasms before ejaculation occurred (Robbins & Jensen, 1978). These multiorgasmic men were able to control ejaculation until the final orgasm and described the final orgasm as the most intense. Dunn and Trost (1989) also found some men to have "dry" or nonejaculatory orgasms, with little loss of erection between orgasms, especially if sexual stimulation continued. Chia and Arava (1996) claim that most men can learn to become multiorgasmic through a combination of physical and spiritual self-development.

### 8.3.5 Female Ejaculation?

In a study of 2,350 professional women in Canada and the United States, 40 percent report a release of fluid at the moment of orgasm (Darling, Davidson, & Conway-Welch, 1990). The nature of this fluid and its source is a continuing controversy. Some researchers believe the fluid is urine that is involuntarily released during orgasm. Yet other findings have shown this "ejaculate" to be high in *prostatic acid phosphatase* (PAP), a chemical known to be secreted by the prostate gland in men. This has led to suggestions that perhaps the fluid comes from the *Skene's glands* (often seen as *homologous* to the male prostate gland). Autopsy studies have revealed the presence of some prostate-like glandular tissue containing substances known to be produced by the male prostate. Still other researchers have found the fluid to be chemically indistinguishable from urine. Still other researchers contend that this fluid is released only when a woman has reached a sufficient state of arousal, and this might explain why "female ejaculation" occurs so irregularly (Darling, Davidson, & Conway-Welch, 1990).

### 8.3.6   The G Spot

Recent studies have suggested that some women have an area of erotic sensitivity on the front wall of the vagina that swells during sexual arousal and, if stimulated further, can lead to a very intense orgasmic experience. This area has been called the **Grafenberg spot**, or **G spot**, after Ernest Grafenberg, the physician who first described it during the 1950s (Ladas, Whipple, & Perry, 1982). Located about halfway between the pubic bone and the cervix (fig. 8.9), its size varies from that of a small bean during its unaroused state to the size of a dime or larger during arousal.

Some scientists believe that such an area exists in only a small percentage of women, and that when it is present, its location is *not* a clearly defined "spot" (Alzate, 1990). Stimulation of the whole anterior wall of the vagina seems to result in more sexual arousal than stimulation of the back wall (Levin, 1993).

A woman or her partner might try to locate this area. Use two clean, lubricated fingers to press gently into the front wall of the vagina. Or during intercourse a penis could stimulate this area in the woman-above or rear-entry positions. When stimulated, the spot might provide a pleasurable feeling, a slight feeling of discomfort, or the feeling of needing to urinate. With more stimulation, the area might swell somewhat, and some women report a strong feeling of pleasure. Further research is needed to prove the existence of a G spot. All that is known at present is that some women are more sensitive to vaginal stimulation (Ladas, 1989). Ultimately, this whole debate might be another sign of the diversity of human sexual responsiveness.

### 8.3.7   Aphrodisiacs: Old-Fashioned and New-Fangled

Aphrodisiacs are substances that are used to produce, intensify, or extend sexual arousal. Sometimes they are meant to produce orgasms or give someone sexual mastery over another. The human search for such substances appears to go back to the beginning of recorded history. The ancient Egyptians recommended consuming dried, powdered crocodile penises for these purposes. In many cultures, objects that resembled sex organs were prepared and ingested. These included oysters, clams, asparagus, stag horns (that's probably where our modern expression "horny" originates), bird beaks, and more recently, the horn of the white rhinoceros. This last creature has been hunted to near extinction because a powder made from its horn is so prized in China and other parts of Asia. Over more recent centuries, Spanish Fly, a powder made from the dried bodies of a particular beetle found in southern Europe, was touted as an aphrodisiac. It actually irritates the urethra and other internal tissues, thus creating feelings of warmth and "excitement" in the genital area. However, many deaths resulted from its use. Today, the active ingredient in Spanish Fly, *cantharidin*, is used to burn off warts.

More recently, the people of Cameroon, in Africa, have noted the effects of *yohimbine* on the vasocongestion of the penis (Brody, 1993), but more controlled studies fail to show a consistent effect (Rowland, Kallan, & Slob, 1997). Today, in our society, books and magazines promote certain foods and herbs to increase libido or sexual capacity (Bullough & Bullough, 1994). Some men inject certain substances directly into the penis to produce a dependable erection. These substances include *papaverine* and *alprostadil* (Crowley & Rogers, 1997).

Some people inhale *amyl nitrate* to ostensibly heighten sensations of arousal and orgasm. These "poppers" or "snappers" dilate blood vessels in the brain and genitals and thus facilitate erection and prolong orgasm. They can also cause dizziness,

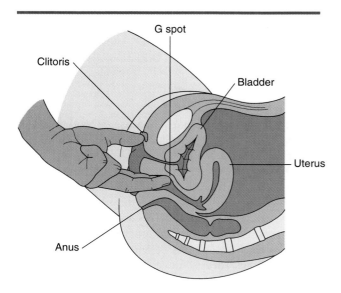

**FIGURE 8.9**   To locate the Grafenberg spot (G spot), a woman or her partner should use two fingers to press gently into the front wall of the vagina.

---

**Grafenberg spot (G spot)**      a sensitive area on the
   (grăf´en-burg)      front wall of the vagina

## "KEGELS" AND INCREASED SEXUAL PLEASURE

The *pubococcygeus muscle* (PC) lies on the pelvic floor in both women and men. When contracted rhythmically during orgasm, the PC muscle can increase sensations of pleasure. Regular exercise can strengthen this muscle. Strengthening the PC muscle can result in stronger and more pleasurable orgasms in men. Greater control of this muscle has allowed some men to delay ejaculation: for some, relaxing the muscle delays ejaculation, while for others, contracting it does the job. Experimenting to see which works could be fun.

For women, PC muscle exercises strengthen orgasms. Some women who did not have orgasms were able to do so after exercising this muscle. Contracting and relaxing this muscle can be self-arousing, and during vaginal penetration with the penis or fingers, a partner will be able to feel the contractions and may be further stimulated by this.

There are some other health benefits involved. The PC muscle supports various internal organs, including the vagina, uterus, and bladder, as well as urinary and anal openings. Strengthening the PC muscle can decrease or even cure urinary incontinence. Dr. Arnold Kegel originally developed these exercises to help women with urinary incontinence, and his patients were very pleased with the sexual "side effects." How does one learn to do their "Kegels"?

*Finding the PC muscle.* Sit on the toilet with legs apart. Start a flow of urine and try to stop it without moving your legs. That's your PC muscle at work, turning your flow on and off. Relax and try it several times.

*Several types of exercises. Slow Kegels:* Tighten the PC muscle as you did to stop the urine. Hold it for a count of three and then relax it. *Quick Kegels:* Tighten and relax the PC muscle as rapidly as you can. *Pull in/push out:* Pull up the whole pelvic floor as though you were trying to suck water into your vagina or penis. Then push out or bear down as if trying to push this imaginary water out. This exercise strengthens a number of abdominal muscles.

*When to do your "Kegels."* Do 10 of each of the above exercises five times every day for a week. If you wish, you can increase each exercise by 5—that is, do 15, 20, etc.—and repeat the whole set.

It's best not to move around while doing your Kegels, which makes them ideal for boring lectures, being stuck in traffic, watching television, talking on the phone, or lying in bed.

When you start, you'll probably have trouble keeping the muscle contracted and find that you work rather slowly. Keep at it and better control will soon follow. Also, remember to breathe naturally during your Kegels. Women can check on their own progress by inserting one or two clean, lubricated fingers into the vagina and contracting the PC muscle.

**Source:** R. F. Valois, and S. K. Kammermann, *Your Sexuality* (New York: McGraw-Hill, 1995), pp. 67–69. Original source: *All about Kegels,* Planned Parenthood and Sexual Counseling Series, 1977, Planned Parenthood of Central and Northern Arizona.

fainting, and migraine-type headaches. It's healthier to use this substance as intended—namely, to treat cardiac pain.

Many believe that psychoactive substances such as alcohol and cocaine have aphrodisiac properties. Controlled studies in which people *falsely believe* they have been drinking alcohol demonstrate that suggestion and social expectations are the stongest factors at work here (Roerich & Kinder, 1991). Alcohol is a central nervous system depressant, and in large quantities it impairs sexual response.

Some individuals report greater sexual responsiveness after using marijuana, but there is no objective evidence to support this. Others report an inhibition of sexual response with marijuana. As with alcohol, the effects of marijuana use depend more on the users' prior experiences and expectations about the drug (Wolman, 1985).

Others believe that cocaine is an aphrodisiac. While a small amount may loosen inhibitions, and the initial rush of intoxication may be pleasurable, the physiological effect of cocaine is to constrict blood vessels. Most regular cocaine users lose the ability to enjoy sex (Weiss & Mirin, 1987).

Sometimes drugs developed for quite other purposes are found to have unforeseen effects on sexual responsiveness. A recent survey (McCoy & Matyas, 1996) of women using various types of oral contraceptives revealed that users of *triphasic pills* (see chapter 15) report more sexual interest, more arousal during intercourse, and greater sexual satisfaction compared to users of monophasic contraceptives.

Norwegian researchers claim to have found a substance in fertilized chicken eggs with reported aphrodisiac properties. It has been marketed as a drug called *Libido* in Norway. At the same time, the Centers for Disease Control and Prevention in Atlanta report that four men died and a seventeen-year-old was hospitalized after consuming a supposed aphrodisiac purchased from a herbalist. The substance, marketed as *Lovestone* or *Rock Hard*, contained the dried skin secretions of a toad and an extract of the foxglove plant.

Where does all of this leave us? There seem to be only three things that consistently work as sexual enhancers: being in love, having a new partner, and the placebo effect. Which works best for you?

## 8.4  THINKING ABOUT SEXUAL DYSFUNCTIONS

As with so many of the issues surrounding sexuality, we have to begin with the understanding that what constitutes a problem in sexual functioning, or a *sexual dysfunction*, is defined by a particular society or social group. For example, in many cultures the typical time between penile insertion and male ejaculation is about 1 minute. In North America, the average time is between 5 and 10 minutes. In certain Asian cultures, insertion and thrusting typically lasts 20 to 30 minutes. Given this range, how can we judge whether a man "comes too quickly" (has the dysfunction known as "premature ejaculation")? To cite another example, in some cultures female orgasm is unknown. But among heterosexual couples in our culture, female orgasm is often considered the criterion for successful lovemaking (Davidson & Moore, 1994a). Again, we see how so many aspects of our sexuality are "socially constructed."

Even *within* our own culture, sexologists emphasize the point that a **sexual dysfunction** may be said to exist *only* if the person or couple is distressed by a particular aspect of their sexual response, rather than on the basis of some "objective criteria."

This section describes what our culture considers to be problems in sexual functioning (sexual dysfunctions). (You can read about another culture's construction of a sexual dysfunction in "Dimensions of Diversity: A Sexual Dysfunction Common in Southeast Asia: *Koro*.") In keeping with Helen Singer Kaplan's (1983) model of human sexual response, we will discuss disorders of sexual *desire*, disorders of sexual arousal (*excitement*), and disorders of *orgasm*. A fourth category of dysfunction has to do with painful

sexual intercourse. For each disorder, we will discuss what is known about its likely origins and then describe how sex therapists attempt to intervene to overcome the problem. We will then take a quick look at some medical conditions and some medical treatments that have an effect on sexual functioning. Lastly, we will examine some important issues that surround the whole idea of seeking help for sexual problems.

The *Diagnostic and Statistical Manual of Mental Disorders*, fourth edition (usually referred to as DSM-IV), (American Psychiatric Association, 1994), lists every category of mental and psychological disorders recognized by the American Psychiatric Association. All of the sexual dysfunctions described in this section are listed in that manual.

If the person has always had a particular problem in sexual functioning, the dysfunction is described as *lifelong*. If there has been a change from previous functioning that was adequate, the term *acquired dysfunction* is applied. This second type is much more common. When the disorder occurs only with a partner (in contrast to during masturbation), or only with certain partners, it is said to be *situational*. If it occurs during any sexual activity (including masturbation), it is said to be *generalized* (American Psychiatric Association, 1994).

## 8.5  TYPES OF SEXUAL DYSFUNCTIONS: ORIGINS AND INTERVENTIONS

### 8.5.1  Disorders of Desire

**Hypoactive sexual desire disorder** (HSD) involves a lack of sexual fantasies and/or desire for sexual activity. Individuals who have this problem might respond physically (adequate lubrication, erection, orgasm) and psychologically when stimulated, but they do not experience an interest in, initiate, or seek genital sexual activity. Among the 18- to 24-year-olds surveyed by the National Health and Social Life Survey (NHSLS; Laumann et al., 1994), 15.7 percent of men and 33.4 percent of women reported that they lacked interest in sex (fig. 8.10).

Although HSD is one of the most commonly diagnosed sexual dysfunctions, there is little agreement among clinicians on what exactly is meant by "low" sexual desire. There is no agreed-upon standard

| **sexual dysfunction** | impaired or incomplete sexual functioning resulting in distress |
| **hypoactive sexual desire disorder** | a disorder characterized by a lack of sexual desire |

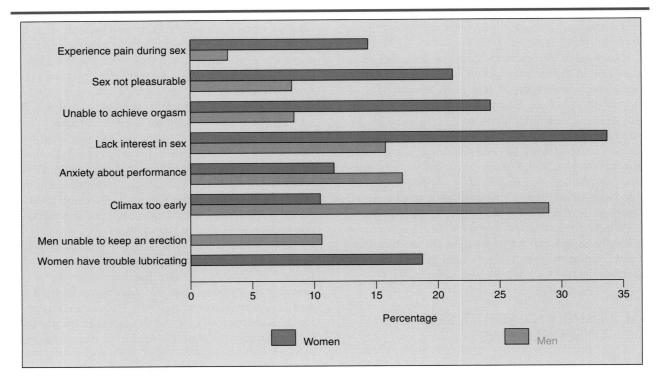

**FIGURE 8.10**   The percentage of women and men reporting sexual difficulties experienced during the past year in the National Health and Social Life Survey.

**Source:** Laumann et al., 1994.

regarding what level of sexual desire is "normal" (Letourneau & O'Donohue, 1993). Such a diagnosis might depend on a definite change in the sexual desire of one or both members of a couple (Rosellini, 1992). However, in most cases where such a change occurs, a therapist or counselor is more likely to assist the couple in accommodating to *each other's needs,* rather than trying to restore the sexual interest of the person with low sexual desire.

A **sexual aversion** is an active and deeply felt repugnance or revulsion at the idea or actuality of genital sexual contact with another person. While those with HSD might be *indifferent* toward sexual interactions, the person with sexual aversion disorder finds sexual contact repulsive, and might experience *sexual phobia* (intense fear) or a *sexual panic state* (Kaplan, 1987).

*Origins:* Since the 1960s and 1970s, the general sexual norms of North American sexuality have leaned in a more "hypersexual" direction. That is, the modern norm is that sex is good, therefore more sex is better (Letourneau & O'Donohue, 1993). Thus, a cultural prescription toward high interest in sex can lead to a "problem" of low sexual desire.

But it is overly simplistic to dismiss the problems of a couple who believe that the sexual interest of one or both of the partners is "too low" and who experience distress about this. It is not helpful to tell them that their distress is "culture bound." A sex therapist has to consider all of the possible factors that influence a particular individual's level of sexual interest and behavior. These often include a combination of physical, interpersonal, intrapersonal, learned, and practical factors.

The incidence of HSD is generally higher among women, and this is usually attributed to women's traditional sexual socialization (ambivalence toward overt sexual expression) and their greater likelihood of a history of sexual assault and abuse (Letourneau & O'Donohue, 1993). Among gay men, the fear of HIV is believed to have contributed to an increase in HSD.

Sometimes HSD is traceable to the effects of certain illnesses or treatments, but its origins are generally believed to be more psychological than physiological. Anxiety and depression are typically identified as the factors underlying HSD (Beck, 1995).

The origins of sexual aversion are also seen as primarily psychological. While *lifelong sexual aversion* is more often observed among men, *acquired*

# DIMENSIONS OF DIVERSITY

## A SEXUAL DYSFUNCTION COMMON IN SOUTHEAST ASIA: *KORO*

Beliefs about "low" sexual desire, how long an erection lasts, or the importance of female orgasms evoke fear and worry among some Westerners. In parts of Southeast Asia, some suffer from fears that their sex organs will retract and disappear into the body and eventually cause death. This is called *koro*, and several "epidemics" of *koro* have been documented. *Koro* is found more often among men than women and occurs mostly in Chinese societies such as China, Taiwan, Hong Kong, and Singapore.

In *koro*, anxiety about the retraction of the sex organs into the body can become so intense that some people take extreme measures, such as tying strings tightly around the penis or securing the penis with a clamping device. The "attack" is usually brief and tends not to recur. Of course, sex organs never really do retract into the body, so interventions are usually successful.

What factors contribute to the prevalence of this disorder? A 1984–85 epidemic of *koro* can be best understood by examining certain social and cultural events. In 1984, fortune-tellers predicted an outbreak of *koro* on Hainan Island off the southern coast of China. The epidemic was limited to the Han people, the dominant ethnic group in China. Members of other Chinese ethnic groups, such as the Li and Miao people (who live with and around the Han people) were not affected. How can this be explained?

First, the Han share the belief and expectation that genitals (or breasts) can actually retract into the body by the actions of a *fox spirit* that pulls the genitals inside the body.

Second, in contrast to the Li and Miao minorities, the Han share certain repressive sex-related attitudes and behaviors. Strong traditions of secrecy and ignorance about sexual matters persist among these rural folk. The Li and Miao allow premarital sex among their young and also encourage young people to choose their own dating and marriage partners. While members of these two minority groups tend to marry early, a couple typically does not live together until several years after marriage, usually after a first child. During these years of living apart, they interact freely with other men and women.

Third, victims of *koro* tended to be much less educated than the general population that surrounds them. Most *koro* victims were found to be adolescents and unmarried young adults.

Fourth, fortune-teller's predictions (fortune-tellers have high status and are seen as very powerful) seemed to influence the appearance of *koro* in this society.

*Koro* is an example of a culture-specific disorder, where the beliefs and traditions of the community affect the health of an individual. The extent to which sociological factors contribute to the incidence of disorders like *koro* in individuals is a focus of debate and ongoing research.

**Adapted from:** S. Cheng, "Epidemic Genital Retraction Syndrome: Environmental and Personal Risk Factors in Southern China," *Journal of Psychology and Human Sexuality* 9(1): 57–70.

---

*sexual aversion* is more often observed among women, and the prognosis for the acquired type is much more favorable (Gold & Gold, 1993).

*Interventions:* Desire problems are considered the most complex sexual dysfunctions to treat, and treatment must be carefully tailored to the particular individual or couple (Rosen & Leiblum, 1995). Some general approaches involve encouraging masturbation and discovering what fantasies are particularly arousing. Improving sexual communication skills has also been found to be very helpful. Exercises that focus on more exciting ways to initiate sexual interactions, and on constructive ways of refusing undesired sexual activity, have been shown to result in greater sexual interest and activity. Expanding the types of sexual activities the individual or couple engages in is also helpful.

Masters and Johnson (1970, 1976) developed an approach that has been found useful for enhancing the sexual interactions of couples, whether they are experiencing particular dysfunctions or not. This approach, called **sensate focus** (fig. 8.11), can be used by couples of all sexual orientations.

| sexual aversion | a feeling of revulsion toward sexual activity |
|---|---|
| sensate focus | a treatment for sexual difficulties that involves focusing on sensations of touch |

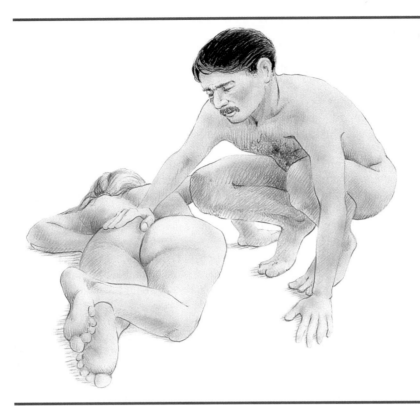

**FIGURE 8.11** Sensate focus. These exercises, designed to teach people to focus on the sensations involved in giving and receiving sensual pleasure through touching, are used in the treatment of both female and male sexual dysfunction.

The bedroom becomes the battleground for couples who cannot resolve relational problems. It can become easy for one partner to delay sex when the other partner is aroused, and it might not take long for such episodes to develop into problems in sexual arousal and response.

The first step is a commitment to *not* engage in intercourse or other genital, orgasm-producing activities during the early stages of this process. Then, with instruction by a trained therapist or via a prescribed videotape, the couple selects a warm, comfortable, and pleasant setting in which to begin the actual sensate focus exercises. One person gently touches and explores a partner's body, but only in nonerogenous areas. The goal is not arousal, but for both partners to focus on his or her own sensations

and perceptions during this *nondemand* or *nongenital* touching. The roles of "toucher" and "touchee" are then reversed. Touching with warmed lotion adds more dimensions to this exploration of sensuality. During subsequent sessions, partners touch and explore each other simultaneously. In later sessions, erogenous areas, such as breasts and genitals, may be touched. Still later a couple might engage in *sensual intercourse,* where both concentrate on the sensations experienced as their genitals make contact in various ways. Again, the purpose of all of this is not to proceed to orgasm but to take the time to experience the *sensuality* of sexual interactions—"to restore the feeling side of sex" (Masters, Johnson, & Kolodny, 1994, p. 39). Sensate focus helps individuals and couples rediscover the sensual aspects of their sexuality (Goodwin & Agronin, 1997).

## 8.5.2   Disorders of Arousal

*Sexual desire* refers to the psychological experience of wanting or seeking sexual activity. Although there is clearly a strong psychological component to what each of us finds sexually arousing, currently the tendency is to approach difficulties in sexual *arousal* in more physiological terms, especially for men. That is, difficulties in arousal tend to be defined in terms of *vasocongestion* (rapid inflow of blood to the genital area) that results from sexual stimulation. Vasocongestion involves the familiar experiences of penile erection and vaginal lubrication.

## Erectile Disorder in Men

**Erectile disorder** in men, or *erectile dysfunction,* is a persistent or recurrent inability to attain or maintain an erection (American Psychiatric Association, 1994). Erectile dysfunction is the most common problem for which men seek sex therapy (Hawton, 1992; Rosen & Leiblum, 1995). Overall, 10.4 percent of male respondents in the NHSLS reported they had difficulty maintaining erections (Laumann et al., 1994).

*Origins:* Recent research and treatment have emphasized the physical aspects of arousal, but psychological factors are also critical in understanding disorders of arousal. For example, some individuals engage in spectatoring during lovemaking: Rather than being fully involved in the sexual activity, the person psychologically separates from the event and carefully watches, monitors, and evaluates his or her sexual responses and actions, as well as those of a partner (Masters & Johnson, 1970). Thus, the person becomes a "spectator" rather than a participant. For example, a spectatoring man evaluates whether his erection is firm enough. A spectatoring woman might worry about whether she is wet enough. All of this serves to interfere with the ongoing physical processes of arousal.

It is important to remember that most men occasionally experience problems with erection, and that these problems become more frequent with age. The most common reasons for occasional erectile difficulties are excessive alcohol, high levels of stress or fatigue, a significant level of depression, low self-confidence, or discord with his partner (Sheehy, 1997). Unfortunately, our society places such a strong emphasis on erection and ejaculation as the central focus of male sexuality, that a temporary problem can lead to a recurring problem. After one problem episode some men become anxious about their ability to "perform," and this will lead to the experience of **performance anxiety**, which will interfere with his response at the next sexual encounter. Thus, a repetitive cycle begins. Remember, just as you cannot "will" or force yourself to sneeze, an erection cannot be "willed" or forced.

There is an ongoing debate about what percentage of erectile disorders are due to psychological factors versus organic (physiological) factors. Estimates of organic origins for these difficulties vary from 50 percent to 85 percent (Morley, 1986; Nordenberg, 1996). Organically based erectile difficulties tend to come on more gradually, be more persistent, and worsen over time. Among young men, injury to the

genitalia is the main cause. The majority of men with organic difficulties are over age 55 (Toufexis, 1988).

*Interventions:* Over the last decade, there have been major innovations in treating erectile disorders in men. Because the major causes of erectile dysfunctions are physical, the treatments are largely biological.

For some men the difficulty stems from abnormally low testosterone levels, and hormones can be administered through skin patches and injections (Schiari et al., 1997). For women who experience arousal dysfunction after removal of their adrenal glands, low doses of testosterone can be effective.

Various *vacuum devices* are available. The penis is placed in an acrylic tube attached to a hand pump. The tube is held tightly against the body to form an airtight seal, and pumping the device forces blood flow into the penis, thus producing an erection. Elastic bands placed at the base of the penis prevent blood from flowing back out. However, these bands interfere with normal ejaculation, and permanent damage to the penile blood vessels can occur if the bands are kept on too long (fig. 8.12a).

For those men whose difficulties arise from blockages in the vascular system, surgery to repair blood-supplying arteries has been effective (fig. 8.12b).

Penile injections are also becoming more commonplace. An injection of *alprostadil* directly into the base of the penis relaxes smooth muscle cells and will produce an erection within ten minutes that can last an hour or more. The injections, which can be painful, cannot be used every day (Althof & Turner, 1992; Rogers & Vourroulias, 1997; Padina-Nathan et al., 1997).

The most expensive and elaborate interventions involve the use of *penile implants.* The inflatable implant involves the surgical placement of two balloon-like cylinders within the cavernous bodies of the penis and also a fluid reservoir near the bladder (fig. 8.12c). Squeezing a hand-held pump, or one placed in the scrotum, forces the fluid into the penis and an erection results. After the sexual encounter, activating a release valve will return the fluid to the reservoir. The semirigid type of implant involves the placement of two silicone rods in the penis (fig. 8.12d). These are less rigid than an erect penis. To simulate an erection, the rods are extended straight out.

| | |
|---|---|
| **erectile disorder** | a recurrent inability to attain or maintain an erection |
| **performance anxiety** | worries about being able to "perform" sexually |

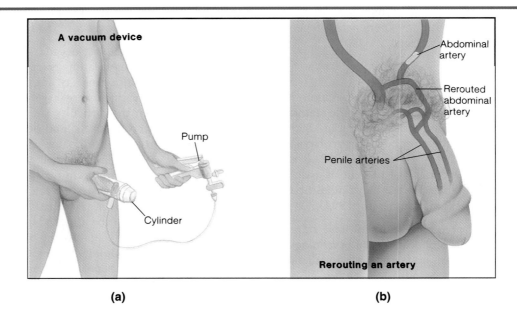

(a)    (b)

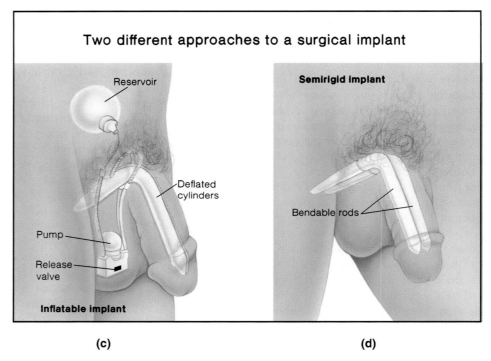

(c)    (d)

**FIGURE 8.12**  Four methods that restore erectile function.

## Arousal Disorder in Women

**Arousal disorder** in women is the persistent or recurrent inability to produce or maintain adequate lubrication and genital swelling (American Psychiatric Association, 1994).

The NHSLS found that 18.8 percent of women had difficulty lubricating (Laumann et al., 1994). Relatively inexpensive vaginal lubricants such as *K-Y*

*Jelly* can be used to facilitate sexual activity that involves vaginal penetration.

*Origins:* In contrast to erectile disorder in men, arousal difficulties among women more often have a psychological basis. Some women have been subjected to rape, sexual assault, or other types of sexual abuse. Childhood sexual abuse has been identified as a significant factor in the histories of many women with arousal disorders (Morokoff & Gillilland, 1993). Other causes can include deep anger at her partner, anxiety about sexual performance, negative feelings about herself, or major depression. These problems can be compounded by an inept or uncaring partner, and she herself might be inhibited about communicating her erotic preferences.

A woman's lack of arousal might not be as evident as that of a man, so she is less likely to report this as a problem. Yet without some positive attention, lack of arousal can lead her to perceive sex as something to be endured. Some women pretend to be aroused so as not to disappoint their partners. On the other hand, some women report they enjoy many aspects of sexual intimacy even though their level of arousal remains low (McConaghy, 1993).

### 8.5.3   Disorders of Orgasm

As with all aspects of sexuality, there is a wide range of diversity when it comes to orgasm. Some people reach orgasm very quickly, while others need an extended period of stimulation. Still others never experience orgasm, regardless of stimulation. It is very typical for partners to differ in the type and duration of stimulation each needs to reach orgasm, and these differences do not constitute a problem. Rather they are part of the territory of exploration in which loving partners can learn to please each other.

However, some individuals and couples do experience orgasm-related difficulties. *Disorders of orgasm* are defined as persistent or recurrent delays in, or absence of, orgasm following normal stimulation of sufficient intensity and duration (American Psychiatric Association, 1994). Orgasm disorders are more common in women than in men.

#### *Orgasmic Disorder in Women*

**Orgasmic disorder** in women is defined as the persistent or recurrent delay in, or absence of, orgasm after what is viewed as a normal excitement phase. Women who have never had an orgasm are described as being **anorgasmic**. Delayed or absent orgasm is the most common reason why women seek the help of a sex therapist (Rosen & Leiblum, 1995). The NHSLS indicated that 24.1 percent of the female respondents were unable to have orgasms (Laumann et al. 1994). Women with orgasm problems typically have erotic feelings, lubricate adequately, and show substantial genital vasocongestion.

Yet they cannot reach the orgasm phase. As with other sexual dysfunctions, orgasm disorders can be lifelong or acquired, situational or generalized.

*Origins:* Contributing factors include a male partner who ejaculates very quickly, negative attitudes toward sex, great discomfort in communicating about

sex, and higher levels of guilt about sexual matters (McConaghy, 1993). In one study comparing orgasmic women with those who had significant orgasmic problems, Kelly, Strassberg, and Kircher (1990) found that anorgasmic women had more negative attitudes toward masturbation, greater sex guilt, and more difficulty communicating with their partners about their preferences for clitoral stimulation. When more attention is given to clitoral stimulation and responsiveness, anorgasmic women might experience more orgasms (fig. 8.13).

One last point: Some women do not feel deprived by not having orgasms with their partners. Some anorgasmic women rate their sexual experiences as quite positive (Raboch & Raboch, 1992). As said before, a sexual response or its absence is a dysfunction only when it interferes with personal or couple satisfaction.

*Interventions:* Anorgasmic women can often learn to have orgasms by concentrating on sexual fantasies while masturbating (Barbach, 1975). The idea is to increase her overall eroticism and for her to discover what works as an "orgasmic trigger" for her. For some women it works to masturbate in a warm bath or bed while reading erotic materials. Use of a vibrator and a regular regimen of Kegel exercises have all been found to increase the likelihood of orgasm for women (Stock, 1993).

#### *Orgasmic Disorder in Men*

Orgasmic disorder in men has also been called *retarded ejaculation, ejaculatory delay,* and *ejaculatory incompetence.* According to the NHSLS, 8.2 percent of men report some difficulty in reaching orgasm (Laumann et al., 1994).

While the problem can be acquired or lifelong, generalized or situational, it is rare that a man has *never* ejaculated (Kaplan, 1974). Some men who find it difficult or impossible to ejaculate with a partner during intercourse have firm erections and have no difficulty ejaculating during masturbation or oral sex.

*Origins:* The origins of male orgasmic disorder are quite varied. He may have become conditioned by a masturbatory pattern that he cannot duplicate with a partner. He might have anxiety about dealing with a partner with whom he does not feel relaxed, trusting, or confident. He might have fears regarding possible

| | |
|---|---|
| **arousal disorder** | a recurrent inability to attain or maintain vaginal lubrication |
| **orgasmic disorder** | delayed or absent orgasm after a normal excitement phase |
| **anorgasmic** | never having had an orgasm |

**FIGURE 8.13** Clitoral stimulation. This position allows for simultaneous stimulation of the clitoris during heterosexual coitus in the nonorgasmic woman. She may stimulate herself, or the man may stimulate her. When she reaches the point of climax, the couple can thrust vigorously and bring on orgasm.

pregnancy. He might come from a religious background that severely restricted sexual expression, or he might have been the victim of sexual abuse or aggression (Dekker, 1993). As with many other sexual dysfunctions, the causes can be quite temporary (fatigue, stress, or alcohol or drug intoxication) and can clear up when he has a more normal lifestyle.

One other form of orgasmic disorder is *retrograde ejaculation*. As shown in figure 8.14, retrograde ejaculation occurs when semen is expelled back into the bladder rather than out through the penis. Retrograde ejaculation results from the reversed functioning of the two urethral sphincters, the tiny rings of muscle that surround the urethra. Usually the *internal* urethral sphincter contracts during erection and ejaculation. This prevents sperm from entering the bladder. The *external* urethral sphincter usually relaxes just before ejaculation, allowing semen to pass through the urethra. In retrograde ejaculation, these sphincters reverse their action and this results in semen being ejaculated into the bladder instead of out through the urethra. This is usually not harmful because the semen is later eliminated through urination. However, if this happens frequently, a man should consult a health care provider to determine if there is an underlying health problem.

### Premature Ejaculation

**Premature ejaculation** refers to persistent or recurrent onset of ejaculation with minimal sexual stimulation and before the person wishes it to occur. Ejaculation occurs before, on, or shortly after penetration, but this pattern is not considered a dysfunction unless it causes distress or interpersonal difficulty (American Psychiatric Association, 1994). This is the most common sexual dysfunction found among men (St. Lawrence & Madakasira, 1992). The NHSLS found that 28.5 percent of the male respondents reported a problem in reaching orgasm too early (Laumann et al., 1994).

Gender roles are a significant factor in considering whether ejaculation is "premature." Note that reaching orgasm quickly is defined as a dysfunction only in men. Women who reach orgasm very quickly are *not* considered to have a dysfunction. Actually, there has been little agreement on when ejaculation is too rapid and what exactly constitutes premature ejaculation (PE). That is, should PE be defined by the number of thrusts after penetration begins, or by the amount of time between penetration and ejaculation (*latency*), or by some combination of the two? PE has also been defined more subjectively as partner satisfaction (Masters & Johnson, 1966). The *DSM-IV* combines voluntary control with latency by defining PE as *persistent or recurrent ejaculation with minimal sexual satisfaction before, on, or shortly after penetration and before the person wishes it* (American Psychiatric Association, 1994).

*Origins:* Most cases of premature ejaculation have psychological causes. Some men are highly sensitive to erotic sensation. Others have learned a pattern of masturbating very quickly out of fear of being caught. For other men, early sexual encounters occurred under pressure or in situations in which they

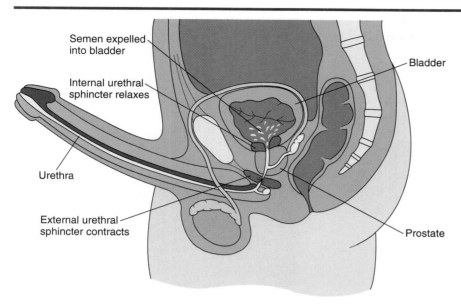

Semen expelled into bladder

Internal urethral sphincter relaxes

Urethra

External urethral sphincter contracts

Bladder

Prostate

**FIGURE 8.14** Retrograde ejaculation. Reversed functioning of the urethral sphincters results in semen being ejaculated into the bladder.

became conditioned to ejaculate very rapidly. Frequent repetition of these experiences maintains the conditioning effect. Inability to control ejaculation often leads to feelings of inadequacy and guilt, especially when a partner's pleasure is curtailed. Some men avoid having these feelings by avoiding intercourse or other forms of partnered sex. Thus, what appears to be a situation of unusually low sexual desire (HSD) is really a fear of premature ejaculation. This may give you some sense of the complexities involved in trying to help those with a sexual dysfunction (Grenier & Byers, 1997).

*Interventions:* Some couples can work together on improving a man's "staying power" by arranging for an ejaculation before insertion is attempted. He can do this himself or his partner can do this as part of their "pleasuring." For a heterosexual couple, in the woman-on-top position, if the man can relax and resist thrusting, this too can prolong his erection.

A more specific technique was developed by urologist James Semans (1956), who believed that for some men the problem of premature ejaculation was caused by the man's lack of awareness regarding when ejaculation was close. He developed the **start-stop technique** in which stimulation continues until the man feels ejaculation coming. Penile stroking then stops. This allows the man to experience the feeling of impending ejaculation and to "learn" that erections can subside and then return easily. This technique can be mastered alone or with a partner (Masters, Johnson, & Kolodny, 1994).

In the **squeeze technique**, a partner is shown how to apply firm pressure to the frenulum with the thumb, and on the other side of the corona with the

second and third fingers until the urge to ejaculate is lost (fig. 8.15). The man will have to show his partner how much pressure to apply. Several days or weeks of training and practice sessions will be needed to perfect this technique.

More recently, medical researchers have learned that small doses of certain antidepressant drugs (*Paxil or Zoloft*, for example) can help men delay ejaculation. However, too high a dose can result in orgasm difficulties (Yudofsky, Hales, & Ferguson, 1991).

### 8.5.4 Pain-Producing Problems

*Dyspareunia*

Some individuals experience considerable pain when they attempt penetrative sexual activity. **Dyspareunia** refers to recurrent and persistent genital pain occurring

| | |
|---|---|
| **premature ejaculation** | a recurrent inability to delay ejaculation, which causes distress |
| **start-stop technique** | a way of treating premature ejaculation by repeatedly stimulating the penis almost to orgasm, then allowing the erection to subside |
| **squeeze technique** | a way of treating premature ejaculation in which a man's partner squeezes the penis at the frenulum until the urge to ejaculate is lost |
| **dyspareunia** (dis″par-rū′ni-ah) | a recurrent genital pain before, during, or after sexual intercourse |

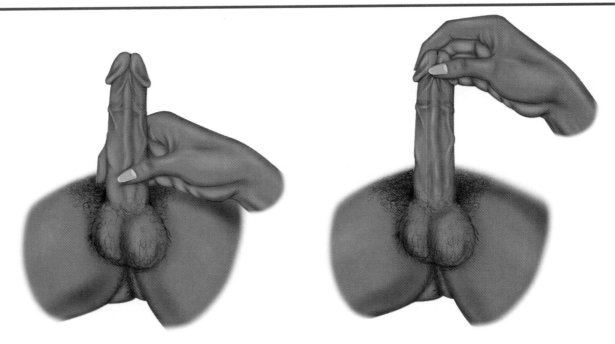

**FIGURE 8.15**    The squeeze technique, which can be applied below the head of the penis or at the base of the penis, can be used in the treatment of premature ejaculation.

before, during, or after sexual intercourse (in both men and women). It may range from a mild discomfort that distracts from sexual enjoyment, to such sharp pain that the person avoids all sexual activity. In the NHSLS, 3 percent of men and 14.4 percent of women reported pain during penetrative sex (Laumann et al., 1994).

*Origins:* The psychological causes of dyspareunia include anxiety about intercourse, sexual guilt, the psychological consequences of sexual trauma, or an unhappy relationship with the sexual partner. In such situations, communication between the partners is critical. Painful intercourse is one difficulty that both partners must address openly and directly. A thorough and sympathetic medical evaluation is the place to begin.

For women, the pain might be due to various physical disorders and diseases that affect the genitals. Insufficient vaginal lubrication is probably the most common cause. This lack of lubrication might be due to insufficient sexual arousal or due to relationship problems. Other common causes include untreated gonorrhea, sensitivity to contraceptive materials (such as latex), or other medical problems (Spector et al., 1993). Recently, a condition called *vulvar vestibulitis* has been identified as a frequent cause of dyspareunia in women (Schover, 1995). Less common causes involve the irritating remnants of a hymen, irritation around the clitoral hood, and infection of the Bartholin's gland or bladder.

In men, there might be testicular or penile pain during or after ejaculation. This pain can result from infection or inflammation of the penis, foreskin, testes, urethra, or prostate gland. Other possible causes include infection of the bladder, seminal vesicles, prostate gland, or urethra. Some men also experience irritation from contraceptive materials. Some uncircumcised men fail to remove the smegma that collects under the foreskin, and this irritates the glans penis. Evaluation by a urologist can help determine if there is an underlying physiological problem.

### Vaginismus

**Vaginismus** refers to involuntary, powerful, spasms of the muscles surrounding the outer third, or *introitus*, of the vagina (Fliegelman, 1990). Whenever penetration is attempted, the vaginal opening closes so tightly that intercourse or other penetrative activity is very difficult or impossible (fig. 8.16). The woman might not be aware that her vaginal muscles are contracting. About 12 to 17 percent of women who visit sex therapy clinics are affected by vaginismus (Spector & Cary, 1990).

In *complete vaginismus*, this muscular contraction occurs upon any attempted penetration of the vagina, whether by a finger, penis, speculum, or tampon. For other women, vaginismus is *situational*.

*Origins:* The causes of vaginismus can be physical or psychological. Vaginismus occurs more often among younger women, in women raised in authoritarian-

# GO ASK ALICE

*Dear Alice,*

*What are the long-term effects of taking Prozac? I've been taking 20 mg/day for almost a year.*

*Happy but at what cost?*

Dear Happy but at what cost?,

In the last several years, *Prozac* has become the most widely prescribed antidepressant in the United States. Besides treating depression, *Prozac* is used to treat obsessive-compulsive and panic disorders. *Prozac* is the oldest drug of this kind, with 20 years of research behind it showing no known long-term side effects. *Prozac* has few side effects when compared to other antidepressant drugs. These side effects may include dry mouth, constipation, urinary retention, sedation, and weight gain.

*Prozac*, however, is associated with insomnia, restlessness, nausea, and tension headaches, which normally go away within one to two weeks from when it was first taken. One possible side effect, which remains for the time *Prozac* is taken, is *Prozac's* affect on your sex life. It often reduces desire, and can delay or interfere with orgasm, in both women and men. Fatigue and memory loss are other possible problems. These side effects subside when you stop taking the drug. In some people, the effectiveness of *Prozac* seems to diminish with time, and an increase in dosage is necessary. In these cases, talk with your prescribing doctor, who may alter your medication.

Stopping *Prozac's* use needs to be supervised by a physician. It is not advised to take this drug if you are pregnant or breastfeeding. So, talk with your doctor for an alternative.

    http:www.mhhe.com/byer6

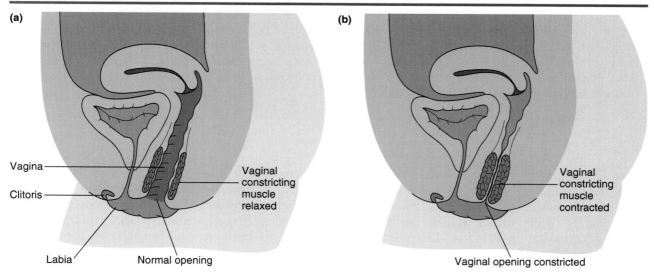

**FIGURE 8.16**    Vaginismus. Involuntary contractions in the muscles surrounding the vaginal opening make intercourse difficult or impossible. **a:** Relaxed vaginal muscles. **b:** Contracted vaginal muscles.

oppressive homes, in women with negative attitudes toward sex, in women who see their husbands as undependable, and among women who have a history of being sexually abused or traumatized (American Psychiatric Association, 1994; Tugrul & Kabakei, 1997). Physical origins include a problem **episiotomy**, pelvic disorders, or infections of the vagina (Beck, 1993).

Like all other sexual dysfunctions, vaginismus is a problem for the couple, if their sexual practices include penetration. The woman with vaginismus

| | |
|---|---|
| **vaginismus** (vaj-in-iz´mus) | involuntary spasms of the muscles of the lower vagina that prevent penetration |
| **episiotomy** (e-pis-i-ot´ō-mē) | a surgical procedure to enlarge the vaginal opening during childbirth by cutting through the perineum |

## GENITAL DISORDERS THAT AFFECT SEXUAL FUNCTIONING

Some individuals are born with malformations of the genitals. These often affect sexual functioning, and so they are mentioned here. There are also several physical conditions that can develop later in life that affect the physical capacity for genital sex.

There are several relatively rare congenital conditions that can have a serious effect on the sexuality of both sexes. In *agenesis*, an organ fails to grow or develop. In females the clitoris may be absent; in males the penis may be absent or, if present, be tiny and nonfunctional. These males might undergo surgery and be reassigned as girls. Male infants who sustain severe traumatic injury to the penis have also been reassigned to the other gender. Recently, there has been a growing controversy about the ethics of such reassignment ("A Tragedy Yields Insight into Gender," 1997). If surgery is not an option, counseling will help with adjustment during adolescence and adulthood. *Hypospadias* is a congenital incomplete fusion of the underside of the penis or clitoris. In a boy the urethra ends at the the site of the abnormal opening. In a girl the urethra opens into the vagina. In *epispadias* there is an incomplete fusion of the upperside of the penis or clitoris. Among males, this split in the penis may result in urine leaving the body through the abdominal

wall above the penis. Although surgery can repair the appearance and urinary function of the penis, the penis might not be functional for intercourse (Money, 1994).

Some congenital conditions that can affect female sexuality include *vaginal atresia* (closure of the vagina or absence of a true vagina). Corrective surgery (usually performed after puberty) involves construction of a vaginal vault. This makes intercourse and other sexual activities possible, but it will not permit vaginal delivery of an infant (Money, 1994).

Among women, a*cute urethral syndrome*, an infection of urethra, and *interstitial cystitis* can be chronic problems. Both of these conditions result in the frequent urge to urinate, burning or pain upon urination, and severe pain during sexual activity or even in response to the light pressure exerted by clothing (Webster, 1996).

*Vaginal atrophy* (shrinkage and narrowing of the inner surfaces of the vagina) can occur as a result of the lowered estrogen levels that come with menopause. *Varicose veins* can develop in the vulva, often as a result of pregnancy. This is experienced as a heavy aching feeling in the pelvis.

---

might feel frustrated and inadequate. Her partner might feel rejected and not understand what is happening. Some men maintain their own ability to function sexually, while others develop an acquired erectile dysfunction in reaction. Lesbian couples rarely complain about vaginismus. For all couples, if penetration is a problem, oral-genital contact and other sexual techniques can be employed (Nichols, 1995).

*Interventions:* The goal of treatment for vaginismus is to eliminate the involuntary muscle spasms. Relaxation training that focuses on the tightening and relaxing of vaginal muscles is usually very helpful. The woman might undergo *desensitization training* by having a series of lubricated dilators gently inserted into the vagina. These will vary from very small to large. The woman progresses at her own pace until she can insert a dilator that is the size of three fingers. Each dilator is left in place for 10 to 15 minutes while she relaxes. There are usually good results within five

or six days of dilator use (LoPiccolo & Stock, 1986). Then, a partner will begin to participate. No attempt at vaginal penetration is made until a partner can insert three fingers without a spasm occurring. For other-sex partners, penile penetration is the final step.

### 8.5.5 Dysfunctions Due to Medical Conditions and Treatments

Some individuals have genital malformations or other conditions that directly affect sexual functioning (see "Healthy Sexuality: Genital Disorders That Affect Sexual Functioning"). However, these are relatively rare. There are many nonsexual medical conditions, especially chronic ones, that have a significant impact on sexual functioning. Moreover, sometimes, even if a medical condition itself has little or no effect on sexuality, various treatments for such conditions do have effects on sexual functioning. Since health care providers often fail to discuss these effects with

**TABLE 8.4**  OTHER COMMON MEDICAL CONDITIONS THAT CAN AFFECT SEXUAL DESIRE, AROUSAL, AND ORGASM

Alcoholism
Anemia
Anxiety disorders
Cerebral vascular accidents (strokes)
Cirrhosis
Coronary disease
Degenerative disc disease (back problems)
Depression
Diabetes
Drug addiction
Hand traumas
Head injuries
Hepatitis
Neurological disorders (multiple sclerosis, cerebral palsy, etc.)
Nutritional deficiencies
Parkinson's disease
Pituitary and hypothalamic insufficiencies due to tumors, etc.
Testosterone deficiency in males
Tuberculosis

patients, it is useful for individuals and couples to be aware of these effects (Mira et al., 1992). Some of the most common conditions and treatments that affect sexual functioning will be discussed here (see table 8.4).

### Desire

Thyroid problems and diabetes are two major causes of lowered sexual desire. Other diseases known to significantly decrease sexual functioning include Parkinson's disease and nonalcoholic liver disease (Kresin, 1993). Medications for cancer, cardiac conditions, hypertension (high blood pressure), gastric conditions, and glaucoma have been shown to have similar effects (Meston, Gorzalka, & Wright, 1997). Some antidepressant drugs, such as imipramine (*Tofranil*), and lithium (used to treat another serious mood disorder) also have been known to result in diminished sexual desire. Exposure to environmental toxins such as lead, pesticides, and herbicides (Agent Orange) can result in loss of libido.

### Arousal

Some common causes of difficulty in arousal are diabetes, scleroderma, kidney disease, arteriosclerosis (hardening of the arteries), hypertension, and neurological disorders. Medications for cardiac conditions and for high blood pressure are known to interfere with vasocongestive processes. For example beta-blockers prevent the sympathetic nervous system from stimulating the cardiac muscles (remember that

sympathetic nervous system action is central in the physical responses of sexual arousal). People who take beta-blockers often experience erectile and lubrication difficulties. Some cardiac patients work out a careful plan with their health care providers to not take their medications for a day or two before engaging in sexual intimacies. Considering the risks involved, open communication between patient and health care provider is critical.

Some antidepressants and antianxiety medications also have a negative effect on vasocongestive processes. Alcohol abuse, cigarette smoking, and the use of narcotics or other illicit drugs have similar consequences (Graber, 1995).

For women, as for men, arousal difficulties can arise from physical as well as psychological factors. Decreasing levels of estrogen can lead to vaginal dryness. Other pelvic, hormonal, vascular, or neurological problems can also lead to arousal difficulties.

### Orgasm

The use of antihypertensive medications and antidepressants can also result in orgasmic difficulties. More lasting physical causes include nervous system damage, multiple sclerosis, and chronic alcohol or drug abuse (Segraves & Segraves, 1993).

## 8.5.6  Seeking Help for Sexual Dysfunctions

Since many sexual dysfunctions have a major physical or organic basis, the place to start in seeking help is with one's medical care provider. Depending on the problem, a visit with a gynecologist or urologist may be helpful. A thorough physical examination will rule out or uncover most medical problems. A second issue is the effect of medications taken for already identified conditions. Third, one must consider the normal physical changes in sexual functioning that occur through aging.

Whether or not physical factors are central in the problem, sexual dysfunctions typically arise in the context of a relationship, and so the psychological and emotional aspects of a dysfunctional sexual relationship need special attention. That is why most sex therapists emphasize treating the couple, rather than a couple partner (Masters, Johnson, & Kolodny, 1994). To read about a couple who saw their problem in sexual terms and consulted a sex therapist, see "Case Study: Judy and Richard Seek the Help of a Sex Therapist." In this case, interpersonal issues clearly underlay this couple's sexual difficulties. The "sex therapy" helped with the erotic component of their relationship, but this couple also worked very hard on the other aspects of their relationship.

## JUDY AND RICHARD SEEK THE HELP OF A SEX THERAPIST

This couple, both in their mid-forties, were well educated and quite accomplished in their respective professions. Early in their relationship, they agreed not to have children. The presenting problem was Judy's disinterest in sexual contact with Richard. Judy was orgasmic, but she described their interactions as mechanical and emotionally unsatisfying. Both viewed their difficulties in terms of *sexual frequency:* Judy saw Richard as making excessive demands for sexual contact, while he saw Judy as having a low desire for sexual contact.

Judy's alcoholic father was deceased, and she had nothing unusual in her sexual history. Richard had a history of breaking off relationships with women soon after they became sexual. In talking about their courtship period, Richard recalled feeling pressured to be emotionally close and then needing to break off with Judy. After repeating this pattern with other women, he would return to Judy. Their sexual relationship would be satisfactory for a while, but Judy would soon lose interest. Richard had previously told Judy about his extramarital affairs, and this brought them close to separating. They reconciled after several sessions of pastoral counseling.

A psychological assessment showed Richard's difficulty in tolerating emotional closeness. He misinterpreted Judy's requests for intimacy as sexual demands. When he would respond to her approaches by mechanically initiating sex, Judy would rebuff him. His subsequent withdrawal led to her pursuing him, and then an angry argument would result. This had become a repetitive cycle.

Treatment began with *sensate focus* exercises. The therapist prescribed that they should not attempt intercourse during their treatment. Both were taught to attend to bodily cues of emotion, to label feelings, and to share these verbally. This ability to communicate verbally was emphasized for both of them because they tended to misinterpret each other's emotional messages. Judy enjoyed the "homework" but Richard found the exercises "odd."

Although Richard had previously denied masturbating, in fact he did so several times a day. This was accompanied by intense fantasies of sex with strangers, and he had acted on these fantasies several times while attending conferences. Revealing this in therapy led to an emotional crisis between Judy and Richard and also evoked powerful fears of HIV infection. After negative HIV test results, Judy agreed to remain in therapy together for three more months. More communication training gradually reduced the number of marital conflicts. The next phase of treatment focused on Richard's fears that emotional intimacy would lead to being "controlled and smothered." It also focused on Judy learning to elicit intimacy verbally rather than by sexual pursuit. Later, the couple was asked to read and discuss several popular "sex manuals," so as to consider greater variation and innovation in their sexual activity. Finally, the ban on having intercourse was lifted, and over the next several months both expressed satisfaction with their improved emotional and sexual relationships. While Richard still fantasized about additional sexual contacts, he had learned to substitute his wife in his masturbatory fantasies. Judy expressed greater interest and investment in maintaining their relationship.

**Adapted from:** J. Gayle Beck, "What's Love Got to Do with It? The Interplay between Low and Excessive Desire Disorders," in *Case Studies in Sex Therapy,* ed. R. C. Rosen & S. R. Leiblum. (New York: Guilford Press, 1995), pp. 46–64.

A primary health care provider is often a good source for a referral to a sex therapist. Your college or university health services department or counseling center might also be a good referral source. The American Association of Sex Educators, Counselors and Therapists (AASECT) has developed a code of ethics, certification criteria, and procedures for sexuality educators, counselors, and therapists.

Only licensed or certified therapists should be considered (Magee, 1997). The licensed professional can be a psychiatrist, psychologist, social worker, or professional counselor. Licenses are granted and regulated by governmental agencies, so this gives clients some legal protection.

What will happen if an individual or couple actually goes to a sex therapist? Most of us are uncomfortable discussing our sexual habits and difficulties with strangers, so some anxiety is perfectly normal. Does the therapist help facilitate greater comfort? Is openness encouraged? Does the therapist appear knowledgeable and at ease in discussing sexual issues?

A good therapist will be clear and direct about realistic goals for treatment. She or he will be able to clearly describe the approach that will be taken (cognitive-behavioral, insight therapy, etc.) and will discuss fees very clearly and openly. It is appropriate for clients to ask where the therapist received specialized training and the nature of this training. A qualified sex therapist will be comfortable discussing the licenses he or she holds.

During an initial visit to a sex therapist, the therapist is likely to listen carefully in order to understand the problems as *the individual or couple perceive them*. A thorough history may be taken and various questionnaires administered. Soon a treatment plan and goals will be developed and discussed. Most sex therapy involves "homework," and the couple must be willing to follow directions in doing this homework. Treatment will be highly individualized to the couple rather than a "cookbook" approach.

### Professional Ethics

Regardless of the therapist's credentials or qualifications, it is *always unethical* for the therapist to become sexually intimate with clients. Unless the therapist is a physician, a physical examination is inappropriate, so it is improper for a therapist to ask the client to disrobe.

In a therapeutic relationship, the client is in a position of vulnerability relative to the more "expert" therapist. Therefore, sexual contact between therapist and client is viewed as exploitative. Female clients can be particularly harmed by such contact (Rutter, 1989). In some states, sexual contact between a professional and a client is illegal and is considered a criminal behavior (Foster, 1996). Without exception, should any sexual advances be made, the client should leave immediately (Powell, 1996). She or he may wish to consult with a lawyer or other knowledgeable person before deciding whether to pursue legal action.

### Sex Therapy for Gay Men and Lesbian Women

Gay men, lesbian women, bisexuals, and others whose sexual lifestyle does not fit mainstream patterns will need to be especially alert to the attitudes and values of the therapist. It is important for lesbian and gay couples to consult with therapists who have "gay-positive" attitudes and who understand those everyday-life and relationship issues that present special challenges for lesbian and gay couples (Friedman, 1991). Unless a person is distressed about his or her sexual orientation, changing a person's sexual orientation should not be a goal of sex therapy. Just as for heterosexual couples, the goal will be to help with problems in sexual functioning (Nichols, 1993).

### A Critical Evaluation of Sex Therapy

The whole notion of sex therapy was pioneered by William Masters and Virginia Johnson in their book *Human Sexual Inadequacy* (1970), and since then the idea has grown to be an active and changing field of research and therapy. Over the years, more controlled studies of various sex therapy approaches have led to the following conclusions:

1. It is more useful to consider the origins of sexual dysfunction as an interaction among cultural, personal, interpersonal, and physical factors rather than as due to one factor versus another (Rosen & Leiblum, 1995).

2. The sensate focus exercises developed by Masters and Johnson have been found to be generally helpful to couples who have any type of sexual dysfunction.

3. Behavioral treatments for erectile difficulties have been found to be generally effective, although other studies have found recurrent difficulties (Everaerd, 1993). Adding biological treatments to the behavioral approaches has resulted in improved results for many erectile problems. However, there have been relatively few long-term studies on the safety and efficacy of these treatments, and their impact on partners has not been assessed (Rosen & Leiblum, 1995).

4. The success rate for treatment of vaginismus is about 80 percent, and the success rate for treatment of premature ejaculation is about 90 percent (Beck, 1993).

5. After a program of directed masturbation, about 95 percent of anorgasmic women were able to have orgasms. About 85 percent of those so treated were able to have orgasms with a partner, but only a minority were able to do so during coitus (LoPiccolo & Stock, 1986).

6. An evaluation of treatment programs for male orgasmic disorder showed generally poor results (Dekker, 1993).

7. Hypoactive sexual desire has consistently been the most difficult dysfunction to treat effectively (Beck, 1995; Hawton, 1991).

## SUMMARY

1. Whether sexual arousal originates from external or internal stimuli, the limbic system and the cerebral cortex are two important brain structures involved in sexual response.

2. The spinal cord mediates the important reflexes involved in sexual response, such as lubrication, erection, and ejaculation.

3. The differing actions of the sympathetic and parasympathetic subdivisions of the autonomic nervous system regulate various aspects of sexual response.

4. Androgens, especially testosterone, have an important but complex role in sexual desire for both women and men.

5. Masters and Johnson developed their sexual response cycle model from laboratory observation and measurement. Some have criticized the model as narrow, sexist, and biased.

6. The processes of vasocongestion and myotonia are central in human sexual response. The four phases of the Masters and Johnson sexual response cycle are *excitement, plateau, orgasm,* and *resolution.* For men, the resolution phase includes a refractory period.

7. Kaplan's alternative triphasic model of sexual response has some advantages, especially in terms of clinical work with sexual dysfunctions. Phases of this model are *desire, excitement,* and *orgasm.*

8. Both sexual response models are based on averages, and the responses of any particular individual can vary considerably from the models.

9. Both culture and gender influence sexual response.

10. Simultaneous orgasm is difficult for most couples. Most women are capable of multiple orgasms, especially through self-stimulation or the use of a vibrator. Some men can develop the capacity for multiple orgasm.

11. Controversy continues to surround the notions of female ejaculation and the existence of a sensitive area on the anterior wall of the vagina (G spot).

12. Throughout recorded history, human beings have sought substances to enhance or prolong sexual response. To date, only three factors appear to have this effect: being in love, having a new partner, and the placebo effect.

13. What constitutes a sexual dysfunction varies across cultures. Even within our own culture, determining when a sexual dysfunction exists is largely subjective.

14. Sexual dysfunctions can be described as lifelong versus acquired, and situational versus generalized.

15. Hypoactive sexual desire disorder is characterized by a lack of sexual fantasies, desire, or interest in sexual activity. Sexual aversion involves a deeply felt repugnance or revulsion toward sexual activity. The origins of the desire disorders are generally hypothesized to be psychological.

16. Psychological interventions in the desire disorders involve various forms of psychotherapy. Masters and Johnson developed a system of sex therapy that can be used to treat most of the sexual dysfunctions.

17. Sensate focus is a treatment technique designed to emphasize the more sensual aspects of sexual activity.

18. The arousal disorders include erectile disorder in men and arousal disorder in females. Important psychological factors involved in the arousal disorders are spectatoring, performance anxiety, negative sexual attitudes, and a history of sexual trauma. Recently there has been an increasing emphasis on physiological interventions for erectile disorder in men.

19. The disorders of orgasm include orgasmic disorder in women and men, male orgasmic disorder, retrograde ejaculation, and premature ejaculation. These disorders are believed to be primarily psychological in origin. Interventions for the orgasmic disorders involve psychological counseling and the encouragement of masturbation. Specialized interventions—such as the squeeze technique, the start-stop technique, and the use of certain antidepressants—are used to treat premature ejaculation.

20. Vaginismus refers to muscle spasms that make penetration of the vagina difficult or impossible. Dyspareunia refers to painful sexual intercourse. The origins of these two conditions can be psychological or physical. Systematic desensitization training can improve or eliminate vaginismus.

21. A variety of medical conditions and their treatments can result in problems in sexual functioning.

22. A physical examination can help determine the source of a sexual dysfunction. Sexual dysfunctions typically occur in the context of a relationship, so psychological counseling is also important.

23. Ethical considerations are important in sex therapy.

24. Individuals with alternative sexual lifestyles need to be particularly alert to a sex therapist's attitudes and understanding regarding their lifestyle and special concerns.

25. A critical evaluation can reveal the strengths and weaknesses of sex therapy.

## CRITICAL THINKING CHALLENGES

1. List the physiological changes that occur in a male or female body during each phase of Masters and Johnson's model of sexual response. Now divide the list into changes that affect the genitals, and those that take place in other parts of the body. Which list is longer? Is our society too focused on the role of the genitals in sexual arousal and response?

2. Mickey and Chris have become very close, and have just begun a sexual relationship. Even though they both enjoy having sex, Mickey is clearly uncomfortable with explicit sexual language and embarrassed about trying new things. What approach would you recommend for Chris to make sure that their sexual explorations are exciting and enjoyable for both of them?

3. Some religious traditions consider masturbation a serious moral transgression. Yet sex therapists often encourage and prescribe masturbation, especially for women, as a way to learn about one's sexual arousal and responses. What are your thoughts about dealing with such conflicting values?

# SEXUAL PLEASURING

9

**AFTER STUDYING THIS CHAPTER, YOU SHOULD BE ABLE TO**

**[1]** Summarize the findings regarding the features, meaning, and purposes of sexual fantasy and private erotic imagery.

**[2]** Describe the relationship between erotic fantasy and solitary as well as partnered sexual activity.

**[3]** Summarize the findings regarding the relationship of masturbation to other important demographic factors and explain the significance of masturbation in human sexual expression.

**[4]** Summarize the gender differences in masturbatory techniques.

**[5]** List and describe how couples arouse each other during shared pleasuring.

**[6]** Summarize the findings regarding changing attitudes (legal and social) toward oral sex and other types of noncoital sexual activities, and then describe the important features of oral-genital sexual activity.

**[7]** Summarize the findings regarding the prevalence of anal sexual activities and explain the special risks involved.

**[8]** List the various common coital postures and describe the advantages and disadvantages of each.

**[9]** Explain the special significance of coitus in heterosexual sexual expression, and how coital preferences reflect cultural values.

**[10]** Summarize the findings of the National Health and Social Life Survey regarding the sexual lives of Americans.

**[11]** Summarize the similarities and differences among gay, lesbian, and heterosexual sexual expression.

**[12]** Describe how adult toys and other sexual aids can enhance sexual pleasure.

**[13]** Describe how personal attitudes, the ambience surrounding sexual activity, and careful attention to the "afterglow" period of a sexual encounter can all enhance sexual pleasure.

## 9.1    ATTITUDES AND APTITUDES

This chapter is about individual sexual expression. For many people in our culture and time, "having sex" evokes associations of passionate feelings, as well as intense psychological and bodily pleasure that culminate in orgasm for both partners. As you have learned, human sexual behavior is much broader than that.

In this chapter, we will describe a range of things that human beings do to arouse and pleasure *themselves* as well as their sexual partners. A major part of the chapter will be devoted to sexual fantasy and masturbation, because for most people those are the most frequent sexual behaviors engaged in *over the course of a lifetime*. Another major part will be devoted to coitus, or heterosexual intercourse, because that is the *most frequent partnered* sexual behavior that human beings engage in. It is also a critical aspect of reproductive sex and heterosexual bonding. We will also discuss same-sex sexual behaviors as well as some ways that individuals attempt to enhance their solitary and partnered sexual pleasure.

What you read in this chapter might challenge some of your most deeply held views and ideals. For example, you might find the discussion about sexual fantasy and masturbation at odds with your personal, religious, or cultural values. Hopefully, you will approach this information with an open mind. At the least, you might clarify your own values about this area of sexual expression, or you might even change your attitudes about these behaviors.

Another issue has to do with respect for personal preferences and the sensitive process of sexual negotiation with a partner. You or your partner might read about a sexual activity that lies outside your usual repertoire or that you thought was rare or deviant. It might sound like a great erotic turn-on to one of you and a totally repellant turn-off to another—and that's the way it is. It's important to respect one's own boundaries and limitations in exploring sexual possibilities, and to recognize that intimate, sexual negotiations with a partner can be difficult. It's impossible to explain why any one of us enjoys "this" but dislikes "that." No one can explain why one person loves butter pecan ice cream and the next person gags at the very thought of tasting it. Some folks don't like ice cream at all, and those who love it find that difficult to understand, but that's what human diversity is all about.

## 9.2    PRIVATE, SOLITARY PLEASURING

### 9.2.1    Erotic Fantasy

In the privacy and safety of our own minds, we play out imaginary scenarios that might or might not be acted upon. We construct such fantasies, or daydreams, from our general creativity, our past experiences, anticipated events, and sometimes our wishes. Some of our fantasies are romantic; others are overtly sexual in content. Scenarios can be pleasant or painful. We might fantasize about real people we know, fictitious characters, faceless, nameless strangers, or cultural idols from the world of sports or the performing arts. When internally generated fantasies are combined with external physical stimulation, sexual arousal and pleasure can be extremely powerful (Dekker & Everaerd, 1993). The National Health and Social Life Survey (NHSLS) revealed that 54 percent of men and 19 percent of women fantasized about sex at least once a day (table 9.1) (Laumann et al., 1994).

Erotic fantasies vary in intensity. Some are fleeting; others are so strong, they crowd out other thoughts. Their frequency and intensity are influenced by our creative imagination and the strength of our wishes, as well as by our need to attend to other, non-erotic concerns. Lying in a hammock on a warm summer afternoon can result in intense erotic fantasies; lying naked on an examination table in your physician's office might not. Researchers have found

The desire to touch and be touched marks a growing closeness both socially and sexually in a relationship.

**TABLE 9.1**    RESPONSES TO THE QUESTION "HOW OFTEN DO YOU THINK ABOUT SEX?"

| | *"Every day" or "Several times a day"* | *"A few times a month" or "A few times a week"* | *"Less than once a month" or "Never"* |
|---|---|---|---|
| Men | 54% | 43% | 4% |
| Women | 19% | 67% | 1% |

**Source:** Data from E. Laumann et al., *The Social Organization of Sexuality* (Chicago: University of Chicago Press, 1994), p. 135.

that the lower the level of a person's sexual guilt and the more permissive her or his sexual attitudes, the longer and more explicit are her or his erotic fantasies (Meuwissen & Over, 1991). Some individuals believe they should consciously limit the content of their erotic fantasies. They may have been raised in a religious tradition that emphasized that fantasizing about an unacceptable or immoral act is equivalent to actually performing that act.

Fantasizing is a learned cognitive skill (Heiman and LoPiccolo, 1988). The potential for erotic fantasy develops early and unfolds over a lifetime (Bell, 1997; Maltz & Boss, 1997). Adolescent sexual fantasies typically begin between the ages of eleven and thirteen, with males beginning earlier than females (Gold & Gold, 1991; Leitenberg & Henning, 1995). First fantasies tend to be about acquaintances, dates, or teachers, but soon begin to involve unconventional content, strangers, and fictitious persons. Some researchers believe that the gender of the individuals who appear in erotic fantasies offers a clue regarding gender identity and the future sexual orientation of the fantasizer: primarily homosexual, bisexual, or heterosexual (Storms, 1981). However, this is still uncertain, as fantasized sexual activities with same-sex and other-sex individuals are common, regardless of the individual's primary sexual orientation.

## Gender Differences in Fantasy Content

In keeping with learned gender roles, women and men tend to have somewhat different kinds of fantasies. Women report softer and more romantic fantasies that are not so focused on explicit sexual encounters (Michael et al., 1994). They might involve submitting to a sexual situation, imaginary same-sex and other-sex lovers, and a wide range of sexual activities. Women's fantasies tend to contain more sensory imagery—imagery of touch, sight, sound, taste, and smell. They are more likely to be focused on the social and psychological aspects of sexual relating, rather than on the physical aspects (Alfonso et al., 1992; Gold & Gold, 1991).

Men report fantasies that tend to focus on body parts and sex acts, as well as explicit images related to sexual intercourse (Michael et al., 1994). A man's

fantasies often involve relatively impersonal sexual encounters in which he is powerful and aggressive. Common themes involve coercing others to have sex with him, or their complying after initially resisting. Here again, gender roles have an influence on erotic imagery, in that men's fantasies focus on active performance, explicit sexual details, and numerous partners (Byrne & Schulte, 1990).

## Fantasies and Sexual Expression

Fantasies are an important aspect of both solitary and shared sexual experiences and typically serve as "orgasmic triggers." An imaginary scenario might involve an ideal lover or sexual situation. Imaginary stimuli are so effective in enhancing arousal that sex therapists often encourage their clients to practice sexual fantasies during masturbation in order to intensify sexual arousal (Heiman & LoPiccolo, 1988).

Masturbation fantasies allow their creator to engage in sexual situations that are impossible or forbidden in real life. They allow us to "test out" various sexual scenarios, create "ideal responses" from a partner, and choose whatever behaviors enhance arousal.

Masturbatory fantasies don't reflect dissatisfaction with a real partner; they are private, personal events that have little to do with one's real partner. Nor do they reflect sexual or marital dissatisfaction, an inadequate personality, or an inactive sex life (Davidson & Hoffman, 1986). The general rule seems to be that those who engage in more frequent sexual activity and those whose sexual lives are more satisfying and happy tend to engage in more erotic fantasizing (Leitenberg & Henning, 1995). Erotic fantasies serve to introduce psychological novelty and variation into sexual activity.

Fantasies are an important part of partnered sexual expression as well. In one survey, 84 percent of respondents indicated they fantasized during intercourse (Cado & Leitenberg, 1990), and another survey found that about the same proportion of women and men report frequent erotic fantasies during

**coitus** (kō'i-tus)    heterosexual intercourse

intercourse (Sue, 1979). African Americans appear to engage in coital fantasies somewhat more frequently compared to whites (Price & Miller, 1984).

Yet some individuals do not feel comfortable with their erotic fantasies. Some feel guilty, and as if they were betraying their real-life partner. College students with such guilt feelings were more likely to believe their fantasies were immoral, abnormal, and a sign of problems in their love relationship (Cado & Leitenberg, 1990).

Another issue has to do with fantasies that involve violent sexual encounters, being forced into sexual activity or sexual scenarios that involve humiliation. Women appear to be more likely to have these fantasies, though men have them too. Women who have such fantasies, and sometimes the partners they tell them to, might conclude that they represent the "secret wishes" of the fantasizer. These conclusions are further fueled by pornographic movies that often portray resistant women who then "enjoy" being brutalized and raped. These beliefs can lead to one of the more prevalent rape myths: that "all women secretly want to be raped." There is no evidence to support any of these conclusions. Remember that the fantasizer is totally and completely in control of all that happens in the scenario. The fantasized "brute" is brutal in exactly the right way and is directed to do precisely and only what the fantasizer wants. Real rape is terrifying because the victim has *very little control* over the rapist. One might say that what is stimulating in such fantasies is not the violence; *it is the fantasizer's power and control over the violence.* For the majority of human beings, sexual fantasies, no matter how strange or unusual, are best viewed as erotic creativity.

One last point. There is some evidence that actually living out sexual fantasies is invariably disappointing (Bullough & Bullough, 1994).

The case has been made here that sexual fantasy is a normal, safe, and potentially useful human activity. This conclusion is well supported by sexological researchers who study erotic imagery among emotionally stable individuals (Whipple, Ogden, & Komisanak, 1992). For the vast majority of human beings, private erotic fantasies are pleasurable, self-enhancing, and just plain fun.

## 9.2.2   Masturbation

Masturbation (genital self-stimulation) is the most frequent form of sexual expression for most people in our culture (Kinsey, Pomeroy, & Martin, 1948; Kinsey et al., 1953; Leitenberg, Detzer, & Srebnik, 1993), especially men. Not only do more men than women masturbate, they do so much more often (Oliver & Hyde, 1993). One survey found that men masturbated almost three times as often as women (Leitenberg, 1993).

**Masturbation** is voluntary, intentional self-stimulation (often to orgasm) of one's own genitals or other sensitive areas of the body. This is most often done by the hands, but other objects can be used to reach gratification. While the term can be used to describe stimulation or manipulation of someone else's genitalia, as in *mutual masturbation,* here we will use the term to refer to self-stimulation. During masturbation, the body goes through exactly the same stages of increasing vasocongestion and myotonia as occur during sexual activity with a partner (Masters & Johnson, 1966).

### Incidence and Frequency

Masturbation is a very common sexual practice. Janus and Janus (1993) found that 81 percent of men and 72 percent of women regularly masturbated. The NHSLS data indicated that 60 percent of men and 40 percent of women had masturbated in the previous twelve months (Laumann et al., 1994). Of these individuals, about one in four men and one in ten women masturbated once a week or more. Men between 18 to 24 masturbated *less* than any other age group, except for men over age 54. This finding was interpreted to mean that men age 18 to 24 might believe that masturbation is what adolescents do, and so it becomes more taboo (Michael et al., 1994). There were some gender differences in masturbation patterns, in that women, as a group, tended to begin masturbating after adolescence, and often *after* having begun having sexual intercourse, rather than before, as men do. Again, contrary to popular notions about the relationship between masturbation and partnered sexual expression, adults between the ages of 24 and 49 were the *most sexually active age group, and those most likely to have regular sexual partners were the ones most likely to masturbate.* In fact, nearly 85 percent of men and 45 percent of women who were living with a sex partner reported they had masturbated in the past year. It's clear, then, that masturbation does not serve as a *substitute* for partnered sex: those having the most partnered sex are the most likely to masturbate (Laumann et al., 1994).

In addition, those most likely to masturbate were white, college-educated, and more "liberal" in their sexual attitudes. As the level of education rose in the NHSLS respondents, so did the incidence of masturbation. By contrast, more than half of all men and more than three-quarters of all women without a high school education had not masturbated in the year prior to the survey. In terms of ethnicity, twice as many African American men reported *not* masturbating in the previous year. Overall, respondents who were less likely to masturbate were less experienced in sexual matters and more conservative and conventional in their sexual attitudes (Michael et al., 1994).

# GO ASK ALICE

*Alice,*

*If we are engaging in mutual masturbation, and I get semen on my hands, how long should I wait before touching my partner's vulva?*

*Handy*

Dear Handy,

Sperm survive only in a warm wet environment, and will die within seconds without it. When all of the semen dries, you are not in any danger of impregnating your partner. However, should your ejaculation land in or close to the vagina when still moist, there is a possibility of fertilization, even if you've never had intercourse. Make sure that moist semen stays away from the vaginal area to be super safe!

*Dear Alice,*

*I masturbate about 2–3 times a week, but I still feel horny all the time. I think about sex during class and other situations. I think this is also affecting my life. I can't help it when I get an erection during class, and it seems so obvious that I'm afraid other people may find out. What should I do? Is this natural? I especially think about this one girl, who I've had a crush on for a few years. I always think about her during class, but then I feel like a dirty scum when I'm around her. Am I just sexually repressed?*

*Horny*

Dear Horny,

Masturbating 2–3 times per week is well within the normal range. It's also normal for men, including young men, to feel horny frequently, and to have sexual fantasies. Horniness can increase or decrease when under stress, and also when inundated by stimuli, including memories.

When you get erections in class, there are ways of remaining discreet. Alice is sure that you already have a few tricks. Erections are a reaction to a sexual signal. Often, if you think about something asexual, or something that is a total turn-off, like your next exam, you can lose your erection.

Think about specific ways of discharging some of your sexual energy, such as masturbating more frequently. In terms of the woman you have a crush on, try talking with her. Sometimes, by acting on your feelings, you can put this looming sexual energy into perspective.

*Dear Alice,*

*I enjoy performing cunnilingus on my partner and she enjoys receiving it as well. Are there any techniques that can help me increase the pleasure she receives from oral sex?*

*Oral Man*

Dear Oral Man,

Your partner is the best resource available to answer this question. Ask her what she likes, and what turns her lights on before you go down on her and while you are doing it. Pay attention to her signals (moans and cries of delight or discomfort) as you try variations of your own style, or ask her about her fantasies. Many women would be thrilled to have you as their partner!

 http://www.mhhe.com/byer6

## Contemporary Perspectives on Masturbation

The Judeo-Christian tradition views only potentially reproductive sexual expression as acceptable, so masturbation is viewed very negatively. Catholic Church doctrine considers masturbation a serious moral offense, and Orthodox Judaism views masturbation as a sexual crime (Gregerson, 1986). During the nineteenth century, Western attitudes toward masturbation shifted from seeing it as a *sin* to seeing it an *affliction* that led to physical deterioration, mental disorder, and even death. Among the general public, there is still a negative attitude toward masturbation, but certain facts are now clear. Masturbation is physically and mentally harmless. It does not lead to physical weakness, mental illness, or moral deterioration.

Masturbation can be as physically satisfying as partnered sex, and some individuals report masturbatory orgasms to be even more intense. Men cannot "run out" of semen if they masturbate: the more semen released, the more produced. Masturbation can help us learn what is personally pleasurable and give us experience with how we respond during sexual arousal and orgasm. In fact, masturbation is a widely recommended form of treatment for women who have difficulty reaching orgasm (Kay, 1992; Goodwin & Agronin, 1997). It can also provide effective relief

| **masturbation** (mas-ter-bā′shun) | self-stimulation of the genitals or other parts of the body for sexual pleasure |
| --- | --- |

from menstrual cramps. However, masturbation is *not* physically necessary for either good mental or physical health.

The NHSLS found that 70 percent of men and 65 percent of women reported they masturbated to "relieve sexual tension." About one-third of the respondents of both genders offered "lack of an available sexual partner" as a reason. About one-quarter of the men said they masturbated "to relax."

How did respondents feel about their masturbatory activities? Again, a gender difference emerged. Among men, the more frequently they masturbated, the higher their report of guilt feelings. Among women, the higher the level of masturbatory frequency, the *lower* their level of guilt feelings (Michael et al. 1994). And how is masturbation related to other aspects of sexual responsiveness? Women who masturbate have been found to have significantly more single and multiple orgasms, greater sexual desire, higher self-esteem, and greater marital and sexual satisfaction; and they become sexually aroused faster than women who do not masturbate (Hurlbert & Whittaker, 1991; Kelly, Strassberg, & Kircher, 1990).

### How Men Masturbate

While there may be variations, most men masturbate by manipulating the penis in some way with their hands. They might begin with a gentle rubbing or tapping action of the flaccid penis, and then build to a mild stroking of the semi-erect penis. Often the penis is grasped with the whole hand, by making a ring with the thumb and index finger, or by the thumb and several fingers. The penis is then stroked along the length of the shaft with pressure ranging from a light touch to a tight grip (fig. 9.1). The amount of pressure used, the number of fingers used, and how much of the shaft is stroked vary among different men. Some rub only the glans, tap the glans, or roll the foreskin back from the glans. As orgasm approaches, the action tends to become more rapid and vigorous, with increasing pressure on the penis. As ejaculation begins, stroking might slow or stop entirely, because continued stimulation of the glans might be unpleasant.

Some men use one hand to caress or grasp the scrotum or caress the anal region, or they might massage their nipples. Beyond a drop or two of Cowper's fluid secreted from the tip of the penis, there is no natural lubricant on the skin of the penis in masturbation. Therefore, some men use a lubricating jelly, cream, oil, or saliva to enhance sensation, or use water and soapsuds when they masturbate while bathing. Some men purchase artificial vaginas, or use a vibrator to stimulate the penis and/or anal area directly, or they might strap a vibrator to the back of

the hand for indirect penile stimulation. A few men attempt to insert objects into the urethral opening, and this can result in infection and injury.

### How Women Masturbate

Masters and Johnson (1966) reported that no two of the women observed in their laboratory masturbated exactly alike. In general, women stimulate the mons, the inner lips, the clitoral area, or the clitoral shaft with circular or back-and-forth movements, or by lightly touching the glans (fig. 9.2). Tugging on the inner lips creates sensations on the clitoris while the fingers penetrate the vagina. Pressure on the very sensitive glans may be unpleasant for many women. Some women use the other hand to caress the breasts, nipples, or anal region. Some women do pelvic thrusting by squeezing the thigh muscles. Despite what is a mainstay of male-oriented pornography, only about 20 percent of women insert objects (such as **dildos**) into the vagina. Vibrators are also popular during masturbation. Applying the vibrator directly on the genital area or through a bedsheet or layer of underwear is common; a smaller number of women who use vibrators prefer the type that straps to the back of the hand to provide indirect stimulation. Some women direct streams of warm water onto the genital area while bathing.

It is commonly believed that women "take longer" to become aroused to the point of orgasm, and this is generally true during partnered sexual activity. During masturbation, a woman can totally direct the location, speed, and intensity of stimulation. Kinsey and colleagues (1953) found that during masturbation, most women can reach orgasm in less than four minutes (about the same amount of time as men require) and some were able to reach orgasm in less than one minute.

## 9.3 SHARED PLEASURING

Shared pleasuring involves interactive give-and-take with another person who has his or her sexual needs, preferences, and insights. Shared sexual interactions range from gentle hugs and kisses to passionate orgasms and strong feelings of emotional vulnerability.

### 9.3.1 The Beginnings of Pleasuring

The term **foreplay** is commonly used in our culture to describe the first stages of lovemaking. It is wise to recognize the psychological biases inherent in that term. It implies that the behaviors described are merely the "play before" the "goal" (penile-vaginal coitus, orgasm, etc). It also implies that unless the

**FIGURE 9.1** Male masturbation not only provides for relaxation and self-knowledge, but also is a source of sexual release.

**FIGURE 9.2** A woman can use masturbation as a relaxed, private, self-exploration in which she teaches herself to respond sexually.

goal is reached, "real sex" has not occurred. Sexologists prefer to use the term *pleasuring* in order to free our thinking and our lovemaking from this goal orientation. For some, caressing, holding, kissing, and intimate conversation can be satisfying ends in themselves. Sometimes it is difficult for one partner to clearly communicate that "kissing and snuggling" is all that is desired at a particular moment, but these communication skills can be very important.

Close body contact is the starting point of all lovemaking. This can begin with dry or oiled massages, or perhaps back or foot rubs. In our culture, it typically includes embracing, as well as the kissing, caressing, touching, and stroking of erogenous areas of the body. Thus touching (tactile stimulation), whether with the hands, mouth or other parts of the body, is very important. This pleasuring can last as long as the couple desires, but researchers typically find that women prefer a longer period of pleasuring than do their male partners (Darling, Davidson, & Cox, 1991; Denny, Fields, & Quadagno, 1984).

While traditional sexual "scripts" portray women as the passive recipients of pleasuring, the so-called "sexual revolution" and women's movement seem to have had an impact in the bedroom (Friday, 1991). In general, women are now more active and reciprocating during this phase of lovemaking. Also,

as was previously suggested, once women discover through the experience of masturbation how they like to be touched or otherwise stimulated, they can be much more adept at helping their partner please them. Soft murmurs and groans of delight, shifting body movements, "hand-riding" their partner's hands, and even quiet whispers can contribute mightily to the experience of pleasuring.

### 9.3.2 Kissing

In our culture erotic kissing can be used to signal and facilitate increased arousal. Members of our society view kissing as a sign of affection and intimacy; kissing between prostitutes and their clients is relatively uncommon. In the simplest form, we press our lips to the lips of the other person. We also use our lips to kiss, stroke, suck, or nibble elsewhere on a partner's body. "French kissing" involves inserting the tongue into a partner's mouth. Sometimes the tongue is thrust in and out or around the person's mouth to simulate sexual intercourse. Kissing is pleasurable

| | |
|---|---|
| **dildo** | an object designed to be placed in the vagina or anus for sexual stimulation |
| **foreplay** | the first stages of lovemaking |

because the lips, tongue, and mouth are packed with sensory nerve endings. Touch, smell, and taste are all involved in kissing.

## 9.3.3 Touching

In terms of what connects people to each other, even before there is language, there is touching. Touch is the sense through which an infant experiences caretaking, comfort, love, and connection. No wonder we sometimes hunger for touch or rely on touch to communicate our most intimate needs and desires.

Through our highly sensitive fingertips, we express affection, arouse our partners, and increase the eroticism of a sexual encounter. Creative and imaginative hand stimulation is part of the art of lovemaking. Small buildups, teasing withdrawals, and further buildups all contribute to increasing arousal. Careful attention to our partner's responses to our touching will increase the pleasure felt by both individuals. Light, slow touch is often preferred over pressure during early excitement. As arousal mounts, touch can be more specific, pressured, and excited.

### Breast Stimulation

The breasts are erotically sensitive in both women and men, though women and gay men are more likely than heterosexual men to enjoy having their breasts stimulated (Masters & Johnson, 1979). In our culture, next to the genitals, the breasts are probably the most erogenous area of the body for women, but this is not universally true (Ecker, 1993).

Breast size is unimportant to their sensitivity. Breast sensitivity varies from woman to woman as well as in the same woman at different times. As with most things sexual and human, some women do not enjoy breast stimulation, and others enjoy it only at certain times.

Breast stimulation is enhanced when both the hands and the mouth are used. Although the nipples are the most sensitive part of the breast in both women and men, caressing other areas is also pleasurable. Some men enjoy nipple stimulation; others do not. Breasts can be kissed, sucked, kneaded with the lips, or tongued. Personal preferences can be communicated to a partner, either through explicit description or by those very helpful, moans, murmurs, and movements.

### Genital Touching

The genitals of both women and men are highly sensitive, and most people are easily aroused when their genitals are caressed. Over 90 percent of men and women report that they stimulate the genitals of their sex partners (Breakwell & Fife-Shaw, 1992). Caressing a partner's genitals can lead to orgasm, or it can be a prelude to oral sex and/or intercourse.

Stroking or kissing the abdomen, buttocks, and inner thighs, gradually getting closer to the genitals, is exciting preparation for more direct genital attention. At first, gentle genital caresses are usually more arousing because genital tissue is sensitive and easily irritated. The pressure and speed of the caresses can be slowly increased as arousal builds. Partners might caress each other's genitals simultaneously or alternate and concentrate on one, then the other, partner's pleasure.

Some sex therapists suggest that partners watch each other masturbate in order to learn each other's preferences regarding stimulation. How does that idea sound to you? For many people, this can be very arousing. For others, it can sound threatening or embarrassing.

Remember, individual and couple preferences are very diverse (Gach, 1997). Remember also that everyone's preferences vary from time to time. Attending carefully to a partner's responses, movements, and verbal communications during lovemaking will usually provide good guidance. Some sexologists believe that when it comes to pleasure with a partner, a useful guideline is "Read my hips!" Want some other helpful hints? Remember that the glans of the penis and clitoris can be extremely sensitive, so indirect stimulation of these areas might be more effective. Remember also that stimulation of the labia and scrotum is generally very pleasurable. Moving a finger or fingers in and out of the vaginal vestibule is very arousing, but only after there is plenty of lubrication, so it's best to approach this activity gradually and with careful attention to a partner's responses. Gripping the penis just behind the corona and stroking it up and down is also very arousing, but again, one must attend carefully to a partner's feedback regarding how tightly to grip and the desired speed of movement. Caressing the perineum and the anal area can also be very arousing, but many people have very strong feelings about anal stimulation, so it might be best to openly ask about this. If anal stimulation is agreed upon, be very sure not to put anything that has been in the anus into the mouth or vagina without carefully washing it first.

Many of us think of caressing each other's genitals (fig. 9.3) as a prelude to oral-genital sex or intercourse, but for some couples such caressing is all that is desired or preferred. This is often referred to as **mutual masturbation.** Because no bodily fluids are exchanged, mutual masturbation can serve as a good "safer sex" technique. It can be a very satisfying activity for heterosexual couples who desire sexual intimacy without having intercourse. Such couples might not feel ready for intercourse or they might have no contraceptives available. Mutual masturbation is a very common technique for gay and lesbian couples.

**FIGURE 9.3** Hand caressing of the female genitals (especially the clitoris) by the male and of the male genitals by the female is an exciting form of stimulation.

## 9.3.4 Oral-Genital Sex

A very erotic form of kissing is genital kissing, or **oral-genital sex.** Attitudes toward the acceptability of oral-genital sex have undergone a major change in the United States since the 1950s (Breakwell & Fife-Shaw, 1992). Long considered a rather deviant activity and associated with homosexual orientation, Kinsey and colleagues (1948, 1953) found that oral-genital sex was practiced by 60 percent of college-educated couples, but by only about 20 percent of persons with only a high-school education. Only 10 percent of persons with only a grade school education included such contacts in their lovemaking. According to the NHSLS (Laumann et al., 1994), 77 percent of men and 68 percent of women had played the active role in oral sex with a partner during their lifetime, and 27 percent of men and 19 percent of women had done so in their last sexual encounter. About 79 percent of men and 73 percent of women had received oral sex during their lifetime. Education level, ethnicity, age, and religious orientation were important predictors of who was more likely to engage in oral sex. Those *least likely* to engage in oral sex were persons who had not graduated from high school, African Americans, persons over fifty years of age, and persons from a conservative Protestant religious orientation (Laumann et al., 1994). Oral-genital sex was ranked as the third most appealing form of sexual activity in the NHSLS (Laumann et al., 1994). An earlier survey, of American men (Billy et al., 1993), revealed some other interesting ethnic differences. Overall, African American men were less likely to engage in oral-genital sex, and white Latinos were less likely to have done so compared to other groups of whites.

Like all sexual activities, oral sex can be very arousing for some people, while others may find the idea disgusting. Some people have negative reactions to oral sex because urination and defecation is associated with the genital area, and there might be fear of contact with disease-causing agents. Others associate unpleasant tastes or odors with such activity, or they are hesitant about taking vaginal secretions or semen into the mouth. Some experience the lack of face-to-face contact as less intimate, while others view oral sex as a sign of a very intimate and special relationship between committed partners. Some heterosexual couples engage in oral sex as a precursor to intercourse, while for others it is the center of their lovemaking. For same-sex couples, oral-genital sex might be their preferred way of making love.

During oral-genital sex, body fluids are exchanged, so precautions against sexually transmitted infections apply. Viruses and bacteria can be transmitted during oral sex, so if the couple is not monogamous, or if they are not absolutely certain that both are free of HIV and other STIs, a male or female condom, or a latex dam, should be used (see chapter 6). One other precaution: Never blow air into a woman's urethral opening or into the penis opening. Doing so can force bacteria into the opening. Blowing air into the vagina during pregnancy is particularly hazardous because a potentially fatal *air embolism* could form.

### Cunnilingus

The word **cunnilingus** comes from the Latin and means "licking the vulva," so it refers to using the tongue and lips to stimulate the female genitals (vulva): clitoris, labia, vaginal vestibule, and vaginal opening (fig. 9.4). Any part of the vulva might be stimulated, but the primary focus is usually the clitoral area. The preferred type of contact is quite variable. Some enjoy pressure on either side of the clitoral shaft, around the hood, or on the glans itself. Others

| | |
|---|---|
| **mutual masturbation** | partners' simultaneous stimulation of each other's genitals |
| **oral-genital sex** | stimulation of a partner's genitals with the mouth and tongue |
| **cunnilingus** (kun-i-lin´gus) | stimulation of a woman's genitals using the mouth and tongue |

**FIGURE 9.4**  Cunnilingus, or oral stimulation of the female genitals, can be a way of expressing deep intimate feelings between partners.

**FIGURE 9.5**  Fellatio, the oral stimulation of the man's genitals, may or may not include ejaculation, but can provide a great deal of pleasure to both partners.

prefer having the inner labia licked or the tongue inserted into the vaginal opening. The type of movement preferred also varies, so good communication is vital.

Many women enjoy cunnilingus because the tongue is moist and gentle, and there is less chance for discomfort than with manual stimulation. As one woman put it: "A tongue offers gentleness and precision and wetness and is the perfect organ for contact. And besides, it produces sensational orgasms!" (Hite, 1976, p. 361).

Some women need to conquer the notion that a partner would not enjoy performing cunnilingus on them. Actually, this activity can be equally arousing for the active partner. Some women have acquired negative attitudes toward their genitals and believe them to be "dirty" and "ugly." Some resort to using unnecessary and often harmful vaginal cosmetics to reassure themselves that they are acceptable. When freshly bathed and disease-free, a woman's genitals are as clean as any other part of her body. Like all partnered sexual behavior, cunnilingus should be mutually agreeable. For beginners, some experimentation might be necessary, and if this particular activity

is not acceptable to either member of a couple, there are lots of other sexual activities from which to choose.

### Fellatio

The term *fellatio* comes from the Latin and means "to suck." **Fellatio** involves oral stimulation of a man's genitals (fig. 9.5). While fellatio techniques vary, the most common approach involves sucking or licking the glans and neck of the penis. Some variations and additions include nibbling the glans, licking the scrotum, or placing part or all of the shaft of the penis into the mouth. To do this, the active partner has to relax the throat muscles, and this might take practice! Any type of sucking or tonguing action might be used. Both partners need to agree whether the active partner will receive ejaculate into the mouth. Some individuals are aroused by doing this, but others prefer not to. The active partner can spit out the ejaculate into a tissue or towel, or switch to manual stimulation just before ejaculation. Again, as in all partnered sexual activity, communication and mutual agreement are vital if fellatio is to be a positive part of lovemaking.

**FIGURE 9.6** Simultaneous oral-genital stimulation.

Fellatio is very pleasurable for many men. It is a very common practice among gay men, and has become normative in heterosexual couples as well. It is the most frequent sexual activity between prostitutes and their clients.

### Mutual Oral-Genital Sex

A couple might opt to have oral-genital contact at the same time. The common term for this is "**69**," or "*soixante neuf,*" which describes the body posture of the two individuals (fig. 9.6). Either partner can be on top of the other, or they can lie side by side. Again, a bit of experimentation and practice is called for. Simultaneous oral-genital contact is exciting for many couples; others find the positioning too acrobatic. Some find that trying to actively please one's partner while being pleasured at the same time calls for too much concentration and can actually interfere with the enjoyment of both partners. Again, partners can negotiate "taking turns" even in this position. Too great a height difference between partners can also be problematic in simultaneous oral sex.

## 9.3.5   Anal Sex

Anal sex is stereotypically associated with gay male sexuality, yet both the Kinsey reports (1948, 1953) and the NHSLS (Laumann et al., 1994) found that such behavior was not limited to gay men. Of the NHSLS respondents, 26 percent of men and 20 percent of women had engaged in anal sex during their lifetime. Ten percent of men and 9 percent of women respondents had done so within the previous twelve months. Anal activities were more common among the better educated and among those with no religious practice. In terms of ethnicity, more Latino men had engaged in anal sex, compared to either white or African American men (Michael et al., 1994). Anal sexual activities were highest among white women, and lowest among African American women; the rate for Latino women was in between those two.

Anal activities can include oral-anal contact (**anilingus**), (commonly referred to as "rimming"), insertion or stimulation with the fingers ("fingering"), gradual insertion of the penis (**anal intercourse**), or insertion of some inanimate object such as a dildo. Anal tissue is very sensitive, and anal stimulation can lead to orgasm in both women and men (Masters & Johnson, 1979).

The public debate about anal sex has become more prominent because of recent court decisions, surveys regarding attitudes toward anal sex, and the laws that seek to punish such activities. Few students realize that in many states, *sexual acts involving oral and anal contact are illegal.* They often constitute what laws refer to as "sodomy." Do you know what the laws are in your state? For an update on this controversial issue, see "At Issue: Private Sexual Behavior and the Law."

The anus lacks any natural lubrication, and it is easily damaged by dry or abrasive objects. Before inserting anything into the anus, lubrication with a water-soluble lubricant (such as *K-Y Jelly*) is important. During anal intercourse, lubricated condoms should always be used.

The anal sphincter muscle normally keeps the anus tightly shut and the muscle contracts even further when the anus is penetrated. Before attempting insertion, some individuals manually dilate the anus with a finger. Slowly the anus becomes more adapted

| | |
|---|---|
| **fellatio** (fe-lā´shē-ō) | using the mouth and tongue to stimulate a man's genitals |
| **"69"** | a sexual position allowing simultaneous oral-genital contact between two partners |
| **anilingus** (ā´´ni-lin´gus) | using the mouth and tongue to stimulate a partner's anus |
| **anal intercourse** | the insertion of the penis into a partner's anus |

# AT ISSUE

## PRIVATE SEXUAL BEHAVIOR AND THE LAW

In approximately half the states that make up the United States, noncoital sex acts are prohibited by law. Often described as "unnatural sex acts" or "laws against nature," these non-coital sex acts include oral sex, anal sex, and sexual contact with animals. They are typically codified as "sodomy."

Despite laws that make certain sex acts between consenting adults illegal, there have been a series of judicial decisions that have sought to protect private sexual behavior. You may recall that the Comstock Laws prohibited the dissemination of contraceptive information. Two famous cases (*Griswold v. Connecticut* and *Eisenstadt v. Baird*) established that preventing people from obtaining contraceptive information violated their constitutional right to privacy. During the 1970s, *Roe v. Wade* established that laws preventing a woman from choosing whether or not to keep a pregnancy violated her right to privacy.

A 1986 Supreme Court case (*Bowers v. Hardwick*) raised similar privacy issues regarding sex acts between consenting adults. A Georgia man was being served a warrant on an unrelated charge. The police officer discovered him committing an act of "sodomy" and charged him with a felony under Georgia law. He was convicted, but this was reversed by a U.S. court of appeals on the grounds that the conviction violated his right to privacy. The Supreme Court subsequently reversed that decision on the grounds that there was no constitutional right to engage in sodomy. In other words, the court could not go around creating rights not found in the Constitution. The man was not prosecuted, so the whole issue was sidestepped.

At about the same time as the Supreme Court decision, a Gallup poll found that 57 percent of those surveyed believed that states should not attempt to regulate sexual acts between consenting homosexual adults. Seventy-four percent believed that states should not regulate non-coital heterosexual acts (Alpern, 1986).

to the penetration and can relax to accommodate a larger object such as a penis. Never force anything into the anus.

The upper parts of the rectum are insensitive to pain. The lining of the rectum is very tender and can be very easily torn and damaged during anal sex. This can lead to pelvic inflammation and other serious problems (Agnew, 1986). For these reasons, attempts to insert large objects, such as a hand (*"fisting"*), can be very dangerous and harmful.

When freshly bathed, the skin around the anus can be as clean as any other body area. Yet bacteria and other organisms are normally present within the anus and rectum. These can cause mouth, vaginal, and urethral infections in both women and men, especially hepatitis B. It is worth repeating that anything that has contact with the anus should be thoroughly washed before it has any contact with the mouth or vagina. A more effective precaution is to use a lubricated condom during anal contact, which should then be removed and disposed of. However, anal intercourse is one of the most damaging acts for a condom. The calculated condom breakage rate is 1 in 105 for anal intercourse, as compared to 1 in 165 for vaginal intercourse (Consumers Union, 1989).

Anal intercourse is also one of the riskiest activities for contracting HIV infection. Infected white blood cells and HIV in ejaculate can easily pass through the rectal lining and into the bloodstream of the receptive partner.

Whether male or female, all who receive anal sex run a greater risk of contracting HIV from an infected partner (Voeller, 1991). Anal sexual practices, including penile-anal, oral-anal, and manual-anal contacts, especially between those who engage in sexual activity with more than one person, all increase the risk of contracting HIV. (See chapter 7 for a more detailed discussion.) Not all gay men practice anal intercourse (Catania et al., 1991); but AIDS prevention programs have been very effective in decreasing unprotected anal intercourse among young gay men (Kegeles, Hays, & Coates, 1996; Vincke, Bolton, & Miller, 1997).

## 9.3.6 Coitus

*Sexual intercourse* or *coitus* (from the Latin word *coire*) refer to the "going together" of the penis and vagina (fig. 9.7). Although the word *intercourse* can be used to refer to nonvaginal forms of sexual activity, such as *interfemoral intercourse* (moving the erect penis between tightly squeezed thighs), *intermammary intercourse* (moving the erect penis in the cleavage between the breasts), or *anal intercourse,* here the discussion will be limited to vaginal intercourse.

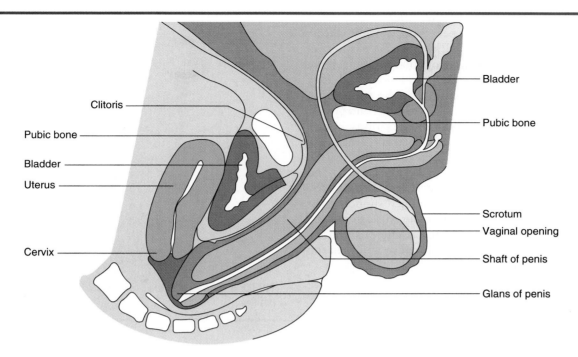

**FIGURE 9.7** Male and female genitals during coitus. Varying body positions can create greater satisfaction because pressure is exerted on different genital organs.

How coitus is carried out depends on a couple's culture, time in history, and their personal preferences (see "Dimensions of Diversity: Coital Positions across Cultures"). It also depends on the age, size, health, and physical condition of the individuals. There is no one "normal" or "natural" position, nor are there "abnormal" or "perverted" positions. Some coital positions are very restful, while others require almost acrobatic abilities. An imaginative couple might use several positions during one extended lovemaking session. Coital practices that both partners enjoy are the ones to use (Goodwin & Agronin, 1997). Once again we're reminded of the importance of communication and negotiation!

There are two basic varieties of coital positioning: face-to-face and rear-entry. The face-to-face postures are much more common in our culture, so we will begin with those.

### Face-to-Face, Man Above

Man-on-top positions are so common in our society that many view these as the only "normal" ones for intercourse. These positions are sometimes referred to as the "missionary position." Advantages of this position include being able to look into each other's eyes, and being able to continue mouth kissing and breast caressing (fig. 9.8), although one researcher found that most couples did not maintain eye contact during intercourse (Schnarch, 1993). The woman is

**FIGURE 9.8** A variation of the man-above face-to-face coital position.

able to lie relaxed and hold and caress the man's body, allowing him to take the initiative and to psychologically feel assertive. Either the man or the woman can gently open the inner lips to guide the penis into the vagina. Pelvic thrusting is easy for the healthy man who is free of disabilities, and he is in control of the speed and intensity of stimulation.

Disadvantages include the man's very high arousal level. He might penetrate quickly, thrust rapidly, and ejaculate so quickly that his partner remains unsatisfied. These are not good positions if the man has poor control over ejaculation, and they contribute to the problems of men who suffer from *premature ejaculation* (lack of voluntary control over the timing of ejaculation). In these positions, a man cannot control the depth of penetration into the vagina, and his weight might be too great for the woman's comfort. She might feel "pinned down" and be unable to move freely, especially if he rests too much of his weight on her. Some men support their weight with their arms and legs, but this can quickly become very tiring. This is not a useful position for intercourse late in pregnancy because it places too much pressure on the fetus.

Man-above positions increase the likelihood of conception (Masters & Johnson, 1966). Because the woman is on her back, the vaginal barrel slopes downward into the blind end or cul-de-sac of the vagina, and with increased sexual arousal this cul-de-sac enlarges. This allows semen to collect in the cul-de-sac after ejaculation. When sexual arousal decreases, the uterus returns to its original position and the cervix dips into the seminal pool formed in the cul-de-sac. This allows for easier movement of the sperm into the uterus (Masters & Johnson, 1966).

There are several variations within the man-above positions. Both partners might lie flat with legs extended. Or the woman might bend her knees and draw them toward her chest with the man between them. Or she can rest her feet on his shoulders or lock them around his back. He can vary how much weight he places on her body.

### Face-to-Face, Woman Above

Around the world, woman-above positions are the most frequently used (Langmyhr, 1976). Advantages include greater pleasure for the woman because she has greater control over the rhythm and angle of penile-vaginal friction (fig. 9.9) and over the depth of penile penetration. By merely flexing her hips, she can shorten the length of the vaginal barrel, placing the tip of the penis deeper into the vagina. Furthermore, many women feel that woman-above positions make them feel more involved, less passive, and less like intercourse is something that is "done" to them.

Woman-above positions are also helpful for the woman who has difficulty reaching orgasm, because she can arrange for penetration to occur in a way that she finds more arousing and she can experiment with the kinds of movements she finds erotic. If the man is having difficulty with erection, woman-above positions allow her to work the semi-erect penis into the vagina and then help enhance full erection. These

**FIGURE 9.9** A variation of the woman-above face-to-face coital position.

positions are also helpful to men who ejaculate too quickly. In these positions, the woman can more easily control the tempo of penile penetrations, and she can slow the rhythm down to regulate his arousal level.

The woman-above positions lead some men to feel they are being forced to "surrender" their dominant role, and they feel psychologically subordinate. Again, communication and negotiation are needed.

Variations of the woman-above positions include the woman sitting upright, astride the man's body, and facing him. This allows for talking, kissing, breast stimulation, and stimulation of the clitoris. Or she can rest her full body on his, or between his spread legs. Woman-above positions require more effort from the woman and can therefore be more restful for the man.

### Face-to-Face, Side-to-Side

In the side-to-side coital positions, both partners lie on their side, facing each other, and fully bear their own weight. Often their legs are intertwined (fig. 9.10).

Advantages of the side-to-side positions include their being very restful and leisurely for both partners. They allow for kissing, breast stimulation, and freedom of movement. These positions are very useful when one or both partners is overweight, or the woman is pregnant. Also, the depth of penile penetration is easy to control by positioning the legs of each partner. Because these positions are less active, they allow for greater ejaculatory control by the man, and so they can be helpful in countering premature ejaculation.

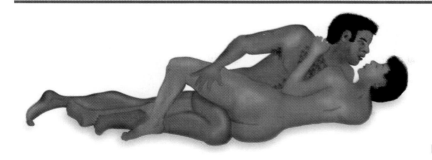

**FIGURE 9.10** Side-to-side coital position.

Some find these positions disadvantageous because penetration by the penis can be more difficult, lying on one arm can be uncomfortable, and there can be less clitoral stimulation.

The lateral coital position is a variation of the side-to-side posture and was recommended by Masters and Johnson (1970) for ejaculatory problems. In this variation, the couple shifts from a woman-above position to a side-by-side position, with the man partially supporting the woman's body. This frees one arm of each partner for caressing, yet provides comfort and support for the woman's free pelvic thrusting.

### Rear-Entry Positions

In rear-entry positions, the man faces the woman's back and enters her vagina from the rear (fig. 9.11). This is usually done with both partners lying on their sides. Other variations include the woman standing and leaning over, or kneeling and resting on her hands and elbows. Still other variations involve the man sitting on a low stool while the woman sits astride him, facing away.

As with the other positions described here, rear-entry positions have both advantages and disadvantages. During rear entry, the woman's hips are likely to be flexed, bringing the thighs forward. Such flexing shortens the vaginal barrel, placing the penis deeper into the vagina. For some women, this is very pleasurable, but for others it is uncomfortable. Rear-entry positions also provide less clitoral stimulation for the woman, but manual stimulation of the clitoral area by either partner can compensate for this. Some men find rear-entry positions especially arousing because they allow full exposure to and contact with the woman's buttocks.

Because rear-entry positions allow both partners to bear their own weight, they require less exertion and are more restful. This is advantageous if the partners are fatigued, debilitated, elderly, or recovering from an illness or surgery. These positions are also more comfortable during late pregnancy and for obese individuals.

**FIGURE 9.11** Rear-entry coital position.

Some people object to rear-entry positions because they resemble the posture for anal intercourse, which they find repugnant. They might also feel it is too "animalistic" because this is the posture that most lower animals assume during copulation. Still others feel the rear-entry positions lack the intimacy of the face-to-face positions.

### Sitting Positions

In the various sitting positions, the man is usually sitting on a chair or bed, while the woman sits astride him and faces *either toward him or away from him* (fig. 9.12). Unless her weight is excessive, these positions can be very restful for both partners. They allow the man to embrace the woman and to caress her breasts and clitoral area. These positions are very useful for men with spinal cord injuries. Also, some women prefer these positions during late pregnancy.

### Other Positions

Numerous other positions are possible (fig. 9.13). Some require extensive agility and athleticism, but they also allow for imagination. For many couples,

**FIGURE 9.12**   Sitting coital positions.

**FIGURE 9.13**   Some other coital positions.

agreeing to experiment with different coital techniques has been part of the formula for a happy and exciting sexual relationship.

## Contemporary Perspectives on Coitus

Coitus is the means by which human beings reproduce. Yet women can become pregnant during only about five days each month. Clearly, human beings engage in coitus for other than reproductive purposes. Sexual intercourse and other sexual intimacies serve to emotionally bond a couple together. Coitus and its equivalents express love, intimacy, trust, and commitment, as well as lust, hostility, and aggression (Sprecher & McKinney, 1993). Coitus can also express our desire for pleasure as well as our need to please someone else.

The National Health and Social Life Survey (Laumann et al., 1994) provided some eye-opening revelations about sex in America. According to the popular media and widely held stereotypes, young, attractive, single, healthy Americans engage in a great deal of shared sexual activity. Other widely held stereotypes are that (a) African Americans have sex more often than other ethnic groups, (b) religious conservatives have less sex than other groups, (c) marital sex is rare and routinized, (d) the young, unattached, and beautiful have the most passionate and frequent sex, and (e) frequent sex with a partner is overwhelmingly important and desireable (Michael et al., 1994).

The truth of the matter is that people are not having that much partnered sex, and the group having the most sex is not the young and single, but the married. According to the NHSLS data, Americans don't have sex as frequently as believed. Only one-third of the respondents reported sex with a partner at least twice a week. Another third reported sex a few times a month, and the final third had partnered sex a few times a year, or not at all during the course of the previous year. There were no differences based on ethnicity, education level, religious orientation, geographic part of the country, political orientation, or gender. The frequency of partnered sex, according to the NHSLS, was determined by how old the person was, whether people were married or cohabiting, and how long the couple had been together. Those between 18 and 24 and those between 50 and 59 had the least-frequent partnered sex. Men and women in

# DIMENSIONS OF DIVERSITY

## COITAL POSITIONS ACROSS CULTURES

Culture influences coital behaviors and which coital positions are preferred. These cultural prescriptions often reflect the status of each gender in that society. In other words, the popularity of woman-above, man-above, or side-by-side positions can tell us something about the relative status of men and women in that society. Among the earliest known cultures, coital positions also reflected religious beliefs. Ancient religions that emphasized a "sky mother" and an "earth father" usually had woman-above as the accepted position. Where there was a "sky father" and an "earth mother," the man-above position predominated (Bullough & Bullough, 1994).

In societies where women have a more privileged social status, they usually have the option of choosing whether or not to participate in coitus. In cultures such as the Hopi and Crow American Indian tribes, and among the South Seas Trobriand Islanders, women's sexual satisfaction is viewed as equally important as men's. Here woman-above positions seem to predominate. In mainstream Western societies, women's social status is less privileged than that of men, and so man-above positions are much more common (Langmyhr, 1976). Some societies practice a variant of the man-above position in which the man squats or kneels between the legs of the prone woman. Because this position was commonly reported among groups living in the Pacific area, it is often referred to as the "Oceanic position." However, a preference for this position has been found among groups as culturally and geographically diverse as the Tallensi of Africa, the Karaja of South America, and the Santals and Lepcha of India (Gregersen, 1986).

In large areas of Africa, side-by-side positions are the norm. The man is supposed to lie on his right shoulder in order to keep his left hand free for sex play. The right hand is normally used for eating, and it is believed that if it is used to touch the sex organs (even one's own), it will become contaminated.

Our lower primate cousins generally use a rear-entry position, but this is seldom preferred among human groups. However, the Nambikwara and Apinaye of South America as well as the Bush people of southern Africa do prefer this posture (Gregerson, 1986).

In India, standing coital positions are often associated with adulterous relationships. These positions are seen in statues and other sculptures carved into the outside walls of Hindu temples (Gregerson, 1986).

The *Kama Sutra,* the classic Indian sex manual, claims to describe 529 possible coital positions, while a Chinese classic limits itself to 30 basic positions, including "gamboling wild horses," "hovering butterflies," and "winding dragon" (Bullough & Bullough, 1994; Verma, 1997).

---

their middle twenties and those married or living with a partner had the most shared sexual activity. Married or cohabiting couples also reported enjoying sexual activity more. Name the last movie or novel in which all the passionate love scenes took place between married folks!

## 9.3.7   Gay and Lesbian Sex

The sexual techniques of same-sex couples include virtually all of the ones already described. Lesbian and gay couples engage in erotic kissing, breast stimulation, genital touching, mutual masturbation, oral-genital sex, and anal sex. Obviously, same-sex pairs cannot engage in coitus, but most of the postures described, as well as their variations, can be utilized by same-sex couples in order to arouse each other.

Because lesbian women and gay men are raised with the same "gender scripts" as their heterosexual sisters and brothers, their approach to sex and lovemaking reflects our culture's gender prescriptions for men and women. However, there are a few distinctive features of same-sex techniques.

In their observations of gay and lesbian couples, Masters and Johnson (1979) were struck by how much more time same-sex pairs, especially lesbians, took in their sexual encounters. Female couples took more time holding, kissing, stimulating the breasts, and erotically touching. Male couples spent more time in nipple stimulation, and in stimulating the frenulum of the penis.

Among both lesbian and gay couples, more frequent oral sex has been found to be related to greater satisfaction with their partners and with their sexual relationship (Blumstein & Schwartz, 1983). Lesbian couples were more likely to engage in *tribadism,* or *genital apposition,* in which the partners position themselves so that they can rub their genital areas together. In general, lesbian women are less genitally oriented and less fixated on orgasm, compared to men. Romance and the other emotional aspects of lovemaking seem to be more central in their sexual

Gay and lesbian couples engage in many of the same sexual practices as heterosexual couples.

Sexual pleasuring can be heightened by using erotic aids and gadgets such as vibrators, oils, dildos, "cock rings," and feathers.

encounters. Again, contrary to male-oriented pornography, dildos and other sex toys are not commonly used by lesbian women, though they have become more popular (as they have among heterosexual couples as well). Nor is rigid role-playing that common. It is much more typical for partners to alternate active and receptive roles.

Like heterosexuals and lesbian women, gay men engage in the whole range of human sexual intimacies described. Anal sex is less common than oral-genital sex (Berger, 1991; Mays et al., 1992). *Interfemoral* intercourse is also practiced. Most gay men alternate in taking the active or receptive role in sex.

## 9.4  ENHANCING SEXUAL PLEASURE

### 9.4.1  Adult Toys and Sexual Gadgetry

The use of sex toys is nothing new. Dildos and other devices date back to the beginnings of human culture. A wide array of devices are available in sex shops, mail-order catalogs, and online stores (Winks & Semans, 1997). These include scented body oils, feathers, furry gloves, vibrators, dildos, penis "extenders," penile rings ("cock rings" or "cock eyes"), artificial vaginas, inflatable dolls with openings to simulate oral, vaginal, and anal areas, and so forth (see "Healthy Sexuality: All about Vibrators and Other Sex Toys"). Also available are various aids for those with more exotic or specialized preferences, especially for those interested in sadomasochistic activities. If you add the thousands of available erotic and pornographic videos, one can get just a glimpse of exactly how extensive and profitable this segment of the "sex industry" really is, both in this country and internationally.

Most of this sexual paraphernalia is harmless and, depending on individual and couple preferences, can add to sexual pleasure. However, some of it can be harmful. Taking proper precautions to avoid viral and bacterial infections has already been mentioned. The extended use of "cock rings" to maintain erections can damage the blood vessels of the penis. Improper or inconsiderate use of dildos can tear or otherwise injure delicate tissue.

### 9.4.2  Ambience, Attitudes, and Afterglow

Whether solitary or shared, a sexual interlude is as much a psychological as a physical experience. Therefore, it is important to acknowledge the psychological and environmental factors that can enhance or detract from sexual pleasure.

Cleanliness and good grooming are the very bottom line in a shared sexual encounter. Most North Americans are raised to have low tolerance for bodily odors and secretions. While smokers often include various tobacco-related rituals into their sexual activity, the smoke-free majority usually find smoking-related odors very unpleasant. A very recent bath or shower, clean and trimmed fingernails (long artificial nails can be rather scary around all that naked skin), and clean undergarments should complete the job here.

Then there is the matter of ambience. A safe, quiet, private place, unlikely to be disturbed by parents, children, roommates, or neighbors, is certainly enhancing. Turn off the sound on the answering machine, and, if your circumstances allow, turn off the telephone. Individual tastes vary, but candlelight, soft music, and a clean and comfortable bed or couch are usually safe bets. Soft, silky, and/or revealing undergarments for both men and women are appealing to most people.

## HEALTHY SEXUALITY

### ALL ABOUT VIBRATORS AND OTHER SEX TOYS

Vibrators can be used for clitoral, vaginal, penile, or anal stimulation. They can be used for solitary pleasuring or incorporated into partnered lovemaking.

No matter their shape, most vibrators are used by women for clitoral, not vaginal, stimulation. There are smooth and ribbed hard plastic cylindrical vibrators as well as softer ones that look more like penises. There are also egg-shaped, bullet-shaped, and butterfly-shaped vibrators (these keep a woman's hands free). Some Japanese vibrators have a longer "branch" for vaginal insertion and a shorter one (often animal-shaped) for clitoral stimulation (Bullough & Bullough, 1994); when the vibrator is turned on, the longer part swivels in the vagina and the shorter part vibrates. Some anal plugs contain vibration-producing motors as well.

Many types of vibrators are available from drugstores and department stores, but their descriptive literature never hints at their possible sexual usage. Others are available at "adult sex shops" and through various mail-order catalogs (Winks & Semans, 1997).

Currently there are three main types of vibrators on the market. The "wand" type has a long cylindrical body and a round vibrating head attached by a flexible neck. A second type is shaped like a small hair-dryer, has several attachments, and is virtually silent. The third type, vibrators that strap over the back of the hand, are strongly favored by men. Almost every sex-toy catalog advertises "ben-wa balls," which are meant to be inserted into the vagina but are rather ineffective.

Dildos are usually penis-shaped objects, from 4 to 12 inches in length, and made of soft plastic or vinyl, or of latex stuffed with cotton. Some are very realistic and come complete with bluish veins and "testicles" that can be manipulated inside a "scrotal" pouch. Some are specially designed for anal insertion, including one shaped like a forearm and fist. Some dildos are hollow and meant to be worn over a flaccid penis. A small number of dildos are carefully crafted from silicone. Some of these are shaped like vegetables, others resemble animals. These are smaller, very smooth, warm quickly to body temperature, and do not have a rubbery odor.

Many women who have not had orgasms are able to have orgasms with a vibrator because they can have complete control over the type, location, and intensity of stimulation. Vibrators also increase the possibility of multiple orgasms for women.

Between uses, vibrators must be kept clean to prevent the growth of transmittable fungi and bacteria on their surfaces. Simple soap and hot water work well. Silicone dildos can be placed in boiling water for a few minutes, but latex rubber might melt. Because vibrators are battery or electrically operated, they should not be totally submerged in water. For greater cleanliness, use a condom over the vibrator or dildo. When switching from anal to vaginal or penile stimulation, change the condom. Thoroughly clean the dildo or vibrator after any anal contact, or serious infections can occur.

---

For partners in longstanding sexual relationships, family, work, and other responsibilities often leave little time for thinking about or acting on romantic impulses. Lovemaking might have to be carefully planned and scheduled in advance. Attention, imagination, and creativity are the key concepts here. Try a furry rug in the living room, or take a long, warm bath or shower together. A weekend or vacation away from the children or other responsibilities can result in some special pleasuring. There are lots of books and videos on the market (in the *most respectable* of stores). You can surprise each other with your individual selections. Just keep the words and eye contact flowing so that *both partners* are involved in enhancing the sexual relationship.

This chapter began by mentioning that our society tends to emphasize orgasm as "the end" of a sexual encounter. One of the things that can enhance lovemaking is the special time after both partners feel physically satisfied (whether or not they have had orgasms). This is usually a time of emotional openness and vulnerability, especially for women. Close body contact, intimate loving conversation, or compliments regarding a partner's technique and/or passion go very well here. Sincere declarations of love and commitment are usually very well received. If love and commitment are not on the agenda, expressions of appreciation and enjoyment can also enhance the total experience of shared pleasuring.

## SUMMARY

1. Like all societies, ours promotes varying attitudes toward different types of sexual activities. Individuals and couples vary in the kinds of sexual acts they prefer or find acceptable.

2. Erotic fantasy is an important and creative aspect of both solitary and partnered pleasuring. When combined with external, physical stimulation, fantasies and private sexual imagery heighten sexual arousal and can serve as "orgasmic triggers." Sexual fantasies reflect culturally prescribed gender roles.

3. Masturbation is the most frequent form of personal sexual expression in our culture, especially among men. Recent research contradicts many conventional beliefs about who masturbates and why.

4. Women and men employ different masturbatory techniques. Women's are more varied.

5. Shared pleasuring typically progresses from close body contact, to kissing, and breast stimulation, and then genital touching.

6. Attitudes toward oral-genital sex have changed in recent decades, and both cunnilingus and fellatio are now relatively normative in our society.

7. Anal sex is more prevalent than generally believed, and there are special health risks involved in such sexual acts.

8. The three basic coital positions all have variations, as well as advantages and disadvantages.

9. The NHSLS has revealed some surprising patterns in the sexual behavior of Americans.

10. Except for coitus, lesbian women and gay men employ virtually all of the same pleasuring techniques as heterosexual couples. Research has revealed a few distinctive features of same-sex lovemaking.

11. Human beings actively seek to enhance their sexual pleasuring, whether solitary or partnered. Many use sex toys and other erotic aids. Careful attention to personal preparation, the ambience that surrounds sexual encounters, and the "afterglow" period of a sexual encounter can also enhance pleasuring.

## CRITICAL THINKING CHALLENGES

1. Do you believe that our culture is too focused on the orgasm as the goal of sexual activity? How would you feel after a long session of lovemaking if you had not reached orgasm? If you had but your partner had not? What factors would influence your feelings in those situations?

2. Some people say that "scientific" research concerning sexual response and techniques, and the publication of sex manuals (like this chapter) take the spontaneity out of sex, by focusing on the mechanics of the process. Others argue that more information can enrich the sexual experience, providing a road map to explore body parts and activities that were previously unknown. What do you think? If you attempted to apply some of the information you've learned in this chapter, what effect would it have?

# SEXUALITY IN DISABILITY AND ILLNESS

**AFTER STUDYING THIS CHAPTER, YOU SHOULD BE ABLE TO**

[1] Explain how the language we use to talk about disabilities affects our perceptions of persons with disabilities or obvious illnesses.

[2] Describe how age at onset of a disability or illness affects a person's sexual socialization.

[3] List and describe the physical and mental capacities required to engage in sexual behavior.

[4] Describe how visual and hearing impairments can affect sexuality.

[5] Explain which of the physical and mental capacities required for sexual behavior are affected by cerebral palsy and multiple sclerosis.

[6] Summarize what is known about sexual functioning after a spinal cord injury.

[7] List and describe two common psychiatric conditions that affect sexual expression.

[8] Explain why sexual expression among those with mental retardation presents a special challenge.

[9] Describe how cardiovascular diseases—especially coronary problems, hypertension, and cerebrovascular accidents—and their treatments have an impact on sexual behavior.

[10] Describe how diabetes affects sexual functioning.

[11] Explain why HIV infection may now be considered a chronic disease that affects sexual expression.

[12] Summarize how cancer and cancer treatments affect sexual expression.

[13] Describe how skin problems, amputations, and ostomies present special difficulties in sexual expression.

[14] Explain how a personal care attendant can facilitate sexual expression among persons with severe disabilities.

## 10.1  THINKING ABOUT PERSONS WITH DISABILITIES AND ILLNESSES

Most college students have a relatively healthy and whole body that can do all sorts of things, including sexual things. If that describes you, take a moment to consider others in your classroom and around your campus. You know there are specially marked parking spaces for the disabled. You might be aware of specially designed restroom facilities, drinking fountains, and ramps. You might notice students, staff, and faculty moving around in wheelchairs, or with the aid of crutches or white canes. Perhaps you have had someone in your classroom signing a lecture to a deaf student. Most of us have had contact with individuals whose physical limitations are obvious to all who take a moment to become aware of them. Then there are those individuals whose disabilities are not at all visible or obvious—those with ongoing or chronic illnesses, or who live with chronic pain, and those who have permanent scars, amputations, and other residuals of surgeries or other treatments. Off

Confinement to a wheelchair need be only a partial restriction for partners who share special feelings for each other. The person with a disability can interact sexually in many effective ways.

campus, you might have friends, neighbors, or relatives who have disabilities such as mental retardation or mental illnesses. If you are fortunate enough to be physically and mentally whole and healthy, it is important to remember that no matter what body part might be missing or not working properly, people with disabilities are whole people with needs and desires just like everyone else. In talking about the relationships among sexuality, disability, and illness, we must always keep in mind that we are dealing with a whole *person* who happens to have some limitation or difficulty. The disability or illness is *not* the whole person. If our bodies are healthy and functioning well, learning about sexuality, disability, and illness can give us a new appreciation of the relative ease of our own sexual expression.

### 10.1.1  Disabilities and Language

It's an old psychological rule that the language we use to talk about something both reflects and influences how we think about it. This is certainly true about disabilities. Rather than helping to open channels of communication, language has often been used to stigmatize people with disabilities. Words such as *deformed, crippled, victims of,* or *suffers from* can insulate us from persons with disabilities. Such words cast the person with a disability as being helpless and hopeless, and as someone to be pitied rather than as a person with the potential to enrich our lives, and to be enriched by knowing us. Such terms strengthen common myths and help excuse discrimination against people with disabilities. Euphemisms such as *physically challenged, mentally different,* and *handicapped* are now considered condescending and unacceptable (Research and Training Center on Independent Living, 1996). Note that we use the phrase *person with a disability* rather than *disabled person.* The first implies a whole person with a particular problem or limitation. The second implies that all aspects of that person are somehow disabled (Kroll & Klein, 1992). (The first is called "person-centered" language.)

### 10.1.2  Disability Onset and Sexual Learning

Some disabilities and illnesses are present at birth or from early childhood, and then the person's socialization can be affected. There might be less opportunity to join with other children in the regular activities of childhood (running at the playground, trips with other kids, private play time away from adults, etc.) and have the peer interaction during which many types of social and sexual learning usually occur. Parents who are concerned about their child's emotional and sexual vulnerability might protect the child from being ridiculed or embarrassed. Family members might try to protect the adolescent from rejection during potential dating opportunities. Thus, the adult with a disability or an illness with an early origin might have no knowledge or memory of how people without disabilities behave or interact in such situations. If the illness or disability began later in life, especially after sexual maturity or after sexual relationships have begun, individuals might feel a profound sense of loss (Charmaz, 1994): loss of their previous sense of who they are and how they functioned before in intimate relationships (DeLoach, 1994). Among adults, there can be additional concerns about fertility, reproductive functions, or the ability to parent adequately.

People with disabilities or illnesses are often perceived as childlike, asexual beings. If you are nondisabled and healthy, imagine someone suddenly hanging a large, unremovable sign around your neck that said in giant letters, "I AM NOT A SEXUAL PERSON." This is often the way persons with disabilities or illnesses are perceived in our society.

People with disabilities represent a cross section of our society, and therefore their sexual preferences vary. Even those who work with persons with disabilities and who do envision them as sexual beings can have common heterosexist assumptions. Lesbian women with disabilities might be routinely given contraceptives (O'Toole & Brigante, 1992), and gay men with disabilities might be given advice about coital positions.

Few injuries change a person's social activities any more dramatically than do those of the spinal cord. For the young person, there is concern over how such injuries my alter his or her social and sexual attractiveness.

### 10.1.3 Physical and Mental Capacities for Sexual Expression

Let's begin by looking at some of the basics of what's required for sexual expression, whether alone or with a partner. First, one must be able to move part or all of the body relatively freely. Second, one must be able to experience a range of sensations. Third, in order to have the physiological processes of arousal and/or orgasm, one's body must be able to undergo vasocongestion and myotonia. Fourth, in considering sexual activity with another person, a person must believe that his or her body can be appealing. Fifth, if the illness or disability requires the use of special equipment, both partners will have to deal with this equipment. Sixth, couples must be able to communicate with each other. Lastly, we should mention that one has to be aware of the societal norms that govern sexual expression and be sure not to violate them (these include such issues as privacy and partner consent). For the person with a disability or illness, one or more of these requirements may be problematic.

As we discuss the various categories of disability and illnesses, it may help you to think about which of the physical requirements just listed would be affected by a particular condition or illness.

The person with a disability or illness has an additional set of psychosexual issues. Powerful feelings of shock, anger, and resentment can all result in high levels of anxiety and/or deep depression. Increased dependence on a partner or others can bring about profound conflicts between formerly loving partners, especially if the partner without a disability becomes the "overseer" or "enforcer" of treatment requirements. All of these have a potential impact on the erotic bond between partners (Feigin, 1994). In this chapter, we will examine some fairly common disabilities and how they can affect sexual expression.

## 10.2 SOME COMMON DISABILITIES AND ILLNESSES THAT AFFECT SEXUALITY

### 10.2.1 Sensory Impairments

Impairments of vision and hearing do not produce any physical limitations on the body's sexual responsiveness. People who are blind or deaf have the same physical and sexual needs, conflicts, and problems as everyone else.

However, if blindness or deafness are present at birth or from an early age, the usual path of social and sexual learning can be seriously affected. The person may lack some basic social skills as well as basic sexual information. Lack of visual cues for the

Signing is vital to the deaf. People who rely on signing have as much capacity in sexual learning and expression as do people who hear.

Although blind people may encounter difficulties in initially meeting someone, blindness does not have to mean social isolation.

blind person and lack of vocal cues for the deaf person can lead to significant communication problems. Moreover, the distorted body image and reduced self-esteem that many such people experience can also contribute to sexual difficulties.

In the absence of ongoing vocal interaction, the deaf person comes to depend on the visual and printed media as a source of sexual learning (FitzGerald & FitzGerald, 1980). This is problematic because the images that appear in such media are often stereotypical and not an accurate reflection of real relationships.

Perhaps the most disabling characteristic of deafness is how it restricts social contact and communication. People with serious hearing impairments typically communicate through *signing* (sign language), and so their friendships might be limited to people who are also able to sign. Most deaf individuals find it easier to maintain romantic relationships only with other deaf individuals or those few hearing individuals who can sign. So deaf people tend to date, have sexual relationships with, and marry individuals who are members of the deaf community (Kroll & Klein, 1992). This is true of both homosexual and heterosexual deaf people.

As we have learned, the sense of touch is critical during lovemaking, and deaf people are fully able to use their hands to touch, embrace, and caress. Body manipulation and even finger-spelling can all facilitate sexual communication.

The initial stages of human courtship involve a great deal of eye contact. Obviously, those who have serious sight impairments cannot employ eye contact to signal interpersonal interest, flirt with the eyes, or look around to see who might be of interest. In our society this can be especially difficult for men, because

they are expected to take the initiative in romantic or sexual encounters. As one newly blind man said:

> Body language, postures, and facial expressions all have a lot to do with the way people communicate. As a blind man, I now had to learn to pick up on these signals without seeing them. (Kroll & Klein, 1992, p.134)

The blind person also lacks visual information about current clothing styles, fashionable colors, hairstyles, body makeup, and other adornments. Without some assistance, the person with visual impairments can find it more difficult to look appealing or attractive, and this is very important in our society.

Some blind persons display *blindisms,* mannerisms common to people who are blind. They might not walk upright or face the person with whom they are speaking. They might exhibit unusual postures and habits, such as sitting or walking differently, rocking, and fiddling with clothing. These mannerisms develop because they help the blind be aware of their environment, but the mannerisms can also alienate sighted individuals.

Sex education for the blind provides another set of challenges. Anatomical models and contraceptive devices that invite touching can be used, but the amount of sexuality-related educational material that is available in braille is still very limited.

Lacking visual cues, the blind person depends more heavily on touch and hearing for sensory input.

## 10.2.2 Neuromuscular Disorders

### Cerebral Palsy

**Cerebral palsy (CP)** is a general term that covers a variety of motor disturbances due to prenatal or congenital brain defects or injuries. Miscommunication between the brain and the muscles results in uncoordinated movements. Depending on the extent and location of the brain damage, different levels and types of disabilities occur. The most common effects of CP are lack of muscle coordination, involuntary tremors, and speech difficulties (Kroll & Klein, 1992). If the person becomes anxious or upset, involuntary muscle spasms can occur. The nature and degree of muscle control and spasticity determine what types of sexual activity or coital positions are possible for the person. While most people with CP have normal intelligence, some have mental retardation.

Establishing and maintaining intimate relationships is difficult for people with CP because the disorder is conspicuous and it affects socialization and general sexual learning. Spasticity can affect the person's ability to engage in sexual activity with a partner. It might be impossible to straighten the legs and body enough to enable adequate physical contact with a partner. Persons with CP have complete sensory abilities (responsiveness to touch, sight, hearing, etc.). Thus they feel the same sensations as anyone without the disorder might feel, including sexual desire and physical arousal (Kroll & Klein, 1992). Sexual relationships with high levels of emotional intimacy and acceptance can help people who have CP with problems of self-image and self-esteem.

### Multiple Sclerosis

**Multiple sclerosis (MS)** is a progressive neurological disease with an unpredictable course and varying levels of disability. In the United States, between 6,000 and 10,000 new cases of MS are diagnosed each year (Seftel, Oates, & Krane, 1991), and the disease affects an estimated 300,000 Americans. MS first strikes people usually between the ages of 20 and 40 (Segal, 1994a). About two-thirds of those diagnosed with MS are women.

MS involves inflammation of the myelin sheath that surrounds nerve fibers. The damaged sheath becomes hardened (*sclerosed*) in many places, and this slows and short-circuits the transmission of nerve impulses. Vision, tactile sensation, muscular strength, and coordination can all be affected. Many aspects of living, including sexuality, can be seriously disrupted by MS (McCabe et al., 1996). There may be a reduction or loss of sexual interest, sexual arousal, genital sensations, or orgasm. Sometimes when people with MS do engage in sexual activity, they report low levels of sexual satisfaction (McCabe et al., 1996).

### Spinal Cord Injury

The **spinal cord** is a bundle of nerve fibers about 17 inches long that connects the brain with the muscles, skin, and internal organs. Although it is encased within the 33 hard, protective vertebrae of the spinal column, the spinal cord is very soft and easily damaged by pressure or trauma. The 33 vertebrae are grouped by location as *cervical* (C), in the neck; *thoracic* (T), in the chest; *lumbar* (L), in the lower back; and *sacral* (S), in the pelvis. Every movement we make, and every sensation we experience, is directly due to the neural messages carried by the spinal cord. The key concept in understanding how *spinal cord injury* (SCI) affects movement and sensation is this: When the spinal cord is damaged, we lose the functions controlled by the nerves *below the level of injury,* so the *higher up* on the spinal cord the **lesion** (area of damage) is located, the more functions and sensations are lost. (Take a look at figure 10.1 to see which nerves control which functions.) Typically the spinal cord does not heal or repair itself, so the damage and the effects of the damage are permanent. Each year about 10,000 new SCI cases occur in the United States. The impact of SCI is devastating, especially because most such injuries are to young adults. The leading causes of SCI are traffic accidents, diving accidents, and falls (Kroll & Klein, 1992). Sport-related accidents, industrial accidents, and stab and bullet wounds are other common causes of SCI.

People with SCI usually experience **paralysis—** the loss of sensation (feeling) and voluntary motion. **Paraplegia** is paralysis in the legs, while **quadriplegia**

| | |
|---|---|
| **cerebral palsy (CP)** (ser′a-bral pol′ze) | any of several disorders of the central nervous system characterized by a lack of muscle coordination |
| **multiple sclerosis (MS)** (skla-rō′sis) | a progressive neurological disease characterized by a lack of coordination and speech difficulties |
| **spinal cord** | a bundle of nerve fibers running through the spinal column and connecting the brain with the rest of the body |
| **lesion** | tissue injury or wound |
| **paralysis** (pa-ral′ĭ-sis) | loss of sensation and voluntary movement in an area of the body |
| **paraplegia** (par-a-plē′jē-a) | paralysis of the lower torso and both legs |
| **quadriplegia** (kwod-ra-plē′jē-a) | paralysis of the arms, legs, and trunk |

# GO ASK ALICE

*Dear Alice,*

*A friend of mine has a spinal cord injury and is paralyzed from the waist down. I was wondering if he is capable of having an erection and ejaculating.*

*Wanting to Be Informed*

Dear Wanting to Be Informed,

With people experiencing paraplegia, sexual functions are generally affected. For a man, sexual problems include having erections, keeping erections, and ejaculating semen. A weak erection may be helped through the application of a tight rubber ring around the base of the penis, removed directly after intercourse. For those unable to have an erection, surgical procedures exist to implant devices into the penis so that they can manually initiate an erection. Ejaculation and the production of semen may be assisted by using a finger-shaped electronic probe placed in the rectum to stimulate the prostate gland and seminal vesicles to produce semen.

Men with spinal cord injuries have erogenous zones, and many paraplegics who have lost all genital sensation are capable of having orgasms through stimulation of other body parts. They also have desires, and are capable of having pleasure and satisfying sexual relationships—sometimes resulting in pregnancy and childbirth.

 http://www.mhhe.com/byer6

refers to paralysis in all four limbs. Quadriplegia typically occurs as the result of neck trauma. If the lesion is complete, both sides of the body below the level of the injury will be affected. From the point of the lesion downward there is an absence of all voluntary movement and sensitivity of the skin to touch and pinprick sensation (American Spinal Injury Association, 1992). If the lesion is incomplete, the paralysis may affect one side of the body more than the other. In addition to the muscular paralysis and inability to feel touch or pain, bladder and bowel functions can be disrupted. People with SCI typically have normal life spans, but the quality of their lives may be significantly affected. Their sexual functioning is but one aspect of this altered quality of life.

*The Sexual Effects of SCI:* For both women and men, the physical processes of vasocongestion and myotonia underlie our sexual functioning. Some aspects of sexual response are controlled by the brain, while others (reflexive responses such as ejaculation) are controlled by the spinal cord. Physiological arousal can be activated by **psychogenic stimuli,** which arise in the *brain* and can include erotic thoughts, fantasies, dreams, sights, sounds, or smells. If the spinal cord is completely severed, signals cannot travel down the spinal cord from the brain to the genitals, so the person cannot experience arousal based on psychogenic stimuli. However, physiological arousal can be activated by **reflexogenic stimuli,** which is produced by direct stimulation of the genitals (touching, rubbing, etc.). So clitoral and penile erection and engorgement of vaginal tissue can occur,

but the person *cannot feel them* (Spark, 1991). (To understand this further, see "Healthy Sexuality: Neural Mechanisms of Erection and Ejaculation.")

Researchers report that about three-fourths of men with SCI can have erections, but fewer than 10 percent are able to ejaculate (Hawton, Catalan, & Fagg, 1992). Injections of papaverine can facilitate erections in certain cases of SCI, but papaverine can have serious side effects (Yarkoney et al., 1995). Some men with SCI can ejaculate by applying a vibrator to the shaft of the penis. Others depend on vacuum tumescence constriction therapy (VTCT) (Aloni et al., 1992). This involves applying a suction device that creates an erection and a constricting band at the base of the penis to maintain vasocongestion. Still others use a rigid or inflatable, surgically implanted penile prosthesis. Usually the rate of partnered sexual activity tends to drop following SCI but about one-third continue to engage in coitus (Alexander, Sipski, & Findley, 1993; Spark, 1991).

There are comparatively few studies about sexual functioning among women with SCI, and those that have been conducted typically emphasize menstrual and reproductive functioning (Kettl et al., 1991). As with men, women's ability to respond sexually after SCI depends on the site and severity of the injury (Seftel, Oates, & Krane, 1991). Genital sensations are typically lost, and the capacity for vaginal lubrication can be disrupted. Most women with SCI retain breast sensations, and the breasts might become much more erotogenic than they were before. One survey of women with SCI revealed that about half were able to have orgasms via stimulation of the breasts, lips,

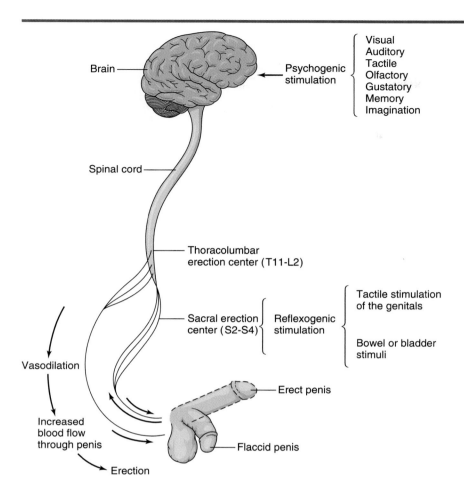

**FIGURE 10.1** The spinal cord is involved in erection (penile and clitoral), with different portions of the spine interacting with different stimuli.

or other parts of the body that are not affected by the spinal cord injury (Kettl et al., 1991). However, the most significant changes were a significant decline in body-image satisfaction and body-esteem. Some women report "psychological orgasms" or "phantom orgasms," which seem comparable to the "phantom pain" amputees report in missing limbs (Perduta-Fulginiti, 1992).

Other impulses from the spinal cord leave at the sacral level and reach skeletal muscles at the base of the penis, which contract to expel sperm from the urethra to the exterior (Tortora & Grabowski, 1993).

Having SCI does not interfere with menstruation or with the ability to conceive, gestate, give birth, or lactate (Whipple, 1990). Childbirth is painless for the woman with SCI. In general, only 37 percent of women with SCI ever receive information about sexual functioning, compared with 66 percent of men, and most studies of the effects of SCI have been conducted with men (Whipple, Gerdes, & Komisaruk, 1996).

*Rethinking Sexual Responsiveness:* Having a spinal cord injury, or relating to someone who does, forces the person or couple to confront their ideas about erotic pleasure, sexual sharing, and intimacy. In a society that places so much emphasis on genital sensations in sex, SCI involves a loss of precisely that experience. Yet people with SCI retain their need and desire for touch, erotic expression, and sharing of pleasure. What happens psychologically and physically after SCI?

If the person's ideas about lovemaking and sexuality are focused on erection, insertion, and orgasm, then sexual fulfillment may be impossible. Some people with SCI avoid all sexual opportunities; others maintain active involvement with a partner. Some heterosexual couples have learned to "stuff" the penis into the vagina. This involves tucking the soft or semifirm penis into the vagina, with the woman

| | |
|---|---|
| **psychogenic stimuli** (sī-kō-jen′ik) | stimuli arising in the brain (thoughts, fantasies, etc.) |
| **reflexogenic stimuli** (ri-flex-ō-jen′ik) | stimuli arising from bodily reflexes (e.g., in response to touch or smell) |

## NEURAL MECHANISMS OF ERECTION AND EJACULATION

Penile and clitoral erection and penile ejaculation are *reflexes*—unlearned, automatic responses to sexual stimulation, over which we have little voluntary control. We can neither will nor demand erection or lubrication. We can, however, set the stage for them to occur by setting up, or exposing ourselves to, effective sexual stimulation.

### Erection

Erections can be caused by either psychogenic stimulation (the brain produces sexual fantasy, or responds to viewing/hearing erotic stimuli) or reflexogenic (direct physical) stimulation to the genitals.

There are two erection centers along the lower spinal cord: the lumbar, at the lower level of the rib cage, and the sacral, which is at the level of the hips (fig. 10.1).

The following can all cause erections:

1. Psychogenic stimulation of both or either the lumbar and the sacral erection centers.
2. Psychogenic and reflexogenic stimulation, acting together or alone, of the sacral erection center.

3. Reflexogenic stimulation of the sacral erection center only. Here, the brain receives no messages, so the person has no pleasurable genital sensations with erection (Spark, 1991).

### Ejaculation

Tactile (touch) stimulation of the penis leads to ejaculation. With intense sexual stimulation, impulses leave the spinal cord at the lumbar level and pass to the genital organs. This causes contractions of the genital ducts that propel sperm and seminal and prostatic fluid into the urethra, where they mix with Cowper's fluid, resulting in the formation of semen (Tortora & Grabowski, 1993).

Other impulses from the spinal cord leave at the sacral level and reach skeletal muscles at the base of the penis, which contract to expel sperm from the urethra to the exterior (Tortora & Grabowski, 1993).

---

doing the hip thrusting in order to contain the penis in the vagina. This reflexogenic stimulation can result in erection. Like all sexual activities, these options have to be negotiated by the particular couple. A performance-oriented man may find it difficult to accept a replacement for genital sex, yet many other parts of the body do remain very arousable (Alexander, Sipski, & Findley, 1993). The mouth, lips, neck, shoulders, and ears remain very responsive for the majority of people with SCI (Seftel, Oates, & Krane, 1991). A couple, whether heterosexual or homosexual, might have to experiment with kissing, oral-genital contact, cuddling, massage, and the use of a vibrator (Szasz & Carpenter, 1989). For a description of the erotic life of a loving couple in which one partner has a spinal cord injury, see "Case Study: A Couple in Which One Partner Is Disabled."

Some people with SCI can concentrate on their sensations from a part of their bodies that has not been neurologically affected by the cord injury, mentally reassign that sensation to their genitals, and experience an orgasm in fantasy. In developing this heightened erotic responsiveness, skin areas in all the neurologically unaffected parts of the body become

erogenous zones: nipples, lips, neck, ears, nose, forehead, elbows, and so on. Using this reassignment method, some men with SCI even report multiple orgasms (Perduta-Fulginiti, 1992). After a spinal cord injury, the need for closeness, intimacy, expression of desire, and love continue. These psychological aspects of sex can become more fulfilling and compensate for the changes in physical ability.

## 10.2.3 Psychiatric Conditions

In the vast majority of cases, psychiatric conditions constitute a category of invisible disabilities. A significant change in sexual behavior is one of the major symptoms of the commonest of problems: *depression*. It is estimated that one in every ten people will have a significant depressive episode in their lifetime (Wade & Tavris, 1995). Also quite common are the problems categorized as *anxiety disorders*. New psychiatric medications and more effective psychological treatments now permit thousands of people who would otherwise be incapacitated to live full and productive lives. The medications prescribed to alleviate these difficulties sometimes have side effects that

## CASE STUDY

## A COUPLE IN WHICH ONE PARTNER IS DISABLED

While in his early twenties, Jaimie was caught under a runaway tractor and his injuries resulted in total paralysis and loss of sensation from the neck down, except for in his right thumb. Today, Jaimie uses an electric wheelchair and can write, eat, and perform some manual tasks with the help of a brace. He drives a lift-equipped van outfitted with special controls. However, his mother serves as a full-time nurse and attendant. Jaimie earned a master's degree in education and teaches at a small-town high school.

Before the accident, he was popular with women, but afterward he had very few social relationships. Loneliness led to self-pity, and this further alienated others.

Marlina and Jaimie met through a friend, and over time both seemed willing to relate socially and romantically. Having experienced her own share of tragedies, Marlina felt unfazed by Jaimie's disability. Their first several months together consisted of soul-searching talks about past sorrows and future dreams. After they fell deeply in love, sexual intimacy became their next challenge. Both Jaimie and Marlina now accept that their way of making love might be different from what most others do, but both believe strongly that the loving feelings are what count.

Jaimie can have sustained erections, but he cannot feel them. They sometimes have intercourse with Marlina straddling Jaimie in his wheelchair. He keeps his catheter tube folded back along his penis, and Marlina says she doesn't even notice it.

However, both agree that oral sex is their most pleasurable and satisfying activity. Marlina positions herself so that Jaimie can place his mouth on her vulva and put his thumb in her vagina. He then performs cunnilingus for an extended time. Marlina's excitement during their lovemaking really arouses Jaimie. At the same time, he states that the sensations he feels with his mouth and tongue are incredibly powerful. In addition, the friction and squeezes he feels in his thumb excite him to the point of orgasm.

Marlina and Jaimie report that most people in their small town treat them as a couple, and they are considering marriage.

---

**Adapted from:** K. Kroll and E.L. Klein, *Enabling Romance* (New York: Harmony Books, 1992), pp.82–85.

---

influence sexual behavior. Busy health care providers might fail to mention these side effects, so it is important for those who use these medications to be aware of them and to discuss them fully with their health care providers.

## 10.2.4   Mental Retardation

**Mental retardation** is a developmental disability manifested by below-average intellectual functioning in work, education, and/or daily living that is present before the age of eighteen (Research and Training Center on Independent Living, 1996).

Some see people with mental retardation or related developmental disabilities as asexual. Others seek to protect individuals with mental retardation from erotic stimuli and sexual expression in order to prevent their sexual activity, marriage, pregnancy, or the possibility of passing on similar defects to children (Patti, 1995). Still others fear the "ungovernable" sexual impulses of the retarded and view these persons as potential sex offenders (Reinisch, 1990). Advocates view persons with mental retardation as sexually disenfranchised (without sexual rights) and victimized by those of average intelligence. However we might view such individuals, we need to recognize that they are exposed to the same sexual images in the media as the rest of us, and to society's conflicting messages about sexuality.

A score of close to 100 on an IQ test is considered "normal" intelligence. About two-thirds of those who are considered retarded have IQs between 35 and 70 (*mildly to moderately retarded*) and live in the general population. Those with an IQ of below 34 are considered *profoundly retarded,* and usually reside in institutions.

Although the intellectual development of people with mental retardation is diminished, their physical development is not. They undergo a normal sexual maturation during adolescence and have a normal capacity for sexual arousal and reproduction, and some are lesbian, gay, or bisexual in orientation. Yet because of the socialization they have experienced, they might have difficulty expressing their sexuality in typical or socially acceptable ways (Bernstein, 1985).

---

| | |
|---|---|
| **mental retardation** | a developmental disability resulting in below-average intellectual functioning |

Today people who are mildly mentally disabled are encouraged to live independent lives.

Parents of children and adolescents who have mental retardation might be concerned about their offspring's vulnerability to sexual coercion and exploitation. Retarded children might not know how to defend themselves, or if they voluntarily choose to be sexual, they might not know how to use contraception effectively or protect themselves from sexually transmitted infections.

Just like their peers with average intelligence, individuals with mild retardation can be educated and directed into satisfactory and responsible intimate relationships (Reinisch, 1990). Yet some individuals with mental retardation face potential problems regarding intimacy and sexuality. They may:

- be overly responsive to attention and give affection indiscriminately.
- show poor judgment and deficient reasoning in developing and carrying on relationships.
- be unable to verbalize their feelings, thoughts, or experiences.
- not be sufficiently mature emotionally to defer gratification.

- do whatever is asked of them without questioning, and consequently are more likely to be exploited.
- have difficulty distinguishing reality from nonreality and more readily believe lies and half-truths.

Like all of us, people with mild mental retardation experience sexual interest and desire, and they might experiment with masturbation, though they might be confused about what is happening to them physically during masturbation. Sex might be one of their few gratifying experiences. Women who are mentally retarded might seek to imitate the seductive femininity they see in the media (Bernstein, 1985).

Contemporary education for people with mental retardation emphasizes independent living and integration into society. Many with *mild retardation* have homes, jobs, and social lives that result in marriages or extended partnering. For many, a marital relationship offers companionship, independence, and sexual fulfillment, as well as increased feelings of accomplishment, security, self-confidence, and personal worth. Many couples with developmental disabilities manage their social and sexual lives very effectively (Yohalem, 1995). Persons with *moderate mental retardation* generally require a more protected and restricted environment for their own safety and comfort. However, they too are capable of learning about their sexuality as well as about masturbation and reproduction. Persons with *profound mental retardation* are limited in their capacity for social learning and will be more restricted in their sexual expression. Because most of these individuals are institutionalized, they have very little privacy for sexual activity. Those who work with this group of individuals recommend that institutions provide a private place (a bathroom or bedroom) where masturbation or permissible sexual contact with others be allowed. Whatever their level of developmental disability, all human beings have a need for closeness, affection, and physical contact. Persons with developmental disabilities need clear, specific directions and training about their sexuality. This permits them to lead lives as safe and fulfilling as their disabilities allow (Ciotti, 1989).

## 10.3 CHRONIC ILLNESS AND SEXUALITY

The nature of medical illness has shifted dramatically over the last several decades. Most of the infectious diseases that used to take so many lives are now controllable. Surgical and technological innovations can now correct formerly fatal problems. More and more of us have or will have lifelong, chronic health problems (Taylor, 1995). Even those infected with HIV now have had to shift from anticipating imminent death to planning for a life of management and medication.

Many illnesses affect sexual expression. Some illnesses directly interfere with the sexual response cycle. Others create pain that interferes with a person's strength or agility (Schlesinger, 1996). Some cultures have unique views on the relationship between health and sexuality (see "Dimensions of Diversity: The Yin-Yang Principle and Chinese Medicine"). Because of the long-term nature of chronic illnesses, one can forget that the person who is sick still has erotic needs; the satisfaction of knowing that loved ones still care and exhibit that caring can have a positive effect on recovery or coping. We will focus here on some of the more common illnesses and conditions that can affect sexual expression.

## 10.3.1  Cardiovascular Disease

**Cardiovascular diseases** include coronary disease, hypertension, and cerebrovascular accidents (stroke). Most people who have these conditions receive much counseling about smoking, diet, and exercise but little advice about sexual activity (American Heart Association, 1996). Nor do they typically receive help with the depression, sense of inadequacy, or relationship difficulties that usually accompany these conditions—and all of these have a powerful effect on sexual expression.

Sexual activity appears to drop significantly for people with cardiac illnesses. For men this decline often begins before the diagnosis of cardiovascular disease, because clogged blood vessels can cause significant erectile problems.

A common misconception prevails among cardiac patients and the general public: namely, that if a person who has had a **myocardial infarction** (heart attack) resumes sexual activity, this can trigger another heart attack (DeBusk, 1996). However, research suggests that persons with a history of *angina* (chest pains) or a prior *infarction* have no greater risk for another heart attack than people with no prior cardiac disease (Jackson, 2000; Stein, 2000). Anxiety, misinformation, and avoidance seem to be the real causes of sexual problems after an infarction. In reality, the "cardiac cost" of sexual activity, including orgasm, is comparable to normal moderate activity (Jackson, 2000; Stein, 2000).

Of course, in situations of severe heart disease or during recovery from an infarction, sexual and many other kinds of activity may be significantly restricted. But with milder types of cardiac problems, there is usually no reason to limit sexual activity: think of it as "mild exercise." Most health providers permit sexual activities a month or two after an infarction. Some useful guidelines for the cardiac patient are to keep well rested and avoid alcohol and extreme temperatures. A low-salt diet and waiting a few hours after a big meal are also good practices for patients who wish to resume their erotic lives. Psychologically speaking, a feeling of safety, comfort, and confidence about sexual activity with a familiar and loving partner will also reduce stress. In fact, one sign of a patient's improving health might be the urge to masturbate. Successful masturbation can also increase the patient's confidence in her or his ability to engage in sexual activity with a partner. However, patients should be aware that the medication used to treat cardiovascular problems may have a powerful impact on sexual response. The patient should consult their health care provider if they think this might be the case.

The person recovering from a **cerebrovascular accident** (stroke) might have a variety of functional and mobility problems. In terms of sexual behavior, one of the most common changes is a loss of sexual desire (Aloni et al., 1993). For others, *sexual disinhibition* or *hypersexuality* can become problems. They might disrobe or masturbate in public, make inappropriate sexual advances to others, or make lewd or obscene comments. These symptoms can have devastating effects on a partner or other family members.

## 10.3.2  Arthritis

While more men than women are affected by cardiovascular disease, more women than men suffer from arthritis. **Arthritis** (meaning "joint inflammation") is a progressive, chronic disease that causes pain, inflammation, and swelling of the joints, often the knees, hips, and lower back. It can lead to reduced joint movement, destruction of the joint, and limb deformity. Joint movement can become very difficult or impossible.

Although arthritis does not directly affect the capacity for sexual arousal and response, it does have a negative impact on self-image and state of mind, and this will reduce the person's interest in sex.

| | |
|---|---|
| **cardiovascular disease** (kar-dē-ō-vas′kya-ler) | any of a group of disorders of the heart and blood vessels |
| **myocardial infarction** (mī-ō-car′dē-al) | heart attack |
| **cerebrovascular accident** | stroke |
| **arthritis** | a progressive disease causing pain and inflammation of the joints |

# DIMENSIONS OF DIVERSITY

## THE YIN-YANG PRINCIPLE AND CHINESE MEDICINE

Every culture has its sexual beliefs and these affect the sexual expression of its people. The Chinese concept of yin-yang has had an extensive influence on Chinese sexology, medicine, philosophy, literature, and art.

According to yin-yang philosophy, all objects and events are the products of two forces or principles. *Yin* is negative, passive, weak, destructive, and traditionally considered the sexual essence of women. *Yang* is positive, active, strong, constructive, and traditionally considered the sexual essence of men. At birth, the body is filled with both principles, but yin tends to increase and yang to decrease. Death is the serious imbalance of these forces. For both sexes, long life is based on retaining as much yang as possible. In intercourse, the man is to delay ejaculation as long as possible, and to allow the woman to reach orgasm. This would preserve his yang force (Gregerson, 1983).

According to the yin-yang principle, desirable sexual expression is based on the harmonious interaction of these male and female principles. However, all of traditional Chinese medicine is based on the yin-yang concept. A patient's physical condition, disease symptoms, as well as herbal and dietary remedies are all classified as yin or yang. Yang is associated with exteriority, excess, and heat. Yin is associated with inferiority, deficiency, and cold. Illness is the imbalance of yin and yang, so all treatment seeks to restore a harmonious balance. Sexual intercourse is seen as an important treatment for health problems because it allows an exchange of yin and yang energies and thus can restore their harmonious balance.

**Source:** R. Ruan and M. Matsumura, *Sex in China* (New York: Plenum Press, 1991).

---

Masturbation can be difficult or impossible. Joint pain or inability to move the hips, knees, and hands can preclude certain sexual activities or coital positions (Ehrlich, 1988). Even light pressure on the body can create severe pain. Women with arthritis might find a rear-entry coital position while lying in bed or on soft furniture the most comfortable. A man might need to choose a position in which he does not bear his partner's weight. Moist heat and medications prior to sexual activity can help relax muscles, reduce pain, and increase flexibility (Bullard, 1988).

### 10.3.3 Diabetes

**Diabetes** is a chronic condition in which insulin deficiency impairs the body's ability to metabolize sugar. Individuals with diabetes either produce an insufficient supply of insulin or they are not adequately responsive to it. For both women and men, this condition affects sexual functioning by interfering with the vasocongestive process. In many cases the problems are due to *nerve damage* (Amarenco, Basc, &Goldet, 1997), while in others it is due to *circulatory* problems (Bemelmens et al., 1994).

For women, the effects of diabetes include reduced sexual desire, poor lubrication (Dunning, 1993), and reduced frequency of orgasm (Spector et al., 1993). Nerve damage reduces sexual arousal, so stimulation to orgasm takes longer and must be more intense. Diabetic women might have a higher incidence of miscarriages, stillbirths, and birth defects in their offspring (Woods, 1984).

About 35 percent of diabetic men have erectile dysfunctions, which is more than triple the rate for healthy men. However, such problems are not inevitable for men with diabetes (Weinhardt & Carey, 1996). Some diabetic men are so fearful of erectile problems, they develop these difficulties solely as a result of anxiety (Turner et al., 1990). Most diabetic men with erectile problems can ejaculate, but they might experience increasingly longer refractory periods. The problems caused by diabetes increase with age.

### 10.3.4 HIV Infection

An extensive discussion of HIV and AIDS is presented in chapter 7. Infection with HIV is a life-threatening condition that all of us have to take into consideration in managing our sexual activities. Those who are *seropositive* (infected with HIV) have both ethical and legal obligations to inform any potential sex partner of their HIV status and to take every precaution against transmitting the virus to a sexual partner. Those who are *seronegative* (not infected with HIV) need to take every precaution to avoid infection by following safer-sex practices.

Until quite recently, infection with HIV generally meant several years of progressively debilitating opportunistic infections and then death. During these years, severe illnesses and others' fears often led to a sense of physical and emotional isolation. Patients who were sick and dying of AIDS often commented about how they longed for the comfort of simple human touch.

Recently developed "drug cocktails" of several medications, especially protease inhibitors, have been shown to reduce the amount of virus circulating in the blood of recently infected individuals, (Fan, 2000). Many who take these new drugs enjoy a new sense of well-being and hope for the future. However, the drug regimens themselves can be difficult, often requiring dozens of pills to be taken at precise times and in specific combinations. Many people experience severe side effects, including constant nausea. These stresses can have a negative impact on intimacy and sexual desire (Fan et al. 2000).

## 10.3.5   Cancers

**Cancer** is all too often a fatal condition, but early detection and improved treatment regimens have produced a substantial population of cancer survivors. In many, if not most, cases, cancer is best thought of as a lifelong *chronic disease*. Some cancers leave permanent disfigurements and physical limitations, while others require lifelong attention to prevent recurrence. As people with cancer and their partners cope with the long-term effects of cancer, the human needs for affection, touch, and erotic expression do not disappear.

Some cancers and cancer treatments have direct physical effects on sexual functioning—affecting the balance or level of sex hormones, damaging the genital or reproductive organs, or damaging the nerves that connect to these organs. The psychological effects are also often profound. Discovery of the cancer can lead to feelings of despair, fear, and anger. Self-esteem might plummet. The patient's body image might be disturbed, and this can be intensified by the conspicuous scars or hair loss that often result from intensive treatments. There is also the constant fear that the cancer will recur (Anderson & Elliott, 1993). All the changes that surround cancer and its treatment also have an effect on the patient's relationships. A loving partner who does not fear contracting the disease and who is not repelled by the effects of the cancer can help bolster and support a cancer patient's esteem and hope.

There are many forms of cancer, but several have a particularly powerful effect on sexual activity and the reproductive potential of women and men. Cancers of the breast, cervix, endometrium, and ovaries can all affect a woman's sexual expression. Cancers of the prostate and testicles have similar effects on men.

## 10.4   DISFIGUREMENTS AND APPLIANCES

Scars and other disfigurements due to accidents, burns, skin diseases, and surgery can have profound effects on a person's sexuality. Remember, genitalia are not all that is involved in sexuality. An individual's body image, self-esteem, and self-awareness as an attractive, appealing person are ultimately much more important than genital functioning (Charmaz, 1994).

### 10.4.1   Skin Problems

Various conditions can disfigure the skin, including burns, birthmarks, and scars. *Psoriasis* is a common, chronic skin disease that can leave the skin itchy and scaly, with silvery patches of powdery residue. This condition is not contagious, but others might be disturbed by seeing or having physical contact with those with this condition.

People are very concerned about the appearance of their skin. Skin quality relates to body image and how touchable a person is. Those who have learned the interpersonal skills necessary to develop satisfying adult relationships earlier in life can make use of these skills to overcome problems due to their own or a partner's disfigurement.

### 10.4.2   Amputations

An **amputation** involves the surgical removal of a limb or part of a limb. About 160,000 amputations are performed each year in the United States, and the majority involve the lower extremities (Williamson & Walters, 1996; Hamilton, 1997). People over age sixty account for about 85 percent of all amputations (Schulz, Williamson, & Bridges, 1991). Adjustment to an amputation is a complex physical and psychological process. The patient must cope with the physical illness that necessitated the amputation as well as the psychological impact of a serious change of body image. Then there is the change in mobility or loss of function that accompanies the loss of a leg or arm. All of these issues have a serious impact on the person's sense of himself or herself as a sexual person. All of the sexual scripts of our society assume

| | |
|---|---|
| diabetes | a condition in which the body does not metabolize sugar properly |
| cancers | diseases characterized by uncontrolled growth of cells |
| amputation | surgical removal of a limb, or part of a limb, of the body |

The amputation of an arm or a leg is conspicuous and may bear strongly upon the person's sense of body image and wholeness. Important to such a person is the reassurance that he or she will remain attractive to significant people.

physical attractiveness free of physical defects or deformities, so amputees often lose their "sexual selves" along with the lost limb (Mooney, 1995). Such a radical change in body image can also lead to a loss of one's sense of femininity or masculinity.

The mechanics of sexual pleasuring, whether alone or with a partner, can present difficulties for amputees. Balance and movement might require awkward adjustments or overt assistance by a partner or even an aide.

If the amputee has a loving sexual partner before the amputation, sexual difficulties can be lessened. A partner's loving acceptance can reassure an amputee of his or her continued desirability. However, the amputee's increased dependence on a partner is often very difficult for both members of a couple to bear. Sexual and marital counseling can be of great help for couples trying to cope with amputation, but such

counseling in relation to an amputation is rarely available (Williamson & Walters, 1996).

### 10.4.3 Ostomies

An **ostomy** is an artificial opening (temporary or permanent) made from the *intestine* or *colon* (bowel) through the person's abdominal wall. This is done in order to bypass the remaining portion of the digestive tract, which might be diseased or might have been removed. This opening serves as an exit site for excretion. The name given to the condition often indicates the site of the opening, such as a *colostomy* (from the colon or bowel) or an *ileostomy* (from the intestine).

All people with an ostomy face similar adjustments, regardless of the specific organ involved. Abdominal openings designed to collect body wastes create feelings of disfigurement and sexual discomfort. Some persons who have undergone ostomies must wear a collecting bag constantly, while others must wear one only periodically. In either case, there is usually emotional and physical discomfort.

For the ostomy patient, an unfamiliar sexual partner can easily elicit anxiety and embarrassment. This is usually lessened with a loving and accepting familiar partner. Sexy garments, worn during sexual activities, can help conceal a pouch or bag. An ostomy can result in a decrease in sexual interest and therefore an overall decline in sexual activity, inhibited arousal and/or ejaculation, and erectile loss due to the severing of essential nerves during surgery. Unfortunately, sexuality information is often omitted when educating the ostomy patient.

## 10.5 SEXUAL FULFILLMENT FOR PEOPLE WITH DISABILITIES

The ability of a person with an illness or disability to express her or his sexuality depends on the physical limitations caused by the disability, the person's overall adjustment to the disability, and the availability of a partner. For the young person, it can also depend on the person's ability to function independently of parents.

Only the person with the disability knows the kinds of sexual expression she or he finds most rewarding. Some experimentation may be necessary to discover what works best or what the person can actually do sexually. Sexual expression may sometimes be difficult, but it can be helpful in living a fulfilling life.

There are many ways to express sexual feelings. Sexual sensations are possible in any area of the body, not just the "erogenous zones." Between adult partners, all that is needed is the consent of both.

There are few rules about what to do in sexual activity (of course, one does not want to do anything to physically or mentally harm oneself or a partner). Physical limitations can be a powerful incentive to explore sexual intimacies other than the socially prescribed ones (such as, for heterosexuals, "penis-in-vagina coitus with man on top"). For the vast majority of individuals with physical disabilities or illnesses, their imaginations and sense of eroticism are usually quite intact.

Some individuals or couples with disabilities might seek the help of a *personal care attendant* (PCA) to assist in preparing one or both partners for sexual activity. The PCA must be prepared to affirm the person or couple's sexuality and their need for sexual fulfillment. A partner who uses the assistance of a PCA might feel a greater sense of independence and self-esteem in a relationship. A loving, resourceful, and motivated couple can find ways of fulfilling their sexual needs and providing pleasure for each other, regardless of the disability.

STIs, and contraception, can result in satisfying partnered relationships.

10. Cardiovascular conditions such as coronary disease, hypertension, and cerebrovascular accidents, as well as the treatments for these problems, can affect sexual behavior.

11. Arthritis impairs mobility and physical comfort. Diabetes impairs the capacity for vasocongestion.

12. With the development of protease inhibitors, HIV has become a chronic, rather than certainly fatal, illness for many who are infected.

13. Cancers and cancer treatments affect many of the physical and mental capacities required for sexual expression.

14. Skin conditions can affect an individual's self-concept as an appealing person.

15. Amputations, ostomies, and the appliances that might accompany them can all affect various aspects of sexual behavior and expression.

16. A personal care attendant can assist individuals and couples who are severely disabled so that they can enjoy erotic expression.

## SUMMARY

1. Individuals with disabilities or illnesses are whole people who happen to have some limitation or difficulty.

2. The language we use in discussing disabilities and illnesses reflects and influences how we think about persons who have such conditions.

3. Disability or illness that occurs early in life can impede the process of sexual learning and other aspects of socialization. Those that occur later in life typically elicit strong feelings of loss.

4. There are at least seven physical and mental capacities that are necessary for sexual activity. Various disabilities and illnesses can affect one or more of these.

5. Sensory impairments mainly affect communication in sexual expression.

6. Cerebral palsy and multiple sclerosis are neuromuscular conditions that affect many of the mental and physical capacities needed for sexual expression.

7. Because so many young people have SCI, there has been considerable research on the effects of SCI on sexual functioning. SCI often motivates individuals to reassess what constitutes satisfying erotic interactions.

8. Depression and the anxiety disorders are common psychiatric conditions that affect sexual expression.

9. Persons with mild or moderate mental retardation typically live in the general population. For these persons, education and training about sexual issues, such as sexual social norms, sexual exploitation,

## CRITICAL THINKING CHALLENGES

1. Propose a "Bill of Sexual Rights" for people with disabilities. How might a disabled person go about claiming their rights? How are those rights affected by various disabilities?

2. Describe the various stimuli that can cause erection, and the mechanisms by which the spinal cord controls these responses. List the spinal locations where injury could result in the possibility of erections. Are there SCI locations where erection ability is likely to be permanently lost?

| | |
|---|---|
| **ostomy** (os′tuh-mē) | a surgically created opening from the intestine or colon through the abdominal wall |

# BIOLOGICAL SEXUAL DEVELOPMENT

# 11

**AFTER STUDYING THIS CHAPTER, YOU SHOULD BE ABLE TO**

[1]  Describe genes and chromosomes.

[2]  Contrast mitosis and meiosis.

[3]  Contrast zygote, embryo, and fetus.

[4]  Describe X and Y chromosomes and explain the genetic determination of the sex of a person.

[5]  Explain how any change in the current ratio of males to females could have major social effects.

[6]  Explain the outcome of various sex chromosome abnormalities.

[7]  Contrast organizing versus activating effects of hormones.

[8]  Explain how an undifferentiated embryo develops into a female or a male.

[9]  Explain the concept of homologous sex organs and cite several examples.

[10]  Explain some ways that a person's apparent sex might differ from his or her genetic sex.

[11]  Explain why the traditional approaches to treating infants born with ambiguous sex organs are being reconsidered.

[12]  Explain prenatal sexual development of the fetal brain.

[13]  Describe the relative timing of sexual maturation of girls compared to boys.

[14]  Describe the physiological changes that take place in males during puberty.

[15]  Describe the physiological changes that take place in females during puberty.

[16]  List the processes that occur during development of the breasts in males and females.

In this and the following chapters, we will examine a series of topics on sexual development. This brief chapter covers biological sexual development—how a fertilized egg becomes a biological female or male. Later chapters will cover gender identity—a person's feeling of being either a male or a female, and the sexual life cycle, from birth through old age.

Now, turning to the biological aspects of sexual development, we will explore the genetic basis for sexuality and how this is translated into a functioning female or male.

## 11.1   THE GENETIC BASIS OF SEXUAL DEVELOPMENT

A human body consists of trillions of microscopic units called **cells.** Within each person's body are many different kinds of cells, but they all carry the same set of genes. The way in which the cells develop their various special forms is one of the most fascinating areas of biological study. This differentiation of cells is governed by the activation and inactivation of specific genes which allow cells to develop in specialized ways.

### 11.1.1   Genes

Genes, the units of heredity, are made from a complex chemical called **DNA (deoxyribonucleic acid)** (fig. 11.1). In general, one **gene** is the portion of a DNA molecule that carries the genetic code for the production of one protein, either an enzyme or a structural protein such as those found in blood, skin, or muscle.

In addition to storing genetic information and directing protein synthesis, DNA molecules have the unique ability to duplicate themselves. Just before a cell divides into two cells, all of the genes are dupli-cated, so each of the two resulting cells receives a full set of genes.

### 11.1.2   Chromosomes

In each cell, the genetic material is broken into specific segments called **chromosomes.** In most human beings, every body cell contains 46 chromosomes (23 pairs of chromosomes). The genes are located in linear order along the chromosomes. A particular gene always occurs at a certain place on a specific one of the 23 types of chromosomes. Because the chromosomes occur in pairs, there are two copies of every gene in most body cells.

Figure 11.2a is a photograph taken during cell division that shows the 46 chromosomes of a human cell. Figures 11.2b and 11.2c are charts, called **karyotypes,** of the chromosomes of a female cell and of a male cell. In karyotypes, the chromosomes are arranged and classified according to their size and shape.

As we can see by the karyotypes in figures 11.2b and 11.2c, most chromosomes in the female and male karyotypes are identical. The **sex chromosomes,** however, are distinguishable between females and males. A female cell contains two large X chromosomes (XX). The karyotype of the cell (or the individual carrying the cell) is indicated by the terminology 46, XX to show the total number of chromosomes (46) and specify the sex chromosomes (XX). A male cell contains one X chromosome and a smaller Y chromosome (XY), indicated as 46, XY.

### 11.1.3   Mitosis (Cell Division)

**Mitosis** is the division of one cell into two. During mitosis, all of the DNA molecules within the parent (original) cell are duplicated, and each of the two newly formed cells receives one exact copy of the parent cell's DNA molecules. To survive, mature, and

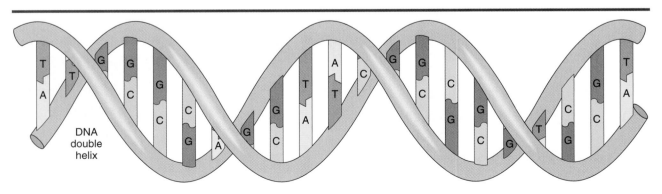

DNA double helix

**FIGURE 11.1**   DNA, the complex chemical molecule of which genes are made. This sketch represents only a small portion of one gene. The difference between different genes lies in the specific sequence of the A:T, T:A, C:G, and G:C pairs.

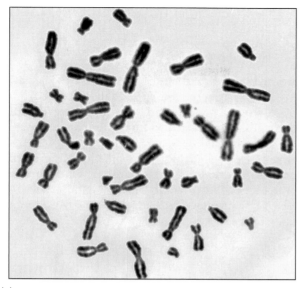

(a)

(b)

(c)

**FIGURE 11.2**

**a:** Human chromosomes from one cell, as seen through a microscope during a cell division **b:** Karyotype of the chromosomes of one cell of a female; shaded square contains two X chromosomes (46, XX)
**c:** Karyotype of the chromosomes of one cell of a male; shaded square contains one X chromosome (the larger one) and one Y chromosome (the smaller one) (46, XY).

function, each of the two new cells must have copies of all of the original DNA molecules of the parent cell. These duplicated DNA molecules contain the same genes as the original molecules in the parent cell; thus, the two offspring cells are genetically identical to each other and to their single parent cell.

The newly formed cells proceed to grow, mature, and differentiate (form into the type of cell they will be in the body, such as skin cell, muscle cell, and so on). All of the cells that make up our body are the result of the cellular reproduction of mitosis, and mitosis occurs continuously within the tissues of our body.

## 11.1.4   Meiosis (Sex Cell Formation)

Human reproduction involves the fusion of two sex cells known as **gametes**; thus, this process is known as sexual reproduction. In a male, the gamete is the sperm; in the female, the gamete is the ovum or egg. Gamete-forming cells are found only in the **gonads**, which are the testes of the male and the ovaries of the female. In sperm or ovum production, there is a division of the number of chromosomes through a process called **meiosis** (fig. 11.3). If meiosis did not reduce the chromosome number by half, the number of chromosomes per cell would double with each generation.

In humans, meiosis results in the formation of four cells. Each of these cells contains 23 chromosomes. In a female, these four cells develop into two or three polar bodies (which die and dissolve) and one ovum. In a male, these four cells develop into four sperm.

| | |
|---|---|
| **cells** | the microscopic basic units of life |
| **DNA** (deoxyribonucleic acid) | the complex chemical that stores genetic information in every cell |
| **gene** | the portion of a DNA molecule that carries the genetic code for the production of one protein |
| **chromosomes** (krŏ′mō-sōmz) | segments of DNA in each cell |
| **karyotype** (kar′ē-ō-tȳp) | a chart showing all of the chromosomes of a person |
| **sex chromosomes** | special chromosomes (X and Y) that determine the sex of a person |
| **mitosis** (mī-tō′sis) | the division of one cell into two (ordinary cell division) |
| **gametes** (gam′ētz) | sex cells (ova and sperm) |
| **gonads** (gō′nădz) | ovaries and testes (primary sex glands) |
| **meiosis** (mī-ō′sis) | sex cell formation, production of sperm or ova |

# GO ASK ALICE

*Dear Alice,*
*Okay, I have looked in just about every place possible. I was just curious about the genetics of genitalia. Is the size of a penis inherited from the father's or mother's side? I have found more than enough info on the size, etc. I just want to know what side of the family my penis came from (no pun intended). Thanks.*
*Reader*

Dear Reader,
After doing some genital gymnastics herself, Alice wound up in Washington, D.C., before finding an answer to your penile pondering. According to

the National Center for Genome Research at the National Institutes of Health, penis size, like height, weight, and general build, probably comes from both mom and pop. Research on size-related genital genetics is scarce because funds and brain power are, understandably, spent on finding treatments and cures for genetic disorders, like human growth hormone deficiency, which can cause stunted penile development. Alice hopes that this information doesn't cause you to lose a bet, or worse yet, start a family feud.

  http://www.mhhe.com/byer6

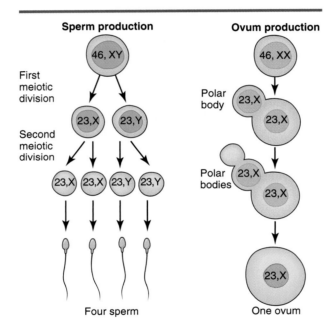

**FIGURE 11.3** Ovum (egg) and sperm production (meiosis). The numbers refer to the number of chromosomes in each cell. In females, meiosis produces one ovum containing 23 chromosomes and two or three polar bodies (these get rid of excess chromosomes). In males, meiosis results in the formation of four sperm, each with 23 chromosomes. Fertilization restores the normal number of 46 chromosomes per cell.

Whereas the original parent cell contained two of each type of chromosome (see fig. 11.2), each sperm or ovum contains only one of each type (see fig. 11.3). For development to take place, an ovum and a sperm must fuse together so that the cell contains a complete set of genes.

The gametes fuse together through fertilization. A human sperm containing 23 chromosomes penetrates a human ovum containing 23 chromosomes. The cell resulting from the union of these two gametes contains 46 chromosomes and is called the **zygote.** All other cells of this new individual develop by mitosis from the zygote.

The process of meiosis assures us that each new generation will be genetically varied from previous generations. Because the ovum and the sperm each contributes only half of a parent's genes, the child that results from fertilization of the ovum by the sperm has a genetic combination that is different from either of his or her parents.

## 11.2  GENETIC DETERMINATION OF ONE'S SEX

As discussed earlier in the chapter, the sex chromosomes in a female cell are two relatively large X chromosomes (XX). The sex chromosomes in a male cell are one large X chromosome and a smaller Y chromosome (XY). Meiosis usually ensures that each ovum or sperm has only *one* sex chromosome—that every ovum contains one X chromosome, and a sperm contains *either* an X chromosome or a Y chromosome.

The sex of an offspring is determined by the sperm that fertilizes the ovum. If the sperm is carrying an X chromosome, fusion of the sperm (X) and the ovum (X) produces an XX combination that results in the development of a female. If the sperm is carrying a Y chromosome, fusion of the sperm (Y) and the ovum (X) produces an XY combination that results in the development of a male (fig. 11.4). Some people, unwilling to leave the sex of their

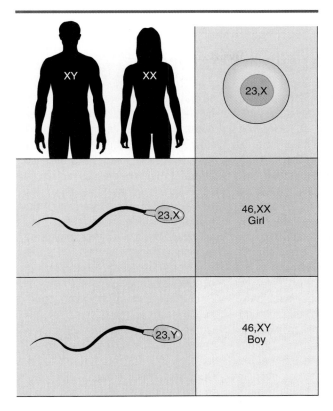

**FIGURE 11.4** Human sex determination. In addition to their other 22 chromosomes, ova normally contain one X chromosome. Each sperm has either an X chromosome or a Y chromosome. The sperm thus determines the genetic sex of a child at the moment of fertilization.

child to chance, take the matter into their own hands. See "At Issue: Gender Selection Raises Ethical Questions."

What causes this differentiation in development? Research has shown that if a Y chromosome is present in the cells of a developing **embryo** (the unborn child during the first eight weeks of development after conception), the embryo develops testes. If the Y chromosome is absent from the cells of the developing embryo, the embryo develops ovaries. Thus, the *presence* of a Y chromosome causes a male to be produced, while the *absence* of a Y chromosome causes a female to be produced. The X chromosome appears to have no effect on initial sexual determination (Moore, 1993).

The Y chromosome is small (see fig. 11.2b) and contains very few genes. For that reason, scientists believe that it is unlikely that all of the genes needed to develop organs as complex as the testes are located on the Y chromosome. The Y chromosome probably contains "switching" or "controller" genes that regulate the expression of genes on some other chromosome, or chromosomes, needed to produce the testes.

The precise mechanisms by which the Y chromosome coordinates the development of the testes are far from clear, but it has been established that the sex hormones are *not* involved. Injecting male hormones into a female mammalian fetus will not produce testes. Similarly, injection of female hormones into a male mammalian fetus will not suppress testes formation or produce ovaries.

## 11.2.1  Sex Chromosome Abnormalities

Occasionally an error occurs in the process of meiosis, creating a sperm or an ovum having either no sex chromosome or two or more sex chromosomes. An individual resulting from such a sperm or ovum will thus have something other than the usual XX or XY sex chromosome combination.

Abnormal chromosome numbers usually result in spontaneous abortion (miscarriage). Griffiths et al. (1993) estimate that of every 100,000 pregnancies, 15,000 end with spontaneous abortions and that about half of those relate to abnormal chromosome numbers. Of the 85,000 live births, about 550 babies have abnormal chromosome numbers. About 150 of those abnormalities (less than 0.2 percent of live births) involve the sex chromosomes.

Several generalizations can be made about sex chromosome abnormalities. First, no person has ever been known to survive without having at least one X chromosome, as the X chromosome carries many genes that are essential to life. Second, regardless of how many X chromosomes are present, if at least one Y chromosome is present, the individual will be genetically male. Table 11.1 catalogs various sex chromosome combinations and provides descriptions of individuals with each combination.

## 11.3  DEVELOPMENT OF THE SEX ORGANS

Development of the human internal and external sex organs into male or female forms is driven by the presence or absence of the Y chromosome. Geneticists have identified on the Y chromosome a gene for "maleness." Referred to as **TDF**, the *testis determining factor*, this gene promotes development of a male. The absence of TDF allows development of a female. There is apparently no specific gene for "femaleness."

| | |
|---|---|
| **zygote** (zī′gōt) | a fertilized ovum |
| **embryo** (em′brē-ōh) | the unborn child during the first eight weeks of development after conception |
| **TDF** | (testis determining factor) a gene that promotes development of a male |

# AT ISSUE

## GENDER SELECTION RAISES ETHICAL QUESTIONS

Traditionally, the sex of a baby has been left to chance and has been a subject of speculation and suspense until the child's birth. The result has been a natural ratio of about 105 boys born for every 100 girls.

There have always been some people who wanted to influence the sex of their baby in a more definite manner, feeling a strong preference for a child of one sex or the other. In earlier times, the methods used were purely superstitious and had no effect on a baby's sex. The pregnant woman (it was believed that the mother determined a baby's sex) might perform certain rituals, think certain thoughts, or eat certain foods in an effort to influence her fetus's sex. In more recent years, methods to influence a baby's sex have been more "scientifically" based—timing of intercourse, or acid or alkaline douches, depending on the sex desired—but only slightly more effective.

Now X and Y sperm separation, followed by artificial insemination, has improved the chances of obtaining a baby of the desired sex. In a method offered by many clinics throughout the United States, sperm swim through a thick layer of albumin protein. The Y sperm swim faster, producing a separation of X and Y sperm. The process, costing $300 to $800 per insemination, improves the chance of having a boy by 30 percent and a girl by 20 percent (Plevin, 1992). There is little doubt that the effectiveness rate will improve as this method is refined and other methods are developed.

It is impossible to predict how many people will practice such gender selection methods; this method will certainly apply only to *planned* conceptions. It is not unreasonable to assume that quite a few people will want to choose the sex of their babies. It is also impossible to predict which sex more people will choose. Perhaps the male/female birth ratio will stay about what it is. But what if it does not?

Even a 5 or 10 percent shift in the birth ratio, in either direction, would probably produce drastic changes in society. Relationships between the sexes are especially likely to be affected. What would hetero-

sexual dating and marriage patterns be like if the ratio between the sexes became 60/40 in either direction? How would members of the more prevalent sex compete with each other for mates of the less numerous sex? How would members of the less prevalent sex make use of the bargaining power inherent in their scarcity? We can only speculate on these questions.

Consider also the ethical side of gender selection. Or is it an ethical issue? We can predict with confidence that at least some of the world's major religions will take a stand against couples acting to determine the sex of their children. Other religions are equally likely not to react to this issue. For their members, and for nonreligious people, the ethics of gender selection will have to be a personal issue. Regardless of the source of our guidance, all of us will at least want to consider the potential effect on society of changing the current balance of the sexes.

## 11.3.1 Organizing Versus Activating Effects of Hormones

Hormones will play a major role in our discussion of how embryos develop into females or males. As you know from earlier chapters, hormones also play important roles in our day-to-day sexual functioning. These two roles illustrate two very different types of effects that hormones can have on people.

One type of hormone action is an **organizing effect,** which refers to how hormones influence early development of some parts of the body, such as the sex organs and the brain. These organizing effects are relatively permanent, such as the lifelong differentiation of sex organs into those of a male or a female.

In contrast, **activating effects** of hormones occur after an organ has developed and influence its activ-

ity at any particular moment. These effects are temporary, in response to the level of a hormone in the body at a given time. For example, the changes in a woman's ovaries and uterus at different phases of her menstrual cycle are in response to the activating effects of her hormones.

## 11.3.2 Gonadal Development

The gonads form within the first two months of embryonic development. Embryonic cells migrate into two **genital ridges** (fig. 11.5), one of which sits atop each rudimentary kidney. Each genital ridge consists of an inner **medulla,** surrounded by an outer **cortex.** If a Y chromosome is present, the medulla of each genital ridge will develop into a testis. If no Y chromosome is present, the cortex of each genital ridge will develop into an ovary (Griffiths et al., 1993).

**TABLE 11.1**    EFFECT OF HUMAN SEX CHROMOSOMES ON DEVELOPMENT OF THE GONAD AND SEXUAL DIFFERENTIATION

| TOTAL NUMBER OF CHROMOSOMES | SEX CHROMOSOMES | GONAD PRODUCED | APPARENT SEX OF INDIVIDUAL | CONDITION PRODUCED | DESCRIPTION |
|---|---|---|---|---|---|
| 46 | XX | Ovary | Female | Normal | |
| 46 | XY | Testis | Male | Normal | |
| 45 | X | Ovary | Female | Turner's syndrome | Ovaries defective or absent; sterile, and external female genitals remain infantile; no pubertal development; no menstrual cycle; rarely attain adult height of more than five feet. (Orten, 1990) |
| 47 | XXX | Ovary | Female | Triple X syndrome | Individuals have no sexual abnormalities, and may have children; some are mentally retarded. (Ratcliffe et al., 1994) |
| 48 and 49 | XXXX and XXXXX | Ovary | Female | | These females are known to exist; no known consistent pattern of traits; mental retardation seems to increase markedly as number of X chromosomes increases. |
| 47 | XXY | Testis | Male | Klinefelter's syndrome | Internal and external genitals are male but testes are very small and do not produce sperm; underdeveloped pubic, facial, and body hair; enlarged breasts; reduced sexual drive; tall; possible mental retardation. (Ratcliffe et al., 1994) |
| 48 and 49 | XXXY and XXXXY | Testis | Male | Variations of Klinefelter's syndrome | Same clinical conditions as Klinefelter's syndrome, but individuals are more severely affected, and severe mental retardation is common. |
| 47 | XYY | Testis | Male | XYY syndrome | Individuals are tall (six feet and over); may show impulsive behavior; sperm production often reduced (may be sterile). (Ratcliffe et al., 1994) |

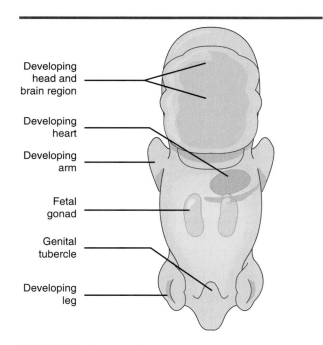

Developing head and brain region

Developing heart

Developing arm

Fetal gonad

Genital tubercle

Developing leg

**FIGURE 11.5**    Fetal gonads in a developing fetus.

If a testis is formed, its interstitial cells will soon begin to secrete testosterone. This hormone binds to androgen receptors, leading to the activation of male-specific gene expression and development of male reproductive organs and secondary male characteristics.

In genetically female individuals, no interstitial cells form in the gonad, no testosterone is produced, and androgen receptors are not activated, allowing the development of female reproductive organs and secondary female characteristics. Thus, it is the presence or absence of the effects of testosterone that determines whether an individual will have male or female sex organs and secondary sex traits. This is clearly demonstrated by the existence of XY females

| | |
|---|---|
| **organizing effect** | how hormones influence early development of some parts of the body |
| **activating effects** | effects of hormones that occur after an organ has developed and influence its activity at any particular moment |
| **genital ridges** | clusters of cells in an embryo that develop into ovaries or testes |
| **medulla** (me-dul´la) | the inner portion of an organ |
| **cortex** | the outer portion of an organ |

(discussed later) who have testes and testosterone, but lack androgen receptors and develop along a completely female pathway.

Up until the third to fourth week of pregnancy, there is no development of the tissues that leads to sexual differentiation (the development of the different sex organs). From the fourth to the sixth week, the genital ridges—tissues that can become either testes or ovaries—develop within the embryo. The changes necessary for this primitive gonad to become either testes or ovaries do not begin until the sixth week of embryonic growth.

### Testicular Development

If a Y chromosome is present in the cells of the developing embryo, its male-determining gene (testis determining factor, TDF) initiates the organization and growth of the male testes during the sixth week of embryonic development. Some cells organize into the seminiferous cords, which become the seminiferous (sperm-producing) tubules of the adult testes. Other cells lying between the seminiferous cords develop into the tissues that form and hold the testes together and into hormone-producing cells known as the interstitial cells.

### Ovarian Development

If a Y chromosome is not present in the cells of the developing embryo, the cells of the genital ridges continue to go through mitosis and proliferate until the seventh week of development. Some of these cells then form small clusters and become the follicles of the ovaries. These cells give rise to oocytes (immature ova) later in development. Other cells become the hormone-producing cells of the follicles. Cells that form around the follicles develop into the tissues forming the ovaries.

Although *initial* formation of the ovaries is dependent upon the absence of a Y chromosome, *complete* ovarian development requires the presence of the two X chromosomes found in most normal women. If the two X chromosomes are not present, a normal number of cells is not produced, and the ovaries do not fully develop. A female with only one X chromosome develops "streak" gonads, which do not function as ovaries. (Turner's syndrome; see table 11.1).

## 11.3.3 Prenatal Development of Other Sex Organs and Structures

The main role of the sex chromosomes in sexual development is completed with the establishment of the male testes or the female ovaries in the **fetus** (the unborn child from the ninth week of development until birth). From this point on, the fetus itself directs the rest of the sexual differentiation. In the male, the testes take over and direct the further development of the male body. In the female, the *absence* of male testes allows for the development of the reproductive structures of the female.

Hormones from the ovaries are not necessary for the development of female sex organs. Two hormones from the testes, though, *are* essential for the development of male sex organs. Within the testes, the interstitial cells start to secrete testosterone, and other cells begin secreting Müllerian inhibiting hormone. The presence of these two hormones ensures the development of male sex organs. In the absence of these two hormones, female sex organs develop.

### Development of Internal Genitals

The internal sex organs of the male or female develop from one of two distinct types of ducts present in the early development of an embryo of either sex. One pair of ducts is called the **Wolffian** (or male) **ducts**. The other pair of ducts is the **Müllerian** (or female) **ducts**. As shown in figure 11.6, both of these genital ducts are initially present in all embryos and have the potential to develop into the internal reproductive structures of either sex.

*Male Development:* The testosterone secreted by the interstitial cells of the testes induces the Wolffian ducts to develop into some of the internal male sex organs—the epididymis, vas deferens, and seminal vesicles. The second testicular hormone, **Müllerian inhibiting hormone,** causes the Müllerian ducts (which would produce female sexual organs) to regress and disappear (see fig. 11.6)

*Female Development:* In a female fetus, the lack of testosterone causes the Wolffian ducts to regress and disappear. In the absence of Müllerian inhibiting hormone, the Müllerian ducts persist, develop, and give rise to the fallopian tubes, uterus, cervix, and the upper part of the vagina (see fig. 11.6). Ovarian hormonal activity is not required for development of the internal female sex organs. Female cells seem to have a built-in mechanism for development of the female internal genitals (Moore, 1993).

### Development of External Genitals

Unlike the development of the internal genitals, the external genitals of both males and females develop from the same embryonic tissues. These embryonic tissues take the form of folds and swellings that develop into female structures, male structures, and structures common to both males and females, such as the bladder. Differentiation begins at about the sixth week after conception and is completed by the twelfth week.

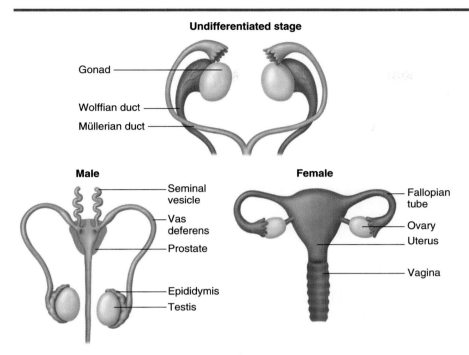

**Undifferentiated stage**

Gonad

Wolffian duct

Müllerian duct

**Male**

Seminal vesicle

Vas deferens

Prostate

Epididymis

Testis

**Female**

Fallopian tube

Ovary

Uterus

Vagina

**FIGURE 11.6** Prenatal development of internal reproductive structures. Early in development, the genital ducts of an embryo have the potential to develop into the internal reproductive structures of either gender. If both testosterone and Müllerian inhibiting hormone (MIH) are secreted by the fetal gonads during the sixth week of development, the Wolffian ducts grow into male structures. Without the presence of both hormones during the critical sixth week of development, the Müllerian ducts grow into female structures.

Because the female and male external genitals develop from similar embryonic tissues, some structures of each sex are said to have homologous (corresponding) counterparts in the other sex. For example, the female clitoris is considered to be homologous to the male penis. Table 11.2 and figure 11.7 show the female and male structures that are homologous.

*Male Development:* Testosterone from the testes in the male fetus causes the folds and swellings of the embryonic tissues to form into the prostate gland, the Cowper's (bulbourethral) glands, the scrotum, the penis, and the urethral tube within the penis (see fig. 11.7)

*Female Development:* In the female, the folds and swellings of the embryonic tissues form the vagina, the labia majora and minora, and the clitoris. This development is shown in figures 11.6 and 11.7.

If the ovaries of a female mammal are removed, these changes still occur, indicating that, as with the development of female internal genitals, no ovarian hormonal activity is required for the development of these female external sex organs (Moore, 1993).

## 11.4 DEVELOPMENT OF AMBIGUOUS GENITALS

In about 1 of every 2,000 births, (Cowley, 1997) a child is born with ambiguous genitals that are not clearly male or female. In other cases, the genitals

**TABLE 11.2**   HOMOLOGOUS SEX ORGANS

| FEMALE ORGANS | MALE ORGANS |
| --- | --- |
| Glans of clitoris | Glans of penis |
| Shaft of clitoris | Shaft of penis |
| Hood of clitoris | Foreskin of penis |
| Labia majora | Scrotal sac |
| Labia minora | Underside of penile shaft |
| Skene's glands | Prostate gland |
| Bartholin's glands | Cowper's glands |
| Ovaries | Testes |

| | |
| --- | --- |
| **fetus** (fē´tus) | the unborn child from the ninth week of development until birth |
| **Wolffian ducts** (wool´fē-an) | a group of cells that develop into the male internal reproductive organs |
| **Müllerian ducts** (mil-air´ē-an) | a group of cells that develop into the female internal reproductive organs |
| **Müllerian inhibiting hormone** | a hormone from the embryonic testes that is necessary for development of male internal organs |

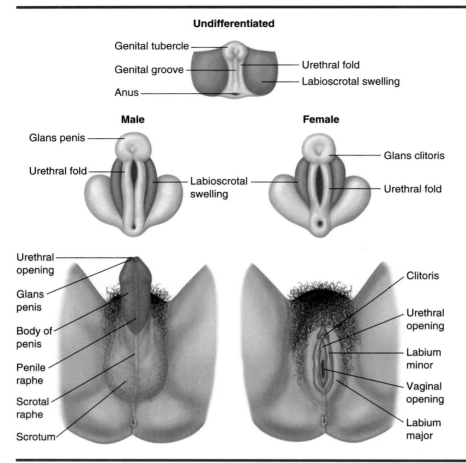

**Undifferentiated**

Genital tubercle

Genital groove

Anus

Urethral fold

Labioscrotal swelling

**Male**

Glans penis

Urethral fold

Labioscrotal swelling

**Female**

Glans clitoris

Urethral fold

Urethral opening

Glans penis

Body of penis

Penile raphe

Scrotal raphe

Scrotum

Clitoris

Urethral opening

Labium minor

Vaginal opening

Labium major

**FIGURE 11.7** Prenatal development of male and female external genitals. Differentiation begins at about the sixth week and is completed by the twelfth week.

may appear normal, but later are discovered to be different from what the sex chromosomes would normally predict.

A commonly used, though usually incorrect, term for such a person is *hermaphrodite*. **True hermaphroditism** is the condition of having both ovaries and testes, an extremely rare occurrence in humans. The true hermaphrodite might have one ovary and one testis or gonads that are mixtures of ovarian and testicular tissue.

More likely, someone having ambiguous genitals is a **pseudohermaphrodite**—the gonads match the sex chromosomes, but the genitals to some degree resemble those of the other sex. This can be caused by prenatal hormone exposure, or (more commonly) by genetic disorders such as androgen insensitivity syndrome or congenital adrenal hyperplasia. A more general term for individuals with genital variations is **intersex**.

### 11.4.1 Androgen Insensitivity Syndrome

Occasionally a female undergoes all of the visible external changes of puberty but fails to begin to menstruate. Sometimes an examination of the chromosomes of such a female reveals the XY sex chromosomes more typical of males. This condition is called **androgen insensitivity syndrome** (AIS).

Androgen insensitivity syndrome is rare, occurring only once in every 65,000 XY births. It is caused by a recessive gene carried on the X chromosome (see "Case Study: Four XY Sisters").

Within the abdomen of XY females are gonads that resemble testes but produce no sperm. They do secrete a level of testosterone that would be normal for a male. However, the body cells that might respond to testosterone lack the necessary testosterone-binding sites to use this hormone. Thus, both before and after birth the potential male differentiation of the internal and external sex organs is blocked. Externally, the genitals develop as those of a female, as would happen in the absence of testosterone. Internally, no uterus develops. Menstruation does not occur and cannot be induced by hormonal treatment following puberty.

External breast development and other body contours appear fully feminine (fig. 11.8). This feminization is caused by estrogen secreted by the adrenal glands at the level normal for a male, but without any competitive action of testosterone. Unable to use testosterone, hair follicles fail to grow masculine facial or body hair. The pubic hair is either absent or sparse.

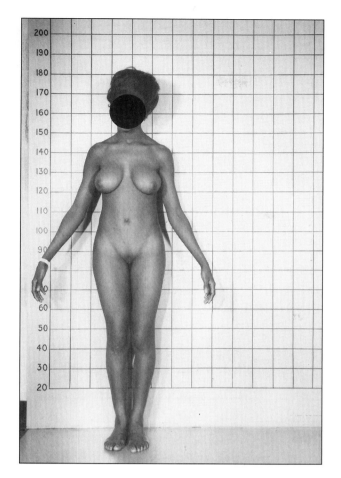

**FIGURE 11.8**   An XY female (androgen insensitivity syndrome). Her XY karyotype is the same as for a normal male. Her gonads are internally located testes that produce no sperm. Because all of her body's cells are insensitive to the testosterone secreted by the testes, the internal reproductive organs are undeveloped (she is sterile). The external genitals and all other body features develop as those of a female. Her gender identity is female.

It is very significant that XY females "feel" fully feminine. This tells us that one's chromosomes alone do not determine gender identity. In the past, it was thought desirable to try to conceal this diagnosis from the XY female. Today such secrecy would be considered unethical and impossible, as the truth would certainly come out in one way or another. XY females also need to be informed of the desirability of having the abdominally located testes removed as there is an increased risk of cancer developing in these testes.

## 11.4.2   Congenital Adrenal Hyperplasia

Atop each of our kidneys lies an **adrenal gland,** the source of a wide variety of important hormones. Among males and females alike, some of these adrenal hormones are androgens—masculinizing hormones. Excessive secretion of these androgens in a female can cause varying degrees of virilization, which is masculinization of the secondary sexual characteristics.

In **congenital adrenal hyperplasia** (CAH, also known as adrenogenital syndrome), an XX fetus develops ovaries normally. Later in prenatal development, the adrenal gland overproduces androgens, which can result in enlargment of the clitoris and other genital effects. In the most extreme case (fig. 11.9), a true penis containing the urethra develops. The labial folds are fused into an empty scrotum. The gonads are ovaries within the abdomen.

When the degree of masculinization is less extreme, the clitoris is enlarged but lacks a urethral tube. There is mild to moderate fusion of the labia, and the openings of the urethra and vagina may be combined into a single opening. Regardless of the degree of virilization of the external genitals, the internal reproductive structures are those of a female.

Since girls with CAH most often have a female gender identity, CAH in an infant usually leads to a female gender assignment. Genital ambiguities are corrected surgically, and adrenal hormone therapy is maintained throughout life. At puberty, menstruation is usually late in onset but otherwise normal. Pregnancy is possible.

| | |
|---|---|
| **hermaphroditism** (her-maf´rō-dit-izm) | the condition of having both ovarian and testicular tissue |
| **pseudohermaphrodite** (sū´´-dō-her-maf´rō-dīt) | a person whose gonads match their sex chromosomes, but whose genitals to some degree resemble those of the other sex |
| **intersex** | individual whose sexual anatomy differs from cultural ideals of male and female |
| **androgen insensitivity syndrome** | a condition in which the body cells that might respond to testosterone lack the necessary testosterone-binding sites to use this hormone; the result is an XY female |
| **adrenal gland** (ad-rē´nal) | a small gland atop each kidney, the source of a wide variety of important hormones |
| **congenital adrenal hyperplasia** | a condition in which high levels of adrenal androgens in an XX fetus result in enlargement of the clitoris and other genital effects |

## FOUR XY SISTERS

These four sisters are genetic males, although each appears and "feels" fully female. They all have androgen insensitivity syndrome (AIS). A fifth sister (not shown) is an XX genetic carrier of the trait and has given birth to a child who also has AIS. The XY sisters are sterile. They each have a vagina but no uterus and, thus, no menstrual periods.

The gene for AIS is X-linked, meaning that it is carried on the X chromosome. This recessive gene causes defective androgen receptors on cells so that a fetus with testes and testosterone still develops into a female. When carried by an XX female, the gene is "invisible," as it has no effect in genetic females.

**Source:** A. Griffiths et al., *An Introduction to Genetic Analysis* (New York: Freeman, 1993).

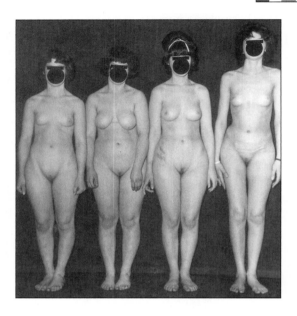

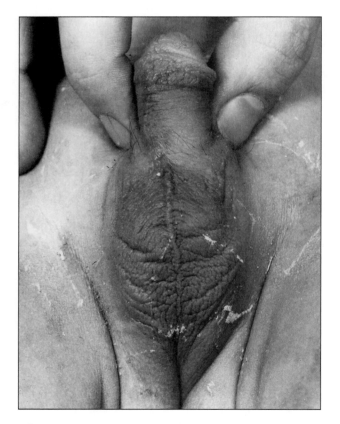

**FIGURE 11.9** Congenital adrenal hyperplasia. Although this individual is genetically XX (normal female), the secretion of abnormally high levels of androgen by the adrenal glands has masculinized the external sex organs. This individual was raised as a male.

## 11.5  NEWBORNS WITH AMBIGUOUS SEX ORGANS

The cause of an infant's having ambiguous genitals is usually unknown. Some cases have genetic causes (such as AIS or CAH), some are due to prenatal hormone exposure, and some cases may have been caused by the mother's drinking during pregnancy (see "Healthy Sexuality: Drinking during Pregnancy Affects Fetal Sexual Development").The sex assignment given such an infant and when it is given have important implications for the infant's future physical and psychological well-being (Kessler, 1990; Slijper et al., 1994).

The standard approach to treating infants with ambiguous genitalia was developed in the 1960s. The strategy was based on a theory that sex assignment would be most successful if done before 18 months of age (Money, 1972). The assigned sex might depend not so much on the sex chromosomes present as on the potential for surgically creating normal-appearing and functioning sex organs (LeMaire, 1988; Slijper et al., 1994). In this protocol, sex assignment was followed by medical treatments including surgical correction of the sex organs and hormone treatments.

While early diagnosis is important to rule out disorders such as AIS (in order to intervene for cancer risk reduction, for example) or CAH, not everyone agrees that ambiguous genitals need to be corrected.

## DRINKING DURING PREGNANCY AFFECTS FETAL SEXUAL DEVELOPMENT

Fetal alcohol syndrome (FAS) is a group of birth defects that occur in infants born to mothers who drink during their pregnancy. At birth, FAS infants are smaller than average, their head is smaller than normal, and facial features include small eyes, fat cheeks, a short nose with a low bridge, thin red lips, and an indistinct groove in the center of the upper lip. Almost half of these infants have heart problems and/or low IQ. FAS is the third leading cause of mental retardation (Kinney, 1994). Case reports also indicate an increased incidence of genital defects in infants with FAS (McGivern & Barron, 1991).

A mother does not have to be a chronic alcohol abuser to expose her fetus to the risks of alcohol during pregnancy. There are documented reports of fetal damage caused by social levels of drinking. The damaging effects of alcohol are greatest during the first three months of pregnancy. During the first weeks the mother might not even be aware that she is pregnant.

How much alcohol is safe to drink during pregnancy? The risk to an embryo or a fetus is in proportion to the amount of alcohol consumed, but some risk exists at any level of alcohol consumption (Kinney, 1994). Our advice is simple: *Don't drink when you're pregnant or at risk of becoming pregnant.*

---

Intersex individuals associated with the Intersex Society of North America argue that differences in genitalia should be viewed as normal variation and treated conservatively, if at all (see "At Issue: Intersexed Decry Genital Mutilation"). Long-term follow-up studies suggest that individuals treated using the traditional approach experience trauma and have serious adjustment problems (Diamond, 1998). The outcome of this type of treatment is illustrated by the classic "John/Joan" case (Colapinto, 2000). An infant boy whose penis was destroyed during circumcision was surgically altered and raised as a girl ("Joan"). Joan was never comfortable as a female, and at age 12 refused to take feminizing hormones. When told the truth at age 14, "John" resumed life as a male, eventually having reconstructive surgery, marrying, and becoming a father through adoption (Colapinto, 2000).

More conservative approaches to treating ambiguous genitalia may be more effective in the long term. One study followed 20 infants diagnosed with micropenis, who were raised as boys without gender reassignment. These individuals were found as adults to be well adjusted, able to experience erection and orgasm, and to form close, sexually satisfying relationships (Reilly & Woodhouse, 1989). The parents of these boys had been well counseled and approached the problem honestly with their child. Had these boys been treated under the "traditional" protocol, their penises would have likely been surgically reduced in size, and they would have been raised as girls with the assistance of hormone treatments. In response to data from studies such as these, and the input of intersex activists, this field is currently experiencing rapid change (Dreger, 1998). New protocols for treating intersex infants based on long-term case studies and new data on the development of gender identity, incorporating honesty and counseling, and considering issues of informed consent, have been proposed (Diamond, 1999; Dreger, 1998; Reiner, 1999).

## 11.6 PRENATAL SEXUAL DEVELOPMENT OF THE BRAIN

Sexual differences are not restricted to the sex organs. Just as the fetal genitals take on a masculine or feminine appearance depending upon the presence or absence of testosterone, the fetal brain becomes masculinized if testosterone is present or remains feminized if testosterone is not present (Damassa & Cates, 1995; Matuszczyk & Larsson, 1995).

Recent brain research has revealed structural differences in the hypothalamus of the brain in relation to biological sex and sexual orientation. At least three areas of the hypothalamus have been reported to show size differences associated with either gender or sexual orientation (Swaab, Gooren, & Hofman, 1995). One area, termed the sexually dimorphic nucleus, contains about twice as many cells in young adult men as in women. No difference in the sexually dimorphic nucleus has been observed between homosexual and heterosexual men, although various researchers have reported such differences in other parts of the hypothalamus (Swaab, Gooren, & Hofman, 1995).

# AT ISSUE

## INTERSEXED DECRY GENITAL MUTILATION

In a press release dated 14 October 1996, the Intersex Society of North America took vigorous issue with the tendency of most physicians involved in neonatal care to surgically "correct" the genitals of infants born not clearly male or female, calling the practice "genital mutilation."

Cheryl Chase, executive director of the Intersex Society of North America, was quoted as saying, "About 1 in 2,000 babies is born with genitals that are 'queer' and the response of American doctors is to cut them off, simply because they judge a clitoris to be 'too large' or a penis to be 'too small.' The infants have no say whatsoever in how their bodies are cut."

Although doctors certainly believe that correcting ambiguous genitals is for the child's own good, Chase says, "Not so. Ask any ISNA member. Intersex genital mutilation has robbed us of our genitals and our sexual feeling. Most who survive IGM are also psychologically scarred for life, while others have committed suicide. Cutting infant genitals to fit heterosexist norms is not medicine, it's mutilation in every sense of the word and it's got to stop."

This opinion does point out the tendency of most people in the prevailing U.S. culture to think dichotomously about gender—a person should be either female or male and anyone not clearly one or the other is defective. This is not a universal view of gender. Some cultures, such as some Native American nations, accept intersex individuals and even have special social roles for them.

The consequences of sexual differentiation in the fetal brain become evident during and after puberty. Physiologically, the brain differentiation (prenatal hormonal organizing effect) influences cyclic sex hormone production, menstrual cycles, and cyclic fertility in the female, while it has a role in preserving the relatively constant level of sex hormone production and fertility in the male.

Psychologically and behaviorly, the brain differences may be significant in the development of gender identity (self-image as a male or female), gender role (behavior as a male or female), and sexual orientation (Grimshaw, Sitarenios, & Finegan, 1995; Meyer et al., 1995). These and other issues related to male and female behavior are addressed in the next chapter.

## 11.7 BIOLOGICAL ASPECTS OF ADOLESCENCE

**Adolescence** can be roughly defined as the period from the onset of puberty until the attainment of adulthood about ages 12 to 20. The term **puberty** is used for the earlier portion of adolescence, during which a person becomes functionally capable of reproduction. Puberty typically occurs between the ages of 9 to 13 in girls and 12 and 16 in boys.

The human reproductive system undergoes a period of remarkable development during fetal life and early infancy. Then its development becomes nearly dormant during early childhood, actively restrained by the hypothalamus within the brain. The onset of puberty is triggered when the hypothalamus stimulates the pituitary gland to release an increased amount of gonadotropic hormones.

Specific mechanisms causing the onset of puberty are complex. Although genetically influenced **neuroendocrine** mechanisms are very important, social, psychological, and nutritional factors also influence the onset of puberty.

Puberty usually spans a period of about four years, but the age at which it begins varies considerably. Puberty is considered to be unusually early if the first physical sign appears before age 8 in girls or 9 in boys and to be delayed if no physical sign has appeared by age 13 in girls or 14 in boys (Hopwood, 1990). Early (precocious) puberty is usually associated with disorders of the hypothalamus. By far the most common cause of delayed puberty is an inherited physiological abnormality. Many studies (e.g., Peterson, Leffert, & Graham, 1995) have addressed the psychological and social effects of precocious or delayed puberty.

Those who mature earlier are less emotionally and intellectually prepared to deal with the events of adolescence. Early puberty in either sex is associated with an increased likelihood for early (many would say premature) sexual experimentation including intercourse (Chilman, 1990).

### 11.7.1 Puberty in Males

In males, the testes are only about 10 percent of their mature size at the time of birth, and little growth occurs until puberty. During the first year or two of puberty, the testes grow rapidly. Then growth slows, and the testes do not reach their maximum size until the age of twenty or twenty-one.

Shortly after the testes begin to develop, the penis starts to grow in length and diameter, and the glands that produce seminal fluid enlarge. Though the penis is capable of erection by contact stimulation from birth, only during puberty does it begin to erect without contact, in response to sexual sights, sounds, or thoughts. Some erections are spontaneous, independent of any sexual stimulus.

During male puberty, there is often a relatively rapid increase in height and weight, along with a broadening of the shoulders. Pubic hair and the beard begin to grow. Hormone levels increase, and the desire for ejaculation becomes urgent. Frequency of masturbation may increase to several times daily. Nocturnal emissions might begin a year or two before the testes are producing mature sperm (Durham, 1989). The average age of first ejaculation, known as **spermarche** or **semenarche**, is 12.9 years.

## 11.7.2   Puberty in Females

Female puberty often begins at a somewhat younger age than male puberty. Researchers believe that the onset of female puberty relates closely to body weight and fat deposition (Alsaker, 1992; Anderson & Crawford, 1992). Athletic girls, particularly those who engage in endurance sports (such as running) and in sports in which there is emphasis on a "thin" body image (such as gymnastics), might undergo puberty later than other girls. This is also true of anorexic girls. All evidence indicates that it is not just total body weight but fat deposition as well that affects the hypothalamic-pituitary-ovarian hormone processes that initiate puberty. Hopwood (1990) found that girls who exhibit delayed puberty because of low fat depositions undergo puberty when a weight gain or cessation of strenuous exercise occurs.

For most girls, however, puberty begins sometime between the ages of nine and thirteen. Its onset is characterized by a marked increase in growth rate accompanied by broadening of the hips, enlargement of the breasts, and the appearance of pubic hair. The ovaries, uterus, fallopian tubes, vagina, and labia all grow rapidly during puberty.

Within one to two years after hip broadening and breast enlargement, underarm hair grows, and the normal, whitish vaginal secretion characteristic of adult females appears. After several additional months, the first menstrual period (**menarche**) occurs. Early menstrual cycles are sometimes **anovulatory** (no ovulation occurs) and irregular. Young women may experience several years of irregular cycles before their menstrual periods become regular and predictable, making "natural" methods of fertility control unreliable for many in this group.

---

## 11.8   BREAST (MAMMARY GLAND) DEVELOPMENT

The mammary glands of both sexes show equal development throughout fetal life. One functional mammary gland bud develops on each side of the chest wall. These buds appear at about the sixth week, and development is complete by the eighth week of pregnancy. The internal milk ducts continue to proliferate and develop until, by the time of birth, fifteen to twenty-five branches are present in each breast. The nipples and areolae (including the areolar glands) arise during the fifth month of fetal development.

The breasts of boys and girls are identical prior to the onset of puberty. At puberty, however, the breast resumes a development pattern that is unique to the sex.

In the female, the areolar region and nipple start to elevate. During the pubertal and adolescent years, the breasts enlarge rapidly. This enlargement is caused by further internal branching of the milk-producing system and by the deposition of fat. By the late teens, the female breast appears as a hemisphere with the areola and the nipple at its apex. Figure 11.10 shows the different stages of female breast development.

The mammary glands of the male also resume development at puberty, reaching their full development when the male is about twenty years of age. At this time, the male mammary glands are about the same size as those of a ten or eleven-year-old female's glands.

| | |
|---|---|
| **adolescence** | the period from the onset of puberty until the attainment of adulthood, about ages 12 to 20 |
| **puberty** (pū´ber-tē) | the earlier portion of adolescence, during which a person becomes functionally capable of reproduction |
| **neuroendocrine** (nū-rō-en´dō-krin) | involving the nervous system and hormones |
| **spermarche** (sperm-ar´kē) | a boy's first ejaculation |
| **semenarche** (sē´menar˝kē) | a boy's first ejaculation |
| **menarche** (men-ar´kē) | the first menstrual period |
| **anovulatory** (an-ov´ū-la-tō-rē) | without ovulation (syn: *anovular*) |

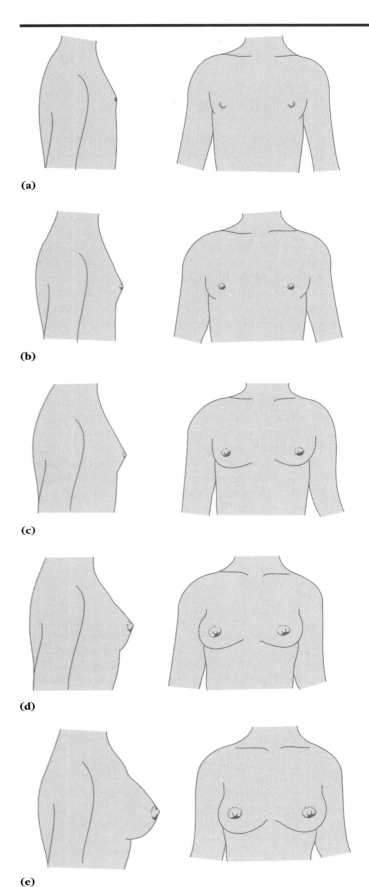

(a)

(b)

(c)

(d)

(e)

**FIGURE 11.10**   Female breast development. **a:** Preadolescent state, with elevation of nipple only **b:** Breast bud stage, in which there is an elevation of the breast and the nipple and enlargement of the areolar diameter. The appearance of the breast bud stage is generally the first sign of puberty, although the appearance of pubic hair might precede it. **c:** The early adolescent stage shows further enlargement and elevation of the breast and areola with no separation of their contours. **d:** In the later adolescent stage, there may be a projection of the areola and nipple to form a secondary mound over the level of the breast. The areolar mound is absent in about 25 percent of females and might be slight in another 25 percent. When it occurs, it often persists well into adulthood. **e:** The mature stage has projection of the nipple only, which is due to recession of the areola to the general contour of the breast.

## SUMMARY

1. There are two kinds of sex chromosomes: X and Y. Females usually have two X chromosomes (XX); males usually have one X and one Y chromosome (XY).

2. Sperm and ova (eggs) are formed by meiosis, a special kind of cell division in which the number of chromosomes is cut from 46 to 23. Fertilization restores the chromosome number to 46.

3. All ova normally carry an X chromosome; a sperm carries either an X or a Y sex chromosome. The sex of a child is determined by whether an X or a Y sperm fertilizes the ovum.

4. The presence of a Y chromosome causes a male to develop; the absence of a Y chromosome causes development of a female.

5. A few people have other than XX or XY sex chromosomes.

6. Homones have two kinds of effects: organizing effects that have permanent results, and activating effects that control day-to-day functioning.

7. The Y chromosome carries a maleness-producing gene called testis determining factor, or TDF. There is apparently no gene for femaleness; in the absence of TDF a female will automatically develop.

8. Between four to six weeks of embryonic development, two clusters of cells called genital ridges develop. Each ridge develops into an ovary if no Y chromosome is present or a testis if a Y chromosome is present.

9. Two sets of ducts lead from the genital ridges: Wolffian (male) ducts and Müllerian (female) ducts.

10. In a male, the testes soon begin secreting two hormones: testosterone and Müllerian inhibiting hormone. The testosterone causes the Wolffian ducts to develop into male internal sex organs while the Müllerian inhibiting hormone causes the female ducts to regress and disappear.

11. Occasionally a child is born with ambiguous genitals (not clearly male or female). In such cases, the gonads usually match the sex chromosomes, but the genitals to some degree resemble those of the other sex.

12. Androgen insensitivity syndrome results when the cells lack testosterone-binding sites. AIS females look and feel fully feminine, but have abdominally located testes, rather than ovaries, and are sterile. There is no uterus or fallopian tubes.

13. External genitals of XX fetuses can be masculinized by excess secretion of androgens by the adrenal glands (congenital adrenal hyperplasia). Resulting genital ambiguities can be surgically and hormonally corrected. Pregnancy is possible.

14. To some degree, the brain is masculinized or feminized prior to birth. The psychological and behavioral significance of this is not yet fully known.

15. Adolescence is marked by the onset of puberty. Physical changes in males and females signal the ability to reproduce.

## CRITICAL THINKING CHALLENGES

1. For many years, the medical standard used when examining an infant with ambiguous genitalia has been that an organ that is 0.9 cm or less in length is a clitoris and an organ 2.5 cm or longer is a penis. Do you feel that these standards are arbitrary? Are such standards needed? How do you think an infant with a 1.7 cm organ should be treated?

2. In DHT-deficiency syndrome, genetically male infants appear female at birth due to a lack of testosterone in early development. However, at puberty, testosterone is produced, which causes the changes associated with normal male puberty—the penis and testes enlarge, the voice deepens, and the male body shape develops. What advice would you give to parents of an infant with this condition?

3. List the sex organs that are homologous in males and females, and the embryonic tissue from which each is derived. Although homologous organs have a common source, do they have similar functions? List the functions of each and consider the differences and similarities.

# GENDER IDENTITY AND GENDER ROLES

# 12

**AFTER STUDYING THIS CHAPTER, YOU SHOULD BE ABLE TO**

[1] Distinguish among the concepts of sex, gender, gender identity, and gender role.

[2] Explain the concept of gender-role ideology, and the general process of gender-role socialization.

[3] Describe the relationship between gender-role socialization and societally based notions of masculinity and femininity.

[4] Describe the process of gender-identity development and its relationship to gender stereotyping and sexism.

[5] Describe the influence of parents, peers, media, education, and religious preference on the process of gender-role socialization.

[6] Summarize the important features of the debate regarding hidden gender biases in contemporary education.

[7] Describe how sociobiology, cognitive social learning theory, and gender schema theory attempt to explain gender-role development.

[8] Summarize the most recent findings regarding hypothesized gender differences in cognitive abilities and aggression.

[9] Describe the positive and negative effects of gender stereotyping and how stereotyping can lead to self-fulfilling prophecies in human interaction.

[10] Briefly summarize the findings regarding the universality of gender stereotypes.

[11] Summarize the major findings regarding gender differences in sexual attitudes and behavior.

[12] Explain the concept of sexual script and describe the important features of contemporary male and female sexual scripts in North American society.

[13] Summarize the important findings regarding gender and sexual scripts in other-sex and same-sex couples.

[14] Define transgenderism and describe the continuum of behaviors associated with this phenomenon.

[15] Explain how transgendered behavior is viewed in our society compared to three other societies.

## 12.1  GENDER AND GENDER IDENTITY

When you were born, someone probably glanced at your external genitals and declared, "Congratulations! You have a baby _____ !" Thus, you were assigned to the boy or the girl category. With this simple pronouncement, a great deal of your life course was set. In this chapter, we will deal with four major issues: First, we will distinguish between **sex** (a biological category) and **gender** (a socially constructed category). Second, we will examine theories about how gender develops and explore a few of the many social and psychological factors that are related to gender in our society. Third, we will explore the relationship between gender and sexuality. Finally, we will learn something about those individuals who experience varying levels of disturbance or confusion regarding their gender. However, before we begin, we should stop to clarify some often misused and misunderstood terms.

### 12.1.1  What's in a Name?

The term sex refers to a person's biological status: female or male. While a great portion of this book refers to the _sex_ that we do, here the term refers to the _sex_ that we are. We are assigned to that status or category based on the appearance of our external genitals. However, from the moment we are assigned to a particular biological category, a complex, lifelong _social_ process begins. Through that process, each one of us begins to learn and internalize all that our culture and our moment in history insist should go with that category. That is, we begin to acquire _gender_. **Gender roles** are the whole array of social and cultural expectations that accompany classification as a girl or boy, woman or man. These typically include a set of interests, preferences, activities, occupations, personality traits, goals, and a myriad of other things. For example, who is supposed to be more interested in business and commerce? In our society, men are, while in parts of West Africa, women are supposed to be involved in trade and commerce. Who is more suited for heavy lifting? Among the nomadic Bedouins in the Middle East, women are said to be, while in our culture heavy lifting is considered appropriate for men. Do men or women have a stronger sex drive? Over the last few hundred years, our own culture has shifted back and forth on this one. Right now, we think of men as being more driven and interested in sexual activity. But this wasn't always so. The general ideals, beliefs, or norms of a particular society regarding what men and women should be like are called that culture's **gender-role ideology.**

We acquire our gender role through the process of **gender-role socialization.** Through this lifelong process, we internalize the societal and cultural _prescriptions_ (what you should do) and _proscriptions_ (what is forbidden) for what is considered gender-appropriate behavior. Another way of saying this is that gender-role socialization is how a person learns to be acceptably _masculine_ or _feminine_ in a particular society. Gender is so important in most societies that individuals are typically required to clearly and continuously announce their gender (researchers call this **gender display**). We demonstrate our knowledge and acceptance of our gender role through our clothing, hairstyle, level of adornment, accentuation of secondary sex characteristics, changing our facial features (in our society, women paint their faces; in other societies, this is strictly a masculine interest), how we talk, and even through our body language. To gauge the importance of gender display, consider what happens when someone violates the rules of gender display in our society. A man dressed in women's clothing, or a woman who exposed her chest, might be arrested.

Among the Wodaabe of Niger, makeup, high levels of ornamentation and elaborate impractical clothing, and even beauty contests are important aspects of the masculine gender role.

Beneath these more social aspects of gender is our more internal and personal *gender identity*. This is a truly central component of who we are. In fact, psychologists refer to a **core gender identity.** This term refers to our basic, innermost sense of ourselves as a male or female, man or woman. If you were asked to finish the sentence, "I am _____" several times, one of the first responses you are likely to give is in terms of your *core gender identity* ("I am a woman" or "I am male"). Later in the chapter, we'll discuss individuals for whom their core gender identity is confused or even conflicts with their biological or genital sex. Such individuals are referred to as *transgendered.*

One more point: Many people have strong but unsubstantiated beliefs about the relationship between *gender identity* and **sexual orientation.** As stated, gender identity refers to our inner sense of being female or male. Sexual orientation refers to the category of people with whom we prefer to relate sexually or intimately. That is, do we prefer people of the same sex as ourselves, or people of the other sex, as sexual/romantic partners? Or are we able to respond erotically to individuals of either sex? Many people assume that if a man does not display a high level of what are considered masculine characteristics, he must have a homosexual orientation. Or if a woman has few or none of the prescribed feminine interests or behaviors, she must be a lesbian. There is no scientific support for this myth. The vast majority of lesbian women and gay men are not confused about their sex or their gender. Most adhere to societal norms regarding femininity and masculinity. Nor do they want to change their anatomy. In other words, there is virtually no relationship between a person's sexual orientation and their gender identity or adherence to gender roles. When some students read this they think, "Sure, I knew this guy Jack, and he was very feminine. Later, I found out he was gay." Remember your critical thinking guidelines (see chapter 1): *Though anecdotes can be vivid and we all have a tendency to rely on our experiences to understand the world, they often give a false picture of the true state of affairs.* Jack represents the exception. Most likely, you know gay men who are masculine and lesbian women who are feminine, and you've never even thought about their sexual orientation.

## 12.2   THE DEVELOPMENT OF GENDER IDENTITY AND GENDER ROLES

Research has shown that by age two, children begin to have an awareness of themselves as boys or girls (the beginning of *gender identity*). By age three or four, they can correctly label themselves as girls or boys. At age four or five, children associate gender with such factors as clothing or play activities rather than genitals. No wonder they believe girls can become boys if they "cut their hair and play with trucks." They also have begun to develop **gender schemas**—that is, they know which toys, clothing, and even playmates are "good" based on gender

| | |
|---|---|
| **sex** | a biological category based on the appearance of the external genitalia (male, female) |
| **gender** | a societally constructed status to which one is assigned (girl or boy, woman or man) |
| **gender roles** | the totality of social and cultural expectations for boys/girls, men/women in a particular society at a particular time in history. Gender roles vary from one society to another. |
| **gender-role ideology** | a particular society's general beliefs and norms regarding how girls and boys or women and men should be (behaviors, traits, etc.) |
| **gender-role socialization** | a lifelong process of acquiring norms of gender-appropriate behavior in a particular society. Learning to be appropriately *feminine* or *masculine*. |
| **gender display** | the use of culture-specific clothing, markings, hair style, etc., to indicate one's gender |
| **core gender identity** | our innermost sense of ourselves as a girl or boy, woman or man. A central component of our sense of "self." |
| **sexual orientation** | one's emotional and erotic preference for partners of a particular sex. *Heterosexuality, homosexuality,* or *bisexuality.* |
| **gender schema (SKĒ-mah)** | a mental organizational network that guides categorizations, behaviors, etc., in terms of gender (e.g., "boy games," "girl games"). |

appropriateness (Martin & Little, 1990). A little later (age five or six), children develop **gender constancy**—that is, they come to understand that gender cannot change and that one remains a girl or boy for life. However, even at this point, most children do not connect gender with a person's genital anatomy. They assign gender on the basis of things like hair length, toy and game preferences, and clothing. At the same time children are developing their gender identity, they are also beginning to understand their culturally prescribed gender role (boys and girls both like to play "dress-up," but she dresses up as a "mommy," while he dresses up like a "spaceman").

With this understanding comes the beginning of the powerful process of **gender stereotyping.** We begin to hold and apply simplified and rigid beliefs about the traits possessed by girls and boys or women and men. This process has been found to be especially rigid among boys and to increase as boys get older (Moller, Hymel, & Rubin, 1992). Once formed, stereotypes are difficult to change because we selectively perceive new information that is in keeping with our stereotypes, and we interpret observed behavior in ways that support our preconceived notions about men and women. Gender stereotypes are also strengthened by the way we *think* and *talk* about men and women. For example, referring to "the opposite sex" implies that women and men have opposite characteristics. In other words, if we believe that members of one gender are passive, then members of the other gender must be active.

Pleck, Sonenstein, and Ku (1993) found that men who strongly subscribe to the idea that men are very different from women had less-intimate relationships and believed that relationships between men and women were adversarial rather than supportive. These ideas can often lead to other problems. For example, part of the feminine stereotype is that women are "emotional" while men are "unemotional." However, if you look at your daily newspaper, you will find it full of male emotional behavior. The anger and rage that result in battering, fighting, and even murder represent emotionality at its height. Yet we do not think about such behaviors in this way. Thus, gender stereotypes distort our views of men and women, and other aspects of reality as well.

Gender stereotyping is just one powerful force that contributes to **sexism.** A sexist is a person who holds negative attitudes toward one gender and subsequently mistreats or discriminates against members of that gender. Holding a stereotype that only women can be effective with children might lead to refusing to hire men as elementary school teachers. Believing that only men are "technological" and "aggressive" might result in policies that prevent women from becoming fighter pilots. Believing that men should be in control of sexual encounters might prevent a woman from insisting that her new lover use a condom.

## 12.2.1 Agents of Gender-Role Socialization

### Parents and Peers

Middle-class American parents often begin the process of their children's gender-role training even before the newborn arrives. The baby's room is painted pink or blue. Decorations are in pastels or stronger colors. Parents and relatives avoid names that do not clearly indicate the child's gender. Today, some parents are aware of the negative aspects of rigid gender-role training and stereotyping. They try to encourage their children to develop the full range of skills that have traditionally been categorized as either masculine or feminine so that they will be prepared for life in a complex society. However, for most, concern about their children's (especially their sons') acceptability continues to move them to purchase cars, computers, and catcher's mitts for their sons, and dolls, dance lessons, and domestic toys for their daughters (Etaugh & Liss, 1992). Children quickly absorb messages about which toys and activities they "should" want and enjoy. Visit your local toy store to observe what kinds of toys are located in the "Boys" and "Girls" sections.

Gender affects how parents and children communicate about sexuality. Nolin and Petersen (1992) studied patterns of sexuality discussions among eighty-four mother-father-child triads. These researchers inquired about communication regarding seventeen topics, such as sexual intercourse, masturbation, the morality of premarital intercourse, and contraception. They found that communication between either parent and daughters was much more far-ranging, in that it covered many more topics. Mothers and sons talked about fewer than half the topics. Father-son discussions covered the fewest number of topics and were especially weak and indirect regarding factual issues and morality. The authors concluded that this apparent lack of parental transmission regarding family sexual norms and values might make boys more susceptible to peer pressure and to engaging in exploitive sexual behavior. Other researchers (Lytton & Romney, 1991) noted that in North American families, there was greater encouragement of achievement, more restrictiveness, and stricter discipline applied to boys. They also found more encouragement of dependence for girls. In general, fathers made more distinctions between sons and daughters than did mothers.

Most of us have observed that children seem to prefer playing and interacting with playmates of their own gender. How do such peer interactions influence gender socialization? Maccoby (1990) found that in gender-segregated groups, boys and girls develop certain gender-typed ways of interacting. Among boys, who tend to prefer rougher games in larger groups, dominance is an ever present concern. This is seen in boys' greater tendency to interrupt each other, use commands, use threats, heckle a speaker, top someone else's story, or call someone names. Girls, who tend to prefer to play with one or two others, are more likely to express agreement in groups, pause to allow another to speak, or acknowledge a point previously made by another. For boys, speech serves egoistic functions (ways of satisfying one's own needs, even at the expense of others), whereas for girls it serves to socially bind together.

These gender-typed ways of interacting carry over into adolescence and adulthood and appear to be strongly related to women's seeking more intimacy and integration in important relationships. It seems that boys' concerns with dominance and turf later become the more limiting and restrictive style of adult men. Scientific findings about gender differences in communication styles have been popularized in such books as Peter Gray's *Men Are from Mars, Women Are from Venus* and Deborah Tannen's *You Just Don't Understand: Women and Men in Conversation.* You read more about gender differences in communication in chapter 2.

## Mass Media

Except for the last seventy years, almost all human children learned the "story of their tribe" from their parents and other adults. That is to say, human children learned who they were and how they should be in the future through face-to-face interaction with adults they knew. Now in most cultures, with the advent of mass media (newspapers, inexpensive books and magazines, movies, radio, and especially television), parents might still be the *earliest,* but they are now relatively *minor,* players in their children's acquisition of cultural beliefs, values, and norms. By the time a child in the United States in 1990 finished high school, he or she had spent more time watching television than engaging in any other activity except sleep (Signorielli, 1990).

While television shows currently present many versions of nontraditional gender roles, there is still a persistence of women as sex objects or victims (Comstock & Paik, 1991). The male stereotypes seen in mass media include the man who seeks only status and success, or who is always tough, confident, and self-reliant. Another common male stereotype is the ever-aggressive, violent, daring, and uninjurable hero. While it's clear that mass media are not the "total mind programmers" some would have us believe, nor are audiences helpless victims of media brainwashing,

media presentations of gender roles do have an impact on the general public.

In movies, television, and magazines, men's bodies are covered and men "do things"—they solve crimes, have adventures, and so on. Overall, women's bodies are constantly "under surveillance" (Douglas, 1994)—they exist to be looked at. They are there, often with much of the body exposed, to be inspected by the camera and audience.

Men often appear in roles in which male aging is associated with increased power and status. Aging women are all but invisible in most media.

Many adolescents in the United States spend a great deal of time watching music videos. This type of media has come under special scrutiny over the last few years because of its hypothesized relationship with increased stereotyping, negative attitudes, and sexual violence toward women.

One study of forty music videos (Sommers-Flannagan, Sommers-Flanagan, & Davis, 1993) found that women appeared half as often as men did, and that when they did appear they were the objects of sexual and other types of aggression. They also appeared most often in implicitly sexual and subservient roles. Body parts were emphasized equally for women and men. A second study found male characters to be more adventuresome, domineering, aggressive, and violent. Females were more affectionate, dependent, nurturant, and fearful compared to males. In the commercials that accompany MTV, females also appeared less often, and wore sexier and skimpier clothing. In keeping with trends in other media, women were more often the object of other people's looking (Signorielli, McLeod, & Healy, 1994).

The lyrics of some rap music, especially "gangsta rap," have been singled out for intense criticism. Music critics, scholars, and leaders of the African American community have expressed deep concern about the influence of the values and view of life reflected in these songs and videos. Images of constant and intense sexual violence against women permeate these songs (Medved, 1992). The feelings and interactions

| | |
|---|---|
| **gender constancy** | a firm understanding that one remains male or female: the last stage of *gender identity development* |
| **gender stereotyping** | the overapplication of simple and rigid beliefs about the traits possessed by girls and women or boys and men |
| **sexism** | negative attitudes toward members of one gender, and their subsequent mistreatment |

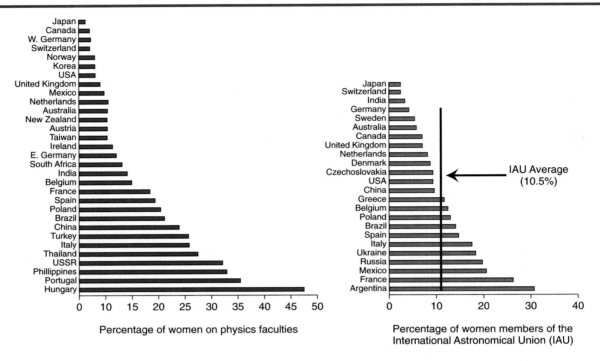

**FIGURE 12.1**   In many rapidly developing countries, achievement in science and mathematics is not associated with the stereotype of masculinity.

between men and women are often presented as exploitive, highly sexualized, and devoid of any affection or respect.

## The School

On the surface, it would appear that today's girls and boys are exposed to the same educational challenges and opportunities. The idea of a "special" curriculum for one gender sounds strange to most of us, yet it wasn't so long ago that many educational leaders and policy makers believed that educating women would seriously damage their brains and reproductive systems (Hall, 1904; Smith, 1905). Today, girls and boys sit in the same classrooms, master the same curriculum, and have access to the same technology, yet the stereotype that boys and men are "naturally" attracted to and excel in math and science remains deeply imbedded in our society's present gender-role ideology (Hyde, Fennema, & Lamon, 1990). Comparisons across countries offer additional insights into how gender affects attraction to mathematics and science. In rapidly developing countries such as the Phillipines, Portugal, and Hungary, women constitute anywhere from 33 to 47 percent of university physics faculty; in already established economies, such as Japan, Canada, and Germany, fewer than 10

percent of university physicists are women. The future may indeed belong to those societies that develop more flexible gender-role ideologies. Take a look at figure 12.1 for some more details about global gender trends in the sciences.

In the United States, the forces that maintain gender inequality continue to be found in the day-to-day interactions that go on in the classroom (see "At Issue: Do Girls and Boys Get the Same Education?").

## Religion

In the United States, about 91 percent of women and 88 percent of men describe themselves as members of a religious group (U.S. Department of Commerce, 1990). Virtually all of these individuals pray to a "male" God, and for many, even imagining a female deity may seem unnatural. Feminine or androgynous images of God may have prevailed at different times and in different places, but Western gender-role ideology is powerfully influenced by the concept of a male deity in Judaism, Christianity, and Islam.

In Orthodox Judaism, only men may initiate divorce, but Jewish law recognizes the rights of both women and men to sexual fulfillment in marriage. Orthodox Judaism also has strict rituals surrounding the "uncleanliness" of women during the menstrual

## AT ISSUE

### DO GIRLS AND BOYS GET THE SAME EDUCATION?

In the vast majority of North American schools, girls and boys are educated in the same classrooms, with the same teachers, and master the same curriculum. The idea that girls should go to homemaking classes while boys should go to the woodworking shop is long gone. However, several recent studies suggest that gender differences in education have little to do with the content of what is formally learned. It has all to do with students' everyday experiences and interactions. These researchers found evidence of gender bias from preschool all the way through college. For example, the Early Education curriculum is more suited to the needs of boys. It emphasizes small muscle development, language enhancement, and impulse control: as a group, girls are already good at these skills.

All through the elementary school grades, textbooks continue to ignore or stereotype girls and women. The experiences and accomplishments of girls and women are underrepresented in the formal curriculum. While girls are equal to or even ahead of boys on almost every standardized measure of achievement and well-being all through the early grades, by the end of high school they are behind on such measures, and the gap widens all through college and into graduate school.

Those who are skeptical of these reports hold that gender, racial, and ethnic bias are simply not tolerated in the classroom: There are official guidelines for avoiding such bias, and administrators are supposed to be alert to any complaints regarding bias.

Researchers insist that although it is true that most teachers and administrators are sensitive to such issues, all through the school years teachers pay less attention to girls. In preschool, boys receive both more instructional time and more hugs. Boys also receive more precise teacher comments, regarding both their academic performance and their conduct. During normal classroom interactions, teachers tolerated boys' shouting out answers but reprimanded girls for doing so. Teachers were also found to continually reinforce rigid gender-role behavior and attitudes in boys, pushing them to be competitive, nonexpressive and dominance oriented. Another study found that overt sexual harassment of girls by boys began during the sixth grade and progressed to high levels during high school. Teachers and administrators often accept such harassment as "normal masculine behavior." A particularly damaging form of harassment involves ridicule about being gay or lesbian.

Critics of these reports respond that such charges are unfair: It is easier to document instances of supposed bias than to document thousands of instances where no such "bias" occurs. Besides, even if there are differences in day-to-day student-teacher interactions, this does not appear to influence academic achievement. Girls tend to perform better than boys in school. Behavioral and learning problems are much more common among boys, and boys typically show lower achievement compared to girls.

Claims of gender bias are based on two reports published by the American Association of University Women (AAUW 1992, 1994). Researchers examined more than a thousand publications about girls and education. These included hundreds of actual research studies, mostly conducted during the 1980s. Myra and David Sadker also published *Failing at Fairness: How America's Schools Cheat Girls* (1994). They conducted actual observations in many classrooms in order to document the gender differences in normal ongoing teacher-student interactions. They also examined archival data documenting actual school performance from elementary school through college and graduate programs.

Traditional gender-role socialization in the schools takes its toll on girls' self-esteem. One study found that 69 percent of elementary school boys and 60 percent of elementary school girls reported they were "happy the way I am." By high school, 46 percent of boys agreed with this statement, but only 29 percent of girls did so. Beginning in the sixth grade, girls rank being liked and being popular as most important. Boys rank independence and competence as most important. These characteristics are central features of traditional gender roles.

cycle. In contrast to Orthodox congregations, Conservative Judaism allows women and men to sit together during religious services, and began ordaining women as rabbis in 1973 and as cantors in 1990 (Renzetti & Curran, 1995). Gays and lesbians are welcome as members of Conservative congregations, but none may be ordained. Reform congregations emphasize equal roles and rights for women and ordain both women and homosexuals.

Historical documents suggest that women had an equal place as missionaries, prophets, and victims of persecution in the fledgling Christian movement, but

Pagan religious traditions such as Wicca coexisted with Christianity for centuries in northern Europe. This pagan "sheela" comes from a twelfth-century Irish church. Display of the female genitals protected worshipers against evil spirits.

as soon as Christianity became better established, women were relegated to second-class status. Many theologians made reference to St. Paul's statements about the "proper" secondary status for women in the church. In general, women were viewed as sexual temptresses who eroded men's rationality and self-control. Women were either the cause of sexual sin, sexless pure virgins, or, they were mothers. Today, almost all Protestant churches ordain women as ministers. In 1992, 31 percent of those enrolled in divinity school in the United States were women (Bedell, 1993). Condemnation of homosexuality continues among many Protestant sects, and controversy swirls around those who have ordained homosexuals as clergy.

Among the Muslim faithful (one-fifth of the world's population), sexuality, like virtually all aspects of life, is governed by the rules of the Qu'ran (Koran). The founder of Islam, Muhammad, stated that a woman had to consent to marriage and that she, and not her father, would receive the brideprice. Women had conjugal rights and could own their own jewelry, keep their earnings, initiate divorce, and receive inheritances (though they could receive only half of what male heirs could receive). Silence, immobility, and obedience are the traditional and highly desirable traits for the Muslim woman (Sabah, 1984). Both women and men have the right to sexual pleasure and gratification, but nonmarital sex is seen as dangerous and extremely harmful both to the individual and to society as a whole. Women are seen as the source of this sexual temptation, and it is held

that their activity must thus be limited and controlled (Timimi, 1995). It was from these concerns that the traditions of *purdah* (virtual confinement to the home) and *chador* (being completely covered and veiled during any public appearance) arose and persist today in more fundamentalist Muslim nations (Renzetti & Curran, 1995).

## 12.2.2  Theories of Gender-Role Development

We now turn to the issue of how scientists try to explain how we develop gender roles. Over the years, there have been many theories that attempt to explain this complex process. No one theory has been shown to be more correct than another, but it has been said that theories are best judged by how *useful* they are, rather than by their ultimate correctness.

### Sociobiological Theory

**Sociobiology** attempts to apply evolutionary theory and principles toward understanding human social behavior, including sexual behavior. This view emphasizes **reproductive success** (success in passing on one's genes). Sociobiologists hypothesize that reproductive success for males involves the insemination of many females. They claim that this explains why males tend to seek many more sexual partners than do women. Since a male's time and energy involvement in reproduction is so short (arousal and ejaculation), males are more likely to pursue casual sex (Bailey et al., 1994). On the other hand, women's eggs are fewer and thus more precious. Accordingly, it makes evolutionary sense for her to be more careful and selective about who she pairs with. Further, she must devote nine months of her bodily functioning to gestation and then provide care for the helpless child for a number of years. Therefore, she is more likely to be attracted to males who have resources for the care and well-being of her offspring (Feingold, 1992). Ostensibly, this can explain why women prefer older men, who are more likely to have amassed economic resources (Kenrick & Trost, 1993; Oliver & Hyde, 1993).

### Psychological Theories

Many psychological theorists have attempted to account for how gender develops and is maintained throughout life. For example, the gender-related ideas of Sigmund Freud dominated psychological thinking for several decades. Although Freud's work is fascinating to read and thought provoking in its emphasis on the importance of sexuality in development, there is virtually no scientific support for Freud's theories regarding gender-role development. Here, we'll take a look at two psychological theories with good research support.

According to cognitive social learning theory, children learn attitudes and values by observing and imitating the behavior of others. What they learn depends partly on the power and prestige of the person observed. Television, movies, and music can be powerful influences on the sexual values and behavior of children and adolescents.

In an early version of **cognitive social learning theory,** Mischel (1966) hypothesized two central processes in gender-role development. First, children are differentially *punished* for gender-role-inconsistent behavior (e.g., criticism for the girl who plays too aggressively) and rewarded for gender-role-consistent behavior (e.g., praise for the boy who explores the woods near his home). A second process involves *observation and modeling* of same-gender adults or other important figures (boys observe male presidents, soldiers, criminals, or doctors, while girls observe female teachers, gymnasts, victims, or nurses). A more recent version of this theory also emphasizes the mental processes that go along with learning, especially *expectations* (Bussey & Bandura, 1992). For example, a boy might anticipate ridicule if he does not pursue athletic activities with his friends. A girl does not expect excitement from her playmates when she collects samples of stagnant pond water to examine under her microscope.

Another useful model is Sandra Bem's **gender schema theory.** A schema is a central organizing idea that is applied to all incoming information. For example, you have developed a "school" schema that includes such factors as learning unfamiliar information, listening to a more knowledgeable person, obeying that person's instructions regarding what to learn and how to show what you've learned, and so on.

Some other schemas include a "family" schema and a "date" schema. According to Sandra Bem's (1984, 1993) gender schema theory, as we grow up, we develop a "gender schema." That is, our culture makes important distinctions between men and women. Children come to know this and then begin to organize new information about themselves and the world according to that distinction or schema. So, the moon, cats, flowers, dancing, physical attractiveness, and love are seen as feminine, while the sun, dogs, sports, physical strength, and sex are seen as masculine. We use our cultural ideas of what is masculine or feminine and organize all sorts of interests, behaviors, traits, and experiences as masculine or feminine. To demonstrate the pervasiveness of gender schemas, it is likely that you can even categorize various kinds of cars as being more masculine or feminine.

Thus, anticipating and arranging for intercourse to occur on a date might be seen as part of a "masculine schema," so a feminine woman does not place a condom in her purse. Instead, a "feminine schema" is activated, so only lipstick and perfume go into her purse.

Individuals who are very prone to organize various aspects of their lives in terms of gender are described as highly **gender schematic;** those for whom gender is not a strong organizing principle are considered *gender aschematic.* This personality trait has been found to be related to all sorts of other factors. For example, gender schematic children tend to remember toys in terms of their gender appropriateness (Levy, 1994). As adults, gender schematic males tend

| | |
|---|---|
| **sociobiology** | a theory suggesting that many social behaviors and conventions (such as gender) have evolutionary significance |
| **reproductive success** | the likelihood that one's offspring will survive, thereby passing on one's genetic endowment |
| **cognitive social learning theory** | a theory suggesting that children acquire gender roles through rewards/punishments, observation/modeling, and expectations regarding outcomes |
| **gender schema theory** | Bem's theory that our gender-related schemas guide our future categorizations, associations, and behaviors |
| **gender schematic** (skē-MA-tik) | the degree to which persons organize aspects of life in terms of gender |

**TABLE 12.1** MAJOR THEORIES OF GENDER-ROLE DEVELOPMENT

| THEORY | CENTRAL CONCEPTS | ILLUSTRATIVE EXAMPLE | THEORISTS |
|---|---|---|---|
| Sociobiology | Reproductive success | For men, more casual sex increases likelihood of passing on genes. For women, one stable mate with resources increases the likelihood of passing on genes. | David Buss, David Kenrick |
| Cognitive social learning theory | Rewards and punishment, observation and modeling, expectations | Praise for gender-typed behavior. Admonishing of cross-gendered behavior. We see and imitate gender-typed models (pilots and stewardesses). We come to anticipate negative outcomes for behavior that does not conform to gender roles. | Walter Mischel, Albert Bandura |
| Gender schema theory | Formation of mental organizational schemes for processing new information | We think of cats as feminine and dogs as masculine. We tend to view sperm as masculine even though half carry an X chromosome. | Sandra Bem |

to see relationships between men and women as adversarial and these men are more likely to treat women in a more sexist manner after exposure to pornography (McKenzie-Mohr & Zanna, 1990). (See table 12.1 for a summary of the theories we have just discussed.)

## 12.2.3 Real and Imaginary Gender Differences

When we think about the "real differences" between men and women, we typically think of obvious anatomical and physiological differences. Clearly, there are physical and functional differences between women and men. Only men can impregnate, and only women can become pregnant and breast-feed a new infant. But what then? Are there actual brain differences in men and women that result in differences in their cognitive abilities? Do men and women naturally have certain social and personality characteristics that make one gender better caretakers for children? Because men are seemingly necessary for such a small (but vital) aspect of reproduction, should they naturally be less involved in child rearing? Or are these gender differences **socially constructed**—that is, are they developed and normalized by a particular society, which then passes them on to the next generation as "natural" roles for women and men?

One area of gender differences is **aggression,** and this difference has been attributed to higher levels of testosterone in males. Even at very young ages, boys engage in more rough and aggressive play than girls. However, research has shown that parents and other adults perceive and interact with female and male infants rather differently from a very young age. For example, in a classic study (Rubin, Provenzano, &

Luria, 1974), adults saw the same film of a particular baby. When adults were told the baby was a boy, they rated it as stronger, larger, more alert, and more active compared to those who were told that same baby was a girl. Perhaps parents and others encourage more aggressive behavior in infants perceived as stronger, firmer, and so on. Furthermore, at home and at school, boys are encouraged to engage in many large-muscle activities (running, ballgames, etc.) but often, girls are not. Such gross motor activities encourage the arousal and large movements associated with aggressive behavior. Recent research suggests that when women and men know that their partner in an interactive game is of the other sex, men do behave more aggressively than women. However, if subjects do not know the sex of their interaction partner, women and men demonstrate equal levels of aggression (Lightdale & Prentice, 1994). Studies of aggression offer an interesting arena in which to observe the relationship between biologically based behavior potential and the power of socially constructed avenues for expression of that potential. Olympic competition offers repeated and dazzling testimony to the fact that traits such as physical strength, nurturance, courage, emotional expressiveness, and even aggressiveness exist in both women and men from all over the globe.

### Gender Differences in Cognitive Abilities

Over the last several decades, there has been great debate regarding whether there are brain-based differences between males and females in three areas: spatial abilities, verbal abilities, and mathematical abilities. **Spatial abilities** involve a variety of capacities for mentally manipulating shapes and images (see fig. 12.2). Such abilities are important for a whole range of tasks and occupations (architecture, pilot,

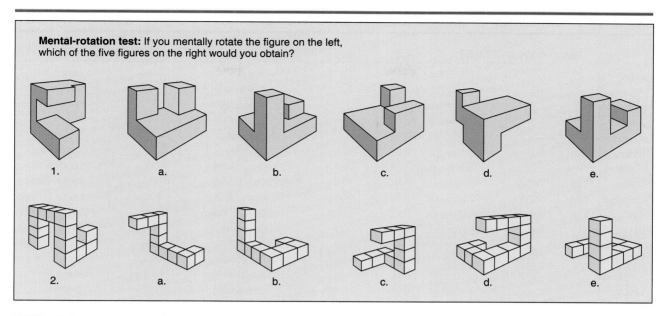

**Mental-rotation test:** If you mentally rotate the figure on the left, which of the five figures on the right would you obtain?

1.    a.    b.    c.    d.    e.

2.    a.    b.    c.    d.    e.

**FIGURE 12.2    Rotating geometric figures in space.** Visual-spatial skills—for example, the ability to rotate geometric figures in space—have been considered part of the male gender-role stereotype. Gender differences in visual-spatial skills are small, however, and can be modified by training.

**Source:** From Rathus, S. A., et al. (1990). *Psychology* (4th ed.). Copyright © 1990 by Holt, Rinehart and Winston, Inc. Reprinted by permission of the publisher.

etc.). Researchers referred to "solid" evidence of male superiority in this area based on differences in brain development (Caplan, MacPherson, & Tobin, 1985). Most recently, it has become clear that gender-typed experiences beginning in earliest childhood have a strong influence on the development of such skills. Even throwing a ball to another person involves practice in spatial judgments. Dressing a Barbie doll does not. Several researchers have demonstrated that providing females with training designed to improve spatial abilities equalizes performance between the genders (Baenninger & Newcombe, 1989; Willis & Schaie, 1988).

The vague term **verbal abilities** is applied to a wide range of factors related to language and communication. Traditional research literature suggested female superiority in this domain, but again, more refined measures and more similar socialization experiences have eradicated this "gap" as well (Feingold, 1992).

A long observed "biologically based gender gap" in mathematics performance has essentially disappeared (Hyde, Fennema, & Lamon, 1990; Shea, 1994). However, more boys than girls continue to be identified as "gifted" in math (Holden, 1987, 1991).

### Gender As a Self-Fulfilling Prophecy

In our society, the stereotypical personality traits for men include such qualities as being ambitious, as-sertive, confident, cruel, dominant, forceful, rational, strong, tough, and unemotional. For women, it includes such qualities as being affectionate, charming, dependent, fickle, flirtatious, gentle, mild, prudish, sentimental, submissive, and whiny (Williams & Best, 1990). Social psychologists have consistently found that if we expect individuals to have certain qualities, then we tend to treat them in ways that bring out those very qualities (Beall & Sternberg, 1993; Geis, 1993). Thus, individuals become exactly the kind of person we expect them to be. To compound the issue, most people tend to hold the same

| | |
|---|---|
| **social construction** | the idea that much of what we experience as real, normal, or natural is "created" based on cultural influences |
| **aggression** | behavior intended to harm, injure, or dominate another |
| **spatial abilities** (SPĀ-shul) | abilities related to the mental manipulation of shapes, images, or physical relationships between objects or their parts |
| **verbal abilities** | abilities related to the creation, use, and manipulation of language |

**TABLE 12.2**    THE 100 ITEMS OF THE CROSS-CULTURAL ADJECTIVE CHECKLIST

| MALE-ASSOCIATED TRAITS | | FEMALE-ASSOCIATED TRAITS | |
|---|---|---|---|
| Active | Loud | Affected | Modest |
| Adventurous | Obnoxious | Affectionate | Nervous |
| Aggressive | Opinionated | Appreciative | Patient |
| Arrogant | Opportunistic | Cautious | Pleasing |
| Autocratic | Pleasure-seeking | Changeable | Prudish |
| Bossy | Precise | Charming | Self-pitying |
| Capable | Progressive | Complaining | Sensitive |
| Coarse | Quick | Complicated | Sentimental |
| Conceited | Rational | Confused | Sexy |
| Confident | Realistic | Curious | Shy |
| Courageous | Reckless | Dependent | Softhearted |
| Cruel | Resourceful | Dreamy | Sophisticated |
| Cynical | Rigid | Emotional | Submissive |
| Determined | Robust | Excitable | Suggestive |
| Disorderly | Serious | Fault-finding | Talkative |
| Enterprising | Sharp-witted | Fearful | Timid |
| Greedy | Show-off | Fickle | Touchy |
| Hardheaded | Steady | Foolish | Unambitious |
| Humorous | Stern | Forgiving | Unintelligent |
| Indifferent | Stingy | Frivolous | Unstable |
| Individualistic | Stolid | Fussy | Warm |
| Initiative | Tough | Gentle | Weak |
| Interests wide | Unfriendly | Imaginative | Worrying |
| Inventive | Unscrupulous | Kind | Understanding |
| Lazy | Witty | Mild | Superstitious |

From J. E. Williams and D. L. Best, "Cross Cultural Views of Women and Men" in *Psychology and Culture*, by W. J. Lonner and R. Malpass (eds.), 1994. Copyright © 1994 by Allyn and Bacon, Inc. Reprinted by permission.

stereotypes, so that even the *target* of a stereotype shares the same beliefs and might begin to act out the stereotypic quality expected.

Some gender stereotypes are more or less universal. John Williams and Deborah Best (1990) examined gender stereotypes in more than thirty countries. They found a relatively high degree of agreement across cultures about the characteristics of women and men. Table 12.2 offers the listing of the one hundred traits that were selected across cultures as being characteristic of men or women. Masculine characteristics were evaluated more positively than feminine characteristics in Japan, South Africa, and Nigeria, while feminine characteristics were more favorable in Italy, Peru, and Australia. In general, masculine stereotypes contain themes of greater strength and more activity compared to feminine stereotypes.

Does it matter if women and men are believed to have certain characteristics? Psychologically speaking, it does. Even though stereotypes are useful in helping us make quick judgments about how to interact with others, they also can keep us from seeing and treating others as unique individuals. The woman who believes that real men are pleasure-seeking and unscrupulous might reject the softhearted and understanding man. The man who insists that real women are dependent and suggestive might ignore the woman who is individualistic and resourceful. For a discussion of one recent development in the area of gendered behavior, see "At Issue: The Men's Movement."

## 12.3   GENDER AND SEXUAL BEHAVIOR

As we discussed, gender affects many aspects of our everyday life. We will now examine how gender influences our attitudes and behavior in romantic and sexual relationships in our society.

### 12.3.1   Gender and Sexual Attitudes

Mary Beth Oliver and Janet Shibley Hyde (1993) conducted a meta-analysis of studies that reported on gender differences in sexual behavior and attitudes.

## AT ISSUE

### THE MEN'S MOVEMENT: REINVENTING A GENDER ROLE?

The second wave of feminism began during the 1970s. The goal of this mass movement was to bring about economic, political, and social equality for both genders. In parallel to these feminists, groups of men began meeting to examine the problematic aspects of traditional masculine roles. It was clear that men had great personal, social, economic, and political power; it was also clear that gender-related emphases on competition, aggressiveness, control, and power-seeking had detrimental effects on men—a higher likelihood of early death due to alcoholism, drug-abuse, homicide, and suicide. Masculine role expectations can be connected to stress-related illnesses, shortened lifespan, poorer family relationships, and lower general life satisfaction (Gilmore, 1990). Some men formed organizations such as the National Organization for Men Against Sexism or the North American Federation of Men's Councils. Men's Studies programs arose in universities, and publications such as *Changing Men: A Journal of Men's Studies* were founded.

One branch of this social phenomenon is devoted to men's individual enlightenment and personal development. The best-selling writings of Robert Bly (*Iron John*) and Sam Keen (*A Fire in the Belly: On Being a Man*) typify this facet of the reexamination of men's roles. Bly suggests that men in our society are wounded by their fathers' lack of emotional involvement with them, and also by the absence of any rituals that initiate boys into manhood. He celebrates masculine ideals such as bravery and independence and also encourages such nonmasculine pursuits as close friendships between men, expressing warm emotions, and closer involvement with children (Erkel, 1990).

Another facet of this movement is made up of "men's rights groups" such as the Domestic Rights Coalition and Fathers United for Equal Rights. These groups seek to rectify situations where they perceive that the legal and social rights of men are being violated. They believe that current divorce and child custody laws are unfair to men. Such groups provide emotional support and legal assistance for divorcing men. They also lobby for changes in family law (Renzetti & Curran, 1995). Further along the continuum is the "no-guilt wing" (Brod, 1987). Spokespersons for this group suggest that men should not feel guilty about "illusory" gender privileges and domination. They actively work to eliminate any gender-related favoritism in public policies such as military exemptions, differences in automobile insurance rates, as well as "happy hours" and "ladies' nights" that offer reduced prices to women.

Some poke fun at the goals of the men's movement. Carol Tavris (1992) would like men to contemplate the possibilities of an Ironing John rather than an Iron John. Others contend that the men's movement continues the tradition of woman-blaming. However, one very positive result of this reexamination of gender roles is that it has led to the involvement of men in opposing violence against women and children. Groups such as Men Against Violence and Men Stopping Violence have formed an alliance with rape crisis centers and battered women's agencies to change the behavior of violent men. Do such groups exist in your community?

The strongest gender difference in *behavior* was found in the incidence of masturbation. Men masturbated much more often and began at an earlier age compared to women. The strongest *attitudinal* gender difference had to do with casual, premarital sex, with men being much more permissive.

Moderate gender differences appeared in the following areas:

- Men were especially more permissive about premarital and extramarital sex in committed relationships.
- Women were more guilty or anxious regarding sexual behavior.

- Men reported a higher incidence and frequency of sexual intercourse with more partners.
- Men tended to be younger than women at the age of their first intercourse.
- More men engaged in same-sex sexual behavior.

No gender differences were found in these areas:

- Attitudes about homosexuality
- Levels of experienced sexual satisfaction
- The overall incidence of kissing
- The overall incidence of oral-genital activity

It is also interesting to note that all of the gender differences became smaller over time—that is, *smaller gender differences were found in more recent studies compared to older studies.*

## 12.3.2 Gender and Responses to Erotica

In a series of classic studies, Julia Heiman (1977) measured blood flow to the genitals of men and women as they listened to various kinds of sexually arousing audiotapes. She found that both women and men were most aroused by erotic and erotic-romantic tapes. Both men and women found a female-centered tape to be the most arousing. Among women, there was a greater discrepancy regarding *self-reports* of arousal versus *objective measures* of arousal. However, in a later study, when women were instructed to "attend to" their bodily signs of arousal, the difference between women's self-reports and their objective measures of arousal disappeared. How might we interpret this finding? In general, our culture teaches women not to pay attention to their physiological arousal, but rather to focus more on the social and romantic aspects of sexual encounters. In other words, there are gender differences in the traditional **sexual scripts** of women and men (Gagnon, 1990a). Sexual scripts cover such issues as what constitutes a sexual behavior; who is an appropriate sexual partner; how frequently sexual activity should occur; when and where sexual behavior should occur; how one is supposed to feel about various sexual behaviors; and so forth. Let's take a closer look at the gender-typed sexual scripts of our own society.

## 12.3.3 Male and Female Sexual Scripts

Sexual scripts are usually thought of in the context of heterosexual sexual expression, but lesbian women, gay men, and bisexuals are all socialized with the same sexual scripts as their heterosexual sisters and brothers. As we will see later on, same-sex couplings can sometimes result in an exaggeration of the sexual scripts associated with women or men.

An excellent source for many insights into the male sexual script is Bernie Zilbergeld's book *The New Male Sexuality* (1992). Based on his work with many clients, Zilbergeld suggests that the following guidelines constitute the sexual script for men in our culture (most apply to both heterosexual and homosexual men). Note how many of these notions are direct extensions of the gender-stereotypic traits associated with men.

1. Men are supposed to know all about sex and be very comfortable talking about, initiating, and proceeding in a sexual encounter. They never feel hesitant or awkward.

2. Sex is the only masculine way of communicating deep feelings. Talking is feminine. The real man doesn't have to stop and talk about sexually transmitted infections or discuss contraception. Nor does he have to verbalize his doubts, fears, or other emotional needs.

---

# GO ASK ALICE

*Dear Alice,*
    *Why is it that, in all the movies and stuff about sex, it is always the woman who feels pressured? I felt pressured my first time and no one would believe me if I told them. Any comments would be helpful.*
    *Sensitive Guy*

Dear Sensitive Guy,
    You bring up the beginnings of a huge debate about gender stereotypes and societal norms in the United States and other countries. Alice has heard from, and knows, men who feel similar to the way you do about your first sexual experience, and often about subsequent sexual experiences. Contrary to commonly held beliefs that men are "too big," "too strong," "too much in control," or "too much into sex" to be pressured into sex, or even sexually assaulted, it happens. Exact numbers are difficult to determine because of a lack of research and official records, and men's unwillingness to discuss it.

    Alice would encourage both men and women to choose when or whether to have sex. Pressure from others can, and does, unfairly influence us in this decision. Also, once a person has chosen to have sex, this does NOT take away his/her right to say "no" at other times during his/her life. Saying "no" to sex often is a way of saying "yes" to ourselves.

    Your question alone helps a great deal in dispelling myths about men's sexuality. Thank you for writing.

 http://www.mhhe.com/byer6

3. Touching, caressing, and hugging are nothing but coital foreplay, and so they should always lead to intercourse.

4. Manly men are always interested in sex and always ready for sex. Wanting to take a walk, read, or even talk is not what men prefer to do.

5. In intimate encounters, men perform, do things, or take action, while women respond and feel.

6. The most important aspect of sex is how hard a penis becomes, what a man does with that penis, and for how long he can do it.

7. Being sexual with someone means that intercourse will occur. Intercourse and orgasm mark the "end" of a sexual encounter.

8. Real men "bring" their partners to powerful and multiple orgasms. If this doesn't happen, it's probably because she's inhibited.

9. An intimate encounter counts as "sex" only if he has an orgasm. It's "good sex" if she has a loud, dramatic orgasm.

10. Men can overcome women's rebuffs, refusals, or reluctance by their persistence or insistence. A more dangerous form of this script is that a man has a *right* to ignore her protests when he is aroused, was sexual with her on a previous occasion, or feels "led on."

11. As demonstrated by pornography, the best sex is fast, silent, and spontaneous. Talking gets in the way of passion.

12. Men never have any sexual problems or difficulties.

Since the 1960s, the sexual script for women in the United States has changed somewhat (Dennis, 1992; Ogden, 1994), but many traditional views persist. Of course, the sexual scripts of women (and men) are also influenced by the gender roles and gender ideology of their particular ethnic group.

1. It's now okay for most women to want sex. However, "good" sex is what occurs in a committed relationship. In the past, this commitment involved marriage, but now good sex can occur in the context of a committed relationship, whether or not marriage is on the horizon (Altman, 1984).

2. Casual sex or sex without love is not okay. A sexual encounter outside the context of a loving relationship is bad, dangerous, and damaging to one's self-concept and to one's reputation (Breay & Gentry, 1990).

3. Women's bodies are sexually exciting, but their genitals are ugly, smelly, and unacceptable.

Many women have never explored or seen their own genitals. Men have the opportunity to see the genitals of many men and women (via the locker room and their having a higher number of sexual partners). Usually, only lesbian women and female health professionals see other women's genitals.

4. Women's sexual arousal is something done for men. Women are not as interested in sex as men are. Women's sexuality is dormant until aroused by a man (Janus & Janus, 1993).

5. A woman doesn't know what pleases her sexually. It is up to a man to help her discover it. She is innocent of the workings of her genitals, and men know what to do to arouse her.

6. Women don't have to communicate verbally about what feels good or doesn't feel good sexually. The man is the "sexpert" and should be able to figure it out without her telling him.

7. Feminine women don't talk about sex easily. That's because they don't have strong sexual desires or feelings.

8. A real woman is always young, thin, beautiful, graceful, and without flaws. Women's bodies should look like those of women appearing on magazine covers, starring in movies, or singing popular songs. Therefore, all the real women you know fall far short of how they should look (Tevlin & Leiblum, 1983).

9. In keeping with their role as nurturers and care takers, women "give" sex to men. Sexual activity happens when *he* wants or needs it. *His* pleasure is more important.

10. The right way to have an orgasm is during intercourse and only as a result of stimulation from the penis. Cunnilingus, masturbation, manual or digital stimulation, and using a vibrator are not really okay.

## 12.3.4 Gender and Sexual Scripts in Other-Sex Couples

There is little doubt that female and male gender roles and their sexual scripts are undergoing rapid change today. This is a very lively issue, not just in societal terms, but also on a personal level as we negotiate all manner of agreements with our sexual and romantic partners. Do they share the expenses of dates? Does she keep her name when they marry? Who is more

| sexual scripts | culture-specific, learned guidelines regarding all aspects of sexual expression |
|---|---|

willing to move for the sake of a partner's career advancement? Do they take turns staying at home with a sick child?

A majority of North American women have paying jobs, and more of them have earnings comparable to those of their male partners. This has shifted the power balance in intimate relationships, and two-career couples must negotiate carefully to balance family and personal needs as well as their respective career demands. In spite of these many changes, women still spend three times as many hours on housework and child care as their husbands (Hughes & Galinsky, 1994). Although most couples attempt to distribute household tasks, women still do most of the domestic work. This creates a particularly difficult burden for poorer women, because a couple's combined income is insufficient to pay for needed domestic services (Crosby, 1991). Improved job opportunities for women have led to both greater power for women and greater freedom for men. Knowing that theirs is not the sole income, men can leave a disliked job, risk a business venture, pursue greater educational opportunities, and experience more of the pleasure and satisfaction of day-to-day family life (Gerson, 1993).

In our society, sexual scripts have shifted somewhat as well (Gagnon, 1990b). Some general trends include the following:

1. Masturbation, or self-pleasuring, is a legitimate and acceptable form of sexual self-expression for both women and men (Laumann et al., 1994).

2. Premarital sexuality is acceptable for both men and women as long as it occurs in the context of a loving, committed relationship. Contemporary literature, movies, and even prime-time television sitcoms take this relatively recent norm for granted. This new norm is often referred to as "permissiveness with affection."

3. Men and women bear equal responsibility for their sexual activities. Contraception and protection from sexually transmitted infections should be intimate, shared responsibilities (Herold & Mewhinney, 1993).

4. Sexual expression solely for the sake of mutual erotic pleasure is acceptable.

5. Both partners have equal rights regarding the opportunity to experience sexual pleasure and orgasm. One partner's sexual pleasure is not more important than the other's.

6. Sexual activities other than intercourse are acceptable. These might include manual-genital and oral-genital stimulation (Gagnon & Simon, 1987).

7. Either partner in an established relationship may initiate sexual activity (Anderson & Aymami, 1993).

## 12.3.5   Gender and Sexual Scripts in Same-Sex Couples

There have been relatively few studies of gender-role behavior within gay male and lesbian relationships. In general, lesbian women acquire the gender-typed social and sexual scripts of women, and gay men acquire those of men (Gagnon, 1990b), and both bring the results of such socialization to their intimate relationships. Clearly, lesbian and gay couples must come to some understanding about how traditionally gender-typed tasks and roles (yard work, child care, etc.) will be carried out, but conventional or stereotypic notions might not help at all with these decisions. On a more intimate level, women are socialized not to be sexual initiators, so who is more likely to express an overt interest in sexual activity in a lesbian couple? If men are socialized not to express their fears about love and work, who, in a gay male couple, will initiate the reciprocal self-disclosure that seems necessary to maintain intimacy?

Lesbian women and gay men follow cultural scripts regarding "dating" to varying degrees. But how does one know who is gay and who is not? Where does one meet potential partners? Men are socialized to express interest in a potential partner; it can be more difficult for lesbian women to express such interest, which is why most lesbian relationships develop out of established acquaintances and friendships. Traditional male gender socialization has emphasized an interest in casual sexual encounters, so it is easy to see why traditional gay male culture has exaggerated this norm. But new norms have developed in this age of HIV and other STIs (Huston & Schwartz, 1996).

The old stereotype is that gay and lesbian couples have "butch-femme" arrangements, with each partner playing the traditional male or female gender role. But such relationships are rare today, especially among younger couples (Schreurs, 1993). One typical arrangement is to merely assign each partner responsibility for specific tasks, but this can result in inequities if one partner gets all the "dirty work" (Huston & Schwartz, 1996). A more egalitarian approach involves each partner doing what he or she does best and distributing undesirable chores equally. Lesbian couples seem more successful in maintaining such egalitarianism in their household roles (Kurdek, 1993). Among gay men, income differences translate into greater power in the relationship, and this power differential will often affect household tasks and decision making.

Little research has been published about the distribution of child-care responsibilities in lesbian and gay relationships, except that in lesbian partnerships the biological mother typically has more power in making major decisions regarding the children

In every kind of family, household tasks and family responsibilities must be distributed and carried out.

(Moore, Blumstein, & Schwartz, 1994). However, a growing number of gay and lesbian couples bear or adopt children after the relationship is established, and this represents another understudied area (Patterson, 1992; Kantrowitz, 1996).

In keeping with gender-role socialization, lesbian women might feel more awkward initiating sexual activity, whereas gay men might feel more awkward refusing or constraining sexual expression (Huston & Schwartz, 1996).

In comparing the sexual attitudes and behaviors of gay men *versus* lesbian women, it appears that lesbian women more often cite the need to express emotional closeness, while gay men emphasize physical motives for sexual activity (Leigh, 1989). Compared to gay men, lesbian women value monogamy more, have fewer sexual partners, have sex less frequently, but kiss more (Schreurs, 1993). Lesbian women and gay men express equal levels of sexual satisfaction in their relationships. Overall, gender-role socialization is a powerful force in same-sex relationships.

## 12.4 VARIATIONS IN GENDER DEVELOPMENT

Nineteenth-century scholars tended to group together all those who violated sex-related gender norms. That is, they did not distinguish among (a) men who used female-related objects (such as clothing) for sexual stimulation, (b) individuals who dressed in the clothing of the other sex, (c) those who mimicked the behavior and roles of the other gender, and (d) those who expressed discomfort or even disgust about their anatomical sex (Bullough & Bullough, 1993). Today, the *general* term applied to the various types and degrees of cross-gendered behavior is **transgenderism.**

### 12.4.1 Is There a Continuum of Transgenderism?

After World War II it became clear that cross-gendered behavior could include an array of behaviors, ranging from a mere *desire* to dress in the clothing associated with the other sex, actually engaging in cross-dressing, attempting to *live out the social roles* of the other sex, or in its most intense form, hormonally altering bodily features, and surgically modifying one's genitalia to resemble those of the other sex (fig. 12.3). The surgical extreme of the transgendered continuum is called **transsexualism,** and the medical interventions are designed to allow the person to more easily live out the gender role of the other sex.

Individuals cross-dress for a number of reasons.

### Occasional Cross-Dressing and Transvestism

Individuals *cross-dress* for various reasons. Historical accounts are filled with many more female **cross-dressers** or **transvestites** (Bullough & Bullough, 1993b). However, since women today have virtually complete freedom to wear "male" clothing, male cross-dressing appears more common. Some men claim it relaxes them in some way, perhaps by releasing them from the behavioral constraints associated with the masculine role. Others do it as entertainment and as a way to make a living, as is the case with female impersonators. For still others (almost exclusively heterosexual men), seeing, touching, and dressing in such clothing brings about sexual excitement. For this last group, contact with the clothing is usually accompanied by masturbation to orgasm, and the clothing is preferred over contact with an actual live partner. Such **fetishistic transvestism** will be discussed in chapter 17 as one of the **paraphilias.**

### Transsexualism

The most prominent characteristic of this group of highly transgendered individuals is that they experience a profound and long-term discrepancy between their *core gender identity* and their *anatomical sex.*

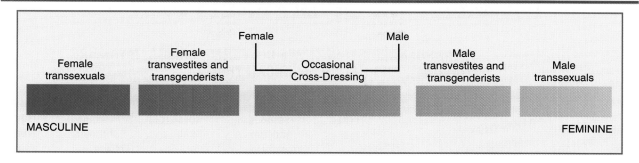

**FIGURE 12.3**   Gender identity disorders and the masculine-feminine continuum. Cross-genderism is not necessarily related to sexual orientation but rather to an emotional or psychological attitude that both men and women may have about their own sexual natures.

Transsexuals typically express feelings that they are "trapped in the wrong body" and a deep sense that some terrible error in physical development has occurred. They might experience revulsion at seeing or touching their genitalia. Many feel alienated from their secondary sex characteristics such as breasts or chest hair. They have frequent thoughts and fantasies about engaging in behaviors associated with the other gender (Morris, 1974). If they are having sex with same-sex partners, they usually insist that their partners not see or touch their genitals. If their partner is of the other sex, they often fantasize about being the same sex as the partner, or mentally reverse their sexes (American Psychiatric Association, 1994). Some live conventional gender-typed lives, while others expend a great deal of energy trying to "pass" as a member of the other gender.

These various forms of transgendered behavior might seem to blur into each other. It continues to be difficult for sexologists to make clear delineations among the various types and degrees of transgendered behavior.

## 12.4.2   Diagnosing a Gender Identity Disorder

Highly transgendered behavior appears in many societies, but it always takes on a *form and meaning that are socially constructed.* You can see how transgendered behavior is interpreted in three very different societies in "Dimensions of Diversity: Transgenderism in Three Cultures." In our society, confusion or deep-seated dissatisfaction with one's assigned gender is considered a *psychological disturbance.* One major category of disorder listed in the fourth edition of the *Diagnostic and Statistical Manual* (APA, 1994), or *DSM-IV,* is called **sexual and gender**

**identity disorders;** this category includes the extreme transgendered behavior under discussion here.

According to the *DSM-IV,* two important factors must be present to conclude that someone suffers from a gender identity disorder. First, there must be a

| | |
|---|---|
| **transgenderism** (cross-gender behavior) | a continuum along which individuals engage in behaviors associated with the other gender |
| **transsexualism** | extreme transgenderism in which an individual seeks to hormonally and surgically alter the appearance of the genitalia and secondary sex characteristics |
| **cross-dressing** (transvestism) (tranz-VEST-izm) | wearing the clothing and adornment associated with the other gender |
| **fetishistic transvestism** (fe-tish-ISS-tik) | cross-dressing associated with erotic arousal and orgasm |
| **paraphilia** (pa-ra-FEL-ya) | strong and repeated erotic arousal via an object or activity that is atypical or unusual |
| **DSM-IV** (dē-es-em-4) | the fourth edition of the Diagnostic and Statistic Manual, a listing of the categories of mental and emotional disturbances and their characteristics |
| **sexual and gender identity disorders** | a DSM-IV category that includes sexual dysfunctions, paraphilias, and gender identity disorders (distress due to cross-gender identification) |

# DIMENSIONS OF DIVERSITY

## TRANSGENDERISM IN THREE CULTURES: SAMOA, MYANMAR (BURMA), AND NATIVE AMERICAN TRIBES

### SAMOA

The tradition of *fa'afafine* began long before Western missionaries arrived in Samoa. A family with no girl children would declare the next child born to be a girl, regardless of sex. Originally, the term *fa'afafine* was applied to these boys who performed girls' household tasks (Mageo, 1992). Today, Samoan transgenderism is somewhat demeaned by men but often supported by an understanding mother (Poasa, 1992).

In general, Samoans do not distinguish sharply between men and women. Both take equal pride in combative behavior, and traditional (premissionary) names were not gender-typed. Outside of school, girls and boys wear the same clothing.

Adult *fa'afafine* apparently engage in casual and promiscuous relationships with men, typically met at bars. HIV infection is associated with men who go "off island," and such men are considered highly questionable or dangerous partners. *Fa'afafine* do not engage in sexual behavior with each other, as this would be socially undesirable "gay" behavior. They see themselves as female and believe their sexual partners regard them as such.

The *fa'afafine* also engage in elaborate beauty contests involving female impersonation. At public gatherings such as showers and weddings, the *fa'afafine* provide entertainment via ribald and overtly sexual jokes. Traditionally, this role was given to young girls, but nowadays girls' ribaldry is disapproved.

*Fa'afafines* often live, work, and dress as women throughout most of their lives. They hold all types of jobs, but congregate in traditionally feminine occupations such as teach-

ers, secretaries, or directors of community programs. At some point, they marry a woman and typically have children. They may be active and honored members of traditional churches and participate in all the women's activities. It is difficult to classify the *fa'afafine* in Western terms.

### MYANMAR (BURMA)

In Myanmar, male transgendered behavior is generally viewed in a positive light because of religious beliefs and cultural heritage (Coleman, Colgan, & Gooren, 1992). Transgendered men are called *acaults,* and their cross-gendered behavior is seen as evidence of possession by the female spirit *Manguedon.* These men are drawn to *Manguedon* and eventually go through a marriage ceremony with her to achieve the status of *acault.* Possession by *Manguedon* typically begins at a young age, and boys are seen as having no choice in this. The presence of *acaults* at public events is associated with good fortune and success, so *acaults* can make a living through the money they receive from businesspeople and public officials.

*Acaults* live as females and express the wish to have the body of a woman. Most restrict their sexual behavior to other males. In Burma, sex between males is illegal and considered morally repugnant, but the *acault* is considered a female. The *acaults* are typically orally and anally receptive, and never have sex with each other. They may live with a man, and this is seen as a heterosexual coupling. In such an arrangement, the *acault* usually takes care of "her husband" financially and sexually. The men who live with *acaults* are somewhat disapproved of be-

cause they are seen as lazy. Note that these men are disparaged because of their laziness, *not* their sexual behavior. The *acaults* are not considered immoral for their difference, and they participate fully in community and religious life. There is no attempt to shield children from knowledge of, or interaction with, *acaults.*

### NATIVE AMERICAN

Native American tribes vary tremendously in their concepts of gender and sexuality, so generalizations across tribes are unwise. However, there were some widespread commonalities. Many Native American tribes included a person called the *berdache* (Day, 1995). The *berdache* was usually biologically male, but sometimes female or of ambiguous sex. This person took on at least some of the occupations, clothing, and behaviors associated with the "other" gender. The *berdache* had a recognized and accepted social status. They served as mediators between men and women, and between the physical and spiritual worlds. Their sexual orientation was variable.

The *berdache* performed the tasks and occupations of the assumed gender (there were many stories of very proficient female *berdache* hunters). In general, *berdaches* were wealthy and productive, because they could combine women's and men's economic activities. They often performed special services at births and deaths, and their role as mediators between disputing men and women was especially significant. Male *berdaches* were typically excluded from warfare, whereas female *berdaches* took on the warrior role. A nineteenth-century European writer describes *berdaches* as "respected as saints"

---

*Transgenderism in Three Cultures: Samoa, Myanmar (Burma), and Native American Tribes—continued*

in their communities. People often became *berdaches* after an instructional dream (especially among the Winnebago and the Iowa tribes). Among others, *berdache* status was assumed after an unusual childhood interest in the work and people of the other sex. The ceremonial role of the *berdache* overlapped with that of the shaman. They had responsibility for healing and the general welfare of the community. Shamans were not necessarily *berdaches*, but *berdaches* were shamans.

*Berdaches* cannot be considered homosexual because their sexuality was not predictable from their role as *berdache*. They cannot be considered transvestites because their choice of clothing varied. Nor should they be labeled with our term *transsexual* because they had no conflict regarding their sex. Most Native American languages used a distinct referent (that is, they did not use *he* or *she*) for the *berdache* (Schnarch, 1992). Also their spiritual essence was considered to be quite distinct from that of women or men. Some Native American mythology considers the first human being to have been a *berdache*. *Berdaches* are best understood to constitute a third gender (female *berdaches*) and a fourth gender (male *berdaches*) in Native American culture.

---

"strong and persistent cross-gender identification." This must include the desire to be, or the insistence that one is, the other sex. Second, there must be "persistent discomfort" about one's assigned sex or a feeling that one's gender role is wrong (APA, 1994, pp. 532–33): this is called **gender dysphoria.** Also, there must be no physical intersex problem, such as pseudohermaphroditism or androgen insensitivity syndrome (see chapter 11).

The terms *transsexual* and *transsexualism* do not appear in the *DSM-IV* because they actually refer to the surgical "treatment" available for individuals who are deeply distressed about their anatomical sex. However, many sexologists continue to use the terms *transsexual* and *transsexualism* to refer to gender identity disorder, and so we will also.

How common is this disorder? It's difficult to estimate accurately, but data from certain European countries suggest that 1 in 30,000 males and 1 in 100,000 females might manifest this behavior (APA, 1994).

The causes of gender identity disorder are unknown. Researchers have been investigating this issue for well over forty years. The pendulum seems to swing back and forth between hypothesizing psychological causes and hypothesizing physiological causes. Yet, at present, no clear-cut origins have been identified.

## 12.4.3 Interventions in Gender Identity Disorder

While different gender disorder clinics vary in the details of their assessment and intervention, there are four basic steps in **sex reassignment surgery (SRS).**

1. *Counseling.* The client meets with a specially trained therapist for six months. The client must communicate that a strong desire to change assigned gender and be rid of present genitalia has existed for at least two years. The therapist must also verify that no other mental disturbances are present.

2. *Hormone treatments.* Appropriate hormone treatments result in the appearance of appropriate secondary sex characteristics, such as breasts for male-to-female transsexuals, or facial and body hair for female-to-male transsexuals. Body weight and contours may shift dramatically.

3. *Gender-role transition.* For a year or two, the client must live successfully as a person of the preferred gender. The client must learn the subtleties of body language, voice inflection, and so forth. This phase is considered critical for many individuals because they discover that a change of gender role often does not solve many of life's problems. During this phase, the social and legal realities of gender change are confronted. Individuals might be fired from their jobs when they inform their employers of their intentions regarding sex reassignment. Names must be changed legally, new birth certificates and new driver's licenses must be obtained. Family relationships and friendships must be renegotiated. Male-to-female transsexuals might be surprised to encounter salary discrimination and sexual harassment as they apply for equivalent jobs as women.

---

| | |
|---|---|
| **gender dysphoria** (dis-FOR-ē-uh) | dissatisfaction with and profound distress about one's gender identity and gender role |
| **sex reassignment surgery (SRS)** | hormonal and surgical alteration of genitalia to resemble those of the other sex |

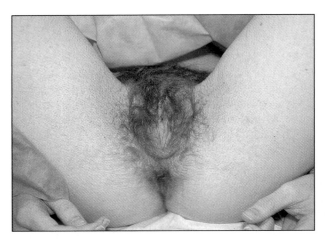

The genitals of a male-to-female transsexual. The vulva and vagina are constructed from the sensitive penile tissue.

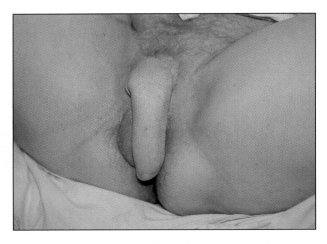

A surgically constructed penis. In female-to-male transsexual surgery the penis is constructed from abdominal tissue or from labial and perineal tissue. This penis is not capable of erection in response to sexual arousal but several artificial devices are available that produce an erection for intercourse.

4. *Sex reassignment* surgery. Surgery is considered the final step, and it costs many thousands of dollars. For anatomical males, the penis and testes are removed and a clitoris, vaginal lips, and an artificial vagina are constructed from the former penile tissue and excess skin. For anatomical females, the process is more complex. The clitoris is augmented into a penis using tissue from elsewhere in the body (usually the forearm). A scrotum is constructed and artificial testes are inserted.

After surgery, transsexuals can experience sexual arousal and perhaps even orgasm. Female-to-male transsexuals can have erections only with penile implants or other artificial devices. Postoperative transsexuals cannot menstruate, impregnate, ejaculate, conceive a child, or give birth to children.

There are comparatively few long-term studies of sex reassignment. The general findings are that only 10 to 15 percent of cases are considered to have unsatisfactory outcomes (Bullough & Bullough, 1993; Green & Fleming, 1990). A study of 141 Dutch transsexuals (Kuiper & Cohen-Kettenis, 1988) indicated that a majority were quite happy with the results and no longer experienced the dysphoria that moved them to such radical intervention. The skill of the surgeon seems important in creating a positive body image. Female-to-male transsexuals seem generally more satisfied than male-to-female transsexuals (Bodlund & Kullgren, 1996).

One of the most intriguing and perhaps confusing aspects of gender identity disorder has to do with the sexual orientation of these individuals. Many preoperative transsexuals have little interest in sexual relationships and seem more focused on anatomical and gender-role issues (Arndt, 1991). Coleman,

Bockting, and Gooren (1993) concluded that postoperative transsexuals might have homosexual, heterosexual, or bisexual orientations. All of this should serve to remind us again that gender identity and sexual orientation are remarkably distinct.

## 12.4.4 Another Perspective on Transgendered Behavior

Transgendered behavior has been described here as a problem or "disturbance" that requires careful diagnosis and "treatment." Not all sexologists share that perspective. Early studies of transgendered individuals were based on deeply troubled individuals who appeared before physicians and psychologists while more recent research has focused on a wider population of transgendered individuals. Some sexologists and writers from the "transgendered community" feel transgendered behavior is merely a normal variation on the more typical gender-conforming behavior of the majority of people within a culture. They believe transgendered behavior should not be seen as disturbed or pathological (Burke, 1996). They also hold that mental health professionals should not function as "gatekeepers" regarding who secures sex-reassignment surgery. Rather, all those who wish to purchase such services should be able to obtain them. After all, no psychological or psychiatric evaluation is required for any other type of elective "cosmetic" surgery. Several organizations, such as the Society for the Second Self and the Australian Seahorse Society help individuals develop a positive identity as transvestites. Transsexuals gain similar support from Aegis, the Gender Identity Project, and the Renaissance Transgender Association.

## SUMMARY

1. Biological sex is distinct from the socially constructed concept of gender. Gender identity is our inner sense of being male or female. General cultural norms regarding appropriate masculine and feminine behavior constitute that culture's gender-role ideology. Gender role is acquired through the process of gender-role socialization.

2. Parents, peers, media, the educational system, and religion are some of the agents of gender-role socialization.

3. Sociobiology, cognitive social learning theory, and gender schema theory attempt to explain gender-role development.

4. Recent research documents the virtual disappearance of gender differences in spatial, verbal, and mathematical abilities. Even well-established differences in cognitive abilities and aggression are subject to environmental influences.

5. Some gender stereotypes are relatively universal, and they can affect many aspects of human interaction.

6. Gender-role ideology affects sexual attitudes and behaviors. There are well-defined sexual scripts associated with each gender, and these have recently undergone modification in our society.

7. There are both differences and similarities in contemporary gender and sexual scripts among other-sex and same-sex couples.

8. *Transgenderism* refers to the array of variations in gender identity. The continuum extends from occasional cross-dressing to interventions designed to achieve congruence among a person's anatomy, gender-role behavior, and gender identity. Some see transgenderism not as a disturbance, but rather as a human variation that occurs in most societies.

## CRITICAL THINKING CHALLENGES

1. Disregarding the division of adjectives into "male-associated" and "female-associated" categories, list the traits in table 12.2 that you think are reflected in your personality. Androgyny is the quality of exhibiting traits associated with both genders, and it has been proposed that androgynous individuals are better able to cope with a wide variety of situations, since they have a larger repertoire of behaviors and responses. How androgynous are you? Did you select traits from both categories, or only one?

2. Do you think our society is limited by having only two genders? List the advantages and disadvantages of having a "third" or indeterminate gender. How would you feel if you were talking with someone you had just met, but you didn't know (and couldn't easily determine) their gender?

3. Read the lists of sexual scripts starting on p. 300. To what degree do you subscribe to or practice the scripts associated with your gender? In what ways do your sexual scripts affect your approach to sexuality? What might you do to actively discard or change one of your sexual scripts?

# CHILDHOOD AND ADOLESCENT SEXUALITY

# 13

**AFTER STUDYING THIS CHAPTER, YOU SHOULD BE ABLE TO**

[1]   Explain the statement "Children are sexual."

[2]   Explain how unhappy childhood sexual experiences can affect adult sexual relationships.

[3]   Describe how experts on sexuality suggest parents should deal with their child's masturbation.

[4]   Distinguish between developmentally appropriate and inappropriate child-to-child sexual activity.

[5]   Explain why erotic material might be a poor basis for the formation of a child's sexual attitudes.

[6]   Explain the importance of parents' showing affection for their children.

[7]   List six key developmental tasks for adolescents.

[8]   Describe why no single theory is likely to explain the development of everyone's sexual orientation.

[9]   List some individual and social factors associated with an early onset of sexual intercourse.

[10]   Describe why adolescence may be especially difficult for lesbian and gay youths.

[11]   List some factors that have contributed to the increased average age for a first marriage.

[12]   List some of the causes and effects of adolescent pregnancy.

[13]   Describe some characteristics of an effective program to reduce the risk of adolescent pregnancy.

From birth to death, sexuality is a basic part of every one of us. This is the first of two chapters that explore our sexuality progressively, as it develops through the course of our lives.

In this chapter, we examine the emerging sexuality of children and adolescents. This information is of value to parents or other concerned adults about the sexuality of young people and on how to best nurture it. In addition, an understanding of one's own childhood and adolescent sexual experiences may reveal how they may be influencing adult sexuality. We also discuss sexuality education—its necessity, content, and sources.

## 13.1    CHILDREN ARE SEXUAL

From the moment of birth, children begin to learn about feelings of love, the pleasure of touch, and the complexity of human relationships. Their experiences and observations form the foundation for their future sexual attitudes, feelings, and decisions (SIECUS, 1995b).

Babies enter the world ready to experience sensations and react to them. They quickly develop a sense of self-awareness and awareness of those around them by the way they are held, spoken to, and cared for. The types of touch they receive (or fail to receive), the toys that they are given, and the human interactions they experience and observe around them form a foundation for future sexual learning and development.

Children develop a powerful interest in and values about sexuality during the first few years of life. Very quickly children learn that there are two sexes, and almost as quickly they develop strong expectations for the behavior of each sex. Before the age of five, they might have questions about pregnancy and childbirth and might engage in genital and sexual play, either alone or with other children. They might mimic the sexual language they hear spoken by older children or by adults. When 236 children aged 4 to 18 years completed a juvenile version of Elaine Hatfield's Adult Passionate Love Scale, even the youngest children reported having experienced passionate love. In fact, young children and adolescents received similar scores. Girls scored significantly higher than boys on the Juvenile Love Scale, with boys aged 10 to 13 years receiving the lowest scores (Hatfield et al., 1988).

Many young children exhibit an endless sexual curiosity, asking countless questions about male and female bodies and reproductive processes. How these questions are responded to sends powerful messages to children about sexuality in general and their own sexuality in particular. Parents and other adult guardians are the most important sexuality educators for children. Honest, thoughtful, and respectful communication about sexuality can provide a basis for a lifetime of healthful sexuality.

Some people doubt the sexual nature of infants and children, preferring to believe that the very young are asexual. Even the thought that children might be sexual elicits feelings of anxiety in many people who have not come to terms with their own sexuality and who find any display of sexuality uncomfortable (Lindblad et al., 1995).

Sigmund Freud believed that, following a period of sexual interest during early childhood, children enter a period of sexual latency (dormancy) lasting from about age five until puberty. A more current interpretation is that children quickly learn that their displays of sexual interest are considered taboo by parents and others, so they hide their sexuality from those who might punish them.

### 13.1.1    Parents and Their Children's Sexuality

Parents who are comfortable with their own sexual selves are more likely to perceive their children's sexuality in its widest and most positive dimension. Less secure parents may have a very restricted and negative view of the implications of sexual development in their children.

Parents' problems in handling their children's sexual development can arise from a number of sources. Parents might want to avoid being confronted with a reawakening of those uncomfortable feelings that occurred during their own entry into puberty. They may hold beliefs that include religious or societal prohibitions regarding sexual expression. Parents might fear loss of control over their children or wish to keep them in a dependent state for the satisfaction of the parents' own emotional needs.

Some adult sexual inhibitions, anxieties, and dysfunctions can be traced to negative parental reactions to their own childhood sexual behavior. For example, someone who was on numerous occasions punished for childhood sex play might years later be unable to respond freely in adult sexual activities (SIECUS, 1995b). Some people, in fact, report that just when they start to respond sexually, the image or voice of a parent appears before them, and they just "turn off."

The emotional damage of unhappy childhood sexual experiences can extend beyond the sexual arena to impair your entire self-concept. For example, children are often spanked, shamed, or scolded for sexual behavior. They are likely to interpret this punishment as meaning that they should not even have sexual feelings. But sexual feelings exist in people of all ages. They are part of us. If you perceive

Parents are their children's most important sexuality educators. Their attitudes and behaviors reveal even more about sexuality than their words do.

that a part of you is bad, evil, or shameful, this can lower your entire opinion of yourself—it damages your self-esteem. As adults, we might understand intellectually that our sexual feelings are perfectly normal and healthy. Yet, at an emotional level, we might still carry residual guilt, shame, or anxiety about our sexuality (McCabe, 1989).

This situation is perpetuated from generation to generation because many parents deal with their children's sexuality in much the same way as their parents dealt with *their* sexuality. Even when we try to deal with childhood sexuality in positive ways, any sexual anxieties, doubts, and inhibitions we might feel are revealed to our children in countless verbal and nonverbal ways. For example, if the voice of a parent conveys anxiety or disgust when a child is discovered masturbating, regardless of the words spoken by the parent, the message is clear. The child internalizes the concept of sex as shameful. In later life, even though it is intellectually understood that it is "OK" to feel sexual and act sexually, the feelings of shame persist at an emotional level. Among the many results are difficulties in adult sexual adjustment and interaction and reluctance to focus attention on their own sexual body parts, as in breast self-examination or in arranging for routine medical examinations

such as Pap smears or rectal prostate examinations (McCabe, 1989).

Even what we leave unsaid can effectively communicate our attitudes. The mere fact that sex is never discussed in some families conveys the idea that it must be a disgusting subject. Cross-cultural studies have shown that children are not born with sexual guilts or anxieties; they acquire them (Tannahill, 1992).

## 13.1.2    The "Right From the Start" Guidelines

Recognizing the lifelong importance of sexual values and attitudes that form during early childhood, the Sexuality Information and Education Council of the United States (SIECUS, 1995b) convened a task force of experts on early childhood development and sexuality to compile a set of guidelines for parents and other adult caregivers of children from birth to age five. Following these "Right From the Start" guidelines can help children form the values and attitudes needed for healthy adolescent and adult sexuality. These are some of the guidelines:

- Sexuality is a natural and healthy part of living that begins at birth and continues throughout life.
- All children should be loved and cared for and should feel safe and protected.
- All children should be respected and valued as unique individuals.
- Children experience their sexuality as a natural part of their development.
- Children begin learning about sexuality as soon as they are born and continue to learn throughout their lives.
- Parents are their children's most important sexuality educators. School and preschool teachers, day care workers, and health professionals can also provide a positive influence in children's development toward sexual health.
- Children learn from how people touch them, talk with them, and expect them to behave as males or females. These messages children receive affect their future attitudes, values, and behaviors.
- Children are naturally curious about how their bodies look and work, and how male and female bodies differ, and about where babies come from.
- Children need to be helped to develop an awareness and appreciation of the human body and how it works.

▌ Children's understanding of sexuality is influenced by their parents, other family members, friends and neighbors, community, and school, as well as the media and other factors.

▌ Relationships should never be coercive or exploitative.

▌ Information about sex-related health risks and abuses should be presented to children within the context of positive information aimed at healthy personal and sexual development, such as human development and relationships, personal skills, and health.

▌ In a pluralistic society like the United States, educators should respect the diversity of values and beliefs about sexuality that may exist in a community and among families.

## 13.2    CHILDHOOD EXPRESSIONS OF SEXUALITY

For the purposes of this discussion, childhood will be considered to extend from about age two to age twelve (or to the approximate onset of puberty). During this period, profound physical and mental changes occur in the child. The older the child, the more specific is the form of sexual expression. Although infants may experience a diffused sort of pleasure from genital stimulation, older children might fantasize about or engage in more specific sexual interaction with other people.

### 13.2.1    Childhood Masturbation

At an early age, often during infancy, children discover that the sex organs can be a source of pleasure. Starting early in infancy, many develop methods of masturbating. Infants probably do not perceive the pleasures of masturbation in a sexual sense as do older children and adults. Yet it must be a pleasant experience, as many infants do stimulate their genitals. Masturbation becomes both more prevalent among children and more frequent in individual children as they age (Lindblad et al., 1995). Unlike infants, older children are also likely to accompany their masturbation with elaborate fantasies that are specifically sexual in content.

Childhood masturbation is a normal and harmless behavior that need be no cause for concern. A child may need to be cautioned against inserting objects into body orifices (openings) or told that masturbation is done in private, but a general prohibition is neither necessary nor desirable (Leung & Robson, 1993; SIECUS, 1995b).

It is important to understand the unspoken messages that are revealed by adult responses toward childhood masturbation. If adults are negative in the way they deal with genital touching, the message is that the child's genitals or sexual feelings are bad or evil. In order for children to develop healthy adolescent and adult sexuality, they need supportive and positive acceptance of their emerging sexuality.

### 13.2.2    Childhood Sex Play

Parents are sometimes shocked to find their young children deeply engrossed in sexual forms of play behavior. Perhaps two or more children of the same sex or both sexes are engaged in examining each other's genitals (playing "doctor" or "show") or in watching each other urinate.

A frequent parental reaction to such play is visible horror, anger, and/or disgust. The children might be scolded, perhaps physically punished, and left feeling confused, guilty, and less positive about themselves. What had seemed like pleasurable body parts and activities are now sources of shame. Such childhood experiences are believed to contribute to the problems of sexual adjustment and function that plague so many adults in our society (Bauserman & Davis, 1996; SIECUS, 1995b).

Parents who observe their children in genital exploration are usually advised to keep their responses nonpunitive. They might ask the child what he or she has learned in the play. Childhood misconceptions might be revealed and clarified at this time. Similarities and differences between the sexes can be productively discussed in this context, as can be the proper time and place for particular behaviors. Nonpunitive limits on public sexual activity can be set. A positive attitude toward the body can be conveyed in these discussions. Parents can encourage a child's questions rather than activities.

There are some startling and frightening occurrences of forceful sexual exploitation by siblings or other children in sharp contrast to normal sexual curiosity. Distinctions between times when sex play is normal development and when it is exploitative can involve the age of each child and whether the sex play is mutually desired or is forced by one child upon the other. Here are some childhood sexual behaviors that are clearly inappropriate and warrant intervention (Wardle, 1995):

▌ Intrusive and/or painful child-to-child sexual activity.

▌ Self-inflicted painful sexual activity.

▌ Oral-genital child-to-child sexual activity.

▌ Engaging in simulated or attempted or completed intercourse while undressed.

▌ Forced penetration with an object or a finger of any orifice of a child.

Children engaging in these behaviors have often been victims of sexual abuse and are simply doing to others what has been done to them. They might not know that it is wrong to invade another child's privacy or to coerce or force another child, because they have experienced such behavior, possibly from someone who plays an important role in their life.

### 13.2.3 Same-Sex Attractions

Many gay and lesbian people remember feeling sexually "different" during their elementary school years or even earlier (Bem, 1996). Parents of lesbian and gay people often express regret that they never considered the possibility that their children might have been feeling same-sex attraction when they were young. This is especially true when parents learn of the feelings of isolation and "differentness" their children may have experienced. Feeling "different" becomes a secret that many children with same-sex attractions keep to themselves, fearing retribution or loss of love from family or friends should their secret become known. For children growing up in blatantly homophobic families or communities this fear may be realistic.

It used to be thought that sexual identities did not emerge until puberty, when hormone changes resulted in greater sex drives. However, Savin-Williams and Diamond (2000) found that gay male teens reported their first same-sex attraction at an average age of 7.7 years, and lesbian teens at 9 years of age. Most of them did not act on their attractions until 3 to 5 years later when they were adolescents. Children need to learn early on that there are different kinds of acceptable attractions between human beings. Not everyone is heterosexual. Although it is still unclear how sexual orientation is determined, evidence is mounting in favor of biological explanations. Adults need to know that there is no reliable way to predict the adult sexual orientation of a child and that every child deserves to feel comfortable with her or his sexuality.

### 13.2.4 Children and Erotic Material

Another potentially difficult family situation is the discovery by parents of erotic (sexually stimulating) material in their child's possession. Children are extremely curious about sexual subjects, and if sex is not a subject of open discussion at home, erotic materials might be sought as an alternate source of information. Erotic books, magazines, and videos are easily attainable by young people.

Some erotic material is a poor basis for the formation of sexual attitudes and is a source of factual misinformation. The material might present a hostile, exploitative, distorted, dehumanized, and degrading approach to sexuality. Physical and emotional abuse

of females is a common theme. People of both genders are portrayed merely as sexual objects. Physical aspects of sexual interaction are exaggerated, while interpersonal relationships are ignored. Other common themes include exaggeration of the significance of physical characteristics, such as breast or penis size. Sadomasochism is quite prevalent. Less commonly, children are portrayed in sexual acts with adults.

Although material that portrays a distorted sexuality can damage **psychosexual** development, parents who overreact to it with fear, anger, visible anxiety, and harsh discipline are not being helpful. This turns a potentially good opportunity for constructive sex education into a damaging, negative childhood experience.

If parents calmly mention the discovery of erotic material, the situation can provide an excellent opportunity for a productive discussion of sexuality. Depending on the type of material found, and the age and understanding of the child, the discussion might include sexual function, sexual orientation, and the nature and quality of relationships.

This might also be an appropriate time to provide a child with sex education books specifically intended for her or his age-group. Most large bookstores carry such books. Examples of the many available for younger children include *How Was I Born?* by Lennart Nilsson (1966) and *Where Did I Come From?* by Peter Mayle (1990). *The What's Happening to My Body Book for Girls* (1988) and *The What's Happening to My Body Book for Boys* (1988), both by Lynda Madaras, and *A Child Is Born* by Lennart Nilsson (1990) are recommended for older children and adolescents.

## 13.3 FAMILY AFFECTION AND CHILDHOOD SEXUALITY

The family is the first and most important social system in a child's life. Ideally, family relationships allow children to learn to form secure attachments and to view themselves as lovable and valuable people who can expect to receive affection and support from the important people in their lives, first as children and later on as adults.

Children can thrive in many different kinds of families. Effective families can include both the biological mother and the biological father, only one parent, one or more grandparents or other extended family, stepparents and stepsiblings, same-gender

---

**psychosexual**    pertaining to the emotional or mental aspects of sexuality

parents, or foster parents. Whatever the family structure, all children have the need and the right to feel proud of their family. The "Right From the Start" Project (SIECUS, 1995b) suggests that adults project the following key family messages to children:

- Children need adults who love and take care of them.
- There are different kinds of families.
- Parents, siblings, grandparents, aunts, uncles, and cousins are all members of a family.
- In some families, aunts, uncles, grandparents, older siblings, or family friends carry out parenting jobs.
- Sometimes close friends are considered part of the family.
- Family members can have fun together.
- Family members need to help one another.
- Some children are part of more than one family.
- Family members who live in different places continue to be a family.
- Each family member can help take care of the family. As children get older, they can do more family jobs.
- Families have rules to help their members live together safely and happily.

Child development authorities believe that the most significant role models in children's lives are their parents or the adults who serve in that capacity. Very early in life, children develop concepts regarding sexuality, love, affection, and caring that are based largely on what they have observed in the adults in their family. Children come to perceive sexuality as either a positive or a negative force, and they develop ideas about appropriate expressions of love and affection. At the same time, the child's own sexuality influences how he or she perceives the behavior of adults. Adults might be unaware of their influence on children or, conversely, knowing that they are role models, might feel uncertain about appropriate expressions of their love, affection, and sexuality. In the following paragraphs, we briefly examine the effects on childhood sexuality of adult displays of affection for their children and for each other.

## 13.3.1 Parent-Child Affection

Feeling loved as a child is important preparation for adult love relationships. Feeling loved makes children believe that they are worthy of being loved and helps them to be able to love. Children who feel loved are more secure, self-confident, and responsive to adult guidance, because they know that the guidance is based on caring and concern.

Ideally, the family provides a baby's first loving experiences through holding, hugging, kissing, bathing, feeding, dressing, and other nurturing. These early intimate experiences are thought to provide the emotional foundation for feeling love and attachment later in life.

Most parents feel a great amount of affection for their children, although this parental love is not always demonstrated. A variety of hypotheses may explain why so many parents fail to be more affectionate with their children. One obvious answer lies in the great demands placed upon the time of many parents. With career pressures, social obligations, keeping a home functioning, and all other adult responsibilities, children sometimes seem to get lost in the shuffle.

However, authorities on child development emphasize that it is important for parents to show affection for their children. Having affectionate parents contributes to a sense of self-esteem that serves us well in all phases of our lives. It helps us to weather the hard knocks of childhood and it contributes to our academic and social success in school and to later career success as an adult. Having had affectionate parents helps us in our relationships with others throughout our lives, because people who are shown plenty of affection as children are better able to display affection to others as adults. In addition, people relate to their children much as their own parents related to them (Woititz, 1992). Problems such as child neglect or other abuse tend to perpetuate themselves from generation to generation.

## 13.3.2 Parents' Partnerships

Parents sometimes wonder how open they should be with their children concerning their own sexual relationships. Many young people find it difficult to think of their parents as being sexual. If the parents are together, their children might never see them kissing each other, and they might seldom hear affectionate verbal exchanges between them. Many parents are so uncomfortable with their sexuality or carry such negative feelings about sexuality in general that they believe that children must be "protected" from any display of sexual feelings. But what better role models for adult partner interaction could children have than a pair of loving, caring parents?

Although children sometimes verbally reject everything their parents stand for, in reality, as we have stated before, parents are the most significant role models in their children's lives. Children tend to pattern their attitudes and behaviors on what they have observed in their parents. If children observe little open display of affection between their

Children learn how to display (or conceal) their affection by the example presented by their parents—whether two biological parents or a biological parent and his or her partner.

parents, they may be inhibited in their own ability to demonstrate affection when they reach adulthood (Woititz, 1992).

Sometimes children, perhaps in response to discussions with their peers, specifically ask to watch their parents have sex. If this situation should arise, it is best for parents to explain that they prefer privacy while having sex and, although they would be happy to discuss sex with their child, they will not demonstrate the process (Van Heeswyk, 1994).

Single parents are often quite uncertain about how open to be about their partnerships around their children. As role models, we probably don't want to confront our children with a series of our casual or short-term relationships. Exposing our children to a stable, loving relationship, especially when the child can feel included in the relationship, provides positive role modeling for family life.

When surveyed on their expectations regarding their single parent's dating behaviors, a group of children emphasized six themes: connectedness, informational certainty, openness, interpersonal acceptance, emotional security, and boundaries (Ferguson & Dickson, 1995).

Problems can arise when children are fond of both of their biological parents and secretly or openly

wish that their parents were together. Mom's new boyfriend or dad's new girlfriend may be the target of resentment and hostility.

Some children grow up in households headed by lesbian or gay partners. One partner might be a biological parent or the family may have been formed by adoption or some other arrangement. Evidence indicates that lesbian or gay partners are just as effective parents as heterosexual partners (Patterson, 1995). (See "At Issue: Gay, Lesbian, and Bisexual Parents.")

## 13.4 ADOLESCENT DEVELOPMENT

Probably no other period in the life cycle involves such rapid and profound physical and emotional changes as adolescence. **Adolescence** can be roughly defined as the period from the onset of puberty until the attainment of adulthood, about ages twelve to twenty. In addition to the major physical and hormonal changes of **puberty** (see chapter 11), adolescence challenges a young person with adjusting to an entirely new body image and a transformed identity as she or he relates to other people. (See "Dimensions of Diversity: Rites of Passage in Adolescence.")

### 13.4.1 Coping with Puberty

The physical changes of puberty in males and females are associated with many new issues and feelings. For boys, the first ejaculation, referred to as **spermarche** or **semenarche,** may elicit feelings of surprise, curiosity, pleasure, confusion, of being more grown up. It does not typically evoke feelings of upset, embarrassment, shame, or fear. In the United States, no one is usually told that ejaculation has occurred (Downs & Fuller, 1991; Stein & Reiser, 1994). In Nigeria, in contrast, friends are usually told of the experience after it happens (Adegoke, 1993).

Details of physical development may seem extremely important to boys going through puberty. The common belief that masculinity can be equated with the size of the penis and testes contributes to this

| adolescence | the period from the onset of puberty until the attainment of adulthood, about ages 12 to 20 |
| puberty (pū´ber-tē) | the earlier portion of adolescence, during which a person becomes functionally capable of reproduction |
| spermarche (sperm-ar´kē) | a boy's first ejaculation |
| semenarche (sĕ´men-ar´´kē) | a boy's first ejaculation |

# AT ISSUE

## LESBIAN, GAY, AND BISEXUAL PARENTS

Recent years have seen an increasing number of lesbian, gay, and bisexual (LGB) people who desire to raise children. The desirability of LGB parenting has been debated in the courts and elsewhere. Let's look at each side of this issue.

On the negative side, assumptions are made about nonheterosexuals and the effect of LGB parenting on children. Rationales stated by courts in both the United States and Canada in denying custody or adoption rights to LGB parents have included the following claims (Fowler, 1995):

- Being raised in an LGB household would impair the psychosocial development of a child.
- The child would suffer from society's stigmatization, harassment, or intolerance.
- Individuals who are lesbian, gay, or bisexual are unable to be good parents.
- The child might be infected by HIV.
- The child might be sexually exploited or molested by LGB parents.

An abundance of literature suggests that these assumptions are invalid.

No one claims that growing up in a household with one or more LGB parents or co-parents is exactly the same experience as growing up in a household with one or more heterosexual parents. But neither has any research shown that the former experience is inferior to the latter (Flaks et al., 1995; Samuels, 1995; Tasker & Golombok, 1995; Fowler, 1995; Victor & Fish, 1995). None of the five listed assumptions has been validated.

In one study, fifteen lesbian couples and the three- to nine-year-old children born to them through donor insemination were compared with fifteen matched heterosexual-parent families. Results showed no significant differences between the two groups of children. No significant differences were found between the couple adjustment of the lesbian and heterosexual couples. The only difference found was that the lesbian couples exhibited more awareness of parenting skills than did the heterosexual couples (Flaks et al., 1995).

Many people have wondered about the effect of parents' nonheterosexual orientation on the sexual orientation of their biological or adoptive children. In light of the strong possibility that sexual orientation is biologically influenced, one might expect a high percentage of the natural sons of gay fathers to be gay. But they are mostly heterosexual in their orientation. In one study, only about 10 percent of adult biological sons raised by gay fathers were gay, only a little higher than the percentage of gay males in the general population (Bailey et al., 1995). Another study showed that neither the daughters nor the sons raised by lesbian mothers have a high incidence of same-gender sexual orientation (Tasker & Golombok, 1995). As adults, these sons and daughters also functioned well in terms of their psychological well-being, their family identity, and their friendships and intimate relationships.

Being an LGB parent is not always easy. The parent's partner might or might not take an active role in parenting or co-parenting, and social support networks might not be as widespread as they are for heterosexual parents. A sector of the lesbian community itself, for example, is unsupportive of lesbian motherhood (Lott-Whitehead & Tully, 1993).

concern. Many males worry that their penises are too small. A few are concerned that they may be too large. Young men need to know that the size of the penis does not reflect their masculinity and is not an important factor in either experiencing or providing sexual gratification. Similarly, muscle size may also seem disproportionately important since size of muscles is so closely related to masculinity in our culture.

Another source of concern for males during puberty is **gynecomastia**—swollen breasts. This condition is so common that it should be viewed as a normal developmental event. Usually disappearing without treatment, gynecomastia is caused by a small amount of glandular growth under stimulation of the high hormone levels of puberty. It does not represent any lack of masculinity and need be no cause for alarm.

Physical concerns of girls during puberty often center on breast development, weight, and menarche (Alsaker, 1992). Breast development either earlier or later than that of friends can be a major source of anxiety. Breast size is also assigned a great importance. Breasts perceived as being larger or smaller than those of peers can cause both anxiety and embarrassment.

Being teased about physical appearance during adolescence has a lasting effect on the body images and self-esteem of many women (Cash, 1995). Almost any aspect of a girl's appearance can be targeted for teasing. Peers are deemed the worst perpetrators

# DIMENSIONS OF DIVERSITY

## RITES OF PASSAGE IN ADOLESCENCE

Rites of passage, in some form, are part of the adolescent experience in every culture, even in the United States. They have existed throughout history and probably contribute to a stable adult personality. Most rites of passage include four elements (Delaney, 1995):

1. a separation from society
2. preparation or instruction from an elder
3. a transition from childhood to adulthood, usually involving a ceremony including spiritual cleansing, physical transformation, prayers and blessings, special attire, food, and traditional music
4. a welcoming back into society with acceptance of the adolescent's changed status

The rite of passage in the Okiek tribe in Kenya, at age fourteen to sixteen, is similar for both genders, though boys and girls are initiated separately. The initiates are first ceremoniously circumcised or excised (female circumcision). Then they live in seclusion from adults of the other sex for 4 to 24 weeks. Certain secret knowledge is imparted by same-sex adults. The most important knowledge concerns the cemaasiit, a mythical beast that haunts the initiates during their time in seclusion. At night its roar can be heard and the initiation is complete when each youth has seen and held the instrument used for producing the roar and produced the sound him- or herself (Kratz, 1990). Then they return back to society.

Here in North America, many Native American nations (tribes) have or once had tribal rites of passage. In the "vision quest," for example, a boy of age fourteen or fifteen is taken into the sweat lodge where his body and spirit are purified by the heat from a wood fire. With him in the sweat lodge is a shaman who advises him and assists him with his prayers. Afterward he is taken to an isolated spot and left there to fast for four days. While there, he prays, thinks about the words of the shaman, and waits for a vision to reveal the path of his life as a man (Heinrich, Corbine, & Thomas, 1990).

Where is the rite of passage for the typical young person in the United States? Cassandra Delaney (1995) suggests that high school education and graduation serve as the rite of passage for most Americans. High school involves isolation from society (during the school day) and instruction by teachers who act in the role of initiators, and ends with a graduation ceremony. Delaney does not see high school as an adequate rite of passage, however, because there is little opportunity for "bonding" with teachers and spirituality and morality are not emphasized in public high schools.

Delaney (1995) speculates that some of the problems experienced by U.S. young people result from their lack of a definitive rite of passage. Lacking any formalized rite of passage, young people attempt to initiate themselves into adulthood by various "first time" activities. These are attempts to imitate adult behavior through smoking, drinking, or sexual activity. Like a rite of passage, these activities are usually done in isolation from the general society, but without the participation of elders. The adolescents' lack of knowledge and judgment lead to harmful consequences of their actions, such as alcohol or tobacco addiction, STI transmission, or undesired pregnancy.

Especially impacted by the lack of a rite of passage are African American and Native American adolescents. Rites of passage played major roles in their ancestral cultures, but those cultures have been severely disrupted and the rites of passage have disappeared with no adequate replacement. As with other U.S. adolescents, their lack of a rite of passage is said to contribute to high rates of alcohol abuse and unwanted pregnancy (Delaney, 1995). No one suggests returning to African or Native American style rites of passage, but there does seem to be a need for a more definitive demarcation between childhood and adulthood and more emphasis on moral guidance of young people by the "elders" of the community.

---

of appearance teasing, but family members, especially brothers, may also be serious offenders (Cash, 1995).

Menarche is a major symbolic event in the lives of most young women. Girls' subjective sense of themselves as maturing women develops along with a process of sexualization whereby young women begin to perceive themselves as sexualized and their bodies as sexual objects. Menarche changes relationships with themselves, males, and families (Lee, 1994).

---

**gynecomastia** (gī-ne-kō-mas′tē-a)  swollen breasts in a male

Several types of menstrual anxieties also are common in adolescent girls. A girl's anxiety level may become quite high if all of her friends have begun menstruating and she has not (Alsaker, 1992). Conversely, menarche in a younger girl who has not been properly prepared for the event can be extremely frightening. Long before the possible onset of menstruation, a girl should know about the process and function of menstruation and the techniques of menstrual protection through the use of pads and/or tampons. She should also understand that irregular periods for a year or so are not abnormal. Unfortunately, many parents are ill-prepared to teach their children about sex or to reinforce the information they learn in school (Hockenberry-Eaton et al., 1996).

In both genders, such aspects of growth as height, weight, and skin problems, especially acne, create anxiety. Insecurities are amplified during this difficult period, and minor physical characteristics might be assigned significance far beyond their true importance. The impact of such anxieties is minimized by a well-developed sense of self-esteem. Parents can perform no more vital service for their child, especially during puberty, than to contribute to their child's developing a strongly positive self-image.

Many of the anxieties of both female and male adolescents (as well as adults) can be traced directly to the advertising industry. We are frequently the targets of advertising campaigns intended to create anxieties, then sell products that promise to relieve those anxieties. Male and female models present unrealistic, blemish-free bodies that are often (especially in printed media) artifically created through photo adjustment or computer imagery. To adolescents, whose bodies are growing and changing, these body types may represent an impossible "ideal." Many people are influenced by such advertising and have diminished self-esteem as a result.

## 13.4.2  Developmental Tasks for Adolescents

Developmental psychologists have identified six key developmental tasks for adolescents (SIECUS, 1995a). Becoming a sexually healthy adult requires successful completion of each task. The six tasks are these:

1. **Physical sexual maturation.** Presumably because of better diet and generally better health conditions, young people reach sexual maturity at younger mean (average) ages than they did in the past. In 1860, the mean age at menarche (first menstruation) was about 17 years. Over the next hundred years the age at menarche dropped steadily until about 1960, when it stabilized and remains today at about 12 to 12.5 years (Neinstein, 1991). The significance of this change is that young people become physically sexually functional at ages where they are less psychologically and socially mature than in the past.

   Puberty brings on many physiological changes. Young women need to adjust to the many effects of cycling hormone levels. Both genders experience increased sex drive. Young men find that sexual maturity brings erections at embarrassing times. Hormonal changes influence the emotions in both genders. All of these changes require adjustment.

2. **Independence.** Independence (autonomy) usually develops gradually and by degrees. The nature of the parent-child relationship changes, with adjustments required by both the adolescent and the parent. It would be a rare family where no conflicts occurred relating to the development of autonomy. The parent and the adolescent might have different schedules or goals in mind for this aspect of development.

3. **Conceptual identity.** Each of us must identify and place ourselves within the multitude of ethnic, cultural, economic, religious, ethical, and political constructs within our society. Possibly more than anywhere else in the world, this task is complicated by the extremely heterogeneous nature of the United States, along with the unusual degree of freedom we enjoy to choose from and move among various identities.

4. **Functional identity.** This refers to how we find our adult roles in society. We try to identify our competencies and, from the bewildering array of options available to us, decide how we will support ourselves and our families as productive members of society. Again, in the United States we tend to have more options than people in many other nations.

5. **Cognitive development.** Adolescents face the challenge of **cognitive** development—learning to think in a different way than in their childhood. Children and younger adolescents are concrete thinkers—they focus on real objects, present needs and desires, and immediate benefits. The emphasis is on *now*. During adolescence, a successful transition to adulthood requires learning how to think abstractly, plan for the future, and judge the impact of current actions on the future. Not everyone, of course, is able to make this transition. We all know adults who are thought of as being "immature" because they still think exclusively in terms of *now*.

6. **Sexual self-concept.** While childhood is not without sexual feelings, attractions, and curiosity, during adolescence sex assumes a much greater prominence in a person's awareness. Most adolescents experience powerful sexual attractions and erotic feelings. Most experiment with sexual behaviors. And most develop a clearer sense of their own gender identity and sexual orientation.

## 13.5 DEVELOPMENT OF SEXUAL ORIENTATION

Exactly what determines sexual orientation, whether heterosexual, bisexual, or homosexual, is still uncertain. Over the years, many theories have come and gone. Biological, psychological, cultural, and subcultural forces are probably all involved in developing sexual orientation (Van Wyk & Geist, 1995). No single theory is ever likely to explain adequately how everyone's sexual orientation develops or even how one specific person's orientation has developed. Human emotions and behavior are far too complex to be explained by simplistic theories. Any valid theory will explain the development of heterosexual orientation as well as bisexual or homosexual orientation. Regardless of how sexual orientation is determined, it appears that for most people the process is begun early in life, probably even before birth.

### 13.5.1 Biological Theories

Considerable evidence suggests that genetic factors affect sexual orientation in both sexes. The evidence of genetic influence is especially strong in males (Bailey & Pillard, 1995). Evidence for a genetic element has been accumulating for many years (Kallman, 1952). Twin studies have long suggested a genetic influence. For example, identical (monozygotic) twins, who are genetically alike, have a greater rate of concordance (similarity) in their sexual orientation than do fraternal (dizygotic) twins, who are not genetically alike (Bailey et al., 1993; King & McDonald, 1992; Whitam, Diamond, & Martin, 1993).

The role of sex hormones in influencing sexual orientation is still unclear. You will remember from chapter 13 that hormones can have organizing or activating effects. Little, if any, activating effect of hormones on sexual orientation during adolescent or adult life is apparent. Hormones might very well, however, exert an organizing effect on sexual orientation during fetal development. Many researchers believe that prenatal hormone-influenced sexual differentiation of the brain does contribute to sexual orientation (Van Wyk & Geist, 1995).

### 13.5.2 Psychological Theories

Even if genes influencing sexual orientation are identified, psychological factors will still be recognized as further influencing how we express our sexuality (Bem, 1996). Many psychological theories on sexual orientation have been proposed, but none has gained universal acceptance. Perhaps a number of these theories are valid for at least some people.

Some theories on sexual orientation have presumed that the normal pattern of development is toward a heterosexual orientation and that a homosexual or bisexual orientation is the result of something going astray in that development. This frame of mind, however, can build a bias into research, making it difficult to formulate and test a theory that adequately explains the development of all sexual orientations. This model leads to the conclusion that same-gender sexual orientation is an exception to the norm (at best) or an illness or disorder (at worst). However, based on the results of many research studies, the American Psychiatric Association no longer lists homosexuality as a disorder in its *Diagnostic and Statistical Manual of Mental Disorders*. There is no evidence that lesbian, gay, or bisexual people differ from heterosexual people on any measure of psychological well-being or mental health (Strickland, 1995).

### 13.5.3 Cultural Theories

In most, if not all, cultures, social pressure is applied for members to engage in heterosexual behavior. Acceptance of homosexuality and even definitions of homosexuality vary from culture to culture. For example, in the United States, voluntary fellatio or anal intercourse between two males is generally considered homosexual behavior for both parties. In other countries, such as Mexico, Brazil, Greece, Turkey, and Morocco, only the passive recipient (insertee) is considered gay; the active inserter is not.

Few cultures (and few people in our own culture) perceive the distinction between gender-role behavior and sexual orientation. People assume that someone who behaves in nonsexual ways that are more characteristic of the other sex must be lesbian, gay, or bisexual. Or they assume that because someone is LGB, he or she must assume the stereotypical gender role of the other sex. None of these assumptions, of course, are valid.

---

**cognitive**  relating to knowing, including both awareness and judgment

An ongoing controversy is whether a person's sexual orientation is flexible and capable of changing over time or is forever fixed once it is determined (Baumrind, 1995). For example, if sexual orientation is permanently fixed, any clinical effort to change a person's orientation, such as from bisexual to heterosexual, would be futile. Indeed, such attempts to change sexual orientation, whether through psychotherapy or religious conversions, are generally more harmful to the individual's self-esteem and psychological well-being than helpful (Haldeman, 2000).

### 13.5.4   Emergence of Sexual Orientation

How and when does a person know whether she or he is heterosexual, bisexual, gay or lesbian? The answer varies from person to person. Some adults can remember being clearly aware of their attraction to someone of either their own sex or the other sex at a very early age. Others, though in their twenties, thirties, or ever older, still are not sure just what their orientation is.

If sexual orientation is mainly biologically determined, then the process is probably completed very early in life, possibly before birth. But it still might take many years before a person is consciously aware of his or her orientation. If sexual orientation is mainly psychologically or culturally determined, then the process could continue throughout life. This would explain why some people who always thought of themselves as heterosexual become aware of a same-gender sexual orientation at an advanced age (Baumrind, 1995).

## 13.6   ADOLESCENT SEXUAL OUTLETS

During the years of adolescence, the relationships of young people typically become gradually more intimate, in both sexual and emotional senses of the word. Each young person progresses at her or his own particular pace, as influenced by individual rates of physical, psychological, and social development, as well as by religious, ethnic, and socioeconomic factors.

### 13.6.1   Fantasy

Sexual fantasies are nearly universal among adolescents (Purifoy, Grodsky, & Giambra, 1992; Reinisch, 1990), and they might or might not be accompanied by masturbation. The subjects of adolescent sexual fantasy include just about every imaginable form of sexual activity with just about every imaginable partner. The partners in adolescent fantasies range from schoolmates and boyfriends or girlfriends to celebrities to purely imaginary people.

Adolescent sexual fantasies can be viewed as part of a developmental process in which behavioral possibilities are explored in a safe manner. Many fantasies serve as rehearsal for later partner activities.

### 13.6.2   Masturbation

Masturbation begins at widely varying ages. As noted earlier in this chapter, some children discover long before puberty that stimulation of their genitals can be a pleasurable experience. In younger children, this pleasure is not perceived as sexual. With the physical and emotional changes of puberty, however, masturbation becomes more sharply identified as a sexual act and increases in both incidence and frequency. For many adolescents, masturbation provides the principal sexual outlet. Twice as many adolescent males as females masturbate, and of adolescents who do masturbate, the males masturbate three times as often as the females (Leitenberg et al., 1993).

Many studies have assessed the possibility of any positive or negative effects of masturbation on other sexual behavior. Such research has to be carefully conducted to avoid drawing false conclusions of cause and effect. Well-designed studies show that childhood or adolescent masturbation is not causally related to disorders of sexual arousal or sexual satisfaction, or other sexual difficulties in adult relationships (Leitenberg et al., 1993; Leung & Robson, 1993). A study of 41 married women who had masturbated to orgasm and 41 who had not showed that the masturbators had more rapid sexual arousal, had significantly more coital orgasms, and had greater sexual desire, higher self-esteem, and greater general marital and sexual satisfaction (Hurlbert & Whittaker, 1991).

Medical authorities have been in agreement for many years that masturbation causes no physical or mental harm, and sex therapists often recommend masturbation as part of sex therapy. Yet for some young people, masturbation is still laden with guilt and anxiety. Several studies have shown that women who feel guilt about their masturbation are less likely than other women to report satisfactory general sexual adjustment, physiological sexual satisfaction (orgasm), and psychological sexual satisfaction (Davidson & Darling, 1993; Davidson & Moore, 1994b; Leung & Robson, 1993). Masturbation guilt can be due to ignorance of the fact that masturbation is harmless. Another source of guilt may be that some religions, including Orthodox Judaism, Roman Catholicism, some Protestant sects, and the Latter-Day Saints (Mormons), teach that masturbation is sinful.

# GO ASK ALICE

*Dear Alice,*

*If a person masturbates once or twice a day, over a long period of time, like 2–3 years, would there be any side effects for this person? Or maybe, are there any long-term side effects?*

*Curious Student about Masturbation*

Dear Curious Student about Masturbation,

Individuals vary tremendously in the frequencies with which they masturbate. There are people who never masturbate, those who masturbate two or three times in their lifetime, and those who masturbate three or more times a day, as well as everything in between. Many people masturbate throughout their lifetime without any side effects other than pleasure. If there is no significant stress in your life (work, school, relationship, family, etc.), and the amount you are masturbating isn't hurting you, why not just enjoy yourself?

*Dear Alice,*

*I don't know if it's stress or what, but lately I feel the urge to masturbate five or six times a day (and I do). This has been going on for about 2 months now. I'm a 24-year-old man who doesn't get it any other way lately. Should I be concerned?*

*Humble*

Dear Humble,

Alice has a few questions for you to think about. What was your usual pattern of masturbation in the past? Did anything else in your life change two months ago? You mentioned stress. Is this stress about being in school, leaving a job, moving, ending a relationship?

There are a few directions you can take at this point. One, crazy as it may sound, is to masturbate more often and see if you feel any differently. Another is to try masturbating one or two times less per day and see how that makes you feel. How about a masturbation schedule? This would give you a framework for the activity so that it doesn't take time away from other things you need to do. Also, it would make you conscious about each time you are masturbating, what triggered the need to release, and whether or not there are discernible patterns.

You might want to change your style of masturbation. Try using a lube so that your penis does not become raw or irritated. Alice would also encourage you to try to get more pleasure from each experience with yourself. Choose one time a day to make it something special, to try to change the nature of your interaction with yourself. All of this is to give you more information about your needs, desires, and wants, and make the masturbation experience more deliberate.

If the real issue is that you are lonely, angry, or resentful that you are not "getting it" (sex, orgasm, relief?) any other way lately, you need to think about that. You might look at other stress outlets. Exercise might make a difference physically.

Psychologically, there might be something you could do to become more available or more receptive to a potential partner. Don't exclude counseling as an option if this continues to be distressing for you.

 http://www.mhhe.com/byer6

## 13.6.3 Sexual Partner Activities

Many young people follow a succession of partner activities beginning with mild sex play and eventually progressing to intercourse.

### Sex Play

**Sex play** (making out) is defined as all activities more physically sexual than kissing but short of penetration or intercourse, typically including manual or oral stimulation, or both, of the breasts and genitals. Sex play might or might not lead to orgasm in either partner.

Sex play is usually seen as a normal step in adolescent development of psychosexual maturity (Leitenberg, Greenwald, & Tarran, 1989). It enables young people to learn their own sexual responses as well as those of their partners. Many couples develop techniques of oral or manual stimulation to mutual orgasm as an alternative to intercourse. This can effectively satisfy the immediate needs for sexual relief and shared intimacy, while also satisfying the desire to reserve intercourse for some future partner or situation, such as marriage or reaching a certain age. Heterosexual couples stimulating to orgasm, however,

| | |
|---|---|
| **sex play** | activities more physically sexual than kissing but stopping short of vaginal intercourse or orgasm; also called making out or petting |

Sex play is a normal step in psychosexual development. It enables young people to learn their own sexual responses as well as those of their partners.

**TABLE 13.1** PERCENTAGE OF HIGH SCHOOL STUDENTS WHO HAVE EVER HAD SEXUAL INTERCOURSE

|  | FEMALES | MALES |
|---|---|---|
| **By Grade in School** | | |
| 9th grade | 32% | 41% |
| 10th grade | 46% | 50% |
| 11th grade | 60% | 57% |
| 12th grade | 66% | 67% |
| **By Ethnicity** | | |
| White, non-Hispanic | 49% | 49% |
| African American | 67% | 81% |
| Hispanic | 53% | 62% |

**Source:** Data from Centers for Disease Control and Prevention, 1996, "Youth Risk Behavior Surveillance-United States, 1995" in *CDC Surveillance Summaries, Morbidity and Mortality Weekly Report,* 45(SS-4), September 27, 1996.

**TABLE 13.2** PERCENTAGE OF CURRENTLY SEXUALLY ACTIVE HIGH SCHOOL STUDENTS WHO USED A CONDOM DURING LAST SEXUAL INTERCOURSE PRIOR TO SURVEY

|  | FEMALES | MALES |
|---|---|---|
| **By Grade in School** | | |
| 9th grade | 59% | 66% |
| 10th grade | 52% | 68% |
| 11th grade | 49% | 57% |
| 12th grade | 43% | 57% |
| **By Ethnicity** | | |
| White, non-Hispanic | 48% | 58% |
| African American | 61% | 72% |
| Hispanic | 33% | 56% |

**Source:** Data from Centers for Disease Control and Prevention, 1996, "Youth Risk Behavior Surveillance-United States, 1995" in *CDC Surveillance Summaries, Morbidity and Mortality Weekly Report,* 45(SS-4), September 27, 1996.

must be careful that the male's semen is kept away from the vaginal opening, because pregnancy can occur even without vaginal penetration by the penis.

Any value judgment regarding adolescent sex play must be based on such considerations as the age and emotional maturity of each individual. The role of sex in the total relationship must also be considered. Is sex play just one of many varied activities of the couple, or is it their only shared activity? Is it contributing to the growth of each individual, or is so much time spent in sex play that growth is inhibited?

### Heterosexual Intercourse

Published incidence figures for adolescent sexual experiences are rather variable, depending on the survey methods and group surveyed. Tables 13.1 through 13.4 present some of the results of a large national school-based survey of adolescent sexual behaviors (Centers for Disease Control and Prevention, 1996g). Over 10,900 students were surveyed in 110 schools selected to fairly represent a cross section of American students who were currently attending school in grades 9 through 12. Native Americans and Asian American/Pacific Islanders were not included because the numbers surveyed were not large enough to ensure validity of the survey.

All contemporary U.S. surveys, compared with those of thirty or forty years ago, show that the mean (average) age of onset of sexual activity has dropped and the total incidence of adolescent intercourse has increased. At the same time, the marriage rate for the younger age groups has dropped sharply. Thus, non-marital intercourse is a much more significant sexual outlet for today's young people than it was for those of previous generations.

### Deciding about Intercourse

Despite today's high incidence of adolescent sexual intercourse, our society is far from unanimous in accepting it. Some people hold conflicting religious or

**TABLE 13.3** PERCENTAGE OF SEXUALLY ACTIVE HIGH SCHOOL STUDENTS WHO USED ALCOHOL OR ANOTHER DRUG AT TIME OF LAST SEXUAL INTERCOURSE

|  | FEMALES | MALES |
|---|---|---|
| **By Grade in School** | | |
| 9th grade | 17% | 38% |
| 10th grade | 18% | 39% |
| 11th grade | 21% | 28% |
| 12th grade | 12% | 29% |
| **By Ethnicity** | | |
| White, non-Hispanic | 18% | 36% |
| African American | 11% | 27% |
| Hispanic | 22% | 28% |

**Source:** Data from Centers for Disease Control and Prevention, 1996, "Youth Risk Behavior Surveillance-United States, 1995" in *CDC Surveillance Summaries, Morbidity and Mortality Weekly Report,* 45(SS-4), September 27, 1996.

**TABLE 13.4** PERCENTAGE OF HIGH SCHOOL STUDENTS WHO HAVE BEEN PREGNANT OR GOTTEN SOMEONE PREGNANT

|  | FEMALES | MALES |
|---|---|---|
| **By Grade in School** | | |
| 9th grade | 5% | 4% |
| 10th grade | 6% | 5% |
| 11th grade | 10% | 5% |
| 12th grade | 10% | 9% |
| **By Ethnicity** | | |
| White, non-Hispanic | 4% | 4% |
| African American | 16% | 14% |
| Hispanic | 13% | 12% |

**Source:** Data from Centers for Disease Control and Prevention, 1996, "Youth Risk Behavior Surveillance-United States, 1995" in *CDC Surveillance Summaries, Morbidity and Mortality Weekly Report,* 45(SS-4), September 27, 1996.

Decisions about sexual behavior should be made without coercion and should reflect each individual's emotional and social maturity and personal values.

other moral beliefs; others cite risks of disease transmission and unwanted pregnancy. Thus, decisions regarding sexual activity are not always easy to make. For many young people, sexual decisions involve emotional turmoil and may never be satisfactorily resolved.

In addition to one's own values, many external forces can also influence sexual decisions. First of all, peers might exert pressure for or against sexual activity, and adolescents value the opinions of their peers highly. Parents also might try to influence their offspring in either direction.

In a study of 176 California Latino adolescents aged 15 to 19 years, girls were less likely to have vaginal intercourse if they had educational goals beyond high school and the presence of parental love. Having vaginal intercourse was positively associated with advancing age and maternal communication about sex. In the boys, the strongest predictors for having vaginal intercourse were feeling close to both parents and having a positive body image (Marchi & Guendelman, 1995).

Often we hear people associating adolescent sexuality with "hormones," and the association appears to be valid. Blood samples were taken from 100 adolescent boys every six months for three years. Testosterone levels were significantly related to having vaginal intercourse, but not to sexual fantasy or noncoital sexual activity (Halpern et al., 1993).

In another study that included 206 adolescent males, an earlier onset of vaginal intercourse was associated with delinquent behavior, alcohol and other drug use, early physical maturity, and parental transitions such as divorce or marriage. A later onset of vaginal intercourse was associated with higher anxiety levels (Capaldi, Crosby, & Stoolmiller, 1996).

The ambivalent sexual attitudes of our society influence an adolescent's decision about becoming sexually active. Our society presents sexuality as simultaneously good and bad. For example, sexual attractiveness is highly valued, and the media tell us that we simply must be perceived as sexually attractive and available. Actual sexual interaction by unmarried individuals still is not accepted by many, however. Also, the double standard of permissiveness for males but restrictiveness for females is still held by many people. There is little wonder that a young person in such a culture might have difficulty in making sexual decisions.

Ultimately, the decision of when to engage in coitus should be made only by the individual. Ideally, the decision will reflect the emotional and social maturity of the individual as well as her or his personal values. Of all the conflicting values of society, religions, peers, parents, and others, we internalize—take as our own—those that are meaningful to us as individuals. A person who understands his or her values has a basis for making decisions about sexual behavior. See "Where Do I Stand? It's Up to You—Decisions about Sex."

### Early Sexual Experiences

Even when they are voluntary and much desired, early sexual experiences can be surrounded by fear and anxiety.

First sexual experiences in the context of a valued personal relationship are likely to be more emotionally rewarding than a sexual initiation with someone with whom no intimacy exists or where there is force or coercion (Sprecher, Barbee, & Schwartz, 1995).

Events that might be considered sexual dysfunctions in an established sexual relationship are no cause for concern in early sexual experiences, in light of the high anxiety levels associated with early sexual experiences. Males, for example, might have difficulty gaining an erection or might experience very rapid ejaculation. In their first sexual experiences, young females might fail to lubricate, might experience vaginismus (spasm of the vaginal muscles), and very possibly will not experience orgasm. Again, none of these male or female experiences should be perceived as problems that are likely to interfere with future sexual interaction. They are entirely predictable in view of the inexperience and high anxiety levels typical of early sexual activities. It is important to note that occasionally first sexual experiences are not voluntary, but involve rape, incest, or other forms of coercion. These experiences are more accurately considered acts of violence and aggression, rather than sex. Counseling is essential to help heal or prevent the far-reaching consequences that can result from the violent and sexual elements of these experiences. A referral to a skilled therapist can be obtained from a school nurse or guidance counselor, health care practitioner, or member of the clergy.

### 13.6.4 Discovering a Lesbian or Gay Orientation

Adolescent sexual fantasies and activity might or might not reflect an individual's true sexual orientation. For many people, a clear-cut sense of sexual orientation manifests itself slowly. In one study of adolescents in grades 7 through 12, 88 percent described themselves as predominantly heterosexual, 1 percent described themselves as either predominantly homosexual or as bisexual, and 11 percent were unsure of their sexual orientation (Remafedi et al., 1992). Uncertainty decreased with age. Twenty-six percent of the 12-year-olds were unsure but by age 18 this had decreased to only 5 percent.

Many lesbian, gay, and bisexual adults remember their adolescence as a time of confusion about their sexuality. Even though, as previously mentioned, a majority of LGB adults recall feeling "different" as children, most did not clearly identify themselves as homosexual until their late teen years. Lesbian women tend to make this identity a year or two later than gay men (Remafedi et al., 1992). In both genders, becoming openly homosexual ("coming out") generally does not occur until adulthood.

Many people who will have a same-gender sexual orientation as adults experience heterosexual activity earlier in life, perhaps motivated by social expectancy, and might even marry and have children (Baumrind, 1995; Rosario et al., 1996). Conversely, many people who are predominantly heterosexual as

Individuals become aware of their sexual orientation at various ages. Some adolescents are certain about their orientation, but many pass through a period of uncertainty.

# WHERE DO I STAND?
## IT'S UP TO YOU—DECISIONS ABOUT SEX

The following material is based on an excellent brochure prepared by the Los Angeles Planned Parenthood–World Population organization. Although the brochure is intended for teenagers, much of it applies to adults as well.

How do you know when you're ready for sex? Many people will tell you what to do, and this can be very confusing. As a teenager, you are physically capable of having and enjoying sex. But there's more involved than physical needs, including your feelings, your relationship, and your view of yourself. Sex is used by people for many purposes. Although most people desire the pleasure of sex, it is often used for other reasons, many of which lead to pain. Sex can be one of life's most pleasurable experiences, or it can be equally as devastating. Because sex can be such a strong force, deciding when you are ready for sex is not a decision to be made in a moment of passion. It is a decision that you alone can make. Because remember—in the end, *it's up to you.*

Answering the following questions should help you in making decisions about your sexual activity.

### You

1. Have you thought about your sexuality?
2. Are you prepared to make sure effective forms of contraception and STI protection are used?
3. In heterosexual relationships, if you don't use contraception, are you prepared to cope with a pregnancy?
4. Even with protection, sexually transmitted diseases are a definite risk. Can you deal with that?
5. There are many types of sexuality; which will you choose?
6. How will you handle it if your sexual experience is unpleasant?
7. If the sexual lifestyle you choose is not legal (for example, prostitution), are you willing to deal with the consequences?
8. Do you use sex to shock people?
9. How will you feel the next day?

### Your Relationship

1. Is there mutual consent to have sex?
2. Is sex being used as a weapon or bribe?
3. Do you or your partner feel like a sex object or feel exploited?
4. Is sex a last resort to hold the relationship together?
5. What kind of commitment are you willing to make to one another?
6. Can you have a good relationship without sex?
7. Do you feel comfortable talking about sex with one another?
8. Will sex enhance your relationship?

### Your Parents

1. How will your parents react?
2. Have you ever discussed sex with your parents? Or their values about sex?
3. Will you have to lie to your parents? Can you cope with that?
4. Are you using sex as a way to hurt your parents?
5. How have your parents' attitudes toward sex influenced you?

### Your Friends

1. Do you feel pressured to have sex?
2. Would you be considered "out of it" if you didn't have sex?
3. Do you need to be sexually active to be popular?
4. Are you tempted to have sex when and if you get high or drunk?
5. Does it really matter what your friends think?

### Back to You

Many of these questions can be answered only by you. To answer them, it is helpful to understand your personal values, needs, and desires, as well as the consequences of your actions. If any of these questions are difficult to answer, perhaps you need more time to think before you make a decision or take an action. These questions should help you in making the best decision for yourself, because, basically, *it's up to you.*

---

Adapted from It's Up to You, Planned Parenthood–World Population, Los Angeles.

adults recall adolescent homosexual experiences of either a transient or a more lasting nature (Eliason, 1995). It is common for adolescents to have crushes or close relationships with peers or older people of their own sex, and association with these people sometimes results in sexual arousal.

Despite the common nature of adolescent homosexual activity, many young people feel uncomfortable about these experiences. Young people are well aware of our society's often negative attitude toward LGB individuals, which can contribute to anxiety about same-gender sexual experiences or feelings that they might have had (Eliason, 1995).

An LGB adolescent who wishes to come out might feel even more anxiety about this than an adult in the same situation. Many adolescents are outspoken in their homophobia, and a lesbian or gay adolescent, frequently hearing derisive remarks about lesbian and gay people, may anticipate receiving little support from heterosexual peers upon coming out. Many lesbian, gay, and bisexual adolescents are victims of antigay violence. Between one-third and one-half of gay adults reported victimization in junior or senior high school, and between one-half and three-fourths reported verbal or physical abuse in college (Ryan & Futterman, 1998). An LGB adolescent might also have heard his or her parents expressing negative feelings about homosexuality, and might be reluctant to come out to such parents when she or he is still dependent on them in so many ways. Each lesbian or gay young person has to make her or his own decision about when and how to come out. The book *Coming Out to Parents* by Mary Borhek (Pilgrim Press, 1993) is a good resource for LGB adolescents and their parents.

Adolescents sometimes confuse gender-role behavior with sexual orientation. A nonstereotypical style of masculinity or femininity does not in any way indicate a homosexual orientation. A male can be sensitive, emotionally expressive, and noncompetitive, all of which contradict the standard male role stereotype, and still be strongly attracted to females as sexual partners. Similarly, a female can be willful, ambitious, independent, and assertive and still prefer male partners. Gender-role behavior and sexual orientation are separate personality elements in each of us.

## 13.7 ADOLESCENT MARRIAGE

The incidence of adolescent marriage has declined in recent years. In 1990, 17 percent of first-time brides were teenagers, down from 30 percent in 1980 and 42 percent in 1970 (National Center for Health Statistics, 1995a). This decline is considered fortunate because adolescent marriages are statistically the least

**TABLE 13.5** DIVORCE RATES FOR EARLY MARRIAGES

| | DIVORCES PER YEAR PER 1,000 MARRIED | |
|---|---|---|
| | *Women* | *Men* |
| Ages 15–19 | 48.6 | 32.8 |
| Ages 20–24 | 46.0 | 50.2 |
| Average for all ages | 18.7 | 19.2 |

**Note:** Divorce rate is for 1,000 married people of age specified per year for the forty-eight states that report divorces by age.

**Source:** Data from National Center for Health Statistics, *Monthly Vital Statistics Report*, 43(9), Supplement, March 22, 1995.

successful of all marriages, as measured by divorce rates (see table 13.5). Adolescent marriage is also associated with lower educational attainment and lower lifetime earnings.

Many social and technological changes seem to have contributed to the decrease in the incidence of adolescent marriage. Some possible factors include the following:

1. Rising career expectations of young women, requiring longer periods of preparation.
2. Relaxation of traditional restrictions on nonmarital sexual activities, which in the past motivated people to marry early in order to experience sexual fulfillment.
3. Improved contraceptive methods and their availability to young people.
4. Greater accessibility of safe abortions.
5. Greater willingness of women to raise children without marrying.
6. Success of programs that discourage premature pregnancy or marriage.

Despite the decline in adolescent marriage, hundreds of thousands of people aged nineteen or under do marry each year (over 200,000 females and almost 88,000 males in the United States in 1990). Why so many early marriages? Pregnancy is still a common motivation for adolescent marriage (see the next section of this chapter).

Various unfulfilled emotional needs are also associated with early marriage. Low self-esteem is foremost among these. Not appreciating their own potential for personal growth and development, many young people are unable to set significant educational and career goals for themselves. They are more interested in anything that promises to provide more immediate identity and fulfillment. Marriage often seems to hold that promise.

Limited awareness of the many options life holds is another shared characteristic of individuals who marry during adolescence. In particular, limited dating experience is quite common. On the average, adolescents who marry have dated fewer people than adolescents who do not marry. Having had few, if any, prior relationships and finally enjoying the attention of someone who seems to believe that they are special, these individuals feel a strong tendency to want to make that relationship "permanent." There is often the feeling that maybe this is the "last chance." In these situations, not only do people marry prematurely, but they often make poor choices of partners since they lack a broad range of prior relationships to use as a basis for comparison.

Regardless of the reasons adolescents choose to marry, few are emotionally, socially, and economically prepared for marriage. Their degree of emotional and social development, for example, might prepare them neither for appropriate partner selection nor for the difficult interpersonal, social, and financial tasks of maintaining a marriage. Another problem of early marriage is that it commonly inhibits the partners' personal growth and development. Each is denied some of the social experiences that contribute to personal development, and some of the options open to a single person of the same age are closed or rendered more difficult.

Many married adolescents find that their educational and economic achievement is also limited. Some fail to complete even high school, as immediate financial need takes them out of school and into low-paying, menial, dead-end jobs. Some are able to complete school or vocational training later on, but many remain in low-paying jobs for long periods of time. Financial difficulties contribute to the high failure rate of such early marriages.

## 13.8   ADOLESCENT PREGNANCY

Organizations such as Planned Parenthood and some schools sponsor effective sexuality programs for young people. These programs usually attempt to reduce the incidence of adolescent pregnancy and marriage by decreasing premature and irresponsible sexual activity. Thanks in part to programs like these, the adolescent pregnancy rate has declined in recent years, based on declines in both abortion and live birth rates for teenagers. Most people agree that this is a fortunate trend.

### 13.8.1   Adolescent Pregnancy Rates

Adolescent pregnancy rates can be estimated by totaling the numbers of live births, and spontaneous and induced abortions. The live birth rate for all women aged 15 through 19 dropped by 12 percent

**TABLE 13.6**   BIRTHS PER 1,000 WOMEN AGED 15–19, UNITED STATES, 1996, BY ETHNICITY

| Ethnicity | Birth Rate |
|---|---|
| All ethnicities | 54.7 |
| White, non-Hispanic | 48.4 |
| African American | 91.7 |
| Native American | 75.1 |
| Asian/Pacific Islander | 25.4 |
| Hispanic | 101.6 |

**Source:** Data from Ventura, et al., 1997.

between 1991 and 1996. For African American women in this age group, the decline was 23 percent. The live birth rate per 1,000 teenagers of all ethnicities, aged 15 through 19 years, in 1996 was 54.7, compared to 62.1 in 1991 (Ventura et al., 1997).

Some ethnic differences in pregnancy rates are apparent (see table 13.6). The adolescent pregnancy rate is especially high among young African American and Hispanic women—over double the rate for white females ages 15 to 19 (Ventura et al., 1997). The 23 percent decline in African American teen births since 1991 represents significant progress for these young women.

The Alan Guttmacher Institute has compared adolescent pregnancy rates in thirty-seven countries and found that the United States incidence is higher than that of almost any other developed country. Although American adolescents are no more sexually active than young people in other industrialized countries, they are much more likely to become pregnant. White adolescent U.S. women have twice the pregnancy rate of comparable British and French girls and six times the rate of Dutch women of the same age (Jones, 1985; Trussell, 1988).

European countries tend to be more open than the United States about sexuality, and their official government policies focus on reducing unprotected intercourse, rather than reducing sexual behaviors (SIECUS, 1995a). Sexual information and reproductive health services in these countries are more available for young people.

### 13.8.2   Costs of Adolescent Childbirth

The costs of adolescent childbirth can be measured in personal, social, and economic terms. The *personal costs* include:

- A young woman's ambitions, which might be fulfilled only with great difficulty, if at all.
- A young woman's potential abilities, which might remain undeveloped or unused.

- A young man might work long hours at low pay to support his child instead of advancing himself through education or training.
- Grandparents might assume much of the responsibility for raising a child at a time in their lives when they would enjoy freedom from parenting duties.
- A child might grow up lacking the benefits and role models of a two-parent home.
- Many children of adolescent mothers might never know their fathers.

*Social costs* of adolescent childbirth can include:

- A need for public assistance for young families.
- Behavioral problems resulting from inadequate parenting skills of very young parents.
- A less educated society because of incomplete education of young parents.

Poverty must play a prominent role in any discussion of adolescent pregnancy. In a vicious cycle, low income acts as a contributing factor to high adolescent pregnancy rates, and adolescent parenthood is a major cause of low-income family units. This cycle can go on for generation after generation. The hopelessness of poverty motivates premature parenthood, which in turn effectively blocks most efforts at rising above poverty. Here are some of the *economic realities* of adolescent parenthood (Kristof, 1994):

- Eighty percent of teenage mothers will live in poverty for the rest of their lives.
- The average income for a never-married mother in 1994 was $9,820.
- The national average annual rent for a one-bedroom apartment in 1994 was $7,068.
- For a mother and one infant, annual food expenses are about $2,250.
- A baby costs $450 per year to clothe.
- Transportation costs vary widely, but most lower-income people spend about $690 to $820 per year on public transportation. Owning a car would cost much more.
- Health care for a young mother and her infant would cost about $720 per year.
- The average cost of day care for one child is $3,100 per year.

## 13.8.3   Incomplete Education

Incomplete education is a common outcome of adolescent pregnancy. In many U.S. cities, only one-fifth to one-third of the women who give birth before completing high school will ever earn high school diplomas. Some are too busy trying to support themselves and their babies in low-paying jobs. Some cannot locate or finance adequate child care. Some simply believe that school is now irrelevant.

Forste and Tienda (1992) analyzed the association of ethnicity with high school completion for teen mothers. African American teen mothers were the most likely to graduate from high school and Hispanic teen mothers were the least, with an intermediate rate for non-Hispanic white mothers.

Programs for pregnant adolescents that combine educational strategies with educational support can greatly improve the school completion rate. These programs combine classes on labor and delivery, nutrition, infant bonding, and infant and child care, with group sessions designed to build feelings of support and self-esteem.

## 13.8.4   Effects on the Children

Many adolescent mothers receive inadequate prenatal care and have little knowledge of how to care for an infant. Their babies have a greater incidence of low birthweight and more developmental disorders than babies of older mothers. Many of these problems stem from the poor prenatal care that many adolescent mothers receive.

Babies of adolescent mothers have high rates of illness and death. As they grow up, they have above-average rates of educational and emotional problems. Many are victims of child abuse or neglect by parents too immature to understand why their baby is crying or who perceive their infant or child as being the cause of their own difficult and unhappy life. Many of these children of children wind up in foster care. Adolescent pregnancy is a self-perpetuating problem. Children of children are prone to becoming adolescent parents themselves.

## 13.8.5   Causes of Adolescent Pregnancy

A multitude of factors contribute to adolescent pregnancies. One of the traditional deterrents to adolescent pregnancy was the great social stigma formerly attached to unmarried motherhood. Today, in many parts of American society, little stigma is attached to being an unmarried mother.

Many pregnant adolescents come from unhappy home situations with absent parents, unloving parents, abusive parents, fighting parents, or chemically dependent parents. Daughters in these homes might perceive motherhood as a way to escape from their unhappiness, move into an adult role, and feel loved by someone.

Researchers are almost unanimous in their belief that popular media influence adolescent sexual attitudes. Monique Ward (1995) analyzed the content of three episodes of each of the twelve prime-time TV programs most preferred by children and adolescents. Discussions about sexuality were common in these episodes. An average of 29 percent of the interactions on each individual episode contained verbal references to sexual issues, with the level exceeding 50 percent for some episodes. The most common messages about sexuality were those in which men commented on women's bodies and physical appearance and in which masculinity was equated with being sexual. The media's focus on sexuality may contribute to sexual activity among adolescents unprepared to prevent or handle a pregnancy.

In recent years, adolescents have become better users of contraceptives, probably in response to the threat of AIDS. In 1995, it was reported that over 70 percent of adolescents used contraception during their first intercourse (National Center for Health Statistics, 1995c). Two-thirds of teenagers are fairly consistent users of condoms (Centers for Disease Control and Prevention, 1992), but many still use no contraceptives or are inconsistent in their use.

Effective contraceptive use by an adolescent or anyone else requires advanced planning. This, in turn, requires you to (1) accept yourself as a sexual being and (2) consciously accept the idea that you are going to be sexually involved and that it is going to be a planned event. Unfortunately many people, due to anxiety or guilt, convince themselves that their sexual activity just "happens" in the heat of passion and is beyond their control. Letting sex "just happen" may save some guilt or anxiety, but causes a lot of unwanted pregnancies.

Having a limited awareness of life's options and opportunities promotes adolescent pregnancy. This is especially true for young women in low-income situations or in families or ethnicities where a woman's role is defined primarily in terms of motherhood. Seeing no other interesting alternatives and perceiving little potential identity for herself other than the role of "mother," a young woman might have little or no motivation to delay pregnancy (Stevens, 1994). She might view motherhood as the answer to her feelings of emptiness and lack of self-actualization. Of course, adolescent motherhood rarely lives up to the fantasies a woman may have entertained about it.

## 13.8.6 Preventing Adolescent Pregnancy

If the majority of Americans agree on the need to reduce the adolescent pregnancy rate, they certainly do not agree on how to accomplish this goal (Center for the Study of Social Policy, 1995). The subject of adolescent pregnancy raises almost every divisive social issue in American politics today. It includes the controversial subjects of school sexuality education, contraceptive availability for adolescents, abortion rights, gender roles, family structure, and welfare programs, to name only a few. Bickering over *how* to deal with adolescent pregnancy has often resulted in not dealing with it at all.

People tend to fall into two camps on how to prevent adolescent pregnancy. Some believe that programs should promote nonmarital sexual abstinence; others believe that programs need to encourage contraceptive knowledge, availability, and use. People in the first group tend to believe that sexuality education should be the responsibility of parents and that teaching young people about birth control is condoning their sexual activity. People in the latter group tend to believe that Americans should learn to accept adolescent sexuality and to follow the lead of European countries that have achieved low adolescent pregnancy rates by promoting effective contraceptive use (Center for the Study of Social Policy, 1995).

Many adults have difficulty accepting adolescents' emerging sexuality. Adults' denial and disapproval of teenage sexual behavior can actually increase young people's risk of pregnancy. Young people sense this disapproval and are often willing to risk pregnancy and disease rather than experience the disapproval of parents or other adults with whom they must interact in order to obtain contraceptives (SIECUS, 1995a).

Most Americans—80 to 86 percent in most surveys (Gordon, 1992)—favor school- and community-based programs to reduce adolescent pregnancy. To be effective, such programs need to give young people, especially females in low-income families, a broader perspective on life's many options, an increased sense of the possibility of improving their position in society, and an awareness of how much better their opportunities are without the impediment of premature parenthood.

It is evident that much adolescent sexual activity takes place outside a mutually loving relationship and is motivated by pressure from others rather than by individual needs or desires. Effective programs must help young people build the self-confidence and assertiveness required to resist outside pressures for sexual involvement. Adolescents are often afraid to stand up for what they believe is right and end up becoming sexually involved in an effort to be liked by others or to reassure themselves of their sexual attractiveness. Moreover, young people often have difficulty in assertively letting others know that they mean what they say. Their nonassertive no to a sexual advance may be taken to mean that all that is needed is a little more persuasion.

# WHERE DO I STAND?
## AN ASSESSMENT OF ADOLESCENT SEXUAL HEALTH

This assessment isn't just intended for adolescents. Its content is also appropriate for adults and can help lead to a greater self-awareness. This assessment may also be useful to parents of adolescents or those who have younger siblings who may wish to evaluate their sexual health. You have permission to make photocopies of this form to pass on to them. Assure them that their responses are confidential unless *they* choose to discuss them with you. This assessment can be an excellent "opener" for a discussion on sexuality. Circle the number that represents the most appropriate response for each question, then total all of your numbers.

|  |  | Almost Always | Sometimes | Almost Never |
|---|---|:---:|:---:|:---:|
| 1. | Do you feel good about your body? | 5 | 3 | 0 |
| 2. | Do you develop rewarding relationships with people of both sexes? | 5 | 3 | 0 |
| 3. | Are you able to express love and intimacy in nongenital ways? | 5 | 3 | 0 |
| 4. | Are you able to avoid being sexually exploited? | 5 | 3 | 0 |
| 5. | Are you careful to never sexually exploit anyone else? | 5 | 3 | 0 |
| 6. | Can you identify and clearly explain your sexual values? | 5 | 3 | 0 |
| 7. | Do you act according to your sexual values? | 5 | 3 | 0 |
| 8. | Do you take full responsibility for your own sexual behavior? | 5 | 3 | 0 |
| 9. | Can you communicate effectively with your family and friends? | 5 | 3 | 0 |
| 10. | Can you ask questions of parents and other adults about sexual issues? | 5 | 3 | 0 |
| 11. | Can you enjoy sexual feelings without necessarily acting upon them? | 5 | 3 | 0 |
| 12. | Are you able to assertively communicate and negotiate sexual limits? | 5 | 3 | 0 |
| 13. | Can you talk with a partner about sexual activity before it occurs, including limits, disease and pregnancy prevention, and the meaning of the sexual activity within that relationship? | 5 | 3 | 0 |
| 14. | Can you communicate desires not to have sex? | 5 | 3 | 0 |
| 15. | Do you respect a partner's desire not to have sex? | 5 | 3 | 0 |
| 16. | If you are sexually active, do you use contraception to avoid pregnancy and condoms to avoid disease transmission? | 5 | 3 | 0 |
| 17. | Do you observe all health-related behaviors such as Pap smears, breast self-examination, or testicular self-examination? | 5 | 3 | 0 |
| 18. | Are you tolerant of people with different sexualities? | 5 | 3 | 0 |
| 19. | Do you understand how the media influence your sexual thoughts, feelings, values, and behaviors? | 5 | 3 | 0 |
| 20. | Do you seek further information on sexuality when you need it? | 5 | 3 | 0 |

**Total points:** _____

*An Assessment of Adolescent Sexual Health—continued*

**Interpretation:**

92–100 points: Great! Your sexuality is enriching your life and your relationships.

84–91 points: Not bad. You might want to make an effort to improve your "problem areas."

76–83 points: You have some unresolved sexual issues to deal with.

75 or fewer points: You need to do some serious work on coming to terms with your sexuality. You are probably lacking some of the skills needed to maintain a rewarding, responsible sexual relationship.

**Source:** Adapted from Sexually Healthy Adolescents, *SIECUS Report,* 21:29, December 1992/January 1993.

Another issue to be addressed is the perception of sexual involvement as a symbol of adulthood. Programs to prevent adolescent pregnancy need to emphasize responsibility and other routes to maturity, such as getting a diploma and becoming established in a career.

Well-planned and carefully executed programs of sexuality education have lowered the adolescent pregnancy rate. It may reassure those who favor adolescent sexual abstinence to know that good programs also serve to delay, rather than hasten, sexual involvement (Center for the Study of Social Policy, 1995). Effective sexuality education programs explore the many motivations for sexual involvement and help a young person to confidently say no to exploitative or inappropriate sexual invitations. Recognizing that many young people will be sexually involved, effective programs also present a thorough coverage of contraception.

## 13.8.7 Dealing with an Adolescent Pregnancy

Without a doubt, supportive parents are the most valuable asset a pregnant adolescent can have. A good parental relationship encourages the young woman to face the reality of pregnancy more promptly. The sooner a woman faces the fact that she is pregnant, the more options she has in dealing with her situation.

About 44 percent of pregnant women under age 15 choose to abort their pregnancies, as do about 32 percent of 16-year-olds and 31 percent of 18-year-old women (Centers for Disease Control and Prevention, 1996a). Even before the 1989 U.S. Supreme Court decision giving the individual states more power to regulate abortion, the percentage of pregnant young women choosing to abort their pregnancies began dropping, as more women chose single motherhood.

If abortion is being considered in the case of an unplanned pregnancy, a decision one way or the other must be made very early in the pregnancy. With delay, abortion becomes more dangerous, more expensive, and psychologically more difficult. Early abortion by a licensed physician is relatively safe—actually, it is less dangerous than carrying the pregnancy to term (Hatcher et al., 1994). The decision to abort must be compatible with the young woman's personal philosophy and values.

If a decision is made not to abort, prenatal care should start promptly. Because they psychologically deny being pregnant, or are accustomed to irregular cycles, or are afraid to tell a parent, few pregnant girls under age fifteen receive any prenatal care at all during the crucial first three months of pregnancy (Noble, Cover, & Yanagishita, 1996). Compounding the problem, many pregnant adolescents continue to use drugs and alcohol, which cause fetal defects.

When an adolescent chooses not to abort a pregnancy, the chances are high that she will keep her baby and, as a single mother, raise the child. In spite of long waiting lists of well-qualified adoptive parents, few give up their babies for adoption. Fewer adolescents marry because of pregnancy than was once the case, as adolescent marriage is viewed as likely to fail (a realistic view), and unmarried motherhood does not carry the stigma that it did some years ago.

Despite preventive programs, adolescent motherhood is likely to be with us for some time. Society can and should do much to assist adolescent mothers and their babies. Schools and other agencies do a great service when they provide well-funded, caring programs to help young mothers finish their education. The ability to earn a decent living is of utmost importance to the mother and her child. A child born to a mother who is teenage, unmarried, and a high school dropout is ten times as likely to live in poverty as a child born to a mother with none of these three characteristics (Annie E. Casey Foundation, 1996).

Many young mothers need parenting training and counseling. Some need housing. Without adequate social services, many young women slip into a cycle of desperation and subsequent pregnancies. Their children represent another generation that is likely to repeat the same pattern of premature parenthood and unfinished education (Annie E. Casey Foundation, 1996).

## 13.8.8 Who Are the Fathers?

Teenage pregnancy is usually defined by the age of the mother, but it is important to recognize that many of the fathers of these babies are not teenagers. More than half (51 percent) of the fathers of children born to females aged 17 years or less are over 20 years of age. On the average the father is 3.6 years older than the mother, and in 20 percent of the cases the father is more than 5 years older than the mother (Landry & Forrest, 1995). When teen pregnancy prevention programs focus solely on teens, they may be missing an important segment of the people involved in this problem.

Another overlooked factor is the growing evidence that many teen pregnancies are the result of nonvoluntary or coercive sex (Boyer & Fine, 1992). To the extent that teen births are a result of nonvoluntary sex, prevention programs that focus on choice might not be appropriate.

## 13.8.9 Adolescent Fathers

Adolescent fathers are often thought of as being irresponsible hit-and-run artists, caring little about their children or the young women they have impregnated. This is no doubt true in some cases, but many young fathers are very concerned and eager to help their partners and offspring (Gregory, 1992). Relationships between adolescent parents tend to be rather durable. Two-thirds of adolescent couples who bear a child together are still in a relationship two years after the conception occurred (Toledo-Dreves, Sabin, & Emerson, 1995).

Young fatherhood has been shown to be, in many cases, as disruptive to an adolescent's life as young motherhood can be. Even though a young father's desire to help may be strong, his means and ability to do so may be quite limited. Teenage fathers usually lack the education or training to obtain well-paying jobs. Many are still in high school. Many will compound their problems by dropping out of school. When they leave school, they head straight into a

Less than half of the fathers of children born to adolescent mothers are teenagers. But those who are, are often bewildered by their situation. Some would like to be responsible for their child and their child's mother but lack the resources to do so. Others, whose fathers were not present as they grew up, have no idea what a father is supposed to do.

low-paying job, a trap few perceive themselves entering. Years later they might still not qualify for more than minimum-wage jobs.

Teenage fathers are usually bewildered by their situation. In many cases, their own fathers were not present as they grew up, and the young men have no idea of what a father is supposed to do. They want to do something, however, because they frequently perceive masculinity as including a responsible father role (Gregory, 1992). Being unable to provide for their child undermines their sense of masculinity. Thus, young fathers and fathers-to-be have proven to be quite receptive to programs designed to assist them in their new roles. Programs like these benefit both young fathers and mothers as well as their children. They offer the hope of breaking the cycle of children producing children.

## SUMMARY

1. Children *are* sexual. Some adult sexual problems can be traced to negative parental reactions to childhood sexuality.

2. Childhood masturbation is normal and harmless. Childhood sex play is a normal learning experience and should not be punished. Sexual exploitation of a child by a sibling or another child does occur and warrants intervention.

3. Some children feel same-sex attractions at an early age. Children need to learn early on that there are different kinds of acceptable sexual attractions between human beings.

4. Children are interested in erotic material, which sometimes presents a distorted, dehumanized, and degrading approach to sexuality.

5. The family is the first and most important social system in a child's life. Children can thrive in many different kinds of families.

6. Parents or those adults who serve in that capacity are the most significant role models for children's concepts of sexuality, love, affection, and caring.

7. The physical and emotional changes of adolescence are rapid and profound. Developmental tasks for adolescents include physical sexual maturation, independence, conceptual identity, functional identity, cognitive development, and sexual self-concept.

8. How sexual orientation, whether heterosexual, bisexual, or homosexual, develops is still uncertain, although there are probably biological, psychological, and cultural influences. People become aware of their sexual orientation at various ages.

9. Adolescent sexual outlets include fantasy, masturbation, and heterosexual and homosexual partner activities.

10. The incidence of adolescent marriage has declined sharply in recent years. Causes of adolescent marriage include pregnancy, low self-esteem, limited awareness of life's options and opportunities, and limited dating experience.

11. Adolescent pregnancy is still a problem. U.S. adolescent pregnancy rates are much higher than the rates of other developed countries, though American adolescents are no more sexually active.

12. Some Americans believe that programs combating adolescent pregnancy should emphasize sexual abstinence, although others believe that programs need to encourage contraceptive knowledge, availability, and use.

## CRITICAL THINKING CHALLENGES

1. Although it is clear that many factors contribute to the development of sexual preference, current research indicates that there is a genetic component. Someday a gene may be isolated that plays an important role in sexual orientation. Would societal attitudes improve if sexual orientation were seen as a biological variation like eye color? Or would people interpret the genetic difference as a birth defect to be rectified? If a genetic test were available for sexual orientation, what would be the possible uses and misuses of such a test?

2. What events constituted a "rite of passage" for you as an adolescent? List the events and behaviors that you feel marked your transition from child to adult.

3. List the ten most important things in a relationship for you, in order of their importance. Where do you rank sex? What things are more or less important to you? How would your relationship be affected if your partner ranked sex higher? Lower?

# ADULT SEXUALITY

# 14

## AFTER STUDYING THIS CHAPTER, YOU SHOULD BE ABLE TO

[1] List six dimensions of intimacy in adult partner relationships.

[2] Describe some gender differences in intimacy.

[3] Describe what constitutes sexual coercion in dating and how to deal with unwanted sexual advances.

[4] List seven causes of abusive dating relationships.

[5] Explain how single parents can manage their dating with respect for the needs of their children.

[6] Explain how a person can avoid loneliness while living alone.

[7] Describe the potential benefits of marriage.

[8] Describe the personal traits associated with successful marriage.

[9] List some special challenges that gay and lesbian partnerships face.

[10] Describe some important issues that must be faced when adjusting to parenthood.

[11] List some factors that contribute to successful blended family relationships.

[12] Explain why so many marriages terminate with divorce.

[13] Explain how a divorcing couple can minimize the difficulties associated with their divorce.

[14] Explain the benefits to college students of learning about sexuality and aging.

[15] Explain the six types of aging and how they interact.

[16] Define ageism and explain how it operates in our society.

[17] State four common myths about sex and aging and refute each of them.

[18] Contrast male climacteric with menopause.

[19] Explain the pros and cons of hormone replacement therapy.

[20] Explain society's expectations for sexuality in older people and how these expectations affect older people.

[21] Explain the age-related changes in sexual response for each gender.

[22] Explain the "double standard" of aging for heterosexual men and women.

[23] Contrast aging in the lesbian and gay communities with aging in the heterosexual community.

This chapter discusses the sexual life cycle through adult life. The emphasis throughout this chapter is on relationships. With few exceptions, the emotional and even the physical well-being of an adult is dependent upon the quality of her or his relationships with other people.

## 14.1   INTIMACY IN ADULT PARTNER RELATIONSHIPS

Intimacy in adult partner relationships includes up to six dimensions. Two are individual: authenticity and openness; three are partnership characteristics: sharing of affection, sharing of knowledge and information, and sharing of tasks; and one is a social characteristic: exclusiveness of the relationship (Van den Broucke, Vandereycken, & Vertommen, 1995). Of course, not every adult relationship achieves all six of these dimensions.

Adult intimate relationships carry many potential benefits. Having intimate partnerships reduces feelings of isolation, depression, and personal distress and is associated with lower death risk from a number of causes (Berkman, 1995; Coriell & Cohen, 1995; Palosaari & Aroo, 1995; Sheffield et al., 1995).

Following successful completion of the six major adolescent developmental tasks discussed in chapter 13, one challenge during early adulthood is to develop intimate relationships with others. These developmental tasks are accomplished most effectively in sequence; more specifically, *intimacy can develop only after identities are established.* Many people who are well beyond adolescence are still unable to establish intimate relationships because they have yet to resolve their identity (Garbarino et al., 1995; Horst, 1995; Winefield & Harvey, 1996). Only after you achieve a sense of identity and feel comfortable enough to risk revealing this identity to another can you develop a new, adult kind of intimacy. This is the kind of intimacy freely chosen by two equal individuals who have both worked through their adolescent developmental tasks and know basically who they are.

Before you resolve your identity, your relationships may be of the searching, self-serving kind. You might share your inner self very little. Communication is superficial at best. When you are at this stage of development, you may be afraid of losing yourself in an intimate relationship because you do not really have yourself to begin with.

In contrast, intimacy is characterized by mutuality (Van den Broucke, Vandereycken, & Vertommen, 1995). Communication is open and honest. Mutuality includes the willingness to make sacrifices and compromises. It also involves mature sexual functioning, in that there is a mutual sharing of sexual pleasures. This emotional intimacy most distinguishes the sexual relationships of young adults from those of adolescents.

Of course, intimacy is not an either/or situation. There are all degrees of intimacy in relationships (Manusov, 1995). Even in a continuing relationship between the same two individuals, the level of intimacy fluctuates from day to day and year to year. As each individual has his or her own emotional ups and downs, the nature and quality of the interaction between the two naturally varies. It would be unrealistic to expect any relationship to exhibit a high level of intimacy at all times. Such unrealistic expectations cause some people to become disenchanted with what are actually very good relationships, perhaps feeling an unwarranted sense of failure.

The opposite of intimacy is **emotional isolation.** Some young adults intentionally isolate themselves from intimate relationships. Their bodies might be rather freely available to others, but their true selves remain closely guarded. Perhaps a young man has been so hurt by a parent or former partner that he is simply unable to take the emotional risk involved in satisfactory interpersonal relationships. Perhaps a young woman is in the midst of an intentional, temporary "moratorium" on intimacy. She may be at a point where problems involved in breaking free of parents or choosing and preparing for a career make it easier for her not to "get involved." For these and other reasons, many young adults engage in superficial sexual relationships, turning away from the challenge of intimacy to become self-absorbed and to exclude others emotionally (Townsend, 1995).

### 14.1.1   Gender Differences in Intimacy

Some gender differences affect intimacy. Men, for example, feel more comfortable with sexual involvement in the absence of emotional involvement, while women in the same situation feel more emotionally vulnerable and have anxiety about their partner's lack of willingness to make an emotional investment in the relationship (Townsend, 1995). The more partners a woman has, the greater these feelings, while the opposite is true in men.

Women tend to express intimacy more verbally, whereas men tend to act out their feelings. Wood and Inman (1993) contend that textbooks (such as this one) have unfairly favored the feminine approach and devalued the masculine approach. They argue that the male approach is equally valid and that failing to recognize this fact impairs research, teaching, and our interpersonal relationships.

Some gender differences in intimacy are said to be influenced by hormonal differences (Ridley, 1993). From menarche to menopause, a woman's fluctuating hormone levels affect her emotions and attitudes about intimacy, which tend to be more communication-focused than men's. Men tend to experience a more steady, genitals-centered need for intimacy. Ridley (1993) suggests that these physically based gender differences cause much difficulty in heterosexual relationships when an assumption is made that there is no difference between men and women.

## 14.2 DATING

Humans are social beings who usually prefer companionship over being alone. We are also sexual beings who usually desire to spend at least some of our time with someone whom we find sexually attractive. When we are not committed to a current partnership, we try to satisfy these needs through dating. Beginning often in junior high school and continuing to the senior citizen center, dating remains a source of both great pleasure and some anxiety for many of us. Sometimes we date "casually" for the pleasure of the moment; sometimes we date "seriously" with partnership in mind.

Some of the issues we face in dating include meeting someone we will enjoy, asking for that first date, dating at work, sexual coercion, date abuse, and single parents' dating issues. Take a minute right now and complete "Where Do I Stand? An Assessment of Attitudes on Relationships."

### 14.2.1 Meeting Someone

In general, the most productive places to meet potential dates are places where people share a common interest with you. Most relationships begin at work, at school, at a place of religion, at a gym or fitness center, or in an organization or group pursuing a shared interest such as hiking, bicycling, art, music, acting, computing, or similar activities. "Friends of friends" are another common source of people to date.

### 14.2.2 Shyness

If you feel shy about meeting potential partners, don't feel alone. One survey found that 64 percent of heterosexual college students felt shy with the other sex (Grossman & McNamara, 1989). Social anxiety (shyness) is apparently a separate trait from general anxiety (Schroeder, 1995). Shy people react differently than others in romantic relationships. Shy women, compared to shy men, are more committed to making a relationship work, whereas shy males are quick to abandon a troubled relationship (Johnson et al., 1995).

When it comes to asking someone to go out with you, be direct. Skip all of the phony lines and cute

come-ons. Simply tell the person what you have in mind and ask whether he or she is interested in sharing that activity with you. If you are shy, try practicing this with a friend first.

### 14.2.3 Dating at Work

As we have mentioned, many relationships develop among coworkers. But workplace romance is a delicate subject. If the individuals involved are at different levels in the chain of command, there is the potential for sexual harassment. In any case, there is the potential for jealousy to create problems.

Employers differ in their policies or nonpolicies regarding romance between their employees. A fairly typical approach is that if a romance is between equals in the organization, if the participants act professionally at work, and if there is no disruption of productivity, management does not get involved (Brown & Allgeier, 1995; Pierce, Byrne & Aquinas, 1996). Nonetheless, if you are contemplating a workplace romance, keep in mind that when the romance ends, you both might still be working there and it might become quite uncomfortable for either or both of you at that point.

Because of common interests, lots of relationships develop among coworkers. But if individuals are at different levels in the organization, there is the possibility of sexual harasssment. Jealousy can also create problems.

---

**emotional isolation**     lacking intimate relationships

# WHERE DO I STAND?
## AN ASSESSMENT OF ATTITUDES ON RELATIONSHIPS

1. Rate on a scale of 0–10, each of the following characteristics of a potential partner for yourself, the importance of
   (0 = not important; 10 = extremely important):

   a. _____ Sexually attractive to you

   b. _____ Wealthy

   c. _____ Viewed as attractive by others

   d. _____ Cheerful

   e. _____ Intelligent

   f. _____ Well educated

   g. _____ Optimistic

   h. _____ Practical

   i. _____ Stable personality

   j. _____ Sexually monogamous

   k. _____ Ethnicity

   l. _____ Religious beliefs or nonbeliefs

   m. _____ Smoker or nonsmoker

   n. _____ Drinker or nondrinker

   o. _____ Age

   p. _____ Educational level attained

2. Which (if any) of these characteristics are so important that you would not consider a partnership with someone who lacked one of them, even if that person possessed all of the other characteristics listed?

3. Which of these traits *in yourself* do you think make *you* a desirable partner? Which do you feel have created problems or might create problems in a relationship? Even so, could you still be a good partner for someone?

4. Do you appear to be more attracted to someone with traits similar to your own or someone whose traits might be complementary to yours? Do you see any potential conflicts between the traits you rate highly and your own traits?

## 14.2.4 Lesbian and Gay Dating

Research on dating has predominantly addressed heterosexual dating. Consequently, there is less published information on lesbian and gay dating (Klinkenberg & Rose, 1994). In exploring gay and lesbian dating patterns, several studies analyzed the personals ads in newspapers. One study compared the ads of homosexual and heterosexual men and women (Gonzales & Meyers, 1993). In their ads, gay men emphasized physical characteristics the most and lesbians the least. Heterosexual women mentioned their attractiveness more often than lesbian women did. Gay men mentioned sexuality most often of the four groups. Heterosexuals of each sex were more likely than homosexuals of their sex to seek long-term relationships. Heterosexuals also made more mention of sincerity and financial security.

Another study compared ads placed by gay men before and after HIV emerged (Davidson, 1991). From 1978 to 1988, there was a significant increase in ads suggesting a concern for health as well as an increase in ads expressing rejection of stereotypical "gay behavior."

How do lesbian and gay dates compare with heterosexual dates? Dean Klinkenberg and Suzanna Rose (1994) explored the dating "scripts" for gay men and lesbian women, finding that gay men's scripts were more sexually oriented and less focused on emotions and intimacy than lesbian womens' scripts. Dating for both gay men and lesbian women was free of many traditional gender-typed roles and

# GO ASK ALICE

*Hi, Alice!*

*I don't know if this is the right place for this question but I'm gonna take my chances. Anyway, a few weeks ago I met this girl who I thought was the most attractive girl I've seen in a long time. So what did I do? I went up to her and talked to her for one mere minute! In that little chit-chat we neglected to introduce ourselves, and nothing substantial was talked about. Later that night, I did some detective work and found out her name and even an address and phone number! Well, two and a half weeks have passed and I still think the same about her but I don't have the guts or a plan of courtship. What should I do? She probably doesn't even remember me! I need your advice because I think I've finally seen my future wife! Well . . . not really . . . .*

*Hopeless*

Dear Hopeless,

What a dilemma! Rule of thumb for dating is that if you're really interested in someone, you should call two to three days after you first meet. Any sooner and you'll seem too eager; any longer and the other person might forget you. So, at the time of your writing, two and a half weeks after you met this woman, it might be too late. Alice's suggestion is to wait until another chance meeting with her, and not to let that one slip by. Probably the minute you stop thinking about her, she'll walk out in your path! Or, take the risk and just call her anyway.

*Dear Alice,*

*I am beginning my sophomore year at college. Last year I was disappointed to not become friendly with any women. I have been back a week and I'm looking to turn my situation around. I would like to start dating once and for all. Any suggestions?*

*More for the Sophomore*

Dear More for the Sophomore,

Alice assumes that you are looking for dating techniques? If so, the first thing you should know is that there is no one consistently successful way to "date." What IS consistent is that there is always some risk involved when you are the initiator of a dating relationship—so you will just have to take that risk and Go For It this semester. And although you shouldn't expect it, be prepared that whomever you ask might say no. This may or may not be a rejection of you per se; it may very well be that she doesn't want to go out with you right now for some reason. Don't let this discourage you—keep the confidence and try someone else with whom you think you might be compatible. When someone does agree to go out with you, choose somewhere you like to go and are comfortable in, and just spend a few hours getting to know each other on the first date. Don't feel that you have to find the "perfect" woman for you immediately (if ever); date a variety of people and learn which qualities you find attractive and which you just can't tolerate. This is a time for exploration—just be safe.

 http://www.mhhe.com/byer6

---

behaviors that characterize heterosexual dating (Klinkenberg & Rose, 1994). Lesbian and gay dates are often very similar to heterosexual dates in terms of activities such as restaurants, concerts, and the theater, but they can also be very different when they center around gay or lesbian bars or clubs.

## 14.2.5 Sexual Coercion

Dating frequently exposes a person to unwanted sexual advances. Many people, mainly women, are pressured into unwanted sexual activity, sometimes by physical force, but more often because of verbal pressure or a partner simply proceeding without asking for consent (Muehlenhard, Andrews, & Beal, 1996).

Sexual coercion in dating relationships has always existed, but until recent years the victims were expected to suffer in silence (McCormick, 1996). Today, sexual coercion is seen as a serious problem, with psychological, social, medical, and legal implications. It strips people of their sexual autonomy and can have long-term emotional and physical consequences. It impairs future ability to experience sexual pleasure and diminishes self-confidence and feelings of well-being.

Coercion exists along a continuum ranging from gentle verbal pressure to have sex to threatened or actual physical violence if sex is refused. Not surprisingly, published statistics on the incidence of sexual coercion vary with survey methods and how coercion is defined (Hogben, Byrne, & Hamburger, 1996). Laumann and associates (1994) reported that 22 percent of American women had been forced to have sex by a man, 1 percent of men had been forced to have sex by a woman, 2 percent of men had been forced to have sex by a man, and 0.3 percent of women had been forced by a woman. In another survey, 22 percent of the women and 16 percent of the men reported that they had been forced to engage in sexual intercourse on a date at least once (Struckman-Johnson, 1988). In a more recent study, 24 percent of men reported the use of sexual pressure or force by women and 4 percent by men (Struckman-Johnson & Struckman-Johnson, 1994).

How can a woman most effectively deal with a man's unwanted sexual advances when "saying no" does not work because the man does not believe her refusal or chooses to ignore it? Muehlenhard, Andrews, and Beal (1996) have extensively researched this question. Here are a few of their findings:

▐ Open communication about sexual limits, stated very early in the date, may be effective in preventing a man from making unwanted sexual advances and in reducing the chance that the man will feel that he has been "led on" when the woman subsequently refuses to have sex with him.

▐ If the man does make unwanted sexual advances, telling him that she cares about him but wants to wait until the relationship is stronger may cause him to stop the advances while still maintaining a positive relationship.

▐ If he still persists, the woman can state that any further advance will be termed sexual assault or rape and that the police will be informed.

▐ If he still does not stop, forceful responses such as screaming, biting, and fighting may work. If they don't work, and rape occurs, remember that the fault lies with the rapist, not the victim.

## 14.2.6 Date Abuse

It may seem difficult to believe, but physical abuse occurs in the dating relationships of 20 to 30 percent of college students (Cate, 1989). In most cases the aggressor is male and the victim female, although the opposite happens more often than you might think. Males who are abused by females are often very reluctant to tell anyone. Abuse also occurs in gay and lesbian partnerships.

Among abused women, the most frequent kinds of abuse are being pushed (reported by 67 percent of abused women), grabbed (52 percent), restrained (41

percent), and hit (40 percent) (Mahlstedt & Keeny, 1993). Abuse can also consist of threatening to do bodily harm or inflicting verbal abuse. Sometimes the scars of a purely psychological abuse take longer to heal than the scars of physical abuse.

Most dating relationships that involve violence also have periods of good times that, unfortunately, serve to keep the couple together. People who are abused while dating are at high risk of being chronically and severely abused and tend not to report the abuse to authorities (Graham et al., 1995).

Why would someone stay with an abusive partner? The "Stockholm Syndrome" (bonding with an abusive partner) is characterized by depression, low self-esteem, loss of sense of self, and the feeling that one cannot survive without the abusive partner's love (Graham et al., 1995).

What causes abuse in dating relationships? A survey of the literature revealed several recurrent themes:

1. *The abuser needs to feel in control (to dominate)* (Gagné & Lavoie, 1993; Hockenberry & Billingham, 1993; Pape & Arias, 1995; Stickel & Ellis, 1993).
2. *The abuser blames the abused for the violence* (Dutton, 1995; Gagné & Lavoie, 1993; LeJeune & Follette, 1994).
3. *Drug and alcohol abuse among couples involved in close relationships is often associated with the physical abuse of one of the partners* (Gagné & Lavoie, 1993; LeJeune & Follette, 1994).
4. *Abusive women are often motivated by a desire for revenge* (Gagné & Lavoie, 1993).
5. *The cycle of violence* Both the abused and the abuser are likely to be from families where children were physically abused and/or spouse abuse occurred. (Dutton, 1995).
6. *Both the abused and the abuser tend to have lower self-esteem than people who are not involved in abuse* (Graham et al., 1995).
7. *Gender-role attitudes* Men who abuse women tend to have rigid, traditional views about gender roles.

Date abuse should not be taken lightly. Should the relationship become long-term, the abuse will likely escalate rather than abate. If professional counseling cannot resolve the abuse or if either party is unwilling to participate in counseling, the abused person should break off the relationship.

Karen Rosen and Sandra Stith (1995) studied young women who had succeeded in extracting themselves from abusive dating relationships. Their subjects had been abused for three months to five

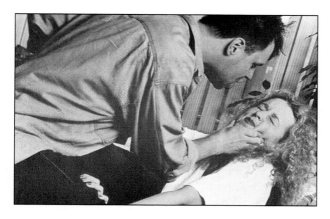

Physical abuse occurs in 20 to 30 percent of college students' dating relationships. Some of the causes include the need to dominate, alcohol and other drug abuse, revenge, low self-esteem, and gender-role attitudes.

years. They had endured grabbing, punching, beatings, and murder threats. Factors that had led to their terminating abusive relationships included, more or less in order, "seeds of doubt," turning points, reappraisals, objective reflections, self-reclaiming actions, and "last straw" events.

The abused may need assistance to end the harmful relationship. Even in the most abusive relationship, strong bonds of dependency must be broken. A self-help group or a counselor can provide the necessary support to help the abused person make difficult decisions and follow through on them.

### 14.2.7 Single Parents' Dating

At some point, most single parents, whether never-married or formerly married, want to fulfill their need for adult companionship through dating. The impact on children of mom's or dad's dating has to be considered. Children in single-parent homes often feel insecure about their parent's dating unless it is carefully explained to them (Pickhardt, 1996).

Early dating should be explained as purely social and recreational, satisfying the parent's need for adult companionship. It does not replace or diminish the parent's desire for her or his child's companionship. Should a relationship become serious and romantic, then the children should be told that this is now a significant relationship, satisfying the parent's need for adult love (Ferguson & Dickson, 1995). Still, the children must understand that it does not in any way replace or diminish the parent's love for his or her child.

Pickhardt (1996) suggests *not* including children on early or social dates because the children might assume that the relationship is serious when it is not. If they begin to develop affection for the parent's companion, a failure of that relationship to flourish can bring them disappointment and a sense of loss.

For teenage children, a parent's dating raises additional concerns. Just when the children are trying to deal with their own sexuality and dating issues, now their parent is dating too. Teenage children are quite aware of the sexual implications of their parent's dating and might worry about whether the person their parent is dating is safe to be with.

Children of any age feel quite threatened by the possibility (real or imagined) of losing their parent or of having to share their parent's love or attention with someone new (Ferguson & Dickson, 1995). And often the children have retained a hope that their biological parents will get back together and a new partner seems certain to "put the last brick in the wall" on that relationship.

A single parent can avoid or minimize many of these problems by carefully talking with her or his children (Ferguson & Dickson, 1995). The parent can provide explanations of the dating and ask frequently for the children's reactions to and questions about the parent's dating.

## 14.3 LIFESTYLES

We North Americans are a diverse group with a diversity of lifestyles. We are straight, bisexual, gay, and lesbian. We live alone, we cohabit, we marry, we divorce, we marry again. This section will examine some of the ways we live.

### 14.3.1 Living Alone

One of the significant changes in American living habits in recent years has been the sharp increase in the number of people living by themselves (Glick, 1994). Who are these people? Some have never been married. Some are divorced, widowed, or married and living separately. Some live alone by choice, some by necessity. Some find it a highly rewarding lifestyle; many do not. Like other lifestyles, living alone has its advantages and disadvantages.

One advantage of living alone is that it offers more freedom than any other lifestyle. There is usually plenty of time to travel, to develop talents and skills, to enjoy hobbies, to relax, to entertain and be entertained, and to discover one's own individuality. For some self-sufficient people, living alone offers the greatest potential for personal fulfillment of all the lifestyles. Many who live alone are not at all bothered by loneliness (Burnley & Kurth, 1992).

Other people, however, find coming home to an empty house or apartment, eating alone, or sleeping alone difficult and depressing (Mastekaasa, 1995).

Some even remain in relationships that are unproductive and unfulfilling only because they cannot conceive that living alone can be anything but a lonely, negative experience. It does not have to be that way. Regardless of whether an individual lives alone by choice or necessity, viewing it as a positive lifestyle is the first step toward making it such.

Loneliness is the most common complaint about living alone. Humans are basically social beings who depend upon each other for fulfillment of many needs. Thus, those who live alone must make a special effort to create an adequate social support system (Glick, 1994). Actually, many people who are married or otherwise living with one or more other people are just as lonely as people who live alone (Burnley & Kurth, 1992). These suggestions for combating loneliness are valid for people who live alone or with someone.

- *Start with a positive attitude.* When you are lonely, it is easy to wallow in self-pity, viewing loneliness as a permanent condition. For many, this attitude has led to alcoholism and other chemical dependencies. Instead, recognize loneliness as only temporary and get started doing something about it.

- *Avoid do-nothing behavior patterns* such as sleeping too much, watching too much TV, abusing alcohol or other drugs, or sitting around and eating. Keep busy! Regardless of their life situations, busy people are always happier than bored, inactive people.

- *Take the initiative in meeting people.* Don't wait for others to come to you; they may be just as shy as you are. Push yourself to be more outgoing.

- *Create companionship.* Create a network of good friends by becoming involved in organizations where people share common interests. The possibilities are virtually endless. Hobby groups, amateur sports leagues, fitness centers, music performance or appreciation groups, religious organizations, community service groups, and professional or career-related organizations are just a sampling of places where companionship is available and where you would be very welcome.

- *Develop intimate relationships.* Going beyond casual companionship, intimate relationships form your emotional support system, seeing you through your difficult times and allowing you to share your joys. Intimate relationships, of which sex is not necessarily a part, can be formed with friends, neighbors, coworkers, relatives, or anyone else. They are one of the best remedies for loneliness.

## 14.3.2 Sharing Accommodations

Rather than live alone, many people prefer some form of roommate or housemate arrangement. Nonsexual shared housing arrangements commonly include one or both genders. In addition to the obvious economic advantages of shared housing, companionship is another big advantage over living alone.

In choosing roommates, make sure that everyone's habits are fairly compatible. Don't overlook smoking habits, similar degrees of neatness or sloth, and attitudes about parties and people sleeping over. A regular source of rent money is mandatory.

## 14.3.3 Cohabitation

**Cohabitation** usually refers to unmarried persons living together in a sexual relationship. Cohabitation is more prevalent today in all socioeconomic strata and all age groups in the United States than it was in the past. About one-third of all people cohabit at some time in their lives (National Center for Health Statistics, 1991).

People who cohabit are heterosexual, lesbian, gay, bisexual, never-married, divorced, and widowed. What all of these people have in common is the desire to live with someone rather than alone. People live together to gain intimacy, companionship, and security, and for economic and convenience reasons. Gay and lesbian people might prefer a more formal marriage arrangement, but same-sex marriage is not legal in most states (see "At Issue: Same-Sex Marriages").

Some differences have been identified between university students who do or do not choose to cohabit. Those who cohabit are older, less religious, hold more liberal sexual attitudes, and have less traditional views of marriage and gender roles (Huffman et al., 1994).

When cohabitation was in the process of becoming more prevalent during the 1960s and 1970s, people tended to wonder what its long-term effects might be. It was often viewed as "trial marriage" that might reduce the incidence of subsequent unhappy marriages. Cohabitation is now usually viewed by its participants as a different kind of relationship. Younger people view cohabitation as being well suited to a time in life when a person is breaking away from close family ties and is developing autonomy (Nicole & Baldwin, 1995). Cohabitation is also attractive to divorced or widowed people who may be reluctant to remarry but who still desire the benefits of living with someone (Mastekaasa, 1994).

Steven Nock (1995a) compared the relationships of 2,493 married couples and 499 heterosexual cohabiting couples. The cohabiting couples expressed lower levels of commitment to their relationships and lower levels of happiness in their relationships

# AT ISSUE

## SAME-SEX MARRIAGES

Same-sex marriage became a political issue in 1990 when a gay male couple and two lesbian couples stepped up to the counter at the Health Department in Honolulu to request marriage licenses. As expected, their applications were denied. The three couples appealed their case to the Hawaii state Supreme Court.

Hawaii's Supreme Court, in May 1993, ruled 3–1 that the state's exclusion of same-sex couples from marital status might be unconstitutional because it amounts to sex discrimination, unless the state can prove a "compelling interest" to prohibit it. A trial took place in September 1996. In a decision announced on 3 December 1996, Judge Kevin S. C. Chang ruled that the state had failed to prove that it had a compelling interest in preventing same-sex marriages. The judge noted that much research has shown that same-sex parents are just as successful in raising children as traditional married couples are.

Same-sex marriage became a national issue because federal law requires all states to recognize a marriage that takes place in any state. One state offering same-sex marriage could basically provide this service for the entire nation. Not surprisingly, some people favor allowing same-sex marriage and others are in opposition. Each side is now scrambling to secure its position.

Gay and lesbian rights organizations are encouraging widespread adoption of the following resolution:

> Because marriage is a basic human right and an individual personal choice, RESOLVED, the State should not interfere with same-gender couples who choose to marry and share fully and equally in the rights, responsibilities, and commitment of civil marriage.

Conservative groups with names such as Family Research Council, Alliance for Traditional Marriage, and Traditional Values Coalition have launched a counter campaign to deny same-sex marriage rights. Their resolution reads:

> WHEREAS marriage is an essential element in the foundation of a healthy society, and WHEREAS government has a duty to protect that foundation, RESOLVED, the State should not legitimize same-sex relationships by legalizing same-sex "marriage" but should continue to reserve the special sanction of civil marriage for one man and one woman as husband and wife.

Legislation banning same-sex marriages was introduced in 37 states during 1995 and 1996 and passed in 16 of those states. In two additional states, same-sex marriages were prohibited by executive order of the governors. At the federal level, the Defense of Marriage Act, signed by President Clinton in September 1996 denies federal benefits to same-sex couples and allows states to ignore the same-sex marriages of another state.

In 1999 the state of Hawaii effectively reversed it's position with the approval of a constitutional amendment banning gay marriages. More recently, however, the Vermont Supreme Court ruled that same-sex couples are entitled to the same benefits and protections as married, heterosexual couples. Activists hope this will be a springboard for legalization of same-sex marriages.

---

compared to the married couples. Hispanic cohabiting couples were less satisfied than either African American or non-Hispanic white couples, which Nock (1995a) attributed to the lack of social support among Hispanic people for cohabitation.

There are certain practical considerations for a cohabiting couple. A couple living together is not usually recognized as an economic unit in the same manner as a married couple. However, they can own property jointly, and they can incur debts and obligations jointly. They file their income tax separately.

Most of the difficult economic questions arise if the living-together relationship is terminated. Depending on how a title to items purchased jointly has been registered or recorded, a fair and equitable division of property may or may not occur. Further, there have been well-publicized cases of "palimony" being granted to one partner when she or he has been financially supported by the other. It is strongly recommended that individuals considering cohabitation engage an attorney to draw up a binding financial agreement to protect the rights of both parties.

## 14.3.4   Marriage

Several long-term trends are apparent in marriage statistics. The first is that more people are going throughout life without ever marrying. The percentage of people expected to marry at least once in their

| cohabitation | usually, unmarried persons living together in a sexual relationship |

lives dropped from 95 percent in the early 1980s to about 71 percent of women and 70 percent of men in the nineties (Clarke, 1995b).

Several changes account for the lower percentage of people now predicted to marry eventually. There is less social pressure to marry; people feel more free to remain single if they so choose. There is less social stigma concerning single motherhood; many women now choose to have children without being married. Opportunities for women to be self-sufficient have improved; fewer women feel the need to marry for financial security.

Another trend is that when people do marry, the average age at which they do so has increased. The median age at first marriage is about 25.0 years for brides and about 26.9 years for grooms, up from 20.5 years and 22.4 years in 1972 (Clarke, 1995b).

Although somewhat fewer people are marrying, and those who do marry later, marriage remains the preferred way of life for many Americans. Let's examine some possible reasons for this.

## Effects of Marriage

In general, it is highly beneficial to be married (Myers, 1992). On the average, married people are happier by self-ratings, healthier, and live longer than people who have never been married or who are divorced or widowed. Marriage improves self-esteem in women (Elliott, 1996). Not surprisingly, people who regard their marriage as happy have a greater sense of general well-being than those who are dissatisfied with their marriage (James, Tucker, & Mitchell-Kernan, 1996).

Let's look more closely at relationships between marriage and longevity. In an American study that followed 1,077 people for over 40 years, those who had been consistently married lived longer than those who had been married, divorced, and remarried, but not longer than those who never married (Tucker et al., 1996). In a British study of men aged 40 to 64 years, all groups of unmarried men had higher death rates than married men. Compared to married men of the same age, never-married men had unusually high rates of violent and accidental deaths; divorced or separated men had higher rates of cancer deaths; and widowed men had higher rates of death from coronary disease (Ben-Shlomo et al., 1993).

Like any statistical association, the association of marriage with health and happiness is subject to interpretation. Another possible interpretation is that healthy, happy people are more likely to get married or stay married than are unhealthy or unhappy people.

Assuming that marriage is a cause of happiness rather than an effect, part of why marriage makes people happy is simply living with someone else rather than living alone. There are definite psychological advantages in having someone to share your joys and sorrows and for general companionship.

There are, however, further psychological benefits of marriage derived from one's sense of mutual commitment and public recognition of that commitment. This is apparently what most distinguishes marriage from cohabitation (Nock, 1995a).

## Personal Readiness for Marriage

Although marriage holds the potential for great happiness, almost half of all marriages end in divorce (National Center for Health Statistics, 1998), and some of the rest are maintained more for convenience than out of desire. Obviously, you need to be very careful about who, when, and even whether you marry.

Marriage is definitely not for everyone. Some people are not yet ready for marriage in terms of their social or emotional maturity. Others have particular personality types or lifestyles that would make it very difficult for their marriage to succeed. Those who hold little expectation of success in marriage are probably not ready to marry, nor are those who would demand perfection in their marriage. There is no totally reliable way to know who is ready for marriage, but the following criteria may be helpful.

*Age:* Certainly not everyone at a particular chronological age has the same degree of maturity. Yet age at the time of marriage is one of the most reliable predictors of the success of a marriage.

Many studies have shown that the level of satisfaction and success in marriage increases with the age of the partners at the time of marriage. Marriages where both partners are quite young, perhaps under age twenty, are particularly likely to be unhappy. U.S. Center for Health Statistics figures reveal that three out of four teenage marriages fail (Clarke, 1995a).

One source of the problems in young marriages is that many people experience considerable growth in their value systems between the ages of sixteen and twenty-four. During this period, a person's interests, tastes, ideals, standards, and goals often undergo a complete change. A couple might grow in different directions, or one might grow while the other remains static. Eventually they may have too little in common to continue their relationship.

*Autonomy:* **Autonomy**, meaning independence and capacity for self-direction, is an important personal characteristic for success in marriage and life in general (Jenkins, 1996). It includes the ability to set one's own goals and to work toward achieving them. In marriage, autonomy enables each partner to function well as an individual and as part of a couple.

Autonomous people achieve greater individual fulfillment and self-actualization (Bordages, 1989). They are able to offer more to a marriage relationship and, through their independence, remain more interesting to their partners. Autonomy prevents you from being an overly dependent "clinging vine," which is unpleasant for both partners in a relationship. To marry before your autonomy develops is to risk never becoming autonomous. You simply transfer your dependencies from your parents to your spouse.

*Emotional Maturity:* In a successful marriage, each partner contributes to the need fulfillment of the other (Russell & Wells, 1994b). One measure of emotional maturity is how well a person has developed the means of satisfying his or her own emotional needs without exploiting others in the process. Anyone with a number of unfulfilled needs is going to have trouble contributing to a partner's need fulfillment.

Even the most enthusiastic supporters of marriage agree that maintaining a smoothly working marital relationship is not often easy. Marriage requires ongoing patience, tolerance, and compromise. All of these require a good measure of emotional maturity.

*Social Maturity:* Social maturity develops through social interaction, such as dating many different individuals. Dating provides a basis for the selection of a marriage mate and helps to satisfy social and sexual curiosity.

Another way of developing social maturity is to experience a period of single, independent life before marriage, a time of freedom between the former dependence on parents and the future responsibilities of marriage. Living away from parents for a time is a good way to get to know oneself, to develop social competency, and to learn to manage one's own affairs. On the other hand, given today's high rents and other living expenses, young people often remain in their parents' homes out of necessity even though they might prefer to be out on their own. Even in this situation, considerable growth is possible as the young person learns to manage her or his financial and social affairs with increasing independence.

*Flexibility:* Successful marriage always requires compromise. Two people cannot always have exactly the same interests, tastes, needs, and desires at the same time. Ideally, two partners are fairly similar in their preferences. Also ideally, each partner is willing to meet the other halfway when compromise is necessary. A good marriage does not result when one partner does all of the compromising and the other does little or none. In this situation, hostilities build quickly and will certainly be expressed—if not

openly, then in numerous other ways, such as sexual problems, financial mismanagement, and extramarital affairs. People who find compromise difficult might seriously consider remaining single.

## Choosing a Marital Partner

For most of us there are literally thousands of people who would be good choices for marital partners. (There is no such thing as a "one and only" love.) At the same time, of course, there are thousands of other people who would be very poor marital choices. The desirability of any potential partner depends on his or her personal traits and how those traits interact with your own.

*Personality Traits:* By far the most important characteristic in a potential marriage partner is her or his personality. Traits that produce happy marriages include optimism, a sense of humor, an honest concern for the needs of others, a sense of ethics, the ability to adjust easily to changes in conditions, and freedom from severe emotional problems such as extreme anxiety, depression, and jealousy. The single most important emotional characteristic and the basis for most other desirable characteristics, however, is well-developed self-esteem. Conversely, the traits most seen in people in therapy for marital problems include high risk-taking; low self-esteem; being shrewd, self-serving, and manipulative; being tense, anxious, worrisome, and suspicious; being fussy and easily frustrated; and having an overriding desire for approval (Craig & Olson, 1995). In another study, hostility and defensiveness were identified as traits causing marital conflicts (Newton et al., 1995).

*Mutual Need Satisfaction:* A happy and lasting marriage is one in which the needs of each individual are adequately fulfilled. Although the idea may not appeal to romantics, the basic reason people marry is to satisfy various needs: love, companionship, sex, self-esteem, security, and so forth. Usually without being consciously aware of what we are doing, we tend to be attracted to people we perceive as being best able to satisfy our needs. Our perception may or may not be accurate. Only through a long period of interaction in a variety of situations (both pleasant and unpleasant) can two people learn whether they are really able to fulfill each other's needs.

At the same time, many marriages fail because one or both partners unreasonably expect the other to fulfill *all* of his or her needs. Many needs just cannot be fulfilled by someone else. For example, it is unrealistic to expect another person to ensure your

---

**autonomy** (aw-ton´ō-mē)  independence and capacity for self-direction

happiness. Certainly, someone else can contribute to your happiness, but true happiness must come from within. Similarly, although a caring partner can contribute to your self-esteem, true feelings of personal adequacy can only arise within yourself.

*Communication:* Effective communication is essential to a smoothly working marital partnership. If either partner is unable to communicate needs, desires, preferences, thoughts, and feelings to the other, serious difficulties are likely to develop.

For example, before marriage a couple needs to discuss money management—where the money is to come from and how it is to be spent. Free and open communication on sexual matters can help prevent conflict in this critical area.

A lack of open communication is usually indicative of a relationship that lacks emotional intimacy. Such a relationship is a weak basis upon which to build a marriage.

*Agreement Concerning Parenthood:* Most people hold strong feelings regarding parenthood. Some place a high value on raising children; others are certain that they wish to remain childless. Some want one child; some want more. Agreement on parenthood is crucial between two people considering marriage. Although many compromises are necessary in every marriage, there is really no satisfactory compromise between someone who strongly desires to raise children and someone who truly wants to remain childless. Any couple thinking about marriage will want to explore this topic in an open, honest manner. If there are to be children, it is desirable for a couple to hold similar feelings on how the children are to be raised, a major source of conflict in many marriages. Many couples who opt for voluntary childlessness find satisfying alternative ways to be involved with young people.

## Marital Adjustments

When two people marry, each assumes a new role, that of "wife" or "husband." This new role requires more personal, social, economic, and sexual adjustments than most unmarried people anticipate.

*Adjustments to Each Other:* Even after several years of cohabitation, the new relationship of marriage usually demands some reevaluation of old patterns of interaction. Marriage usually implies a new level of commitment (Nock, 1995a). Where before partners may have felt they could easily walk out the door if they wanted to, now there may be an uncomfortable feeling of being tied down. Some of the difficult adjustments in many marriages concern patterns of dominance, dependence versus independence, self-assertion versus compromise, and prioritizing one's own needs versus the possibly conflicting needs of one's partner.

*Social Adjustments:* People, even relatives and old friends, suddenly relate to a newly married person in a different manner. Social activity now more often involves the couple as a unit rather than as individuals. At the same time as marriage creates new social opportunities, it may also seem to limit one's social activities. Newly married people often find that they, as individuals, are no longer included in activities and primarily single social groups in which they might still wish to be involved.

In-law relationships also may call for some adjustments. Parents may have difficulty in accepting a new son- or daughter-in-law or in releasing their hold on their own son or daughter.

*Economic Adjustments:* Though state laws vary, a married couple is usually viewed as being an economic unit beyond the economic roles of each individual. For example, in "community property" states, the earnings of either partner are considered to belong equally to both and financial obligations made by either partner are binding upon both. Conflicts arise when partners are reluctant to pool their earnings or when one partner disapproves of the other's spending habits (Burgoyne & Lewis, 1994). Serious disagreements over money often reflect more basic conflicts in the partnership, such as questions of dominance and dependency (Siegel, 1990; Smith, 1992).

*Sexual Adjustments:* The sexual success of a marriage depends both on the individual characteristics of the partners and on how the partners interact with each other. Significant individual characteristics include self-esteem, assertiveness, concern for the partner, and freedom from sexual anxieties or inhibitions. People whose childhood and adolescent sexual experiences were of a positive nature tend to make a more successful adult sexual adjustment than those with a history of negative sexual experiences (Bauserman & Davis, 1996).

Significant characteristics of the partnership include open and honest communication, shared emotional intimacy, and freedom from hostilities and conflicts, such as struggles for dominance. A good sexual relationship is generally assured if the two partners are relatively free of individual emotional conflicts or sexual inhibitions and enjoy a mutually rewarding total relationship.

## 14.3.5 Gay and Lesbian Partnerships

Lesbian and gay people look to their partnerships to fulfill the same needs—emotional and sexual intimacy, companionship, security, self-esteem, and so

Much of what is true of heterosexual partnerships is true of gay and lesbian couples as well. Lesbian and gay people look to their partnerships to fulfill the same needs as straight people do.

forth—as straight people do. Most of what is true of heterosexual partnerships is true of lesbian and gay partnerships as well. Here we will mention a few differences.

## Gender Differences versus Orientation Differences

Are differences between heterosexual and homosexual partnerships the result of sexual orientation or of the gender of the partners? Quite a few studies have addressed this issue, and the answer appears to be "both of the above."

Some attitudes toward sex are apparently more influenced by orientation and some more by gender. In one study, gay men and lesbian women exhibited more positive attitudes on communication with a sex partner and commitment issues, more sexual self-understanding, and less sexual guilt (Crowden & Koch, 1995). In the same study, however, gender was the main determining factor on attitudes related to sexual performance concerns, with males more concerned than females, regardless of sexual orientation.

Another major study indicated that lesbian women and lesbian couples have more in common with heterosexual women than with gay men, leading to the conclusion that gender is more important than orientation in lesbian sexuality (Schreurs, 1993). The same study also found that lesbian couples have sex less often than either gay male couples or heterosexual couples, but are more satisfied with their sex life.

Comparing women in lesbian and heterosexual couples, Rosenbluth and Steil (1995) found that the unequal power that characterizes many heterosexual couples (the male being more powerful) leads to different communication patterns for the woman and the man. Lesbian couples are able to use more direct and bilateral communication strategies, while heterosexual women must more often use indirect communication. The outcome is that heterosexual couples, in addition to having less effective communication, have a lower level of intimacy than lesbian couples.

## Lack of Role Models

Some differences between heterosexuals and homosexuals might relate to a lack of role models for successful lesbian or gay relationships (Berzon, 1992a; Isensee, 1990). Many heterosexual people grow up with role models of successful heterosexual partnerships, but few gay or lesbian people grow up with homosexual role models. Many people's exposure to lesbian and gay couples living and coping together on a daily basis is very limited, and the media don't offer much help either. We see few gay and lesbian partnerships portrayed realistically.

## Homophobia

**Homophobia** is the fear of homosexuality. Among heterosexuals, homophobia results in an aversion to or prejudice against homosexual people.

Internalized homophobia clouds some lesbian and gay partnerships. Whenever a group is discriminated against, some of its members might internalize a negative self-image. Most individual members of ethnic groups that suffer from discrimination at least grow up with their families and ethnic communities for support, but, once again, most gay and lesbian people grow up in heterosexual families in primarily heterosexual communities. After so many years of hearing antigay and antilesbian comments, some gays and lesbians accept the idea that perhaps their sexuality is inferior to heterosexuality (Berzon, 1992a; Isensee, 1990). This feeling, along with what is sometimes a realistic fear of retaliation from homophobic employers, coworkers, family members, and others, forces many lesbian and gay people to keep their relationships secret. The resulting social isolation cuts off many avenues of support enjoyed by heterosexual partnerships and reinforces the internalized homophobia.

## Social Influences

Males and females, regardless of their sexual orientation, are socialized differently and this difference is reflected in their relationships, especially in same-sex partnerships (Berzon, 1992a). Males are conditioned by society to be strong, competitive, independent, and sexually aggressive. Relationship skills are secondary

| | |
|---|---|
| **homophobia** | fear of homosexuality |

to the ability to win, earn, achieve, make sexual conquests, and appear strong. Put two males together in a partnership, and they may spend a lot of energy competing with each other. The competition can be over almost anything—physical strength, sexual attractiveness or ability, intelligence, income—but the outcome is the same: the competition prevents the development of emotional intimacy in the relationship.

Females, in contrast, are socialized with emphasis on relationship skills. They are conditioned to equate being okay with acquiring and hanging on to a mate. Thus, many lesbian couples put a lot of emphasis on nurturing the relationship. This often gives lesbian women more stable relationships than those of gay males, but also sometimes creates an overdependency on the relationship for personal validation (Berzon, 1992a). The thought of losing a partner can be very threatening and jealousy can be a problem.

### Conflicts about Openness

Lesbian and gay couples can experience conflict when partners are at different stages in the coming-out process (Toder, 1992). The partner who is more open about her or his sexual orientation may become frustrated with the partner who prefers to be more secretive. Conflicts may arise over participation in the gay or lesbian social community, or over relationships with family members (Ben-Ari, 1995).

Becoming involved in the local gay or lesbian community is very beneficial to a same-sex partnership (Berzon, 1992a; Isensee, 1990; Toder, 1992). For those still struggling to accept their sexual orientation, socializing with other lesbian or gay people and getting to know them as whole people helps overcome any internalized homophobia and reduce any sense of differentness or isolation. For those who have lacked role models for gay or lesbian partnerships, the gay or lesbian community can provide many examples of long-term loving partnerships. There is opportunity to exchange ideas and gain insights on ways of dealing with the issues that are unique to same-sex partnerships. And, finally, each individual can gain a new sense of pride as an out-of-the-closet gay man or lesbian woman and bring this pride to their couple relationship.

## 14.3.6 Sexual Dynamics in Partnerships

The desire for sexual activity varies considerably among different people. Some strongly desire sexual pleasure daily or more often. Others are satisfied with much less frequent activity.

For most individuals, sexual interest in a partner is greater when the partners are getting along well and reduced when they are in a state of conflict. Fur-ther, the sexual interest of any individual tends to vary with his or her own emotional and hormonal state. Most people are more sexually interested and responsive during periods of emotional well-being (Nelson, Hill-Barlow, & Benedict, 1994). Some, however, respond to stress and anxiety by increased desire for sexual release (Morokoff & Gillilland, 1993). All of these variables ensure that in almost any relationship there will be times when one partner desires sexual activity but the other is uninterested.

### Frequency of Sexual Activity

Frequency of sexual activity can become a major source of conflict in a relationship. Ideally, each partner can compromise to some extent, and a mutually satisfactory frequency of sexual activity can be achieved. This does not always happen, though. Sometimes the giving or withholding of sexual favors is used as a bargaining device—a barter. Some relationships deteriorate into a struggle for dominance; each partner wants to be the one to initiate sexual activity and might refuse to take part if the other takes the initiative. Obviously, in situations such as these, sexual frequency is not the real issue. It is merely the battleground on which basic relationship conflicts are fought. If those conflicts can be resolved, issues of sexual frequency usually resolve themselves (Hurlbert & Apt, 1994).

### Time of Sexual Activity

Many of us are primarily morning people or night people. This can cause some people to have a definite preference for sexual activity at a particular time—early morning, afternoon, or late at night. Males, whose testosterone level is highest in the morning, often prefer to have sex upon awakening. Females often prefer evening sex, though there are many exceptions to these generalizations.

Generally, if the overall relationship is sound, a couple can agree on a mutually acceptable time for sexual pleasuring. As with sexual frequency, however, basic power conflicts between a couple may emerge as disagreements on when sexual activity should occur.

### Choice of Sexual Activities

Not all couples can agree on just what specific sexual activities and techniques they want to enjoy. Some people are eager to try almost any form of sexual activity. Others, perhaps coming from more sexually restrictive backgrounds, feel comfortable with a more limited sexual repertoire.

As with the previously discussed conflicts, those concerning specific sexual practices are usually not too disruptive to a strong total relationship. In a relationship with such basic conflicts as struggles for dominance, however, issues such as oral or anal sex, choice of positions, contraceptive choices, and countless other technical matters can be severe impediments to pleasant lovemaking. Like money, sex is a common battlefield where the core conflicts in a relationship are fought out (Henderson-King & Veroff, 1994).

### Nonsexual Attention

In some relationships, one partner ignores the other partner's needs for attention and affection except when sex is desired. This often results in the ignored partner feeling used and may create general hostility in the relationship.

Most people, especially women, are more easily aroused in the context of an emotionally intimate relationship (Giles, 1994; Hurlbert & Apt, 1994). It is important for partners to spend time together in nonsexual activities, such as relaxed dining, conversation, and enjoying shared interests. Both partners can feel acceptance as total people rather than mere sexual objects. Nonsexual activities improve and strengthen not only the sexual relationship but the total relationship as well.

## 14.3.7 Monogamy and Nonmonogamy

Sexual exclusivity (**monogamy**) often becomes an issue in "committed" relationships, including cohabitation, marriage, and gay and lesbian partnerships. The expectation of sexual exclusivity is typical, unless other agreements have been made. Regardless of this expectation, the fact is that within a few years, some relationships become **nonmonogamous**—one or both partners has outside sexual partnerships ("affairs").

Statistics on affairs are notoriously unreliable. Some people lie to cover up affairs they have had, while others fabricate affairs that never took place. In a large national survey of affairs by married people, about 21 percent of all men surveyed and 11 percent of all women surveyed had *ever* been unfaithful. The percentage rose with increasing age (more time to have had an affair), peaking at 37 percent of men aged 54 to 63 and 20 percent of women aged 44 to 53 (Adler, 1996). Infidelity rates for the most recent twelve-month period were 4.7 percent for men and 2.1 percent for women. Higher rates of affairs were associated with remarried people, lower income levels, urban residence, and *either* less than high school education *or* having a postgraduate degree (Adler, 1996).

In another large survey (the National AIDS Behavioral Survey), among married people, extramarital sex within the last year was reported by 2.9

Various statistics are published on the incidence of extramarital sex. One alarming study showed that condoms are used in only 12 percent of affairs, indicating a great potential for disease transmission.

percent of men and 1.5 percent of women in a national sample (Choi, Catania, & Dolcini, 1994). Among those who reported extramarital sex, only 8 percent always used condoms with their primary partners and only 12 percent always used condoms with their secondary partners, indicating a great potential for disease transmission.

Even in the age of HIV, gay men are less likely than lesbian women or heterosexual men or women to hold the expectation of monogamy. A British survey of 387 gay men revealed that the most common partnership arrangement was an "open" (nonexclusive) relationship (Hickson et al., 1992).

There is some controversy in the lesbian community over monogamy. Some members of the radical lesbian-feminist community believe that nonmonogamy is more liberated and healthy for women than monogamy (Toder, 1992). The basic argument is that enforced monogamy has long been used to regulate women's behavior as the "property" of men. Further, monogamy is seen as fostering jealousy, possessiveness, and dependency and creating closed units of two women, thus setting artificial and unnecessary limits on their growth and personal development through limiting their relations with other women.

| | |
|---|---|
| **monogamy** (ma-nog´a-mē) | having only one sexual partner |
| **nonmonogamy** (non´ma-nog´a-mē) | having more than one sexual partner |

## Attitudes on Affairs

Gender differences exist in how people feel about infidelity. Heterosexual men place more importance on their partner's sexual faithfulness than on their own, while women place an equal value on faithfulness for both partners (Regan & Sprecher, 1995). A survey of 566 undergraduates compared their reactions to sexual infidelity (having sex with another person) versus emotional infidelity (loving another person). Men reacted more strongly to sexual infidelity of a partner while women reacted more strongly to emotional infidelity (Buss et al., 1992).

In another study of college students, men rated infidelity as more acceptable in both dating and marriage relationships than did women. Both genders rated infidelity as more acceptable when dating than when married. Self-esteem ratings were higher in both genders for students who had not been unfaithful than for those who had (Sheppard, Nelson, & Andreoli-Mathie, 1995).

Finally, interviews of 45 young (ages 23–36 years) married adults on their attitudes about extramarital sex revealed the following (Wiederman & Allgeier, 1996):

▌ 62 percent had discussed with their spouse the acceptability of an affair and, of those, 96 percent had agreed on goal of mutual monogamy.

▌ 87 percent said that extramarital sex would never be acceptable for themselves; 78 percent said that it would never be acceptable for their partners.

▌ Among the 22 percent who said that their partner's affair would be acceptable, the circumstances of acceptability included his or her love for another person, physical separation for a long time, problems in the marriage, or a close friendship in which boundaries became blurred.

▌ Only about one-third felt that there was no likelihood of their spouse ever having an extramarital affair, and only about one-third believed that there was no chance that they would themselves ever have an affair.

▌ The most likely reason a spouse would have an affair: dissatisfied with the marriage.

▌ The most upsetting reason for a spouse's affair: fell out of love and seeking new relationship.

▌ The least upsetting reason for a spouse's affair: one-night stand, did it on a whim.

## Motivations for Affairs

Affairs are motivated by all of the factors that move us toward any sexual relationship plus some additional factors. The motivating forces for any *particular* affair, however, are often difficult to identify. The participants might not recognize their true motives or might be reluctant to reveal their motives. In most cases, a number of forces are likely to be involved.

Therapist Emily M. Brown has identified five types of affairs (AASECT, 1996; Brown, 1991):

1. *Conflict avoidant affairs.* Both partners have poor conflict resolution skills, so their differences are never resolved. They never fight, but eventually the partner most dissatisfied with ongoing unresolved conflict has an affair.

2. *Intimacy avoidant affairs.* These couples fight constantly as a way of avoiding intimacy. The affair is just one more weapon the partners use against each other.

3. *Compulsive sexual behavior.* People with compulsive sexual behavior might have dozens of short-term affairs. They are motivated by the excitement of the conquest of a new partner and the novelty of sex with someone new. Their affairs lack intimacy and seldom last very long.

4. *The split-self affair.* This affair is characteristic of older people and might go on for many years. One partner—most often a man—values the primary relationship, but feels that it does not meet all of his needs. He enters into a long-term serious affair. Brown says that this affair represents the ultimate lack of commitment, because the individual never chooses between his or her two partners.

5. *The out-the-door affair.* Affairs are sometimes used as a means of ending a relationship, though they are not the reason that the relationship disintegrates. This affair contributes to an angry, hostile split-up.

Gender differences were also noted by Mullen and Martin (1994) in a survey in New Zealand. Men, when their partner was unfaithful, were more concerned about the potential loss of the partner. Women were more concerned about the effect of their partner's infidelity on the quality of the primary relationship. Men tended to cope with their partner's infidelity by using denial and avoidance; women were more likely to vocalize their distress and to try to make themselves more attractive to their wayward partner. High rates of jealousy were associated with heavy drinkers and people with low self-esteem.

## Dealing with Affairs

On the surface, affairs seem to be a major factor in the breakup of many relationships. Most authorities, however, view affairs as one of the *results* of the deterioration of a relationship, rather than one of the causes (AASECT, 1996). Severe partner incompatibilities, interpersonal conflicts, personality disorders, and chronic hostility all serve to produce the kinds of situations in which affairs are likely to occur. Such troubled relationships often lack the resources to deal constructively with affairs and, thus, break up when the affair of one partner is discovered.

Rather than automatically assuming that the discovery of an affair must lead to termination of a relationship, couples in this situation might try counseling. There is little chance that counseling will be successful unless both partners are involved, because there is no such thing as an uninvolved partner in a troubled relationship (Kell, 1992).

## 14.4  PARENTHOOD

Becoming a parent is not something to leave to chance. Having a baby ought to be a planned event. Every child has the right to be born to a parent or parents who desire parenthood and at a time when they want to become parents. Every adult has the right to remain childless if that is his or her preference.

A number of factors are important when considering parenthood. Successful parenthood requires emotional stability, adaptability, and a well-developed ability to cope with difficult situations. Parenthood should be compatible with your career goals. Someone whose career requires extensive time away from home might not be able to give a child the time and attention needed. Some people say that the little time they spend with their children is "quality time," but there must also be adequate time. Careful consideration must be given to the financial aspects of parenting. It costs far more to raise a child than most childless people would expect. Your income must be adequate and, above all, steady so as to provide a secure home for a child. One final item: The decision to have a child should reflect the feelings of the potential parents of the child, not their friends, not the potential grandparents. The decision to remain childless requires no explanation to anyone.

### 14.4.1  Adjusting to Parenthood

Becoming a parent is a unique mixture of joy and life changes. Being a parent can bring deep pleasure, intimacy, and personal growth. In caring for and playing with children, you discover new dimensions to living and loving. At the same time, parenthood can also require many adjustments in your lifestyle and daily routine. Your first baby usually demands the greatest adjustment, but each additional child requires further adjustments (O'Brien, 1996).

During the first few months of parenthood, you learn what it means to be a parent. Many people find this to be a period of fragmentation and disorganiza-

tion. Many new skills and ways of coping must be learned (O'Brien, 1996). Fatigue is a near-universal problem for the first few months, with night after night of interrupted sleep.

Some new parents are reluctant or resentful about giving up activities they used to enjoy. Feelings of isolation are common in the first few months. This may be especially true if a parent who is accustomed to going to work is now staying home with the baby. Particularly during this adjustment period, maintaining social contacts is important for a parent's emotional health.

After the first few months of parenthood, life smooths out as long-term adjustments are successfully made. Still, several long-term issues complicate daily life in some families. For most parents, balancing parenthood with all the other concerns of adult life is difficult. There is seldom enough time to do everything you would like to do. With so many demands upon your time and attention, it is easy for jealousy to develop among family members competing for each other's affection (McHale, 1995).

Ways can be found to break through the barriers set up by busy lives and jealousy. This often involves a departure from our culture's expectations about men's and women's roles in the family (McHale, 1995). The belief that mothers do their part by caring for children while fathers do theirs by making money contributes to jealousy. Each parent might see the other as having an easier, more interesting, or otherwise better life. Many couples have found that the most effective solution to this problem is to share the responsibilities of parenthood more equally (McHale, 1995). Even if one parent spends more hours working outside the home than the other, that parent can relieve the parent who does most of the parenting by making definite commitments of time and interest to the job of parenting.

Finally, long-term conflict between parents often arises from differences in opinion on how strict family discipline ought to be. Compromises may have to be worked out, perhaps with the help of a family counselor.

It takes hard work and self-awareness to be a successful parent. For those who choose to be parents, the challenge is great but so are the potential rewards.

### 14.4.2  Parenting

Being a parent to any children you might have is probably the most important, and possibly the most difficult, task of your life. Almost all parents have a strong love for their children and the desire to be a good parent, but many do not receive enough information or training in parenting to know how to handle the challenging situations that arise in every home (Allan, 1994; Gross et al., 1995).

Lacking any formal training in parenting, most parents have only the model of their own parents for guidance in how to parent. Not only were their own parents similarly untrained in parenting, but a generation later, many formerly effective parenting strategies no longer work (Buntain-Ricklefs et al., 1994; Covell et al., 1995; Hemenway, Solnick, & Carter, 1994; Kennedy, 1995).

In many families, parents and children are engaged in ongoing struggles for power and control, making family life joyless for everyone. Conflicts drain everyone's time and energy. In two-parent families, parenting conflicts often drive wedges between the parents as each attempts to parent in the way he or she believes to be best (McHale, 1995).

Many resources are available to help parents learn effective skills and cope with problems and conflicts. Many colleges and communities offer effective courses and programs on parenting skills. Individuals and couples who are contemplating parenthood, or are faced with the job of parenting (whether planned or unplanned), are encouraged to seek out information, resources, and support as you begin this new phase of life. A bookstore, the Internet, a church or community center are good places to start. Learning effective parenting techniques, rather than relying on past experience, role models, or instinct, can make all the difference for personal satisfaction, successful families, and well-adjusted children.

## 14.4.3   Lesbian and Gay Parents

Many lesbian and gay people love and enjoy raising children. Some raise children they fathered or gave birth to in prior heterosexual partnerships. Some adopt children or become foster parents. Some lesbian women bear children through artificial insemination or in vitro fertilization; a few arrange temporary liaisons with a man specifically for the purpose of becoming pregnant.

Some straight people question the ability of gay and lesbian people to be effective parents and role models for their children. What kind of success do lesbian and gay people have as parents? Actually, this issue was studied and resolved many years ago (Kirkpatrick, Smith, & Roy, 1981; Pennington, 1987; Scallen, 1981; Wyers, 1984). Gay and lesbian people are at least as good at parenting as heterosexual people are. Children raised by lesbian or gay parents are at no increased risk of gender identity confusion or any identifiable emotional or behavioral pathology.

The sexual orientation of the adults raising a child doesn't appear to influence the sexual orientation of the child. After all, most lesbian and gay people were raised by straight parents. Children raised by homosexual parents are no more likely to have a homosexual orientation than are children raised by heterosexual parents.

It wouldn't be accurate to say that homosexual and heterosexual parents are identical. A few differences have been identified in parenting styles of homosexual and heterosexual parents (Scallen, 1981). For example, gay fathers were found to place more emphasis on a nurturing style of parenting, while straight fathers were found to place more emphasis on providing material or economic benefits to their children. But in general, the similarities between homosexual and heterosexual parents are more striking than the differences.

A few special issues do concern homosexual parents:

▌ In the past, a parent's homosexuality was often used as a reason for denying custody. This is less likely to happen today, but is still a possibility in some places.

▌ Children need to be given a broad view of what constitutes a family, such as "A family is people who live together and love and take care of each other" (Abbitt & Bennett, 1992). Relatively few of today's families consist of a biological mother, a biological father, and their child or children.

▌ Child care isn't always available at gay and lesbian events (nor at primarily heterosexual events, for that matter), and many members of the gay and lesbian communities are still unaware of the needs and problems of lesbian and gay parents.

▌ To what extent should a gay or lesbian parent's partner be involved in parenting? This question has to be resolved by each individual couple, taking into consideration how the partner feels about children and the stability of the partnership.

▌ Jealousy is a common problem when one of two partners has a child; the partner and the child must compete for the parent's attention.

▌ When and how much should children be told about their homosexual parent's sexual orientation and the nature of his or her partnership? Experts usually recommend being open and honest, providing a positive view of homosexuality to help counteract the great amount of negative opinions every child is certain to hear from peers (Abbitt & Bennett, 1992).

▌ How open in their affection should the parent and her or his partner be? Our answer here is the same as we give to straight parents: Don't bring home a steady parade of new partners; it confuses children and sets a bad example. Keep your sexual activity private but be open in your display of love and affection.

Remember that you are your child's main role model for growth into a caring, loving adult.

### 14.4.4 Stepfamilies and Blended Families

With today's great diversity of lifestyles and living arrangements, there can be confusion about just what constitutes a stepfamily, or **blended family**. A stepfamily usually includes two adults, who are emotionally and/or legally committed to each other. One or both of these adults has one or more children from previous partners, and they may have one or more children together.

Many studies have focused on factors that contribute to successful stepfamily and blended-family relationships. Among their findings are the following:

- Flexibility, regularity in household routines, and effective parent-adolescent and stepparent-adolescent communication are all associated with the satisfaction of adolescents living in remarried-family households (Henry & Lovelace, 1995).

- Stepfamilies function better when stepparents avoid forcing their families into the biological family model, recognizing the different roles that stepparents need to maintain and the need for special bonds between biological parent and child (Kelley, 1992).

- Adolescents with stepfathers adjust better when there are lower levels of parental punishment, more parental rewards, consistency in discipline, more parent-stepparent agreement on parenting issues, more traditional beliefs regarding marriage and family life, and when the adolescents are less angry about their mother's remarriage (Fine, Donnelly, & Voydanoff, 1991).

- Children experience greater emotional well-being when they perceive warmth from their parents and stepparents (Fine, Voydanoff, & Donnelly, 1993).

Many blended-family problems can be avoided or resolved by the parents' learning about the predictable problems and ways of avoiding them. Most bookstores carry current books on this topic, and there are many useful resources available on the Internet. Self-help groups such as the Stepfamily Association of America (602 East Joppa Road, Baltimore, MD 21204), the Stepfamily Foundation (333 West End Avenue, New York, NY 10024), and the Step-

Living in a blended family can present some complexities not experienced in most other families. Stepfamilies function better when stepparents avoid forcing their families into the biological family model, recognizing the special characteristics of blending families.

family Association of Illinois (P.O. Box 3124, Oak Park, IL 60303) can also be very useful.

## 14.5  DIVORCE

In 1997, almost half of all marriages ended in divorce (National Center for Health Statistics, 1998). Focusing on married people only, the annual divorce rate for married *women* is highest for 15- to 19-year-olds, while the rate for married *men* peaks in the 20- to 24-year-old age group, (Clarke, 1995a). First marriages last longer than subsequent marriages. The mean (approximate average) duration at the time of divorce for first, second, and third marriages, respectively, is 11.0 years, 7.7 years, and 5.4 years for women and 10.9 years, 7.8 years, and 6.0 years for men (Clarke, 1995a).

### 14.5.1  Why Divorce Rates Are High

A number of factors are believed to contribute to high divorce rates, although it is virtually impossible to determine the relative importance of each factor. One factor is the liberalization of divorce laws during the 1970s. Many states abandoned the traditional approach of granting a divorce to the "innocent" party because of the objectionable behavior (usually extramarital sex) of the "guilty" party. Now, in these states, neither party is recognized as guilty, and "no-fault" divorces are granted for what the laws describe

| **blended family** | a committed relationship in which one or both partners has children from previous relationships |
| --- | --- |

as "irreconcilable differences." Actually a substantial percentage of divorcing people really have been romantically involved with someone other than their spouse in the period leading up to the divorce (South & Lloyd, 1995).

Increased expectations for marital and sexual fulfillment have probably had an even greater impact on divorce rates than has liberalization of divorce laws (South & Lloyd, 1995). People today are less willing than in the past to stay in an unfulfilling marriage simply because of religious or social pressures or as a matter of economic convenience. The media have created an idealized concept of marital bliss against which many people measure the success of their own marriages.

Changes in childbearing patterns also have contributed to the rising divorce rates. According to U.S. Census Bureau data, people now tend to start families later, have fewer children, and more often remain voluntarily childless. By delaying children for a few years, the still-childless couple can more easily part company if their marriage does not succeed. When children are involved, the fewer their number, the more easily divorce can be accomplished.

Some ethnic differences are evident in divorce rates. African Americans have the highest rates, white Americans have somewhat lower rates, and other ethnic groups have much lower rates (see table 14.1). When attitudes of Anglo-, Chinese, and Korean Americans toward divorce were compared, Anglo-Americans had the most positive attitudes and Korean Americans had the least positive (Tien, 1986). "Dimensions of Diversity: Divorce in Ireland" contrasts Irish divorce laws with American laws.

A Canadian study by Krishnan (1994) associated women's attitudes toward divorce with several characteristics. More negative attitudes about divorce were found in employed women, less educated women, and highly religious women. The effect of women's employment was especially strong in predicting negative attitudes about divorce.

## 14.5.2  Marriage and Increasing Life Expectancies

The addition of 20 to 25 years of life expectancy during this century has had an impact on our ideas regarding marriage and divorce. Even though people don't marry as young as they once did, a young couple entering into marriage is making a significantly longer commitment than in the past. Not only do people live longer now, they also have higher expectations for happiness in marriage than was once the case (South, 1995; South & Lloyd, 1995).

Most people today expect to live 75 or 80 years or more, compared with about 50 years in the past. If you are 30 years old and unhappy in a marriage, the thought of another 50 years with the same partner might be too much to face. It appears that many people who in the past might have stayed in an unhappy marriage today feel strongly motivated to divorce and remarry.

## 14.5.3  Divorce Challenges

Regardless of relaxed legal and social attitudes, divorce is almost always very challenging for all concerned. Divorce often involves persistent psychological problems for one or both spouses and any children they may have.

Less is published about divorced men's concerns than divorced women's concerns, although this in itself does not mean that divorced men have fewer problems. For divorced men, finances, social relationships, contacts with former spouses, self-confidence, and loneliness are major areas of concern. Contrary to common belief, matters of practical living (cooking, cleaning, etc.) are least troublesome, according to Mitchell-Flynn and Hutchinson (1993).

Compared to men, women make more specific plans for a divorce and implement their plans. During the decision-making process, women think more about divorce and talk more to their friends about it (Crane, Soderquist, & Gardner, 1995). Social support is important for divorcing people. Yet two studies found that separated women have smaller support networks than married women, more conflict with support network members, and a higher turnover rate of friends (Hughes, Good, & Candell, 1993; Nelson, 1995).

Looking at some positive aspects of divorce for women, one survey of 148 divorced women with children found that they generally practiced healthy lifestyles, and 44 percent reported improved health

**TABLE 14.1**    DIVORCE RATES BY ETHNICITY AND GENDER, PER 1,000 MARRIED PEOPLE

|  | WHITE AMERICANS | AFRICAN AMERICANS | OTHER RACES |
|---|---|---|---|
| Men | 19.1 | 24.6 | 12.7 |
| Women | 19.1 | 22.8 | 13.1 |

**Source:** Data from S. C. Clarke, "Advance Report of Final Divorce Statistics, 1989 and 1990" in *Monthly Vital Statistics Report*, 43 (no. 9, supplement), March 22, 1995.

behaviors since their divorce. Healthy behavior was strongly associated with education level (Duffy, 1995). Another study describes divorce as a means for women to reassert their autonomy (Hackstaff, 1993). And still another attributed women's successful postdivorce recovery to their spiritual strength (Nathanson, 1995).

### 14.5.4   Divorce Alternatives

Divorce alternatives should be explored before any irrevocable decision to terminate marriage is made. This suggestion is based not on any traditional moralistic or religious grounds but on the pragmatic reasoning that staying married is often the happiest solution for everyone concerned. Although there are situations in which the damage done by staying together is greater than that of breaking up, this is definitely not always the case.

Professional marital therapy (counseling) is one alternative that should be considered before any decision to divorce is finalized. Although therapy can be expensive, its cost is small when compared with the financial costs of divorce and trivial when compared with the emotional costs of most divorces (Bray & Jouriles, 1995).

With surprising frequency, seemingly insolvable problems are successfully resolved through counseling. Many marital conflicts reflect the individual psychological problems of one or both spouses (Kincaid

& Caldwell, 1995). The problem might not be one spouse's inability to live with the other; it might be a problem of living with oneself. If an individual in this situation were to divorce and remarry without counseling, the same problems would be likely to develop in the new marriage.

### 14.5.5   Dealing with Divorce

If, after exploring alternatives, a couple decides that divorce really is the best course of action, the partners should try to plan carefully together the details of the divorce. This discussion should cover such topics as the timing of the divorce, money matters, and child custody (Kincaid & Caldwell, 1995).

The timing of the divorce can be important. A delay may allow for improvement in a couple's financial situation, a move to an area where the couple has supportive relatives, or the children's growing a bit older so that they are better able to understand what is happening and are less disturbed by the divorce.

If possible, the divorcing couple should also try to reach some basic agreements on finances and child custody before engaging any lawyers. These matters can often be resolved more successfully, and with less conflict, between the spouses if third parties are not involved. However, by the time divorce takes place, many relationships have deteriorated to a point where cooperation between spouses is unlikely.

## DIMENSIONS OF DIVERSITY

### DIVORCE IN IRELAND

In November, 1995, following a tense national struggle between tradition and reform, the voters of Ireland, by the narrowest of margins, legalized divorce for the first time since 1937. Historians say that the divorce prohibition was originally included in the constitution as a means of assuring Vatican support for the Irish Republic. The constitution also recognizes the Catholic Church as "the guardian of the faith professed by the great majority of the citizens." In an election in 1986, a proposed deletion of the antidivorce article from Ireland's 1937 constitution was defeated by a 2-to-1 margin.

The 1995 campaign to allow divorce was headed by Mags O'Brien, one of some 80,000 Irish citizens who were legally separated but forbidden by law from divorcing. Campaigning against allowing divorce was a conservative alliance supported by the Roman Catholic Church.

With 92 percent of Ireland's people Catholics, it was Catholics themselves who went against church teachings to approve the divorce amendment. Catholics in Italy and Spain previously followed the same course. In all of Europe now, only Malta still forbids divorce.

The 1995 election signaled a major change in Irish social priorities and increased willingness to separate church from state and to respect the rights of minorities. Only in recent years has family planning become acceptable, homosexuality been decriminalized, and abortion information become available.

By American standards, divorce will still be difficult to obtain in Ireland. Couples will have to prove that they have lived apart for four of the past five years and that their marriage is irreparable before they may divorce.

**Source:** W.D. Montalbano, "Irish Voters Overturn Ban on Divorce," *Los Angeles Times,* 26 November 1996, p. A1.

Along with working out all the *material* details of the divorce, each spouse may want to consider personal counseling to help him or her sort out all of the *emotional* details of the divorce. Counseling can help minimize the psychological damage associated with the divorce and prepare the parting couple for new relationships. Predictable emotions surrounding divorce include guilt, anger, fear, anxiety, depression, and loneliness (Kincaid & Caldwell, 1995; Walters-Champman, Price, & Serovich, 1995). Counseling can reassure the spouses that their feelings and emotions are normal and not indicative of any emotional illness and that these feelings will decrease with time.

## 14.5.6   Learning from Experience

Most divorced people do remarry. In fact, only 54 percent of today's marriages involve two never-before-married people (Clarke, 1995a). Divorce rates in second and subsequent marriages are higher than in first marriages, however (Clarke, 1995b). The bright side of the story is that many second marriages are extremely successful.

Many people are able to identify the factors that caused conflicts in their first marriage and so are able to avoid similar problems in their second marriage. After a first marriage, most people are likely to have a better idea of what traits they want a potential mate to possess (Nock, 1995b). They might be more sensitive to developing conflicts and be able to act more effectively to resolve those conflicts before they damage the relationship. And, of course, the individuals are now "older and wiser" than at the time of their first marriage. When a divorcing person is unable to pinpoint the problems that destroyed the marriage, a professional counselor can often help to identify these factors and to suggest ways of avoiding the same problems in a future marriage (Hartin, 1990).

## 14.6   SEXUALITY AND THE OLDER ADULT

Aging is a lifelong process taking place every day in every one of us. It is not something that is going to happen "later." Our attitudes toward aging influence how we live our lives. Living with an extreme fear of growing old isn't healthy, nor is ignoring the effects of daily health habits on the speed of our aging.

Senior citizens are forming an increasing percentage of the U.S. population. Most of us have older friends and relatives, and we want to be able to relate to them and understand their sexual concerns. Our society's attitudes and political policies as they relate to the sexuality of seniors are a critical concern for them and, in time, will be of equal concern to each of us. When we understand and express our concern about the sexual needs of older people while we are younger, we pave the way for a more rewarding sexual future for ourselves.

## 14.7   SIX TYPES OF AGING

**Aging** is the process of growing older. Augustine DiGiovanna (1994) has identified six types of aging: chronological, biological, cosmetic, social, psychological, and economic. Each of these types of aging influences and is influenced by each of the others (see fig. 14.1). Each has implications for our sexuality.

**Chronological aging** is the passage of time since a person's birth. Your **chronological age** is how long you have lived. Chronological age is not a reliable measure of "oldness," because two people of the same chronological age may have aged at different rates and have very different biological ages (DiGiovanna, 1994). There are cultural expectations regarding the sexual capabilities of people of any particular chronological age (Deacon, Minichiello, & Plummer, 1995). In general, older people are expected to be less sexually interested and less sexually capable than younger people. Sadly, many older people internalize these values and become sexually inactive at an age when they could still be enjoying a rich and rewarding sex life.

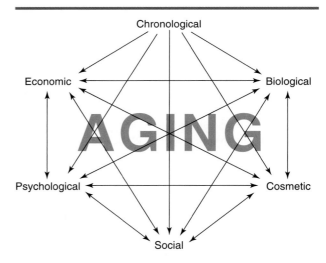

**FIGURE 14.1**   There are six types of aging, each of which interacts with each of the others in obvious or subtle ways. Each has sexual implications. Note that none of the others affects chronological aging; it is simply the passage of time.

**Source:** "Interactions Among Types of Aging," adapted from *Human Aging*, by Augustine DiGiovanna, 1994, p. 8. Reprinted by permission of McGraw-Hill, Inc.

**Biological aging,** which is sexually more significant than chronological aging, consists of age-related changes in a person's anatomy and physiology.

The biological aging of different people proceeds at very different rates. Some of this difference relates to lifestyle factors that are very much within our ability to control. Heavy drinking, smoking, other substance abuse, poor diet, and lack of exercise all take a terrible toll in terms of a person's biological age. Both sexual attractiveness and sexual ability are influenced by biological aging. If we want long, full sex lives, we do have to take care of ourselves.

**Cosmetic aging** refers to the changes in outward appearance that occur with advancing age. Even though cosmetic aging is not a reliable indicator of chronological or biological age, it can have a powerful influence on a person's life (DiGiovanna, 1994). If we believe that we appear "old," we might think of ourselves as "old" and withdraw from various physical, social, or sexual activities. We might also begin to neglect our appearance, causing ourselves to appear even "older."

**Social aging** consists of age-related changes in the interactions people have with each other. Each culture has its expectations for the sexual and other behavior of people of different ages (Deacon, Minichiello, & Plummer, 1995). Social aging is tied to various "milestones" in a person's life—graduating from high school, graduating from college, becoming a parent, becoming a grandparent, entering the work force, retiring, and so on—each of which changes society's expectations of us. Such status changes affect self-perception as well as how others think of us, including sexual perceptions.

**Psychological aging** consists of age-related changes in how people think and act. It results partly from the biological aging of the brain, as well as from chronological, social, cosmetic, and economic aging (this is a good example of how the different types of aging influence each other). As we go through life, we tend to change our perceptions of situations and how we react in a certain situation. This is certainly true sexually—think about how your own sexual perceptions and reactions have changed over the past few years.

**Economic aging** consists of age-related changes in a person's financial status. Up to a point, a person's economic position tends to improve with age, then, typically, to decline. The effects here of the other types of aging can be profound. For example, biological, chronological, social, cosmetic, and psychological aging can all reduce a person's earning ability. The sexual implications of economic aging include impaired sexual functioning or loss of sexual interest during periods of financial stress. Also, people who, at an advanced age, are still working long hours to make ends meet have less time and energy remaining for sexual activities.

## 14.8   AGEISM

The term **ageism,** coined by Robert Butler (1975) refers to the stereotyping of and discrimination against people simply because of their age. Many of the world's cultures hold their seniors in a position of high esteem. American society, however, highly values youth, physical attractiveness, sexuality, sensuality, productivity, progress, speed, and independence. It associates none of these with the older population. Older people in the United States are often viewed as unattractive, asexual, slow, and nonproductive (Hodson & Skeen, 1994). The media help to perpetuate this stereotype. Advertising, in particular, tells us *we must not appear old.* Skin creams promise to hide "those ugly age spots and wrinkles." We must color our hair to "get rid of that *ugly* gray." It's hard for older people to think very positively of themselves in such an atmosphere. Take a moment now and complete "Where Do I Stand? Attitudes about Aging and Sexuality."

## 14.9   MYTHS ABOUT SEX AND AGING

As we have mentioned, our society does not associate advancing age with sexual attractiveness, interest, or activity. Fallacies are widespread among younger people, and, sadly, many older people believe in these

| | |
|---|---|
| aging | the process of growing older |
| chronological aging | the passage of time since a person's birth |
| chronological age | how long a person has lived |
| biological aging | age-related changes in a person's anatomy and physiology |
| cosmetic aging | the changes in outward appearance that occur with advancing chronological age |
| social aging | age-related changes in the interactions people have with each other |
| psychological aging | age-related changes in how people think and act |
| economic aging | age-related changes in a person's financial status |
| ageism | stereotyping of and discrimination against people simply because of their age |

erroneous ideas, too. Let's examine some common myths about sex and aging (Deacon, Minichiello, & Plummer, 1995; Hodson & Skeen, 1994).

**Myth** *Sex is for the young. Older people are no longer interested in sex and no longer engage in sexual activity.*

**Fact** Most people remain sexually active until very advanced ages, with a partner if one is available and/or through self-pleasuring. Sex is important for older people for the same reasons it is important for younger people—it is a source of great physical and emotional pleasure. Society's false expectations for seniors are based partially on associations of attractiveness and romance with youth. Another association is made between sexuality and the possibility of reproduction, leading to the false expectation that a woman would not be interested in sex after menopause.

**Myth** *Older people are not able to enjoy sex.*

**Fact** Many young people define "sex" very narrowly as meaning heterosexual vaginal intercourse, and most older people are, in fact, quite capable of vaginal intercourse. Even the relatively few older people whose physical condition precludes vaginal intercourse can find many creative and rewarding ways to enjoy sexual pleasure. Cuddling, caressing, and oral and manual stimulation are all pleasant sexual activities enjoyed by older people. Although younger people might believe that a sexual experience is incomplete unless both partners have orgasms, older people tend to find sexual activities satisfying whether one, both, or neither partner comes. Also, among older women in particular, same-sex partnerships become more common.

**Myth** *Older people are physically unattractive and therefore sexually undesirable.*

**Fact** If judged by the unrealistic standards of perfection portrayed by the popular media, we're probably all pretty unattractive. Most older people have gained enough emotional maturity and wisdom to understand that our society's standards of appearance are very superficial and that the real beauty of a person lies within. Older people find each other very attractive.

**Myth** *The idea of older people having sex is shameful.*

**Fact** Anyone who thinks that sex is only for the young probably *is* young. We are sexual from birth to death. Sex remains an important and legitimate source of pleasure for people of any age. Some people are still influenced by the very old and thoroughly disproved idea that sex is only for reproduction and that once people reach an age where reproduction is impossible, sex should be discontinued. There is simply no scientific basis for this belief.

## 14.10   SEXUALITY IN MIDLIFE

During midlife the variable speed of biological aging, as influenced by people's living habits, becomes quite evident. At any gathering of middle-aged individuals, it is easy to observe people of the same chronological age who are at least twenty years apart in biological age. The effects of excessive stress, poor diet, inadequate exercise, smoking, drinking, and other substance abuses become very obvious at this time.

Both genders experience hormonal declines during midlife. In either sex, these hormonal changes and their effects are called the **climacteric.**

### 14.10.1   Male Climacteric

In contrast to female climacteric (menopause), when estrogen production fairly abruptly and almost totally ceases, male climacteric includes a gradual, partial decline in the amount of bioavailable testosterone in a man's blood. Not only is less testosterone produced by the testes, but a growing proportion of it is inactivated by bonding with a protein (Cowley, 1996; Schiavi et al., 1991).

During this period there is often a gradual decrease in the urgency of sexual desires. The refractory period following ejaculation might increase. Declining available testosterone levels also result in a reduction in both the force of ejaculation and the volume of ejaculate. Despite these changes, orgasm remains intensely pleasant (Schiavi et al., 1990). Control of ejaculation is often improved, enabling longer intercourse and greater partner satisfaction.

Sperm production declines somewhat during midlife, stabilizing at about age sixty. Even then, most men still produce adequate sperm to father children (Cowley, 1996).

Because of the many adverse effects of declining testosterone levels in aging men, testosterone replacement therapy is recommended by some physicians for some of their male patients. It can decrease bone and muscle loss while improving sexual function and a man's general sense of well-being (Swerdloff et al., 1992). Testosterone skin patches are available by prescription at a cost of about $100 per month (Cowley, 1996). As with every medication, benefits must be

# WHERE DO I STAND?
## ATTITUDES ABOUT AGING AND SEXUALITY

Attitudes toward aging influence not only our later lives, but our younger years as well. What are your attitudes toward aging and the sexuality of older people? Circle the number for the response to each statement that most closely fits your attitude.

|  |  | Strongly Agree | Somewhat Agree | Strongly Disagree |
|---|---|:---:|:---:|:---:|
| **1.** | I expect to have an active sex life when I'm 70 years old. | 2 | 1 | 0 |
| **2.** | It's hard for me to picture my parents or people their age having sex. | 0 | 1 | 2 |
| **3.** | It's really hard for me to picture my grandparents or people their age having sex. | 0 | 1 | 2 |
| **4.** | Older people have a lot of good ideas. | 2 | 1 | 0 |
| **5.** | I believe that by living healthfully, I can slow my own aging process. | 2 | 1 | 0 |
| **6.** | I can see some advantages in being old. | 2 | 1 | 0 |
| **7.** | I would rather die young than be old. | 0 | 1 | 2 |
| **8.** | Being around old people makes me nervous. | 0 | 1 | 2 |
| **9.** | Growing old is a natural part of life. | 2 | 1 | 0 |
| **10.** | I enjoy being around old people. | 2 | 1 | 0 |
| **11.** | I will start to think about aging when I get older. | 0 | 1 | 2 |

**Total points:** _____

**Interpretation:**

20–22 points: Your positive attitudes about sexuality and aging will help you have a healthy, sexually rewarding life.

16–19 points: Your attitudes about sexuality and aging are about typical of the population; there is plenty of room for improvement.

15 or fewer points: Your negative views of aging will cause problems for you as you grow older; read this chapter very carefully.

---

weighed against potential risks, such as inducing sterility and stimulating more rapid growth of prostate tumors.

DHEA (dehydroepiandrosterone), available without prescription in health food stores for $5 to $10 per month, is produced by the adrenal glands of people of both sexes. Its rate of production declines with age. Taken orally, DHEA has effects similar to, but milder than, testosterone. DHEA has many users who believe that it improves their mood, memory, energy, and sex drive (Cowley, 1996).

## 14.10.2   Menopause

None of the male midlife changes are of the magnitude of the hormonal changes a woman experiences in menopause. **Menopause** (cessation of menstruation) usually occurs somewhere between ages forty-

five and fifty. Although a woman starts her reproductive years with many thousands of immature ovarian follicles, eventually most of them degenerate. By the time of menopause, few remain to be stimulated by FSH and LH.

Not only are no more mature ova produced, but ovarian production of estrogen and progesterone also sharply decreases at menopause. Without enough of these hormones to stimulate the endometrium, menstrual periods stop.

| | |
|---|---|
| **climacteric** (kli-mak´ter-ik) | hormonal changes during midlife and their effects |
| **menopause** | permanent cessation of menstruation |

# GO ASK ALICE

*Dear Alice,*
    *Does a man's sexual drive start to decrease at a certain age?*
        *Reaching 30*

Dear Reaching 30,

For both women and men, sexual desire or drive decreases gradually with age. However, testosterone, the hormone which primarily controls sexual drive in men, never stops being produced entirely. This is why it is not uncommon for men in their 70s and 80s to have an active libido. However, there are certain reasons why a man's libido may be affected for temporary periods of time at any point in their life cycle: stress, fatigue, preoccupation with work, side effects of medications, medical conditions, dissatisfaction with a relationship, and lack of desire for a partner, among others.

A man's sexual life does change with age, however, even as desire is maintained. From ages 20–35, men tend to masturbate less often, and they have fewer wet dreams. Some men in this age group notice that their penises are not as hard as they once were, and that they require direct stimulation to get hard. Around ages 40–50, in order to get an erection, a man may require direct stimulation, and his erection may not be as full or firm as before. It is easier for his penis to lose its hardness and, once lost, more difficult to regain. Men's angle of erection may change—a penis that once pointed up may now just stick straight out; one that once pointed straight out may now still be stiff but point slightly down. The need for orgasm is less pronounced than in younger years. The force of the ejaculation is less, as is the amount ejaculated. As men reach their 50s through 70s, physical and mental arousal become much more critical to erection. It takes longer to ejaculate, and men find they don't need to ejaculate every time. Semen may seem to seep out rather than "shoot out."

What's important to remember is that these changes are normal bodily aging processes. Just as you wouldn't expect an Olympic runner to maintain his Olympic speed at age 60, you shouldn't expect to maintain adolescent levels of sexual arousal 20–30 years later. However, the penis and the rest of the body NEVER lose their capacity for giving and receiving pleasure! Alice hopes you enjoy a lifetime of good sex—don't start worrying at age 30!!

    http://www.mhhe.com/byer6

---

Early in menopause, periods may become either more or less frequent than before and menstrual bleeding may be either lighter or heavier. Some women have no changes in their periods at all until menstruation just suddenly stops. For some women, periods might stop for several months and then start up again.

Other specific physiological changes that occur in a woman at climacteric include thinning of the vaginal walls, reduced elasticity of the vagina, slowing of the vaginal lubrication response, and atrophy (decrease in size) of the ovaries and uterus. All of these are caused by declining estrogen levels (Williams, 1995).

Many women find the climacteric quite uneventful. Others may experience some unpleasant symptoms, such as headaches, insomnia, dizziness, irritability, weight gains, and "hot flashes" or "flushes." These symptoms result from the hormonal imbalances occurring during this time (Williams, 1995).

The changes in the vaginal tissues are also hormonally produced. Because of decreasing amounts of estrogen, the vaginal lining becomes thinner and changes to a lighter color. These changes, along with decreased vaginal flexibility and reduced lubrication during sexual response, can result in uncomfortable or painful intercourse at times (Williams, 1995). To alleviate these problems, millions of women are taking hormone replacement therapy (HRT), as prescribed by their physicians.

## Hormone Replacement Therapy

Following menopause, many women now take **hormone replacement therapy (HRT)**—estrogen and progestin (synthetic progesterone), which replace the hormones no longer produced by their ovaries. These hormones can be taken orally on a daily basis or they can be absorbed from a skin patch. Hormone replacement therapy offers several potential benefits, but involves some potential risk. It can alleviate hot flashes, deterioration of skin tone, thinning of the vaginal lining, and reduced vaginal lubrication. HRT can help to maintain sexual interest and response. More importantly, it can also help prevent osteoporosis (weakening of the bones due to calcium loss) and cardiovascular disease (Hennekens, 1996).

No medical treatment is totally free of risk, and the risk in any treatment must be considered relative to its benefit. Experts do not agree on the risk-benefit ratio of HRT. The majority of physicians appear to view the ratio as favorable, in light of how HRT helps prevent both osteoporosis and cardiovascular disease. These benefits, however, need to be weighed against a possible increase in the risk of breast cancer or other cancers. A woman may want to discuss the pros and cons of HRT with her physician before beginning this therapy (Rostosky & Travis, 1996).

### 14.10.3 Sex in Middle Age

In the past, middle-aged people were expected to lose interest in sex. Today it is understood that sexuality is a vital part of the lives of most middle-aged people. Middle-aged women, in particular, often have strong sex drives (Koster & Garde, 1993). Factors associated with decreased sexual desire, which does occur in 27 to 30 percent of middle-aged women, are lack of an intimate relationship, having an emotionally nonsupportive spouse or an alcoholic spouse, having vaginal dryness, and experiencing major depression (Hallstrom & Samuelsson, 1990; Mansfield, Voda, & Koch, 1995).

For most women, middle age can bring new sexual satisfaction for a number of reasons. For heterosexual women, after menopause there is little fear of pregnancy and after age fifty almost no fear at all. Their male partners might develop increased ejaculatory control with increased age. Also, with children leaving home and more money available, privacy increases, and financial problems are often reduced. These changes promote shared pleasant experiences and improved communication that enhance sexual expression (Blattberg & Hogan, 1994).

Nevertheless, there are differences between youthful and middle-aged sexuality. Between the ages of forty-six and fifty-five, most men and women become aware of a decline in their sexual responses. Although middle-aged people experience satisfying sexual relationships, sexual response is usually slower, and more imaginative sex play may be necessary for arousal. Although this often enhances the intimacy between partners, the natural slowing of the sexual response can provoke anxiety in either or both genders, and especially in men (Panser et al., 1995; Schiavi, 1990; Schiavi et al., 1990; Schiavi, Mandeli, & Schreiner-Engle, 1994).

A middle-aged male might begin to fear that he will not be able to attain or maintain erection, and he may at times actually experience erectile difficulties. Many erectile problems in middle age are the result of anxiety or other psychological problems, rather than a physical effect of aging. The middle-aged male might be sexually bored, or anxious over financial or career decisions. More physical causes include fatigue and excessive alcohol use. Heavy drinking is an espe-

Despite some visible evidence of aging and some slowing of sexual responses, most middle-aged people remain quite sexually interested and active.

cially common cause of erectile dysfunction. Once erectile difficulty appears, some middle-aged males withdraw voluntarily from any sexual activity rather than risk the ego-shattering experience of periodic erectile dysfunction (Panser et al., 1995; Schiavi, Mandeli, & Schreiner-Engle, 1994).

A middle-aged female might also feel anxiety about the natural slowing of the sexual response—especially in a male partner. If her male partner is having erectile problems, she might identify herself as the cause of those problems and form a negative self-image of herself as undesirable or "past her prime." The facts are, however, that a woman can be orgasmic and a satisfying sexual partner at any age, and the sexually experienced middle-aged woman is often more—not less—likely to reach orgasm than a younger woman (Lieblum, 1990).

### 14.10.4 Midlife Divorce

About half of all marriages end in divorce, and many of these divorces occur during midlife. In fact, about 26 percent of all divorcing women and 29 percent of all divorcing men are between ages thirty-five and fifty-four (Clarke, 1995a).

Divorce in midlife occurs in response to such stresses as differential growth of the partners, midlife career and identity crises, and extramarital affairs. Historical trends can also be at work. Many of today's divorcing middle-aged people married at a time when people were expected to marry young, have

| hormone replacement therapy (HRT) | taking estrogen and progestin following menopause to replace hormones formerly produced by the ovaries |

children, and stay married "for the children" at any cost. Now, in midlife, these people are finding that divorce has become a more accepted solution to an unpleasant marriage.

Divorce at any time, however, is painful. It is usually followed by loneliness, self-doubt, mood swings, and the need for many practical adjustments in living arrangements (Wright & Maxwell, 1991). Women divorcing during midlife often experience a greatly reduced standard of living. A recently divorced middle-aged woman may also find that she must begin dating at just the time when she begins to have doubts about her attractiveness. Both genders may feel out of touch with the whole dating scene.

### 14.10.5 Midlife Widowhood

The death of one's partner is one of the greatest emotional and social losses an individual can suffer in the normal course of the life span. It is an emotional emergency that the individual must live through, and then it becomes a social status—widowhood or widowerhood—that she or he must live with, often without adequate emotional preparation.

Depression, suicide, and increased death rates have all been associated with widowhood (Bowling & Windsor, 1995; Gilbar & Dagan, 1995; Levy, Martinkowski, & Derby, 1994; Li, 1995). Reports seem to conflict on which gender handles bereavement better, depending on how the difficulty is measured.

Bowling and Windsor (1995) indicate that widowed men are at greater risk of dying than are widowed women, and Li (1995) reported an increased risk of suicide for widowed men but not for widowed women. Gilbar and Dagan (1995) found significantly more psychological distress and greater difficulty in psychosocial adjustment in widows than in widowers.

Some of the problems of the middle-aged widow are unique. The middle-aged widow is often the first of her friends to lose her partner. The couple's friends are usually all couples, and the new middle-aged widow now feels like the "fifth wheel" at any social occasion. The middle-aged widow is also less willing than older widows to resign herself to a life without partner companionship and sexual activity. This often causes her female friends who still have partners to feel threatened, and although they exhort her to socialize, friends "forget" to include her in social activities unless they have a potential partner present. Another problem for heterosexual women is that the middle-aged widow is often unable to find suitable single men her age, especially widowed men, who understand her experience.

### 14.10.6 "Gay Widowhood"

The HIV/AIDS epidemic has taken a terrible toll in the gay male community. Many thousands of gay men of all ages have experienced the death of a partner, increasing the phenomenon of "gay widowhood." Every culture has its mourning rituals, which help its members deal with the profound meaning of their loss. But for gay men (and lesbian women) the lack of recognition in the larger, primarily heterosexual, society of the importance of gay and lesbian relationships can be demoralizing (Berger & Kelly, 1992). Many straight people (family, friends, coworkers) simply do not perceive the death of a gay or lesbian lover as being the equivalent of the death of a heterosexual spouse. Needed emotional support or time off from work might not be given.

Within the gay or lesbian community, "gay widows" find plenty of support. The concept of "chosen family" operates in a way that is largely unknown in the heterosexual community (Berger & Kelly, 1992).

## 14.11 SEXUALITY AND OLDER ADULTS

In 1900, only about 4 percent of the U.S. population was 65 years old or older. By the year 2040, this group will constitute 20 to 25 percent of the population. This is not just speculation; this projection is based on the known number of people of each age in our current population, according to U.S. census figures. Because there are now far fewer premature deaths of people in their thirties, forties, and fifties, most currently young and middle-aged people can look forward to someday joining the ranks of older adults.

### 14.11.1 Attitudes on Sex and Older Adults

Unfortunately, our society does not really expect older people to be interested in sex (Hodson & Skeen, 1994). We may joke about sexual older people, but these jokes seem funny only because they contradict our image of older people as asexual. Older people are, in reality, very sexual. Society, however, does not deal well with this sexuality; families and senior-care facilities might ignore or deny the sexual needs of older people. Worse still, many older people may accept society's expectations as valid and either unnecessarily discontinue their sexual activity or experience unnecessary guilt and doubts about their continued sexual activity.

### 14.11.2 Sexual Interest and Activity among Older People

Many college students and other young adults have great difficulty believing that their parents and grandparents are still sexually active. Many young people

**TABLE 14.2** SEXUAL INTEREST AND ACTIVITY IN OLDER ADULTS

| | AGED 50–59 | AGED 60–69 | AGED 70 AND OLDER |
|---|---|---|---|
| Sexually active* | | | |
| Women | 93% (N** = 801) | 81% (N = 719) | 65% (N = 324) |
| Men | 98% (N = 823) | 91% (N = 981) | 79% (N = 598) |
| Sexually active, reporting sexual activity at least once a week* | | | |
| Women | 73% (N = 743) | 63% (N = 582) | 50% (N = 211) |
| Men | 90% (N = 804) | 73% (N = 893) | 58% (N = 473) |
| Sexually active, reporting a high level of sexual enjoyment* | | | |
| Women | 71% (N = 743) | 65% (N = 582) | 61% (N = 211) |
| Men | 90% (N = 804) | 86% (N = 893) | 75% (N = 471) |

*Includes sex with a partner or alone (masturbation).

** N = number of people surveyed.

**From:** *Love, Sex, and Aging* by Edward M. Brecher and the Editors of Consumer Report Books. Copyright © 1984, Little, Brown and Company.

believe that sexual activity should diminish after middle age and is probably very unusual among older people (Deacon, Minichiello, & Plummer, 1995). (See "Case Study: A Living History Interview with a Parent or Grandparent.") Some older people have helped perpetuate this myth by hiding their sexuality from their children and grandchildren.

Only in recent years has much research explored the sexuality of our older population. Even the famous Kinsey studies of the 1940s and 1950s largely ignored older people. One comprehensive project was sponsored by the Consumers Union, publisher of *Consumer Reports* magazine, and conducted by Edward Brecher (1984). Questionnaires were mailed to people across the United States who were between ages 50 and 93. Some of the findings of this survey are summarized in table 14.2.

The Brecher study revealed that sexual fantasies are common among older people. Over half reported engaging in fantasy during sex with a partner, and over three-quarters reported engaging in sexual fantasy while masturbating. Many of their fantasies were similar to those of younger people—attractive partners, romantic situations. Other fantasies were replays of actual experiences that occurred years earlier with a previous partner, or in which one's current partner was substituted. Some of the fantasies were of being young again—looking or performing as one did many years ago. Many older men and women also reported using erotic materials as sources of sexual fantasies.

Another, more recent survey (table 14.3) focused only on sexual activity with a partner and, unlike the study summarized in table 14.2, excluded masturbation. Here, considerable gender difference was evident in the incidence of sex with partners for people of 70

**TABLE 14.3** PERCENTAGE OF PEOPLE STILL SEXUALLY ACTIVE WITH PARTNERS, BY AGE

| | SEXUALLY ACTIVE WITH PARTNERS | |
|---|---|---|
| Age | Women | Men |
| 70–74 | 30% | 65% |
| 75–79 | 22% | 53% |
| 80–84 | 9% | 48% |

**Source:** Data from E. Laumann, J. Gagnon, R. Michael, and S. Michaels. *The Social Organization of Sexuality.* (Chicago: University of Chicago Press, 1994).

to 84 years of age (Laumann et al., 1994). The lower rate for women was attributed to the scarcity of available partners for women above 70 years of age.

The quality of relationships is very important to the degree of sexual activity and enjoyment of older people (Brecher, 1984). Apparently, as physical attractiveness fades, intimacy, communication, and shared experiences become increasingly important sexual stimuli. Now let's look at some of the more specific changes in sexual response as people grow older.

## 14.11.3 Male Sexual Response and Aging

Males typically reach their peak of sexual function in their late teens or early twenties. Their sexual function then begins a gradual, progressive decline. A male tends to go through periods of relative plateau in sexual function, as well as periods of more rapid decline associated with his general physical and emotional health and overall aging. Male sexual decline is

## CASE STUDY

### A LIVING HISTORY INTERVIEW WITH A PARENT OR GRANDPARENT

This case history is a little different because you are going to write it. There is no better way for you to gain an appreciation of sexuality among older people (at least until you are an older person) than to interview a parent, grandparent, or other older person about their sexual values and feelings. It's also a good way to get better acquainted with the person you interview. The following are some suggested questions:

▌ At what age did you start dating?

▌ What was dating like at that time?

▌ Can you show me any pictures of yourself at different ages?

▌ What were your expectations for your life?

▌ (If your interviewee is gay or lesbian):

　▌ At what age did you first become aware of your sexual orientation?

　▌ At what age did you come out?

　▌ Did family members have trouble dealing with your homosexuality?

▌ (If your interviewee has ever been married):

　▌ How did you and _____ meet?

　▌ What were your expectations for marriage?

　▌ How did your actual marriage compare to your expectations?

▌ How important is (was) sex in your marriage?

▌ (If your interviewee has been widowed):

　▌ How old were you when _____ died?

　▌ How did you adjust to his or her death?

　▌ (If interviewee remarried):

　　▌ How did you meet your new spouse?

　　▌ How did that marriage compare to your previous marriage?

　　▌ Is (was) sex as important in your second marriage as in the first?

▌ (If your interviewee has been divorced):

　▌ How long were you married before you got divorced?

　▌ How did the divorce come about?

　▌ (If interviewee remarried):

　　▌ How did you meet your new spouse?

　　▌ How did that marriage compare to your previous marriage?

　　▌ Is (was) sex as important in your second marriage as in the first?

▌ In general, how satisfied are you with your sex life today?

▌ What would you do different if you had your life to live again?

---

visible in many ways (Panser et al., 1995; Schiavi, 1990; Schiavi et al., 1990; Schiavi, Mandeli, & Schreiner-Engle, 1994):

▌ Urgency of sex drive decreases. Sex is still important, but a reduced frequency of sexual activity is typical.

▌ Most older men take longer to gain an erection. More physical stimulation of the penis may be needed. More elaborate fantasies may be necessary to produce arousal.

▌ When fully erect, the penis is not as hard as it was in youth.

▌ Erection more frequently disappears prior to orgasm.

▌ Ejaculation may require more stimulation than in the past, and intercourse may be more prolonged.

▌ Intercourse more often terminates without ejaculation.

▌ Ejaculation is less forceful than before, and the volume of semen is reduced.

▌ The time it takes to have another erection is longer and may even require as much time as twenty-four to forty-eight hours.

As shown in tables 14.2 and 14.3, despite these changes, most men remain sexually interested and active until very advanced ages (Brecher, 1984). Sex remains important as a source of physical pleasure and for self-esteem. Incidentally, most men also remain fertile and capable of fathering children until very advanced ages, as evidenced by the children of Charlie Chaplin, Bing Crosby, Cary Grant, and Pablo Picasso.

### 14.11.4  Female Sexual Response and Aging

Female sexual response also slows with age. Responses in both sexes are controlled by the same nerves and involve the same circulatory changes. Thus, age-related changes in the female that are similar to those that occur in the male are as follows (Antonovsky, Sadowsky, & Maoz, 1990; Kellett, 1991; Segraves & Segraves, 1995; Sherwin, 1991):

- The vagina lubricates more slowly, and the amount of lubrication decreases. Lubrication changes, however, are less obvious than male erectile changes and are easier to compensate for, perhaps with a vaginal lubricant.

- During sexual arousal, the labia of older women do not become as engorged with blood as they do in younger women. Consequently, they do not press as tightly against the penis during intercourse, and a partner might perceive the vagina as "looser."

- The vaginal and uterine contractions of orgasm are often reduced in number in older women, thereby reducing perceived orgasmic intensity. In some older women, orgasmic contractions can be painful because of the hormonal changes of menopause. This problem can be relieved by the use of a vaginal estrogen cream.

- Sexual interest might increase following menopause, as fear of pregnancy is no longer a factor.

In summary, although people of both genders undergo definite changes in their sexual responses with advancing age, most continue to desire sexual activity and find it highly rewarding.

## 14.12  AGE-RELATED ADJUSTMENTS IN LOVEMAKING

Aging can necessitate some adjustments in a couple's sexual activity. Illness, for example, can bring about a temporary loss of sexual interest or ability. Even severe illnesses, however, usually don't mean the end of all sexual activity, but may require different ways of giving and receiving sexual pleasure (Rose & Soares, 1993; Shaw, 1994).

Open and effective communication is extremely important when physical limitations affect lovemaking. For example, one partner might be reluctant to initiate sex because of arthritic or other pain. But because the cause of concern is not communicated, the other partner might interpret the lack of sexual activity as a personal rejection.

A partner for whom pain is a problem can let the other partner know what feels good and what hurts during sex. Each partner can ask for what he or she wants in a clear and positive way. Before making love, partners can agree on a signal that tells when something hurts. If one favored position for sex has become uncomfortable, there are many other positions to be tried.

People sometimes fear returning to sexual activity after an illness or surgery, especially surgery such as a mastectomy or a colostomy that has changed their body's appearance or way of functioning. Goodwin (1987) suggests a gradual resumption of lovemaking—first touching and nonsexual caressing, gradually leading to sexual touching and stimulation. If the health of one partner makes intercourse impossible, partners can still lie together and hold each other and let feelings flow between them.

Rose and Soares (1993) describe a full range of adaptations, including sexual accommodations, fantasy romance, projected sexuality, voluntary and involuntary sexual retirement, and revitalization. They point out that sometimes sexual losses as well as sexual capacities must be recognized in counseling the frail elderly.

Many older couples have the advantage of being able to choose any time of day for sexual activity. Making love in the morning is often recommended because the partners are more rested and older men are more likely to have a firm erection in the morning (Butler & Lewis, 1993). Creating a relaxed, sexy mood can also enhance the sexual activity of older (as well as younger) people. A warm bath or shower together before sex can help, as can exchanging massages, having romantic lighting, and listening to music together.

## 14.13  RELATIONSHIPS AMONG OLDER PEOPLE

Some people experience all or most of their older years with a longtime partner. Others, through divorce, death, or breakups of partnerships, must find new partners at advanced ages or live without a sexual partner.

In healthy long-term relationships, sex remains important. Many seniors report that their sexual relationships are "better than ever." Longtime partners often feel more comfortable exploring new and different pleasuring techniques with each other than they did in the past. They may have more time for sexual pleasuring and more privacy and freedom from the difficulties of raising children.

Other long-term relationships do not fare as well (Quirouette & Gold, 1992). There are many factors that can diminish sexual interest, activity, and/or pleasure between long-term partners. Long-standing unresolved conflicts can intensify until hostility blocks out sexual desire. Allowing feelings to surface, acknowledging their validity, and discussing them together can often renew sexual desire.

Sexual interest and pleasure aren't just for younger people. Many seniors report that their sexual relationships are "better than ever." Long-term partners might feel more comfortable exploring new and different pleasuring techniques than they did in the past and might have more time available for sexual pleasuring.

Sometimes after both partners retire from their careers they feel that they are spending too much time together. Each person feels emotionally crowded. For couples of any age, having some separate interests, activities, and friends helps keep the partners and their relationship alive and interesting (Butler & Lewis, 1993).

Because women have a longer average life expectancy than men and often pair with men who are older than themselves, most heterosexual women will experience the loss of a partner through death. After a time of grieving, most women feel continuing needs for love, affection, companionship, and sexual expression. The same is true for men whose partners die first.

Because of the longer life expectancy of women compared to men, heterosexual women over age 60 have more difficulty finding new partners than older men do. Only one-quarter of widows remarry within five years of the loss of their spouse, and the majority never remarry (Wortman & Silver, 1993). Lesbian women are in a more advantageous position as they grow older, since partners who are their own age will have a similar life expectancy, and they move in a world that becomes increasingly female with each passing year.

When older people separate or divorce, additional adjustments are necessary, especially for the partner who did not initiate the breakup (Wright & Maxwell, 1991). In addition to grieving over the end of the relationship, this partner might experience a period of low self-esteem and lack of sexual confidence. The feeling of rejection, added to possible age-related feelings of unattractiveness, might cause reluctance to enter into a new relationship.

Privacy issues can be a significant problem for older men and women who wish to pursue a sexual relationship (or even personal sexual expression, such as masturbation). Many seniors live in group settings or with their adult children and their families. While some situations can be conducive to intimacy (an apartment with a separate entrance, or a condominium in a senior community), others severely limit opportunities for privacy. Nursing homes may fail to provide for an individual's (or a couple's) need for privacy for sexual expression.

### 14.13.1 Partner Availability for Older Heterosexual People: The Double Standard of Aging

Finding a sexual partner is more difficult for an older woman than it is for an older man. Through widowhood, divorce, or by choice, great numbers of older heterosexual women are unmarried. They are twice as likely to be unmarried as older men. Newly single men over 65 are *seven times* more likely to remarry than women over 65 (Goodwin, 1987).

What accounts for this difference? For starters, the ratio of women to men increases with each additional year of age as more males than females die. In the over-65 category, women greatly outnumber men. In 1992, over 48 percent of all women over age 65 were widowed, while only 15 percent of men over 65 were widowed (Butler & Lewis, 1993).

But female-to-male ratio is only the beginning of the story. When older men remarry, they usually marry younger women (Kenrick & Keefe, 1992). Our youth-worshiping culture especially penalizes older women. Even the slightest sign of age in a woman is seen by some as reducing her sexual desirability. Something as simple as a few wrinkles or gray hairs, or mature body contours, can cause a woman to feel less desirable and cause some men to agree with her. Our society's "ideal" woman, in terms of sexual attractiveness, is just barely through puberty.

In contrast, signs of age in males are often perceived as adding to sex appeal. Wrinkles, gray hair, even baldness can be interpreted as "sexy." Signs of aging suggest that a man may have accumulated some interesting experiences and possibly some wealth.

Our society feels more comfortable with the pairing of an older man and a younger woman than with the opposite, although a significant number of older women do pair with younger men. On the whole, however, as a heterosexual woman grows older her

With the double standard of aging (men can show their age, women can't) society tends to "understand" the pairing of an older man with a younger woman more readily than it "understands" couples in which the woman is older than the man.

range of potential sexual partners narrows, while as a man grows older his options increase (Kenrick & Keefe, 1992).

New relationships don't just "happen." People of any age who are alone have to take an active role in establishing a new partnership. Here are some suggestions for older people of either gender who would like to find new relationships (Butler & Lewis, 1993):

- Get involved with groups of people who share your common interests (sports, hobbies, travel, books, gourmet foods, hiking, biking, nature, birdwatching, music, dancing, theater, art, gambling, fine wine, volunteer work, etc.).

- If you're an older woman, don't feel that you still have to wait for a man to take the initiative. It is very acceptable today for a woman to pick up the phone and ask a man to share an activity. He has the option of refusing, just as you do when a man asks you.

- Senior centers and clubs can be found in almost every community.

- Many tour and cruise companies promote special travel arrangements for older single people.

- If you have religious beliefs, become active in your church.

- Go to high school and college reunions.

- Commercial singles clubs and computer dating services are suitable for older people as well as for young people.

- Let your friends know that you are looking for someone. People love to be matchmakers and can often introduce you to just the right person.

## 14.14 AGING IN THE LESBIAN AND GAY COMMUNITIES

Conflicting accounts appear on the relative ease of aging in the lesbian, gay, and bisexual (LGB) communities versus the heterosexual community (Berzon, 1992b; Berger & Kelly, 1992; McDougall, 1993). Some authorities, such as Berger and Kelly (1992) and McDougall (1993), suggest that LGB individuals may be at an advantage in coping with aging. Several reasons are cited.

One of the most difficult adjustments to advancing age is learning to cope with the stigma that our society attaches to older people (as being less attractive, less capable, and less valuable). Heterosexuals, especially if they are white, might face such stigma for the first time when they grow older. But older LGB men and women have dealt with negative stereotyping and stigma for many years. Most have learned how to value themselves and to survive as self-respecting people despite the stereotyping (McDougall, 1993).

Another advantage held by older LGB individuals is that as young adults, most developed a higher degree of independence and self-sufficiency than many heterosexuals did. Many LGB young people had to face the possibility that their homosexuality could have alienated their family and friends Thus, LGB individuals tend to become more self-sufficient, in emotional as well as practical ways. This independence serves them well as they reach advanced ages and friends and lovers die (Berger & Kelly, 1992).

Older LGB people are less likely than older heterosexuals to feel confined to rigid gender roles. Older heterosexuals who have spent much of their lives in partnerships might be unable to perform

Gay and lesbian people might have some aging advantages over heterosexual people. They are often more independent, more experienced in dealing with stigma and stereotyping, and more flexible in gender roles.

some essential life duties that they have depended on their partners to take care of. When their partners are unable to perform those duties, they are at a loss (Berger & Kelly, 1992).

Lesbian women and gay men who are out (more open about their orientation) are reported to be more comfortable about their aging than those who are more closeted (Quam, 1992). This does not necessarily indicate a cause-and-effect relationship, because people who are more comfortable with their sexual orientation might also feel more comfortable about their advancing age.

Like heterosexual people, LGB people are likely to remain sexually active at advanced ages. In a study of 100 lesbian women over age 60 (Kehoe, 1989), 66 were still sexually active. Of those 34 who were not currently sexually active, two-thirds said it was not by choice.

Isensee (1990) suggests that the normal decline in a man's sexual abilities—slower erection, longer refractory period, and so on—are more difficult for gay male couples to accept than for heterosexual couples, because of a greater emphasis on sex in the gay male culture. He suggests that gay partners talk to each other about how they feel about these changes. A de-

cline in sexual frequency or intensity need not be viewed as indicating any loss of interest in the relationship or decrease in the partners' depth of feeling for each other.

Very few mainstream "senior centers" or other agencies for the aged cater to the needs of older LGB adults (Martin & Lyon, 1992; Berger & Kelly, 1992). Almost all senior centers are designed with only heterosexuals in mind. But older lesbian, gay, and bisexual people also need to find new friends, support groups, and life-enriching programs. Fortunately, most large cities and many smaller ones have an abundance of social and political organizations where older members of the LGB communities are made very welcome.

## 14.15 SOCIETY'S RESPONSE TO THE SEXUALITY OF OLDER PEOPLE

Contrary to the myths about aging that are accepted as truth by many people, older people are still sexual beings with sexual thoughts and needs that often persist to very advanced ages. Yet the sexual needs of older men and women are often ignored by family members, caregivers, and society in general (Hodson & Skeen, 1994; Deacon, Minichiello, & Plummer, 1995).

It should not be assumed that the normal physiological changes associated with advancing age, or even the pathological changes that occur in some older people, reduce the desire, ability, or opportunity to enjoy sexual activities. Alternative interpretations and expressions of sexuality may be one of the greatest benefits of growing older, especially in the absence of socially and culturally adverse attitudes and expectations about the sexuality of older people (Deacon, Minichiello, & Plummer, 1995).

The attitudes and expectations of health care providers regarding aging and sexual function can have a special impact on their older clients. Physicians, nurses, and other care providers need to assess their own beliefs and values about the sexuality of older people and how these beliefs and values are reflected in their communication with older clients. Health care workers in particular are in a position to understand that aging does not need to impair the ability to give and receive affection. Promoting the total well-being of their clients includes discussion of sexual health and adjustment. Caregivers may need to initiate this discussion, because some older people will be shy or embarrassed to mention sexual concerns (Gender, 1992).

We all may need to change some of our ways of thinking so that we don't see sexual activity and romance as being only for the young. Older people also have needs and abilities for intimacy, friendship, and sexual fulfillment. They might also have more time to pursue these ambitions. Older people are sexual beings in as valid a sense as are young people. It is to the personal advantage of those of us who are still younger to accept this fact, because eventually each of us, with luck, will be one of those older adults.

## SUMMARY

1. Intimacy in adult relationships includes at least six dimensions: authenticity, openness, sharing of affection, sharing of knowledge and information, sharing of tasks, and exclusiveness of the relationship.

2. In a continuing relationship, the level of intimacy varies from day to day and year to year.

3. People of all ages and sexual orientations enjoy dating to fulfill needs for companionship and the company of a sexually attractive person.

4. The most productive places to meet potential dates are places where people share a common interest. Workplace romance is a complicated subject, with the potential for sexual harassment or uncomfortable situations.

5. Gay and lesbian dating is free of many of the gender-typed roles and behaviors of heterosexual dating.

6. Physical abuse occurs in 20 to 30 percent of college dating relationships.

7. Singles now make up a large portion of the adult U.S. population. Millions of people live alone, either by choice or by necessity. The advantage is great freedom. The potential disadvantage is loneliness.

8. Cohabitation is prevalent in all socioeconomic strata and all age groups.

9. About 71 percent of American women and 70 percent of men can be predicted to marry at least once. The average age at the time of first marriage is about 25.0 for women and 26.9 for men. On the average, married people are happier, healthier, and live longer than those who have never married, who are divorced, or who are widowed.

10. Lesbian women and gay men look to their partnerships to fulfill the same needs as straight people do. Special challenges include a lack of role models, internalized homophobia, social influences, and conflicts concerning outness.

11. Most people in emotionally committed relationships expect monogamy, but nonmonogamy is very common.

12. Few people are adequately prepared for the challenges of parenting. Parents are encouraged to make use of the many resources available to learn effective parenting techniques.

13. Increasing numbers of gay men and lesbian women are parenting, and are just as effective as parents as heterosexual people are.

14. Blended families (his kids, her kids, and maybe their kids) face many challenges not experienced in most other families.

15. At current divorce rates, about half of all marriages will end in divorce. Divorce can be made easier by careful timing, agreement on finances and child custody, and counseling to help with the emotional aspects.

16. There are six types of aging: chronological, biological, cosmetic, social, psychological, and economic.

17. Ageism is the stereotyping of and discrimination against people simply because of their age. Ageism is prevalent in the U.S. society.

18. Four common myths about sex and aging are that sex is for the young, that older people are not able to enjoy sex, that older people are physically unattractive and therefore sexually undesirable, and that it is shameful for older people to have sex.

19. During midlife, both genders experience hormonal declines referred to as the climacteric.

20. Sexual activity is a vital part of the lives of most middle-aged people. Sexual response for them is usually slower, which can cause anxiety, particularly for a male. Women are often more orgasmic in middle age than when they were younger.

21. By the year 2040, 20 to 25 percent of the population will be over age sixty-five. Our society does not really expect older people to be interested in sex and does not deal well with their sexuality.

22. Specific sexual changes in older males include decreased urgency of sex drive, a slower and less rigid erection, ejaculation that might require more stimulation and is less forceful, reduced semen volume, and a longer refractory period.

23. Specific sexual changes in older females include reduced and slower vaginal lubrication, thinning of the vaginal lining, and reduced number of orgasmic contractions.

24. In healthy long-term relationships, sex remains important at very advanced ages and might be perceived as being "better than ever." Relationships with unresolved conflicts do not fare as well.

25. Some authorities suggest that lesbian women and gay men may have an advantage over heterosexual people in coping with aging, because they have more experience with coping with stigma and stereotyping, greater independence, and greater flexibility on gender roles.

26. Barriers to sexual fulfillment in older people are more likely to be social than physical. Older people are sexual in as valid a sense as younger people, a fact that society has yet to accept.

## CRITICAL THINKING CHALLENGES

1. Mary Krueger (1996) argues that sexist assumptions about female sexuality are one cause of sexual coercion and acquaintance rape. Our society is uncomfortable with the idea of women as sexual agents with their own erotic needs. In a culture that denies women the freedom to say yes to sex, "no" does not always really mean no. Krueger believes that eliminating male sexual aggression from dating relationships will require elimination of sexist assumptions first. Do you agree with this position? What would be effective means of pursuing these goals?

2. What kinds of support organizations and social groups are available in your community for newly divorced individuals? For single adults? For older adults?

3. If you were responsible for the care of an aging person, how would you go about making sure their needs for privacy for sexual expression are being met? How would you broach the subject? What kinds of arrangements would you make if they lived in your home? In an institution or retirement community? How would you feel when considering their sexuality?

# FERTILITY MANAGEMENT

**AFTER STUDYING THIS CHAPTER, YOU SHOULD BE ABLE TO**

[1] Explain why managing one's fertility is important in today's world.

[2] Briefly summarize some significant historical developments relevant to fertility control.

[3] List and define some important terms relevant to understanding modern contraceptive methods.

[4] List and describe the factors that enter into choosing a particular contraceptive technique.

[5] Define abstinence and explain the various menstrual charting techniques. Briefly indicate the advantages and disadvantages of these "low-tech" techniques.

[6] Explain why withdrawal is not considered an effective contraceptive technique.

[7] List and describe the various barrier methods of contraception. Briefly list the advantages and disadvantages of this approach to contraception.

[8] Describe the modern IUD, how it prevents pregnancy, and the advantages and disadvantages of this contraceptive method.

[9] Describe the various types of oral contraceptives, how they work to prevent pregnancy, and the advantages and disadvantages of this popular contraceptive method.

[10] Explain the advantages of progestin-only contraceptives, particularly implants such as Norplant, or the use of Depo-Provera.

[11] Distinguish between male and female sterilization techniques and describe the advantages and disadvantages of this approach to contraception.

[12] List and describe the various postcoital contraceptive options now available.

[13] Define abortion and briefly summarize the nature of the controversy that surrounds pregnancy termination.

[14] List and describe the various methods of abortion.

[15] Summarize important points regarding the safety of abortions and the process of decision making that surrounds pregnancy termination.

## 15.1 THINKING ABOUT FERTILITY MANAGEMENT

In some human societies, the creation of as many children as possible is a central value. This was true even in our own society when North America was an agrarian (agriculture-based) society. Today, relatively few societies can afford this perspective. The general trend is that as a society becomes more industrialized and as women particularly become more educated, attempts to limit and manage the birth rate increase. In our culture, the vast majority of adults devote considerable time, attention, and resources to controlling and managing the circumstances under which children are conceived and birthed. On a personal and interpersonal level, the decision to birth a child is often seen as a sign of intimacy and as a lifelong commitment between two people to the care and raising of that child. For the single woman, there is often an awareness that a pregnancy may mean a change in the course of the rest of her life. On a global level, access to reliable contraception is the key to maintaining a healthy planet for all of our children (Grant, 1994). The control of reproduction is a very personal and intimate aspect of relating sexually to another person. It is also an issue that needs attention all through a couple's relationship, whether that relationship lasts for one night or for a lifetime.

### 15.1.1 Some Basic Concepts in Contemporary Fertility Management

The very general term *fertility management* was deliberately chosen as the title of this chapter in order to communicate that there are several issues involved in controlling reproduction. The term **contraception** involves overt actions taken to prevent conception. Sometimes the term **birth control** is used interchangeably with *contraception,* but it implies that a couple or individual is using techniques to limit the number of children who are birthed. Thus, birth control is more equivalent to **family planning.** All of these techniques offer control over whether and when pregnancies occur. Should these contraceptive methods fail and a pregnancy occur, a woman or couple is faced with the decision whether to maintain the pregnancy and birth a child, or to terminate the pregnancy through an **elective abortion.**

Another important concept allows us to better evaluate the effectiveness of a particular contraceptive method. For every method discussed here you will see reference to the *perfect use failure rate.* This number refers to the number of pregnancies that are likely to occur in a year (per hundred uses of the

An unplanned pregnancy can change a person's plans and goals. Annually, 1 in 8 women aged fifteen to nineteen in the United States becomes pregnant. Perhaps if men became pregnant, they would be more careful.

method during sexual intercourse) if the method were used absolutely perfectly, that is, without error. More practical is the *typical use failure rate.* This refers to the number of pregnancies that are likely to occur with typical use—that is, with a normal number of errors, memory lapses, incorrect or incomplete usages, etc. In other words, this is the failure rate for real people.

### 15.1.2 A Brief History of Contraception

There is evidence that in ancient Egypt women inserted crocodile dung and honey into their vaginas to block and soak up sperm. In ancient Greece, eating various body parts of a mule was thought to prevent pregnancy (you might recall that mules are sterile). Consumption of the seeds of the Queen Anne's lace plant was known to irritate the uterine lining and interfere with implantation. This method is still used in parts of India and isolated areas of the Appalachian Mountains in North Carolina (Riddle, Estes, & Russell, 1994).

In eighteenth-century Europe, withdrawal, vaginal absorbents, postcoital douching, and condoms made of sheep intestines were among the contraceptive techniques known to the affluent and to prostitutes (Bullough & Bullough, 1994). The legendary Casanova boasted about his use of penile "sheaths," which he referred to as "English riding coats." Abortion and **infanticide** (the killing of newborns) were also employed to control family size. During the nineteenth century early versions of the diaphragm, **spermicides** (chemicals that destroy sperm), condoms, and cervical caps began to appear. Female sterilization techniques were also developed. The twentieth century saw the development of the IUD and improved methods of male and female sterilization. Most significant of all, the oral contraceptive was developed. The reliability, effectiveness, and relative safety of this innovation resulted in major changes in sexual mores in the Western world beginning in the 1960s.

However, the historical path through these advances was not an easy one. It was not until 1965 that the United States Supreme Court (*Griswold v. Connecticut*) overturned the last major law forbidding the availability of contraceptive information and devices for married couples. In 1972 the Supreme Court finally decriminalized (*Eisenstadt v. Baird*) the laws against the use of contraception by single people.

During the early 1900s, nurse-activist Margaret Sanger (1883–1966) was deeply disturbed by the terrible suffering and deaths of poverty-stricken mothers who attempted to abort their many unwanted pregnancies. Sanger became determined to distribute contraceptive materials to these women. However, in the America of 1912, the Comstock Laws made it a crime for even health professionals to dispense such materials. Taking on the dangerous cause of reproductive rights for women, Sanger founded the National Birth Control League and opened a birth control clinic in Brooklyn, New York. Repeated clinic closures, arrests, and harassment by the authorities forced her to flee to Europe. Eventually, strong support by the American public and media allowed her to return to the United States. She remained a lifelong worker on behalf of family planning, and her organization later became Planned Parenthood of America. She also provided financial and organizational backing for people like Gregory Pincus, one of the developers of the oral contraceptive (Reed, 1984).

### 15.1.3 Choosing a Contraceptive Method

The ideal contraceptive method would meet the following criteria.

1. *Safety.* The most important factor in choosing a method of birth control is safety. No device should create health risks for either partner. In preventing pregnancy it should pose minimal side effects.

2. *Effectiveness.* Effectiveness should be maximal in preventing pregnancy. Unfortunately, the ideal birth control method has yet to be developed, and no currently used method is effective for everyone all of the time. Yet a person should strive to choose the method that is personally safest and most effective.

3. *Ease of use.* Some devices, such as the intrauterine device (IUD), are placed into the body by a professional and left there for an extended period of time. Other devices, such as the condom, diaphragm, and pill, are self-administered. Some devices must be inserted into or placed at the site of use prior to the beginning of sex play, rather than handled during the lovemaking.

4. *Acceptability.* The method chosen should be acceptable in terms of partners' medical history, physical comfort, religious viewpoints, and personal preferences.

5. *Reversibility.* Many users of birth control methods prefer one that is reversible, which means that when its use is discontinued the user's prior fertility is restored. A person might wish to retain the option of a future pregnancy.

6. *Affordability and availability.* The chosen birth control method should be at a cost the user can afford. Some contraceptive devices (such as pills and diaphragms) are available only by prescription from a physician, whereas others (such as condoms, foam, and suppositories) are available over the counter (without prescription) from a pharmacy.

A contraceptive that meets all these criteria perfectly has yet to be developed. Each of the contraceptive methods described here varies on all of these

| | |
|---|---|
| **contraception** (kon-tra-sep´shun) | the prevention of conception, or pregnancy |
| **birth control** | regulation of conception, pregnancy, and birth |
| **family planning** | planning for whether and when to have children |
| **elective abortion** | intentional expulsion of embryo or fetus |
| **infanticide** (in-fan´ti-sīd) | killing a newborn child |
| **spermicide** | sperm-killing chemical agent |

# WHERE DO I STAND?

## CONTRACEPTIVE COMFORT AND CONFIDENCE SCALE

In assessing your answers to these questions, you will be helping yourself decide whether the method of control you are using or considering is a realistic choice. (Members of a couple should answer these questions separately.)

Method of birth control you are considering using:    _____

Length of time you used this method in the past:    _____

Check **Yes** or **No** for each of the following questions:

|  |  | Yes | No |
|---|---|---|---|
| 1. | Have I had problems using this method before? | _____ | _____ |
| 2. | Have I or my partner ever become pregnant while using this method? | _____ | _____ |
| 3. | Am I afraid of using this method? | _____ | _____ |
| 4. | Would I really rather not use this method? | _____ | _____ |
| 5. | Will I or my partner have trouble remembering to use this method? | _____ | _____ |
| 6. | Will I or my partner have trouble using this method correctly? | _____ | _____ |
| 7. | Do I still have unanswered questions about this method? | _____ | _____ |
| 8. | Does this method make menstrual periods longer or more painful? | _____ | _____ |
| 9. | Does this method cost more than I can afford? | _____ | _____ |
| 10. | Could this method cause me or my partner to have serious complications? | _____ | _____ |
| 11. | Am I opposed to this method because of my religious or moral beliefs? | _____ | _____ |
| 12. | Is my partner opposed to this method? | _____ | _____ |
| 13. | Am I using this method without my partner's knowledge? | _____ | _____ |
| 14. | Will using this method embarrass my partner? | _____ | _____ |
| 15. | Will using this method embarrass me? | _____ | _____ |
| 16. | Will I or my partner enjoy intercourse less because of this method? | _____ | _____ |
| 17. | If this method interrupts lovemaking, will I avoid it? | _____ | _____ |
| 18. | Has a nurse or physician ever told me or my partner NOT to use this method? | _____ | _____ |
| 19. | Is there anything about my or my partner's personality that could lead me or my partner to use this method incorrectly? | _____ | _____ |
| 20. | Am I or is my partner at risk of being exposed to HIV or STIs if I use or my partner uses this method? | _____ | _____ |

Most persons will have a few "yes" answers. "Yes" answers mean that problems might arise. If you have more than a few "yes" responses, you may want to talk with a physician, counselor, partner, or friend to help you decide whether to use this method or how to use it so that it will really be effective for you. In general, the more "yes" answers you have, the less likely you are to use this method consistently and correctly at every act of intercourse.

**Source:** Adapted from Hatcher et al. 1994, p. 130.

factors. The best we can do is offer you the most accurate and up-to-date information about options available now and in the near future. It will be up to you and your partner to make an informed decision in selecting the method that meets most of your priorities. (To help determine what contraceptive methods are best for you, see "Where Do I Stand? Contraceptive Comfort and Confidence Scale.") The advice and support of a contraception professional is also desirable.

The contraceptive technique that is "best" is likely to depend on factors such as stage of life, sexual lifestyle, physical health, and religious orientation. No one particular method meets everyone's needs. For example, a monogamous couple in their early twenties attend colleges half a continent apart. They have limited incomes and see each other only during school year breaks. Condoms and spermicidal foam might make the most sense for this couple. A married couple with two children are agreed that they want no more children. Permanent sterilization is likely to allow them to enjoy their sexual relationship without contraceptive paraphernalia and concerns. Which contraceptive technique makes the most sense for you today? Will it make equal sense in fifteen years?

## 15.2 "LOW-TECH" AND "NO-WAY" METHODS

### 15.2.1 Abstinence

The term *abstinence* can mean different things to different individuals or couples. Some people use the term to refer to refraining from any type of sexual expression, whether partnered or solitary—that is, **celibacy.** Others use the term *abstinence* to mean refraining only from partnered sex. Sexologists view voluntary abstinence as a normal and acceptable lifestyle choice. There are no known negative physical or psychological effects of voluntary abstinence no matter the length of time. According to the NHSLS (Laumann et al., 1994), 14 percent of male and 10 percent of female respondents (ages 18–59) reported they had not engaged in sexual activity in the year prior to the survey. Individuals and couples might choose sexual abstinence for any number of reasons, and they might remain abstinent for a short time or a lifetime. These reasons could include fear of STIs, religious commitments, geographic separation, medical problems, or just a personal preference.

In terms of fertility management, **abstinence** involves refraining from penile-vaginal contact. Abstinence implies no possibility of pregnancy.

### Advantages and Disadvantages

Advantages:

- no possibility of an unwanted pregnancy
- avoidance of genital exposure to STIs
- might intensify sexual desire
- no costs involved

Disadvantages:

- might create feelings of loneliness
- might lead to sexual frustration

## 15.2.2 Fertility Awareness Methods

Observing the monthly menstrual cycle and recording it on a regular basis is known as **menstrual cycle charting** or fertility awareness. The goal of this method is to pinpoint when a woman ovulates and then identify her fertile days (those days when an ovum is in the fallopian tubes and thus can be fertilized). The success of this method as a contraceptive technique depends on *periodic abstinence*—that is, abstaining from intercourse during these fertile days. An understanding of these methods can also be used to *increase the likelihood that conception will occur.* Couples or individuals eager to become pregnant can chart the ovulatory cycle and pinpoint the optimal time to introduce sperm into the vagina, whether through intercourse or through artificial insemination.

The variety of techniques that depend on menstrual cycle charting are sometimes referred to as *natural family planning* (NFP). This does not imply that other methods are somehow "unnatural"; it only means that this method depends on the naturally occurring rhythm of the menstrual and ovulatory cycles.

### Charting the Menstrual Cycle

All of the various menstrual charting methods are based on three assumptions (and they can be faulty assumptions): (1) that ovulation occurs 14 days (plus or minus 2 days) *before* the beginning of menstruation (but not necessarily 14 days after the onset of the last menstrual period); (2) that sperm deposited into the vagina remain viable for only 2 to 3 days; and (3) that unless fertilized by sperm within 12 to 24 hours after ovulation, the ovum degenerates.

The charting methods include the calendar method, the basal body temperature method, the cervical mucus method, and the sympto-thermal method.

*Calendar Method:* The calendar rhythm method is the oldest and most widely practiced *fertility awareness* method worldwide, as well as the most common one in the United States (Hatcher et al., 1994; Frank-Hermann et al., 1991).

| | |
|---|---|
| celibate (sel′i-bat′) | not engaging in solitary or partnered sexual expression |
| abstinent | refraining from sexual intercourse |
| menstrual cycle charting | recording of monthly menstrual events to aid in inducing or preventing pregnancy |

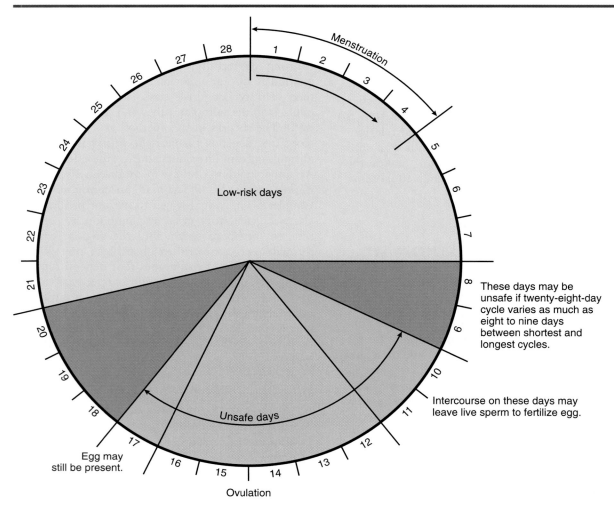

**FIGURE 15.1** The calendar (rhythm) method based on avoiding intercourse when the sperm might meet the ovum. The figure indicates days on which the chances of conception are greater.

First, a woman must record the length of at least eight menstrual cycles to determine the average length of her cycle. The first day of her period is considered day 1 of each new cycle. Second, she needs to subtract 18 days from the length of the shortest cycle to find the *first* fertile (unsafe) day and 11 days from the length of the longest cycle to find the *last* fertile day. For example, if her cycles average 28 days, the first unsafe day is the 10th day, and the last unsafe day is the 17th day (fig. 15.1). Another example: If a woman's shortest cycle was 26 days and the longest was 31 days, the first unsafe day of her cycle is day 8 (26 − 18 = 8), and the last unsafe day of each cycle is day 20 (31 − 11 = 20). For contraception, the couple must abstain from sexual intercourse from day 8 until day 20.

*Basal Body Temperature:* Basal body temperature (BBT) is defined as one's lowest body temperature upon awakening. A drop in BBT of several tenths of a degree might precede ovulation by 12 to 24 hours, followed by a sustained rise when ovulation is occurring or has occurred (due to progesterone released by the corpus luteum) (Stewart et al., 1987; MacDonald, Dombroski, & Casey, 1991) (see fig. 15.2). Although the upward shift indicates ovulation or *postovulation,* there is little warning of the shift—that is, there is no way to *predict* the day of ovulation. By recording the BBT for several months, a woman might be able to identify when ovulation occurs.

When using the **basal body temperature (BBT) method,** a woman must record her temperature every day, immediately upon rising and before any physical exercise or urinating. A special BBT thermometer should be used, or one can purchase new electronic thermometers with memories or an electric resistance meter that can accurately pinpoint a woman's fertile period (Goldberg, 1994). The BBT method is useful

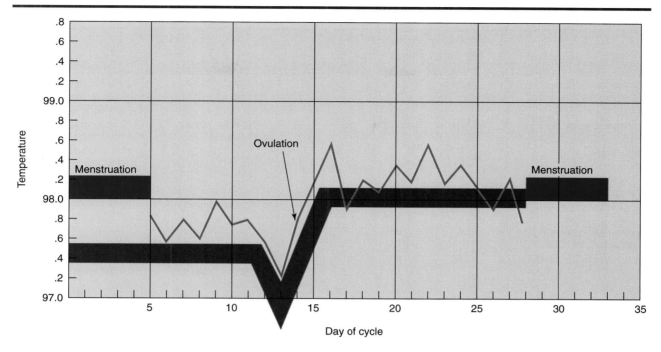

**FIGURE 15.2** Basal body temperature method. Resting, or basal, temperature is taken each morning and recorded for several months. A woman then times intercourse to avoid the days of ovulation each month. A drop in the basal body temperature may precede ovulation by 12 to 24 hours, followed by a progressive rise during the next several days postovulation.

for contraceptive purposes but not for optimizing conception. This is because it is difficult to predict fertile days with this technique.

*Cervical Mucus Method:* To use the **cervical mucus method** (also called the *ovulation* or *Billings method*), a woman must attend to the changing quality of her cervical mucus during the various phases of her menstrual cycle. Cervical mucus secretions are usually cloudy, but near ovulation they become clear, slippery (like raw egg white), and stretch between the fingers in a thin strand of two inches or more. This stretchability is called *spinnbarkheit*. This altered discharge usually coincides with a feeling of increased vaginal wetness or stickiness. The last day of spinnbarkheit is called the *peak day,* and ovulation typically occurs the day *after* the peak day. A woman is fertile from the time the clear mucus appears until the fourth day after the peak day. Menstruation typically begins 11 to 16 days after the peak day. For contraception, intercourse must be restricted to the days well *after* ovulation (Hatcher et al., 1994). This technique can be used for either contraceptive purposes or to increase the likelihood of conception.

*The Sympto-Thermal Method:* The **sympto-thermal method (STM)** combines the BBT with the ovulation method. Here, a woman attends to the changes in cervical mucus *before* ovulation and BBT to confirm

that ovulation is occurring. The fertile period ends either at the end of the third day of elevated temperature or the fourth day after peak mucus, whichever is later. Unprotected intercourse is avoided until the termination of the fertile period. The sympto-thermal method can be used either for family planning or to maximize the possibility of conception.

## Effectiveness and Cost

The typical use failure rate is about 20 percent during the first year of use. The perfect use failure rate ranges from 9 percent for the calendar method down to about 1 percent for the basal body temperature method (table 15.1). When couples confine unprotected intercourse to the postovulation period only, the lowest failure rate is achieved. The ovulation

| basal body temperature (BBT) method | recording daily basal body temperature to determine time of ovulation |
|---|---|
| cervical mucus method | observing changes in cervical mucus secretions to determine time of ovulation |
| sympto-thermal method (STM) | combining methods of basal body temperature and cervical mucus to determine time of ovulation |

**TABLE 15.1**    FAILURE RATES OF BIRTH CONTROL METHODS

| Method | Typical Use Failure Rate % | Perfect Use Failure Rate % | Cost* | Advantages | Disadvantages |
|---|---|---|---|---|---|
| Chance (no protection) | 85.00 | 85.00 | 0 | No preparation; no hormones or chemicals | High risk of pregnancy; provides little peace of mind if pregnancy is not wanted |
| Spermicidal agents (foams, creams, jellies, and vaginal suppositories) | 21.00 | 6.00 | $0.85 | Easy to obtain and use; no prescription | Continuing expense; requires high motivation, presence of mind to use correctly and consistently with each intercourse |
| Periodic abstinence (calendar, cervical mucus, sympto-thermal, basal body temperature) | 20.00 | 9.00 3.00 2.00 1.00 | 0 | No preparation or cost; no hormones or chemicals | May be frustrating to full enjoyment of intercourse; low effectiveness |
| Withdrawal (*coitus interruptus*) | 19.00 | 4.00 | 0 | No hormones or chemicals; acceptable to those who object to devices or hormones/ chemicals | Requires much motivation and cooperation between partners |
| Cervical cap (with spermicide) parous (previously given birth) nulliparous (no previous birth) | 36.00 18.00 | 26.00 9.00 | $20** | Can be left in place for several days; uses no hormones; no side effects | Can be dislodged by intercourse; requires skill in insertion; can cause vaginal or cervical trauma |
| Diaphragm (with spermicide) | 18.00 | 6.00 | $22** | Easy to obtain and use; uses no hormones; no side effects; helps consistently prevent disease | Continuing expense; requires high motivation to use correctly and with each intercourse |
| Condom (without spermicide) female (*Reality*) male | 21.00 12.00 | 5.00 3.00 | $2.50 $0.50 | No side effects; easy to use; easy to obtain; helps prevent disease if contains nonoxynol-9; no prescription required | Continuing expense; must use every time; can interrupt continuity of lovemaking |
| Pill Progestin only (minipill) Combined (oral contraceptive) | 3.00 | 0.50 0.10 | $10–20/cycle | Highly effective; easy to use | Daily use required; continuing cost; slight medical risk; some side effects |
| IUD Progestasert T Copper T 380A | 2.00 0.80 | 1.50 0.60 | $120** | Needs little attention; no expense after insertion | Side effects; possible expulsion; might perforate uterine wall; some incidence of pelvic inflammatory disease |
| Depo-Provera | 0.30 | 0.30 | $35/injection | No day-to-day attention required; long-lasting protection | Some risk of infertility after using; side effects |
| Norplant (6 capsules) | 0.09 | 0.09 | $350/kit** | No day-to-day attention; low hormone levels for high protection; might protect against pelvic inflammatory disease | Tenderness at site; menstrual changes |
| Female sterilization | 0.40 | 0.40 | +/−$1,200** | Permanent relief from pregnancy worries | Low success of surgical reversal; possible surgical/medical/ psychological complications |
| Male sterilization | 0.15 | 0.10 | +/−$250– 400*** | Permanent relief from pregnancy worries | Low success of surgical reversal; possible surgical/medical/ psychological complications |
| Abstinence | 0.00 | 0.00 | | No chance of pregnancy | May require much motivation |

*A unit cost; will vary with location; may be less in public clinics.
** Plus practitioner's cost of fitting, insertion, or removal.
*** Public sector; private sector is more expensive.

**Source:** From R. Hatcher, et al., *Contraceptive Technology*, 17th revised edition, 1994. Copyright © 1994 Irvington Publishing. Reprinted by permission.

method and sympto-thermal methods are viewed as effective when taught carefully, well understood, and properly used (Moffat, 1993).

Costs will vary depending on whether barrier methods are used as a backup and the expense of charts, thermometers, and other equipment. How well do you believe you and your partner would fare with any of these methods?

## Advantages and Disadvantages

### Advantages:

▌ helps a woman know her own body

▌ no hormones or chemicals are used or put into the body

▌ potentially minimal cost

▌ can be useful for those who do not have access to other contraceptives or who have ethical, religious, or medical reasons for not using other techniques

### Disadvantages:

▌ typical use failure rate is high

▌ requires consistent motivation on the part of both partners regarding ban on intercourse during fertile period

▌ requires careful record keeping

▌ requires careful attention to monthly changes in bodily cycles

▌ no protection from STIs

▌ frustration if noncoital sexual expression is not acceptable during fertile periods

▌ many women vary widely in the length of their menstrual and ovulatory cycles

## 15.2.3 Withdrawal: A "No-Way" Way

**Withdrawal,** or removal of the penis from the vagina just before ejaculation, may be the oldest of attempts to avoid pregnancy. The Latin term for this technique is *coitus interruptus,* but more common terms include *pulling out* and *taking care.* Experts agree that it is very ineffective as a method of avoiding pregnancy, yet it continues to be used a great deal. (See "Healthy Sexuality: Mythical and Magical Contraceptive Techniques.") Nevertheless, in Turkey and many other parts of the world, it is the most prevalent approach to family planning (Durbin, 1996).

### Use

Withdrawal depends on both timing and physical distance. A man must be very sensitive to the first signs of impending ejaculation and be prepared to terminate intercourse at that moment. He must also quickly move his penis away from the labia, because

if sperm are deposited there, they can continue moving up into the vagina and into the cervix. Because of such motility, it is crucial that no sperm come into contact with a woman's genitals.

As a birth control technique, withdrawal is further compromised by the fact that the preejaculatory fluid ("pre-cum") secreted from the Cowper's gland might contain a great deal of sperm (Ilaria et al., 1992; Pudney et al., 1992). Quite obviously, withdrawal is not a very reliable contraceptive technique.

Withdrawal also runs counter to many of the psychological and physical urges of the coital couple. Women might prefer that thrusting continue in order to reach orgasm. Many men would prefer deep penetration at the moment of ejaculation. Thus withdrawal can curtail sexual satisfaction for both partners.

### Effectiveness

The typical failure rate for withdrawal is 19 percent. The perfect use rate is difficult to estimate (Trussell et al., 1990). In the case of an accidental ejaculation in or near the vagina, even an immediate application of spermicide would be too late to keep some sperm from entering the vagina.

### Advantages and Disadvantages

#### Advantages:

▌ no preparations are necessary

▌ no cost

▌ no hormones or chemicals are required

▌ can be done at any time and in any circumstance

▌ the man assumes responsibility

#### Disadvantages:

▌ relatively high failure rate

▌ it is difficult for many men to predict their ejaculation

▌ preejaculatory fluid can carry sperm

▌ no protection from STIs

▌ requires unfailing discipline and consistency

▌ requires continuing motivation and self-control

▌ interferes with spontaneity in intercourse

▌ ever-present fear of failure

▌ terminating intercourse prior to climax can be disturbing and can create sexual tensions in both partners

| withdrawal | removal of penis from vagina prior to ejaculation |

## HEALTHY SEXUALITY

### MYTHICAL AND MAGICAL CONTRACEPTIVE TECHNIQUES

**NURSING AN INFANT:**   Breast-feeding will delay fertility immediately after childbirth, but it is not an effective contraceptive technique because there is no way to determine when ovulation resumes.

**DOUCHING:**   Some believe that postcoital douching will protect against pregnancy. However, sperm can enter the uterus within one minute after ejaculation. In fact, postcoital douching can sometimes aid sperm in reaching the cervix.

**WITHDRAWAL:**   Many sexologists believe that withdrawal should not be listed as a contraceptive technique, because the pregnancy rate for those using this method is just slightly better than using no contraceptives at all.

**TEEN TALES:**   Teenagers (and way too many adults) seem to have an array of mistaken ideas about preventing pregnancy. Most of these "tales" were collected from teenagers as they sat in prenatal care and abortion clinics.

- Having intercourse while standing up, or jumping up and down immediately after intercourse, will allow sperm to fall out of the vagina.
- If a woman doesn't have an orgasm, she can't become pregnant.
- A first intercourse can never lead to pregnancy.
- Douching with a cola drink can prevent pregnancy.

## 15.3   BARRIER METHODS

**Barrier methods** of contraception are designed to prevent sperm and ova from meeting. Attempts to do this date back to antiquity, and until the development of oral contraceptives they were the most effective method of birth control.

The most commonly used barrier device is the male condom. The other three barrier methods are used by women: the female condom, the diaphragm, and the cervical cap.

Except for the possible allergic reaction to the materials used to make the barrier devices, there are few side effects to their use (Goldberg, 1994). When barrier devices are used along with a spermicide containing nonoxynol-9, there is a considerable measure of protection from most STIs, including HIV.

### 15.3.1   The Male Condom

**Condoms** for men consist of a sheath that covers the penis during intercourse. They are commonly referred to as "rubbers," "prophylactics," and "safes." Next to oral contraceptives, condoms for men are the most widely used contraceptive device in North America. Most condoms are made of latex rubber; about 5 percent are made from lamb intestines. This last type is commonly referred to as "skins" or "natural membranes." Condoms are worn rather tightly

over the erect penis, and are fitted with a ring at the open end to keep them from slipping off the penis. If the condom is being used for protection against STIs, as well as for contraception, it is important to remember that skin condoms contain pores large enough for viruses such as HIV, hepatitis B, and herpes to pass through. The Food and Drug Administration does not permit skin condom packages to carry the "for disease prevention" labeling found on packages of latex condoms (Hatcher et al., 1994).

Over a hundred brands of condoms for men are sold in North America. American-made latex condoms differ little in their shape, but do offer variety in their texture (ribbing or stripping along the shaft).

Lubricants might or might not be present, and since 1982 many contain a spermicide such as nonoxynol-9 both inside and outside the condom. Such spermicidal-coated condoms have been shown to be highly effective in killing sperm within the condom and are estimated to be 99.9 percent effective in reducing the risk of spreading STIs (including HIV) (Kestelman & Trussell, 1991). No studies have shown a positive effect in the prevention of HIV for spermicide when used without condoms (Stone & Peterson, 1992). Latex condoms have either a plain end or a reservoir end, which is a nipplelike extension at the tip that holds the ejaculated sperm. Some condoms are tinted; most are a neutral color. Sometimes the dyes used to tint condoms will stain or cause burning and irritation for both partners. As public

## HEALTHY SEXUALITY

### USING THE CONDOM FOR MEN

To use the condom for men successfully for contraception (fig. 15.3), remember to:

1. Apply a condom every time before having vaginal or anal intercourse.
2. Handle the condom carefully to prevent snagging it with fingernails or rings.
3. Put the condom on the penis before any ejaculate is lost and before the penis touches the vaginal area.
4. Unroll the condom all the way to the base of the penis, leaving about one-half inch of empty space at the tip of the condom, unless the condom comes with a reservoir end to collect the ejaculate.
5. Lubricate the penis to ease entry into the vagina if a nonlubricated condom is used. Use *K-Y Jelly*, a spermicide, or saliva; *never* use an oil-based petroleum product (such as *Vaseline*), baby oil, vegetable oil, butter, or suntan oil; they can damage the condom.
6. Withdraw the penis soon after ejaculation and before erection is lost to prevent loss of ejaculate. When withdrawing, pinch the ring near the vagina to reduce the risk of pregnancy and STIs.
7. Check the condom for tears or leaks before discarding. If a leak or tear is found, or ejaculate is accidentally spilled into the vagina, apply some spermicide into the vagina immediately to minimize the risk of pregnancy.
8. Dispose of the condom after use. *Never reuse a condom.*
9. Store condoms in a cool, dry place. Do not store them in a wallet or in your car's glove box, because heat can cause rubber to deteriorate.
10. Each condom packet contains a manufacturer's date or an expiration date. An expiration date is marked as such, else it is a manufacturer's date. Do not use past the expiration date; do not use after five years past the manufacturer's date.

---

awareness and the popularity of condoms have increased, condom manufacturers continue to improve their appeal and effectiveness.

### Effectiveness and Cost

For best results in using the male condom, follow the instructions presented in "Healthy Sexuality: Using the Condom for Men." The male condom has a typical failure rate of about 12 percent and a perfect use failure rate of 3 percent. The use of foam or some other type of barrier method in conjunction with the condom enhances its effectiveness. If additional spermicide is used, it should be applied inside the vagina (Kestelman & Trussell, 1991). Do not store condoms in a wallet or the glove compartment of a car—heat can make condoms unusable.

If condoms are purchased in packages over the counter at the local pharmacy, cost can be as little as 50¢ per condom. Typical annual cost for regular condom use might be about $50 plus the cost of spermicide. (Cost will vary, depending on how frequently condoms are used.)

### Advantages and Disadvantages

*Advantages:*

- easily available to either partner at any drugstore
- completely reversible (that is, to conceive a child, just stop using the condom—there is no waiting period)
- relatively inexpensive
- no side effects, except for relatively rare allergic reactions
- protection from STIs
- contains no hormones

| | |
|---|---|
| **barrier methods** | types of contraceptives designed to prevent the sperm and egg from meeting |
| **condom** (kon´dum) | contraceptive sheath worn over the erect penis or in the vagina to prevent sperm from entering the vagina and uterus |

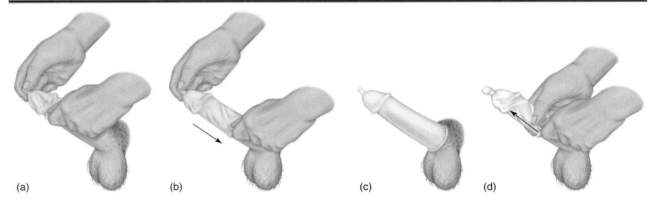

(a)                    (b)                         (c)            (d)

**FIGURE 15.3**  Using the condom for men. **a:** Begin unrolling the condom onto the tip of the penis; leave about one-half inch of empty space at the tip of the condom if the condom does not have a built-in reservoir to collect ejaculate. **b:** Unroll the condom to the base of the penis. **c:** When the condom is completely on, a water-based lubricant can be applied if the condom is not of the lubricated variety. **d:** After intercourse, carefully roll the condom back off of the penis, being careful not to spill any of the ejaculate, and dispose of the condom promptly.

▮ actively shared responsibility

▮ can be used anywhere, anytime

▮ use can be incorporated into pleasuring activities

*Disadvantages:*

▮ requires motivation and consistency for effective use

▮ some are allergic to latex or spermicide

▮ might lead to some loss of penile sensation

▮ prompt withdrawal of the penis after ejaculation is necessary, with careful removal of the condom

▮ condom might slip off penis during vigorous thrusting

▮ putting the condom on might disrupt lovemaking

## 15.3.2    The Female Condom

The **female condom** was approved by the Food and Drug Administration for over-the-counter sale in 1993. The female condom is a pouch that is worn inside the vagina (fig. 15.4). *Reality,* the most common brand available, is made of polyurethane, a clear, soft, impermeable material that is stronger than latex and less likely to tear or break. Resembling the material used in food storage bags, lubricated polyurethane (unlike the latex in male condoms) is not susceptible to deterioration when exposed to oil-based products, nor does it deteriorate during storage. It is designed with two flexible rings connected by the polyurethane sheath. One ring, at the closed end of the sheath, fits loosely over the cervix similar to a diaphragm. The other ring, at the open end of the sheath, remains out-side the vagina and covers the labial area. Because it covers the vulval area, it greatly reduces exposure to microorganisms that cause STIs. The female condom comes in only one size.

### Use

Designed to fit the contours of the vagina, the female condom allows the penis to move freely inside the sheath. It can be inserted up to eight hours before intercourse (Hatcher et al., 1994). It should not be used with a male condom, because they will not both stay in place (Goldberg, 1994). Like its male counterpart, it is designed to be discarded after one act of intercourse (Fackelman, 1992b).

### Effectiveness and Cost

The typical failure rate is 21 percent, and the perfect use failure rate is 5 percent. To be effective, there must not be any contact between the partners' genitals and no seminal fluids can touch the female genitals. Each condom costs about $2.50, and annual cost is estimated to be about $250 plus the cost of any backup spermicides.

### Advantages and Disadvantages

*Advantages:*

▮ no side effects except for rare allergic reactions

▮ completely and immediately reversible

▮ available over the counter at local pharmacies

▮ no involvement of health care professionals

▮ offers moderate protection from STIs

▮ relatively inexpensive

### Disadvantages:

▌ some loss of sensitivity

▌ use requires motivation and consistency

▌ not as effective as male latex condom in protecting against STIs

## 15.3.3   Diaphragm

The vaginal **diaphragm** is a shallow, round dome made of soft latex or gum rubber, about two to four inches in diameter. Its rim is sealed over a flexible metal spring or coil to hold it in place. The diaphragm is placed inside the vagina and is designed to completely cover the cervix of the uterus (fig. 15.5). It is held in place by the pressure of its rim against the narrow vaginal wall. A recent improvement in the diaphragm design includes a rim-attached soft latex flange designed to create a seal with the vaginal wall.

The diaphragm prevents pregnancy by blocking sperm from entering the cervix, and it helps destroy sperm by holding spermicidal jelly or creams near the cervix. The diaphragm might not always block the cervical canal, so the spermicide kills off any sperm that have moved across the rim of the diaphragm.

Until the 1960s, the diaphragm was the most common and effective contraceptive method to which women had access. Today, about 5 percent of all women who use contraceptives use the diaphragm (Hatcher et al., 1994).

### Use

Women vary regarding the length and width of their vaginas, and diaphragms are available in a range of sizes and in several different styles. Since a diaphragm of the wrong size can slip out of place or be dislodged during intercourse, a woman must be fitted for a diaphragm by a physician or nurse-practitioner. After instruction, most women can insert a diaphragm with ease and comfort. When properly fitted and inserted, a diaphragm cannot be felt by either partner. Once the diaphragm is in place, the user should check to be sure that the cervix is completely covered (fig. 15.5).

Prior to inserting the diaphragm, it should be checked for holes and cracks, because over time latex will deteriorate and leak. Then the inside surface of the diaphragm and its rim should be covered with spermicidal foam or cream. Such products are easily available over the counter at drug stores.

A diaphragm can be inserted up to six hours before intercourse or other penis-vagina contact. Since sperm can survive in the vagina for several hours, even in the presence of a spermicide, the diaphragm must be left in place for six to eight hours *after* intercourse. However, if left in place for longer than 24

hours, there is a risk of *toxic shock* (a rare but life-threatening condition caused by the toxins of a bacterium) (Hatcher et al., 1994). If intercourse is repeated within this time frame, more cream or foam should be inserted into the vagina, but the diaphragm should be left in place.

After removal, the diaphragm should be washed with warm water and mild soap, rinsed, dried, and stored in its plastic container away from light and heat.

The size and fit of a diaphragm should be routinely checked by a physician every year or two. Childbirth, miscarriage, abortion, or any significant change in weight can necessitate a new diaphragm. Even with normal wear, it is recommended that a diaphragm be replaced every three years (Hatcher et al., 1994).

### Effectiveness and Cost

When used with a spermicide, the typical failure rate of the diaphragm is 18 percent. The perfect use failure rate is 6 percent for the first year of use. The cost of a diaphragm is about $20, plus anywhere from $50 to $150 for fitting. The cost of spermicide is about $85 per year.

### Advantages and Disadvantages

#### Advantages:

▌ can be inserted up to six hours before sexual pleasuring begins

▌ no hormones are involved

▌ once properly fitted, a diaphragm can be used for several years

▌ once purchased and fitted, the only additional costs are for spermicide

▌ significantly reduces the risk of PID (pelvic inflammatory disease)

#### Disadvantages:

▌ must be sized and fitted by a health care professional

▌ requires motivation, some skill, and careful attention to properly care for, prepare, insert, and remove diaphragm

▌ must be attended to after each act of intercourse

| | |
|---|---|
| **female condom** | contraceptive sheath worn inside the vagina |
| **diaphragm** (dī´a-fram) | dome-shaped rubber device worn over cervix to prevent sperm from entering |

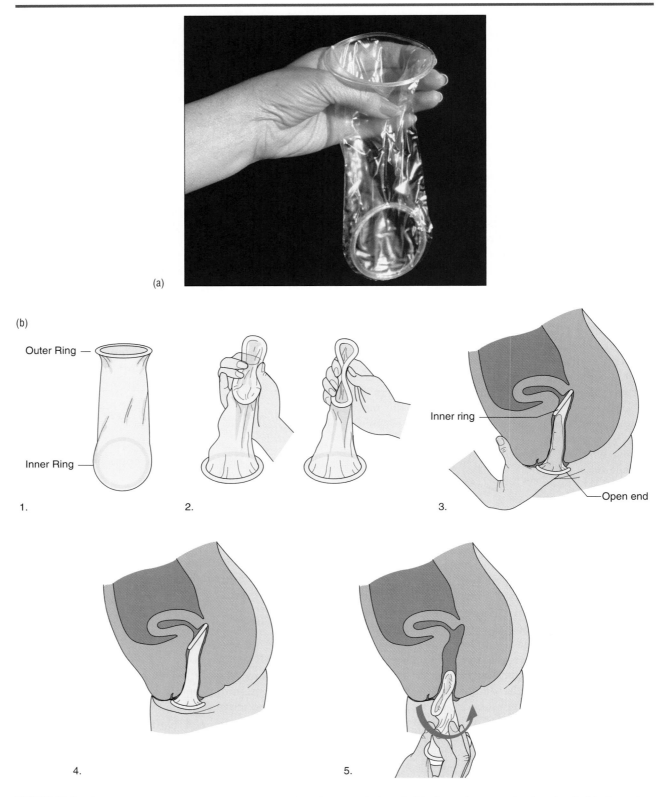

**FIGURE 15.4a:** The condom for women is a soft, loose-fitting polyurethane sheath with a flexible ring at the open end and another flexible ring at the closed end that fits over the cervix. **b:** Inserting the condom. (1) Remove the condom from package. (2) Hold the inner ring between thumb and fingers and squeeze. (3) Squeezing the inner ring, insert the sheath by gently pushing it toward the small of the back. (4) Make sure the sheath is not twisted. When the condom is properly inserted, the outer ring should rest on the labia around the vaginal opening, and the inner ring (closed end) should surround the cervix. (5) To remove the condom, squeeze and twist the outer ring. Pull out gently and dispose in the trash.

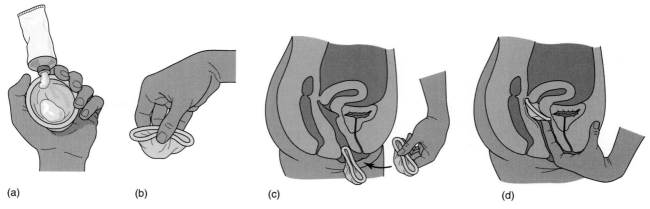

(a)                    (b)                    (c)                    (d)

**FIGURE 15.5**   The diaphragm is a soft latex dome with a rim enclosing a coil. **a:** Spermicide is applied around the rim. **b:** The diaphragm is pinched between the thumb and fingers. **c:** Then it is inserted into the vagina and **d:** positioned over the cervix.

- offers little protection against STIs
- some users may be allergic to latex and spermicides
- must be left in place at least six hours after intercourse
- taste of spermicide may interfere with enjoyment of oral sex

## 15.3.4   Cervical Cap

The **cervical cap** is a small, thimble-shaped, soft rubber device (resembling a miniature diaphragm) that fits snugly over the cervix. About one and one-half inches in diameter, it comes in several diameters (fig. 15.6). A groove on the inner lip of the cap helps to form an airtight seal around the cervix that holds it in place until removal. A metal version has been used in Europe, but the rubber version was approved for sale in the United States in 1988.

### Use

The cap must be fitted by a health professional. To use, the cap is filled to one-third level with spermicide before insertion. Once in place, it provides continuous protection for 48 hours, even with repeated intercourse. The cap must be left in place for at least six to eight hours after intercourse. Wearing the cap for longer than 48 hours increases the risk of toxic shock syndrome. After intercourse, the woman should check the cap with her finger to make certain it was not dislodged by the penis. If it is found to be out of place, extra cream or jelly should be inserted with an applicator.

Odor problems can occur if the cap is not removed frequently enough. Some women remove the cap every day or two to allow the flow of cervical fluids and to avoid toxic shock. The cap should not be used during the menstrual flow, because the seal of the cap can be broken by the flow. If it is used during this time, the cap should be removed daily to allow

| | |
|---|---|
| **cervical cap** (ser´vi-kal) | small plastic or rubber cuplike contraceptive positioned over the cervix |

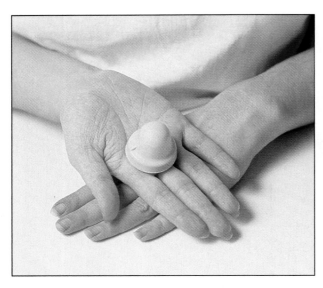

**FIGURE 15.6** The cervical cap is like a miniature diaphragm, but it only covers the cervix.

the secretions to flow. After use, the cap should be washed with mild soap or plain water and stored away from heat.

Insertion of the cervical cap requires instruction and takes some practice. When being inserted, the cap is pushed back along the vaginal canal to the cervix, where the rim is pressed snugly around the cervix until it forms a seal. To remove the cap, the rim is tilted away from the cervix, breaking the suction. The cervical cap is more difficult to insert than the diaphragm.

### Effectiveness and Cost

For nonparous women (women who have never given birth), the typical use failure rate is 18 percent, and the perfect use failure rate is 9 percent. For the parous woman (women who have given birth), the typical use failure rate is 36 percent, and the perfect use failure rate is 26 percent. These percentages assume that a spermicide is being used with the cap. Compared to other barrier methods, cervical caps have very high failure rates.

The cap costs about $20, plus anywhere from $50 to $100 for fitting. A typical year's supply of spermicide costs about $85 per year. The cap should be replaced every three years.

### Advantages and Disadvantages

*Advantages:*

■ effects are immediately and completely reversible

■ relatively inexpensive

■ no hormones are involved

■ no side effects, except for relatively rare latex and spermicide allergies

■ less spermicide is needed compared to diaphragm

■ can be inserted up to two days before intercourse

■ once inserted, can be left in place for two days

*Disadvantages:*

■ more difficult to insert and remove than diaphragm

■ odor development and possible toxic shock if left in place too long

■ offers little protection against STIs

■ greater initial costs

■ cost of replacement every three years

■ cost of spermicide

## 15.4 VAGINAL SPERMICIDES

**Vaginal spermicides** contain chemicals that kill sperm. They also create a mechanical barrier that keeps sperm out of the cervix. Spermicides come in various forms, including foam (resembles shaving cream), gel, suppositories (these dissolve in the vagina), creams, jellies, and a paper-thin vaginal contraceptive film (VCF). Their active ingredient (usually nonoxynol-9) kills sperm as well as many other microorganisms, thus providing some protection against STIs. No matter the form, vaginal spermicides are best used in combination with another barrier method, such as a condom or diaphragm.

### Use

Spermicides in the form of aerosol foams are the most effective and easiest to use. The foam is placed high into the vagina either by an applicator or in the form of foaming tablets that melt at body temperature (fig. 15.7). The foam spreads quickly and evenly over the cervical opening and forms a relatively good barrier. Gels and creams are also placed high into the vagina with an applicator. The *suppository* is a glycerin-based spermicide contained in a cylinder about an inch or so long that is placed high into the vagina near the cervix. The glycerin liquefies at body temperature, spreading a foaming spermicide around the upper vagina. *Vaginal film* is a small thin sheet of film that is inserted into the vagina, either alone or with a condom or diaphragm, to cover the cervical opening.

As stated above, spermicides are most effective when combined with another barrier technique. They have little value when used after intercourse or with

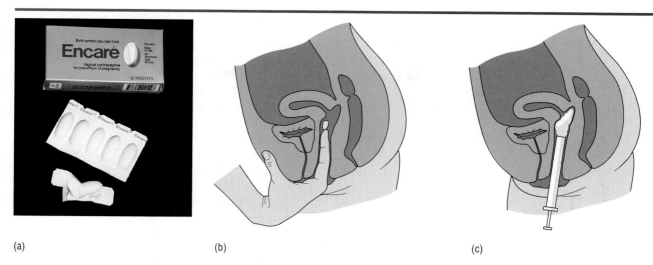

(a)                              (b)                              (c)

**FIGURE 15.7    a:** Vaginal spermicides: A vaginal suppository; vaginal contraceptive film. **b:** Suppositories should be inserted deep in the vagina, and intercourse should be timed according to the manufacturer's instructions accompanying the suppository; suppositories can take a few minutes to dissolve. **c:** Contraceptive foam is inserted with a plastic applicator that must be placed deep into the vagina so that the foam covers the cervical opening.

postcoital douching. Even if the douche contains a spermicide, it is not effective because sperm can enter the cervical canal as quickly as fifteen seconds after ejaculation.

Because the vaginal lining absorbs most of the spermicidal material, there is no reason for vaginal douching after spermicide use. Douching serves only to increase the chances of vaginal infection. Recent statistics indicate that only 2 percent of all women using contraceptives use spermicides (Hatcher et al., 1994).

### Effectiveness and Cost

Spermicides have a typical use failure rate of 21 percent and a perfect use failure rate of 6 percent during the first year of use. The cost of spermicides is about $85 per year.

### Advantages and Disadvantages

*Advantages:*

- easily available at any pharmacy
- does not require a health care professional
- no hormones are involved
- no side effects known
- provide additional lubricating effect
- some protection against STIs and PID (pelvic inflammatory disease)
- immediately and completely reversible

*Disadvantages:*

- can irritate genital tissues (usually overcome by changing brands)

- some increased risk of yeast infections
- residual taste may interfere with oral sex

## 15.5   INTRAUTERINE DEVICES

The **intrauterine device (IUD),** is a small (one to one-and-a-half inch) device that is inserted inside the uterus. Made of soft plastic, it is inserted by a health professional through the cervical canal and carefully positioned within the uterus, where it can remain in place for several years.

At one time it was thought that the IUD prevented implantation of a fertilized ovum in the endometrium of the uterus. Newer research suggests the IUD works by immobilizing sperm as they migrate from the vagina to the fallopian tubes. It also seems to speed transport of the ovum through the fallopian tube (Goldberg, 1994; Hatcher et al., 1994).

After a decade of uterine injuries, deaths, and lawsuits, IUDs such as the Dalkon Shield were taken off the market in the United States. Newer, safer models have been introduced and approved for use. Today, there are three types of IUDs available in the United States. These are the *Copper T (ParaGard T380A),* the *Progestasert* (fig. 15.8), and the *Mirena Intrauterine System* (available in 2001).

| | |
|---|---|
| **vaginal spermicide** | sperm-killing agents placed in the vagina |
| **intrauterine device (IUD)** (in-tra-ū′ter-in) | contraceptive device placed within the uterus |

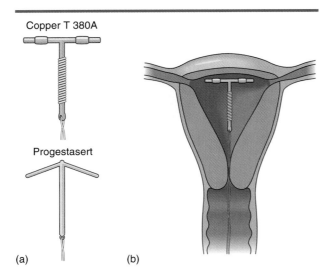

**FIGURE 15.8** **a:** Types of IUDs. **b:** An IUD (T380A) in position.

The *Copper T* is made of plastic, with a covering of fine copper wire wrapped around the stem of the T and a copper sleeve over each arm. A string is attached to the end of the stem. After insertion, the copper on the wires takes about two years to slowly dissolve into the fluids of the uterus. This interferes with certain enzymes and biochemical processes.

The *Progestasert T* is a medicated IUD that contains a supply of progestin in a reservoir in the stem of the T. After insertion, the progestin is gradually released into the uterus over a year's time. The device must be replaced annually to renew its action.

### Insertion

IUDs are usually inserted into the uterus by a health professional during the menstrual period, when the cervix is dilated. Insertion at this time also allows greater certainty that the woman is not pregnant.

Once inserted, it can be left in place for an extended period. During this time, no other contraceptive protection is necessary. A string protrudes from the cervix and it allows the woman to confirm that the IUD is in place. Prior to intercourse, she should feel the string to be certain the device has not been inadvertently expelled. This is best done in a squatting position. If she cannot feel the thread or it seems longer than before, she needs to have it checked by her health care provider. In the meantime, it is important to use some other type of contraception.

When the woman wishes to become pregnant, her health care provider removes the IUD. Within a month to a year, the uterus will return to normal functioning, and most women will then be able to become pregnant. Occasionally a pregnancy will occur with the IUD still in its proper place. Should that occur, a physician will have to determine if the IUD

should be left in place or removed (Hatcher et al., 1994). It seems that most obstetricians or nurse-midwives have at least one story of a baby being born with its mother's IUD grasped securely in its hand.

### Effectiveness and Cost

The effectiveness of the IUD depends on the type used. The Progestasert T has a typical use failure rate of 2.0 percent and a perfect use failure rate of 1.5 percent, while the Copper T 380A has a typical failure rate of 0.8 percent and a perfect use failure rate of 0.6 percent.

An IUD costs approximately $120, plus $40 to $50 for insertion and lab tests. Annual costs depend on how long the device can be safely left in place. For example, annual replacement of the Progestasert costs about $160, while the Copper T 380A costs about $20 per year if it is retained for eight years.

### Advantages and Disadvantages

*Advantages:*

- once inserted, it requires little attention
- nothing must be done either before or after intercourse
- little to no cost after initial insertion
- no manipulation of bodily hormones
- completely, though not immediately, reversible
- progestin- or progesterone-releasing IUD decreases menstrual blood loss

*Disadvantages:*

- relatively high initial cost for purchase and insertion
- periodic replacement required
- need to check string before intercourse
- no protection against STIs
- up to 20 percent of users spontaneously expel the IUD within the first year
- risk of uterine wall perforation at time of insertion
- possible risk of ectopic pregnancy with IUD in place
- if pregnancy occurs with IUD in place, spontaneous abortion might occur
- some increased risk of PID for women with multiple male sex partners

## 15.6 COMBINATION ORAL CONTRACEPTIVES

**Oral contraceptives** (OCs) are contraceptive hormones taken by mouth. They are commonly referred to as "birth control pills" or "the pill." They are the most popular contraceptive method used by women in North America, especially women in their late teens and early twenties (Hatcher et al., 1994).

Combined or *combination* OCs contain both synthetic *estrogen* and *progestin,* a synthetic progesterone. Each of these hormones performs a specific bodily function. The synthetic estrogen inhibits ovulation, alters the secretions within the uterus, accelerates ovum transport, and causes the degeneration of the corpus luteum. The progestin thickens the cervical mucus (hampering sperm motility), inhibits capacitation, inhibits ovulation, and hampers implantation (Hatcher et al., 1994).

Today, OCs commonly contain a relatively small amount of progestin. Pills with an estrogen dosage of 30 micrograms or less are known as low-dosage estrogen pills. Many physicians recommend low estrogen dosage to reduce estrogen-related complications. Some OCs, called biphasic and triphasic pills, step up estrogen and progestin concentrations progressively during the ovulatory cycle.

The estrogen component of the pill is responsible for most of the pill-associated complications that might lead a woman to discontinue using the pill. Higher estrogen dosages are more effective in preventing contraceptive failure and bleeding irregularities, but they can cause nausea, fluid retention, and breast tenderness. Since side effects vary with the type of synthetic estrogen used, some women obtain relief by changing brands of pills. Too low an estrogen content leads to breakthrough bleeding and missed menstrual periods (Hatcher et al., 1994).

### Packaging and Use

Different brands of pills are packaged in 21- and 28-pill packages, with different forms and dosages of hormones. In 21-day packs, one active (hormone-containing) pill is taken daily, starting on the fifth day after the start of menstruation, for three weeks. During the fourth week, no pills are taken and menstruation is allowed to occur. After seven days, a new pill pack is started.

With the 28-day pack, the pack is again started on the fifth day from the start of menstruation. The first 21 pills are active and the last 7 are inactive, often containing iron supplements to replace iron lost in menstruation. After the last pill in the pack is taken, a new pack is started the next day. The 28-day pack helps insure against forgetting when to start a new pack.

If a woman is using an OC and wishes to become pregnant, it is recommended that she finish the pack she is then using and simply not start another pack. She may wish to use another reliable method of contraception for two or three normal menstrual periods off the pill so that when she becomes pregnant, her date of delivery can be accurately calculated. According to the American College of Obstetricians and Gynecologists (1987), "There is no evidence that oral contraceptive use decreases subsequent fertility. After oral contraceptive use is stopped, there may be a short delay of one to two months in the reestablishment of menses and ovulation." When OCs are discontinued, ovulation usually, but not always, resumes promptly.

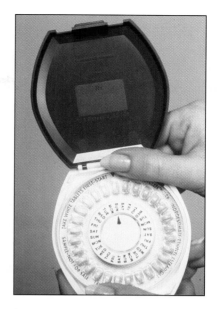

Oral contraceptives are easy to take and are highly reversible.

Before beginning the use of OCs, a woman needs a thorough physical exam, including a detailed medical history. The health care provider then selects the brand of OC best suited to her on the basis of her medical history, age, and physical characteristics. A woman's pill use should be reevaluated during the first three to six months that she is using the pill.

It is important that a woman take only the type of pill prescribed for her, since different dosages and combinations of hormones have different effects. It is very unwise to accept OCs from a health care provider who has not examined the woman, or to "share" OCs with a friend. Because the pill is given only by prescription, annual visits to a health care provider are necessary for prescription renewal.

### Effectiveness and Cost

The typical use failure rate for OCs is 3.0 percent and the perfect use failure rate is 0.1 percent during the first year of use. The annual cost is estimated to be about $130 to $260.

| oral contraceptives (OCs) | contraceptive hormones taken by mouth; birth control pills |
|---|---|

## Advantages and Disadvantages

*Advantages:*

▌ very effective contraception

▌ easily taken

▌ very safe for most women to take (OCs are one of the most intensely studied medications ever prescribed)

▌ completely reversible with no loss of fertility upon stopping

▌ tends to decrease menstrual cramps and pain, shorten the length of the menstrual flow, and reduce the amount of blood lost, and often eliminates midcycle ovulatory pain (*mittelschmerz*)

▌ reduces the chances of developing ovarian and endometrial cancers

▌ can be taken all through the reproductive years

▌ enhances spontaneity and sexual pleasure for most couples

▌ offers other health benefits regarding problems such as anemia, endometriosis, and rheumatoid arthritis

*Disadvantages:*

▌ pill must be taken daily

▌ relatively expensive

▌ hormonal actions may cause headaches, depression and, mood changes

▌ hormonal actions may cause menstrual changes, such as missed periods, scanty bleeding, and spotting

▌ increases risk of circulatory problems for women who are smokers, overweight, over age 50, diabetic, hypertensive, or who have elevated cholesterol levels

▌ can cause a decrease in milk production if taken during breast-feeding

▌ provides no protection against STIs, including HIV

## 15.7 PROGESTIN-ONLY CONTRACEPTIVES

Some of the most exciting new choices in birth control are progestin-only methods. These hormone methods use only *progestin* (a synthetic progesterone) and contain no synthetic estrogens. The advantage of this is that most of the health concerns of the combined oral contraceptives relate to the estrogen portion of those pills (Pollack, 1991).

Progestin-only contraceptives can be administered orally (*minipills*), by injection, via implants, or through intrauterine devices. Similarly to other types of OCs, progestin inhibits ovulation, thickens the cervical mucus (thus inhibiting sperm movement), thins the endometrium (thus inhibiting implantation), and causes the early degeneration of the corpus luteum (Hatcher et al., 1994).

### 15.7.1 Norplant

The long-lasting contraceptive **Norplant** (brand name) is implanted under the skin. The implant consists of six progestin-filled silicone rubber tubules, each about the size of a matchstick. In place, these cylinders provide a steady, low-level release of the hormone into the bloodstream, thus avoiding the *high-low* surges of hormones of the oral contraceptives that are taken daily. Norplant use avoids all of the negative estrogen-related side effects. Norplant has been tested all over the world for the past twenty years (Frost, 1994). Norplant is the contraceptive of choice for Indonesian family planning programs (Noble, 1996).

### Use

Norplant is implanted under the skin on the inside of a woman's upper arm in a fan-shaped configuration (fig. 15.9). It is effective in preventing conception within 24 hours after insertion. One insertion of the implant is effective for up to five years. Should a woman wish to become pregnant within those five years, the tubes can be removed at any time. For most women, full fertility is restored within 48 hours after removal. For continuous contraception, new tubules may be inserted every five years.

### Effectiveness and Cost

Because Norplant is surgically implanted, there is no opportunity for incorrect use, so both perfect use and typical use failure rates are the same: 0.09 percent for the first year of use. Implantation costs $650 to $850. The average annual cost is $130 to $170 if the devices are retained for the full five years.

### Advantages and Disadvantages

*Advantages:*

▌ highly effective long-term contraception

▌ protection from estrogen-related side effects

▌ complete and virtually immediate reversibility when removed

▌ no day-to-day attention is required

▌ no circulatory system complications

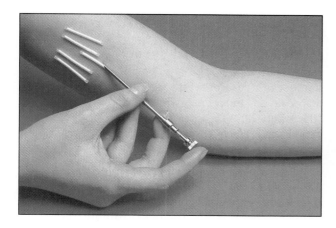 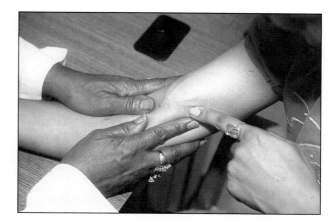

**FIGURE 15.9** The long-lasting contraceptive device. Norplant, consists of six matchstick–sized silicone tubes, which are implanted beneath the skin of the upper arm. Contraception is provided by the hormone contained in and released from the tubes over a period of 60 months.

- especially useful if no more children are wanted but sterilization is not desired
- no adverse effects on lactation
- light or absent menstruation
- decreased menstrual cramps and pain

*Disadvantages:*

- both insertion and removal require minor surgical procedure
- higher initial cost
- may be slightly visible under skin
- no protection from STIs
- interaction with certain other drugs can increase failure rates
- possible weight gain or bloated feeling
- possible breast tenderness (treatable)
- some women have experienced great pain and difficulty during removal and have sustained scarring and nerve damage from the surgery

## 15.7.2  Depo-Provera

Already in use in more than ninety countries, including the United States, **Depo-Provera** (brand name) is used by more than 15 million women worldwide. Also known as DMPA (for its chemical name), Depo-Provera is an injectable progestin-only contraceptive that does not require a surgical implantation. The popularity of Depo-Provera has been its convenience and reliability. It is injected intramuscularly by a health care professional once every three months.

### Effectiveness and Cost

Given only by injection, the perfect and typical use failure rates for the first year are only 0.3 percent. DMPA is so effective that there is a two-week "grace period" at the end of every three months of use during which the user can be late for the next shot without losing protection. Each injection of DMPA costs about $35, for an annual cost of $140 plus any other lab costs.

### Advantages and Disadvantages

*Advantages:*

- highly effective contraception
- no need for surgical implantation or removal
- no estrogen is administered
- one-third to one-half of users have no menstrual bleeding
- no daily attention required
- offers extended protection against pregnancy
- useful in cultures where the woman wants a contraceptive without her partner's knowledge
- no adverse effects on lactation
- no circulatory system complications
- no known negative drug interactions
- might protect against endometrial and ovarian cancer

*Disadvantages:*

- must return to health care provider every three months for an injection
- return to fertility delayed an average of six to twelve months if and when use is discontinued

| | |
|---|---|
| **Norplant** (nor´plant) | trade name for a progestin-only contraceptive device placed beneath the skin of the arm |
| **Depo-Provera** (de´po pro-ver´a) | trade name for a progestin-only contraceptive injection |

# GO ASK ALICE

*Dear Alice,*

*Is there any way for a woman to combine her birth control pills to get the same effect as PCC (postcoital contraception)? Could I take three or four or even all of my birth control pills at once in order to get the same effect?*

*Desperate*

Dear Desperate,

Postcoital contraception, or the morning after pill, is now called emergency contraception. Emergency contraception needs to be taken within 72 hours of unprotected intercourse (or birth control failure or rape), but the sooner it is taken, the better. Emergency contraception has been around for about 20 years now, but the Food and Drug Administration (FDA) recently announced that certain birth control pills, those containing ethinyl estradiol and norgestrel (or levonorgestrel), are considered safe and effective for use as emergency contraception. Emergency contraception consists of two doses of hormone pills, with the first dose taken as soon as possible, and the second dose taken 12 hours later.

Emergency contraception provides a short, strong burst of hormones which prevents pregnancy in 75% of cases. Some women may feel nauseous from using emergency contraception, but this is temporary. Since the dosage and number of pills ad-ministered vary by the type of pill used, talk with your health care provider for the details. You can also call the Emergency Contraception Hotline at (888) Not-2-LATE for information on where you can get emergency contraception in your area.

*Hey Ho!*

*I am a male undergrad who has never had sex before, but I am currently in a relationship in which I may soon. This sounds silly, but after sex, is there a graceful way to remove and discard a condom without ruining the moment?*

*A "Sheathed" Panoose*

Dear "Sheathed" Panoose,

Congratulations on being committed to using a condom the first time! That way, you will be in the habit of regularly using a condom for intercourse. . . . You deserve a pat on the back. As far as taking off the condom the first time you have sex, it is so potentially awkward anyway but taking the condom off adds nothing extra-unusual. It can help to take the condom off with a joke, or a sigh, or a moan; to keep a trash pail or a tissue or napkin handy to put the used condom in; and, to cuddle back up with your partner after taking it off.

 http://www.mhhe.com/byer6

---

- once injected, DMPA cannot be discontinued immediately
- no protection from STIs
- possible side effects, such as menstrual cycle disturbances, breast tenderness, weight gain, and depression
- bone density can decrease with long-term use

## 15.7.3 Minipill

The **minipill** is a low-dose progestin-only pill. Available in packets of 35 to 42 pills, one is taken daily, without a break, for as long as contraception is desired. Unlike use of the combination pill, there are no pill-free or hormone-free intervals.

Progestin-only pills are most effective if ovulation is consistently inhibited, so the pill must be taken at the same time daily. Women on the minipill are likely to be **amenorrheic** for long periods.

### Effectiveness and Cost

The minipill is very effective, with a typical use failure rate of 3.0 percent and a perfect use failure rate of 0.5 percent. Older women and women nursing an infant have a lower failure rate compared to other women. The cost of the minipill ranges from $100 to $300 for a full year's supply.

### Advantages and Disadvantages

*Advantages:*

- highly effective contraception
- relatively easy daily use
- no estrogen-related side effects

■ no menstrual periods, and therefore few or no premenstrual symptoms

*Disadvantages:*

■ some pharmacies do not stock the minipill

■ since fewer women use the minipill, there is less clinical knowledge and experience regarding their use

■ no protection against STIs

■ requires consistent motivation to take pill at same time daily

■ continuing expense

■ slightly greater risk of pregnancy compared to combination OCs

■ increases risk of ectopic pregnancy and ovarian cysts

## 15.7.4   Other Progestin-Only Contraceptives

The progestin-containing IUD has already been discussed. Various other devices containing progestin and progesterone are under development. These include vaginal rings, suppositories, subdermal implants, injectable *microspheres* (pellets), and skin creams.

## 15.8   SURGICAL/MEDICAL METHODS

### 15.8.1   Sterilization

Since 1982, sterilization has been the predominant method of fertility management in the United States, due to population increase, and it has become one of the most widely used methods of family planning in the world (Hatcher et al., 1994). Aside from total abstinence, sterilization is the most effective method of contraception. **Sterilization** is a surgical interruption of the reproductive tract that prevents the discharge of sex cells. This method is safe and generally considered permanent. It has great appeal to couples who do not want to have children at all or do not want additional children.

Sterilization must be considered very carefully. Some who have undergone sterilization have later wished, for any number of reasons, to regain their reproductive ability. Reversals are sometimes successful, but restoration of fertility cannot be guaranteed. Reversible methods of contraception are more desirable for persons who might wish to have children in the future.

### *Tubal Sterilization*

For women, virtually all the sterilization techniques involve interrupting the fallopian tubes (**tubal**

sterilization) (fig. 15.10). This will prevent the sperm and ovum from uniting. In the operating room, a surgeon will make an incision in the abdominal wall or enter the abdomen through the vagina.

In a *minilaparotomy* a two-inch incision is made in the lower abdomen near the pubic hairline. The surgeon lifts the fallopian tubes and, using clips, a plastic ring, or an electric current, seals the tubes. A *laparoscopy* involves making a small incision near the navel and inserting a miniaturized, flexible telescopic instrument called a *laparoscope* to see the fallopian tubes and close them off. Surgical complications are very rare and occur in only 1.7 percent of cases (Goldberg, 1994). In the United States over 10 million women of childbearing age have undergone tubal sterilization (Peterson et al., 1997). Many more women seek sterilization than are accepted for the procedure, with very few women (about 3 percent) seeking reversal (Goldberg, 1994).

In a study comparing the effects of tubal sterilization, male vasectomy, and no surgical interventions on the marital sexuality of women, no detrimental effects were found for the tubal sterilization. In fact, there was an increase in the frequency of intercourse one year after sterilization compared to the other groups (Shain et al., 1991).

### *Effectiveness and Cost*

The overall failure rate for tubal sterilization (perfect and typical use rates are the same) is 0.4 percent in the first year. Very rarely, a sterilization procedure might fail due to regrowth or reconnection of the severed tubes. When a pregnancy does occur there is a substantial risk it will be an ectopic pregnancy (Peterson et al., 1997).

The cost of a tubal sterilization varies, depending on where it is performed. Typically it runs between $1,200 to $2,500.

### *Advantages and Disadvantages*

*Advantages:*

■ a highly effective family-planning technique

■ permanent

| | |
|---|---|
| minipill | progestin-only contraceptive pill |
| amenorrheic | not having a menstrual period |
| sterilization | surgical procedure that leaves a person unable to cause pregnancy or become pregnant |
| tubal sterilization | sterilization of a woman by interrupting the fallopian tubes to prevent the passage of ova or sperm |

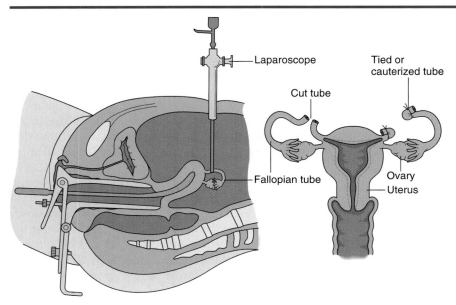

Laparoscope

Tied or cauterized tube

Cut tube

Fallopian tube

Ovary

Uterus

**FIGURE 15.10** In a tubal sterilization by laparoscopy, the physician inserts a narrow instrument through an incision in the abdominal wall and cauterizes, cuts, or clamps a small section of each fallopian tube to block the movement of sex cells and prevent ova from joining with sperm.

■ very cost effective when cost is spread over the years following surgery

■ requires no supplies or attention

■ no significant long-term side effects

■ partner cooperation not required

■ no interruption in lovemaking

■ no effect on ability to enjoy all sexual activities

*Disadvantages:*

■ permanent

■ a major medical procedure requiring a surgeon, operating room, etc.

■ if not done properly, higher risk for ectopic pregnancy

■ no protection against STIs

■ high initial expense

## Vasectomy

For men, sterilization, or **vasectomy,** involves a minor surgical procedure that consists of cutting and tying the two *vas deferens,* the tubules that carry sperm from each testis to the penis. The procedure requires only small cuts on each side of the scrotum, and can be performed in a physician's office under local anesthesia (fig. 15.11).

A vasectomy has no effect on the ability to have an erection, produce ejaculate, or enjoy orgasm. The volume of ejaculate remains relatively unchanged because most of what constitutes semen comes from the seminal vesicles and the prostate gland, neither of which is affected by the surgery. Sperm cells make up only 3 percent of semen. After vasectomy, sperm cells remain in the epididymis and vas deferens, where they disintegrate and are absorbed by the body.

Sperm do not disappear from the semen immediately after vasectomy. Millions of sperm are stored in the vas deferens *above* the site of the surgery, and it takes several ejaculations to rid the vas deferens of these sperm. Only after two negative sperm counts can a man be considered sterile. Thus he must depend on some other method of contraception for six to eight weeks after the vasectomy.

Successful reversal of a vasectomy depends on many factors, but if microscopic surgery was used in the vasectomy, impregnation rates after reversal of vasectomy have ranged from 16 to 79 percent (Belker et al., 1993). Nonetheless, because reversal cannot be guaranteed, a vasectomy must be considered permanent, so it is important that such a decision be considered very carefully. Some men choose to store their sperm in sperm banks in case unforeseen circumstances lead them to wish for a child in the future.

## Effectiveness and Cost

The typical use failure rate is 0.15 percent, and the perfect use failure rate is 0.1 percent for the first year. Failure of the technique is rare, but can occur from regrowth of the vas deferens, mistakenly closing off the wrong structure, or failure to observe that the man had more than two vas deferens (human diversity is everywhere!).

Because vasectomy is an outpatient procedure, costs run between $250 to $1,000, depending on where it is performed.

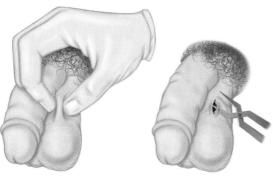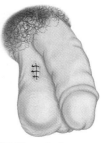

(1) The vas deferens is located.

(2) A small incision in the scrotum exposes the vas.

(3) A small section of the vas is removed, and the ends are cut and/or cauterized.

(4) The incision is closed.

(5) Steps 1–4 are repeated on the other side.

**FIGURE 15.11**  A vasectomy.

## Advantages and Disadvantages

*Advantages:*

- highly effective family-planning technique
- relieves partner of contraceptive responsibility
- permanent
- a one-time, relatively simple, outpatient procedure
- very safe
- over time, very inexpensive

*Disadvantages:*

- no protection against STIs
- generally irreversible
- not immediate, must temporarily depend on other forms of contraception
- regret and desire to reverse procedure occur in 4 to 10 percent of patients

## 15.9  POSTCOITAL CONTRACEPTION

On occasion, some people might face a contraceptive emergency and the risk of an unwanted pregnancy: for instance, when a woman has been forced to have intercourse, a condom has broken or slipped off, or the woman has forgotten to take her OCs. The intercourse has occurred. What can be done now?

The overall risk of pregnancy from a single unprotected act of intercourse on any day of the menstrual cycle ranges from about 0 to 26 percent, depending on when in the cycle the intercourse takes place. As you have learned, the risk of pregnancy is highest during the three days prior to ovulation and the day of ovulation. During this four-day interval, the risk for pregnancy from one coital act rises to between 15 and 26 percent (Hatcher et al., 1994).

### 15.9.1  Options for Postcoital Contraception

*Emergency contraceptive pills:* The most widely used emergency treatment method is a combination of synthetic estrogen and progestin. This approach consists of two doses taken 12 hours apart. The first dose should be taken as soon as possible (it is best not to wait until "the morning after"). If treatment is delayed longer than 72 hours, it may not be effective. Some women report nausea and vomiting after taking these pills (Hatcher et al., 1994).

*Mifepristone (RU-486):* Mifepristone is an antiprogesterone drug that blocks the action of progesterone coming from the woman's ovaries. Without progesterone, the endometrium is unsuitable for implantation from a blastocyst. Given in a single dose within 72 hours after unprotected intercourse, the drug has excellent effectiveness, and side effects such as nausea and vomiting are rare (Webb & Morris, 1993).

*Postcoital IUD insertion:* Here, a copper intrauterine device is inserted within five to seven days after an ovulatory cycle in which unprotected

| | |
|---|---|
| **vasectomy** (vas-ek´tō-mē) | sterilization of a man by interrupting the vas deferens to prevent the passage of sperm |

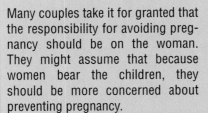

## "MUST I BE RESPONSIBLE?"

Many couples take it for granted that the responsibility for avoiding pregnancy should be on the woman. They might assume that because women bear the children, they should be more concerned about preventing pregnancy.

Yet taking total responsibility can be burdensome for a woman. She will always be the one to schedule appointments, take time from work and studies, undergo and pay for examinations, be fitted for contraceptive devices, have prescriptions filled, or pay for supplies. She must remember to take the pill daily, be sure the IUD, cervical cap, diaphragm, or foam is in place, or keep charts of her menstrual cycle. She might wish for freedom from the health hazards associated with the pill or IUD. Shouldering the bulk of the responsibility can create resent-

ments that interfere with loving feelings. And the male's lack of involvement can result in his feeling distant and isolated.

An even worse scenario involves the couple who both assume that the other partner has taken the responsibility for contraception and feel embarrassed to ask about this. For this couple, this lack of communication can mean that no preparations have taken place.

For many couples, contraception can be a *shared responsibility*. Some share by having each partner use one form of contraception. For example, he uses a condom, while she uses a diaphragm. Aside from the sense of shared responsibility, this can improve the effectiveness of the methods chosen. The following could be some additional steps:

- Find ways of making love without intercourse. This is often called "outercourse," and can include a whole array of pleasurable activities. Be imaginative.
- Share the costs of contraceptive devices and monthly supplies.
- Help keep track of the days of the month, or when menstrual periods begin.
- Take the initiative in permanent, lifelong relationships by undergoing sterilization.
- Accompany your partner to clinic or other appointments related to fertility management.

intercourse has occurred. However, there are some drawbacks. It is not recommended if there is risk of STD infection. Nor is it recommended for women with multiple sex partners, women who have never been pregnant, or women with a history of PID or ectopic pregnancy.

You may have noticed that with the exception of the male condom and vasectomy, all of these contraceptive techniques are the responsibility of women. Many couples believe that because sex involves a shared relationship, contraception should be a shared responsibility. Some interesting ideas about this issue are offered in "At Issue: 'Must I Be Responsible?'"

## 15.10 ABORTION

**Abortion** involves the removal or expulsion of a growing embryo or fetus from the uterus, before the fetus can survive independently. A fetus may become *viable* (able to survive independently of the mother's body) between the twentieth and twenty-eighth week of pregnancy. A naturally occurring abortion is com-

monly called a miscarriage or spontaneous abortion. These usually occur because of some fetal abnormality. An estimated 15 percent of all pregnancies end in spontaneous abortion between the fourth and twentieth weeks of gestation (Cunningham et al., 1993). An *induced* or *elective abortion* is the intentional expulsion of the embryo or fetus. About 23 percent of all pregnancies in the United States are terminated by elective abortion (Koonin et al., 1996). For a worldwide perspective on abortion, see "Dimensions of Diversity: Abortion, a Global Perspective."

The matter of elective abortion is controversial in our society. It is a volatile issue for political candidates, and some people who oppose elective abortions have acted with violence against physicians who perform abortions and clinics where abortions are available. (See "At Issue: The Abortion Debate.") Few are neutral on the subject of abortion, and the mere mention of the word quickly brings up strong emotions and statements.

Although a woman's right to terminate a pregnancy was clearly established in 1973 (*Roe v. Wade*), since then there have been many attempts to restrict

# DIMENSIONS OF DIVERSITY

## ABORTION, A GLOBAL PERSPECTIVE

**GERMANY:** Before unification, East German women had complete access to abortion services, whereas West German women could have a legal abortion only in cases of rape or severe hardship. Since unification, a compromise law allows abortion within the first trimester with state-sponsored counseling. The government may fund such abortions for poor women.

**TURKEY:** Abortion is available to women up until the tenth week of pregnancy. In 1992, 18 percent of all pregnancies were aborted.

**BRAZIL:** It is estimated that 30 percent of all pregnancies are terminated through illegal abortions.

**POLAND:** In 1992, the Polish Parliament put an end to legal abortions except in the case of rape, incest, or danger to the mother's life. Illegal and self-induced abortions are very widespread. It is estimated that 50 percent of all pregnancies end in abortion.

**SOUTH KOREA:** In a 1985 survey, it was found that abortion accounted for about one-third of the rate of fertility reduction. Many of the abortions appear to be for sex selection, because data reveal a disproportionate number of male births. A 1986 law forbade the identification of fetal sex, except in limited cases.

**JAPAN:** Abortion is legal up to 22 weeks of pregnancy, but may be performed after that to protect the life of the woman. Partner's consent is usually required. The government does not fund any abortions.

**LATVIA:** Abortion is the major form of birth control. In 1994, 32,500 abortions were performed compared to 24,256 live births.

**FRANCE:** Abortion is government funded in approved clinics up through the tenth week for women distressed about their pregnancy. A one-week waiting period, counseling in alternatives to abortion, and government promotion of contraceptive information is mandated.

**LATIN AMERICA:** Abortion is illegal in all countries except Cuba and Barbados. There is ongoing debate about legalizing abortions in many countries.

**ITALY:** Women may terminate pregnancies upon request through the first trimester, and for medical or psychological reasons through the fifth month. Government funding is available.

**Sources:** Data from various issues of *Population Today,* Population Reference Bureau, Washington, DC.

---

that right. Pressures and fears have led to fewer abortion clinics, fewer physicians willing to perform them, and mandated waiting periods (Gest et al., 1992).

The motivations for terminating a pregnancy are as varied as the individuals who consider this option. The pregnancy might be unwanted and/or unplanned. A sudden dramatic change in life circumstances might transform a planned pregnancy into an unwanted one.

## 15.10.1   History

Elective abortions are nothing new. In the thirteenth century, St. Thomas Aquinas declared that male embryos had no soul until forty days following conception and that female embryos had no soul until 90 days had passed (Rodman, Sarvis, & Bonar 1987), and that therefore abortion was acceptable during those time periods. Early American law followed English Common Law and allowed abortions until the pregnant woman felt "quickening"—fetal movement—in the fourth or fifth month of pregnancy. In 1869, Pope Pius IX declared that the soul enters the *zygote* (fertilized ovum) at conception, and around this time abortion became illegal in the United States. However, it was still allowable to terminate a pregnancy that threatened a woman's life (Wills, 1990). It is important to note that many religious traditions have no doctrines regarding the acceptability of pregnancy termination.

Up until the 1973 *Roe v. Wade* decision, women seeking to terminate a pregnancy in the United States had to seek an illegal abortion. Affluent women could afford to travel to a country where abortion

| | |
|---|---|
| **abortion** | expulsion or removal of an embryo or fetus from the uterus before it can survive independently |

## AT ISSUE

### THE ABORTION DEBATE

Whether a woman should be able to abort an embryo or fetus she is carrying is a highly controversial issue. Adding to the heat of the debate has been the use of emotionally loaded labels such as *pro-choice* or *pro-life*.

Those who favor a woman retaining this choice are generally identified as "pro-choice." Simply stated, pro-choice individuals believe that the decision to keep or terminate a pregnancy is a private, very personal matter, and that a woman should have the right to make this choice. They hold that she has an undeniable right to control her own body. They believe this reproductive right entitles her to the services of trained professionals for both advice and the carrying out of her decision. They also believe that the pregnant woman should not be subject to interference from the state or church as she makes her decision. They hold that a pregnant woman has a right to easy access to a qualified physician who is an expert at performing a medically safe abortion,

regardless of the woman's ability to pay for the procedure. Supporters of women's reproductive rights also believe that if she decides to keep the pregnancy, she has a right to adequate prenatal care.

Those who do not favor abortion are called "pro-life" or "right-to-life" supporters. They hold that a new individual is formed from the moment a sperm fertilizes an egg. They contend that the developing embryo or fetus is a separate growing organism, and not just part of the woman's body. They hold that the developing embryo is human and therefore entitled to legal protection, including the right to life. They reject the idea of elective abortion whether for personal need, convenience, or population control. They argue that abortion poses physical and emotional hazards to women, and that it constitutes a denial of basic moral principles.

At the core of this argument is the debate over when life actually begins, or, stated differently: When

does a person actually come to exist? Pro-choice advocates believe that the embryo or fetus is a potential person even before it is viable (Leo, 1992).

Arguments, protests, bombings, courtroom confrontations, and the like regarding abortion might shortly become an artifact in the history of sexuality, as new drugs such as mifepristone (formerly known as RU-486) become available in the United States. These drugs prevent implantation of the conceptus, thus avoiding the need to later abort a developing embryo or fetus. A woman who decides that she does not want to continue her pregnancy can obtain a prescription for such a drug and resolve her difficulty in the privacy of her own home. However, because of the availability of mifepristone and other drugs such as *methotrexate* and *misoprostol*, it is predicted that abortion later in pregnancy will be a very rare event.

---

was legal, while poor women had to rely on primitive, unsanitary, dangerous procedures. Women who were unable to locate and pay for help tried to abort themselves. During the 1960s and 1970s several states tried to relax these restrictions and allow medically safe abortions. Such states became meccas of safety for thousands of women seeking legal and safe abortions (Guttmacher & Kaiser, 1986).

In the famous 1973 *Roe v. Wade* decision, the United States Supreme Court found that a woman's right to privacy overrides the state's interest in regulating sexual conduct. The court also stated that a fetus represented a "potential life," rather than "a person," and thus did not have a "right to life." The court further ruled that (a) elective abortions within the first three months of pregnancy were a private matter between a woman and her physician, (b) second-trimester and third-trimester abortions may be regulated so as to protect the health of the woman,

and (c) during the third trimester, if the fetus is viable, the state may prohibit abortion, except if the mother's health or life is threatened.

In 1976, the Hyde Amendment banned Medicaid funding for abortions for poor women, unless the pregnancy resulted from rape or incest or threatened the woman's life. This law was upheld by the U.S. Supreme Court in 1980 (*Harris v. McRae*). In 1983, the Supreme Court overturned an Ohio law that required a physician to inform abortion patients about potential pain to the fetus. This decision also reaffirmed the *Roe v. Wade* decision and stated that a state could not require a waiting period before an abortion, nor could a state demand that early abortions be done in a hospital. However, the court did uphold the rights of states to require parental or judicial consent for juvenile abortions, and the requirement of the presence of a second physician if the viability of the fetus was open to question.

The national debate over abortion continues.

During the 1980s and 1990s, several laws were passed that restricted abortion through various means, but these restrictions could not place "an undue burden" on a woman. During the mid 1990s, legal confrontations centered on the rights of abortion protesters to block access to clinics. In 1994, the Freedom of Access to Clinic Entrances Act became law; this law allowed imposing prison time for both violent and nonviolent abortion clinic disruption. The abortion debate continues. While antiabortion advocates would like to see national legislation making abortion illegal and establishing the rights of an unborn fetus, pro-choice supporters see abortion as a social necessity and a basic reproductive right for women. Exercising this right would require unobstructed access to abortion services.

## 15.10.2 Incidence and Prevalence of Abortion

Abortion is a global issue. Almost three-fourths of the people in the world live in countries that permit elective abortions. In 1995 there were about 5.1 million pregnancies and 1.2 abortions in the United States (Centers for Disease Control, 1997). The 1994 abortion *rate* (number of abortions per 1,000 women age 15 through 44) was 13 for whites and 40 for African Americans (Koonin et al., 1997). Among states reporting on abortion for Latinos, the abortion rate was 29 for Latinos and 18 for non-Latinos.

The abortion rate for American teenagers is much higher than for their European counterparts; this is related to the fact that European teenagers have received more extensive sexuality education. Overall, the annual *abortion-to-live-birth ratio* (the number of abortions to 1,000 live births) in the United States has been declining after 1987. Single parenthood for women has become more acceptable, and women have greater economic opportunities. This appears to be contributing to the trend for women to keep more of their unplanned pregnancies.

According to statistics from the Centers for Disease Control and Prevention (Koonin et al., 1997), most women who elect to terminate their pregnancies are unmarried (78 percent) and 20–24 years of age (54 percent). Twenty percent were 19 years old or younger. Most (54 percent) have had a previous live birth, and about 90 percent have had two or fewer previous live births. A small proportion (17 percent) have had at least two previous abortions (Koonin et al., 1997).

Most women who choose to abort their pregnancies have several reasons for doing so, including feeling too young to take on the responsibility, a desire to complete their education, and economic hardship. Others offered health concerns, partner-related difficulties, and not wishing to add to their families as important reasons for terminating their pregnancies.

Choosing to terminate an unwanted pregnancy is a serious, highly personal decision. It often involves examining and weighing personal values and priorities. Even after a decision is made to keep or terminate a pregnancy, the woman or her partner might still feel ambivalence and have strong feelings such as anger, a sense of loss, regret, and depression before an abortion. After the abortion is complete, the most commonly reported feelings are relief, a feeling of having reached a resolution, and a sense of self-efficacy (Dagg, 1991). Adverse psychological effects are reported by a small number of women (Major & Cozzarelli, 1992).

## 15.10.3 Methods of Abortion

Surgical abortion methods include vacuum aspiration, dilation and curettage, dilation and evacuation, and hysterotomy (see table 15.2).

**Vacuum aspiration** (also referred to as vacuum curettage or suction curettage) accounts for 99 percent of all abortions performed in the United States (Koonin et al., 1997). This procedure is commonly performed up to the fourteenth week of pregnancy (Cunningham et al., 1993). It involves dilation of the woman's cervical canal and insertion into the uterus of a small, plastic tube-type curette attached to a suction pump. The contents of the uterus are quickly sucked out (fig. 15.12). Although vacuum aspiration is one of the safest of all surgical procedures, frequent

side effects include light bleeding and menstrual-type cramps.

**Dilation and curettage** (often referred to as "D&C") can also be used up until the fourteenth week of pregnancy (Cunningham et al., 1993). The physician first dilates the cervical canal and then inserts a small, metal, spoon-shaped curette into the uterus. The fetus and endometrial tissue are scraped loose and removed. The D&C is usually performed under general anesthesia in a hospital. This procedure has largely been replaced by the quicker and safer aspiration techniques, but aside from pregnancy terminations, this method is also used in cases of spontaneous abortion and suspected uterine malignancies.

**Dilation and evacuation** (sometimes referred to as "D&E") is a second trimester method that combines dilation and curettage with aspiration techniques. Used up until the sixteenth week of pregnancy, this procedure is performed in a hospital under general anesthesia (Cunningham et al., 1993) and requires a one- or two-day stay.

In this technique, a wide dilation of the cervix is followed by removal of fetal parts by forceps. Then a vacuum aspiration is performed with a larger suction curette to remove the placenta and any remaining residue. The uterine wall is then scraped with a metal curette. This procedure is associated with a greater risk of cervical injury and perforation of the uterine wall.

**Hysterotomy** (sometimes called a *laparotomy*) is also a second trimester procedure. It involves taking the fetus from the uterus through an abdominal incision. This surgical procedure is usually used

**TABLE 15.2** RATES OF ABORTION PROCEDURES

The most common abortion procedure overall and during the first trimester is curettage (suction or sharp). Almost 52 percent of all abortions are terminated at less than nine weeks of pregnancy, and almost 89 percent are terminated at less than thirteen weeks of pregnancy. The table below shows the percentage of induced abortions in the United States by type of procedure.

| METHOD | PERCENTAGE | | | | | | |
|---|---|---|---|---|---|---|---|
| | *8 Weeks or Less* | *9 to 10 Weeks* | *11 to 12 Weeks* | *13 to 15 Weeks* | *16 to 20 Weeks* | *21 Weeks or More* | *All Periods* |
| Curettage (suction or sharp) | *99.8 | 99.9 | 99.7 | 98.7 | 90.1 | 82.7 | 99.1 |
| Intrauterine saline instillation | 0.0** | 0.0** | 0.1 | 0.5 | 3.6 | 2.1 | 0.2 |
| Intrauterine prostaglandin instillation | 0.0** | 0.0** | 0.0** | 0.2 | 2.4 | 6.9 | 0.2 |
| Hysterotomy/hysterectomy | 0.0** | 0.0** | 0.0** | 0.0** | 0.1** | 0.0 | 0.0** |
| Other*** | 0.2 | 0.1* | 0.2 | 0.6 | 3.8 | 8.3 | 0.5 |
| TOTAL | 100.0 | 100.0 | 100.0 | 100.0 | 100.0 | 100.0 | 100.0 |

*includes dilation and evacuation
**less than and including 0.05 percent
***includes instillation

**Source:** Data from L. Koonin et al., "Abortion Surveillance-United States, 1992" by *CDC Surveillance Summaries*, May 3, 1996; and *Morbidity and Mortality Weekly Report*, 1997, page 95.

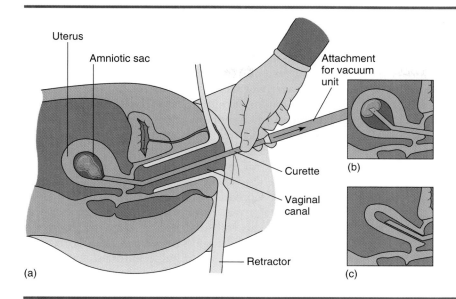

Uterus
Amniotic sac
Attachment for vacuum unit
Curette
(b)
Vaginal canal
Retractor
(a)
(c)

**FIGURE 15.12**  Vacuum aspiration or suction abortion. **a:** Removal of fetal material. **b, c:** As fetal material is removed, the uterus contracts back to its original size.

if a medical procedure has failed. Hysterotomy is major surgery and requires several days of hospitalization.

There are two nonsurgical medical techniques of abortion. As of this date, they have not been confirmed to be as safe as the vacuum aspiration method.

**Mifepristone (RU-486)** blocks the action of progesterone and therefore causes the uterine lining to slough off, as it would during a normal menstrual period. Without progesterone, a pregnancy cannot continue. Mifepristone is given in combination with misoprostol (a *prostaglandin*), a drug that induces expulsion of uterine contents.

A single dose of mifepristone administered within the first six weeks after conception is followed several days later by a dose of misoprostol. In 90 to 95 percent of cases, the pregnancy is effectively terminated at home within several hours. If termination is incomplete, surgical procedures (such as D&C) are required. Beyond this point in the pregnancy, mifepristone is less and less effective. Known side effects include nausea, vomiting, and abdominal cramping.

**Intrauterine injections** are chemicals used to induce second-trimester abortions. Hypertonic saline, hypertonic urea, or prostaglandin E2, either alone or in combination, are injected into the amniotic sac within the uterus. This procedure is called *instillation,* and these substances immediately terminate development of the fetus. The fetal remains are expelled by childbirth-like uterine contractions that are usually induced by prostaglandins or oxytocin.

Since pregnancy can be confirmed at four weeks, and since vacuum aspiration is generally possible through the fourteenth week, it is rarely necessary to resort to an instillation abortion. Intrauterine instillation methods account for less than 1 percent of all abortions in the United States (Koonin et al., 1997).

### 15.10.4  Safety of Abortions

Legal abortions are quite safe. The rate of complications is less than 1 in 200 cases (Hakim-Elahi, Tovell, & Burnhill, 1990). The death rate is 0.8 per 100,000

| | |
|---|---|
| **vacuum aspiration** | removal of embryo or fetus from the uterus through a curette tube by vacuum suction |
| **dilation and curettage (D&C)** (dī-lā'shun kū-re-tohz) | abortion procedure in which cervix is dilated and the embryo or fetus is removed by scraping of the uterine walls with a metal curette |
| **dilation and evacuation (D&E)** | abortion procedure in which cervix is dilated, the fetus parts removed by forceps, and a curette used to remove the placenta and remaining products |
| **hysterotomy** (his-ter-ot'ō-mē) | incision through the abdominal wall to remove a fetus |
| **mifepristone (RU-486)** (mi-fuh-pri'stōn) | a chemical administered to cause sloughing of the uterine lining, preventing continued pregnancy |
| **intrauterine injection** | injection by needle through the abdominal wall into amniotic sac to induce abortion |

abortions. Both of these ratios are lower than those for live birth difficulties. The complications that do rarely occur include perforation of the uterine wall, damage to the cervix that reduces its ability to retain a future fetus, hemorrhaging, infections, and *peritonitis* (inflammation of the lining of the abdominal cavity). Problems are reduced if (Hatcher et al., 1994):

- ▌ the pregnancy is confirmed early
- ▌ referral for pregnancy termination is made early
- ▌ the woman is healthy
- ▌ the woman is clear about wanting the abortion
- ▌ the woman has no STIs
- ▌ local anesthesia is used
- ▌ the uterus is carefully and completely emptied
- ▌ the aspirated or curetted tissue is carefully examined to rule out an ectopic pregnancy
- ▌ the woman understands the signs of postprocedure problems
- ▌ prompt follow-up care is available on a 24-hour basis

## 15.10.5 Decision-Making Regarding Pregnancy Termination

In a world in which sexually active couples used perfect contraceptives, all pregnancies were risk free, and all pregnancies were welcomed with joy, there would be no need to terminate a pregnancy. But such a world simply does not exist.

A decision about whether to keep or abort a pregnancy is an extremely personal one and is best undertaken with great care and only after weighing other options. It would be helpful if a loving partner were involved to support the woman in whatever she chooses to do, but this is often not possible.

As soon as a woman suspects she is pregnant, she can begin considering her options. To do this, she will need to have an accurate recollection of when she had her last menstrual period. The two months (about eight weeks) after conception are a critical time period. If she chooses to keep the pregnancy, good prenatal care needs to begin during that time. If she chooses to terminate the pregnancy, it is safest to begin arranging this as quickly as possible. She may want to explore options such as keeping her infant or placing it up for adoption. She may need to reexamine her relationship to her sexual partner, consider what she wants to communicate to her family and friends, and arrange as supportive an environment as she can (Torres & Forrest, 1988; Russo, Horn, & Schwartz, 1992).

For many women, the decision to have an abortion can be a very emotional one, and they may have many feelings both before and after the procedure. A woman might feel anxious and apprehensive, or she might fear her partner will abandon her. She might feel angry toward her partner for impregnating her, or she might feel alone and depressed. A supportive partner and supportive friends and family who are available to listen, and not judge, can help the woman feel positive about herself and her decision. On a practical level, abortions carried out as early as possible tend to cause much less stress than later ones (Major & Cozzarelli, 1992; Dagg, 1991). A regular health care provider can provide all the necessary information she will need about where and how the procedure can be done. The woman is likely to want to know about safety, any discomfort she might expect, and how to pay for these services. She might need detailed information about how to avoid future unwanted pregnancies.

The woman's partner might share some of her same feelings. He might have his own preferences about the pregnancy, but might not have been consulted. He might feel guilty about the burden being placed on her, and confused about how to be with his partner through this process (Russo, Horn, & Schwartz, 1992). Counseling for both individuals might help if both wish it.

## 15.11 IN CONCLUSION

An old Spanish proverb says, "Saber es poder"—knowledge is power. Your new knowledge about fertility management can give you great power in controlling and enjoying your sexual potential.

## SUMMARY

1. Control of fertility is an important issue on the personal, interpersonal, and global level.

2. It is important to understand the implications of several terms and concepts in the area of fertility management. The relative effectiveness of the various contraceptive methods is evaluated in terms of typical use failure rate and perfect use failure rate.

3. Attempts to regulate fertility date back to the earliest human civilizations. In spite of some social and political obstacles, highly effective contraceptive technology has been developed and made available during the twentieth century.

4. There are complex personal issues that make one contraceptive technique or another optimal for a particular person or couple at a particular time.

5.  Abstinence and menstrual cycle charting are two traditional approaches to contraception. There are advantages and disadvantages for each. Withdrawal is a traditional, highly ineffective approach.

6.  Barrier methods include the condom (male and female), diaphragm, and cervical cap, each with its own advantages and disadvantages. Vaginal spermicides are best used with another barrier method and provide both a barrier and chemical spermicidal action.

7.  There are currently three approved IUDs available in the United States, and this approach also has its advantages and disadvantages.

8.  The various types of oral contraceptives differ in terms of their hormone content. OCs are a very popular contraceptive method. They work mainly by inhibiting ovulation. There are numerous advantages and disadvantages for these contraceptives as well.

9.  Norplant, Depo-Provera, and the minipill are examples of highly effective progestin-only contraceptives. The first is an implant, the second is an injectable, the third is taken orally.

10. Male and female sterilization are popular, permanent approaches to contraception. Female sterilization involves major surgery; vasectomy is a minor outpatient procedure. Neither procedure affects sexual interest or response.

11. Recently, an array of postcoital contraceptives have been developed.

12. Abortion is a controversial approach to terminating unwanted or unplanned pregnancies that has a long history. United States court decisions have established women's rights to choose abortion, but conflict and controversy continue.

13. There are several methods for terminating pregnancies. First trimester abortions are simpler, safer, and less traumatic compared to those performed later.

14. The decision-making process regarding the choice to keep or abort a pregnancy is very sensitive and complex. Early, rather than later, abortions and a supportive environment have a positive impact on the woman who elects to terminate a pregnancy.

## CRITICAL THINKING CHALLENGES

1.  For anyone who is, or might become, sexually active, the effects of a pregnancy can significantly change future plans. If faced with your or your partner's pregnancy, what is your likely course of action regarding keeping or aborting that pregnancy? What factors would influence your decision?

2.  Safety, effectiveness, ease of use, acceptability, reversibility, and affordability are listed as important criteria for choosing a contraceptive. Put these features in order of their importance to you. Which contraceptive method would be ideal for you? Which method would you choose if your ideal method were unavailable?

# CONCEPTION, PREGNANCY, AND CHILDBIRTH

# 16

**AFTER STUDYING THIS CHAPTER, YOU SHOULD BE ABLE TO**

[1] Discuss the ways in which a newborn child can affect the lifestyle of the parents.

[2] Explain the activities of the sperm and ovum that lead to conception.

[3] Compare the definitions of the terms *embryo* and *fetus.*

[4] List the four positive signs of pregnancy.

[5] Describe how a pregnant woman can estimate the date of her expected delivery.

[6] Discuss the events that occur in the development of the embryo/fetus during the first trimester.

[7] Define the word *quickening.*

[8] Discuss ways in which a pregnant woman should adjust her diet.

[9] Discuss the causes of fetal alcohol syndrome in a newborn.

[10] Distinguish between a managed birth and a natural birth.

[11] Describe the events that occur during the three stages of labor.

[12] Define the words *preterm* and *term.*

[13] Discuss the meaning of the terms *low birthweight, very low birthweight,* and *extremely low birthweight.*

[14] Describe the advantages of breast-feeding a newborn.

[15] List five kinds, or causes, of birth defects.

For many people, pregnancy and childbirth are among the most joyful experiences they have in their lives. This is especially true when the baby is wanted and the pregnancy and birth are relatively healthy and normal. However, pregnancy and childbirth can involve difficult decisions when a couple is unable to conceive, when the parents have social problems like poverty, drugs, or familial problems, or when ethical issues involving the rights of the fetus and those of the parents come up.

Pregnancy and childbirth involve biological, psychological, and social considerations. As you read this chapter, notice what assumptions you have about how these events "should" proceed, and see if you can consider some other points of view. One thing you might notice is that this chapter is written with the general assumption that the "pregnant couple" is a woman and a man. But childbirth arrangements come in an increasingly great variety. The pregnant couple might be two lesbian women, who have a variety of options available for impregnation; or two gay men, who have arranged with a woman to bear a child for them; and so on. Likewise, an unpartnered woman who is willingly pregnant can have arrived at that condition by a variety of routes.

Couples who find satisfaction in their relationship and their work are more likely to realize the greatest rewards from parenthood.

## 16.1 THE DECISION TO BECOME A PARENT

Ideally, a pregnancy and the birth of a healthy baby are the responsibility of both parents. A baby's health depends not only on the health of the parents at the moment of conception, but on their lifestyle beforehand. The baby will affect, and be affected by, the parents' way of living—those things we have come to take for granted. It will intrude into the parents' time, may cost them more than expected, will alter how they spend their leisure time, might sharpen their ambitions, and will affect their relationships with family and friends. Since a person's lifestyle before conception can affect the health of the unborn child, potential parents need to look at their use of alcohol, drugs, and prescriptions, whether or not they smoke, what they eat, and the conditions of their workplace.

If a pregnant woman has chronic long-term conditions such as asthma, epilepsy, diabetes, or heart disease, her pregnancy might be affected. Women with viral STIs risk transmitting the virus to their babies. If either parent has a history of a genetic disease, or if such a condition is known within either extended family, counseling will help prospective parents understand their risk of passing the disease to a child.

The decision to become a parent should be given careful thought, along with the counsel of the par-

ents' health care provider. You can help determine your readiness to become a parent by answering the questions in "Where Do I Stand? To Be or Not to Be a Parent." A baby has the right to be born to parents who really want a child. A careful consideration of the factors of parenthood will influence how satisfied you will be as a mother or as a father, and how well you will be able to parent.

### 16.1.1 Parenthood by Choice

Before the 1950s, when birth control devices became widely available, sexually active men and women had little choice about whether or not to become parents. Existing birth control methods were unreliable, and abortion was often illegal or dangerous. Today, however, parenthood is more often a matter of choice. We can, to a large extent, decide whether to have children, when to have them, how many to have, and the space of time between them. As a result, the birthrate in America has dropped in the past forty years, to an average of two children per married couple.

However, many married couples still feel overt and subtle pressure to have children. They might be told that they are "selfish" or "unnatural" if they don't want to become parents. The decision to remain child-free can be a difficult one, especially when

# WHERE DO I STAND?
## TO BE OR NOT TO BE A PARENT

Deciding to have a child should ideally be a joint decision, and the result of a candid discussion in which a couple assesses the effect that pregnancy and childbirth will have on their lives. You and your partner should separately write a sentence or two in response to each of the following questions. Next, read through what you have written and indicate, by a check in the proper column, whether each response amounts to a yes, a no, or a not sure response.

|  | Yes | No | Not Sure |
|---|---|---|---|
| Do we really want to have a child? | _____ | _____ | _____ |
| Are we ready to accept the responsibility of having a child? | _____ | _____ | _____ |
| Are we willing to give up much of the freedom we now have and some of the things we enjoy doing for the sake of a child? | _____ | _____ | _____ |
| Are we prepared to alter our monthly budget so that we can accommodate the needs of a child? | _____ | _____ | _____ |
| Can we handle the emotional obligations of taking care of a child for the next 18 years? | _____ | _____ | _____ |
| Are we willing to accept the responsibility of making decisions affecting someone else's life? | _____ | _____ | _____ |
| Do we feel uncomfortable bringing a child into our current social and economic situation? | _____ | _____ | _____ |
| Are we prepared to live with a child who challenges (and perhaps rejects) our social values, view of life, religious outlook, and political philosophy? | _____ | _____ | _____ |

**Scoring:**

Compare your answers with those of your partner. A discussion about the realistic expectations of parenthood can quiet some fears and be a starting point for a decision.

**From:** R. Valois and S. Kammerman, "To Be or Not to Be Parents" in *Your Sexuality, A Personal Inventory.* Copyright © 1984 McGraw-Hill Company, New York, NY. Reprinted by permission.

---

friends, family, and society seem to expect that every couple wants to become parents. But remaining child-free has many potential advantages. People without children have more time and financial resources to pursue other goals. They have more flexibility in their work and social lives. And there may be more time and energy for adult intimacy, without the stress of having to negotiate who does what for the children (Cowan & Cowan, 1992).

Another trend made possible by the availability of reliable birth control is that of delaying having children until a woman is in her thirties or forties. Since the 1970s the number of women over thirty having their first child has risen steadily, and demographers expect the trend to continue, especially for parents in middle- and upper-income groups (White-

head, 1990). Thanks to the women's movement, women have many more career options that they may want to pursue before having children. The average age at first marriage is also increasing as women and men take longer to find their mate. In addition to allowing more time for the establishment of a career and relationship before having a family, delaying parenthood can make a couple more financially and emotionally prepared for the demands of children.

## 16.1.2 Becoming Pregnant

Becoming pregnant is an important moment in the life of a woman, and her life situation at that time has special bearing on her reactions to it. Since those situations vary so widely, her reactions to a pregnancy can range all the way from exhilaration to fear and disappointment. A woman's reaction to learning she is pregnant can depend on whether the pregnancy was planned or unplanned, her relationship with the father, her socioeconomic status, her physical health, and her feelings about pregnancy and motherhood.

Pregnancy brings many changes to a woman, which involve all aspects of her life—physically, emotionally, socially, and spiritually. The timing might or might not be ideal in terms of her finances, employment, schooling, or age. She and her partner might live in an apartment or house that has an extra bedroom, or she might be sharing limited living quarters with her family or a friend. She might have a partner with whom she feels secure and who shares her excitement, or she might feel alone, wondering whether the event will sustain or break her relationship with her partner, whose affection she might value very much. Some women will have to make difficult decisions about whether to have an abortion, put the baby up for adoption, or keep and raise the baby themselves.

A woman's relationships with others can change when she becomes pregnant. It can be a stressful event for couples, especially if the pregnancy was not planned. During this time communication becomes especially important as couples negotiate the many plans and decisions that must be made to prepare for the birth of a child. A woman's relationship to her own family of origin might change as well. She might for the first time see herself as a true adult, joining the ranks of her own mother and other parents in the family. And a woman's relationship to her own body will change through the pregnancy. This can be a time of reevaluating old habits and caring for her body in a new way, for the sake of the next generation (see "Healthy Sexuality: Before Conception").

The woman's partner faces many of the same challenges as she does. The responsibility for providing for the needs of a totally dependent person might make the partner apprehensive. He might wonder what changes this new baby will have on their relationship, his work, and other aspects of his life. He might feel especially close to his partner during this time, yet he might be anxious that the new baby will take her time and attention away from him.

The partner can be a full participant in the pregnancy and birthing process if the couple chooses. Sharing in visits to the practitioner, attending birthing classes, participating in the birthing process, and actively interacting with the newborn help in becoming a nurturing caregiver. If both partners see the need to provide mutual support for each other, they can lay the groundwork for becoming a strong family.

## 16.2 FIRST EVENTS OF PREGNANCY

In this section we will discuss pregnancies that result from sexual intercourse. There are other ways for people to become parents; these options will be covered later in this chapter.

### 16.2.1 Egg and Sperm Form

As discussed in chapters 4 and 5, women and men produce sex cells. Beginning around age twelve, the woman begins releasing sex cells (**eggs, ova**) from her ovary about every 28 days. As soon as an ovum bursts out of its follicle in the ovary, it is drawn into the flared opening of the nearby fallopian tube. As the *cilia,* or tiny hairs, along the lining of the walls of the tube move and the muscles of the tube expand and contract, the ovum is moved toward the uterus, a journey that requires several days.

The male sex cells, or **sperm,** are much smaller than the ova, but much more numerous. As they pass through the ducts in the man's penis, they mix with secreted fluids to become **semen** (*seminal fluid*). Propelled into the vagina with some force, the sperm move into the uterus and fallopian tubes to the egg, which is already in the fallopian tube (fig. 16.1). There may be upward of 200 million sperm in each ejaculation (Cunningham et al., 1993). Although sperm can live from 48 to 72 hours in the woman's body, many are killed by the acidic environment of the vagina. As a sperm moves through the uterus and fallopian tubes, it undergoes **capacitation**—changes in the membrane of the sperm that enable it to enter the ovum (Van De Graaff & Fox, 1995). Of the several hundred million sperm deposited into the vagina, most are killed by vaginal acidity or trickle out of the vagina. Only 100 to 200 are likely to reach the ovum. There sperm secrete an enzyme that softens the gelatinlike covering of the ovum, allowing one sperm to enter. Some sperm might reach the site of the ovum within five minutes after ejaculation, although four to six hours is average (Cunningham et al., 1993).

### 16.2.2 Conception

Upon meeting an ovum, one sperm passes through the ovum's softened covering toward its nucleus. The moment when this sperm unites with the nucleus of the ovum is the moment of **fertilization** or **conception.** Fertilization, which usually takes place in the outer third of the fallopian tube, results in a fertilized egg, or a **zygote.** This marks the beginning of **pregnancy,** the sequence of events that ends with birth. Based on whether the sperm is carrying an X chromosome or a Y chromosome to unite with the X chromosome of the ovum, a female or male is conceived. After about

## HEALTHY SEXUALITY

### BEFORE CONCEPTION

Individuals who are thinking about having a baby can increase their odds for a healthy pregnancy and child by watching their health right now. Things that are not ordinarily considered unhealthy can be damaging during an early pregnancy—before they realize the woman is pregnant. Having a few drinks at a party, using a hot tub, spraying chemicals on the lawn, or taking antihistamines for a cold are risks partners might not be taking if they knew the woman was pregnant.

Potential parents can take steps that will help:

■ See a health care provider before stopping using birth control or trying to become pregnant. She or he will want to give important early counsel.

■ See a genetic counselor if either partner is aware of any hereditary disease in his or her family.

■ Check with a health care provider or pharmacist about any medications being taken, including over-the-counter drugs.

■ Stop smoking, and stop drinking alcohol.

■ Reduce or eliminate caffeine intake.

■ Avoid X rays and environmental chemicals, such as lawn and garden chemicals.

■ Begin a program of moderate regular exercise if you're not already engaged in one.

■ Maintain a normal weight; lose weight, if necessary.

■ If dental X rays are needed in a dental checkup, get them now.

---

one day, cell division begins and the zygote enters the **cleavage stage.** Over the next two to three days, as it continues moving through the fallopian tube, the cell divides to form two, four, eight cells, and so on, to become a solid ball of cells called a *morula*.

### 16.2.3   Implantation

As cell division progresses, the morula continues moving down the fallopian tube. After about three days it reaches the uterus. At this time, the morula becomes a hollow ball of cells called a **blastocyst.**

For the next two or three days, the blastocyst floats in the cavity of the uterus. As cell division speeds up, one side of the blastocyst forms an inner mass of embryonic cells that eventually becomes the *embryo* proper. The blastocyst then attaches itself to the endometrium (uterine lining) and sinks down into the lining, which then closes over it. This is **implantation.**

As cell division speeds up, one side of the embryo forms a depression or indentation. This is the first indication that specialized cells, tissues, and organs will be appearing. A fold called the *neural groove* develops, which later becomes the nervous system. (The nervous system is derived from the same embryonic tissue as the skin, which explains why certain disease agents, such as herpes viruses, attack both the skin and the nervous system.) The neural groove becomes

a tube, and the head end of the tube enlarges to form a rudimentary brain. Blood vessels develop and spread out, and soon the primitive beginnings of the head, heart, and limbs are evident. The **embryonic stage** extends from the second week through the eighth week of development. The term **embryo** is

| | |
|---|---|
| **eggs** | female sex cells |
| **ova** (ō′va) | female sex cells |
| **sperm** | male sex cells |
| **semen** (sē′men) | male ejaculate |
| **capacitation** (kah-pas-i-tā′shun) | changes in sperm that occur in the uterus and fallopian tubes |
| **fertilization** | union of egg and sperm |
| **conception** | union of egg and sperm |
| **zygote** (zī′gōt) | fertilized egg |
| **pregnancy** | sequence of events beginning with fertilization and ending with birth |
| **cleavage stage** (klē′vej) | first cell divisions of zygote |
| **blastocyst** (blas′tō-sist) | an early embryo |
| **implantation** | embedding of blastocyst in uterine wall |
| **embryonic stage** (em-bri-on′ik) | weeks 2 through 8 of early embryo |
| **embryo** (em′bri-ō) | developing child through week 8 |

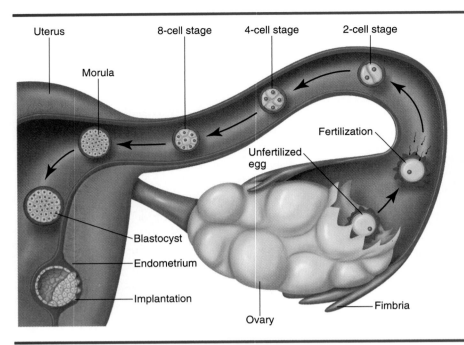

**FIGURE 16.1**   Stages in the development of the early embryo. The unfertilized egg is released from the ovary and moves into the fallopian tube, where it is fertilized by a sperm cell. As the fertilized egg is moved by the cilia through the tube toward the uterus, the egg divides to form a two-cell stage, a four-cell stage, and an eight-cell stage. As cell division continues, the embryo becomes a hollow blastocyst that is implanted into the endometrial lining of the inside of the uterus.

used to describe the developing child through the eighth week of development; after this time until birth it is referred to as a **fetus** (fig. 16.2).

## 16.2.4   Hormone Secretion

At this stage of development, the outer cells of the blastocyst are secreting the hormone **human chorionic gonadotropin (hCG)**. (Because hCG also ends up in a pregnant woman's blood and urine, its presence or absence is a common indicator in most pregnancy tests.) Beginning soon after fertilization, the secretion of hCG increases to a peak level in about fifty to sixty days.

When present, hCG causes the corpus luteum to be maintained through the early stages of pregnancy, thereby stopping menstrual periods. hCG is also thought to help protect the blastocyst against rejection by the woman's immune system.

## 16.2.5   Placental and Fetal Membrane Formation

The embryo continues to develop through the embryonic stages. The outer wall of the blastocyst develops into two fetal membranes, the outer **chorion** and an inner **amnion**. The chorion on one side of the blastocyst forms fingerlike outgrowths called the **chorionic villi**, which project into the maternal endometrium to form the placenta, an organ that attaches the embryo to the uterine wall. During this time, the **placenta**, or *afterbirth*, a complex, spongy structure (fig. 16.3), is responsible for exchanging nutrients, gases, and wastes between blood of the pregnant woman and that of her embryo/fetus. Nutrients and oxygen pass from the

body of the woman to the fetus, and fetal wastes return to her system. The blood of the pregnant woman and fetus do not mix, but remain separated by a thin membrane through which these materials diffuse. Unfortunately, harmful chemicals and disease agents from the blood of the woman are often able to cross the placenta and move into the fetus.

The placenta, when fully formed, is a reddish-brown disc about eight inches in diameter by one inch thick weighing one to two pounds. Eventually the placenta connects to the fetus by a ropelike **umbilical cord.**

The part of the chorion not forming the placenta fuses with the amnion to become a fluid-filled **amniotic sac** (commonly called the "bag of waters") surrounding the embryonic cells. In this **amniotic fluid** the embryo/fetus can freely move and grow, protected against any jarring movements of the woman's body.

| | |
|---|---|
| **fetus** (fē′tus) | developing child after week 8 |
| **human chorionic gonadotropin (hCG)** (kō-re-on′ik gon-a-dō-trō′pin) | a hormone produced by the chorion of the embryo-fetus |
| **chorion** (kō′re-on) | outer cells of blastocyst wall |
| **amnion** (am′ne-on) | inner cells of blastocyst wall |
| **chorionic villi** (kō-re-on′ik vil′lī) | fingerlike outgrowths of chorion |
| **placenta** (pla-sen′ta) | organ uniting fetus to uterine wall |
| **umbilical cord** (um-bil′i-kal) | cord attaching fetus to placenta |
| **amniotic sac** (am-ni-ot′ik) | fluid-filled sac between amnion and fetus |
| **amniotic fluid** | watery contents of amniotic sac |

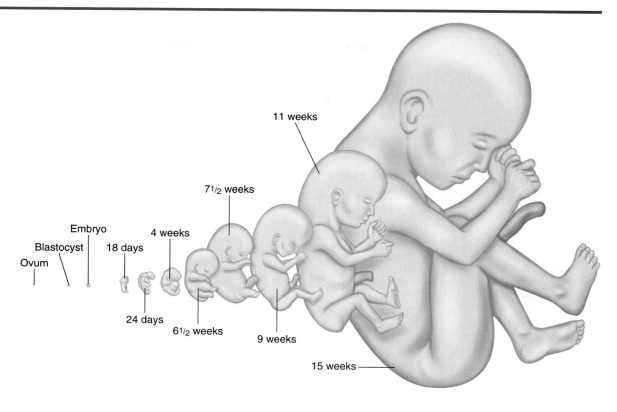

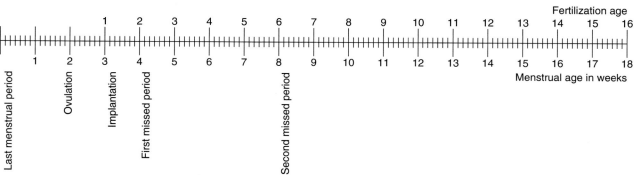

**FIGURE 16.2**  Embryo and fetal growth. The actual sizes of the embryo and fetus are shown, from the ovum through the fifteenth week. The calendar shows the events of early pregnancy.

## 16.3    DETERMINING PREGNANCY

There are certain signs that may give a woman a clue that she is pregnant, even before she sees a health care provider. These signs include:

*Amenorrhea:* A missed or light period about two weeks after fertilization might indicate pregnancy, although it is not an absolute sign (it can also be caused by illness, stress, bereavement, surgery, or jet lag).

*Frequent urination:* Even though in small quantities.

*Fatigue:* Feeling the need for more sleep.

*Nausea:* "Morning sickness" can occur at any time, especially when the pregnant woman does not eat often enough.

*Breast change:* The nipples might become sensitive, even sore, to the touch and deepen in color.

*Smell:* The sense of smell might become more acute, and common odors might make the woman nauseated.

When a woman suspects she is pregnant, she should seek confirmation as early as possible. Early prenatal care is essential to help avoid causes of

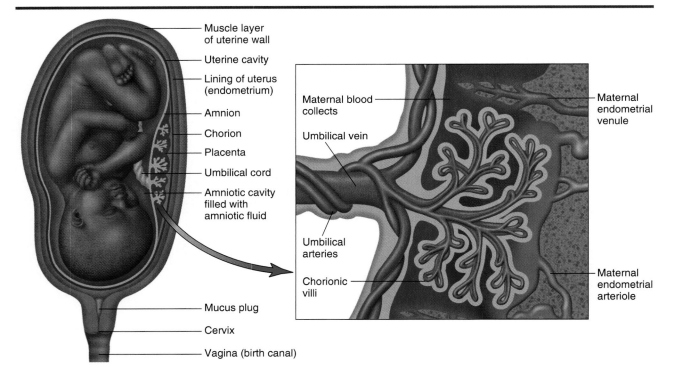

**FIGURE 16.3**    The fetus and uterus and a section of the placenta. The placenta provides for an exchange of materials between mother and fetus. Through blood vessels in the umbilical cord, nutrients and oxygen pass from the mother to the fetus, and wastes pass from the fetus to the mother.

congenital defects in the baby, and for the health of the mother. If a woman has any plans for aborting, an early abortion is preferable to one performed later, since the risk to a woman in later abortions is significantly higher.

There are a variety of tests available to confirm pregnancy, including these:

> *Blood tests:* Performed by your health care provider, blood tests can accurately detect the presence of hCG (the pregnancy hormone) within two weeks after conception. hCG is produced by the blastocyst, not by the mother.
>
> *Urine tests:* hCG can also be detected in the urine.

More than 90 percent accurate, these tests may be performed by a professional or as a home pregnancy test. Home pregnancy test kits are easy to use but the results may be less reliable than laboratory test results, due to the chance that the directions might not be followed exactly.

More reliable than pregnancy tests is an internal examination by a woman's physician once there are obvious signs of a suspected pregnancy (usually four weeks or more after conception). The cervix and uterus become softer and the vagina and cervix may change slightly in color. The uterus may be slightly enlarged.

Most reliable are tests confirming the four positive signs of pregnancy. All arise from the fetus: *fetal heartbeat, perception of fetal movement, sonographic (ultrasound) recognition of the fetus,* and *ability to see the fetal skeleton using X rays.*

Hearing and counting the fetal heartbeat is unmistakable evidence of pregnancy. The pulse rate will be about twice as fast as the woman's pulse. Fetal movements are commonly felt after the fifth month of pregnancy by placing the hand over the abdomen. (The first detectable movement of the fetus is called the "quickening.") Movements have been felt as early as the tenth week. *Sonography* (ultrasound imaging) will confirm pregnancy as early as six weeks of development. Furthermore, sonograph technicians can estimate the fetal age quite accurately from the length of the embryo. X rays will reveal the fetal skeleton sometime after the fourteenth week of pregnancy. However, the radiation hazard to both the fetus and the woman limits the use of X rays to only those few cases in which its use is absolutely essential.

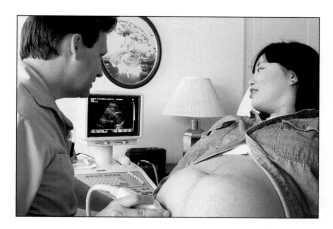

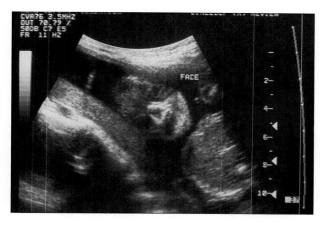

(a)                                                                          (b)

Ultrasonography. **a:** Sound waves are reflected from the body tissues of the pregnant woman. **b:** Structures of the fetus observed through an ultrasound scan.

## 16.4  DURING PREGNANCY

A full-term pregnancy from conception to birth lasts about 266 days, or 38 weeks. Ovulation usually occurs about midway between periods of menstrual flow, so conception usually commences about the middle of the menstrual month *after* a woman's last flow, or her *last menstrual period (LMP).* By adding 14 days, or the two weeks between the LMP and conception, to the 266 days, we have a total of 280 days.

Using 280 days, pregnancy can be divided into *40* weeks, or into *ten* **lunar** (moon) **months** (each of 28 days, or four weeks). Using the calendar, the approximately nine months also can be divided into *three trimesters* of 13 weeks each.

### 16.4.1  Establishing a Due Date

To determine the date when her baby is due to be born, a woman can calculate from the beginning of her **last menstrual period (LMP).** Preferred by obstetricians, this calculation will tell a woman the *gestational age* of her fetus. *Embryologists* often cite the *ovulatory* or *fertilization age,* which starts with the time of ovulation.

Using calendar months, delivery can be estimated by adding seven days to the date of the first day of the LMP and counting back three months. For example:

| LMP | 20 March |
|---|---|
| add seven days | 27 March |
| subtract three months | 27 December (previous year) |
| add one year | 27 December (current year) |

But do not be surprised if birth does not occur on the expected day. Eighty-five percent of babies born from normal pregnancies are delivered within a week before or after the date predicted (Stoppard, 1993).

### 16.4.2  First Trimester (One through Three Lunar Months)

#### The Mother

Each woman reacts to pregnancy differently. Her body is adjusting to pregnancy, although she might not look and feel pregnant (fig. 16.4). As her hormones start affecting her, sex desires might increase or decrease, or she might experience mood swings. It is not unusual for women to have a new sense of well-being and energy. Foods might taste different, and some women have unusual food cravings. A woman might gain two to four pounds during this time. Others might begin feeling somewhat nauseous a month or so into their pregnancy. Although it can occur any time of the day, such nausea is commonly called "morning sickness." Many women find that frequent small meals of bland foods help minimize the discomfort of morning sickness. Fortunately, such symptoms usually disappear a month or two after they begin (Striegel-Moore et al., 1996).

Due to the developing embryo and placenta, the woman's body is working harder. Her heart rate rises and her breathing becomes more rapid as she exchanges oxygen and carbon dioxide with the fetus. Her breasts become larger and heavier and more

| **lunar month** (lū′ner) | a 28-day month |
|---|---|
| **last menstrual period (LMP)** | last menstrual period before a pregnancy |

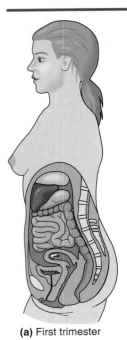

**(a)** First trimester

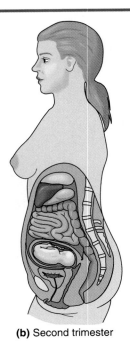

**(b)** Second trimester

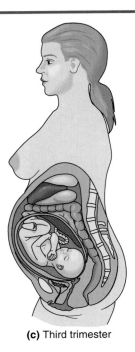

**(c)** Third trimester

**FIGURE 16.4** Changes in a woman's body during pregnancy. Through the three trimesters, the shape of the pregnant woman's body changes dramatically.

# GO ASK ALICE

*Alice,*
*How can you tell whether you have had a miscarriage?*
*Bleeding at the Wrong Time*

Dear Bleeding at the Wrong Time,
One in six pregnancies result in miscarriage, and 75% of those happen before the first twelve weeks of pregnancy. This makes miscarriage a fairly common event. Miscarriage is also called spontaneous abortion, and is often thought to be due to genetic or physical defects in the fetus. In many first trimester miscarriages, the woman does not even know that she is pregnant, since the miscarriage may often seem like a heavier than usual menstrual flow. Late miscarriages may involve uncomfortable cramping and profuse bleeding.

So, in answer to your question, the only way to know for sure if you have had a miscarriage is to previously have had a positive pregnancy test.

 http://www.mhhe.com/byer6

tender to the touch, and the areola around the nipple becomes darker. As a woman's uterus slowly enlarges, it will increasingly press against her bladder, causing her to urinate more often. Bowel movements might be irregular and vaginal secretions might increase.

## The Embryo-Fetus

The embryo's growth and development begin shortly after fertilization. By the end of the fourth week (LMP), the embryo is about an eighth of an inch long and its body tapers off into a small pointed tail. The brain, spinal cord, nervous system, and throat have begun to develop. The mouth, eyes, ears, and nose are forming and the arms and legs are budding out.

The head is large in proportion to the rest of the body. Although incompletely formed, the heart is beating and pumping blood through simple vessels.

At the end of the eighth week (LMP), the embryo is about 1.5 inches long. The face appears human, with eyes, ears, and nose visible. Limbs become distinct—arms with hands and fingers, legs with feet and toes. Testicles begin to form in the male; ovary formation occurs a bit later in the female. Muscles are forming and slight movements may begin.

By the end of the twelfth week (LMP), the fetus is about 3 inches long and weighs about 1.5 ounces. The fetus responds to stimulus and moves easily, although the mother does not yet feel its movement. As

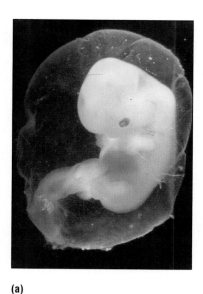  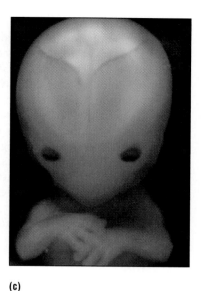

(a)  (b)  (c)

Fetal development. **a:** At 6 to 7 weeks. **b:** During the third month. **c:** At about 4 months.

teeth are forming under the gums, fingers and toes are well formed and nails are present. Closed eyelids cover the eyes. All major organs have formed and have limited functioning. The genitals in both the male and female are now recognizable.

### 16.4.3 Second Trimester (Four through Six Lunar Months)

#### The Mother

By now a woman's pregnancy is well established. Symptoms from early pregnancy, such as "morning sickness," usually lessen or disappear, and many women have a feeling of well-being.

As the breasts and nipples continue to increase in size, the nipples and areolae become darker. The nipples begin to secrete colostrum. As the fetus grows, the skin over the woman's abdomen stretches and the abdomen begins to protrude and she will need to wear looser, maternity-style clothing. In the fourth month she might, for the first time, feel the fetus move, a development called the "quickening."

During this trimester the woman will likely gain approximately 12 pounds, with about 2 pounds of this gain being fetal weight, and other 10 pounds consisting of placenta/amniotic fluid, along with her own weight gain (Stoppard, 1993).

#### The Fetus

By the sixteenth week (LMP) eyebrows and eyelashes become visible. The fetus' entire body structure is formed and the skin is covered with a fine downlike hair. Sucking motions may begin. The sex of the fetus can be identified by a careful sonographic examina-

tion of the genital organs. The fetus is now about 5.5 inches long and weighs 4 to 6 ounces.

At the end of week 20 (LMP), scalp hair is visible. The skin has a bright pinkish hue and is covered by a cheeselike substance that will remain until after birth. Fetal movements are strong and the heartbeat can be heard with a stethoscope. The fetus is now about 8 inches long and weighs about 11 ounces.

By week 24 (LMP) the eyelids have separated and are open, and the skin is wrinkled and red. The fetus is 10 to 12 inches long and weighs 1.0 to 1.5 pounds. A fetus born at this period usually will not survive (Cunningham et al., 1993).

### 16.4.4 Third Trimester (Seven through Ten Lunar Months)

#### The Mother

The woman's size is increasing rapidly as the fetus grows. As the uterus pushes forward, the woman might begin walking with her head and shoulders back to maintain balance, and walking becomes more awkward to her. As the fetus moves toward the pelvis late in her pregnancy, the woman's feelings of breathlessness might lessen due to decreased pressure on the diaphragm. She might feel increased tiredness, might not sleep well at night, and might need increased rest.

Fetal movements can become strong and bothersome, especially when the woman tries to relax. As the fetus puts more pressure on the bladder, frequent urination may be necessary. Heartburn during this trimester is not uncommon.

A woman's weight gain during the third trimester is about 10 pounds, depending on race, size of parents, socioeconomic status of the mother, and the sex of the fetus. Boys tend to be about 3 ounces heavier than girls (Cunningham et al., 1993). (For total weight gain during pregnancy, see section 16.5 "Prenatal Care"). The enlarged uterus and fetus put pressure on the blood vessels in the lower back, which can cause cramps and varicose veins in the woman's legs and hemorrhoids in her rectum.

Late in pregnancy, uterine contractions might become more frequent and might be mistaken for labor. During the last few weeks, the head of the fetus usually lowers ("drops") into the pelvis, until it is positioned against the pelvic bones. Sometimes this "dropping" does not occur until the beginning of labor, especially if a woman has had previous births.

### The Fetus

By the end of week 28 (LMP), the head and body are more proportionate and the eyes are open. The down-like hair disappears over most of the fetus' body. The surface of the skin is still reddish and wrinkled. The testes of the male have descended into the scrotum. The fetus now weighs about 2.5 pounds and is about 11 inches long. The fetus has rotated and repositioned the head downward toward the cervix of the uterus. An infant born at this time will usually survive if given intensive care (Cunningham et al., 1993).

At the end of week 32 (LMP) the fetus weighs 3.5 to 4 pounds and is 14 to 16 inches long. Most infants born at this point will survive. The fetus tends to fall asleep when rocked but may be startled by loud noises. If so, soft speaking by the woman usually calms the fetus down.

By the end of the final eight weeks (LMP) the fetus has reached 18 to 20 inches in length and 6.5 to 8 pounds in weight. The skin has lost its wrinkled appearance due to the accumulation of body fat. Its skin color is pinkish-blue, even in fetuses of dark-skinned parents (Van De Graaff & Fox, 1995). Term is 40 weeks after the onset of the last menstrual period (LMP), or 38 weeks after conception.

## 16.4.5  Sexual Intimacies between Partners during Pregnancy

During pregnancy there are many psychological, emotional, and physical changes that influence a woman's attitude toward and enjoyment of sex. Much higher levels of two hormones in her body, progesterone and estrogen, may be responsible for most of this. Once the embryo has implanted into the uterine lining, the embryo and placenta become primary sources of these hormones. In fact, the level of progesterone can rise to levels ten times higher than before conception, and the amount of estrogen produced in one day can equal the amount produced by the ovaries of a nonpregnant woman in three years (Stoppard, 1993).

Commonly, there is a decline of interest in sex in the first trimester, an increase in the second trimester, followed by a decline again in the third trimester. A pregnant woman might find sex more arousing and satisfying than before conception. The higher levels of progesterone and estrogen cause changes in her breasts and sex organs, making them more sensitive and responsive. Her vagina and labia become slightly stretched and swollen, hastening sexual arousal. Her enlarging breasts are more sensitive and also more responsive to caressing and kissing by her partner. The vagina lubricates more rapidly, making penetration easier, and orgasm can be more intense.

Unless her health care provider counsels a pregnant woman to the contrary, there is no physical reason to forego sex during pregnancy. In fact, good sex during pregnancy is not only very enjoyable but tends to bond the woman closer to her partner. As long as there is the desire, there is no need for partners to stop sex until the onset of labor. The uterine contractions during orgasm can help prepare the uterus for labor. If, however, either partner has an STI, or if either partner has any other sexual partners or a history of intravenous drug abuse, the use of condoms is recommended to avoid any possible infection of the vagina.

If vaginal or uterine bleeding occurs, couples should avoid vaginal penetration unless a health care provider approves. Rupture of the amniotic sac, dilation of the cervix, or indications of premature labor are further reasons to avoid penetration. Blowing air into the vagina, as might be done during cunnilingus, can lead to maternal death from *air embolisms* (air bubbles in a blood vessel).

Some couples find that pregnancy is a good time to explore new lovemaking positions—side by side, rear entry, or sitting—that may be more comfortable at this time. Pregnancy can also be a time to try other sensual and sexual pleasures such as oral sex, mutual masturbation, massage, or erotically kissing and stroking each other.

## 16.5  PRENATAL CARE

It is impossible to overemphasize the importance of **prenatal** care to both the pregnant woman and her developing child. Prenatal care involves not only the medical advice and supervision of a physician or other practitioner, but also the healthful habits of the woman herself. The health care provider can play an important role in early detection of unexpected problems. The woman can play an even more important role in prevention of many potential complications.

## 16.5.1   Choosing a Practitioner

The pregnant woman has many choices regarding the health care professionals who will help her in her pregnancy, labor, and delivery, and regarding where this takes place. Babies can be delivered by a family physician, by an obstetrician-gynecologist, or by midwives. The choice of practitioner for prenatal care influences the physical well-being of both mother and child and also the emotional rewards of the whole experience of pregnancy and birth. Further, this choice usually determines where and how the birth will take place.

Many women choose their family physician to confirm their pregnancies and to care for them during pregnancy. If the family physician is chosen to deliver the baby, she or he will likely want to do the delivery in a hospital, although some are agreeable to alternatives such as a home delivery or special birthing centers. **Obstetrician-gynecologists (Ob-Gyns)** are physicians who specialize in women's health issues and who have passed examinations to document their knowledge, competency, and skills in the medical and surgical care of women.

In the United States today there are two main types of practicing midwives: certified nurse-midwives and lay midwives. **Certified nurse-midwives (CNMs)** are registered nurses who are trained and experienced in providing health care for pregnant women from early pregnancy through labor and delivery. Depending on the licensing requirements of the state in which they practice, CNMs might have a private practice, or they might work in private physicians' practices, freestanding birthing centers, hospitals, health departments, or sometimes homes. Mothers receiving postnatal midwife care have rated it highly in terms of help in dealing with infant feeding, postnatal depression, and preparation for parenthood (Shields et al., 1997). In most states, they practice in collaboration with a physician to whom they can refer if birthing complications occur.

Another type of midwife is the *lay midwife*. Lacking the nursing education of certified nurse-midwives, lay midwives usually receive their training from other lay midwives. Lay midwives are more apt to be found in poorer rural or inner-city areas. They mainly practice in homes and might or might not have physician support. Because they lack medical training, their level of competence varies considerably. Most states do not license lay midwives.

Many physicians coordinate with a team of health care professionals to provide care for the pregnant woman. The team might include *childbirth educators* to help educate prospective parents, *labor* and *delivery nurses, postpartum nurses* to provide care after delivery, neonatal nurses to care for the newborn, social workers to provide information and counseling, and nutritionists to give advice on dietary needs.

## 16.5.2   Nutrition

The diet of a pregnant woman has lifelong implications for her baby. Appropriate nutrition is essential in the development of the fetus and for as long as the mother nurses her infant.

During her pregnancy a woman may be at nutritional risk if she has had a recent miscarriage or stillbirth, there is less than 16 months between her pregnancies, she smokes or uses alcohol or drugs, is allergic to certain key foods (such as milk and wheat), is under age 18, is carrying more than one fetus, has been subject to a great deal of stress or any physical injury, is a strict vegetarian, or is anemic, underweight, run-down, or eating an inadequate or unbalanced diet (Institute of Medicine, 1990).

A well-balanced diet is the best source of vitamins and minerals. During her pregnancy a woman's diet should provide sufficient amounts of the basic food groups and extra amounts of protein, calcium, iron, and vitamins A, B, C, and D. Fresh, whole foods like fruits and vegetables, milk products, and lean meats are the best sources of vitamins and minerals. A wide range of nutrients is found in milk or milk products (fresh low-fat milk, buttermilk, yogurt, or cottage cheese). She is advised to avoid multivitamins and mineral supplements, except those recommended by her health care provider. (Institute of Medicine, 1990). Pregnant women are often prescribed special prenatal vitamins, which contain extra iron and folic acid. The National Academy of Science, through the Institute of Medicine (1990), advises a pregnant woman to gain 25 to 35 pounds of weight during her pregnancy to further insure adequate nutrition for herself and her fetus.

## 16.5.3   Exercise

Many women today have an interest in maintaining an exercise-fitness program. Exercise during pregnancy improves a woman's stamina and strength and helps her body adapt to the demands of pregnancy.

| | |
|---|---|
| **prenatal** (prē-nā′tl) | before birth |
| **obstetrician-gynecologist (Ob-Gyn)** (ob-ste-trish′an gī-ne-kol′ō-jist) | physician specialist dealing with pregnancy and women's health matters |
| **certified nurse-midwife (CNM)** | a registered nurse who is specially trained to deliver babies |

Maintaining an exercise routine during pregnancy improves a woman's stamina and strength, and conditions her muscle tone so that her body returns to its original shape more quickly after delivery.

Well-conditioned women who engage in aerobics or run regularly have shorter labors and fewer cesarean deliveries, although such exercise does result in reduced birthweight due to less fat mass (Clapp & Capeless, 1990). Exercise during pregnancy can condition a woman's muscle tone so that her body returns more quickly to its original shape sooner after delivery.

The American College of Obstetricians and Gynecologists (1986) recommends that if a pregnant woman is accustomed to aerobic exercise before pregnancy, she be allowed to continue those routines during pregnancy without starting new exercise programs or intensifying existing ones. They further recommend that if she has been sedentary (inactive) before pregnancy, she engage in no activity more strenuous than walking during pregnancy.

Rhythmic, moderate activity is well advised and safe for both mother and fetus (McGlynn, 1993). Recommended activities (as long as you have been doing it regularly beforehand) include swimming, walking, and dancing. Activities to avoid include jogging, backpacking, and sit-ups (Stoppard, 1993).

### 16.5.4 Teratogens

The subject of birth defects is one of special concern. The causes for some birth defects are unknown. Other birth defects can be caused by known factors or agents that adversely affect an embryo or fetus during its rapid growth and development. Such agents, called **teratogens,** include various drugs, microorganisms, and high-level ionizing radiation.

Along with nutrients, wastes, and gases, the placenta allows many drugs to pass freely from the pregnant woman's blood to that of the fetus. Thus, substances taken in by the woman can also affect her fetus. For instance, when a pregnant woman drinks alcohol, she is also exposing her fetus to it. Many people in our culture have become so accustomed to relying on drugs to cope with life situations that it does not occur to them that the effect on a fetus might be as great or greater than on them. The following are some known teratogenic agents.

### Alcohol

The number one fetal teratogen by far is alcohol (Tortora & Grabowski, 1993). Long suspected of being a teratogen, only in recent years has the relationship between maternal alcohol intake and characteristic fetal malformations been shown. Known as **fetal alcohol syndrome (FAS),** the symptoms include growth retardation, facial malformations, and central nervous system dysfunctions, including mental retardation and behavioral disorders. Many infants are born with less serious, yet significant, damage described as *fetal alcohol effects (FAE).* The effects of FAE can include learning disabilities and behavioral abnormalities (Aase, Jones, & Clarren, 1995).

When alcohol crosses the placental barrier, it reaches a level in the fetus equal to that in the body of the woman. Because the body of the fetus is small and its detoxification system immature, alcohol remains in fetal blood long after it has disappeared in the woman's blood. Reducing the number of cells produced and damaging those that are produced, alcohol interferes with many developmental events in the fetus (Beattie, 1992). Alcohol consumption can also cause low birthweight (National Center for Health Statistics, 1993).

The damage evident at birth persists; children with FAS never fully recover (Spohr, Wilms, & Steinhausen, 1993). Not just a childhood disorder, FAS has a long-term progression into adulthood (Streissguth et al., 1991). Unfortunately, FAS can only be prevented; it cannot be treated (Committee on Nutritional Status During Pregnancy and Lactation, 1990).

Although the number of defects rises with increasing amounts of alcohol, and the effects of maternal problem drinking are well documented, even the effects of light to moderate drinking during pregnancy can be damaging. As little as one to two drinks a day can have measurable effects (Whitney & Rolfes, 1996). FAS and related effects can be avoided by complete abstention from alcohol by women who realize they are pregnant or, better yet, by women who are about to become pregnant (Committee on Substance Abuse and Committee on Children with Disabilities, 1993). There is now evidence that exposure of pre-ovulatory human eggs to alcohol is at least as harmful as is the exposure of a recently fertilized embryo (Kaufman, 1997).

All containers of beer, wine, and liquor carry this warning: *Government warning: (1) According to the Surgeon General, women should not drink alcoholic beverages during pregnancy because of the risk of birth defects.* The best advice to women who are pregnant, planning to become pregnant, or who might be pregnant and not know it, is *don't consume alcohol.*

### Cigarette Smoking

Cigarette smoking during pregnancy is one of the most damaging factors to the health of an unborn baby. The associated risks include:

- Miscarriage and stillbirth, damage to the placenta, low birthweight, and an increased chance of fetal abnormalities (Stoppard, 1993).

- Smoking restricts the blood supply to the growing fetus and thus limits oxygen and nutrition delivery and waste removal. The nicotine constricts blood vessels and carbon monoxide (CO) in the blood reduces oxygen-carrying capacity.

- Smokers tend to eat less nutritious food during pregnancy than nonsmokers, which impairs fetal nutrition (Haste et al., 1990).

- Smoking during pregnancy can harm the intellectual and behavioral development of the child later in life (Olds, Henderson, & Tatelbaum, 1994; Fergusson, Horwood, & Lynskey, 1993).

Smoking during pregnancy is particularly common among white mothers. They are not only more likely than African American mothers to smoke, but those who do smoke, smoke much more. Hispanic women are much less likely to smoke than non-Hispanic women; smoking is relatively rare among Asian women (National Center for Health Statistics, 1993).

Cigarette smoking may be teratogenic, causing cardiac abnormalities and *ancephaly* (absence of a cerebrum). It appears to be a significant factor in the development of cleft lip and palate, and a positive relationship has been shown both between cigarette smoking and passive (secondhand) smoke and the occurrence of *sudden infant death syndrome (SIDS)* (Klonoff-Cohen et al., 1995). Infant gastrointestinal troubles are more common in nursing mothers who smoke (Tortora & Grabowski, 1993). It is best for women who smoke before pregnancy to find a way to curtail the habit *before* becoming pregnant.

### Drugs

Both legal *medications* (prescription, and OTC) and *street* (illegal) *drugs* taken by a woman and/or her partner can significantly affect her and her fetus during pregnancy. It is crucial that a woman tell her physician all of the drugs she is taking if there is any chance she is or plans to become pregnant.

### Medications

There are legal drugs, both prescription and OTC, that might be safe for a woman to take when she is not pregnant, but that can adversely affect her and her unborn child if taken during pregnancy. Especially critical are drugs that, if taken during the embryonic period (from week 2 through week 8), can cause developmental malformations. Certain drugs that would cause congenital malformations if taken during this period would not have the same effect if taken late in pregnancy. Unless directed to do so by her physician, it is important that a pregnant woman not use aspirin or ibuprofen during the last three months of pregnancy because these can cause problems in the unborn child and/or during delivery (Whitney & Rolfes, 1996).

Although some medications are prescribed, others such as OTC drugs are commonly taken without the knowledge and advice of a physician or are taken before a woman realizes that she is pregnant. Aspirin is a widely used OTC drug. Aspirin and other drugs that contain salicylate are not recommended through pregnancy, especially during the last three months, except under a physician's supervision. Acetylsalicylate, found in many painkillers, can prolong pregnancy and cause excessive bleeding before and after delivery.

Due to the long list of commonly used drugs that can adversely affect the pregnant mother and/or the fetus, the American Pharmaceutical Association advises women to "avoid the use of drugs, in general, at any stage of pregnancy" (Cunningham et al., 1993).

### Street (Illegal) Drugs

Use of street (illegal, illicit) drugs such as cocaine, marijuana, heroin, and morphine should be stopped long before a woman conceives. Unfortunately, the use of illicit drugs may be common among pregnant women. In one study, 15 percent of pregnant women,

| | |
|---|---|
| **teratogens** (ter-at′ō-jenz) | organisms or substances that adversely affect the embryo-fetus |
| **fetal alcohol syndrome (FAS)** (fē′tl, sin′drōm) | cluster of physical effects on fetus due to mother drinking alcohol during pregnancy |

regardless of ethnicity or socioeconomic status, tested positive for illicit drugs (Chasnoff, Landress, & Barrett, 1990).

Any woman who uses *cocaine*, or "crack," in her childbearing years greatly reduces her chances of producing a healthy baby. Cocaine used by a pregnant woman subjects the fetus to a higher risk of retarded growth, attention and orientation problems, a tendency to stop breathing, crib death, and malformed or missing organs, as well as an increase in miscarriage, premature birth, and stillbirth. Use by the mother affects her heart action and causes strokes, seizures, sudden death, and aortic rupture (Petitti & Coleman, 1990). Even though the woman withdraws from use of cocaine during pregnancy, her fetus will go through withdrawal inside her uterus (Alroomi et al., 1988).

Other illicit drugs can also adversely affect an unborn child. Marijuana interferes with the normal production of male sperm. Heroin, morphine, and other opiates can damage the chromosomes in the ovum and sperm, causing abnormalities.

Illicit drug use is very common in the United States. It is estimated that 70 percent to 90 percent of Americans age 15 to 40 use mood-altering drugs, and many of these users are women of childbearing age (Richards, 1985). Besides this, illicit drug users commonly abuse more than one drug, which can increase the risk of adverse affects.

The sharing of syringes during illicit drug use presents a high risk of transmitting *human immunodeficiency virus (HIV)*. HIV not only affects the unborn child, but HIV-positive newborns rarely survive beyond the first few years of life.

Once again, illicit drug use has no place either with partners who are prospective parents or with women who are or might become pregnant. If a woman is pregnant, or planning to become pregnant, she should inform her health care provider and take only those drugs he or she prescribes or approves.

### Diseases

A great many diseases assume an increased importance in pregnancy. Only a few are included here; others are discussed in chapter 6.

*Rubella (German Measles):* One of the diseases most devastating to the fetus is **rubella,** commonly known as German measles. A disease usually of minor importance in a nonpregnant person, the virus can cross the placenta and have severe congenital effects on a fetus, especially when the infection occurs during the first trimester of pregnancy. The degree of risk drops later in pregnancy. Fortunately, immunization has greatly reduced the number of babies born with congenital rubella syndrome. Rubella vaccine is one of the standard childhood immunizations and should provide lifelong protection. The problem is that the rubella vaccine contains a live virus, and therefore it might cause the same problem as when contracting the disease. Women receiving the vaccine are cautioned against conceiving for six months.

*Toxoplasmosis:* **Toxoplasmosis** is caused by *Toxoplasma gondii*, a protozoan (one-celled animal). It can be transmitted by eating infected undercooked meat or by food, water, or dust contaminated with cat droppings. The parasite is carried in the mother's blood and crosses the placenta into the fetus. Adults might experience only flu like symptoms, but fetal infection can be much more severe, with possible damage to the brain or eyes, or fetal death.

To prevent toxoplasmosis during pregnancy, cook all meats thoroughly, avoid cleaning cat litter pans, prevent cats from hunting rodents (their source of infection), and avoid contact with cats of unknown feeding habits. Wear gloves while gardening and wash hands thoroughly afterward.

### Other Teratogens

Ionizing radiation can be a potent teratogen. Radiation presents a risk to the developing ovum *before* ovulation, as well as to the embryo or fetus afterward. The dangers include microcephaly (small head in relation to the rest of the body), skeletal malformations, and mental retardation. X rays of the teeth or extremities do not generally expose the fetus to significant levels of radiation. Caution in the use of all diagnostic X rays is advised, especially during the first trimester of pregnancy. If a woman knows or suspects she is pregnant, she should inform the physician or X ray technician. The benefits of using ionizing radiation must always be weighed against the risks.

Exposure to excessive heat can adversely affect an unborn child, particularly its nervous system. Heat can have the same effect as a high fever, such as when the body becomes overheated for an extended period of time. Especially implicated are hot tubs and saunas. Pregnant women are advised to avoid saunas and whirlpools, particularly during the first trimester, and to keep bath temperatures moderate (Milunsky et al., 1992).

## 16.6 CHILDBIRTH

Having a baby is one of the most powerful and memorable experiences a person can have. With good preparation much of the uncertainty and fear can be reduced. To prepare for childbirth, it is important to have a health care provider who is readily available to the pregnant woman, one whom she feels she can trust. Partners can learn about the delivery process and how they can both be active participants by attending classes on how both partners can share in the birthing process.

## 16.6.1 Birthing Choices

Women are taking greater control of their own health. The response of the medical profession has generally been enthusiastic to the needs and decisions of women. Many women ask to have their children more naturally, whether in the home or in a hospital, yet with access to full medical care if unexpected problems arise during childbirth. Other women prefer to give birth in a clinic or hospital. The choice of *when* and *how* to deliver will depend on the clinic and practitioner the woman chooses.

### Natural Birth

Although a natural birth is what some women desire, not all birthing places or practitioners are prepared to accommodate such a wish. Many woman want a birth in which they feel familiar with the whole process, where they can take the body positions they find most comfortable, where there is no undue pressure to take pain-relieving drugs, and where there is no unnecessary medical intervention. After all, the woman's body is exquisitely designed to give birth.

Overall, the ideas on natural birth have centered on a woman knowing her own body and responding to its lead. Of particular interest has been the concept of **prepared childbirth,** or *prepared delivery* (often referred to as *natural childbirth*), for which partners prepare themselves by taking prebirthing classes. Two popular approaches are the Bradley method and the Lamaze method.

In the Bradley and Lamaze methods, the woman and someone who will accompany her at the delivery (a partner or friend), referred to as a *coach,* prepare themselves through special classes for the eventual delivery. This preparation includes learning about the birthing process, various breathing and relaxation techniques, and how to push to assist in the delivery. Good nutrition and exercise during pregnancy are also emphasized.

The rationale for prepared childbirth stems from the fact that much (though not all) of the pain in childbirth results from muscle tension caused by fear. This fear can be reduced by a thorough knowledge of the birthing process and by having familiar, supportive people present at the delivery. Often some form of psychological relearning is used to lower the pain expectation and raise the pain tolerance. The Bradley and Lamaze methods differ in how the pain is managed, either facing and accepting the pain or seeking

In prepared childbirth, the woman and someone who will accompany her at delivery (her "coach") attend classes to learn about the birth process and how to breathe and push to assist in the delivery.

distraction from it. With pain thus managed, delivery can proceed with a minimal use of pain-relieving drugs.

If the Lamaze, Bradley, or a similar "nontraditional" birthing method is desired, a practitioner must be chosen accordingly. Many practitioners favor and use a combination of these methods, yet some do not.

### Managed Birth

In a managed birth, labor is actively controlled by the practitioner and the procedures of the hospital or clinic. Managed birth is still the norm in many hospital births and is essential for women who face complications.

Each hospital has its own routines for labor and delivery. A visit to the hospital beforehand—meeting with the staff and looking into the labor and delivery rooms—helps a woman feel more comfortable with the surroundings.

Once admitted and after initial preparations and examinations, the woman is usually taken to a room where the staff monitors her progress in labor. Labor proceeds naturally or with medications. For the actual delivery the same room may be used as a birthing room, and where family and friends may attend the delivery. Electronic monitoring of the mother to be

| | |
|---|---|
| **rubella** (roo-bel′la) | viral-caused disease affecting embryo-fetus; German measles |
| **toxoplasmosis** (tox-ō-plas-mō′sis) | protozoan-caused disease affecting embryo-fetus |
| **prepared childbirth** | natural childbirth using breathing-relaxation techniques |

and fetus is standard procedure. Or the woman might be taken to a delivery room that, although sterile, is well equipped with all types of means for intervention, should it be needed, such as birth induction and cesarean section. Such interventions are not often needed, and many people think these procedures are overused. However, a managed hospital delivery might provide a woman with reassurances so that she knows she has access to the best of care.

Freestanding birthing centers (usually not within a hospital, but often near a hospital) have become very popular as sites for childbirth. Birthing centers provide a comfortable, relaxed environment where friends and family members often participate in the birthing experience.

A baby may be delivered by a physician or by a midwife. Certified nurse-midwives may, under direction of a physician, supervise uncomplicated deliveries. Deliveries in birthing centers are less likely than hospital deliveries to include episiotomy.

Birthing centers are more likely to offer delivery options. Many woman are finding that being free to move around as they want to and to take any birthing position they find comfortable, such as sitting, squatting, or standing, is their first choice. Such positions can provide comfort and reduce the need for episiotomy, cesarean section, or the use of forceps.

Some use birthing pools of warm water where a woman can soak to ease her pain, when contractions become intense, and where birth may even be completed. It is not intended that the baby be delivered underwater. In fact, a baby born underwater is in danger of injury or death if not lifted out of the water immediately so it can gasp for air and be cuddled.

The most fundamental difference between birthing centers and traditional hospitals is not in the surroundings but in the fact that the woman who is delivering is more empowered. She decides when to walk, sit, bathe, receive a massage, or ask for help. Most women who deliver in birthing centers are enthusiastic boosters of this form of childbirth.

### Home Birth

Some women opt for a home birth in order to have their baby in familiar surroundings and without the medical atmosphere of a hospital. Some birthing practitioners try to discourage this. If her practitioner says no to such a request, the woman might be able to find another who will agree, or she might contact the American College of Nurse-Midwives. It is essential that a physician or certified nurse-midwife be present in a home childbirth. Home births present certain risks not faced in a hospital or clinic, but some of this risk can be reduced by proper prenatal planning with the practitioner.

### Leboyer Method

Some psychologists believe that an infant's birth experience can have long-lasting effects. Frederick Leboyer, a French physician, introduced a birthing technique for reducing the trauma a newborn experiences. Focusing primarily on the birth experience of the infant, he made a serious effort to ease the transition from the warm, dark, quiet womb (uterus) to the "cold, cruel world." Lights in the delivery room are dimmed and people talk in hushed voices. Immediately after delivery the baby is put onto the mother's abdomen. The umbilical cord is not cut until it stops pulsating (ensuring a maximum return of blood to the baby from the placenta). The baby is then placed in a body-temperature bath, which simulates the uterine environment and gives a soothing effect.

## 16.6.2 Pain Management

Whether or not a woman attends prepared childbirthing classes, labor invariably involves pain. Yet a woman can build up her confidence by preparing for the intensity of contractions, by understanding her own limits of pain tolerance, and by learning about different methods of pain relief. Use of drugs for pain relief should not be seen as a sign of cowardice, and might even be essential for a safe delivery (Stoppard, 1993).

*Analgesics* (pain-reducing drugs) used to reduce the pain of labor contractions are either narcotics such as *Demerol* or nonnarcotics such as *Nubain*. However, timing in the use of these drugs is important. The drugs can cause breathing problems for the baby if it is born with the drug in its system. Thus, *Demerol* should not be given within two hours of birth and *Nubain* should not be given within one hour (Stehlin, 1994). Narcotics cross the placenta into the fetal blood and can depress the newborn's respiration and might affect its ability to suckle.

In the event analgesics do not provide sufficient relief, an epidural or a general anesthetic may be the next choice. *Epidurals* are anesthetic drugs, injected into the lower back, that cause loss of pain sensation in the lower half of the body by blocking the pain messages the nerves around the spine normally send to the brain, but allow the woman to stay awake. The amount of numbness depends on the amount of the drug used. Since drugs used in epidural anesthesia cannot enter the fetal blood, the newborn tends to be alert and to be breathing well soon after birth (Stoppard, 1993). The problem with the use of epidurals is that although they help relieve pain, they also have a tendency to arrest labor. Worst of all, epidurals take away the bearing-down reflex that is necessary to push the baby out. Also, since epidurals are administered only by an *anesthesiologist* (a physician who specializes in administering drugs), birthing centers must transfer their patients to a hospital if an epidural is necessary (Stehlin, 1994). A *general anesthetic,* which may be administered by needle into a vein or by inhalation, can be necessary in deliveries in which there are unexpected complications. The mother does not stay awake, all sense of pain is gone, and she will have no recollection of her baby being born. After the mother regains consciousness she, as well as the newborn, must recover from the effects of the anesthetic.

Drug use in childbirth presents special problems because some of the drugs used cross the placenta and affect the fetus or infant. With drugs that cross the placenta, it must be assumed that the fetus will receive some of the drug that is given to the birthing mother, often within minutes of its administration. In fact, the concentration of the drug in the blood of the fetus is often as high as or higher than in the blood of the mother.

Concern has been expressed that critical early mother-infant relationships may be adversely affected by depressant drugs. A chemically depressed infant and a mother who might also feel the residual effects of these drugs may not be able to respond as well to each other during this special bonding period. Because of these and other factors, many women today choose prepared childbirth as a way of avoiding, or at least limiting, the use of drugs in childbirth.

## 16.6.3 Labor

The entire process of childbirth is referred to as **labor,** or *parturition.* Late in the third trimester the fetus positions itself deep in the pelvic cavity, a process called *lightening,* or engagement (fig. 16.5). The fetal body rotates and the head engages deep within the mother's pelvic girdle, a process referred to as "dropping."

Painless uterine contractions called *Braxton-Hicks contractions* indicate that delivery is close. Although these contractions can occur throughout pregnancy, they become much more common in the late phases.

As the uterine contractions intensify, they put pressure on the cervix, which shortens from a neck-like structure to a narrow ring. Known as *cervical effacement,* this funneling occurs shortly before, and as a part of, early labor.

Labor occurs in three stages. The first stage of labor starts with the beginning of uterine contractions and lasts until the cervix is fully dilated. The second stage is the birth of the baby. The third stage is the delivery of the afterbirth (placenta).

### First Stage of Labor

The first stage of labor is the longest and can last from eight to fourteen hours for the first birth and four to eight hours for subsequent deliveries (Kilpatrick & Laros, 1989). At first the uterine contractions are short and mild and occur at intervals of 10 to 20 minutes. As labor progresses, the contractions become more frequent (every 3 to 5 minutes), more intense, and longer lasting. The contractions immediately preceding full cervical dilation can be quite painful.

Prepared childbirth classes can greatly help a woman to relax during labor, make the pain bearable, and reduce the need for drugs or other medical intervention. The following suggestions for the woman can help make labor more pleasant.

1. Choose comfortable surroundings. When you feel comfortable, with familiar people around you, you are better able to relax.
2. Choose support people with whom you feel comfortable. The presence of others, their touch and support, can give you comfort, strength, and confidence. Too many people or the wrong people can do just the opposite.
3. Breathe deeply. Deep breathing can help you relax.
4. Change position and move around. Positions in which your spine is upright, as in walking, can help you relax and relieve pain. Being on your hands and knees can also help.
5. Eat and drink (not alcohol!). This will give you strength and prevent dehydration. (Eating is not allowed if a general anesthetic will be administered.)
6. Express your emotions. Emotions are likely to be strong at this point and expressing them in any way—shouting, moaning, laughing, singing, etc.—can help you relax.
7. Take baths and showers (no baths if the amniotic sac has broken). The water is relaxing and soothing.
8. Ask your support people to touch, massage, and hold you.

### Late Stage 1 Labor: The Transition Phase

In late stage 1 labor (transition stage), the cervix completes dilation and stretches over the baby's head. Contractions during transition are the longest and most intense of labor. They are from 50 to 90 seconds long and occur every 2 to 3 minutes. There is very little time for rest between them. During transition, a woman must remain alert and fully concentrate on each contraction. The amniotic sac (bag of waters)

---

**labor** birthing process

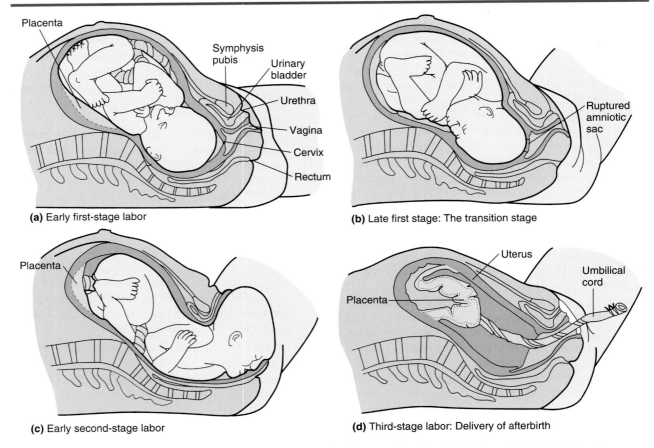

**(a)** Early first-stage labor

**(b)** Late first stage: The transition stage

**(c)** Early second-stage labor

**(d)** Third-stage labor: Delivery of afterbirth

**FIGURE 16.5**    The stages of labor. **a:** First stage: The cervix is dilating. **b:** Late first stage (transition stage): The cervix is fully dilated, and the amniotic sac has ruptured, releasing amniotic fluid. **c:** Second stage: The birth of the infant. **d:** Third stage: Delivery of the placenta (afterbirth).

will probably rupture during transition if it has not already done so. This phase of labor is definitely the hardest and most uncomfortable, but it is usually fairly short. Transition averages between 30 and 60 minutes (Stoppard, 1993).

## Second Stage of Labor (Delivery of the Baby)

With the cervix fully open, the baby begins to move down into the vagina (normally head first). Each labor contraction moves the head down farther. The first sight of the baby's head is called *crowning*. Before crowning the physician or midwife might perform an episiotomy. Just before the head emerges from the vagina, it rotates to the side to pass the front part of the pelvic bone. With the next few contractions the neck and shoulders emerge. The body of the baby is then quickly expelled. The remaining amniotic fluid gushes out. The baby is cleaned and quickly checked. Its vital signs such as breathing and color are checked. The umbilical cord is clamped off several inches from the navel, and the baby soon begins

to breathe. The second stage of labor averages about 50 minutes in length in a first delivery and 20 minutes in later ones (Kilpatrick & Laros, 1989).

## Third Stage of Labor (Delivery of the Placenta)

Uterine contractions stop briefly following the birth of the baby and then begin again at regular intervals until the placenta (afterbirth) is separated and expelled. Placental separation takes about 2 to 3 minutes and its expulsion another 5 or 6 minutes. The clean removal of any placental remnants is important to avoid later hemorrhaging. The practitioner repairs the episiotomy and any other damage to the uterus and vagina. During this time, called *postpartum*, the uterus begins returning to its original size.

### 16.6.4   Episiotomy

An **episiotomy** is an incision through the skin and muscles in the *perineum*, the area between the vagina and the anus. The incision is made late in the first

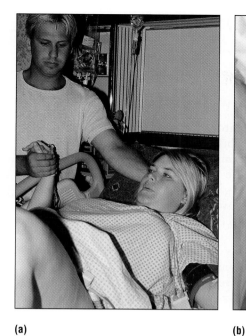
(a)

(b)

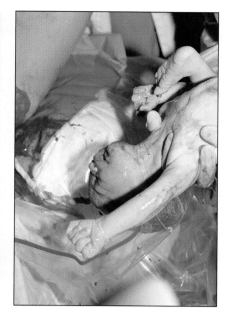
(c)

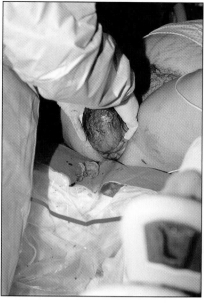
(d)

The process of childbirth. **a:** The first stage of labor. **b, c:** The second stage of labor. **d:** Holding the newborn.

stage of labor before the head of the child emerges. The procedure may be necessary if:

- ▌ the baby's head is too large for the opening
- ▌ the baby is in distress
- ▌ the baby is in an irregular position
- ▌ there is need for a forceps delivery
- ▌ the perineum has not stretched sufficiently

The enlargement helps the labor move more quickly and may help prevent potential tearing of the tissue in the perineal area during the second stage of labor. A straight, neat incision heals better than a tear, with less scar tissue and a reduced chance of infection.

Episiotomies are performed in about two-thirds of all births in this country and in about 80 to 90 percent of first births. It is the most widely performed operation in the West (Stoppard, 1993), but the procedure is not so widely used in other countries.

Some health care professionals believe this to be an overdone, often unnecessary surgical procedure. If done too early in birthing, or done improperly, it can unnecessarily damage tissue and lead to slow postpartum healing. If the woman has wishes regarding an episiotomy being done in her delivery, she

| **episiotomy** (e-piz-ē-ot′ō-mē) | an incision in the area between the vagina and the anus made during labor to enlarge the opening to ease delivery |

should make her feelings known to her practitioner (Stoppard, 1993). Relaxation, proper breathing and pushing, a manual stretching of the perineum, and use of alternate positions by the woman in delivery can greatly reduce the need for many episiotomies.

## 16.6.5 Cesarean Section

When a normal vaginal delivery is considered dangerous or impossible, a fetus is delivered through a small horizontal incision in the abdominal and uterine walls known as a **cesarean section, or C-section.** Around 15 to 20 percent of all deliveries in the United States are by cesarean section (Stoppard, 1993). Often the need for cesarean section is apparent before labor begins and plans can be made for it. Such a cesarean section is spoken of as an *elective* cesarean section. An elective cesarean section might be advisable when:

- the fetus is improperly aligned
- the fetal head is too large to pass through the pelvic opening
- the mother has had a prior cesarean
- there are multiple fetuses
- there is fetal distress, the fetus is having respiratory or cardiac distress, or the umbilical cord is compressed
- certain medical conditions, such as active herpes type 2 infection, is present

Some practitioners resort to a cesarean section to avoid the risk of being sued if a difficult delivery causes complications, as in a breech birth or a difficult forceps delivery (see "At Issue: Too Many Cesarean Sections?"). A cesarean section is major surgery, yet does not require a long hospital stay. In most cases, the mother remains awake during a cesarean delivery, and her partner can be with her in the operating room. Cesarean deliveries do not prevent a mother from nursing her newborn. A mother should feel no sense of failure for not being able to deliver vaginally; a cesarean section is no less significant than a vaginal delivery. Having had a cesarean section does not preclude a mother from delivering vaginally in the future. Although it was once feared that the scar tissue from a prior cesarean section might open up during a later labor, experience has shown this to not necessarily occur.

## 16.6.6 Premature Birth

The pace of development of the unborn baby is geared to the expectation of its being born full term, or 40 weeks LMP. If, for any reason, the fetus is delivered before full term, he or she may not be prepared for life outside the uterus.

A fetus or newborn infant is said to be at **term** if born between the 38th and 42nd weeks LMP. A birth before the 38th week is *preterm,* one after 42 weeks is *postterm.*

## 16.6.7 Low Birthweight

The best indicator of adequate fetal growth is *birthweight.* A newborn weighing 5.5 pounds or less (less than 2,500 grams [g]) has a *low birthweight* (known as a **premature infant**). If the birth weight is 3.3 pounds (1,500 g) or less it is of *very low birthweight,* and if the birthweight is 2.2 pounds (1,000 g) or less, it is of *extremely low birthweight* (Cunningham et al., 1993). About 1 in 14 babies born in the United States is of low birthweight, and about 1 in 100 weighs 3 pounds or less (Stoppard, 1993; Scott, 1990). Underweight babies are forty times more likely than others to die in the first four weeks of life (Scott, 1990).

The factors influencing birthweight include gender (male babies weigh more than female babies), order (firstborns weigh less), and race (e.g., white babies weigh more at term than African American babies) (Cunningham et al., 1993). Other factors that can put a woman at risk are age (under age 17 and over age 34), socioeconomic status (poverty), marital status (unmarried), and education (uneducated) (Scott, 1990).

The majority of *neonatal* deaths (deaths during the first six weeks after birth) are in newborns whose birthweight is under 3.3 pounds (1,500 g). Unfortunately, the proportion of these newborns has increased. It's believed this has happened in part due to the increase in multiple births resulting from techniques that assist reproduction. The primary factor for this increase is the epidemic of premature births among the poor (McCormick, 1994). The proportion of low birthweight infants differs among ethnic groups, ranging from about 60 per 1,000 newborns for white mothers to approximately 120 per 1,000 newborns for African American women. Although social and environmental factors may bear on this, lack of access to medical care is likely a major factor (Cunningham et al., 1993) (see "Dimensions of Diversity: African American Infant Death Rate More Than Double That of Whites and Rising").

Survival rates gradually increase with birthweight (see table 16.1). Notice that the chances for survival increase significantly with newborns above 1,000 g birthweight. Newborn survival is possible at 500 g to 750 g (and survival of a 380-g infant has been reported), although it's believed that these newborns were actually of greater gestational age and thus of advanced maturity (Cunningham et al., 1993).

# AT ISSUE

## TOO MANY CESAREAN SECTIONS?

Delivery by cesarean section in this country has become more common during the past two decades. The rate increased from 4.5 percent of all births in 1965 to almost 25 percent in 1988 (Taffel et al., 1991), but leveled off thereafter (Centers for Disease Control, 1993b). Even so, cesarean section is still one of the most commonly performed surgeries in this country. There are several reasons for this.

One reason is that the rate of deliveries with complications has been rising. It is known that older women are having children, and that more of all births are first births. Both of these kinds of births have higher rates of complication. Adding to this is the fear of litigation. There is increasing concern physicians are sued for difficult childbirth cases that could have been avoided by cesarean section (Cunningham et al., 1993).

Another reason is that many women who had a previous cesarean section elect to have a subsequent cesarean section for its convenience and its relative safety.

Yet there are socioeconomic factors that can have a significant role in the rates of cesarean sections. The rates are higher among women from areas with a higher median family income than among women from areas with lower median family incomes (Gould, Davey, & Stafford, 1989). And the rates of vaginal births after a prior cesarean section are lower in for-profit hospitals with patients with private insurance than in higher-volume hospitals for indigent patients (Stafford, 1990). Also, rates are generally lowest for uninsured women, intermediate for women with Medicaid coverage, and highest for women with private insurance, especially fee-for-service coverage (Braveman et al., 1995).

There is little question that women of low family income who come from cities and rural areas do not have access to the better community-based preventive care. So, although women of financial means have greater access to cesarean sections, perhaps what women of low socioeconomic backgrounds are calling for is not greater access to cesarean section deliveries, but to improved community-based preventive care. The emotional benefits of a prepared delivery through a knowledge of the birthing process, the reduction of fear of childbirth, and the support of familiar people can also reduce the rates of cesarean section. In a 1991 study (Kennell et al.) of women giving birth for the first time, those who received continuous emotional support from an experienced companion had a significantly lower rate of cesarean delivery (8%) than those without such support (13%).

---

The development of *neonatal* intensive care in recent years has significantly lowered the death rate of low birthweight infants in the United States. This care includes controlling oxygen, temperature, humidity levels, and intravenous feeding. The lower the birthweight, the longer the period of care. The care can be extremely expensive (several thousand dollars per day) and of long duration (sometimes a week to several months). Even with such care, there is a higher frequency of long-term severe handicaps in low birthweight babies, such as learning deficit, cerebral palsy, low IQ, and a wide range of health and behavioral problems (Hack et al., 1994).

A woman's health is important to the fetus; if she has an infection, high blood pressure, or anemia, it can affect fetal weight. A pregnant woman's nutritional habits, other behavior such as smoking or drug use, and whether she is carrying twins or triplets can lead to low birthweight. Teenage mothers might not have the physical maturity to provide for adequate

**TABLE 16.1**  SURVIVAL RATES FOR NEWBORNS ACCORDING TO BIRTHWEIGHT

| BIRTHWEIGHT (g) | SURVIVAL PERCENTAGE |
|---|---|
| 500–750 | 43 |
| 751–1,000 | 72 |
| 1,001–2,500 | 96.8–99.5 |
| 2,501–4,000 | 99.8–99.9 |
| over 4,000 | 100 |

**Source:** Data from G. Cunningham et al., *Williams Obstetrics,* 19th edition, 1993, Appleton-Lange, Norwalk, CT.

| | |
|---|---|
| **cesarean section** **(C-section)** (se-zair′ē-an) | surgical childbirth through the abdominal wall |
| **term** | fetus at 38 to 42 weeks of development; mature fetus |
| **premature infant** | a low birthweight infant |

# DIMENSIONS OF DIVERSITY

## AFRICAN AMERICAN INFANT DEATH RATE MORE THAN DOUBLE THAT OF WHITES AND RISING

The United States has had a relatively unfavorable international standing in terms of *infant mortality* (the death of children between birth and their first birthday), and the U.S. infant mortality rate still remains higher than for most other Western industrialized nations. This is due in large part to the substantial racial disparity of infant survival and associated socioeconomic inequality that has existed in the United States for a long period.

The good news is that according to the National Center for Health Statistics, a record number of newborns in the United States are surviving to their first birthday. Overall, for the whole population, the rate is down from 8.9 per 1,000 births in 1991 to 7.9 in 1994. Overall the decline in infant mortality was due largely to improved treatment for premature and low birthweight infants.

Yet African American infants are increasingly faring *worse* than white infants. In 1950 the infant mortality rate for African Americans was 43.9 per 1,000 compared to 26.8 per 1,000 for whites, or a ratio of 1.6 infant deaths among African Americans for every one white. By contrast, in 1992 the infant mortality rate for African Americans had dropped to 10.7 per 1,000 newborns, compared to 5.1 per 1,000 for whites, or a ratio of 2.3 African American infant deaths for every one white. The widening gap of African American infant mortality compared to that of whites, which is expected to continue through the first decade of the next century, is thought to correlate to a widening educational inequality between African Americans and whites across all educational levels. Many experts believe that the disparity in infant mortality has more to do with socioeconomic status, which is lower on the average for African Americans, than it does with race. If you were a researcher, how would you go about investigating the factors that lead to increased infant mortality?

**Source:** From G. Singh and S. Yu, "Infant Mortality in the United States: Trends, Differentials, and Projections, 1950 Through 2010" in *American Journal of Public Health,* 85 (1995):957–964.

---

fetal development. A mother might be under stress, or receive inadequate prenatal care and nutrition (Scott, 1990).

## 16.7    AFTER CHILDBIRTH

Immediately after the birth of a child there are adjustments for everyone involved. The mother wants to relax in the presence of her partner and baby and enjoy the feeling of accomplishment and joy. She will want to concentrate on her baby and on learning to know it and on giving her baby the chance to see her, hear her voice, and feel her skin. Her partner, too, can have the chance to hold the newborn and to begin knowing it.

### 16.7.1    Psychological Effects

In the time after childbirth a special emotional attachment between the mother and her child called *bonding* occurs. This special feeling of identification and intimacy occurs from a perception of unique odors between mother and child, from the sound of each other's voice, from a visual perception of each other, from the warmth between their bodies, and in the touching of each other's skin that occurs. Even fathers are sometimes coached to expose the skin of their chests to the bare body of the newborn in order to create the special touch bonding between them (Stoppard, 1993).

Soon after birth there can be an emotional letdown that follows the excitement and fears that most women experience during pregnancy and delivery. The discomforts of early motherhood, the fatigue the mother is feeling from loss of sleep during labor, and anxieties over her abilities to care for her infant once back home from the hospital may leave her tearful, anxious, or irritable. In addition, she may find it difficult to adjust to the abrupt drop in the levels of estrogen and progesterone to which her body has become accustomed. For some, this *postpartum* (after-birth) adjustment is uneventful; for others it is distressing. As many as 80 percent of mothers feel to some extent the "baby blues"—those adjustments to the mundane day-to-day tasks after the highs of pregnancy (Stoppard, 1993). These feelings may coincide with the beginning of the mother's milk production.

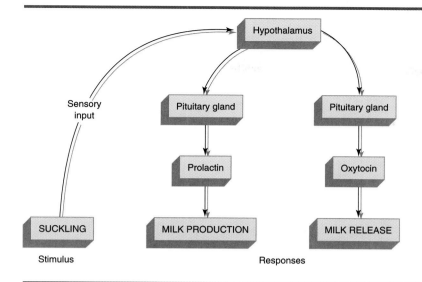

**FIGURE 16.6**  Control of lactation. Lactation occurs in two stages: *Milk production* is stimulated by prolactin, and *milk release* is stimulated by oxytocin. The stimulus of suckling triggers a nerve reflex to the hypothalamus that increases secretion of prolactin and oxytocin. Oxytocin also causes uterine contraction, helping the uterus return to normal following a pregnancy, another advantage of breast-feeding.

About 10 percent of mothers actually experience postpartum depression, which is something more severe than the "blues." The blues as a mild disorder is self-limited, usually lasting only 2 to 3 days, but sometimes as long as 10 days. Should postpartum blues persist or worsen, then the woman might have developed depression, in which case it is essential that the mother get medical help promptly. With treatment such emotional lows should be resolved in several weeks.

There are many adjustments to the new baby. The nightly feedings and diaper changes, along with the attention everyone else thinks a woman and her newborn should have, may seem overwhelming. The new mother may feel exhausted and vulnerable. This is a good time for family and friends to give her help and reassurances.

## 16.7.2  Physical Effects

After delivery, the mother's body must undergo many physical adjustments. Her body is adjusting to the loss of a fetus. The uterus shrinks back to its normal size in about six weeks. During the first several weeks the uterine lining grows back and produces a bloody discharge called *lochia.* The stretched vagina shrinks, although it will be soft and slack for a while. The mother may need to start a program of leg lifts and abdominal exercises to help restore muscle tone, shape, and size.

If the mother has had an episiotomy or a cesarean section with her delivery, she will need to give them time to heal. She should not be surprised if she experiences hemorrhoids after birth due to the strain of labor and delivery. If pains from any causes persist, she should talk it over with her health care provider.

## 16.7.3  Breast-Feeding

During pregnancy, estrogens and progesterone from the placenta cause the mammary glands in the breast to become functional. They are now able to secrete and eject milk, in a process called **lactation.** Estrogens stimulate the duct system to grow and branch, and large quantities of fat to be deposited around them. Progesterone causes the development of the milk-producing glands (fig. 16.6). Due to all of this activity, the breasts may double in size (Hole, 1994). The same hormones that affect the mother's breast can also affect the child's. Some newborn breasts, even those of males, might secrete a little milk for a few days.

Usually no milk production occurs during pregnancy. The woman's body needs a supply of the hormone prolactin before lactation can begin (fig. 16.6). True milk production begins two to three days following birth.

Around the fifth week of pregnancy, the anterior pituitary starts releasing prolactin in increasing amounts. The action of this hormone is temporarily blocked however, by the high levels of progesterone being produced by the placenta. At childbirth the placenta is expelled and progesterone levels fall rapidly, and the prolactin is free to stimulate the secretion of milk. In the several days between birth and the beginning of milk production, the breasts produce

---

**lactation** (lak-tā′shun)    production and secretion of milk

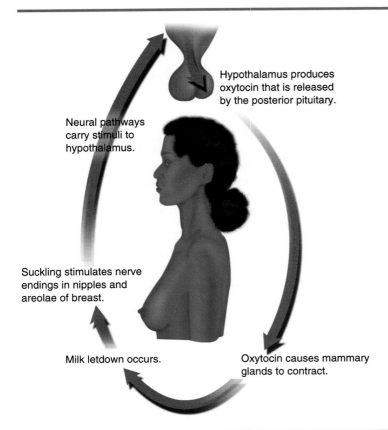

Hypothalamus produces oxytocin that is released by the posterior pituitary.

Neural pathways carry stimuli to hypothalamus.

Suckling stimulates nerve endings in nipples and areolae of breast.

Milk letdown occurs.

Oxytocin causes mammary glands to contract.

**FIGURE 16.7**   Suckling reflex. Suckling sets in motion the sequence of events that lead to mild letdown, the flow of milk into ducts of the breasts.

**colostrum,** a thin, watery fluid rich in proteins, but low in sugars and fat. It is also very high in infection-fighting antibodies. Following delivery, another pituitary hormone, oxytocin, stimulates the contraction of the milk glands and the ducts leading away from them. Without the prolactin and oxytocin working in tandem, there is no milk ejection.

How do the breasts "know" when to eject milk? When the nipple or areola of a breast is suckled, or otherwise mechanically stimulated, nerve impulses travel from it to the hypothalamus, which signals the pituitary gland to release oxytocin (fig. 16.7). Carried by the blood, oxytocin reaches the breast in about thirty seconds and contractions of the milk glands begin. Milk flows into the milk ducts (called the *milk "let-down"*), where it may be drawn out of the nipple by the suckling child. The more suckling, the more oxytocin released, and the more milk there is for the child. Milk ejection can also be stimulated by the cry of an infant or by its physical closeness to the mother. However, ejection can be inhibited if the mother feels fright or stress (Cunningham et al., 1993; Stoppard, 1993). In most instances, even if the supply of milk at first appears insufficient, that supply becomes adequate if suckling is continued.

If, during milk production, the breasts are not emptied of milk regularly, the hypothalamus might stop the continued secretion of prolactin by the pituitary. If so, milk production ceases in about a week (Cunningham et al., 1993).

Before the end of her pregnancy the woman will need to decide whether to feed her baby breast milk, infant formula, or both. Of these options, breast-feeding is the most widely practiced method of feeding newborns. Although it became fashionable several decades ago for mothers to bottle-feed their infants, according to a recent survey nearly two-thirds of mothers are again breast-feeding their one-year-old infants, compared with less than 50 percent twenty-five years ago (Cunningham et al., 1993). As a way for the mother's body to nourish her infant, breast-feeding is a natural extension of pregnancy.

There are many advantages to breast-feeding. Breast milk contains all of the essential nutrients needed by the body. Unlike cow's milk or formula, it is rich in disease-fighting antibodies. Colostrum, the liquid produced by the breasts before milk production begins, is especially high in antibodies. It helps prevent infant diarrhea and many other neonatal

Breast-feeding offers an infant superior nutrition, protection from disease, and fewer allergies. It is economical and convenient, helps the mother of a newborn lose weight, helps shrink her uterus, and contributes to bonding between mother and baby.

infections. Breast milk is readily available, clean, and always at the right temperature. There are no bottles to warm, wash, and sterilize.

For these reasons, health care providers and dietitians believe breast-feeding is sufficiently important to encourage mothers to do it even if for only a short time. A few months or even weeks are long enough to provide an infant with the disease-fighting protection that breast-feeding offers (Whitney & Rolfes, 1996).

To breast-feed, it is necessary for the mother to maintain adequate nutrition both for herself and her infant in order to provide the needed stamina, patience, and self-confidence her nursing infant deserves.

Women who breast-feed usually lose weight faster than women who do not. Breast-feeding amounts to a transfer of calories from mother to baby, making it much easier for her to lose weight. Breast-feeding also releases the hormone oxytocin, which causes uterine contractions that help the uterus to return to its normal state.

Breast-feeding also helps build emotional closeness between mother and baby. The breast-feeding mother and her baby have a very special relationship. Those mothers who are more relaxed in the care of their infants tend to breast-feed them for a longer period of time (Vandiver, 1997). The La Leche League is an international organization offering support and information to parents interested in breast-feeding.

### Breast-Feeding and Fertility

The mother's menstrual cycles and fertility are usually blocked temporarily when she is breast-feeding.

The high prolactin levels associated with breast-feeding are thought to inhibit the release of FSH and LH and, thus, ovulation. How long this suppression of ovulation lasts depends on the intensity, duration, and frequency of nursing episodes. If there are nightly feedings, for instance, fertility may quickly return (Labbock, 1989).

In a lactating woman whose menstrual periods have returned, fertility may have already returned. The longer it takes for her period to return, the likelier it is that ovulation will occur before there is any sign of menstrual bleeding (Labbock, 1989). So, throughout her period of breast-feeding, even before her menstrual periods resume, she should use a non-hormonal form of contraception during all sexual intercourse to prevent pregnancy (Hatcher et al., 1994).

### Breast-Feeding and HIV

Human immunodeficiency virus (HIV) can be transmitted by an infected mother to her infant through breast milk (Hatcher et al., 1994). Where safe alternatives to breast milk are available, as in the United States, HIV-infected mothers are advised to avoid breast-feeding.

## 16.7.4    Sexual Activity after Childbirth

Physicians often recommend refraining from intercourse for several weeks after childbirth to allow episiotomy incisions to heal and the uterus and vagina to return to prepregnancy states. Usually, intercourse is physically safe within three to four weeks following delivery, but it needs to be based on the mother's desire and comfort. In the mean-time couples can enjoy other kinds of sensual and sexual pleasure, including massage, oral-genital sex, and mutual masturbation. Because breast-feeding suppresses estrogen production, the mother might experience vaginal dryness. If so, she may need to use a vaginal lubricant prior to intercourse.

Women usually become fertile again within a few months after giving birth to a baby. Women who are breast-feeding usually remain infertile longer than those who are not breast-feeding, because the hormonal activity causing *lactation* (milk production) suppresses the menstrual cycle. Yet pregnancy sometimes occurs during lactation. Breast-feeding or the absence of menstrual bleeding should not, however, be taken as an indication that ovulation has not resumed.

---

**colostrum** (kō-los′trum)    the premilk fluid produced by the breasts after delivery

Pregnancy too soon following childbirth is often undesirable for physical, emotional, and economic reasons. Use of an effective conception control method is essential as soon as intercourse resumes. For women who are not breast-feeding, oral contraceptives are often recommended and can be started as soon as three weeks following delivery (Cunningham et al., 1993). A woman who is breast-feeding should not use oral contraceptives unless her physician approves them.

## 16.8 PROBLEMS DURING PREGNANCY

Most women have uneventful pregnancies, yet others encounter distressing problems. The following are several of the more common problems.

### 16.8.1 Preeclampsia

Some pregnant women experience elevated blood pressure, or *pregnancy-induced hypertension (PIH)*. Seen in about 15 percent of all pregnant women, it occurs more commonly in women having their first baby, women over age 35, and women carrying multiple fetuses (Stoppard, 1993). Preeclampsia apparently results from impaired kidney functioning. If PIH is accompanied by protein in the urine and swelling of the face, hands, and feet, the condition is referred to as **preeclampsia.** In severe cases, painful headaches and blurred vision may occur.

Typically the signs of preeclampsia occur after the twentieth week, although they can start earlier in pregnancy. For this reason it is important that a woman's blood pressure be checked during each prenatal visit. If preeclampsia is evident, a woman should expect to be admitted to a clinic or hospital for observation.

### 16.8.2 Birth Defects

One of the last things an expectant mother wants to think about is the possibility of something having gone awry in the development of her unborn baby. Fortunately, the incidence of fetal problems is quite rare, especially with the excellent care many women receive. Yet it is not realistic to avoid this subject entirely.

**Birth,** or *congenital,* **defects** are defects present at birth in a newborn. Recognizable developmental problems occur in approximately 3 to 5 percent of all newborns (Shepard, 1986). The breakdown among kinds, or causes, and the approximate percentage of each is as follows (Beckman & Brent 1986):

- genetic (single genes or chromosomes)—20 to 25 percent
- fetal infections (rubella, toxoplasmosis, etc.)—3 to 5 percent
- maternal diseases (diabetes, alcohol abuse, etc.)—4 percent
- drugs and medications—less than 1 percent
- multiple factors or unknown causes—65 to 70 percent

Chromosomal problems often occur in miscarriage, stillbirths, and preterm infants (as found from autopsies). Some of these disorders are lethal (fatal) before birth, some afterward. Birth defects are the leading cause of infant deaths before age one (Oakley, 1986). Chromosomal disorders, for example, occur in 1 out of every 170 newborns.

It's important that prospective parents become aware of the prospect that their newborn might have some impairment. In a society that prizes beauty and perfection, parents with a newborn possessing a birth defect deal with many questions in their own minds as to who or what was responsible. Some parents are able to accept and love the child; others have trouble coping with and accepting the condition.

### How to Detect Birth Defects

Pregnant women over the age of 35, parents who have already given birth to a child with birth defects, and parents with a history of genetic or chromosomal disorders may want to confirm the absence of birth defects in an unborn child. There are tests that can provide parents with some basis for deciding whether to continue or terminate a pregnancy. The following are several prenatal diagnostic tests that may be used.

*Amniocentesis:* **Amniocentesis** is a procedure in which a small amount of amniotic fluid, which contains fetal cells and dissolved substances, is withdrawn from the amniotic sac. A needle is passed through the woman's abdominal and uterine walls, guided by ultrasonic imaging (fig. 16.8). About 1/2 ounce of fluid is withdrawn and then subjected to microscopic examination and biochemical testing. Usually performed at 16 to 18 weeks' gestation, the procedure can detect several hundred chromosomal disorders and biochemical defects.

*Chorionic Villus Sampling (CVS):* **Chorionic villus sampling (CVS),** also known as *chorionic villus biopsy,* can detect the same conditions as amniocentesis, but has several additional advantages. It is a widely accepted first-trimester alternative to amniocentesis, allowing an earlier decision on whether or not to continue the pregnancy. Fluid is withdrawn through a *catheter* (tube) that is inserted into the uterus via the vagina and cervix under the guidance

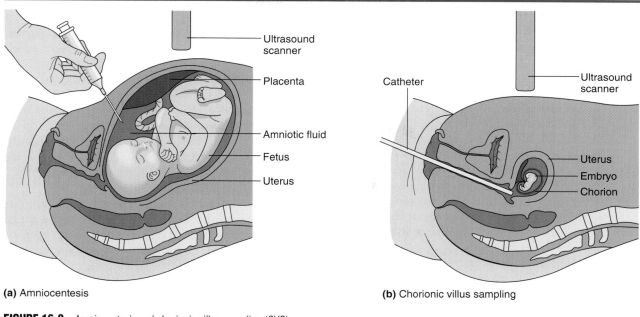

**(a)** Amniocentesis

**(b)** Chorionic villus sampling

**FIGURE 16.8** Amniocentesis and chorionic villus sampling (CVS).

of ultrasound imaging (fig. 16.8). A sample of the chorionic villus can then be removed and treated the same way as it is in an amniocentesis.

*Ultrasound Examination:* In **ultrasonography**, high-frequency ultrasound waves are beamed into the body and reflected off fetal tissue. The reflection of these waves is used to form an image of the fetus. Sonography is a common diagnostic technique used to determine true fetal age (when the time of conception is uncertain), fetal position, fetal viability, and multiple pregnancies, as well as for directing instruments used in other tests. It can also be used to determine the sex of the fetus.

*Alpha-Fetoprotein (AFP) Screening: Alpha-fetoprotein screening* is a blood test that measures a substance produced by the fetal liver and gastrointestinal tract. Found in a woman's blood throughout pregnancy, the relative levels may indicate neurological problems. For example, levels two to three times higher than the average sample may indicate problems such as hydrocephalus or spina bifida; levels that are too low might indicate Down syndrome.

## 16.8.3 Genetic Counseling

Genetic counseling aims to determine the risk individuals run in passing on an inheritable disease or condition to their child. Secondly, it can help individuals decide, based on this information, whether to proceed and conceive.

The genetic counselor will question the individual or couple on their health and discuss their family background. A family tree may be constructed detailing blood relationships and all known diseases and causes of death. The information provided by a genetic counselor usually consists of the *probability* (such as one-quarter or one-half) that a child born to the individuals would have a specific genetic defect. Trained in genetics and psychology, the counselor will assess the degree of risk and help in making a decision.

When a child with a defect has been born, genetic counseling can often determine whether the disorder has a genetic origin or is the result of an isolated developmental accident. It can help relieve feelings of guilt, anxiety, and uncertainty following the birth of a child and inform the parents of the possibilities of defects in subsequent children.

| | |
|---|---|
| **preeclampsia** (prē-ē-klamp'si-a) | elevated blood pressure during pregnancy |
| **birth defect** | fetal developmental defect present at birth |
| **amniocentesis** (am-nē-ō-sin-tē'sis) | needle removal of amniotic fluid |
| **chorionic villus sampling** (**CVS**) (kō-ri-on'ik vil'us) | needle removal of chorionic villus tissue |
| **ultrasonography** (ul-tra-son-og'ra-fē) | high-frequency sound-wave imaging of fetus |

## 16.8.4 Miscarriage and Stillbirth

**Miscarriages** are spontaneous abortions of embryos too young to live outside the uterus. In the United States this definition is generally limited to the termination of pregnancy before 20 weeks of gestation or to the delivery of a fetus weighing less than 500 grams. A **stillbirth** is one in which there are no signs of life in the fetus at or after birth (Cunningham et al., 1993).

Although it is often reported that 25 percent of pregnancies miscarry, in healthy, fertile females the rate during the first trimester is probably no more than 10 percent (Cunningham et al., 1993). More than 80 percent of miscarriages occur in the first 12 weeks of pregnancy (Harlap, Shiono, & Ramcharan, 1980).

Miscarriages increase in frequency with maternal and paternal age. The tendency toward later childbearing has increased the number of miscarriages that occur as well as the degree of concern over each miscarriage (Wilson et al., 1986). Women over age 35 have about double the miscarriage rate of women under age 24. The amount of anxiety caused by a miscarriage tends to increase as the number of remaining years in which a woman can conceive declines (Harlap et al., 1980).

Physical exertion, including sexual activity, seems to have no adverse effect on a healthy pregnancy. The most common symptom of miscarriage is bleeding, which occurs in 95 percent of cases (Stoppard, 1993).

An early miscarriage might be the result of an embryo or fetal problem, such as a chromosomal abnormality or a developmental abnormality. Maternal causes include uterine abnormalities, hormonal imbalance, and infection. Although exposure to certain chemical substances such as lead, formaldehyde, and benzene can cause miscarriage (Barlow & Sullivan, 1982), exposure to video display terminals and accompanying electromagnetic fields, or exposure to short waves and ultrasound, such as physiotherapists work with, do not increase the risk of miscarriage (Taskinen, Kyyronen, & Hemminki, 1990).

### Psychological Effects

Much more attention is being given to the psychological aspects of miscarriage and stillbirth. The emotional pain of losing a fetus is not relieved by friends who simply tell a couple to try again (Beck, 1988).

When a woman experiences a miscarriage or stillbirth, it is not uncommon for her to be deeply distressed. She may experience a whole range of emotions—anger, grief, despair, guilt, jealousy, and isolation. She might find no one to really turn to—friends and family want to be sympathetic, but do not know what to say. Her practitioner might be at a loss for words, and might, in fact, become the target of the woman's anger. The woman might feel intense jealousy toward people who have had healthy babies. Perhaps worst of all is a sense of parental guilt, which is usually without any foundation.

After all, this unborn baby that was so real to the mother-to-be is gone—it is a death, and she needs time to mourn her loss. As in any significant loss, there is a predictable depression. A woman's adjustment after a loss through miscarriage or stillbirth is not only emotional, but also physical. Her body experiences the sudden withdrawal of pregnancy hormones.

And her partner is also grieving. Sometimes partners shut each other out because they do not want to add to the other's grief. It's important for both of them to vent their emotions, to cry together, and to talk through their feelings. They both need healing, and denying the grief might only impede that healing. Some hospitals make counseling services available to people who have had a miscarriage.

Blaming no one, including the parents, can help hasten the healing process. Making contact with other parents who have experienced loss may help. Some couples draw closure to their loss by having a private memorial service or formally burying the stillborn child. For support in facing a pregnancy loss, you may wish to contact a pregnancy loss center or the Compassionate Friends support group for people who have lost children.

## 16.9 FERTILITY PROBLEMS

Both men and women are generously supplied biologically with great numbers of sex cells for possible parenthood. Yet about one couple in every twelve who tries to conceive fails (Randal, 1994). Couples unable to conceive after a year or more of regular sexual intercourse are said to be **infertile**. The number of childless infertile couples has increased from 14.4 percent in 1965 to 18.5 percent now (Begley et al., 1995). The problem lies entirely with the man in about 1/3 of the cases, entirely with the woman in about another 1/3, and in 15 percent to 20 percent of cases the fertility of both partners is too low. In the remaining cases, no explainable cause can be found (Randal, 1994).

### 16.9.1 Causes of Infertility

About 20 percent of all infertility is caused by sexually transmitted infections, in particular *chlamydia* and *gonorrhea* (Randal, 1994). Even successfully treated infections in either gender can leave fertility-blocking scar tissue if treatment has not been prompt.

# GO ASK ALICE

*Alice,*

*I recently heard that women can still menstruate even when they are pregnant. In other words, women shouldn't believe that they're not pregnant if they receive their period. From what I understand of the process, I find this to be incorrect. Do you have any answers?*

*Expecting*

Dear Expecting,

Menstruation stops when a woman is pregnant. However, in some cases, a woman might have "break-through bleeding" (uterine bleeding suggestive of a period) with less blood or that lasts fewer days than usual and still be pregnant. Your confusion is understandable because these signs can lead women to believe they are not pregnant. However, various kinds of bleeding can occur in early pregnancy. Women can get some spotting in their first trimester:

- When the fertilized egg implants in the uterus;
- If the pregnancy is abnormal in any way (i.e., ectopic pregnancy [implantation outside of the uterus, such as in a fallopian tube], a threatening miscarriage); or,
- From "break-through" bleeding as part of their menstrual cycle (this is extremely rare).

If a woman had unprotected intercourse and is concerned about being pregnant, then she can take advantage of emergency contraception within 72 hours of the unprotected sex. If it's after 72 hours and she has not taken emergency contraception, then she can take a home pregnancy test seven to ten days after unprotected intercourse.

Common signs of pregnancy usually include:

- Frequent urination
- Swelling, tenderness, or tingling in the breasts
- Fatigue
- Nausea or vomiting
- Feeling bloated or crampy
- Increased or decreased appetite
- Changes in digestion (constipation or heartburn)
- Mood changes

Since the outcome(s) is unknown, bleeding and pregnancy are always taken seriously. If a woman is "spotting" or having what appears to be even a light menstruation, and **knows** she is pregnant, then she needs to see a health care provider or Ob-Gyn to make sure that she is okay.

 http://www.mhhe.com/byer6

---

A number of reasons for infertility tend to relate to one of the partners. Here are lists of some of these causes.

Possible sources of infertility in *males* include the following:

- too low a sperm production, for reasons such as having had mumps as an adolescent, undescended testes, drugs and other chemicals, or excessive exposure of the testes to heat
- low sperm motility, possibly relating to the nature of the seminal fluid or use of certain drugs
- blockage of the vas deferens by scar tissue resulting from prior surgery, sexually transmitted or other infections, or a prior vasectomy
- severe sexual dysfunction, such as impotence or premature ejaculation
- poor nutrition or generally poor health
- a *varicocele* (swollen veins in the scrotum)

Possible sources of infertility in *females* include the following:

- failure to ovulate due to a hormonal imbalance or exercising too vigorously (Randal, 1994)
- scar tissue in the fallopian tubes from sexually transmitted or other infections, IUDs, or a prior tubal ligation
- *endometriosis,* a condition that can cause tubal blockage
- structural disorders of the uterus or cervix
- extreme obesity

| | |
|---|---|
| **miscarriage** | spontaneous abortion |
| **stillbirth** | birth of a dead fetus |
| **infertile** | unable to conceive |

- anorexia or another eating disorder, or rapid weight loss that has left the woman too thin (Randal, 1994)
- poor nutrition or generally poor health
- cervical mucus of incorrect consistency or pH

*Shared* fertility problems may include the following:

- a woman's immune response against sperm, either of a specific man or of men in general
- lack of knowledge of when you are fertile and how to time intercourse during this period
- delay of pregnancy until the thirties, since infertility increases with age

Regardless of its cause, infertility can be very distressing for both partners. Having children is an important part of most people's life plan. Being unable to do so can produce feelings of depression, sadness, guilt, anger, and sexual inadequacy. Fortunately, with the help of fertility experts and advancing technology, many couples are able to overcome infertility.

## 16.9.2    Evaluating Infertility

An evaluation for possible infertility includes assessing the couple's knowledge of the menstrual calendar and instructing them in the timing of intercourse. A medical history is completed and a physical examination is commonly given. This exam may include blood tests to confirm that ovulation is occurring, BBT charting to show that ovulation is taking place in the right intervals, semen analysis, an *endometrial biopsy* (the taking and examining of a small sample of endometrial tissue) to check the ability of the endometrium to accept implantation, and a *laparoscopy* to confirm that the fallopian tubes are open.

## 16.9.3    Assisting Conception

Not too many years ago, couples who were unable to conceive could only resign themselves to infertility or decide to adopt a child. Although many couples still respond in the same ways to infertility, others choose to seek out medical help to assist them in becoming biological parents. About 15 percent of American women have received some type of infertility service. Fertility treatments in clinics across the nation are successful about 20 percent of the time (Centers for Disease Control and Prevention, 1997c).

Many infertile couples need merely low-tech intervention (for instance, the man needs to wear loose boxer shorts to reduce scrotal temperatures). In some couples a woman might be prescribed drugs such as *Clomid* or *Pergonal* to stimulate ovulation. Some fertility drugs induce the release of more than one egg at

a time, leading to multiple births that can complicate pregnancy and endanger infant survival.

Another medical way of enhancing or restoring fertility is corrective surgery to correct a varicocele, or microsurgery to remove scar tissue from the fallopian tubes or from the vas deferens.

For other couples the best hope lies in *assisted reproductive technology (ART)*. The following are the most common high-tech procedures:

- *In vitro fertilization (IVF)*

Meaning "in glass," *in vitro* fertilization is performed in a shallow glass or porcelain dish in the laboratory (fig. 16.9); thus the designation "test-tube" babies. In principal, the method involves the removal of eggs from the ovaries, fertilization with the partner's sperm in the laboratory, and transfer of the embryos into the uterus. This method is useful when a woman's fallopian tubes are blocked. IVF is used in 70 percent of ART procedures. Approximately 11 percent of ART procedures include *intracytoplasmic sperm injection (ICSI),* in which sperm is injected directly into a woman's egg. This procedure is most often used in cases of male infertility (Centers for Disease Control and Prevention, 1997c).

- *Gamete intrafallopian transfer (GIFT)*

In this variation on IVF, a fiber-optic instrument called a *laparoscope,* inserted through a small incision in a woman's abdomen, is used to place the unfertilized eggs and sperm into a fallopian tube, where fertilization occurs. The fertilized egg then passes into the uterus to implant as it would naturally. GIFT is used in about six percent of ART procedures (Centers for Disease Control and Prevention, 1997c).

- *Tubal ovum transfer*

The woman's eggs are retrieved and put into the fallopian tube close to where it opens into the uterus. The couple then has intercourse or the woman is artificially inseminated. This technique is used where GIFT cannot be used due to damaged fallopian tubes.

- *Intrauterine insemination (IUI)*

In this procedure, frozen sperm from a partner or unknown donor is introduced by *catheter* (a tiny tube) directly into the uterus, bypassing the cervix and the upper vagina.

- *Zygote intrafallopian transfer (ZIFT)*

A variation of GIFT, in ZIFT the sperm are allowed to fertilize eggs in the laboratory dish, then the fertilized eggs, or zygotes, are transferred into the fallopian tube. ZIFT is used in only about two percent of ART procedures (Centers for Disease Control and Prevention, 1997c).

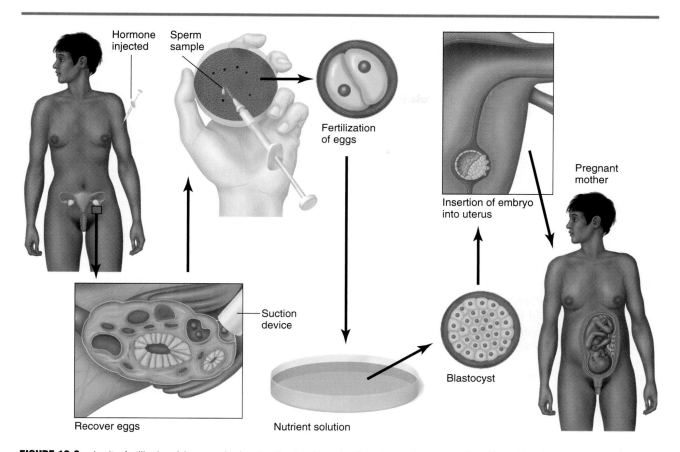

**FIGURE 16.9**    *In vitro* fertilization. A hormone is given to stimulate the maturation of several ova at one time. About thirty-three to thirty-four hours later, a slender fiber-optic instrument is inserted into the abdomen through a small incision. One or more ova are removed from the ovaries by suction and placed with sperm from the male partner, along with chemicals simulating the conditions within the fallopian tube. After fertilization, the embryos are transferred to a nutrient solution to grow for two to four days. At the blastocyst stage, one or several embryos are transferred into the uterus through a plastic tube. The embryo settles into the endometrium (implants), and pregnancy proceeds normally. Multiple births can occur.

### ▌ *Sperm donation*

The simplest method of assisted conception is the artificial insemination of a woman by her partner's sperm. This method is used when the partner's sperm count is low or where the male cannot ejaculate due to spinal cord injury, cancer, or surgery, but can ejaculate with the help of electric stimulation. Known as *artificial insemination by partner (AIP)*, in this method sperm are collected and combined, then inserted (inseminated) artificially by syringe into the vagina near the cervix close to the time of expected ovulation. Success rates for sperm donation range from 50 to 65 percent (Randal, 1994). Another option if the partner's sperm do not result in successful conception, or if a woman does not have a male partner, is known as *donor insemination (DI)*. Single women and lesbian couples are using artificial insemination in greater numbers in order to become parents. They might use sperm from a donor known to them, and that man might later take an active role in

the life of the child. Or they might use the sperm of an unknown donor. Due to concern with possible HIV infection, donor sperm is now collected and tested, then frozen for at least 180 days to allow for retesting for possible infection before use (Randal, 1994). Counseling should always be sought out to clear up any personal or medical questions regarding sperm donation.

## 16.9.4    Other Techniques

*Embryo lavage.* A fertile donor provides the eggs. At the proper time in her menstrual cycle she is artificially inseminated by the would-be father's sperm. If conception occurs, the early embryo is washed out of her reproductive tract and transferred to the woman who is unable to produce eggs.

*Pregnancy after menopause.* Eggs that have been collected from younger women are combined with sperm. After multicelled embryos have developed, they are transferred into the uterus of a postmenopausal woman. Although the woman is too old to produce ova, her uterus is able to bear children through her fifties and beyond. There was a splash in the media in 1997 when a 63-year-old woman gave birth to a child. Many people thought that this woman was too old to be allowed to have a baby, and that reproductive technologies should have strict age limits. What do you think?

*Frozen embryos.* Drugs can be administered to a woman to induce her ovaries to produce and release a dozen or more ova, which can then be collected, fertilized, and frozen for later thawing and use. Not all frozen embryos survive the freezing and thawing process. Approximately 14 percent of all ART procedures use only frozen embryos (Centers for Disease Control and Prevention, 1997c).

*Tubal embryo stage transfer (TEST).* In this variant of ZIFT, the embryos, rather than zygotes, are transferred into the fallopian tube.

*Opening blocked fallopian tubes.* Fallopian tubes that have been blocked by scar tissue or other obstructions can be opened. Microsurgery may be used, or a balloon catheter can be inserted and inflated to clear the passageway for the natural migration of ova and sperm.

*Microinjection.* In this variant of IVF, a thin needle is used to insert a single sperm through an egg's outer membrane.

*Intracytoplasmic sperm injection (ICSI).* A physician using a microscopic pipette injects a single sperm from a man's semen into an egg. The zygote is then introduced into the uterus.

### 16.9.5   Surrogate Motherhood

*Surrogate motherhood,* where a woman bears a child on behalf of another, is being arranged in many places today. Although how it is done may appear simple, it is an issue of increasing legal, emotional, and ethical complexities.

#### Types of Surrogacy

In a *full surrogacy,* the surrogate conceives by an infertile woman's partner and carries out the pregnancy. She might be artificially inseminated with his sperm or might have intercourse with him. In *partial surrogacy,* an egg from the woman who is unable to conceive is fertilized with her partner's sperm and then implanted into the uterus of the surrogate mother (Stoppard, 1993). In some cases the surrogate mother carries an unborn child conceived using sperm and ovum from anonymous donors (Platte, 1996).

#### Problems with Surrogacy

In principle, after the child is born through surrogacy it is given to the couple who "contracted" for the sur-

rogacy, who then legally adopt it. But a problem can arise if, contrary to the "contract," the surrogate mother does not want to part with the baby after she has carried it and given birth to it, especially if she is its biological (genetic) mother. Costly legal action has been necessary in some cases for the contracting "parents" to gain custody of the infant. Or the surrogate mother might only want to maintain contact with the child, which the new parents may oppose.

Another possibility is where the parents, in spite of the contract, do *not* want to accept the child they contracted for. After contracting and before adopting, they might divorce and no longer want the child. In some such cases courts have ordered the divorced parents to provide child support (Platte, 1996). Or the child may have been born impaired, a prospect the parents had not planned for. Who then is responsible for the physical and financial care of the child? What is done if the surrogate mother has engaged in drug use that has harmed the fetus?

For these and any other reasons, it is crucial for the sake of all involved that anyone contemplating becoming a participant in such a contract obtain the best legal, medical, ethical, and psychological counseling. Even so, surrogacy contracts are not well regulated in some states (Platte, 1996).

### 16.10   ADOPTION

Another alternative for couples in which one or both individuals are infertile is adoption. Adoption is also an increasingly popular option for single people and gay couples who want to become parents. About 60,000 children are adopted in the United States each year, and of these, about half are infants of the same race as the adoptive parents. Some hopeful couples are successful in getting one of the over 8,000 babies adopted from abroad each year (Stone, 1995).

Until about 1970, most young women with unwanted pregnancies placed their babies for adoption. But legalized abortion and the increasing acceptance of motherhood outside of marriage has dramatically changed this. Only about 5 to 6 percent of mothers now put their children up for adoption (Andolsek, 1990). For the adopting couples, the expense may be surprising. Total cost, for legal fees, other costs for the couple and the pregnancy, and birthing expenses for the biological mother, ranges between $10,000 and $20,000 (Stone, 1995).

Adoptions can be pursued through several avenues. Most commonly, adoptions are handled through state-licensed *private* or *public adoption agencies,* usually nonprofit social services that handle approximately 70 percent of all adoptions. Some of these children are under the agency's direct care, and other children are from foster-care homes. An agency adoption may be the best option for adopting an older child, a minority child, or a child with special needs, although agencies also help in the adoption of infants and foreign children. Signing up with an adoption agency will not, however, guarantee your receiving a child or when. Commonly the wait, after a request for adoption, is several years. Some states, such as Arizona, allow private licensed for-profit adoption agencies to operate, and some of these agencies are being run very successfully and are reducing the waiting time for couples to as little as a year or less.

Another way to adopt a child is through an *independent* or *private adoption*. The individuals wishing for a child make arrangements with a woman who wants to release her child, often with the help of a physician, cleric, or attorney serving as an intermediary. Each state has its own laws concerning independent adoptions, and it is important for the adopting couple to know all the state laws for both their state and that of the birth parents. In all independent adoptions, for instance, the birth parents can give their consent to the adoption only *after* the birth of the child, and in some states independent arrangements are prohibited due to concern over cases in which the adoptive home was not suitable, babies were not suitably matched with the adopting couple, or the couple was not properly protected against an unacceptable adoption (Consumer Reports, 1996).

Yet another adoption route is an *international adoption*. Increasingly frequently done in this country, about 2/3 of these children are adopted as infants and about 1/3 are adopted between the ages of one and four, often from foreign orphanages. Both state and federal requirements must be met in international adoptions, and most foreign adoptions are handled through adoption agencies, although some are independent adoptions (Consumer Reports, 1996).

Many adoptions bring the happiness anticipated to otherwise childless couples. In studies on children adopted as infants, adopted children and adolescents are perceived as well adjusted, happy, and less apt than other children and adolescents to engage in destructive behavior. This is believed to be due in part to the strong relationship between parents who adopt and to their philosophical acceptance of adoption (Benson, Sharma, & Roehlketartain, 1995).

Yet there can be many problems with seeking an adoption. Some biological mothers change their minds after the adoptive parents take the child home, and sometimes the biological father objects. In a few celebrated cases adopted children have been removed from adoptive homes several years after adoption. What can be done if the birthing mother's expenses have been paid, but the child is congenitally deformed? What if the adoptive parents change their minds? These and other questions need to be anticipated. A useful resource for answering such questions is Adoptive Families of America, 3333 Highway 100 North, Minneapolis, MN 55422 (phone 1-800-372-3300).

## SUMMARY

1. Preparation for having a healthy baby begins before conception, and includes the mother having a physical examination, adjusting her body weight if necessary, eating more carefully, discontinuing all illegal drug use, and quitting smoking and drinking.

2. Conception (fertilization of the ovum by a sperm) usually occurs in the fallopian tube. The fertilized ovum develops into the blastocyst, which enters the uterus and then after two or three days implants into the endometrium.

3. After the first two weeks of development the conceptus is referred to as an embryo; after the eighth week until delivery it is known as a fetus.

4. Exchange of materials between maternal and fetal blood takes place through the membranes of the placenta. Blood is carried to and from the embryo or fetus to the placenta and back through blood vessels in the umbilical cord.

5. A full-term pregnancy usually lasts about 266 days from conception or 280 days from the beginning of the last menstrual period. The 280 days are divided into 10 four-week lunar months or 3 thirteen-week trimesters.

6. During the first trimester the mother might develop "morning sickness," and the fetus is 3 inches long. In the second trimester the mother begins to show, and the fetus reaches 1.0 to 1.5 pounds and is 10 to 12 inches long. In the third trimester the fetus settles into the pelvis, and the fetus reaches 18 to 20 inches and 6.5 to 8 pounds.

7. Adequate maternal nutrition is essential for the development of the fetal brain, bones, and all other body parts. For women whose weight is normal before pregnancy, a gain of 25 to 35 pounds during the pregnancy is ideal.

8. Any alcohol consumption during pregnancy can cause fetal damage. Even light to moderate drinking can cause a group of defects collectively called fetal alcohol syndrome (FAS). Women who smoke during pregnancy often bear smaller babies that have a higher infant death rate.

9. Childbirth is divided into three stages. The first stage starts with the beginning of labor and lasts until the cervix is fully dilated. The second stage is the birth of the baby. The third stage is the delivery of the placenta.

10. Cesarean section is delivery of a baby through an incision in the abdominal and uterine walls,

performed when vaginal delivery is impossible or would be hazardous to the woman or fetus.

11. Term is 38 to 42 weeks of fetal development. Newborn weight of less than 5.5 pounds is low birthweight, and known as being premature. Care of preterm infants is expensive, and lifelong limitations afflict many surviving preterm infants.

12. There are many advantages to breast-feeding an infant.

13. The incidence of miscarriage increases with a woman's age.

14. Infertility continues to be a problem for many couples. Infertility is treated using artificial insemination, ovulation-stimulating hormones, *in vitro* fertilization, and surrogate motherhood.

15. About 60,000 children are adopted in the United States each year. Children can be adopted through a private or public adoption agency, an independent or private adoption, or an international adoption.

## CRITICAL THINKING CHALLENGES

1. The type of medical care we can afford can affect our health care decisions. Do you know whether your health insurance provides for a cesarean section, if elected or needed?

2. Surrogacy is a complicated and controversial issue. How would you feel about donating your sperm or ovum to another couple? Would you feel you had become a parent? Would you prefer to be an anonymous donor or to have a more open relationship with the family? List the pros and cons of both situations.

# VARIATIONS IN SEXUAL BEHAVIOR

# 17

**AFTER STUDYING THIS CHAPTER, YOU SHOULD BE ABLE TO**

[1]  Explain the social and psychological implications of using various labels for rare or unusual sexual behavior.

[2]  Describe the ways in which paraphilic behavior resembles more typical sexual behavior and the ways in which it is fundamentally different.

[3]  Describe the important features of exhibitionism and related paraphilic behaviors, and then summarize the known characteristics of those who engage in such behaviors.

[4]  Describe the important features of pedophilia and distinguish between exclusive versus nonexclusive pedophiles, fixated versus regressed pedophiles, and homosexual versus heterosexual pedophiles.

[5]  Describe the important features of the continuum of sadomasochism (and related behaviors) and relate this to the details of the case study presented here.

[6]  Describe the distinguishing features of fetishism, partialism, and fetishistic transvestism.

[7]  Describe the important features of voyeurism, frotteurism, and eleven other even rarer paraphilias.

[8]  Explain the strengths and weaknesses of classifying paraphilic behavior as coercive or noncoercive.

[9]  Summarize the strengths and weaknesses of various approaches to explaining paraphilic behavior.

[10]  Summarize major treatment programs designed to treat paraphilic behavior.

## 17.1   WHAT'S IN A NAME?

As in previous chapters, we need to take some time to discuss how we label things. Psychologists have shown us that what we name things affects how we think and feel about them. In this chapter we will be discussing types of human sexual expression that are unusual in that they represent the behavior of only a small group of people. However, these relatively rare modes of sexual expression elicit very powerful reactions from others. These reactions may range from puzzlement, to ridicule or disgust, all the way to demands for extreme and prolonged punishment.

After much thought, this chapter came to be called "Variations in Sexual Behavior." This rather neutral language is designed to set the stage for you to form your own *informed* attitudes about the unusual sexual behavior described here. Let's look at some other labels for this type of behavior and take note of the attitudes and perspectives that go with each label.

The term **sexual perversion** suggests sexual behavior that is twisted or sick in an evil way. Calling someone perverted certainly implies disdain. The terms **sexual deviance** and **sexual deviation** are sometimes applied to these behaviors. This implies a more willful violation of social norms, perhaps in the same category as prostitution or criminal behavior. Some very neutral labels include **sexual variation** and **atypical sexual expression**. These terms imply that while such behavior is rare or unusual, it also resembles more common forms of sexual expression.

Another common label for the behaviors under discussion here is **paraphilia**: *para* = meaning "beside or beyond," and *philia* meaning "love" or "attraction." This label connotes a sense of sexual or psychological disturbance or illness. If one accepts the premise that such behavior is, in fact, a sign of mental or psychological disturbance, then that implies it could or should be "treated," that is, the behavior should change or be made to change. We will see that there are some who question whether it is appropriate or even desirable to intervene in some forms of paraphilic behavior. They see these behaviors as an issue of strong individual preference and as one more type of human diversity (Brame, Brame, & Jacobs, 1996).

Formally, *paraphilic behavior* refers to the repetitive use of unusual/bizarre images or behaviors for sexual excitement. The *DSM-IV* (APA, 1994) defines paraphilias as "recurrent, intense sexually arousing fantasies, sexual urges, or behaviors generally involving (1) nonhuman objects, (2) the suffering or humiliation of oneself or one's partner, or (3) children or other nonconsenting persons" (APA, 1994, pp. 522–23). Acknowledging the value judgments inherent in any of these labels, the term *paraphilia* will be used here. The authors of this book have opted for the more psychological term for a number of reasons. First, although paraphilic behaviors such as transvestism, fetishism, and even sadomasochism are generally quite harmless, at their extremes they do cause psychological and sometimes physical damage to those who engage in these behaviors. Second, voyeurism, exhibitionism, frotteurism, and pedophilia are serious violations of social norms in our society. They can also result in serious psychological and emotional damage to the targets of such behavior. Moreover, the lives of those who act on their unusual sexual urges are often ruined due to repeated incarcerations.

In this chapter, we will begin by exploring the concept of paraphilic behavior and the way behavioral scientists and sexologists think about them. Next we will examine the important features of the most common paraphilias and look at various theories regarding their origin. Then we will review several approaches aimed at changing, or at least reducing, those paraphilic behaviors that cause distress in those who exhibit them, or that harm other people. Finally, we will discuss some critical thinking issues that surround our knowledge about the paraphilias.

## 17.2   THINKING ABOUT THE PARAPHILIAS

While it may comfort most of us to think of these unusual sex-related behaviors as "strange and unnatural," one way to look at the paraphilias is that they are *extreme exaggerations* of what is fairly typical sexual behavior. For example, most of us experience sensual or overtly erotic pleasure in touching or kissing objects associated with a beloved (a photograph, for example). We may like to smell or wear a love partner's clothing. These behaviors are very typical indeed, and seem to have some resemblance to fetishistic behavior. Couples might like to undress in front of each other or display their naked bodies to each other. In fact, the National Health and Social Life Survey (Laumann et al., 1994) found that watching a partner undress was the second most preferred sexual activity among the heterosexual Americans surveyed. Thus, both *exhibiting* one's own naked body and *observing* a partner's nudity is very common in sexual relationships. Very attractive young women are sexual icons in our culture, and it is considered quite acceptable for men (and some women) to spend billions of dollars each year for the opportunity to stare at women's naked bodies on stage or in magazines, films, and videos. Women spend billions of dollars and thousands of hours each year on clothing, cosmetics, and surgery all designed to help them look as young as possible. Is this an attempt to come close to a "childlike" appearance and appeal to men's *pedophilic* interests? Men and women dressed in the clothing associated with the other gender (*transvestism*) has been a common comedic theme in our culture from the very beginnings of Western theater (Bullough & Bullough, 1993). Finally, a good many people enjoy bites, squeezes, restraining hugs, and so on as a regular part of their passionate lovemaking repertoire (you probably know all about "hickies")—is this sadomasochism?

It's probably helpful to open our minds by recognizing that mild versions of the behaviors described as paraphilic are familiar to many of us, yet paraphilic behavior is fundamentally different in some major ways. First, for the majority of human beings, all the "more typical" behaviors described above occur in the context of a romantic or sexual relationship with another consenting partner, or they are culturally approved. Even the antics of the cross-dressed comedian have a social function: entertainment. However, for the fetishist, it is an *object* that is arousing, *not* the person associated with the object. That is, it is the lock of red hair that is arousing, *not* the woman who has the red hair. For the *fetishistic transvestite* it is his own handling or wearing of women's clothing that results in arousal and orgasm. For the exhibitionist, voyeur, or frotteur, a *nonconsenting person* is required for arousal. The sadomasochist typically seeks a consenting partner, but it is the *power or powerlessness* that is sexually arousing for the sadomasochist. For the true pedophile, fantasies and physical contact with children are arousing.

Second, paraphilic urges have a demanding, insistent, and compulsive quality to them (Brody, 1990). The paraphilic experiences these urges and fantasies as uncontrollable (Money & Lamacz, 1989). Acting on them results in a tremendous release of tension and anxiety. Afterward, the cycle of gradually increasing tension and anxiety begins again. Lastly, with the exception of sadomasochism, all of the paraphilias described here appear to be exclusively male behaviors. In fact, paraphilic behavior has been described as a disturbance in masculine development (Levine, Risen, & Althof, 1990).

There are many jokes and humorous stories about exhibitionists, but real-life encounters are often disrupting and frightening.

## 17.3 THE MOST COMMON PARAPHILIAS

### 17.3.1 Exhibitionism

About one-third of all reported sex offenses involve **exhibitionism,** yet it is estimated that only about 20 percent of exhibitionistic incidents are reported to police. The main feature of this paraphilia is

| | |
|---|---|
| **sexual perversion** | abnormal or disturbed sexual behavior |
| **sexual deviance** | purposeful violation of sexual norms, as in prostitution |
| **sexual variation** | a neutral term, implying a "difference" in sexual expression or behavior |
| **atypical sexual expression** | a neutral term applied to relatively rare sexual expression or behavior; implies that such behavior resembles more typical or common forms of sexual behavior |
| **paraphilia** (pa-rah-fēl′yuh) | recurrent, intensely arousing sexual fantasies, urges, or behaviors that involve (a) nonhuman objects, (b) suffering or humiliation, or (c) nonconsenting others. Implies psychological disturbance, and therefore a need for treatment |
| **exhibitionism** | exposure or display of the male genitals to a nonconsenting person |

# GO ASK ALICE

*Dear Alice:*

*Occasionally, I expose myself on public transportation. I show myself mostly to high school girls, but sometimes to adult women. I position myself so only the person viewing me can see me. A few times I've masturbated while exposing myself. I like what I'm doing, but know I should not be doing it. I don't think I'm harming anyone. Are the women annoyed or upset? Are they being harmed?*

*Exposed*

Dear Exposed,

YOU are being harmed. Your behavior is illegal, and the more you engage in it, the greater the likelihood of arrest. Exposing oneself is a sex crime and can be punished with a jail sentence. Consider that your job, your family relationships, and your reputation are at stake. If you cannot play out your needs/fantasies with a consenting partner in a "safe" way, you need assistance. You need to change your behavior to avoid arrest, a jail sentence, blackmail, or someone's rage. See a qualified counselor who will refer you for appropriate treatment.

  http://www.mhhe.com/byer6

exposure of the male genitals to a stranger, usually a girl or woman. Many exhibitionists admit that the shock, surprise, or indignation of their victim is what is arousing, while others fantasize that their victim will become sexually aroused by viewing the exhibitionist's genitals. Indifference or scorn are emotionally painful to the exhibitionist. In terms of their sexual attitudes, exhibitionists are known to be generally puritanical, prudish, and exceedingly modest. Their heterosexual relationships are usually immature and marked by sexual dysfunctions (Arndt, 1991).

Interestingly, exhibitionists often make little effort to avoid arrest, or they might do things that increase the likelihood of apprehension. They often repeat their behavior in the same place, and one study found that exhibitionists had an average of three arrests over seven years (Arndt, 1991). This risk-taking seems an important element of the exhibitionist's sexual arousal. Guilt and shame follow soon afterward. After each episode, exhibitionists are usually convinced they will never do it again. This is typically followed by another cycle of increasing fantasy and rising tension.

Clearly, nudity and genital display are a regular part of most adults' sexual repertoire, but the exhibitionist seems unable to control the urge, nor does he limit this activity to the bedroom or other more acceptable places. Most importantly, the display itself is the goal, not sexual behavior with the observer/victim. Is the nude dancer or strip teaser a marginally approved female exhibitionist? Most sexologists would respond in the negative because, unlike true exhibitionism, this behavior always involves a consenting audience. Also, the goal of such behavior is earning a living, or entertainment, not the stripper's sexual arousal. Nor does the nude dancer experience a relief of intense tension when she or he performs.

Exhibitionistic behavior sometimes occurs along with developmental disability (mental retardation) and senile dementia, but this is easily distinguishable from true paraphilic behavior (Abel & Osborne, 1992). For some men, exhibitionism follows some trauma or loss. A more impulsive type of exhibitionist exposes himself habitually, and he might also engage in voyeurism and transvestism. Just before the exhibitionistic act, these men typically report an increase in negative feelings and mounting tension, along with fearfulness and nervousness. Exhibiting seems to relieve this tension and anxiety. Most arrested exhibitionists were found to also be engaging in more typical sexual relating around the time of their offense, so sexual deprivation is not viewed as a causal factor (Arndt, 1991). Nor is alcohol usually involved. Typically, the exhibitionist stands outdoors or sits in an automobile, about twelve feet from his victim, so closer sexual contact is impossible. Unlike transvestites or pedophiles, exhibitionists express great hostility toward others with similar interests. Exhibitionism is virtually unknown among homosexuals (Arndt, 1991).

Obscene telephone calls (**telephone scatologia**) are considered a form of exhibitionism. The caller's lewdness is often aggressive or threatening. It is clear that shocking the recipient is more important than *merely saying* overtly sexual things, because these

## HEALTHY SEXUALITY

### DEALING WITH OBSCENE TELEPHONE CALLERS

What should you do if you or your children receive an obscene telephone call? Quietly hanging up is usually effective. Try to remember that the paraphilic is excited by the recipient's shock, fright, or even disgust, so a lack of response is disappointing to the caller. If the phone quickly rings again, ignore it, turn on your answering machine, or lift the receiver and hang up again. If the calls continue, your telephone company can trace their origin and the police should take action. The caller *is* committing a crime. Your own caller identification service will also aid in tracing the caller. Although, as some suggest, it might feel good to blow a loud whistle into the phone, the caller might do the same to you.

callers do not leave obscene messages on telephone answering machines. For more on obscene phone callers, see "Healthy Sexuality: Dealing with Obscene Telephone Callers." A more recent version of this paraphilia is called **computer scatophilia** (Bullough & Bullough, 1994).

### 17.3.2 Pedophilia

Exhibitionism is the most frequently reported paraphilia, but pedophilic acts may actually be more common (Bradford, Boulet, & Pawlak, 1992). The **pedophile** fantasizes about, and attempts to engage in, sexual activity with prepubescent children, that is, someone younger than thirteen years old. Those who are attracted to girls usually prefer eight- to ten-year-olds; those who are attracted to boys typically approach slightly older boys. Some may be attracted to children of either sex. Anywhere from 60 to 90 percent of pedophilic incidents involve little girls, yet those involving boys seem to capture more of the headlines. Although there is some evidence to support the notion that brain impairment and neurological damage underlie pedophilic behavior, it is not very strong (Langevin, 1992).

Pedophiles may be classified as "*exclusive*" (relating sexually *only* to children) or "*nonexclusive*" (relating sexually to both adults and children). Another categorization (Groth, Hobson, & Gary, 1982) classifies some pedophiles as "fixated" at an earlier stage of development. This person typically prefers boys and relates to youngsters as "one boy to another." Fixated pedophiles typically have been attracted to children since they themselves were adolescents. "Regressed" pedophiles prefer girls and relate to them as if the girls were adults. Regressed pedophiles typically do not begin their paraphilic behavior until adulthood (McConaghy, 1993).

### Heterosexual Versus Homosexual Pedophilia

The terms *heterosexual* and *homosexual* as used here indicate whether the child victim is of a sex different from that of the offender, or of the same sex as the offender. They do *not* describe the adult sexual orientation of the offender. This is an important point, because many people mistakenly believe that gay men and lesbian women are more likely than heterosexual men to sexually abuse children. Regardless of the sex of their child victims, most men who molest children are heterosexual in their adult sexual orientation. Most gay men are sexually interested in other adult males and actively reject homosexual pedophiles. Child sexual abuse is virtually unknown among lesbians. Typically, women accused of child sexual abuse are either demonstrably mentally ill or engage in this behavior to please a male partner (Carroll & Wolpe, 1996).

About half of those convicted for heterosexual pedophilic crimes have committed their first act before age sixteen. For the other half, this behavior typically follows some disturbance in their relationships with women, or occurs along with an increasing concern about their sexual potency. They are often

| | |
|---|---|
| **telephone scatologia** (skat-ō-lō′jē-uh) | a form of exhibitionism involving making lewd or sexually aggressive telephone calls to a nonconsenting person |
| **computer scatophilia** | a form of exhibitionism involving sending lewd or sexually aggressive computer messages to a nonconsenting person |
| **pedophilia** (peh-dō-fēl′yuh) | sexual contact or activity with prepubescent children |

concerned with negative evaluations by women. Many heterosexual pedophiles have a history of exhibitionism and voyeuristic behavior during adolescence (Longo & Groth, 1983). Alcohol is involved in about 30 to 50 percent of reported pedophilic incidents, and pornography is implicated in about one-third of such reports. About one-third of heterosexual pedophiles have a history of having been sexually abused themselves as children (Bard et al., 1987).

Homosexual pedophiles tend to come from highly dysfunctional families. A large number were victims of childhood sexual abuse and many fantasized about or had actual sexual contact with animals. They tend to frequent female prostitutes and rely on masturbation as a preferred sexual outlet. They are shunned by most adult gay men. They prefer masculine boys over effeminate boys. Contrary to the stereotype of the pedophile as a "dirty old man," the typical age at first arrest is 28 to 35.

Interpersonally, pedophiles generally tend to be shy and unassertive. However, a recent review of the research literature on the personalities of pedophiles failed to reveal any strong consistencies in personality traits (Okami & Goldberg, 1992). Another study (Kalichman, 1991) found that as the age of their pedophilic victims decreased, there was an associated increase in the level of mental disturbance on the part of the pedophile. Pedophiles as well as rapists are more likely to describe their parents as rejecting and controlling, but neither group was subjected to harsher discipline than that experienced by nonoffending college students (Bass & Levant, 1992).

Occasionally pedophiles will form "child sex rings" in which some legitimate authority figure will involve a group of children in sexual activities and the production of pornographic materials. Attempts to recruit children and share pornography via the Internet have led to arrests and to failed legislative attempts to control what appears on the Internet (Quittner, 1995a).

Pedophiles might approach children within or outside their own families. Unless he also has sadistic interests, the pedophile usually attempts to be attentive to the child's needs, and might use gifts and favors to keep the child from reporting the sexual activity (Okami & Goldberg, 1992). If these fail, threats of force or actual force might be used. Children who are lonely or uncared for are more vulnerable to pedophiles than are other children (Arndt, 1991).

Often the pedophile expresses very distorted cognitions (beliefs or attitudes) that allow him to justify his activities to himself. Four such distorted cognitions have been identified: (1) the belief that the sexual contact benefits the child (this might be couched in terms of their "educational benefit"); (2) the belief that the children enjoy the sexual activities; (3) assuming little responsibility for the sexual contact (they often claim it "just happened"); (4) a perception that the child actively sought or elicited the sexual contact ("she looked at me seductively") (Arndt, 1991; McConaghy, 1993). Pedophilia evokes strong negative feelings in the general public. Consider your response to the activities of NAMBLA (North American Man/Boy Love Association), as described in "At Issue: NAMBLA."

Researchers distinguish among *incest offenders,* child molesters, and pedophiles. The incest offender molests one or more children, adolescents, or *adults* within his own family. The child molester might sexually abuse a particular vulnerable child or children, but does not have an overall erotic preference for children in general.

## 17.3.3 Sadomasochism

In **sadomasochism,** sexual arousal is associated with suffering or humiliation. This is the sole paraphilia in which numbers of women are involved, but men outnumber women at a ratio of about twenty to one (Arndt, 1991). The term **sadism** is based on the written works of the Marquis de Sade (1774–1814), whose stories involved inflicting suffering or humiliation on others in a *sexualized context.* The term **masochism** is based on the works of Leopold von Sacher-Masoch (1835–95). His writings describe men who were aroused by women beating or whipping them.

Most people assume that sadists are dedicated to inflicting pain or humiliation, while masochists always prefer to be the recipient of such activity. However, recent studies suggest that the same person might engage in either role over time (Brame, Brame, & Jacobs, 1996). Therefore, the inclusive term *sadomasochism* seems more accurate. Such interests usually begin during childhood, and the acting out of such fantasies is typically chronic. There is some evidence that for arousal to continue to occur, the severity of the sadomasochistic stimulation must be increased over time (Morrison, 1995).

It is far too simplistic to conclude that "sadists like to hurt people and masochists like to be hurt." For the sadomasochist, the suffering and humiliation must occur in a sexual ("eroticized") context. The sadist does not go around trying to hurt or injure strangers in everyday life. Outside of the eroticized sadomasochistic "scene," the masochist does not seek or enjoy pain, discomfort, or humiliation.

Writers in the area of sadomasochism suggest that it is not the actual suffering and humiliation that is sexually arousing. They claim that for the sadist, what is arousing is the sense of *complete control and*

## AT ISSUE

### NAMBLA: DIVERSITY, DEPRAVITY, OR DISORDER?

NAMBLA, the North American Man/Boy Love Association, was founded in 1978 and describes itself as a "civil rights/political organization" that supports consensual "intergenerational relationships." Organizational literature indicates that it seeks to educate society about the "true nature" of these relationships. They claim not to engage in any illegal activities, such as providing sexual contacts between adults and children. There are presently chapters in New York City, Boston, and San Francisco. Their activities include "educating the public, consciousness raising, providing emotional support for members," and assisting "incarcerated boy-lovers."

Gay and lesbian groups such as the Human Rights Campaign Fund, P-FLAG (Parents, Families, and Friends of Lesbians and Gays), and the International Lesbian and Gay Association have dissociated themselves from NAMBLA, insisting that NAMBLA supports pedophilic activities and is "not a gay organization." These groups have adamantly refused to be a part of any umbrella group or event that includes NAMBLA. Major urban Gay Pride Celebration committees have refused to let NAMBLA participate and have made public statements repudiating the group and its goals.

NAMBLA has issued a series of position papers. One such paper seeks abolition of all age-of-consent laws. Another opposes the military draft. A third opposes laws that force physicians to inform parents if a minor seeks contraceptive or abortion services. Other papers call for increased funding for AIDS education and access by minors to sex education and contraception. In addition, NAMBLA distributes a reading list of novels and short stories that idealize romantic/sexual relationships between adult men and boys. They also publish a list of selected research reports on pedophilia, all of which find no harm or negative aftereffects of sexual contact between adult men and male children or adolescents. The group contends that it is sexual *coercion or force* that harms children, not consensual sexual contact with adults.

NAMBLA was recently approved by New York State as a "legitimate nonprofit organization." This status allows NAMBLA to receive charitable donations and public grants. In San Francisco there was public outrage when it was learned that NAMBLA was meeting in a public library. This confrontation quickly became an issue of free speech: The library may not discriminate against groups wishing to use its facilities, provided no illegal activities are occurring. Doesn't NAMBLA meet to discuss or plan illegal activities? No police action can be taken until the illegal acts are committed. Local parents demanded that the library post notices about what groups are meeting there.

---

*domination* over another person. The pain or cruelty present in a sadomasochistic encounter symbolizes that power and control (Bronski, 1991; Thompson, 1991). For the masochist, it is the *complete submission* to the will of another person that is arousing (Brame, Brame, & Jacobs, 1996).

"S&M" is the common term for such paraphilic interests. The person in the sadist role is usually called the "top," while the person in the masochist role is called the "bottom." Specific activities include bondage, blindfolding, spanking, whipping, the use of restraints, or various ways of humiliating the partner. Members of the "S&M community" point out that those whose erotic interests are lumped together under the label *sadomasochism* actually have very individual preferences. For instance, the person who finds being bound or spanked arousing might dislike the application of painful stimuli. They make distinctions among those who pursue "bondage and disci-

pline" (B&D) or "domination and submission" (D&S). Others might engage in **hypoxyphilia,** a dangerous practice which involves the attempt to

| | |
|---|---|
| **sadomasochism** (sā-dō-ma'sō-kizm) | sexual arousal via inflicting or being the recipient of pain, suffering, or humiliation. Complete control and domination (or their complete absence) are important features |
| **sadism** | sexual arousal or orgasm via inflicting of pain, restraint, or humiliation on another |
| **masochism** | sexual arousal or orgasm via being the recipient of pain, restraint, or humiliation |
| **hypoxyphilia** (hi-pox-i-fēl'yuh) | sexual arousal or orgasm via oxygen deficiency to the brain |

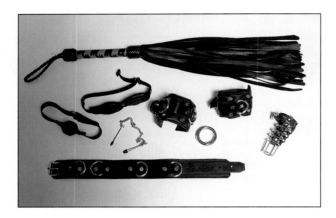

A wide array of sadomasochistic paraphernalia is available from sex shops and catalogs.

enhance orgasm by reducing oxygen to the brain through the use of plastic bags or chest compression. Whatever the specific activities engaged in, sadomasochistic arousal appears to depend on several themes: (a) The top experiences complete control over another person, (b) the bottom experiences freedom from responsibility for any erotic activity by giving control to the top, (c) the bottom must trust the top to go only as far as they have mutually agreed to go, (d) there is a great reliance on the acting out of fantasies related to pain and humiliation, and (e) the partners often engage in their activities in the context of an elaborate, mutually agreed-upon ritual (master/slave, torturer/prisoner, teacher/schoolchild, etc.) (Brame, Brame, & Jacobs, 1996; Weinberg, 1987).

How widespread are such paraphilic activities? What kind of people engage in such behaviors? It is difficult to tell. In the Janus and Janus (1993) survey, 14 percent of the male respondents and 11 percent of female respondents reported some experience with sadomasochistic activities. According to a survey conducted among the readers of an S&M magazine (Moser & Leavitt, 1987), most readers were heterosexual, well-educated, and switched roles relatively easily. Sadomasochistic interests appear to occur among persons of all sexual orientations. There is a fairly well developed S&M subculture that includes clubs and social organizations. These include the National Leather Association, the Eulenspiegel Society, SAMOIS (a lesbian S&M group), and the Society of Janus. There are "leather lifestyle contests" in the gay male community (Bronski, 1991). Local newspapers carry personal ads, and there are specialized chat rooms on the Internet (Rose & Thomas, 1995). Though sadomasochists previously were secretive, greater openness has been noted more recently. Some

consider the growing popularity of "fashion statements" such as extensive tatooing, leather garments, branding, and multiple body piercings (including lips, nipples, labia, penis, etc.) to be signs of this increasing openness to this form of sexual expression.

Sadomasochistic behavior is carried out along a continuum. Some couples engage in "minor sadism" and might beat each other with a soft object or use silken scarves as restraints. Spanking, whipping, bondage, or humiliating the partner are all considered examples of minor sadism. The S&M community claims to live by the adage "Safe, Sane, and Consensual" and views their activities as *recreational sex* (Brame, Brame, & Jacobs, 1996). To read about a couple who include sadomasochistic activities as part of their erotic lives, see "Case Study: Domination and Submission."

At the other extreme is the sadistic murderer who experiences orgasm only with his victim's extended suffering and dying. Some pedophiles have sadistic interests and mutilate or murder their victims.

### 17.3.4   Fetishism

The **fetishist** prefers or requires the presence of an inanimate object or body part for sexual arousal. The fetish object might be touched or rubbed and is used as an accompaniment to fantasy or masturbation or during intercourse. Prostitutes are often called upon to satisfy the fetishistic needs of their customers, and some prostitutes manage to establish "specialties" in this area.

Some materials and objects are more common than others as fetishes: **Media fetishes** include leather, rubber, fur, or silk. **Form fetishes** include particular objects such as shoes, garters, boots, or underwear. Others are truly rare or seem more bizarre: safety pins or auto exhaust pipes (Arndt, 1991). Table 17.1 lists the most commonly encountered fetish objects.

Another form of fetishistic behavior is called *partialism*. Here a particular body part serves as fetish object: hands, feet, buttocks, hair, and so on.

### 17.3.5   Transvestism

In chapter 12, it was pointed out that men cross-dress (**transvestism**) for many reasons. Some do it for fun or entertainment. For men with gender identity disorder, the wearing of feminine garments elicits feelings of great calm, psychological congruence, and a sense of feeling right about expressing one's true, "inner," feminine self. However, for the **fetishistic transvestite**, looking at, handling, and wearing women's apparel elicits sexual arousal, erotic fantasy, masturbation, and orgasm (Brown, 1995; Talamini, 1982). In

**TABLE 17.1**   MOST COMMON FETISHES (*N* = 48)

| | |
|---|---|
| Clothes | 58% |
| Rubber | 23% |
| Parts of the body | 15% |
| Footwear | 15% |
| Leather | 10% |
| Clothes of soft materials | 8% |
| Other | 18% |

**Source:** Data from A. J. Chalkey & E. E. Powell (1983). The clinical description of forty-eight cases of sexual fetishism. *British Journal of Psychiatry*, 142, 292–295.

contrast to the gender-identity-disordered transsexual, the transvestic fetishist generally does *not* wish to alter his anatomy and live as a woman. It is interesting to note that the *DSM-IV* considers fetishistic transvestism to occur only among heterosexual males (APA, 1994). If cross-dressing occurs in the context of a gender identity disorder, it is *not considered a paraphilia*. Recent research findings of fetishistic transvestism among homosexually and bisexually oriented individuals have cast some doubt on this classification (Bullough & Bullough, 1996).

Fetishistic cross-dressing typically begins during adolescence. The variety of transvestic behaviors ranges from the occasional wearing of women's underclothing in private, to full dress and makeup with appearances in public. This transvestite might become involved with the transvestic subculture. This could include membership in organizations such as Tri-Ess (Society for the Second Self) or the Renaissance Educational Association (Garber, 1992). To make matters more complex: Sometimes, after several years of fetishistic cross-dressing, erotic arousal might decrease, only to be replaced with feelings of gender dysphoria (see chapter 12) and the subsequent pursuit of surgical and hormonal intervention to change his genitalia (Arndt, 1991).

As the vast majority of these cross-dressers are heterosexual men, their wives and family members have also been studied (Wysocki, 1993). Some wives are initially accepting and allow their husbands to wear female attire during sexual activities. Wives with greater self-esteem and greater feelings of control over their lives are generally more accepting of their husband's paraphilic interests (Weinberg & Bullough, 1988). However, the general finding is that wives become more disapproving over time, and eventually these marriages end in separation and divorce. When not cross-dressed, transvestic men appear appropriately masculine in their behavior and interests.

Although television talk shows give the impression transvestism, whether fetishistic or transsexual, is widespread, most experts estimate that only 1.5 to 2 percent of American men cross-dress (Arndt, 1991).

## 17.3.6   Voyeurism

In **voyeurism**, sexual excitement is generated by observing naked women, those who are undressing, or those engaged in sexual activity. There seem to be three elements necessary for the preferred voyeuristic experience. First, those observed must be strangers. Second, they must not consent to being observed. And third, the voyeur must have a sense of personal risk while observing (for example, perching high in a tree). The sense of danger and the violation of another person's privacy provide the stimulating fantasy for the voyeur (Adams & McNaulty, 1993). The voyeur masturbates while observing, or later, while fantasizing about the encounter. Ultimately, it is not simply someone else's nakedness that is arousing, for the voyeur does not go to nudist camps or nude dance bars.

In our culture, men eyeing or staring at scantily clad or naked women is considered normative masculine behavior. When women ogle men, most consider it to be a humorous gender reversal, though the target might feel as offended as his female counterpart. It is interesting to note that across all human cultures female genitals are never exposed and young girls are always given covering clothing before little

| | |
|---|---|
| **fetishism** | sexual arousal or orgasm via the preferred or required presence or use of an inanimate object or body part (partialism) |
| **media fetish** | eroticizing of an object based on the material from which it is made (silk, leather, etc.) |
| **form fetish** | eroticizing of an object based on its shape (high-heeled shoes, garters, etc.) |
| **transvestism** (tranz-vest′izm) | dressing and self-adornment that is associated with the other gender |
| **fetishistic transvestism** | sexual arousal or orgasm via handling or dressing in clothing associated with the other gender |
| **voyeurism** (voy′your-izm) | sexual arousal or orgasm via observing nonconsenting strangers who are naked or engaging in sexual activities |

## DOMINATION AND SUBMISSION: TRUDI AND LANCE

Lance is in his late forties and describes himself as "primarily heterosexual" and, in terms of his sado-masochistic activities, "primarily a bottom." His wife, Trudi, is also in her late forties and describes their S&M interests as "more of a head game" that centers on a reversal of traditional gender roles.

Lance reports that he began fantasizing about sadomasochistic activities during childhood, and he associates this with frequent physical punishment at home. He attended Catholic school, and although he was never hit or spanked there, he was aware of feeling intimidated by the nuns and of becoming aroused by certain aspects of Catholic rituals. He was once exposed to a pornographic S&M magazine but felt no connection with the activities portrayed there.

During adolescence he had arousing fantasies of having a woman or girlfriend spank him. He never acted on these fantasies, but he reports that several girlfriends were aroused by his spanking them. He reports fantasizing about being in their place.

Trudi reports growing up in a family that "treated women as doormats" and says that she always "wanted to be in charge" but never had a place to express herself. She believes that she wanted something "better than what [her] family had," but did not know exactly what.

Trudi and Lance married during their twenties and began "playing" about six months into the marriage. Lance encouraged Trudi to pursue her interest in riding horses, and over time he gave her fifty-six whips. Lance frequently commented about how "naughty" he had been and suggested her using the whips to correct him. Trudi enjoyed Lance's pleasure over her boots and spurs. Their games began to center around punishment for his "misdeeds" and role-

plays about power in which he was forced to do something humiliating. Spanking represented authority, and over-the-knee spanking became important to both of them. Sometimes their play involves forcing Lance to cross-dress or wear diapers.

Trudi indicates that what is most arousing for her is Lance's "surrendering of total power" and his being "totally submissive and very vulnerable" to her. She notes that Lance must play a very dominating role in his business life, and their total role reversal helps him deal with that. Lance believes that S&M has had a positive effect on his life in that it has been a way to love his wife much more deeply. He sees these activities as creating a bond of trust and understanding between them.

Trudi reports that she doesn't particularly seek orgasm in the course of their games, but often has one. Sometimes she forbids Lance to have an orgasm until she decides he may do so, and this is also very arousing for both of them. Lance indicates that S&M play that does *not* lead to intercourse or orgasm is "enormously powerful and fulfilling." He describes it as "another way to love,…a choice."

Trudi believes that their S&M activities have allowed her to become more assertive in her work life and to be tolerant of differences among people. She also believes that she experiences an "alternate high" from their power play. Lance perceives that their S&M activities allow Trudi to enjoy and express herself. He believes that, for them as a couple, these activities stimulate their "sense of adventure."

**Source:** Adapted from G. G. Brame, et al., *Different Loving*, 1996. Villard Press, a division of Random House, New York, NY.

---

boys are (Bullough & Bullough, 1993). This would seem to imply a recognition that men's tendency to become aroused at female nudity must be controlled in some way.

Most often, the voyeur is about age twenty-four at first conviction, but he has been engaging in such behavior since about age fifteen. Typically, no drugs or alcohol are involved in his paraphilic behavior, nor does he show any serious mental disorder. Some have a history of poor heterosexual relationships; others do not. In general, voyeurs tend to be less sexually experienced compared to other paraphilics, and they

are less likely to be married. They often have low self-esteem and tend to be interpersonally inadequate (Arndt, 1991).

## 17.3.7   Frotteurism

In **frotteurism,** the main interest is in touching or rubbing the penis against a nonconsenting person. This is often accompanied by fantasies regarding a relationship with his victim. Crowded places such as buses, subways, and elevators are typical sites for this behavior. Some frotteurs touch or fondle the victim

# DIMENSIONS OF DIVERSITY

## OTHER PARAPHILIAS: FROM A TO Z

**Asphyxiophilia:** (Hypoxiphilia) Cutting off oxygen to the brain in order to elevate carbon dioxide levels. This increases euphoria during orgasm or masturbation. Unfortunately, this often leads to accidental self-strangulation or hanging. Investigators typically find fetishes or transvestic articles present at the death scene, suggesting that other paraphilic interests are involved as well.

**Coprophilia:** Sexual arousal based on the smell or handling of feces.

**Infantilism:** Sexual arousal from impersonating or being treated as a baby. Sometimes this is incorporated into sadomasochistic activity.

**Klismophilia:** Sexual arousal based on receiving enemas.

**Mysophilia:** Smelling, tasting, or contact with bodily dirt: dirty socks, underwear, used tampons, etc.

**Necrophilia:** Sexual attraction to and arousal by corpses.

**Pyrophilia:** Arousal via lighting fires or watching things burn.

**Stigmatophilia:** Arousal by undergoing piercing or tatooing.

**Troilism:** Sexual arousal from watching one's partner having sexual relations with another person.

**Urophilia:** Sexual arousal focused on urine or urination.

**Zoophilia:** Human history and mythology is replete with references to human and animal sexual contact, and this is often referred to as **bestiality.** This behavior typically occurs among rural adolescent boys who have access to farm animals (Cerrone, 1991). More urban equivalents involve using pets in sexual activity. Another version involves sexual arousal while watching animals copulate. This paraphilia occurs more often among patients with significant mental disorder (Alvarez & Freinhar, 1991).

---

with their hands. This behavior is most commonly seen among males between fifteen and twenty-five years of age. One study found that 70 percent of frotteurs were also involved in exhibitionism, voyeurism, or rape (Freund & Blanchard, 1986).

## 17.4  UNDERSTANDING THE PARAPHILIAS

### 17.4.1  Coercive Versus Noncoercive Paraphilias

One suggested approach to understanding the paraphilias is to categorize them as *coercive* or *noncoercive*. Coercive paraphilias involve a nonconsenting person, and these would include exhibitionism, voyeurism, frotteurism, and pedophilia. Noncoercive paraphilias are typically solitary or involve a consenting partner. These could include fetishism, transvestism, and sadomasochism. However, even these paraphilias could become coercive. For example, the fetishist might break into someone's home to steal the fetish object. The *partialist* might attempt to touch the feet of women studying in libraries. The transves-

tic fetishist might insist that his partner participate in sexual activity while he wears feminine clothing, wigs, etc., and this might be repugnant to her. For a list of some of the rarer paraphilias, see "Dimensions of Diversity: Other Paraphilias." After reading their descriptions, can you classify them as coercive or noncoercive?

### 17.4.2  Multiple Paraphilias

One fact that has emerged from recent research is that individuals who demonstrate one paraphilic interest are likely to engage in other paraphilic activities (Arndt, 1991; Bradford, Boulet, & Pawlak, 1992). That is, the exhibitionist is also likely to have engaged in frotteurism, and so on. A second, related fact is that the typical paraphilic engages in his paraphilic behavior very frequently—especially those who engage in pedophilia, exhibitionism, and masochism (Abel & Osborn, 1992).

---

**frotteurism**
(frō-tūr′izm)    sexual arousal or orgasm via touching or rubbing against a nonconsenting person

# DIMENSIONS OF DIVERSITY

## PARAPHILIC BEHAVIOR IN THREE CULTURES: CHINA, IRELAND, AND JAPAN

**CHINA:** In China, from about the eleventh to the early twentieth century, we can see an example of institutionalized fetishism or partialism in the traditional custom of tightly binding the feet of five- or six-year-old girls. This forced the smaller toes under the sole and crushed the ball of the foot and the heel together. This process eventually resulted in an adult foot that was only three to five inches in length.

This custom may have originated with the fetishistic desires of a particular emperor-poet who made his favorite concubine bind her feet and dance for him (Gross & Bingham, 1980). The custom took on an erotic flavor, and spread among the aristocracy and eventually down to the lowest levels of society. Even prostitutes with normal feet were at a disadvantage. Wealthy men selected their wives and concubines from among girls and women who had

bound feet. Through the centuries, innumerable erotic poems and love stories were written glorifying the "golden lily," or "lotus feet." Tiny bound feet became the height of sensual beauty. Traditional Chinese erotic drawings show women naked except for socks or little slippers covering tiny deformed feet. Such feet became a national fetish, and poor parents bound their daughters' feet in the hope of attracting wealthier husbands.

Foot binding was an excruciating experience for the first year or so. After that, the foot usually lost all feeling, but unbearable pain returned as soon as the bandages were loosened or removed for cleaning. This too seemed to enhance the erotic appeal to men. Walking was very difficult and often impossible for women with bound feet (Gregerson, 1983).

**IRELAND:** A British restaurant company recently sought to open a new branch of their very popular School Dinners eatery in Belfast, Ireland. Like most upscale dining establishments, this one too offered a specialized atmospheric theme. Waitresses would wear British school uniforms, modified to include short skirts and lace tights. They would also whip the rear ends of customers who failed to consume everything on their dinner plates. The original restaurant has apparently operated in London for the past fourteen years. Belfast's major newspaper was concerned that the restaurant would lead to the molestation of underage girls. The mayor of Belfast called the restaurant concept "immoral" and stated: "This is not fun, this is filth." He called for the resignation of two local councilmen who had smilingly posed in publicity shots with the waitresses.

The councilmen responded by calling the mayor a "fuddy-duddy." A Belfast judge ended the debacle by prohibiting the restaurant from opening ("Whip-Bearing Waitresses Banned from Belfast," 1995).

**JAPAN:** Every day, about 15 million people ride the subways in Tokyo. During rush hours, the "shiri oshi," or "tushy pushers," pack commuters onto trains so that doors may close. Such crowding apparently attracts innumerable Japanese frotteurs. Reports that men fondle, rub against, or actually try to undress women are commonplace. Women riding on Japanese subway trains complain that being pawed or groped by molesters is all too common. In this nation where male dominance is the norm, police simply will not take this problem seriously. Japanese women feel they have no way to seek justice against those who commit such acts ("Sexual Groping Common on Japanese Trains," 1996).

Have there been comparable examples of bodily damage and mutilation in our own culture? Refer to chapter 2 and the fashionable corsets of the seventeenth and eighteenth centuries. Consider also our society's emphasis on thinness and breast size in women.

Japanese officials have been unresponsive to complaints of frotteurism, but Korean officials have begun running some women-only trains during crowded rush hours.

### 17.4.3 Relationship between Paraphilic Behavior and Sexual Violence

Most people want to know whether paraphilics are just harmless nuisances or dangerous offenders. This is not a simple question to answer, and the answers we have are far from complete. Fetishism and transvestism seem generally harmless, and sadomasochists seek a consenting partner. However, some sadistic rapes result in torture, mutilation, and death. While the exhibitionist and voyeur appear initially threatening, ultimately they are treated as nuisances by the criminal justice system. However, a substantial proportion of convicted pedophiles and rapists have a history of exhibitionism (Abel, Becker, & Cunningham-Rathner, 1988; Longo & Groth, 1983).

### 17.4.4 Other Issues in Paraphilic Behavior

One of the confusing issues in understanding the paraphilias is that such behavior is not a simple "preference" in the way that being attracted to men with very hairy bodies or finding oral-genital contact more arousing than intercourse might be. Many paraphilics are disgusted or repelled by their own behavior (Adams & McNaulty, 1993), yet feel compelled to repeat it.

Another puzzling aspect of the paraphilias is that 95 percent of those diagnosed as paraphilic are male (Levine, Risen, & Althof, 1990). How might this fact be interpreted? One way to conceptualize the paraphilias is that they might actually represent a gender identity disorder. That is, they represent a disorder in the development of appropriate masculinity.

Some sexologists think about the paraphilias as a disturbance in the basic human function of *emotional and sexual bonding.* Paraphilics have failed in the task of becoming emotionally attached to others capable of reciprocating this attachment. Their capacity to love appears to be seriously impaired (Levine, Risen, & Althof, 1990; Money & Lamacz, 1989).

Does behavior that we would describe as paraphilic occur in all human societies? Unfortunately, there has been little research on this question, so it is difficult to find examples of such behavior. For a description of paraphilic behavior in three very different cultural contexts, see "Dimensions of Diversity: Paraphilic Behavior in Three Cultures."

## 17.5 THEORETICAL PERSPECTIVES ON PARAPHILIC BEHAVIOR

In studying about paraphilic behavior, most students want to know how a person comes to have such un-usual sexuality. In spite of almost one hundred years of speculation and research on this question, the answers seem as far away as ever.

Those who have taken a *biological approach* have focused on hormone levels, brain malfunctions, or neurochemical imbalances. Research findings have been murky. Yet, as we will see later, some paraphilics do respond to antiandrogenic drugs (drugs that reduce levels of male hormones). Others respond to some of the newer antidepressant medications. These findings suggest that there may well be a neurochemical basis for at least some of these behaviors. Others have hypothesized some prenatal changes in the biochemistry of the developing brain, but little evidence supports this (Brown, 1995). It is difficult to isolate possible neuroanatomical bases for paraphilic behavior because, like all significant behavior, paraphilic behavior and any accompanying chemical abuse, head injury, or mental illness can actually alter the structure and functioning of the brain and nervous system. Thus, it is hard to tell which came first, the neuroanatomical abnormality or the paraphilia (Langevin, 1992).

Psychoanalysts generally describe paraphilic behavior as a defense against castration anxieties, but there is no scientific evidence to support any of the formulations of Freud or his followers.

**Behaviorists** assume that paraphilic behaviors are learned through experience with the environment. This is a relatively optimistic view in that it implies that if such behaviors are *learned,* they can be *unlearned* through the use of other learning techniques. Behavioral treatments are a mainstay of attempts to eliminate or at least control paraphilic urges and activities. But how are paraphilic interests learned?

Behaviorists usually make reference to the **classical conditioning** and **operant conditioning** models. First, sexual arousal or orgasm becomes *associated* with a particular stimulus (classical conditioning). The stimulus could be an object or a behavior. Later, the person fantasizes about the stimulus, or the stimulus is somehow involved in masturbation and orgasm,

| | |
|---|---|
| **behaviorism** | a psychological perspective that emphasizes learning (changes in behavior via interaction with the environment) |
| **classical conditioning** | learning via repeated association of one behavior with another |
| **operant conditioning** | the learning of a behavior via its repeated reinforcement, or its unlearning via its punishment |

which provides further *reinforcement* (operant conditioning). In the simplest of examples: a young boy masturbates while playing with his father's rubber boots, or perhaps while watching his sister kiss her boyfriend, and so sexual arousal becomes *associated* with rubber boots or observing others in erotic activity (classical conditioning). Later the boy masturbates while fantasizing about his previous experience and experiences orgasm, and so fantasizing about/wearing rubber boots or observing others is *reinforced* (operant conditioning). With repetition, the rubber boots or the act of observing others becomes preferred or required for sexual arousal. Similarly, sadomasochism is explained by sexual arousal experienced while being spanked or otherwise physically punished. In a truly classic test of the learning approach, Rachman (1966) paired slides of boots with sexually arousing slides of nude women. With repetition, the male subjects experienced some arousal when shown slides of the boots alone.

So far, this seems like a convincing explanation, but there are too many loose ends. For example, why do so many objects, materials, or behaviors associated with masturbation *never* become fetishes? Why don't cotton bed sheets, flannel pajamas, or warm bath water ever become fetish objects? Some point to Seligman's (1971) hypothesis regarding an evolution-based *biological readiness* to respond to certain environmental stimuli. Just as humans are more likely to fear bugs rather than flowers, humans might be more biologically prepared to become erotically conditioned to silky fabrics rather than wool, but this seems too weak an explanation.

Another problem is that studies of sadomasochists reveal that most never experienced sexual arousal during punishment or other painful childhood experiences (Arndt, 1991). Lastly, a critical review of the conditioning approach to human sexual arousal showed only "tenuous" support for such a process (O'Donohue & Plaud, 1994).

Another developmental approach describes how significant childhood experiences create a **"lovemap"** in the brain (Money & Lamacz, 1989). These experiences determine the particular stimuli and activities that become sexually arousing to a particular person. According to this approach, these lovemaps become "vandalized" by childhood experiences of sexual abuse, incest, extreme punitiveness around sexual curiosity, or emotional neglect and physical abuse. The paraphilias emerge from this damaged development.

Others describe the paraphilias as "courtship disorders" (Freund & Blanchard, 1986). In its most basic form, a sexual encounter involves several steps before intercourse can occur. These steps include first

locating a suitable adult sexual partner. The voyeur and frotteur do this inappropriately, and the same might be said about the pedophile. Next, a male must approach and interact with the potential partner. He must then display the right signals to interest the prospective partner and arouse himself. The signals may be colorful feathers, antlers, muscles, or just a steady job. The fetishist and fetishistic transvestite have trouble with this one. They display inanimate objects or cross-gendered clothing. In the animal kingdom, the goal of courtship is genital union. In the paraphilias, this goal is typically lost, and the paraphilic compulsively repeats his repertoire of distorted courtship behaviors (Freund & Watson, 1990).

A feminist perspective emphasizes the sociocultural factors that promote the sexism that seems so central in the paraphilias. Girls and women are virtually the exclusive targets of male paraphilic behavior (only the homosexual pedophile seeks male targets), and females do experience significant personal threat and violation as a result of such behavior. Accordingly these threats serve to keep women in a subordinate position in society. Every responsible parent feels a need to instill a fear in daughters about "strange men," and such gender-role socialization influences how that daughter operates in a world that she learns is dominated by males. She must be careful of men, lest she "provoke" some threat or sexual aggression from them. The encouragement of paraphilic interests through specialized pornography (and some would say even through common types of advertising) continues traditions of male threat and domination (Arndt, 1991). This material, and its normalization in our society, ostensibly leads to a minimized and distorted view of the harm such behavior causes girls and women (Travin & Protter, 1993). See table 17.2 for a summary of the theories we've just discussed.

## 17.6    CHANGING PARAPHILIC BEHAVIOR

There are several factors that make the treatment of paraphilic behavior very problematic. First, the paraphilic often does not view his or her behavior as the problem. The paraphilic may see *society's response* to his or her behavior as the real problem. This implies that many paraphilics are not highly motivated to change their behavior, and therefore they might not cooperate with pharmacological or psychological interventions. (Try to think of something that really arouses you. Would you be willing to give that up

**TABLE 17.2** THEORETICAL PERSPECTIVES ON PARAPHILIC BEHAVIOR

| PERSPECTIVE | CENTRAL CONCEPT(S) | EVALUATION |
|---|---|---|
| Biological | Hormone level abnormalities, brainstem malfunctions, neurochemical imbalances. | Mixed findings, generally inconclusive. Difficulty in knowing whether abnormality preceded or followed paraphilic behavior, especially if chemical abuse is involved. |
| Psychoanalytic | Castration fears. | No supporting scientific evidence. |
| Behavioral | Paraphilic behavior is learned via association (classical conditioning) and reinforcement (operant conditioning). | This model is used to design and implement treatments designed to change or control paraphilic behavior. |
| Lovemap | Early trauma (abuse, incest, etc.) vandalizes the template (lovemap) of what particular stimuli arouse an individual. | Some correlational support. |
| Courtship disorder | Disruption in the normal processes of locating a suitable partner, approaching and interacting with that partner, appropriate display of sexual interest, and genital union. | Minimal research support. |
| Feminist | Paraphilias as dominance and aggressive behaviors that subordinate women and limit their freedom. | Minimal research support. |

completely?) Second, there are ethical issues. Is the goal of the treatment to impose society's goals on the person? What about his or her own personal goals? Third, the treatments developed to date are minimally to moderately effective. Fourth, there is an issue of perceived responsibility. Often sex offenders claim they cannot control their impulses and behaviors, and so should not be punished for them. Before any type of behavior change can begin, the offender must give up this cognitive stance.

## 17.6.1 Types of Treatment Programs

### Biological Treatments

In Europe, surgical and chemical castration have been used. Such techniques are not utilized in North America, on ethical and humanitarian grounds, nor are they particularly effective (Becker et al., 1995).

In North America, antiandrogenic drugs such as *Depo-Provera* (medroxyprogesterone acetate, or MPA) have been used with "nonexclusive" paraphilics, that is, those who can function sexually without the paraphilic object or behavior. There has been some good success with this group. The general result of this treatment is a significant decrease in sexual tension and paraphilic fantasies and preoccupations. "Exclusive" paraphilics typically experience a total shutdown of any erotic interests and subsequently become depressed and hostile (Arndt, 1991).

MPA works by suppressing the activity of male hormones, thereby reducing sexual fantasy, drive, and arousal (Langevin, 1994). However, the person's basic sexual orientation does not change. For example, while taking MPA, the pedophile's basic attraction to children does not change, but he is less likely to act on it. *Cyproterone acetate* (CPA) is another antiandrogenic compound that does seem to change the overall pattern of arousal (Bradford & Pawlak, 1987). Moderate effectiveness has been noted when the treatment is combined with counseling.

Some recently developed antidepressants (known as *serotonin reuptake inhibitors*) such as fluoxetine (Prozac) have been shown to be effective in reducing those paraphilias that have more of an **obsessive-compulsive** flavor, such as exhibitionism, fetishism, and voyeurism (Federoff, 1993; Kafka, 1994; Masand, 1993).

### Psychological Treatments

Conventional individual psychotherapy has *not* been found to be effective with paraphilic behavior. More effective and commonly used group approaches involve **cognitive behavioral therapy**. Specific techniques include *covert sensitization*. Here, undesirable behaviors are paired with *aversive imagery* (visualizing very unpleasant things). For example, a photograph of a

| | |
|---|---|
| **lovemap** | representation in the brain/mind of what is arousing to a particular individual |
| **obsessive-compulsive disorder** | a group of psychological disorders characterized by a very high level of anxiety that is reduced by repetitive behaviors |
| **cognitive behavioral therapy** | psychological treatment that emphasizes changing self-defeating thoughts and behaviors |

child is paired with images of an angry adult discovering the pedophile. Fantasies of pedophilic behavior are paired with images of being shackled or incarcerated. Covert sensitization has been found to be helpful in overcoming the pedophile's distorted cognition that he cannot control his impulses and behaviors (Travin & Protter, 1993). *Orgasmic reconditioning* involves having the person masturbate to paraphilic images. Just before orgasm, he switches to more acceptable imagery.

Based on the idea that the paraphilic has inadequate social skills to pursue and maintain a relationship with an adult woman, *social skills training* attempts to teach, practice, and reinforce appropriate interpersonal skills.

As was noted earlier, paraphilic behaviors are often associated with periods of stress. Treatment programs that emphasize *stress management* have also had limited success with paraphilics (Travin & Protter, 1993)

*Relapse prevention strategies* are designed to help the offender recognize and avoid situations where paraphilic urges are likely to arise and overwhelm the offender. The offender is trained to recognize "high-risk situations" such as negative emotional states, interpersonal conflicts, and social pressures. The offender is then supposed to apply the new coping mechanisms that he has been taught. Another facet of this approach involves developing empathy for victims. That is, the sex offender is guided in imagining how the target of his paraphilic behavior felt and might have been affected.

Some treatment programs have adopted and modified a *twelve-step* approach. This group-oriented technique originated in Alcoholics Anonymous and has been somewhat effective.

## 17.6.2 Evaluating the Effectiveness of Treatment Programs

In general, group approaches have been found to be more effective than individual treatment approaches. Success is increased if the offender is well motivated and cooperative (Langevin, 1994). In the few longer-term studies that have been carried out, the general finding is that the longer sex offenders are monitored, the higher their recidivism rates (Furby, Weinrott, & Blackshaw, 1989).

## 17.7 THINKING CRITICALLY ABOUT THE PARAPHILIAS

In the last twenty years, the amount of research devoted to paraphilic behavior, especially pedophilia, has increased considerably (Okami & Goldberg,

1992). Yet there are many areas in which confusion and controversy continue. Below are some of the issues involved in the many unanswered questions about paraphilic behavior as well as a sampling of some of the unresolved controversies that surround this type of human sexual expression.

First, what do we clearly know about the paraphilias? Only six facts seem truly established and generalizable.

1. Paraphilic behavior is rare to nonexistent among women. There is still no satisfactory explanation for this fact.
2. Most paraphilics display more than one paraphilic interest or behavior. This was only recently recognized and suggests that the paraphilias are *not* just a type of preferred sexual expression. Instead, there appears to be a *generalized* disturbance in sexual expression that may manifest itself in several ways over a lifetime.
3. There is a continuum of behavior involved in each of the paraphilias. Expression can range from mild to moderate to extreme, and might or might not exist along with more typical forms of sexual expression.
4. It is problematic to categorize some paraphilias as harmless or *noncoercive,* as the demanding and compulsive nature of the paraphilias results in a strong potential for coercion and therefore harm to others.
5. Paraphilias occur across all sexual orientations.
6. *Fantasy* appears to be an outstanding element in all types of paraphilic expression. Paraphilic behavior might be a type of sexual expression in which internal, psychological factors are more powerful than external stimuli.

A second series of issues has to do with what kind of sexual expression is considered disturbed or unacceptable. Acceptable sexual expression varies according to sociohistorical norms. One recent example that demands some critical thinking is the idea that a person can become "addicted" to sex. This notion suggests that the "too frequent" pursuit of sexual release, whether partnered or solitary, can become a consuming, mood-altering drive, similar to what is experienced by the alcoholic and other drug abusers. This idea was promoted in the early 1990s by both television talk shows and "sexperts." Books such as *Sexual Addiction, Out of the Shadows: Understanding Sexual Addiction,* and *Looking for Love in All the Wrong Places* became best-sellers. All of these books describe a condition called "compulsive sexual behavior" (CSB) or, in the more popular volumes, "sexual addiction." This condition is characterized by very frequent sexual behavior that places the person in danger of contracting STIs and other sexuality-related illnesses. CSB can also result in social and legal difficulties, and can be accompanied by emotional pain. Coleman (1992) discusses five subtypes of such behavior: compulsive cruising and multiple partners, compulsive fixation on an unattainable partner, compulsive masturbation, compulsive multiple love relationships, and compulsive sexuality in a relationship. These repetitive behaviors are ostensibly driven by anxiety rather than by sexual desire.

The older *DSM-III-R* (APA 1987) seemed to lend support to this idea by describing a condition characterized by "distress about a pattern of repeated sexual conquests or other forms of nonparaphilic sexual addiction, involving a succession of people who exist only as things to be used" (APA 1987, p. 296).

Scholars specializing in the history of human sexuality note the many decades of psychomedical concern about conditions involving "too much sex with too many partners." Pseudoscientific writings include in these conditions *erotomania* (excessive sexual desire in women), *nymphomania* (excessive sexual activity in women), *satyriasis* (excessive sexual activity in men), *promiscuity* (indiscriminate or casual sexual activity), Don Juanism (obsessive seduction of women, named after a fourteenth-century Spanish nobleman), Don Juanitaism (you can guess this one), and the Casanova complex (promiscuity in men, named after an eighteenth-century Italian nobleman) (Coleman, 1992). These terms fell out of fashion after the "sexual revolution" of the 1960s. Most professionals in the field of sexuality have come to view them as judgmental and culture-bound. Also, because these terms were much more often used to pathologize women's sexual behavior (especially *nymphomania*), they are also considered damaging examples of the sexual double standard.

Note that all such conditions have disappeared from the current *DSM-IV* (APA, 1994). In this fourth edition, attention is focused on problems such as low sexual desire, difficulty in becoming adequately aroused, or difficulty in reaching orgasm. In other words, concern has shifted from "too much sex with too many partners" to "too little, ineffective, or unsatisfying sex." Thus, we see how our perceptions regarding "disturbed sexual behavior" can sometimes reflect nothing more than current social norms and concerns.

## SUMMARY

1. The use of different terminology in examining these relatively unusual sexual behaviors reflects differing attitudes and value judgments about them. The psychological term *paraphilia* is used in this chapter.

2. Students have had different degrees of life experience with paraphilic behavior. Most often, girls and women are the targets of such behavior.

3. Some features of paraphilic behavior appear to resemble extreme exaggerations of more typical sexual expression. However, paraphilic behaviors differ from more typical sexual behavior in that they (a) are not focused on consenting, shared, adult sexual expression (sadomasochism may be the exception), (b) have a demanding, compulsive quality to them, and (c) are almost exclusively male behaviors.

4. The most commonly encountered paraphilias are exhibitionism, pedophilia, sadomasochism, fetishism, transvestism, voyeurism, and frotteurism.

5. To further understand the nature of the paraphilias, one must consider several issues. First, can they be adequately classified as coercive versus noncoercive? Second, most paraphilics engage in multiple paraphilias. Third, the paraphilias do not appear to be a simple "preference" in sexual expression. Fourth, paraphilic behavior occurs almost exclusively among males. Fifth, paraphilic behavior appears to be symptomatic of a disturbance in the ability to bond emotionally with another person.

6. There are many theories regarding the origin of paraphilic behavior: biological, psychological, developmental, feminist, and "courtship disorder." No current theory can fully account for paraphilic behavior.

7. Current biologically based treatments for paraphilic behavior include antiandrogenic drugs and recently developed antidepressants. Psychologically based group treatments include various forms of cognitive behavioral therapy, social skills training, stress management, relapse prevention strategies, and a modified twelve-step approach. Adequate research has not yet been done to evaluate the effectiveness of the various treatment approaches.

8. Several controversial issues surround the paraphilias, and these lend themselves to a critical analysis. First, in spite of the growth in research about the paraphilias, relatively little is clearly established about their nature. Second, a historical perspective on what sexual behaviors have been considered pathological in the past also contributes to a more critical and healthily skeptical view of paraphilic behavior.

## CRITICAL THINKING CHALLENGES

1. Read "At Issue: NAMBLA." Whatever your reaction to NAMBLA, remember that the First Amendment to the Constitution was specifically designed to protect the free-speech rights of groups whose views are abhorrent or unpopular. How do you view the rights, goals, and activities of NAMBLA?

2.  One hundred years ago, masturbation was considered to be a serious disturbance and medical interventions, including surgery, were considered appropriate for this "illness." Until the 1980s, a preference for same-sex partners was also considered to be an indication of mental illness. Of course, both of these behaviors are now considered normal. As a greater understanding of the paraphilias accumulates, do you think our society will also adopt a very different attitude toward the paraphilias? Or do you think the nature of paraphilic behavior is in some way fundamentally different?

# COMMERCIAL AND COERCIVE SEX

## 18

**AFTER STUDYING THIS CHAPTER, YOU SHOULD BE ABLE TO**

[1] List and describe four principles that help explain how sexual imagery in advertising can influence behavior.

[2] Explain how advertisers often make use of stereotypes, as well as our visceral responses to sexual stimuli, to sell products.

[3] Distinguish among erotica, pornography, and obscenity and summarize several important court cases relevant to these distinctions.

[4] Summarize the messages about human sexuality that pornography promotes.

[5] Explain the controversies surrounding child pornography.

[6] Summarize the findings regarding the relationship between pornography and sexual violence.

[7] List and describe the main types of female and male prostitutes.

[8] Explain the relationship between prostitution and the spread of HIV.

[9] List and describe seven pervasive attitudes that make dealing with coercive and violent sexual behavior problematic.

[10] Describe four types of sexual harassment, what is known about their prevalence and impact, and what to do if you experience sexual harassment.

[11] Describe the special issues surrounding sexual harassment in academic settings and between professionals and their clients.

[12] Distinguish between rape and sexual assault, describe the important features of five types of rape or sexual assault, and summarize what one should do if raped or sexually assaulted.

[13] Summarize the findings regarding the impact of rape and sexual assault on survivors.

[14] Summarize what is known about why particular individuals rape or sexually assault.

[15] Describe how our society attempts to prevent rape and to deal with the rapist.

[16] Distinguish among child sexual abuse, pedophilia, incest, and child molestation.

[17] Summarize what is known about the prevalence and signs of child sexual abuse.

[18] Summarize the findings regarding the characteristics of child sexual abusers and the response of their victims.

[19] Describe the impact of child sexual abuse on survivors, including the controversy about recovered memories.

[20] Describe how our society attempts to prevent and treat child sexual abuse and how offenders are dealt with.

## 18.1  OVERVIEW

Many human relationships involve the exchange of money or goods in return for some activity or service, even some very intimate personal services. An employer pays money to employees in exchange for their labor. We pay certain individuals for their skills, attention, and willingness to please us personally: a hairdresser for example. We exchange money for the time spent in intimate interaction with certain professionals: a therapist or minister. Yet we do not exchange money in return for friendship, caring, or involvement. For these human interactions to be "real" or meaningful, they must be freely offered and voluntarily shared. What about sexual arousal and activity? Where do we place our personal sexual expression? Can we make our sexual expression a purely physical act, separate from a social/emotional relationship? Can sex be meaningful or pleasurable if it is bought or sold?

When sex is removed from its emotional, *intimate* context, it can take on new characteristics. Sex-related behavior can be treated as a commodity: something to be bought, sold, and bargained for in the marketplace. In *advertising*, many products are sold by associating them with sexually arousing imagery or suggestions of sexual behavior. *Pornography* involves the production and selling of depictions of others engaging in sexual activity. These images are designed for the specific purpose of sexual arousal. In the extreme form of sex as a commodity, actual shared sexual experiences can be sold and bought through *prostitution*.

In some of the most troublesome and disturbing areas of human sexual expression, some individuals use their power or even overt violence to coerce or force others into sexual activity. In our society, as in many others, sexual coercion and the use of force are all too common. We will explore three major types of coercive or violent sexual expression: sexual harassment, sexual assault or rape, and child sexual abuse.

## 18.2  SEX IN ADVERTISING

The old adage "Sex Sells" is forever being tested by the advertising industry. Actually, the principles of truth in advertising should require the adage to declare "Sexual Fantasies Sell," but that's not as catchy as the traditional saying. Exactly how do advertisers use sexual innuendo and sex-related imagery to market their products?

Four principles explain how such advertising works. The first principle is that of *association*. The pleasant, mild sexual arousal that accompanies hearing or seeing the sexy ad is associated with the product. When the product is seen or heard in real life, the person should reexperience that mild arousal. In other words the person has been **classically conditioned.** She or he has *learned* to automatically respond with arousal at the sight or mention of the product. It is doubtful that this effect lasts for any length of time.

Advertisers also depend on the psychological process called **identification.** When we observe attractive, sexy models using or enjoying the product, we might picture ourselves with that product and, on some level, believe or at least hope that we will look as attractive or alluring as that model. In other words, we come to identify with that model.

Another way advertisers play on our fantasies is through *suggestion*. The ads suggest that if we purchase that car, drink that beer, or wear that panty hose, those very attractive models will somehow come into our lives with the product.

A fourth way advertisers use sexual imagery to encourage us to purchase certain products is **embedment.** *Embedment* refers to placing sexual words or images within an advertisement in such a way that the viewer is not consciously aware of their presence. Supposedly these sexual words and images are perceived in the viewers' unconscious. This approach is relatively rare. Although popular writers and the public seem to be titillated at the idea of being manipulated in this way, the scientific findings indicate extremely weak effects (Balay & Shevrin, 1988; Widing et al., 1991).

### 18.2.1  Responding to Sexual Imagery

#### Gender

Gender is a strong predictor of how people will respond to explicit sexual imagery in advertisements. In general, men respond more positively to such overt visual or auditory imagery. They tend to feel more energized. Women respond more negatively, in that they report greater tension and fatigue (La Tour, 1990).

In spite of the old adage, today's big companies and ad agencies have read the mountain of research and rightfully concluded that a softer sell sells more. Even the auto industry, one of the strongest bastions of the use of images of scantily attired, skinny young women (draped suggestively around new car models), has shifted to "real-looking" women and men to display their cars.

#### Stage of Life

Advertisers must also consider the life stage of the consumer. As baby boomers age, they are probably more responsive to images of family and romance than to those of sexual innuendo (Schiller, Landler, &

Most Americans believe that they are immune to the influences of such imagery and that "others" are more vulnerable.

Siler, 1991), and baby boomers are the ones with the income. As baby boomers are now advancing into their fifties and beyond, what kinds of sex-related imagery do you predict will now become more common?

In general, advertising research suggests that when sexual imagery is used in an ad, consumers often pay more attention to the arousing model or message and less attention to the product name or its features. The product name or features may never even register in consumers' memories (Severn, Belch, & Belch, 1990). When the sexy ads are an expression of the product—lingerie, suntan lotions, and perfumes—sexual imagery works, but when the sexual imagery has nothing to do with the nature of the product, people mentally turn them off (Foltz, 1985).

A few years ago, a series of Calvin Klein ads in which barely pubescent boys and girls posed provocatively sparked a great controversy regarding sexual innuendo in ads. A storm of public and official protests, as well as charges of child pornography, led many to drop these ads, but images of ambiguously gendered young people, with a body shape best described as that of a "thin tube," remain very popular. Recently, this look has permeated fashion advertisements. A recent *Vogue* cover girl at seventeen years old, was five feet, ten inches tall and weighed 120 pounds. This is a patently unhealthy ideal. Most contemporary models are thinner than 95 percent of the female population (Jacobson & Mazur, 1995).

Thus we see that sexual imagery in advertising is used to convince potential consumers that if they purchase the product shown, they will somehow magically become or possess the unrealistically alluring people seen in those ads.

## 18.2.2 Advertising and Gender-Role Stereotypes

You might recall from an earlier chapter that a **stereotype** is a set of characteristics believed to be possessed by all members of a particular group. A **gender stereotype** refers to the personal and behavioral characteristics believed to be possessed by women or men in our culture—for example, that all women are dependent, computer klutzes, and nurturant, and that all men are assertive, mathematical whizzes, and insensitive. While we form these stereotypes from many sources, many researchers have studied how advertising both reflects and maintains stereotypic notions about women and men. Some of these stereotypes have to do with women as *symbols of sexuality*, and others have to do with the social and sex-related roles played out by each gender. These factors often overlap in advertising.

Advertising often presents a distorted or even false picture of women and men and their sexualities. Next, we will consider an area where women, men, and sometimes children are reduced to mere body parts and the complexity of sexual interaction reduced to mere genital activity, often in a context of raw power and submission.

## 18.3 PORNOGRAPHY

### 18.3.1 What's in a Name?

Once again we will begin by defining some important terms. However, things are a bit more complicated here. Even if the public and experts can agree on the general meaning of these terms, fierce court battles have been fought over some of these definitions and

| | |
|---|---|
| **classical conditioning** | learning via repeated *association* of one behavior with another |
| **identification** | internalizing the qualities, characteristics, values, etc., of another into one's self concept or identity |
| **embedment** | the placement or hiding of sexual words or pictures in the background of an advertisement |
| **stereotype** | a belief that all members of a group possess certain traits, qualities, or characteristics |
| **gender stereotype** | a belief that all men or all women possess certain traits, qualities, or characteristics |

what kinds of material exemplify these concepts. When human sexual expression bumps up against the law, a profound battle often ensues.

Writing, pictures, films, or videos that are created for the specific purpose of sexual arousal are considered **pornography**. Some define pornography as sexually explicit material that is *degrading* or *demeaning*, no matter whether the persons being debased are women, children, or men (Griffin, 1981). If the material has a sexual content, but is created for other purposes, such as for artistic expression, then it is considered to be **erotica**. Thus, the creator's *intentions* are an issue, not just the explicitness of the material.

Sometimes it is very difficult to draw the line between erotica and pornography. The First Amendment of the United States Constitution, which guarantees the rights of free speech and expression, protects the creation of some sex-related materials. However, a 1957 Supreme Court decision (*Roth v. United States*) made it clear that the rights of free speech and expression do not cover the creation of material that is **obscene**. This court decision established three criteria for determining obscenity. First, the dominant theme of the material must be an appeal to "prurient interests." **Prurient interest** was defined as "shameful and morbid interest in nudity, sex, or excretion, and which goes beyond customary limits of candor." Second, the material had to be "patently offensive" to current community standards. Third, the material had to be without any redeeming social value.

In 1973, another important court case (*Miller v. California*) determined somewhat different criteria for obscenity. First, the "average person" must find that the work appeals to prurient interests. Second, the work shows sexual acts defined as obscene by state law. Third, the work lacks any artistic, political, or scientific value. Fourth, to be judged obscene, the dominant theme of the material and its content must be taken as a whole rather than out of context. In 1987 (*Pope v. Illinois*), it was determined that a "reasonable person" rather than an "average person" is a better judge of whether something appeals to prurient interests.

What does this have to do with you? One reason why you need to understand this controversy has to do with the line between artistic expression and what is considered obscene. In 1990, an exhibit of the works of well-known photographer Robert Mapplethorpe was judged obscene by the officials of Cincinnati, Ohio. As a result, the exhibit was closed and the director of the Contemporary Arts Center of Cincinnati was incarcerated. He was subsequently acquitted of charges of pandering to obscenity and the illegal use of minors. Who should decide what you should be able to see?

In this section of the chapter, we will deal with the issue of pornography. We will first take a brief look at pornography from a historical perspective. Then we will learn a bit about pornography as a very lucrative part of the sex industry, as well as about the various types of pornography. Next we will take a look at the thematic content of pornography and examine the messages it contains about women, men, children, sexuality, power, and violence. Finally, we will examine two important questions related to pornography. First, what is the impact of pornography on its consumers and others? Second, we will examine whether the use of pornography is related to sexual violence. Most people agree that this is an important question, and we will see why it is such a difficult question to answer.

## 18.3.2   A Brief History of Pornography

The earliest examples of sex-related artwork or artifacts were probably fertility symbols. Later in human history, sexually oriented objects were probably used to ward off evil spirits. Modern pornography dates back to the sixteenth century, when sexually explicit materials were meant and used not to arouse others sexually, but rather as social, political, or religious satire or criticism (Hunt, 1993). A corrupt king or church leader might be shown engaging in some lewd act. By the eighteenth century, this material came to be used solely for sexual excitation. Access to early pornography was limited to a social elite who shared the contents of their "secret museums" with each other. Most scholars agree that the spread of pornography appears related to increases in literacy, general education, and democratization (Elmer-Dewitt, 1995). Today, pornographic images flood our everyday life. We don't even have to seek out such materials anymore. Pornography can now enter our homes with the mere flick of the "on" switch of our VCRs and personal computers (Tierney, 1994).

In most eighteenth- and nineteenth-century pornographic stories and novels, the narrator is a female prostitute (Hunt, 1993), like the narrator in *Fanny Hill,* published in 1748. She is usually an independent person who is financially successful and who ridicules traditional notions of female virtue and domesticity. In twentieth-century North America, *Esquire* magazine began publishing erotic stories and photographs for "sophisticated men" during the 1930s. This was followed by the publication of the first edition of *Playboy* in 1953. This magazine contained attractively posed female nudes. During the 1960s, a series of more explicit "men's magazines" became available. These included *Penthouse, Hustler,* and *Oui* and contained even more explicit photographs that included pubic hair and genitalia. More

Up until the twentieth century, pornography was used mainly for the purpose of political and social satire.

recent magazines, with such names as *Smut* and *Screw*, push the limits even more. These publications seem to cross the line between what is considered generally considered **soft porn** into what is usually termed **hard-core pornography.** This latter term refers to very explicit materials with a minimum of context surrounding the display of various sexual acts and close-ups of genitalia. There is an emphasis on the violation and degradation of women. Hard-core films were referred to as "stag films" or "blue films." The first nickname probably refers to the notion that these films are primarily of interest to single, young males. The second nickname refers to the bluish tinge prominent in many of these films, caused by inadequate or inept lighting. The hard-core film industry hit its peak during the 1970s.

Today, the pornography industry has been forever changed by the development of the videocassette (see "Dimensions of Diversity: 'The Money Shot'"). Now, about 2,400 new "adult videos" are produced each year in an almost $3 billion business (Faludi, 1995; Kelly, 1996). The content, production values, and intended market for these videos have also changed. These videos are now elaborately staged in interesting settings. Scenery, acting, and plots have been developed. These changes are all geared to appeal to the new market for such materials: *couples*. According to the adult video industry, about 70 percent of adult videos are rented by women on weekends (Kelly, 1996). Most of these new consumers are in relationships and the films are used as stimulants or enhancers for the couple's sex life. Sexually explicit materials that degrade or subordinate women have given way to videos with more emphasis on sexual and gender equality (Brosius, Weaver, & Staub, 1994; Cowan & Dunn, 1994). A new wrinkle in the adult

video market involves amateurs who make videos of themselves engaging in sexual acts at home and then attempt to sell them.

The personal computer makes access to pornography relatively easy. Today, interactive X-rated computer games, self-help software for those who suffer from sexual dysfunctions, and chat rooms that cater to paraphilic interests proliferate on the Internet (Rose & Thomas, 1995). Newspaper accounts of the Internet being used by pedophiles and child pornographers have also incensed the general public. For some more about these issues, see "At Issue: Cyberporn."

It appears that a significant majority of the American public believe that adults have the right to obtain sexually explicit materials. A majority also believe that it is acceptable for adults to see materials that display genitalia and all types of sexual activity (Winick & Evans, 1994).

### 18.3.3 The Pornography Industry

Pornography is a $7 billion international business (Jacobson & Mazur, 1995). Although most people equate the term *pornography* with magazines, films, and videos, the pornography industry is much broader than that. Sex shops, catalog companies, telephone sex lines, audiotapes, and computer-based pornography are all part of this segment of the sex industry. As we saw earlier, many people consider some advertising, especially in the fashion industry, to border on the pornographic. Further, many prostitutes are often involved in the creation of pornography. The majority of pornographic materials are created by men for the consumption of heterosexual men.

| | |
|---|---|
| **pornography** | sexually explicit writings, pictures, etc., created for the purpose of sexual arousal |
| **erotica** | writings or other artistic creations that are sexually arousing or sensual |
| **obscenity** | sexually explicit writings, pictures, etc., that are offensive or repulsive |
| **prurient interests** | excessive or morbid interest in nudity, sexual function, or excretion that well exceeds socially acceptable limits |
| **soft porn** | explicit material designed to sexually arouse, but lacking in graphic close-ups of genitals, ejaculation, degradation, etc. |
| **hard-core pornography** | explicit material designed to sexually arouse that includes graphic close-ups of genitals, ejaculation, degradation, etc. |

# DIMENSIONS OF DIVERSITY

## "THE MONEY SHOT": THE CULTURE OF THE PORNOGRAPHIC VIDEO

The workaday problems and personal struggles of those who make and appear in popular and profitable X-rated videos offer a distorted and corrupt reflection of our own workaday world. But the final "product" of this industry is the portrayal of sexual acts.

The World Modeling Talent Agency is a major provider of "talent" for America's video porn industry. The new "products" of the video porn industry are displayed at the annual Consumer Electronics Show, and the industry has its own trade publication, *The Adult Video News.* At the annual Adult Video News Awards, honors are given in such categories as "Best Specialty Tape: Spanking" and "Best Anal-Themed Feature."

At present, the video pornography industry is sharply divided and competition is fierce. A few giant companies dominate the field, and they produce very profitable upscale videos with costumed actors, identifiable plots, and interesting settings. At the other end of the spectrum are scores of small-scale producers that release endless videos of "harsh sex." In the upscale format, a small number of female stars predominate. At one point, one such successful woman had a huge fan club, operated several 900 lines, a mail-order catalogue clothing business, and

marketed custom-made videos selling from $300 to $5,000. Other "stars" have been invited to mainstream television talk shows and have become quasi celebrities.

One of the very few men to make it in this relatively new image-oriented world of video porn is Jeff Stryker. His image can be seen on video box covers, magazines, sexual aids, playing cards, greeting cards, calendars, T-shirts, compact disks, and an expensive line of clothing *(Thierry Mugler's)*. He even has a mass-marketed mold of his penis, "Jeff Stryker's Realistic." It is one inch longer than his real penis and sells for $59. His videos are about evenly divided among the gay and heterosexual markets, but in keeping with his image, he always plays the "top." When he cannot perform sexually in front of the crew and cameras, a "stand-in" penis is quickly called in from the World Talent Agency. Stryker's recent attempts to start his own video company as well as another firm to market his product lines failed. However, he was able to win a custody battle with his wife and now has his young son living with him. He has no pornography in the house and refuses to even subscribe to cable television. He states he would like his son never to know what his father does for a living, and

hopes to accomplish this by buying and building a house on vast acreage in rural Missouri.

In the dingy, downscale video format, penises, erections, and ejaculations are the mainstays. In this world, "one-day wonders" are the rule (the amount of time devoted to shooting one complete feature). Traditional male porn actors have two qualifications: they must be able to produce and maintain full erections for extended periods of time, and they must be able to ejaculate on command. External, visible, and copious male ejaculation is the all-important "money shot" that defines the end of every hard-core scene, and male pornography performers are paid by the scene. However, the male sexual organ is notoriously unreliable, and in the increasingly pressurized world of video pornography, many a shooting is delayed for hours or even days as cast and crew "wait for wood." Inability to "have wood" means a quick replacement by one of the scores of men waiting at the World Talent Modeling Agency. Male porn performers at the high end of the market are always terrified at the specter of "no wood" and their subsequent drop to the low end of their industry. In the world of video porn, "Guys are a dime a dozen" (Faludi, 1995).

However, a considerable proportion of it is "specialized." These "specialty lines" include child pornography, gay pornography, and materials that cater to various paraphilic interests, especially sadomasochism and transvestism. Lebegue (1991) found that half of all paraphilia-oriented magazines observed were devoted to sadomasochism, while incest was the theme of about 21 percent of these magazines.

### 18.3.4 Pornography's Portrayal of Human Sexuality

Worldwide, the vast majority of pornographic materials involve heterosexual acts (Weaver, 1994). These materials focus on the power of male arousal, depict it as central to sexuality, and are preoccupied with overt sexual activity. Pornography excludes all other aspects

**AT ISSUE**

## CYBERPORN: THE CURRENT CONTROVERSY

The *Communications Decency Act of 1995* attempted to keep "obscene, lewd, lascivious, filthy or indecent" material off the Internet (Levy, 1995). Legal challenges arose immediately because the law was so broad and so vague that uploading some classic literary works would become felonies, as would distributing certain information about contraception and abortion. The central question was whether cyberspace should be as controlled as radio and television, *or* as free as telephones, magazines, newspapers, and private conversations. Cyberspace experts point out that the Internet is more comparable to a river of ongoing conversation among 30 million computers and thus should not and cannot be subject to the same restrictions as other electronic media.

Trading sexually explicit images is one of the largest recreational uses of computer networks. (Yet such images constitute only 3 percent of all messages on Usenet newsgroups). Because standard pornography is so easily available elsewhere, "specialty" materials are in greater demand on the Internet. Paraphilic images, especially those involving pedophilia, sado-masochism, and bestiality, are common. Most of the images are simply taken from preexisting print sources, but now these are available in one's own home. Knowledge of children's heavy involvement with computers has led some child molesters to use this means to contact children. But how should children be protected from such material? Is parental guidance enough? Can software be developed that would allow such material to be screened away from children?

In June 1996, a federal three-judge panel produced a 175-page memorandum (it appeared online within minutes) extending free-speech protections to cyberspace. The decision noted that because the Internet is in its infancy, still evolving, and one of the most democratic of communications channels, it probably deserved even greater free-speech protection than broadcast and print media (Nadler & Fong, 1996). They came to this conclusion after spending several weeks surfing around the Net alone and under the guidance of experts. They searched for pornography and tested programs that allow parents to screen or block certain materials. They con-cluded that parents, not government, should take responsibility for limiting their children's access to materials on the Net. To protect children, the panel called for voluntary content rating by PICS (Platform for Internet Content Selection) as well as filtering and blocking software. SurfWatch and Canada's Net Nanny are examples of such software. Groups representing social and religious conservatives vowed to continue their fight for increased restrictions.

In 1997, the U.S. Supreme Court declared the Communications Decency Act to be unconstitutional and a serious threat to free speech. Noting the tremendously democratic potential of the Internet as a forum where every citizen's voice can be heard, the Court concluded that communications on the Internet deserve the highest level of protection. After learning how to surf the Internet, the Supreme Court Justices determined that the Internet is not as invasive as radio or television and that there are other ways to protect children from the pornography on the Internet. The Court found, in particular, that it is extremely difficult to "accidentally" encounter pornography on the Internet (Levy, 1997).

---

of human relationships between sexual partners. Intercourse occurs in every setting imaginable. Acts include sex between women, group sex, anal intercourse, oral-genital contact, and copious, visible, external, ejaculations. Generally, the only human feelings present in pornographic encounters are "fear and lust" (Weaver, 1994, p. 218). No attention is paid to communication, affection, or the more tender emotions, nor is there any concern about the consequences of such sexual activity. In nonviolent pornography, women are typically portrayed as eager and hysterically euphoric in all sexual encounters. The desires and prowess of men are emphasized, and women are portrayed as promiscuous and submissive. Violent pornography repeatedly depicts women as enjoying being raped and otherwise hurt and humiliated. Unless it is sadistically oriented material, her protests and distress are always transformed into arousal and pleasure. Thus, violent pornography trivializes rape, exaggerates the prevalence of paraphilic practices, and decreases sensitivity to women. Many believe that pornography promotes callousness toward the suffering of child victims of sexual abuse and trivializes the mistreatment of women. Pornography certainly ignores the fact that sexual assault is a serious crime.

Recently, Zillman (1994) did an analysis of standard-fare pornography and identified three themes as typically present in such materials:

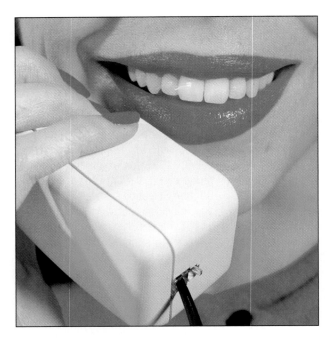

Some view "telephone sex" as a form of safe sex. The easy access to such services has led some telephone companies to take measures to prevent calls from minors.

1. Sexual acts occur between strangers who have just met. After these sexual acts, they depart as strangers.
2. Bodies (people) are interchangeable. Consecutive encounters occur with new and numerous partners.
3. All sexual acts lead to extreme euphoria.

Other researchers analyzing the content of pornography (Mosher & MacIan, 1994) note the absence of foreplay, cuddling, or afterplay. Nor are there expressions of love or affection. Male feelings expressed in pornography include excitement, surprise, anger, and disgust. Female feelings are joy, fear, distress, and shame. On a more positive note, according to an analysis of sexually explicit videos created to enhance the sexual expression of couples, a major theme of these sexually explicit videos is that the purpose of sexual activity is pleasure for *both partners* (Mooney & Siefer, 1991). However, a theme that has crossed over from traditional pornographic films is that there are many partners interested in sex and they are all easily available. A second theme is that all partners experience a high level of sexual desire. Finally, the videos demonstrate a diversity of more unusual sexual activities and exaggerate their frequency in real life (Brosius, Weaver, & Staub, 1994).

One view of pornography is that it is entertainment and that it offers positive images of sexual plea-

sure and abandon. It has been hypothesized that pornography can have educational and therapeutic benefits and help eradicate puritanical attitudes (Kelly, Dawson, & Musialowski, 1989). Others view pornography as degrading and demeaning the roles and bodies of women (Griffin, 1981). Also pornography can promulgate overtly false information about the sexuality of women and men.

### 18.3.5 Child Pornography

About twenty thousand pieces of child pornography ("kiddie porn") are smuggled into the United States each year, mainly from Scandinavia (Kelly, 1996). The children in this material are usually runaways from sexually and physically abusive families. Sometimes, though, parents encourage or force their children into this work. A 1977 federal law made child pornography illegal. This led to the production of child pornography by amateurs who utilize young runaways, emotionally troubled youngsters, and their own children for such purposes. The portrayal of children as suitable objects for male sexual pleasure is disturbing to most adults in our society, and such activity is considered a form of sexual abuse. Scientific research has demonstrated that children are profoundly harmed by their experiences in the creation of child pornography (Burgess, 1984). The 1984 Child Protection Law made the trading or giving of child pornography as a gift a crime. The Child Protection and Obscenity Act of 1988 threatens harsh penalties for those who produce, distribute, or sell child pornography.

### 18.3.6 Evaluating the Impact of Pornography on its Consumers

In 1986, a new Commission on Obscenity and Pornography (popularly known as the "Meese Commission") concluded that there is indeed a relationship between exposure to sexually violent materials and aggression toward women and children (Linz, Donnerstein, & Penrod, 1987). Researchers described how pornography facilitated belief in "rape myths." These myths include the notions that women really want to be forced into sexual activity and that they ultimately enjoy sexual violence. The writers also concluded that such material desensitizes men to the seriousness of rape, and results in their perceiving rape victims as less injured or deserving of sympathy. They also found that rapists were more likely to have been exposed to hard-core pornographic material, and concluded that all pornographic material was harmful to children. The report was criticized as lacking objectivity in that it tended to ignore research that was contrary to its stated position. Also, many of the members of the commission had previously been involved in antipornography activities.

# GO ASK ALICE

*Dear Alice:*

*I enjoy reading pornographic magazines, but I don't want to go through the embarrassment of buying them over the counter. Is there any way I can get these magazines privately? I'm also curious about live nude shows. Are these safe places to go? Are they expensive?*

*Debbie Does*

Dear Debbie Does,

You can order pornographic magazines privately through the mail by using catalogs. Buy a title you like over-the-counter and use the subscription card inside. Or, you can go to one of the "safer sex shops" in your city. Most of their materials are erotic, not pornographic.

Live nude shows are expensive. While "free admission" may be a lure, once inside, there is usually a drink minimum, and you are expected to give money to the dancers regularly. If you don't do this, you may be pressured to leave. About safety, if there's no exchange of blood, semen, and/or vaginal secretions (and there shouldn't be), you're safe from all STIs. However, security for customers varies from club to club. If you mean safety from being arrested, that chance always exists if prostitution is also taking place on the premises.

 http://www.mhhe.com/byer6

---

The debate about the impact of pornography can also be understood in terms of two conflicting psychological theories. **Social learning theory** suggests that pornography provides distorted and harmful models of human sexual expression.

Learning theorists believe that consumers, especially young men, model some of the attitudes and behaviors seen in pornographic materials in their relationships with women. Some men come to believe it is part of their sexual nature to dominate, mistreat, and use women solely for their own pleasure (both sexual and nonsexual). According to this theory, women exposed to pornography learn that male sexual needs and power are all-important. Their reluctance, refusal, or fear to do or feel what is illustrated in pornography is taken as a sign of their own sexual inhibition. They learn that submission, pain, and mistreatment are all appropriate sexual roles for women.

An opposing perspective is offered by **catharsis theory**. According to this perspective, if men observe pornography and vicariously experience the domination and violence against women shown in such materials, they will be *less likely* to actually behave that way. Their sexual tensions will be released by looking at and perhaps masturbating to pornographic materials (Kelly, Dawson, & Musialowsky, 1989). This ultimately benefits women and children. At least one study (Scott & Schwalm, 1988) found that nonaggressive pornography may reduce aggressive tendencies among men, but overall scientific support for this second perspective is scarce indeed. Support for the first model is mixed.

After showing pornographic or innocuous entertainment films to students and nonstudents for various periods of time, Zillman and Bryant (1984) and Zillman (1994) found that those exposed to the pornographic materials

1. were more lenient in their punishments for rapists.
2. showed more indifference toward women and children who were sexually assaulted.
3. perceived promiscuity as more natural and common.
4. evidenced greater acceptance of premarital and extramarital sex.
5. indicated greater acceptance of the idea that health risks are a myth, and that only sexual restraint poses a health risk.
6. expressed more negative feelings about marriage.
7. believed more strongly that sex-related issues are more acceptable as grounds for divorce.
8. indicated a reduced desire to have children, especially female children.
9. revealed more sexual dissatisfaction, especially in relation to the behavior of their partners.
10. indicated a greater interest in trying unusual sexual practices.

| | |
|---|---|
| **social learning theory** | a theory emphasizing the learning of social roles, behaviors, etc., via rewards/punishments and observation/imitation |
| **catharsis** | a release of emotional tension that refreshes or returns the organism to a normal state |

Thus, although some claim that pornography has little effect on its consumers' attitudes and behavior, and is harmless fantasy and entertainment, others say that it seriously affects consumers' attitudes toward women, particularly relationships between women and men, both inside and outside the bedroom. This takes us to a central question regarding pornography: What is the relationship between pornography and sexual violence?

## 18.3.7 Does Pornography Contribute to Sexual Violence?

A good amount of research has been devoted to studying the relationship between the use of pornography and sexual behavior, especially violent sexual behavior (Cline, 1994). In general, the findings indicate that pornography has little effect on consumers' overall sexual behavior. After viewing pornography, male consumers tend to masturbate more. In terms of their shared sexual activity, they generally do not change their usual sexual repertoire to include activities seen in pornographic materials. After exposure to pornographic material, female consumers tend to engage in intercourse with their usual partners somewhat more often. Several studies (Malamuth, 1981; Malamuth, Heim, & Feshbach, 1980) found greater sexual arousal, in both women and men, in response to materials depicting mutually desired sex than to depictions of rape. But all viewers showed increased arousal if the rape victim was shown to have an orgasm. However, both in the laboratory and in more natural settings, violent pornography has been shown to result in more aggressive behavior toward women (Malamuth & Check, 1981; Malamuth & Donnerstein, 1984; Weaver, 1994). Edward Donnerstein and his colleagues (Linz, 1989; Linz & Donnerstein, 1992) have made a major contribution to our understanding of this effect by showing that it is the *violence* in violent pornography that results in increased aggression. They showed that *nonsexual, violent material* leads to increased aggression against women by the men who have seen such material. It might be the violence permeating much of contemporary mass media, whether in action films, slasher movies, or television programming, that is a contributing factor to violence against women and children.

Field studies have suggested that although pornographic images and materials are increasing in our society, violent pornographic images may be decreasing (Fisher & Grenier, 1994; Scott & Cuvelier, 1993). There is also the possibility that the problem lies in the fact that *some individuals* already have preexisting tendencies to harm women and they are very vulnerable to the effects of pornography (Check & Malamuth, 1985; McKenzie-Mohr & Zanna, 1990).

Yet these conclusions have been seriously challenged by other researchers who claim that, at the very least, pornography clearly results in the overriding of female autonomy and it disinhibits men in their expression of aggression toward women. Pornography continues to be a major channel of sexual socialization and indoctrination for young men in our society (Duncan, 1990; Duncan & Donnelly, 1991). The ongoing controversy about this issue demands some serious critical thinking.

## 18.4 PROSTITUTION

The most significant factor regarding prostitution in North America is its relative decline (Bullough & Bullough, 1996). Current estimates are that there are anywhere from 84,000 to 2 million female prostitutes in the United States (Ward, Carter, & Perrin, 1994). It is also clear that most prostitutes leave "the life" after four or five years (Potterat et al., 1990). Fewer men now visit prostitutes, and they do so less frequently. A major reason for this is that rates for premarital sexual relationships among both men and women are rapidly approaching the same level. A second reason is that more women now have access to better-paying employment. A third reason is probably concern over HIV infection. Furthermore, husbands who are interpersonally or sexually incompatible with their wives may now divorce, rather than substitute the services of a prostitute. Fifty years ago, Kinsey and his colleagues (1948) found that about 69 percent of the white males in their sample had visited prostitutes. They concluded that even this figure represented a decline from previous generations and attributed the decline to increasing sexual activity on the part of unmarried women. Nonetheless there are few North American communities, whether urban or rural, where prostitution is unknown, and some researchers believe there is actually an increase in male prostitution (Earls & David, 1989). In contemporary Western industrialized society, several types of prostitutes are well recognized.

### Female Prostitutes
The *streetwalker* is the most visible and most numerous type of prostitute. Most often they are poor young women who are outfitted in gaudy or revealing clothing, and they solicit customers from among the men walking or driving by.

Some prostitutes work bars and hotels. They must usually pay the bar manager 40 to 50 percent of their earnings, and they encourage customers to run up a large bar tab before negotiating fees for sexual activity.

*Call girls* are typically from a more middle-class background and have more education than the streetwalker. Call girls are typically well-dressed and well-educated. They provide conversation and companionship, and can be presented as a "date" publicly. They will cater to the special interests of customers and will provide sexual activities in the customer's hotel room or in an apartment.

No matter what her level of operation, the prostitute is surrounded by an extensive circle of individuals who depend on her work to earn part or all of their own living. The *panderer* is a "broker" between the streetwalker or house prostitute and potential customers. In return for securing customers, he might demand a percentage of her earnings. The *pimp* functions as master, enforcer, bail and drug provider. The successful pimp accumulates a "stable" of prostitutes who give him all of their earnings. He then uses this money to live ostentatiously, and purchase drugs and attention-attracting wardrobes for the prostitutes. He might pay rent and other expenses for an apartment for the prostitute. Traditionally, a *madam* is a woman who operates a brothel, or whorehouse. During the 1980s, Sydney Biddle Barrows, descendent of a prominent American family with a genealogy said to date back to the Pilgrims, was often referred to as the "Mayflower Madam." She was arrested for operating an "escort service" that was a front for prostitution. Her case attracted national and international headlines because she ran the escort service according to the latest business principles learned through her Ivy League education. During the 1990s, Heidi Fleiss, the "Hollywood Madam," provided call girls for many well-known stars and entertainment executives.

Some have called for the *legalization* or at least the *decriminalization* of prostitution (Rio, 1991). Legalization implies that the state will collect taxes, issue licenses, require adherence to health laws, and otherwise regulate prostitution just as it regulates other types of business organizations. This is the path taken in certain counties in the state of Nevada. Decriminalization simply means the repeal of all laws against the exchange of sex for gain among consenting adults (Basow & Campanile, 1990) Organizations made up of former and working prostitutes advocate for better police and legal protection for prostitutes as well as improved health care. These groups desire to have prostitution viewed as "legitimate, dignified work" that is not different from the offering of other personal services.

Some see prostitution as an expression of women's right to control their own bodies. They also believe that the legitimization of prostitution is another step toward ending the double standard regarding male and female sexual behavior. They see legalization or decriminalization as ending male control over women's sexuality. However, others view prostitution as the continued exploitation and degradation of women and their bodies.

## Male Prostitutes

Like the streetwalker, *hustlers* are the most visible of male prostitutes. These are young men who cater to other men. A proportion of transvestites or presurgery transsexuals support themselves totally or partially by prostitution (*drag prostitutes*). They often attempt to fool customers into believing they are women and solicit money from them in return for performing fellatio or passive anal sex.

In male prisons young men (*punks*) often trade sexual favors for protection from other prisoners as well as for cigarettes, drugs, and other gifts. These men

Streetwalkers are merely the most visible segment of the prostitution industry.

Another type of streetwalker

may or may not consider themselves homosexual, and they may or may not continue their prostitution outside of prison.

Like his female counterpart, the *call boy* is well paid for his services. The kept boy often lives in the same household with an affluent older man, or "sugar daddy." He might have an official role in the household, such as driver or gardener.

*Gigolos* are attractive men who cater mainly to the social and sometimes sexual needs of wealthy older women.

## 18.4.1   The Psychology of Prostitution

Novels and movies are replete with male fantasies of the prostitute's life. One typical version of the fantasy prostitute is the "whore with a heart of gold." She is often depicted as a fun-loving, generous woman who loves sex or men so much that she has chosen a life of prostitution. The fantasy prostitute always exists as an independent woman, without parents or siblings and certainly without children. The hero marries her at the end of the story. Her clients are portrayed as attractive or of high social status.

The reality is quite different. The street prostitute typically lives a shortened life of drugs, violence, jail, and disease. Whatever their ethnic group, a majority come from backgrounds of poverty (Edgley, 1989) and early sexual and physical abuse (Simons & Whitbeck, 1991). One study (Earls & David, 1990) found that several factors distinguished the family backgrounds of both female and male prostitutes from the backgrounds of socially comparable nonprostitutes. These factors included a high incidence of childhood physical abuse, sexual contact with a family member, and the occurrence of that sexual contact at a very early age. Running away from home at an early age is often an attempt to escape from this abuse. These runaways find themselves without resources on the streets of urban centers. Thus, for many of these young women, prostitution is merely a way of surviving. Most are of average intelligence, but except for call girls, they are not very well educated. Many child and teenage prostitutes have been neglected or abandoned by parents or relatives, and a number of them show high levels of psychological disturbance. A study of adult Belgian prostitutes also revealed similarly high levels of psychological disturbance (DeSchampheleire, 1990).

Overall, there is little information about the male hustler. One group of researchers collected data on the psychological characteristics of 211 hustlers from the streets of New Orleans (Simon et al., 1992). Their profiles were compared to psychiatric outpatients and nonpatients. Contrary to police and press impressions of hustlers as violent and chaotic individuals, these researchers found them to be "calm, cooperative, insightful and extremely open" (Simon et al., 1992). The disturbance level of these participants was well below that of psychiatric outpatients, and only two of the hustlers showed any disturbance that even approached diagnosable levels. The authors concluded that, given recurring problems with police, physical violence from customers, chronic substance abuse, a lack of job skills, and the ever-present threat of contracting a fatal disease, these young men functioned remarkably well.

Alcohol and other chemical abuse are high among hustlers, and many accept these substances in place of money. Intravenous drug use is high and needle sharing is common (Morse et al., 1992). Cates and Markley (1992) studied a group of Indiana male prostitutes who described themselves as having chosen this type of work. The group studied by these researchers had regular jobs and hustled part-time to supplement their income through prostitution.

Until recently, the customers ("johns" or "tricks") were the invisible characters in studies of prostitution. They were seldom arrested, and when they were arrested, there was great concern about damage to their reputations. In general, the prostitute has been viewed as the "deviant" and her customer has been viewed as "normal."

Two studies of female street prostitutes identified two distinct groups of male clients. The larger group was an essentially white suburban group who drove in to the central city for the purpose of engaging in sex with prostitutes. A second group consisted of local residents who were mostly African American. A majority of men from both groups had repeated contacts with the same individual or small group of prostitutes (Freund, Lee, & Leonard, 1991; Freund, Leonard, & Lee, 1989).

A study of a small group of customers of male prostitutes in New Orleans revealed that 40 percent were married and identified themselves as heterosexual. About 53 percent identified themselves as bisexual, and only 1 of the total of 15 customers surveyed identified himself as homosexual (Morse et al., 1992).

## 18.4.2   Prostitution and HIV

Regardless of gender, the prostitute is very vulnerable to both contract and transmit HIV and other STIs. In developing countries, where HIV is overwhelmingly a heterosexual problem, prostitution *is* the major factor in the spread of HIV. But no matter where she or he lives, the prostitute typically has many partners, and this makes exposure to HIV via blood and semen very likely. Intravenous drug use is rampant among North American prostitutes and needle sharing is commonplace. Once infected, they are very likely to

# DIMENSIONS OF DIVERSITY

## PROSTITUTION IN THREE CULTURES

### THAILAND: THE SEX BARS OF BANGKOK

The brothels and sex bars of Bangkok make a substantial contribution to Thailand's economy. They are also at the center of its HIV epidemic. Anywhere from 20 to 70 percent of Thai sex workers are seropositive (Grove, 1996). Nonetheless, the young sex workers of Bangkok provide life's basic necessities for their impoverished families all over rural Thailand.

Thai, Japanese, Australian, European, and American men are the usual patrons of the sex bars and shows. Customers pay about $12 to $15 to enter. Sitting with a "bar girl" requires purchasing her drinks and paying an additional fee to have sex with her. The women wear numbers around their necks so they can be "ordered" by patrons, and the price for sexual acts varies from $20 to $40. Quick sex occurs in small rooms, but oral sex may be performed in public view. The women are paid about $80 per month and supplement this with their prostitution activities and by performing in the bars. Stage performances consist of women performing sexual tricks, such as inserting and releasing ping-pong balls or strings of razor blades from their vaginas. Pairs or trios of performers assume various coital positions on stage. Gay bars have comparable young male performers.

Many sex workers have children, and Thai culture emphasizes a mother's responsibility to provide for her family (Muercke, 1992). Traditionally, she would do this by farming, but her work as a prostitute is viewed within this tradition. Sex work is socially disapproved, but it is seen as terrible work done for a worthwhile purpose. Prostitutes earn considerably more than domestic or factory workers. Most sex workers seek to return to their native villages and families, but the specter of HIV makes this highly unlikely (Manderson, 1992).

### RUSSIA: EXPANDING ITS EXPORTS

In some areas of the new Russia, unemployment among women runs as high as 75 percent, so many young women are tempted by the opportunity to travel and live abroad. Some know they are being recruited for prostitution, while others naively believe they will work as dancers, waitresses, and hostesses all over Western Europe ("Organized Export of Prostitutes from CIS Is Flourishing," 1993). Organized crime networks rotate the women through a circuit of Western cities via falsified tourist visas. When these documents are confiscated, the women are left isolated and frightened in a strange land. Gang enforcers beat and disfigure women who want out of the sex industry.

Turkey's Black Sea region has been invaded by thousands of "Natashas," with a resulting upsurge of divorce, gonorrhea, and syphilis. In the Middle East, planeloads of Russian women disembark in Dubai, earn hard currency for the duration of their fourteen-day visas, and then return home, carrying television sets and other Western luxuries. Meanwhile, in Tel Aviv, Israel, the number of brothels has gone from 30 to 150 over the last five years, most of them staffed with Russians. Media ads hawk the "hot new Russians." Some are poor immigrants, but most are there on temporary tourist visas. In Asia, many Chinese and Japanese bars tout the presence of new blonde, blue-eyed Russian "hostesses." Even in rundown, wartorn Kac, Serbia, a Ukrainian woman proudly boasts of the money she can make to support her parents and baby daughter who remain back home (Hornblower, 1993).

### AMSTERDAM: THE "WALLETJES"

In the Netherlands, prostitution is both open and legal. The streets of Amsterdam's well-policed red-light district consist of many windowed establishments in which women and young men sit, making themselves available to passersby. Some walk the street in revealing clothing or costumes that imply more paraphilic sexual services. There are also sex shows and shops selling erotica. The Erotic Museum contains erotic objects from previous ages and from all over the world. The Prostitution Information Center is available to help visitors locate special services such as sex workers who can accommodate disabled individuals. It also publishes a price list for specific sexual acts (Kelland, 1995). Amsterdam Call Girls is a sex workers collective. Sex club owners are contemplating publishing a Michelin-style guidebook, and government officials are considering a pension plan for sex workers. It is estimated that thirty thousand people work in the Dutch sex industry, and presently there is some ambiguity about the laws governing them. Prostitution is legal, but the sex clubs and brothels in which many work are not. Laws now under consideration would legalize these establishments, provide tougher penalties for those who abuse minors or push adults into prostitution, and make condom use compulsory. Prostitutes will enjoy pensions and other benefits, but will have to begin paying heavy income taxes (Conradi, 1995). A trade union, FNV, is attempting to assist sex workers to adapt to their new legalized status. Similar bills have been quashed in the past, but there is a new impetus for passage.

pass the virus to their sexual partners as well as to customers, who might then infect their wives and other sexual partners. An added problem is that street prostitutes tend to continue their sexual activities even after testing positive for HIV (Bellis, 1990; Morse et al., 1992). The male prostitute is considered a powerful bridge in the infection of heterosexual women. Many of the customers of male prostitutes are bisexual or heterosexual and have wives or female lovers with whom they do not use condoms (Morse et al., 1992).

Frequency of condom use appears varied. A study of New York City street and bar hustlers (Pleak & Meyer-Bahlburg, 1990) reported that condoms were used 85 percent of the time in anal intercourse. However, they were less likely to engage in these safer sex techniques with their male lovers and least of all with their female partners. Another study of hustlers in New Orleans (Morse et al., 1992) revealed that fewer than half their customers requested a condom. These men reported that even when the prostitute was the active partner in anal intercourse, 67 percent of their customers did not request a condom. A comparable study of female street prostitutes in a northeastern industrial city found that condoms were used in 72 percent of vaginal ejaculations and in 33 percent of oral ejaculations (Freund, Lee, & Leonard, 1991).

A sample of 182 mostly African American streetwalkers in San Francisco revealed that 7.7 percent tested positive for HIV (Dorfman, Derish, & Cohen, 1992). A comparable study of a large sample of New Orleans street and bar hustlers found 17 percent to test positive for HIV (Morse et al., 1991; Morse et al., 1992; Simon et al., 1992). A sampling of street hustlers in Atlanta found almost 30 percent to test positive for HIV (Elifson, Boles, & Sweat, 1993). Finally, researchers studying a small group of transvestite prostitutes found that 68 percent tested positive for HIV (Elifson et al., 1993).

## 18.5 COERCIVE AND VIOLENT SEXUAL BEHAVIOR

Surveys of the general population such as the National Health and Social Life Survey (Laumann et al., 1994) lead to the sad prediction that if your class is typical, several members are likely to be survivors of child sexual abuse or sexual assault. Some will have experienced, or will know someone who has experienced, sexual harassment, either in school or at work. This is an important fact to keep in mind as you read about and discuss these topics. For many students, this material merely covers the dark side of human sexual behavior, whereas for others it touches on personal life experiences that are profoundly painful and

disturbing. For still others, a family member, friend, romantic partner, or spouse may have been deeply affected by an experience of sexual coercion or violence. Thus, it is important to be sensitive to the feelings and reactions of others as you discuss these topics in class.

This section will discuss men as the perpetrators of sexual coercion and violence, and females and young boys as their targets or victims. Women *do* sexually abuse and assault others, but this is rare (Laumann et al., 1994). Many adult men also suffer directly or indirectly from the effect of such violations (Remer & Ferguson, 1995). If not survivors themselves, they cope with the suspicions and fears of the women they meet and become involved with. Their partners, daughters, sisters, wives, and mothers all have been affected by the threat of coercive and violent sexual behavior.

### 18.5.1 Making the Invisible Man Visible

Issues of sexual coercion and sexual violence were essentially absent from the research and clinical literature about sexuality until the 1970s (Leidig, 1992). Today, there is a mountain of information to help both professionals and laypeople understand the nature of sexual coercion and violence and how one can try to protect oneself and one's family from it (Muehlenhard, 1994). This effort, spearheaded by survivors of sexual violence and by feminist psychologists (Ward, 1995), has been referred to as a sucessful attempt to make the invisible man visible. Since the 1970s, the formerly vague figure of the predatory male—whether sexual harasser, rapist, or child molester—have become much clearer and more distinct. The general public has undergone a profound education about the nature and prevalence of coercive and violent sexuality. In spite of this greater awareness, there are certain ways of thinking about coercion and violence that make dealing with these problems very difficult (Leidig, 1992). Some of these problematic attitudes are these:

1. *Minimization.* No matter their gender, some individuals refuse to take coercive sexual behavior seriously and might actively demean the person who "makes such a big deal" over such behavior. They might ignore or reject someone who appears to be suffering after an experience of sexual coercion or violence.

2. *Directionality.* Because sexual coercion and violence are mainly perpetrated by males upon women and children, it is often difficult to talk openly about these problems. Men might feel defensive or ashamed, and women might feel

angry or overly protective of the men who are present during discussions.

3. *Trivialization.* Sexual coercion and violence are often joked about by both women and men. It is even normalized by frequent and eroticized presentations by various media, especially in pornography (Scully & Marolla, 1985).

4. *Collusion.* Often women are blamed for male coercion and sexual violence. For example, a mother might be blamed for her husband's incestuous behavior, or a wife might be blamed for her husband's rape of another women. It is very important to place responsibility for these harmful behaviors directly on the adults who carry them out.

5. *Blaming the victim.* Women might be blamed for dressing or behaving "provocatively," or little girls punished for behaving "seductively." Again, this diverts responsibility from the perpetrator. Social psychologists understand that when we lapse into blaming the victim, we are just trying to convince ourselves that "it couldn't happen to me because I don't dress that way, act that way, or live in that part of town." Nevertheless, blaming the victim prevents us from really confronting the scope and significance of sexual coercion and violence (Ellis, 1994).

6. *"Female masochism."* Some continue to hold on to outmoded ideas that women connect sexual pleasure with physical and emotional pain. These notions are believed by many to be dead, but they sometimes persist where one least expects them: among health care professionals, among mental health workers, and even in the legal system.

7. *Psychopathology.* Many prefer to believe that men who harass, molest, or rape are mentally ill. This idea protects us from having to face the fact that the causes of sexual coercion and violence are embedded in our social norms, and especially in our society's **gender-role ideology** (see chapter 12). Studies of incarcerated sex offenders suggest that a small proportion are mentally ill, but they are only about 2 percent of men who engage in coercive or violent sexual behavior (Leidig, 1992; Scully & Marolla, 1985).

## 18.6   SEXUAL HARASSMENT

Unwelcome sexual advances, requests for sexual favors, and other verbal or physical conduct of a sexual nature constitute sexual harassment when (1) submission to such conduct is made explicitly or

Sexual harassment occurs in many settings, but most often in settings where there are clear differences in power and authority.

implicitly a term or condition of an individual's employment, (2) submission to or rejection of such conduct is used as a basis for employment decisions affecting such individuals, or (3) such conduct has the purpose or effect of unreasonably interfering with an individual's work performance or creating an intimidating, hostile, or offensive working environment. (Equal Employment Opportunity Commission, 1980, pp. 74676–77)

The term **sexual harassment** did not come into use until the early 1970s. Today this term is fairly common, and the Anita Hill/Clarence Thomas hearings of 1991 gave the American public a general sense of what it implies. While the definition above clearly applies to work situations, the concept of sexual harassment has gradually been extended beyond the workplace. It now includes sexual coercion in academic settings and in professional-client relationships.

Currently, there are four types of behaviors that may be considered sexual harassment. In the first, someone with power over another person communicates to that less powerful person that her or his sexual favors are expected in return for employment, promotion, raises, grades, or academic success. This overt attempt at sexual coercion is often referred to as *quid pro quo* harassment. The second type of sexual harassment includes the creation of *"hostile environment."* This could include being subjected to unwanted sexual remarks, pictures, or sexually degrading employment policies. For example, male

| **gender-role ideology** | society's *general* beliefs and norms regarding how girls and boys or women and men should be (behavior, traits, etc.) |
| **sexual harassment** | sexual coercion that occurs in situations of unequal power |

## HEALTHY SEXUALITY

### IF YOU ARE THE TARGET OF SEXUAL HARASSMENT

Both women and men may experience sexual harassment, but most targets are women. It is important to understand that there is a pervasive belief that women create their own sexual problems, because "blaming the victim" is a very strong part of our culture's *gender-role ideology* (see chapter 12). Also, perpetrators often don't believe they are doing anything wrong. They often truly believe that the target's reaction is extreme. Most women and men try to deal with sexual harassment by ignoring it (Powell, 1991), but this is seldom effective and can lead to an escalation. Women with higher self-esteem deal with the problem assertively. Powell (1996) offers the following general guidelines to minimize sexual harassment in the workplace.

1. Be professionally pleasant rather than overly friendly.
2. When work problems arise, don't try to "smooth things over" with extra smiles, touches, or cuddles.
3. Avoid playful flirtatiousness.
4. Respond only to appropriate comments.

If the person persists and you feel you are being sexually harassed, Powell (1996) recommends you do the following:

1. Avoid being alone with the harasser.
2. Create and maintain a careful descriptive record of incidents as well as any formal or informal complaints you lodge, including those with the harasser. These records should include

where the incident occurred.

time and date of occurrence.

what exactly happened.

what was said.

how you felt.

names of any witnesses or others who have been harassed by this person at this company or institution. It is very likely there are other workers or students who have been harassed.

3. Use your judgment about the best way to proceed in the particular organization. In some places it is legal to make secret recordings of the harassing comments, in others it is not. In some organizations it is best to arrange a talk with the harasser, or to write a letter. In other situations it is best to proceed through official channels such as a supervisor, department chair, affirmative action officer, or union representative. If a conversation or letter is determined to be the best approach, it should cover three items:

A description of what happened: for example, "You often say things about my body or clothing."

A description of the effect on you: "I feel threatened and cannot concentrate during class."

A description of what changes you would like to happen: e.g., "I want you to stop making sexual remarks and to stop touching me."

From Elizabeth Powell, *Sex on Your Terms*. Copyright © 1996 by Allyn and Bacon. Adapted by permission.

---

servers in a restaurant are told to wear long trousers, a shirt, and a tie, while female servers are told to bare their legs to the thigh and display cleavage. A third category of sexually harassing behaviors involves *"aggressive acts"* by supervisors, coworkers, instructors, and so on. These could include anything from unwanted touching or fondling to full-scale sexual assault. A fourth type of sexual harassment is referred to as *"third-party effects."* How would you feel if you knew that someone else in your class was guaranteed an A in the course and admission to a prestigious graduate program or job interview just because she or he had a sexual relationship with your professor? In the workplace, a sexual relationship between a supervisor and a particular employee has a negative effect on all the other "third parties" in the department or company. For some practical advice regarding sexual harassment on the job, see "Healthy Sexuality: If You Are the Target of Sexual Harassment."

### 18.6.1 Prevalence and Impact of Sexual Harassment in the Workplace

While estimates vary, several large-scale surveys suggest that almost half of all working women will encounter some type of sexual harassment, as will about 15 percent of working men (Charney & Russell,

# GO ASK ALICE

*Dear Alice:*

*My girlfriend just broke up with me after one year of relationship. She gave me no reason. She says she has no time to give anyone. Last night I called her every half hour, but she didn't want to pick up the phone. This morning, she told me that if I keep calling her, or keep showing up at her house, or try to follow her, she will call the police and sue me. My question is: is it against the law if I am trying to get in touch with her by being the same place she is? Is it against the law if I wait for her at her front door?*

*Home Alone*

Dear Home Alone,

It seems clear that your ex-girlfriend doesn't want to see you, talk to you or anything else right now. You need to leave her alone right now. She has been definite and clear about her wishes. You absolutely need to back off and stay away from her. By continuing to call her, you are HARASSING her. This is considered stalking, and is illegal. If she gets an order of protection and you keep persisting in these behaviors, you could be arrested. What you are describing is very serious. You need to leave your ex-girlfriend alone for awhile, or maybe forever.

 http://www.mhhe.com/byer6

---

1994; Fitzgerald, 1993). Rates of sexual harassment against women are generally higher in areas where women are underrepresented, such as firefighting, mining, and medicine. However, it is estimated that fewer than 7 percent of all those affected ever report the problem. While about 90 percent of those affected experience some psychological and/or physical symptoms, fewer than 12 percent ever seek counseling or other assistance (Charney & Russell, 1994). In a survey of Japanese women, 70 percent reported at least one incident of sexual harassment at the workplace, as did 50 percent of women surveyed in several European countries (Castro, 1992). Research suggests that there is a widespread gender difference in perceiving certain behaviors and situations as sexual harassment. Men tend to label an interaction as sexual harassment only if *the woman's reactions are negative.* Women tend to call an observed interaction sexual harassment based on the *man's conduct or actions,* regardless of the woman's reactions (Williams & Cyr, 1992).

It is clear that sexual harassment has far-reaching negative consequences. These include emotional distress, disrupted family relationships, job loss, decreased morale and job satisfaction, increased absenteeism, and disturbed interpersonal relationships at work (Barak, 1994). Targets of harassment are more likely to experience anxiety, depression, headaches, sleep disturbance, gastrointestinal disorders, weight change, nausea, and sexual dysfunction. Some victims report elevated fears of rape (Fitzgerald, 1993). Victims are often blamed for provoking the harasser by their dress or demeanor. Complainants are often disbelieved by management, administrators, or other officials, especially when the perpetrator is of high status. Read about one working student's actual experiences in "Case Study: One Experience of Sexual Harassment."

## 18.6.2  Sexual Harassment in Academia

Romantic relationships between teachers and their students have long been a well-recognized fact of life on most American college campuses (Epperson & Rochman, 1995). However, with the growing understanding of sexual harassment, and the growing number of successful sexual harassment lawsuits against professors and institutions, many educational institutions and the academicians within them are working hard to define the line between the right to privacy and exploitive relationships in academia. Administrators recognize that there is a power differential between teacher and student, and when a sexual relationship also exists, there is the potential for exploitation and favoritism. Some institutions have enacted total bans on relationships between students and teachers, but they have found these policies too problematic. Most now merely "discourage" such relationships. When they occur, sexual relationships between faculty and students can demoralize other students, fracture academic departments, and seriously impair the functioning of the student and faculty member involved.

## ONE EXPERIENCE OF SEXUAL HARASSMENT

*Rebecca A. Whicker*

I had worked for my new boss approximately three weeks when it happened. I went into his office to discuss a memorandum with him. He was seated behind his desk, and I stood in front of the desk and turned the memo around so he could read it. He said he couldn't see it, got up, and came around the desk. He stood behind me pressing his body into my backside. I immediately left his office and sat at my desk, shaking. I was stunned, and had no idea what to do. I always thought I could handle a situation like this on my own, and had even remarked smugly about the Clarence Thomas/Anita Hill sexual harassment hearings, thinking Dr. Hill should have been able to handle her problem on her own. I was soon to learn what it was like to walk a mile in her shoes.

I was afraid to make a formal complaint of sexual harassment. I lived in a small southern town and worked for a very "public" company. If word leaked out that an Executive Vice President of this company sexually harassed one of his employees, the local press would be all over it. I would lose my job and never work in that town again. My ten years of hard work with that company had gotten me a good salary, and no local firm could compete with it.

Finally, I reported the incident to a Vice President who already knew of several similar incidents involving my boss. No action was taken. My stress and discomfort level skyrocketed each day I went to work. I reported the incident to another executive, and many weeks later I had a meeting with the "brass." After hearing my story, the company president minimized the incident and expressed surprise that I would make such a fuss. After another executive urged action, the president conceded to reporting the matter to the corporate attorneys, having the harasser counseled, and making him apologize to me. It was also suggested that I be moved away from my boss, to a lower position, at a lower salary. I protested and they agreed to maintain my salary at the new position under two conditions: I had to go through a phony "job interview" process and the incident was never to be discussed again. All records would disappear. I felt angry, bitter and betrayed. I had worked so hard to earn some status and respect and these were taken away in a few minutes at that meeting.

How did this all end? The harasser insisted he did not remember the incident. Nevertheless, I finally received a cursory apology. I later learned that several other women in the company had been subjected to various indignities: his hand up their skirts, an offer for a drive home when a husband was out of town, and at least two pinches on the behind. The harasser did not lose his job, and received large raises for his "good performance." He remained in his position for four more years. After one more incident of sexual harassment, the Board of Directors gave the president an ultimatum: either fire the harasser or lose his own job. The perpetrator was asked to resign on grounds other than sexual harassment.

---

However, in creating and enforcing antiharassment policies, administrators must be sure they are not damaging the important tradition of academic freedom. For example, worried faculty might shy away from classroom discussions of theories of gender inferiority, or administrators might censor artistic exhibits involving male or female nudity for fear of creating a "hostile environment." It is also important to distinguish between *feeling* sexually harassed and the actual *harassing conduct* of another. For example, some students or faculty might *feel* uncomfortable when they view, read, or discuss material related to homosexuality or watch videos about coitus or abortion. They might view such class activities as threatening or coercive (Stern, 1993). As difficult as it may be, the instructor's *intentions* have to be considered in determining whether sexual harassment has occurred.

Another aspect of sexual harassment involves lesbian women and gay men. Bias and discrimination against gay and lesbian people is called **heterosexism.** Some students, faculty, and administrators feel comfortable about making derogatory remarks or threats against lesbian women and gay men (**gay bashing**). D'Augelli (1992) conducted a survey at a large university and found that about half of his 315 gay and lesbian respondents had experienced verbal insults on more than one occasion, while about one-third reported never having been insulted. Seven percent reported they had been threatened with physical violence on more than one occasion.

## 18.6.3 Sexually Exploitive Professionals

In the professions, most cases of sexual exploitation take place between a powerful male professional and a female client. The second most common scenario involves a male professional and a male client. The

A satirical view of traditional attitudes toward accusations of rape and sexual assault.

MAXINE! COMIX. Copyright © Marian Henley. Reprinted by permission of the artist.

rarest instances occur between female professionals, and clients of either sex (Levine, Risen, & Althof, 1994). Relationships that occur in the professional-client "forbidden zone" can severally damage both the client and the professional in terms of self-concept, guilt, identity, and the ability to trust oneself and others (Rutter, 1989).

### Therapist-Client Relationships

Virtually all of the professional organizations that oversee therapists and counselors are clear that once a professional relationship is begun, any "dual relationship," especially a sexual or romantic relationship, is *unethical*. Furthermore, such relationships are *illegal* in at least fifteen states (Foster, 1996).

### Physician-Patient Relationships

Physician misconduct with patients is probably less common than therapist misconduct with a client, yet it has a similarly negative impact on patients. The American Medical Association and the Canadian Medical Association clearly prohibit sexual activity with patients (Abel, Barrett, & Gardos, 1992; Carr & Robinson, 1990).

### Clergy-Layperson Relationships

Recently, there has been growing attention to sexual misconduct between clergy and church members. Many clergy appear to be poorly educated or trained on how to deal with their own feelings about church members (Foster, 1996). Even though these relationships are between consenting adults, there still exists an imbalance of power between the clergyperson and the church member, as in other professional relationships.

What should you say to a mental health professional, physician, nurse, dentist, attorney, or cler-

gyperson who suggests anything sexual? In the words of Elizabeth Powell in her very useful book *Sex on Your Terms* (1996): "Good-bye!"

## 18.7  RAPE AND SEXUAL ASSAULT

Look at the title of this section. Aren't rape and sexual assault the same thing? Many students are surprised to learn that in many states or provinces, the crime of rape is defined rather narrowly as *forcible penetration of the vagina by the penis*. Decades of research have shown us that in crimes of sexual violence, many other acts are committed that do not fit this description. There might be anal penetration, fellatio, mutilation of the genitals, breasts, or other parts of the body, penetration of orifices with objects, or the victim (regardless of gender) might be made to do or endure other degrading acts (Rozee, 1993). Thus, the broader term *sexual assault* is often used by researchers (Muehlenhard et al., 1992).

Students are also often surprised (and sometimes outraged) to learn that the first laws against rape treated it as a "property crime" (Brownmiller, 1975). That is, when a girl or woman was sexually assaulted, the law assumed that damage had been done to a father's or husband's property and *he* should be compensated for that damage. Other legal and religious traditions around such assaults included the punishment or execution of the woman along with

| heterosexism | attitudes and behaviors that denigrate and stigmatize nonheterosexual behavior |
| gay-bashing | verbal insults or physical threats and harm aimed at gay and lesbian people |

her assailant. Many of us find such ideas repellant, but we are still left with some remnants of these sexist views. For example, up until the 1970s, many states required the testimony of an eyewitness before the complaints of a woman claiming to be raped would be considered by authorities (Donat & D'Emilio, 1992)! Even today, the ethnicity, social class, dress, demeanor, and even occupation of a woman enters into how her claim of rape will be treated. In a survey of 248 women, Wyatt (1992) found that a similar proportion of African American and white women in her sample reported attempted or completed rapes (25 percent and 20 percent, respectively), and the psychological impact of sexual assault was equivalent for members of both groups. However, African American women were significantly less likely to disclose the assault to others, including authorities. This researcher interpreted this finding in terms of how the rape complaints of black women have traditionally been trivialized or ignored.

### 18.7.1 Types of Rape and Sexual Assault

*Acquaintance/Date Rape*

When most people hear the term *rape,* their usual image is of a stranger appearing out of the dark and accosting a woman he doesn't know. This is actually a relatively rare occurrence. In about 80 percent of rapes or sexual assaults, the perpetrator is known to the victim (Ellis, 1994; Koss, 1992). Take a look at table 18.1 to examine some findings regarding the perpetrators of acquaintance rape. One study of campus rapes revealed that 84 percent of the women who had been sexually assaulted knew their attackers (Finley & Corty, 1993). Yet many researchers believe that only about 16 percent of acquaintance rapes are reported (Benson, Charlton, & Goodhart, 1992; National Victims Center, 1992). The following are some of the reasons for this underreporting.

**TABLE 18.1** PERPETRATORS OF ACQUAINTANCE RAPE*

| Perpetrators | Percentage of Acquaintance Rape |
| --- | --- |
| Husbands | 9% |
| Fathers/stepfathers | 11% |
| Other relatives | 16% |
| Boyfriends | 10% |
| Friends, coworkers | 29% |

*This data is based on incidents of acquaintance rape reported to authorities. What differences would you predict in these figures if they included both reported and unreported instances of acquaintance rape?

**Source:** From M. P. Koss, "Date Rape: Victimization by Acquaintance" in *Harvard Mental Health Letter,* 9(3), 5–6, 1992. Reprinted with permission of Harvard School Health Publications Group, Boston, MA.

1. Her experience might not fit into her **intrapersonal sexual script** of what a "real" rape is, even though she experiences all of the same physical and psychological trauma as those who experience a stranger rape (Kahn, Mathie, & Torgler, 1994).

2. She might blame herself or be aware that others are likely to blame her for "going there," "saying this," or "wearing that" (Kormos & Brooks, 1994).

3. She might be unable to recall the assault clearly because of alcohol or drug use.

4. She might mistrust the police and legal system.

5. She might fear reprisals from the rapist, his friends, or his family.

6. She might fear the publicity that can accompany accusations of rape.

There is a body of research that indicates that one of the bases for acquaintance rape is miscommunication between the genders (Sawyer, Desmond, & Lucke, 1993). Men have been found to interpret many kinds of friendly behavior as sexual invitations when women had no such intent (Abbey, 1987; Berkowitz, 1992).

How common are rape and sexual assault? Several studies suggest that between one-fourth and one-third of college women surveyed report at least one experience of forced sexual contact (Caron & Brossoit, 1992; Reilly et al., 1992) and about one-third of male respondents indicated they had forced sex upon a woman at some time. A great many of these assaults are related to high alcohol use by college men and women. Incidents of sexual assault, especially by groups, or "gang rape," are particularly associated with campus fraternities and athletic teams (Frintner & Rubinson, 1993; Sanday, 1990). For some guidelines for preventing heterosexual acquaintance rape, see "Healthy Sexuality: Reducing the Likelihood of Acquaintance Rape."

*Statutory Rape*

The term *statutory rape* refers to sexual relations with a female who is below the legal age of consent. This age of consent varies from twelve to sixteen years in different states and Canadian provinces. Beginning in the 1960s, changes in sexual norms led to a somewhat more accepting view of adult sexual activity with young teens, but this attitude appears to be changing. Recent studies indicate that in the United States, 60 percent of babies born to unmarried teen mothers were fathered by adult males. California has the nation's highest teen pregnancy rate and has recently begun a program to prosecute men who have sex with underage girls. Connecticut and Florida are considering similar programs (Gleick, 1996). Do you know the age of consent in your state or province?

### Stranger Rape

Stranger rape is the type of rape that the general public believes is most prevalent. Most rape prevention efforts are aimed at this relatively infrequent occurrence. Groth and Hobson (1983) described three types of rape. In the *anger rape,* the perpetrator seems more focused on venting his rage and contempt against women than in any sexual gratification. His victim is usually injured physically and subjected to severe degradation. The assailant usually does not have an orgasm. These attacks are usually impulsive and typically triggered by a conflict with a spouse or lover.

The *power rapist* focuses on complete power and control over his target. Such attacks are usually planned and repetitive and tend to increase in frequency over time. The assailant uses just enough force to make his target submissive. The power rapist usually feels he is an economic and social failure and seeks to assert his masculinity and sense of worth.

In a *sadistic rape,* ritualistic violence, often involving bondage, torture, and genital mutilation, is committed against a victim. The rapist's aggression is eroticized. Such assaults are preplanned, and often the perpetrator has a history of heavy use of violent pornography.

Whether perpetrated by an acquaintance or by a stranger, rapes and sexual assaults are not always as easily distinguishable as the previous classification suggests.

### Marital Rape

Does a wife have a legally protected right to refuse sexual relations with her husband? Up until quite recently, she did not. The traditional *marital rape exemption* dates back to a seventeenth-century legal concept according to which a wife had contracted, through matrimony, for sex with her husband and could not retract this. On the basis of this concept, the first marital rape exemption law was passed in Massachusetts in 1857, and all other states followed. Today, all fifty states have eliminated the legal exemption for marital rape. Most marital rapes take place in marriages where wife battering and other forms of domestic violence occur (Frieze, 1983). In 1995, Muslim delegates to the United Nations had marital rape *excluded* from a human rights resolution on violence against women (Kelly, 1996).

### Male Rape

The National Health and Social Life Survey (Laumann et al., 1994) found that 1.5 percent of female respondents said they had forced a man to have sex at least once. While many find the idea of male rape trivial or even humorous, the reality of male rape is as gruesome as its female counterpart. Male rape is often perpetrated by two or more adult heterosexual males against an adolescent or young adult male, who might be gay or heterosexual (Hickson et al., 1994). The primary purpose is to humiliate and degrade the victim. The victim is typically anally penetrated, forced to perform fellatio, or perhaps mutilated in some way. Compared to rape against females, male rape often results in a higher level of physical damage to the victim's body (McMullen, 1990). A few cases of one or more females restraining and forcing a male into sexual activity have also been reported (Sarrel & Masters, 1982).

Male rape occurs fairly frequently in prisons (Ben-David & Silfen, 1993; McMullen, 1990). The young inmate might be attacked by a gang of older convicts. A victim often perceives himself to have one of two choices: become the common property of these gangs or place himself under the protection of an older, tough convict who will offer protection from other inmates in exchange for sexual favors.

## 18.7.2 The Impact of Rape and Sexual Assault

The National Health and Social Life Survey (Laumann et al., 1994) found that about 22 percent of women surveyed reported they had engaged in sex against their will after they had been threatened or felt they had no choice. However, only 2.8 percent of male respondents indicated they had ever forced sex on someone. This discrepancy suggests that many men did not understand how coercive their demands were or the impact of their behavior on women.

What happens to an individual during and after an experience of forced sex? Immediately after a rape or sexual assault (the *crisis period*), the survivor's physical state is of initial concern. Stab wounds, bleeding, bruises, and other injuries need immediate attention. Drugs may be administered to prevent the possibility of pregnancy, and tests for all STIs, including HIV, must be given. Psychologically, the victim might display all of the signs and symptoms of rape trauma syndrome (Burgess & Holmstrom, 1974), which is a type of post-traumatic stress disorder (Becker & Kaplan, 1991). The survivor might experience flashbacks to the assault and have recurrent,

| intrapersonal sexual script | scripts are culture-bound, learned guidelines regarding any aspect of sexual expression. For example, most people believe that rapes are committed by strangers. |
|---|---|

## HEALTHY SEXUALITY

### REDUCING THE LIKELIHOOD OF ACQUAINTANCE RAPE: A GUIDE FOR MEN AND WOMEN

**For Men**

1. Be able to hear and respect a "no" from a prospective sexual partner. Your desires may be strong, but you can control your behavior.
2. Do not assume that because you have spent a great deal of money on a date, she "owes" you sexual activity.
3. Do not assume that sexy clothing or flirtatiousness automatically implies a willingness to have sex. Recognize that traditional gender-role socialization encourages women to look as sexy and appealing as possible. But it also teaches them to be less willing to engage in casual sex.
4. Be direct. Ask her what she wants to do regarding sex. If she is unclear, back off.
5. Do not assume that having sexual relations on a previous occasion entitles you to sex on a later occasion.
6. Avoid the overuse of alcohol and other drugs. Remember that a situation in which a woman *cannot freely give consent* constitutes rape or sexual assault. Both partners should be able to think and communicate effectively.

**For Women**

1. Know that you have a right to set limits in an intimate encounter. To do so effectively, you must know your limits.
2. Be assertive. Clearly state your interests and/or limits.
3. Be aware that men might interpret flirtatiousness and revealing clothing as sexual invitations. You have been raised to make yourself as appealing and attractive to men as you possibly can, but this aspect of gender-role socialization can backfire.
4. If you are not interested in sex, avoid vulnerable situations.
5. Trust your feelings. If you feel there is danger of forced sex, you are probably right. Take steps to decrease or avoid the danger.
6. Avoid the overuse of alcohol and drugs. You should be able to think and communicate effectively.

From Elizabeth Powell, *Sex on Your Terms.* Copyright © 1996 by Allyn and Bacon. Adapted by permission.

intrusive memories of the event. Other responses include emotional numbness, high levels of anxiety, depression, lowered self-esteem, social adjustment problems, agitation, and hyperalertness.

The second phase—the *recovery phase*—usually involves a long-term reorganization of the survivor's life. This may include a change of residence, a change of job, and changes in family and social relationships. The survivor must regain her sense of basic security and trust in others, and she might need a means of expressing her anger. In many cities and on many campuses, Take Back the Night marches and demonstrations serve to help survivors heal by sharing their experiences with others and to educate the public about the nature and prevalence of rape and sexual assault. A small number of survivors appear to have a *silent rape reaction.* They may insist on quickly trying to "forget what happened and put it behind me." Often these survivors have an explosive reaction several months or years later.

The existence of rape and sexual assault in our society affects all women. Some writers have referred to

this pervasive sense of threat as "the hum" (Rozee-Koker, Wynne, & Mizrahi, 1989). The idea here is that the threat and fear of sexual aggression is *always* in the background of all women's lives, and that they have unknowingly adapted to it. The "hum" restricts a woman's freedom of movement. It affects the kinds of jobs and work hours she will consider, the kinds of clothing she will wear, how late she studies at the library, where she parks her car, how often she buys a new car rather than repairs an old one, and hundreds of other everyday considerations. The "hum" pushes her to pay more for housing that she believes is "safer" and for extra lighting and security devices, and often shapes how she relates and responds to *all* men. Are any aspects of your life, or your partner's life, affected by "the hum"? You may want to explore this in class.

### 18.7.3 Psychological Recovery from Rape and Sexual Assault

Experience has shown that individual counseling immediately after the assault and then group support

# AT ISSUE

## THE SEXUAL VICTIMIZATION OF COLLEGE WOMEN

Our understanding of the prevalence and nature of violence against college women in the United States was expanded greatly by the publication of a study conducted in 1997 entitled "The Sexual Victimization of College Women" (Fisher et al., 2000). Not only are college women at greater risk for sexual assault and rape, but they are less likely to characterize their victimization as a crime.

This study is unique in that it correlated the results of two different survey methods. One sample of 4,446 randomly selected respondents participated in the National College Women Sexual Victimization Study (NCWSV), which used a series of behaviorally specific questions to assess a range of possible sexual victimizations. Rather than asking if a respondent "had been raped," the NCWSV described an incident graphically (e.g., someone "made you have sexual intercourse by using force or threatening to harm you . . . by intercourse I mean putting a penis in your vagina"). These questions were then followed by a detailed incident report. Another group participated in a more traditional survey approach.

The NCWSV study found that in a 6-month period, 2.8 percent of college women sampled had experienced either a completed or an attempted rape, some more than once. These results suggest that in a calendar year, nearly 5 percent of college women are victimized in this manner. Put another way, for every 1,000 women attending college, there may well be 35 incidents of rape in a given academic year. Projected over the nation's female student population of several million, these numbers suggest that rape victimization is a problem of large proportions.

Most often, the offender was a boyfriend, ex-boyfriend, classmate, friend, acquaintance, or coworker and was known to the victim. 12.8 percent of completed rapes, 35 percent of attempted rapes, and 22.9 percent of threatened rapes occurred on a date. Most incidents of sexual victimization occurred in the evening, in the victim's home. College women were victimized both on- and off-campus.

Although two-thirds of victims told someone about the sexual victimization (usually a friend), fewer than 5 percent of completed and attempted rapes were reported to law enforcement officials. In some cases, the victim felt the incident was not serious enough to report, or wasn't sure a crime had been committed. In others there were barriers to reporting, including fear of hostility from the assailant or the police, fear of not being believed, or concerns about others learning of the incident.

Other results from the NCWSV study suggest that many students will encounter sexist and harassing comments, receive obscene phone calls, and may be stalked or experience some form of coerced sexual contact. The study also showed that women who live on campus, are unmarried, get drunk frequently, and have experienced prior sexual victimization are more likely to be sexually victimized than others. College officials should use this information to improve education and knowledge of sexual assault. College women would be wise to use this information to develop safe habits and strategies to avoid circumstances in which sexual assault can occur.

**Source:** B. S. Fisher, F. T. Cullen, & M.G. Turner. (2000). The Sexual Victimization of College Women. U. S. Department of Justice publication. NCJ 182369.

sessions with other survivors are very helpful to rape and sexual assault survivors (Calhoun & Atkeson, 1991). Long-term goals include help with the relational and sexual problems that remain after the rape. Many survivors experience a loss of interest in any physical contact and certainly in sexual activity. Most fair-sized towns and cities have a *rape crisis program* that can respond fairly quickly to a victim of rape or sexual assault. Do you know what services are available on your campus or in your community?

True recovery from rape or sexual assault is characterized by several important features (Frazier & Schauben, 1994; Koss, 1992):

1. The survivor is able to think about the assault when she or he wants to, without being beset by intrusive flashbacks, memories, or nightmares.

2. The survivor can remember the assault with appropriate emotions rather than with numbing or false detachment.

3. The survivor can identify and endure the emotions associated with the assault without becoming overwhelmed by them.

4. The survivor's level of depression, anxiety, and sexual dysfunction drop to at least a tolerable level.

Such demonstrations are held in virtually every major urban area. They raise awareness about sexual violence and provide an opportunity for survivors to continue their recovery.

5. Survivors end their social and emotional isolation by reestablishing relationships with others.

6. Survivors assign some meaning to the rape or sexual assault, and their self-esteem becomes stronger than their tendency to self-blame.

## 18.7.4    Understanding Rape and Sexual Assault: Why Do Men Rape?

We can examine the rapist and the occurrence of rape and sexual assault on at least three levels of analysis. We can study the *individual rapist* and his typical characteristics. This will take us down the path of examining personal histories and the personality factors or pathology that led a *particular person* to commit rape. However, when we see how widespread rape and sexual assault are, and the fact that most rapists are not mentally disturbed, then we must take a broader view and examine the *social-psychological factors* that make these destructive behaviors so very prevalent in our society. That is, we need to examine how *individuals are influenced by the social forces that shape their attitudes and behavior toward sexuality, women, men, power, and their personal emotional needs*. At still another level, we can examine the *cultural norms* that *generally encourage or discourage* coercive and violent sexual expression.

### The Individual Level

Most studies are done with incarcerated rapists, so it is difficult to talk about the psychological makeup of "the rapist." Stranger rapes are more likely to be reported, and only a small number of such perpetrators are ever arrested and an even smaller number are ever convicted and sentenced. Therefore, it is very unlikely that incarcerated rapists are truly representative of those who commit rape.

Many researchers report that a substantial proportion of incarcerated rapists are socially and interpersonally inadequate and that they lack empathy for others (Marshall et al., 1995), yet other recent research has contradicted this (Fisher & Howells, 1993). A second subgroup of convicted rapists consists of **antisocial individuals** with a history of violent behavior. A third subgroup abuses alcohol, and their sex crimes appear related to a loss of inhibition. A fair proportion of convicted rapists have a childhood history of sexual abuse, and some report they must merge sex and violence in order to experience genital arousal. Many demonstrate deficits in impulse control and anger control as well as a lack of basic sexual knowledge (Becker, Harris, & Sales, 1993). According to Malamuth and his colleagues (1991), the rapist typically comes from a hostile home environment. He often has a history of delinquency and sexual promiscuity. He defines his masculinity in terms of hostility and aggression, especially toward women. Other individual factors that are identified as risk factors in sexual aggression include the active and frequent pursuit of power over others (especially women), the use of one's physical strength to get what one wants (Lonsway & Fitzgerald, 1994), and being a member of a *hypersexual peer group* where his status depends on "scoring" with women. Feminists have pointed out that rape and sexual assault enable men to act out their needs for power and domination, rather than sex (Brownmiller, 1975), but clearly sexual gratification is also involved.

### The Social-Psychological Level

A number of social factors contribute to the conditions that make rape and sexual assault so prevalent in our society (Benson, Charlton, & Goodhart, 1992):

1. Men are socialized to believe that sex is the only method of meeting their human needs for intimacy and closeness (Finkelhor & Lewis, 1988).

2. There is a sexualization of subordination. In our society, persons considered to be suitable sex objects have qualities that lend themselves to subordination. Men choose sexual partners who are smaller, younger, more physically vulnerable, more inexperienced, often less educated, and more economically dependent. (Before you shake your head and insist that this isn't true for you and your social group, stop and think about *general patterns* in our society.)

3. Because the development of empathy is not encouraged in men, and because young males

are seldom in the roles of caretakers or nurturers, they often do not understand the effect of their behavior on others (Ring & Kilmartin, 1992).

4. Our society continues to encourage **misogynistic** attitudes toward girls and women. These views are presented repeatedly in everyday interpersonal interactions, our mass media, and, most powerfully, in pornography (Boeringer, 1994; Perse, 1994).

5. To be considered very masculine in our society means to adopt an aggressive, invasive style. The extreme of hypermasculinity involves antisocial conduct, including sexual assault (Scully & Marolla, 1985).

6. Needs for power and control, or needs to express anger or neediness, are often channeled into sexual behavior by men in our society (Zilbergeld, 1992).

7. In our society, gender-role socialization results in notions that women are always passive and that men should always be eager and ready for sex. Also, men are supposed to initiate and control sexual interactions, whereas women are supposed to be less interested in sex. This leads to men feeling they must always "push" for sexual activity and women feeling they must always be more reticent or unclear about their sexual interests (Ellis, 1994).

8. Men's sexual urges are supposed to be intense and uncontrollable, so women are given the responsibility not to provoke men's sexual arousal unless they plan to "give in" (Zilbergeld, 1992).

9. Other norms, such as men bearing the expense of dates and other courtship activities, can lead both men and women to believe that men are entitled to "something in return" (Muehlenhard & Linton, 1987).

10. In our society, several rape-related myths are prevalent, and those who commit rape and sexual assault are much more accepting of these beliefs. Rape myths include (Burt, 1980; Lonsway & Fitzgerald, 1994) these:

    a. No woman can really be raped. She could resist if she really didn't want to have sex.

    b. Women say no so men won't think they are "easy." She really doesn't mean it.

    c. Many women falsely accuse men of rape.

    d. All women secretly want to be raped, and once they "get into it" they enjoy being forced to have sex.

    e. "It can't happen to me." Women want to believe that rape happens to other women who are less careful, behave provocatively,

or are members of other social groups (Norris, Nurius, & Dimeff, 1996). Men want to believe that their behavior is within the bounds of gender appropriateness and they couldn't possibly be accused of rape or sexual assault.

### The Cultural Level

Anthropologist P. R. Sanday (1981) carried out a classic study in which she attempted to discover the factors that differentiate *rape-prone* from *rape-free* societies. Rape-prone societies had the following characteristics:

1. There were adversarial relations between the sexes: it was a general belief that there was an ongoing "battle between the sexes" for control of one over the other.

2. Women had lower status compared to men.

3. Negative attitudes toward women were promoted by male socialization.

4. There was a glorification of male violence (Grubin, 1993).

5. There was an abundance of "male only" gathering places (workplaces, recreational facilities, warrior groups, etc.).

6. Males had much greater economic and political power.

7. Men demeaned and rejected "women's work."

Rape-free societies tended to have the following features:

1. Women and men shared economic power and political authority.

2. Women and men contributed equally to the well-being of the community.

3. Both genders were raised to equally value nurturance.

4. Both genders were raised to avoid violence and aggression.

## 18.7.5 Societal Attempts to Deal with Rape and the Rapist

Most rape prevention strategies are aimed at women and imply successful avoidance of stranger rape. They tend to emphasize awareness of one's surroundings and constant alertness. To reduce the likelihood of home break-ins, they recommend extra lights, locks, and other security devices. Relatively few

| antisocial personality | individuals capable of committing any act or crime, seemingly without remorse |
| misogyny (mis-ah'jen-ē) | hatred of women |

Men Against Rape, now called Men Can Stop Rape, is a pioneer group empowering men to join women as allies in the stopping of rape and promoting gender equality.

© Bob Christeson

programs are aimed at educating men to counter peer attitudes and behaviors known to be associated with sexual assault (Caron & Brossoit, 1992). A few college campuses have instituted rape awareness and prevention programs aimed at college men, but these are not well attended (Ring & Kilmartin, 1992). Is there a rape/sexual assault prevention program on your campus? How would you go about evaluating its effectiveness?

In considering how to deal with attempted or completed rape and rapists, three things should be kept in mind. First, rape and sexual assault are crimes, and the criminal justice system is often involved. For the perpetrator, this means the possibility of imprisonment and other punishment. For the survivor, this means she or he may be treated in ways that are stressful and perhaps demeaning, rather than personally supportive. (For some practical advice about what to do in the aftermath of a sexual assault, see "Healthy Sexuality: If You or Someone You Know Has Been Raped or Sexually Assaulted.") Third, remember that the vast majority of rapists are not mentally ill (Scully & Marolla, 1985). While researchers do not claim to understand all the reasons why a man rapes, it is clear he does this partly because he has internalized certain ideas and feelings about himself, sex, women, and men.

Perhaps the terms *reeducation* and *resocialization* are more appropriate than *treatment* when it comes to dealing with the rapist. When rapists are remanded to "treatment programs," they usually attend groups aimed at understanding what sexual assault does to its victims. Other goals include helping them see the women as people rather than objects to be used to satisfy their wants and needs. They also work on their interpersonal skills and ways of coping (Becker & Kaplan, 1993).

## 18.8 SEXUAL ABUSE OF CHILDREN

### 18.8.1 What's in a Name

Before we proceed, let's clarify the meaning of some important terms. **Child sexual abuse** could include inappropriate looking or leering at the child, showing the genitals, sexual touching, masturbation, oral-genital contact, and anal or vaginal penetration (Walker, 1988). In our culture, **incest** includes sexual interactions between offspring and their parents, grandparents, uncles, or aunts, or between siblings. Different cultures have varying conceptions of what constitutes incest, but all cultures do recognize limitations on who is appropriate as a sexual partner. How would you evaluate sexual interactions between first cousins or second cousins? There are differing perspectives on this last issue. In any case, you should realize that it is not necessary for one of the individuals to be a child to consider the sexual activity as incest. However, here we will limit our discussion to incest involving children.

Some scholars use the terms **pedophilia** and **child molestation** interchangeably; others distinguish between the two. Pedophiles have an *overall sexual preference for and an intense and persistent attraction to children* (young boys, young girls, or both). This person is considered to have a **paraphilia** (see chapter 17). Some adults have an overall sexual attraction to adults but have selected a particular child or particular children to molest. This person is labeled a *child molester*. However, these distinctions are not very clear-cut, as the child molester might repeat his behavior with many other children. Girls are more likely to be abused between 6 and 12 years of age, and the abuser is more likely to be a family member, neighbor, or friend of the family. Table 18.2 presents some recent data on the relationship of child molesters to their victims. Boys are more likely to be abused between 7 and 10 years of age, and their abuser is more likely to not be a family member and to perpetrate the crime in a public place.

What about sex play? Sex play among children who are close in age is a normal and healthy part of development. However, when there is an age or developmental difference of several years between those engaging in such play, then sexual abuse might, in fact, be occurring.

### 18.8.2 Incest

The most frequently reported type of incest is father-daughter, but surveys of the general population have found sibling incest to be more common. Yet this last is the least reported type of incest (Canavan, Meyer, & Higgs, 1992). Researchers can describe the general

## HEALTHY SEXUALITY

### IF YOU OR SOMEONE YOU KNOW HAS BEEN RAPED OR SEXUALLY ASSAULTED

1. Get to a safe place and call your local rape crisis hotline. You will be advised to go to a hospital or clinic. You will also be asked if you want to report the assault to the police. While most workers suggest that you report the crime, it is important for the survivor to regain some control, because that is exactly what has been violated by the rapist. If you do choose to notify the police, a specially trained police officer (usually a woman) and a rape crisis worker will meet you at the hospital or clinic.

2. Do not change clothes, wash in any way, brush your teeth, or even comb your hair. Try not to use the toilet.

3. As difficult as it may be, do not try to clean your oral, vaginal, or anal area in any way.

4. Do not move, clean, or destroy any clothing or other materials that the perpetrator may have touched or used.

5. Try to describe the rapist. If he or they were strangers, concentrate on details: voice, mannerisms, and so forth. Be prepared to provide the details of the assault. The police will try to be sensitive to your state of mind, but an immediate and thorough investigation is necessary if there is to be any possibility of apprehending the rapist.

6. Be prepared for a physical examination, either by your personal physician or by a physician at the hospital. You will be treated to prevent any STIs and pregnancy.

---

characteristics of families in which father-daughter incest has occurred (Arndt, 1991).

1. The father functions as a domineering and traditional patriarchal tyrant who heavily controls the activities of females in the family.

2. Both father and mother adhere to very traditional gender roles and instill these in their children.

3. The father is very emotionally dependent on the mother.

4. The mother is a full-time homemaker and economically dependent on the father.

5. The father has poor impulse control.

6. The mother is emotionally isolated and/or suffers from poor health, so the daughter has taken over many of the mother's parental and emotional roles.

Other studies reveal that incest is more likely to occur in homes where there is spouse abuse, alcoholism, physical abuse, or economic stress. When the incest occurs with young, preschool daughters, the perpetrator is more likely to be passive and dependent. Fathers who molest adolescent daughters tend to be domineering and rather authoritarian. It is relatively rare for incestuous fathers to be mentally disturbed or to engage in other criminal behavior, though they are often very suspicious of others. One study found mothers in incestuous families to have married young, to be sexually uninformed and naive, to be economically dependent on their husbands, and

to have come from very traditional, very hierarchical families (Johnson, 1992).

Father-daughter or father-stepdaughter incest often begins during childhood, though sometimes it begins after puberty. A typical progression is for playful activity to spill over into sexual touching, and then to oral contact or coitus. The child usually does not comprehend the meaning of these activities and often cooperates because of the extra attention. The father seldom uses force or threats, but rather takes advantage of his authority and the child's trust in him. This betrayal or exploitation of parental authority and innocent trust is what leads to the psychological damage that results from incest.

Later in life, the incest survivor typically has great difficulty experiencing love, especially sexual love, as based on mutuality and affection. The fundamental

| | |
|---|---|
| **child sexual abuse** | sexual contact with a prepubescent person |
| **incest** | sexual activity between closely related individuals |
| **pedophilia** (pe-dō-fēl′yuh) | a general erotic preference for children |
| **child molestation** | sexual abuse of a child by an adolescent or adult |
| **paraphilia** (pa-ra-fēl′yuh) | recurrent sexual arousal that involves nonhuman objects, suffering/humiliation, or nonconsenting others |

**TABLE 18.2** RELATIONSHIP TO CHILD SEXUAL ABUSE VICTIMS OF THEIR ABUSERS (PERCENTAGES)

| | Female Victims | Male Victims |
|---|---|---|
| Stranger | 7% | 4% |
| Teachers | 3 | 4 |
| Family friend | 29 | 40 |
| Mother's boyfriend | 2 | 1 |
| Older friend of respondent | 1 | 4 |
| Other relative | 29 | 13 |
| Older brother | 9 | 4 |
| Stepfather | 7 | 1 |
| Father | 7 | 1 |
| Other | 19 | 17 |
| Number of cases | 289 | 166 |

**Source:** From Laumann et al., *The Social Organization of Sexuality,* 1994. Copyright © 1994 The University of Chicago Press, Chicago, IL. Reprinted by permission.

trust in their parents that children need and depend on for healthy emotional and sexual development is damaged or destroyed by incest, and this damage carries over into many interpersonal aspects of the survivor's adult life. There might also have been physical pain involved in the incestuous activity, and this too can become strongly intertwined in the survivor's experience of sex. For many survivors, life experiences that are usually surrounded with positive feelings (affection, love, sex, emotional intimacy, parental trust and protection, and the integrity of one's own body) are all tainted with feelings of betrayal, exploitation, secrecy, shame, and invasion. Some people who experienced incest as children appear to successfully cope as adults, but many have moderate to severe difficulties in many areas of their adult lives (Ussher & Dewberry, 1995).

### 18.8.3 Prevalence of Child Sexual Abuse

In the National Health and Social Life Survey (Laumann et al., 1994), 12 percent of male and 17 percent of female respondents reported unwanted sexual touching during childhood. These figures are substantially lower than those in previous reports. For example, Finkelhor (1994) estimated that 20 to 30 percent of girls and 10 to 16 percent of boys had been sexually molested during childhood. Again we see how differing definitions of what constitutes "sexual abuse" and weaknesses in survey sample selection can provide very different pictures of the prevalence of problematic sexual behavior.

Although the vast majority of child sexual abusers are male, there has been a growing awareness that some females sexually abuse children, but little information is available. Moreover, researchers have begun

to examine the incidence of child sexual abuse all over the world. Table 18.3 offers some insight into the scope of this problem on an international scale. Most of the available data comes from English-speaking and Northern European countries, but three Spanish-speaking countries and Greece are included here. It is difficult to draw any conclusions from such studies because very different definitions of child sexual abuse are used in different countries, and methods of data collection also vary widely. However, this international overview is important in helping us realize that child sexual abuse is not limited to North America.

### 18.8.4 Signs and Symptoms of Child Sexual Abuse

There is also great controversy over what the signs and symptoms are of child sexual abuse. Some children can clearly report attempts to abuse them sexually. However, for very young children, it is sometimes difficult to determine what has really happened. The development of anatomically correct dolls has helped in evaluating whether child sexual abuse has actually occurred, but there are serious questions as to the accuracy and reliability of what children report as they interact with these dolls (Realmuto, Jensen, & Wescoe, 1990). Observing highly sexualized behavior that seems inappropriate to the child's age (such as a young child attempting oral-genital contact with another youngster), unexplained fearfulness and phobic behavior, unusual nightmares, vague bodily complaints, difficulty concentrating at school, depression, and suicidal thoughts may all suggest sexual abuse, but a medical examination by a specially trained physician will help in judging whether such abuse has occurred (American Academy of Pediatrics, 1991; Gibbons & Vincent, 1994). Experts in the field generally agree that evaluating child sexual abuse should be a team effort, and that *no one finding* should ever be used to make such a determination. This team should include specially trained medical personnel, counselors, social workers, police officers, prosecutors, and others.

### 18.8.5 The Psychology of Child Sexual Abuse

Unfortunately, child molesters are not identifiable before they commit their crimes. Child molesters come from all walks of life and have the appearance of being law-abiding and respectable. Whether pedophile, child molester, or incestuous relative, perpetrators typically demonstrate a set of distorted cognitions (beliefs and attitudes) that allow them to carry on their activities (Neidigh & Krop, 1992; Travin & Protter, 1993). These distorted beliefs include the following notions: (1) The child enjoys the sexual activity. (2) The adult's actions will not hurt or affect the child in any way. (3)

**TABLE 18.3**    PREVALENCE RATES OF CHILD SEXUAL ABUSE IN TWENTY NATIONS

| | PREVALENCE PER 100 | |
|---|---|---|
| | *Females* | *Males* |
| Austria | 36 | 19 |
| South Africa | 34 | 29 |
| The Netherlands | 33 | * |
| Costa Rica | 32 | * |
| New Zealand | 32 | * |
| Australia | 28 | * |
| United States | 27 | 16 |
| Spain | 23 | 15 |
| Norway | 19 | 9 |
| Belgium | 19 | * |
| Canada | 18 | 8 |
| Greece | 16 | 6 |
| Denmark | 14 | 7 |
| Great Britain | 12 | 8 |
| Switzerland | 11 | 3 |
| Germany | 10 | 4 |
| Sweden | 9 | 3 |
| France | 8 | 5 |
| Ireland | 7 | 5 |
| Finland | 7 | 4 |

* Statistics are not available.

**Source:** Reprinted from D. Finkelhor, "The International Epidemiology of Child Abuse" in *Child Abuse and Neglect,* 18, 1994, pp. 409–417. Copyright © 1994, with kind permission from Elsevier Science Ltd, The Boulevard, Langford Lane, Kidlington OX5 1GB, UK.

The perpetrator's actions do not feel bad to him, so they must not be wrong. (4) No one will ever know. (5) The child is flirting and teasing and wants the sexual activity to occur. (6) Because the child likes or loves the perpetrator, the sexual activity is okay. (7) The child did not object, so it must be okay with her or him. (8) Because there is no force involved, this activity is wanted by both persons. (9) The child is asleep, and so won't know what is happening. (10) The perpetrator is providing a type of sex education for the child. (11) The sexual offenses are the fault of his spouse or others (Abel, 1989).

Most child sexual abusers are adolescent or adult heterosexual males (even if their child victims are boys). The general public persists in believing that gay males are more likely to molest young boys, but there is no evidence to support this. The small number of women convicted of child sexual abuse tend to be of very low intelligence and manifest substantial mental illness (Rowan, Rowan, & Langelier, 1990).

A good percentage of pedophiles, child molesters, and incest perpetrators were sexually abused during their own childhoods (Freund & Kuban, 1994). For many pedophiles, negative mood states and events lead to an increase in deviant sexual fantasies. These fantasies are soon followed by pedophilic behavior (McKibben, Proulx, & Lusignan, 1994). Some research indicates that nonabusing adults might be also be aroused by sexual imagery involving children, but that, in contrast to the pedophile or child molester, they are able to inhibit their behavior (Haywood & Grossman, 1994).

Why don't children just tell their mothers or another adult what's going on? Many young children simply do not understand the significance or inappropriateness of what is happening. They might innocently enjoy the special attention or rewards. When children do realize that something is wrong, they might experience great shame or fear of reprisals. It is not unusual for the perpetrator to threaten that if the victim tells anyone terrible things will happen (e.g., the child will go to jail, or the parents will divorce and the family will be separated). When incest or child sexual abuse is discovered, the perpetrator may indeed be incarcerated and a family torn apart. The child-victim might come to feel this is all her or his fault. Sometimes an incested child might accurately perceive that his or her continued submission is the only thing that keeps the family together. A child might also continue to acquiesce in order to protect younger siblings from the sexually abusive parent or other adult. When a child tells her or his mother about the sexual abuse and fails to be believed or the mother communicates that she lacks the emotional strength to take action to protect the child, the first parental betrayal is then compounded by a second major betrayal. Incest survivors and sexual abuse survivors often express great rage toward their weak and submissive mothers.

## 18.8.6    The Impact of Child Sexual Abuse

Even when the molester is not the child's parent, evidence indicates that psychological damage occurs along a continuum (Wyatt, 1991). First, one cannot assume that childhood sexual abuse *always* leads to dysfunction (Kilpatrick, 1992). However, in many situations, the survivor experiences a general lack of trust in others, especially in close relationships (can you see why?). These difficulties regarding trust and closeness often carry over into relationships with their own spouses and children (Carson et al., 1990).

Depression, a pervasive sense of guilt or shame, low self-esteem, anxiety disorders (Mancini, Van Ameringen, & Macmillan, 1995), chemical abuse, some eating disorders (Jones & Emerson, 1994), chronic gynecological difficulties, preoccupation with suicide, and sexual dysfunctions have all been associated with childhood sexual abuse (Schetky, 1993). Other researchers have pointed out the increased vulnerability of childhood sexual abuse survivors to

## AT ISSUE

# CRITICAL THINKING ABOUT RECOVERING REPRESSED MEMORIES OF CHILDHOOD SEXUAL ABUSE

The vast majority of those who have been sexually abused as children clearly recall those events. However, a painful controversy has erupted over whether some sexual abuse survivors could *repress* such memories and then *recover* them during therapy.

It is healing for women and men who have been sexually abused to be believed and helped, and to finally have justice. Therapists facilitate these processes. However, like all of us, therapists can find it difficult to distinguish between factual knowledge and popular but misleading ideas. The controversy about "recovered memories" of childhood sexual abuse demands critical thought. The story is a complex one, but well worth your time and effort.

As you have read, as adults, survivors of childhood sexual abuse often (but not always) manifest many serious symptoms and dysfunctions. A small number of therapists, dealing with clients who had these same symptoms and dysfunctions, concluded that these problems were *caused* by forgotten childhood sexual abuse. They began to "help" some of their clients *recover memories* of childhood sexual abuse by parents or others. The techniques these therapists used to help recover these memories were sometimes based on erroneous ideas regarding the nature of human memory. It was assumed that past events are "recorded" and "stored" in the human memory like some sort of videotape library, and that therapists could help the client find the "sexual abuse tape," play it, have "recall" of those traumatic events, and facilitate client recovery. However, some of these techniques could *unintentionally* implant "memories" of events that never really happened.

Based on their "recovered memories," some clients were encouraged to confront their abusers. Sometimes criminal proceedings were initiated against alleged abusers. Therapists stood by their clients as they sought justice (L. Brown, 1995). Family members who insisted they were falsely accused formed the *False Memory Syndrome Foundation,* an advocacy group of accused parents who seize upon any information that questions the legitimacy of recovered memories. The group also seeks to repeal laws that encourage criminal prosecutions based on recovered memories.

What does the research show? Here are some examples of the relevant findings. As you can see, no easy conclusion is possible:

1. When researchers repeatedly asked children about an event that had not occurred (the fictitious event involved going to the hospital after their fingers had been caught in a mousetrap), one-third of the children became convinced the event had really happened and could "remember" details of this traumatic incident (Ceci, 1994). This implies that memories of traumatic events can be implanted or suggested.

2. Survivors of Dutch concentration camps, in which torture was commonplace, years later had forgotten that they themselves had been tortured, and they even misidentified their torturers (Wagenaar & Groeneweg, 1990). This implies that traumatic events can be "repressed" or forgotten.

3. Family members were asked to convincingly recount stories of

how a particular adult family member was lost in a shopping mall when she or he was a child. After repeated tellings, 25 percent of the adults who heard these stories "recalled" this event (Loftus, 1993; Loftus & Ketcham, 1994). Apparently, adults can have "memories" of events that are repeatedly suggested by significant others.

4. A researcher located women who had been admitted to emergency rooms for *physical-abuse-related* injuries when they were children. Thirty-eight percent of the women were not able to recall the reported abuse. Those who were abused by someone they knew or at a very young age were *least* likely to recall the hospital visit (Williams, 1994). It appears adults can "repress" or forget traumatic events during childhood.

The battle rages on. Therapists have been sued; $500,000 was awarded to a father who had been falsely accused of molesting his daughter (Gorman, 1995). Therapists insist that scientists don't understand the nature of trauma and its effect on memory (van der Kalk, 1995). Researchers insist that practitioners don't understand that memories are "reconstructed" from disconnected and changeable bits and pieces of experience and imagination (Ceci & Loftus, 1994). In the popular press, a writer insists that "a wrongful conviction of child abuse can be reversed. The damage from a wrongful acquittal probably cannot" (Vachs, 1996). Is it really as simple as that?

later *revictimization* (Kluft, 1993). Compared to women who were not sexually abused as children, survivors appear to be more likely to experience adult rape, masochistic behavior, involvement with abusive men, prostitution, and psychiatric illness.

However, it is important to understand that *not all childhood sexual abuse survivors manifest these problems, nor are all those who have these difficulties necessarily childhood sexual abuse survivors.* (Use your critical thinking skills to consider this last fact.) The degree of difficulty or disturbance seems to depend on how early the abuse began, how invasive, forceful, or violent the abuse was (McConaghy, 1993), how close the perpetrator was to the survivor, and how effectively and supportively the mother or other caretakers responded to knowledge of the molestation (Beitchman et al., 1992; Roesler, 1994).

Sexually abused boys are more likely to become aggressive, manifest some sexual identity confusion, and be involved in other abusive relationships as either abuser or the abused (Schwartz, 1994). For example, one recent study of serial rapists found that 31 of the 41 incarcerated participants reported childhood sexual abuse, and over half of these reported being the victim of incest themselves (McCormack, 1992). Similarly, abused girls tend toward increased levels of depression (Finkelhor, 1990).

Is it possible that childhood sexual abuse is so invasive or traumatic that the survivor **represses** these memories? Over the last few years, a heated controversy has ensued over whether **recovered memories** of childhood sexual abuse are accurate and reliable or whether they actually have been unknowingly suggested to psychotherapy clients by naive and perhaps overzealous therapists. To understand the debate over this difficult problem, see "At Issue: Critical Thinking about Recovering Repressed Memories of Childhood Sexual Abuse."

## 18.8.7 Attempts to Prevent and Respond to Child Sexual Abuse

### Prevention

School-based programs that sensitize children to the differences between affectionate touching and "bad touch" have apparently been effective in helping children cope with attempts to molest them (Goleman, 1993). Other programs attempt to support children who have experienced molestation. Teaching children that the abuse was not their fault, and that they do not have to keep "bad secrets," has also been found to be helpful.

### Helping Sexual Abuse Survivors

The first intervention must be to separate and protect the abused child from the offender. The therapist or social worker should be well trained and experienced in working with sexually abused children *and their families* (Maddock & Larson, 1995). Sexually abused children can be very hostile and aggressive at first, but this soon gives way to great guilt and shame. Those who have been violently abused might be quite disturbed emotionally. For survivors who enter treatment as an adolescent or adult, group techniques involving support from others who have been similarly abused have been found to be effective in reestablishing trust (Hack, Osachuk, & DeLuca, 1994).

### Treating Sexual Offenders

Individual and insight-oriented therapies have not been found to be effective with child sexual abusers (Arndt, 1991). Programs that emphasize impulse control, recognition of "risky" situations, empathy for victims, and general sexuality education appear to have greater success (Marshall & Pithers, 1994), but long-term studies are rare. Psychopharmacological interventions, such as the use of drugs that reduce obsessive-compulsive behaviors (Camp & Thyer, 1993), and certain antiandrogenic compounds can be effective in reducing repeat offenses (Langevin, 1994).

## SUMMARY

1. Advertising, pornography, and prostitution are three areas in which sexuality is treated as a marketable commodity.

2. Advertising that includes sexual imagery can be considered to be selling sexual fantasies designed to increase the likelihood of purchase of a product. Such imagery works through classical conditioning, identification, suggestion, or, very rarely, embedding.

3. Research evaluating the effectiveness of sexual imagery in advertising presents a mixed picture. Advertising also serves to maintain gender-stereotyped behavior. These stereotypes are often gross distortions of reality.

4. Pornography refers to material designed to elicit sexual arousal. Pornography may be distinguished from erotica and obscenity. Most pornography in the twentieth century has been aimed at young men, but recently the videocassette has expanded the market for pornographic materials to couples, and this has changed that industry. Computer pornography is a new phenomenon.

| | |
|---|---|
| **repression** | the pushing of traumatic memories out of awareness and into the unconscious |
| **recovered memories** | memories of traumatic events, recalled through hypnosis, regression, or other techniques |

5. Pornography contains many negative and distorted messages about human sexuality.

6. Research evaluating the impact of pornography on social and sexual relationships, and especially its relationship to sexual violence, presents a complex, mixed picture. The general finding is that violence, whether in sexual or nonsexual materials, stimulates the highest levels of aggression toward women and children.

7. Although on the increase in developing countries, prostitution is in decline in North America. There is a social hierarchy among female and male prostitutes.

8. The myriad of individuals who depend on the work of the female prostitute is large, leading some to call for the legalization or at least decriminalization of prostitution.

9. Types of male prostitutes include hustlers, drag prostitutes, punks, call boys, kept boys, and gigolos. Types of female prostitutes include streetwalkers and call girls.

10. Regardless of gender, prostitutes are active agents in the transmission of HIV among several populations.

11. Sexual harassment, rape/sexual assault, and child sexual abuse are difficult and all too common experiences for many in our society.

12. Certain attitudes contribute to the difficulty of dealing with issues of sexual coercion and violence. These include minimization, directionality, trivialization, collusion, blaming the victim, notions of female masochism, and the psychopathologizing of the perpetrators of sexual violence.

13. Four types of sexual harassment are generally recognized: quid pro quo, creation of a hostile environment, commission of aggressive acts, and third-party effects.

14. Other areas in which sexual harassment is an issue include harassment of lesbian women and gay men, harassment in academia, and harassment of clients by sexually exploitive professionals.

15. *Sexual assault* is a broader and more accurate term than *rape*. Acquaintance or date rape is the most prevalent type of sexual assault, and it is a particular problem on college campuses.

16. There are several types of the more stereotypical, but rarer, stranger rape: anger rape, power rape, and sadistic rape. Statutory rape, marital rape, and male rape have also been studied.

17. Concern for the physical health of the rape victim is primary during the rape crisis stage. Long-term recovery involves psychological healing.

18. The question of why men rape can be examined on the individual, social-psychological, or cultural level. Each level of analysis gives partial insight into why sexual violence occurs. Society attempts to deal with rape and the rapist through prevention programs and incarceration, and occasionally through reeducation and resocialization.

19. It is important to distinguish among incest, pedophilia, and child molestation. There is ongoing debate about the prevalence and detection of child sexual abuse.

20. His cognitive distortions allow the child sexual abuser to continue his activity. The features that distinguish child sexual abusers from other men are not clear, and it is not always simple to determine whether child sexual abuse has actually occurred.

21. A relatively large number of disturbances and dysfunctions have been associated with childhood sexual abuse, but suffering from these disturbances and dysfunctions does not imply that childhood sexual abuse has occurred.

22. Programs aimed at preventing childhood sexual abuse, treating survivors of childhood sexual abuse, and treating those who sexually abuse children have varying degrees of success.

## CRITICAL THINKING CHALLENGES

1. Consumerism, the idea that goods and services can be purchased, is a cornerstone of our society. Some would say that we are purchasing a sexual fantasy when we pay a large sum of money for that bottle of "Jungle Passion" perfume. Are we just paying for some individual's labor when we purchase a magazine or video illustrating people engaging in sexual acts? Can shared sexual activity be a "personal service" that can be purchased like a commodity?

2. One of the unique features of the Internet is its unregulated nature as a forum for free speech. However, publishers and consumers have also found it to be an abundant resource for child and adult pornography. Do you think the potential value of free speech on the Internet outweighs the potential for harm? Do you think there should be regulation of "adult" sites on the Internet? What kinds of protections would you use or endorse to protect children from exposure to inappropriate material?

3. Attempts to determine whether pornography contributes to sexual violence against women and children have revealed this to be a complex issue. Below are statements commenting on pornography's impact on sexual attitudes and behavior. Apply the principles of critical thinking to evaluate the weaknesses of each claim, and suggest a way to test each for validity.

   "My patients who depend on pornography require an escalation in its violence or bizarreness to continue to experience arousal."

   "The police files of my state contain 20,000 cases of sexual assault in which perpetrators used pornography to arouse themselves before seeking a victim."

   "Half the rapists studied used pornography regularly."

   "All ten of the convicted pedophiles in this study were found to have extensive collections of child pornography."

# GLOSSARY

## A

**abortion:** Expulsion or removal of an embryo or fetus before it is capable of independent life. 398

**abstinent:** Refraining from sexual intercourse. 377

**accessory glands:** The glands that produce the seminal fluid portion of the semen. 120

**acquired immune deficiency syndrome (AIDS):** A severe disruption of the body's immune mechanism caused by viral (HIV) infection of certain lymphocytes (white blood cells) needed to initiate immune responses. 170

**activating effects:** Effects of hormones that occur after an organ has developed and influence its activity at any particular moment. 274

**adolescence:** The period from the onset of puberty until the attainment of adulthood, about ages twelve to twenty. 282, 317

**adrenal gland:** A small endocrine gland atop each kidney, the source of a wide variety of important hormones. 88, 126, 279

**agape:** The giving love. Agape is the generous love that puts others before self. 62

**ageism:** Stereotyping of and discrimination against people based on their age. 359

**aggression:** Any behavior intended to harm, injure, or dominate another person. 296

**aggressive behavior:** Attempting to accomplish your goals or fulfill your needs at the expense of others' rights, needs, or feelings. 45

**aging:** The process of growing older. 358

**ambivalence:** Being simultaneously attracted to and repulsed by a person, object, or action. 54

**amenorrhea:** The absence of menses. 94

**amenorrheic:** Not having a menstrual period. 394

**amniocentesis:** Penetration of the abdominal and uterine walls and amniotic sac with a needle in order to remove amniotic fluid. 434

**amnion:** The innermost fetal membrane, serving as the amniotic sac and containing amniotic fluid; also called the bag of waters. 412

**amniotic fluid:** The watery contents of the amniotic sac. 412

**amniotic sac:** See *amnion*.

**ampulla:** Expansion near end of vas deferens. 119

**amputation:** Surgical removal of a limb of the body. 265

**anabolic steroids:** Synthetic testosterones that stimulate the growth of muscle mass. 129

**anilingus:** Oral stimulation of a partner's anal area. 243

**anal intercourse:** Sexual intercourse by inserting the penis into the anus. 243

**androgen-insensitivity syndrome:** A condition in which the body cells that might respond to testosterone lack the necessary testosterone-binding sites to use this hormone. The result is an XY female. 278

**androgens:** Hormones that promote the development of male or malelike sexual structures and characteristics. 88, 126, 202

**androgynous:** Exhibiting both male and female traits; being both feminine and masculine. 55

**anecdotal reports:** Stories of individual experiences or observations that might or might not be representative. 24

**aneurysm:** Saclike bulge in an artery. 162

**anorgasmic:** Never having had an orgasm. 223

**anovulatory:** Without ovulation (syn: *anovular*). 283

**antibodies (immunoglobulins):** Y-shaped protein molecules produced by B lymphocytes to destroy or inactivate specific antigens. 138, 175

**antigen:** Any substance that stimulates an immune response. 137, 173

**antisocial personality:** Individuals who are impulsive and indifferent to others. They are capable of committing any act or crime, seemingly without guilt or remorse (sociopaths, psychopaths). 484

**aphrodisiac:** Substance believed to increase sexual responsiveness, pleasure, or capacity. 8

**applied practitioner:** A professional who applies scientific knowledge to assist others (e.g., a sex therapist). 15

**areola:** The darkened ring surrounding the nipple of the breast. 83

**arousal disorder:** A recurrent inability to attain or maintain vaginal lubrication. 222

**arthritis:** A progressive disease causing joint inflammation and pain. 263

**asceticism:** A philosophy advocating extreme self-denial, self-discipline, and often celibacy. 10

**assertiveness:** Making your needs and desires known to others. 44

**asymptomatic:** Having no symptoms. 137

**asymptomatic carrier:** A person who harbors a pathogen without experiencing symptoms. 137

**attitude:** A relatively stable positive or negative evaluation of some "object" (person, group, idea, behavior, etc.). 22

**atypical sexual expression:** A neutral term applied to relatively rare sexual expression or behavior. Implies that such behavior resembles more typical or common forms of sexual behavior. 444

**autonomic nervous system:** The part of the nervous system that controls involuntary body functions, including glands, involuntary muscles, and the heart. 202

**autonomy:** Independence and capacity for self-direction. 346

## B

**B lymphocytes (B cells):** Lymphocytes that produce a type of immunity called humoral immunity. 174

**barrier methods:** Contraceptives designed to be a physical barrier that prevents sperm and ovum from meeting. 382

**basal body temperature (BBT) method:** A technique for determining ovulation by recording daily basal body temperature. 378

**behavioral psychologists** or **learning theorists:** Psychologists who see behavior as conditioned by reward and punishment. 60

**behaviorism:** A psychological perspective that emphasizes learning (changes in behavior via interaction with the environment) via association, rewards, or punishments. 455

**biological aging:** Age-related changes in a person's anatomy and physiology. 359

**birth control:** Any device used for the regulation of conception, pregnancy, and birth. 374

**birth defect:** Fetal developmental defect present at birth; congenital defect. 434

**bisexual:** Having or desiring sex partners of both sexes. 66

**blastocyst:** An early stage in embryonic development in which the embryo consists of a hollow ball of cells. 411

**blended family:** Family unit made up of adults and their offspring from previous marriages or relationships. 4, 355

# C

**cancer:** Diseases characterized by uncontrolled growth of cells. 265

*Candida albicans:* A yeast that causes common vaginal infections. 100

**Candidiasis (yeast infection):** Infection by *Candida albicans.* 100, 163

**capacitation:** See *sperm capacitation.* 410

**cardiovascular disease:** Any disease affecting the heart or blood vessels. 263

**carpopedal spasms:** Contractions of the muscles of the hands and feet during sexual arousal. 206

**castration:** Removal of the testicles. 202

**catharsis:** A release of emotional tension that refreshes or returns the organism to a normal state. 469

**cause-and-effect relationships:** How changes in one variable affect, or cause change in, a second variable (e.g., the effects of sleep deprivation on sexual responsiveness. 18

**cavernous bodies:** See *corpora cavernosa.* 110

**celibate:** Not engaging in either solitary or partnered sex. 377

**cell-mediated immunity:** Immunity produced by T cells; its target is usually the cell of a pathogen or an abnormal human cell. 174

**cells:** The microscopic basic units of life. 270

**cerebral cortex:** A part of the brain involved in thinking, memory, and language. 200

**cerebral palsy (CP):** A limited paralysis caused by disturbances of the brain present at the time of birth; any of several disorders of the central nervous system. 257

**cerebrovascular accident:** Stroke. 263

**certified nurse-midwife (CNM):** A registered nurse who has been specially trained in the delivering of babies. 419

**cervical cap:** A small plastic or rubber cuplike contraceptive device positioned over the cervical opening. 387

**cervical mucus method:** A technique for determining ovulation by observing changes in cervical mucus secretions from the vagina. 379

**cervix:** The neck of the uterus. 79

**cesarean section (C-section):** Surgical childbirth through the abdominal wall. 428

**chancre:** A lesion that appears at the exact spot where infection with syphilis took place. 160

**child molestation:** Sexual abuse of a child by an adolescent or an adult. 486

**child sexual abuse:** Sexual contact with a prepubescent person. Because children are not considered able to give free consent, these activities are viewed as abusive. 486

*Chlamydia:* The bacterium that causes genital chlamydia infections. 156

**chorion:** The outermost membrane in the early embryo. 412

**chorionic villi:** Fingerlike vascular projections of the chorion that become a part of the fetal placenta. 412

**chorionic villus sampling (CVS):** Needle removal of small amounts of placental tissue for prenatal detection of fetal abnormalities. 434

**chromosomes:** The rodlike physical carriers of the genes. 270

**chronological aging:** The passage of time since a person's birth. 358

**circumcision:** The surgical removal of part or all of the foreskin of the penis. 115

**circumscribing:** Restricting areas of communication to "safe" topics. 72

**classical conditioning:** Learning via repeated association of one stimulus with another, especially a behavior. 455, 462

**cleavage stage:** The first cell divisions of the fertilized ovum, or zygote. 411

**climacteric:** Hormonal changes during midlife and their effects; the group of physical changes that occur during an older person's period of declining sexual functions. 128, 360

**clinical case study:** An in-depth psychological or physical study of an individual patient. 19

**clinical population:** Patients/group seeking, or identified as needing, treatment for some condition. 19

**clitoris:** The erectile projection located in the front part of the vaginal vestibule. 77

**coercion:** To bring about by force, threat, or deceit rather than by informed free choice. 33

**cognitive:** Relating to knowing, including both awareness and judgment. 320

**cognitive behavioral therapy:** Psychological treatment that emphasizes changing self-defeating thoughts and behaviors. 457

**cognitive social learning theory:** A theory suggesting that children acquire gender roles or other behaviors through rewards/ punishments, observation/modeling, and expectations regarding outcomes. 295

**cohabitation:** Unmarried persons living together in a sexual relationship. 344

**coitus:** Heterosexual intercourse. 234

**coitus interruptus:** Withdrawal of the penis from the vagina before ejaculation. 7

**collaborating:** Working together. 40

**colostrum:** The thin yellowish premilk fluid produced by the mother's breasts within a few days following childbirth. 432

**communicable diseases:** Diseases that can be transmitted from person to person (also called infectious diseases). 136

**communicable period:** When a disease is transmissible from person to person. 137

**companionate love:** A less emotionally intense form of love involving friendly affection and deep attachment. 62

**computer scatophilia:** Sexual arousal via the creation and sending of lewd and obscene messages over computer lines. Considered a paraphilic behavior. 447

**conception:** The union of a sperm and an ovum. 410

**condom:** A contraceptive sheath-like device worn over the erect penis or in the vagina to prevent sperm from entering the vagina and uterus. 382

**conflict:** Any situation in which the wants, needs, or intentions of one person are incompatible with the wants, needs, or intentions of another person. 39

**congenital:** Present at birth. 162

**congenital adrenal hyperplasia (CAH):** A condition in which high levels of adrenal androgens in an XX fetus result in enlargement of the clitoris and other genital effects. 279

**contagious:** Capable of being transmitted readily from one person to another. 137

**contraception:** The prevention of conception. 374

**control group:** In an experiment, the group that is *not* exposed to some treatment or variable. 18

**core gender identity:** Our innermost psychological sense of ourselves as a girl or boy, woman or man. A central component of our sense of "self." 289

**corpora cavernosa:** The upper two erectile bodies in the shaft of the penis. 110

**corpus luteum:** "Yellow body" formed from follicle after ovulation. 83

**corpus spongiosum:** The lower erectile body in the shaft of the penis. 110

**correlation:** A relationship or association between two naturally occurring variables. 19

**cortex:** The outer portion of an organ. 274

**cosmetic aging:** The changes in outward appearance that occur with advancing chronological age. 359

**Cowper's glands:** Two glands located exterior to the prostate that produce preejaculatory fluid; the bulbourethral glands. 121

**cremaster muscle:** Surrounds spermatic cord. 117

**critical thinking:** Awareness and avoidance of biases and presumptions in evaluating information, claims, and arguments. Using facts and logical reasoning to reach conclusions. 21

**cross-dressing (transvestism):** Wearing the clothing and adornment associated with the other gender. May be done for entertaining, sexual arousal, or as an expression of gender dysphoria. 22, 304, 450

**cryptorchidism:** Failure of testes to descend into scrotum during development. 116

**cultural diversity:** People with a variety of histories, ideologies, traditions, values, lifestyles, and languages living and interacting together. 28

**cunnilingus:** The oral stimulation of a woman's genitals. 241

**cystitis:** Inflammation of the urinary bladder. 100

**cytomegalovirus (CMV):** A common virus that causes mild or asymptomatic infections in most people, but severe infections in HIV patients. 182

# D

**dartos muscle:** muscle in scrotum. 117

**denial:** Keeping anxiety-producing realities out of one's conscious awareness. 166

**Depo-Provera:** The trade name for a progestin-only contraceptive injection (intramuscular). 393

**depression:** A feeling of sadness and apathy. 166

**detumescence:** The subsiding of tumescence (swelling). 202

**diabetes:** A condition in which the body does not metabolize sugar properly; characterized by excessive urination and caused by an insulin deficiency. 264

**diaphragm:** A dome-shaped rubber contraceptive device worn in the vagina over the cervix to prevent sperm from entering. 385

**differentiating:** In partnership disintegration, moving from a strongly shared identity to a more individual identity. 71

**dilation and curettage (D&C):** A surgical procedure in which the cervix is dilated and the inner uterine lining scraped with a metal curette; sometimes used as an abortion procedure during the second trimester. 402

**dilation and evacuation (D&E):** A second trimester abortion procedure in which the cervix is dilated and the fetus removed with a combination of forceps and vacuum aspiration. 402

**dildo:** An object designed to be placed in the vagina or anus for sexual stimulation. 238

**DNA (deoxyribonucleic acid):** The complex chemical that stores genetic information in every cell. 270

**dogma:** A principle or doctrine believed by its advocates to be absolutely true. 10

**DSM-IV:** Fourth edition of the *Diagnostic and Statistic Manual,* a listing of the categories of mental and emotional disturbances and their characteristics. 305

**dysmenorrhea:** painful menses. 94

**dyspareunia:** Recurrent genital pain occurring before, during, or after sexual intercourse. 225

# E

**economic aging:** Age-related changes in a person's financial status. 359

**egg:** The sex cell of a woman; see also *ova.* 410

**ejaculation:** The emission and expulsion of semen from the erect penis. 122, 209

**ejaculatory duct:** The last section of vas deferens before it joins with the urethra. 119

**ejaculatory inevitability:** The point at which ejaculation must occur. 210

**elective abortion:** Intentional expulsion of an embryo or fetus. 374

**embedment:** The placement or hiding of sexual words or pictures in the background of an advertisement. 462

**embryo:** The unborn child through the eighth week of development after conception. 273, 411

**embryonic stage:** The second week through the eighth week of embryo development. 411

**emission:** The discharge of seminal fluid from the accessory glands and filling of the urethral bulb; the first phase of ejaculation. 122, 209

**emotional isolation:** Lacking intimate relationships. 338

**empirical data:** Information or knowledge derived from scientific observation or experimentation. 3

**encephalitis:** Inflammation of the brain. 151

**endocrine glands:** Glands that produce and secrete hormones into the blood. 85, 125

**endometriosis:** The growth of endometrial tissue outside of the uterus. 97

**endometrium:** The tissue lining the inner wall of the uterus. 79

**epididymis:** The tightly coiled genital duct located on the side of each testis in which sperm are stored. 118

**episiotomy:** An incision made in the perineum during childbirth to enlarge the vaginal opening to ease delivery. 227, 426

**erectile bodies:** Bodies of tissue in the penis, capable of becoming erect. 110

**erectile disorder:** A recurrent inability to attain or maintain an erection. 221

**erection:** The firming, swelling, and elevation of the penis. 113

**eros:** The erotic love style. Erotic love is intense, passionate, and sensual. 62

**erotica:** Writings or other artistic creations that are sexually arousing or sensual. 464

**estrogens:** Ovarian sex hormones that promote the development of a woman's reproductive tract and her bodily characteristics. 87

**ethnocentric:** Assuming that the ways of one's own culture are "best" and judging other cultures by how closely they approximate one's own. 30

**ethnocentrism:** The belief that one's own ethnic group is superior to others. 4

**eunuch:** A castrated male (testicles removed). 10

**exhibitionism:** Sexual arousal via the display of one's genitals to a nonconsenting person. A type of paraphilic behavior. 445

**experiment:** A research method in which one of two or more equivalent groups is exposed to a treatment to measure its effect on some variable of interest. 18

**experimental group:** The group in an experiment that is exposed to some treatment or variable. 18

**expulsion:** The second phase of ejaculation in which semen is expelled from the penis. 122, 209

**external sex organs:** Sex organs visible on the outside of the body. A woman's vulva; a man's penis and scrotum. 76

## F

**fallopian tubes:** The ducts that connect the ovaries to the uterus for the passage of ova. 82

**family planning:** Planning for whether and when to have children. 374

**fellatio:** Oral stimulation of a man's genitals. 121, 242

**female condom:** A contraceptive sheath worn inside the vagina. 384

**female genital mutilation:** Surgical removal of the clitoris and all or part of the labia (a cultural ritual). Clitoridectomy. 5

**female reproductive cycle:** The monthly events occurring in the ovary and uterus. 89

**feminism:** Belief in the social, economic, and political equality of the sexes. 14

**fertilization:** The union of a sperm and an ovum. 410

**fetal alcohol syndrome (FAS):** The cluster of physical effects seen in children due to the mother drinking alcohol during pregnancy. 420

**fetishism:** Sexual arousal or orgasm via the presence (preferred or required) or use of an inanimate object or body part (partialism). A paraphilic behavior. 450

**fetishistic transvestism:** Cross-dressing associated with erotic arousal and orgasm (among heterosexual men). A paraphilic behavior. 304, 450

**fetus:** The unborn child from the ninth week of development until birth. 276, 412

**flaccid:** Relaxed, not erect. 110

**flirting:** Using indirect tactics to signal interest to a potential partner. 31

**follicle-stimulating hormone (FSH):** The pituitary hormone that acts on the ovarian follicle in the ovary and on the sperm-producing cells of the testes. 87, 125

**foreplay:** Any sexual activity that is a part of arousal and the first stages of lovemaking. 238

**form fetish:** Eroticizing of an object based on its shape: high-heeled shoes, garters, etc. 450

**frotteurism:** Sexual arousal or orgasm via touching or rubbing against a non-consenting person. A paraphilic behavior. 452

## G

**gametes:** Sex cells (sperm and ova). 271

**gay-bashing:** Verbal insults or physical threats and harm aimed at gay men and lesbian women. 478

**gender:** A societally constructed status to which one is assigned (boy or girl, woman or man). Distinguishable from the biological category of sex (male or female). 22, 288

**gender constancy:** The firm understanding that one remains male or female: the last stage of *gender identity development*. 290

**gender display:** The use of culture-specific clothing, markings, hairstyle, etc., to indicate one's gender. 288

**gender dysphoria:** Dissatisfaction with and profound distress about one's gender identity and gender role. Preference for the identity and role of the other gender. 307

**gender-role ideology:** A particular society's *general* beliefs and norms regarding how girls and boys or women and men should be (behaviors, traits, etc.). 288

**gender roles:** The totality of social and cultural expectations for boys/girls, men/women in a particular society at a particular time in history. 288, 475

**gender-role socialization:** A lifelong process of acquiring norms of gender-appropriate behavior in a particular society. Learning to be appropriately *feminine* or *masculine*. 288

**gender schema:** A mental organizational network that guides categorizations, behaviors, etc., in terms of gender (e.g., "boy games," "girl games"). 289

**gender schema theory:** Bem's theory that our gender-related schemas guide our future categorizations, associations, and behaviors. 295

**gender schematic (aschematic):** The degree to which persons organize aspects of life in terms of gender. 295

**gender stereotyping:** The overapplication of simple and rigid beliefs about the traits possessed by girls and women or boys and men. 290, 463

**generalized:** The degree to which a characteristic or claim is applicable to other individuals or groups. 16

**genital ducts:** Ducts that carry sperm and semen. 118

**genital ridges:** Clusters of cells in an embryo that develop into ovaries or testes. 274

**genitals:** External and internal sex organs. 76

**glans:** The head, or tip, of the clitoris or penis. 77

**glans penis:** The head of the penis. 110

**gonadotropin-releasing hormone (GnRH):** A hypothalamic hormone that directs the release of pituitary sex hormones. 86, 125

**gonadotropins:** The pituitary hormones that stimulate activity in the gonads, or the testes and ovaries. 125

**gonads:** The sex glands; a woman's ovaries, a man's testes. 271

**gonorrhea:** Infection with *Neisseria gonorrhoeae*. 157

**Grafenberg spot (G spot):** A sensitive area on anterior (front) wall of vagina in some women. 215

**gynecological examination:** A medical examination that focuses on female reproductive health. 97

**gynecology:** The medical specialty that deals with female reproductive health. 97

**gynecomastia:** Swollen breasts in a male. 318

## H

**hard-core pornography:** explicit material designed to sexually arouse that includes graphic close-ups of genitals, ejaculation, degradation, etc. 465

**hepatitis:** Inflammation of the liver. 154

**hermaphroditism:** The condition of having both ovarium and testicular tissue. 278

**hetaerae:** Courtesans. An educated and cultured class of female sexual companions for affluent Greek men in ancient Greece. 9

**heterosexism:** Attitudes and behaviors that denigrate and stigmatize nonheterosexual behavior. Some prefer the term *homophobia*. 478

**heterosexual:** Having or desiring partners of the other sex. 66

**homogeneous:** Uniform in structure. All of the same kind. 184

**homophobia:** The fear of homosexuality. 349

**homosexual:** Having or desiring partners of one's own sex. 66

**hormone replacement therapy (HRT):** Taking estrogen and progestin following menopause to replace hormones formerly produced by the ovaries. 362

**hormones:** The chemicals produced by and released into the blood by the endocrine glands to serve as internal chemical regulators in the body. 85, 125

**human chorionic gonadotropin (hCG):** A hormone produced by the chorion of the embryo-fetus. 88, 412

**human immunodeficiency virus (HIV):** The virus that causes AIDS. 176

**humanistic psychology:** A psychological model that emphasizes a person's conscious feelings and intellectual processes and the development of one's maximum potential. 61

**humoral immunity:** The immune response produced by the release of antibodies by B lymphocytes. 174

**hymen:** A membrane that may surround the vaginal opening. 78

**hypertension:** An elevated blood pressure, as can occur during sexual arousal and response. 208

**hyperventilation:** Rapid breathing, as can occur during sexual arousal and response. 208

**hypoactive sex desire disorder:** The deficiency or absence of sexual fantasies and desires for sexual activity. 217

**hypothalamus:** The lower portion of front of brain, from which the pituitary gland is suspended. 86, 125

**hypoxyphilia (asphyxiophilia):** Sexual arousal or orgasm from purposely depriving the brain of oxygen. 449

**hysterectomy:** The partial or complete removal of the uterus. 102

**hysterotomy:** An incision through the abdominal and uterine walls for the removal of a fetus before it is capable of independent life as a second trimester abortion procedure, or as a birthing procedure to remove a fully formed fetus (a cesarean section). 402

## I

**identification:** Internalizing the qualities, characteristics, values, etc., of another into one's self-concept or identity. 462

**immunity:** An array of highly specific bodily defenses against pathogens. 137

**implantation:** The early pregnancy embedding of the blastocyst in uterine wall. 411

**incest:** Sexual activity between closely related individuals (blood relatives or those related by marriage). 486

**incubation period:** Interval between infection and appearance of disease symptoms. 137

**infanticide:** Killing a newborn child. 375

**infatuation:** A state of strong sexual attraction to someone based mainly on his or her resemblance to a lover fantasy. 57

**infertility:** The inability or diminished ability to produce children. 436

**inguinal hernia:** A portion of small intestine is forced through abdominal wall. 116

**inhibin:** A hormone that inhibits the production of FSH, LH, and GnRH. 89, 126

**internal sex organs:** Those sex organs located inside the body. 78

**intersex:** Individual whose sexual anatomy differs from cultural ideals of male and female. 278

**interstitial cells:** Cells in the testes that produce and secrete testosterone. 118

**interstitial cell-stimulating hormone (ICSH):** The pituitary hormone that acts on interstitial cells of testes to stimulate the production of testosterone. 125

**intimacy:** A sense of closeness including emotional, intellectual, social, and spiritual bonds. 57

**intrapersonal sexual script:** Culture-bound, learned guidelines regarding any aspect of sexual expression. 480

**intrauterine device (IUD):** A contraceptive device placed in the uterus and left there for up to several years. 389

**intrauterine injection:** Injection by needle of substances through the abdominal and uterine walls into the amniotic sac that surrounds the fetus to induce an abortion. 403

**"I" statements:** Statements of how a person is feeling without placing blame for those emotions. 37

## J

**jealousy:** Fear of losing someone's exclusive love. 71

## K

**Kaposi's sarcoma (KS):** A cancer of the connective tissues. 181

**karyotype:** A chart showing all of the chromosomes of a person. 270

## L

**labia majora:** The outer genital lips that surround the vaginal vestibule. 76

**labia minora:** The inner genital lips that surround the vaginal vestibule. 76

**labor:** The birthing process. 425

**lactation:** The production and secretion of milk from the mammary glands of the breasts. 431

**last menstrual period (LMP):** The last menstrual period before a pregnancy. 415

**latent:** Dormant, not evident. 162

**lesion:** An area of damaged tissue; a wound or infection. 149, 257

**libido:** The sex drive. 202

**limbic system:** A group of structures in the brain involved with emotions and motivation. 200

**lobules:** Compartments in testis. 117

**lovemap:** A representation in the brain/mind of what is arousing to a particular individual. 456

**ludus:** The playful love style. Ludus is associated with lack of commitment. Love is just for fun, a game to be played. 62

**lunar month:** A 28-day month. 415

**luteinizing hormone (LH):** A pituitary sex hormone that stimulates the production and release of ovarian hormones and ova; identical to interstitial cell stimulating hormone (ICSH) in a man. 87

**lymph nodes:** Rounded structures along lymph vessels that produce certain white blood cells and serve as filters to keep pathogens and cancer cells from entering the bloodstream. 173

**lymphatic system:** The body system that conveys excessive fluid from the tissues to the bloodstream and houses the immunity-producing white blood cells called lymphocytes. 173

**lymphocytes:** White blood cells involved in producing immunity. 138, 174

# M

**mammary glands:** The milk-producing glands in a woman's breast. 83

**mammography:** An X-ray examination of a woman's breast. 105

**mania:** The obsessive love style. Manic lovers experience swings of mood ranging from ecstasy to despair. 62

**masochism:** Sexual arousal or orgasm via being the recipient of pain, restraint, or humiliation. A paraphilic behavior. 448

**masturbation:** Self-stimulation of the genitals to obtain erotic gratification. 236

**media fetish:** Eroticizing of an object based on the material from which it is made: silk, leather, etc. 450

**medulla:** The inner portion of an organ. 274

**meiosis:** Sex cell formation, production of sperm or ova. 271

**menarche:** The onset of menstruation. 89, 283

**menopause:** The permanent cessation of menses. 89, 361

**menstrual cycle charting:** The technique of determining ovulation by charting the monthly menstrual events to aid in inducing or preventing pregnancy. 377

**menstrual flow:** Menstrual discharge; menses. 89

**mental retardation:** A developmental disability characterized by below-average intellectual functioning. 261

**mifepristone (RU-486):** A chemical administered to cause sloughing of the uterine lining, preventing continued pregnancy. 403

**minipill:** A progestin-only contraceptive pill. 394

**miscarriage:** Spontaneous abortion. 436

**misogyny:** Hatred of women. 485

**mitosis:** The division of one cell into two (ordinary cell division). 270

**monogamy:** Having only one sexual partner. 351

**mons pubis:** The fatty, hairy pad over the pubic bone. 76

**Müllerian ducts:** A group of cells that develop into the female internal reproductive organs. 276

**Müllerian inhibiting hormone:** A hormone from the embryonic testes that inhibits development of female internal organs. 276

**multiple sclerosis (MS):** A progressive disease of the central nervous system, characterized by lack of coordination and speech difficulties. 257

**mutation:** A change in DNA which affects the function or sequence of a gene. 177

**mutual masturbation:** Partners' simultaneous stimulation of each other's genitals. 240

**myocardial infarction:** Heart attack. 263

**myotonia:** Muscle tension. 204

# N

***Neisseria gonorrhoeae:*** The bacterium that causes gonorrhea. 157

**neuroendocrine:** Involving the nervous system and hormones. 282

**nipple:** The tip of the breast. 83

**nits:** Lice eggs. 165

**nocturnal emission:** The expulsion of semen during sleep; a "wet dream." 124

**nonmonogamy:** Having more than one sexual partner. 351

**Norplant:** The trade name for a progestin-only contraceptive implant placed beneath the skin of a woman's arm. 392

**NSU or NGU:** Urethritis of an unknown cause.(Nonspecific urethritis; nongonococcal urethritis.) 160

# O

**obscenity:** Sexually explicit writings, pictures, etc., that are offensive or repulsive. 464

**observation:** The describing or recording of ongoing, visible behavior. 18

**obsessive-compulsive disorder:** A group of psychological disorders characterized by very high levels of anxiety. The anxiety is typically related to repetitive thoughts (obsessions) and is reduced by repetitive behaviors (compulsions). 457

**obstetrician-gynecologist (Ob-Gyn):** A physician who specializes in the care of pregnant women and women's reproductive health matters. 419

**operant conditioning:** The learning of a behavior via repeated reinforcement or its unlearning via punishment. 455

**opportunistic infections:** Infections that the bodily defenses would normally hold in check; these pathogens require a special opportunity to produce disease. 181

**oral contraceptives (OC):** Contraceptive hormones taken by mouth. Birth control pills. 390

**oral-genital sex:** Stimulation of a partner's genitals using the mouth and tongue. 241

**organizing effect:** How hormones influence early development of some parts of the body. 274

**orgasm:** The peak, or climax, of sexual arousal and response; characterized by a series of highly pleasurable muscular contractions of the pelvic floor and the sudden discharge of accumulated sexual tensions, and, in males, ejaculation. 123, 207

**orgasmic disorder:** Delayed or absent orgasm after a normal excitement phase. 223

**orgasmic platform:** The narrowing of part of the vagina during sexual arousal due to vasocongestion. 206

**ostomy:** A surgically created opening from the intestine or colon through the abdominal wall. 266

**ova:** A woman's sex cells or eggs (singular, *ovum*). 82, 410

**ovaries:** A woman's gonads. 82

**ovulation:** The discharge of an ovum from the ovary. 82

**oxytocin:** hormone that promotes release of milk. 87

# P

**pandemic:** A disease that is epidemic at the same time in many parts of the world. 170

**Pap test:** A diagnostic examination of cervical tissue of the uterus for the detection of premalignant and malignant cells. 101

**paralysis:** Loss of sensation and voluntary movement in an area of the body. 257

**paraphilia:** Recurrent, intensely arousing sexual fantasies, urges, or behaviors that involve nonhuman objects, suffering, or nonconsenting others. 304, 444, 486

**paraphrasing:** Restating what has just been said, and putting it into the listener's own words. 44

**paraplegia:** The paralysis of the lower torso and both legs. 257

**paresis:** A term denoting all of the mental and physical effects of syphilitic degeneration of the nervous system. 162

**passionate love:** A strong emotional state of confused feelings: tenderness and sexuality, elation and pain, anxiety and relief, altruism and jealousy. 62

**passive behavior:** Denying your own needs and rights. 44

**pathogens:** Disease-causing agents, commonly called "germs." 136

**pederasty:** Sexual contact between adult men and adolescent boys. 8

**pedophilia:** A general erotic preference for children. 447, 486

**pelvic examination:** A medical examination of a woman's genital-rectal organs. 98

**pelvic inflammatory disease (PID):** Extensive bacterial infection of the female pelvic organs, particularly the uterus, cervix, fallopian tubes, and ovaries. 156

**penile strain gauge:** Device used to measure penile engorgement during sexual arousal. 18

**penis:** The external male reproductive organ through which urine and semen pass; becomes erect during sexual arousal. 110

**performance anxiety:** Worries about being able to "perform" sexually. 221

**perineum:** The body area located between the anus and vaginal opening in women and between the anus and scrotum in men. 76, 110

**phagocytes:** White blood cells that engulf and kill pathogens. 176

**phallus (phallic):** The penis (related to the penis). 6

**pituitary gland:** An endocrine gland beneath the hypothalamus that produces hormones, including gonadotropins. 87, 125

**placenta:** The organ that unites the fetus to the uterine wall during pregnancy. 412

**plateau phase:** The second phase of Masters and Johnson's sexual response cycle, the phase of sustained sexual arousal. 205

**plethysmography:** Measurement of the size or state of an organ based on the amount of blood flowing through it (e.g., plethysmograph of the vagina during arousal). 16

*Pneumocystis carinii:* Fungus that causes pneumonia in many AIDS patients. 181

**pornography:** Sexually explicit writings, pictures, etc., created for the purpose of sexual arousal. 464

**pragma:** Practical love. Pragma is pragmatic and logical, rather than emotional. 62

**preeclampsia:** Elevated blood pressure in a woman during pregnancy, characterized by protein in the urine and swelling of the extremities. 434

**pregnancy:** The condition of carrying a developing embryo or fetus in the uterus; the sequence of events beginning with fertilization and ending with birth. 410

**premature ejaculation:** An ejaculation that occurs sooner than one or both partners desire it. 224

**premature infant:** Commonly, an infant born prior to 38 weeks of pregnancy, most often accompanied by low birth weight. 428

**premenstrual syndrome (PMS):** The physical discomforts some women experience prior to the beginning of menstruation. 93

**prenatal:** Before birth. 419

**prepared childbirth:** A method of childbirth using breathing-relaxation techniques; natural childbirth. 423

**prepuce:** The penile foreskin. 110

**progesterone:** An ovarian sex hormone that promotes the repair of the uterus to receive the blastocyst. 87

**prolactin:** A pituitary hormone that promotes milk secretion by the milk-producing glands of a woman's breast. 87

**prolactin inhibiting hormone:** hormone produced by the hypothalamus that regulates prolactin secretion. 86

**prostaglandins:** Fatty acid substances that stimulate muscle contraction. 94, 120

**prostate gland:** A gland surrounding the neck of the urinary bladder in men that produces the prostatic fluid portion of seminal fluid. 120

**protease:** An enzyme that splits a protein molecule. 184

**protease inhibitors:** Drugs that block the action of protease, which is needed to complete the assembly of new HIV particles. 184

**prurient interest:** Excessive or morbid interest in nudity, sexual function, or excretion that well exceeds socially acceptable limits. 464

**pseudohermaphrodite:** A person whose gonads match their sex chromosomes, but whose genitals to some degree resemble those of the other sex. 278

**pseudoscience:** A theory or practice that has no scientific basis. 14

**psychoanalysis:** A psychological model that emphasizes past experiences and the unconscious mind as motivating forces for human feelings and behavior. 60

**psychogenic stimuli:** Stimuli arising in the brain (thoughts, fantasies, etc.). 258

**psychological aging:** Age-related changes in how people think and act. 359

**psychosexual:** Pertaining to the emotional or mental aspects of sexuality. 315

**puberty:** The earlier portion of adolescence, during which a person becomes functionally capable of reproduction. 282, 317

**pubic lice:** Small, gray insects that live as external parasites on the body, especially in the pubic hair. 165

## Q

**quadriplegia:** Paralysis of the arms, legs, and torso. 257

## R

**random assignment:** Assigning research participants to groups in such a way that each participant has an equal chance of being in any group. 18

**recovered memories:** Memories of traumatic events, recalled through hypnosis, regression, or other techniques. 491

**reflexogenic stimuli:** Stimuli arising from bodily reflexes (e.g., in response to touch or smell). 258

**refractory period:** The period of time following an ejaculation during which a man cannot have an erection or an orgasm. 212

**relaxin:** A hormone produced by the ovary and placenta that relaxes the pubic symphysis and uterine cervix in childbirth. 89

**replicate:** To redo or reproduce a study to determine if the findings are dependable or occurred by chance. 3

**representative sample:** A survey target group that has the important (relevant) characteristics of the whole population. 17

**repression:** The pushing of traumatic memories out of awareness and into the unconscious; a controversial concept. 491

**reproductive rights:** Legal and political control over various aspects of reproduction. 14

**reproductive success:** The likelihood that one's offspring will survive, thereby passing on one's genetic endowment. 294

**research:** Scholarly or scientific study designed to increase knowledge. 15

**resolution phase:** The phase of the sexual response cycle in which loss of sexual arousal occurs; the fourth phase of Masters and Johnson's sexual response cycle. 211

**response rate:** The proportion of those contacted in a survey who actually respond. 16

**retrograde ejaculation:** Reverse ejaculation of semen into the urinary bladder. 124

**retroviruses:** Viruses containing RNA that converts to DNA upon entering a host cell. 176

**rubella:** A viral disease affecting the embryo-fetus; German measles. 422

## S

**sadism:** Sexual arousal or orgasm via inflicting of pain, restraint, or humiliation on another. A paraphilic behavior. 448

**sadomasochism:** Sexual arousal via inflicting or being the recipient of pain, suffering, or humiliation. Complete control, domination (or their complete absence) are important features. Paraphilic behaviors. 448

**sample:** A portion that represents a whole population (in a scientific study). 15

**sample of convenience:** A survey target group that is easily available or from whom it is easy to collect data. 17

**scabies:** Infection of the skin by tiny burrowing mites. 165

**scrotum:** The loose pouch behind the penis that contains the testes. 116

**self-actualization:** Using our full inherent potential as human beings. 61

**self-report bias:** The tendency to offer a generally favorable description of one's own behavior or attitude. 15

**semen:** A man's ejaculate. 121, 410

**seminal fluids:** That portion of semen produced and secreted by the accessory glands. 120

**seminal vesicles:** The two accessory glands near the prostate gland that produce and secrete seminal fluid. 120

**seminiferous tubules:** The ducts in the testes from which sperm cells are produced. 118

**sensate focus:** A treatment for sexual difficulties that involves focusing on sensations of touch. 219

**seroconversion:** The process of becoming positive on an HIV antibody test. 180

**seronegative:** Having a negative test for HIV antibodies. 180

**seropositive:** Having a positive test for HIV antibodies. 180

**sex:** A biological status, typically based on the appearance of one's genitals (male or female). Also, genital contact between individuals for the purpose of pleasure and/or reproduction. 22, 288

**sex chromosomes:** Special chromosomes (X and Y) that help determine the sex of a person. 270

**sex flush:** A temporary reddish color of the skin resulting from sexual excitement. 205

**sex glands:** Glands that produce and secrete sex hormones. 125

**sexism:** Behavior, conditions, or attitudes that foster stereotypes of social roles based on gender. 45, 290

**sex play:** Activities more physically sexual than kissing but stopping short of vaginal intercourse or orgasm; also called making out or petting. 323

**sex reassignment surgery (SRS):** Hormonal and surgical alteration of genitalia to resemble those of the other sex. 307

**sexual and gender-identity disorders:** A *DSM-IV* category that includes sexual dysfunctions, paraphilias, and gender identity disorders (distress due to cross-gender identification). 305

**sexual aversion:** A feeling of revulsion toward sexual activity. 218

**sexual deviance (deviation):** Purposeful violation of sexual norms, as in prostitution. 444

**sexual double standard:** Belief that certain behaviors (especially sexual) are acceptable for one gender but not for the other. 22

**sexual dysfunctions:** Sexual disturbances that interfere with a full or complete sexual response cycle. 217

**sexual harassment:** sexual coercion that occurs in situations of unequal power. 475

**sexual orientation:** Whether a person is attracted to people of the same, the other, or both sexes. 66, 289

**sexual perversion:** Abnormal or disturbed sexual behavior. 444

**sexual response cycle (SRC):** The cycle of sexual arousal and response. 202

**sexual scripts:** Culture-specific, learned guidelines regarding all aspects of sexual expression (e.g., "dating," "foreplay," etc.). 300

**sexual variation:** A neutral term, implying a "difference" in sexual expression or behavior. Some prefer this term over *paraphilia*. 444

**sexually transmitted infections (STIs):** Infections that can be transmitted by sexual contact; other methods of transmission are sometimes possible. 136

**"sixty-nine" ("69"):** A sexual position allowing simultaneous oral-genital contact between two partners. 243

**social aging:** Age-related changes in the interactions people have with each other. 359

**social construction:** The idea that much of what we experience as real, normal, or natural is "created" based on cultural influences. 296

**social learning theory:** a theory emphasizing the learning of social roles, behaviors, etc., via rewards/punishments and observation/imitation. 469

**sociobiology:** a theory suggesting that many social behaviors and conventions (such as gender) have evolutionary significance. 294

**soft porn:** Explicit material designed to sexually arouse, but lacking in graphic close-ups of genitalia, ejaculation, degradation, etc. 465

**spatial abilities:** Abilities related to the mental manipulation of shapes, images, or physical relationships between objects or their parts. 296

**spectatoring:** A psychological process in which a person becomes a "spectator" to his or her own sexual performance; occurs in some sexual dysfunctions. 213

**spermarche:** A boy's first ejaculation. 283, 317

**spermatic cord:** The cord that suspends the testes in the scrotum. 116

**spermatogenic cells:** Cells in testes that produce sperm cells. 118

**spermatozoa:** Sperm cells. 118

**sperm capacitation:** The process in which sperm acquire the capacity to fertilize an ovum. 121, 410

**sperm cells:** A man's sex cells; his gametes. 410

**spermicide:** A sperm-killing chemical agent. 375

**sphincter:** Muscle that surrounds an opening which closes when muscle contracts. 122

**spinal cord:** A bundle of nerve fibers running through the spinal column and connecting the brain with the rest of the body. 257

**spirochete:** A spiral bacterium. 160

**spongy body:** The lower erectile body in the shaft of the penis. 110

**squeeze technique:** A way of treating premature ejaculation. The man's partner squeezes the penis at the frenulum until the urge to ejaculate is lost. 225

**stagnating:** Not advancing or developing. 72

**start-stop technique:** A way of treating premature ejaculation by stimulating the penis almost to orgasm, then allowing the erection to subside. 225

**stem cells:** Immature lymphocytes capable of developing into various types of immune cells. 174

**stereotype:** a belief that all members of a group possess certain traits, qualities, or characteristics. 463

**sterilization:** The surgical interruption of the reproductive tract in a woman or man that leaves a person incapable of conception. 395

**stillbirth:** The birth of a dead fetus. 436

**storge:** The companionate love style. Storge is a slowly developing, "comfortable" form of love. 62

**survey:** A method of studying a topic by forming specific questions and asking them of a specific group. 16

**sustentacular cells:** Cells in seminiferous tubules that nourish developing sperm. 118

**sympto-thermal method (STM):** A technique of determining ovulation by combining the methods of basal body temperature and cervical mucus. 379

**syphilis:** Infection of the body by the spirochete *Treponema pallidum.* 160

**systemic:** Pertaining to the whole body. 160

# T

**T lymphocytes (T cells):** Lymphocytes that produce a type of immunity called cell-mediated immunity. 174

**target cells:** Cells with specific receptors for a hormone. 85

**TDF (testis determining factor):** A gene that promotes development of a male. 273

**telephone scatologia:** A form of exhibitionism involving making lewd, obscene, or sexually aggressive phone calls to a nonconsenting person. 446

**teratogen:** An organism or substance that adversely affects the embryo-fetus. 420

**testes:** A man's sex glands that produce sperm and testosterone; a man's gonads. 116

**testosterone:** A man's primary sex hormone; the most important androgen. 126

**toxic shock syndrome (TSS):** A condition caused by bacterial toxins. 100

**toxoplasmosis:** A protozoan-caused disease affecting the embryo-fetus. 422

**trachoma:** A chronic eye infection caused by the bacterium *Chlamydia trachomatis.* 156

**transgenderism (cross-gender behavior):** Continuum along which individuals engage in behaviors associated with the other gender. 304

**transmission:** The transfer of a pathogen from one person to another. 137

**transplacental:** Across the placenta. 179

**transsexualism:** Intense and prolonged psychological discomfort with one's sexual anatomy, often to the degree that one seeks surgery to "correct" the condition. 22, 304

**transudate:** A plasma fluid. 204

**transvestism (transvestite):** See *cross-dressing.*

***Treponema pallidum:*** the spirochete that causes syphilis. 160

***Trichomonas vaginalis:*** A protozoan that causes vaginal infection. 164

**tubal sterilization:** The sterilization of a woman by surgically interrupting the fallopian tubes to prevent the passage of ova or sperm. 395

**tumescence:** Swelling, such as that caused by vasocongestion. 202

# U

**ultrasonography:** High-frequency sound-wave imaging of the fetus. 435

**umbilical cord:** The cord attaching the fetus to the placenta. 412

**urethra:** The duct from the urinary bladder to a woman's vaginal vestibule or through a man's penis. 78, 110

**urethritis:** Inflammation of the urethra. 158

**urinary meatus:** opening of urethra on glans. 120

**urinary tract infection (UTI):** inflammation of the urinary bladder. 101

**urogenital system:** The system of urinary and reproductive organs. 130

**urology:** The medical specialty treating urogenital organs and their conditions. 130

**uterus:** The organ in which the embryo-fetus develops; the womb. 79

# V

**vaccine:** A preparation composed of one or more antigens used to stimulate the development of immunity. 138

**vacuum aspiration:** A first-trimester abortion technique for the removal of the embryo or fetus from uterus through a curette tube by vacuum suction, or aspiration. 402

**vagina:** The internal genital structure leading from the vestibule to the uterus. 79

**vaginal orifice:** The external opening of the vagina into the vestibule. 78

**vaginal photoplethysmograph:** Device used to measure engorgement of the vaginal walls during arousal. 18

**vaginal spermicide:** A chemical sperm-killing agent placed in the vagina to prevent conception. 388

**vaginismus:** Involuntary muscle spasms of the lower third of the vaginal canal that prevent penile penetration. 226

**vaginitis:** Vaginal inflammation. 163

**variable:** Any factor that can vary in level, size, or intensity. 18

**vas deferens:** The genital duct that carries sperm from the epididymis to the inside of the man's body. 119

**vasectomy:** The sterilization of a man by surgically interrupting his vas deferens to prevent the passage of sperm. 119, 396

**vasocongestion:** The filling of blood vessels, such as those in erectile tissue, in response to sexual arousal. 204

**venereal disease (VD):** An older term for a sexually transmitted infection. 136

**verbal abilities:** Abilities related to the creation, use, and manipulation of language. 297

**vestibule:** The cavity between the genital lips. The vaginal vestibule. 78

**volunteer bias:** Behavioral and attitudinal differences that exist between those who are likely to volunteer and those who are not. 16

**voyeurism:** Sexual arousal via observation of nonconsenting others who are undressing, nude, or engaging in sexual activity. A paraphilic behavior. 450

**vulva:** A woman's external sex organs or genitals. 76

**vulvitis:** An inflammation of the vulva. 99

# W

**withdrawal:** The removal of the penis from the vagina prior to ejaculation (an ineffective method of contraception); as used relative to sexually transmitted infections, a shutting off of social contacts. 166, 381

**Wolffian ducts:** A group of cells that develop into the male internal reproductive organs. 276

# Y

**"you" statements:** Statements that accuse or place blame on another person. 37

# Z

**zygote:** A fertilized ovum. 272, 410

# REFERENCES

A tragedy yields insight into gender. (1997). *Newsweek* (24 March):66.

Aase, J., Jones, K., & Clarren, S. (1995). Do we need the term "FAE"? *Pediatrics* 95:428–430.

Abbey, A. (1987). Misperceptions of friendly behavior as sexual interest: A survey of naturally occurring incidences. *Psychology of Women Quarterly* 11:173–194.

Abbitt, D., & Bennett, R. (1992). On being a lesbian mother. In B. Berzon (Ed.), *Positively Gay*. Berkeley, CA: Celestial Arts.

Abel, G. G. (1989). Paraphilias. In H. I. Kaplan & B. Sadock (Eds.), *Comprehensive Textbook of Psychiatry* (vol. 1, 5th ed.). Baltimore: Williams & Wilkins.

Abel, G. G., Barrett, D. H., & Gardos, P. S. (1992). Sexual misconduct by physicians. *Journal of the Medical Association of Georgia* 81:237–246.

Abel, G. G., Becker, J. V., & Cunningham-Rathner, J. (1988). Multiple paraphiliac diagnoses among sex offenders. *Bulletin of the American Academy of Psychiatry and Law* 2:153–168.

Abel, G. G., & Osborne, C. (1992). The paraphilias: The extent and nature of sexually deviant and criminal behavior. *Psychiatric Clinics of North America* 15 (3):675–687.

Ackerman, D. (1994). *A Natural History of Love*. New York: Vintage.

Adams, H. E., & McNaulty, R. D. (1993). Sexual disorders. In P. B. Sutker and H. E. Adams (Eds.), *Comprehensive Handbook of Psychopathology* (pp. 563–579). New York: Plenum Press.

Adams, V. (1980). Sex therapies in perspective. *Psychology Today* (August):35–36.

Adler, J. (1996). Adultery: A new furor over an old sin. *Newsweek* (30 September):54–60.

Adler, N.E., David, H. P., Major, B. P., Roth, S., Russo, N. F., & Wyatt, G. E. (1992). Psychological factors in abortion: A review. *American Psychologist* 47 (10):1194–1204.

Agnew, J. (1986). Hazards associated with anal erotic activity. *Archives of Sexual Behavior* 15:307–314.

Aguillaume, C., & Tyrer, L. (1995). Current status and future projections on use of RU-486. *Contemporary Obstetrics and Gynecology* (June):23–40.

AIDS activist battles for baboon marrow transplant. (1995). *AIDS Weekly* (24 July):17–18.

Ainsworth, M. (1978). *Patterns of Attachment: A Psychological Study of the Strange Situation*. Hillsdale, NJ: Erlbaum.

Aitken, R., Paterson, M., & Koothan, P. (1993). Contraceptive vaccines. *British Medical Bulletin* 49:88–99.

Alapack, R. (1991). The adolescent first kiss. *Humanistic Psychologist* 19 (1):48–67.

Alexander, C. J., Sipski, M. L., & Findley, T. W. (1993). Sexual activities, desire and satisfaction in males pre- and post-spinal cord injury. *Archives of Sexual Behavior* 22:217–228.

Alexander, G., Swerdloff, R., Wang, C., & Davidson, T. (1997). Androgen-behavior correlations in hypogonadal men and eugonadal men: I. Mood and response to auditory sexual stimuli. *Hormone and Behavior*: 110–119.

Alexander, N. (1996). Barriers to sexually transmitted diseases. *Scientific American Science and Medicine* 3 (2):32–41.

Alger, L. (1989). Chlamydial infection as a cause of preterm delivery. *Medical Aspects of Human Sexuality* (April):71.

Alicke, M., Braun, J., Glor, J., & Klotz, M. (1992). Complaining behavior in social interaction. *Personality and Social Psychology Bulletin* 18 (3):286–295.

Allan, J. (1994). Parenting education in Australia. *Children and Society* 8 (4):344–359.

Allen, B. (1995). Gender and computer-mediated communication. *Sex Roles* 32 (7–8):557–563.

Aloni, R., Heller, L., Kerer, O., Mendelson, E., & Davidoff, G. (1992). Non-invasive treatment for erectile dysfunction in the neurologically disabled population. *Journal of Sex and Marital Therapy* 18 (3):243–249.

Aloni, R., Ring, H., Rozenthul, N., & Schwartz, J. (1993). Sexual function in male patients after stroke: A follow-up study. *Sexuality and Disability* 11 (2):121–128.

Alpern, D. (1986). A Newsweek poll: Sex laws. *Newsweek* (14 July):38.

Alroomi, L., Davidson, J., Evans, T., Galea, P., & Howat, R. (1988). Maternal narcotic abuse and the newborn. *Archives of Disabled Children* 63:81.

Alsaker, F. (1992). Pubertal timing, overweight, and psychological adjustment. *Journal of Early Adolescence* 12 (4):396–419.

Althof, S., & Turner, I. (1992). Self-injection therapy and external vacuum devices in the treatment of erectile dysfunction: Methods and outcome. In R. Rosen and S. Leiblum (Eds.), *Erectile Disorders*. New York: Guilford.

Altman, M. (1984). Everything they always wanted to know. In C. S. Varce (Ed.), *Pleasure and Danger: Exploring Female Sexuality* (pp. 115–130). Boston: Routledge & Kegan Paul.

Alvarez, W. A., & Freinhar, J. P. (1991). A prevalence study of bestiality zoophilia in psychiatric in-patients, medical in-patients, and psychiatric staff. *International Journal of Psychosomatics* 38 (1–4):45–47.

Alzate, H. (1990). Vaginal erogeneity, the "G spot" and "female ejaculation." *Journal of Sex Education and Therapy* 16:137–140.

Amarenco, G., Bosc, S., & Goldet, R. (1997). Clinical and electrophysiological study of penile neuropathy—A series of 186 cases. *Neurophysiologie Clinique* 27(1):51–58.

Ambady, N., Hallahan, M., & Rosenthal, R. (1995). On judging and being judged accurately in zero-acquaintance situations. *Journal of Personality and Social Psychology* 69 (3):518–529.

American Academy of Pediatrics. (1989). Report of the task force on circumcision. *Pediatrics* 84 (August): 388–391.

American Academy of Pediatrics. (1989a). Report of the task force on circumcision. *Pediatrics* 84 (August):388–391.

American Academy of Pediatrics. (1991). Guidelines for the evaluation of sexual abuse of children. *Pediatrics* 87 (2):254–260.

American Association of Sex Educators, Counselors, and Therapists. (1993). *Code of Ethics*. Mt. Vernon, IA: AASECT.

American Association of Sex Educators, Counselors, and Therapists. (1996a). AIDS conference offers hope. *Contemporary Sexuality* 30 (8):1–11.

American Association of Sex Educators, Counselors, and Therapists. (1996b). Intimacy and the Internet. *Contemporary Sexuality* 30 (9):1–11.

American Association of University Women. (1992). *How Schools Shortchange Girls: A Study of Major Findings on Girls and Education*. Washington, DC: AAUW.

American Association of University Women. (1994). *Shortchanging Girls: Shortchanging America*. Washington, DC: AAUW.

American Cancer Society. (1996). *Cancer Facts and Figures—1996*. New York: American Cancer Society.

American Cancer Society. California Division, and Public Health Institute, California Cancer Registry. (1997). *California Cancer Facts and Figures, 1998*. Oakland, CA: American Cancer Society. California Division, September.

American College of Obstetrics and Gynecology. (1986). Women and exercise. *Technical Bulletin* No. 87 (September).

American College of Obstetrics and Gynecology. (1987). Oral contraceptives. *ACOG Bulletin* No. 106 (July).

American Heart Association. (1996). *1996 Heart and Stroke Facts Statistics*. Dallas: American Heart Association.

American Psychiatric Association. (1987). *Diagnostic and Statistical Manual of Mental Disorders* (3d ed.). Washington, DC: APA.

American Psychiatric Association. (1994). *Diagnostic and Statistical Manual of Mental Disorders* (4th ed.). Washington, DC: APA.

American Psychological Association. (1992). Ethical principles of psychologists and code of conduct. *American Psychologist* 47 (12):1597–1611.

American Public Health Association. (1994). *Resolution 6917: Sex Education in School Systems*. APHA Public Policy Statements, 1948–present. Washington, DC: APHA.

American Social Health Association. (1994). The natural way. *The Helper* 16 (4):11.

American Social Health Association. (1995). Diagnostic update. *The Helper* 17 (1):1–9.

American Spinal Injury Association. (1992). *American Spinal Injury Association: Standards or Neurological and Functional Classification of Spinal Cord Injury*. New York: American Paraplegia Association.

Anderson, B. L., & Elliot, M. L. (1993). Sexuality for women with cancer: Assessment, theory and treatment. *Sexuality and Disability* 11 (1):7–37.

Anderson, J., & Crawford, C. (1992). Modeling costs and benefits of adolescent weight control as a mechanism for reproductive suppression. *Human Nature* 3 (4):299–334.

Anderson, P. B., & Ayamami, R. (1993). Reports on the female initiating of sexual contact: Male and female differences. *Archives of Sexual Behavior* 22:335–343.

Andolsek, K. (1990). *Obstetric Care: Standards of Prenatal, Intrapartum, and Postpartum Management*. Philadelphia: Lea & Febiger.

Annie E. Casey Foundation. (1996). *Kids Count Data Book*. Baltimore: The Annie E. Casey Foundation.

Antonovsky, H., Sadowsky, M., & Maoz, B. (1990). Sexual activity of aging men and women: An Israeli study. *Behavior, Health, and Aging* 1 (3):151–161.

Arndt, W. B. (1991), *Gender Disorders and the Paraphilias*. Madison, CT: International Universities.

Aron, A., & Aron, E. N. (1994). Love. In A. L. Weber & J. H. Harvey (Eds.), *Perspectives on Close Relationships*. Boston: Allyn & Bacon.

Athanasiou, R., Shaver, P., & Tavris, C. (1970). Sex. *Psychology Today* (July):39–52.

Atlas, G. (1994). Sensitivity to criticism: A new measure of responses to everyday criticism. *Journal of Psychoeducational Assessment* 12 (3):241–253.

Aube, J., & Koestner, R. (1995). Gender characteristics and relationship adjustment: Another look at similarity-complementarity hypotheses. *Journal of Personality* 63 (4):879–904.

AuBuchon, P. G., & Calhoun, K. S. (1985). Menstrual cycle symptomatology: The role of social expectancy and experimental demand characteristics. *Psychosomatic Medicine* 47:35–45.

Baba, T., Trichel, A., An, L., Liska, V., Martin, L., Murphey-Corb, M., & Ruprecht, R. (1996). Infection and AIDS in adult Macaques after nontraumatic oral exposure to cell-free SIV. *Science* 272:1486–1489.

Baenninger, M., & Newcombe, N. (1989). A role of experience in spatial test performance: A meta-analysis. *Sex Roles* 20:327–343.

Bailey, J. M., Bobrow, D., Wolfe, M., & Mikach, S. (1995). Sexual orientation of adult sons of gay fathers. *Developmental Psychology* 31:124–129.

Bailey, J. M., Gaulin, S., Agyei, Y., & Gladue, B. A. (1994). Effects of gender and sexual orientation on evolutionarily relevant aspects of human mating psychology. *Journal of Personality and Social Psychology* 66 (6):1081–1093.

Bailey, J. M., & Pillard, R. C. (1995). Genetics of human sexual orientation. *Annual Review of Sex Research* 6:126–150.

Bailey, J. M., Pillard, R. C., Neale, M. C., & Agyei, Y. (1993). Heritable factors influence female sexual orientation. *Archives of General Psychiatry* 50:217–223.

Balay, J., & Shevrin, H. (1988). The subliminal psychodynamic activation method: A critical review. *American Psychologist* 43 (3):161–174.

Baldwin, J. D., & Baldwin, J. I. (1989). The socialization of homosexuality and heterosexuality in a non-western society. *Archives of Sexual Behavior* 18:13–34.

Ball, F., Cowan, P., & Cowan, C. (1995). Who's got the power? Gender differences in partners' perceptions of influence during marital problem-solving discussions. *Family Process* 34 (3):303–321.

Bancroft, J. (1984). Hormones and human sexual behavior. *Journal of Sex and Marital Therapy* 10:3–21.

Barak, A. (1994). A cognitive behavioral educational work-shop to combat sexual harassment in the workplace. *Journal of Counseling and Development* 72:595–602.

Barbieri, R. (1988). New therapy for endometriosis. *New England Journal of Medicine* 318:512–514.

Bard, L. A., Carter, D. L., Cerce, D. D., & Knight, R. A. (1987). A descriptive study of rapists and child molesters: Developmental, clinical and criminal characteristics. *Behavioral Sciences and the Law* 5:203–220.

Barlow, S., & Sullivan, F. (1982). *Reproductive Hazards of Industrial Chemicals: An Evaluation of Animal and Human Data*. New York: Academy.

Basow, S. A., & Campanile, F. (1990). Attitudes toward prostitution as a function of attitudes toward feminism in college students. *Psychology of Women Quarterly* 14 (1):135–141.

Bass, B. A., & Levant, M. D. (1992). Family perception of rapists and pedophiles. *Psychological Reports* 71 (1):211–214.

Baumeister, L., Flores, E., & Marin, B. (1995). Sex information given to Latina adolescents by parents. *Health Education Research* 10 (2):233–239.

Baumrind, D. (1995). Commentary on sexual orientation: research and social policy implications. *Developmental Psychology* 31 (1):130–136.

Bauserman, R., & Davis, C. (1996). Perceptions of early sexual experiences and adult sexual adjustment. *Journal of Psychology and Human Sexuality* 8 (3):37–59.

Beall, A. E., & Sternberg, R. J. (Eds.) (1993). *The Psychology of Gender*. New York: Guilford.

Beattie, J. (1992). Alcohol exposure and the fetus. *European Journal of Clinical Nutrition* 46:S7–S17.

Beck, J. (1993). Vaginismus. In W. O'Donahue & J. Geer (Eds.), *Handbook of Sexual Dysfunctions: Assessments and Treatment* (pp. 381–397). Boston: Allyn & Bacon.

Beck, J. G. (1995). Hypoactive sexual desire disorder: An overview. *Journal of Consulting and Clinical Psychology* 63:919–927.

Beck, J., Bozman, A., & Qualtrough, T. (1991). The experience of sexual desire: Psychological correlates in a college sample. *Journal of Sex Research* 28:443–456.

Beck, M. (1988). Miscarriages. *Newsweek* (15 August):46–52.

Becker, J. V., & Kaplan, M. S. (1991). Rape victims: Issues, theories and treatment. *Annual Review of Sex Research* 2:267–292.

Becker, J. V., Alpert, J. L., Bigfoot, D. S., Bonner, B. L., Geddie, L. F., Henggeler, S. W., Kaufman, K. L., & Walker, C. E. (1995). Empirical research on child abuse treatment: Report by the Child Abuse and Treatment Working Group, American Psychological Association. *Journal of Clinical Child Psychology* 24:23–46.

Becker, J. V., Harris, C. D., & Sales, B. D. (1993). Juveniles who commit sexual offenses: A critical review of research. In G. C. N. Hall et al. (Eds.), *Sexual Aggression: Issues in Etiology, Assessment and Treatment*. Washington, DC: Taylor & Francis.

Becker, J. V., & Kaplan, M. S. (1993). Cognitive behavioral treatment of the juvenile sex offender. In H. E. Barbaree et al. (Eds.), *The juvenile sex offender:*264–277.

Beckman, D., & Brent, R. (1986). Mechanisms of known environmental teratogens: Drugs and chemicals. *Clinical Perinatology* 13:649.

Bedel, K. B. (1993). *1993: Year of American and Canadian Churches*. New York: National Council of Churches.

Begley, S., Brant, M., Springen, K., & Rogers, A. (1995). The baby myth. *Newsweek* (4 September):38–47.

Beitchman, J. H., Zucker, K. J., Hood, J. E., DaCosta, G. A., Akman, D., & Cassaira, E. (1992). A review of the long-term effects of child sexual abuse. *Child Abuse and Neglect* 16 (1):101–118.

Belker, A., Konnak, J., Sharlip, J., & Thomas, A. (1993). Intraoperative observations during vasovasectomy in 334 patients. *Journal of Urology* 149:524–527.

Bell, A. P., Weinberg, M. S., & Hammersmith, S. K. (1981). *Sexual Preference: Its Development in Men and Women*. Bloomington, IN: Indiana University.

Bellis, D. J. (1990). Fear of AIDS and risk reduction among heroin-addicted female street prostitutes: Personal interviews with 72 southern California subjects. *Journal of Alcohol and Drug Education* 35 (3):26–37.

Bem, D. (1996). Exotic becomes erotic: A developmental theory of sexual orientation. *Psychological Review* 103 (2):320–335.

Bem, S. L. (1984). Androgyny and gender schema theory: A conceptual and empirical integration. In T. B. Sonderegger (Ed.), *Nebraska Symposium on Motivation: Psychology and Gender* (vol. 38). Lincoln: University of Nebraska.

Bem, S. L. (1993). *The Lenses of Gender: Transforming the Debate on Sexual Inequality*. New Haven, CT: Yale University.

Bemelmens, B., Meuleman, E., Doesberg, W., Notermans, S., & Debruyne, F. (1994). Erectile dysfunctions in diabetic men: The neurological factor revisited. *Journal of Urology* 151:884–889.

Ben-Ari, A. (1995). Coming out: A dialectic of intimacy and privacy. *Families in Society* 76 (5):306–314.

Ben-David, S., & Silfen, P. (1993). Rape death and resurrection: Male reaction after disclosure of the secret of being a rape victim. *Medicine and Law* 12 (1–2):181–189.

Ben-Shlomo, Y., Smith, G., Shipley, M., & Marmot, M. (1993). Magnitude and causes of mortality differences between married and unmarried men. *Journal of Epidemiology and Community Health* 47 (3):200–205.

Benenson, A. S. (1995). *Control of Communicable Diseases Manual* (16th ed.). Washington, DC: American Public Health Association.

Benson, D., Charlton, C., & Goodhart, F. (1992). Acquaintance rape on campus: A literature review. *Journal of American College Health* 40:157–165.

Benson, P., Sharma, A., & Roehlketartain, E. (1995). *Growing Up Adopted: A Portrait of Adolescents and Their Families*. Minneapolis: Search Institute.

Berger, A. (1991). Of mice and men: An introduction to mouseology: Or anal eroticism and Disney. *Journal of Homosexuality* 21:155–165.

Berger, R. (1990). Passing: Impact on the quality of same-sex couple relationships. *Social Work* 35 (4):328–332.

Berger, R., & Kelly, J. (1992). The older gay man. In B. Berzon (Ed.),

*Positively Gay.* Berkeley, CA: Celestial Arts.

Bergmann, M. (1995). On love and its enemies. *Psychoanalytic Review* 82 (1):1–19.

Berkman, L. (1995). The role of social relations in health promotion. *Psychosomatic Medicine* 57 (3):245–254.

Berkowitz, A. (1992). College men as perpetrators of acquaintance rape and sexual assault: A review of recent research. *Journal of American College Health* 40:175–181.

Bernstein, N. (1985). Sexuality in mentally retarded adolescents. *Medical Aspects of Human Sexuality* (November):50–61.

Bertolli, J. (1996). Estimating the timing of mother to child transmission of human immunodeficiency virus in a breast-feeding population in Kinshasa, Zaire. *Journal of Infectious Disease* 174:722–726.

Berzon, B. (1992a). Building successful relationships. In B. Berzon (Ed.), *Positively Gay.* Berkeley, CA: Celestial Arts.

Berzon, B. (1992b). Why are older gays and lesbians treated like pariahs? *The Advocate* (28 January).

Billy, J., Tanfer, K., Grady, W., & Klepinger, D. (1993). The sexual behavior of men in the United States. *Family Planning Perspectives* 25:52–60.

Blackwood, E. (1986). *The Many Faces of Homosexuality: Anthropological Approaches to Homosexual Behavior.* New York: Harrington Park.

Blanchard, R. (1992). Nonmonotonic relation of autogynephilia and heterosexual attraction. *Journal of Abnormal Psychology* 101 (2):271–276.

Blanchard, R. (1993a). The she-male phenomenon and the concept of partial autogynephilia. *Journal of Sex and Marital Therapy* 19 (1):69–76.

Blanchard, R. (1993b). Partial versus complete autogynephilia and gender dysphoria. *Journal of Sex and Marital Therapy* 19 (4):301–307.

Blattberg, K., & Hogan, J. (1994). Marital distress across the mid-life transition among middle-class Caucasian women. *Psychological Reports* 75 (1, part 2):497–498.

Bloom, D., & Shernoff, M. (1986). *I Can't Cope with My Fear of AIDS.* New York: Gay Men's Health Crisis.

Blumstein, P. W., & Schwartz, P. (1983). *American Couples: Money, Work, Sex.* New York: William Morrow.

Boeringer, S. (1994). Pornography and sexual aggression: Association of violent and nonviolent depictions with rape and rape proclivity. *Deviant Behavior* 15:289–304.

Bogaert, A. F. (1996). Volunteer bias in human sexuality research: Evidence for both sexuality and personality differences in males. *Archives of Sexual Behavior* 25 (2):125–140.

Bordages, J. (1989). Self-actualization and personal autonomy. *Psychological Reports* 64 (3, part 2):1263–1266.

Bowlby, J. (1969). *Attachment and Loss* (vol. 1). New York: Basic.

Bowlby, J. (1973). *Attachment and Loss* (vol. 2). New York: Basic.

Bowlby, J. (1980). *Attachment and Loss* (vol. 3). New York: Basic.

Bowling, A., & Windsor, J. (1995). Death after widow(er)hood: An analysis of mortality rates up to 13 years after bereavement. *Omega Journal of Death and Dying* 31 (1):35–49.

Boyer, D., & Fine, D. (1992). Sexual abuse as a factor in adolescent pregnancy and child maltreatment. *Family Planning Perspectives* 24 (1):4–11.

Boyer, J. (1997). Protection of chimpanzees from high-dose heterologous HIV-1 challenge by DNA vaccination. *Nature Medicine* 3:526–532.

Bozzette, S. (1995). A randomized trial of three antipneumocystis agents in patients with advanced HIV infection. *New England Journal of Medicine* 332:693–699.

Bradford, J. M., Boulet, J., & Pawlak, A. (1992). The paraphilias: A multiplicity of deviant behaviors. *Canadian Journal of Psychiatry* 37 (2):104–108.

Bradford, J. M., & Pawlak, A. (1987). Sadistic homosexual pedophilia: Treatment with cyproterone acetate: A single case study. *Canadian Journal of Psychiatry* 32 (1):22–30.

Brame, G. G., Brame, W. D., & Jacobs, J. (1996). *Different Loving: An Exploration of the World of Sexual Dominance and Submission.* New York: Villard.

Braveman, P., Egerter, S., Edmonston, F., & Verdon, M. (1995). Racial/ethnic differences in the likelihood of cesarean delivery, California. *American Journal of Public Health* 85:625–630.

Breakwell, G. M., & Fife-Shaw, C. (1992). Sexual activities and preferences in a United Kingdom sample of 16 to 20-year-olds. *Archives of Sexual Behavior* 21 (3):271–293.

Breay, E., & Gentry, M. (1990, April). *Perceptions of a Sexual Double Standard.* Paper presented at the meeting of the Eastern Psychological Association, Philadelphia.

Brecher, E. (1984). *Love, Sex, and Aging.* Boston: Little, Brown/Consumer Reports.

Brehm, S. (1992). *Intimate Relationships* (2d ed.). New York: McGraw-Hill.

Brinton, L., Reeves, W., Brenes, M., Herrera, R., Gaitan, E., Tenoria, F., de Britton, R., Garcia, M., & Rawls, W. (1989). The male factor in the etiology of cervical cancer among sexually monogonous females. *International Journal of Cancer* 44:109–203.

Brod, H. (1987). A case for men's studies. In H. Brod (Ed.), *The Making of Masculinities.* Boston: Allyn & Bacon.

Brody, J. E. (1990). Scientists trace aberrant sexuality. *New York Times* (23 January):C1, C12.

Brody, J. E. (1993). A new look at an old quest for sexual stimulants. *New York Times* (4 August):C12.

Bronski, M. (1991). The mainstreaming of S/M. *Outweek* 89:32–37.

Brosius, H. B., Weaver, J. B., & Staub, J. F. (1994). Exploring the social and sexual "reality" of contemporary pornography. *Journal of Sex Research* 30 (2):161–170.

Brown, E. (1991). *Patterns of Infidelity and Their Treatment.* New York: Brunner-Mazel.

Brown, G., & Rundell, J. (1993). A prospective study of psychiatric aspects of early HIV disease in women. *General Hospital Psychiatry* 15 (3):139–147.

Brown, G. R. (1995). Cross-dressing men often lead double lives. *Menninger Letter* (April):4–5.

Brown, L. (1995). The therapy client as plaintiff: Clinical and legal issues for the treating therapist. In J. L. Alpert (Ed.), *Sexual Abuse Recalled: Treating Trauma in the Era of the Recovered Memory Debate* (pp. 337–360). Northvale, NJ: Jason Aronson.

Brown, T., & Allgeier, E. (1995). Managers' perceptions of workplace romances: An interview study. *Journal of Business and Psychology* 10 (2):169–176.

Brownmiller, S. (1975). *Against Our Will: Men, Women, and Rape*. New York: Simon & Schuster.

Budland, O., & Kullgren, G. (1996). Transsexualism—General outcome and prognostic factors: A five year follow-up study of nineteen transsexuals in the process of changing sex. *Archives of Sexual Behavior* 25 (3):303–316.

Bullard, D. (1988). The treatment of desire disorders in the medically ill and physically disabled. In S. Leiblum & R. Rosen (Eds.), *Sexual Desire Disorders*. New York: Guilford.

Bullough, B., & Bullough, V. L. (1996). Female prostitution: Current research and changing interpretations. *Annual Review of Sex Research* 7:158–180.

Bullough, B., & Bullough, V. (1997). Are transvestites necessarily heterosexual? *Archives of Sexual Behavior* 26 (1):1–12.

Bullough, V. L. (1976). *Sexual Variance in Society and History*. Chicago: University of Chicago.

Bullough, V. L. (1990). History and the understanding of human sexuality. *Annual Review of Sex Research* 1:75–92.

Bullough, V. L. (1996). Our feminist foremothers. *Journal of Sex Research* 33 (2):91–98.

Bullough, V. L., & Brundage, J. (Eds.) (1982). *Sexual Practices and the Medieval Church*. Buffalo, NY: Prometheus.

Bullough, V. L., & Bullough, B. (1987). *Women and Prostitution: A Social History*. Buffalo, NY: Prometheus.

Bullough, V. L., & Bullough B. (1994). *Human Sexuality: An Encyclopedia*. New York: Garland.

Bullough, V. L., & Bullough, B. (1993). *Cross Dressing, Sex and Culture*. Philadelphia: University of Pennsylvania.

Buntain-Ricklefs, J., Kemper, K., Bell, M., and Babonis, T. (1994). Punishments: What predicts adult approval. *Child Abuse and Neglect* 18 (11):945–955.

Burgess, A. W. (Ed.) (1984). *Child Pornography and Sex Rings*. Lexington, MA: Lexington.

Burgess, A. W., & Holmstrom, L. L. (1974). Rape trauma syndrome. *American Journal of Psychiatry* 131 (9):981–986.

Burgoyne, C., & Lewis, A. (1994). Distributive justice in marriage: Equality or equity. *Journal of Community and Applied Social Psychology* 4 (2):101–114.

Burk, R. D., et al. (1996). Sexual behavior and partner characteristics are the predominant risk factors for genital human papillomavirus infection in young women. *Journal of Infectious Diseases* 174 (4):679–689.

Burke, P. (1996). *Gender Shock: Exploring the Myths of Male and Female*. New York: Anchor.

Burnley, C., & Kurth, S. (1992). Never married women: Alone and lonely? *Humboldt Journal of Social Relations* 18 (2):57–83.

Burris, S. (1996). Human immunodeficiency virus-infected health care workers: The restoration of professional authority. *Archives of Family Medicine* 5:102–106.

Burt, M. R. (1980). Cultural myths and support for rape. *Journal of Personality and Social Psychology* 38:217–230.

Buss, D., & Dedden, L. (1990). Derogation of competitors. *Journal of Social and Personal Relationships* 7 (3):395–422.

Buss, D., Larsen, R., Westen, D., & Semmelroth, J. (1992). Sex differences in jealousy. *Psychological Science* 3 (4):251–255.

Bussey, K., & Bandura, A. (1992). Self-regularity mechanisms governing gender development. *Child Development* 63 (5):1236–1250.

Butler, R. (1975). *Why Survive?: Being Old in America*. New York: Harper & Row.

Butler, R., & Lewis, M. (1993.) *Love and Sex After 60*. New York: Ballantine.

Byrne, D., & Schulte, L. (1990). Personality dispositions as mediators of sexual responses. *Annual Review of Sex Research* 1:93–117.

Cado, S., & Leitenberg, H. (1990). Guilt reactions to sexual fantasies during intercourse. *Archives of Sexual Behavior* 19:49–64.

Calhoun, K. S., & Atkeson, B. M. (1991). *Treatment of Rape Victims: Facilitating Social Adjustment*. New York: Pergamon.

Cameron, W. (1990). Sexual transmission of HIV and the epidemiology of other STDs. *AIDS* 4:S99–S103.

Camp, B. H., & Thyer, B. A. (1993). Treatment of adolescent sex offenders: A review of empirical research. *Journal of Applied Social Sciences* 17 (2):191–206.

Canavan, M. M., Meyer, W. J., & Higgs, D. C. (1992). The female experience of sibling incest. *Journal of Marital and Family Therapy* 18 (2):129–142.

Capaldi, D,. Crosby, L., & Stoolmiller, M. (1996). Predicting the timing of first sexual intercourse for at-risk adolescent males. *Child Development* 67 (2):344–359.

Caplan, P. J., MacPherson, G. M., & Tobin, P. G. (1985). Do sex-related differences in spatial abilities exist? A multilevel critique with new data. *American Psychologist* 40 (7):786–799.

Carani, C., Zini, D., Baldini, A., & Della Casa, L. (1990). Effects of androgen treatment in impotent males with normal and low levels of free testosterone. *Archives of Sexual Behavior* 19:223–234.

Carli, L., LaFleur, S., & Loeber, C. (1995). Nonverbal behavior, gender, and influence. *Journal of Personality and Social Psychology* 68 (6):1030–1041.

Carlson, M. (1994). Old enough to be your mother. *Time* (10 January):41.

Carlson, N. R. (1995). *Foundations of Physiological Psychology* (3d ed.). Needham Heights, MA: Allyn & Bacon.

Caron, S. L., & Brossoit, L. (1992). Rape/sexual assault on the college campus: Some questions to think about. *Journal of College Student Development* 33:182–183.

Carr, M., & Robinson, G. E. (1990). Fatal attraction: The ethical and clinical dilemma of patient-therapist sex. *Canadian Journal of Psychiatry* 35 (2):122–127.

Carroll, J. L., & Wolpe, P. R. (1996). *Sexuality and Gender in Society*. New York: HarperCollins.

Carson, D. K., Gertz, L. M., Donaldson, M. A., & Wonderlich, S. A. (1990). Family-of-origin characteristics and current family relationships of female adult incest victims. *Journal of Family Violence* 5 (2):153–171.

Cash, T. (1995). Developmental teasing about physical appearance: Retrospective descriptions and relationships with body image. *Social Behavior and Personality* 23 (2):123–129.

Castro, J. (1992). Sexual harassment: A guide. *Time* (20 January):37.

Catania, J., Coates, T., Stall, R., Bye, L., Kegles, S., Capell, F., Henne, J., McKusick, L., Morin, S., Turner, H., & Pollack, L. (1991). Changes in condom use among homosexual men in San Francisco. *Health Psychology* 10:190–199.

Cate, R. (1989). Detecting premarital abuse. *Medical Aspects of Human Sexuality* (May):104–110.

Cates, W., et al. (1999). Estimates of the incidence and prevalence of sexually transmitted diseases in the United States. *Sexually Transmitted Disease* 26 (suppl):S2–S7.

Ceci, S. J. (1994). *Cognitive and social factors in children's testimony.* Paper presented at the annual meeting of the American Psychological Association (August).

Ceci, S. J., & Loftus, E. F. (1994). Memory work: A royal road to false memories? *Applied Cognitive Psychology* 8:351–364.

Center for Population Options. (1993). *Condom Availability in Schools: A Guide for Programs.* Washington, DC: Center for Population Options.

Center for the Study of Social Policy. (1995). *Building New Futures for At-Risk Youth.* Washington, DC: Center for the Study of Social Policy.

Centers for Disease Control and Prevention. (1987). Pregnancy adolescent group for education and support—Illinois. *Morbidity and Mortality Weekly Report* (28 August).

Centers for Disease Control and Prevention. (1988). Universal precautions for prevention of transmission of HIV, hepatitis B, and other blood borne pathogens in health care settings. *Morbidity and Mortality Weekly Report* 37 (24 June): 377.

Centers for Disease Control and Prevention. (1990a). Black-white differences in cervical cancer mortality—United States, 1980–1987. *Morbidity and Mortality Weekly Report* 39:245–248.

Centers for Disease Control and Prevention. (1990b). Surveillance for HIV-2 infection in blood donors—United States, 1987–1989. *Morbidity and Mortality Weekly Report* 39:829–831.

Centers for Disease Control and Prevention. (1993a). 1993 sexually transmitted disease control guidelines. *Morbidity and Mortality Weekly Report* 42 (No. RR-14), entire issue.

Centers for Disease Control and Prevention. (1993b). Rates of cesarean delivery—United States,

1991. *Morbidity and Mortality Weekly Report* 42:285–289.

Centers for Disease Control and Prevention. (1995a). First 500,000 AIDS cases—United States, 1995. *Morbidity and Mortality Weekly Report* 44 (24 November):849–853.

Centers for Disease Control and Prevention. (1995b). Update: AIDS among women—United States. *Morbidity and Mortality Weekly Report* 44 (10 February):81–84.

Centers for Disease Control and Prevention. (1996b). AIDS associated with injecting-drug use, United States, 1995. *Morbidity and Mortality Weekly Report* 45 (17 May):392–398.

Centers for Disease Control and Prevention. (1996c). Contraceptive method and condom use among women at risk for HIV infection and other sexually transmitted diseases—Selected U.S. Sites, 1993–1994. *Morbidity and Mortality Weekly Report* 45 (38):820–823.

Centers for Disease Control and Prevention. (1996d). Provisional cases of selected notifiable diseases for weeks ending October 12, 1996. *Morbidity and Mortality Weekly Report* 45 (41):894–895.

Centers for Disease Control and Prevention. (1996e). Provisional Public Health Service recommendations for chemoprophylaxis after occupational exposure to HIV. *Morbidity and Mortality Weekly Report* 45 (7 June):468–472.

Centers for Disease Control and Prevention. (1997a). Abortion surveillance—United States, 1995. *Morbidity and Mortality Weekly Report* 46 (SS-3) (5 December):1133–1137.

Centers for Disease Control and Prevention. (1997b). Update: Syringe-exchange programs—United States, 1996. *Morbidity and Mortality Weekly Report* 46 (24):565–568.

Centers for Disease Control and Prevention. (1997c). *1995 Assisted Reproductive Technology Success Rates: National Summary and Fertility Clinic Reports.* National Center for Chronic Disease Prevention and Health Promotion, Centers for Disease Control and Prevention, U.S. Department of Health and Human Services (December) 1997.

Cerrone, G. H. (1991). Zoophilia in a rural population: Two case studies. *Journal of Rural Community Psychology* 12 (1):29–39.

Cervical cancer deaths preventable. (1996). *Contemporary Sexuality* 30 (5):(May).

Chalker, R. (1994). Updating the model of female sexuality. *SIECUS Report* 22:1–6.

Charmaz, K. (1994). Identity dilemmas of chronically ill men. *Sociological Quarterly* 35 (2):269–288.

Charney, D. A., & Russell, R. C. (1994). An overview of sexual harassment. *American Journal of Psychiatry* 151 (1):10–17.

Chasnoff, I., Landress, H., & Barrett, M. (1990). The prevalence of illicit drug or alcohol use during pregnancy and discrepancy in mandatory reporting in Pinellas Co., Florida. *New England Journal of Medicine* 322:1202–1206.

Check, J. V. P., & Malamuth, N. M. (1985). An empirical assessment of some feminist hypotheses about rape. *International Journal of Women's Studies* 8 (4):414–423.

Chia, M., & Arava, D. A. (1996). *The Multiorgasmic Male.* San Francisco: Harper.

Chilman, C. (1990). Family life education: Promoting healthy adolescent sexuality. *Family Relations* 39:123–131.

Choi, K., Catania, J., & Dolcini, M. (1994). Extramarital sex and HIV risk behavior among U.S. adults: Results from the National AIDS Behavioral Survey. *American Journal of Public Health* 84 (12):2003–2007.

Christenfeld, N. (1995). Does it hurt to say um? *Journal of Nonverbal Behavior* 19 (3):171–186.

Chung, W., & Choi, H. (1990). Erotic erection versus nocturnal erection. *Journal of Urology* 143:294–297.

Ciotti, P. (1989). Growing up different. *Los Angeles Times* (9 May, pt. 5):5, 1, 4, 10.

Clancy, P. (1986). The acquisition of communicative style in Japanese. In B. Scheffelin & E. Oaks (Eds.), *Language acquisition and socialization across cultures.* Cambridge: Cambridge University.

Clapp, J., & Capeless, E. (1990). Neonatal morphometrics after endurance exercise during pregnancy. *American Journal of Obstetrics and Gynecology* 163:1805.

Clarke, S. C. (1995a). Advance report of final divorce statistics, 1989 and 1990. *Monthly Vital Statistics Report* 43 (no. 9, supplement) (22 March).

Clarke, S. C. (1995b). Advance report of final marriage statistics, 1989 and 1990. *Monthly Vital Statistics Report* 43 (no. 12, supplement) (14 July).

Clement, U. (1990). Surveys of heterosexual behavior. *Annual Review of Sex Research* 1:45–74.

Cline, V. B. (1994). Pornography effects: Empirical and clinical evidence. In D. J. Zillman & A. C. Huston (Eds.), *Media, children and the family* (pp. 229–247). Hillsdale, NJ: Erlbaum.

Cloven, D. H., & Roloff, M. (1993). The chilling effect of aggressive potential on the expression of complaints in intimate relationships. *Communication Monographs* 60 (3):199–219.

Cloven, D. H., & Roloff, M. E. (1994). A developmental model of decisions to withhold relational irritations in romantic relationships. *Personal Relationships* 1:143–164.

Colapinto, J. (2000). *As Nature Made Him: The Boy Who Was Raised as a Girl.* New York: HarperCollins.

Cole, E., & Rothblum, E. (1990). Commentary on "Sexuality and the Midlife Woman." *Psychology of Women Quarterly* 14 (4):509–512.

Coleman, E. (1992). Is your patient suffering from compulsive sexual behavior? *Psychiatric Annals* 22 (6):320–325.

Coleman, E., Bockting, W. O., & Gooren, L. (1993). Homosexual and bisexual identity in sex-reassigned female-to-male transsexuals. *Archives of Sexual Behavior* 22 (1):37–50.

Coleman, E., Colgan, P., & Gooren, L. (1992). Male cross-gender behavior in Myanmar (Burma): A description of the acault. *Archives of Sexual Behavior* 21 (3):313–321.

Committee on Nutritional Status during Pregnancy and Lactation. (1993). *Nutrition during Pregnancy.* Washington, DC: National Academy.

Committee on Substance Abuse and Committee on Children with Disabilities, American Academy of Pediatrics. (1993). Fetal alcohol syndrome and fetal alcohol effects. *Pediatrics* 91:1004–1006.

Comstock, G., & Paik, H. J. (1991). *Television and the American Child.* Orlando, FL: Academic.

Congleton, G. K., & Calhoun, L. G. (1993). Post-abortion perceptions: A comparison of self identified distressed and non-distressed populations. *International Journal of Social Psychiatry* 39 (4):255–265.

Conradi, P. (1995). Dutch sex industry prepares to become a red-tape district. *New York Sunday Times* (6 August):16.

Consumer Reports. (1996). Another alternative: If you are contemplating adoption. *Consumer Reports* (February):55.

Consumers Union. (1989). Can you rely on condoms? *Consumer Reports* (March):135–142.

Cooper, M. (1990). "I saw what you said": Nonverbal communications and the EAP. *Employee Assistance Quarterly* 5 (4):1–12.

Corbitt, G. (1990). HIV infection in Manchester, 1959. *Lancet* 336:51.

Corea, G. (1992). *The Invisible Epidemic: The Story of Women and AIDS.* New York: HarperCollins.

Coriell, M., & Cohen, S. (1995). Concordance in the face of a stressful event. *Journal of Personality and Social Psychology* 69 (2):289–299.

Covell, K., Grusec, J., & King, G. (1995). The intergenerational transmission of maternal discipline and standards for behavior. *Social Development* 4 (1):32–43.

Cowan, G., & Dunn, K. F. (1994). What themes in pornography lead to perceptions of the degradation of women? *Journal of Sex Research* 31 (1):11–21.

Cowan, P., & Cowan, C. 1992. *When Partners Become Parents.* New York: HarperCollins.

Cowley, G. (1997). Gender limbo. *Newsweek* (19 May):64–66.

Cowley, G., & Rogers, A. (1997) Rebuilding the Male Machine. *Time* (17 November):66–67.

Cowley, G., & Rosenberg, D. (1992). A needle instead of a knife. *Newsweek* (13 April):62.

Cox, D. J. (1988). Incidence and nature of male genital exposure behaviors as reported by college women. *Journal of Sex Research* 24 (1):227–234.

Cox, D. J., Tsang, K., & Lee, A. (1982). A cross-cultural comparison of the incidence and nature of male exhibition among female college students. *Victimology: An International Journal* 7:231–234.

Craig, R., & Olson, R. (1995). Sixteen PF profiles and typologies for patients seen in marital therapy. *Psychological Report* 77 (1):187–194.

Crane, D., Soderquist, J., & Gardner, M. (1995). Gender differences in cognitive and behavioral steps toward divorce. *American Journal of Family Therapy* 23 (2):99–105.

Crosby, F. J. (1991). *Juggling: The Unexpected Advantages of Balancing Career and Home for Women and Their Families.* New York: Free.

Crowden, C., & Koch, P. (1995). Attitudes related to sexual concerns: Gender and orientation comparisons. *Journal of Sex Education and Therapy* 21 (2):78–87.

Crowley, G., et al. (1996). Testosterone: Aging men. *Newsweek,* 16 September, pp. 68–75.

Cutler, W., Garcia, C., & McCoy, N. (1987). Perimenstrual sexuality. *Archives of Sexual Behavior* 16:225–234.

Cyrus, I. (1996). Does your date want to know?: Sexual relationships and HIV disclosure. *The Volunteer* 13 (3):1–14.

D'Augelli, A. R. (1992). Lesbian and gay male undergraduates' experiences of harassment and fear on campus. *Journal of Interpersonal Violence* 7 (3):383–395.

D'Emilio, J., & Freedman, E. B. (1988). *Intimate Matters: A History of Sexuality in America.* New York: Harper & Row.

Dabbs, J. (1990). Salivary testosterone measurements: Reliability across hours, days, and weeks. *Physiology and Behavior* 48:83–86.

Dagg, P. (1991). The psychological sequelae of therapeutic abortion— Denied and completed. *American Journal of Psychiatry* 148:578–585.

Dalton, K. (1987). *Once a Month.* Ramona, CA: Hunter House.

Damassa, D., & Cates, J. (1995). Sex hormone-binding globulin and male sexual development. *Neuroscience and Biobehavioral Reviews* 19 (2):165–175.

Dannenberg, A. (1996). Suicide and HIV infection: Mortality followup of 4147 HIV seropositive military service applicants. *Journal of the American Medical Association* 276:1743–1746.

Danner, S. (1995). A short-term study of the safety, pharmacokinetics, and efficacy of Ritonavir, an inhibitor of HIV-1 protease, to treat HIV-1 infection. *New England Journal of Medicine* 333:1528–1533.

Darling, C., Davidson, J., & Cox, R. (1991). Female sexual response and the timing of partner orgasm. *Journal of Sex and Marital Therapy* 17:3–21.

Darling, C. A., Davidson, J. K., & Jennings, D. A. (1991). The female sexual response revisited: Understanding the multiorgasmic experience in women. *Archives of Sexual Behavior* 20:527–540.

David, H. P. (1994). Reproductive rights and reproductive behavior: Clash or convergence of private values and public policies? *American Psychologist* 49 (4):343–349.

Davidson, A. (1991). Looking for love in the age of AIDS: The language of gay personals, 1978–1988. *Journal of Sex Research* 28 (1):125–137.

Davidson, J., & Darling, C. (1989). Perceived differences in the female orgasmic response: New meanings for sexual satisfaction. *Family Practice Research Journal* 8:75–84.

Davidson, J., & Darling, C. (1993). Masturbatory guilt and sexual responsiveness among post-college age women: Sexual satisfaction revisited. *Journal of Sex and Marital Therapy* 19 (4):289–300.

Davidson, J., & Hoffman, L. (1986). Sexual fantasies and sexual satisfaction: An empirical analysis of erotic thought. *Journal of Sex Research* 22:184–205.

Davidson, J., & Moore, N. (1994a). Guilt and lack of orgasm during sexual intercourse: Myth versus reality among college women. *Journal of Sex Education and Therapy* 20 (3):153–174.

Davidson, J., & Moore, N. (1994b). Masturbation and premarital sexual intercourse among college women: Making choices for sexual fulfillment. *Journal of Sex and Marital Therapy* 20 (3):178–199.

Davies, G., Li, X., & Newton, J. (1993). Release characteristics, ovarian activity and menstrual bleeding pattern with a single contraceptive implant releasing 3-ketodesogestrel. *Contraception* 47:251–261.

Davis, C. M., Black, J., Lin, H., & Bonillas, C. (1996). Characteristics of vibrator use among women. *Journal of Sex Research* 33 (4):313–320.

Davis, S. (1990). Men as success objects and women as sex objects: A study of personal advertisements. *Sex Roles* 23:43–50.

Day, S. M. (1995). American Indians: Reclaiming cultural and sexual identity. *SIECUS Report* 23 (3):6–7.

Deacon, S., Minichiello, V., & Plummer, D. (1995). Sexuality and older people: Revisiting the assumptions. *Educational Gerontology* 21 (5):497–513.

DeBusk, R. (1996). Sexual activity triggering myocardial infarction: One less thing to worry about. *Journal of the American Medical Association* 275:1447–1448.

De Cock, K. (1996). Presentation at the XI International Conference on AIDS (11 July), Vancouver, BC.

de Dreu, C. (1995). Coercive power and concession making in bilateral negotiation. *Journal of Conflict Resolution* 39 (4):646–670.

de Dreu, C., Nauta, A., & Van de Vliert, E. (1995). Self-serving evaluations of conflict behavior and escalation of the dispute. *Journal of Applied Social Psychology* 25 (23):2049–2066.

Dekker, J. (1993). Inhibiting male orgasm. In W. O'Donahue & J. Geer (Eds.), *Handbook of Sexual Dysfunctions: Assessment and Treatment* (pp. 279–30l). Boston: Allyn & Bacon.

Dekker, J., & Everaerd, W. (1993). Imagery and sexual arousal. *Sexual and Marital Therapy* 8:283–285.

Delaney, C. (1995). Rites of passage in adolescence. *Adolescence* 30:891–897.

Delaney, J., Lupton, M. J., & Toth, E. (1988). *The Curse: A Cultural History of Menstruation.* Urbana, IL: University of Illinois.

DeLoach, C. P. (1994). Attitudes toward disability: Impact on sexual development and forging of intimate relationships. *Journal of Applied Rehabilitation Counseling* 25 (1):18–25.

Denenberg, R. (1993). Female sex hormones and HIV. *AIDS Clinical Care* 5:69–71, 76.

Dennis, W. (1992). *Hot and Bothered: Sex and Love in the Nineties.* New York: Viking.

Denny, N., Fields, J., & Quadagno, D. (1984). Sex differences in sexual needs and desires. *Archives of Sexual Behavior* 13:233–245.

DeSchampheleire, D. (1990). MMPI characteristics of professional prostitutes: A cross-cultural replication. *Journal of Personality Assessment* 54:343–350.

de Silva, P., & Marks, M. (1994). Jealousy as a clinical problem: Practical issues of assessment and treatment. *Journal of Mental Health (UK)* 3 (2):195–204.

deWeerth, C., & Kalma, A. (1995). Gender differences in awareness of courtship initiation tactics. *Sex Roles* 32 (11–12):717–734.

Diamond, M. (1998). Intersexuality: recommendations for management. *Archives of Sexual Behavior* 27 (6):634–641.

Diamond, M. (1999). Pediatric management of ambiguous and traumatized genitalia. *Journal of Urology* 162 (3 Pt. 2):1021–1028.

DiGiovanna, A. (1994). *Human Aging: Biological Perspectives.* New York: McGraw-Hill.

Doherty, R. W., Hatfield, E., Thompson, K., & Choo, P. (1994). Cultural and ethnic influences on love and attachment. *Personal Relationships* 1:391–398.

Donat, P. L. N., & D'Emilio, J. (1992). A feminist redefinition of rape and sexual assault: Historical foundations and change. *Journal of Social Issues* 48 (1):9–22.

Donnerstein, E. I., Linz, D. G., & Penrod, S. (1987). *The Question of Pornography: Research Findings and Policy Implications.* New York: Free.

Dorfman, L. E., Derish, P. A., & Cohen, J. B. (1992). Hey girlfriend: An evaluation of AIDS prevention among women in the sex industry. *Health Education Quarterly* 19:25–40.

Douglas, S. J. (1994). *Where the Girls Are: Growing Up Female with the Mass Media.* New York: Time.

Downey, J., & Damhave, K. (1991). The effects of place, type of comment, and effort expended on the perception of flirtation. *Journal of Social Behavior and Personality* 6 (1):35–43.

Dreger, A. D. (1998). "Ambiguous sex"— or ambivalent medicine? *The Hastings Center Report* 28:24–35.

Drew, W. L. (1994a). Hepatitis viruses. In K. Ryan (Ed.), *Sherris Medical Microbiology* (3d ed.). Norwalk, CT: Appleton & Lange.

Drew, W. L. (1994b). Sexually transmitted diseases. In K. Ryan (Ed.), *Sherris Medical Microbiology* (3d ed.). Norwalk, CT: Appleton & Lange.

Drigotas, S. M., & Rusbult, C. E. (1992). Should I stay or should I go? A dependence model of breakups. *Journal of Personality and Social Psychology* 62:62–87.

Droney, J., & Brooks, C. (1993). Attributions of self-esteem as a function of duration of eye contact.

*Journal of Social Psychology*, 133 (5):715–722.

Duffy, M. (1995). Factors influencing the health behavior of divorced women with children. *Journal of Divorce and Remarriage* 22 (304):1–12.

Duncan, D. F. (1990). Pornography as a source of sex information for university students. *Psychological Reports* 66 (2):442.

Duncan, D. F., & Donnelly, J. W. (1991). Pornography as a source of sex information at a private northeastern university. *Psychological Reports* 68 (3):782.

Dunn, M., & Trost, J. (1989). Male multiple orgasms: A descriptive study. *Archives of Sexual Behavior* 18:377–399.

Dunning, P. (1993). Sexuality and women with diabetes. *Patient Education and Counseling* 21 (1–2):5–14.

Durbin, S. (1996). Spotlight: Turkey. *PopulationToday*, March, p. 7.

Durham, R. (1989). *Human physiology.* Dubuque, IA: Brown.

Dutton, D. (1995). Intimate abusiveness. *Clinical Psychology Science and Practice* 2 (3):207–224.

Earls, C. M., & David, H. (1989). A psychosocial study of male prostitution. *Archives of Sexual Behavior* 18:401–420.

Earls, C. M., & David, H. (1990). Early family and sexual experience of male and female prostitutes. *Canada's Mental Health* 38:7–11.

Ecker, N. (1993). Culture and sexual scripts out of Africa. *SIECUS Report* 22 (2):16.

Edgley, C. (1989). Commercial sex: Pornography, prostitution and advertising. In K. McKinney & S. Sprecher (Eds.), *Human sexuality: The societal and interpersonal context* (pp. 370–424). Norwood, NJ: Ablex.

Ehrlich, G. (1988). Sexual concerns of patients with arthritis. *Medical Aspects of Human Sexuality,* March, pp. 104–107.

Einhorn, L., & Polgar, M. (1994). HIV-risk behavior among lesbians and bisexual women. *AIDS Education and Prevention* 6 (6):514–523.

Eliason, M. (1995). Accounts of sexual identity formation in heterosexual students. *Sex Roles* 32 (11–12):821–834.

Elifson, K. W., Boles, J., & Sweat, M. (1993). Risk factors associated with HIV infection among male

prostitutes. *American Journal of Public Health* 83 (1):79–83.

Elifson, K. W., Boles, J., Posey, E., Sweat, M., Darrow, W., & Elsca, W. (1993). Male transvestite prostitutes and HIV risk. *American Journal of Public Health* 83 (2):260–261.

Elliott, M. (1996). Impact of work, family, and welfare receipt on women's self-esteem in young adulthood. *Social Psychology Quarterly* 59 (1):80–95.

Ellis, G. M. (1994). Acquaintance rape. *Perspectives in Psychiatric Care* 30 (1):11–16.

Ellis, H. (1906). *Studies in the Psychology of Sex.* London: Davis.

Elmer-Dewitt, P. (1995). Cyberporn. *Time* (3 July):38–45.

Epperson, S. E., & Rochman, B. I. (1995). Romancing the students. *Time* (3 April):58–59.

Erkel, R. T. (1990). The birth of a movement. *Family Networker* 14 (3):26–35.

Etaugh, C., & Liss, M. B. (1992). Home, school and playroom: Training grounds for adult gender roles. *Sex Roles* 26 (3–4):129–147.

Everaerd, W. (1993). Male erectile disorder. In W. O'Donohue & J. H. Geer (Eds.), *Handbook of Sexual Dysfunctions* (pp. 201–224). Boston: Allyn & Bacon.

Fackelmann, K. (1992a). Herpes, HIV, and the high risk of sex. *Science News* 141:68.

Fackelmann, K. (1992b). Sex protection: Balancing the equation. *Science News* (14 March):168–169.

Fackelmann, K. (1994). AZT lowers maternal HIV transmission rate. *Science News* 145:134.

Fake aphrodisiac kills four. (1996). *Contemporary Sexuality* 30 (1):7.

Faludi, S. (1995). The money shot. *New Yorker* (30 October):64–87.

Fan, H., Conner, R. F., and Villarreal, L. P. (2000). *AIDS: Science and Society* (3d ed.). Sudbury, MA: Jones and Bartlett.

Fan, M. S., et al. (1994). Sexual attitudes and behavior of Chinese university students in Shanghai. *Journal of Sex Education and Therapy* 20 (4):277–286.

Farah, M. (1984). *Marriage and Sexuality in Islam.* Salt Lake City: University of Utah.

Farley, D. (1994). Preventing TSS. In *Current Issues in Women's Health* (2d ed.). An FDA Consumer Special Report, January. DHHS Pub. No.

(FDA)94-1181. Public Health Service, U.S. Department of Health and Human Services.

Fedoroff, J. P. (1993). Serotogenic drug treatments of deviant sexual interests. *Annals of Sex Research* 6 (2):105–121.

Feigin, R. (1994). Spousal adjustment to a post marital disability in one partner. *Family Systems Medicine* 43:95–103.

Feingold, A. (1992). Gender differences in mate selection preferences: A test of the paternal investment model. *Psychological Bulletin* 112:125–139.

Ferguson, S., & Dickson, F. (1995). Children's expectations of their single parents' dating behaviors. *Journal of Applied Communication Research* 23 (4):308–324.

Fergusson, D., Horwood, L., & Lynskey, M. (1993). Maternal smoking before and after pregnancy: Effects on behavioral outcomes in middle childhood. *Pediatrics* 92:815–822.

Fine, M., Donnelly, B., & Voydanoff, P. (1991). The relation between adolescents' perceptions of their family lives and their adjustment in stepfather families. *Journal of Adolescent Research* 6 (4):423–436.

Fine, M., Voydanoff, P., & Donnelly, B. (1993). Relations between parental control and warmth and child well-being in stepfamilies. *Journal of Family Psychology* 7 (2):222–232.

Finkelhor, D. (1990). Early and long-term effects of child sexual abuse: An update. *Professional Psychology: Research and Practice* 21:325–330.

Finkelhor, D. (1994). The international epidemiology of child sexual abuse. *Child Abuse and Neglect* 18:409–417.

Finkelhor, D., & Lewis, J. A. (1988). An epidemiological approach to the study of child molestation. In R. A. Prentky & V. J. Quinsey (Eds.), *Human Sexual Aggression: Current Perspectives* (pp. 64–78). New York: New York Academy of Sciences.

Fisher, B. S., Cullen, F. T., & Turner, M. G. (2000). *The Sexual Victimization of College Women.* U.S. Department of Justice Pub. No. NCJ 182369.

Finley, C., & Corty, E. (1993). Rape on campus: The prevalence of sexual assault while enrolled in college. *Journal of College Student Development* 34:113–117.

Fischer, J., & Heesacker, M. (1995). Men's and women's preferences regarding sex-related and nurturing traits in dating partners. *Journal of College*

*Student Development* 36 (3):260–269.

Fisher, D., & Howells, K. (1993). Social relationships in sexual offenders. *Sexual and Marital Therapy* 8 (2):123–136.

Fisher, W., Branscombe, N., & Lemery, C. (1983). The bigger the better? Arousal and attributional responses to erotic stimuli that depict different size penises. *Journal of Sex Research* 19:377–396.

Fisher, W. A., & Grenier, G. (1994). Violent pornography, antiwoman thoughts, and antiwoman acts: In search of reliable effects. *Journal of Sex Research* 31 (1):23–38.

Fitzgerald, L. F. (1993). Sexual harassment: Violence against women in the workplace. *American Psychologist* 48(10):1070–1076.

FitzGerald, M., & FitzGerald, D. (1980). The potential effects of deafness upon sexuality. *Sexuality and Disability* 3:177–181.

Flaks, D., Ficher, I., Masterpasqua, F., & Joseph, G. (1995). Lesbians choosing motherhood: A comparative study of lesbian and heterosexual parents and their children. *Developmental Psychology* 31 (1):105–114.

Fleming, D. T., et al. (1997). Herpes simplex virus type 2 in the United States, 1976 to 1994. *New England Journal of Medicine* 337 (16):1105–1111.

Fliegelman, E. (1990). Vaginismus. *Medical Aspects of Human Sexuality* (June):15–19.

Flieger, K. (1990). Testosterone: Key to masculinity and more. *FDA Consumer* (May):27–31.

Foltz, K. (1985). A kinky Calvinism. *Newsweek* (11 March):65.

Forste, R., & Tienda, M. (1992). Race and ethnic variation in the schooling consequences of female adolescent sexual activity. *Social Science Quarterly* 73 (1):12–30.

Foster, S. (1996). The sexual exploitation of women by men in power. *Counseling Today* 38 (6):1, 11–12.

Fowler, J. (1995). Homosexual parents: Implications for custody cases. *Family and Conciliation Courts Review* 33 (3):361–376.

Franchis, R., Meucci, G., & Vecchi, M., et al. (1993). The natural history of asymptomatic hepatitis B. *Annals of Internal Medicine* 118:191–194.

Francoer, R. T. (1990). Sexual archetypes in Eastern cultures can be helpful in creating sex-positive views. *Contemporary Sexuality* 22 (2):6.

Frank-Herrmann, P., Freudl, G., Baur, S., Bremme, M., Doring, G., Godehardt, E., & Sottong, U. (1991). Effectiveness and acceptability of the symptothermal method of natural family planning in Germany. *American Journal of Obstetrics and Gynecology* 165:2052–2054.

Franks, P., Shields, C., Campbell, T., & McDaniel, S. (1992). Association of social relationships with depressive symptoms. *Journal of Family Psychology* 6 (1):49–59.

Franzoi, S. (1996). *Social Psychology.* Madison, WI: Brown & Benchmark.

Frazier, P. A., & Schauben, L. J. (1994). Causal attributions and recovery from rape and other stressful life events. *Journal of Social & Clinical Psychology* 13 (1):1–14.

Freud, S. (1963). *Three Essays on the Theory of Sexuality* (U. Strachey, Ed. and Trans.). New York: Basic. (Originally published 1905)

Freund, K., & Blanchard, R. (1986). The concept of courtship disorder. *Journal of Sex and Marital Therapy* 12:79–92.

Freund, K., & Kuban, M. (1994). The basis of the abused abuser theory of pedophilia: A further elaboration on an earlier study. *Archives of Sexual Behavior* 23 (5):553–563.

Freund, K., & Watson, R. (1990). Mapping the boundaries of courtship disorder. *Journal of Sex Research* 27 (4):589–606.

Freund, M., Lee, N., & Leonard, T. (1991). Sexual behavior of clients with street prostitutes in Camden, New Jersey. *Journal of Sex Research* 28:579–591.

Freund, M., Leonard, T., & Lee, N. (1989). Sex behavior of resident street prostitutes in Camden, New Jersey. *Journal of Sex Research* 26 (4):460–478.

Friday, N. (1991). *Women on Top: How Real Life Has Changed Women's Sexual Fantasies.* New York: Simon & Schuster.

Friedman, R. (1991). Couple therapy in gay couples. *Psychiatric Annals* 21:485–490.

Friend, R. (1990). Older lesbian and gay people: A theory of successful aging. *Journal of Homosexuality* 20 (3–4):99–118.

Frieze, I. H. (1983). Causes and consequences of marital rape. *Signs* 8:532–553.

Friis, S. (1997). Cervical intraepithelial neoplasia, anogenital cancer, and other cancer types in women after hospitalization for condylomata acuminata. *Journal of Infectious Disease* 175:743–748.

Frintner, M. P., & Rubinson, L. (1993). Acquaintance rape: The influence of alcohol, fraternity membership and sports team membership. *Journal of Sex Education and Therapy* 19 (4):272–284.

Fromm, E. (1956). *The Art of Loving.* New York: Harper & Row.

Frost, J. (1994). The availability and accessibility of the contraceptive implant from family planning agencies in the United States, 1991–1992. *Family Planning Perspective* 26:4–10.

Furby, L., Weinrott, M. R., & Blackshaw, L. (1989). Sex offender recidivism: A review. *Psychological Bulletin* 105:3–30.

Gagné, M., & Lavoie, F. (1993). Young people's view on the causes of violence in adolescents' romantic relationships. *Canada's Mental Health* 41 (3):11–15.

Gagnon, J. H. (1990a). The explicit and implicit use of the scripting perspective in sex research. *Annual Review of Sex Research* 1:1–43.

Gagnon, J. H. (1990b). Gender preference in erotic relations: The Kinsey scale and sexual scripts. In D. P. McWherter, S. A. Sanders, & J. M. Reinisch (Eds.), *Homosexuality/ heterosexuality: Concepts of sexual orientation* (pp. 177–207). New York: Oxford University.

Galetto-Lacour, A. (1996). Prognostic value of viremia in patients with long-standing HIV infection. *Journal of Infectious Disease* 173:138–193.

Gangestad, S., Thornhill, R., & Yeo, R. (1994). Facial attractiveness, developmental stability, and fluctuating symmetry. *Ethology and Sociobiology* 15 (2):73–85.

Ganon, J. H., & Simon, W. (1987). The sexual scripting of oral genital contacts. *Archives of Sexual Behavior* 16:1–25.

Garbarino, J., Gaa, J., Swank, P., & McPherson, R. (1995). The relation of individuation and psychosocial development. *Journal of Family Psychology* 9 (3):311–318.

Garber, M. (1992). *Vested Interests: Cross-Dressing and Cultural Anxiety.* New York: Harper Perennial.

Garner, J. (1996). Guideline for isolation precautions in hospitals. *Infection*

*Control and Hospital Epidemiology* 17:53–80.

Garry, R. (1988). Documentation of an AIDS virus infection in the United States in 1968. *JAMA* 260:2085–2087.

Gay, J. (1986). "Mummies and babies" and friends and lovers in Lesotho. In E. Blackwood (Ed.), *The Many Faces of Homosexuality. Anthropological Approaches to Homosexual Behavior* (pp. 97–116). New York: Harrington Park.

Geis, F. L. (1993). Self-fulfilling prophecies: A social psychological view of gender. In A. E. Beall & R. J. Sternberg (Eds.), *The psychology of gender* (pp. 9–54). New York: Guilford.

Gender, A. (1992). An overview of the nurse's role in dealing with sexuality. *Sexuality and Disability* 10 (2):71–79.

Gergen, K. J. (1985). The social constructionist movement in modern psychology. *American Psychologist* 40:266–275.

Gerson, K. (1993). *No Man's Land: Men's Changing Commitments to Family and Work.* New York: Basic.

Gest, T., Lord, M., Johnson, C., Cooper, M., & Roberts, S. (1992). Sound and fury signifying little. *U.S. News and World Report* (13 July):32–38.

Ghalwash, M. (1997). (Associated Press), Egyptian Court Bans Operation on Females. *Inland Valley Daily Bulletin* (29 December):A-9.

Gibbons, M., & Vincent, C. (1994). Childhood sexual abuse. *American Family Physician* 49:125–136.

Gilbar, O., & Dagan, A. (1995). Coping with loss: Differences between widows and widowers of deceased cancer patients. *Omega Journal of Death and Dying* 31 (1):207–220.

Gilbert, N. (1995). Realities and mythologies of rape. *Society* (May/June):4–10.

Giles, J. (1994). A theory of love and sexual desire. *Journal for the Theory of Social Behavior* 24 (4):339–357.

Gilfoyle, T. J. (1992). *City of Eros: New York City, Prostitution, and the Commercialization of Sex, 1790–1920.* New York: Norton.

Gilmore, D. D. (1990). *Manhood in the Making: Cultural Concepts of Masculinity.* New Haven: Yale University.

Glass, L. (1992). *He Says, She Says.* New York: Putnam.

Gleick, E. (1996). Putting the jail in jailbait. *Newsweek* (29 January): pp. 33–34.

Glick, P. (1994). Living alone during middle adulthood. *Sociological Perspectives* 37 (3):445–457.

Gold, S., & Gold, R. (1991). Gender differences in first sexual fantasies. *Journal of Sex Education and Therapy* 17:207–216.

Gold, S. R., & Gold, R. G. (1993). Sexual aversions: A hidden disorder. In W. O'Donohue and J. H. Geer (Eds.), *Handbook of Sexual Dysfunctions* (pp. 83–102). Boston: Allyn & Bacon.

Goldberg, M. (1994). Choosing a contraceptive. In *Current Issues in Women's Health* (2d ed.). An FDA Consumer Special Report, January. DHHS Pub. No. (FDA) 94-1181. Public Health Service, U.S. Department of Health and Human Services.

Goleman, D. (1993). Abuse-prevention efforts aid children. *New York Times* (6 October):C13.

Golod, S. (1993). Sex and young people. In I. Kon & J. Riordan (Eds.), *Sex and Russian Society* (pp. 135–151). Bloomington: Indiana University.

Gonzales, M., & Meyers, S. (1993). "Your mother would like me": Self-presentation in the personals ads of heterosexual and homosexual men and women. *Personality and Social Psychology Bulletin* 19 (2):131–142.

Goodale, I., Domar, A., & Benson, H. (1990). Alleviation of premenstrual syndrome symptoms with the relaxation of response. *Obstetrics and Gynecology* 4:649–655.

Goodwin, A. (1987). Sexuality in the second half of life. In P. Doress (Ed.), *Ourselves, Growing Older.* New York: Simon & Schuster.

Goodwin, A., & Agronin, M. (1997). *A Woman's Guide to Overcoming Sexual Fear and Pain.* Oakland, CA: New Harbinger.

Gordon, L. (1976). *Woman's Body, Woman's Right: A Social History of Birth Control in America.* New York: Grossman.

Gordon, S. (1992). Values-based sexuality education. *SIECUS Report* 20 (6):1–4.

Gorman, C. (1995). Memory on trial. *Time* (17 April):54–55.

Gould, J., Davey, B., & Stafford, R. (1989). Socioeconomic differences in rates of cesarean section. *New England Journal of Medicine* 321:233.

Graber, B. (1995). Medical aspects of sexual arousal disorders. In W. O'Donohue & J. H. Geer (Eds.), *Handbook of Sexual Dysfunctions* (pp. 103–156). Boston: Allyn & Bacon.

Graham, D., Rawlings, E., Ihms, K., & Latimer, D. (1995). A scale for identifying "Stockholm Syndrome" reactions in young dating women. *Violence and Victims* 10 (1):3–22.

Grammer, K. (1990). Strangers meet: Laughter and nonverbal signs of interest in opposite-sex encounters. *Journal of Nonverbal Behavior* 14(4):209–236.

Grammer, K., & Thornhill, R. (1994). Human facial attractiveness and sexual selection: The role of symmetry and averageness. *Journal of Comparative Psychology* 108 (3):233–242.

Grant, L. (1994). The timid crusade. *NPG Forum* (January):1–12.

Green, R., & Fleming, D. T. (1990). Transsexual surgery follow-up: Status in the 1990s. *Annual Review of Sex Research* 1:163–174.

Gregersen, E. (1983). *Sexual Practices: The Story of Human Sexuality.* New York: Franklin Watts.

Gregersen, E. (1986). Human sexuality in cross-cultural perspective. In D. Byrne & K. Kelly (Eds.), *Alternative Approaches to the Study of Sexual Behavior* (pp. 35–47). Hillsdale, NJ: Erlbaum.

Gregory, S. (1992). Teaching young fathers the ropes. *Time* (10 August):49.

Grenier, G., & Byers, E. (1997). The Relationship Among Ejaculatory Control, Ejaculatory Latency, and Attempts to Prolong Heterosexual Intercourse. *Archives of Sexual Behavior* 26(1):27–47.

Griffiths, A., Miller, J., Suzuki, D., Lewontin, R., & Gelbart, W. (1993). *An Introduction to Genetic Analysis.* New York: Freeman.

Grifflin, S. (1981). *Pornography and Silence: Cultures' Revenge Against Nature.* New York: Harper & Row.

Grimes, D. (1992). The safety of oral contraceptives: Epidemiologic insights from the first 30 years. *American Journal of Obstetrics and Gynecology* 166:1950–1954.

Grimshaw, G., Sitarenios, G., & Finegan, J. (1995). Mental rotation at 7 years: Relations with prenatal testosterone levels and spatial play experiences. *Brain and Cognition* 29 (1):85–100.

Gross, D., Fogg, L., & Tucker, S. (1995). The efficacy of parent training for promoting positive parent-toddler relationships. *Research in Nursing and Health* 18 (6):489–499.

Gross, S. H., & Bingham, M. W. (1980). *Women in Traditional China*. St. Louis Park, MN: Glenhurst.

Grossman, K., & McNamara, J. (1989). Screening procedure for use with a self-help book to overcome dating anxiety. *Psychological Reports* 65 (2):385–386.

Groth, N. A., & Hobson, W. F. (1983). The dynamics of sexual assault. In L. Schlesinger and E. Revitch (Eds.), *Sexual Dynamics of Antisocial Behavior*. Springfield, IL: Thomas.

Groth, N. A., Hobson, W. F., & Gary, T. S. (1982). The child molester: Clinical observations. *Journal of Social Work and Human Sexuality* 1:129–144.

Grove, N. (1996). The many faces of Thailand. *National Geographic* 189 (2):82–104.

Grubin, D. (1993). Sexual offending: A cross-cultural comparison. *Annual Review of Sex Research* 3:201–217.

Gruen, R., Gwadz, M., & Morrobel, D. (1994). Support, criticism, emotion, and depressive symptoms. *Journal of Social and Personal Relationships* 11 (4):619–624.

Guerrero, L., & Anderson, P. (1994). Patterns of matching and initiation: Touch behavior and touch avoidance across romantic relationship stages. *Journal of Nonverbal Behavior* 18 (2):137–153.

Gutman, H. G. (1976). *The Black Family in Slavery and Freedom*. New York: Pantheon.

Guttmacher, A., & Kaiser, I. (1986). The genesis of liberalized abortion in New York: A personal insight. In J. Butler & D. Walbert (Eds.), *Abortion, Medicine, and the Law* (3d ed., pp. 229–246). New York: Facts on File.

Hack, M., Taylor, H., Klein, N., Eiben, R., Schatschneider, D., & Mercuri-Minich, N. (1994). School-age outcomes in children with birth weights under 750 g. *New England Journal of Medicine* 12:755–759.

Hack, T., Osachuk, T., & DeLuca, R. (1994, April). Group treatment for sexually abused preadolescent boys. *Families in Society* 75 (1):217–228.

Hackstaff, K. (1993). The rise of divorce culture and its gendered foundations. *Feminism and Psychology* 3 (3):363–368.

Hadley, M. (1996), *Endocrinology* (4th ed.). Upper Saddle River, NJ: Prentice Hall.

Haffner, D. (1995/96). The essence of consent is communication. *SIECUS Report* 24 (2):2–3.

Hakim-Elahi, E., Tovell, H., & Burnhill, M. (1990). Complications of first trimester abortion: A report of 170,000 cases. *Obstetrics and Gynecology* 76:129–135.

Haldeman, D. (2000). Therapeutic responses to sexual orientation: Psychology's evaluation. In B. Greene & G. L. Croom (Eds.), *Education, Research, and Practice in Lesbian, Gay, Bisexual, and Transgendered Psychology: A Resource Manual* (pp. 244–262). Thousand Oaks, CA: Sage.

Hall, G. S. (1904). *Adolescence: Its Psychology and Its Relation to Physiology, Anthropology, Sociology, Sex, Crime, Religion and Education* (vols. 1–2). New York: Appleton.

Hallstrom, T., & Samuelsson, S. (1990). Changes in women's sexual desire in middle life: The longitudinal study of women in Gothenburg. *Archives of Sexual Behavior* 19 (3):259–268.

Halpern, C., Udry, J., Campbell, B., & Suchindran, C. (1993). Testosterone and pubertal development as predictors of sexual activity: A panel analysis of adolescent males. *Psychosomatic Medicine* 55 (5):436–447.

Hamilton, R. (1997). "Big Steps Forward for Amputees." *FDA Consumer* 31(2):6–11.

Hanassab, S., & Tidwell, R. (1993). Change in the premarital behavior and sexual attitudes of young Iranian women: From Tehran to Los Angeles. *Counseling Psychology Quarterly* 6 (4):281–289.

Hansell, D. (1993). *Legal Answers About AIDS*. New York: Gay Men's Health Crisis.

Harlap, S., Shiono, P., & Ramcharan, S. (1980). A life table of spontaneous abortions and the effects of age, parity, and other variables. In I. Porter & E. Hook (Eds.), *Human Embryonic and Fetal Death*. New York: Academy.

Harrison, F. (1978). *The Dark Angel: Aspects of Victorian Sexuality*. New York: Universe.

Hartin, W. (1990). Remarriage: Some issues for clients and therapists. *Australian and New Zealand Journal of Family Therapy* 11 (1):36–42.

Haste, F., Brooke, O., Anderson, H., Bland, H., Shaw, J., Griffin, A., & Peacock, J. (1990). Nutrient intakes during pregnancy: Observations on the influence of smoking and social class. *American Journal of Clinical Nutrition* 51:29–36.

Hatano, Y. (1991). Change in the sexual activities of Japanese. *Journal of Sex Education and Therapy* 17 (1):1–14.

Hatfield, E., & Rapson, R. L. (1996). *Love and Sex: Cross Cultural Perspectives*. Boston: Allyn & Bacon.

Hatfield, E., Schmitz, E., Cornelius, J., & Rapson, R. (1988). Passionate love: How early does it begin? *Journal of Psychology and Human Sexuality* 1 (1):35–51.

Hatfield, E., & Sprecher, S. (1995). Men's and women's preferences in marital partners in the United States, Russia, and Japan. *Journal of Cross-Cultural Psychology* 26 (6):728–750.

Hauth, J. C. (1995). Reduced incidence of preterm delivery with metronidazole and erythromycin in women with bacterial vaginosis. *New England Journal of Medicine* 333:1732–1736.

Hawton, K. (1992). Sex therapy [Special Issue: The changing face in behavioral psychotherapy]. *Behavioral Psychotherapy* 19:131–136.

Hawton, K., Catalan, J., & Fagg, J. (1992). Sex therapy for erectile dysfunction: Characteristics of couples, treatment outcome, and prognostic factors. *Archives of Sexual Behavior* 2:161–175.

Hayes, A. (1995). Age preferences for same- and opposite-sex partners. *Journal of Social Psychology* 135 (2):125–133.

Haywood, T. W., & Grossman, L. S. (1994). Denial of deviant sexual arousal and psychopathology in child molesters. *Behavior Therapy* 25 (2):327–340.

Hazen, C., & Shaver, P. (1987). Romantic love conceptualized as an attachment process. *Journal of Personality and Social Psychology* 52 (3):511–524.

Heider, K. G. (1979). *Grand Valley Dani: Peaceful Warriors*. New York: Holt, Rinehart & Winston.

Heiman, J., & LoPiccolo, J. (1988). *Becoming Orgasmic*. New York: Prentice Hall.

Heinrich, R., Corbine, J., & Thomas, K. (1990). Counseling Native Americans. *Journal of Counseling and Development* 69:128–132.

Hemenway, D., Solnick, S., & Carter, J. (1994). Child-rearing violence. *Child Abuse and Neglect* 18 (12):1011–1020.

Henderson-King, D., & Veroff, J. (1994). Sexual satisfaction and marital well-being in the first years of marriage. *Journal of Social and Personal Relationships* 11 (4):509–534.

Hennekens, C. (1996). Postmenopausal estrogen and progestin use and the risk of cardiovascular disease. *New England Journal of Medicine* 335 (7):453.

Henry, C., & Lovelace, S. (1995). Family resources and adolescent family life satisfaction in remarried family households. *Journal of Family Issues* 16 (6):765–786.

Herdt, G. H. (Ed.) (1984). *Ritualized Homosexuality in Melanesia.* Berkeley: University of California.

Herold, E. S., & Mewhinney, D. M. (1993). Gender differences in casual sex and AIDS prevention: A survey of dating bars. *Journal of Sex Research* 30 (1):36–42.

Heyl, B.S. (1974). The madam as entrepreneur. *Sociological Symposium* 11:61–87.

Hickson, F., Davies, P., Hunt, A., & Weatherburn, P. (1992). Maintenance of open gay relationships: Some strategies for protection against HIV. *AIDS Care* 4 (4):409–419.

Hickson, F., Davies, P., Hunt, A., Weatherburn, P., McManus, T., & Coxon, A. (1994). Gay men as victims of nonconsensual sex. *Archives of Sexual Behavior* 23 (3):281–294.

Hite, S. (1976). *The Hite Report.* New York: Macmillan.

Hite, S. (1982). *The Hite Report: A Study on Male Sexuality.* New York: Ballantine.

Ho, G. Y. F., et al. (1998). Natural history of cervicovaginal papillomavirus infection in young women. *New England Journal of Medicine* 338 (7):423–428.

Hockenberry, S., & Billingham, R. (1993). Psychological reactance and violence within dating relationships. *Psychological Reports* 73 (3, part 2):1203–1208.

Hockenberry-Eaton, M., Richman, M., Di Iorio, C., & Rivero, T. (1996). Mother and adolescent knowledge of sexual development: The effects of gender, age, and sexual experience. *Adolescence* 31 (121):35–47.

Hodge, R. W. & Ogawa, N. (1992). *Fertility Change in Contemporary Japan.* Chicago: University of Chicago.

Hodson, D., & Skeen, P. (1994). Sexuality and aging: The hammerlock of myths. *Journal of Applied Gerontology* 13 (3):219–235.

Hoerder, D. (1994). Changing paradigms in migration history: From "to America" to world-wide systems. *Canadian Review of American Studies* 24 (2):105–126.

Hogben, M., Byrne, D., & Hamburger, M. (1996). Coercive heterosexual sexuality in dating relationships of college students: Implications of differential male-female experiences. *Journal of Psychology and Human Sexuality* 8 (1/2):69–78.

Holden, C. (1987). Female math anxiety on the wane. *Science* 236:660–661.

Holden, C. (1991). Is "gender gap" narrowing? *Science* 253 (23):959–960.

Holden, C. (1994). Teen sex survey back on track. *Science* 263 (154):1688.

Hole, J. (1994). *Human Anatomy and Physiology.* (6th ed.). Dubuque, IA: Brown.

Holmes, J. (1989). Compliments and compliment responses in New Zealand English. *Anthropological Linguistics* 28:485–508.

Hooker, E. (1957). The adjustment of the male overt homosexual. *Journal of Projective Techniques* 21:18–31.

Hooker, E. (1993). Reflections of a 40-year exploration: A scientific view on homosexuality. *American Psychologist* 48 (4):450–453.

Hopwood, N. (1990). The onset of human puberty. In J. Bancroft & J. Reinisch (Eds.), *Adolescence and Puberty.* New York: Oxford University.

Hornblower, M. (1993). The skin trade. *Time* (21 June):44.

Horst, E. (1995). Reexamining gender issues in Erikson's stages of identity and intimacy. (1995). *Journal of Counseling and Development* 73 (3):271–278.

How to lower risk for patients with heart disease. (1995). *Geriatrics* 50 (8):16.

Huffman, T., Chang, K., Rausch, P., & Schaffer, N. (1994). Gender differences and factors related to the disposition toward cohabitation. *Family Therapy* 21 (3):171–184.

Hughes, D. L., & Galinsky, E. (1994). Gender, job and family conditions, and psychological symptoms. *Psychology of Women Quarterly* 18:251–270.

Hughes, R., Good, E., & Candell, K. (1993). A longitudinal study of the effects of social support on the psychological adjustment of divorced mothers. *Journal of Divorce and Remarriage* 19 (1–2):37–56.

Hunt, L. (Ed.) (1993). *The Invention of Pornography: Obscenity and the Origins of Modernity, 1500–1800.* New York: Zone.

Hurlbert, D. (1991). The role of assertiveness in female sexuality: A comparative study between sexually assertive and sexually nonassertive women. *Journal of Sex and Marital Therapy* 17 (3):183–190.

Hurlbert, D., & Apt, C. (1993). Female sexuality: A comparative study between women in homosexual and heterosexual relationships. *Journal of Sex and Marital Therapy* 19 (4):315–327.

Hurlbert, D., & Whittaker, K. (1991). The role of masturbation in marital and sexual satisfaction: A comparative study of female masturbators and nonmasturbators. *Journal of Sex Education and Therapy* 17 (4):272–282.

Huston, M., & Schwartz, M. (1996). Gendered dynamics in the romantic relationships of lesbians and gay men. In J. Woods (Ed.), *Gendered Relationships* (pp. 163–175). Mountain View, CA: Mayfield.

Hyde, J. (1991). *Half the Human Experience: The Psychology of Women* (4th ed.). Lexington, MA: Heath.

Hyde, J. S., Fennema, E., & Lamon, S. J. (1990). Gender differences in mathematics performance: A meta-analysis. *Psychological Bulletin* 107:139–155.

Ilaria, G., Jacobs, J., Polsky, H., Koll, B., Baron, P., Machow, C., Armstrong, D., & Schlegel, P. (1992). Detection of HIV-1 DNA sequences in preejaculatory fluid. *Lancet* 340:1469.

India seeks to control population by discouraging child marriage. (1997). *Contemporary Sexuality* 31 (2):7–8.

Indian Council of Medical Research Task Force on Hormonal Contraception. (1993). Phase III clinical trial with Norplant II (two covered rods): Report on 5 years of use. *Contraception* 48:120–132.

Institute of Medicine, Subcommittee on Nutritional Status and Weight Gain During Pregnancy. (1990). *Nutrition during Pregnancy.* Washington, DC: Academy.

Isensee, R. (1990). *Love between Men.* Los Angeles: Alyson.

Jackson, G. (2000). Sexual intercourse and stable angina pectoris. *American Journal of Cardiology* 20:35F–37F.

Jacob, K. A. (1981). The Mosher report. *American Heritage,* 57–64.

Jacobs, J. (1992). Facilitators of romantic attraction and their relation to lovestyle. *Social Behavior and Personality* 20 (3):227–233.

Jacobson, M. F., & Mazur, L. A. (1995). *Marketing Madness.* Boulder, CO: Westview.

James, A., Tucker, M., & Mitchell-Kernan, C. (1996). Marital attitudes, perceived mate availability, and subjective well-being among partnered African American men and women. *Journal of Black Psychology* 22 (1):20–36.

Jamison, P., & Gebhard, P. (1988). Penis size increase between flaccid and erect states. *Journal of Sex Research* 1:177–183.

Janus, S. S., & Janus, C. L. (1993). *The Janus Report on Sexual Behavior.* New York: Wiley.

Japanese practice mourning ritual for abortion. (1996, March). *Contemporary Sexuality* 30 (3):4.

Jayne, C. (1981). A two-dimensional model for female sexual response. *Journal of Sex and Marital Therapy* 7:3–30.

Jeffries, V. (1993). Virtue and attraction: Validation of a measure of love. *Journal of Social and Personal Relationships* 19 (1):99–117.

Jenkins, S. (1996). Self-definition in thought, action and life path choices. *Personality and Social Psychology Bulletin* 22 (1):99–111.

Jensen, E. R. (1996). The fertility impact of alternative family planning distribution channels in Indonesia. *Demography* 33 (2):153.

Joesoef, M. (1996). Douching and sexually transmitted diseases in pregnant women in Surabaya, Indonesia. *American Journal of Obstetrics and Gynecology* 174:115–119.

Johnson, J., Aikman, K., Danner, C., & Elling, K. (1995). Attributions of shy persons in romantic relationships. *Journal of Clinical Psychology* 51 (4):532–536.

Johnson, J. T. (1992). *Mothers of Incest Survivors: Another Side of the Story.* Bloomington: Indiana University.

Johnston, L., Ward, T., & Hudson, S. M. (1997). Deviant sexual thoughts: Mental control and the treatment of sexual offenders. *Journal of Sex Research* 34 (2):121–130.

Jolles, C. (1989). Gynecologic cancer associated with pregnancy. *Seminars in Oncology* 16:417–424.

Jones, E. (1985). Teen pregnancy in developed countries. *Family Planning Perspectives* 2:53–62.

Jones, J. (1994). Embodied meaning: Menopause and the change of life. *Social Work in Health Care* 19 (3–4):43–65.

Jones, W. P., & Emerson, S. (1994). Sexual abuse and binge eating in a nonclinical population. *Journal of Sex Education and Therapy* 20 (1):47–55.

Kafka, M. P. (1994). Sertraline pharmaco-therapy for paraphilias and paraphilia-related disorders: An open trial. *Annals of Clinical Psychology* 6 (3):189–195.

Kahn, A., Mathie, V. A., & Torgler, C. (1994). Rape scripts and rape acknowledgement. *Psychology of Women Quarterly* 18:53–66.

Kalb, C. (1996). How old is too old? *Newsweek* (5 May):64.

Kalichman, S. C. (1991). Psychopathology and personality characteristics of criminal sexual offenders as a function of victim age. *Archives of Sexual Behavior* 20:187–197.

Kallman, F. J. (1952). Twin and sibship study of overt male homosexuality. *American Journal of Human Genetics* 4:136–146.

Kantor, L. M., & Haffner, D. W. (1995). Responding to "The failure of sex education." *SIECUS Report* 23 (3):17–18.

Kantrowitz, B. (1996). Gay families come out. *Newsweek* (4 November):50–57.

Kao, J. (1996). Transmission of hepatitis C virus between spouses. *American Journal of Gastroenterology* 91:2087–2090.

Kaplan, H. (1974). *The New Sex Therapy: Active Treatment of Sexual Dysfunctions.* New York: Simon & Schuster.

Kaplan, H. (1979). *Disorders of Sexual Desire.* New York: Brunner/Mazel.

Kaplan, H. (1983). *The Evaluation of Sexual Disorders.* New York: Brunner/Mazel.

Kaplan, H. (1987). *The Illustrated Manual of Sex Therapy.* New York: Brunner/Mazel.

Kaplan, H. S., & Owett, T. (1993). The female androgen insensitivity syndrome. *Journal of Sex and Marital Therapy* 19:3–25.

Katner, H. (1987). Evidence for a Euro-American origin of human immunodeficiency virus. *Journal of the National Medical Association* 79:1068–1072.

Katz, W. L. (1968). *The American Negro: His History and Literature.* New York: Arno.

Kaufman, M. "The Tetrogenic Effects of Alcohol Following Exposure During Pregnancy, and Its Influence on the Chromosome Constitution of the Pre-Ovulatory Egg." *Alcohol and Alcoholism* (June 1997):1375–1384.

Kay, D. Masturbation and mental health: Uses and abuses. *Sexual and Marital Therapy* 7:97–107.

Kegeles, S., Hays, R., & Coates, T. (1996). The Mpower Project: A community-level HIV prevention intervention for young gay men. *American Journal of Public Health* 86:1129–1136.

Kehoe, M. (1989). Lesbians over 60 speak for themselves. *Journal of Homosexuality* 16 (3–4).

Kell, C. (1992). The internal dynamics of the extramarital affair: A counseling perspective. *Sexual and Marital Therapy* (2):157–172.

Kelland, K. (1995). Dutch sex trade urges end to brothel bar. *Reuters North American Wire Service* (4 June).

Kellett, J. (1991). Sexuality of the elderly. *Sexual and Marital Therapy* 6 (2):147–155.

Kelley, P. (1992). Healthy stepfamily functioning. *Families in Society* 73 (10):579–587.

Kelly, G. F. (1996). *Sexuality Today: The Human Perspective* (5th ed.). Madison, WI: Brown & Benchmark.

Kelly, K., Dawson, L., & Musialowski, D. M. (1989). The three faces of sexual explicitness: The good, the bad and the useful. In D. Zillman & J. Bryant (Eds.), *Pornography: Research advances and policy considerations* (pp. 57–85). Hillsdale, NJ: Erlbaum.

Kelly, M. P., Strassberg, D. S., & Kircher, J. R. (1990). Attitudinal and experiential correlates of anorgasmia. *Archives of Sexual Behavior* 19 (2):165–167.

Kennedy, J. (1995). Teachers, student teachers, paraprofessionals, and young adults' judgments about the acceptable use of corporal punishment in the rural South.

*Education and Treatment of Children* 18 (1):53–64.

Kennedy, S., & Over, R. (1990). Psychophysiological assessment of male sexual arousal following spinal cord injury. *Archives of Sexual Behavior* 1:15–27.

Kennel, J., Klaus, M., McGrath, S., Robertson, S., & Hinkley, C. (1991). Continuous emotional support during labor in a U.S. hospital: A randomized controlled trial. *Journal of the American Medical Association* 2197:265.

Kenner, A. (1993). A cross-cultural study of body-focused hand movement. *Journal of Nonverbal Behavior* 17 (4):263–279.

Kenrick, D., & Keefe, R. (1992). Age preferences in mates reflect sex differences in human reproductive strategies. *Behavioral and Brain Sciences* 15 (1):75–133.

Kenrick, D., Keefe, R., Bryan, A., & Barr, A. (1995). Age preferences and mate choice among homosexuals and heterosexuals: A case for modular psychological mechanisms. *Journal of Personality and Social Psychology* 69 (6):1166–1172.

Kenrick, D. T., & Trost, M. R. (1993). The evolutionary perspective. In A. E. Beall & R. J. Sternberg (Eds.), *The psychology of gender* (pp. 148–172). New York: Guilford.

Kessler, S. (1990). The medical construction of gender: Case management of intersexed infants. *Signs* 16 (1):3–26.

Kestelman, P., & Trussell, J. (1991). Efficacy of the simultaneous use of condoms and spermicides. *Family Planning Perspectives* 23:226–227, 232.

Ketti, P., Zarfoss, S., Jacoby, K., Garman, C., Hulse, C., Rowley, F., Cory, R., Sredy, M., Bixler, E., & Tyson, K. (1991). Female sexuality after spinal cord injury. *Sexuality and Disability* 9:287–295.

Kilpatrick, A. C. (1992). *Long Range Effects of Child and Adolescent Sexual Experiences: Myths, Mores and Miracles.* Hillsdale, NJ: Erlbaum.

Kilpatrick, S., & Laros, R. (1989). Characteristics of normal labor. *Obstetrics and Gynecology* 74:85.

Kincaid, S., & Caldwell, R. (1995). Marital separation: Causes, coping, and consequences. *Journal of Divorce and Remarriage* 22 (3–4):109–128.

King, C., & Miskovic, J. (1996). Ethical issues: A survey of perioperative nurses. *Seminars in Perioperative Nursing* 15:84–91.

King, M., & McDonald, E. (1992). Homosexuals who are twins. *British Journal of Psychiatry* 160:407–409.

Kinney, J. (1994). *Loosening The Grip: A Handbook of Alcohol Information* (5th ed.). St. Louis: Mosby.

Kinsey, A. C., Pomeroy, W. B., & Martin, C. E. (1948). *Sexual Behavior in the Human Male.* Philadelphia: Saunders.

Kinsey, A. C., Pomeroy, W. B., Martin, C. E., & Gebhard, P. H. (1953). *Sexual Behavior in the Human Female.* Philadelphia: Saunders.

Kirkpatrick, L.A., & Hazen, C. (1994). Attachment styles and close relationships. *Personal Relationships* 1:123–142.

Kirkpatrick, M., Smith, C., & Roy, R. (1981). Lesbian mothers and their children: A comparative study. *American Journal of Orthopsychiatry* 51:545–551.

Kitcher, P. (1996). *Lives to Come.* New York: Simon & Schuster.

Klassen, W. (1993). The sacred kiss in the New Testament. *New Testament Studies* 39 (1):122–135.

Klein, J. (1996). The predator problem. *Newsweek* (26 April):32.

Kleinke, C., & Taylor, C. (1991). Evaluation of opposite-sex person as a function of gazing, smiling, and forward lean. *Journal of Social Psychology* 131 (3):451–453.

Klinkenberg, D., & Rose, S. (1994). Dating scripts of gay men and lesbians. *Journal of Homosexuality* 26 (4):23–35.

Klonoff-Cohen, H., Edelstein, S., Lefkowitz, E., Srinivasan, I., Kaegi, D., Chang, J., & Wiley, K. (1995). The effects of passive smoking and tobacco exposure through breast milk on sudden infant death syndrome. *Journal of the American Medical Association* 273:795–798.

Kluft, R. P. (1993). *Incest-Related Syndromes of Adult Psychopathology.* Washington, DC: American Psychiatric.

Kochman, T. (1981). *Black and White Styles in Conflict.* Chicago: University of Chicago.

Kockott, G., & Fahmer, E. M. (1988). Male-to-female and female-to-male transsexuals: A comparison. *Archives of Sexual Behavior* 17 (6):539–546.

Koff, E., & Rierdan, J. (1995). Preparing girls for menstruation: Recommendations from adolescent girls. *Adolescence* 30 (120):795–811.

Kolaric, G., & Galambos, N. (1995). Face-to-face interactions in unacquainted female-male adolescent dyads: How do girls and boys behave? *Journal of Early Adolescence* 15 (3):363–382.

Kolodny, R., Masters, W., & Johnson, V. (1979). *Textbook of Sexual Medicine.* Boston: Little, Brown.

Koonin, L., Smith, J., Ramick, M., & Green, C. (1995). Abortion surveillance—United States. *CDC Surveillance Summaries* (3 May). *Morbidity and Mortality Weekly Report* 46 (December 1997):1133–1137.

Koop, C. E. (1996). HIV and AIDS: Facts that could save your life. Via the Internet.

Kormos, K. C., & Brooks, C. I. (1994). Acquaintance rape: Attributions of victim blame by college students and prison inmates as a function of relationship status of victim and assailant. *Psychological Reports* 74 (2):545–546.

Koss, M. P. (1992). Date rape: Victimization by acquaintances. *Harvard Mental Health Letter* 9 (3):5–6.

Koss, M. P. (1993). Rape: Scope, impact, intervention and public policy responses. *American Psychologist* 48 (10):1062–1069.

Koster, A., & Garde, K. (1993). Sexual desire and menopausal development: A prospective study of Danish women born in 1936. *Maturitas* 16 (1):49–60.

Koutsky, L. (1997). Epidemiology of genital human papillomavirus infection. *American Journal of Medicine* 102 (suppl 5A):3–8.

Kratz, C. (1990). Sexual solidarity and the secrets of sight and sound. *American Ethnologist* 17:449–467.

Kresin, D. (1993). Medical aspects of inhibited sexual desire disorder. In W. O'Donohue & J. H. Geer (Eds.), *Handbook of Sexual Dysfunctions* (pp. 15–51). Boston: Allyn & Bacon.

Krishnan, V. (1994). The impact of wives' employment on attitude toward divorce. *Journal of Divorce and Remarriage* 22 (1–2):87–101.

Kristof, K. M. (1994). Welfare or no, teen pregnancy spells poverty. *Los Angeles Times* (28 August):D4.

**Kroll, K., & Klein, E.** (1992). *Enabling Romance.* New York: HarperCollins.

**Kuiper, B., & Cohen-Kettenis, P.** (1988). Sex reassignment surgery: A study of 141 Dutch transsexuals. *Archives of Sexual Behavior* 17:439–457.

**Kurdek, L. A.** (1993). The allocation of household labor in gay, lesbian and heterosexual married couples. *Journal of Social Issues* 49 (3):127–139.

**Kyman, W.** (1995). The first step: Sexuality education for parents. *Journal of Sex Education and Therapy* 21 (3):153–157.

**Labbock, M.** (1989). Breastfeeding and fertility. *Medical Aspects of Human Sexuality* (March):43–56.

**Lackritz, E.** (1995). Estimated risk of transmission of HIV by screened blood in the United States. *New England Journal of Medicine* 333:1721–1725.

**Ladas, A.** (1989). False information about female anatomy causes great unhappiness. *Contemporary Sexuality* 21:5–11.

**Ladas, A., Whipple, B., & Perry, J.** (1982). *The G Spot.* New York: Holt, Rinehart, & Winston.

**Landry, D., & Forrest, J.** (1995). How old are U.S. fathers? *Family Planning Perspectives* 27 (4):159–161.

**Langevin, R.** (1992). Biological factors contributing to paraphilic behavior. *Psychiatric Annals* 22 (6):307, 309–314.

**Langmyhr, G.** (1976). Varieties of coital positions: Advantages and disadvantages. *Medical Aspects of Human Sexuality* (June):128–139.

**Langston, C.** (1995). Excess intrauterine fetal demise associated with maternal HIV infection. *Journal of Infectious Disease* 172:1451–1460.

**Lapins, J.** (1996). Mucocutaneous manifestations of 22 consecutive cases of primary HIV-1 infection. *British Journal of Dermatology* 134:257–261.

**Larson, J.** (1992). "You're my one and only": Premarital counseling for unrealistic beliefs about mate selection. *American Journal of Family Therapy* 20 (3):242–253.

**La Tour, M. S.** (1990). Female nudity in print advertising: An analysis of gender differences in arousal and ad response. *Psychology and Marketing* 7:65–81.

**Laumann, E. O., Gagnon, J. H., Michael, R. T., & Michaels, S.** (1994). *The Social Organization of Sexuality.* Chicago: University of Chicago.

**Lebegue, B.** (1991). Paraphilias in U.S. pornography titles: "Pornography made me do it." (Ted Bundy). *Bulletin of the American Academy of Psychiatry and the Law* 19 (1):43–48.

**Lebra, T. S.** (1986). *Japanese Patterns of Behavior.* Honolulu: University of Hawaii.

**Lee, E.** (1994). Spotlight: Jordan. *Population Today* 22, (September):7.

**Lee, J.** (1988). Love styles. In R. Sternberg & M. Barnes (Eds.), *The Psychology of Love.* New Haven, CT: Yale University.

**Leidig, M. W.** (1992). The continuum of violence against women: Psychological and physical consequences. *Journal of American College Health* 40:149–155.

**Leigh, B. C.** (1989). Reasons for having and avoiding sex: Gender sexual orientation and relationship to sexual behavior. *Journal of Sex Research* 26:199–209.

**Leigh, B., & Aramburu, B.** (1996). The role of alcohol and gender in choices and judgments about hypothetical sexual encounters. *Journal of Applied Social Psychology* 26 (1):20–30.

**Leitenberg, H., Detzer, M., & Srebnik, D.** (1993). Gender differences in masturbation and the relation of masturbation experience in preadolescence and/or early adolescence to sexual behavior and sexual adjustment in young adulthood. *Archives of Sexual Behavior* 22:87–98.

**Leitenberg, H., Greenwald, E., & Tarran, M.** (1989). The relation between sexual activity among children during preadolescence and adolescence and sexual adjustment in early adulthood. *Archives of Sexual Behavior* 18:299–313.

**Leitenberg, H., & Henning, K.** (1995). Sexual fantasy. *Psychological Bulletin* 117:469–496.

**LeJeune, C., & Follette, V.** (1994). Taking responsibility: Sex differences in reporting dating violence. *Journal of Interpersonal Violence* 9 (1):133–140.

**LeMaire, W.** (1988). Management of a newborn with ambiguous genitalia. *Medical Aspects of Human Sexuality* (January):633–646.

**Lemp, G., Hirozawa, A., Givertz, D., & Nieri, G.** (1994). Seroprevalence of HIV and risk behaviors among young homosexual and bisexual men: The San Francisco/Berkeley Young Men's Survey. *Journal of the American Medical Association* 272 (6):449–454.

**Lemp, G., Jones, M., Kellogg, T., & Niere, G.** (1995). HIV seroprevalence and risk behaviors among lesbians and bisexual women in San Francisco and Berkeley, California. *American Journal of Public Health* 85 (11):1549–1552.

**Leo, J.** (1992). The quagmire of abortion rights. *U.S. News and World Report* (13 July):16.

**Leon, J., Parra, F., Cheng, T., & Flores, E.** (1995). Love styles among Latino community college students in Los Angeles. *Psychological Reports* 77 (2):527–530.

**Leshner, A.** (1978). *An Introduction to Behavioral Endocrinology.* New York: Oxford University.

**Letournea, E., & O'Donohue, W.** (1993) Sexual desire disorders. In W. O'Donohue and J. Geer (Eds.), *Handbook of Sexual Dysfunctions: Assessment and Treatment* (pp. 53–81). Boston: Allyn & Bacon.

**Leung, A., & Robson, W.** (1993). Childhood masturbation. *Clinical Pediatrics* 32 (4):238–241.

**Lever, J., Kanouse D., Rogers, W., & Carson, S.** (1992). Behavior patterns and sexual identity of bisexual males. *Journal of Sex Research* 29 (2):141–167.

**Levin, R. J.** (1993). The mechanism of human female sexual arousal. *Annual Review of Sex Research* 3:1–48.

**Levine, S. B., Risen, C. B., & Althof, S. E.** (1990). Essay on the diagnosis and nature of paraphilia. *Journal of Sex and Marital Therapy* 16 (2):89–102.

**Levine, S. B., Risen, C. B., & Althof, S. E.** (1994). Professionals who sexually offend: Evaluation procedures and preliminary findings. *Journal of Sex and Marital Therapy* 20 (4):288–302.

**Levy, G. D.** (1994). Aspects of preschoolers' comprehension of indoor and outdoor gender-typed toys. *Sex Roles* 30 (5–6):391–405.

**Levy, L., Martinkowski, D., & Derby, J.** (1994). Differences in patterns of adaptation in conjugal bereavement: Their sources and potential significance. *Omega Journal of Death and Dying* 29 (1):71–87.

**Levy, S.** (1995). Indecent proposal: Censor the net. *Newsweek* (3 April):53.

Levy, S. (1997). On the net, anything goes. *Newsweek* (7 July):28–29.

Li, G. (1995). The interaction effect of bereavement and sex on the risk of suicide in the elderly. *Social Science and Medicine* 40 (6):825–828.

Lieblum, S. (1990). Sexuality and the midlife woman. *Psychology of Women Quarterly* 14 (4):495–508.

Lightdale, J. R., & Prentice, D. A. (1994). Rethinking sex differences in aggression: Aggressive behavior in the absence of social roles. *Personality and Social Psychology Bulletin* 20:34–44.

Lim, D. 1998. *Microbiology*, 2d ed. Boston: WCB/McGraw-Hill.

Lindblad, F., Gustafsson, P., Larsson I., & Lundin, B. (1995). Preschoolers' sexual behavior at daycare centers: An epidemiological study. *Child Abuse and Neglect* 19 (5):569–577.

Linz, D. G. (1989). Exposure to sexually explicit materials and attitudes toward rape: A comparison of study results. *Journal of Sex Research* 26 (1):50–84.

Linz, D. G., & Donnerstein, E. (1992). Research can help us explain violence and pornography. *Chronicle of Higher Education* 39 (6):B3–B4.

Linz, D. G., Donnerstein, E., & Penrod, S. (1987). The findings and recommendations of the Attorney General's Commission on Pornography: Do the psychological "facts" fit the political fury? *American Psychologist* 42:946–953.

Little, R., Anderson, K., Erwin, C., Worthington-Roberts, B., & Clarren, S. (1989). Maternal alcohol use during breastfeeding and infant mental and motor development at one year. *New England Journal of Medicine* 7:425–430.

Loftus, E. (1993). The reality of repressed memories. *American Psychologist* 48 (5):518–537.

Loftus, E., & Ketcham, K. (1994). *The Myth of Repressed Memory*. New York: St. Martin's.

Longo, R. E., & Groth, A.–N. (1983). Juvenile sex offenses in the histories of adult rapists and child molesters. *International Journal of Offender Therapy and Comparative Criminology* 27:150–155.

Lonsway, K. A., & Fitzgerald, L. F. (1994). Rape myths: In review. *Psychology of Women Quarterly* 18:133–164.

LoPiccolo, J., & Stock, W. (1986). Treatment of sexual dysfunction.

*Journal of Consulting and Clinical Psychology* 54:158–167.

Los Angeles County Department of Health Services. (1995). Genital chlamydia infection. *Public Health Letter* 17 (October):25–28.

Lott-Whitehead, L., & Tully, C. (1993):The family lives of lesbian mothers. *Smith College Studies in Social Work* 63 (3):265–280.

Lykklen, D., & Tellegen, A. (1993). Is human mating adventitious or the result of lawful choice? A twin study of mate selection. *Journal of Personality and Social Psychology* 65 (1):56–68.

Lytton, H., & Romney, D. M. (1991). Parents' differential socialization of boys and girls: A meta-analysis. *Psychological Bulletin* 109 (2):267–296.

Maccoby, E. E. (1990). Gender and relationships: A developmental account. *American Psychologist* 45 (4):513–520.

MacDonald, P., Dombroski, R., & Casy, M. "Recurrent Secretion of Progesterone in Large Amounts: An Endocrine/Metabolic Disorder Unique to Young Women?" *Endocrinology Review* 12 (1997):372.

Madaras, L., & Patterson, J. (1984). *Woman Care: A Gynecological Guide to Your Body*. New York: Avon.

Maddock, J. W., & Larson, N. R. (1995). *Incestuous Families: An Ecological Approach to Understanding and Treatment*. New York: Norton.

Magana, J. R., & Carrier, J. M. (1991). Mexican and Mexican-American male sexual behavior and spread of AIDS in California. *Journal of Sex Research* 28:425–441.

Magee, R. (1997). "Ethical Issues in Couple Therapy." In D. Marsh and R. Magee (Eds)., *Ethical and Legal Issues of Professional Practice with Families*, (pp. 112–126). New York: Wiley.

Mageo, J. M. (1992). Male transvestism and cultural change in Samoa. *American Ethnologist* 19 (3):443–459.

Mahlstedt, D., & Keeny, L. (1993). Female survivors of dating violence and their social networks. *Feminism and Psychology* 3 (3):319–333.

Major, B., & Cozzarelli, C. (1992). Psychosocial predictors of adjustment to abortion. *Journal of Social Issues* 48:121–142.

Malamuth, N., & Check, J. V. (1981). The effects of mass media exposure on acceptance of violence against women: A field experiment. *Journal of Research in Personality* 15:436–446.

Malamuth, N., & Donnerstein, E. (1984). *Pornography and Sexual Aggression*. New York: Academic.

Malamuth, N., Sockloskie, R.J., Koss, M. P., & Tanaka, J. S. (1991). Characteristics of aggressors against women: Testing a model using a national sample of college students. *Journal of Consulting and Clinical Psychology* 59 (5):670–681.

Malamuth, N. M. (1981). Rape fantasies as a function of exposure to violent sexual stimuli. *Archives of Sexual Behavior* 10:33–48.

Malamuth, N. M., Heim, N., & Feshbach, S. (1980). Sexual responsiveness of college students to rape depictions: Inhibitory or disinhibitory effects? *Journal of Personality and Social Psychology* 38:399–408.

Maltz, W., & Boss, S. (1997). *In the Garden of Desire*. New York: Broadway.

Mancini, C., Van Ameringen, M., & Macmillan, H. (1995). Relationship of childhood sexual and physical abuse to anxiety disorders. *Journal of Nervous and Mental Disease* 183 (5):309–314.

Manderson, L. (1992). Public sex performance in Patpong and explorations of the edges of imagination. *Journal of Sex Research* 29 (4):451–475.

Mango, C. (1993). The oral matrix. *Arts in psychotherapy* 20:403–410.

Mansfield, P., Voda, A., & Koch, P. (1995). Predictors of sexual response changes in heterosexual midlife women. *Health Values, the Journal of Health Behavior, Education, and Promotion* 19 (1):10–20.

Manusov, V. (1995). Reacting to changes in nonverbal behaviors: Relational satisfaction and adaptation patterns in romantic dyads. *Human Communication Research* 21 (4):456–477.

Marchi, K., & Guendelman, S. (1995). Gender differences in the sexual behavior of Latino adolescents: An exploratory study in a public high school in the San Francisco Bay area. *International Quarterly of Community Health Education* 15 (2):209–226.

Markowitz, M. (1995). A preliminary study of Ritonavir, an inhibitor of

HIV-1 protease, to treat HIV-1 infection. *New England Journal of Medicine* 333:1534–1539.

Marshall, W. L., Hudson, S. M., Jones, R., & Fernandez, Y. M. (1995). Empathy in sex offenders. *Clinical Psychology Review* 15 (2):99–113.

Marshall, W. L., & Pithers, W. A. (1994). A reconsideration of treatment outcomes with sex offenders. *Criminal Justice and Behavior* 21 (1):10–27.

Martens, M., & Faro, S. (1989). Update on trichomonas: Detection and management. *Medical Aspects of Human Sexuality* (January):73–79.

Martin, C. L., & Little, J. K. (1990). The relation of gender understanding to children's sex-typed preferences and gender stereotypes. *Child Development* 61:1427–1439.

Martin, D., & Lyon, P. (1992). The older lesbian. In B. Berzon (Ed.), *Positively Gay*. Berkeley, CA: Celestial Arts.

Masand, P. S. (1993). Successful treatment of sexual masochism and transvestic fetishism associated with treating depression with fluoxetine hydrochloride. *Depression* 1 (1):50–52.

Mason, H., Marks, G., Simoni, J., & Ruiz, M. (1995). Culturally sanctioned secrets? Latino men's nondisclosure of HIV infection to family, friends, and lovers. *Health Psychology* 14 (1):6–21.

Massachusetts Department of Education. (1996). *Massachusetts youth risk behavior survey results for 1995*. Boston: Massachusetts Department of Education.

Mastekaasa, A. (1994). The subjective well-being of the previously married: The importance of unmarried cohabitation and time since widowhood or divorce. *Social Forces* 73 (2):665–692.

Mastekaasa, A. (1995). Age variations in the suicide rates and self-reported subjective well-being of married and never-married persons. *Journal of Community and Applied Social Psychology* 5 (1):21–39.

Masters, J., & Johnson, V. (1970). *Human Sexual Inadequacy*. Boston: Little, Brown.

Masters, J., & Johnson, V. (1979). *Homosexuality in Perspective*. Boston: Little, Brown.

Masters, W. H., & Johnson, V. E. (1966). *Human Sexual Response*. Boston: Little, Brown.

Masters, W., Johnson, V., & Kolodny, R. (1988). *Human Sexuality* (3d ed.). Glenview, IL: Scott, Foresman.

Masters, W., Johnson, V., & Kolodny, R. (1994). *Heterosexuality*. New York: HarperCollins.

Matsumoto, D., & Kudoh, T. (1993). American-Japanese cultural differences in attributions of personality based on smiles. *Journal of Nonverbal Behavior* 17 (4):241–243.

Matuszczyk, J., & Larsson, K. (1995). Sexual preference and feminine and masculine sexual behavior of male rats, prenatally exposed to antiandrogen or antiestrogen. *Hormones and Behavior* 29 (2):191–206.

May, R. (1969). *Love and Will*. New York: Norton.

Mays, V., Cochran, S., Bellinger, G., & Smith, R. (1992). The language of Black gay men's sexual behavior: Implication for AIDS risk reduction. *Journal of Sex Research* 29:425–434.

McAninch, J., & Wessels, H. (1995). Penis study challenges need for risky surgery. *Watertown (NY) Daily Times*, 21 May, pp. G1, G7.

McCabe, M. (1989). The contribution of sexual attitudes and experiences during childhood and adolescence to adult sexual dysfunction. *Sexual and Marital Therapy* 4 (2):133–141.

McCabe, M., MacDonald, E., Deeks, A., Vowels, L., & Cobain, M. (1996). The impact of multiple sclerosis on sexuality and relationships. *Journal of Sex Research* 33:241–248.

McConaghy, N. (1993). *Sexual Behavior: Problems and Management*. New York: Plenum.

McConnell, J. (1989). *Understanding Human Behavior* (6th ed.). New York: Holt, Rinehart & Winston.

McCormack, A., Rokous, F. E., Hazelwood, R. R., & Burgess, A. W. (1992). An exploration of childhood development of serial rapists. *Journal of Family Violence* 7 (3):219–228.

McCormick, D. (1992). *Erotic Literature: A Connoisseur's Guide*. New York: Continuum.

McCormick, M. (1994). Survival of very tiny babies—Good news and bad news. *New England Journal of Medicine* 12:802–803.

McCormick, N. (1996). *Foreword to Sexual Coercion in Dating Relationships*. Binghamton, NY: Hayworth.

McCormick, N. B. (1996). Our feminist future: Women affirming sex research in the late 20th century. *Journal of Sex Research* 33 (2):99–102.

McCoy, N. L., & Matyas, J. (1996). Oral contraceptives and sexual desire in university women. *Archives of Sexual Behavior* 25 (1):73–90.

McDougall, G. (1993). Therapeutic issues with gay and lesbian elders. *Clinical Gerontologist* 14 (1):45–57.

McFarlane, J. M., & Williams, T. M. (1994). Placing premenstrual syndrome in perspective. *Psychology of Women Quarterly* 18:339–373.

McGivern, R., & Barron, S. (1991). Influence of prenatal alcohol exposure on the process of neurobehavioral sexual differentiation. *Alcohol Health and Research World* 15 (2):115–125.

McGlynn, G. (1993). *Dynamics of Fitness, A Practical Approach* (3d ed.). Dubuque, IA: Brown & Benchmark.

McHale, J. (1995). Coparenting and triadic interactions during infancy: The roles of marital distress and child gender. *Developmental Psychology* 31 (6):985–996.

McIntosh, E., & Tate, D. (1990). Correlates of jealous behaviors. *Psychological Reports* 66 (2):601–602.

McKenzie-Mohr, D., & Zanna, M. P. (1990). Treating women as sexual objects: Look to the (gender schematic) male who has viewed pornography. *Personality and Social Psychology Bulletin* 16 (2):296–308.

McKibben, A., Proulx, J., & Lusignan, R. (1994). Relationships between conflict, affect and deviant sexual behaviors in rapists and pedophiles. *Behavior Research and Therapy* 32 (5):571–575.

McLaren, A. (1981). "Barrenness against nature": Recourse to abortion in preindustrial England. *Journal of Sex Research* 17:224–237.

McMullen, R. J. (1990). *Male Rape: Breaking the Silence on the Last Taboo*. London: Gay Men's.

Medved, M. (1992). *Hollywood vs. America: Popular Culture and the War on Traditional Values*. New York: HarperCollins.

Mellors, J. (1996). Prognosis in HIV-1 infection predicted by the quantity of virus in plasma. *Science* 272:1167–1170.

Mennella, I., & Beauchamp, G. (1991). The transfer of alcohol to human milk. *New England Journal of Medicine* 14:981–985.

Mertz, G. (1992). Risk factors for the sexual transmission of genital herpes. *Annals of Internal Medicine* 116:197–202.

Meston, C., Gorzalka, B., & Wright, J. (1997) "Inhibition of Subjective and Physiological Sexual Arousal in Women with Clonidine." *Psychosomatic Medicine* 59(4):399–407.

Meuwissen, I., & Over, R. (1991). Multidimensionality of the content of female sexual fantasy. *Behavior Research and Therapy* 17:207–216.

Meuwissen, I., & Over, R. (1992). Sexual arousal across phases of the human menstrual cycle. *Archives of Sexual Education* 21:101–119.

Meyer, B., Heino, F., Ehrhardt, A., Rosen, L., & Gruen, R. (1995). Prenatal estrogens and the development of homosexual orientation. *Developmental Psychology* 31 (1):12–21.

Michael, R. T., Gagnon, J. H., Laumann, E. O., & Kolata, G. (1994). *Sex in America*. Boston: Warner.

*Miller v. California*, 413 U.S. 15 (1973).

Milunsky, A., Ulcickas, M., Rothman, K., Willett, W., Jick, S., & Jick, H. (1992). Maternal heat exposures and neural tube defects. *Journal of the American Medical Association* 7:882–885.

Mira, J. J., Perez, M. J., Orozco, D., & Gea, J. (1992). Primary care nurses' awareness of sexual problems of people with chronic disease. *Sexual and Marital Therapy* 7 (1):19–28.

Mischel, W. (1966). A social learning view of sex differences in behavior. In E. E. Maccoby (Ed.), *The Development of Sex Differences* (pp. 56–81). Stanford, CA: Stanford University.

Mishra, R. (1991). Steroids and sports are a losing proposition. *FDA Consumer* (September):25–27.

Mitchell-Flynn, C., & Hutchinson, R. (1993). A longitudinal study of the problems and concerns of urban divorced men. *Journal of Divorce and Remarriage* 19 (1–2):161–182.

Moffat, S. (1993). Natural option. *Los Angeles Times* (7 January):E-1, E-7.

Moller, L. C., Hymel, S., & Rubin, K. H. (1992). Sex typing in play and popularity in middle childhood. *Sex Roles* 26:331–353.

Money, J. (1987). Treatment guidelines: Antiandrogen and counseling of paraphiliac sex offenders. *Journal of Sex and Marital Therapy* 13:219–223.

Money, J. (1972). Strategy, ethics, behavior modification, and homosexuality. [editorial]. *Archives of Sexual Behavior*, (June) 2 (1):79–82.

Money, J. (1994). *Sex Errors of the Body and Related Syndromes: A Guide to Counseling Children, Adolescents and Their Families* (2d ed.). Baltimore: Brookes.

Money, J., & Lamacz, M. (1989). *Vandalized Lovemaps: Paraphilic Outcome of Seven Cases in Pediatric Sexology*. Buffalo, NY: Prometheus.

Mooney, E., & Siefer, J. H. (1991). Setting standards of sexually explicit material. *Contemporary Sexuality* 25 (5):5–6.

Mooney, R. (1995). *The Handbook: Information for New Upper Extremity Amputees, Their Families, and Friends*. Lomita, CA: Mutual Amputee Aid Foundation.

Moore, K. (1993). *Before We Are Born* (4th ed.). Philadelphia: Saunders.

Moore, M. (1995). Courtship signaling and adolescents: Girls just wanna have fun? *Journal of Sex Research* 32 (4):319–328.

Moore, M., Blumstein, P., & Schwartz, P. (1994). *The Power of Motherhood: A Contextual Evaluation of Family Resources*. Manuscript submitted for publication to the *Journal of Marriage and the Family*.

Morley, J. E. (1986). Impotence. *American Journal of Medicine* 80:897–905.

Morokoff, P. J., & Gilliland, R. (1993). Stress, sexual functioning, and marital satisfaction. *Journal of Sex Research* 30:43–53.

Morris, J. (1974). *Conundrum*. New York: New American Library.

Morrow, G., Clark, E., & Brock, K. (1995). Individual and partner love styles: Implications for the quality of romantic involvements. *Journal of Social and Personal Relationships* 12 (3):363–387.

Morse, E. V., Simon, P. M., Balson, P. M., & Osofsky, H. J. (1992). Sexual behavior patterns of customers of male street prostitutes. *Archives of Sexual Behavior* 21:347–357.

Morse, E. V., Simon, P. M., Balson, P. M., Osofsky, H. J., & Gaumer, R. (1992). The male street prostitute. *Social Science and Medicine* 32:535–539.

Mosher, D. L., & MacIan, P. (1994). College men and women respond to X-rated videos intended for male or female audiences: Gender and sexual scripts. *Journal of Sex Research* 31 (2):99–114.

Moss, E. (1995). Treating the lovesick patient. *Israel Journal of Psychiatry and Related Sciences* 32 (3):167–173.

Motley, M., & Reeder, H. (1995). Unwanted escalation of sexual intimacy: Male and female perceptions of connotations and relational consequences of resistance messages. *Communication Monographs* 62 (4):357–382.

Moyes, J. (1996). A world of anguish in an inch of glass. *The Independent* (3 August):48.

Muehlenhard, C. (1995/96). The complexities of sexual consent. *SIECUS Report* 24 (2):4–7.

Muehlenhard, C., Andrews, S., & Beal, G. (1996). Beyond "just saying no": Dealing with men's unwanted sexual advances in heterosexual dating contexts. *Journal of Psychology and Human Sexuality* 8 (1–2):141–168.

Muehlenhard, C., & Hollabaugh, L. C. (1988). Do women sometimes say no when they mean yes? The prevalence and correlates of women's token resistance to sex. *Journal of Personality and Social Psychology* 54:872–879.

Muehlenhard, C. L. (1994). Controversy about rape: Research and activities. *Journal of Sex Research* 31 (2):143–153.

Muehlenhard, C. L., & Linton, M. (1987). Date rape and sexual aggression in dating situations: Incidence and risk factors. *Journal of Counseling Psychology* 34 (2):186–196.

Muehlenhard, C. L., Powch, J. G., Phelps, J. L., & Giusti, L. M. (1992). Definitions of rape: Scientific and political implications. *Journal of Social Issues* 48 (1):23–44.

Muercke, M. A. (1992). Mother sold food, daughter sells her body. *Social Science and Medicine* 35 (7):891–901.

Mullen, P., & Martin, J. (1994). Jealousy: A community study. *British Journal of Psychiatry* 164:35–43.

Murray, S., & Holmes, J. (1993). Seeing virtues in faults: Negativity and the transformation of interpersonal narratives in close relationships. *Journal of Personality and Social Psychology* 65 (4):707–722.

Myers, D. (1992). *The Pursuit of Happiness*. New York: William Morrow.

Nadler, D. M., & Fong, K. C. (1996). Good call on internet smut. *National Law Journal* 18 (48):A19.

Nathanson, I. (1995). Divorce and women's spirituality. *Journal of Divorce and Remarriage* 22 (3–4):179–188.

National Center for Health Statistics. (1991a). Cohabitation, marriage, marital dissolution, and remarriage: United States, 1988. *Advance Data, U.S. Department of Health and Human Services, No. 194*, DDHS Pub. No. (PHS)91-1250, 4.

National Center for Health Statistics. (1993). *Monthly Vital Statistics Report* 40 (12).

National Center for Health Statistics. (1995a). Advance report of final marriage statistics, 1989 and 1990. *Monthly Vital Statistics Report* 43 (no. 12, supplement) (14 July).

National Center for Health Statistics. (1995b). Advance report of final natality statistics, 1993. *Monthly Vital Statistics Report* 44 (no. 3, supplement) (21 September).

National Center for Health Statistics. (1995c). *Contraceptive use in the United States: 1982–1990*.(14 February).

National Center for Health Statistics. (1996b). Births, marriages, divorces and deaths for February 1996. *Monthly Vital Statistics Report* 45 (2). Hyattsville, MD: Public Health Service (13 September).

National Center for Health Statistics. (1998). *Monthly Vital Statistics Report*, 46(6), (28 January).

National Victims Center. (1992). *Rape in America: A Report to the Nation*. Fort Worth, TX: National Victims Center.

Neidigh, L., & Krop, H. (1992). Cognitive distortion among child sexual offenders. *Journal of Sex Education and Therapy* 18 (3):208–215.

Neinstein, L. S. (1991). *Adolescent Health Care: A Practical Guide* (2d ed.). Baltimore: Williams & Wilkins.

Nelson, E., Hill-Barlow, D., & Benedict, J. (1994). Addiction versus intimacy as related to sexual involvement in a relationship. *Journal of Sex and Marital Therapy* 20 (1):35–45.

Nelson, G. (1995). Women's social support networks and social support following marital separation. *Journal of Divorce and Remarriage* 23 (1–2):149–169.

Nettles, S. M., & Scott-Jones, D. (1987). The role of sexuality and sex equity in the education of minority adolescents. *Peabody Journal of Education* 64 (4):183–197.

Newell, M. L. (1996). Detection of virus in vertically exposed HIV-antibody-negative children. *Lancet* 347:213–214.

Newton, T., Kiecolt-Glaser, J., Glaser, R., & Malarkey, W. (1995). Conflict and withdrawal during marital interaction: The roles of hostility and defensiveness. *Personality and Social Psychology Bulletin* 21 (5):512–524.

Nezlek, J. B., & Pilkington, C. J. (1994). Perceptions of risk in intimacy and social participation. *Personal Relationships* 1:45–62.

Nichols, M. (1990). Lesbian relationships: Implications for the study of sexuality and gender. In D. McWhirter, S. Sanders, & J. Reinisch (Eds.), *Homosexuality/Heterosexuality: Concepts of Sexual Orientation* (pp. 350–364). New York: Oxford University.

Nichols, M. (1995). Sexual desire disorder in a lesbian-feminist couple: The intersection of therapy and politics. In R. C. Rosen and S. R. Leiblum (Eds.), *Case Studies in Sex Therapy*. New York: Guilford.

Nichols, M. P., & Schwartz, R. C. (1995). *Family Therapy: Concepts and Methods*. Boston: Allyn & Bacon.

Nicole, F., & Baldwin, C. (1995). Cohabitation as a developmental stage. *Journal of Mental Health Counseling* 17 (4):386–396.

Noble, J. (1996). Spotlight: Indonesia. *Population Today* 24:7.

Noble, J., Cover, J., & Yanagishita, M. (1996). *The World's Youth 1996*. Washington, DC: Population Reference Bureau.

Nock, S. (1995a). A comparison of marriages and cohabiting relationships. *Journal of Family Issues* 16 (1):53–76.

Nock, S. (1995b). Spouse preferences of never-married, divorced, and cohabiting Americans. *Journal of Divorce and Remarriage* 22 (3–4):91–108.

Nolin, M. J., & Petersen, K. K. (1992). Gender differences in parent-child communication about sexuality. *Journal of Adolescent Research* 7:59–79.

Nordenberg, T. (1996). The facts about aphrodisiacs. *FDA Consumer*, (January–February):10–15.

Norris, J., Nurius, P. S., & Dimeff, L. A. (1996). Through her eyes: Factors affecting women's perceptions of and resistance to acquaintance sexual aggression threat. *Psychology of Women Quarterly* 20:123–145.

O'Brien, M. (1996). Child-rearing difficulties reported by parents of infants and toddlers. *Journal of Pediatric Psychology* 21 (3):433–446.

O'Donohue, W. T., & Plaud, J. J. (1994). The conditioning of human sexual arousal. *Archives of Sexual Behavior* 23 (3):321–344.

O'Toole, C. J., & Brigante, J. L. (1992). Lesbians with disabilities. *Sexuality and Disability* 10:163–172.

Oakley, G. (1986). Frequency of human congenital malformations. *Clinical Perinatology* 13:545.

Ochs, E. (1992). Indexing gender. In A. Duranti and C. Goodwin (Eds.), *Rethinking Context: Language as an Interactive Phenomenon*. Cambridge: Cambridge University.

Ogden, G. (1994). *Women Who Love Sex*. New York: Pocket Books.

Okami, P., & Goldberg, A. (1992). Personality correlates of pedophilia: Are they reliable indicators? *Journal of Sex Research* 29:297–328.

Olds, D., Henderson, C., & Tatelbaum, R. (1994). Intellectual impairment in children of women who smoke cigarettes during pregnancy. *Pediatrics* 93:221–227.

Oliver, M. B., & Hyde, J. S. (1993). Gender differences in sexuality: A meta-analysis. *Psychological Bulletin* 114:29–51.

Once rejected AIDS treatment resurfaces. (1994). *AIDS Weekly*, 25 April, p. 2.

Organized export of prostitutes from CIS is flourishing. (1993). *Current Digest of the Post-Soviet Press* (2 June):17.

Orten, J. (1990). Coming up short: The physical, cognitive, and social effects of Turner's syndrome. *Health and Social Work* 15 (2):100–106.

Otten, M. W., Zaidi, A. A., Peterman, T. A., & Witte, J. J. (1994). High rate of HIV seroconversion among patients attending urban sexually transmitted disease clinics. *AIDS* 8:549–553.

Padma-Nathan, H., Hellstrom, W., Kaiser, F., & Labasky, R. (1997). Treatment of Men with Erectile Dysfunction with Transurethral Alprostadil. *New England Journal of Medicine* 336(1):1–7.

Palosaari, U., & Aroo, H. (1995). Parental divorce, self-esteem, and depression: An intimate relationship as a protective factor in young adulthood. *Journal of Affective Disorders* 35 (3):91–96.

Pan, S. (1993). A sex revolution in current China. *Journal of Psychology and Human Sexuality* 6 (2):1–14.

Panel urges risky baboon transplant for AIDS patient. (1995). *American Medical News* (7 August):51.

Panser, L., Rhodes, T., Girman, C., & Guess, H. (1995). Sexual function of men ages 40 to 79 years: The Olmsted County study of urinary symptoms and health status among men. *Journal of the American Geriatrics Society* 43 (10):1107–1111.

Pantaleo, G. (1996). *Overview: Viral replication and the immunopathology of HIV. Improving survival in people living with HIV infection.* Paper presented at XI International Conference on AIDS, Vancouver, BC (8 July).

Papadopoulos, C. (1989). *Sexual Aspects of Cardiovascular Disease.* New York: Praeger.

Papalia, D., & Olds, S. (1987). *A Child's World: Infancy through Adolescence* (4th ed.). New York: McGraw-Hill.

Pape, K., & Arias, I. (1995). Control, coping, and victimization in dating relationships. *Violence and Victims* 10 (1):43–54.

Parks, C., & Hulbert, L. (1995). High and low trusters' responses to fear in a payoff matrix. *Journal of Conflict Resolution* 39 (4):718–730.

Parks, C., Henager, R., & Scamahorn, S. (1996). Trust and reactions to messages of intent in social dilemmas. *Journal of Conflict Resolution* 40 (1):134–151.

Parks, C., & Vu, A. (1994). Social dilemma behavior of individuals from highly individualist and collectivist cultures. *Journal of Conflict Resolution* 38 (4):708–718.

Parlee, M. B. (1993). Psychology of menstruation and premenstrual syndrome. In F. L. Denmark & M.A. Paludi (Eds.), *Psychology of Women: A Handbook of Issues and Theories* (pp. 325–377). Westport, CT: Greenwood.

Patterson, C. J. (1992). Children of lesbian and gay parents. *Child Development* 63 (5):1025–1042.

Patterson, C. J. (1994). Lesbian and gay families. *Current Directions in Psychological Science* 3 (2):62–64.

Patterson, C. J. (1995). Families of the baby boom: Parents' division of labor and children's adjustment. *Developmental Psychology* 31 (1):115–123.

Patti, P. J. (1995). Sexuality and expression in persons with mental retardation. *SIECUS Report* 23 (4):17–20.

Paul, J., Stall, R., Crosby, G., & Barrett, D. (1994). Correlates of sexual risk-taking among gay male substance abusers. *Addiction* 89 (8):971–983.

Peck, M. S. (1978). *The Road Less Traveled.* New York: Simon & Schuster.

Pennington, S. B. (1987). Children of lesbian mothers. In F. W. Bozett (Ed.), *Gay and Lesbian Parents.* New York: Praeger.

Perduta-Fulginiti, P. (1992). Sexual functioning of women with complete spinal cord injury: Nursing implications [Special Issue: Nursing Roles and Perspectives]. *Sexuality and Disability* 10:103–118.

Perriens, J. (1995). Pulmonary tuberculosis in HIV-infected patients in Zaire: A controlled trial of treatment for either 6 or 12 months. *New England Journal of Medicine* 332:779–784.

Perse, E. M. (1994). Uses of erotica and acceptance of rape myths. *Communication Research* 21 (4):488–515.

Persky, H., Dreisbach, L., Miller, W., O'Brien, C., Khan, M., Lief, H., Charney, N., & Strauss, D. (1982). The relation of plasma androgen levels to sexual behaviors and attitudes of women. *Psychosomatic Medicine* 44:305–319.

Perusse, D. (1994). Mate choice in modern societies: Testing evolutionary hypotheses with behavioral data. *Human Nature* 5 (3):255–278.

Peterson, H., Xia, Z., Hughes, J., Wilcox, L., Tylor, L., & Trussell, J. "The Risk of Ectopic Pregnancy After Tubal Sterilization." *The New England Journal of Medicine* (13 March 1997):762–767.

Peterson, K. S. (1995). A million men, a single message: Black dads hope to restore spirit of African-American male. *USA Today* (15 October):D5.

Petitti, D., & Coleman, C. (1990). Cocaine and the risk of low birth weight. *American Journal of Public Health* 80:25–28.

Piccinin, S., Chislett, L., & McCarrey, M. (1989). A ten-hour social skills training program on giving and receiving criticism. *Journal of College Student Psychotherapy* 4 (1):53–63.

Pickhardt, C. E. (1996). *Keys to single parenting.* Hauppage, NY: Barron's.

Pierce, C., Byrne, D., & Aquinis, H. (1996). Attractions in organizations: A model of workplace romance. *Journal of Organizational Behavior* 17 (1):5–32.

Platte, M. (1996). Man ordered to pay support for girl born to surrogate. *Los Angeles Times* (9 February):A-3, 29.

Pleak, R. R., & Meyer-Bahlburg, H. F. L. (1990). Sexual behavior and AIDS knowledge of young male prostitutes in Manhattan. *Journal of Sex Research* 27 (4):557–587.

Pleck, J. H., Sonenstein, F. I., & Ku, L. C. (1993). Masculinity ideology: Its impact on adolescent men's heterosexual relationships. *Journal of Social Issues* 49 (3):11–29.

Plevin, N. (1992). Parents take a thorny ethical path in quest to select sex of children. *Los Angeles Times* (14 June):B-7.

Poasa, K. (1992). The Samoan fa'afafine: One case study and discussion of transsexualism. *Journal of Psychology and Human Sexuality* 5 (3):39–51.

Pollack, A. (1991). Norplant, what you should know about the new contraceptive. *Medical Aspects of Human Sexuality* (January):38–42.

*Pope v. Illinois,* 107 S. Ct. 1918 (1987).

Portnoy, E. (1993). The impact of body type on perceptions of attractiveness by older individuals. *Communication Reports* 6 (2):101–108.

Potterat, J. J., Woodhouse, D. E., Muth, J. B., & Muth, S. Q. (1990). Estimating the prevalence and longevity of prostitute women. *Journal of Sex Research* 27 (2):233–243.

Powell, E. (1991). *Talking Back to Sexual Pressure.* Minneapolis: CompCare.

Powell, E. (1996). *Sex on Your Terms.* Boston: Allyn & Bacon.

Price, J., & Miller, P. (1984). Sexual fantasies of black and white college students. *Psychological Reports* 54:1007–1014.

Propp, K. (1995). An experimental examination of biological sex as a status cue in decision-making groups and its influence on information use. *Small Group Research* 26 (4):451–474.

Pudney, J., Oneta, M., Mayer, K., Seage, G., & Anderson, D. (1992). Pre-ejaculatory fluid as potential vector for sexual transmission of HIV-1 (Letter). *Lancet* 340:1470.

Purifoy, F., Grodsky, A., & Giambra, L. (1992). The relationship of sexual daydreaming to sexual activity, sexual drive, and sexual attitudes for women across the life-span. *Archives of Sexual Behavior* 21:369–375.

Quam, J. (1992). Age-related expectations of gay and lesbian older adults. *Gerontologist* (June).

Quanfeng, S. (1994). Late-night talk show: Giving listeners what they want. *China Today* (June):56–57.

Quirouette, C., & Gold, D. (1992). Spousal characteristics as predictors of well-being in older couples. *International Journal of Aging and Human Development* 34 (4):257–269.

Quittner, J. (1995a). Vice raid on the net. *Time* (3 April):63.

Quittner, J. (1995b). How parents can filter out the naughty bits. *Time* (3 July):45.

Raboch, J., & Raboch, J. (1992). Infrequent orgasms in women. *Journal of Sex and Marital Therapy* 18:114–120.

Rachman, S. (1966). Sexual fetishism: An experimental analogue. *Psychological Record* 16:293–296.

Randal, J. (1994). Trying to outsmart infertility. In *Current Issues in Women's Health* (2d ed.). An FDA Consumer Special Report, January. DHHS Pub. No. (FDA)94-1181. Public Health Service, United States Department of Health and Human Services.

Ratcliffe, S., Masera, N., Pan, H., & McKie, M. (1994). Head circumference and IQ of children with sex chromosome abnormalities. *Developmental Medicine and Child Neurology* 36 (6):533–544.

Ray, A. L., & Gold, S. R. (1996). Gender roles, aggression and alcohol use in dating relationships. *Journal of Sex Research* 33 (1):47–55.

Razack, S. (1994). What is to be gained by looking white people in the eye? Culture, race, and gender in cases of sexual violence. *Signs* 19 (4):894–923.

Realmuto, G. M., Jensen, J. B., and Wescoe, S. (1990). Specificity and sensitivity of sexually anatomically correct dolls in substantiating abuse. *Journal of the American Academy of Child and Adolescent Psychiatry* 29 (5):743–746.

Reed, J. (1984). *The Birth Control Movement and American Society: From Private Vice to Public Virtue.* Princeton, NJ: Princeton University.

Regan, P., & Sprecher, S. (1995). Gender differences in the value of contributions to intimate relationships. *Sex Roles* 33 (3–4):221–238.

Reilly, J. M., & Woodhouse, C. R. J. (1989). Small penis and the male sexual role. *Journal of Urology* 142:569–571.

Reilly, M. E., Lott, B., Caldwell, D., & DeLuca, L. (1992). Tolerance for sexual harassment related to self-reported victimization. *Gender and Society* 6 (1):122–138.

Reiner, W. G. (1999). Assignment of sex in neonates with ambiguous genitalia. *Current Opinion in Pediatrics* 11 (4):363–365.

Reinisch, J. (1990). *The Kinsey Institute New Report on Sex.* New York: St. Martin's.

Reis, H. T., & Franks, P. (1994). The role of intimacy and social support in health outcomes: Two processes or one? *Personal Relationships* 1:185–197.

Rekart, M. (1996). *High risk behavior in young gay males.* Report to Eleventh International Conference on AIDS, 8 July.

Remafedi, G., et al. (1992). Demography of sexual orientation in adolescents. *Pediatrics* 89:714–721.

Remer, R., & Ferguson, R. A. (1995). Becoming a secondary survivor of sexual assault. *Journal of Counseling and Development* 73 (4):407–413.

Renzetti, C. M., & Curran, D. J. (1995). *Men, Women and Society.* Boston: Allyn & Bacon.

Research and Training Center on Independent Living. (1996). *Guidelines for Reporting and Writing About People with Disabilities* (5th ed.). Lawrence, KS: Research and Training Center on Independent Living.

Rice, D. (1995). ELVIS, the diagnostic test. *The Helper* 17 (4):10.

Richards, L. (1985). Demographic trends and drug abuse, 1980–1985. *NIDA Research Monograph* 35.

Washington, DC: Department of Health and Human Services.

Richardson, S. (1997). Crushing HIV. *Discover*, January, pp. 28–30.

Richman, D. (1996). Primary infection: Guidelines for antiretroviral therapy; bringing the state of the art to clinical practice. *Paper presented at the Eleventh International Conference on AIDS*, Vancouver, BC (10 July).

Riddle, J., Estes, J., & Russell, J. (1994). Birth control in the ancient world. *Archeology* (March/April):29–35.

Ridley, J. (1993). Gender and couples: Do men and women seek different kinds of intimacy? *Sexual and Marital Therapy* 8 (3):243–253.

Ring, T. E., & Kilmartin, C. (1992). Man to man about rape: A rape prevention program for men. *Journal of College Student Development* 33:82–84.

Rio, L. M. (1991). Psychological and sociological research and the decriminalization or legalization of prostitution. *Archives of Sexual Behavior* 20 (2):205–218.

Roan, S. (1994). 4,600 deaths that a simple yearly test might prevent. *Los Angeles Times* (4 October):E-1, E-4.

Robbins, M., & Jensen, G. (1978). Multiple orgasm in males. *Journal of Sex Research* 14:21–26.

Robins, A., Dew, M., Davidson, S., & Penkower, L. (1994). Psychosocial factors associated with risky sexual behavior among HIV-seropositive gay men. *AIDS Education and Prevention* 6 (6):483–492.

Robinson, J., Plichta, B., Weisman, C., Nathanson, C., & Ensminger, M. (1992). Dysmenorrhea and use of oral contraceptives in adolescent women attending a family planning clinic. *American Journal of Obstetrics and Gynecology* 166:578–583.

Rodman, H., Sarvis, G., & Bonar, J. (1987). *The Abortion Question.* New York: Columbia University.

Rodrigues, J., & Moji, K. (1995). Factors affecting choice of sterilization among low-income women in Paraiba, Brazil. *Journal of Biosocial Science* 27:339–345.

*Roe v. Wade,* 410 U.S. 113 (1973).

Roenrich, L., & Kinder, B. N. (1991). Alcohol expectancies and male sexuality: Review and implications for sex therapy. *Journal of Sex and Marital Therapy* 17:45–54.

Roesler, T. A. (1994). Reactions to disclosure of childhood sexual abuse. *Journal of Nervous and Mental Disease* 182 (11):618–624.

Rogers, A. & Vourvoulias, B. (1997). In Pursuit of Upward Mobility. *Time* (17 November):65.

Roiphe, K. (1993). *The Morning After: Sex, Fear and Feminism on Campus.* Boston: Little, Brown.

Romberg, R. (1985). *Circumcision: The Painful Dilemma.* South Hadley, MA: Bergin & Garvey.

Rosario, M., Meyer-Bahlburg, H., Hunter, J., Exner, T., Gwadz, M., & Keller, A. (1996). The psychosexual development of urban lesbian, gay, and bisexual youths. *Journal of Sex Research* 33 (2):113–126.

Rose, C., & Thomas, C. (1995). *net.sex.* Indianapolis, IN: SAMS.

Rose, M., & Soares, H. (1993). Sexual adaptations of the frail elderly. *Journal of Gerontological Social Work* 19 (3–4):167–178.

Rosellini, L. (1992). Sexual desire. *U.S. News and World Report,* 6 July, pp. 61–66.

Rosen, K., & Stith, S. (1995). Women terminating abusive dating relationships: A qualitative study. *Journal of Social and Personal Relationships* 12 (1):155–160.

Rosen, R. C., & Leiblum, S. R. (Eds.) (1995a). *Case Studies in Sex Therapy.* New York: Guilford.

Rosen, R. C., & Leiblum, S. R. (1995b). Treatment of sexual disorders in the 1990s: An integrated approach. *Journal of Consulting and Clinical Psychology* 63 (6):877–890.

Rosenberg, H., Ventura, S., & Maurer, J. (1996). Births and deaths: United States, 1995. *Monthly Vital Statistics Report* 45 (3, supp. 2): 1–40.

Rosenbluth, S., & Steil, J. (1995). Predictors of intimacy for women in heterosexual and homosexual couples. *Journal of Social and Personal Relationships* 12 (2):163–175.

Ross, M., & Paul, J. (1992). Beyond gender: The basis of sexual attraction in bisexual men and women. *Psychological Reports* 71 (3, part 2): 1283–1290.

Rossignol, A., & Bonnlander, H. (1990). Caffeine containing beverages, total fluid consumption, and premenstrual syndrome. *American Journal of Public Health* 9:1106–1110.

Rostosky, S., & Tavris, C. (1996). Menopause research and the

dominance of the biomedical model 1984–1994. *Psychology of Women Quarterly* 20:285–312.

Rotenberg, K., & Korol, S. (1995). The role of loneliness and gender in individual's love styles. *Journal of Social Behavior and Personality* 10 (3):537–546.

*Roth v. United States,* 354 U.S. 476 (1957).

Rothman, B. K. (1991). *In Labor: Women and Power in the Birthplace.* New York: Norton.

Rotolo, J., & Lynch, J. (1991). Penile cancer: Curable with early detection. *Hospital Practice* (15 June):131–138.

Rowan, E. L., Rowan, J. B., & Langelier, P. (1990). Women who molest children. *Bulletin of the American Academy of Psychiatry and Law* 18 (1):79–83.

Rowe, P. (1991). Research on intrauterine devices. Annual Technical Report, 1991. Geneva, Switzerland: Special Programme of Research, Development and Research Training in Human Reproduction, *World Health Organization* (1992):127–137.

Rowland, D., Kallan, K., & Slob, A. (1997). "Yohimbine, Erectile Capacity and Sexual Response in Men." *Archives of Sexual Behavior* 26 (1):49–62.

Rozee, P. D. (1993). Forbidden or forgiven? Rape in cross-cultural perspective. *Psychology of Women Quarterly* 17 (4):499–514.

Rozee-Koker, P., Wynne, C., & Mizrahi, K. (1989, April). Workplace safety and fear of rape among professional women. *Paper presented at the meeting of the Western Psychological Association,* Reno, NV.

Ruan, F. F., & Bullough, V. (1992). Lesbianism in China. *Archives of Sexual Behavior* 21 (3):217–226.

Rubin, J. Z., Provenzano, F. J., & Luria, Z. (1974). The eye of the beholder: Parents' views on sex of newborns. *American Journal of Orthopsychiatry* 44:512–519.

Rudd, N. (1996). Appearance and self-presentation in gay consumer cultures: Issues and impact. *Journal of Homosexuality* 32 (1–2):109–134.

Russell, R., & Wells, P. (1994b). Personality and quality of marriage. *British Journal of Psychology* 85 (2):161–168.

Russo, N., Horn, J., & Schwartz, R. (1992). U.S. abortion in context: Selected characteristics and

motivations of women seeking abortions. *Journal of Social Issues* 48:183–202.

Russo, N. F., & Zierk, K. L. (1992). Abortion, childbearing and women's well being. *Professional psychology, Research and Practice* 23 (4):269–280.

Rust, P. (1992). The politics of sexual identity: Sexual attraction and behavior among lesbian and bisexual women. *Social Problems* 39 (4):366–386.

Rutter, P. (1989). *Sex in the Forbidden Zone: When Men in Power—Therapists, Doctors, Clergy, Teachers, and Others—Betray Women's Trust.* Los Angeles: Tarcher.

Ryan, C., & Futterman, D. (1998). *Lesbian and Gay Youth: Care and Counseling.* New York: Columbia University Press.

Ryan, J. (1994). *Sherris Medical Microbiology* (3d ed.). Norwalk, CT: Appleton & Lange.

Rybo, G., Anderson, K., & Odlind, V. Hormonal intrauterine devices. *Annals of Medicine* 25:143–147.

Rytting, M., Ware, R., & Hopkins, P. (1992). Type and the ideal mate: Romantic attraction or type bias? *Journal of Psychological Type* 24:3–12.

Sabah, F. A. (1984). *Women in the Muslim Unconscious.* New York: Plenum.

Sadker, M., & Sadker, D. (1994). *Failing at Fairness: How America's Schools Cheat Girls.* New York: Scribner's.

Samuels, A. (1995). The good-enough father of whatever sex. *Feminism and Psychology* 5 (4):511–530.

Sanday, P. R. (1981). The socio-cultural context of rape: A cross-cultural study. *Journal of Social Issues* 37 (4):5–27.

Sanday, P. R. (1990). *Fraternity Gang Rape: Sex, Brotherhood and Privilege on Campus.* New York: New York University.

Sarrel, P., & Masters, M. (1982). Sexual molestation of men by women. *Archives of Sexual Behavior* 11:117–131.

Savin-Williams, R. C. & Diamond, L. M. (2000). "Sexual Identity Trajectories among Sexual-Minority Youths: Gender Comparisons." *Archives of Sexual Behavior* 29 (6):607–627.

Sawyer, R. G., Desmond, S. M., & Lucke, G. M. (1993). Sexual communication and the college student: Implications for date rape. *Health Values: Journal* of *Health Behavior, Education and Promotion* 17 (4):11–20.

Scallen, R. M. (1981). An investigation of paternal attitudes and behaviors in homosexual and heterosexual fathers. *Dissertation Abstracts International* 41:3809.

Schetky, D. H. (1993). A review of the literature on the long-term effects of childhood sexual abuse. In R. P. K. Luft (Ed.), *Incest-Related Syndromes of Adult Psychopathology.* Washington, DC: American Psychiatric Press, Inc.

Schiavi, R. (1990). Sexuality and aging in men. *Annual Review of Sex Research* 1:227–249.

Schiavi, R., Mandeli, J., & Schreiner-Engle, P. (1994). Sexual satisfaction in healthy aging men. *Journal of Sex and Marital Therapy* 20 (1):3–13.

Schiavi, R., Schreiner-Engle, P., Mandeli, J., and Schanzer, H. (1990). Healthy aging and male sexual function. *American Journal of Psychiatry,* 147 (6):766–771.

Schiavi, R., Schreiner-Engle, P., Mandeli, J., Schanzer, J., & Cohen, E. (1990). Chronic alcoholism and male sexual dysfunction. *Journal of Sex and Marital Therapy* 16:23–33.

Schiavi, R., Schreiner-Engle, P., White, D., & Mandeli, J. (1991). The relationship between pituitary-gonadal function and sexual behavior in healthy aging men. *Psychosomatic Medicine* 53 (4):363–374.

Schiavi, R., White, D., Mandeli, J., & Levine, A. (1997). Effect of testosterone administration on sexual behavior and mood in men with erectile dysfunction. *Archives of Sexual Behavior* 26(3):231–241.

Schiffman, M. (1992). Recent progress in defining the epidemiology of human papillomavirus infection and cervical neoplasia. *Journal of National Cancer Institute* 84:394–398.

Schiller, Z., Landler, M., & Siler, J. F. (1991). Sex still sells—But so does sensitivity. *Business Week* (18 March):100.

Schimmack, U. (1996). Cultural influences on the recognition of emotion by facial expressions. *Journal of Cross Cultural Psychology* 27 (1):37–50.

Schlesinger, L. (1996). Chronic pain, intimacy and sexuality: A qualitative study of women who live with pain. *Journal of Sex Research* 33 (3):249–256.

Schmit, J. (1996). Resistance-related mutations in the HIV-1 protease gene

of patients treated for one year with the protease inhibitor Ritonavir. *AIDS* 10:995–999.

Schnarch, B. (1992). Neither man nor woman: Berdache—A case for non-dichotomous gender construction. *Anthropologica* 34 (1):105–121.

Schnarch, D. (1993). *The Sexual Crucible.* New York: Norton.

Schoen, E., Anderson, G., Bohon, C., Hinman, F., Poland, R., & Wakeman, E. (1989). Report on the task force on circumcision. *Pediatrics* 84:388–391.

Schover, L. R. (1995). It's not all in your head: Integrating sex therapy and surgery in treating a case of chronic vulvar pain. In R. C. Rosen and S.R. Leiblum (Eds.), *Case Studies in Sex Therapy* (pp. 295–310). New York: Guilford.

Schreurs, K. G. (1993). Sexuality in lesbian couples: The importance of gender. *Annual Review of Sex Research* 4:49–66.

Schroeder, J. (1995). Self-concept, social anxiety, and interpersonal perception skills. *Personality and Individual Differences* 19 (6):955–958.

Schulz, R., Williamson, G., & Bridges, M. (1991). *Limb Amputation among the Elderly: Psychosocial Factors Influencing Adjustment.* Washington, DC: AARP Andrus Foundation.

Schwartz, B., Garenta, S., Broome, C., Reingold, A., Hightower, A., Perlman, J., & Wolf, P. (1989). Nonmenstrual toxic shock syndrome associated with barrier contraceptives: Report of a case-control study. *Reviews of Infectious Diseases* 2:S43–S49.

Schwartz, M. (1994). Negative impact of sexual abuse on adult male gender: Issues and strategies of intervention. *Child and Adolescent Social Work Journal* 11 (3):179–194.

Scott, J. (1990). Low birth weight's high cost. *Los Angeles Times* (31 December):A1, A20, A21.

Scott, J. E., & Curvelier, S. J. (1993). Violence and sexual violence in pornography: Is it really increasing? *Archives of Sexual Behavior* 22 (4):357–371.

Scott, J. E., & Schwalm, L. A. (1988). Rape rates and the circulation rates of adult magazines. *Journal of Sex Research* 24:241–250.

Scully, D., & Marolla, J. (1985). Riding the bull at Gilley's: Convicted rapists describe the rewards of rape. *Social Problems* 32:251–263.

Sedikides, C., Oliver, M. B., & Campbell, W. K. (1994). Perceived benefits and costs of romantic relationships for women and men: Implications for exchange theory. *Personal Relationships* 1:5–21.

Seftel, A. D., Oates, R. D., & Krane, R. J. (1991). Disturbed sexual functioning in patients with spinal cord disease. *Neurologic Clinics* 9:757–778.

Segal, M. (1994a). Multiple sclerosis: New treatment reduces relapses. *FDA Consumer* (June):12–16.

Segraves, R., & Segraves, B. (1995). Human sexuality and aging. *Journal of Sex Education and Therapy* 21 (2):102.

Segraves, R. T., and Segraves, K. B. (1993). Medical aspects of orgasm disorders. In W. O'Donohue & J. H. Geer (Eds.), *Handbook of Sexual Dysfunctions* (pp. 225–252). Boston: Allyn & Bacon.

Seligman, M. E. P. (1971). Phobias and preparedness. *Behavior Therapy* 2:307–320.

Sell, R., Wells, J., & Wypij, D. (1995). The prevalence of homosexual behavior and attraction in the United States, the United Kingdom, and France: Results of national population-based samples. *Archives of Sexual Behavior* 24 (3):235–248.

Semans, J. (1956). Premature ejaculation: A new approach. *Southern Medical Journal* 49:353–358.

Serour, F., Samra, Z., Kushel, Z., Gorenstein, A., & Dan M. (1997). Comparative Periurethral Bacteriology of Uncircumcised and Circumcised Males. *Geritourinary Medicine* 93(4):288–290.

Severn, J., Belch, G. E., & Belch, M. A. (1990). The effects of sexual and non-sexual advertising appeals and information level on cognitive processing and communication effectiveness. *Journal of Advertising* 19:14–22.

Sexual culture in Brazil creates AIDS risk. (1995). *Contemporary Sexuality* 29 (4):5.

Sexual groping common on Japanese trains. (1996). *Contemporary Sexuality* 30 (2).

Shain, R., Miller, W., Holden, A., & Rosenthal, M. (1991). Impact of tubal sterilization and vasectomy on female marital sexuality: Results of a controlled longitudinal study. *American Journal of Obstetrics and Gynecology* 164:763–771.

Shapurian, R., & Hojat, M. (1985). Sexual and premarital attitudes of

Iranian college students. *Psychological Reports* 57:67–74.

Shaver, P., Hazen, C., & Bradshaw, D. (1988). Love as attachment: The integration of three behavioral systems. In R. Sternberg & M. Barnes (Eds.), *The Psychology of Love*. New Haven, CT: Yale University.

Shaver, P. R., Wu, S., & Schwartz, J. C. (1991). Cross-cultural similarities and differences in emotion and its representation: A prototype approach. In M.S. Clark (Ed.), *Review of Personality and Social Psychology* (vol. 13, pp. 175–212). Beverly Hills, CA: Sage.

Shaw, J. (1994). Aging and sexual potential. *Journal of Sex Education and Therapy* 20 (2):134–139.

Sheehy, G. (1997). Beyond Virility, and New Vision. *Time* (17 November):69.

Sheer, V. (1995). Sensation seeking predispositions and susceptibility to a sexual partner's appeals for condom use. *Journal of Applied Communication Research* 23 (3):212–229.

Sheer V., & Cline, R. (1995). Individual differences in sensation seeking and sexual behavior: Implications for communication intervention on HIV/AIDS prevention among college students. *Health Communication* 7 (3):205–223.

Sheffield, M., Carey, J., Patenaude, W., & Lambert, M. (1995). An exploration of the relationship between interpersonal problems and psychological health. *Psychological Reports* 76 (3, Pt. 1):947–956.

Shepard, T. (1986). Human teratogenicity. *Advances in Pediatrics* 33:225.

Sheppard, V., Nelson, E., & Andreoli-Mathie, V. (1995). Dating relationships and infidelity: Attitudes and behaviors. *Journal of Sex and Marital Therapy* 21 (3):202–212.

Sherwin, B. (1991). The psychoendocrinology of aging and female sexuality. *Annual Review of Sex Research* 2:181–198.

Sherwin, B., Gelfand, M., & Brender, W. (1985). Androgen enhances sexual motivation in females: A prospective crossover study of sex steroid administration in the surgical menopause. *Psychosomatic Medicine* 47:339–351.

Shields, N., Reid, M., Cheyne, H., & Holmes, A. "Impact of Midwife-Managed Care in the Postnatal Period: An Exploration of Psychosocial Outcomes." *Journal of Reproductive and Infant Psychology* (May 1997):91–108.

Shuit, D. (1996). Penile enlargement patients sue, say they were disfigured. *Los Angeles Times* (4 March):B1, B3.

SIECUS (Sexual Information and Education Council of the United States). (1995a). *Facing Facts: Sexual Health for America's Adolescents*. New York: SIECUS.

SIECUS (Sexual Information and Education Council of the United States). (1995b). *Right From the Start: Guidelines for Sexuality Issues, Birth to Five Years*. New York: SIECUS.

Siegel, J. (1990). Money and marriage: A transparency to the struggles of intimacy. *Journal of Independent Social Work*, 4 (4):51–60.

Signorielli, N. (1990). Children, television and gender roles: Messages and impact. *Journal of Adolescent Health Care* 11 (1):50–58.

Signorielli, N., McLeod, D., & Healy, E. (1994). Gender stereotypes in MTV commercials: The beat goes on. *Journal of Broadcasting and Electronic Media* 38 (1):91–101.

Sikstrom, B., Hellberg, D., Nilsson, S., Brihmer, C., & Mardh, P. (1996). Sexual risk behavior in women with cervical human papillomavirus infection. *Archives of Sexual Behavior* 25 (4):361–372.

Simon, P. M., Morse, E. V., Osofsky, H. J., Balson, P. M., & Gaumer, R. (1992). Psychological characteristics of a sample of male street prostitutes. *Archives of Sexual Behavior* 21 (1):33–44.

Simons, R. L., & Whitbeck, L. B. (1991). Sexual abuse as a precursor to prostitution and victimization among adolescents and adult homeless women. *Journal of Family Issues* 12:361–379.

Sinding, S. W., & Siegel, S. J. (1991). Birth rate news. *New York Times* (19 December):A31.

Singh, D. (1995). Female judgment of male attractiveness and desirability for relationships: Role of waist to hip ratio and financial status. *Journal of Personality and Social Psychology* 69 (6):1089–1101.

Singh, G., Kochanek, K., & MacDorman, M. (1996). Advance report of final mortality statistics, 1994. *Monthly Vital Statistics Report* 45 (1, supp. )(30 Sept). Hyattsville, MD: National Center for Health Statistics.

Singh, G., & Yu, S. (1995). Infant mortality in the United States: Trends, differentials, and projections, 1950 through 2010. *American Journal of Public Health* 85:957–964.

Slijper, F., Drop, S., Molenaar, J., & Scholtmeijer, R. (1994). Neonates with abnormal genital development assigned the female sex: Parent counseling. *Journal of Sex Education and Therapy* 20 (1):9–17.

Small, M. (1992). The evolution of female sexuality and mate selection in humans. *Human Nature* 3 (2):133–156.

Smith A. L. (1905). Higher education of women and race suicide. *Popular Science Monthly* 66:467–468.

Smith, D. (1981). Spinal cord injury. In D. Bullard & S. Knight (Eds.), *Sexuality and Physical Disability*. St. Louis: Mosby.

Smith, L. (1992). How couples misuse money. *Family Therapy* 19 (2):131–135.

Smith, R. A. (1995). *Challenging Your Preconceptions*. Pacific Grove, CA: Brooks/Cole.

Snyder, H. (1991). To circumcise or not. *Hospital Practice* (15 January):201–207.

Sobo, E. J. (1994). Menstruation: An ethnophysiological defense against pathogens. *Perspectives in Biology and Medicine* 38 (1):36–37.

Some teenagers say they might not seek health care if they could not be assured of confidentiality. (1993). *Family Planning Perspectives* (July/August).

Sommers-Flanagan, R., Sommers-Flanagan, J., & Davis, B. (1993). What's happening on music television? A gender role content analysis. *Sex Roles* 28 (11–12):745–753.

Soto-Ramirez, L. (1996). HIV-1 Langerhans' cell tropism associated with heterosexual transmission of HIV. *Science* 271 (1 March): 1291–1293.

South, S. (1995). Do you need to shop around? Age at marriage, spousal alternatives, and marital dissolution. *Journal of Family Issues* 16 (4):432–449.

South, S., & Lloyd K. (1995). Spousal alternatives and marital dissolution. *American Sociological Review* 60 (1):21–35.

Spark, R. (1991). *Male Sexual Health: A Couple's Guide.* Mt. Vernon, NY: Consumer Reports Books.

Spector, I., & Carey, M. (1990). Incidence and prevalence of the sexual dysfunctions: A critical review of the empirical literature. *Archives of Sexual Behavior* 19:389–408.

Spector, I., Leiblum, S., Carey, M., & Rosen, R. (1993). Diabetes and female sexual function: A critical review. *Annals of Behavioral Medicine* 15:257–264.

Spence, A., & Mason, E. (1992). *Human Anatomy and Physiology.* (4th ed.). St. Paul, MN: West.

Speroff, L., & Darney, P. (1992). *A Clinical Guide for Contraception.* Baltimore: Williams & Wilkins.

Spiegel, C. (1991). Bacterial vaginosis. *Clinical Microbiology Reviews* 4:485–498.

Spohr, H., Willms, J., & Steinhausen, H. (1993). Prenatal alcohol exposure and long-term developmental consequences. *Lancet* 341:907–910.

Sporer, A. (1991). Male sexuality. In J. Leyson (Ed.), *Sexual Rehabilitation of the Spinal Cord Injured Patient.* Clifton, NJ: Humana.

Sprecher, S., Aron, A., Hatfield, E., Cortese, A., Potapova, E., & Levitskaya, A. (1994). Love: American style, Russian style, and Japanese style. *Personal Relationships* 1:349–369.

Sprecher, S., & McKinney, K. (1993). *Sexuality.* Newbury Park, CA: Sage.

Sprecher, S., Sullivan, Q., & Hatfield, E. (1994). Mate selection preferences: Gender differences examined in a national sample. *Journal of Personality and Social Psychology* 66 (6):1074–1080.

St. Lawrence, J., & Madakasira, S. (1992). Evaluation and treatment of premature ejaculation: A critical review. *International Journal of Psychiatry and Medicine* 22:77–97.

St. Louis, M. E., & Wasserheit, J. N. (1998). Elimination of syphilis in the United States. *Science* 281:353-354.

Stafford, R. (1990). Alternative strategies for controlling rising cesarean section rates. *Journal of the American Medical Association* 263:683.

Staples, R., & Johnson. J. (1993). *Black Families at the Crossroads: Challenges and Prospects.* San Francisco: Jossey-Bass.

Stark, E. (1989). Teen sex: Not for love. *Psychology Today* (May):10–11.

Stebleton, M., and Rothenberger, J. (1993). Truth or consequences: Dishonesty in dating and HIV/AIDS related issues in a college-age population. *Journal of American College Health* 42 (2):51–54.

Steen, S., & Schwartz, P. (1995). Communication, gender, and power: Homosexual couples as a case study. In M. Fitzpatrick & A. Vangelisti (Eds.), *Explaining Family Interactions* (pp. 310–343). Thousand Oaks, CA: Sage.

Stehlin, D. (1994). Medication and labor: Birthing babies in the '90s. In *Current Issues in Women's Health* (2d ed.). An FDA Consumer Special Report, January. DHHS Pub. No. (FDA)94-1181. Public Health Service, U.S. Department of Health and Human Services.

Stein, R. A. (2000). Cardiovascular response to sexual activity. *American Journal of Cardiology* 20:27F–29F.

Steinhart, C. R., Ash, S. R., Gingrich, C., Sapir, D., Keeling, G. N., & Yatvin, M. B. (1996). Effect of whole body hyperthermia on AIDS patients with Kaposi's sarcoma: A pilot study. *Journal of Acquired Immune Deficiency Syndromes and Human Retrovirology* 11 (3):271–282.

Stern, C. S. (1993). Colleges must be careful not to write bad policies on sexual harassment. *Chronicle of Higher Education* (10 March):B1–B2.

Sternberg, R. (1988a). *The Triangle of Love.* New York: Basic Books.

Sternberg, S. (1996). New tests mark big leap in HIV diagnosis. Three-drug combination appears to eradicate HIV in the blood. *Science News* (20 July):36.

Stevens, J. (1994). Adolescent development and adolescent pregnancy among late age African American female adolescents. *Child and Adolescent Social Work Journal* 11 (6):433–453.

Stewart, F., Guest, F., Stewart, G., & Hatcher, R. (1987). *Understanding Your Body.* New York: Bantam.

Stickel, S., & Ellis, K. (1993). Dating relationships of entering first-year students: A baseline study of courtship violence. *Journal of College Student Development* 34 (6):439–440.

Stine, G. (1993) *Acquired Immune Deficiency Syndrome: Biological, Medical, Social, and Legal Issues.* Englewood Cliffs, NJ: Prentice Hall.

Stock, W. (1993). Inhibited female orgasm. In W. O'Donohue and J. H. Geer (Eds.), *Handbook of Sexual Dysfunctions* (pp. 253–277). Boston: Allyn & Bacon.

Stone, A. (1995). Finding a way through the adoptive maze. *Business Week* (12 June):104–106.

Stone, I., & Peterson, H. (1992). Spermicides, HIV, and the vaginal sponge. [editorial]. *Journal of the American Medical Association* 268:521–523.

Stoppard, M. (1993). *Conception, Pregnancy, and Birth.* New York: Dorling Kindersley.

Storms, M. (1981). A theory of erotic orientation development. *Psychological Review* 88:340–353.

Strange, C. (1996). Coping with arthritis in its many forms. *FDA Consumer* (March):17–21.

Streissguth, A., Aase, J., Clarren, S., Randels, S., LaDue, R., & Smith, D. (1991). Fetal alcohol syndrome in adolescents and adults. *Journal of the American Medical Association* 15:1961–1967.

Strickland, B. R. (1995). Research on sexual orientation and human development. *Developmental Psychology* 31 (1):137–140.

Struckman-Johnson, C. (1988). Forced sex on dates: It happens to men, too. *Journal of Sex Research* 24:234–241.

Struckman-Johnson, C., & Struckman-Johnson, D. (1994). Men pressured and forced into sexual experience. *Archives of Sexual Behavior* 23:93–114.

Stubbs, K. R. (1992). *Sacred Orgasms.* Berkeley, CA: Secret Garden.

Sue, D. (1979). Erotic fantasies of college students during coitus. *Journal of Sex Research* 15:299–305.

Suggs, R. C. (1966). *Marquesan Sexual Behavior.* New York: Harcourt, Brace & World.

Suman, G. (1990). The role of physical attractiveness and eye contact in sexual attraction. *Journal of Personality and Clinical Studies* 6 (1):109–112.

Swaab, D., Gooren, L., & Hofman, M. (1995). Brain research, gender, and sexual orientation. *Journal of Homosexuality* 28 (3–4):283–301.

Swerdloff, R., Wang, C., Hines, M., & Gorski, R. (1992). Effect of androgens on the brain and other organs during development and aging. *Psychoneuroendocrinology* 17 (4):375–383.

Szasz, G., & Carpenter, C. (1989). Clinical observations in vibratory stimulation of the penis of men with spinal cord injury. *Archives of Sexual Behavior* 18:461–474.

Taffel, S., Placek, P., Moien, M., & Kosary, C. (1991). 1989 U.S. cesarean section rate studies—VBAS rises to nearly one in five. *Birth* 18:73.

Talamini, J. T. (1982). *Boys Will Be Girls: The Hidden World of the Heterosexual Male Transvestite*. Lanham, MD: University.

Tanagho, E., Lue, T., & McClure, R. (1988). *Contemporary Management of Impotence and Infertility*. Baltimore: Williams & Wilkins.

Tannahill, R. (1992). *Sex in History* (rev. ed.). Scarborough House Publishers.

Tannen, D. (1990). *You Just Don't Understand*. New York: William Morrow.

Tannen, D. (1994). *Talking From 9 to 5*. New York: William Morrow.

Tanner, W. M., & Pollack, R. H. (1988). The effects of condom use and erotic instructions on attitudes toward condoms. *Journal of Sex Research* 25:537–541.

Tasker, F., & Golombok, S. (1995). Adults raised as children in lesbian families. *American Journal of Orthopsychiatry* 65 (2):203–215.

Taskinen, H., Kyyronen, D., & Hemminki, K. (1990). Effects of ultrasound shortwaves and physical exertion on pregnancy outcome in physiotherapists. *Journal of Epidemiology and Community Health* 44:196.

Tavris, C. (1992). *The Mismeasure of Woman*. New York: Simon & Schuster.

Taylor, S. E. (1995). *Health Psychology* (3d ed.). New York: McGraw-Hill.

Temple, S., & Robson, P. (1991). The effect of assertiveness training on self-esteem. *British Journal of Occupational Therapy* 54 (9):329–332.

Tevlin, H. E., & Leiblum, S. R. (1983). Sex-role stereotypes and female sexual dysfunction. In I. V. Franks & E. D. Rothblum (Eds.), *Stereotyping of Women: Its Effects on Mental Health* (pp. 129–148). New York: Springer.

Thompson, H., King, L., & Knox, E. (1975). Report of the Ad Hoc Task Force on Circumcision. *Pediatrics* 56:610–611.

Thornburg, H., & Aras, Z. (1986). Physical characteristics of developing adolescents. *Journal of Adolescent Research* 1:47–78.

Tiefer, L. (1991). Historical, scientific, clinical, and feminist criticisms of "the human sexual response cycle" model. *Annual Review of Sex Research* 2:1–23.

Tiefer, L. (1994). Sex is not a natural act. *Zeitschrift fur Sexualferschung* 7:36–42.

Tiefer, L. (1995). *Sex Is Not a Natural Act*. Boulder, CO: Westview Press.

Tien, J. (1986). Attitudes toward divorce across three cultures. *Asian American Psychological Association Journal* (pp. 55–58).

Tierney, J. (1994). Porn, the low-slung engine of progress. *New York Times* (9 January):Section 2, pp. 1, 18.

Timimi, S. B. (1995). Adolescence in immigrant Arab families [Special Issue: Adolescent treatment: New frontiers and new dimensions]. *Journal of Psychotherapy* 32 (1):141–149.

Tissot, S. A. D. (1766/1985). *Onanism*. New York: Garland.

Toder, N. (1992). Lesbian couples in particular. In B. Berzon (Ed.), *Positively Gay*. Berkeley, CA: Celestial Arts.

Toledo-Dreves, V., Zabin, L., & Emerson, M. (1995). Durations of adolescent sexual relationships before and after conception. *Journal of Adolescent Health* 17 (3):163–172.

Torres, A., & Forrest, J. (1988). Why do women have abortions? *Family Planning Perspectives* 20:7–9.

Tortora, G., & Grabowski, S. (1998). *Principles of Anatomy and Physiology* (6th ed.). New York: HarperCollins.

Toufexis, A. (1988). It's not all in your head. *Time* (5 December):94–95.

Townsend, J. (1993). Sexuality and partner selection: Sex differences among college students. *Ethology and Sociobiology* 14 (5):305–329.

Townsend, J. (1995). Sex without emotional involvement: An evolutionary interpretation of sex differences. *Archives of Sexual Behavior* 24 (4):173–206.

Townsend, J., Kline, J., & Wasserman, T. (1995). Low-investment copulation: Sex differences in motivations and emotional reactions. *Ethology and Sociobiology* 16 (1):25–51.

Travin, S., & Protter, B. (1993). *Sexual Perversion: Integrative Treatment Approaches for the Clinician*. New York: Plenum Press.

Triandis, H. C. (1995). *Individualism and Collectivism*. Boulder, CO: Westview Press.

Triandis, H. C. (1996). The psychological measurement of cultural syndromes. *American Psychologist* 51 (4):407–415.

Trussell, J. (1988). Teenage pregnancy in the United States. *Family Planning Perspectives* 5:262–272.

Trussell, J., Hatcher, R., Cates, W., Stewart, F., & Kost, K. (1990). Contraceptive failure in the United States: An update. *Studies in Family Planning* 21:51–54.

Tucker, J., Friedman, H., Wingard, D., & Schwartz, J. (1996). Marital history at midlife as a predictor of longevity: Alternative explanations to the protective effect of marriage. *Health Psychology* 15 (2):94–101.

Tucker, M., & Mitchell-Kernan, C. (1995). Social structural and psychological correlates of interethnic dating. *Journal of Social and Personal Relationships* 12 (3):341–361.

Tugrul, C. & Kabakci, E. (1997). Vaginismus and its correlates. *Sexual and Marital Therapy* 12(1):23–24.

Turgeon, M. L. (1996). *Immunology and serology in laboratory medicine*. St. Louis: Mosby.

Turner, L., Froman, S., Althof, S., Levine, S., Tobias, J., Kursh, E., Bodner, D., & Resnick, J. (1990). Intracavernous injections in the management of diabetic impotence. *Journal of Sex Education and Therapy* 16:126–136.

Twohey, D., & Ewing, M. (1995). The male voice of emotional intimacy. *Journal of Mental Health Counseling* 17 (1):54–62.

Tyler, A., & Boxer, D. (1996). Sexual harassment? Cross cultural/cross linguistic perspectives. *Discourse and Society* 7 (1):107–133.

Udry, J. R. (1993). The politics of sex research. *Journal of Sex Research* 30 (2):103–110.

Udry, J. R., et al. (1985). Serum androgenic hormones motivate sexual behavior in adolescent boys. *Fertility and Sterility* 43:90–94.

U.S. Department of Commerce. (1990). *Statistical Abstract of the United States*. Washington, DC: U.S. Government Printing Office.

U.S. Public Health Service. (1997). *HIV Prevention Bulletin: Medical Advice for Persons Who Inject Illicit Drugs*. Atlanta: U.S. Department of Health and Human Services, Public Health Service.

*United States v. One Package*, 86 F. 2d 737 (1936).

Ussher, J. M., & Dewberry, C. (1995). The native and long-term effects of childhood sexual abuse: A survey of adult women survivors in Britain. *British Journal of Clinical Psychology* 34 (2):177–192.

Vachs, A. (1996). If we really want to protect children. *Parade: The Sunday Newspaper Magazine* (3 November):4–5.

Vance, E. B., & Wagner, N. W. (1976). Written descriptions of orgasm: A study of sex differences. *Archives of Sexual Behavior* 6:87–98.

Van De Graaff, K., & Fox, S. (1995). *Concepts of Human Anatomy and Physiology* (4th ed.). Dubuque, IA: Brown.

Van den Broucke, S., Vandereycken, W., & Vertommen, H. (1995). Marital intimacy: Conceptualization and assessment. *Clinical Psychology Review* 15 (3):217–233.

van der Kalk, B. (1995). The body, memory, and the psychobiology of trauma. In J. L. Alpert (Ed.), *Sexual Abuse Recalled: Treating Traumas in the Era of the Recovered Memory Debate* (pp. 29–60). Northvale, NJ: Jason Aronson.

Vandiver, T. "Relationship of Mothers' Perceptions and Behaviors to the Duration of Breastfeeding." *Psychological Reports* (June 1997):1375–1384.

Van Heeswyk, P. (1994). Parental intercourse—The official secret act: Trying not to think about sex in adolescence. *Journal of Child Psychotherapy* 20 (2):231–241.

Van Howe, R. (1997). Variability in penile appearance and penile findings: A prospective study. *British Journal of Urology* 80(5):776–782.

Van Wyk, P., & Geist, C. (1995). Biology of bisexuality: Critique and observations. *Journal of Homosexuality* 28 (3–4):357–373.

Ventura, S., Peters, K., Martin, J. & Maurer, J. 1997. Births and Deaths, 1996. *Monthly Vital Statistics Reports*, 46(1), Supplement 2 (11 September).

Verma, V. (1997). *The Kamasutra for Women*. New York: Kodansha.

Victor, S., & Fish, M. (1995). Lesbian mothers and the children: A review for school psychologists. *School Psychology Review* 24 (3):456–479.

Vincke, J., Bolton, R., & Miller, M. (1997). Younger versus older gay men: Risks, pleasures and dangers of anal sex. *AIDS Care* 9(2):217–225.

Voeller, B. (1991). AIDS and heterosexual anal intercourse. *Archives of Sexual Behavior* 20:233–276.

Vyras, P. (1996). Neglected defender of homosexuality: A commemoration. *Journal of Sex and Marital Therapy* 22 (2):121–129.

Wade, C., & Tavris, C. (1996). *Psychology* (4th ed.). New York: HarperCollins.

Wagenaar, W. A., & Goeneweg, J. (1990). The memory of concentration camp survivors. *Applied Cognitive Psychology* 4 (2):77–87.

Walker, L. E. A. (Ed.) (1988). *Handbook on Sexual Abuse of Children*. New York: Springer.

Wallis, C. (1986). The career woman's disease. *Time* (28 April):62.

Walters-Champman, S., Price, S., & Serovich, J. (1995). The effects of guilt on divorce adjustment. *Journal of Divorce and Remarriage* 22 (3–4):163–177.

Ward, A. (1990). The role of physical contact in childcare. *Children and Society* 4 (4):337–351.

Ward, C. A. (1995). *Attitudes toward Rape: Feminist and Social Psychological Perspectives*. London: Sage.

Ward, D. A., Carter, T. J., & Perrin, R. D. (1994). *Social Deviance: Being, Behaving and Branding*. Boston: Allyn & Bacon.

Ward, M. (1995). Talking about sex: Common themes about sexuality in the prime-time television programs children and adolescents view most. *Journal of Youth and Adolescence* 24 (5):595–615.

Wardle, F. (Ed.) (1995). *Child-to-Child Sexual Behavior in Child Care Settings: Final Report of the Symposium*. Denver: Children's World Learning Centers.

Watzlawick, P. (1984). *The Invented Reality: How Do We Know What We Believe We Know?* New York: W. W. Norton.

Weaver, J. B. (1994). Pornography and sexual callousness: The perceptual and behavioral consequences of exposure to pornography. In D. Zillman, J. Bryant, and A. C. Huston (Eds.), *Media, Children, and the Family: Social Scientific, Psychodynamic and Clinical Perspectives* (pp. 215–228). Hillsdale, NJ: Erlbaum.

Weaver, R. (1993). *Understanding Interpersonal Communication* (6th ed.). Glenview, IL: Scott, Foresman.

Webb, A., & Morris, J. (1993). Practice of postcoital contraception—The results of a national survey. *British Journal of Family Planning* 18:113–118.

Webster, D. C. (1996). Sex, lies and stereotypes: Women and interstitial cystitis. *Journal of Sex Research* 33 (3):197–203.

Weinberg, T. S. (1987). Sadomasochism in the United States: A review of recent sociological literature. *Journal of Sex Research* 23:50–69.

Weinberg, T. S., & Bullough, V. L. (1988). Alienation, self-image, and the importance of support groups for the wives of transvestites. *Journal of Sex Research* 24:262–268.

Weinhardt, L., & Carey, M. (1996). Prevalence of erectile disorder among men with diabetes mellitus: Comprehensive review, methodological critique, and suggestions for future research. *Journal of Sex Research* 33:205–214.

Weiss, R. D., & Mirin, S. M. (1987). *Cocaine*. Washington, DC: American Psychiatric Press.

Wells, B. (1986). Predictors of female nocturnal orgasm. *Journal of Sex Research* 23:421–437.

Whatt, G. E., Peters, S. D., & Guthrie, D. (1988a). Kinsey revisited: Part I. Comparison of the sexual socialization and sexual behavior of White women over 33 years. *Archives of Sexual Behavior* 17:201–239.

**Whip-bearing waitresses banned from Belfast.** (1995). *Contemporary Sexuality* 29 (12).

Whipple, B. (1990). Female sexuality. In J. Leyson (Ed.), *Sexual Rehabilitation of the Spinal Cord Injured Patient* (pp. 19–38). Clifton, NJ: Humana.

Whipple, B., Ogden, G., & Komisaruk, B. (1992). Physiological correlates of imagery-induced orgasm in women. *Archives of Sexual Behavior* 21:121–133.

Whipple, B., Gerdes, C., & Komisaruk, B. (1996). Sexual response to self-stimulation in women with complete spinal cord injury. *Journal of Sex Research* 33:231–240.

Whitney, E., & Rolfes, S. (1996). *Understanding Nutrition* (7th ed.). St. Paul, MN: West.

Widing, R. E., Hoverstaad, R., Coultier, R., & Brown, G. (1991) The VASE scales: Measures of viewpoints about sexual embeds in advertising. *Journal of Business Research* 22 (1):3–10.

Wiederman, M. (1993). Evolved gender differences in mate preferences: Evidence from personal advertisements. *Ethology and Sociobiology* 14 (5):331–351.

Wiederman, M., & Allgeier, E. (1992). Gender differences in mate selection criteria: Sociobiological or socioeconomic explanation? *Ethology and Sociobiology* 13 (2):115–124.

Wiederman, M., & Allgeier, E. (1996). Expectations and attributions regarding extramarital sex among young married individuals. *Journal of Psychology and Human Sexuality* 8 (3):21–35.

Wiest, W. M. (1977). Semantic differential profiles of orgasm and other experiences among men and women. *Sex Roles* 3:399–403.

Williams, A. (1997). Estimates of infectious disease risk factors in U.S. blood donors. *Journal of the American Medical Association* 277:967–972.

Williams, G., & Kleinke, C. (1993). Effects of mutual gaze and touch on attraction, mood, and cardiovascular reactivity. *Journal of Research in Personality* 27 (2):170–183.

Williams, J. E., & Best, D. E. (1990). *Sex and Psyche: Gender and Self Viewed Cross-Culturally*. Newbury Park, CA: Sage.

Williams, K. B., & Cyr, R. R. (1992). Escalating commitment to a relationship: The sexual harassment trap. *Sex Roles* 27 (1–2):47–72.

Williams, L. M. (1994). Recall of childhood trauma: A prospective study of women's memories of child sexual abuse. *Journal of Consulting and Clinical Psychology* 62 (6):1167–1176.

Williams, M. E. (1995). *The American Geriatrics Society's Complete Guide to Aging and Health*. New York: Harmony Books.

Williamson, G., & Walters, A. Perceived impact of limb amputation on sexual activity: A study of adult amputees. *Journal of Sex Research* 33:221–230.

Willis, S. L., & Schaie, K. W. (1988). Gender differences in spatial ability in old age: Longitudinal and intervention findings. *Sex Roles* 18:189–204.

Wills, G. (1990). *Under God*. New York: Simon & Schuster.

Wilson, R., Kendrick, V., Wittmann, B., & McGillivray, B. (1986). Spontaneous abortion and pregnancy outcome after normal first trimester ultrasound examination. *Obstetrics and Gynecology* 67:352.

Winefield, H., & Harvey, E. (1996). Psychological maturity in early adulthood: Relationships between social development and identity. *Journal of Genetic Psychology* 157 (1):93–103.

Winick, C., & Evans, J. T. (1994). Is there a national standard with respect to attitudes toward sexually explicit media material? *Archives of Sexual Behavior* 23 (4):405–419.

Winks, C., & Semans, A. (1997). *The New Good Vibrations Guide to Sex*. San Francisco: Cleis.

Winston, R., & Handyside, A. (1993). New challenges in human in-vitro fertilization. *Science* 260:932–936.

Wiswell, T., & Geschke, D. (1989). Risks from circumcision during the first month of life compared with those of uncircumcised boys. *Pediatrics* 83:1011–1015.

Wiswell, T., Miller, G., & Gelston, H. (1988). The effect of circumcision status on periurethral bacterial flora during the first year of life. *Journal of Pediatrics* 113:442–446.

Witte, K., & Morrison, K. (1995). Using scare tactics to promote safer sex among juvenile detention and high school youth. *Journal of Applied Communication Research* 23 (2):128–142.

Wittich, A., & Salminen, E. (1997). Genital mutilation of young girls traditionally practiced in militarily significant regions of the world. *Military Medicine* 162(10):677–679.

Woititz, J. (1992). *Healthy Parenting*. New York: Simon & Schuster.

Wolman, T. (1985). Drug addiction. In M. Farber (Ed.), *Human Sexuality* (pp. 277–285). New York: Macmillan.

Wood, J., & Inman, C. (1993). In a different mode: Masculine styles of communicating closeness. *Journal of Applied Communication Research* 21 (3):279–295.

Woods, M. (1984). *Sexuality in Health and Illness* (3d ed.). St. Louis: Mosby.

Wortman, C., & Silver, R. (1993). Successful mastery of bereavement and widowhood: A life-course perspective. In P. Baltes & M. Baltes (Eds.), *Successful Aging: Perspectives From the Behavioral Sciences*. Cambridge: Cambridge University Press.

Wright, C., & Maxwell, J. (1991). Social support during adjustment to later-life divorce: How adult children help parents. *Journal of Divorce and Remarriage* 15 (3–4):21–48.

Wyatt, G. E. (1991). Child sexual abuse and its effects on sexual functioning. *Annual Review of Sex Research* 2:249–266.

Wyatt, G. E. (1992). The sociocultural context of African-American and white American women's rape. *Journal of Social Issues* 48 (1):77–91.

Wyatt, G. E., & Dunn, D. (1991). Examining predictors of sex guilt in multiethnic samples of women. *Archives of Sexual Behavior* 20 (5):471–485.

Wyatt, G. E., Peters, S. D., & Guthrie, D. (1988b). Kinsey revisited: Part II. Comparison of the sexual socialization of Black women over 33 years. *Archives of Sexual Behavior* 17:289–332.

Wyers, N. L. (1984). *Lesbian and Gay Spouses and Parents: Homosexuality in the Family*. Portland, OR: Portland State University.

Xu, X., & White, M. (1990). Love matches and arranged marriages: A Chinese replication. *Journal of Marriage and the Family* 52 (August): 709–722.

Xu, X., & White, M. K. (1990). Love matches and arranged marriages: A Chinese replication. *Journal of Marriage and the Family* 52 (3):709–722.

Yarkoney, G., Chen, D., Palmer, J., Roth, E., Rayner, S., & Lovell, L. (1995). Management of impotence due to spinal cord injury using low-dose papaverien. *Paraplegia* 33:77–79.

Yeager, K., Agostini, R., Nattiv, A., & Drinkwater, B. (1993). The female athlete triad: Disordered eating, amenorrhea, osteoporosis. *Medicine and Science in Sports and Exercise* 25:775–777.

Yohalem, L. (1995). Why do people with mental retardation need sexuality education? *SIECUS Report* 23:14–16.

Yudofsky, S. C., Hales, R. E., & Ferguson, T. (1991). *What You Need to Know About Psychiatric Drugs*. New York: Ballantine.

Zilbergeld, B. (1992). *The New Male Sexuality*. New York: Bantam Books.

Zillman, D. (1994). Erotica and family values. In D. Zillman, J. Bryant, & A. C. Huston (Eds.), *Media and Children in the Family* (pp. 199–213). Hillsdale, NJ: Erlbaum.

Zillman, D., & Bryant, J. (1984). Effects of massive exposure to pornography. In N. M. Malamuth and E. Donnerstein (Eds.), *Pornography and Sexual Aggression* (pp. 115–138). New York: Academic Press.

Zimmerman, R., Sprecher, S., Langer, L., & Holloway, C. (1995). Adolescents' perceived ability to say "no" to unwanted sex. *Journal of Adolescent Research* 10 (3):383–399.

Zinn, M., & Eitzen, D. (1990). *Diversity in Families* (2d ed.). New York: HarperCollins.

Zucker, K. J., Bradley, S. J., & Sullivan, C. B. L. (1993). Gender identity disorder in children. *Annual Review of Sex Research* 3:73–119.

# CREDITS

## PHOTOGRAPHS

### CHAPTER 1

Page 4: © Deborah Davis/PhotoEdit; p. 5: © W.B.Spunbarg/PhotoEdit; p. 6: Jim Cartier/Photo Researchers, Inc.; p. 7: © AP Photo/Doug Mills; p. 8: "private collection"; p. 8: © George Holton/Photo Researchers, Inc.; p. 8: Scala/Art Resource, NY; p. 11: © Collection of The New-York Historical Society; p. 12: National Library of Medicine; p. 13: © Bettmann/CORBIS; p. 13: Sophia Smith Collection; p. 14(both): National Library of Medicine; p. 17: © Archive Photos; p. 18: © Bettmann/CORBIS; p. 18 a, b: Behavioral Technology, Inc., Salt Lake City, UT

### CHAPTER 2

Page 26: © Ami Katz/Unicom Stock Photos; p. 33: © Michael Newman/PhotoEdit; p. 37: © Marc Romanelli/The Image Bank; p. 39: © Michael Newman/PhotoEdit; p. 47: © Jonathan Nourok/PhotoEdit; p. 50: © Jonathan Nourok/PhotoEdit

### CHAPTER 3

Page 54: © Michael Newman/PhotoEdit; p. 57: © Stewart D. Halperin; p. 61: © Archive Photos; p. 67: © Bill Bachmann/The Image Works; p. 69: © Rag Productions/FPG International; p. 73: © Jeff Greenberg/Unicom Stock Photos

### CHAPTER 4

Page 85 a–d: © Baron Wolman Photography; p. 97: Michael Newman/Photo Edit; p. 99: © Dion Ogust/The Image Works; p. 105: © SIU/Visuals Unlimited; ; p.107 a, b: American Society of Plastic Surgeons

### CHAPTER 5

Page 112a: With permission of The McGraw-Hill Company Publishers; p. 112b: © Dion Ogust/The Image Works; p. 131: © Alan Carey/The Image Works

### CHAPTER 6

Page 139: © Robert Fox/Impact Visuals; p. 146 a–f: © Gay Men's Health Crisis, NYC/photography by Naakkve; p. 150: © Oliver Meckes/Photo Researchers, Inc.; p. 150: © Biophoto Associates/Photo Researchers, Inc.; p. 155: © Dr. P. Marazzi/Science Photo Library/Photo Researchers, Inc.; p. 158: Centers for Disease Control; p. 161(top left): © M. Abbey/Photo Researchers, Inc.; p. 161(bottom left): Centers for Disease Control; p. 161(right): Centers for Disease Control; p. 165(left): Centers for Disease Control; p. 165(right): © E. Gray/Science Photo Library/Photo Researchers, Inc.

### CHAPTER 7

Page 181: © A. Ramey/PhotoEdit; p. 183: Courtesy SmithKline Beecham; p. 186: © Michael Krasowitz/FPG International; p. 188: © Barros & Barros/The Image Bank; p. 190: © Mark Richards/PhotoEdit; p. 195: © Mike Malyszko/FPG International

### CHAPTER 8

Page 220: © Barbara Peacock/FPG International

### CHAPTER 9

Page 234: © Britt J. Erianson-Massens/The Image Bank; p. 250 left: © Amy Eira/PhotoEdit; p. 250(right): © Phyllis Christopher/Good Vibrations

### CHAPTER 10

Page 254: © David W. Hamilton/The Image Bank; p. 255: © Bob Daemmrich/The Image Works; p. 256 left: © Marc Romanelli/The Image Bank; p. 256 right: © Mitch Wojnarowicz/The Image Works; p. 262: © Michael Greenlar/The Image Works; p. 266: © Doug Lee/Peter Arnold, Inc.

### CHAPTER 11

Page 271a: March of Dimes; p. 279: © Dr. John Money, Johns Hopkins Medical Institutes; p. 280: Leonard Pinsky, McGill University; p. 280: © Dr. John Money, Johns Hopkins Medical Institutes

### CHAPTER 12

Page 288: © Victor Englebert/Photo Researchers, Inc.; p. 294: Royal Commission on the Historical Monuments of England; p. 295: © Myrleen Ferguson Cate/PhotoEdit; p. 303a: © Bill Bachmann/The Image Works; p. 303b: © MarkRichards/PhotoEdit; p. 304: © Ron Chapple/FPG International; p. 308: Courtesy Dr. Daniel Greenwald Tampa, FL; p. 308: Courtesy Dr. Daniel Greenwald, Tampa, FL

### CHAPTER 13

Page 313: © David W. Hamilton/The Image Bank; p. 317: © Frozen Images/The Image Works; p. 324: © Michael Newman/PhotoEdit; p. 325: © JeffGreenberg/Unicorn Stock Photos; p. 326: © Donna Binder/Impact Visuals; p. 334: © Tony Freeman/PhotoEdit

### CHAPTER 14

Page 339: © Arthur Tilley/FPG International; p. 343: © Esbin-Anderson/The Image Works; p. 349: © Ron Chapple/FPG International; p. 351: © Andreas Pistolesi/The Image Bank; p. 355: © M. Bridwell/PhotoEdit; p. 363: © Ron Chapple/FPG International; p. 368: © Janeart Ltd./The Image Bank; p. 369a: © Juan Alvarez/The Image Bank; p. 369b: © JimCummins/FPG; p. 370: © (364428), Image Network

### CHAPTER 15

Page 374: Courtesy of Planned Parenthood Association of Utah; p. 386a: Courtesy The Female Health Company; p. 387: © SIU/Photo Researchers, Inc.; p. 388: © Gary Parker/Science Photo Library/Photo Researchers, Inc.; p. 389a: © SIU/Visuals Unlimited; p. 391: © M. Long/Visuals Unlimited; p. 393a: © John Griffin/The Image Works; p. 393b: © 1997 Marty Katz/All Rights Reserved; p. 401a: © Steven Rubin/The Image Works; p. 401b: © Fred Chase/Impact Visuals

### CHAPTER 16

Page 408: © Ken Huang/The Image Bank; p. 415a: © Ken Huang/The Image Bank; p. 415b: © Eric R Berndt/Unicorn Stock Photos; p. 417 a, c: © Petit Format/Nestle/Science Source; p. 417b: © C. Edelman/Petit Format/Nestle; p. 420: © Elyse Lewin/The Image Bank; p. 423: © Gary Buss/FPG International; p. 427(all): © Therisa Stack/Tom Stack & Associates; p. 433: © Dion Ogust/The Image Works

## CHAPTER 17

Page 445: © James L. Shaffer; p. 450:
© Cindy Charies/PhotoEdit; p. 454:
© Layma/Photo Researchers, Inc.;
p. 454: © Eugen Gebhardt/FPG
International

## CHAPTER 18

Page 463: © David Young-Wolff/
PhotoEdit; p. 465: From: *The Family Sex
and Marriage in England 1500–1800* by
Lawrence Stone, published by Harper &
Row, Publishers #37 Indecent exposure,
1800; p. 468: © David McGlynn/FPG
International; p. 471(left): © Michael
Goldman/FPG International; p. 471(right):
© Michael Newman/PhotoEdit; p. 475:
© Montes De Oca/FPG International;
p. 484: © Mark Richards/PhotoEdit;
p. 486: Unknown

# LINE ART, BOXES, EXCERPTS

## GO ASK ALICE BOXES

Page 60; p. 159, question 1; p. 179,
question 2; p. 227; p. 272; p. 300; p. 477
All from Go Ask Alice. © 1998 by The
Trustees of Columbia University in
the City of New York. Reprinted by
permission of Henry Holt and Company,
Inc.; p. 9; p. 78; p. 159, question 2;
p. 179, question 2; p. 211; p. 323; p. 341;
p. 362; p. 416; p. 437; p. 446; p. 469
All from the Go Ask Alice
(www.goaskalice.columbia.edu) Health
Question and Answer Website of
Columbia University Health Service.
Reprinted by permission.

## CHAPTER 3

Fig. 3.1: From *The Psychology of Love*,
edited by Robert J. Sternberg and Michael
L. Barnes. Copyright © 1988 Yale
University Press, New Haven, CT.
Reprinted by permission.

## CHAPTER 4

Fig. 4.1: From Kent M. Van De Graaf and
Stuart Ira Fox, *Concepts of Human
Anatomy and Physiology*, 4th edition.
Copyright © 1995 McGraw-Hill
Companies, Inc., Dubuque, Iowa. All
Rights Reserved. Reprinted by permission;
Fig. 4.2: From David Shier, et al., *Hole's
Human Anatomy & Physiology*, 7th
edition. Copyright © 1996 McGraw-Hill
Companies, Inc., Dubuque, Iowa. All
Rights Reserved. Reprinted by permission;
Fig. 4.4: From Kent M. Van De Graaf and
Stuart Ira Fox, *Concepts of Human
Anatomy and Physiology*, 4th edition.
Copyright © 1995 McGraw-Hill
Companies, Inc., Dubuque, Iowa. All

Rights Reserved. Reprinted by permission;
Fig. 4.8: From David Shier, et al., *Hole's
Human Anatomy & Physiology*, 7th
edition. Copyright © 1996 McGraw-Hill
Companies, Inc., Dubuque, Iowa. All
Rights Reserved. Reprinted by permission;
Fig. 4.9: From Sylvia Mader, *Human
Reproductive Biology* © 1992 McGraw-
Hill Companies, Inc., Dubuque, Iowa. All
Rights Reserved. Reprinted by permission;
Fig. 4.10: From John W. Hole, Jr., *Human
Anatomy and Physiology, 6th edition*.
Copyright © 1993 McGraw-Hill
Companies, Inc., Dubuque, Iowa. All
Rights Reserved. Reprinted by permission;
Fig. 4.12: From Sylvia Mader, *Human
Reproductive Biology* © 1992 McGraw-
Hill Companies, Inc., Dubuque, Iowa. All
Rights Reserved. Reprinted by permission;
Fig. 4.13: From David Shier, et al., *Hole's
Human Anatomy & Physiology*, 7th
edition. Copyright © 1996 McGraw-Hill
Companies, Inc., Dubuque, Iowa. All
Rights Reserved. Reprinted by permission.
Text (BSE): Reprinted by permission of the
American Cancer Society.

## CHAPTER 5

Fig. 5.1a: From David Shier, et al., *Hole's
Human Anatomy & Physiology*, 7th
edition. Copyright © 1996 McGraw-Hill
Companies, Inc., Dubuque, Iowa. All
Rights Reserved. Reprinted by permission;
Fig. 5.1b: From Kent M. Van De Graaf
and Stuart Ira Fox, *Concepts of Human
Anatomy and Physiology*, 4th edition.
Copyright © 1995 McGraw-Hill
Companies, Inc., Dubuque, Iowa. All
Rights Reserved. Reprinted by permission;
Fig. 5.6: From Kathleen D. Mullen, et al.,
*Connections for Health*, 2nd Edition.
Copyright © 1990 McGraw-Hill
Companies, Inc., Dubuque, Iowa. All
Rights Reserved. Reprinted by permission;
Cross Section of Seminiferous Tubule from
Sylvia Mader, *Human Reproductive
Biology* © 1992 McGraw-Hill Companies,
Inc., Dubuque, Iowa. All Rights Reserved.
Reprinted by permission; Fig. 5.7: From
David Shier, et al., *Hole's Human
Anatomy & Physiology*, 7th edition.
Copyright © 1996 McGraw-Hill
Companies, Inc., Dubuque, Iowa. All
Rights Reserved. Reprinted by permission;
Fig. 5.8: From David Shier, et al., *Hole's
Human Anatomy & Physiology*, 7th
edition. Copyright © 1996 McGraw-Hill
Companies, Inc., Dubuque, Iowa. All
Rights Reserved. Reprinted by permission;
Fig. 5.9: From Elaine N. Marieb, *Human
Anatomy and Physiology*, 4th edition.
Copyright © 1997, Benjamin Cummings.
All Rights Reserved. Reprinted by
permission.

## CHAPTER 8

Fig. 8.3: From W. H. Masters and V. E.
Johnson, *Human Sexual Response*, 1966,

Little, Brown, and Company; Fig. 8.4:
From W. H. Masters and V. E. Johnson,
*Human Sexual Response*, 1966, Little,
Brown, and Company; Fig. 8.10: From
Laumann, et al., *The Social Organization
of Sexuality*, 1994. Copyright © 1994
University of Chicago Press. Reprinted by
permission.

## CHAPTER 11

Fig. 11.1: From Kent M. Van De Graaf
and Stuart Ira Fox, *Concepts of Human
Anatomy and Physiology*, 4th edition.
Copyright © 1995 McGraw-Hill
Companies, Inc., Dubuque, Iowa. All
Rights Reserved. Reprinted by permission;
Fig. 11.5: From Gary F. Kelly, *Sexuality
Today: The Human Perspective*, 7th
edition. Copyright © 2001 McGraw-Hill
Companies, Inc., New York, New York.
All Rights Reserved. Reprinted by
permission.

## CHAPTER 12

Fig. 12.2: Figure from *Psychology*, Fourth
Edition by Spenser A. Rathus, copyright ©
1990 by Holt, Rinehart and Winston,
reproduced by permission of the publisher;
pp. 300–301: From *The New Male
Sexuality* by Bernie Zilbergeld, PH.D.
Copyright © 1992 by Bernie Zilbergeld.
Used by permission of Bantam Books, a
division of Bantam Doubleday Dell
Publishing Group, Inc.; Fig. 12.3: From
Gary F. Kelly, *Sexuality Today: The
Human Perspective*, 7th edition.
Copyright © 2001 McGraw-Hill
Companies, Inc., New York, New York.
All Rights Reserved. Reprinted by
permission.

## CHAPTER 15

Page 376: Where Do I Stand?: From
R. Hatcher, et al., *Contraceptive
Technology*, 17th revised edition, 1994.
Copyright © 1994 Irvington Publishing,
Reprinted by permission.

## CHAPTER 16

Fig. 16.5: From Kent M. Van De Graaf
and Stuart Ira Fox, *Concepts of Human
Anatomy and Physiology*, 4th edition.
Copyright © 1995 McGraw-Hill
Companies, Inc., Dubuque, Iowa. All
Rights Reserved. Reprinted by permission;
Fig. 16.7: From Sylvia Mader, *Human
Reproductive Biology* © 1992 McGraw-
Hill Companies, Inc., Dubuque, Iowa. All
Rights Reserved. Reprinted by permission.

## CHAPTER 18

Page 466 Dimensions of Diversity: From
Susan Faludi, "The Money Shot: The
World of Pornographic Video" in The
New Yorker, October 30, 1995. Reprinted
by permission.

# NAME INDEX

Note: Page numbers in *italics* indicate illustrations; page numbers followed by *t* indicate tables.

# SUBJECT INDEX

Note: Page numbers in *italic* indicate illustrations, page numbers followed by *t* indicate tables.